Architectures of Global AI Governance

Architectures of Global AI Governance

From Technological Change to Human Choice

MATTHIJS M. MAAS

Senior Research Fellow, Institute for Law & AI, Cambridge, MA, USA
Associate Fellow, Leverhulme Centre for the Future of Intelligence, University of Cambridge, Cambridge, UK

OXFORD
UNIVERSITY PRESS

OXFORD
UNIVERSITY PRESS

Great Clarendon Street, Oxford, OX2 6DP,
United Kingdom

Oxford University Press is a department of the University of Oxford.
It furthers the University's objective of excellence in research, scholarship,
and education by publishing worldwide. Oxford is a registered trademark of
Oxford University Press in the UK and in certain other countries.

Published in the United States of America by Oxford University Press
198 Madison Avenue, New York, NY 10016, United States of America.

British Library Cataloguing in Publication Data
Data available

Library of Congress Control Number: 2025937516

ISBN 9780198877837

DOI: 10.1093/9780191988455.001.0001

Printed and bound by
CPI Group (UK) Ltd., Croydon, CR0 4YY

The manufacturer's authorised representative in the EU for product safety is
Oxford University Press España S.A., Parque Empresarial San Fernando de Henares,
Avenida de Castilla, 2 – 28830 Madrid (www.oup.es/en or product.safety@oup.com).
OUP España S.A. also acts as importer into Spain of products made by the manufacturer.

MIX
Paper | Supporting responsible forestry
FSC® C013604

To Wilfried Maas (1957–2024)
and to Kai (2022–)
For teaching me the value of choice
when the world changes

Acknowledgements

How do we govern a changing technology, in a changing world, using governance instruments that may themselves be left changed?

One good answer is: with each other.

In writing this book I have had the fortune to spend years exploring an issue I both deeply care about and am unendingly fascinated by. Throughout this process, I have been especially lucky to work with and learn from a large and supportive community. I am deeply grateful to so many people for their support, feedback—and patience.

Stretching over many years, my thinking on AI and its governance has benefited tremendously from work by, and conversations and exchanges with, many people, including Cecil Abungu, Ashwin Acharya, Sumaya Nur Adan, Michael Aird, Marco Almada, Markus Anderljung, Bill Anderson-Samways, Jacob Arbeid, Renan Araujo, Shahar Avin, Joslyn Barnhart, Seth Baum, Haydn Belfield, Lyria Bennett Moses, John Bliss, Emma Bluemke, Ingvild Bode, Jan Brauner, Roger Brownsword, Miles Brundage, Justin Bullock, Duncan Cass-Beggs, Alan Chan, Peter Cihon, Di Cooke, Carla Zoe Cremer, Rebecca Crootof, Allan Dafoe, John Danaher, Ashley Deeks, Jeffrey Ding, Noemi Dreksler, Connor Dunlap, Sophie-Charlotte Fischer, Carrick Flynn, John Fogle, Kevin Frazier, Gideon Futerman, Iason Gabriel, Denise Garcia, Benjamin Garfinkel, Katja Grace, Ross Gruetzemacher, Oliver Guest, Carlos Ignacio Gutierrez, Rose Hadshar, Hiski Haukkala, Keith John Hayward, Seán Ó hÉigeartaigh, Lennart Heim, Jeffrey Heninger, Lewis Ho, Jeroen Hopster, Shin-Shin Hua, Cullen O'Keefe, Luke Kemp, Kyle Kilian, Leonie Koessler, Noam Kolt, Victoria Krakovna, David Krueger, Karin Kuhlemann, Martina Kunz, Kristian Lauta, Harry Law, Gavin Leech, Jade Leung, John-Clark Levin, Gregory Lewis, Lucy Lim, Hin-Yan Liu, Garrison Lovely, Suvradip Maitra, Kayla Matteucci, Andrew Mazibrada, Zvi Mowshowitz, Rune Nyrup, Tobi Olasunkanmi, Michael Page, Kenneth Payne, Carina Prunkl, Neil Renic, Regina Rini, Léonard van Rompaey, Anders Sandberg, Lewin Schmitt, Jonas Schuett, Nathan Sears, Elizabeth Seger, Toby Shevlane, Konrad Seifert, Rumtin Sepasspour, Henry Shevlin, Morgan Simpson, Jacob Livingston Slosser, Maxime Stauffer, Merlin Stein, Charlotte Stix, Andrew Strait, Thomas Streinz, Janna Tay, Sue Anne Teo, Lena Trabucco, Robert Trager, Maaike Verbruggen, José Jaime Villalobos, Karina Vold, Gabriel Weil, Christoph Winter, Misha Yagudin, Baobao Zhang, and many, many others.

For sparking and nourishing my interest in these topics, and for supporting my career in this field from an early stage, I am especially grateful to Seán Ó hÉigeartaigh and Seth Baum, as well as to my PhD supervisors at the University of Copenhagen Faculty of Law, Hin-Yan Liu and Kristian Lauta: they both provided detailed and patient guidance throughout my process of writing the original dissertation which serves as the kernel of this book. For their excellent critical engagement with the argument during my PhD defence I am also indebted to Lyria Bennett Moses, Ingvild Bode, and Mikael Rask Madsen.

The Centre for the Study of Existential Risk at the University of Cambridge organized the 2016 conference where I met Dr Liu, which directly enabled my career change back into academia. Both during my PhD and later in my time as a postdoctoral research associate at CSER, I have profited immensely from conversations with many fellow scholars there, including Shahar Avin, Haydn Belfield, Adrian Currie, Seán Ó hÉigeartaigh, Catherine Rhodes, Martina Kunz, Shin-Shin Hua, Jess Whittlestone, Sabin Roman, Lara Mani, Luke Kemp, Sam Clarke, Lalitha Sundaram, SJ Beard, Jochem Rietveld, Mia Sannapureddy, Freya Jephcott, Tom Hobson, and Alex McLaughlin. I would like to especially thank Jess Whittlestone and Jess Bland for excellent guidance and conversations about my research, and Natalie Jones for sharing with me her invaluable experience on preparing an academic book proposal. I am also indebted to many people at the Centre for the Future of Intelligence, CSER's sister centre within the Institute for Technology and Humanity, in particular for conversations with and work by Miri Zilka, Kanta Dihal, Stephen Cave, Henry Shevlin, John Burden, Kerry McInerney, Rune Nyrup, Harry Law, Myesha Jemison, and José Hernández-Orallo. I also gained tremendously from the rich intellectual environment and conversations at King's College, Cambridge, and am furthermore indebted to the immense hospitality of Joel, Miriam, Jacob, and Moshe Peck, whose warmth and humanity saw me through the depths of the pandemic, and Steen Korsgaard and Conny Balsgård Thomsen, for their warmth, patience, and support as I finished up the manuscript.

I am also especially grateful to my colleagues at the Institute for Law and AI, including Alfredo Parra, Christoph Winter, José Jaime Villalobos, Mackenzie Arnold, Matteo Pistillo, Daisy Newbold-Harrop, Suzanne van Arsdale, Charlie Bullock, Eric Martínez, Cullen O'Keefe, Laurens Prins, Jackson Gardner, Matt Reardon, Jaxson Khan, Sophia Rubio, and Chloe Clayton-Green. They have given me an amazing intellectual environment, and I am constantly amazed by the rigour, breadth of expertise, sense of purpose, and kindness that they bring to the field. I am especially grateful for the patient support they've given me throughout the process of reworking and comprehensively updating this book manuscript, in a year when AI governance did not stand still for a single week.

In writing this book, I have had the privilege of having different versions of this book reviewed by many people, all of whom have been enormously generous with their time and attention. For providing detailed feedback on the original dissertation manuscript, I owe thanks to Roger Brownsword, Miles Brundage, Laura Emily Christiansen, Peter Cihon, Jeffrey Ding, James Fox, David J. Galbreath,

Eugenio Vargas Garcia, Ross Gruetzemacher, Olle Häggström, Gavin Leech, John-Clark Levin, Sam Lusk, Wilfried Maas, Suvradip Maitra, Sebastian Porsdam Mann, Andrew Mazibrada, Eugenie Carolina van der Meulen, Alessandro Monti, Robert de Neufville, Joe Parrino, Carina Prunkl, Max Reddel, Beatriz Martinez Romera, Léonard van Rompaey, Luisa Scarcella, Zachary Shaw, Jonas Schuett, Jaime Sevilla, Charlotte Siegmann, Lena Trabucco, Theodora Valkanou, Magnus Vinding, Jess Whittlestone, and Kim Zwitserloot. Furthermore, between 2022 and 2025 I very comprehensively reworked, expanded, and updated this book. In that period, I received many more comments, especially from Cecil Abungu, Sumaya Nur Adan, James Baker, Noam Kolt, Carlos Ignacio Gutierrez, José Jaime Villalobos, Donato Mancini, Zershaaneh Qureshi, Harry Law, Kevin Frazier, Matteo Pistillo, Suzanne van Arsdale, Richard Fisher, Elliot Davies, Luke Kemp, Jonathan Maas, and Wilfried Maas. Their comments have made this work immensely better. Any remaining errors are all my own.

In terms of the process of writing this book, I am also grateful to Thomas Basbøll, who taught me the best writing methodology that I was never able to fully implement (but which nonetheless left its mark); Sing Yun Lee, for approaching the design of the book's cover art with amazing creative skill; and Donato Mancini, for excellent copy-editing support on a number of key sections of the book during the final months of writing. Any remaining mixed metaphors are entirely on me. I am also grateful to my editorial team at OUP, in particular Peter Daniell, Jacqueline Larabee, and Lindsay Glick, for making this a smooth and engaging process, and for their understanding and patience during several rough periods during the writing; and to OUP's production team, including Kristy Barker, Louise Karam, and Titus Prathish, for their meticulous copy-editing and expert professional guidance throughout all stages of the production process.

My family deserves the original and conclusive credit. They have supported me throughout the years of writing this book, and throughout all life, patiently putting up with endless drafts. To my mother, Patricia, and my brothers, Jonathan and Olivier—I owe so much to you. And to my father, Wilfried, who was this book's biggest fan from the very start: thank you for helping me see this through; I wish you could have seen the result; I miss you.

Finally, I am so grateful to Christina Korsgaard and to our Kai: you both have made the years writing this book among the happiest of my life.

Contents

Tables

Abbreviations

AAAI	Association for the Advancement of Artificial Intelligence
AAJI	Advanced Artificiatl Judicial Intelligence
ABM	Anti-Ballistic Missile (Treaty)
ADM	Automated Decision-Making (systems)
AGI	Artificial General Intelligence
AI	Artificial Intelligence
AIA	Artificial Intelligence Act *(EU Regulation)*
AIAB	AI Advisory Body (also 'High-Level Advisory Body on AI', HLAB)
AIDA	AI and Data Act *(Canadian regulation)*
AIDD	AI Incident Database
AISI	AI Safety Institute
ASEAN	Association of South East Asian Nations
ATT	Arms Trade Treaty
AUKUS	*[Trilateral security partnership between Australia, UK, US]*
AWS	Autonomous Weapons Systems
BMEWS	Ballistic Missile Early Warning System
CAAI	China Administration of AI *(proposed)*
CAC	Cyberspace Administration of China
CAHAI	Council of Europe Ad Hoc Committee on Artificial Intelligence
CAIS	Comprehensive AI Services / Centre on AI Safety
CASS	Chinese Academy of Social Sciences
CBM	Confidence-Building Measures
CBRN	Chemical, Biological, Radiological and Nuclear
CCGAI	Coordinating Committee for the Governance of AI *(proposed)*
CCTV	Closed-Circuit Television
CCW	Convention on Certain Conventional Weapons
CEB	(UN) Chief Executives Board for Coordination
CERN	European Organization for Nuclear Research
CIL	Customary International Law
CoC	Code of Conduct
CoE	Council of Europe
CS	Computer Science
CSTO	Collective Security Treaty Organization
CTBT	Comprehensive Test Ban Treaty
DARPA	Defense Advanced Research Projects Agency
DART	Dynamic Analysis and Replanning Tool
DETF	Digital Economy Task Force
DUFM	Dual-Use Foundation Models
EOD	Earth Observation Data

EU	European Union
FATF	Financial Action Task Force
FGCS	Fifth Generation Computer Systems
FIGO	Formal Intergovernmental Organisation
FLOPS	Floating Point Operations Per Second
FMF	Frontier Model Forum
FOBS	Fractional Orbital Bombardment System
FSB	Financial Stability Board
G7	Group of Seven
G20	Group of Twenty
GATS	General Agreement on Tariffs in Services
GATT	General Agreement on Tariffs and Trade
GAN	Generative Adversarial Network
GDC	Global Digital Compact
GDPR	General Data Protection Regulation
GGE	Group of Governmental Experts
GIS	Geographic Information Systems
GOHAI	Global Organization for High-Risk AI *(proposed)*
GPAI	Global Partnership on AI
GPAIS	General-Purpose AI System
GPT	General-Purpose Technology/Generative Pretrained Transformer
GPT-*[n]*	Generative Pretrained Transformer- *[n]* (series of OpenAI LLMs)
GPU	Graphics Processing Units
HBP	Human Brain Project
HLAB	High-Level Advisory Body on AI (also 'AI Advisory Body', AIAB)
HLAI	Human-Level AI
HLEG	High-Level Expert Group on Artificial Intelligence
HLMI	High-Level Machine Intelligence
IAEA	International Atomic Energy Agency
IAIA	International Autonomous Incidents Agreement *(proposed)*
IAIO	International Artificial Intelligence Organisation *(proposed)*
ICAO	International Civil Aviation Organization
ICBM	Intercontinental Ballistic Missile
ICC	International Criminal Court
ICJ	International Court of Justice
ICRAC	International Committee for Robot Arms Control
ICTY	International Criminal Tribunal for the Former Yugoslavia
IDI	*Institut de Droit International*
IEC	International Electrotechnical Commission
IEEE	Institute for Electrical and Electronics Engineers
IGF	Internet Governance Forum
IHL	International Humanitarian Law
IHRL	International Human Rights Law
IIGO	Informal Intergovernmental Organization
IL & IR	International Law & International Relations

ILC International Law Commission
ILO International Labour Organization
IMO International Maritime Organization
IMS International Monitoring System
INF Intermediate-Range Nuclear Forces (Treaty)
IoT Internet of Things
IPAI Intergovernmental Panel on AI *(proposed)*
IPAIS International Panel on AI Safety *(proposed)*
IPCC Intergovernmental Panel on Climate Change
ISO International Organization for Standardization
ISR Intelligence, Surveillance, and Reconnaissance
ISTAR Intelligence, Surveillance, Target Acquisition, Reconnaissance
IT Information Technology
ITER International Thermonuclear Experimental Reactor
ITS Intelligent Treaty Systems
ITU International Telecommunications Union
LAWS Lethal Autonomous Weapons Systems
LLM Large Language Model
LTPA Long-Term Planning Agent
MAGIC Multinational AGI Consortium *(proposed)*
MAIM Mutual Assured AI Malfunction *(proposed strategy)*
MAIRI Multilateral Artificial Intelligence Research Institute *(proposed)*
MAV Maritime Autonomous Vehicles
MHC Meaningful Human Control
ML Machine Learning
MLLM Multi-Modal Language Model
MTCR Missile Technology Control Regime
MTOPS Million Theoretical Operations Per Second
NAT Normal Accident Theory
NGAD Next-Generation Air Dominance
NGO Non-Governmental Organization
NIST National Institute of Standards and Technology
NLP Natural Language Processing
NPT Nuclear Non-Proliferation Treaty
NSG Nuclear Suppliers Group
OECD Organisation for Economic Co-operation and Development
OHCHR Office of the High Commissioner of Human Rights
OoD Out-of-Distribution [*inputs to neural networks*]
OSET Office of the Secretary-General's Envoy on Technology
OST Outer Space Treaty
PAI Partnership on AI
PGIAI Partnership for Global Inclusivity on AI
PLA People's Liberation Army
REAIM Responsible and Ethical AI in the Military Domain
RFM Robot Foundation Model

RL	Reinforcement Learning
RLAIF	Reinforcement Learning from AI Feedback
RLHF	Reinforcement Learning from Human Feedback
SALT	Strategic Arms Limitation Talks
SCI	Strategic Computing Initiative
STS	Science and Technology Studies
TAI	Transformative AI
TBT	Agreement on Technical Barriers to Trade
TPU	Tensor Processing Units
UAV	Unmanned Aerial Vehicle
UDHR	Universal Declaration of Human Rights
UN	United Nations
UNCLOS	United Nations Convention on the Law of the Sea
UNGA	United Nations General Assembly
UNEP	United Nations Environment Programme
UNESCO	United Nations Educational, Scientific and Cultural Organization
UNICRI	UN Interregional Crime and Justice Research Institute
UNIDIR	United Nations Institute for Disarmament Research
UNODC	United Nations Office on Drugs and Crime
UNU	United Nations University
VCLT	Vienna Convention on the Law of Treaties
VLM	Vision Language Model
WAMI	Wide-Area Motion Imagery
WHO	World Health Organization
WSIS	World Summit on Information Society
WTO	World Trade Organization

Introduction: AI and Change

Prologue

New technologies emerge in many forms. Many arrive on the scene with a flourish of initial public attention before they settle into the background. Some are normalized and become a regular part of the everyday world for us or for our children. Other technologies fail to live up to their initial promise or potential.

Few technologies fundamentally change the human condition in a way that is both broad and deep. Artificial intelligence (AI) will likely be one such transformative technology. In the past decade AI technology has made remarkable progress; within the next, it will come into its own as a major force of global change, for good or ill.

AI has been described as a 'coming wave',[1] with its transformative potential as a generally enabling technology compared by some to fire, electricity, the internal combustion engine, nuclear power (or weapons), or computing.[2] If machine intelligence turns out to be even half as impactful as these past technologies, it will still be one of the key developments of this century. Indeed, its stakes could be even greater, with some arguing that AI will soon constitute one of the most important global challenges facing the world[3] and that, if handled poorly, the most severe outcomes could well be irreversible or even catastrophic for human societies worldwide.[4]

[1] Mustafa Suleyman and Michael Bhaskar, *The Coming Wave: Technology, Power, and the Twenty-First Century's Greatest Dilemma* (Crown 2023).

[2] Lauren Goode, 'Google CEO Sundar Pichai Says AI Is More Profound than Electricity or Fire' (*The Verge*, 19 January 2018) <https://www.theverge.com/2018/1/19/16911354/google-ceo-sundar-pichai-ai-artificial-intelligence-fire-electricity-jobs-cancer> accessed 12 September 2018; Shana Lynch, 'Andrew Ng: Why AI Is the New Electricity' [2017] *Stanford Graduate School of Business* <https://www.gsb.stanford.edu/insights/andrew-ng-why-ai-new-electricity> accessed 22 October 2018; Michael C Horowitz, 'Artificial Intelligence, International Competition, and the Balance of Power' [2018] *Texas National Security Review* <https://tnsr.org/2018/05/artificial-intelligence-international-competition-and-the-balance-of-power/> accessed 17 May 2018; Greg Allen and Taniel Chan, 'Artificial Intelligence and National Security' (Harvard Kennedy School, Belfer Center for Science and International Affairs 2017) <http://www.belfercenter.org/sites/default/files/files/publication/AI%20NatSec%20-%20final.pdf> accessed 19 July 2017.

[3] Yoshua Bengio and others, 'Managing Extreme AI Risks amid Rapid Progress' (2024) 384 Science 842.

[4] Yoshua Bengio and others, 'International AI Safety Report' (2025) DSIT 2025/001 <https://www.gov.uk/government/publications/international-ai-safety-report-2025>; Tom Davidson, 'The Danger of Runaway AI' (2023) 34 Journal of Democracy 132; Atoosa Kasirzadeh, 'Two Types of AI Existential Risk: Decisive and Accumulative' [2025] Philosophical Studies <http://arxiv.org/abs/2401.07836> accessed 20 February 2024; Karina Vold and Daniel R Harris, 'How Does Artificial Intelligence Pose an

Architectures of Global AI Governance. Matthijs M. Maas, Oxford University Press. © Matthijs M. Maas 2025.
DOI: 10.1093/9780191988455.003.0001

For some, these prospects are grounds for anticipation and excitement; for others, they are cause for concern, caution. or even alarm. For all, the stakes involved should be grounds for making deliberate, informed, and effective choices. To choose well in the face of a transformative technology, and to govern it in a deliberate, informed and effective way, is to reckon with questions of change in technology, in society, and in law and governance.

Effective tools of governance will be key in making these choices well, and in determining whether AI becomes a driver of societal progress or decline. Yet while the challenges of AI are widely viewed as increasingly urgent on the global stage, current governance debates struggle to make progress, especially at the global level. Disciplinary gaps along with a disconnect between the changing pace of the technology and international legal approaches to regulating technology mean that governance efforts in response to AI technology are often reactive, fragmented, and grounded in shallow analogies to past technologies or legacy institutions. Unless these knots are untied, effective AI governance may not be established, in time or at all, to allow the world to meet the profound social changes AI will entail.

Humanity is at a crossroads with AI: there is an urgent need to make choices that ensure that regulators and global governance institutions alike are up to the task of governing it well. Will they—will we—succeed? How can we (re)design our global governance institutions to meet the challenges and promises of this increasingly advanced technology?

Summary of the Book

In this book, I aim to explore these questions. The book argues that global governance for AI can and must do better than it has to date, and that it can do so by drawing on the concepts of *sociotechnical change*, *governance disruption*, and *regime complexity*, drawn from established fields such as technology law and global governance scholarship.

These frameworks, the book argues, help ensure that global governance institutions and norms for AI can be adapted or scaled in response to three vectors of ongoing global change: (1) changes in the *sociotechnical problems* to be addressed by governance; (2) changes in the *tools* of governance; (3) changes in the *environment* of governance. These frameworks, the book argues, ground richer analytical descriptions, explanations, and projections of key trends in the emerging global

Existential Risk?' in C Veliz (ed), *Oxford Handbook of Digital Ethics* (Oxford University Press 2021); Yoshua Bengio, 'AI and Catastrophic Risk' (2023) 34 Journal of Democracy 111; Jan Kulveit and others, 'Gradual Disempowerment: Systemic Existential Risks from Incremental AI Development' (arXiv, 29 January 2025) <http://arxiv.org/abs/2501.16946> accessed 31 January 2025; see also the survey of AI researchers in Katja Grace and others, 'Thousands of AI Authors on the Future of AI' (arXiv, 5 January 2024) <http://arxiv.org/abs/2401.02843> accessed 8 January 2024.

architecture of AI governance under these conditions. Simultaneously, they help AI governance advocates and practitioners give greater weight to a range of new approaches and strategies to ensure that institutions and policies will be more *effective* in responding to AI's diverse societal impacts, more *resilient* to future AI-driven disruption to laws, and more *coherent* in terms of the different institutions and norms in the AI governance regime complex. Through this approach, we can adapt our global governance proposals for advanced AI in a manner that is more robust to ongoing and future changes in AI technology, in law, and in international politics.

As such, this book is not just an investigation into how to govern AI, nor just a study of how AI may change governance. It is an exploration of what AI can tell us about the changing nature of global cooperation, today and into the future. How can we govern this changing technology, in a changing world, while using global governance instruments that may themselves become subject to technology-driven change?

This book is split into three parts: it comprehensively explores the foundations of AI governance (Part I); introduces three conceptual lenses for understanding the challenges facing this architecture (Part II); and synthesizes these in a practical framework for analysing and shaping global AI governance (Part III).

Background: The Advanced AI Governance Challenge

AI is significantly reshaping the world. But what is AI? Many debates over the global governance of AI frequently start from, and rapidly flounder on, attempts to pin down a single definition, a challenge compounded by the widely diverse perspectives, framings, and analogies applied to the technology,[5] as well as by the dizzying range of terms for AI systems—including many concepts which are operationalized in different or inconsistent ways.[6] AI researchers have characterized 'AI' as a scientific field focused on 'making machines intelligent, [where] intelligence is that quality that enables an entity to function appropriately and with foresight in its environment'.[7] Yet, in a practical, technical perspective, 'AI' has served as an umbrella term for a motley range of techniques—ranging from traditional

[5] For a survey of framings, see Matthijs Maas, 'AI Is Like . . . A Literature Review of AI Metaphors and Why They Matter for Policy' (Institute for Law & AI 2023) AI Foundations Report 2 <https://law-ai.org/ai-policy-metaphors> accessed 25 February 2025.

[6] Matthijs Maas, 'Concepts in Advanced AI Governance: A Literature Review of Key Terms and Definitions' (Institute for Law & AI 2023) AI Foundations Report 3 < https://law-ai.org/advanced-ai-gov-concepts> accessed 25 February 2025; Elliot Jones, 'Explainer: What Is a Foundation Model?' (Ada Lovelace Institute 2023) <https://www.adalovelaceinstitute.org/resource/foundation-models-explainer/> accessed 31 August 2023. For further discussion of definitions of AI, see also Chapter 1.

[7] Nils J Nilsson, *The Quest for Artificial Intelligence: A History of Ideas and Achievements* (Cambridge University Press 2010) xiii. For a classic overview, see Stuart Russell and Peter Norvig, *Artificial Intelligence: A Modern Approach* (4th edn, Pearson 2020).

rule-based symbolic AI approaches to the more modern data-driven machine learning (ML) approaches which have been responsible for the surge in AI progress this last decade, all the way to the contemporary 'foundation models',[8] such as transformer-based large language models (LLMs),[9] which have over the past few years enabled the swift rise of so-called generative AI[10] and general-purpose AI systems (GPAIS).[11]

In this book, however, I will approach this technology in a broader societal perspective, which considers it as a stack of artefacts, processes, and practices at different levels of abstraction, covering: (1) a diverse suite of computational *techniques* which improve the accuracy, speed, and/or scale of machine decision-making across diverse information-processing or decision-making contexts; which produce (2) *capabilities* that can be used to support, substitute for, or improve upon, human performance in tasks in many domains, such as (among others) data classification or generation, pattern recognition, prediction, optimization, anomaly detection, or autonomous decision-making; which enable (3) useful *applications* across domains and industries; which drive (4) diverse *societal impacts*.

At whichever level we consider AI—techniques, capabilities, applications, or societal impacts—it is increasingly clear that recent years are seeing a rate of system capability progress that is surprising, steep, and (so far) sustained. To be clear, many of today's AI systems remain subject to a range of limitations, and face increasingly steep and restrictive resource requirements. Yet even so, they have at long last begun to demonstrate remarkable capabilities in, and across, many key tasks and domains.[12]

[8] Rishi Bommasani and others, 'On the Opportunities and Risks of Foundation Models' [2021] arXiv:2108.07258 [cs] <http://arxiv.org/abs/2108.07258> accessed 18 August 2021 (defining 'foundation models' as 'models trained on broad data at scale [. . .] that are adaptable to a wide range of downstream tasks').

[9] Helen Toner, 'What Are Generative AI, Large Language Models, and Foundation Models?' (*Center for Security and Emerging Technology*, 12 May 2023) <https://cset.georgetown.edu/article/what-are-generative-ai-large-language-models-and-foundation-models/> accessed 25 May 2023.

[10] Laura Weidinger and others, 'Sociotechnical Safety Evaluation of Generative AI Systems' (arXiv, 18 October 2023) 6 <http://arxiv.org/abs/2310.11986> accessed 20 October 2023 (defining 'generative AI' as 'models that input and output any combination of image, audio, video, and text. This includes transformer-based systems, such as large language models, diffusion-based systems, and hybrid architectures').

[11] See Carlos I Gutierrez and others, 'A Proposal for a Definition of General Purpose Artificial Intelligence Systems' (2023) 2 Digital Society 36 (defining 'general-purpose AI systems' as '[a]n AI system that can accomplish or be adapted to accomplish a range of distinct tasks, including some for which it was not intentionally and specifically trained').

[12] For overviews of trends in AI system performance and application, see generally Nestor Maslej and others, 'The AI Index 2024 Annual Report' (AI Index Steering Committee, Human-Centered AI Initiative, Stanford University 2024) <https://aiindex.stanford.edu/report/?sf187707917=1> accessed 16 April 2024; Epoch, 'AI Trends' (*Epoch*, 11 April 2023) <https://epochai.org/trends> accessed 10 January 2024. For definitions and explanations of AI in a legal context, see Jacob Turner, *Robot Rules: Regulating Artificial Intelligence* (Springer Berlin Heidelberg 2018) 7–21; David Lehr and Paul Ohm, 'Playing with the Data: What Legal Scholars Should Learn About Machine Learning' (2017) 51 UC Davis Law Review 653; Jonas Schuett, 'Defining the Scope of AI Regulations' (2023) 15 Law, Innovation and Technology 1.

As a result, AI has come into its own as a widely applicable set of technologies, with applications in virtually all sectors.[13] While the performance of today's AI systems is not without problems and limits, fewer and fewer people today doubt that AI's development and proliferation will ultimately come to impact every aspect of human society. Indeed, the emergence of increasingly capable and advanced AI systems are, one could suggest, a landmark moment in history. After all, if many human achievements and successes are the result of our 'intelligent' or adaptive behaviour (broadly and functionally defined), then the creation of technologies that manage to automate—or even merely mimic,[14] in a philosophical perspective—even some parts of this capacity is likely a major development,[15] sufficient to drive significant upheaval in all societies that take up this technology.

The Spectrum of AI's Global Challenges

While many hail the benefits that AI could bring to humanity, there is growing public and expert concern about the technology's diverse impacts and challenges.[16]

[13] See Richard Van Noorden and Jeffrey M Perkel, 'AI and Science: What 1,600 Researchers Think' (2023) 621 Nature 672, and previously Maithra Raghu and Eric Schmidt, 'A Survey of Deep Learning for Scientific Discovery' [2020] arXiv:2003.11755 [cs, stat] <http://arxiv.org/abs/2003.11755> accessed 29 June 2020. See also the discussion of various breakthroughs in Chapter 1.

[14] Melanie Mitchell and David C Krakauer, 'The Debate Over Understanding in AI's Large Language Models' (2023) 120 Proceedings of the National Academy of Sciences e2215907120.

[15] Ross Gruetzemacher and Jess Whittlestone, 'The Transformative Potential of Artificial Intelligence' (2022) 135 Futures 102884. However, a counterargument could also be made that AI is in fact far from our first 'intelligence technology', given that past (social) technologies such as markets or bureaucracies have also managed to embed, externalize, and (in some cases) exceed some aspects of human cognition. Allan Dafoe, 'AI Governance: Overview and Theoretical Lenses' in Justin B Bullock and others (eds), *The Oxford Handbook of AI Governance* (Oxford University Press 2023).

[16] For a range of relevant opinion surveys, see also: Noemi Dreksler and others, 'What Does the Public Think About AI? An Overview of the Public's Attitudes towards AI and a Resource for Future Research' (Centre for the Governance of AI 2025) <https://www.governance.ai/research-paper/what-does-the-public-think-about-ai>; Centre for Data Ethics and Innovation, 'International Survey of Public Opinion on AI Safety' (UK Government, Department for Science, Innovation and Technology and Centre for Data Ethics and Innovation 2023) <https://www.gov.uk/government/publications/international-survey-of-public-opinion-on-ai-safety> accessed 11 December 2023; Noemi Dreksler and others, 'Preliminary Survey Results: US and European Publics Overwhelmingly and Increasingly Agree That AI Needs to Be Managed Carefully' (*GovAI Blog*, 17 April 2023) <https://www.governance.ai/post/increasing-consensus-ai-requires-careful-management> accessed 19 April 2023; however, global opinion surveys do show significant regional variation in perceptions and concerns, as seen in Peter John Loewen and others, 'Global Public Opinion on Artificial Intelligence' (Schwartz Reisman Institute for Technology and Society 2024) <https://srinstitute.utoronto.ca/public-opinion-ai> accessed 19 April 2024; other domestic surveys also show rising concerns. For instance, in the US context, see: AI Policy Institute, 'Poll Shows Overwhelming Concern About Risks From AI as New Institute Launches to Understand Public Opinion and Advocate for Responsible AI Policies' (9 August 2023) <https://theaipi.org/poll-shows-overwhelming-concern-about-risks-from-ai-as-new-institute-launches-to-understand-public-opinion-and-advocate-for-responsible-ai-policies/> accessed 10 August 2023; Baobao Zhang and Allan Dafoe, 'U.S. Public Opinion on the Governance of Artificial Intelligence', *Proceedings of the AAAI/ACM Conference on AI, Ethics, and Society* (ACM 2020) <http://dl.acm.org/doi/10.1145/3375627.3375827> accessed 12 February 2020; Ross Gruetzemacher and

Indeed, concerns over these risks may be rapidly growing in recent years.[17] As a technology aimed at automating various human activities either in part or in full, AI, almost by definition, has the potential to reach into virtually any sphere of human activity. The use of AI systems is driving considerable social changes—both for better and for worse—across a staggering array of domains.[18]

Many of these concerns have been exacerbated and scaled up by the ascent of large language models (LLMs), and their application in 'generative AI' tools.[19] Globally, concerns are growing over the contributions AI might make to pervasive economic and social instability,[20] including through large-scale work displacement and possible changes in the nature of work itself.[21] Concurrently, the rise in new military AI systems, which include but are certainly not limited to 'lethal autonomous weapons systems' (LAWS), has raised concerns over these weapons' incompatibility with the laws of war and norms of human dignity; risks of terrorist weaponization; their impacts on the dynamics of interstate crisis instability and even (nuclear) escalation;[22] or their effects on the dynamics of domestic and civil conflict.[23] Furthermore, AI technology is projected to contribute to widespread challenges in political economy, global power relations, surveillance,

others, 'Implications for Governance in Public Perceptions of Societal-Scale AI Risks' (arXiv, 10 June 2024) <http://arxiv.org/abs/2406.06199> accessed 26 July 2024.

[17] For example, one 2023 opinion survey of 3,500 experts across 50 countries, and 20,000 members of the general public in 15 countries, found that concerns over AI had jumped to the 4th-highest rank (from 14th-highest in 2022), and that 64% of risk experts and 70% of the general public believed 'there should be a break in research into AI and other disruptive technologies'. AXA, 'Future Risks Report 2023' (AXA 2023) 5 <https://www.axa.com/en/press/publications/future-risks-report-2023-report> accessed 1 August 2024.

[18] Usman Anwar and others, 'Foundational Challenges in Assuring Alignment and Safety of Large Language Models' 73–104 <https://llm-safety-challenges.github.io/challenges_llms.pdf> accessed 25 February 2025; Iason Gabriel and others, 'The Ethics of Advanced AI Assistants' (Google DeepMind 2024) <https://storage.googleapis.com/deepmind-media/DeepMind.com/Blog/ethics-of-advanced-ai-assistants/the-ethics-of-advanced-ai-assistants-2024-i.pdf> accessed 25 February 2025.

[19] Laura Weidinger and others, 'Taxonomy of Risks Posed by Language Models', *2022 ACM Conference on Fairness, Accountability, and Transparency* (ACM 2022) <https://dl.acm.org/doi/10.1145/3531146.3533088> accessed 8 May 2023.

[20] Nick Bostrom, Allan Dafoe, and Carrick Flynn, 'Public Policy and Superintelligent AI: A Vector Field Approach' in SM Liao (ed), *Ethics of Artificial Intelligence* (Oxford University Press 2019).

[21] Mary L Gray and Siddharth Suri, *Ghost Work: How to Stop Silicon Valley from Building a New Global Underclass* (Houghton Mifflin Harcourt 2019); Carl Benedikt Frey and Michael A Osborne, 'The Future of Employment: How Susceptible Are Jobs to Computerisation?' (2017) 114 Technological Forecasting and Social Change 254. Though for a more optimistic view, see John Danaher, *Automation and Utopia: Human Flourishing in a World without Work* (Harvard University Press 2019).

[22] Nehal Bhuta and others (eds), *Autonomous Weapons Systems: Law, Ethics, Policy* (Cambridge University Press 2016); Jürgen Altmann and Frank Sauer, 'Autonomous Weapon Systems and Strategic Stability' (2017) 59 Survival 117; Matthijs Maas, Kayla Lucero-Matteucci and Di Cooke, 'Military Artificial Intelligence as a Contributor to Global Catastrophic Risk', *The Era of Global Risk* (Open Book Publishers 2023) <https://www.openbookpublishers.com/books/10.11647/obp.0336/chapters/10.11647/obp.0336.10> accessed 9 August 2023.

[23] Lance Y Hunter and others, 'The Fourth Industrial Revolution, Artificial Intelligence, and Domestic Conflict' (2023) 37 Global Society 375.

authoritarianism,[24] and cyber-power,[25] among broader changes to the fabric of international relations.[26] Finally, recent years have seen concern over a set of cross-spectrum societal-scale risks that, many expect, will result from the deployment of increasingly capable general-purpose AI systems at the frontier of the field.[27] Such systems—which may acquire a wide range of new capabilities matched with increasing levels of autonomy—could contribute to a range of significant and potentially global catastrophic risks, deriving from their potential misuse, misalignment, or loss of control over autonomous systems, or from their broader systemic impacts.[28] While still emerging, these risks have become of increasing global and national concern to many governments and international organizations alike.[29]

[24] Allan Dafoe, 'AI Governance: A Research Agenda' (Center for the Governance of AI, Future of Humanity Institute 2018) <https://www.fhi.ox.ac.uk/govaiagenda/> accessed 25 February 2025; Dafoe (n 15).

[25] Joe Devanny, 'Artificial Intelligence and Cyber Power: Foreign Policy Implications' (2024) 63 Research Publications <https://digitalcommons.fiu.edu/jgi_research/63> accessed 25 February 2025.

[26] Stephane J Baele and others, 'AI IR: Charting International Relations in the Age of Artificial Intelligence' (2024) 26 International Studies Review viae013.

[27] These have also been described as 'highly capable foundation models' or 'frontier AI'. See Elizabeth Seger and others, 'Open-Sourcing Highly Capable Foundation Models: An Evaluation of Risks, Benefits, and Alternative Methods for Pursuing Open-Source Objectives' (Centre for the Governance of AI 2023) <https://www.governance.ai/research-paper/open-sourcing-highly-capable-foundation-models>; Markus Anderljung and others, 'Frontier AI Regulation: Managing Emerging Risks to Public Safety' (arXiv, 11 July 2023) <http://arxiv.org/abs/2307.03718> accessed 7 August 2023. However, note that there remains some contestation over the term 'frontier AI', and over how it would be best defined or operationalized in the context of regulation. See Jones (n 6); Helen Toner and Shelton Fitch, 'Regulating the AI Frontier: Design Choices and Constraints' (*Center for Security and Emerging Technology*, 26 October 2023) <https://cset.georgetown.edu/article/regulating-the-ai-frontier-design-choices-and-constraints/> accessed 25 November 2023; Maas, 'Concepts in Advanced AI Governance' (n 6) 50–52. See also Chapter 2.

[28] Bengio and others (n 4); Bengio and others (n 3). Michael K Cohen and others, 'Regulating Advanced Artificial Agents' (2024) 384 Science 36. See also Lewis Ho and others, 'International Institutions for Advanced AI' (arXiv, 10 July 2023) <http://arxiv.org/abs/2307.04699> accessed 11 July 2023. ('the potential dangerous capabilities of powerful and general-purpose AI systems create global externalities in their development and deployment'). For other discussions of the risks from advanced, general-purpose AI systems, see also Pegah Maham and Sabrina Küspert, 'Governing General Purpose AI: A Comprehensive Map of Unreliability, Misuse and Systemic Risks' (Stiftung Neue Verantwortung 2023) <https://www.stiftung-nv.de/de/publikation/governing-general-purpose-ai-comprehensive-map-unreliability-misuse-and-systemic-risks>; Yoshua Bengio, 'International Scientific Report on the Safety of Advanced AI: Interim Report' (Department for Science, Innovation & Technology, and AI Safety Institute 2024) 2024/009 <https://www.gov.uk/government/publications/international-scientific-report-on-the-safety-of-advanced-ai> accessed 21 May 2024.

[29] Department for Science, Innovation & Technology, 'New Commitment to Deepen Work on Severe AI Risks Concludes AI Seoul Summit' (*GOV.UK*, 22 May 2024) <https://www.gov.uk/government/news/new-commitmentto-deepen-work-on-severe-ai-risks-concludes-ai-seoul-summit> accessed 24 May 2024; Government Office for Science, 'Future Risks of Frontier AI: Which Capabilities and Risks Could Emerge at the Cutting Edge of AI in the Future?' (UK Government Office for Science 2023) <https://assets.publishing.service.gov.uk/media/653bc393d10f3500139a6ac5/future-risks-of-frontier-ai-annex-a.pdf> accessed 25 February 2025; Jim Mitre and Joel B Predd, 'Artificial General Intelligence's Five Hard National Security Problems' (RAND Corporation 2025) <https://www.rand.org/pubs/perspectives/PEA3691-4.html> accessed 13 February 2025.

Developments in Global AI Governance

Many national and global polls indicate rising public concern over AI development and its potential risks.[30] There have been growing calls from civil society, policymakers, and, indeed, AI companies themselves, demanding the implementation of policies and regulation to adequately address these challenges.[31]

The technology has also made its way to the top of international and multilateral agendas. In 2023, UN Secretary-General António Guterres identified AI as a technology that would have a 'dramatic impact on sustainable development, the world of work, and the social fabric',[32] and a range of global governance efforts and institutional initiatives for the technology now date back almost a decade.

Yet the difficulty of addressing these challenges internationally is compounded by the (perceived) strategic stakes of AI, and by rising tensions around digital governance as well as over the architecture of global cooperation more broadly.[33] AI, it has been argued, will be 'the biggest geopolitical revolution in human history'.[34] It has been suggested that whichever nation leads in AI technology will dominate global politics for decades to come.[35]

[30] Loewen and others (n 16); Centre for Data Ethics and Innovation (n 16); Dreksler and others (n 16); Zhang and Dafoe (n 16); AI Policy Institute (n 16).

[31] AI Now Institute, 'Zero Trust AI Governance' (Accountable Tech, AI Now Institute, EPIC 2023) <https://ainowinstitute.org/publication/zero-trust-ai-governance>; David McCabe, 'Microsoft Calls for A.I. Rules to Minimize the Technology's Risks' *The New York Times* (25 May 2023) <https://www.nytimes.com/2023/05/25/technology/microsoft-ai-rules-regulation.html> accessed 10 January 2024; Courtney Rozen, 'AI Leaders Are Calling for More Regulation of the Tech. Here's What That May Mean in the US' *Washington Post* (31 July 2023) <https://www.washingtonpost.com/business/2023/07/27/regulate-ai-here-s-what-that-might-mean-in-the-us/f91462c8-2caa-11ee-a948-a5b8a9b62d84_story.html> accessed 10 January 2024. See also Microsoft, 'Global Governance: Goals and Lessons for AI' (Microsoft 2024) <https://aka.ms/AIGlobalGovernanceBook> accessed 25 February 2025.

[32] António Guterres, 'Secretary-General's Remarks to the Security Council on Artificial Intelligence | United Nations Secretary-General' (*United Nations Secretary-General*, 18 July 2023) <https://www.un.org/sg/en/content/sg/speeches/2023-07-18/secretary-generals-remarks-the-security-council-artificial-intelligence> accessed 18 September 2023.

[33] Thorsten Jelinek, Wendell Wallach, and Danil Kerimi, 'Policy Brief: The Creation of a G20 Coordinating Committee for the Governance of Artificial Intelligence' [2020] AI and Ethics <https://doi.org/10.1007/s43681-020-00019-y> accessed 30 October 2020; Ian Bremmer and Mustafa Suleyman, 'The AI Power Paradox' [2023] *Foreign Affairs* <https://www.foreignaffairs.com/world/artificial-intelligence-power-paradox> accessed 24 August 2023.

[34] Kevin Drum, 'Tech World: Welcome to the Digital Revolution' [2018] *Foreign Affairs* 46.

[35] For instance, Indermit Gill has suggested that 'whoever leads in artificial intelligence in 2030 will rule the world until 2100'. Indermit Gill, 'Whoever Leads in Artificial Intelligence in 2030 Will Rule the World until 2100' (*Brookings*, 17 January 2020) <https://www.brookings.edu/blog/future-development/2020/01/17/whoever-leads-in-artificial-intelligence-in-2030-will-rule-the-world-until-2100/> accessed 22 January 2020. Note, however, that an often-repeated claim by Russian President Vladimir Putin, that 'whoever rules AI rules the world', may have been taken out of context: rather than an official statement of Russian foreign policy, this appears to have been an off-the-cuff comment which Putin made in the context of giving young Russian schoolchildren feedback on their science projects. Interview with Robert Wiblin, Keiran Harris, and Allan Dafoe, 'The Academics Preparing for the Possibility that AI Will Destabilise Global Politics' (18 March 2018) <https://80000hours.org/podcast/episodes/allan-dafoe-politics-of-ai/> accessed 12 August 2020.

As such, it should be no surprise that in just a short few years, dozens of nation-states have articulated national AI strategies,[36] and have begun investing vast sums in AI research, application, and the underlying computing hardware infrastructure. Both the US and China, considered global AI powers, consider the technology a lynchpin of their future strategic dominance.[37] Beyond them, a set of challenger states that are relatively new to the AI scene—among them France, Saudi Arabia, South Korea, Singapore, and the United Arab Emirates—have all begun coordinated efforts to develop their own AI industries and become rising powers in the technology.[38] While not all national AI investment programmes have persisted,[39] many of these states are eager to secure their place among the lead innovators in this technology.

[36] For an overview, see: OECD, 'OECD's Live Repository of AI Strategies & Policies' (*OECD AI Policy Observatory*) <https://oecd.ai/en/dashboards> accessed 8 January 2024. For an analysis, see Fernando Filgueiras, 'Artificial Intelligence Policy Regimes: Comparing Politics and Policy to National Strategies for Artificial Intelligence' (2022) 3 Global Perspectives <https://online.ucpress.edu/gp/article/3/1/32362/119790/Artificial-Intelligence-Policy-Regimes-Comparing> accessed 19 May 2022.

[37] In the US, this was initially articulated (in 2016) under the Obama administration: Office of Science and Technology Policy, 'The National Artificial Intelligence Research and Development Strategic Plan' (National Science and Technology Council 2016) <https://obamawhitehouse.archives.gov/sites/default/files/whitehouse_files/microsites/ostp/NSTC/national_ai_rd_strategic_plan.pdf> accessed 26 February 2017. Meanwhile, in 2017 China's State Council issued a plan that anticipated China becoming the world leader in the AI field by 2030: China's State Council, 'A Next Generation Artificial Intelligence Development Plan' (Rogier Creemers and others trs, New America Cybersecurity Initiative 2017) <https://na-production.s3.amazonaws.com/documents/translation-fulltext-8.1.17.pdf> accessed 23 October 2017.

[38] Mark Bergen, 'Microsoft to Invest €4 Billion in French Cloud and AI Services' *Bloomberg.com* (13 May 2024) <https://www.bloomberg.com/news/articles/2024-05-13/microsoft-to-invest-4-billion-in-french-cloud-ai-services> accessed 6 June 2024; Commission de l'Intelligence Artificielle, 'Our AI: Our Ambition for France' (2024) <https://www.info.gouv.fr/upload/media/content/0001/09/02cbcb40c3541390be391feb3d963a4126b12598.pdf> accessed 10 April 2024; Noah Greene, 'Will France Be the AI Hub of Continental Europe?' (*Tech Policy Press*, 2 April 2024) <https://techpolicy.press/will-france-be-the-ai-hub-of-continental-europe> accessed 6 June 2024; Adam Satariano and Paul Mozur, '"To the Future": Saudi Arabia Spends Big to Become an A.I. Superpower' *The New York Times* (25 April 2024) <https://www.nytimes.com/2024/04/25/technology/saudi-arabia-ai.html> accessed 6 June 2024; Reuters, 'South Korea to Invest $7 Billion in AI in Bid to Retain Edge in Chips' *Reuters* (9 April 2024) <https://www.reuters.com/technology/south-korea-invest-7-bln-ai-bid-retain-edge-chips-2024-04-09/> accessed 6 June 2024; Sheila Chiang, 'Singapore's AI Ambitions Get a Boost with $740 Million Investment Plan' (*CNBC*, 19 February 2024) <https://www.cnbc.com/2024/02/19/singapores-ai-ambitions-get-a-boost-with-740-million-investment-plan.html> accessed 6 June 2024; Billy Perrigo, 'The UAE Is on a Mission to Become an AI Power' (*TIME*, 20 March 2024) <https://time.com/6958369/artificial-intelligence-united-arab-emirates/> accessed 6 June 2024.

[39] For instance, one notable case of policy reversal came from the United Kingdom. In March 2023, the UK Conservative government under Rishi Sunak announced a national GBP 900 million exascale supercomputer investment dedicated to AI development, along with a GBP 500 million AI Research Resource computing reserve. Dan Milmo and Alex Hern, 'UK to Invest £900m in Supercomputer in Bid to Build Own "BritGPT"' *The Guardian* (15 March 2023) <https://www.theguardian.com/technology/2023/mar/15/uk-to-invest-900m-in-supercomputer-in-bid-to-build-own-britgpt> accessed 8 January 2024. However, less than a year later, the UK's new Labour government reversed course, abandoning the projects. Zoe Kleinman, 'Government Shelves £1.3bn UK Tech and AI Plans' *BBC* (2 August 2024) <https://www.bbc.com/news/articles/cyx5x44vnyeo> accessed 5 August 2024.

Likewise, in the military domain, a range of influential countries have steadily scaled up their AI investments,[40] as well as establishing various strategic partnerships to facilitate the development of AI weapons and military support systems.[41] As a result, some claim we are seeing a new global 'arms race' in all but name, or even an impending 'Cold War' to be fought within the domain of AI,[42] while others anticipate the rise of 'techno-nationalism' around AI.[43]

Even if AI's technological trajectory were not, eventually, to fulfil these ambitious promises, and even if zero-sum framings of global AI development as a race might be misconceived or even hazardous,[44] such depictions increasingly shape global debates, setting the terms for governance efforts.[45]

[40] Justin Haner and Denise Garcia, 'The Artificial Intelligence Arms Race: Trends and World Leaders in Autonomous Weapons Development' (2019) 10 Global Policy 331.

[41] Lena Trabucco and Matthijs M Maas, 'Technology Ties: The Rise and Roles of Military AI Strategic Partnerships' (10 November 2023) <https://papers.ssrn.com/abstract=4629283> accessed 10 November 2023; Zoe Stanley-Lockman, 'Military AI Cooperation Toolbox: Modernizing Defense Science and Technology Partnerships for the Digital Age' (Center for Security and Emerging Technology 2021) <https://cset.georgetown.edu/wp-content/uploads/CSET-Military-AI-Cooperation-Toolbox.pdf> accessed 23 August 2021.

[42] Edward Moore Geist, 'It's Already Too Late to Stop the AI Arms Race—We Must Manage It Instead' (2016) 72 Bulletin of the Atomic Scientists 318; Haner and Garcia (n 40); Kai-Fu Lee, *AI Superpowers: China, Silicon Valley, and the New World Order* (Houghton Mifflin Harcourt 2018); Nicholas Thompson and Ian Bremmer, 'The AI Cold War That Threatens Us All' [2018] *Wired* <https://www.wired.com/story/ai-cold-war-china-could-doom-us-all/> accessed 20 November 2018; Michael Auslin, 'Can the Pentagon Win the AI Arms Race?' [2018] *Foreign Affairs* <https://www.foreignaffairs.com/articles/united-states/2018-10-19/can-pentagon-win-ai-arms-race> accessed 20 November 2018; Julian E Barnes and Josh Chin, 'The New Arms Race in AI' *Wall Street Journal* (2 March 2018) <https://www.wsj.com/articles/the-new-arms-race-in-ai-1520009261> accessed 22 November 2018.

[43] Claudio Feijóo and others, 'Harnessing Artificial Intelligence (AI) to Increase Wellbeing for All: The Case for a New Technology Diplomacy' (2020) 44 Telecommunications Policy 101988. See also Ian Hogarth, 'AI Nationalism' (*Ian Hogarth*, 13 June 2018) <https://www.ianhogarth.com/blog/2018/6/13/ai-nationalism> accessed 23 July 2018.

[44] For a range of critiques of the 'arms race' framing, on empirical, conceptual and normative grounds, see for instance Stephen Cave and Seán S ÓhÉigeartaigh, 'An AI Race for Strategic Advantage: Rhetoric and Risks', *Proceedings of the 2018 AAAI/ACM Conference on AI, Ethics, and Society* (ACM 2018) <https://dl.acm.org/doi/10.1145/3278721.3278780> accessed 12 December 2020; Seán Ó hÉigeartaigh, 'The Most Dangerous Fiction: The Rhetoric and Reality of the AI Race' in Max Rangeley and Nicholas Fairfax (eds), *The Artificial Intelligence Revolution* (Springer Nature 2025) <https://papers.ssrn.com/abstract=5278644> accessed 5 June 2025; and previously: Heather M Roff, 'The Frame Problem: The AI "Arms Race" Isn't One' (2019) 75 Bulletin of the Atomic Scientists 3; Remco Zwetsloot, Helen Toner, and Jeffrey Ding, 'Beyond the AI Arms Race: America, China, and the Dangers of Zero-Sum Thinking' [2018] *Foreign Affairs* <https://www.foreignaffairs.com/reviews/review-essay/2018-11-16/beyond-ai-arms-race> accessed 20 November 2018; Elsa Kania, 'The Pursuit of AI Is More Than an Arms Race' [2018] *Defense One* <https://www.defenseone.com/ideas/2018/04/pursuit-ai-more-arms-race/147579/> accessed 26 April 2018; Arthur Holland Michel, 'Recalibrating Assumptions on AI: Towards an Evidence-Based and Inclusive AI Policy Discourse' (Chatham House 2023) 22–27 <https://www.chathamhouse.org/2023/04/recalibrating-assumptions-ai> accessed 11 June 2024; Kerry McInerney, 'Yellow Techno-Peril: The "Clash of Civilizations" and Anti-Chinese Racial Rhetoric in the US–China AI Arms Race' (2024) 11 Big Data & Society 2.

[45] This should be somewhat nuanced. Already in 2020, a report by the Center for Security and Emerging Technology reviewed coverage of AI in 4,000 English-language articles over a seven-year period, and found that while a growing number of these framed AI development as a competition, these represented a declining proportion of all articles about AI, suggesting narratives around AI are becoming more diverse. Andrew Imbrie and others, 'Mainframes: A Provisional Analysis of Rhetorical Frames in AI' (Center for Security and Emerging Technology 2020) <https://cset.georgetown.edu/research/mainframes-a-provisional-analysis-of-rhetorical-frames-in-ai/> accessed 18 August 2020.

Nonetheless, the stakes of AI have also prompted significant energy and attention for renewed international cooperation in order to govern this technology well, and bend its impacts towards peace, human rights, safety, and welfare. Nonetheless, at the international level, debates around the global governance of AI are relatively novel, having only started in the early 2010s and not picking up sustained momentum until around 2016.[46] However, the pace of such initiatives has increased rapidly since; according to an ongoing inventory of AI regulatory initiatives maintained by the Council of Europe, international organizations (IOs) overtook national authorities as the main source of AI regulation initiatives in 2020, with national authorities launching 170 policy initiatives between 2015 and 2022, and IOs establishing 210 initiatives in the same period.[47]

Much of this activity initially proceeded along parallel tracks for military and (narrow, conventional) civilian AI. Early debates in AI governance focused predominantly on the military domain, and the threats from LAWS.[48] This is perhaps not surprising, given how the spectre of 'killer robots' is one that is both particularly visceral within the popular imagination as well as an issue that is located squarely in the domain of international peace and security, a founding concern of the global legal order.[49] However, there has also been substantial growth in broader global AI governance efforts for conventional, narrow AI systems. This includes an explosive increase in the number of AI ethics codes issued,[50] an accompanying rise in discussions exploring many important questions in the global governance of AI,[51] and a wide range of governance initiatives ranging from private governance

[46] For a history of these governance developments, see also Chapter 3.

[47] Council of Europe, 'Datavisualisation of AI Initiatives' (*Artificial Intelligence*, 2023) <https://www.coe.int/en/web/artificial-intelligence/national-initiatives> accessed 8 January 2024; Jonas Tallberg and others, 'The Global Governance of Artificial Intelligence: Next Steps for Empirical and Normative Research' (2023) 25 International Studies Review viad040, 5–6. Note, however, that the OECD AI Policy Observatory has registered more than 1,000 AI policy initiatives, across 69 countries and territories. See OECD, 'OECD's Live Repository of AI Strategies & Policies' (n 36).

[48] Bhuta and others (n 22); Human Rights Watch, *Losing Humanity: The Case against Killer Robots* (Human Rights Watch 2012) <https://www.hrw.org/sites/default/files/reports/arms1112_ForUpload.pdf> accessed 25 February 2025; Thomas Burri, 'International Law and Artificial Intelligence' (2017) 60 German Yearbook of International Law 91.

[49] Colin B Picker, 'A View from 40,000 Feet: International Law and the Invisible Hand of Technology' (2001) 23 Cardozo Law Review 151.

[50] Anna Jobin, Marcello Ienca, and Effy Vayena, 'The Global Landscape of AI Ethics Guidelines' [2019] Nature Machine Intelligence 1; Jessica Fjeld and others, 'Principled Artificial Intelligence: Mapping Consensus in Ethical and Rights-Based Approaches to Principles for AI' <https://dash.harvard.edu/handle/1/42160420> accessed 16 January 2020; Yi Zeng, Enmeng Lu, and Cunqing Huangfu, 'Linking Artificial Intelligence Principles' [2018] arXiv:1812.04814 [cs] <http://arxiv.org/abs/1812.04814> accessed 30 January 2019.

[51] For overviews, see James Butcher and Irakli Beridze, 'What Is the State of Artificial Intelligence Governance Globally?' (2019) 164 The RUSI Journal 88; Angela Daly and others, 'Artificial Intelligence Governance and Ethics: Global Perspectives' (2019) <https://arxiv.org/ftp/arxiv/papers/1907/1907.03848.pdf> accessed 28 June 2019; Daniel Schiff and others, 'What's Next for AI Ethics, Policy, and Governance? A Global Overview' (ACM 2020) <https://econpapers.repec.org/paper/osfsocarx/8jaz4.htm> accessed 12 January 2020.

initiatives and industry partnerships, standard-setting organizations, various UN initiatives and instruments,[52] and major non-binding principles from the OECD,[53] the G20,[54] and UNESCO,[55] as well as recently concluded negotiations on binding legal frameworks for AI, in the forms of the EU AI Act and the Council of Europe Framework Convention on Artificial Intelligence and Human Rights, Democracy, and the Rule of Law.[56] There have also been steps towards the establishment of new organizations and institutions, such as the 2020 Global Partnership on AI (GPAI).[57]

Moreover, the period from 2023 to 2025 and onwards has seen a flurry of multilateral and institutional activity in response to the acute global attention for the potential extreme risks and impacts of increasingly advanced and general-purpose AI systems, including the 2023 UK AI Safety Summit and the Bletchley Declaration,[58] the 2024 Seoul Declaration and Statement of Intent,[59] new provisions on

[52] Eugenio V Garcia, 'Multilateralism and Artificial Intelligence: What Role for the United Nations?' in Maurizio Tinnirello (ed), *The Global Politics of Artificial Intelligence* (CRC Press 2020) <https://papers.ssrn.com/sol3/papers.cfm?abstract_id=3779866> 25 February 2025.

[53] OECD, 'Recommendation of the Council on Artificial Intelligence' <https://legalinstruments.oecd.org/en/instruments/OECD-LEGAL-0449> accessed 28 May 2019.

[54] G20, 'G20 Ministerial Statement on Trade and Digital Economy' <https://www.mofa.go.jp/files/000486596.pdf> accessed 25 May 2020.

[55] UNESCO, 'Recommendation on the Ethics of Artificial Intelligence' <https://unesdoc.unesco.org/ark:/48223/pf0000381137> accessed 6 September 2023.

[56] European Council, 'Artificial Intelligence (AI) Act: Council Gives Final Green Light to the First Worldwide Rules on AI' (21 May 2024) <https://www.consilium.europa.eu/en/press/press-releases/2024/05/21/artificial-intelligence-ai-act-council-gives-final-green-light-to-the-first-worldwide-rules-on-ai/> accessed 22 May 2024; Council of Europe, 'Council of Europe Adopts First International Treaty on Artificial Intelligence' (*Council of Europe, Newsroom*, 17 May 2024) <https://www.coe.int/en/web/portal/-/council-of-europe-adopts-first-international-treaty-on-artificial-intelligence> accessed 22 May 2024.

[57] Global Partnership on Artificial Intelligence, 'Joint Statement from Founding Members of the Global Partnership on Artificial Intelligence' <https://www.gov.uk/government/publications/joint-statement-from-founding-members-of-the-global-partnership-on-artificial-intelligence>.

[58] UK Government, 'The Bletchley Declaration by Countries Attending the AI Safety Summit, 1-2 November 2023' (*GOV.UK*, 1 November 2023) <https://www.gov.uk/government/publications/ai-safety-summit-2023-the-bletchley-declaration/the-bletchley-declaration-by-countries-attending-the-ai-safety-summit-1-2-november-2023> accessed 3 November 2023.

[59] 'Seoul Declaration for Safe, Innovative and Inclusive AI by Participants Attending the Leaders' Session: AI Seoul Summit, 21 May 2024' (*Department for Science, Innovation & Technology, GOV.UK*, 21 May 2024) <https://www.gov.uk/government/publications/seoul-declaration-for-safe-innovative-and-inclusive-ai-ai-seoul-summit-2024/seoul-declaration-for-safe-innovative-and-inclusive-ai-by-participants-attending-the-leaders-session-ai-seoul-summit-21-may-2024> accessed 22 May 2024; 'Seoul Statement of Intent toward International Cooperation on AI Safety Science, AI Seoul Summit 2024 (Annex)' (*Department for Science, Innovation & Technology, GOV.UK*, 21 May 2024) <https://www.gov.uk/government/publications/seoul-declaration-for-safe-innovative-and-inclusive-ai-ai-seoul-summit-2024/seoul-statement-of-intent-toward-international-cooperation-on-ai-safety-science-ai-seoul-summit-2024-annex> accessed 22 May 2024; Department for Science, Innovation & Technology, 'Global Leaders Agree to Launch First International Network of AI Safety Institutes to Boost Cooperation of AI' (*GOV.UK*, 21 May 2024) <https://www.gov.uk/government/news/global-leaders-agree-to-launch-first-international-network-of-ai-safety-institutes-to-boost-understanding-of-ai> accessed 22 May 2024.

general-purpose AI systems in the EU AI Act,[60] the 2023 G7 Hiroshima AI Process,[61] and major new national regulatory initiatives in the US and China.[62]

Many proposals have been made for the way forward. In the field's early years, many focused on how existing international law might be directly applied to AI,[63] or how we might extend or adapt the mandates of existing organizations.[64] However, since 2022 there have been renewed calls for the establishment of entirely new international organizations specifically for AI. These proposals range widely.[65] Among them, we have seen designs for an International Panel on Artificial Intelligence Safety (IPAIS),[66] an AI Observatory,[67] an International AI Organization (IAIO) to certify state jurisdictions compliance with international standards,[68] international consortia for the testing and evaluation of advanced AI systems,[69] or broad-based

[60] Benjamin Larsen and Sabrina Küspert, 'Regulating General-Purpose AI: Areas of Convergence and Divergence across the EU and the US' (*Brookings*, 21 May 2024) <https://www.brookings.edu/articles/regulating-general-purpose-ai-areas-of-convergence-and-divergence-across-the-eu-and-the-us/> accessed 22 May 2024; Cornelia Kutterer, 'Regulating Foundation Models in the AI Act: From "High" to "Systemic" Risk' (*MIAI*, 11 January 2024) <https://ai-regulation.com/regulating-foundation-models-in-the-ai-act-from-high-to-systemic-risk/> accessed 31 January 2024.

[61] OECD, 'G7 Hiroshima Process on Generative Artificial Intelligence (AI): Towards a G7 Common Understanding on Generative AI' (OECD 2023) <https://www.oecd-ilibrary.org/science-and-technology/g7-hiroshima-process-on-generative-artificial-intelligence-ai_bf3c0c60-en> accessed 13 September 2023.

[62] Executive Office of the President, 'Executive Order on the Safe, Secure, and Trustworthy Development and Use of Artificial Intelligence' (*The White House*, 30 October 2023) <https://bidenwhitehouse.archives.gov/briefing-room/presidential-actions/2023/10/30/executive-order-on-the-safe-secure-and-trustworthy-development-and-use-of-artificial-intelligence/> accessed 3 November 2023. Cyberspace Administration of China, 'Interim Measures for the Management of Generative Artificial Intelligence Services' (*China Law Translate*, 13 July 2023) <https://www.chinalawtranslate.com/generative-ai-interim/> accessed 13 January 2024.

[63] Martina Kunz and Seán Ó hÉigeartaigh, 'Artificial Intelligence and Robotization' in Robin Geiß and Nils Melzer (eds), *The Oxford Handbook of the International Law of Global Security* (Oxford University Press 2021); Mark Chinen, *The International Governance of Artificial Intelligence* (Edward Elgar Publishing 2023).

[64] Rumtin Sepasspour, 'A Reality Check and a Way Forward for the Global Governance of Artificial Intelligence' [2023] 79 Bulletin of the Atomic Scientists 304. <https://doi.org/10.1080/00963402.2023.2245249>; Jelinek, Wallach, and Kerimi (n 33).

[65] Matthijs M Maas and José Jaime Villalobos, 'International AI Institutions: A Literature Review of Models, Examples, and Proposals' (Institute for Law & AI 2023) 1 <https://law-ai.org/international-ai-institutions>; Ho and others (n 28).

[66] Mustafa Suleyman and others, 'Proposal for an International Panel on Artificial Intelligence (AI) Safety (IPAIS): Summary' (*Carnegie Endowment for International Peace*, 27 October 2023) <https://carnegieendowment.org/2023/10/27/proposal-for-international-panel-on-artificial-intelligence-ai-safety-ipais-summary-pub-90862> accessed 29 November 2023.

[67] Geoff Mulgan and others, 'The Case for a Global AI Observatory (GAIO)' (*Carnegie Council for Ethics in International Affairs*, 6 June 2023) <https://www.carnegiecouncil.org/media/article/the-case-for-a-global-ai-observatory-gaio-2023> accessed 3 September 2023.

[68] Robert Trager and others, 'International Governance of Civilian AI: A Jurisdictional Certification Approach' (arXiv, 29 August 2023) <http://arxiv.org/abs/2308.15514> accessed 31 August 2023.

[69] Ross Gruetzemacher and others, 'An International Consortium for AI Risk Evaluations' (2023) <https://openreview.net/forum?id=HoIEKQhiRs> accessed 17 December 2023; Jason Hausenloy, Andrea Miotti, and Claire Dennis, 'Multinational AGI Consortium (MAGIC): A Proposal for International Coordination on AI' (arXiv, 13 October 2023) <http://arxiv.org/abs/2310.09217> accessed 3 November 2023; see also more generally Shayne Longpre and others, 'A Safe Harbor for AI

benefit and access-providing organizations.[70] Notably, these proposals often draw an analogy to or are outright modelled on the template of one or another extant international organization,[71] such as the International Atomic Energy Agency (IAEA),[72] the European Organisation for Nuclear Research (CERN),[73] the International Civil Aviation Organisation (ICAO),[74] or the Intergovernmental Panel on Climate Change (IPCC).[75]

Indeed, many of these proposals have gained uptake at a high political level. Global figures ranging from UN Secretary-General António Guterres to OpenAI's CEO Sam Altman, and from former UK Prime Minister Rishi Sunak to a range of former heads of state, have all supported the idea of establishing an AI equivalent of the IAEA.[76] European Commission President Ursula von der Leyen has advocated for a new AI risk-monitoring body modelled on the IPCC,[77] as well as an

Evaluation and Red Teaming' (arXiv, 7 March 2024) <http://arxiv.org/abs/2403.04893> accessed 2 April 2024.

[70] Ho and others (n 28).

[71] ibid; Maas and Villalobos (n 65); see also Siegele, 'A Global Agency to Oversee AI Is a Tall Order' [2023] *The Economist* <https://www.economist.com/the-world-ahead/2023/11/13/a-global-agency-to-oversee-ai-is-a-tall-order> accessed 10 January 2024. See also Microsoft (n 31) (reviewing the examples of ICAO, CERN, IAEA, IPCC, and a cluster of organizations active in financial governance, specifically the Bank for International Settlements, Basel, the Financial Stability Board, and the Financial Action Task Force).

[72] Sam Altman, Greg Brockman, and Ilya Sutskever, 'Governance of Superintelligence' (*OpenAI*, 22 May 2023) <https://openai.com/blog/governance-of-superintelligence> accessed 23 May 2023; Eoghan Stafford and Robert F Trager, 'The IAEA Solution: Knowledge Sharing to Prevent Dangerous Technology Races' (Centre for the Governance of AI 2022) <https://www.governance.ai/research-paper/knowledge-sharing-to-prevent-dangerous-technology-races>; Harry Law and Lewis Ho, 'Can a Dual Mandate Be a Model for the Global Governance of AI?' [2023] Nature Reviews Physics 1; Mark Robinson, 'The Establishment of an International AI Agency: An Applied Solution to Global AI Governance' [2025] *International Affairs* iiaf105.

[73] Gary Marcus, 'Two Models of AI Oversight—and How Things Could Go Deeply Wrong' [2023] Communications of the ACM <https://cacm.acm.org/blogs/blog-cacm/273791-two-models-of-ai-oversight-and-how-things-could-go-deeply-wrong/fulltext> accessed 19 September 2023; Andrea Miotti, 'We Can Prevent AI Disaster Like We Prevented Nuclear Catastrophe' [2023] *Time* <https://time.com/6314045/prevent-ai-disaster-nuclear-catastrophe/> accessed 18 September 2023. For a discussion of the CERN analogy, and how it has been used in global AI governance debates, see also Kevin Kohler, 'CERN for AI: An Overview' (*AI Analogies*, 7 May 2024) <https://machinocene.substack.com/p/cern-for-ai-an-overview> accessed 23 May 2024.

[74] Brad Smith, 'Advancing AI Governance in Europe and Internationally' (*Microsoft—EU Policy Blog*, 29 June 2023) <https://blogs.microsoft.com/eupolicy/2023/06/29/advancing-ai-governance-europe-brad-smith/> accessed 10 January 2024; summarizing: Microsoft, 'Governing AI: A Blueprint for the Future' (Microsoft 2023) <https://cdn-dynmedia-1.microsoft.com/is/content/microsoftcorp/microsoft/msc/documents/presentations/CSR/Governing-AI-A-Blueprint-for-the-Future.pdf> accessed 25 February 2025; Trager and others (n 68).

[75] Joseph Bak-Coleman and others, 'Create an IPCC-like Body to Harness Benefits and Combat Harms of Digital Tech' (2023) 617 Nature 462; Suleyman and others (n 66).

[76] Altman, Brockman, and Sutskever (n 72); Michelle Nichols, 'UN Chief Backs Idea of Global AI Watchdog like Nuclear Agency' *Reuters* (12 June 2023) <https://www.reuters.com/technology/un-chief-backs-idea-global-ai-watchdog-like-nuclear-agency-2023-06-12/> accessed 10 January 2024; Mary Robinson, 'The Elders Urge Global Co-Operation to Manage Risks and Share Benefits of AI' (31 May 2023) <https://theelders.org/news/elders-urge-global-co-operation-manage-risks-and-share-benefits-ai> accessed 31 May 2023.

[77] Marine Strauss, 'EU's von Der Leyen Speaks to European Lawmakers' *Reuters* (13 September 2023) <https://www.reuters.com/world/europe/eus-von-der-leyen-speaks-european-lawmakers-2023-09-13/> accessed 10 January 2024.

'European AI Research Council' modelled on CERN, with a potential budget of €100 billion;[78] Before his passing, the late Pope Francis called for a legally binding international treaty on AI,[79] reflecting a concern with the technology that has also been taken up by his successor Pope Leo XIV. Many of these ideas are now avidly pursued by governments and in international bodies.[80]

These ideas are in the air, and—at the time of writing—they are gaining traction within international fora.[81] Others have reacted and pushed back, arguing that new institutions are not at all needed, since AI issues can be adequately governed within existing international initiatives.[82] At the same time, in early 2025, many AI governance initiatives—along with many other areas and institutional structures of international law generally—received significant shocks as a result of pivots in the geopolitical priorities of the US.[83]

Under these challenging technological and political conditions, governments will likely decide within the next few years on whether to establish any global body for AI and—if so—what kind of organization should be pursued, or—if not—how to instead organize the global governance architecture for AI. Are we ready to make such decisions?

[78] Jacob Wulff Wold, 'Von Der Leyen Gives Nod to €100 Billion "CERN for AI" Proposal' *Euractiv* (25 July 2024) <https://www.euractiv.com/section/digital/news/von-der-leyen-gives-nod-to-e100-billion-cern-for-ai-proposal/> accessed 30 July 2024 (noting that this budget—slated over five to seven years—would 'exceed the European Commission's entire seven-year research budget for Horizon Europe, which is €95.5 billion').

[79] Philip Pullella, 'Pope Francis Calls for Binding Global Treaty to Regulate AI' *Reuters* (14 December 2023) <https://www.reuters.com/technology/pope-calls-binding-global-treaty-artificial-intelligence-2023-12-14/> accessed 10 January 2024.

[80] Inter-Agency Working Group on Artificial Intelligence (IAWG-AI), 'United Nations System White Paper on Artificial Intelligence Governance: An Analysis of Current Institutional Models and Related Functions and Existing International Normative Frameworks within the United Nations System That Are Applicable to Artificial Intelligence Governance' (United Nations Chief Executives Board for Coordination 2024) CEB/2024/1/Add.1 <https://unsceb.org/sites/default/files/2024-11/UNSystemWhitePaperAIGovernance.pdf> accessed 14 January 2025.

[81] High-Level Advisory Body on Artificial Intelligence, 'Governing AI for Humanity: Final Report' (United Nations 2024) <https://www.un.org/sites/un2.un.org/files/governing_ai_for_humanity_final_report_en.pdf>. Inter-Agency Working Group on Artificial Intelligence (IAWG-AI) (n 80). See also Allison Stanger and others, 'Terra Incognita: The Governance of Artificial Intelligence in Global Perspective' <https://www.annualreviews.org/content/journals/10.1146/annurev-polisci-041322-042247> accessed 18 April 2024; Mark Coeckelbergh, 'The Case for Global Governance of AI: Arguments, Counter-Arguments, and Challenges Ahead' [2024] AI & Society <https://doi.org/10.1007/s00146-024-01949-5> accessed 4 May 2024.

[82] Huw Roberts and others, 'Global AI Governance: Barriers and Pathways Forward' [2024] International Affairs iiae073; Cameron F Kerry, 'The Good, the Not-so-Good, and the Ugly of the UN's Blueprint for AI' (*Brookings*, 29 August 2024) <https://www.brookings.edu/articles/the-good-the-not-so-good-and-the-ugly-of-the-uns-blueprint-for-ai/> accessed 2 September 2024; Emma Klein and Stewart Patrick, 'Envisioning a Global Regime Complex to Govern Artificial Intelligence' (Carnegie Endowment for International Peace 2024) <https://carnegieendowment.org/research/2024/03/envisioning-a-global-regime-complex-to-govern-artificial-intelligence?lang=en> accessed 13 June 2024.

[83] Giulia Torchio and Francesco Tasin, 'The Paris Summit: Au Revoir, Global AI Safety?' (*European Policy Centre*, 14 February 2025) <https://epc.eu/en/Publications/The-Paris-Summit-Au-Revoir-global-AI-Safety~61ea68> accessed 19 February 2025; see generally Monica Hakimi and Jacob Katz Cogan, 'The End of the U.S.-Backed International Order and the Future of International Law' [2025] American Journal of International Law 1.

The Hurdles to Global Governance, and a Window of Opportunity for AI

Clearly, this is an active and exciting time for AI governance. However, the field remains at a vulnerable and uncertain juncture. Many AI governance initiatives are still relatively incipient and fragmented, while AI is developing rapidly, and its adoption proceeds apace. It remains unclear what trajectory existing global governance regimes may take in the coming years, whether or not they will be able to keep pace with the technology, and what is the need for, feasibility of, or optimal design for any new international institutions within that landscape.

All this matters, because in spite of AI's high public profile—or because of it—regulatory success is certainly not guaranteed. To be sure, the idea of multilateralism as dead or irrecoverable may, even today, be premature. As noted by Benvenisti and Downs, '[h]istorically, reports about the death of international law are invariably premature'.[84] While international law has a chequered history, it is one that includes periods where it saw landmark achievements—including shifts in norms which were well in excess of initial expectations—that are often invisible today only because they have become largely normalized.[85] Today, many parts of the international legal architecture, and many global governance regimes, still operate quietly in the background, with most states still meeting most of their binding international commitments,[86] even in high-stakes contexts.[87] Even in the current period of crisis,[88] such systems will continue to be necessary and relevant—even if they may need to evolve in response.

However, guarded optimism should not distract us from the real challenges that face the global governance architecture generally, or the global governance of AI specifically. In spite of the considerable—and often under-appreciated—achievements

[84] Eyal Benvenisti and George W Downs, 'Comment on Nico Krisch, "The Decay of Consent: International Law in an Age of Global Public Goods"' (2014) 108 AJIL Unbound 1, 2.

[85] See notably Oona A Hathaway and Scott J Shapiro, *The Internationalists: How a Radical Plan to Outlaw War Remade the World* (Simon & Schuster 2017) (arguing that the 1928 Kellogg-Briand Pact to outlaw war, often remembered critically for failing to avert the Second World War, nonetheless precipitated a significant change in the international legal status of war which, not just immediately but also in the post-War world, drove lasting shifts in State perceptions of—and incentives around—wars of conquest and gunboat diplomacy, significantly affecting the subsequent occurrence of these historically ubiquitous practices and providing more leeway for the use of third-party sanctions while maintaining neutrality and setting the foundations for the modern UN system). See also Oona Hathaway and Scott J Shapiro, 'What Realists Don't Understand About Law' (*Foreign Policy*, 9 October 2017) <https://foreignpolicy.com/2017/10/09/what-realists-dont-understand-about-law/> accessed 17 April 2019 ('this [sceptical] reaction reveals a misunderstanding about how law works. When it is most effective, the law doesn't induce states to act contrary to incentives; it changes those incentives themselves').

[86] This recalls Louis Henkin's observation (though made of a different era) that 'almost all nations observe almost all principles of international law and almost all of their obligations almost all of the time'. Louis Henkin, *How Nations Behave: Law and Foreign Policy* (Columbia University Press 1979) 47; cited in Rebecca Crootof, 'Jurisprudential Space Junk: Treaties and New Technologies' in Chiara Giorgetti and Natalie Klein (eds), *Resolving Conflicts in the Law* (Brill | Nijhoff 2019) 109.

[87] See again Hathaway and Shapiro (n 85).

[88] Hakimi and Cogan (n 83).

of international law in many domains over the past decades and centuries, it is also painfully clear that global governance actors do not always rise to emergent challenges in time—or at all.

For example, even as recent decades have seen a global proliferation in new international institutions and agreements,[89] the coverage of global issues remains partial. Numerous pressing global problems simply remain mostly or entirely ungoverned—under-institutionalized,[90] locked into a 'non-regime' state.[91]

Among such pressing issues that remain in relative international regulatory limbo are challenges such as coral reef degradation,[92] the accumulation of space junk, the recognition of professional qualifications for migrants, and the regulation of potential chemical endocrine disruptors;[93] global plastic pollution;[94] foreign surveillance activities and intelligence collection activities affecting state leaders or foreign private citizens;[95] many forms of cyber operations[96] and cyber-attacks;[97] the security of the internet-critical global submarine cable infrastructure,[98] and the

[89] Karen J Alter and Kal Raustiala, 'The Rise of International Regime Complexity' (2018) 14 Annual Review of Law and Social Science 329. See also Chapter 6.

[90] See Jean-Frédéric Morin and others, 'How Informality Can Address Emerging Issues: Making the Most of the G7' (2019) 10 Global Policy 267, 2.

[91] Dimitrov and colleagues have called this a 'nonregime' state. Radoslav S Dimitrov and others, 'International Nonregimes: A Research Agenda' (2007) 9 International Studies Review 230 (defining 'nonregimes' as 'transnational policy arenas characterized by the absence of multilateral agreements for policy coordination among states').

[92] Rado S Dimitrov, 'Confronting Nonregimes: Science and International Coral Reef Policy' (2002) 11 The Journal of Environment & Development 53.

[93] See also Anne van Aaken, 'Is International Law Conducive To Preventing Looming Disasters?' (2016) 7 Global Policy 81, 84 (on the WHO's failure to discuss chemical endocrine disruptors).

[94] Daniel Bodansky, 'The Most Important Negotiation You've (Probably) Never Heard Of' (*EJIL: Talk!*, 21 November 2024) <https://www.ejiltalk.org/the-most-important-negotiation-youve-probably-never-heard-of/> accessed 11 December 2024 (reviewing however contemporary progress in the work of the Intergovernmental Negotiating Committee on Plastic Pollution).

[95] Ashley Deeks, 'An International Legal Framework for Surveillance' (2015) 55 Virginia Journal of International Law 291 (however also discussing subsequent developments at UN bodies, judicial tribunals, and beyond to bring such practices under control).

[96] For instance, on disruptive hacking campaigns, see Kristen E Eichensehr, 'Not Illegal: The SolarWinds Incident and International Law' [2022] European Journal of International Law chac060. Though for a counterargument, see Antonio Coco, Talita Dias, and Tsvetelina van Benthem, 'Illegal: The SolarWinds Hack under International Law' (2022) 33 European Journal of International Law 1275 (arguing that this operation was likely illegal under international law rules on sovereignty and non-intervention, as well as under general due diligence duties and international human rights law).

[97] Mette Eilstrup-Sangiovanni, 'Why the World Needs an International Cyberwar Convention' (2018) 31 Philosophy & Technology 379. Note: while many have argued that general norms of existing international law apply to cyberspace—such as, notably, norms of international humanitarian law—it has also been countered that, even where those broad norms exist, they have largely not been effective in shaping the behaviour even of non-state actors, let alone states. See Nori Katagiri, 'Why International Law and Norms Do Little in Preventing Non-State Cyber Attacks' (2021) 7 Journal of Cybersecurity <https://doi.org/10.1093/cybsec/tyab009> accessed 16 March 2021.

[98] Abra Ganz and others, 'Submarine Cables and the Risks to Digital Sovereignty' (12 January 2024) 4–7 <https://papers.ssrn.com/abstract=4693206> accessed 24 June 2024 (noting that although there exists an international forum to discuss relevant technical, legal, and environmental information, in the form of the International Cable Protection Committee (ICPC), the organization can only make non-binding recommendations, and international regulatory frameworks are broadly insufficient). See also Kevin Frazier, 'Policy Proposals for the United States to Protect the Undersea Cable System' (2021) 13 Journal of Law, Technology, & the Internet 12–18 <https://scholarlycommons.law.case.edu/

supervision of cross-border financial institutions under global monetary and financial governance,[99] among others.

This highlights how there are often numerous hurdles that must be overcome before an emergent issue such as AI becomes well governed at the global level. States can be slow to be moved to action on regulating a longstanding issue or a new technology: the 1982 signing of the UN Convention on the Law of the Sea followed half a century of failed attempts to create a treaty regime for the ocean.[100] The same has been true for international responses to new technology. Modern anti-personnel landmines have existed since at least the US Civil War,[101] but the first concerted international legal effort to ban their use did not occur until 1977, and it would take two more decades before there was a measure of success in the form of the 1997 Ottawa Mine Ban Treaty.[102] This highlights that even where there is genuine state interest in multilateral or institutional solutions, negotiating the creation of new instruments is an extremely slow process, which can take many years,[103] and often will stretch into decades.[104]

In other cases, major state efforts to coordinate and consolidate many different rules and regimes into a single integrated and coherent global regime soon floundered, as in the case of the 2017 French initiative to negotiate a new Global Pact for the Environment to unify international environmental law.[105] Despite initially

jolti/vol13/iss1/1> accessed 25 February 2025. (reviewing gaps in UNCLOS and other sources of international law, which afford only limited or non-binding protection to undersea cable systems).

[99] Emilios Avgouleas, 'Effective Governance of Global Financial Markets: An Evolutionary Plan for Reform' (2013) 4 Global Policy 74; Rosa M Lastra, 'Do We Need a World Financial Organization?' (2014) 17 Journal of International Economic Law 787. However, note that the past few years have seen steps towards reforming global financial governance. See Wafa Abedin and others, 'Reforms for a 21st Century Global Financial Architecture: Independent Expert Reflections on the United Nations "Our Common Agenda"' (Global Economy and Development at Brookings 2024) <https://www.brookings.edu/articles/reforms-for-a-21st-century-global-financial-architecture/> accessed 16 April 2024.

[100] Kirsten Sellars, *A 'Constitution for the Oceans': The Long Hard Road to the UN Convention on the Law of the Sea* (Cambridge University Press 2025).

[101] Lorraine Boissoneault, 'The Historic Innovation of Land Mines—And Why We've Struggled to Get Rid of Them' (*Smithsonian Magazine*, 24 February 2017) <https://www.smithsonianmag.com/innovation/historic-innovation-land-minesand-why-weve-struggled-get-rid-them-180962276/> accessed 7 May 2024.

[102] Picker (n 49) 184–185.

[103] For a survey and analysis, see Nicole M Simonelli, 'Bargaining over International Multilateral Agreements: The Duration of Negotiations' (2011) 37 International Interactions 147.

[104] For another example, one can consider how the international community has taken nearly 20 years to move from initial informal debate to the final negotiation of a new treaty on marine biodiversity, namely in the form of the 2023 Biodiversity Beyond National Jurisdiction (BBNJ) Agreement (also known as the High Seas Treaty). For discussion, see: Rachel Tiller and others, 'Shake It Off: Negotiations Suspended, but Hope Simmering, after a Lack of Consensus at the Fifth Intergovernmental Conference on Biodiversity beyond National Jurisdiction' (2023) 148 Marine Policy 105457; Elizabeth Mendenhall, Rachel Tiller, and Elizabeth Nyman, 'The Ship Has Reached the Shore: The Final Session of the "Biodiversity Beyond National Jurisdiction" Negotiations' (2023) 155 Marine Policy 105686.

[105] John H Knox, 'The Global Pact for the Environment: At the Crossroads of Human Rights and the Environment' (2019) 28 Review of European, Comparative & International Environmental Law 40; Margaret Young, 'Global Pact for the Environment: Defragging International Law?' (*EJIL: Talk!*, 29

rapid uptake by the UN General Assembly, the programme quickly ran into diplomatic impediments.[106] In yet other cases, states have seemingly delivered on the creation of institutional arrangements, but in fact merely aimed at creating 'face-saving' but ultimately 'empty' institutions: suboptimal, ill-designed institutions with mandates that may deprive them of much or any capacity for effective policy formulation or implementation.[107]

Another risk is for institutional arrangements to leave notable gaps or loopholes in their coverage of all important dimensions of an issue. For instance, while international climate governance has made steps in setting targets for national reductions in greenhouse gas emissions, it has struggled to agree targets for reducing emissions that derive from international aviation and maritime transport activities.[108] Such challenges can be especially acute in fast-changing issue domains: it has been argued that the World Trade Organization-led international trade governance architecture has been ill-equipped for addressing issues such as the cross-border trade in digital products, or questions of the carbon emissions embodied in traded goods and services.[109]

Even when some issues and domains are indeed effectively governed and institutionalized at the global level, these regimes can face—or even incite—relentless contestation,[110] and persistent governance 'gridlock'.[111] In other domains, such

August 2018) <https://www.ejiltalk.org/global-pact-for-the-environment-defragging-international-law/> accessed 25 September 2023.

[106] José Juste Ruiz, 'The Rise and Fall of the Global Pact for the Environment' (2022) 1 Review of International and European Economic Law 28. Lucien Chabason and Elisabeth Hege, 'Failure of the Global Pact for the Environment: A Missed Opportunity or a Bullet Dodged?' (*IDDRI*, 28 May 2019) <https://www.iddri.org/en/publications-and-events/blog-post/failure-global-pact-environment-missed-opportunity-or-bullet> accessed 12 December 2023.

[107] On 'empty' institutions (discussing the United Nations Forum on Forests, the Copenhagen Accord on Climate Change, and the UN Commission on Sustainable Development), see Radoslav S Dimitrov, 'Empty Institutions in Global Environmental Politics' (2020) 22 International Studies Review 626. On 'face-saving' institutions (discussing the 1980 UN Convention on Certain Conventional Weapons) see Giovanni Mantilla, 'Deflective Cooperation: Social Pressure and Forum Management in Cold War Conventional Arms Control' (2023) 77 International Organization 564.

[108] Indeed, these types of emissions were excluded by the Kyoto Protocol (under Article 2.2), which instead delegated the negotiation of sector-specific regulations to the International Civil Aviation Organization (ICAO) and the International Maritime Organization (IMO). Progress at these venues since then has been limited, however. See Beatriz Martinez Romera, *Regime Interaction and Climate Change: The Case of International Aviation and Maritime Transport* (Routledge 2017).

[109] Emily Jones and Christopher Adam, 'New Frontiers of Trade and Trade Policy: Digitalization and Climate Change' (2023) 39 Oxford Review of Economic Policy 1.

[110] K Egeland, 'The Road to Prohibition: Nuclear Hierarchy and Disarmament, 1968–2017' (University of Oxford 2017) <https://ora.ox.ac.uk/objects/uuid:b03d68ab-4748-4de7-a2e9-15616de6a05c> accessed 16 December 2022. That is not to say that such contestation is always counter-productive. For instance, for a discussion of how the NPT along with other global arms control institutions have, as a consequence of such contestation, gradually evolved over time, in ways that have replaced or supplemented old forms of institutional inequality, see Caroline Fehl, 'Unequal Power and the Institutional Design of Global Governance: The Case of Arms Control' (2014) 40 Review of International Studies 505.

[111] Thomas Hale and David Held, *Beyond Gridlock* (Polity Press 2017).

as arms control, past successes and landmark achievements in diplomacy have steadily frayed in recent years because of reinflamed great power rivalry.[112]

Concerningly, global governance for digital technologies is plagued by similar issues. Indeed, global cyberspace governance, intuitively perhaps one of the closest technological analogues for the governance of AI, has seen a number of remarkable multi-stakeholder successes but has also, as mentioned, seen non-regime gaps on issues such as cyber espionage,[113] and has been subject to ongoing contestation, especially in areas of cybersecurity and cyberwarfare.[114]

As if that were not already enough, new governance initiatives today may face even steeper political thresholds and hurdles than those in the past, since many of these issue-specific trends are bracketed by broader shifts and trends in global governance,[115] including a rise in reliance on non-binding international agreements,[116] and growing pressures on multilateralism.

The above discussion clearly suggests there are clear political hurdles that will need to be overcome. Will AI governance initiatives manage to do so? If so, what forms or strategies should policymakers and actors aim for? The world may well have entered a sensitive and fleeting window of opportunity to get it right. The historical record suggests that while institutional decisions or (mis) steps taken at an early stage in governance may eventually be corrected later, these initial choices do create strong path dependencies:[117] they can, and often do, impact the viability, operation, form, and effectiveness of governance on a given issue for decades afterwards. For instance, in 1946 the Baruch Plan famously proposed establishing a centralized global approach to regulating nuclear weapons and power. In spite of remarkable contemporary enthusiasm for the ideals of world federalism, however, the proposal failed, and in doing so marked—or at least accelerated—the beginning of the Cold War.[118] In 1970, the

[112] Amy J Nelson, 'Innovation Acceleration, Digitization, and the Arms Control Imperative' (Social Science Research Network 2019) SSRN Scholarly Paper ID 3382956 <https://papers.ssrn.com/abstract=3382956> accessed 29 May 2020.

[113] Eichensehr (n 96).

[114] Daniel W Drezner, 'Technological Change and International Relations' (2019) 33 International Relations 286. See also Eneken Tikk and Mika Kerttunen, 'The Alleged Demise of the UN GGE: An Autopsy and Eulogy' (Cyber Policy Institute 2017) <https://cpi.ee/wp-content/uploads/2017/12/2017-Tikk-Kerttunen-Demise-of-the-UN-GGE-2017-12-17-ET.pdf> accessed 25 February 2025.

[115] See also Chapters 6 and 7.

[116] Curtis Bradley, Jack Landman Goldsmith, and Oona A Hathaway, 'The Rise of Nonbinding International Agreements: An Empirical, Comparative, and Normative Analysis' (2023) 90 The University of Chicago Law Review <https://lawreview.uchicago.edu/print-archive/rise-nonbinding-international-agreements-empirical-comparative-and-normative-analysis> accessed 6 September 2023.

[117] Stephanie C Hofmann and Andrew Yeo, 'Historical Institutionalism and Institutional Design: Divergent Pathways to Regime Complexes in Asia and Europe' (2024) 30 European Journal of International Relations 306 (examining the evolution of security regime complexes in Europe and Asia, depending on the institutional design of the initial focal institutions).

[118] John Simpson, 'The Nuclear Non-Proliferation Regime: Back to the Future?' [2004] Disarmament Forum 12; F Bartel, 'Surviving the Years of Grace: The Atomic Bomb and the Specter of World Government, 1945–1950' (2015) 39 Diplomatic History 275; see also the seminal work by

US diplomat George Kennan proposed the establishment of an 'International Environmental Agency', seeing it as an initial step towards an International Environmental Authority.[119] Since then, the merits of a centralized body for bringing coherence to the fragmented instruments and norms of environmental governance have continued to be a vexing subject in the field of environmental law.[120]

As such, while early governance decisions (or the lack of them) may not be irreversible, they often have long-lasting effects, and the reversal of mistaken decisions can be as arduous a process as their establishment was in the first place. All governance decisions therefore merit careful—and early—consideration. This means that for AI technology, there is a need for thinking about institutional design and regime complex organization at an early stage, lest these choices are later forced by crises, in ways that might lock in poor or suboptimal design decisions. It is important that we get AI governance right, and that we do so soon—as we may not have many future chances to do so.

Towards Advanced AI Governance: The Evolving Debate

In the face of these challenges, and what may be a closing global window of opportunity, how has scholarship responded to the challenges posed by AI?

Given the high-profile visibility of AI in public discourse, the past years have seen a great deal of work on the topic. Since AI technology has applications in so many sectors, and touches on so many abiding philosophical questions, it is not surprising that such work has been undertaken from a wide range of disciplines and perspectives.

Indeed, much early work on AI focused on the conceptual, philosophical, and ethical issues related to 'robots'.[121] This focus gradually expanded, aptly broadening the analysis from 'robots', to 'algorithms', to 'responsible AI', as well as from the final artefact itself to the broader infrastructure of artefacts, actors, and practices involved in the development, dissemination, and deployment of AI systems.[122] The time horizon under analysis also broadened, coming to encompass

Joseph Preston Baratta, *The Politics of World Federation: From World Federalism to Global Governance* (Greenwood Publishing Group 2004).

119 George F Kennan, 'To Prevent a World Wasteland: A Proposal' (1970) 48 *Foreign Affairs* 401.

120 See for instance Frank Biermann, *A World Environment Organization: Solution or Threat for Effective International Environmental Governance?* (Steffen Bauer ed, 1st edn, Routledge 2005).

121 Patrick Lin, Keith Abney, and George A Bekey, *Robot Ethics: The Ethical and Social Implications of Robotics* (MIT Press 2011); Patrick Lin, Keith Abney, and Ryan Jenkins (eds), *Robot Ethics 2.0: From Autonomous Cars to Artificial Intelligence* (Oxford University Press 2017).

122 Virginia Dignum, *Responsible Artificial Intelligence: How to Develop and Use AI in a Responsible Way* (1st edn, Springer 2019).

both possible 'near-term' impacts of AI as well as 'long-term' impacts that might emerge in the future:[123] for instance, among others, Barrat,[124] Bostrom,[125] Tegmark,[126] Callaghan and others,[127] and Clarke and Whittlestone[128] have considered the longer-term ramifications of advanced AI, considering the transformative and potentially existential risks that could arise if or when such systems were to attain very advanced or even superhuman capabilities.

For their part, legal professionals and scholars have also certainly got down to work on AI-related issues. In response to AI's societal challenges, many legal scholars have started exploring issues around the regulation of AI. Much of this exploration has been nationally focused, aiming to compare the national regulatory strategies for AI used in different jurisdictions.[129] Other research took a law-centric approach:[130] for instance, Turner[131] and Chesterman[132] offer detailed introductions and overviews to many questions in AI regulation, through various questions (such as around AI 'personhood') within domestic legal systems. Likewise, Wishmeyer and Rademacher[133] and Barfield and Pagallo[134] discuss the regulation of AI from a range of legal approaches (e.g. free speech doctrine, criminal law, anti-discrimination law, data protection and privacy, tax law, legal rights, etc.), providing valuable thematic overviews.

However, work on the international or global governance of AI is relatively novel,[135] with major early research agendas only being formulated around 2018.[136] Within a short period, however, recent years have seen the growth and

[123] S Matthew Liao, *Ethics of Artificial Intelligence* (Oxford University Press 2020); David J Gunkel (ed), *Handbook on the Ethics of Artificial Intelligence* (Edward Elgar 2024).

[124] James Barrat, *Our Final Invention: Artificial Intelligence and the End of the Human Era* (9.1.2013 edn, Thomas Dunne Books 2013).

[125] Nick Bostrom, *Superintelligence: Paths, Dangers, Strategies* (Oxford University Press 2014).

[126] Max Tegmark, *Life 3.0: Being Human in the Age of Artificial Intelligence* (1st edn, Allen Lane 2017).

[127] Victor Callaghan and others (eds), *The Technological Singularity - Managing the Journey* (1st edn, Springer-Verlag Berlin Heidelberg 2017).

[128] Sam Clarke and Jess Whittlestone, 'A Survey of the Potential Long-Term Impacts of AI: How AI Could Lead to Long-Term Changes in Science, Cooperation, Power, Epistemics and Values', *Proceedings of the 2022 AAAI/ACM Conference on AI, Ethics, and Society* (Association for Computing Machinery 2022) <https://doi.org/10.1145/3514094.3534131> accessed 2 August 2022.

[129] Araz Taeihagh, 'Governance of Artificial Intelligence' [2021] Policy and Society 1; Roxana Radu, 'Steering the Governance of Artificial Intelligence: National Strategies in Perspective' (2021) 40 Policy and Society 178; Huw Roberts and others, 'The Chinese Approach to Artificial Intelligence: An Analysis of Policy, Ethics, and Regulation' (2021) 36 AI & Society 59; Huw Roberts and others, 'Achieving a "Good AI Society": Comparing the Aims and Progress of the EU and the US' (2021) 27 Science and Engineering Ethics 68.

[130] Matthijs M Maas, 'Aligning AI Regulation to Sociotechnical Change' in Justin B Bullock and others (eds), *The Oxford Handbook of AI Governance* (Oxford University Press 2022).

[131] Turner (n 12).

[132] Simon Chesterman, *We, the Robots? Regulating Artificial Intelligence and the Limits of the Law* (Cambridge University Press 2021).

[133] Thomas Wischmeyer and Timo Rademacher (eds), *Regulating Artificial Intelligence* (Springer International Publishing 2020).

[134] Woodrow Barfield and Ugo Pagallo (eds), *Research Handbook on the Law of Artificial Intelligence* (Edward Elgar Publishing 2018).

[135] Roberts and others, 'Global AI Governance' (n 82) 3.

[136] Dafoe (n 24).

consolidation of an academic field—and even, potentially, an epistemic community or advocacy network—of 'AI governance'. There are various ways to define this budding field—for instance, as one concerned with

> the study and shaping of local and global governance systems—including norms, policies, laws, processes, and institutions—that affect the research, development, deployment, and use of existing and future AI systems, in ways that help the world choose the role of advanced AI systems in its future, and navigate the transition to that world.[137]

Within a matter of years, this field has produced a growing body of work to chart both existing and emergent global AI governance initiatives,[138] to draw lessons from historical experiences with the regulation of new technologies,[139] and to sketch potential strategies for the road ahead.[140]

Specifically, researchers have examined various governance levers[141] and considering their reach and limits in productively regulating AI's global impacts.[142] These include mechanisms such as the AI ethics principles,[143] technical

[137] See also Maas, 'Concepts in Advanced AI Governance' (n 6) 54 (reviewing various technical, policy, and strategy-focused definitions of this field, and on that basis distilling this definition). See also Matthijs Maas, 'Advanced AI Governance: A Literature Review of Problems, Options, and Proposals' (Institute for Law & AI 2023) AI Foundations Report 4 <https://law-ai.org/advanced-ai-gov-litrev>. But see also other definitions, for instance in Jess Whittlestone and Samuel Clarke, 'AI Challenges for Society and Ethics' in Justin B Bullock and others (eds), *The Oxford Handbook of AI Governance* (Oxford University Press 2022) 1 ('the role of AI governance is ultimately to take practical steps to mitigate this risk of harm while enabling the benefits . . .'), or in Dafoe (n 15) 2 ('AI governance refers (1) descriptively to the policies, norms, laws, and institutions that shape how AI is built and deployed, and (2) normatively to the aspiration that these promote good decisions (effective, safe, inclusive, legitimate, adaptive) . . . In one formulation, the field of AI governance studies how humanity can best navigate the transition to advanced AI systems').

[138] Peter Cihon, Matthijs M Maas, and Luke Kemp, 'Fragmentation and the Future: Investigating Architectures for International AI Governance' (2020) 11 Global Policy 545; Lewin Schmitt, 'Mapping Global AI Governance: A Nascent Regime in a Fragmented Landscape' (2022) 2 AI and Ethics 303.

[139] See also the review in Maas, 'Advanced AI Governance' (n 137) 58–85 (providing a review and taxonomy of work that aims to derive lessons from historical cases for understanding AI's development, impacts, and options for its governance).

[140] Stanger and others (n 81); Anwar and others (n 18); Cohen and others (n 28).

[141] See also Maas, 'Advanced AI Governance' (n 137) 102 (defining a 'lever of governance' as 'a tool or intervention that can be used by key actors to shape or affect (1) the primary outcome of advanced AI development; (2) key strategic parameters of advanced AI governance; (3) other key actors' choices or key decisions').

[142] A more detailed discussion of the strengths and drawbacks of various different levers and tools is provided in Chapter 3. For related reviews, see also Chinen (n 63). See also 'Artificial Intelligence and the Challenge for Global Governance: Nine Essays on Achieving Responsible AI' (Chatham House 2024) <https://www.chathamhouse.org/2024/06/artificial-intelligence-and-challenge-global-governance> accessed 12 June 2024.

[143] For overviews, see Jobin, Ienca, and Vayena (n 50); Jessica Fjeld and others, 'Principled Artificial Intelligence: A Map of Ethical and Rights-Based Approaches' (Berkman Klein Center for Internet & Society at Harvard University 2019) <https://ai-hr.cyber.harvard.edu/images/primp-viz.pdf>; Zeng, Lu, and Huangfu (n 50). Mélanie Gornet and others, 'Mapping AI Ethics: A Meso-Scale Analysis of Its Charters and Manifestos', *Proceedings of the 2024 ACM Conference on Fairness, Accountability, and Transparency* (Association for Computing Machinery 2024) <https://dl.acm.org/doi/10.1145/3630106.3658545> accessed 13 June 2024.

standards,[144] AI certification schemes,[145] or other forms of soft law[146] that have already sprung up around AI. Other work has focused on incorporating AI into the existing general norms of public international law,[147] such as the existing human rights regime,[148] international security and export control regimes,[149] or international economic and global trade governance,[150] among many others.

[144] Peter Cihon, 'Standards for AI Governance: International Standards to Enable Global Coordination in AI Research & Development' (Center for the Governance of AI, Future of Humanity Institute, University of Oxford 2019) Technical Report <https://www.fhi.ox.ac.uk/wp-content/uploads/Standards_-FHI-Technical-Report.pdf> accessed 18 April 2019; Philippe Lorenz, 'AI Governance through Political Fora and Standards Developing Organizations' (Stiftung Neue Verantwortung 2020) <https://www.stiftung-nv.de/de/publikation/ai-governance-through-political-fora-and-standards-developing-organizations> accessed 25 February 2025.

[145] Peter Cihon and others, 'AI Certification: Advancing Ethical Practice by Reducing Information Asymmetries' (2021) 2 IEEE Transactions on Technology and Society 200. Certification Working Group, 'Artificial Intelligence Certification: Unlocking the Power of AI through Innovation and Trust' (Schwartz Reisman Institute for Technology and Society, Responsible AI Institute, and World Economic Forum 2024) <https://srinstitute.utoronto.ca/news/ai-certification-ecosystem> accessed 25 February 2025; Philip Matthias Winter and others, 'Trusted Artificial Intelligence: Towards Certification of Machine Learning Applications' [2021] arXiv:2103.16910 [cs, stat] <http://arxiv.org/abs/2103.16910> accessed 1 October 2021.

[146] Wendell Wallach and Gary E Marchant, 'An Agile Ethical/Legal Model for the International and National Governance of AI and Robotics' 7; Gary Marchant, '"Soft Law" Governance Of Artificial Intelligence' (*AI Pulse*, 25 January 2019) <https://aipulse.org/soft-law-governance-of-artificial-intelligence/> accessed 26 February 2019.

[147] Kunz and Ó hÉigeartaigh (n 63); Turner (n 12) ch 7. Burri (n 48); Chinen (n 63); Georgios I Zekos, 'AI and International Law' in Georgios I Zekos (ed), *Economics and Law of Artificial Intelligence: Finance, Economic Impacts, Risk Management and Governance* (Springer International Publishing 2021) <https://doi.org/10.1007/978-3-030-64254-9_12> accessed 23 March 2021; Talita de Souza Dias and Rashmin Sagoo, 'AI Governance in the Age of Uncertainty: International Law as a Starting Point' (*Just Security*, 2 January 2024) <https://www.justsecurity.org/90903/ai-governance-in-the-age-of-uncertainty-international-law-as-a-starting-point/> accessed 9 June 2024; JG Castel and Mathew E Castel, 'The Road to Artificial Superintelligence—Has International Law a Role to Play?' (2016) 14 Canadian Journal of Law & Technology <https://ojs.library.dal.ca/CJLT/article/download/7211/6256> accessed 25 February 2025.

[148] Eileen Donahoe and Megan MacDuffee Metzger, 'Artificial Intelligence and Human Rights' (2019) 30 Journal of Democracy 115; Lorna McGregor, Daragh Murray, and Vivian Ng, 'International Human Rights Law as a Framework for Algorithmic Accountability' (2019) 68 International & Comparative Law Quarterly 309; Kate Jones, 'AI Governance and Human Rights: Resetting the Relationship' (Chatham House 2023) Research Paper <https://www.chathamhouse.org/2023/01/ai-governance-and-human-rights> accessed 12 June 2024; Silja Vöneky, 'How Should We Regulate AI? Current Rules and Principles as Basis for "Responsible Artificial Intelligence"' in Alexander Bruns and others (eds), *Legal Theory and Interpretation in a Dynamic Society* (1st edn, Nomos Verlagsgesellschaft 2021); Vinodkumar Prabhakaran and others, 'A Human Rights-Based Approach to Responsible AI' (arXiv, 6 October 2022) <http://arxiv.org/abs/2210.02667> accessed 8 August 2023.

[149] Burri (n 48); Kenneth Anderson and Matthew C Waxman, 'Law and Ethics for Autonomous Weapon Systems: Why a Ban Won't Work and How the Laws of War Can' [2013] Law and Ethics for Autonomous Weapon Systems; André Brunel, 'A Proposal for a Semiconductor Export Control Treaty' (2023) 19 Journal of Business & Technology Law <https://digitalcommons.law.umaryland.edu/jbtl/vol19/iss1/2> 25 February 2025; Reinmar Nindler, 'The United Nation's Capability to Manage Existential Risks with a Focus on Artificial Intelligence' (2019) 21 International Community Law Review 5.

[150] Joshua P Meltzer, 'Toward International Cooperation on Foundational AI Models: An Expanded Role for Trade Agreements and International Economic Policy' [2024] Harvard Data Science Review <https://hdsr.mitpress.mit.edu/pub/14unjde2/release/1> accessed 4 June 2024. Han-Wei Liu and Ching-Fu Lin, 'Artificial Intelligence and Global Trade Governance: A Pluralist Agenda' (2020) 61 Harvard International Law Journal <https://papers.ssrn.com/abstract=3675505> accessed 26 September 2020.

Going beyond these existing architectures, others have begun to propose new initiatives and centralized international agencies, empowered to coordinate national regulatory approaches,[151] license AI systems,[152] jointly develop advanced AI,[153] or enforce caps on the capabilities of advanced systems or (as proxy) on the computational resources used in their training.[154] Yet others have explored new governance innovations within existing informal governance bodies,[155] or even under schemes involving private regulatory markets[156] or regimes founded on natural law.[157]

A different line of work instead examines not instruments, but rather the roles played by various key actors[158] in shaping and constituting the AI governance landscape. Such work has explored how different states[159]—whether traditional 'great power' states[160] or various state coalitions in the West,[161] in the Global South,[162] or

[151] Olivia J Erdélyi and Judy Goldsmith, 'Regulating Artificial Intelligence: Proposal for a Global Solution' (2022) 39 Government Information Quarterly 101748; Turner (n 12) ch 6.

[152] Trager and others (n 68).

[153] Hausenloy, Miotti and Dennis (n 69).

[154] Andrea Miotti and Akash Wasil, 'An International Treaty to Implement a Global Compute Cap for Advanced Artificial Intelligence' (30 October 2023) <https://papers.ssrn.com/abstract=4617094> accessed 3 November 2023; Tolga Bilge, 'Treaty on Artificial Intelligence Safety and Cooperation (TAISC)' (2023) <https://taisc.org/taisc> accessed 20 October 2023.

[155] Wallach and Marchant (n 146); See also generally Gary E Marchant and Wendell Wallach, 'Coordinating Technology Governance' (2015) 31 Issues in Science & Technology 43.

[156] Gillian K Hadfield and Jack Clark, 'Regulatory Markets: The Future of AI Governance' <https://arxiv.org/ftp/arxiv/papers/2304/2304.04914.pdf> 25 February 2025. See also Dean W Ball, 'A Framework for the Private Governance of Frontier Artificial Intelligence' (arXiv, 15 April 2025) <http://arxiv.org/abs/2504.11501> accessed 1 June 2025; Philip Moreira Tomei, Rupal Jain and Matija Franklin, 'AI Governance through Markets' (arXiv, 29 January 2025) <http://arxiv.org/abs/2501.17755> accessed 1 June 2025.

[157] Y Weng and T Izumo, 'Natural Law and Its Implications for AI Governance' (2019) 2 Delphi—Interdisciplinary Review of Emerging Technologies 122.

[158] See also Maas, 'Advanced AI Governance' (n 137) 87 (defining 'key actors' as 'actors whose key decisions will have significant impact on shaping the outcomes from advanced AI, either directly (first-order), or by strongly affecting such decisions made by other actors (second-order)').

[159] Some of this has examined states' domestic relations to strategic assets, or 'general-purpose technologies'. See for instance Jeffrey Ding and Allan Dafoe, 'The Logic of Strategic Assets: From Oil to Artificial Intelligence' [2020] arXiv:2001.03246 [cs, econ, q-fin] <http://arxiv.org/abs/2001.03246> accessed 15 January 2020; Jade Leung, 'Who Will Govern Artificial Intelligence? Learning from the History of Strategic Politics in Emerging Technologies' (University of Oxford 2019) <https://ora.ox.ac.uk/objects/uuid:ea3c7cb8-2464-45f1-a47c-c7b568f27665> accessed 25 February 2025.

[160] Eric Schmidt, 'AI, Great Power Competition & National Security' (2022) 151 Daedalus 288; Andrew Imbrie and Elsa B Kania, 'AI Safety, Security, and Stability Among Great Powers: Options, Challenges, and Lessons Learned for Pragmatic Engagement' (Center for Security and Emerging Technology 2019) CSET Policy BRief <https://cset.georgetown.edu/publication/ai-safety-security-and-stability-among-great-powers-options-challenges-and-lessons-learned-for-pragmatic-engagement/ > accessed 25 February 2025; Allison Duettmann and others, 'Artificial General Intelligence: Coordination & Great Powers' [2018] Foresight Institute; Leopold Aschenbrenner, 'Situational Awareness: The Decade Ahead' (2024) <https://situational-awareness.ai/> accessed 25 February 2025.

[161] Andrew Imbrie and others, 'Agile Alliances: How the United States and Its Allies Can Deliver a Democratic Way on AI' (Center for Security and Emerging Technology 2020) <https://cset.georgetown.edu/wp-content/uploads/CSET-Agile-Alliances.pdf> accessed 25 February 2025; Trabucco and Maas (n 41).

[162] Sumaya Nur Adan, 'The Case for Including the Global South in AI Governance Discussions' (*GovAI Blog*, 20 October 2023) <https://www.governance.ai/post/the-case-for-including-the-glo

in Asia[163]—may participate in such governance. It also considers the relative and shifting roles of private (technology) companies,[164] AI researchers and expert epistemic communities,[165] trans-national issue networks of norm entrepreneurs,[166] or various actors across the global AI supply chain[167]—from chip manufacturers[168] to compute cloud providers,[169] and from digital open-source AI model marketplaces[170] to downstream providers and users—and how they could or should participate in shaping and enforcing governance efforts for AI.

To be clear, the field of AI governance is a young, interdisciplinary and methodologically diverse field, one that has a long way to go to fully mature and come into its own. Indeed, there may still be missing conceptual puzzle pieces, 'scattered throughout many disciplinary domains and policy areas'.[171] What are these missing

bal-south-in-ai-governance-conversations> accessed 23 October 2023; Cecil Abungu, Michelle Malonza, and Sumaya Nur Adan, 'Can Apparent Bystanders Distinctively Shape an Outcome? Global South Countries and Global Catastrophic Risk-Focused Governance of Artificial Intelligence' (*arXiv.org*, 7 December 2023) <https://arxiv.org/abs/2312.04616v1> accessed 7 January 2024; Malou Estier, Belinda Cleeland, and Maxime Stauffer, 'Safe and Beneficial Artificial Intelligence for Small-Island Developing States' (Simon Institute for Longterm Governance 2023) <https://www.simoninstitute.ch/blog/post/safe-and-beneficial-artificial-intelligence-for-small-island-developing-states/> accessed 7 November 2023.

[163] Emmie Hine, 'Governing Silicon Valley and Shenzhen: Assessing a New Era of Artificial Intelligence Governance in the United States and China' (2024) 3 Digital Society 50; Sihao Huang, 'Beijing's Vision of Global AI Governance' (*ChinaTalk*, 23 October 2023) <https://www.chinatalk.media/p/beijings-vision-of-global-ai-governance> accessed 21 February 2025.

[164] Jessica Cussins Newman, 'Decision Points in AI Governance' (Center for Long-Term Cybersecurity 2020) 12–29 <https://cltc.berkeley.edu/wp-content/uploads/2020/05/Decision_Points_AI_Governance.pdf> accessed 3 September 2020 (exploring the role of AI ethics advisory committees or shifting AI publication norms).

[165] Haydn Belfield, 'Activism by the AI Community: Analysing Recent Achievements and Future Prospects', *Proceedings of the AAAI/ACM Conference on AI, Ethics, and Society* (ACM 2020) <https://dl.acm.org/doi/10.1145/3375627.3375814> accessed 24 August 2020; Matthijs M Maas, 'How Viable Is International Arms Control for Military Artificial Intelligence? Three Lessons from Nuclear Weapons' (2019) 40 Contemporary Security Policy 285.

[166] Şerif Onur Bahçecik, 'Civil Society Responds to the AWS: Growing Activist Networks and Shifting Frames' (2019) 10 Global Policy 365; Elvira Rosert and Frank Sauer, 'How (Not) to Stop the Killer Robots: A Comparative Analysis of Humanitarian Disarmament Campaign Strategies' (2020) 42 Contemporary Security Policy 4; Belfield (n 165).

[167] Jennifer Cobbe, Michael Veale, and Jatinder Singh, 'Understanding Accountability in Algorithmic Supply Chains', *2023 ACM Conference on Fairness, Accountability, and Transparency* (2023) <http://arxiv.org/abs/2304.14749> accessed 29 September 2023; Girish Sastry and others, 'Computing Power and the Governance of Artificial Intelligence' (2024).

[168] Onni Aarne, Tim Fist, and Caleb Withers, 'Secure, Governable Chips: Using On-Chip Mechanisms to Manage National Security Risks from AI & Advanced Computing' (Center for a New American Security 2024) <https://www.cnas.org/publications/reports/secure-governable-chips> accessed 25 February 2025.

[169] Lennart Heim and others, 'Governing Through the Cloud: The Intermediary Role of Compute Providers in AI Regulation' (Oxford Martin AI Governance Initiative 2024) <https://cdn.governance.ai/Governing-Through-the-Cloud_The-Intermediary-Role-of-Compute-Providers-in-AI-Regulation.pdf> accessed 25 February 2025.

[170] Robert Gorwa and Michael Veale, 'Moderating Model Marketplaces: Platform Governance Puzzles for AI Intermediaries' (SocArXiv 2023) preprint <https://osf.io/6dfk3> accessed 25 November 2023.

[171] Dafoe (n 15) 3.

puzzle pieces? Arguably, there are still important bottlenecks which hinder the development and effective advancement of effective AI governance proposals, while these proposals themselves would gain much from clarification and exploration. As such, this book will focus on three of the most critical hindrances to effective global AI governance.

Three Facets of Change

In governing AI, we encounter a specific challenge that arises in the context of the regulation of any new technology: how can we account for future social, technological, and legal change? Can we scale up or adapt our legal systems, and if so, along what dimensions, and in what ways?

Specifically, we face questions about how we can or should design our AI governance approaches, to ensure that they track and respond to (1) the relation between technological change and *societal* changes, (2) the relation between technological change and changes in our *legal* tools; and (3) the relation between external changes in the governance landscape and changes in the *political conditions* for governance regimes for AI. To make sense of these developments, and to understand our collective understanding of the significance of AI in them, there is much to be gained by developing novel analytical concepts, or transferring such analytical frameworks from other disciplines.[172]

After all, many of these questions are not new, nor are they unique to AI. Indeed, scholars in the field of law, regulation, and technology have long wrestled with them. For instance, Roger Brownsword, Eloise Scotford, and Karen Yeung have previously identified three general themes around the idea of technological 'disruption', namely:

> (1) technology's disruption of legal orders; (2) the wider disruption to regulatory frameworks more generally, often provoking concerns about regulatory legitimacy; and (3) the challenges associated with attempts to construct and preserve regulatory environments that are 'fit for purpose' in a context of rapid technological development and disruption.[173]

However, while such questions have received extensive attention in this field, they remain, with occasional exceptions, under-theorized or under-integrated in the

[172] See also Ingvild Bode, 'AI Technologies and International Relations: Do We Need New Analytical Frameworks?' [2024] The RUSI Journal 1.

[173] Roger Brownsword, Eloise Scotford, and Karen Yeung, 'Law, Regulation, and Technology: The Field, Frame, and Focal Questions' in Roger Brownsword, Eloise Scotford, and Karen Yeung (eds), *The Oxford Handbook of Law, Regulation and Technology*, vol 1 (Oxford University Press 2017) 4.

field of global AI governance. This is a problem, because it is particularly in the field of AI that governance may encounter three especially strong drivers of change.

Sociotechnical Change: Aligning Regulation to Societal Changes from AI

In the first place, AI governance proposals should better consider *when, how, and why technological change drives (global) societal changes that warrant particular regulatory interventions.* In general, many recent AI governance proposals focus on specific new applications or visceral incidents involving AI, but elide a comprehensive or explicit account of when, how, or why new capabilities produce or enable societal changes.[174] Ryan Calo has noted how general this problem is: 'even technically-savvy lawyers—and many policy-savvy technologists—consistently struggle with technology as social fact.'[175] As a consequence, policy discussions often get stuck in intractable debates over how to properly define AI, what are the correct 'essential qualities' of the technology,[176] and whether or not these are sufficiently exceptional or new to warrant entirely new laws.[177] Consequently, policies and laws are often formulated in siloed ways that focus on local problems caused by specific use cases of AI (e.g. autonomous drones, facial recognition, autonomous vehicles, chatbots), or from the perspective of particular conventional legal subjects (e.g. privacy law, contract law, the law of armed conflict).[178] As a result they pay less attention to either the interrelation or interaction of these issue areas.

On the one hand, there is some sense in taking a piecemeal approach: national expertise bodies and international institutions alike often have clear, predefined areas of expertise.[179] Yet, on the other hand, this approach limits our ability to understand the sources of AI's symptomatic challenges.[180] Lacking an

[174] Among other critiques of prominent governance proposals. See also Neel Guha and others, 'AI Regulation Has Its Own Alignment Problem: The Technical and Institutional Feasibility of Disclosure, Registration, Licensing, and Auditing' (2024) 92 George Washington Law Review 1473.

[175] Ryan Calo, 'The Scale and the Reactor' (9 April 2022) <https://papers.ssrn.com/abstract=4079851> accessed 23 May 2023.

[176] Ryan Calo, 'Robotics and the Lessons of Cyberlaw' (2015) 103 California Law Review 513, 549.

[177] Rebecca Crootof and BJ Ard, 'Structuring Techlaw' (2021) 34 Harvard Journal of Law & Technology 347, 348–349. See also the discussion in Chapter 4.

[178] ibid 1 ('Technological breakthroughs challenge core legal assumptions and generate regulatory debates. Practitioners and scholars usually tackle these questions by examining the impacts of a particular technology within conventional legal subjects—say, by considering how drones should be regulated under privacy law, property law, or the law of armed conflict. While individually useful, these siloed analyses mask the repetitive nature of the underlying questions and necessitate the regular re-invention of the regulatory wheel').

[179] Morin and others (n 90).

[180] See Margot E Kaminski, 'Authorship, Disrupted: AI Authors in Copyright and First Amendment Law' (2017) 51 UC Davis Law Review 589; Léonard van Rompaey, 'Discretionary Robots: Conceptual Challenges in the Legal Regulation of Machine Behaviour' (University of Copenhagen 2020).

understanding of when, or why, AI technology actually translates into sufficiently new or relevantly problematic societal changes renders AI governance efforts vulnerable to capture by particularly visceral or emblematic use cases that may, however, also be edge cases that do not (fully) represent the ways that AI affects society. The costs of this can be key: more widespread but less visible or visceral societal changes remain unaddressed. Alternatively, this approach may focus attention on isolated or demonstrated AI harms, without comparing these harms to the baseline of activities that are already feasible without AI, thereby failing to properly account for the actual 'marginal risk' of these technologies,[181] undercutting meaningful assessments of their novelty as well as their benefits and costs. Finally, this siloed approach creates the risk that governance responses may, at best, duplicate one another, and, at worst, work at cross-purposes.[182]

AI governance proposals should be grounded in a better understanding of the vectors of cross-sector change, of how new capabilities or developments might change the array or portfolio of problems that need addressing, and of how to reckon with the increasingly cross-domain impacts of multi-modal foundation models and the general-purpose AI systems they support. It is valuable therefore to approach AI governance through the lens of '*sociotechnical change*',[183] a concept which focuses on when, how, and why changes in technologies actually expand human capabilities in ways that give rise to new activities, ways of being, or new types of relationships.[184] Or, as I will roughly define the concept:

> ***Sociotechnical change***: the processes by which changes in technologies extend the capabilities of some or all actors—allowing them new ways of carrying out old conduct or enabling new types of conduct altogether—in ways that (1) can have unanticipated disruptive impacts on society, which (2) may give rise to one or another *rationale* for regulation; and which (3) shape the particular texture and problem logics of the regulatory *target* for those regulatory interventions.

This framework facilitates a better examination of when AI-enabled behaviour actually creates new problems or negative externalities that may provide precise

[181] Sayash Kapoor and others, 'On the Societal Impact of Open Foundation Models' <https://crfm.stanford.edu/open-fms/>; Harry Law, 'The Marginal Risk of AI' (*Learning from Examples*, 30 March 2024) <https://www.learningfromexamples.com/p/the-marginal-risk-of-ai?publication_id=1838544> accessed 7 May 2024; Amanda Askell, 'In AI Ethics, "Bad" Isn't Good Enough' (*Amanda Askell*, 14 December 2020) <https://askell.io/posts/2020/12/bad-isnt-good-enough> accessed 3 May 2024.

[182] Turner (n 12) 218–221.

[183] See Lyria Bennett Moses, 'Recurring Dilemmas: The Law's Race to Keep Up With Technological Change' (2007) 21 University of New South Wales Faculty of Law Research Series <http://www.austlii.edu.au/au/journals/UNSWLRS/2007/21.html> accessed 3 July 2018; Lyria Bennett Moses, 'Regulating in the Face of Sociotechnical Change' in Roger Brownsword, Eloise Scotford and Karen Yeung (eds), *The Oxford Handbook of Law, Regulation, and Technology* (Oxford University Press 2017).

[184] This draws on the account in Lyria Bennett Moses, 'Why Have a Theory of Law and Technological Change?' (2007) 8 Minnesota Journal of Law, Science & Technology 589, 591–592.

rationales for governance—and how that technology is consequently best approached as a target for governance.

Governance Change: How AI Disrupts Global Governance

In the second place, those who study or craft AI governance must consider with greater precision *how AI technology changes the doctrinal applicability, tools, processes and assumptions of (global) governance* itself.

In recent years, numerous governance proposals for AI have been tabled. Many of these, however, are relatively reactive and static, responding to one or another prominent form or use of the technology at a particular moment, without anticipating how future changes may result in renewed legal uncertainty or disruption. In addition, such proposals often fail to factor in technology-driven changes to the processes and tools of governance itself, or even changes to the very conditions for governance. However, again, most proposals for the global governance of AI still reason in relative isolation from actually legally disruptive uses of AI, and their impacts on (international) law,[185] which is a problem because, as noted by Colin Picker, new technological innovations have a long history of driving the 'creation, modification, or destruction of international law, or the derailment of the creation of new international law'.[186] This one-way approach underappreciates both important challenges and opportunities for the global governance of AI.

In particular, AI governance should be based on a better account of three related but distinct dynamics of legal disruption: (1) how technological change (in AI) will create ambiguities or conflicts in existing laws or regimes, in ways that demand the ongoing *development* of international law and governance to remain clear and effective; (2) how new (AI) technologies can support the automation of various processes within international law and governance, resulting in (beneficial or adverse) *displacement* of older legal instruments or norms; and (3) how new (AI) technologies may drive shifts in the political foundations for international law, resulting in the erosion or even the *destruction* of regimes.

To be sure, independent bodies of work exist, within fields such as technology law ('TechLaw')[187] that have explored these questions in turn. After all, the idea that new technologies are not just rationales, objects, and targets for regulation, but can also change the operation and processes of existing legal systems (and even

[185] Though for an exception, see Allan Dafoe and others, 'Cooperative AI: Machines Must Learn to Find Common Ground' (2021) 593 Nature 33.

[186] Picker (n 49) 156.

[187] BJ Ard and Rebecca Crootof, 'The Case for "Technology Law"' (*Nebraska Governance & Technology Center*, 16 December 2020) <https://ngtc.unl.edu/news/case-technology-law/> accessed 16 March 2021; Crootof and Ard (n 177).

the goals of regulators), is hardly new. Reflections on what a given new technology reveals about the changing face of law have extensive precedent. For instance, in early debates in the field of cyberlaw, Lawrence Lessig famously examined legal questions involving the new technology of cyberspace, not merely to discuss the relative efficacy of different approaches to regulating certain issues (e.g. content zoning or copyright) on the internet, but rather to ground and illustrate his broader reflections on the changing nature and workings of the different 'regulatory modalities' of laws, norms, markets, and architectures ('code').[188] Likewise, Roger Brownsword has used studies of behaviour-shaping technologies and geoengineering in order to reflect, respectively, upon the rising role of non-normative 'technological management' and on 'regulatory responsibilities' for the core global commons.[189] AI technologies fit naturally within this tradition: after all, the Internet 'merely' led to the informatization of infrastructure and public space, in ways that have already significantly altered how regulation operates. In turn, AI systems may enable the increasing 'intelligentization' or 'cognitization' of these infrastructures,[190] suggesting that this technology may in time have an impact on the practices and dynamics of law and governance that is even more far-reaching than any seen before.

As noted, the current field of AI governance has not yet considered in depth the dynamics of how technological change can disrupt existing legal systems.[191] Rather, the focus has still largely been on establishing institutions or regimes in the first place. While some AI policy proposals have begun to signal a greater awareness of the importance of making regulation more resilient or future-proof,[192]

[188] Lawrence Lessig, 'The Law of the Horse: What Cyberlaw Might Teach' (1999) 113 Harvard Law Review 501; Lawrence Lessig, *Code: And Other Laws of Cyberspace, Version 2.0* (2nd rev. edn, Basic Books 2006) <http://codev2.cc/download+remix/Lessig-Codev2.pdf> accessed 25 February 2025.

[189] Roger Brownsword, *Law, Technology and Society: Re-Imagining the Regulatory Environment* (1st edn, Routledge 2019); Roger Brownsword, 'Law and Technology: Two Modes of Disruption, Three Legal Mind-Sets, and the Big Picture of Regulatory Responsibilities' (2018) 14 Indian Journal of Law and Technology 1.

[190] This plays on terminology used by the Chinese PLA. See Elsa Kania, 'Chinese Military Innovation in Artificial Intelligence' (Testimony before the U.S.-China Economic and Security Review Commission Hearing on Trade, Technology, and Military-Civil Fusion, 7 June 2019) <https://www.uscc.gov/sites/default/files/June%207%20Hearing_Panel%201_Elsa%20Kania_Chinese%20Military%20Innovation%20in%20Artificial%20Intelligence_0.pdf> accessed 1 June 2025.

[191] Previously set out in Matthijs M Maas, 'International Law Does Not Compute: Artificial Intelligence and the Development, Displacement or Destruction of the Global Legal Order' (2019) 20 Melbourne Journal of International Law 29. A version of this model is also developed at greater length in Hin-Yan Liu and others, 'Artificial Intelligence and Legal Disruption: A New Model for Analysis' (2020) 12 Law, Innovation and Technology 205.

[192] Anson Ho, 'Future-Proof: Monitoring the Development, Deployment, and Impacts of Artificial Intelligence' (2023) 22 Journal of Science Policy & Governance <http://www.sciencepolicyjournal.org/article_1038126_jspg220305.html> accessed 6 November 2023; Helen Toner and others, 'Skating to Where the Puck Is Going: Anticipating and Managing Risks from Frontier AI Systems' (Center for Security and Emerging Technology 2023) <https://cset.georgetown.edu/publication/skating-to-where-the-puck-is-going/> accessed 1 December 2023; Guillem Bas and others, 'The EU AI Act: A Pioneering Effort to Regulate Frontier AI?' (2024) 27 Inteligencia Artificial 55; See generally Maxime

these proposals often lack a strong account of how future technological changes will create uncertainty for law and governance, or of the different avenues by which legal regimes might respond.

Second, AI governance needs to better reckon with the ways in which AI tools may be integrated into international legal lawmaking processes. In other fields, there has also been plenty of work exploring the uses and risks of legal automation—such as the use of AI and other digital technologies in legal systems,[193] in domestic administrative law,[194] and in the general technological management of citizen behaviour.[195] A small but growing body of work even has recently begun to explore this phenomenon at the level of international law,[196] including work on the use of AI tools in support of international criminal courts,[197] or arms control monitoring and verification.[198] However, such work continues to be somewhat underexplored within proposals for the governance of AI technology.

Finally, the AI governance field needs to account for the ways in which new uses of AI systems may change basic geopolitical conditions—affecting the balance and distribution of global power[199]—in ways that may lead to the erosion or even destruction of the political conditions for governance more generally. Recent work suggests that digital technologies may have a range of disruptive effects on the

Stauffer and others, 'The FAIR Framework—A Future-Proofing Methodology' (*Simon Institute for Longterm Governance*, 26 April 2023) <https://www.simoninstitute.ch/blog/post/the-fair-framework-a-future-proofing-methodology/> accessed 3 November 2023.

[193] This literature is extensive. But see for instance Roger Brownsword, 'In the Year 2061: From Law to Technological Management' (2015) 7 Law, Innovation and Technology 1; Karen Yeung, '"Hypernudge": Big Data as a Mode of Regulation by Design' (2017) 20 Information, Communication & Society 118; Benjamin Alarie, 'The Path of the Law: Towards Legal Singularity' (2016) 66 University of Toronto Law Journal 443; Anthony J Casey and Anthony Niblett, 'Self-Driving Laws' (2016) 66 University of Toronto Law Journal 429; Christopher Markou and Simon Deakin, 'Is Law Computable? From Rule of Law to Legal Singularity' in Christopher Markou and Simon Deakin (eds), *Is Law Computable? Critical Perspectives on Law + Artificial Intelligence* (Hart 2020) <https://papers.ssrn.com/abstract=3589184> accessed 15 May 2020; Brian Sheppard, 'Warming Up to Inscrutability: How Technology Could Challenge Our Concept of Law' (2018) 68 University of Toronto Law Journal 36; Christoph Winter, Nicholas Hollman, and David Manheim, 'Value Alignment for Advanced Artificial Judicial Intelligence' (2023) 60 American Philosophical Quarterly 187.

[194] Karen Yeung and Martin Lodge (eds), *Algorithmic Regulation* (Oxford University Press 2019).

[195] Brownsword, *Law, Technology and Society: Re-Imagining the Regulatory Environment* (n 189).

[196] Burri (n 48); Ashley Deeks, 'High-Tech International Law' (2020) 88 George Washington Law Review 575. Thomas F McInerney, 'The Emergence of Intelligent Treaty Systems and the Future of International Law' [2022] University of Illinois Journal of Law, Technology & Policy 259. See also the more detailed discussion of this work in Chapter 5.

[197] Gabrielle McIntyre and Nicholas Vialle, 'The Use of AI at the ICC: Should We Have Concerns? Part I' (*Opinio Juris*, 11 October 2023) <https://opiniojuris.org/2023/10/11/the-use-of-ai-at-the-icc-should-we-have-concerns-part-i/> accessed 15 November 2023.

[198] Niklas Schörnig, 'AI for Arms Control: How Artificial Intelligence Can Foster Verification and Support Arms Control' (Peace Research Institute Frankfurt 2022) <https://www.hsfk.de/publikationen/publikationssuche/publikation/ai-for-arms-control> accessed 23 August 2022; Thomas Reinhold and Niklas Schörnig, *Armament, Arms Control and Artificial Intelligence: The Janus-Faced Nature of Machine Learning in the Military Realm* (Springer Nature 2022).

[199] Schmidt (n 160).

continued viability of legal regimes, in domains such as international security governance,[200] arms control,[201] or the environment.[202]

AI technology is likely to affect not just the substance of various international regimes, but also their processes, and potentially even their political scaffolding. It is unlikely that these disruptive effects will plague the governance of other domains without affecting the global regulation of AI. Rather, they will also affect the base conditions and actual efficacy of the very governance instruments being proposed to regulate AI, in ways that will render particular strategies more or less viable or attractive. To boot, in this book I will approach the concept of governance disruption in a way that operationalizes it as:

> ***Governance disruption***: a form of sociotechnical change by which new technologies and their resulting changes in artefacts, actors or activities challenge or transform existing systems of law or governance, at the level of (1) their substance, doctrine or assumptions (requiring the urgent development of those laws), (2) their processes of law-creation, adjudication, monitoring, or enforcement (resulting in the potential displacement of those practices through automation or wholesale substitution), or (3) their political foundations (resulting in their potential erosion or even destruction).

Understanding how and where AI can disrupt systems of governance, what kinds of problems or uncertainties this creates, and how legislators can or should adequately respond are all key challenges to address.[203] Scholars and legislators alike will need to reckon with these dynamics. This is not just because they matter for how to design appropriate AI regulations and institutions, but also because they reveal interesting and important lessons about the changing nature of contemporary technology governance specifically, and of twenty-first-century international law in general.

Regime Complexity: The Changing Environment for AI Governance

Third, this field must better consider *how AI governance regimes are shaped by underlying changes in the broader global governance environment.* At present, many

[200] Amandeep S Gill, 'The Changing Role of Multilateral Forums in Regulating Armed Conflict in the Digital Age' (2020) 102 International Review of the Red Cross 261.

[201] Nelson (n 112); Giacomo Persi Paoli and others, 'Modernizing Arms Control: Exploring Responses to the Use of AI in Military Decision-Making' (UNIDIR 2020) <https://unidir.org/publication/modernizing-arms-control> 25 February 2025. See generally, Richard Danzig, 'An Irresistible Force Meets a Moveable Object: The Technology Tsunami and the Liberal World Order' (2017) 5 Lawfare Research Paper Series <https://assets.documentcloud.org/documents/3982439/Danzig-LRPS1.pdf> accessed 1 September 2017.

[202] Peter Dauvergne, 'The Globalization of Artificial Intelligence: Consequences for the Politics of Environmentalism' [2020] Globalizations 1.

[203] Crootof and Ard (n 177).

proposals for AI governance take their cue from past multilateral treaties, or previously established international institutions. For instance, recent years have seen calls for a 'Digital Geneva Convention';[204] diverse calls for an international ban on LAWS inspired by global bans on blinding lasers and anti-personnel mines;[205] and a plethora of recent calls for new international institutions for AI that have frequently invoked the IPCC, the IAEA, or other models such as the ICAO, IMO, or FATF.[206] Yet beyond the question of which of these designs would be most substantively appropriate for the diverse bucket of challenges created by AI, it is also unclear how well-aligned such designs are with the broader context and trajectory of the global governance system, which is itself undergoing considerable historical change.

Indeed, in many other domains, international institutions have exhibited a diverse ecology and patterns of evolution over time, as organizational missions shift and as other fora emerge to address distinct aspects of a given governance challenge. As such, while it is certainly valuable to understand and draw up 'ideal' global governance blueprints for AI,[207] in practice the establishment and operation of any AI governance processes will not occur in a vacuum. Indeed, Karen Alter and Kal Raustiala have argued that new cooperative efforts in global governance necessarily occur within a complex and dense global governance architecture. As such, they argue that all too often,

> [g]lobal governance solutions . . . must take one of two approaches: (a) International actors can attempt to create an encompassing regime that can address all dimensions of the problem, or (b) international actors can accept that policy solutions will be crafted, coordinated, and implemented within a larger regime complex... although the first option might be more efficient and effective, it is rarely the solution adopted.[208]

[204] Brad Smith, 'The Need for a Digital Geneva Convention' (*Microsoft on the Issues*, 14 February 2017) <https://blogs.microsoft.com/on-the-issues/2017/02/14/need-digital-geneva-convention/> accessed 17 April 2019.

[205] Human Rights Watch, 'Precedent for Preemption: The Ban on Blinding Lasers as a Model for a Killer Robots Prohibition: Memorandum to Convention on Conventional Weapons Delegates' (Human Rights Watch 2015) <https://www.hrw.org/news/2015/11/08/precedent-preemption-ban-blinding-lasers-model-killer-robots-prohibition> accessed 28 April 2017. But for critiques of the accuracy of this comparison, see Rosert and Sauer (n 166); Rebecca Crootof, 'Why the Prohibition on Permanently Blinding Lasers Is Poor Precedent for a Ban on Autonomous Weapon Systems' (*Lawfare*, 24 November 2015) <https://www.lawfaremedia.org/article/why-prohibition-permanently-blinding-lasers-poor-precedent-ban-autonomous-weapon-systems> accessed 7 September 2020; Rebecca Crootof, 'The Killer Robots Are Here: Legal and Policy Implications' (2015) 36 Cardozo Law Review 1837.

[206] Maas and Villalobos (n 65); Ho and others (n 28).

[207] Dafoe (n 24) 48–51 (emphasizing the need for research into 'values and principles', 'institutions and mechanisms', and 'positive visions').

[208] Alter and Raustiala (n 89) 337.

To bear this out, the past few decades have been marked by significant changes in the global institutional landscape. These include patterns of institutional proliferation;[209] the ongoing fragmentation of international law, resulting in complex inter-regime impacts and externalities;[210] and growing patterns of contested multilateralism.[211] Others have identified trends of legal stagnation and have argued that, in areas such as international environmental governance or cyberspace,[212] global governance is increasingly marked by a shift towards informality. Among other things, this underscores that fact that the landscape in which AI governance finds itself today differs in important ways from the landscape of the past, when previous landmark institutions or regimes were established.

All of this is not to suggest that historical lessons can no longer be valuable,[213] nor that governance for AI must do away with everything old and blithely adopt the new. As discussed above, it is certainly not the case that the role (or rule) of traditional international law in global affairs has been eclipsed.[214] Nonetheless, many traditional, formal international institutions might be increasingly ill-suited, or uneasily positioned, to address complex cross-sectoral issues such as AI.[215] As a result, it is important to consider how well any proposed AI governance mechanisms, institutions, or arrangements might slot into, and interact with, the complex, evolving architecture of global governance.[216]

To study how AI governance will be shaped by the trends, trajectories, and changes in the global governance architecture, this book draws on the extensive scholarship in global governance studies at the intersection of international law

[209] Kal Raustiala, 'Institutional Proliferation and the International Legal Order' in Jeffrey L Dunoff and Mark A Editors Pollack (eds), *Interdisciplinary Perspectives on International Law and International Relations: The State of the Art* (Cambridge University Press 2012).

[210] Martti Koskenniemi and Study Group of the International Law Commission, 'Fragmentation of International Law: Difficulties Arising from the Diversification and Expansion of International Law' (United Nations—General Assembly 2006) A/CN.4/L.682 <http://legal.un.org/ilc/documentation/english/a_cn4_l682.pdf> 25 February 2025; Frank Biermann and others, 'The Fragmentation of Global Governance Architectures: A Framework for Analysis' (2009) 9 Global Environmental Politics 14.

[211] Julia C Morse and Robert O Keohane, 'Contested Multilateralism' (2014) 9 The Review of International Organizations 385; Amitav Acharya, 'The Future of Global Governance: Fragmentation May Be Inevitable and Creative Global Forum' [2016] Global Governance 453; Michael Zürn, 'Contested Global Governance' (2018) 9 Global Policy 138.

[212] J Pauwelyn, RA Wessel, and J Wouters, 'When Structures Become Shackles: Stagnation and Dynamics in International Lawmaking' (2014) 25 European Journal of International Law 733. On cyberspace governance, see also Joseph S Nye, 'The Regime Complex for Managing Global Cyber Activities' (Global Commission on Internet Governance 2014) 1 <https://dash.harvard.edu/bitstream/handle/1/12308565/Nye-GlobalCommission.pdf> accessed 3 September 2019.

[213] Indeed, they can at least provide precedent about the plausibility of achieving governance even on contested, high-stakes technologies. See Maas, 'How Viable Is International Arms Control for Military Artificial Intelligence?' (n 165).

[214] See Karen J Alter, 'The Future of International Law' (2017) 101 iCourts Working Paper Series <https://papers.ssrn.com/abstract=3015177> accessed 11 June 2020; Benvenisti and Downs (n 84).

[215] Morin and others (n 90).

[216] Tallberg and others (n 47).

and international relations.[217] In the context of this book's approach to global AI governance, I will in particular focus on the concept of 'regime complexity',[218] which, drawing on existing articulations, I define as:

> ***Regime Complexity***: the governance architecture on a given issue area, consisting of (1) at least three international or transnational institutions or actors that (2) jointly address a specific issue area, (3) whose mandates, functions, and/or memberships overlap (4) in ways that may result in various beneficial or problematic interactions; this complex consequently (5) has significant implications for the efficacy, resilience or coherence of governance functions by its actors, as well as the prospects for establishing new institutions.

Theoretically, the regime complexity lens enables us to engage in a more refined discussion of the development and prospects of AI governance regimes, in terms of the specific origins of individual institutions, the topology of the regime complex, potential drivers of regime architecture towards fragmentation or integration, the consequences of either trajectory, and strategies to mitigate adverse consequences and improve the efficacy, coherence, and resilience of the regime.

For this, the framework of regime complexity provides a valuable tool for debates around AI governance. At present, it remains unclear whether AI will be effectively governed, or if recent legal initiatives might fizzle out, leaving the topic in a non-regime state of limbo or gridlock. If some lasting governance system does emerge in the coming years, it is unclear whether this will continue to take the shape of decentralized or fragmented regimes, or whether an effective centralized treaty or institution may emerge in time. We will need better ways not only of understanding the relative likelihood of these scenarios, but also of how best to conduct ourselves within each. In turn, such a study also provides a valuable examination to the literature on regime complexity, which has mostly focused on retroactive studies of already developed and mature regime complexes—by allowing the analysis of the emergence and early evolution of an emerging regime complex.[219]

On This Book

This book explores the conceptual and practical implications of technological, legal and political change for global AI governance. In it, I argue that to effectively

[217] See generally Wayne Sandholtz and Christopher A Whytock, *Handbook on the Politics of International Law* (Edward Elgar Publishing 2017); Jeffrey L Dunoff and Mark A Pollack, 'Reviewing Two Decades of IL/IR Scholarship' in Jeffrey L Dunoff and Mark A Pollack (eds), *Interdisciplinary Perspectives on International Law and International Relations* (Cambridge University Press 2012).

[218] Alter and Raustiala (n 89).

[219] Tallberg and others (n 47); Johannes Geith, Magnus Lundgren and Jonas Tallberg, 'The Emerging Regime Complex for Artificial Intelligence' [2025 forthcoming] *Global Studies Quarterly*.

adapt or 'scale' law and governance for the global challenges of increasingly advanced AI in ways that account for these structural changes, it will be necessary to draw on a broader analytical toolkit.

The Core Argument

The core argument of this book is that, in approaching the global governance of AI, we need to think about three facets of structural change, including:

(1) Changes in AI capabilities which drive *sociotechnical changes* in global society, and how these provide distinct regulatory rationales and targets for global governance instruments;
(2) Changes in AI capabilities which *drive disruption* (doctrinal, substantive, procedural, or political) in the instruments of international law and global governance;
(3) Changes in the *broader governance* architecture that encompasses any specific AI governance regime.

Individually, any one of these three topics warrants close consideration in any studies or proposals for global AI governance. Taken together, they provide a set of foundational considerations with which AI governance scholars and policymakers alike must engage, if they are to reckon effectively with this technology. By providing broader frameworks within which to consider specific AI issues for (international) law, we can gain a deeper understanding of the real issues at stake, the likely effectiveness of different responses, and shared themes across regimes dealing with nominally different issue areas.[220]

In developing this argument, I follow a broad 'pragmatic, analytically eclectic, tool-kit approach',[221] one that draws on a range of theories, models, and cases from adjacent disciplines and fields. I draw connections between three existing bodies of work—on law and sociotechnical change; on technology-driven legal disruption, and on regime complexity theory—and apply these to pressing problems in the field of advanced AI governance.[222] In discussing sociotechnical change and

[220] See also Crootof and Ard (n 177) 354 ('being able to situate a particular techlaw question within a broader framework helps us better understand the fundamental issues, better evaluate the likely effectiveness of different legal responses, and better conduct tech-specific and subject-specific analyses').

[221] Dunoff and Pollack (n 217) 653; cf. Andrea Bianchi, *International Law Theories: An Inquiry into Different Ways of Thinking* (Oxford University Press 2016) 125. On the role of 'eclectic theory' in the study of international relations, see generally Peter Katzenstein and Rudra Sil, 'Eclectic Theorizing in the Study and Practice of International Relations' in Christian Reus-Smit and Rudra Sil (eds), *The Oxford Handbook of International Relations* (2008).

[222] Having outlined these contributions, it is also important to clarify what this book does not aim to do. First, while the three conceptual lenses have many contact points and are commensurable, the aim is not to provide a comprehensive or unified framework that must necessarily be adopted in its entirety.

governance disruption, I draw on recent scholarship in various strands of technology law.[223] In discussing and applying the concept of regime complexity, this book gains from the extensive work of global governance and international regime scholars working at the intersection of international law and international relations.

As such, this book diverges from the usual case-study approach. Rather than analysing a few cases in exhaustive detail, I draw instead on a broad review of current work on AI and its global governance, along with case studies from adjacent fields in technology law and global governance for various issues. The aim is not to understand a few examples in depth, but rather to understand the phenomena of AI governance in a wide perspective: to investigate broad patterns in how AI technologies challenge, disrupt, or affect global governance.

The Aims and Contributions

This book has three aims. I seek: (1) to contribute to the practice of global AI policymaking; (2) to contribute to a deeper and more informed academic study of AI governance going forward; and (3) to contribute in turn to scholarship on technology law and global governance.

My first aim in this book, accordingly, is to contribute to improved decision-making around the global governance of advanced AI, by helping inform debates over the benefits or drawbacks of currently proposed governance solutions. Whether or not the present work leads directly to conclusive outcomes, it promises at least to enable better conversations among different approaches and policy proposals. Further conceptual clarity will help AI governance researchers and practitioners consider and design governance architectures for AI which are more effective, coherent, legitimate, and resilient. Rather than necessarily entailing abstract theoretical debate of little practical utility, exercises of conceptual clarification and cross-fertilization have, at their best, been fundamental to much past work at the intersection of law, regulation, and technology.[224] For instance, Colin

Rather, the goal is to provide a set of exploratory perspectives and tools on AI governance which, taken individually, can help inform more nuanced, targeted and resilient governance strategies for AI. One need not accept or adopt all three lenses at the same time but can simply focus productive analysis on one among them. Second, this is not meant to be a detailed or exhaustive application of each of these lenses. Rather, it is intended as an initial exploration to highlight their promises and limits, as a demonstration of their promise, and as an indication that they warrant further exploration and application.

[223] Among others, see Roger Brownsword, Eloise Scotford, and Karen Yeung (eds), *The Oxford Handbook of Law, Regulation and Technology* (Oxford University Press 2017); Bennett Moses, 'Why Have a Theory of Law and Technological Change?' (n 184); Crootof and Ard (n 177).

[224] For instance, in reflecting on these topics, Roger Brownsword and others have noted that 'debates over these terms, and about the conceptualization of the field or some parts of it, can significantly contribute to our understanding'. Brownsword, Scotford, and Yeung (n 173) 6.

Picker has noted that a high-level view of the strategic dynamics between technology and international law can be critical for policymakers:

> [e]ven though policy makers must be closely concerned with the 'nitty gritty' of their international regimes and negotiations, . . . [they] have much to gain from taking a macro or holistic view of the issues raised by technology. Macro-examinations can provide larger theoretical understandings and can reveal previously hidden characteristics that are simply not discernible from the 'trenches'. Viewing technology from '40,000 feet up' reveals certain patterns, pitfalls, and lessons for policy.[225]

Following Picker, and other scholars, this book aims to link a high-level view of (AI) technology and global governance with practical, actionable questions. It sets out the theories and concepts used in technology governance, illustrates them with historical and contemporary cases, and finally elicits their most relevant lessons for current AI governance debates. Ideally, this exercise will contribute to greater strategic clarity and coherence in the field, improving the quality of interventions and refining policy debates on these important and urgent issues.[226]

To be clear, the analysis in this book is not meant to provide strong predictions about the direction of governance, but rather to sketch a series of possible scenarios and avenues. Present pervasive uncertainty over the future of AI governance only renders it all the more important that we explore various scenarios and trajectories as well as their strategic and normative implications. Even if one considers it unlikely that a centralized governance regime will emerge for AI, should circumstances shift in the coming years such that such a model suddenly becomes viable, then it will be of particular importance to ensure that this regime is well designed and fit for purpose, since poor institutional design could lock in catastrophic outcomes. Conversely, in a fragmented AI regime complex consisting of many parallel and overlapping institutions, one should expect to see clusters and various (conflictive or cooperative) interactions between different institutions. The intent of my analysis is to help navigate such choppy questions, by exploring dependencies and implications today.

225 Picker (n 49) 151–152.

226 In doing so, it is important to distinguish between three potential aims or goals for the field and epistemic community: (1) 'strategic clarity', achieving a sensible and grounded theory of change on the basis of a detailed and robust model of both the technical landscape and the policy world around advanced AI, with a resulting roadmap for how to select, evaluate, or prioritize present-day or near-term interventions; (2) 'strategic consensus', where (almost) everyone in a given epistemic community shares this same perspective or judgment; and (3) 'strategic coherence', when policy interventions or initiatives by different individuals or subcommunities in the field do not interfere with, counter, or erode one another (even if there remains underlying disagreement). Notably, while basic strategic clarity is invaluable for formulating robustly beneficial policies for advanced AI, it is unclear whether outright strategic consensus is always necessary or desirable, as a portfolio approach of many actors with different views (i.e. coherence, but lacking consensus) may be preferable.

Second, this book aims to contribute to a deeper and more informed academic study of future AI governance. By making systematic use of concepts, theories, and insights from other areas of scholarship in technology law and global governance, we can gain a better understanding of key dimensions of global governance for AI.[227] Such conceptual clarity will help improve our analysis. In doing so, it will help us answer previously neglected questions and highlight potentially fruitful avenues for further research. For instance, it can complement descriptive research on the global governance of AI with more explanatory insights.[228] My intent is to consolidate and disentangle some of this field, and to promote greater clarity about underexplored questions or conspicuous gaps in the literature. In addition, by providing a detailed and structured account of developments and problems in AI governance, it should also provide an accessible starting point for those entering this diverse field.

Third, this book aims to contribute to its own underpinning fields of scholarship—in technology law, and international law and international relations—by applying and testing the fit and limits of their frameworks within the new sociotechnical contexts of AI development and governance. Doing so can offer a great opportunity to further develop these concepts and theories in turn.[229] For instance, to technology law scholarship, it contributes a more detailed exploration of how dynamics of technological governance disruption play out not just at the domestic level but also at the international level. It also contributes to the scholarship on regime complexity by applying these frameworks to a new issue domain, AI, that has not been widely studied in that field.[230] In doing so, it also helps in the exploration of dynamics of regime complex creation. After all, while there is extensive research on mature regime complexes, there is to date only limited research on the creation and evolution of regime complexes as these processes unfold at an early stage: the case of AI governance offers a valuable opportunity to track the evolution of such a regime complex from an early stage.[231] Moreover, by considering the phenomenon of AI-driven governance disruption, this book also aims to contribute new insight into long-running theoretical debates over the relative role of rationalist (interest-based), constructivist (norms-based), and a set of

[227] Tallberg and others (n 47) 3 (arguing that 'making more systematic use of social science concepts and theories will help us to gain a better understanding of various dimensions of the global governance of AI').

[228] ibid 9 ('Thus far, existing research on the global governance of AI has been primarily concerned with descriptive tasks and largely fallen short in engaging with explanatory questions').

[229] ibid 3 ('exploring AI as a regulatory issue offers a critical opportunity to further develop concepts and theories of global governance, as they confront the particularities of regulatory dynamics in this important area').

[230] See also Geith, Lundgren, and Tallberg (n 219).

[231] Tallberg and others (n 47). Another example of such a study is found in studies of the emerging regime complex for marine-biodiversity governance. Arne Langlet and Alice Vadrot, 'Negotiating Regime Complexity: Following a Regime Complex in the Making' (2024) 50 Review of International Studies 231.

re-emerging 'material' (that is, artefactual or architectural) factors in shaping the constitution and maintenance of global governance systems.[232]

Structure of the Book

This book is composed of seven chapters, divided across three parts.

Part I (Chapters 1–3) provides a comprehensive overview and discussion of the foundations for advanced AI governance.

Chapter 1 discusses recent developments in AI technology and their stakes. To understand why and how to regulate AI, we first need to understand the how we got here—and where these trends may go. It draws on recent technical research into the strengths, limits, and use preconditions of AI. It argues that while this technology is today still immature in important ways, it is already functional enough for wide adoption, which will necessarily entail societal impacts. Rather than fall into dichotomous debates over whether the promises of AI are exaggerated, the chapter argues that AI is best considered a high-variance technology, with some applications that may still fall short of promises, but where a small share of peak systems is increasingly positioned to drive far-reaching societal impact. I then explore arguments and uncertainties around how this importance could develop in the coming years, considering whether, how, or under what conditions we could expect change (in technological capabilities, applications, and societal impacts) to derive from either further progress in frontier AI systems, or from straightforward algorithmic proliferation. On this basis, I conclude that, even under excessively conservative assumptions about further fundamental progress, AI's global impact will likely be extreme before the end of the decade.

Chapter 2 explores foundational questions for global AI governance. It first argues that global governance is needed for many of these issues. It sketches the range of AI's challenges, distinguishing between the three focus areas of conventional AI, military AI, and advanced AI governance. It then draws on typologies of global public goods to argue that many of these issues may gain from, or even require, some form of global cooperation. It then argues that effective global regulation is indeed feasible. Drawing on models of transnational regulation of digital markets, as well as novel accounts of compute governance, it makes the case that enforceable policy levers already exist by which to regulate AI. This implies that if global agreements to regulate AI were reached, they would be enforceable. The

[232] On the interrelation of these three accounts, and their different historical roles and influence within the field of International Relations, see also broadly Daniel Deudney, 'Turbo Change: Accelerating Technological Disruption, Planetary Geopolitics, and Architectonic Metaphors' (2018) 20 International Studies Review 223. See also Nathan Alexander Sears, 'International Politics in the Age of Existential Threats' [2020] Journal of Global Security Studies 1. See also Chapter 4.

key hurdle instead may be achieving adequate global cooperation and agreement about such regulations in the first place.

Chapter 3 surveys the history of AI governance initiatives over the past decade and a half, reviewing how global governance for military, conventional, and advanced AI systems has proceeded in distinct tracks for each. Specifically, it reviews various influential moments, landmark initiatives and instruments, and discusses the strengths and limits of the resulting AI governance architecture. It then considers a variety of proposals for the way forward, from several perspectives. It concludes that in spite of promising steps, AI governance remains incipient and fragmented today, and there is pervasive uncertainty about the best paths forward.

Throughout Part II (Chapters 4–6), the book explores three facets of change in the AI governance architecture, with each chapter introducing, applying, and exploring lessons from a distinct conceptual lens.

Chapter 4 argues that AI governance should focus more on sociotechnical change, to explore how and when governance should relate to the constantly changing array of capabilities and uses of AI. It distinguishes six situations in which AI-enabled behaviours become relevant *rationales* for global governance. It then discusses how such societal impacts of AI can be best approached as governance *targets*, by distinguishing six types of 'problem logics' that have similar regulatory features across distinct AI architectures or application domains.

Chapter 5 provides an account of governance disruption, addressing how and why AI can produce intended or unintended change in the global governance system itself. It explores three main varieties of potential governance disruption by AI: (1) Under governance development, the sociotechnical changes produced by AI result in situations of substantive legal uncertainty or ambiguity, requiring change in governance to address the new challenges. (2) Under governance displacement, AI technologies can support—or even substitute for—key processes or practices of the global legal order, from rule creation or adjudication to compliance monitoring. (3) Under scenarios of governance destruction, the use of AI can erode the effectiveness, legitimacy, or coherence of the global legal order as such.

Chapter 6 adopts the lens of regime complexity to better understand how overarching changes in the global institutional ecology—whether exogenous or AI-induced—will affect AI governance. The chapter provides a background on regime theory, while previewing some of the debates around the consequences and desirability of the fragmentation or centralisation of a regime complex. Finally, it proposes that the regime complexity lens facilitates exploration of a governance regime at five key levels or stages of analysis.

Part III, the final section of the book, draws these three lenses together to set out frameworks for choice in the face of technological change. Chapter 7 integrates the three lenses to explore key conceptual, strategic, and political questions in AI governance. It argues that these lenses offer insight into five questions that can be asked of diverse existing, emerging, or proposed AI governance systems, in terms of (1) origins of an AI regime, (2) normative and institutional topology, (3) evolution over time, (4) legal, political, and institutional consequences to fragmentation or integration, and (5) strategies to better ensure the efficacy, resilience, and coherence of the AI regime complex in the face of these conditions.

Finally, in the Conclusion, I briefly review the argument, reflect on the strengths and limits of the frameworks presented and the arguments made, and work out implications of this for pressing questions in AI global governance. I reflect on what this tells us about how to govern AI, how AI changes governance, and what we can learn about the changing nature of global cooperation and about the urgency of human choice in the face of technological change. Let us begin.

PART I
FOUNDATIONS OF CHANGE

1
The Stakes of AI: Progress, Trajectories, Impacts

1.1 Introduction

What are the global stakes of artificial intelligence? How important is AI on the world stage? For any new technology it is often hard to assess, in the heat of the moment, what are its actual prospects and implications for human affairs. This has been especially the case for computational systems. In 1842, writing of Charles Babbage's Analytical Engine, Ada Lovelace observed:

> In considering any new subject, there is frequently a tendency, first, to overrate what we find to be already interesting or remarkable; and, secondly, by a sort of natural reaction, to undervalue the true state of the case, when we do discover that our notions have surpassed those that were really tenable.[1]

Today, nearly two centuries later, we face these same challenges when considering our generation of advanced analytical engines—the remote descendants of Babbage's contraption, ones far more capable and mature. How are we to evaluate these machines?

These past years have seen extraordinary attention for AI technology amongst industry, policymakers, scientists, and the general public. Yet there is still a wide range of views on the technology's precise stakes—and the question of whether (or why) these systems require new governance. On the sceptical side, some have questioned the utility and prospects of (at least today's) AI systems, arguing that this industry is built on hyped and flawed technologies,[2] setting the stage for a bubble that must eventually collapse.[3] Others argue that while today's AI technology is

[1] Ada Lovelace, 'Sketch of The Analytical Engine Invented by Charles Babbage By L. F. MENABREA of Turin, Officer of the Military Engineers; With Notes upon the Memoir by the Translator ADA AUGUSTA, COUNTESS OF LOVELACE' <https://www.fourmilab.ch/babbage/sketch.html> accessed 13 May 2024.

[2] Inioluwa Deborah Raji and others, 'The Fallacy of AI Functionality', *2022 ACM Conference on Fairness, Accountability, and Transparency* (Association for Computing Machinery 2022) <https://doi.org/10.1145/3531146.3533158> accessed 30 November 2022.

[3] Michael I Jordan, 'Artificial Intelligence—The Revolution Hasn't Happened Yet' (2019) 1 Harvard Data Science Review <https://hdsr.mitpress.mit.edu/pub/wot7mkc1/release/8> accessed 23 June 2020; Luciano Floridi, 'AI and Its New Winter: From Myths to Realities' (2020) 33 Philosophy & Technology 1; Luciano Floridi, 'Why the AI Hype Is Another Tech Bubble' (Social Science

Architectures of Global AI Governance. Matthijs M. Maas, Oxford University Press. © Matthijs M. Maas 2025.
DOI: 10.1093/9780191988455.003.0002

still flawed, it is already adequately functional to serve as an important 'generative'[4] or 'general-purpose technology',[5] one which may have a comparable impact to the invention of computers or the internet. Some have even argued that the eventual stakes of the AI revolution are even higher, and that continued progress will make this a technology with revolutionary or transformative societal impacts.[6] Among these, there are those who have even suggested that the significance of AI capability advances within the coming years and decades will be so pervasive and far-reaching as to eclipse those of any other technologies yet developed, massively compressing the pace of technological progress and ushering in a profound new 'intelligence age'.[7]

Who is right? Why should we be concerned over scoping the stakes of this emerging technology ahead of time? While all these perspectives remain contested, if some of the higher-end estimates are even partially correct, the world will be due for historically unprecedented disruption and shocks. They imply that this technology will not only give rise to the usual set of novel social challenges that require some form of new governance, but that in fact the stakes of handling AI may

Research Network, 18 September 2024) <https://papers.ssrn.com/abstract=4960826> accessed 21 February 2025.

[4] A Feder Cooper and others, 'Report of the 1st Workshop on Generative AI and Law' (arXiv, 13 November 2023) <http://arxiv.org/abs/2311.06477> accessed 17 November 2023.

[5] Tyna Eloundou and others, 'GPTs Are GPTs: Labor Market Impact Potential of LLMs' (2024) 384 Science 1306; Avi Goldfarb, Bledi Taska, and Florenta Teodoridis, 'Could Machine Learning Be a General Purpose Technology? A Comparison of Emerging Technologies Using Data from Online Job Postings' (2023) 52 Research Policy 104653; Manuel Trajtenberg, 'AI as the Next GPT: A Political-Economy Perspective' (National Bureau of Economic Research 2018) Working Paper 24245 <http://www.nber.org/papers/w24245> accessed 22 October 2018; Jade Leung, 'Who Will Govern Artificial Intelligence? Learning from the History of Strategic Politics in Emerging Technologies' (University of Oxford 2019) <https://ora.ox.ac.uk/objects/uuid:ea3c7cb8-2464-45f1-a47c-c7b568f27665> accessed 27 February 2025; but see also Simone Vannuccini and Ekaterina Prytkova, 'Artificial Intelligence's New Clothes? From General Purpose Technology to Large Technical System' (2021) SWPS 2021–02 <https://papers.ssrn.com/abstract=3860041> accessed 23 November 2021.

[6] Ben Garfinkel, 'The Impact of Artificial Intelligence: A Historical Perspective' in Justin B Bullock and others (eds), *The Oxford Handbook of AI Governance* (Oxford University Press 2023); Ross Gruetzemacher and Jess Whittlestone, 'The Transformative Potential of Artificial Intelligence' (2022) 135 Futures 102884; Ben Buchanan and Andrew Imbrie, *The New Fire: War, Peace, and Democracy in the Age of AI* (MIT Press 2022). For one industry perspective, see also Dario Amodei, 'Machines of Loving Grace: How AI Could Transform the World for the Better' (11 October 2024) <https://darioamodei.com/machines-of-loving-grace> accessed 21 October 2024.

[7] The phrase is by Sam Altman, 'The Intelligence Age' (23 September 2024) <https://ia.samaltman.com/> accessed 26 September 2024. However, see also Max Tegmark, *Life 3.0: Being Human in the Age of Artificial Intelligence* (Knopf 2017). Such perspectives have been particularly influential in Silicon Valley, and within the labs developing the most advanced AI systems. See notably: Leopold Aschenbrenner, 'Situational Awareness: The Decade Ahead' (2024) <https://situational-awareness.ai/>; Holden Karnofsky, 'How to Make the Best of the Most Important Century?' (*Cold Takes*, 14 September 2021) <https://www.cold-takes.com/making-the-best-of-the-most-important-century/> accessed 6 April 2022. See also Fin Moorhouse and Will MacAskill, 'Preparing for the Intelligence Explosion' (Forethought 2025) <https://www.forethought.org/research/preparing-for-the-intelligence-explosion> accessed 14 March 2025.

be higher than they have been for any other technologies in the past. Conversely, if such views are mistaken, then we may be directing our attention to the wrong questions—risking that we regulate the wrong things or activities, or that we overregulate, or that the perception of imminent AI breakthroughs induces undue recklessness, zero-sum thinking, or miscalculation among policymakers.[8] While the impacts of this might at times be more reversible than other societal harms, they are nonetheless real social costs.

Given this, we need a more grounded perspective on the stakes of AI. Rather than rely on heuristics of categorical hype or its inverse, we require an engagement with many potential and plausible scenarios for the field of AI technology, the better to understand their assumptions, and the better to match strategies to stakes. These debates start from many deceptively simple questions: What is artificial intelligence? How important will this technology be, really? Which kinds of meaningful change, if any, will AI create? Through what evidence can we evaluate or inform such judgements? To answer these questions requires an engagement with a sprawling range of technical developments, and many perspectives on this rapidly changing and often uncertain landscape of technological innovation. More often than not, this does not yield unambiguous answers. This is history in the making, after all. However, for those of us interested in AI technology's societal impacts and their governance, it is not only feasible but necessary to grapple with the range of different positions, views, and lines of evidence at hand, if we are to meet the challenge ahead.

As such, in this chapter, I aim to offer a grounded review of developments, debates, and disagreements over the future of AI technology—their assumptions, arguments, and views—in order to develop a better understanding of the stakes the world finds itself facing. To do so, I will briefly discuss the recent history and developments in AI technology, in particular examining what outstanding limits and problems might still beset today's AI systems. We then turn to the potential future trajectory of AI, by considering and weighting various lines of evidence that may help us think through the prospects, or limits, of two scenarios: (1) further capability progress at the AI frontier, or (2) further algorithmic proliferation of today's algorithmic state of the art. On this basis, we will offer some practical, epistemic, and strategic reflections.

[8] Trent Kannegieter, 'AI Timelines and National Security: The Obstacles to AGI by 2027' (*Lawfare*, 2 August 2024) <https://www.lawfaremedia.org/article/ai-timelines-and-national-security--the-obstacles-to-agi-by-2027> accessed 12 August 2024. See also Haydn Belfield and Christian Ruhl, 'Why Policy Makers Should Beware Claims of New "Arms Races"' (*Bulletin of the Atomic Scientists*, 14 July 2022) <https://thebulletin.org/2022/07/why-policy-makers-should-beware-claims-of-new-arms-races/> accessed 10 January 2024.

1.2 Progress: Does AI Actually Matter Today?

How important is AI? Does AI actually matter? Is this technology so unlike others that it should be the subject of unusually intense global, political, and regulatory attention?

It is important to raise such questions, because a technology's novelty, societal impact, or legal exceptionality can at times be too easily taken for granted, especially by non-experts.[9] However, there are certainly reasons to be cautious. As AI sceptics often recount, the field of AI has been subject to multiple previous cycles of hype and disillusionment throughout its 70-year history.[10] These latter periods resulted in so-called AI winters: periods, such as in the 1970s and 1990s, when once-lavish research funding dried up after initially high expectations were not met.[11]

Could the same be true today? Some have argued that in spite of the high-profile successes from the past years, the core breakthroughs necessary for a sustained 'AI revolution' have still not yet occurred.[12] Sceptics claim that other, deeper breakthroughs are needed to create truly general or robust AI systems.[13] Is recent AI progress for real, or is much of it a 'mirage',[14] one which will likely result in yet another bust and a new winter?[15] Even if recent progress is real, will it actually translate into widespread usage and changes for society, or will its uptake remain relatively limited? Even if its usage and impacts are significant, why would we expect the

[9] On the limits of the 'exceptionalist' legal approach to technology, see Jack M Balkin, 'The Path of Robotics Law' (2015) 6 California Law Review Circuit 17; Rebecca Crootof and BJ Ard, 'Structuring Techlaw' (2021) 34 Harvard Journal of Law & Technology 347. See also Section 4.2.

[10] Peter Smith and Laura Smith, 'This Season's Artificial Intelligence (AI): Is Today's AI Really That Different from the AI of the Past? Some Reflections and Thoughts' [2023] AI and Ethics <https://doi.org/10.1007/s43681-023-00388-0> accessed 10 January 2024. For histories of the field, see Pamela McCorduck, *Machines Who Think: A Personal Inquiry into the History and Prospects of Artificial Intelligence* (25th anniversary update, AK Peters 2004); Daniel Crevier, *AI: The Tumultuous Search for Artificial Intelligence* (Basic Books 1993); Nils J Nilsson, *The Quest for Artificial Intelligence: A History of Ideas and Achievements* (Cambridge University Press 2010).

[11] Stuart Russell and Peter Norvig, *Artificial Intelligence: A Modern Approach* (3rd edn, Pearson 2016) 24–28. See also the study on the DARPA strategic computing initiative: Alex Roland and Philip Shiman, *Strategic Computing: DARPA and the Quest for Machine Intelligence, 1983–1993* (MIT Press 2002). See also the brief historical review in Stephan De Spiegeleire, Matthijs Maas, and Tim Sweijs, *Artificial Intelligence and the Future of Defense: Strategic Implications for a Small Force Provider* (HCSS 2017) 31–34. However, some have contested the characterization of these periods as winters. See Thomas Haigh, 'There Was No "First AI Winter"' (2023) 66 Communications of the ACM 35; Harry Law, 'An Introduction to AI History' (*Learning From Examples*, 7 August 2023) <https://learningfromexamples.substack.com/p/an-introduction-to-ai-history> accessed 11 September 2023.

[12] See also Jordan (n 3).

[13] Gary Marcus, 'The Next Decade in AI: Four Steps Towards Robust Artificial Intelligence' [2020] arXiv:2002.06177 [cs] <http://arxiv.org/abs/2002.06177> accessed 22 June 2020. Jérémie Sublime, 'The AI Race: Why Current Neural Network-Based Architectures Are a Poor Basis for Artificial General Intelligence' (2024) 79 Journal of Artificial Intelligence Research 41.

[14] Rylan Schaeffer, Brando Miranda, and Sanmi Koyejo, 'Are Emergent Abilities of Large Language Models a Mirage?' (arXiv, 28 April 2023) <http://arxiv.org/abs/2304.15004> accessed 1 May 2023.

[15] See for instance Floridi, 'AI and Its New Winter' (n 3); Luciano Floridi, 'Why the AI Hype Is Another Tech Bubble' (Social Science Research Network, 18 September 2024) <https://papers.ssrn.com/abstract=4960826> accessed 18 November 2024.

regulation of these technologies or of their impacts to pose a particularly novel challenge for existing instruments of international law and global governance?

It is important to be cautious and sober in assessing the prospects for significant AI impacts. After all, while it is often argued that legal scholarship and regulatory action lag behind technological innovation,[16] legal scholars have on occasion also jumped the gun on attempting to work with or regulate new technologies which they did not yet fully grasp. For instance, Gregory Mandel has discussed how legal scholars and courts alike have at times been too easily 'wowed' by new evidentiary technologies, being too eager to admit into court fingerprinting or DNA identification techniques when these were both still at a premature stage of development.[17]

A similar tendency might have sparked legal scholars' eagerness to pursue the regulation of various emerging technologies at a premature stage. For instance, Colin Picker has charted how, during the 1960s and 1970s, international legal scholars may have been too early in attempting to regulate then imminently anticipated advances in deep terrestrial mining, weather control technology, or deep seabed mining. In reality, of these three innovations, the latter took many more decades to realize, and the former two arguably remain out of reach even today.[18] Such cases recall the warnings of Judge Frank Easterbrook, who in a now-famous critique of the early 'cyberlaw' project cautioned:

> We are at risk of multidisciplinary dilettantism, or, as one of my mentors called it, the cross-sterilization of ideas. Put together two fields about which you know little and get the worst of both worlds . . . Beliefs lawyers hold about computers, and predictions they make about new technology, are highly likely to be false.

[16] For an influential discussion of this regulatory 'pacing problem', see Gary E Marchant, 'The Growing Gap Between Emerging Technologies and the Law' in Gary E Marchant, Braden R Allenby, and Joseph R Herkert (eds), *The Growing Gap Between Emerging Technologies and Legal-Ethical Oversight: The Pacing Problem* (Springer Netherlands 2011) <https://doi.org/10.1007/978-94-007-1356-7_2> accessed 28 January 2019. This assumption is shared by many, see also Ryan Hagemann, Jennifer Huddleston, and Adam D Thierer, 'Soft Law for Hard Problems: The Governance of Emerging Technologies in an Uncertain Future' (2018) 17 Colorado Technology Law Journal 94. Others, however, argue that the commonly alleged gap between technology and law is overstated. Lyria Bennett Moses, 'Agents of Change: How the Law "Copes" with Technological Change' (2011) 20 Griffith Law Review 763, 763–764 (discussing and critiquing the metaphor of the 'hare and the tortoise', common in debates around the regulation of technology, arguing that it too quickly assumes that law will always be the loser in the race against technology). See also Crootof and Ard (n 9) 14. ('The facile but persistent claim that "law cannot keep up with new technologies" ignores the myriad ways in which law shapes most technological developments').

[17] Gregory N Mandel, 'Legal Evolution in Response to Technological Change' in R Brownsword, E Scotford, and K Yeung (eds), *The Oxford Handbook of Law, Regulation and Technology* (Oxford University Press 2017) 225, 235–239.

[18] C Wilfred Jenks, 'The New Science and the Law of Nations' (1968) 17 The International and Comparative Law Quarterly 327, 338–339 ('we may . . . within the next few years need a Sonic Boom Treaty, a Center of the Earth Treaty, a Cybernetics Treaty and a Molecular Biology Treaty'). As quoted in Colin B Picker, 'A View from 40,000 Feet: International Law and the Invisible Hand of Technology' (2001) 23 Cardozo Law Review 151, 194. On proposed international regulation for weather control, see also Edith Brown Weiss, 'International Responses to Weather Modification' (1975) 29 International Organization 805.

> This should make us hesitate to prescribe legal adaptations for cyberspace. The blind are not good trailblazers.[19]

Nonetheless, all this does not mean that investigation of the implications of emerging technologies is not warranted: rather, it simply means that we should be humble. As with any emerging technology, there remains considerable confusion around AI. But that does not mean that an investigation of the different lines of available evidence and arguments is futile. It is rather all the more necessary to address these uncertainties and to explore and demystify the state of the art—in technology, and in our knowledge of it—in relative detail. The importance of AI should not be assumed, nor should it be dismissed out of hand; it should simply be critically examined. The point may be less about whether AI does or does not categorically matter than specifically about when, how, and why it is likely to matter—and under which assumptions.

As such, the remainder of this chapter will trace the history and potential futures of AI, by exploring the ongoing debates over whether or how AI technology matters—and whether we might expect changes to arise out of it, or what kind of changes.

1.2.1 Progress and Promise: A New AI Summer?

The past decade, and especially the period since 2022's public debut of ChatGPT and other generative AI, has seen no shortage of excitement around this technology's promise. This might give the impression that this is all a very new technology. But in fact, of course, computing, robotic technologies, and the discipline of AI have a long and storied history. Even so, there can be no doubt that this past decade is remarkable and distinct, in terms of the amount of rapid and sustained progress the field has undergone.[20]

There are, of course, many distinct and valid ways of telling the history of AI,[21] whether by focusing on the gradual rise and fall of different approaches and schools of thought around the creation of AI,[22] by studying the specific artefactual

[19] Lawrence Lessig, 'The Law of the Horse: What Cyberlaw Might Teach' (1999) 113 Harvard Law Review 501, 207.

[20] For some accessible overviews, see also Max Roser, 'The Brief History of Artificial Intelligence: The World Has Changed Fast—What Might Be Next?' (*Our World in Data*, 6 December 2022) <https://ourworldindata.org/brief-history-of-ai> accessed 6 December 2022; Seb Krier, 'AI from Superintelligence to ChatGPT' (*Works in Progress*, 8 December 2022) <https://www.worksinprogress.co/issue/ai-from-superintelligence-to-chatgpt/> accessed 9 December 2022.

[21] Indeed, there are many different ways of telling the history of computers—with even a question as simple as 'what was the first computer?' sensitively dependent on a range of assumptions. Gavin Leech, 'Disambiguating the First Computer' (*Argmin Gravitas*, 28 August 2017) <https://www.gleech.org/first-computers> accessed 27 February 2025.

[22] See Nilsson (n 10); McCorduck (n 10); Rodney A Brooks, *Cambrian Intelligence: The Early History of the New AI* (The MIT Press 1999) <https://direct.mit.edu/books/book/4667/Cambr

or algorithmic breakthroughs in AI capabilities and their underlying techniques, barriers or drivers,[23] by chronicling the specific political and scientific history of major national AI development initiatives or programmes,[24] or with an eye to historical shifts in public narratives around this technology,[25] and in the evolving imaginaries of its anticipated future paths.[26]

These are all valid and important perspectives on AI's origins. However, one fruitful historiographical approach that usefully contextualizes the vibrancy of recent decades in AI has focused on the changing affordances of the underlying material infrastructure, focusing on historical improvements in computing power and data storage as they have translated into the performance of leading AI models.[27] Indeed, these computational improvements can be empirically linked to distinct eras of progress in the field, in the leading AI architectures, and in the technology's societal impacts. To boot, we can distinguish between a Pre-Deep Learning era (1950s–2010), a Deep Learning era (2010–2016), and a Large-Scale era (2016–present) that is itself gradually giving rise to an emerging General Purpose era (2022–present).[28]

Significantly, while a detailed recounting of the capability breakthroughs associated with each era is beyond the scope of this book, it is noticeable that, from

ian-IntelligenceThe-Early-History-of-the-New> accessed 12 June 2024; Crevier (n 10). See also Law, 'An Introduction to AI History' (n 11).

[23] See for instance Colin Garvey, 'Broken Promises and Empty Threats: The Evolution of AI in the USA, 1956–1996' [2018] Technology's Stories <http://www.technologystories.org/ai-evolution/> accessed 7 March 2022; Sara Hooker, 'The Hardware Lottery' (2021) 64 Communications of the ACM 58. For an overview of technical developments in AI capabilities, placed in the broader context of ten 'hard problems' for the AI field to resolve from here on out, see also Gavin Leech and others, 'Ten Hard Problems in Artificial Intelligence We Must Get Right' (arXiv, 6 February 2024) <http://arxiv.org/abs/2402.04464> accessed 20 February 2024.

[24] Roland and Shiman (n 11); Colin Garvey, 'Artificial Intelligence and Japan's Fifth Generation' (2019) 88 Pacific Historical Review 619.

[25] See generally Stephen Cave, Kanta Dihal, and Sarah Dillon (eds), *AI Narratives: A History of Imaginative Thinking about Intelligent Machines* (Oxford University Press 2020); Adrienne Mayor, *Gods and Robots: Myths, Machines, and Ancient Dreams of Technology* (Princeton University Press 2018). For a specific exploration of narrative shifts, see also Paolo Bory, 'Deep New: The Shifting Narratives of Artificial Intelligence from Deep Blue to AlphaGo' (2019) 25 Convergence 627.

[26] For specific explorations, see Harry Law, 'Computer Vision: AI Imaginaries and the Massachusetts Institute of Technology' [2023] AI and Ethics <https://doi.org/10.1007/s43681-023-00389-z> accessed 9 June 2024 (discussing the ways in which, during the 1960s, computer scientists at MIT constructed visions of the future to direct the AI and computing research agendas); see also Olessia Kirtchik, 'The Soviet Scientific Programme on AI: If a Machine Cannot "Think", Can It "Control"?' [2023] BJHS Themes 1.

[27] Developed in: Jaime Sevilla and others, 'Compute Trends across Three Eras of Machine Learning' [2022] arXiv:2202.05924 [cs] <http://arxiv.org/abs/2202.05924> accessed 15 February 2022. For an accessible primer on the role of compute in driving AI progress, see also Matteo Pistillo and others, 'The Role of Compute Thresholds for AI Governance' (2025) 1 George Washington Journal of Law & Technology <https://gwjolt.org/files/volume_1/GW%20JOLT%201_1%20Winter.pdf> accessed 27 February 2025.

[28] This slightly adapts the framework presented in Sevilla and others (n 27), adding in an additional 'general-purpose' era that is less related to the compute inputs, and rather to the resulting systems' significant capabilities. For another history of the modern field of AI, see also Leech and others (n 23).

around 2015–2016, the AI industry has increasingly entered a 'large-scale era', as a distinct line of AI systems saw development. These differed from those developed in the broader AI field, in that they were trained by large tech corporations using computing resources approximately 2 to 3 orders of magnitude larger than those used in other systems that followed the previous Deep Learning-era trends in annual compute increases.[29] Over time, the wild success of the (2017) Transformer architecture[30] and the AlphaGo line of deep reinforcement learning (RL) systems, as well as the emergence of the large-scale generative pre-trained transformer (GPT) line of models, drastically accelerated the growth in AI systems, and especially language models larger than any seen before.[31]

As a result, the period from 2019 onwards has begun to see even more considerable improvements in domains from computer vision to games, language-based tasks, scientific research, and media generation. Large language models began to show increasing performance across various task testing benchmarks, on capabilities from knowledge and reasoning to text comprehension[32] and even forms of 'common sense',[33] though many of these capabilities (and their underlying test frameworks) also continue to be hotly contested. As a result, AI progress in this period has come to far exceed what either AI experts[34] or generalist forecasters[35] predicted even relatively shortly ahead of time. With this, AI systems have begun to surpass humans at a wide range of tasks—and the rate at which humans are being surpassed in new tasks has since been increasing.[36]

[29] Sevilla and others (n 27).

[30] Ashish Vaswani and others, 'Attention Is All You Need' (arXiv, 5 December 2017) <http://arxiv.org/abs/1706.03762> accessed 13 September 2022; Alec Radford and others, 'Language Models Are Unsupervised Multitask Learners' 24; Alec Radford and others, 'Improving Language Understanding by Generative Pre-Training' 12.

[31] Leech and others (n 23) 7.

[32] Shen Zheng and others, 'GPT-Fathom: Benchmarking Large Language Models to Decipher the Evolutionary Path towards GPT-4 and Beyond' (arXiv, 19 December 2023) <http://arxiv.org/abs/2309.16583> accessed 11 January 2024.

[33] Andy Zeng and others, 'Socratic Models: Composing Zero-Shot Multimodal Reasoning with Language' (arXiv, 27 May 2022) <http://arxiv.org/abs/2204.00598> accessed 29 August 2022.

[34] Ajeya Cotra, 'Language Models Surprised Us' (*Planned Obsolescence*, 29 August 2023) <https://www.planned-obsolescence.org/language-models-surprised-us/> accessed 11 January 2024. This is also illustrated by the shortening of experts' expected future timelines to advanced types of AI systems, as measured by various successive surveys over time. See Katja Grace and others, 'When Will AI Exceed Human Performance? Evidence from AI Experts' (2018) 62 Journal of Artificial Intelligence Research 729 (conducted in 2016); Zach Stein-Perlman, Benjamin Weinstein-Raun, and Katja Grace, '2022 Expert Survey on Progress in AI' (AI Impacts 2022) <https://aiimpacts.org/2022-expert-survey-on-progress-in-ai/> accessed 8 August 2022 (conducted in 2022); Katja Grace and others, 'Thousands of AI Authors on the Future of AI' (arXiv, 5 January 2024) <http://arxiv.org/abs/2401.02843> accessed 8 January 2024 (conducted in 2023).

[35] Jacob Steinhardt, 'AI Forecasting: Two Years In' (*Bounded Regret*, 19 August 2023) <https://bounded-regret.ghost.io/scoring-ml-forecasts-for-2023/> accessed 23 August 2023.

[36] Douwe Kiela and others, 'Plotting Progress in AI' (*Contextual AI*, 31 July 2023) <https://contextual.ai/plotting-progress-in-ai/> accessed 7 September 2023; Henshall, '4 Charts That Show Why AI Progress Is Unlikely to Slow Down' (*Time*, 2 August 2023) <https://time.com/6300942/ai-progress-charts/> accessed 7 September 2023.

Finally, one might characterize the years since 2022 as marking a new general-purpose era in AI, starting with the release of a series of increasingly multimodal and capable AI systems throughout 2022, before especially kicking off with the publicly high-profile release of ChatGPT in November 2022, GPT-4 in March 2023,[37] and many successor and competitor models of different 'model families' in the years since. Consequently, this period has become marked by significant scale-ups in investments as well as attention by the global public, and by states and policymakers.[38]

A few trends stand out in this era: first off, as the training of foundation models has required significant amounts of compute and data, this has significantly shifted the political economy of advanced AI development. The cost of training a language model frequently exceeds tens of millions of dollars in compute alone,[39] and the leading models will cost significantly more: the training costs of GPT-4 are reported to have been between USD 63 million[40] and over USD 100 million.[41] Indeed, since 2015, the cost of compute used to train large-scale systems has grown at a rate of around 0.2 orders of magnitude per year.[42] If that trend continues, it implies that the largest training runs will cost well in excess of a billion dollars by 2027.[43] This has already raised significant economic thresholds to participating at the frontier of AI development,[44] with consequent significant implications for the shape and design of regulatory regimes aimed at regulating these models.[45]

The rise of these models has also led to a polarization of the political economy of AI development. On the one hand, the prohibitive resource costs of training

[37] OpenAI, 'GPT-4 System Card' (OpenAI 2023) <https://cdn.openai.com/papers/gpt-4-system-card.pdf> accessed 15 March 2023. For a survey of MLLMs, see Shukang Yin and others, 'A Survey on Multimodal Large Language Models' (2024) 11 National Science Review nwae403.

[38] See generally Nestor Maslej and others, 'The AI Index 2024 Annual Report' (AI Index Steering Committee, Human-Centered AI Initiative, Stanford University 2024) <https://aiindex.stanford.edu/report/?sf187707917=1> accessed 16 April 2024.

[39] Or Sharir, Barak Peleg, and Yoav Shoham, 'The Cost of Training NLP Models: A Concise Overview' (arXiv, 19 April 2020) <http://arxiv.org/abs/2004.08900> accessed 11 January 2024.

[40] Maximilian Schreiner, 'GPT-4 Architecture, Datasets, Costs and More Leaked' (*THE DECODER*, 11 July 2023) <https://the-decoder.com/gpt-4-architecture-datasets-costs-and-more-leaked/> accessed 8 December 2023.

[41] Will Knight, 'OpenAI's CEO Says the Age of Giant AI Models Is Already Over' [2023] *Wired* <https://www.wired.com/story/openai-ceo-sam-altman-the-age-of-giant-ai-models-is-already-over/> accessed 18 April 2023.

[42] Ben Cottier, 'Trends in the Dollar Training Cost of Machine Learning Systems' (*Epoch*, 31 January 2023) <https://epochai.org/blog/trends-in-the-dollar-training-cost-of-machine-learning-systems> accessed 1 February 2023.

[43] Ben Cottier and others, 'The Rising Costs of Training Frontier AI Models' <https://epochai.org/blog/how-much-does-it-cost-to-train-frontier-ai-models> accessed 27 February 2025.

[44] However, for a countervailing argument, see also Nathan Benaich and Alex Chalmers, 'Alchemy Is All You Need' (*Air Street Capital*, 4 April 2024) <https://press.airstreet.com/p/alchemy-is-all-you-need> accessed 19 April 2024 (arguing that 'most economically useful foundation model applications do not require high powered multi-trillion parameter frontier models').

[45] Paul Scharre, 'Future-Proofing Frontier AI Regulation: Projecting Future Compute for Frontier AI Models' (Center for a New American Security 2024) <https://www.cnas.org/publications/reports/future-proofing-frontier-ai-regulation> accessed 12 April 2024.

such systems have led to an increasing homogenization and concentration of the development of the most cutting-edge AI systems.[46] At the same time, once developed and trained and made publicly accessible, many of these models can be disseminated relatively easily. This can occur either because weaker language models can be cheaply improved by fine-tuning them on outputs from stronger (proprietary) models[47] or because some of these leading foundation models are disseminated through open-source channels. To be sure, some have critiqued the wide usage of the 'open-source' label to describe the way that many modern generative AI systems are created and deployed.[48] For instance, Liesenfeld and Dingemanse have argued that many of these are not truly open-source across all relevant dimensions, since providers often seek to evade scientific and regulatory scrutiny by withholding information on training and fine-tuning data, making these models 'open-weight' at best.[49]

Finally, while most of the public and expert focus in the early years of this era focused on 'generative AI', conceived as a chatbot—that is, an interface that can serve

[46] Johannes Schneider, 'Foundation Models in Brief: A Historical, Socio-Technical Focus' (arXiv, 17 December 2022) <http://arxiv.org/abs/2212.08967> accessed 8 January 2023; Nicolas Moës and Frank Ryan, 'Heavy Is the Head that Wears the Crown: A Risk-Based Tiered Approach to Governing General Purpose AI' (The Future Society 2023) <https://thefuturesociety.org/wp-content/uploads/2023/09/heavy-is-the-head-that-wears-the-crown.pdf> accessed 27 February 2025; Dieuwertje Luitse and Wiebke Denkena, 'The Great Transformer: Examining the Role of Large Language Models in the Political Economy of AI' (2021) 8 Big Data & Society 20539517211047734.

[47] However, for a critique of the performance of such systems, see Arnav Gudibande and others, 'The False Promise of Imitating Proprietary LLMs' (arXiv, 25 May 2023) <http://arxiv.org/abs/2305.15717> accessed 3 October 2023.

[48] David Gray Widder, Sarah West, and Meredith Whittaker, 'Open (For Business): Big Tech, Concentrated Power, and the Political Economy of Open AI' (17 August 2023) <https://papers.ssrn.com/abstract=4543807> accessed 27 February 2024.

[49] Andreas Liesenfeld and Mark Dingemanse, 'Rethinking Open Source Generative AI: Open Washing and the EU AI Act', *Proceedings of the 2024 ACM Conference on Fairness, Accountability, and Transparency* (Association for Computing Machinery 2024) <https://dl.acm.org/doi/10.1145/3630106.3659005> accessed 13 June 2024. See also Elizabeth Gibney, 'Not All "Open Source" AI Models Are Actually Open: Here's a Ranking' [2024] Nature <https://www.nature.com/articles/d41586-024-02012-5> accessed 24 June 2024. Indeed, under some classic definitions of the term, LLaMA-2 would not be considered as true 'open-source-software' (OSS), since it was released with licence caveats 'that the model cannot be used commercially by downstream developers with over 700 million monthly users, and the outputs cannot be used to train other large language models'. Elizabeth Seger and others, 'Open-Sourcing Highly Capable Foundation Models: An Evaluation of Risks, Benefits, and Alternative Methods for Pursuing Open-Source Objectives' (Centre for the Governance of AI 2023) 8 <https://www.governance.ai/research-paper/open-sourcing-highly-capable-foundation-models> accessed 27 February 2025. For other definitions of 'open-source' in the context of AI, see also Open Source Initiative, 'The Open Source AI Definition—Draft v. 0.0.6' (*Open Source Initiative*, 9 March 2024) <https://opensource.org/ai/drafts/the-open-source-ai-definition-draft-v-0-0-6> accessed 19 April 2024. Mike Linksvayer and Peter Cihon, 'GitHub Response to NTIA Request for Comment on "Dual-Use Foundation Artificial Intelligence Models With Widely Available Model Weights"' 4 <https://downloads.regulations.gov/NTIA-2023-0009-0264/attachment_1.pdf>. ('To be "open source," a model must be released under licensing terms that permit anyone to read, modify, (re) distribute, and use the model for any purpose'). For another framework, see Matt White and others, 'The Model Openness Framework: Promoting Completeness and Openness for Reproducibility, Transparency and Usability in AI' (arXiv, 21 March 2024) <http://arxiv.org/abs/2403.13784> accessed 19 April 2024.

as a useful augmenting tool in producing new media, but which is otherwise passive or inert—ongoing work in the field is already making fast progress in taking the step towards increasingly autonomous and capable AI 'agents'. While there are, inevitably, many definitions, one view defines AI agents as systems that can pursue 'an ambiguous, open-ended, complex goal that requires interpretation, judgment, creativity, decision-making, and acting across multiple domains, over an extended time period'.[50] Other accounts argue that AI systems can be considered 'agentic' if they are capable of pursuing difficult goals in complex environments without detailed instruction; if they can be instructed in natural language and then act autonomously; or if they are capable of using design patterns such as tool use (e.g. Web search) or planning.[51]

Accordingly, while previous waves of AI research often focused on training agents within isolated game environments, the broad and general-purpose performance of LLMs has led to a surge of attention to the development and deployment of these agents.[52] To be sure, there are still barriers to the widespread use of thoroughly open-ended agents, with many early frontier models showing a subpar performance at generating executable plans,[53] suggesting that the road to the development and diffusion of truly open-ended agents has some hurdles to clear. Nonetheless, the 'task-completion time horizon' of AI models—as measured on a set of (coding, cybersecurity, and reasoning) tasks which take humans a certain amount of time to complete—has been exponentially lengthening over time, at a doubling rate of seven months between 2019 and 2024, extending to competent or even superior performance at tasks that would take humans an hour or more.[54]

[50] Mustafa Suleyman, 'My New Turing Test Would See If AI Can Make $1 Million' (*MIT Technology Review*, 14 July 2023) <https://www.technologyreview.com/2023/07/14/1076296/mustafa-suleyman-my-new-turing-test-would-see-if-ai-can-make-1-million/> accessed 12 October 2023; Mustafa Suleyman and Michael Bhaskar, *The Coming Wave: Technology, Power, and the Twenty-First Century's Greatest Dilemma* (Crown 2023) ch 4; Noam Kolt, 'Governing AI Agents' (2 April 2024) 12 <https://papers.ssrn.com/abstract=4772956> accessed 2 April 2024.

[51] Sayash Kapoor and others, 'AI Agents That Matter' (arXiv, 1 July 2024) 2 <http://arxiv.org/abs/2407.01502> accessed 10 July 2024.

[52] Lei Wang and others, 'A Survey on Large Language Model Based Autonomous Agents' (2024) 18 Frontiers of Computer Science 186345.

[53] Subbarao Kambhampati and others, 'LLMs Can't Plan, But Can Help Planning in LLM-Modulo Frameworks' (arXiv, 11 June 2024) <http://arxiv.org/abs/2402.01817> accessed 17 August 2024. See generally Nathan Beniach and Alex Chalmers, 'Open-Endedness Is All We'll Need' (*Air Street Capital*, 18 July 2024) <https://press.airstreet.com/p/open-endedness-is-all-well-need> accessed 17 August 2024.

[54] Garrison Lovely, 'AI Could Soon Tackle Projects that Take Humans Weeks' [2025] Nature <https://www.nature.com/articles/d41586-025-00831-8> accessed 20 March 2025. Discussing Thomas Kwa and others, 'Measuring AI Ability to Complete Long Tasks' (arXiv, 18 March 2025) <http://arxiv.org/abs/2503.14499> accessed 20 March 2025. These models were tested on task sets collated in: Hjalmar Wijk and others, 'RE-Bench: Evaluating Frontier AI R&D Capabilities of Language Model Agents against Human Experts' (arXiv, 22 November 2024) <http://arxiv.org/abs/2411.15114> accessed 19 March 2025; David Rein and others, 'HCAST: Human-Calibrated Autonomy Software Tasks' <https://metr.org/hcast.pdf> accessed 20 March 2025. For previous discussion, see also Tharin Pillay, 'AI Models Are Getting Smarter. New Tests Are Racing to Catch Up' [2024] *TIME* <https://time.com/7203729/ai-evaluations-safety/> accessed 19 March 2025.

Such trends would imply the development of AI systems capable of completing tasks that would take a human a month to complete, within just a few years. Even under more conservative scenarios, then, as agentic systems become more capable at a range of domains, are set to constitute the next step in the evolution of general-purpose foundation models,[55] giving rise to significantly greater impacts on public life and global affairs within the next 2–10 years.[56]

Given all this, we may have much reason to expect that AI technology has now well come into its own. Beyond impressive displays in games, these systems—both older, 'narrow' AI algorithms and the newer generations of generative AI and advanced, general-purpose AI systems[57]—are increasingly seeing use across diverse domains, from finance to healthcare, policing to art, science to government, and beyond. Moreover, contrary to previous (once-) 'futuristic technologies' such as nuclear power or gene editing, which were cloistered in far-away industrial installations or labs, many of us interact directly with AI systems in our daily lives, through applications from online product recommendation algorithms to social media content management systems, and from translation services, to cleaner robots, to romantic chatbots.[58]

Given these successes in both capabilities and impacts, one might expect that we are now at long last in the midst of the long-awaited AI revolution, and that AI will soon transform almost every domain of human activity.

1.2.2 Limits and Problems: A Coming AI Autumn?

Yet is that really so? Are we at long last in a sustained AI summer? While progress in AI is certainly remarkable and has exceeded expectations, this does not mean that the technology at present is without limits, shortfalls, or caveats. It is not to say that there are no limits both in application or in the underlying technology. There are a range of challenges and critiques here.

[55] Wang and others (n 52). See also Lilian Weng, 'LLM Powered Autonomous Agents' (23 June 2023) <https://lilianweng.github.io/posts/2023-06-23-agent/> accessed 7 June 2024. For an informal discussion see also Will Knight, 'Forget Chatbots. AI Agents Are the Future' [2024] *Wired* <https://www.wired.com/story/fast-forward-forget-chatbots-ai-agents-are-the-future/> accessed 24 June 2024.

[56] Michael K Cohen and others, 'Regulating Advanced Artificial Agents' (2024) 384 Science 36; Seth Lazar, 'Frontier AI Ethics: Anticipating and Evaluating the Societal Impacts of Generative Agents' (arXiv, 10 April 2024) <http://arxiv.org/abs/2404.06750> accessed 17 April 2024 (discussing these as 'Generative Agents'). For a discussion, see also Section 2.2.2.3.

[57] Section 2.2.1 will further develop the distinction between issue clusters relating to narrow ('conventional') AI, and increasingly general-purpose and highly capable ('advanced') AI.

[58] Roser, 'The Brief History of Artificial Intelligence' (n 20). In this way, it is arguably distinct from previous technologies that featured prominently in e.g. bioethics debates. For instance, human cloning saw extensive debate long before it affected (m)any people directly. Paul Root Wolpe, 'We Have Met AI, and It Is Not Us' (2020) 11 AJOB Neuroscience 75.

Some of these challenges relate to the application of AI systems throughout industry and society. Many AI applications suffer from a *mis-branding problem*. The lack of a clear definition for AI means that many products can be presented and sold as AI-based—in order to afford these solutions a greater veneer of objectivity, accuracy, or modernity—when in fact they are merely rebranded applications of well-established statistical techniques or decades-old algorithms.[59] In some egregious cases, alleged 'AI' products are even operated by humans, a practice which has been called 'fauxtomation'.[60]

Moreover, AI applications can suffer from a *hidden labour* challenge. For many conventional, narrow AI systems, the collation of the requisite training data for many AI approaches often still relies on tacit human labour practices, such as poorly paid 'clickwork' and 'ghost work', or scraping user information from social media or dating websites.[61]

Other AI applications occasionally manifest an 'AI *snake oil*' problem,[62] where proposed uses of AI are categorically flawed because they are based on the presumed existence of certain patterns or correlations that do not exist, or at least cannot be sufficiently predicted or validated. This, many have argued, has been the case with AI systems that were promoted as being capable of detecting micro-expressions;[63] recruitment firms that claimed to predict job performance solely from an applicant's photo or short video;[64] or, more controversially, applications

[59] Virginia Eubanks, *Automating Inequality: How High-Tech Tools Profile, Police, and Punish the Poor* (St Martin's Press 2018). This seems to be an ironic reversal of the aforementioned 'AI effect', where things are now called 'AI' that have worked for years.

[60] Astra Taylor, 'The Automation Charade' [2018] *Logic Magazine* <https://logicmag.io/failure/the-automation-charade/> accessed 12 May 2020. And in a specific sector, see Maaike Verbruggen, 'AI & Military Procurement: What Computers Still Can't Do' (*War on the Rocks*, 5 May 2020) <https://warontherocks.com/2020/05/ai-military-procurement-what-computers-still-cant-do/> accessed 12 May 2020. See also Maureen Ebben, 'Automation and Augmentation: Human Labor as Essential Complement to Machines' in Shalin Hai-Jew, *Maintaining Social Well-Being and Meaningful Work in a Highly Automated Job Market* (2020) <https://digitalcommons.usm.maine.edu/facbooks/298/> accessed 22 June 2020.

[61] Mary L Gray and Siddharth Suri, *Ghost Work: How to Stop Silicon Valley from Building a New Global Underclass* (Houghton Mifflin Harcourt 2019). See also Kate Crawford and Vladan Joler, 'Anatomy of an AI System' (AI Now Institute 2018) <http://www.anatomyof.ai> accessed 22 June 2020.

[62] Arvind Narayanan, 'How to Recognize AI Snake Oil' (2019) <https://www.cs.princeton.edu/~arvindn/talks/MIT-STS-AI-snakeoil.pdf> accessed 27 February 2025.

[63] Louise Marie Jupe and David Adam Keatley, 'Airport Artificial Intelligence Can Detect Deception: Or Am I Lying?' [2019] Security Journal <https://doi.org/10.1057/s41284-019-00204-7> accessed 8 October 2019. That does not mean however that such systems cannot infer sensitive (and even tacit) psychological or mental information by observing samples of our online behaviour. For a broad discussion, see Christopher Burr and Nello Cristianini, 'Can Machines Read Our Minds?' [2019] Minds and Machines <https://doi.org/10.1007/s11023-019-09497-4> accessed 27 June 2019. Though notably, one 2023 breakthrough involved an AI system that was capable of reconstructing images from brain activity. Yu Takagi and Shinji Nishimoto, 'High-Resolution Image Reconstruction with Latent Diffusion Models from Human Brain Activity' (bioRxiv, 1 December 2022) <https://www.biorxiv.org/content/10.1101/2022.11.18.517004v2> accessed 11 January 2024; Kamal Nahas, 'AI Re-Creates What People See by Reading Their Brain Scans' [2023] *Science* <https://www.science.org/content/article/ai-re-creates-what-people-see-reading-their-brain-scans> accessed 11 January 2024.

[64] Manish Raghavan and others, 'Mitigating Bias in Algorithmic Hiring: Evaluating Claims and Practices' [2019] arXiv:1906.09208 [cs] <http://arxiv.org/abs/1906.09208> accessed 1 July 2020.

that claimed to predict various protected attributes, or even criminality, based off photos of an individual's face.[65]

There have also been deeper critiques, however, of the direction of AI research. For many years, research has identified many challenges faced by conventional, narrow ML algorithms. More controversially, recent years have seen pervasive disagreement and contestation over the capabilities of the most recent generations of advanced, general-purpose AI systems. After all, in recent years, while large language models and other foundation models have shown seemingly impressive general-purpose skills across various tasks, these models also have displayed notable outstanding gaps in performance across many specific tasks or domains.[66]

Beyond potentially inhibiting their usefulness and take-up, critics argue that these challenges may reflect deeper problems for this current research programme for AI. Indeed, some claim that, far from temporary growing pains of an immature early technology, these extant challenges may well be indicative of fundamental limits to the overall LLM architecture and research programme as it stands today.[67]

For one, many models in these early generations have become infamous for their susceptibility towards 'hallucinations'—generating content that is factually untrue or fabricated, but presenting it as accurate or true, creating significant challenges around the reliability of some of these systems' outputs and users' ability to trust factual claims.[68] Indeed, such hallucinations can occur even when models are solely trained on factually correct information.[69]

Even beyond such reliability issues, many LLMs continue to display remarkably uneven or at best ambiguous performance across different tasks and contexts.[70]

[65] Mel Andrews, Andrew Smart, and Abeba Birhane, 'The Reanimation of Pseudoscience in Machine Learning and Its Ethical Repercussions' [2024] Patterns <https://www.cell.com/patterns/abstract/S2666-3899(24)00160-0> accessed 7 August 2024. See also Coalition for Critical Technology, 'Abolish the #TechToPrisonPipeline' (*Medium*, 29 June 2020) <https://medium.com/@CoalitionForCriticalTechnology/abolish-the-techtoprisonpipeline-9b5b14366b16> accessed 3 September 2020.

[66] This is not new, of course. For instance, already in 2020, benchmarks of 57 standardized tests, GPT-3 outperformed many other AI systems, but showed limited performance on many tasks. Dan Hendrycks and others, 'Measuring Massive Multitask Language Understanding' [2020] arXiv:2009.03300 [cs] <http://arxiv.org/abs/2009.03300> accessed 9 September 2020.

[67] For a broader accessible discussion of some of these barriers, and the potential implications for AI policy, see also Kannegieter (n 8).

[68] Vipula Rawte, Amit Sheth, and Amitava Das, 'A Survey of Hallucination in Large Foundation Models' (arXiv, 11 September 2023) <http://arxiv.org/abs/2309.05922> accessed 12 June 2024. However, ongoing work has also indicated a number of lines of progress in detecting and addressing LLM hallucinations. See Karin Verspoor, '"Fighting Fire with Fire" — Using LLMs to Combat LLM Hallucinations' (2024) 630 Nature 569; Sebastian Farquhar and others, 'Detecting Hallucinations in Large Language Models Using Semantic Entropy' (2024) 630 Nature 625.

[69] This is because of a phenomenon called 'knowledge overshadowing'—whereby models are queried to return an answer that meets multiple criteria, with the result that some of those conditions overshadow others. Yuji Zhang and others, 'Knowledge Overshadowing Causes Amalgamated Hallucination in Large Language Models' (arXiv, 10 July 2024) <http://arxiv.org/abs/2407.08039> accessed 5 August 2024.

[70] Chengwei Qin and others, 'Is ChatGPT a General-Purpose Natural Language Processing Task Solver?' (arXiv, 19 November 2023) <http://arxiv.org/abs/2302.06476> accessed 7 January 2024.

For instance, LLMs still display a significant performance drop in the context of low (training data)-resource languages, such as some African languages.[71] Furthermore, these models' performance can degrade when they are evaluated on counterfactual tasks that differ from the usual assumptions for those tasks,[72] or on compositional tasks that require breaking problems down into different steps.[73] Indeed, it has been argued that, because of the way LLMs are trained (i.e. to solve next-word prediction over internet text), they display higher accuracy when prompted with 'more probable' tasks or outputs. For instance, they are more successful at decoding a simple cipher when the decrypted output is a common word sequence than when the solution is a rare or unusual sequence.[74]

Furthermore, some of these models also suffer from other strange failure modes, such as a 'reversal curse'—whereby a model trained on 'A is B' fails to automatically infer that 'B is A'[75]—or a 'generative AI paradox'—whereby generative models trained to reproduce expert-like outputs can produce outputs at a level of sophistication that these systems, themselves, are not subsequently able to understand.[76] Moreover, while multi-modal language models (MLLMs) such as GPT-4o or Google's Gemini have scored high on many image-recognition and visual-understanding benchmarks, other tests have noticed they struggle with many low-level vision tasks (e.g. identifying whether two circles overlap, or whether two lines intersect) that come extremely naturally to humans,[77] as well as with multi-image comprehension and spatial understanding.[78]

Consequently, some argue that models such as GPT-4 still fall far short of developing robust abstraction abilities—either at all, or certainly at human-like levels.[79]

[71] David Ifeoluwa Adelani and others, 'IrokoBench: A New Benchmark for African Languages in the Age of Large Language Models' (arXiv, 5 June 2024) <http://arxiv.org/abs/2406.03368> accessed 10 June 2024.

[72] Zhaofeng Wu and others, 'Reasoning or Reciting? Exploring the Capabilities and Limitations of Language Models Through Counterfactual Tasks' (arXiv, 28 March 2024) <http://arxiv.org/abs/2307.02477> accessed 15 July 2024.

[73] Nouha Dziri and others, 'Faith and Fate: Limits of Transformers on Compositionality' (arXiv, 31 October 2023) <http://arxiv.org/abs/2305.18654> accessed 19 December 2023.

[74] R Thomas McCoy and others, 'Embers of Autoregression: Understanding Large Language Models through the Problem They Are Trained to Solve' (arXiv, 24 September 2023) <http://arxiv.org/abs/2309.13638> accessed 19 December 2023.

[75] Lukas Berglund and others, 'The Reversal Curse: LLMs Trained on "A Is B" Fail to Learn "B Is A"' (arXiv, 22 September 2023) <http://arxiv.org/abs/2309.12288> accessed 19 December 2023.

[76] Peter West and others, 'The Generative AI Paradox: "What It Can Create, It May Not Understand"' (arXiv, 31 October 2023) <http://arxiv.org/abs/2311.00059> accessed 19 December 2023.

[77] Pooyan Rahmanzadehgervi and others, 'Vision Language Models Are Blind' (arXiv, 25 July 2024) <http://arxiv.org/abs/2407.06581> accessed 12 August 2024.

[78] Fanqing Meng and others, 'MMIU: Multimodal Multi-Image Understanding for Evaluating Large Vision-Language Models' (arXiv, 5 August 2024) <http://arxiv.org/abs/2408.02718> accessed 12 August 2024.

[79] Melanie Mitchell, Alessandro B Palmarini, and Arseny Moskvichev, 'Comparing Humans, GPT-4, and GPT-4V on Abstraction and Reasoning Tasks' (arXiv, 13 November 2023) <http://arxiv.org/abs/2311.09247> accessed 18 November 2023.

More generally, many of these problems are often taken to show that contemporary LLMs are not yet capable of general reasoning,[80] and lack the full ability to apply careful, stepwise thinking to novel situations. Many LLMs (especially at smaller scales but also at larger ones) display flawed performance in reasoning tasks involving planning,[81] long chains of reasoning,[82] and causal reasoning,[83] as well as in following simple rules in user interactions,[84] forecasting and prediction of future events,[85] or 'intrinsic self-correction' of their own reasoning without external feedback.[86] The sceptical perspective holds that, given these problems, we must deduce that these systems are not truly capable of general reasoning—and perhaps will never be. Indeed, in this perspective, instances where such models do appear to perform well on reasoning tasks must occur because those tasks are relatively simple extensions of examples found in these models' extremely large training data sets.

Nonetheless, research has continued apace, and recent generations of general-purpose models have frequently overturned previous assumptions about their limits. They often not only outcompete specially trained narrow systems, but also—with the right prompts—exceed the capabilities of other, fine-tuned language models.[87] Moreover, contrary to widespread public perceptions that foundation models must necessarily be limited to perform within the range of human performance represented in their training data, it has been shown that under particular conditions these models can in some cases achieve 'transcendence' of

[80] Jiankai Sun and others, 'A Survey of Reasoning with Foundation Models' (arXiv, 25 January 2024) <http://arxiv.org/abs/2312.11562> accessed 26 June 2024.

[81] Karthik Valmeekam and others, 'On the Planning Abilities of Large Language Models—A Critical Investigation' (2023) <https://openreview.net/forum?id=X6dEqXIsEW> accessed 27 February 2024.

[82] Abulhair Saparov and He He, 'Language Models Are Greedy Reasoners: A Systematic Formal Analysis of Chain-of-Thought' (arXiv, 1 March 2023) <http://arxiv.org/abs/2210.01240> accessed 26 June 2024 (studying InstructGPT and GPT-3, and finding that 'LLMs are quite capable of making correct individual deduction steps, and so are generally capable of reasoning, even in fictional contexts. However, they have difficulty with proof planning: When multiple valid deduction steps are available, they are not able to systematically explore the different options').

[83] Emre Kıcıman and others, 'Causal Reasoning and Large Language Models: Opening a New Frontier for Causality' (arXiv, 28 April 2023) <http://arxiv.org/abs/2305.00050> accessed 3 May 2023.

[84] Norman Mu and others, 'Can LLMs Follow Simple Rules?' (arXiv, 8 March 2024) <http://arxiv.org/abs/2311.04235> accessed 1 July 2024.

[85] Philipp Schoenegger and Peter S Park, 'Large Language Model Prediction Capabilities: Evidence from a Real-World Forecasting Tournament' (arXiv, 17 October 2023) <http://arxiv.org/abs/2310.13014> accessed 24 July 2024.

[86] Jie Huang and others, 'Large Language Models Cannot Self-Correct Reasoning Yet' (arXiv, 14 March 2024) <http://arxiv.org/abs/2310.01798> accessed 26 June 2024. Some have argued that this ability to self-critique and correct wrong guesses remains absent (or at least unproven) in LLMs. Subbarao Kambhampati, 'Can Large Language Models Reason and Plan?' (2024) 1534 Annals of the New York Academy of Sciences nyas.15125.

[87] Harsha Nori and others, 'Can Generalist Foundation Models Outcompete Special-Purpose Tuning? Case Study in Medicine' (arXiv, 27 November 2023) <http://arxiv.org/abs/2311.16452> accessed 3 December 2023.

their training data, outperforming any and all human experts that generated their data.[88]

This is an active and ongoing debate. However, these complexities suggest that, while the common account of LLM models as merely 'stochastic parrots'[89] that perform only shallow statistical inference may be oversimplified,[90] it also would be a significant stretch to suggest that the current generation of models should be considered clearly fully general or human-equivalent in a relevant way.

One problem here may of course lie with the threshold or goal of the field: in an important sense, humans are not fully general reasoners either. For example, most humans cannot, for instance, mentally visualize or play easily defined games that take place in higher-dimensional space—or at least cannot do so without tools or interfaces.[91] Nonetheless, today's LLMs still do display a set of limits—and we face the problem that we are unsure, at present, whether these prevalent limitations in reasoning capabilities of LLMs are fundamental, or if they are transient and likely to evaporate (further) as a result of continued scaling up of these models, or as a result of improved training methods.[92]

Effectively resolving these debates is made more difficult, moreover, by a set of outstanding challenges in the scientific field of AI research with regard to the testing and evaluation of models. As a result, many have increasingly suggested that many highly touted advances in AI have not always been representative or have not held up under scrutiny.[93]

Indeed, there exist many problems around properly testing AI system performance:[94] AI researchers often attempt to measure such traits by evaluating an AI

[88] Edwin Zhang and others, 'Transcendence: Generative Models Can Outperform the Experts that Train Them' (arXiv, 21 June 2024) <http://arxiv.org/abs/2406.11741> accessed 27 June 2024 (illustrating how an LLM trained on 1000 Elo chess game transcripts was able to play at 1500 Elo).

[89] Emily M Bender and others, 'On the Dangers of Stochastic Parrots: Can Language Models Be Too Big? &#x1f99c', *Proceedings of the 2021 ACM Conference on Fairness, Accountability, and Transparency* (Association for Computing Machinery 2021) <https://doi.org/10.1145/3442188.3445922> accessed 7 March 2021.

[90] Or at least strictly inaccurate, given that modern language models, starting with ChatGPT, are not solely conducting next-word prediction based on the internet, but rather have had at least some of their weights adjusted through reinforcement learning from human feedback. Dean W Ball, 'The Era of Predictive AI Is Almost Over' (2024) 77 *The New Atlantis* 26. See also Jack Wiseman, 'The Parrot Is Dead' (Inference, 11 April 2025) <https://inferencemagazine.substack.com/p/the-parrot-is-dead> accessed 5 June 2025.

[91] Though for one attempt at presenting a higher-dimensional game world for humans to operate, see Chris Suellentrop, 'One Man's Quest to Build a Mind-Warping 4-D Videogame' [2014] *Wired* <https://www.wired.com/2014/11/4d-game/> accessed 26 June 2024.

[92] See also Usman Anwar and others, 'Foundational Challenges in Assuring Alignment and Safety of Large Language Models' 28 <https://llm-safety-challenges.github.io/challenges_llms.pdf>.

[93] Matthew Hutson, 'Eye-Catching Advances in Some AI Fields Are Not Real' (*Science | AAAS*, 27 May 2020) <https://www.sciencemag.org/news/2020/05/eye-catching-advances-some-ai-fields-are-not-real> accessed 29 May 2020. For instance, it is also claimed that advances in algorithmic accuracy over the past years reflected flaws in the experimental setup of those papers. Kevin Musgrave, Serge Belongie, and Ser-Nam Lim, 'A Metric Learning Reality Check' [2020] arXiv:2003.08505 [cs] <http://arxiv.org/abs/2003.08505> accessed 29 May 2020.

[94] Melanie Mitchell, 'How Do We Know How Smart AI Systems Are?' (2023) 381 Science eadj5957.

system's ability to pass one or more specific tests.[95] Classically, a lot of attention was given to famous tests such as the Turing test; however, in spite of that test's cultural status, most of its variations have for decades been considered inadequate for evaluating meaningful general intelligence in AI systems. This is in part because of philosophical disagreements over whether conversational skills that manage to socially deceive an interlocutor are even at all revealing of a system's 'thinking status', but it is also because AI scientists cannot agree on clear criteria for passing the Turing test; moreover, some systems have managed to perform well at versions of this test using techniques that are not generalizable to other problems.[96] Nonetheless, many new benchmark tests continue to be developed for AI, in particular aiming to test system performance across multiple tasks at once.[97]

However, even these more modern testing and benchmarking approaches face key challenges.[98] For instance, there have been problems with how tests are applied and scored[99] and with how their results are reported, which can often lead to misleading impressions of a model's capabilities or performance both in an absolute sense and relative to the state of the art.[100] Indeed, one 2024 review identified

[95] At least those that focus on an empirical assessment, rather than a prescriptive account of how (by what pathways) AI is to be constructed. See for instance Blaise Agüera y Arcas and Peter Norvig, 'Artificial General Intelligence Is Already Here' [2023] *Noema* <https://www.noemamag.com/artificial-general-intelligence-is-already-here> accessed 11 October 2023 ('For each criticism, we should ask whether it is prescriptive or empirical. A prescriptive criticism would argue: "In order to be considered as AGI, a system not only has to pass this test, it also has to be constructed in this way." We would push back against prescriptive criticisms on the grounds that the test itself should be sufficient—and if it is not, the test should be amended'). See also Blaise Agüera y Arcas, 'Do Large Language Models Understand Us?' (2022) 151 Daedalus 183.

[96] Melanie Mitchell, 'The Turing Test and Our Shifting Conceptions of Intelligence' (2024) 385 Science eadq9356. See also Henry Shevlin and others, 'The Limits of Machine Intelligence' (2019) 20 EMBO reports e49177, 3; Jose Hernandez-Orallo, 'Beyond the Turing Test' (2000) 9 Journal of Logic, Language and Information 447. An early philosophical objection to the Turing test on these grounds was given by Ned Block, who argued that, as a behaviourist test that focused solely on external system behaviour, the Turing test allowed for trickery, in ways that did not match common intuitions over actual intelligence. Ned Block, 'Psychologism and Behaviorism' (1981) 90 The Philosophical Review 5, 21. ('So long as the programmers have done their job properly, [this] machine will have the capacity to emit a sensible sequence of verbal outputs, whatever the verbal inputs, and hence it is intelligent according to the neo-Turing Test conception of intelligence. But actually, the machine has the intelligence of a toaster. *All the intelligence it exhibits is that of its programmers*', emphasis in original).

[97] Hendrycks and others (n 66).

[98] Ernest Davis, 'Benchmarks for Automated Commonsense Reasoning: A Survey' (2023) 56 ACM Computing Surveys 81 (reviewing 139 benchmarks developed to test the commonsense knowledge and reasoning abilities of AI). Significantly, and problematically, these challenges around evaluation not only inhibit our ability to understand overall progress in AI system capabilities, but also undermine our avenues for designing effective, robust and reliable evaluation suites for their safety. Anthropic, 'Challenges in Evaluating AI Systems' (*Anthropic*, 4 October 2023) <https://www.anthropic.com/index/evaluating-ai-systems> accessed 12 October 2023.

[99] See for instance Eric Martínez, 'Re-Evaluating GPT-4's Bar Exam Performance' [2024] Artificial Intelligence and Law <https://doi.org/10.1007/s10506-024-09396-9> accessed 10 April 2024. (suggesting that a highly reported GPT-4 statistic—that it passed a US bar exam with a 90th percentile score—may have been based on an erroneous score conversion).

[100] Ryan Burnell and others, 'Rethink Reporting of Evaluation Results in AI' (2023) 380 Science 136. For a useful guide, see also Lawrence Chan, 'Can You Trust An AI Press Release?' [2024] *Asterisk* <https://asteriskmag.com/issues/07/can-you-trust-an-ai-press-release> accessed 12 August 2024 (discussing how benchmarks and evaluation methods can be cherry-picked, how picking the appropriate

43 different 'questionable research practices' in the machine learning field, which likely undermine reported results in the evaluation of LLMs on public benchmarks.[101] These include practices relating to data contamination, the cherry-picking of results, and the misreporting of results, along with 'irreproducible research practices' that make it highly difficult or even impossible for other AI researchers to reproduce, audit, or build upon publicly reported research.[102]

There is a major risk that many tests used to evaluate AI systems—and in particular many evocative professional tests normally taken by humans—are enormously subject or susceptible to such data leakage and contamination problems.[103] While studies suggests that, at least for some (e.g. mathematics) benchmarks, data contamination may not strongly plague the most advanced generation of models,[104] many other domains of machine learning remain susceptible to this challenge.[105] Such messy and uneven practices to mitigate these practices will continue to impede effective evaluation of AI systems.

Nonetheless, any discussion of AI's important testing troubles should come with a number of caveats.

In the first place, even while individual benchmarks face problems, at the level of the overall field there has notably been a historical shift, from older benchmarks which challenged specialized and custom-built narrow AIs to compete against the general population of humans to today's benchmarks that challenge general-purpose AI models to compete with the best human experts on complex problems. This overall shift in the state and orientation of benchmarks is unlikely to be a pure measurement artefact.[106]

Second, while the (inappropriate) application of professional tests configured for humans still continues, many of the leading benchmarks applied to advanced AI systems have focused on sets of questions that require highly advanced

existing competitor model against which to rate a new system's performance can be difficult because publicly available models improve over time, how headline scores can hide significant and important differences, and how many benchmarks don't measure what we care about).

[101] Gavin Leech and others, 'Questionable Practices in Machine Learning' (arXiv, 16 July 2024) <http://arxiv.org/abs/2407.12220> accessed 18 July 2024. For another, similar analysis, see also Adrian de Wynter, 'Awes, Laws, and Flaws From Today's LLM Research' (*arXiv.org*, 27 August 2024) <https://arxiv.org/abs/2408.15409v2> accessed 8 October 2024; Anka Reuel and others, 'BetterBench: Assessing AI Benchmarks, Uncovering Issues, and Establishing Best Practices' (arXiv, 20 November 2024) <http://arxiv.org/abs/2411.12990> accessed 19 February 2025.

[102] Leech and others (n 101).

[103] Sayash Kapoor and Arvind Narayanan, 'Leakage and the Reproducibility Crisis in Machine-Learning-Based Science' (2023) 4 Patterns 100804.

[104] Hugh Zhang and others, 'A Careful Examination of Large Language Model Performance on Grade School Arithmetic' (arXiv, 3 May 2024) <http://arxiv.org/abs/2405.00332> accessed 7 June 2024 (however finding that such overfitting issues do affect some open-source models).

[105] Kapoor and Narayanan (n 103).

[106] Holden Karnofsky, 'AI Has Been Surprising for Years' (*Carnegie Endowment for International Peace*, 6 January 2025) <https://carnegieendowment.org/research/2025/01/ai-has-been-surprising-for-years?lang=en> accessed 20 January 2025.

expertise in areas such as biology, physics, chemistry, and physics.[107] Importantly for public debate, these tests are far less 'legible' to the general public, who may not be well positioned to assess progress on such domain on the basis of first-hand interactions.[108] Yet such progress does imply that it is increasingly harder to provide a clear or stable answer to the question of what cognitive tasks humans can do that AI systems reliably cannot.[109]

Third, the inadequacy of existing tests and benchmarks of course does not preclude scientific progress towards the design or operationalization of useful tests for understanding when particular forms of advanced AI are in reach.[110] Indeed, by designing tests that seek (implicitly or explicitly) to compare AI systems against human performance, we may also ourselves be committing a category error, missing the fact that, even if large language models fail to robustly meet a human-centric standard of intelligence, this might simply show that such tests fail to capture how particular systems may be 'smart' in their own idiosyncratic ways.[111]

Fourth, and more significantly, the prevalence of badly designed or overtly static[112] benchmarks may cut both ways, potentially contributing to not just overestimation but also underestimation of AI capabilities. For example, brief interactions with publicly and freely available chatbots, such as the older (but freely accessible) GPT-3.5, have often given inexperienced or incidental users the impression that the technology systematically fails many straightforward tasks when in fact such failures may be relatively contingent artefacts of a model's idiosyncratic sensitivities to prompt phrasing, such that it performs well on such tasks when prompts are rephrased in different (but reasonable) ways.

Indeed, just as we should be cautious of anthropomorphism in approaching the performance of AI models, we should also beware anthropocentric biases that might inappropriately lead us to dismiss the performance of LLM systems as 'not

[107] David Rein and others, 'GPQA: A Graduate-Level Google-Proof Q&A Benchmark' (arXiv, 20 November 2023) <http://arxiv.org/abs/2311.12022> accessed 21 February 2025; Elliot Glazer and others, 'FrontierMath: A Benchmark for Evaluating Advanced Mathematical Reasoning in AI' (arXiv, 20 December 2024) <http://arxiv.org/abs/2411.04872> accessed 21 February 2025; Long Phan and others, 'Humanity's Last Exam' (arXiv, 19 February 2025) <http://arxiv.org/abs/2501.14249> accessed 21 February 2025.

[108] Garrison Lovely, 'Why AI Progress Is Increasingly Invisible' (*TIME*, 8 January 2025) <https://time.com/7205359/why-ai-progress-is-increasingly-invisible/> accessed 20 February 2025.

[109] Karnofsky (n 106).

[110] Laura Weidinger and others, 'Toward an Evaluation Science for Generative AI Systems' (arXiv, 13 March 2025) <http://arxiv.org/abs/2503.05336> accessed 14 March 2025. See also Meredith Ringel Morris and others, 'Levels of AGI for Operationalizing Progress on the Path to AGI', *Proceedings of the 41st International Conference on Machine Learning* (PMLR 2024) <http://arxiv.org/abs/2311.02462> accessed 13 November 2023; Wanjun Zhong and others, 'AGIEval: A Human-Centric Benchmark for Evaluating Foundation Models' (arXiv, 13 April 2023) <http://arxiv.org/abs/2304.06364> accessed 18 April 2023.

[111] Robert Long, 'Are We Smart Enough to Know How Smart AIs Are?' [2023] *Asterisk* <https://asteriskmag.com/issues/03/are-we-smart-enough-to-know-how-smart-ais-are> accessed 11 October 2023.

[112] Kiela and others (n 36).

genuinely competent', for instance when apparent failures are only due to auxiliary factors, or when the LLM deploys mechanistic strategies that differ from those of humans.[113] That does not mean that the technology does not have flaws—nor that these idiosyncratic sensitivities should be swept under the rug as irrelevant to the question of a system's 'intelligence'. However, it does suggest, as Samuel Bowman has noted, that 'simply observing that an LLM fails at a task in some setting is not reliable evidence that that LLM doesn't have the skills or knowledge to do that task'.[114] Indeed, this is reflected in the aforementioned debates over the challenges to testing and evaluating these systems.

More importantly, this means that the difficulty of evaluation should not only temper excessive claims of apparent significant system performance, but also caution against rapid 'underclaiming'.[115] Indeed, if we lack good evaluation suites for AI systems, this implies that our processes can throw false negatives as well as false positives: just as poorly designed tests might lead us to perceive breakthroughs where none exist, we might also be in a situation where we are left unable to reliably identify when a given system might be (close to) achieving specific, critical capabilities.[116] This implies that, rather than merely trying to compensate for overclaiming tendencies through pervasive post hoc scepticism of reported results, a better (if harder) road forward will continue to involve the nurturing of a more mature and rigorous scientific domain of AI system evaluation.[117]

1.2.3 AI as High-variance Technology: The Stakes of Stochastic Portfolios

What does all this mean? One sceptical perspective might hold that, notwithstanding a few vivid successes, the core AI technology is in fact flawed, or so limited that it will not sustain progress; that the industry has been mostly overblown, or even that a new AI winter may shortly be upon us.

[113] Raphaël Millière and Charles Rathkopf, 'Anthropocentric Bias and the Possibility of Artificial Cognition' (*arXiv.org*, 4 July 2024) <https://arxiv.org/abs/2407.03859v1> accessed 27 September 2024.

[114] Samuel R Bowman, 'Eight Things to Know about Large Language Models' 7 <https://cims.nyu.edu/~sbowman/eightthings.pdf> accessed 27 February 2025.

[115] Samuel Bowman, 'The Dangers of Underclaiming: Reasons for Caution When Reporting How NLP Systems Fail' in Smaranda Muresan, Preslav Nakov, and Aline Villavicencio (eds), *Proceedings of the 60th Annual Meeting of the Association for Computational Linguistics (Volume 1: Long Papers)* (Association for Computational Linguistics 2022) <https://aclanthology.org/2022.acl-long.516> accessed 11 January 2024.

[116] Toby Shevlane and others, 'Model Evaluation for Extreme Risks' (arXiv, 24 May 2023) <http://arxiv.org/abs/2305.15324> accessed 25 May 2023; Kayla Matteucci and others, 'AI Systems of Concern' (arXiv, 9 October 2023) <http://arxiv.org/abs/2310.05876> accessed 10 October 2023.

[117] See John Burden, 'Evaluating AI Evaluation: Perils and Prospects' (arXiv, 12 July 2024) <http://arxiv.org/abs/2407.09221> accessed 15 July 2024 (proposing to draw inspiration from cognitive sciences—'which have a longstanding tradition of assessing general intelligence across diverse species'—in evaluating general-purpose AI systems).

Yet while an injection of caution would be welcome in many public debates around AI, shifting the pendulum to excessive scepticism might be a wrong lesson to draw. The reality of AI may be messier, and reflect something more like 'Amara's Law'—the adage that holds that 'we tend to overestimate the effect of a technology in the short run and underestimate the effect in the long run'.[118] If we are to govern adequately for change, we need to consider the implications of AI's uneven progress today, and how these may be affected by future change.

As discussed, in public and policymaker debates, 'AI' is often still treated as a single label. This can easily prime such observers to expect or ascribe to the technology a uniform level of performance, whether high or low. Yet as discussed, the single label of AI is far too coarse to capture the granularity or heterogeneity of techniques, capabilities, applications, and inputs to AI.

Given this, a better view might be that AI today is a diverse, heterogeneous, and high-variance portfolio. Rather than being a monolithic technology that either works flawlessly anywhere or must be completely over-hyped everywhere, AI technologies, techniques, and applications make up a high-variance field—a 'jagged frontier'[119]—that includes both systems that achieve constrained or flawed performance, with those that display remarkably high (or adequate) performance on other tasks or in other contexts. Both cases and instances need to be reckoned with, not only to understand AI as a technology, but also to meaningfully address its impacts.

As such, while we must reckon with the well-chronicled risks and harms deriving from AI hype,[120] these must also be set against the danger that we might under-hype or 'underclaim' the performance of AI systems: while often well-meant, this may ultimately harm experts' credibility, limit our ability to mitigate AI's existing harms and prepare for future ones,[121] and generally erode political support from states for any type of global regulatory action at all.[122]

There is therefore no single neat judgement to be made about AI. More interesting and productive than the binary question of whether AI is transformative or entirely overblown may be the more heterogeneous question of *where* and *how*

[118] The adage is named after American futurologist Roy Amara. Susan Ratcliffe (ed), 'Roy Amara 1925–2007: American Futurologist', *Oxford Essential Quotations* (Oxford University Press 2016) <http://www.oxfordreference.com/view/10.1093/acref/9780191826719.001.0001/acref-9780191826719> accessed 13 September 2018.

[119] Fabrizio Dell'Acqua and others, 'Navigating the Jagged Technological Frontier: Field Experimental Evidence of the Effects of AI on Knowledge Worker Productivity and Quality' (Harvard Business School Technology & Operations Mgt Unit 2023) Working Paper 24–013 <https://papers.ssrn.com/abstract=4573321> accessed 15 May 2024.

[120] Jeffrey Funk, 'What's Behind Technological Hype?' (2019) 36 Issues in Science and Technology 36, 38; Kevin LaGrandeur, 'The Consequences of AI Hype' [2023] AI and Ethics <https://doi.org/10.1007/s43681-023-00352-y> accessed 9 June 2024.

[121] Bowman (n 115).

[122] Nathan Gabriel Wood, 'Regulating Autonomous and AI-Enabled Weapon Systems: The Dangers of Hype' [2024] AI and Ethics <https://doi.org/10.1007/s43681-024-00448-z> accessed 9 June 2024 (discussing the challenges of both over- and under-hype).

AI matters—and how the answers to these questions might change in the coming years.[123] To what extent should we expect either further AI capability progress, or rapid proliferation? What kinds of change would these produce? These questions are important not only when talking about the prospects for AI today, but also when debating its importance going forward.

1.3 Trajectories: How Much Will AI Matter in the Near Future?

As such, I will now turn to two distinct, though commensurable, arguments for why we might expect considerable societal impact and change from AI technology.

I first discuss the possibility of change deriving from further AI progress, with the aim of clearing up some of the confusion around this contested topic, and to argue that, while there is pervasive uncertainty around anticipating or forecasting such breakthroughs, these might be grounds not for comfort but for caution and further study. I then turn to the parallel (if complementary) scenario of societal change deriving from further algorithmic proliferation, to argue that even if one assumes that AI capability progress may slow or hit unexpected barriers, we may nonetheless expect the rapid dissemination and usage of various already existing AI applications within the coming years, with disruptive global effects.

1.3.1 Further Progress at the AI Frontier: Between Hype and Counterhype

In the first place, we should explore whether, how, or under what conditions we might expect further societal impact and change from AI on the basis of ongoing and future progress in its underlying capabilities. Could we expect a continuation of the current AI summer?

After a decade of progress that has been surprisingly rapid (if not spotless), how far and how fast might we expect AI technology to advance within the coming years? To be certain, there is outstanding uncertainty over future capability progress in advanced general-purpose AI systems.[124] Yet while there remains some disagreement amongst AI researchers over the exact pathways or routes of development, a surprisingly large number of such experts expect significant breakthroughs over

[123] See also Allan Dafoe, 'AI Governance: A Research Agenda' (Center for the Governance of AI, Future of Humanity Institute 2018) 15–24 <https://www.fhi.ox.ac.uk/govaiagenda/> accessed 27 February 2025 (sketching components of mapping the technical landscape, and progress across it).

[124] Yoshua Bengio, 'International Scientific Report on the Safety of Advanced AI: Interim Report' (Department for Science, Innovation & Technology, and AI Safety Institute 2024) 2024/009 18–33 <https://www.gov.uk/government/publications/international-scientific-report-on-the-safety-of-advanced-ai> accessed 21 May 2024.

the coming decades, or even within the coming years. Surveys of AI experts show that, on aggregate, they give a 50 per cent chance to some form of 'High-Level Machine Intelligence' (HLMI) being achieved by the 2060s, with many disruptive performance levels being reached throughout the intermediate period.[125] Notably, more recent surveys find closer timelines (even accounting for their publication date).[126]

This suggests that, however important or disruptive we consider AI to be today, its importance—and its stakes—will only grow in the years to come. Nonetheless, the question of future progress in AI remains surrounded by deep uncertainties, as well as pervasive public misunderstandings and misperceptions. As such, it is worthwhile briefly delving into it, to clarify the assumptions, uncertainties, and parameters.

1.3.1.1 Lodestars and Thresholds: how advanced might AI become?

Many classic and conventional AI systems are 'narrow', in that they perform well only within the specific tasks that they have been trained for. Accordingly, they cannot be transferred well to new contexts, and they lack a broader human sense of context. Nonetheless, as discussed, advanced AI systems have become increasingly general-purpose in recent years. Many AI researchers assume that—whether progress comes fast or slow—further developments may eventually yield increasingly advanced forms of AI systems, which can precipitate considerable or even transformative social changes.[127]

What would such systems look like? Notions of advanced AI come under a wide diversity of headers and terms.[128] Classically, researchers have focused on the

[125] In these surveys, HLMI is defined as 'unaided machines [that] can accomplish every task better and more cheaply than human workers': Grace and others, 'When Will AI Exceed Human Performance?' (n 34) 731. For previous surveys, see also Vincent C Müller and Nick Bostrom, 'Future Progress in Artificial Intelligence: A Survey of Expert Opinion', *Fundamental Issues of Artificial Intelligence* (Springer 2016) 553 ('[a median estimate of] a one in two chance that high-level machine intelligence will be developed around 2040-2050, rising to a 9 in 10 chance by 2075'). See also Seth D Baum, Ben Goertzel, and Ted G Goertzel, 'How Long until Human-Level AI? Results from an Expert Assessment' (2011) 78 Technological Forecasting and Social Change 185.

[126] Grace and others, 'Thousands of AI Authors on the Future of AI' (n 34); Ross Gruetzemacher, David Paradice and Kang Bok Lee, 'Forecasting Transformative AI: An Expert Survey' [2019] arXiv:1901.08579 [cs] <http://arxiv.org/abs/1901.08579> accessed 17 April 2019. Interestingly, even the most 'optimistic' expert estimates appear further out than those given by the general public, which in one 2019 (US) survey assigned a 54% likelihood of developing HLMI within the next 10 years. Baobao Zhang and Allan Dafoe, 'Artificial Intelligence: American Attitudes and Trends' (Center for the Governance of AI and Future of Humanity Institute 2019) <https://www.ssrn.com/abstract=3312874> accessed 16 December 2019.

[127] Edward Parson and others, 'Artificial Intelligence in Strategic Context: An Introduction' (*AI Pulse*, 8 February 2019) <https://aipulse.org/artificial-intelligence-in-strategic-context-an-introduction/> accessed 26 February 2019.

[128] Matthijs Maas, 'Concepts in Advanced AI Governance: A Literature Review of Key Terms and Definitions' (Institute for Law & AI 2023) AI Foundations Report 3 <https://law-ai.org/advanced-ai-gov-concepts> accessed 27 February 2025.

anticipated form, architecture, design, or nature of future advanced AI systems.[129] These definitions focus on AI systems that can match the reasoning versatility or cross-domain goal achievement performance of humans. While older distinctions focused on 'strong' AI,[130] or 'AI+',[131] recent work has focused instead on thresholds such as 'human-level AI' (HLAI)[132] or 'high-level machine intelligence' (HLMI).[133] Most of all, debates in recent years have often become centred on the idea of 'artificial general intelligence' (AGI).[134] This concept remains significantly contested,[135] and there is no clear single agreed-upon definition.[136] One common approach describes AGI as a future type of AI system that would demonstrate 'the ability to achieve a variety of goals, and carry out a variety of tasks, in a variety of different contexts and environments',[137] achieving performance as well as a human in many or all domains.

At any rate, there are increasingly many active research and industry efforts pursuing advanced AI models, and even explicitly AGI. As early as 2017, a survey identified dozens of projects worldwide pursuing the development of AGI or

[129] See again Gruetzemacher and Whittlestone (n 6) 2 ('it is plausible that more advanced AI systems could precipitate dramatic societal changes . . . Several different terms have been used to refer to the possibility of . . . humanlike AI systems with the potential to lead to such changes. . . . These notions all imply that most of our concern should be afforded to systems which are human-like or sufficiently general in their capabilities').

[130] John R Searle, 'Minds, Brains, and Programs' (1980) 3 Behavioral and Brain Sciences 417, 417. Russell and Norvig (n 11) 1020; Ray Kurzweil, *The Singularity Is Near* (Viking Press 2005) 260.

[131] David J Chalmers, 'The Singularity: A Philosophical Analysis' (2010) 17 Journal of Consciousness Studies 7, 11.

[132] John McCarthy, 'From Here to Human-Level AI', *Proceedings of the Fifth International Conference on Principles of Knowledge Representation and Reasoning* (Morgan Kaufmann Publishers Inc 1996) <https://citeseerx.ist.psu.edu/viewdoc/download?doi=10.1.1.384.8219&rep=rep1&type=pdf> accessed 26 June 2020. Nils J Nilsson, 'Human-Level Artificial Intelligence? Be Serious!' [2005] *AI Magazine* 8.

[133] Grace and others, 'When Will AI Exceed Human Performance?' (n 34).

[134] Ben Goertzel and Cassio Pennachin (eds), *Artificial General Intelligence* (Springer Berlin Heidelberg 2007). However, the original use of the term 'artificial general intelligence' is likely in: Mark Gubrud, 'Nanotechnology and International Security' (1997). Fifth Foresight Conference on Molecular Nanotechnology <https://legacy.foresight.org/Conferences/MNT05/Papers/Gubrud/index.html> accessed 11 March 2025.

[135] Melanie Mitchell, 'Debates on the Nature of Artificial General Intelligence' (2024) 383 Science eado7069.

[136] For instance, Morris and others have surveyed nine common definitions for AGI, which variably define it as: (1) a system with the ability to pass the Turing test; (2) a system with consciousness (Searle's Strong AI'); (3) a system which surpasses the *processes* of the human brain in complexity and speed; (4) a system which surpasses the *performance* of humans on cognitive tasks; (5) a system with the ability to learn new tasks (rather than specialization to one task); (6) a system that outperforms humans at most economically valuable work; (7) a system that is flexible, general and resourceful; (8) systems with the ability to accomplish complex, multi-step tasks in the open world; (9) systems such as state-of-the-art LLMs. See Morris and others (n 110) 2–3 (citing sources). For other discussions of these and other definitions, their conditions, and their implications, see also Maas (n 128) 24–34, 61–65; Kevin Kohler, 'AGI: Definitions, Tests, and Levels' (*AI Analogies*, 23 May 2024) <https://machinocene.substack.com/p/agi-an-overview?publication_id=2076501> accessed 23 May 2024.

[137] Ben Goertzel, 'Artificial General Intelligence: Concept, State of the Art, and Future Prospects' (2014) 5 Journal of Artificial General Intelligence 1, 2. See also Shane Legg and Marcus Hutter, 'Universal Intelligence: A Definition of Machine Intelligence' (2007) 17 Minds and Machines 391.

AGI-like systems[138]—an estimate that was updated by 2020 to 72 active AGI research projects spread across 37 countries.[139] Of course, the prospects for success of many of these efforts (especially relative to frontier labs) remain questionable, at best, given the limited resources available to many. However, not all AI labs face those constraints, and, significantly, almost all leading AI labs—including OpenAI,[140] DeepMind,[141] Anthropic,[142] x.AI,[143] and DeepSeek[144]—as well as many large tech companies—including Microsoft[145] and Meta[146]—have in recent years expressed a clear ambition to develop AGI and similar forms of advanced AI systems. That is not to say that this ambition is uncritically accepted in, or shared by, the AI research community at large.[147] Nonetheless, the goal has even come to the attention within policy contexts, with the *2024 Report to Congress* of the US–China Economic and Security Review Commission explicitly recommending that Congress establish and fund a massive programme dedicated to acquiring an AGI capability.[148]

138 Seth D Baum, 'A Survey of Artificial General Intelligence Projects for Ethics, Risk, and Policy' (Global Catastrophic Risk Institute 2017) 17–1 <https://papers.ssrn.com/abstract=3070741> accessed 17 January 2018.

139 McKenna Fitzgerald, Aaron Boddy, and Seth D Baum, '2020 Survey of Artificial General Intelligence Projects for Ethics, Risk, and Policy' (Global Catastrophic Risk Institute 2020) Global Catastrophic Risk Institute Technical Report 20–1 <https://gcrinstitute.org/2020-survey-of-artificial-general-intelligence-projects-for-ethics-risk-and-policy/> accessed 13 December 2021.

140 Sam Altman, 'Planning for AGI and Beyond' (*OpenAI*, 24 February 2023) <https://openai.com/index/planning-for-agi-and-beyond/> accessed 6 March 2023; Sam Altman, Greg Brockman and Ilya Sutskever, 'Governance of Superintelligence' (*OpenAI*, 22 May 2023) <https://openai.com/blog/governance-of-superintelligence> accessed 23 May 2023.

141 Morris and others (n 110).

142 See broadly Anthropic, 'Core Views on AI Safety: When, Why, What, and How' (*Anthropic*, 8 March 2023) <https://www.anthropic.com/index/core-views-on-ai-safety> accessed 10 March 2023; See also the coverage in Kevin Roose, 'Inside the White-Hot Center of A.I. Doomerism' *The New York Times* (11 July 2023) <https://www.nytimes.com/2023/07/11/technology/anthropic-ai-claude-chatbot.html> accessed 11 January 2024.

143 Sean Michael Kerner, 'Elon Musk Reveals xAI Efforts, Predicts Full AGI by 2029' (*VentureBeat*, 14 July 2023) <https://venturebeat.com/ai/elon-musk-reveals-xai-efforts-predicts-full-agi-by-2029/> accessed 21 February 2025.

144 'DeepSeek (@deepseek_ai)—Unravel the Mystery of AGI with Curiosity' (*X (formerly Twitter)*, 28 January 2025) <https://x.com/deepseek_ai> accessed 21 February 2025.

145 Sébastien Bubeck and others, 'Sparks of Artificial General Intelligence: Early Experiments with GPT-4' (arXiv, 22 March 2023) <http://arxiv.org/abs/2303.12712> accessed 23 March 2023.

146 Alex Heath, 'Mark Zuckerberg's New Goal Is Creating Artificial General Intelligence' (*The Verge*, 18 January 2024) <https://www.theverge.com/2024/1/18/24042354/mark-zuckerberg-meta-agi-reorg-interview> accessed 19 January 2024. Meta has since articulated a goal to pursue 'superintelligent AI'. Cade Metz and Mike Isaac, 'Meta Is Creating a New A.I. Lab to Pursue "Superintelligence"' *The New York Times* (10 June 2025) <https://www.nytimes.com/2025/06/10/technology/meta-new-ai-lab-superintelligence.html> accessed 11 June 2025.

147 See Borhane Blili-Hamelin and others, 'Stop Treating "AGI" as the North-Star Goal of AI Research' (arXiv, 7 February 2025) <http://arxiv.org/abs/2502.03689> accessed 19 February 2025. Indeed, in a 2025 survey by the Association for the Advancement of Artificial Intelligence (AAAI), a majority (77%) of polled respondents prioritized 'designing AI systems with an acceptable risk-benefit profile over the direct pursuit of AGI'. See Association for the Advancement of Artificial Intelligence, 'AAAI 2025 Presidential Panel on the Future of AI Research' (Association for the Advancement of Artificial Intelligence 2025) 66 <https://aaai.org/wp-content/uploads/2025/03/AAAI-2025-PresPanel-Report-FINAL.pdf> accessed 19 March 2025.

148 US–China Economic and Security Review Commission, '2024 Annual Report to Congress' (2024) 27 <https://www.uscc.gov/annual-report/2024-annual-report-congress> accessed 27 February 2025.

To be sure, there remains considerable debate over advanced AI, and especially the idea of AGI. Some have rejected out of hand the very possibility of such systems,[149] or have objected that the very concept of 'AGI' is meaningless, because even human intelligence is not properly 'general', and rather performs differently across many dimensions.[150]

However, putting semantics aside, there is a surprising amount of agreement among AI researchers that it would be *theoretically* possible to build forms of advanced AI at the level of 'high-level machine intelligence'.[151] Rather, many disagree on two other counts. In the first place, some suggest that while this technology is possible in principle, the current paradigm of scaling up (Transformer-based) foundation models with more compute and data is not on the right track to such systems.[152] They argue that other scientific pathways still hold the key to such systems,[153] potentially in conjunction with the existing approach.[154] In the second place, and relatedly, there is little consensus over *when* the development of such advanced AI systems might happen, with estimates ranging from the technology being a decade out to centuries away.[155]

As such, while questions of the prospects for—and timelines of—future progress in AI are deeply uncertain, it is still valuable to discuss the ways in which different people have approached this question. Indeed, there have been various models developed that aim to explore future development ceilings, pathways, and trajectories for AI.[156] These draw on various lines of evidence that range from (expert) judgement-based predictions, from an 'outside' view, and from an 'inside'

[149] Jobst Landgrebe and Barry Smith, *Why Machines Will Never Rule the World: Artificial Intelligence without Fear* (1st edn, Routledge 2022); though see also the reply in William J Rapaport, 'Is Artificial General Intelligence Impossible?' <https://cse.buffalo.edu/~rapaport/Papers/lands.pdf> accessed 27 February 2025.

[150] Kevin Kelly, 'The Myth of a Superhuman AI' (*Backchannel*, 25 April 2017) <https://backchannel.com/the-myth-of-a-superhuman-ai-59282b686c62> accessed 13 May 2017. Though for a response, see Stuart Russell, *Human Compatible: Artificial Intelligence and the Problem of Control* (Viking 2019) 166. However, for a satirical essay collecting some often raised claims made in support of the idea that smarter-than-human AI is categorical impossible, see Ben Garfinkel and others, 'On the Impossibility of Supersized Machines' [2017] arXiv:1703.10987 [physics] <http://arxiv.org/abs/1703.10987> accessed 12 November 2018.

[151] Grace and others, 'When Will AI Exceed Human Performance?' (n 34).

[152] Marcus (n 13).

[153] For different taxonomies and surveys of proposed approaches to building advanced AI, see also Goertzel and Pennachin (n 134) 22; William Hannas and others, 'China's Advanced AI Research: Monitoring China's Paths to "General" Artificial Intelligence' (Center for Security and Emerging Technology 2022) 4–5 <https://cset.georgetown.edu/publication/chinas-advanced-ai-research/> accessed 9 September 2022. As well as Maas (n 128) 36–37. (listing 11 proposed pathways, paradigms and approaches).

[154] Edward Hughes and others, 'Open-Endedness Is Essential for Artificial Superhuman Intelligence', *Proceedings of the 41st International Conference on Machine Learning, Vienna, Austria. PMLR 235, 2024* (arXiv 2024) <http://arxiv.org/abs/2406.04268> accessed 9 June 2024.

[155] Grace and others, 'When Will AI Exceed Human Performance?' (n 34) 729.

[156] Keith Wynroe, David Atkinson, and Jaime Sevilla, 'Literature Review of Transformative Artificial Intelligence Timelines' (*Epoch*, 17 January 2023) <https://epochai.org/blog/literature-review-of-transformative-artificial-intelligence-timelines> accessed 30 January 2023.

view.[157] Let us review these, starting from the most indirect sources of evidence, and gradually converging on more direct lines of evidence.

1.3.1.2 Judgement-based predictions: expert surveys and generalist forecasts

In approaching the debates around AI capability ceilings and rates of further progress, a basic background point of evidence is to (temporarily) suspend either object-level (inside-view) or referent-level (outside-view) analysis, and simply 'defer to the experts'.[158] To be clear, this should not substitute for attempted examination of those more direct sources of evidence. Yet it can provide a basic background source of information.

Within this work, scholars have attempted to gather estimates of future AI development patterns that are based on general expert opinion, as measured through opinion surveys or expert elicitation techniques (e.g. Delphi method).[159] As discussed, various surveys have shown that experts believe that various forms of advanced AI (e.g. 'AGI', 'HLMI') within the next few decades,[160] though there is significant variance among respondents. For instance, in an influential 2017 survey, around a quarter of respondents expected the development of AGI within 20 years (i.e., by 2037)—but another quarter believed this would not happen for at least 100 years.[161] A 2019 survey of 300 AI experts suggested a 20 per cent probability of achieving 'human-level machine intelligence' by 2036, a 50 per cent probability by 2060, and an 85 per cent probability by 2100.[162] This distribution was

[157] The distinction between an 'inside view' and an 'outside view' analysis used here derives from the classical psychological work by Kahnemann, Tverskey, and Lovallo on planning and forecasting biases. In this model:

> [a]n inside view forecast is generated by focusing on the case at hand, by considering the plan and the obstacles to its completion, by constructing scenarios of future progress, and by extrapolating current trends. The outside view . . . essentially ignores the details of the case at hand, and involves no attempt at detailed forecasting of the future history of the project. Instead, it focuses on the statistics of a class of cases chosen to be similar in relevant respects to the present one. The case at hand is also compared to other members of the class, in an attempt to assess its position in the distribution of outcomes for the class.

Daniel Kahneman and Dan Lovallo, 'Timid Choices and Bold Forecasts: A Cognitive Perspective on Risk Taking' (1993) 39 Management Science 17, 25. The insight that outside-view forecasts are often more accurate underlies the methodology called 'reference class forecasting'. In more recent work on 'superforecasting' of various events, there is an emphasis on first taking the outside view, and only then to modify the conclusion using the inside view. Philip E Tetlock and Dan Gardner, *Superforecasting: The Art and Science of Prediction* (reprint edn, Broadway Books 2016). I thank Olle Häggström for highlighting this link, and reminding me of the appropriate sequence.

[158] Wynroe, Atkinson, and Sevilla (n 156); Max Roser, 'AI Timelines: What Do Experts in Artificial Intelligence Expect for the Future?' (*Our World in Data*, 6 December 2022) <https://ourworldindata.org/ai-timelines> accessed 12 December 2022.

[159] Ross Gruetzemacher and others, 'Forecasting AI Progress: A Research Agenda' (2021) 170 Technological Forecasting and Social Change 120909.

[160] For an adjacent, broader survey, see also Julian Michael and others, 'What Do NLP Researchers Believe? Results of the NLP Community Metasurvey' 31.

[161] Grace and others, 'When Will AI Exceed Human Performance?' (n 34).

[162] Baobao Zhang and others, 'Forecasting AI Progress: Evidence from a Survey of Machine Learning Researchers' (arXiv 2022) arXiv:2206.04132 <http://arxiv.org/abs/2206.04132> accessed 13 June 2022. Note, in terms of terminology, this survey draws together the notions of 'High-Level Machine

echoed in a 2022 survey, which found that the median AI researcher gave a 50 per cent chance of HLMI being developed within 37 years (2059).[163]

Notably, these estimates have dropped significantly since then, in the wake of the high-profile success of generative AI since 2023. For instance, a late-2023 survey of over 2,700 researchers who published at top conferences, found that researchers think the chance of unaided machines outperforming humans in every possible task is 10 per cent by 2027 and 50 per cent by 2047, with the latter estimate being 13 years earlier than that suggested by the 2022 survey.[164]

Beyond surveys of AI experts, other judgement-based studies have sought to draw on other sources of expertise. For instance, a range of scholars and institutions have attempted to distil AI development trajectory estimates from information aggregation mechanisms such as generalist forecaster predictions, especially those made on prediction platforms or within forecasting competitions.[165] For instance, in one 2022 forecasting tournament, 31 superforecasters were asked by what date they expected the philosopher Nick Bostrom—author of the book *Superintelligence*—to affirm the existence of an AGI system. The median superforecaster thought there was a 1 per cent chance that this would happen by 2030, a 21 per cent chance by 2050, and a 75 per cent chance by 2100.[166]

What should we make of expert predictions that these forms of advanced AI might be some decades away? To be clear, while providing salient evidence, it should be kept in mind that such approaches can face some methodological challenges. In general, there have been deep challenges around conducting effective long-range forecasts, and the track record of past predictions around AI is chequered at best.[167]

Intelligence' and 'human-level machine intelligence', using them somewhat interchangeably to refer to 'when machines would be able to collectively perform almost all economically relevant tasks'.

[163] Stein-Perlman, Weinstein-Raun, and Grace (n 34).

[164] Grace and others, 'Thousands of AI Authors on the Future of AI' (n 34).

[165] See for instance the forecasting platform Metaculus: Anthony Aguirre, 'Will There Be Human–Machine Intelligence Parity before 2040?' (*Metaculus*, 1 December 2016) <https://www.metaculus.com/questions/384/humanmachine-intelligence-parity-by-2040/> accessed 18 October 2022; Matthew Barnett, 'When Will the First General AI System Be Devised, Tested, and Publicly Announced?' (*Metaculus*, 23 August 2020) <https://www.metaculus.com/questions/5121/date-of-artificial-general-intelligence/> accessed 18 October 2022; Steinhardt (n 35).

[166] Ezra Karger and others, 'Forecasting Existential Risks: Evidence from a Long-Run Forecasting Tournament' (Forecasting Research Institute 2023) FRI Working Paper 1 <https://forecastingresearch.org/s/XPT.pdf> 27 February 2025; Will Henshall, 'When Might AI Outsmart Us? It Depends Who You Ask' [2024] *TIME* <https://time.com/6556168/when-ai-outsmart-humans/> accessed 23 January 2024. See also: Daniel Kokotajlo and others, 'AI 2027' (AI Futures Project 2025) <https://ai-2027.com/> accessed 10 June 2025.

[167] Indeed, many past predictions of AI progress have proven wildly unreliable. See: Stuart Armstrong and Kaj Sotala, 'How We're Predicting AI—Or Failing To' in Jan Romportl and others (eds), *Beyond AI: Artificial Dreams* (University of West Bohemia 2012) <https://intelligence.org/files/PredictingAI.pdf> accessed 27 February 2025; Stuart Armstrong, Kaj Sotala, and Sean S OhEigeartaigh, 'The Errors, Insights and Lessons of Famous AI Predictions—and What They Mean for the Future' (2014) 26 Journal of Experimental & Theoretical Artificial Intelligence <http://www.fhi.ox.ac.uk/wp-content/uploads/FAIC.pdf> accessed 18 February 2017.

There are also, of course, many methodological challenges around the use of surveys, which can be notoriously sensitive to slight differences in phrasing,[168] and need to be carefully scoped to avoid selection bias in respondent samples. For instance, it has been suggested that at least some influential early surveys of AI progress may have suffered from methodological issues relating to sample size and response bias[169]—although many of these shortfalls were better addressed in subsequent surveys, which nonetheless returned similar outcomes.[170] Nonetheless, as in many other social scientific fields, the possibility of such methodological issues continues to pose challenges to gaining a thorough understanding of views in a field.[171]

More fundamentally, there may be concerns that an approach based on eliciting 'expert judgement' does not work well in the context of evaluating the future of AI development. AI progress may be an idiosyncratic area where even domain experts find it hard to anticipate (or conversely, rule out) sudden progress or developments *ex ante*.[172] This might be because many of the contexts that have been critical to developing reliable and useful forecasting expertise (such as the ability for experts to get rapid feedback) are absent in long-range forecasting of A(G)I scenarios.[173] Indeed, if it turns out to be the case that the development of such advanced AI systems requires fundamentally new technical insights, it is even possible that there are today no relevant experts on these future AI architectures, implying that these expert elicitation processes cannot, by definition, generate accurate or well-formed predictions. That is, there may be a category error here, where one can only consult AI experts today that are experts on contemporary machine learning approaches. Querying today's most visible AI experts may implicitly assume that the contemporary approaches they are experts in, will in fact play a role in (e.g. scale to) the development of future advanced AI systems,[174] which is

[168] For instance, surveys have found significant differences on reported timelines for AI capabilities, based on relatively minor differences in phrasing. Grace and others, 'When Will AI Exceed Human Performance?' (n 34) 731.

[169] See Melanie Mitchell, 'Do Half of AI Researchers Believe That There's a 10% Chance AI Will Kill Us All?' (*AI: A Guide for Thinking Humans*, 23 April 2023) <https://aiguide.substack.com/p/do-half-of-ai-researchers-believe> accessed 25 May 2023.

[170] See for instance Grace and others, 'Thousands of AI Authors on the Future of AI' (n 34) 22. ('Compared to the 2022 survey [Grace et al., 2022], which was distributed to a randomly-selected half of the researchers who published in 2021 at NeurIPS or ICML, the 2023 survey was distributed to more than three times as many recipients, and to recipients from a wider range of AI specialties').

[171] Indeed, such challenges should be taken into consideration not just when evaluating surveys of AI experts, but also in surveys of public opinion around AI. Harry Law, 'Do Most People Really Want to Slow Down AI?' (*Learning from Examples*, 31 August 2023) <https://learningfromexamples.substack.com/p/do-most-people-really-want-to-slow> accessed 11 September 2023.

[172] On the specific case of the difficulty of predicting AI progress (or ruling it out) even for AI experts, cf. Eliezer Yudkowsky, 'There's No Fire Alarm for Artificial General Intelligence' (*Machine Intelligence Research Institute*, 14 October 2017) <https://intelligence.org/2017/10/13/fire-alarm/> accessed 13 December 2020.

[173] Armstrong and Sotala (n 167) 52–75.

[174] On the problem of relying on (aggregate) expert judgement in conditions where there may not be a relevant reference class of experts, see generally M Granger Morgan, 'Use (and Abuse) of Expert

itself a not uncontroversial assumption. At the same time, this critique should not be taken too far: one does not need to assume a strong form of the scaling hypothesis to take the more defensible expectation that current approaches will remain at least somewhat relevant to future AI. At the very least, appealing to the experts in the most successful present-day disciplines seems like a defensible, even sensible, starting position for investigation, so long as it is not confused with a definitive answer.

Similarly, while prediction mechanisms based on generalist forecasters can be a valuable and underappreciated epistemic tool for many challenges, hurdles affect the use of this method also. In some cases, there may be difficulties in appropriately resolving questions,[175] and risks of misinterpreting forecasters depending on poor operationalization of the original questions.

However, while many of these challenges might ground reasonable objections to (or caution around) putting too much stock in any specific point-estimates for dates by which advanced AI will be developed, we should also not discard them entirely. After all, while one can quibble over the particular accuracy or inaccuracy of the dates mentioned, the larger point that should not be lost may be a qualitative one: a sizeable number of AI experts see the scenario of very advanced AI systems being developed in the coming decades as a serious possibility.

Even if exact timelines are not known, however, the expectation of further transformative progress occurring in AI—very conceivably in the next decade; likely within our lifetimes; almost certainly within our children's lifetimes—should ground a degree of caution and serious engagement with these scenarios. If nothing else, this should ground further analytical engagement with the question of AI progress, either from an outside view or a direct inside view.

1.3.1.3 Outside-view evidence: historical extrapolation and induction

Taking one step beyond indirect judgement-based forecasts, we can move to take an outside view on the question of advanced AI, based on extrapolation from historical trends, or on reference class comparisons or analogies with other technologies. Once again, this does not focus much on specific considerations around AI and AI progress. Rather, these approaches ask more general, comparative

Elicitation in Support of Decision Making for Public Policy' (2014) 111 Proceedings of the National Academy of Sciences 7176. On the other hand, as noted by Sotala and Yampolskiy, '[t]he lack of expert agreement suggests that expertise in the field does not contribute to an ability to make reliable predictions. If the judgment of experts is not reliable, then, probably, neither is anyone else's. This suggests that it is unjustified to be highly certain of AGI being near, but also of it not being near.' Kaj Sotala and Roman V Yampolskiy, 'Responses to Catastrophic AGI Risk: A Survey' (2015) 90 Physica Scripta 018001, 8.

[175] For an accessible discussion, see Nuño Sempere, 'Hurdles of Using Forecasting as a Tool for Making Sense of AI Progress' (*Measure Is Unceasing*, 7 November 2023) <https://nunosempere.com/blog/2023/11/07/hurdles-forecasting-ai/> accessed 8 November 2023.

questions in order to try to put the future of AI development within a broader ontological or historical perspective. There are various approaches and considerations to this.

1.3.1.3.1 Extrapolation from AI capabilities, economic history, or AI inputs

Perhaps the most famous—and controversial—methodology in debates around the future of AI has involved the extrapolation of various historical trends out into the future.[176]

Before discussing concrete instances and versions of this approach as it is applied to AI, it is worth clarifying the status and usage of this methodology. This is because, in many modern AI debates, usage of trend extrapolation has at times come under fire, or has been decried or dismissed as an invalid, naive approach—or even 'baseless speculation'.[177] In this sceptical perspective, such approaches skirt the hard work of actually grappling with the underlying causes and processes of a trend being modelled, and unreflexively draw straight (or, as is often the case, exponentially curved) lines on graphs, in a way that is fundamentally unwarranted.

In one sense, these disagreements get to core epistemic commitments and assumptions. After all, a mere trend line through data points can be considered as a theory with some inductive support, but lacking a mechanism.[178] The question over whether a theory based (primarily or exclusively) on previous observations justifies expectations of more such observations in the future is well established in the philosophy of science as the 'problem of induction'.[179] More pragmatically, however, while a degree of scepticism regarding trend extrapolation may be understandable—given the sloppy ways in which this low-effort methodology might be applied by some—a blanket dismissal of the methodology may be unnecessarily dismissive. After all, forms of trend extrapolation have long been used as one of several approaches to enable decision-making under uncertainty. It has been used to model certain long-range trends in population growth[180] as well as across domains of technology forecasting.[181] Indeed, it has been argued that

[176] Shahar Avin, 'Exploring Artificial Intelligence Futures' (2018) 2 Journal of AI Humanities 169, 182.

[177] Arvind Narayanan and Sayash Kapoor, 'AI Scaling Myths' (*AI Snake Oil*, 27 June 2024) <https://www.aisnakeoil.com/p/ai-scaling-myths> accessed 30 July 2024.

[178] I thank Shahar Avin for discussion and observations on this point. Any remaining errors are my own.

[179] Leah Henderson, 'The Problem of Induction' in Edward N Zalta and Uri Nodelman (eds), *The Stanford Encyclopedia of Philosophy* (Winter 2022, Metaphysics Research Lab, Stanford University 2022) <https://plato.stanford.edu/archives/win2022/entries/induction-problem/> accessed 17 August 2024.

[180] J Scott Armstrong, 'Extrapolation for Time-Series and Cross-Sectional Data' in J Scott Armstrong (ed), *Principles of Forecasting: A Handbook for Researchers and Practitioners* (Springer US 2001).

[181] Peng-Hung Tsai and others, 'Quantitative Technology Forecasting: A Review of Trend Extrapolation Methods' (2023) 20 International Journal of Innovation and Technology Management 2330002.

extrapolation may be particularly warranted in situations where 'many forecasts are required, little is known about the situation, the situation is stable, and expert forecasts might be biased'.[182]

The question, of course, is whether, or in which situations, trend extrapolations are appropriate for evaluating AI. As such, the relative reliability of these approaches may depend very strongly on what is being extrapolated, and how. This can be seen by considering the range of ways that trend extrapolation has been used in forecasting AI progress.

Perhaps the most controversial, naive approach to extrapolation has involved the direct extrapolation of AI performance on different benchmarks over time (or at different compute budgets) into the future.[183] There are also other uses of extrapolation which have sought to theorize the future of AI, in a way that even abstracts away from the direct capabilities of the models in question. For instance, some have sought to extrapolate long-run historical trends in economic growth, to ask whether, given patterns in macro-scale economic history,[184] we should expect some forms of extreme economic growth to occur in the coming century, deriving from some source that is plausibly technological.[185] While this can provide a valuable baseline for indirect analysis, one can still challenge the specific assumptions used,[186] or the lack of a theorized mechanism.

More nuanced approaches, then, have sought to not just extrapolate on the basis of observed or assumed trends in AI capabilities (or their macro-scale economic impacts), but rather to focus on trends in underlying mechanisms or drivers of progress. For instance, one approach has examined historical trends in the efforts and resources dedicated to creating advanced AI: the argument here is that if the field of AI has managed to achieve steady progress throughout

[182] Armstrong (n 180) 217.

[183] For instance, in one (controversial) account, Leopold Aschenbrenner suggested that the leap in capabilities between the GPT-2 and GPT-4 models—separated by four years and an approximately ~100,000 effective compute scaleup—was equivalent to the difference in capabilities between a human 'preschooler' and a 'smart high-schooler'—and that accordingly we should expect a similarly sized qualitative leap in performance to yield transformative expert-level AI systems as early as the year 2027: Aschenbrenner (n 7) 9. However, this approach has been critiqued, because its characterization of the relative levels of performance and competence of these models may not hold. See Kannegieter (n 8); Gary Marcus, 'AGI by 2027?' (*Marcus on AI*, 5 June 2024) <https://garymarcus.substack.com/p/agi-by-2027> accessed 17 August 2024.

[184] David Roodman, 'Modeling the Human Trajectory' (*Open Philanthropy*, 15 June 2020) <https://www.openphilanthropy.org/blog/modeling-human-trajectory> accessed 31 August 2020; Daniel Kokotajlo, 'Precedents for Economic N-Year Doubling before 4n-Year Doubling' (*AI Impacts*, 14 April 2020) <https://aiimpacts.org/precedents-for-economic-n-year-doubling-before-4n-year-doubling/> accessed 5 September 2020.

[185] Tom Davidson, 'Could Advanced AI Drive Explosive Economic Growth?' (Open Philanthropy Project 2021) <https://www.openphilanthropy.org/could-advanced-ai-drive-explosive-economic-growth> accessed 10 February 2022.

[186] See for instance David Thorstad, 'Against the Singularity Hypothesis' (Global Priorities Institute, University of Oxford 2022) No. 19-2022 <https://globalprioritiesinstitute.org/against-the-singularity-hypothesis-david-thorstad/> accessed 1 November 2022 (arguing that the scenario rests on 'implausible growth assumptions').

its history—despite working from relatively modest resources throughout most of this period—then the fact that corporate investment and academic talent dedicated to developing this technology has recently exploded should, all else being equal, presage an acceleration in the field's progress.[187] For instance, Tom Davidson has attempted to model future AI progress on the basis of 'semi-informative priors'—that is, only basic information about how long people have historically attempted to build truly transformative AI and with what resources—and comparing this investment against those made in other, comparable research fields (in STEM, or proving difficult mathematical conjectures) in order to understand how long it took major problems in those fields to be completed, given the levels of funding and effort dedicated to them.[188] On the basis of this outside-view approach, he expects a 1–18 per cent chance of systems such as AGI being developed by 2036, although this estimate is caveated by significant uncertainty and methodological challenges.[189]

Of course, the direct use of trend extrapolation to make specific predictions hardly exhausts the potential use of historical patterns and comparison in considering the future of AI.

1.3.1.3.2 Meta-induction from the historical topology of science and the record of past predictions

To explore the outside-view approach further, we can therefore cast a broader net, and ask more general comparative questions around the topology of scientific progress. That is, in considering the future of AI, what can we learn from the accelerating historical rate of development in the development of new technologies?[190] Conversely, what can we learn from the historical barriers to technology development, including unexpected delays in development,[191] in suggesting ways in which the development of truly advanced AI might be further in the future than optimists might assume?

Such comparisons are interesting not just in a substantive sense, in what they might weakly tell us about how the development dynamics for AI. They are also interesting in clarifying our epistemic situation: what is the chance that we are

[187] Max Roser, 'Artificial Intelligence Has Advanced Despite Having Few Resources Dedicated to Its Development—Now Investments Have Increased Substantially' [2023] Our World in Data <https://ourworldindata.org/ai-investments> accessed 11 January 2024.

[188] Tom Davidson, 'Semi-Informative Priors over AI Timelines' (Open Philanthropy Project 2021) <https://www.openphilanthropy.org/research/semi-informative-priors-over-ai-timelines/> accessed 13 June 2022.

[189] ibid.

[190] Max Roser, 'Technology over the Long Run: Zoom Out to See How Dramatically the World Can Change within a Lifetime' (*Our World in Data*, 6 December 2022) <https://ourworldindata.org/technology-long-run> accessed 12 December 2022.

[191] Matthijs Maas, 'Paths Untaken: The History, Epistemology and Strategy of Technological Restraint, and Lessons for AI' (*Verfassungsblog*, 9 August 2022) <https://verfassungsblog.de/paths-untaken/> accessed 12 August 2022. This theme is discussed further in Section 4.3.2.

over-optimistic or over-pessimistic about the future of AI, in comparison to how often others have made similar errors in the past?

In a sense, this approach approaches the question of future AI progress on the basis of meta-induction over the track record of past predictions of past progress. There are a broad and a narrow version of this.

In the broad version, one considers the general historical track record of past technological predictions in general, especially those made by famous futurists. Such an analysis is challenging, however, as the performance of different historical futurists seems to have varied significantly.[192] Indeed, there is interpretative contestation over the actual track record of some predictors, especially with predictions made on the basis of trend extrapolation. For instance, Ray Kurzweil, perhaps the most famous user of this approach, in 2010 graded his own predictive track record, arguing that out of 147 predictions he made in 1999, 127 were 'correct or essentially correct', yielding a predictive accuracy as high as 86 per cent.[193] Other reviews however have suggested this may be unusually charitable, and his real predictive record might have been as low as 7 per cent.[194]

A more narrow version of this approach would be to look at the more specific historical track record of past predictions made around AI development.[195] Such an analysis likewise suggests that many AI experts in the past have been overly optimistic about the prospects for advanced AI. For instance, Herbert Simon predicted in 1960 that 'machines will be capable, within 20 years, of doing any work that a man can do'.[196] There are many other such cases.[197] Indeed, one review of

[192] On the track record of past futurists' predictions, see also Lukeprog, 'Futurism's Track Record' (*LessWrong*, 2014) <https://www.lesswrong.com/posts/6ycPKhdmDgWsoyvKd/futurism-s-track-record> accessed 16 August 2022; Holden Karnofsky, 'The Track Record of Futurists Seems . . . Fine' (*Cold Takes*, 30 June 2022) <https://www.cold-takes.com/the-track-record-of-futurists-seems-fine/> accessed 16 August 2022. Karnofsky's analysis is based off a study of predictions made by the 'Big Three' SF authors (Arthur C Clarke, Robert Heinlein, and Isaac Asimov), conducted in: Arb Research, 'Scoring the Big 3's Predictive Performance' (Arb 2022) <https://arbresearch.com/files/big_three.pdf> accessed 20 October 2022. For a critical response, however, see also Dan Luu, 'Futurist Prediction Methods and Accuracy' (14 September 2022) <https://danluu.com/futurist-predictions/> accessed 15 September 2022 (reviewing the track record of many other influential futurists to argue that the predictive track record of many is quite bad, and that more recent analyses around the future of AI 'fundamentally use the same techniques as the futurists analyses we looked at here and then add a few things on top that are also things that people who make accurate predictions do').

[193] Ray Kurzweil, 'How My Predictions Are Faring' 5 <https://www.thekurzweillibrary.com/images/How-My-Predictions-Are-Faring.pdf> accessed 27 February 2025. This claim has been commonly quoted since. See Peter H Diamandis, '86% Accuracy Rate In Tech Predictions' (11 September 2017) <https://www.diamandis.com/blog/86-accuracy-rate-in-tech-predictions> accessed 17 August 2024.

[194] Luu (n 192).

[195] Armstrong, Sotala, and OhEigeartaigh (n 167); AI Impacts, 'Accuracy of AI Predictions' (*AI Impacts*, 4 June 2015) <https://aiimpacts.org/accuracy-of-ai-predictions/> accessed 18 December 2020; AI Impacts, 'Similar Predictions' <http://www.aiimpacts.org/ai-timelines/predictions-of-human-level-ai-dates/similar-predictions> accessed 16 August 2022; Luke Muehlhauser, 'What Should We Learn from Past AI Forecasts?' (*Open Philanthropy Project*, 2016) <http://www.openphilanthropy.org/focus/global-catastrophic-risks/potential-risks-advanced-artificial-intelligence/what-should-we-learn-past-ai-forecasts> accessed 20 February 2017.

[196] Herbert A Simon, *The New Science of Management Decision* (Harper & Brothers 1960).

[197] Armstrong and Sotala (n 167).

academic publications between 1960 and 2023 has found a repeated tendency of society to overestimate the imminent capabilities of AI systems.[198]

However, this does not mean that experts are always overly optimistic. Indeed, there have been a range of cases where even domain experts overestimated the intractability of apparent barriers to progress, and underestimated the imminence or speed of scientific breakthroughs.

1.3.1.3.3 Pessimistic extrapolation from past barriers to scientific progress

How often, and under what circumstances, have high hopes been disappointed? How often have scientists been blindsided by sudden advances? To understand this, we must review notable episodes in scientific history, to identify the prevalence or frequency of past cases of excessive optimism (i.e. 'hype') or excessive pessimism (i.e. counter-hype or 'underclaiming'[199]) over technological progress. From this perspective, we can consider distinct external observations both against and in favour of expecting considerable further scientific progress—both in general, and in AI.

For instance, from a sceptical perspective, we might find reason to expect forms of advanced AI (such as 'AGI') to be even further away than it appears to the average AI researcher. Such a position could find support in the observed difficulty of technological forecasting,[200] the chequered historical track record of predictions made by futurists,[201] and the common and perhaps intuitive assumption that, if or when technology forecasters err, they will usually err on the side of overoptimism.

There are certainly examples to support this attitude: nuclear fusion is proverbially always 'just 20 years away'.[202] The same goes for long-promised technologies such as near-vacuum (hyperloop) travel or nitrogen-fixing cereals.[203] In this view, this optimism bias might be especially hazardous for future-oriented researchers in adjacent, non-technical disciplines. For instance, as discussed, during the 1960s and 1970s, legal scholars jumped the gun on trying to regulate then-anticipated advances in weather control technology or deep seabed mining, which in the event did not come to pass, or at least took many more decades, respectively.[204]

[198] Ritesh Singh, Swati Singh, and Amulya Singh, 'Landmark Events, Major Trends, and the Future of AI Research: History, Promise, Hype', *2024 2nd International Conference on Artificial Intelligence and Machine Learning Applications Theme: Healthcare and Internet of Things (AIMLA)* (IEEE 2024) <https://ieeexplore.ieee.org/document/10531477/> accessed 6 June 2024.

[199] Bowman (n 115).

[200] Luke Muelhauser, 'How Feasible Is Long-Range Forecasting?' (*Open Philanthropy*, 10 October 2019) <https://www.openphilanthropy.org/research/how-feasible-is-long-range-forecasting/> accessed 25 June 2022.

[201] Luu (n 192).

[202] Michael Brooks, 'Forever 20 Years Away: Will We Ever Have a Working Nuclear Fusion Reactor?' [2014] *NewStatesman* <https://www.newstatesman.com/sci-tech/2014/11/forever-20-years-away-will-we-ever-have-working-nuclear-fusion-reactor> accessed 4 September 2020.

[203] Vaclav Smil, *Invention and Innovation: A Brief History of Hype and Failure* (The MIT Press 2023) 109–134.

[204] Picker (n 18) 194.

As such, from a pessimistic perspective, a review of scientific history might lead us to expect that a range of unexpected barriers will emerge, which we cannot yet perceive, but which will likely slow down AI progress in the near to medium-term, or at least keep very transformative (or certainly AGI-type) capabilities out of reach.

That is, there may be both specific and general *scientific barriers*. Scientific progress has historically been hard-won at best.[205] Many fields have been held back for some time until appropriate conceptual breakthroughs were made. Moreover, recent years have seen even stronger suggestions that this is not just a temporary problem of individual scientific fields, but that, when taken as a whole, the general rate of scientific progress has slowed down over the past decades—possibly because a lot of scientific low-hanging fruit has been plucked, or because the task of training larger cohorts of junior researchers up to the expanding edge of knowledge is placing increasing time demands on older generations of senior scientists.[206]

In principle, such factors would be expected to slow down science across the board.[207] For instance, one survey has suggested that 'the number of researchers required today to achieve the famous doubling every two years of the density of computer chips is more than 18 times larger than the number required in the early 1970s'.[208] Such diminishing results are even more striking when considering that today's computer chip designers already have at their disposal better tools (including AI tools) than were available to earlier generations. As such, whether one expects that further AI advances are (at present, or from here on out) more bottlenecked by continued increases in computing hardware power or by peak insights from a few researchers, one might find reasons in either case to expect further friction on fundamental AI progress.

Of course, from an optimist's perspective, even if critical scientific and conceptual barriers remain to further AI progress, it is unclear why we should expect such

[205] Of course, from an 'inside view' perspective, this trend is derived from the history of human science, and may not fully account for the possibility that AI systems (including some early present-day systems) could be brought to bear on resolving scientific questions. On the other hand, scientists throughout history have arguably had some benefit from advancing (artefactual and conceptual) tools. I thank Olle Häggström for raising this point.

[206] Nicholas Bloom, 'Are Ideas Getting Harder to Find?' (2020) 110 The American Economic Review 1104. For an exploration, see also Tyler Cowen and Ben Southwood, 'Is the Rate of Scientific Progress Slowing Down?' 43. Previously, Benjamin Jones has argued that 'would-be innovators require more training and specialization to reach the frontier of a given field. Research teams are also getting bigger, and the number of patents per researcher has declined.' Benjamin F Jones, 'The Burden of Knowledge and the "Death of the Renaissance Man": Is Innovation Getting Harder?' (2009) 76 The Review of Economic Studies 283.

[207] However, this brackets complex debates over how to appropriately measure scientific progress. See also Nicklas Lundblad and Dorothy Chou, 'The Red Queen Problem' (*AI Policy Perspectives*, 30 May 2024) <https://www.aipolicyperspectives.com/p/the-red-queen-problem> accessed 17 August 2024.

[208] Bloom (n 206).

scientific insights to remain fundamentally intractable for many more years and decades, given that some of the world's wealthiest companies and most powerful countries have now begun to funnel extensive funding and top talent into the pursuit of AI technology. Yet while large investments may perhaps be necessary or at least conducive to scientific progress, they are of course no guarantee of it. Even large state or corporate investments are no guarantee that either engineering achievements or fundamental conceptual breakthroughs can be brute-forced. One need only consider the meagre results delivered by the Human Brain Project (HBP), a 1 billion-euro flagship project which fell far short of its initial 2009 claims that it would be able to simulate a human brain within a decade.[209] The ITER fusion reactor programme is projected to average just under $2 billion per year during 12 years of construction,[210] yet many argue success remains elusive.[211] Indeed, just prior to the second AI winter, DARPA's 1983–1993 Strategic Computing Initiative spent about $1 billion in pursuit of what we would now call AGI, but failed.[212] That does not mean that scientific problems are impervious to large sums of funding, of course; and some major projects have managed to achieve breakthroughs even under budget.[213] Nonetheless, if the fundamental 'surface area' of the scientific problem remains small, extensive resources may produce sharply diminishing returns in the absence of a more informed theoretical understanding of where or how to apply them productively.[214]

Second, there may be unexpected *political barriers,* because no scientific field or technology is insulated from its external political and social context. High-profile industrial failures or accidents involving AI systems could sour the public or governments. For example, the Three-Mile Island nuclear power plant meltdown has been argued to have significantly slowed down the development

[209] See Tim Requarth, 'The Big Problem With "Big Science" Ventures—Like the Human Brain Project' (*Nautilus*, 22 April 2015) <http://nautil.us/blog/the-big-problem-with-big-science-venturesl ike-the-human-brain-project> accessed 21 January 2020; Ed Yong, 'The Human Brain Project Hasn't Lived Up to Its Promise' (*The Atlantic*, 22 July 2019) <https://www.theatlantic.com/science/arch ive/2019/07/ten-years-human-brain-project-simulation-markram-ted-talk/594493/> accessed 21 January 2020.

[210] Henry Fountain, 'A Dream of Clean Energy at a Very High Price' *The New York Times* (27 March 2017) <https://www.nytimes.com/2017/03/27/science/fusion-power-plant-iter-france.html> accessed 26 June 2020.

[211] Daniel Jassby, 'Fusion Reactors: Not What They're Cracked Up to Be' (*Bulletin of the Atomic Scientists*, 19 April 2017) <https://thebulletin.org/2017/04/fusion-reactors-not-what-theyre-cracked-up-to-be/> accessed 1 September 2020.

[212] Roland and Shiman (n 11).

[213] National Human Genome Research Institute, 'Human Genome Project FAQ' (*Genome.gov*, 24 February 2020) <https://www.genome.gov/human-genome-project/Completion-FAQ> accessed 26 June 2020.

[214] See also the discussion of the concept of a scientific 'problem surface', and comparing the present prospects of 'AGI' to the Apollo Program or the Manhattan Project, which were both at a state where they were able to roadmap engineering sub-problems much better. John-Clark Levin and Matthijs M Maas, 'Roadmap to a Roadmap: How Could We Tell When AGI Is a "Manhattan Project" Away?' (2020) <http://dmip.webs.upv.es/EPAI2020/papers/EPAI_2020_paper_11.pdf> accessed 27 February 2025.

of nuclear power in the US.[215] A similar public souring on nuclear energy resulted after the 2011 Fukushima nuclear disaster.[216] More broadly, recent years have seen a 'techlash' against the conduct of digital technology companies in a range of sectors.[217] A high-profile and sustained public campaign against the technology or its principals could occur.[218] If this focuses primarily on certain controversial downstream applications (e.g. facial recognition), this might not extend to slowing underlying AI research. But if the backlash is broader, it could conceivably slow, stall, or redirect AI progress. Indeed, Andrew Grotto has drawn a comparison with the historical differences in US and EU attitudes to GMOs, suggesting that, if mishandled, AI technology may experience a similar backlash and subsequent strict regulatory response as GMO crops in the EU.[219]

1.3.1.3.4 Optimistic extrapolation from past rapids in scientific progress

Moreover, while technological forecasting may often be coloured by an optimism bias, this does not necessarily mean that categorical or general scepticism is the better or more historically informed heuristic. Working alongside and counter to the usual sources of excessive futurist optimism, there are also many cognitive biases that we should expect to contribute to undue pessimism or scepticism. These include a common post hoc perception of innovations as 'irreducibly complex', with an overtly linear model and narrow sequence of steps that are necessary

[215] Jeffrey Heninger, 'Muddling Along Is More Likely than Dystopia' (*AI Impacts*, 20 October 2023) <https://blog.aiimpacts.org/p/muddling-along-is-more-likely-than?utm_medium=android> accessed 26 October 2023. Although for a sceptical account, which argues that the role of the Three-Mile Island meltdown in spurring opposition to US nuclear industry is generally overstated, see Nathan Hultman and Jonathan Koomey, 'Three Mile Island: The Driver of US Nuclear Power's Decline?' (2013) 69 Bulletin of the Atomic Scientists 63.

[216] Younghwan Kim, Minki Kim, and Wonjoon Kim, 'Effect of the Fukushima Nuclear Disaster on Global Public Acceptance of Nuclear Energy' (2013) 61 Energy Policy 822. However, see also Nuclear Energy Agency and OECD, *Impacts of the Fukushima Daiichi Accident on Nuclear Development Policies* (OECD Publishing 2017) 3 <https://www.oecd-ilibrary.org/nuclear-energy/impacts-of-the-fukushima-daiichi-accident-on-nuclear-development-policies_9789264276192-en> accessed 17 September 2020 (arguing that 'policy changes driven by the Fukushima Daiichi accident have slowed the development of nuclear energy, but countries' policy re-evaluations of nuclear power linked to the accident generally appear to have subsided').

[217] Darrell M West, 'Techlash Continues to Batter Technology Sector' (*Brookings*, 2 April 2021) <https://www.brookings.edu/articles/techlash-continues-to-batter-technology-sector/> accessed 11 January 2024.

[218] Indeed, this may already be underway. See PauseAI, 'PauseAI Proposal' <https://pauseai.info/proposal> accessed 28 August 2023.

[219] Andrew Grotto, 'Genetically Modified Organisms: A Precautionary Tale For AI Governance' [2019] AI Pulse <https://aipulse.org/genetically-modified-organisms-a-precautionary-tale-for-ai-governance-2/> accessed 26 February 2019. Another comparison could be drawn with the landscape of geo-engineering research. See Adrian Currie, 'Geoengineering Tensions' (2018) 102 Futures 78. See also Jeffrey Heninger, 'Why Has Geoengineering Been Rejected?' (AI Impacts 2022) <http://aiimpacts.org/wp-content/uploads/2023/04/Why-Has-Geoengineering-Been-Rejected.pdf> accessed 27 February 2025.

or sufficient to achieving a particular invention.[220] This is exacerbated by a tendency, even by subject experts, to underestimate the compounding effects of improvements in scientific tools.[221]

As a result of these biases, subject-matter experts in various domains have on various historical occasions perceived—and provided plausible rationales for—the existence of categorical or intrinsic barriers to further progress, which soon proved ethereal or merely modest. For instance, in the first edition of his 2001 book *On the Internet*, Hubert Dreyfus built on his previous critique of AI to argue against the very possibility of searching the internet, claiming that without embodied knowledge online search would hit an intractable wall, and that

> All search techniques on the Web are crippled in advance by having to approximate a human sense of meaning and relevance grounded in the body, without a body and therefore without commonsense. It follows that search engines are not on a continuum at the far end of which is located the holy grail of computerized retrieval of just that information that is relevant given the interests of the user; they are not even on the relevance dimension.[222]

These sections were quietly dropped from the book's second edition, published after Google's 2004 IPO.[223]

Indeed, it is arguable that similar phantom barriers have arguably been at play around modern large language models, with the very prospect of such conversationally proficient systems rejected as impossible (or at least as '(strong) AI-complete') for decades. For instance, as recently as 2016, it was claimed that 'no one is any closer to implementing a contextually nimble machine learning system that could, say, engage us in an exegesis of a poem than when Alan Turing first proposed this thought experiment for machine intelligence in 1950'.[224]

[220] Gwern Branwen, 'Complexity No Bar to AI' (1 June 2014) <https://www.gwern.net/Complexity-vs-AI> accessed 9 June 2020, Appendix: Technology Forecasting Errors: Functional Fixedness in Assuming Dependencies ('Many people use a mental model of technologies in which they proceed in a serial sequential fashion and assume every step is necessary and only all together are they sufficient, and note that some particular step is difficult or unlikely to succeed and thus as a whole it will fail & never happen. But in reality, few steps are truly required. Progress is predictably unpredictable: A technology only needs to succeed in one way to succeed, and to fail it must fail in all ways. There may be many ways to work around, approximate, brute force, reduce the need for, or skip entirely a step, or redefine the problem to no longer involve that step at all').

[221] Yudkowsky (n 172).

[222] Hubert Dreyfus, *On the Internet* (1st edn, Routledge 2001) 21–25, 25-26. I owe this example to Daniel Estrada.

[223] For a contemporary rebuttal of Dreyfus's argument, see also Ian Stoner, 'In Defense of Hyperlinks: A Response to Dreyfus' (2004) 7 Techné: Research in Philosophy and Technology <https://scholar.lib.vt.edu/ejournals/SPT/v7n3/stoner.html> 27 February 2025.

[224] Aaron Plasek, 'On the Cruelty of Really Writing a History of Machine Learning' (2016) 38 IEEE Annals of the History of Computing 6, 6.

All this suggests that, just as we must consider unexpected barriers that might occur and derail progress, we must also consider the potential for unexpected (further) rapids. Historically, there have been diverse cases of sudden, even discontinuous progress occurring across various technological benchmarks.[225] In some cases, such technological advances took not only the general public but even close domain experts by surprise. As late as four years after the first flight of the Wright Flyer, some esteemed US intellectuals still publicly contended that heavier-than-air flight was impossible.[226] Indeed, this case shows how even the eventual inventors themselves may harbour considerable uncertainty over an impeding technology: in 1901, a mere two years before personally building that first heavier-than-air flyer, Wilbur Wright told his brother that he believed powered flight was 50 years away.[227]

Moreover, we do not always recognize signals of technological breakthrough, even after they have already occurred or are ongoing, as illustrated by contemporary scepticism, even during late stages of their development or testing, regarding the possibility of launching rockets outside the Earth's atmosphere,[228] nuclear fission,[229] nuclear bombs,[230] or penicillin.[231] Indeed, these lessons might

[225] Katja Grace, 'Discontinuous Progress in History: An Update' (*AI Impacts*, 13 April 2020) <https://aiimpacts.org/discontinuous-progress-in-history-an-update/> accessed 11 May 2020 (reviewing 37 technological trends to identify 10 'large robust discontinuities'—events that "abruptly and clearly contributed more to progress on some technological metric than another century would have seen on the previous trend". These include among others the Pyramid of Djoser (2650 BC—structure height trends), the *SS Great Eastern* (1858—ship size trends), the first and second telegraph (1858, 1866—speed of sending a message across the Atlantic Ocean), the first non-stop transatlantic flight (1919—speed of passenger or military payload travel), first nuclear weapons (1945—relative effectiveness of explosives), first ICBM (1958—average speed of military payload), and the discovery of $YBa_2Cu_3O_7$ as a superconductor (1987—warmest temperature of superconduction)).

[226] See collected quotes in: Baron Schwartz, 'Heavier-than-Air Flight Is Impossible' (4 June 2017) <https://web.archive.org/web/20200714082759/https://www.xaprb.com/blog/flight-is-impossible/> accessed 6 June 2020.

[227] Donald B Holmes, *Wilbur's Story* (Lulu Enterprises 2008) 91. As cited in Yudkowsky (n 172).

[228] For instance, in 1929, a Massachusetts newspaper published the sarcastic headline 'Moon rocket misses target by 238,7991/2 miles'. It later published an apology. Lihi Gibor, 'The Brilliant Rocket Scientist to Come Before His Time' (*Davidson Institute*, 12 November 2016) <http://davidson.weizmann.ac.il/en/online/sciencehistory/brilliant-rocket-scientist-come-his-time> accessed 8 June 2020.

[229] In 1939, three years before he personally oversaw the first critical uranium chain reaction, Enrico Fermi estimated with 90% confidence that it was impossible to use uranium in a fission chain reaction. Richard Rhodes, *The Making of the Atomic Bomb* (Simon & Schuster 1986) 280. Likewise, in 1962, Edward Teller related how '[t]he possibilities of developing an atomic weapon and the desirability of doing it secretly were discussed at a Princeton University conference in which I participated in March 1939 . . . Bohr said this rare variety could not be separated from common uranium except by turning the country into a gigantic factory. Bohr was worried that this could be done and that an atomic bomb could be developed—but he hoped that neither could be accomplished. Years later, when Bohr came to Los Alamos, I was prepared to say, "You see . . ." But before I could open my mouth, he said: "You see, I told you it couldn't be done without turning the whole country into a factory. You have done just that."' Edward Teller, *The Legacy of Hiroshima* (Doubleday 1962) 210–211.

[230] Jean Harrington, 'Don't Worry—It Can't Happen' (1940) 162 Scientific American 268.

[231] As an illustration of our difficulty in perceiving transformative capability, Allan Dafoe has noted how 'it took about 10 years from Fleming's discovery of penicillin to the production of a compelling proof-of-concept and recognition by a major funder (Rockefeller) that this was worth seriously investing in': Dafoe (n 123) n 11, referring to Robert Bud, *Penicillin: Triumph and Tragedy* (Oxford University Press 2009) 23–34. Though for a critical analysis, exploring whether, or in what ways

be particularly pertinent to AI progress, given how many experts were surprised by the progress of language models and generative AI throughout 2022–2023.[232]

That is not to suggest that such sudden breakthroughs or advances are at all the scientific norm, of course. Nonetheless, along with the historical track record of both excessive optimism and excessive pessimism, it can be useful to consider the epistemic structure of societies' relation to different failures of technological prediction. Prima facie, in cases where excessively optimistic predictions of a new technology repeatedly fail (i.e. a type-I, false-positive error), we would expect to see more high-profile and protracted scientific and public debates held over a longer period of time than in cases where a predicted technology arrives more or less on schedule, or where an unexpected breakthrough occurred (i.e. a type-II, false-negative error), where by its nature there may have been little public anticipation of that breakthrough in the preceding years. If that is so, we would expect frustrated technological predictions to generally be more memorable and produce a bigger cultural footprint over a longer period of time than would successful predictions or unexpected breakthroughs. This outsized footprint in turn may shape or skew our idea of technological prediction as being categorically over-optimistic, even if over-optimistic (false-positive) predictions of a technology's development are in fact roughly as common as overly pessimistic (false-negative) ones.

All this is not to suggest that advanced AI must surely arrive out of the blue to prove the sceptics wrong. Outside-view arguments based on distinct technologies are far from enough to settle such debates. Rather, it is to emphasize our pervasive epistemic uncertainty—an uncertainty that is only occluded, but not resolved, if we reach for either categorical futurist optimism or sceptical counter-hype. From an outside perspective, it can be hard to understand what other cases should be considered as part of the appropriate reference class for debates around AI development. Instead, it is simply far from obvious which trajectory or scenario we should expect to be more accurate. Thoughtful people have at least entertained each, but we remain unsure.

1.3.1.4 Inside-view evidence: scaling laws, resource barriers; architectures

As such, we can now turn to approaches and arguments that are the most prominent focus of most contemporary debates around AI—those taking a so-called inside view on recent developments and future trends in AI.

Such debates often ask: even if considerably more advanced AI capabilities are possible, how would they be achieved? What are the arguments or evidence

penicillin should be considered a 'discontinuous' scientific breakthrough, see AI Impacts, 'Penicillin and Syphilis' (*AI Impacts*, 2 February 2015) <https://aiimpacts.org/penicillin-and-syphilis/> accessed 21 September 2020.

[232] Cotra (n 34).

available or presented? These often focus on attempted direct evaluations of progress, such as through the significance and implications of specific ongoing AI breakthroughs for further development, or attempts to operationalize and measure the generality of existing AI systems.[233]

Unfortunately, there is no clear answer to many of these debates, with many scientists and scholars taking different sides. On the one hand, the previously discussed shortfalls in existing AI systems have led some to be sceptical of future progress. On the other hand, there have been advances on addressing existing limits to AI, with progress on various fronts pushing the performance envelope forward. Optimists might point out that empirically, and in the face of considerable scepticism, AI progress has been considerable over the past years and that even on conservative readings, current trends in AI inputs (compute, data) of the AI 'production function' can be expected to continue for at least some more years. Yet should we expect the mere increase in training data or computing power to be sufficient to sustain progress? This is a critical question, which continues to severely divide experts in the field of AI.

As previously discussed, some AI researchers continue to hold that, the recent remarkable progress notwithstanding, many current approaches in machine learning are at some deep level limited or at least insufficient. They argue that something fundamentally new is needed if we are ever to approach more general or human-like AI systems.[234] Others have increasingly argued that the path of AI progress may well be more continuous, and might involve the simple application of greater computational power or data. Richard Sutton has influentially referred to this as 'The Bitter Lesson'—the insight that it is ultimately not carefully crafted human domain knowledge distilled in bespoke machines, but rather 'general methods that leverage computation [that] are ultimately the most effective, and by a large margin'.[235] Indeed, since OpenAI researchers discovered evidence of these scaling laws in 2019,[236] these patterns have broadly held across many orders of magnitude in scaling.

[233] John Burden and Jose Hernandez-Orallo, 'Exploring AI Safety in Degrees: Generality, Capability and Control', *Proceedings of the Workshop on Artificial Intelligence Safety (SafeAI 2020)* (2020); Pablo Antonio Moreno Casares and others, 'How General-Purpose Is a Language Model? Usefulness and Safety with Human Prompters in the Wild' (2022) 36 Proceedings of the AAAI Conference on Artificial Intelligence 5295; José Hernández-Orallo and others, 'General Intelligence Disentangled via a Generality Metric for Natural and Artificial Intelligence' (2021) 11 Scientific Reports 22822.

[234] See also Gary Marcus and Ernest Davis, *Rebooting AI: Building Artificial Intelligence We Can Trust* (Pantheon 2019). Sublime (n 13). For another review, see AI Impacts, 'Evidence against Current Methods Leading to Human Level Artificial Intelligence' (*AI Impacts*, 12 August 2019) <https://aiimpacts.org/evidence-against-current-methods-leading-to-human-level-artificial-intelligence/> accessed 1 October 2019.

[235] Richard Sutton, 'The Bitter Lesson' (13 March 2019) <http://www.incompleteideas.net/IncIdeas/BitterLesson.html> accessed 18 May 2020; though for a response, see also Rodney Brooks, 'A Better Lesson' (19 March 2019) <https://rodneybrooks.com/a-better-lesson/> accessed 18 May 2020.

[236] Jared Kaplan and others, 'Scaling Laws for Neural Language Models' [2020] arXiv:2001.08361 [cs, stat] <http://arxiv.org/abs/2001.08361> accessed 3 February 2020.

The idea that simply continuing this approach will prove sufficient to eventually deliver advanced AI, or even AGI, is called the 'scaling hypothesis'. While it still remains a minority position among academic AI researchers,[237] it has come to achieve some successes and significantly greater prominence in recent years.[238] This is because through scaling, (seemingly) qualitative increases in AI performance have been achieved in large language models,[239] without deep conceptual breakthroughs. Instead, all that seemed necessary was to scale up existing machine learning approaches and Transformer-based large language models with more training data, parameter size, and computing power.[240] Most notably, OpenAI's GPT-series of language models has viscerally illustrated how apparently qualitative increases in performance at text processing and generation could be achieved through such simple grind.[241] The empirical results suggests that rather than hitting diminishing returns, neural language models continue to gain in performance as they are made larger and more efficient.[242] Indeed, reviews of trends in large language model performance across five orders of magnitude of parameter scaling suggest that compute-based extrapolations are a promising way to forecast AI capabilities.[243] While there may be limits to further scaling at some point, it is unclear where we should expect these to occur.

Of course, as discussed, the scaling hypothesis remains contested. Many argue that the noticeable capability shortfalls, hallucinations, and idiosyncratic reasoning failures displayed by today's LLM models are not growing pains, but

[237] Michael and others (n 160) 2 ('A large majority of respondents are against the hypothesis that scaling up current systems and methods could solve "practically any important problem" in NLP, and this view is perceived as much more popular than it is . . . Yet, narrow majorities of respondents also regard recent progress in large-scale modeling as progress towards AGI, and think AGI should concern NLP researchers'). See also Association for the Advancement of Artificial Intelligence (n 147) 66 ('The majority of respondents (76%) assert that "scaling up current AI approaches" to yield AGI is "unlikely" or "very unlikely" to succeed').

[238] Gwern Branwen, 'On GPT-3—Meta-Learning, Scaling, Implications, and Deep Theory' <https://www.gwern.net/newsletter/2020/05> accessed 21 September 2020; Jack Clark, 'Import AI 215: The Hardware Lottery; Micro GPT3; and, the Peace Computer' (*Import AI*, 21 September 2020) <https://mailchi.mp/jack-clark/import-ai-215-the-hardware-lottery-micro-gpt3-and-the-peace-computer?e=524806dd16> accessed 21 September 2020.

[239] Bubeck and others (n 145).

[240] Matthew Hutchinson and others, 'Accuracy and Performance Comparison of Video Action Recognition Approaches' [2020] arXiv:2008.09037 [cs] 6 <http://arxiv.org/abs/2008.09037> accessed 24 August 2020 (showing how, in the context of video action recognition, simpler approaches which scale better outperform more complex algorithms).

[241] Radford and others, 'Language Models Are Unsupervised Multitask Learners' (n 30); Tom B Brown and others, 'Language Models Are Few-Shot Learners' [2020] arXiv:2005.14165 [cs] <http://arxiv.org/abs/2005.14165> accessed 29 May 2020.

[242] Kaplan and others (n 236). See also previous work on scaling relationships in deep learning: Joel Hestness and others, 'Deep Learning Scaling Is Predictable, Empirically' [2017] arXiv:1712.00409 [cs, stat] <http://arxiv.org/abs/1712.00409> accessed 20 September 2020.

[243] David Owen, 'Extrapolating Performance in Language Modeling Benchmarks' (Epoch 2023) <https://epochai.org/blog/extrapolating-performance-in-language-modelling-benchmarks> accessed 7 January 2024.

indicative of the deep limits and inadequacies of the scaling approach.[244] Others, instead, have even argued that today's large language models may, for all their outstanding flaws, already reach a level of performance that is sufficiently good that, as Arcas and Norvig suggest, 'decades from now, they will be recognized as the first true examples of artificial general intelligence',[245] representing at least an imperfect or emerging form of general AI.[246] Even if such a move represents a moving of the goalposts on 'AGI', the underlying question should be not so much about definitions, but rather an empirical one about capabilities.

This question ultimately will turn on technical debates over whether systems built on the current architectures still have significant space to be enhanced and developed; on scientific questions over whether the scaling approach may become complemented by other, additional methodologies or approaches—such as by an additional avenue of scaling up of inference-time computing to improve model reasoning capabilities;[247] but also on important economic, societal, and strategic questions. What resources would it take to achieve transformative capability gains, in terms of data, computing, and energy? Do we have these resources available in sufficient quantities? Will anyone have—or maintain—the willingness to spend those resources on continued scaling, amidst potentially exorbitant costs?[248]

For space constraints, this book will bracket further discussion of the details of these important debates. Instead, it suffices to note that a set of scenarios of further future progress at the AI frontier—whether through scaling, or new approaches—remain likely enough to warrant serious consideration. These scenarios are not uncertain and contested, but they are likely robust even to many potential short-term barriers or intermediate developmental plateaus. In such cases, the global stakes of AI cannot be overstated.

1.3.2 Further Algorithmic Proliferation: Pervasive AI Is Already Here

So far, we have explored the arguments and prospects around future trajectories of AI. However, one does not need to assume further scientific or technological developments in order to argue that AI technology will be of far-reaching and growing

[244] For an accessible discussion of some of the identified limits, in the context of the scaling, see Kannegieter (n 8).

[245] Arcas and Norvig (n 95).

[246] Morris and others (n 110) (describing it as 'emerging').

[247] See DeepSeek-AI and others, 'DeepSeek-R1: Incentivizing Reasoning Capability in LLMs via Reinforcement Learning' (arXiv, 22 January 2025) <http://arxiv.org/abs/2501.12948> accessed 20 February 2025; and for discussion of some of the implications, see: Toby Ord, 'Inference Scaling Reshapes AI Governance' (arXiv, 12 February 2025) <http://arxiv.org/abs/2503.05705> accessed 19 March 2025; Lennart Heim, 'Inference Compute: GPT-O1 and AI Governance' (22 September 2024) <https://blog.heim.xyz/inference-compute/> accessed 18 February 2025. This is also discussed in more detail in Section 1.3.2.

[248] See also Levin and Maas (n 214).

importance in the coming years. Indeed, even if one were to take a conservative assumption that fundamental AI progress is likely to slow down or halt soon,[249] the state and configuration of the existing technology stack is already such that AI will have considerable societal impact in the coming years.

This is for a range of reasons, relating to both the technological capabilities of leading foundation models, as well as falling supply-side barriers and growing demand; the aggregate effects of these can be considered or compared on the basis of historical pattern of innovation proliferation—suggesting that AI might see relatively rapid global (horizontal) diffusion, as well as domestic (vertical) diffusion, because infrastructure overhangs can facilitate the increasingly quick deployment of AI systems into pre-existing architectures or platforms across society.[250] Let us discuss these briefly in turn.

1.3.2.1 Capability overhangs: the penumbra of post-deployment model enhancements

In the first place, whereas older (and narrow) AI systems were often frozen in their capabilities after training and deployment, today's advanced AI systems are not, or at least not in any way that is very societally relevant. Indeed, while it is true that the resource-intensive nature of the pre-training process ensures that a core general-purpose foundation model is relatively static, there are many ways in which these systems' capabilities can still be enhanced post-deployment by users, in ways that add on, unlock, or leverage new—and at times unexpected—skills. This suggests that not only are we uncertain about the potential capabilities of future foundation models yet to be trained, but we have likely not even explored the full envelope of the capabilities of AI systems that are already in use today. Just as there is a jagged capability frontier with remarkable gaps in some of these models' capabilities, there is also a capability shadow or penumbra of latent capabilities that are not immediately apparent upon initial model training.

1.3.2.1.1 Post-training and post-deployment enhancements

For instance, depending on how a model is released or made accessible to users, new and often significant capabilities can be further elicited or unlocked in a range of ways.[251] These avenues include: (1) 'fine-tuning' the model through minor

[249] For clarity, Section 1.3.2 will primarily entertain scenarios where, in particular, the scaling approach fails to deliver fundamental capability improvements. However, it does assume some continued AI research, especially in domains such as post-deployment augmentations of systems.

[250] What Susskind has called the 'digital lifeworld'. Jamie Susskind, *Future Politics: Living Together in a World Transformed by Tech* (Oxford University Press 2018).

[251] This draws together a range of existing taxonomies of these techniques. See Tom Davidson and others, 'AI Capabilities Can Be Significantly Improved Without Expensive Retraining' (arXiv, 12 December 2023) <http://arxiv.org/abs/2312.07413> accessed 6 January 2024. (distinguishing between tool-use, prompting methods, scaffolding, solution selection, and data generation); Grégoire Mialon and others, 'Augmented Language Models: A Survey' (arXiv, 15 February 2023) <http://arxiv.org/abs/2302.07842> accessed 7 January 2024. Markus Anderljung and others, 'Frontier AI

additional training on data relevant to particular domains, contexts, or tasks, using quantities of data that are far smaller than those needed for pre-training;[252] (2) the use of so-called chain-of-thought prompting,[253] which involves simply telling a model to think through its problems step by step in order to improve the way it solves problems; (3) enabling LLMs to use external tools, or utilize internet access;[254] (4) utilizing automated prompt engineering techniques, which use other LLMs to generate and search over new prompts that elicit improved performance; (5) using standardized foundation model programs to integrate these foundation models into more complex systems; or (6) scaffolding language models, modifying them in ways that, for instance, turn them into autonomous agents,[255] allow them to produce code snippets that are able to iteratively improve upon themselves,[256] or leverage self-play between two adversarial versions of one language model in order to continuously and broadly improve these systems' reasoning capabilities.[257]

The fact that there are such a wide range of approaches to further enhance capabilities implies that there is a large scientific and engineering 'contact surface'

Regulation: Managing Emerging Risks to Public Safety' (arXiv, 11 July 2023) 12 <http://arxiv.org/abs/2307.03718> accessed 7 August 2023 (distinguishing between fine-tuning, chain-of-thought prompting, external tool-use, automated prompt engineering, and foundation model programs); Helen Toner and others, 'Skating to Where the Puck Is Going: Anticipating and Managing Risks from Frontier AI Systems' (Center for Security and Emerging Technology 2023) 1 <https://cset.georgetown.edu/publication/skating-to-where-the-puck-is-going/> accessed 1 December 2023 (noting that 'five ways in which existing AI systems are currently being augmented are multimodality, tool use, deeper reasoning and planning, larger and more capable memory, and increased interaction between AI systems'). See also Danny Woodside and Helen Toner, 'Multimodality, Tool Use, and Autonomous Agents: Large Language Models Explained, Part 3' (*Center for Security and Emerging Technology*, 8 March 2024) <https://cset.georgetown.edu/article/multimodality-tool-use-and-autonomous-agents/> accessed 17 April 2024.

[252] As a result, such fine-tuning costs are very low, 'typically <1% and sometimes <0.01% of the pre-training cost'. Davidson and others (n 251) 2.

[253] Jason Wei and others, 'Chain-of-Thought Prompting Elicits Reasoning in Large Language Models' (arXiv, 10 January 2023) <http://arxiv.org/abs/2201.11903> accessed 12 December 2023. However, others have critiqued the interpretation that chain-of-thought prompts show that a model has learned general algorithmic procedures, and instead argue that the performance improvements yielded through this approach primarily derive from carefully engineering specific problem prompts. Kaya Stechly, Karthik Valmeekam, and Subbarao Kambhampati, 'Chain of Thoughtlessness? An Analysis of CoT in Planning' (arXiv, 5 June 2024) <http://arxiv.org/abs/2405.04776> accessed 26 June 2024.

[254] Tianle Cai and others, 'Large Language Models as Tool Makers' (arXiv, 10 March 2024) <http://arxiv.org/abs/2305.17126> accessed 29 May 2023. Will Knight, 'Chatbots Are Entering Their Stone Age' [2024] *Wired* <https://www.wired.com/story/chatbots-are-entering-the-stone-age/> accessed 24 June 2024.

[255] For an illustrative toy model, see also AI Digest, 'LMs Can Be Modified to Act Autonomously' (*AI Digest*, 2023) <https://theaidigest.org/progress-and-dangers#lms-can-be-modified-to-act-autonomously> accessed 11 January 2024. For a discussion of the implications of such agent-like systems for society and law, see Cohen and others (n 56); Kolt (n 50).

[256] Eric Zelikman and others, 'Self-Taught Optimizer (STOP): Recursively Self-Improving Code Generation' (2023) <https://openreview.net/forum?id=22cDNOtFGV> accessed 7 January 2024.

[257] Pengyu Cheng and others, 'Self-Playing Adversarial Language Game Enhances LLM Reasoning' (arXiv, 16 April 2024) <http://arxiv.org/abs/2404.10642> accessed 29 April 2024.

along which research efforts can boost capabilities. Moreover, some of these post-training enhancement approaches, such as prompt engineering, have proven very potent: one study in the medical context suggests that, through appropriate prompt engineering, a generalist foundation model can outperform leading fine-tuned (medical) specialist models.[258] In another Google experiment, a simple extension of (OpenAI's) GPT-4 model with the 'Naptime' software vulnerability detection tool instantly allowed the LLM to pass a difficult security benchmark.[259]

Prompting strategies can also improve the performance and reliability of these models,[260] for instance by requiring LLM agents to decompose a given task into different subtasks and to continuously introspect upon the suitability and results of actions as they proceed through that plan.[261] In doing so, these techniques can be used to address many of the previously discussed shortfalls of LLMs, reducing their propensity to hallucinate,[262] or improving their ability to reason.[263] That is not to say that all these approaches exert enough leverage: for instance, tests on GPT-4 showed that post-training for agentic capabilities exerted a larger effect on the models' agentic capabilities than did a large amount of 'agent scaffolding' through the provision of various toolsets.[264] Nonetheless, in aggregate, these various post-training enhancements can improve model benchmark performance in ways equivalent to a 5x–20x increase in training compute.[265] Moreover, some of these techniques allow other actors not only to unlock or access improved capabilities, but also to bypass or override AI systems' content controls, such as when users can use adversarial prompts to bypass safety filters and jailbreak these models.[266]

[258] Nori and others (n 87) (comparing GPT-4 against Med-PaLM 2).

[259] Sergei Glazunov and Mark Brand, 'Project Zero: Project Naptime: Evaluating Offensive Security Capabilities of Large Language Models' (*Project Zero*, 20 June 2024) <https://googleprojectzero.blogspot.com/2024/06/project-naptime.html> accessed 8 July 2024.

[260] Chenglei Si and others, 'Prompting GPT-3 to Be Reliable' (arXiv, 14 February 2023) <http://arxiv.org/abs/2210.09150> accessed 7 January 2024.

[261] Haoyu Wang and others, 'Devil's Advocate: Anticipatory Reflection for LLM Agents' (arXiv, 29 May 2024) <http://arxiv.org/abs/2405.16334> accessed 4 June 2024.

[262] Giorgio Roffo, 'Exploring Advanced Large Language Models with LLMsuite' (1 July 2024) <http://arxiv.org/abs/2407.12036> accessed 5 August 2024 (discussing a variety of solutions, such as Retrieval Augmented Generation [RAG], Program-Aided Language Models [PAL], and other frameworks; Verspoor [n 68].

[263] Tianhua Zhang and others, 'Natural Language Embedded Programs for Hybrid Language Symbolic Reasoning' (arXiv, 28 March 2024) <http://arxiv.org/abs/2309.10814> accessed 26 June 2024.

[264] METR, 'Measuring the Impact of Post-Training Enhancements' <https://metr.github.io/autonomy-evals-guide/elicitation-gap/> accessed 27 February 2025.

[265] Davidson and others (n 251).

[266] Stephen Casper and others, 'Open Problems and Fundamental Limitations of Reinforcement Learning from Human Feedback' [2023] Transactions on Machine Learning Research (12/2023) <http://arxiv.org/abs/2307.15217> accessed 7 August 2023. For instance, for examples of attack vectors, see Sahar Abdelnabi and others, 'Not What You've Signed Up For: Compromising Real-World LLM-Integrated Applications with Indirect Prompt Injection', *Proceedings of the 16th ACM Workshop on Artificial Intelligence and Security* (Association for Computing Machinery 2023) <https://dl.acm.org/doi/10.1145/3605764.3623985> accessed 12 December 2023. See also Javier Rando and others, 'Red-Teaming the Stable Diffusion Safety Filter' (arXiv, 10 November 2022) <http://arxiv.org/abs/2210.04610> accessed 7 January 2024. And see Kellin Pelrine and others, 'Exploiting Novel GPT-4

All this creates what Jack Clark has called a 'capability overhang' for large language models. Clark has argued that because modern AI systems 'have a large capability surface [and] our techniques available for exploring the models are very juvenile',[267] we should expect new general-purpose AI models that are released to be more capable—or, to be exact, to prove more capable of becoming even more capable—than is immediately apparent, simply because there are many potential capabilities that we have not thought to test for, or which can be easily scaffolded in or grafted on top of a model.[268]

Moreover, these capability overhangs further augment the space for improving AI capabilities, as they offer more points for research activities to improve overall system performance by enhancing these tools and infrastructures, driving overall progress, even if the approach based on directly scaling training-compute runs into insurmountable data, compute, or energy resource walls.

1.3.2.1.2 The inference scaling paradigm

Moreover, there are signs that the right choice of scaffolding or enhancement techniques may by itself be sufficient for advanced foundation models to reach transformative capabilities in critical domains—such as scientific research and, especially AI research—either directly or by facilitating a new approach to the synthesis and generation of high-quality training data which would allow the pre-training of new base models beyond the limits implied by a 'data wall' based only on raw data on the indexed internet.

For instance, it has been increasingly suggested that the 2024 arrival of 'reasoning' models has marked a major new additional scaling paradigm, one that builds on top of and complements the scaling of pre-training of the base models.[269] This inference scaling paradigm draws on insights from reinforcement learning in order to improve the ability of large language AI models to conduct complex reasoning tasks, by scaling up the computing power dedicated to such inference. For instance, models such as OpenAI's o1 have been designed to spend more time

APIs' (arXiv, 21 December 2023) <http://arxiv.org/abs/2312.14302> accessed 7 January 2024 ('We find that fine-tuning a model on as few as 15 harmful examples or 100 benign examples can remove core safeguards from GPT-4, enabling a range of harmful outputs').

[267] Jack Clark, 'Import AI 310: AlphaZero Learned Chess like Humans Learn Chess; Capability Emergence in Language Models; Demoscene AI' (*Import AI*, 28 November 2022) <https://jack-clark.net/2022/11/28/import-ai-310-alphazero-learned-chess-like-humans-learn-chess-capability-emergence-in-language-models-demoscene-ai/> accessed 11 January 2024; James Vincent, 'ChatGPT Proves AI Is Finally Mainstream—and Things Are Only Going to Get Weirder' (*The Verge*, 8 December 2022) <https://www.theverge.com/2022/12/8/23499728/ai-capability-accessibility-chatgpt-stable-diffusion-commercialization> accessed 11 December 2023.

[268] Of course, one might question whether this is more appropriately described as 'improving a systems' capabilities' or rather as 'revealing latent capabilities' that the system already had. However, from a sociotechnical perspective, that point may be moot: what matters is that the impact of these systems within society will grow.

[269] Ord (n 247).

'thinking' and searching for the right solution.[270] Indeed, these systems, along with more recent entrants such as DeepSeek R1,[271] can dedicate inference-time computation rather than merely rely on pre-training compute, to spend more time on the exploration of the space of solutions to a challenging problem they are presented with, which becomes particularly valuable in domains where its generated answers can be easily and automatically evaluated or verified.[272] Continued progress in this domain is rapidly sufficing to not only significantly increase these models' performance, but also allows a far more effective allocation of inference-compute resources to the task or domain at hand (rather than leveraging general training-compute resources, as in the brute-force scaling approach). In doing so, these methods are significantly transforming the economics of developing and using the most disruptive AI capabilities,[273] as it is no longer (only) necessary to scale up the size of the model or its training compute in order to achieve situationally significant levels of performance. They are also creating challenges for existing regulatory and governance frameworks based on training-compute thresholds.[274]

Finally, it has been suggested that the continued scaling of inference-during-training can help in the production of synthetic data for pre-training, breathing new life into that scaling paradigm; or that it may even enable very rapid capability gains through a training method of 'iterated distillation and amplification', whereby one can repeatedly improve the capabilities of model A through inference scaling, before distilling these capabilities into a new, smaller and cheaper model B, by having that model trained to emulate model A's outputs. This process—which resembles the method through which AlphaGo Zero was once rapidly boosted to a superhuman level—could enable a substantial further acceleration of the rate of AI progress, although it remains unclear whether such a method would scale beyond potential plateaus or engineering efforts.[275]

[270] OpenAI, 'Learning to Reason with LLMs' (12 September 2024) <https://openai.com/index/learning-to-reason-with-llms/> accessed 3 October 2024.

[271] DeepSeek-AI and others (n 247).

[272] See for instance: Bradley Brown and others, 'Large Language Monkeys: Scaling Inference Compute with Repeated Sampling' (arXiv, 30 December 2024) <http://arxiv.org/abs/2407.21787> accessed 20 March 2025; Charlie Snell and others, 'Scaling LLM Test-Time Compute Optimally Can Be More Effective than Scaling Model Parameters' (arXiv, 6 August 2024) <http://arxiv.org/abs/2408.03314> accessed 9 August 2024; however, note that not all domains lend themselves to easy automatic evaluation of performance, which could create one brake on AI performance. Helen Toner, '2 Big Questions for AI Progress in 2025-2026' (Rising Tide, 23 April 2025) <https://helentoner.substack.com/p/2-big-questions-for-ai-progress-in> accessed 23 April 2025.

[273] See Aidan McLaughlin, 'AI Search: The Bitter-Er Lesson' (*Notion*, 10 June 2024) <https://yellow-apartment-148.notion.site/AI-Search-The-Bitter-er-Lesson-44c11acd27294f4495c3de778cd09c8d> accessed 20 June 2024 (drawing a comparison to the way that some 2019–2020 deep learning-based chess algorithms were nonetheless outclassed by the much smaller, symbolic AI-based Stockfish, as it was able to leverage better search techniques).

[274] See José Hernández-Orallo and Seán Ó HÉigeartaigh, 'Implications of DeepSeek V3 and R1 for the EU Code of Practice' (*LCFI—Leverhulme Centre for the Future of Intelligence*, 6 February 2025) <https://www.lcfi.ac.uk/news-events/blog/post/implications-of-deepseek-v3-and-r1-for-the-eu-code-of-practice> accessed 18 February 2025. But for a more confident perspective on the continued relevance of such approaches, see Heim (n 247).

[275] Ord (n 247).

1.3.2.2 Historical patterns and rates of technology adoption and diffusion

There are also important considerations with regards to improving supply-side factors, as well as growing demand factors in terms of model useability. Many longstanding practical barriers to deployment of existing AI technologies are on track to steadily fall.[276] This suggests that, even if—as discussed—current trends in usage of inputs such as high-quality data and computing power may become a prohibitive brake on the further scaling of new generations of advanced AI systems at the frontier, there will nonetheless be many more users who are in a position to develop, access, or run significantly capable models that are increasingly close to that frontier.

Indeed, many AI capabilities have already proliferated relatively quickly across the world. Even if widespread applications of conventional and advanced AI tools will lag their original breakthroughs by a number of years, this should be cause for concern, as it suggests that a certain degree of societal disruption is already baked in, even if underlying AI progress were to hit a wall. For instance, early empirical studies on the use of generative AI-based conversational assistants indicate pervasive usage, especially within already digital societies: one 2023–2024 survey of 100,000 Danish professionals across 11 professions, found that half of workers had used the ChatGPT application, with 32 per cent 'currently using it' and 6 per cent having a paid subscription.[277] Other studies suggest that such generative AI usage is beginning to yield productivity gains in many of these industries,[278] though such gains continue to vary across domains, and often are facilitated by additional training.

What might we learn about further and future rates of proliferation and diffusion, when considering this in light of the historical diffusion rates of general-purpose technologies? Notably, the historical track record suggests that—just as underlying technological developments are not inevitable, but can be delayed or even abandoned as a result of various factors[279]—the diffusion of already invented technologies is not predetermined or frictionless. We can see this by considering both historical patterns of domestic adoption of key (consumer) technologies and rates of global diffusion of strategic technologies.

[276] Epoch, 'AI Trends' (*Epoch*, 11 April 2023) <https://epochai.org/trends> accessed 10 January 2024.

[277] Anders Humlum and Emilie Vestergaard, 'The Adoption of ChatGPT' (The University of Chicago, Becker Friedman Institute for Economics 2024) Working Paper 2024-50 <https://bfi.uchicago.edu/wp-content/uploads/2024/04/BFI_WP_2024-50-3.pdf> 27 February 2025 (though additionally finding that adoption rates varied somewhat across occupation—from 79% for software developers to 34% for financial advisors—age, experience, and gender).

[278] Erik Brynjolfsson, Danielle Li and Lindsey R Raymond, 'Generative AI at Work' (National Bureau of Economic Research, April 2023) <https://www.nber.org/papers/w31161> accessed 4 January 2024.

[279] Maas (n 191). See also the later discussion, in Section 4.3.2, of the societal determinants of technological change, and the conditions under which they result in technological delay or even restraint.

1.3.2.2.1 Historical rates in domestic adoption of consumer technologies

Let us first consider rates of domestic adoption. For instance, Emmie Hine has noted how the adoption of even innovations that appear obviously useful, may turn out far more protracted. She notes how historical studies of US household usage of signature technologies that are ubiquitous today—such as the vacuum, dryer, refrigerator, or air conditioning—show a protracted process of steady but slow diffusion throughout society, in trends that stretched many decades.[280] The same pattern has held, to a lesser extent, for communication technologies such as cell phones, PC, and internet—although that initial set of digital technologies did then set the stage for a much swifter adoption of smartphones and tablets.[281] Indeed, it took more than 20 years for 20 per cent of US retail to move online.[282] In some cases—such as in virtual reality—slow or rocky rates of domestic adoption resulted because of initial perceptions of a lack of perceived utility, and a failure of progress to advance fast enough to maintain consumer interest.[283]

Given this choppy record, many influential models of the evolution of technological innovations, such as the Gartner Hype Cycle model, have at times been critiqued for offering at best incomplete accounts of empirical patterns in attention and 'hype' relative to the actual take-up of technologies.[284] Indeed, even other general-purpose technologies, such as electricity or the first generation of computing systems, critically required a longer period of investment in complementary and intangible goods, in domains such as operator skills and business operations, in order to fully deliver on productivity gains.[285] As a result, for instance, electrification itself took many decades to be fully adopted even in the societies that pioneered its invention. There was a 40-year gap between the building of the first central power stations in the 1880s and the productivity impact of electrification becoming apparent in statistics.[286]

[280] These cases are discussed in Emmie Hine, 'ER 24: On Fast and Slow Takeoffs' (*The Ethical Reckoner*, 25 March 2024) <https://ethicalreckoner.substack.com/p/er-24-on-fast-and-slow-takeoffs> accessed 24 June 2024; drawing on Our World in Data, 'Share of United States Households Using Specific Technologies' (*Our World in Data*, 2017) <https://ourworldindata.org/grapher/technology-adoption-by-households-in-the-united-states> accessed 5 August 2024.

[281] Hine (n 280); drawing on: Our World in Data (n 280).

[282] Benedict Evans, 'The AI Summer' (9 July 2024) <https://www.ben-evans.com/benedictevans/2024/7/9/the-ai-summer> accessed 23 July 2024.

[283] Hine (n 280).

[284] Ozgur Dedehayir and Martin Steinert, 'The Hype Cycle Model: A Review and Future Directions' (2016) 108 Technological Forecasting and Social Change 28.

[285] Martin Neil Baily, Erik Brynjolfsson, and Anton Korinek, 'Machines of Mind: The Case for an AI-Powered Productivity Boom' (*Brookings*, 10 May 2023) <https://www.brookings.edu/articles/machines-of-mind-the-case-for-an-ai-powered-productivity-boom/> accessed 16 May 2024; See generally Erik Brynjolfsson, Daniel Rock, and Chad Syverson, 'The Productivity J-Curve: How Intangibles Complement General Purpose Technologies' (2021) 13 American Economic Journal: Macroeconomics 333.

[286] Paul David, 'The Dynamo and the Computer: An Historical Perspective on the Modern Productivity Paradox' (1990) 80 American Economic Review 355.

A relative sceptic could, on the basis of these historical patterns, argue that even if AI capabilities are advancing fast in lab settings, it will take many decades before they are fully rolled out and integrated across society. If that were the case, it would suggest that AI's societal impact may eventually be large, but not that this process will be particularly rapid or come in the (very) near future.[287]

However, there are also counter-arguments to this view and interpretation of historical patterns. For one, while some past technologies took a long time to see widespread dissemination, other technologies, such as steam engines, saw remarkably fast and broad domestic take-up across British industries during the 1800s.[288] More importantly, there is an overarching trend, over several centuries, showing a steady decrease in the time-to-pervasiveness of many broad-use technologies. For instance, Indermit Gill has noted how historically 'the time between invention and widespread use was cut from about 80 years for the steam engine to 40 years for electricity, and then to about 20 years for IT'.[289] This pattern holds both among countries and in terms of domestic market penetration: while it took more than 30 years for a quarter of all US homes to get a telephone, it took only seven years for a similar fraction to receive internet access.[290] Indeed, there is a reason why tablets and smartphones experienced even faster rates of adoption and diffusion, as they could leverage pre-existing digital infrastructures. In some cases, newer technologies were even able to bypass the need for certain (previous) infrastructures: for instance, in some regions, such as Africa, mobile phone technology comprehensively leapfrogged the installation of older legacy systems such as landline phones.[291]

If this historical pattern of acceleration holds, we should give greater weight to the rollout rates of more recent (digital) technologies when predicting the adoption of AI. Moreover, while it is true that the continued scaling of advanced AI

[287] Hine (n 280).

[288] Sean Bottomley, 'Stationary Steam Power in the United Kingdom, 1800–70: An Empirical Reassessment' [2024] The Economic History Review <https://onlinelibrary.wiley.com/doi/abs/10.1111/ehr.13375> accessed 3 October 2024.

[289] Indermit Gill, 'Whoever Leads in Artificial Intelligence in 2030 Will Rule the World until 2100' (*Brookings*, 17 January 2020) <https://www.brookings.edu/blog/future-development/2020/01/17/whoever-leads-in-artificial-intelligence-in-2030-will-rule-the-world-until-2100/> accessed 22 January 2020 (arguing that 'There are reasons to believe that the implementation lag for AI-related technologies will be about 10 years'), referring to Diego Comin and Martı Mestieri, 'Technology Adoption and Growth Dynamics' 38; Diego Comin and Martí Mestieri, 'If Technology Has Arrived Everywhere, Why Has Income Diverged?' (2018) 10 American Economic Journal: Macroeconomics 137.

[290] Rita Gunther McGrath, 'The Pace of Technology Adoption Is Speeding Up' [2013] *Harvard Business Review* <https://hbr.org/2013/11/the-pace-of-technology-adoption-is-speeding-up> accessed 3 July 2020; Drew DeSilver, 'Chart of the Week: The Ever-Accelerating Rate of Technology Adoption' (*Pew Research Center*, 14 March 2014) <https://www.pewresearch.org/fact-tank/2014/03/14/chart-of-the-week-the-ever-accelerating-rate-of-technology-adoption/> accessed 3 July 2020; Michael DeGusta, 'Are Smart Phones Spreading Faster than Any Technology in Human History?' [2012] *MIT Technology Review* <https://www.technologyreview.com/2012/05/09/186160/are-smart-phones-spreading-faster-than-any-technology-in-human-history/> accessed 3 July 2020. As cited in Hagemann, Huddleston, and Thierer (n 16) 58–59.

[291] Jenny C Aker and Isaac M Mbiti, 'Mobile Phones and Economic Development in Africa' (2010) 24 The Journal of Economic Perspectives 207.

systems may rapidly require significant new infrastructure buildout, it also appears likely that many consumer-facing AI systems will be more akin to smartphones (in that they can leverage pre-existing digital infrastructure) than to electricity (which needed the rollout of entirely new infrastructure).

Given all this, there is still some reason to expect that, barring a massive deflation in, distraction from, or disillusionment in public interest in AI, the pervasive rollout of many AI technologies will occur much faster than did electrification or many older consumer technologies in their time, taking perhaps no more than a decade. Indeed, such a view is supported by early data, showing that in the US, adoption rate of generative AI over 2022–2024 has been almost twice as fast as the historical adoption rates of personal computers and the internet.[292]

1.3.2.2.2 Historical rates in global diffusion of strategic technologies

We can also consider historical patterns around the rates of global diffusion of strategic technologies. Once again, it is clear that global horizontal transfers of technology have been subject to various constraints throughout history.[293] Deliberate strategies and policies intended to erect proliferation barriers have especially reared their head in cases where the technology concerned served as a (perceived) strategic asset to states.[294] Such constraints leveraged both active controls and passive barriers to independent development of the capability in question.

Yet in spite of this, a wide range of technologies do diffuse globally along distinct patterns. As Daniel Drezner has noted, the rapidity with which new technologies disseminate across the international stage tends to depend on whether the technology's production and deployment involves high or low fixed costs, and whether or not they have considerable civilian applications.[295] In Drezner's

[292] Alexander Bick, Adam Blandin, and David J Deming, 'The Rapid Adoption of Generative AI' (National Bureau of Economic Research, September 2024) <https://www.nber.org/papers/w32966> accessed 3 October 2024.

[293] See also Sonia Ben Ouagrham-Gormley, *Barriers to Bioweapons: The Challenges of Expertise and Organization for Weapons Development* (Oxford University Press 2014) (on the remarkably constrained proliferation of bioweapon programmes); Lisa Langdon Koch, 'Holding All the Cards: Nuclear Suppliers and Nuclear Reversal' (2022) 7 Journal of Global Security Studies ogab034 (of nuclear weapons); Max Smeets, *No Shortcuts: Why States Struggle to Develop a Military Cyber-Force* (Oxford University Press 2022) (of offensive military cyber-capabilities); Peter Westwick, 'Lessons from Stealth for Emerging Technologies' (*Center for Security and Emerging Technology*, March 2021) <https://cset.georgetown.edu/publication/lessons-from-stealth-for-emerging-technologies/> accessed 26 October 2022 (of stealth technology); Andrea Gilli and Mauro Gilli, 'Why China Has Not Caught Up Yet: Military-Technological Superiority and the Limits of Imitation, Reverse Engineering, and Cyber Espionage' (2019) 43 International Security 141 (of the US F-22/A Raptor jet fighter). For a deeper historical perspective on proliferation constraints on military technology, going much further back in time, see Elizabeth Smithrosser, 'How to Get Good Horses in Medieval China' (*Medievalists.net*, 9 June 2020) <https://www.medievalists.net/2020/06/horses-medieval-china/> accessed 15 June 2020 (discussing the challenges faced by the Chinese state in procuring good warhorses during the Northern Song period, in the face of embargoes from the Liao and Xixia empires).

[294] See generally Jeffrey Ding and Allan Dafoe, 'The Logic of Strategic Assets: From Oil to AI' [2021] Security Studies 1.

[295] Reproduced from Daniel W Drezner, 'Technological Change and International Relations' (2019) 33 International Relations 286, 291–292.

Table 1.1 Drezner's typology of technological innovation

	Public sector dominance	*Private-sector dominance*
High fixed costs	**Prestige tech**	**Strategic tech**
Low fixed costs	**Public tech**	**General-purpose tech**

Reproduced from Daniel W Drezner, 'Technological Change and International Relations' (2019) 33 International Relations p. 292. Copyright © 2019 by Daniel W Drezner. Reproduced with Permission of Sage Publications.

analysis, this produces four types of technological innovations: strategic tech, prestige tech, public tech, and general-purpose tech (see Table 1.1).

In this typology, '*strategic tech*' technologies have high fixed costs but significant civilian applications (e.g. the civilian aircraft sector or 5G networks). They accordingly invite great power intervention to promote national champions and avoid dependence on foreign suppliers.[296] '*Prestige tech*' innovations have large fixed costs and only limited civilian applications (e.g. nuclear weapons, Concorde, manned space exploration), and therefore tend to be developed predominantly by governments.[297] '*Public tech*' innovations have low fixed costs but limited private-sector opportunities or interests (e.g. public health innovations, such as pre-pandemic vaccines research). This means that they require government investments to seize their public good qualities.[298] Finally, '*general-purpose tech*' involves technologies with low fixed costs and large private-sector applications (e.g. drones or AI), meaning that private-sector activity predominantly drives the technology's direction of development.[299] Drezner argues that these factors have implications for the speed of (horizontal) diffusion: '[t]he more that a technology approaches the general-purpose category, the more quickly it will diffuse across the globe. The lower the fixed costs—whether material, organizational, or societal in nature—the more rapidly a technology should diffuse from leader to laggards.'[300]

What does that suggest for AI? Of course, AI is a diverse technology, and not all of its applications will meet the same criteria. To be sure, many if not most AI applications are characterized by low fixed costs and private-sector dominance, which suggests they are general-purpose technology that will see relatively rapid dissemination. On the other hand, there may be exceptions where, in spite of the private-sector dominance, the fixed costs of AI are relatively high—given

[296] ibid 291.

[297] Notably, the label 'prestige' does not imply that these technologies serve solely symbolic functions. Indeed, in some cases such as with nuclear weapons, governments derive obvious (if controversial) benefits from pursuing them. However, they function as prestige goods because of their exorbitant costs. ibid 292.

[298] ibid 291.

[299] ibid 291–292.

[300] ibid 292.

the increasing computational demands of training up top frontier AI systems—producing AI applications that might be categorized as strategic technology, which suggest attempted export controls and intervention by major states, and relatively constrained (in the near term) proliferation of the most cutting-edge of AI systems.

This model also suggests there may be other particular applications of AI that will also diffuse more slowly. As Ayoub and Payne have noted, '[the] ubiquitous access to advanced algorithms gives a misleading impression of the ease with which military relevant AI may proliferate between states'.[301] Indeed, certain military applications of AI may in fact involve large fixed costs in terms of adjacent or substrate technologies (e.g. pre-existing fleets of long-range drone weapons delivery platforms for LAWS; satellite command networks) which are not conjured out of nothing—even if many countries today admittedly own and operate large military drone fleets.[302]

Alternatively, effective deployment may require large technical changes in to-be-adopted civilian technologies, as well as large organizational and cultural changes in the adopting (military) organization.[303] Finally, notwithstanding a growing trend in the militarisation of domestic policing practices,[304] many of these weapons also have little civilian application, suggesting that LAWS might be most akin to prestige technology, which might proliferate relatively slowly. However, even in such cases, many of the underlying AI capabilities which LAWS leverage (e.g. pattern recognition, autonomous operation) could still qualify as general-purpose technology, with low fixed costs and considerable civilian applications. Our answer may therefore often depend on the precise AI application under consideration. However, this also suggests that, while there are some domains in which the diffusion of AI capabilities may be slow, the bottleneck to its spread may be less in AI capabilities themselves, and more in substrate technologies (e.g. delivery systems) or the computing hardware needed to train leading, frontier AI systems.

[301] Kareem Ayoub and Kenneth Payne, 'Strategy in the Age of Artificial Intelligence' (2016) 39 Journal of Strategic Studies 793, 809.

[302] One 2019 survey found more than 17 countries operating armed drones, and some 100 countries running some kind of military drone program. Dan Gettinger, 'The Drone Databook' (The Center for the Study of the Drone at Bard College 2019) <https://dronecenter.bard.edu/files/2019/10/CSD-Drone-Databook-Web.pdf> 27 February 2025. Nonetheless, there has long been extensive debate over the exact drivers and rate of drone proliferation. Michael C Horowitz, Sarah E Kreps, and Matthew Fuhrmann, 'Separating Fact from Fiction in the Debate over Drone Proliferation' (2016) 41 International Security 7.

[303] Michael C Horowitz, 'Artificial Intelligence, International Competition, and the Balance of Power' [2018] *Texas National Security Review* <https://tnsr.org/2018/05/artificial-intelligence-international-competition-and-the-balance-of-power/> accessed 17 May 2018.

[304] For instance, Arthur Holland Michel has chronicled how the 'Gorgon Stare' Wide-Area Motion Imagery (WAMI) surveillance system, which was developed to identify improvised explosive devices in Iraq, was deployed in Baltimore in 2016 to support investigative law enforcement operations. Arthur Holland Michel, *Eyes in the Sky: The Secret Rise of Gorgon Stare and How It Will Watch Us All* (HMH Books 2019).

1.3.2.3 Infrastructure overhang and rollout rates

This brings us to an additional point, which is that if the proliferation and application of AI capabilities is bottlenecked primarily by the availability of some substrate technologies, then in certain cases we might expect it to be not very constrained at all. This argument invokes a form of what we might call 'infrastructure overhang': the broad availability of pre-existing supporting infrastructure that allow a rapid rollout and user scale-up of a technology.[305] Critically, whereas electrification required the up-front rollout of physical infrastructure in order to reach users, AI may not face these same problems. Indeed, the marginal deployment costs of (already trained) systems, and with them the barriers to AI diffusion, might be far lower than they were for these other technologies, given that in many cases supporting digital infrastructures have already been independently developed or established.

For instance, for all that AI companies at times face challenges in procuring clean and adequate data sets, it is also not the case that they have to always start from scratch. Rather, states have a long history of seeking to make the world more 'legible';[306] as such, both governments and private actors have—for better or worse—spent the last decades collating diverse and comprehensive datasets. These pre-existing databases create troves of structured training data. Conversely, on the rollout level, mobile phones and personal computing enable the rollout of AI services to society.[307] Indeed, this can already be seen in the growth of 'AI-as-a-service' products.

As a result of this, even AI applications that do not focus on virtual behaviour can nonetheless be rolled out surprisingly quickly. It has proven relatively easy, for instance, to graft intrusive AI surveillance capabilities onto extant surveillance infrastructures consisting of 'dumb' CCTV systems.[308] Such AI use can scale up as far along as the pre-existing infrastructure, as seen in reports that China has begun to

[305] It should be noted that this notion of 'infrastructure overhang' is distinct from the idea of 'hardware overhang'—the situation in which 'when human-level software is created, enough computing power may already be available to run vast numbers of copies at great speed': Nick Bostrom, *Superintelligence: Paths, Dangers, Strategies* (Oxford University Press 2014) 73. More generally, this reflects situations where the societal impact of even seemingly small algorithmic improvements may prove sudden and extreme, because existing computing hardware is more than adequate to rapidly scale them. The notion of 'infrastructure overhang' is similar, but points more to the idea that algorithmic improvements can benefit (in both training and deployment rates) from pre-existing digital infrastructures.

[306] See generally Scott, J.C., *Seeing Like A State—How Certain Schemes to Improve the Human Condition Have Failed* (Yale University Press 1998).

[307] That is not to say that coverage is ubiquitous. For instance, while 93% of the world's population live within physical reach of mobile broadband or internet, only 53.6% actually use the internet, showing a significant digital divide. ITU, 'Measuring Digital Development: Facts and Figures 2019' (ITU 2019) <https://www.itu.int/en/ITU-D/Statistics/Documents/facts/FactsFigures2019.pdf> accessed 10 July 2020.

[308] Sahil Chinoy, 'We Built an "Unbelievable" (but Legal) Facial Recognition Machine' *The New York Times* (16 April 2019) <https://www.nytimes.com/interactive/2019/04/16/opinion/facial-recognition-new-york-city.html> accessed 23 April 2019.

roll out AI capabilities to some of its estimated 200 million cameras nationwide.[309] As such, just as the computing revolution was able, in its time, to draw on the already widely established infrastructures of electrification to facilitate rapid and ubiquitous dissemination, AI systems may in turn leverage those pre-existing computing infrastructures to facilitate rapid dissemination.

Of course, even if the digital infrastructure exists, such rollout may not be without friction or economic costs. As discussed before, there may still be various unanticipated brakes or limits on the rollout of this technology. For instance, in general, most discussions of the economics of frontier LLM or foundation models have focused on the immense up-front costs of training that system, rather than the subsequent costs of running these systems in operation, as those inference costs are usually just a fraction of those costs. Yet early analysis has shown that, when run at any reasonable industrial scale, the per-query inference costs of ChatGPT-like systems significantly exceed those of traditional search engines,[310] suggesting this could not normally be scaled up entirely smoothly, or in a way that is necessarily cost-competitive to those tools. Such costs asymmetries may become particularly constraining in the case of 'reasoning' models and AI agents, which may utilize significant inference-compute resources in their operations.

Nonetheless, many prospective AI usage domains can benefit from an existing infrastructure overhang, which can enable the rapid deployment of new AI capabilities or their layering on to existing technologies. It also illustrates how we need not even look too far into the future to see many large-scale impacts of AI using even narrow capabilities: in some cases, we need not even look to the future at all. The use of machine learning for simple facial recognition is well established by now. However, the ability to layer pattern-recognition capabilities onto existing architectures of surveillance means that establishing a comprehensive surveillance society is no longer a qualitative leap, but simply a matter of scaling up investment. Barring strong political and regulatory action to the contrary, similar infrastructural patterns may enable the downhill flow of many other disruptive or challenging AI applications.

1.4 Reflections: What Does This Mean?

Throughout this chapter, and especially in the sections just preceding, we have reviewed a wide range of arguments in favour or against expecting a significant global impact from AI technology. These arguments are diverse, and highlight the

[309] Paul Mozur, 'Inside China's Dystopian Dreams: A.I., Shame and Lots of Cameras' *The New York Times* (15 October 2018) <https://www.nytimes.com/2018/07/08/business/china-surveillance-technology.html> accessed 18 February 2019.

[310] Dylan Patel and Ahmad, 'The Inference Cost of Search Disruption—Large Language Model Cost Analysis' (*SemiAnalysis*, 9 February 2023) <https://www.semianalysis.com/p/the-inference-cost-of-search-disruption> accessed 9 January 2024.

heterogeneity and complexity of technology assessment in this space. They show that, rather than the question being one of whether AI matters, a better question is to ask *how* it matters, and how its stakes will evolve.

1.4.1 How Will AI Matter?

Given this, three broad conclusions can be drawn. First off, AI as it exists today is neither unbounded magic nor outright farce, and instead is best seen as *a high-variance technology portfolio*. As an incipient general-purpose technology, it still faces tremendous barriers and growing pains; nonetheless, it is seeing enough viable applications that this technology domain should be sufficient to warrant societal and regulatory attention. This much may not be very controversial, although it is valuable to investigate and remain aware of the underlying debates and considerations.

Second, in spite of prevailing public misconceptions, *there remains uncertainty around the potential imminence, speed, or ceiling of future AI progress*, with judgement-based arguments derived from expert predictions, outside-view arguments grounded in (historical) comparison or extrapolation, and inside-view arguments focused on the workings, capabilities, and trajectories of AI systems, all able to support both an expectation of further future breakthroughs, but also some caution or scepticism. On balance, continued progress for at least the coming years seems plausible. More pragmatically, our extant uncertainty illustrates the importance of undertaking further study, and formulating anticipatory governance strategies.

Third, even if one adopted an unnecessarily pessimistic expectation around further fundamental AI progress, *AI already matters today*: disruptive AI capabilities and algorithmic applications already exist, or will likely diffuse relatively quickly over the coming years, in ways that make these technologies more than sufficient to drive global change in many if not all domains.[311] For all intents and purposes, disruptive AI systems are already out there—and may soon be here. The technology is already heralding a new chapter in law and governance, and this makes it a fruitful and indeed critical topic for legal scholars to engage with—in a way that is open to yet further progress—today.

1.4.2 Governing under Uncertainty

Direct questions over the magnitude and rate of future AI progress are key not only in setting an approximate ceiling to capabilities or impact, but also for

[311] Parson and others (n 127); Dafoe (n 123).

tailoring the adaptability we want from our institutions and governance structures.[312] In this context, we can anticipate there to be significant stakes around making AI go well.

This is not, and should not be, a narrow agenda. Indeed, the past years have seen efforts and initiatives by various AI academics to highlight the challenges around AI technology as a key global issue,[313] arguing that 'we must anticipate the amplification of ongoing harms, as well as novel risks, and prepare for the largest risks well before they materialize'.[314]

In doing so, the fact that accurate assessment and predictions are difficult might be less ground for comfort than for caution. Articulating better roadmaps of progress and potential early warning signs[315] are important foundations for AI policy. These goals matter not just for those who are interested in the societal impacts of systems such as AGI, but also for many intermediate and less sophisticated AI models that affect people today and in the near future. Their impacts matter, and may themselves scale up as more powerful (including, perhaps, AGI-like) systems come into view; and many of these may need early policy action to avoid the lock-in of interests or governance gridlock.

What does it mean to govern under uncertainty? One implication is to focus less on attempting to make and base our policies on specific predictions over AI capabilities and their impacts—recognizing that we have been frequently surprised by both,[316] and that simultaneously these are becoming less legible to policymakers and the public.[317] Rather than prediction, then, a better foundation for AI policy is to emphasize resilience and risk management under a range of scenarios and trajectories.

[312] As discussed in Peter Cihon, Matthijs M Maas, and Luke Kemp, 'Should Artificial Intelligence Governance Be Centralised? Design Lessons from History', *Proceedings of the AAAI/ACM Conference on AI, Ethics, and Society* (ACM 2020) 231, 233 <https://dl.acm.org/doi/10.1145/3375627.3375857> accessed 12 February 2020.

[313] Yoshua Bengio and others, 'Managing AI Risks in an Era of Rapid Progress' (arXiv, 26 October 2023) <http://arxiv.org/abs/2310.17688> accessed 3 November 2023; Center for AI Safety, 'Statement on AI Risk' (30 May 2023) <https://www.safe.ai/statement-on-ai-risk> accessed 5 June 2023. Note that, while sometimes depicted as an industry initiative, the letter was initiated by academic AI researchers. See Alan Chan, 'Let's Talk about the CAIS Statement on Extinction Risk from AI' (*Alan's Substack*, 4 June 2023) <https://coordination.substack.com/p/lets-talk-about-the-cais-statement> accessed 5 June 2023.

[314] Bengio and others (n 313) 2.

[315] For one discussion of warning signs, see also Carla Zoe Cremer and Jess Whittlestone, 'Artificial Canaries: Early Warning Signs for Anticipatory and Democratic Governance of AI' (2021) 6 International Journal of Interactive Multimedia and Artificial Intelligence 100. Their reference to 'canaries' refers to the set of criteria in Oren Etzioni, 'How to Know If Artificial Intelligence Is About to Destroy Civilization' [2020] *MIT Technology Review* <https://www.technologyreview.com/2020/02/25/906083/artificial-intelligence-destroy-civilization-canaries-robot-overlords-take-over-world-ai/> accessed 23 June 2020.

[316] Karnofsky (n 106).

[317] Lovely (n 108).

1.4.3 Shared Stakes and Shared Agendas

In this context, much has previously been made over the public disagreements between AI researchers or law scholars who focus on the impacts of today's algorithmic systems, and those who focus on the longer-term impacts of more advanced AI systems on the horizon.[318] However, while this framing of the field as riven by scientific dispute and conflict may be appealing to some audiences, it is in reality a narrative that is both descriptively misleading—erasing the plurality of views on AI[319]—as well as pragmatically counterproductive to the goal of serving the public interest.[320] As noted by Arbel, Tokson, and Lin:

> This debate . . . has become counterproductive. Working from mistaken premises about the zero-sum nature of AI concern, it presents a false choice. In reality, AI should be regulated because it causes immediate harms *and* threatens long-term catastrophe . . . Recognition of short-term and long-term AI risk is complementary, with each type of risk strengthening the case for meaningful regulation . . . Regulating AI with a view towards immediate harms can lay the groundwork for future regulation of more dangerous AI . . . Litigation addressing immediate AI harms can bring malfunctioning systems to public attention before they cause widespread damage . . . On the other side, acknowledging the long-term catastrophic risks of AI can help justify systemic AI regulation in the present day.[321]

An improved understanding of the technical landscape of AI over the coming years is key to informing societal choices,[322] even if one is (unusually) confident that the resulting map will not include human-level AI or AGI on it.

[318] Rebecca L Johnson, 'What Are Responsible AI Researchers Really Arguing About?' in David J Gunkel (ed), *Handbook on the Ethics of Artificial Intelligence* (Edward Elgar Publishing 2024) 49–67. Paolo Bory, Simone Natale and Christian Katzenbach, 'Strong and Weak AI Narratives: An Analytical Framework' [2024] AI & Society <https://doi.org/10.1007/s00146-024-02087-8> accessed 21 October 2024; Kelsey Piper, 'There Are Two Factions Working to Prevent AI Dangers. Here's Why They're Deeply Divided' (*Vox*, 10 August 2022) <https://www.vox.com/future-perfect/2022/8/10/23298108/ai-dangers-ethics-alignment-present-future-risk> accessed 19 April 2024.

[319] Carina Prunkl and Jess Whittlestone, 'Beyond Near- and Long-Term: Towards a Clearer Account of Research Priorities in AI Ethics and Society', *Proceedings of the AAAI/ACM Conference on AI, Ethics, and Society* (ACM 2020) <http://dl.acm.org/doi/10.1145/3375627.3375803> accessed 12 February 2020; Thorin Bristow, Luke Thorburn, and Diana Acosta-Navas, 'Views on AI Aren't Binary—They're Plural (Extended Abstract)' (2024) 7 Proceedings of the AAAI/ACM Conference on AI, Ethics, and Society 225.

[320] Yonathan A Arbel, Matthew Tokson, and Albert Lin, 'Systemic Regulation of Artificial Intelligence' (2024) 56 Arizona State Law Journal 545, 35–37 <https://papers.ssrn.com/abstract=4666854> accessed 28 February 2024; Garrison Lovely, 'Can Humanity Survive AI?' (*Jacobin*, 22 January 2024) <https://jacobin.com/2024/01/can-humanity-survive-ai/> accessed 26 February 2024.

[321] Arbel, Tokson, and Lin (n 320) 36.

[322] Dafoe (n 123) 15–33.

To be sure, in the midst of pervasive uncertainty, there is a need to further improve our available forecasting methodologies in order to better understand, as well we can, the range of possible and plausible trajectories in AI's development, use conditions (e.g. investment, data, hardware, talent), capabilities (e.g. cyberwarfare, text generation), use cases, and impacts over the coming years and decades. While difficult, this remains an active and urgent research area.[323]

However, while we wait for clarity, there is no need to make responsible action dependent on such methodological advances.[324] Given the stakes of AI, it is important to tailor our governance responses to the epistemic situation we find ourselves in.[325] Assuming a sceptical stance regarding AI which anticipates little to no future progress may be appealing as a means to balance some of the extreme hype around AI technology. Yet it may be an imperfect heuristic both scientifically and politically. What debate in the AI space needs is fewer over-confident statements of impossibility or inevitability, and more good-faith attempts to wrestle with the best available information and estimates, and the benefits and drawbacks of different regulatory strategies, under admitted circumstances of deep epistemic uncertainty on many outstanding questions.[326]

Along with attempting to increase our knowledge and tools, we may have to engage frankly with questions of appropriate epistemic strategies. It may well be impossible to be perfectly calibrated on AI futures. Given this, what would be the differential costs of different prediction errors? Regardless of one's expectations about AI development and deployment timelines, what might be the costs of excessive optimism or excessive scepticism—of over-preparation or under-preparation?[327] What other biases or incentives might pull us away from considering all scenarios?[328] These are not simple questions either, but they may be key in

[323] Miles Brundage, 'Modeling Progress in AI' [2015] arXiv:1512.05849 [cs] <http://arxiv.org/abs/1512.05849> accessed 30 April 2017; Dafoe (n 123). This is an active research area. See also Ross Gruetzemacher and others, 'Forecasting AI Progress: A Research Agenda' [2020] arXiv:2008.01848 [cs] <http://arxiv.org/abs/2008.01848> accessed 11 August 2020. It should be noted that for specific technological subsets (such as defence technology), forecasts have reportedly achieved reasonable accuracy, which might be explained because of the very long procurement timelines for major weapons systems, and strong strategic pressures on systems' marginal performance. Alexander Kott and Philip Perconti, 'Long-Term Forecasts of Military Technologies for a 20–30 Year Horizon: An Empirical Assessment of Accuracy' [2018] arXiv:1807.08339 [cs] <http://arxiv.org/abs/1807.08339> accessed 18 December 2018.

[324] Maria Nordström, 'AI under Great Uncertainty: Implications and Decision Strategies for Public Policy' (2022) 37 AI & Society 1703.

[325] See Adrian Currie, 'Existential Risk, Creativity & Well-Adapted Science', *Studies in the History & Philosophy of Science* (2019) 76 <https://doi.org/10.1016/j.shpsa.2018.09.008> 27 February 2025; Adrian Currie and Shahar Avin, 'Method Pluralism, Method Mismatch, & Method Bias' (2019) 19 Philosopher's Imprint <http://hdl.handle.net/2027/spo.3521354.0019.013> accessed 9 April 2019.

[326] See also Jess Whittlestone and Samuel Clarke, 'AI Challenges for Society and Ethics' in Justin B Bullock and others (eds), *The Oxford Handbook of AI Governance* (Oxford University Press 2022) 10 (emphasizing the importance of 'making decisions under uncertainty and disagreement').

[327] I thank Miles Brundage for good observations on this point.

[328] See for instance Lucius Caviola and others, 'Crying Wolf: Warning about Societal Risks Can Be Reputationally Risky' (14 June 2024) <https://osf.io/gtr53> accessed 20 June 2024.

reaching more nuanced debate around the considerations and estimates that could or should inform societal debate around its relation to AI.

Indeed, engagement with all of these scenarios may be democratically warranted, even if one strongly expects that advanced AI systems, such as 'AGI', are very far away: after all, as argued by Seth Lazar and Alex Pascal,

> why worry about [AGI] now? Because the people building the most advanced AI systems are explicitly and aggressively working to bring it about, and think they'll get there in 2–5 years. Even some of the most publicly skeptical AI researchers don't rule out AGI within this decade. If we, the affected public, do not shape this techno-quest now, we may miss the chance to do so at all. We face a fundamental question: is the very pursuit of AGI the kind of aim democracies should allow?[329]

Likewise, Jonathan Zittrain has noted that, in the face of emerging AI agents, '"too early to tell" is, in this context, a good time to take stock, and to maintain our agency in a deep sense. We need to stay in the driver's seat rather than be escorted by an invisible chauffeur acting on its own inscrutable and evolving motivations, or on those of a human distant in time and space.'[330] This will be key if we are to maintain our agency and exert proper human choice over the future of technology.

Beyond matters of principle, engaging in early policy debates also matters practically, because there might be many scientific and policy foundations that would need to be established today, given important path-dependencies for regulation.[331] As Martina Kunz and Seán Ó hÉigeartaigh note, '[i]t is still highly uncertain if and when general intelligence comparable to that of humans might be achieved in artificial systems, but taking into account the magnitude of the consequences and a certain degree of inertia and path dependency of international governance, it is worth considering potential risks and mitigation strategies early on'.[332] There is no need for us to reach absolute certainty

[329] Seth Lazar and Alex Pascal, 'Can Democracy Survive Artificial General Intelligence?' (*Tech Policy Press*, 13 February 2024) <https://techpolicy.press/can-democracy-survive-artificial-general-intelligence> accessed 27 May 2024; See also Blili-Hamelin and others (n 147).

[330] Jonathan Zittrain, 'We Need to Control AI Agents Now' (*The Atlantic*, 2 July 2024) <https://www.theatlantic.com/technology/archive/2024/07/ai-agents-safety-risks/678864/> accessed 2 July 2024. See also Alan Chan and others, 'Harms from Increasingly Agentic Algorithmic Systems', *2023 ACM Conference on Fairness, Accountability, and Transparency* (ACM 2023) 654 <https://dl.acm.org/doi/10.1145/3593013.3594033> accessed 24 October 2023 ('If we think it is categorically impossible for AI systems to have agency, we will never be able to accurately recognize when we are giving up our agency to them').

[331] Stephen Cave and Seán S Ó hÉigeartaigh, 'Bridging Near- and Long-Term Concerns about AI' (2019) 1 Nature Machine Intelligence 5.

[332] Martina Kunz and Seán Ó hÉigeartaigh, 'Artificial Intelligence and Robotization' in Robin Geiß and Nils Melzer (eds), *The Oxford Handbook of the International Law of Global Security* (Oxford University Press 2021) 14.

or clarity over which of these forms of advanced AI can or will be developed, or on what timelines. Rather, well-established risk management principles can warrant some engagement with many different scenarios even under some uncertainty about each individual scenario.[333] In such cases, a portfolio approach can be both warranted, supporting effective scenario planning and the creation of contingency plans that allows society to be prepared for multiple possible outcomes.[334]

To be clear, this need not (and should not) mean neglecting or diminishing policy attention for the impacts of existing AI systems,[335] especially as these impacts are already severe and may continue to scale up as AI systems both become more widely implemented and create hazards for existing communities. However, policymakers may need to increasingly combine this with a consideration of the emerging risks from advanced and capable systems at the frontier of the field.[336] In the meantime, there are already a range of shared policy priorities that different communities might converge on, from ensuring that regulators have the knowledge and resources to keep up to date with the technology, and avoid being outrun by industry, to ensuring greater investment in AI measurement science in order to evaluate AI-related dangers of any sort; and from ensuring improved incident tracking and transparency and disclosure requirements to ensuring there are clear allocations of AI liability.[337]

More generally, all this suggests that governance will increasingly have to engage proactively, rather than wait out developments to study the emerging risks of new technologies. In the face of diverse technological developments, from synthetic biotechnology to geo-engineering, there has been an extensive and emerging literature emphasizing the importance of 'Responsible Innovation' for technology

[333] See for instance Henrik Skaug Sætra and John Danaher, 'Resolving the Battle of Short- vs. Long-Term AI Risks' [2023] AI and Ethics <https://doi.org/10.1007/s43681-023-00336-y> accessed 6 September 2023; Huw Price and Matthew Connelly, 'AI Governance Must Deal with Long-Term Risks as Well' (2023) 622 Nature 31; Jan Brauner and Alan Chan, 'AI's Long-Term Risks Shouldn't Distract from Present Risks' [2023] *TIME* <https://time.com/6303127/ai-future-danger-present-harms/> accessed 12 October 2023.

[334] See for instance Anton Korinek, 'Scenario Planning for an A(G)I Future' (*IMF*, December 2023) <https://www.imf.org/en/Publications/fandd/issues/2023/12/Scenario-Planning-for-an-AGI-future-Anton-korinek> accessed 15 May 2024.

[335] For previous work aiming to clarify and address these debates, see also Prunkl and Whittlestone (n 319); Charlotte Stix and Matthijs M Maas, 'Bridging the Gap: The Case for an "Incompletely Theorized Agreement" on AI Policy' (2021) 1 AI and Ethics 261; Cave and Ó hÉigeartaigh (n 331); Seth D Baum, 'Reconciliation between Factions Focused on Near-Term and Long-Term Artificial Intelligence' (2018) 33 AI & Society 565. For another analysis, see also Peter S Park and Max Tegmark, 'Divide-and-Conquer Dynamics in AI-Driven Disempowerment' (arXiv, 9 October 2023) <http://arxiv.org/abs/2310.06009> accessed 16 October 2023.

[336] Markus Anderljung and Anton Korinek, 'Frontier AI Regulation: Safeguards Amid Rapid Progress' (*Lawfare*, 4 January 2024) <https://www.lawfaremedia.org/article/frontier-ai-regulation-safeguards-amid-rapid-progress> accessed 6 January 2024; Toner and others (n 251).

[337] Zachary Arnold and Helen Toner, 'AI Regulation's Champions Can Seize Common Ground—or Be Swept Aside' (*LawFare*, 27 August 2024) <https://www.lawfaremedia.org/article/ai-regulation-s-champions-can-seize-common-ground-or-be-swept-aside> accessed 8 October 2024.

governance, which includes the principle of appropriate anticipation.[338] Some have argued that such principles should be considered beyond national technology regulation, and should also increasingly inform global governance. For instance, Rosemary Rayfuse notes that whereas the international law system has generally been reactive in regulating new technologies, in the face of emerging technologies such as AI, 'international law is being called upon to regulate not just the past and present development and deployment of technologies, but also the uncertain futures these technologies pose'.[339] This has been echoed by other recent proposals to 'couple international law's traditional reactive paradigm with a more proactive, forward-looking approach', particularly when addressing emerging global challenges such as AI.[340] The drive towards anticipation in AI governance—while acknowledging the conditions of uncertainty—could therefore align with a broader shift in the orientation of global governance towards uncertain but high-stakes technological developments more broadly.

1.5 Conclusion: The Stakes of AI

AI is not the first technology to raise deep societal questions.[341] However, the global challenge of governing AI technology well—under conditions of uncertainty and change—will be a major challenge facing societies over the coming decades. In this sense, our ability, or inability, to collectively manage our relationship to emerging technologies such as AI may prove a key objective and test of our global governance systems and norms. Are we ready?

[338] See generally Richard Owen and others, 'A Framework for Responsible Innovation', *Responsible Innovation* (John Wiley & Sons, Ltd 2013) <https://onlinelibrary.wiley.com/doi/abs/10.1002/9781118551424.ch2> accessed 21 August 2019; Jack Stilgoe, Richard Owen, and Phil Macnaghten, 'Developing a Framework for Responsible Innovation' (2013) 42 Research Policy 1568; And specific to AI, see Miles Brundage, 'Artificial Intelligence and Responsible Innovation' in Vincent C Müller (ed), *Fundamental Issues of Artificial Intelligence* (Springer International Publishing 2016).

[339] Rosemary Rayfuse, 'Public International Law and the Regulation of Emerging Technologies' in Roger Brownsword, Eloise Scotford, and Karen Yeung (eds), *The Oxford Handbook of Law, Regulation and Technology* (Oxford University Press 2017) 500–501.

[340] Michal Saliternik and Sivan Shlomo Agon, 'Proactive International Law' (2024) 75 UC Law Journal 661.

[341] See for instance Daniel Deudney, 'Turbo Change: Accelerating Technological Disruption, Planetary Geopolitics, and Architectonic Metaphors' (2018) 20 International Studies Review 223, 223. (suggesting that, historically, 'the emergence and global spread of a modern civilization devoted to expanding scientific knowledge and developing new technologies has radically increased the rate, magnitude, complexity, novelty, and disruptiveness of change', and that we have entered this state since the emergence of nuclear weapons, or even of industrial (fossil-fuel) based civilization).

2

Scaling Law for AI: Issues, Necessity, and Feasibility

2.1 Introduction

As AI systems have become increasingly advanced and capable, recent years have seen the emergence of a range of fields and communities focused on the governance of this technology and its impacts.[1] These AI governance communities are disparate in their methodological tools and specific issue focus areas, but are united by their broad focus on 'the study and shaping of local and global governance systems—including norms, policies, laws, processes, and institutions—that affect the research, development, deployment, and use of existing and future AI systems, in ways that help the world choose the role of advanced AI systems in its future, and navigate the transition to that world'.[2]

Do we even need such a field? More to the point: do we need policies or regulations for AI technology? Finally, do we need such regulations or actions at the *global* level? One might concede that AI technology will likely become increasingly powerful, pervasive, or both, but still be sceptical of this. For instance, one could object that global governance for AI is not really necessary, because AI does not really create significant problems or, if it does, these will simply sort themselves out, or will be adequately addressed through national regulation. Conversely, one might argue that global governance for AI is simply not feasible—for instance, because it is a digital technology that is so easily disseminated around the world, and so hard to monitor or track, that no global rules, norms, or standards could reasonably exert control over it.

In this chapter, I discuss and critically evaluate these arguments. I review the structure and technical and political features of three types of global governance

[1] Allan Dafoe, 'AI Governance: A Research Agenda' (Center for the Governance of AI, Future of Humanity Institute 2018) <https://www.fhi.ox.ac.uk/govaiagenda/>; Allan Dafoe, 'AI Governance: Overview and Theoretical Lenses' in Justin B Bullock and others (eds), *The Oxford Handbook of AI Governance* (Oxford University Press 2023) <https://doi.org/10.1093/oxfordhb/9780197579329.013.2> accessed 4 October 2023; Jess Whittlestone and Samuel Clarke, 'AI Challenges for Society and Ethics' in Justin B Bullock and others (eds), *The Oxford Handbook of AI Governance* (Oxford University Press 2022) 14.

[2] Matthijs Maas, 'Concepts in Advanced AI Governance: A Literature Review of Key Terms and Definitions' (Institute for Law & AI 2023) AI Foundations Report 3, 54 <https://law-ai.org/advanced-ai-gov-concepts> accessed 27 February 2025 (discussing various technical, policy, and strategy-focused definitions of this field, and on that basis distilling this definition).

Architectures of Global AI Governance. Matthijs M. Maas, Oxford University Press. © Matthijs M. Maas 2025.
DOI: 10.1093/9780191988455.003.0003

issues around AI technologies, and argue that, in order to meaningfully address these global public good challenges, some forms of global cooperation or governance will be necessary. Reviewing models for the global regulation of digital technologies, I furthermore suggest that while political challenges and barriers to establishing AI regimes exist, such arrangements, once created, can avail themselves of many regulatory levers which enable the effective governance of many crucial objects and components across the development and deployment 'stack' of AI systems. This suggests that some global enforcement of norms, standards, or agreements on AI would be feasibly enforceable, provided that agreement can be reached on establishing such a regime in the first place. Scaling international law for the challenges of AI is both necessary and urgent if the world is to meet AI's diverse challenges in a timely manner.

2.2 Global AI Governance Issues: Axes, Issue Clusters, Focus Areas

In understanding where, how, and why AI systems constitute global governance issues, where do we start? In the literature, many methods have been used to disentangle AI's societal challenges, in order to help the public and regulators gain a grasp on the range of challenges to be addressed. In framing our approach to the global governance of AI, then, we can first make a number of distinctions that, implicitly and explicitly, have informed or framed many existing studies as well as policy initiatives in the field. Specifically, we can differentiate AI uses at the global level along both technical and political dimensions, resulting in four broad issue clusters. These can be condensed into three overlapping focus areas for global governance—corresponding to the governance of (civilian, narrow) conventional AI, military AI, and (civilian, general-purpose) advanced AI.

2.2.1 Technical and Political Axes of Global AI Governance

The way that AI issues feature on the global governance level can be distinguished along two axes:[3] a technical distinction between conventional and advanced AI;

[3] For a similar distinction, see also Eleonore Fournier-Tombs and others, 'A Global Architecture for Artificial Intelligence' (United Nations University—Centre for Policy Research 2023) Technical Note 10 <https://unu.edu/publication/global-architecture-artificial-intelligence> accessed 10 December 2023 (distinguishing between two dimensions of global AI governance—civilian vs military, and high-risk vs low-risk). Note, there have also been other ways of organizing the space of global governance issues raised by AI. For instance, Cullen O'Keefe has proposed a minilateral global governance initiative—a 'Chips for Peace' framework—as a 'package of interrelated and mutually reinforcing policies aimed at addressing three grand challenges in AI policy', specifically (1) catastrophic harm

and a political distinction between civilian and military uses of either form.[4] These give rise to four clusters of global governance issues (see Table 2.1).

2.2.1.1 The *technical* axis: conventional or advanced AI

Along the technical axis or dimension, we can distinguish between 'conventional' and 'advanced' AI systems.[5] These need to be distinguished in the context of either evaluating or regulating these systems' impacts.[6]

Roughly, one might use the term 'conventional' AI to broadly refer to a range of AI architectures and systems that (1) are narrow in their capabilities, and where (2) the level of performance in those capabilities can often be good (at a functional level),[7] but does not exceed (expert) human performance at that task.[8] To be clear, this term is not ideal,[9] and the frame should not be taken to mean that such

prevention; (2) shared global prosperity; and (3) coordination among states. Cullen O'Keefe, 'Chips for Peace: How the U.S. and Its Allies Can Lead on Safe and Beneficial AI' (*Lawfare*, 10 July 2024) <https://www.lawfaremedia.org/article/chips-for-peace--how-the-u.s.-and-its-allies-can-lead-on-safe-and-beneficial-ai> accessed 15 July 2024.

[4] I emphasize that this taxonomy is not exhaustive, and other dimensions or axes could be added to discuss different issue clusters. For instance, Maurice Chiodo and colleagues have focused on two distinct regulatory axes—corresponding to 'Big/Small AI Impacts' and 'Big/Small AI Teams'—in order to classify a grid of AI types. Maurice Chiodo and others, 'Regulating AI: A Matrix for Gauging Impact and Its Legal Implementation' (2024) University of Cambridge Faculty of Law Research Paper 4765104 <https://papers.ssrn.com/abstract=4765104> accessed 27 May 2024. However, I suggest that, especially at the international level, the technical and political axes proposed here more usefully carve the space of global AI governance issues at its joints.

[5] For a similar distinction, see also the 'Guidance for Safe Foundation Model Deployment' by the Partnership on AI (PAI), which distinguishes between (1) 'specialized narrow purpose' AI, (2) 'advanced narrow & GPAI', and (3) 'Paradigm-shifting or frontier' AI. Partnership on AI, 'PAI's Guidance for Safe Foundation Model Deployment: A Framework for Collective Action' (2023) <https://partnershiponai.org/wp-content/uploads/1923/10/PAI-Model-Deployment-Guidance.pdf>.

[6] Aylin Caliskan and Kristian Lum, 'Effective AI Regulation Requires Understanding General-Purpose AI' (*Brookings*, 29 January 2024) <https://www.brookings.edu/articles/effective-ai-regulation-requires-understanding-general-purpose-ai/> accessed 12 June 2024.

[7] Although see also Inioluwa Deborah Raji and others, 'The Fallacy of AI Functionality', *2022 ACM Conference on Fairness, Accountability, and Transparency* (Association for Computing Machinery 2022) <https://doi.org/10.1145/3531146.3533158> accessed 30 November 2022.

[8] Meredith Ringel Morris and others, 'Levels of AGI for Operationalizing Progress on the Path to AGI', *Proceedings of the 41st International Conference on Machine Learning* (PMLR 2024) 6 <http://arxiv.org/abs/2311.02462> accessed 13 November 2023. Note, this operationalization excludes (and considers as 'advanced') AI systems that are narrow but display super-human performance in their domain, such as AlphaZero or Alphafold. This is in part because those systems do display paradigm-shifting (that is, non-human and therefore potentially genuinely novel) performance at specific tasks, which makes them distinctly useful, as well as potentially risky. This can, for instance, be seen in debates over the potential advances in AI-enabled biological tools, many of which can be relatively narrow but highly capable—yet many of which may also require policy interventions that are distinct from those warranted by general-purpose AI systems. James Smith and others, 'How the UK Government Should Address the Misuse Risk from AI-Enabled Biological Tools' (Centre for Long-Term Resilience 2024) <https://www.longtermresilience.org/post/how-the-uk-government-should-address-the-misuse-risk-from-ai-enabled-biological-tools> accessed 10 April 2024.

[9] For one, it should not be taken to undervalue the sophistication of these systems. Alternate labels—such as 'focused', 'basic', 'intermediate', or 'specialized' AI—could be considered, though each have their drawbacks or ambiguities. I thank Cecil Abungu for discussions around this framework.

systems are unsophisticated, old, outdated, or of little use. Indeed, as discussed in Chapter 1, such technologies continue to see development, progress, and disruptive applications across many domains, and the continued proliferation of these algorithms alone would suffice to drive significant global impacts.

By contrast, one can consider various types of 'advanced' AI systems. As the field of AI has entered its Large-Scale and General-Purpose eras,[10] recent years have seen significant public and policy attention to these new AI systems. Conceptually, this is a broad category that encompasses many other concepts or frames for sophisticated AI,[11] such as 'general-purpose AI systems',[12] 'highly capable foundation models',[13] 'frontier AI models',[14] 'generative AI',[15] or 'AGI'. However, many of these terms remain themselves loose and in flux, and have been defined or operationalized in different and at times inconsistent ways.[16]

Take, for instance, the term 'frontier AI': recent years have seen a rich and ongoing debate over whether this category of systems is most appropriately defined (in regulatory contexts) in terms of (1) a given AI system's cutting-edge performance exceeding the capabilities of the previous state of the art in the field of AI;[17] (2) the amount of compute used in a model's training, compared against a set compute threshold; (3) its achievement of particular capabilities sufficient to pose risks to public safety;[18] or simply (4) the overall level of risk created by a model, in terms

[10] Jaime Sevilla and others, 'Compute Trends Across Three Eras of Machine Learning' [2022] arXiv:2202.05924 [cs] <http://arxiv.org/abs/2202.05924> accessed 15 February 2022. See Chapter 1.

[11] At the level of underlying techniques, this category includes a range of large, data- and compute-intensive AI models, such as transformer-based large language models and diffusion-based image-generation systems.

[12] Carlos I Gutierrez and others, 'A Proposal for a Definition of General Purpose Artificial Intelligence Systems' (2023) 2 Digital Society 36.

[13] Elizabeth Seger and others, 'Open-Sourcing Highly Capable Foundation Models: An Evaluation of Risks, Benefits, and Alternative Methods for Pursuing Open-Source Objectives' (Centre for the Governance of AI 2023) <https://www.governance.ai/research-paper/open-sourcing-highly-capable-foundation-models> accessed 27 February 2025.

[14] Markus Anderljung and others, 'Frontier AI Regulation: Managing Emerging Risks to Public Safety' (arXiv, 11 July 2023) <http://arxiv.org/abs/2307.03718> accessed 7 August 2023; UK Government, 'AI Safety Summit: Introduction' (*GOV.UK*, 25 September 2023) <https://www.gov.uk/government/publications/ai-safety-summit-introduction/ai-safety-summit-introduction-html> accessed 25 September 2023; Elliot Jones, 'Explainer: What Is a Foundation Model?' (Ada Lovelace Institute 2023) <https://www.adalovelaceinstitute.org/resource/foundation-models-explainer/> accessed 31 August 2023.

[15] Laura Weidinger and others, 'Sociotechnical Safety Evaluation of Generative AI Systems' (arXiv, 18 October 2023) 6 <http://arxiv.org/abs/2310.11986> accessed 20 October 2023; Jones (n 14).

[16] Maas, 'Concepts in Advanced AI Governance' (n 2).

[17] Jonas Schuett and others, 'From Principles to Rules: A Regulatory Approach for Frontier AI' in P Hacker and others (eds), *The Oxford Handbook of the Foundations and Regulation of Generative AI* (Oxford University Press, forthcoming) (defining 'frontier AI systems' as 'general-purpose AI systems that match or exceed the capabilities present in the most advanced systems').

[18] Helen Toner and Shelton Fitch, 'Regulating the AI Frontier: Design Choices and Constraints' (*Center for Security and Emerging Technology*, 26 October 2023) <https://cset.georgetown.edu/article/regulating-the-ai-frontier-design-choices-and-constraints/> accessed 25 November 2023; Anderljung and others (n 14); Maas, 'Concepts in Advanced AI Governance' (n 2).

of a given likelihood of a given quantity of societal harm or economic damage.[19] Moreover, in some definitions used for policy, this category has even been extended to some narrow AI systems that perform at a super-human level within that specific domain.[20]

Given the ambiguity around many of these terms, in this book I focus on the category of 'advanced' AI systems, as a broad conceptual category that refers to all AI systems that, at any stage in their development or use,[21] are or become capable of either (a) broad, general-purpose performance across many tasks, achieving a high, roughly near-human level of task performance;[22] or (b) narrow but significantly super-human performance within particular domains of sociotechnical interest.[23] This aims to capture that subset of AI systems that are most likely to create novel and disruptive sociotechnical impacts.[24]

Consequently, throughout most of this book, I will use the term 'advanced AI' rather than more specific terms such as 'large language model' or 'frontier AI'. This is in order to cast a relatively broad net over many AI systems of societal import—from large language models to generative science tools, from highly capable foundation models to capable 'Long-Term Planning Agents' (LTPAs),[25] as well as any other such AI systems with capabilities of sociotechnical concern.[26] This broad framing has additional benefits, in that it sidesteps the existing ambiguities over

[19] Leonie Koessler, Jonas Schuett, and Markus Anderljung, 'Risk Thresholds for Frontier AI' (arXiv, 20 June 2024) <http://arxiv.org/abs/2406.14713> accessed 26 June 2024.

[20] For example, the 2023 Bletchley Declaration defines the 'frontier' of AI as 'those highly capable general-purpose AI models, including foundation models, that could perform a wide variety of tasks—as well as relevant specific narrow AI that could exhibit capabilities that cause harm—which match or exceed the capabilities present in today's most advanced models'. UK Government, 'The Bletchley Declaration by Countries Attending the AI Safety Summit, 1–2 November 2023' (*GOV.UK*, 1 November 2023) <https://www.gov.uk/government/publications/ai-safety-summit-2023-the-bletchley-declaration/the-bletchley-declaration-by-countries-attending-the-ai-safety-summit-1-2-november-2023> accessed 3 November 2023.

[21] That is, including potential post-training capability gains achieved through scaffolding, tool use, or inference scaling. See also Section 1.3.2.1.

[22] Lewis Ho and others, 'International Institutions for Advanced AI' (arXiv, 10 July 2023) n 1 <http://arxiv.org/abs/2307.04699> accessed 11 July 2023.

[23] A similar taxonomy is drawn in Department for Science, Innovation & Technology, 'Frontier AI: Capabilities and Risks—Discussion Paper on the Need for Further Research into AI Risk' (Department for Science, Innovation & Technology 2023) 5 <https://www.gov.uk/government/publications/frontier-ai-capabilities-and-risks-discussion-paper/frontier-ai-capabilities-and-risks-discussion-paper> accessed 20 March 2024.

[24] There are, of course, alternative productive ways of classifying AI models of significant impact. For instance, Anthony Aguirre and Ben Cummings have proposed a tiered set of safety standards for AI models, based on the degree to which models possess one, two, or all of the three features of 'high autonomy (independence of action)', 'high generality (breadth of scope)', and 'high intelligence (task competence)'. See: Ben Cumming, 'Safety Standards Delivering Controllable and Beneficial AI Tools' (Future of Life Institute 2025) <https://futureoflife.org/document/safety-standards-delivering-controllable-and-beneficial-ai-tools/> accessed 18 February 2025.

[25] Michael K Cohen and others, 'Regulating Advanced Artificial Agents' (2024) 384 Science 36.

[26] See Kayla Matteucci and others, 'AI Systems of Concern' (arXiv, 9 October 2023) <http://arxiv.org/abs/2310.05876> accessed 10 October 2023; Toby Shevlane and others, 'Model Evaluation for Extreme Risks' (arXiv, 24 May 2023) <http://arxiv.org/abs/2305.15324> accessed 25 May 2023.

how best to operationalize many of the more specific terms, debates over how those terms relate to one another,[27] and the need to wrangle with the loaded cultural connotations that come with some of these existing terms.[28] Finally, this term also reduces the risk of tying regulatory targets to a moving threshold of model sophistication. For instance, Elizabeth Seger and others have noted some of the drawbacks of defining 'frontier' models as those that make up (only) the cutting-edge of the AI field, because

> the frontier of cutting-edge AI moves forward as AI research progresses. This means that some highly capable systems of concern—those capable of exhibiting dangerous capabilities with the potential to cause significant physical and societal-scale harm—will sit behind the frontier of AI capability. Even if these models are behind the frontier, we should still exercise caution in deciding to release such models, all else being equal.[29]

Likewise, others have critiqued the validity or meaningfulness of defining such systems—and more broadly, regulatory instruments aimed at minimizing their risk—on the basis of the computing power used in their training, because the exact relation between increasing compute used in AI training and the resulting models' risk profile remains highly uncertain and unpredictable.[30]

Given all this, while the conceptual clusters of conventional and advanced AI do not resolve these debates, they may at least allow us to sidestep some of them. Rather than chasing an ever-receding moving target of 'sufficiently novel' systems under an exceptionalist approach,[31] or (solely) focusing on the compute inputs, they may enable a better focus on AI models observed and likely capabilities, uses, and potential societal impacts.

2.2.1.2 The *political* dimension: civilian or military uses

In addition to this technical distinction, there is a political dimension to global AI governance debates. This distinction is between those applications of AI systems

[27] Toner and Fitch (n 18).

[28] See also Maas, 'Concepts in Advanced AI Governance' (n 2) 49–52 (arguing that 'frontier' AI, while a suitable term in some ways, has its risks, since 'to many audiences, the framing of AI research in a "frontier" may rather imply operating within a wild, unregulated space; one subject to constant, continued, decentralized expansion rather than considered and deliberated navigation'). Note that this does not mean that these terms should be abandoned; however, within this analysis they may be productively subsumed within the larger frame of 'advanced' AI. I thank Kevin Frazier for prompting these clarifications.

[29] This has been one critique of some operationalizations of the concept of 'frontier AI'. See for instance Seger and others (n 13) n 6.

[30] Sara Hooker, 'On the Limitations of Compute Thresholds as a Governance Strategy' (arXiv, 8 July 2024) <http://arxiv.org/abs/2407.05694> accessed 15 July 2024.

[31] See also Chapter 4 for a critique of a technology-centric 'exceptionalist' approach to AI regulation, which focuses overly much on debates over whether a technology is sufficiently 'new' to warrant regulation.

(both conventional and advanced) that give rise to civilian issues, and those applications (both conventional and advanced) that become implicated in military uses or (international) security challenges.[32] This distinction has marked and separated many global AI governance debates to date.[33]

AI system applications in the civilian domain are, as discussed in Chapter 1, tremendously broad, and include the deployment of diverse AI system capabilities in applications across virtually any sector, by actors ranging from private companies to government departments to consumers.

Conversely, AI system applications in the security and military domains comprise a narrower set of AI systems, including (1) AI systems developed or procured by the state for sensitive military purposes and (2) AI systems, such as 'dual-use foundation models', which, even if they are developed by private actors, may drive considerable national or international security impacts, and therefore have become the focus of state action.[34] While most work in this space has to date focused on the potential military applications of narrow AI systems, militaries have in recent years become increasingly interested in the use of (or the threats posed by) large language models and other general-purpose AI systems.[35]

To be clear, these should be considered smooth dimensions rather than hard, exclusive categories. This categorization is an analytical tool that inevitably glosses over real-world ambiguities and a degree of overlap on both technological and

[32] However, note that other definitions of what makes something a 'military' system may focus less on the use domain of AI, and rather on the principal that develops it. For instance, 'civilian AI' has been defined by Trager and others as 'all AI except that built under the direct authority of the state for sensitive purposes such as military or intelligence services'. Robert Trager and others, 'International Governance of Civilian AI: A Jurisdictional Certification Approach' (arXiv, 29 August 2023) 2 <http://arxiv.org/abs/2308.15514> accessed 31 August 2023.

[33] See Denise Garcia, *The AI Military Race: Common Good Governance in the Age of Artificial Intelligence* (Oxford University Press 2023) 8 ('To create common good governance frameworks, it is essential to make a distinction between the global attempts at creating governance mechanisms within the civilian realm and the uses of AI in the military realm'); Fournier-Tombs and others (n 3) 10 ('The final decision point for policymakers is the scope of AI systems under discussion . . . there has been a proposal that any entity tasked with AI governance focus only on *civilian AI*, leaving military uses of AI to other processes. However, rather than choosing between civilian and military AI, a possibility is to establish separate but overlapping bodies').

[34] See Executive Office of the President, 'Executive Order on the Safe, Secure, and Trustworthy Development and Use of Artificial Intelligence' (*The White House*, 30 October 2023) <https://www.whitehouse.gov/briefing-room/presidential-actions/2023/10/30/executive-order-on-the-safe-secure-and-trustworthy-development-and-use-of-artificial-intelligence/> accessed 3 November 2023., Section 3(k) (defining a 'dual-use foundation model' as 'an AI model that is trained on broad data; generally uses self-supervision; contains at least tens of billions of parameters; is applicable across a wide range of contexts; and that exhibits, or could be easily modified to exhibit, high levels of performance at tasks that pose a serious risk to security, national economic security, national public health or safety, or any combination of those matters', and giving various examples of such risks).

[35] Notably, on 10 January 2024, OpenAI's 'usage policies' page dropped previous bans on 'weapons development' and use in 'military and warfare' applications. Sam Biddle, 'OpenAI Quietly Deletes Ban on Using ChatGPT for "Military and Warfare"' (*The Intercept*, 12 January 2024) <https://theintercept.com/2024/01/12/open-ai-military-ban-chatgpt/> accessed 14 January 2024.

Table 2.1 Technical and political dimensions of global AI governance issues

		Technical *distinction (capabilities v performance level)*	
		Conventional AI ***Narrow*** *capabilities (up to human-level performance)*	***Advanced AI*** ***General-purpose*** *capabilities at roughly human-level performance* *OR* ***Paradigm-shifting*** *narrow capabilities at super-human performance*
Political *distinction (applications)*	***Civilian*** **domain uses**	**A. Conventional AI applied in Civilian Domain** (e.g. predictive profiling algorithms, facial recognition AI, etc.)	**C. Advanced AI applied in Civilian Domain** (e.g. GPAIS, 'highly capable foundation models', 'frontier' LLMs)
	Military **domain uses**	**B. Conventional AI applied in Military Do main** (e.g. conflict prediction AI; autonomous weapons)	**D. Advanced AI applied in Military Domain** (e.g. military LLMs; 'dual-use foundation models')

political dimensions. Nonetheless, we can start to identify four AI issue clusters (see Table 2.1),[36] which can help us consider the most appropriate regulatory actors or tools for each issue cluster.

In this approach, we can distinguish between (A) the use of conventional AI systems in civilian domains, (B) the use of conventional AI in the military domain, (C) the use of advanced AI in the civilian domain, and (D) the use of advanced AI in the military domain. However, while there is a significant body of work exploring the general risks of advanced AI systems, only relatively little of this focuses on such systems used in military contexts.[37] When such governance does emerge, it may

[36] By comparison, Dafoe has offered a distinct taxonomy of four clusters of AI risks, distinguishing between (1) inequality, turbulence, authoritarianism, (2) great-power war, (3) the problems of control, alignment and political order, and (4) value erosion from competition. Dafoe, 'AI Governance' (n 1) 2–3.

[37] Though for one exception, see Juan-Pablo Rivera and others, 'Escalation Risks from Language Models in Military and Diplomatic Decision-Making', *Proceedings of the 2024 ACM Conference on Fairness, Accountability, and Transparency* (Association for Computing Machinery 2024) <https://dl.acm.org/doi/10.1145/3630106.3658942> accessed 13 June 2024 (studying the role of five different off-the-shelf LLMs used as AI agents in simulated wargames, and finding that all result in forms of

(initially) hew closely to the governance of other military uses of AI. Accordingly, in this book, I will mostly bracket a discussion of global governance for advanced AI in the military domain (D), to focus on the other categories which have all been subject to a greater amount of norm-setting and governance attempts.[38]

2.2.2 Three Focus Areas for Global AI Governance

On this basis, I suggest we can draw a working distinction between three main focus areas in the global governance of AI technology:

1. Conventional AI Governance (A): mitigating the diverse, *broad-spectrum but domain-specific societal impacts* resulting from the (increasingly) pervasive use of different narrow AI systems in many civilian domains.
2. Military AI Governance (B & D): mitigating the diverse *international security impacts* resulting from the adoption of different types of AI systems (both conventional as well as general-purpose) in diverse military roles.
3. Advanced AI Governance (C): mitigating the *cross-spectrum societal-scale risks* resulting from the deployment of increasingly capable general-purpose AI systems, frontier AI, and highly capable foundation models, especially in terms of their potential misuse, misalignment, or systemic effects.[39]

This distinction is not perfect but it can be an analytically useful starting point, sociologically, from a historical perspective, and analytically.

escalation and difficult-to-predict escalation patterns). See also a rare, older exception in Alexey Turchin and David Denkenberger, 'Military AI as a Convergent Goal of Self-Improving AI' in Roman Yampolskiy (ed), *Artificial Intelligence Safety and Security* (CRC Press 2018) <https://philpapers.org/rec/TURMAA-6> accessed 5 March 2025.

[38] This is not to say that such governance for the military uses of advanced AI systems is redundant: indeed, it may be sorely needed very soon, especially as these technologies mature, proliferate, and enter use.

[39] Government Office for Science, 'Future Risks of Frontier AI: Which Capabilities and Risks Could Emerge at the Cutting Edge of AI in the Future?' (UK Government Office for Science 2023) <https://assets.publishing.service.gov.uk/media/653bc393d10f3500139a6ac5/future-risks-of-frontier-ai-annex-a.pdf> accessed 5 March 2025. See also Ho and others (n 22) ('the potential dangerous capabilities of powerful and general-purpose AI systems create global externalities in their development and deployment'). See also Pegah Maham and Sabrina Küspert, 'Governing General Purpose AI: A Comprehensive Map of Unreliability, Misuse and Systemic Risks' (Stiftung Neue Verantwortung 2023) <https://www.stiftung-nv.de/de/publikation/governing-general-purpose-ai-comprehensive-map-unreliability-misuse-and-systemic-risks> accessed 5 March 2025. See also the taxonomy of risks in Yoshua Bengio, 'International Scientific Report on the Safety of Advanced AI: Interim Report' (Department for Science, Innovation & Technology, and AI Safety Institute 2024) 2024/009 <https://www.gov.uk/government/publications/international-scientific-report-on-the-safety-of-advanced-ai> accessed 21 May 2024.

Sociologically, these distinctions roughly track how these three AI risk clusters have, until fairly recently, been mostly studied separately, by distinct epistemic communities.[40] While recent years have seen increasing convergence on these debates, understanding this distinction remains of genealogical and intellectual interest.

In a historical perspective, the political distinction between civilian and military applications reflects the way that new technologies have often received different responses or treatment under global governance, as states and international institutions have generally taken different approaches to the regulation of military and civilian technologies.

Analytically, this distinction could help focus governance debates on more appropriate sets of regulatory levers and targets. This is because these three clusters of AI issues have often been linked to different regulatory responses. For instance, whereas conventional AI systems might at times be adequately (though not necessarily optimally) regulated at the application level, advanced general-purpose AI systems require, it has often been argued, upstream regulation or developer liability.[41] Likewise, whereas the regulation of military AI systems might rely on non-proliferation regimes, norms of use, and/or verification regimes, it has been suggested that the supply chain for (civilian) advanced AI development could instead lend itself well to regulation through a mix of lab-internal Responsible-Scaling Policies,[42] global regimes that rely on compute governance or jurisdictional

[40] Henrik Skaug Sætra and John Danaher, 'Resolving the Battle of Short- vs. Long-Term AI Risks' [2023] AI and Ethics <https://doi.org/10.1007/s43681-023-00336-y> accessed 6 September 2023; Shazeda Ahmed and others, 'Building the Epistemic Community of AI Safety' <https://drive.google.com/file/d/1HIwKMnQNYme2U4__T-5MvKh9RZ7-RD6x/view?usp=drivesdk> accessed 5 March 2025.

[41] AI Now Institute, 'General Purpose AI Poses Serious Risks, Should Not Be Excluded From the EU's AI Act' (*AI Now Institute*, 13 April 2023) <https://ainowinstitute.org/publication/gpai-is-high-risk-should-not-be-excluded-from-eu-ai-act> accessed 16 April 2023.

[42] See Department for Science, Innovation & Technology, 'Emerging Processes for Frontier AI Safety' (Department for Science, Innovation & Technology 2023) <https://www.gov.uk/government/publications/emerging-processes-for-frontier-ai-safety/emerging-processes-for-frontier-ai-safety> accessed 12 April 2024; ARC Evals, 'Responsible Scaling Policies (RSPs)' (*ARC Evals*, 26 September 2023) <https://evals.alignment.org/blog/2023-09-26-rsp/> accessed 26 October 2023. For examples of such policies from different leading labs, see also Anthropic, 'Anthropic's Responsible Scaling Policy, Version 1.0' <http://anthropic.com/responsible-scaling-policy>; OpenAI, 'OpenAI's Approach to Frontier Risk' (26 October 2023) <https://openai.com/global-affairs/our-approach-to-frontier-risk> accessed 13 January 2024; OpenAI, 'Preparedness Framework (Beta)' (OpenAI 2023) <https://cdn.openai.com/openai-preparedness-framework-beta.pdf> accessed 5 March 2025; Anca Dragan, Helen King, and Allan Dafoe, 'Introducing the Frontier Safety Framework' (*Google DeepMind*, 17 May 2024) <https://deepmind.google/discover/blog/introducing-the-frontier-safety-framework/> accessed 17 May 2024. A more indirect approach to evaluation is offered by Google DeepMind: Laura Weidinger and others, 'Holistic Safety and Responsibility Evaluations of Advanced AI Models' (arXiv, 22 April 2024) <http://arxiv.org/abs/2404.14068> accessed 1 May 2024. Though for a more cautious assessment of these policies, see Paul Christiano, 'Thoughts on Responsible Scaling Policies and Regulation' (*AI Alignment Forum*, 25 October 2023) <https://www.alignmentforum.org/posts/dxgEaDrEBkkE96CXr/thoughts-on-responsible-scaling-policies-and-regulation> accessed 13 January

certification, or (national-level) reporting and auditing approaches,[43] among others.

Indeed, we can consider some main themes for all three categories of challenges (see Table 2.2), in terms of the technologies, capabilities, and applications engaged, the main drivers of ongoing change or proliferation for each of these, and the different histories of governance.[44]

Let us briefly discuss all three categories in turn.

2.2.2.1 Conventional AI's cross-spectrum impacts

For many years already, a wide variety of algorithms and AI systems have been used and have seen widespread scrutiny. If highly capable and resource-intensive foundation models are considered the technical 'frontier' of the AI wave, these conventional AI systems have served as its 'flood'. They make up the historical vanguard of AI's sociotechnical impacts, first instantiating the diverse societal challenges that all too often remain unaddressed, and which may grow in scale as these tools proliferate.

As discussed in Chapter 1, many of these AI systems remain relatively limited in their capabilities: that is, they are certainly limited in their generality or adaptability to many tasks, if not their relative performance at particular tasks compared to humans.[45] This is especially so when they are compared to the increasingly general and competent performance seen at the frontier of large-scale foundation models and other forms of advanced AI. At the same time, conventional AI systems should not be characterized as either unsophisticated or outdated: advances continue to be made in many of the underlying fields as well.

Moreover, even for systems that only show moderate or human-competitive performance in narrow domains, conventional AI systems can be nonetheless suitable for particular tasks. This, compared with their relative affordability, means that such models will continue to play a role in the AI landscape—even if they are at times eclipsed from the public eye compared to more general-purpose

2024. For another evaluation of Anthropic's RSP, against the guidance of DSIT, see also Bill Anderson-Samways and others, 'Responsible Scaling: Comparing Government Guidance and Company Policy' (Institute for AI Policy and Strategy (IAPS) 2024) <https://www.iaps.ai/research/responsible-scaling> accessed 21 May 2024.

[43] Anderljung and others (n 14); Avital Balwit, 'How We Can Regulate AI' [2023] *Asterisk* <https://asteriskmag.com/issues/03/how-we-can-regulate-ai> accessed 28 August 2023; Yonadav Shavit, 'What Does It Take to Catch a Chinchilla? Verifying Rules on Large-Scale Neural Network Training Via Compute Monitoring' <https://paperswithcode.com/paper/what-does-it-take-to-catch-a-chinchilla>; Trager and others (n 32). Though for critiques of some of these, see also Neel Guha and others, 'AI Regulation Has Its Own Alignment Problem: The Technical and Institutional Feasibility of Disclosure, Registration, Licensing, and Auditing' (2024) 92 George Washington Law Review 1473.

[44] For a more in-depth discussion of the recent history (and possible futures) of global AI governance, see also Chapter 3.

[45] Although even here there is also a critique that the performance of many AI systems that are pushed into service is frequently overstated. See Raji and others (n 7).

Table 2.2 Three categories of AI global governance challenges

Category	AI systems stack				Need for global governance — *History of governance*
	Techniques — *Usage thresholds*	**Capabilities** — *Drivers of vertical (capability) proliferation*	**Applications** — *Drivers of horizontal (access) proliferation*	**Societal impacts**	
Conventional AI	Various narrow algorithms — *Varying preconditions for use (data, compute)*	**Narrow** but adequate (at times super-human) performance at specific tasks —*Cont'd improvements in specific domains*	Highly **diverse** across industries and domains of life — *Falling access and use thresholds for many usage domains*	**Full-spectrum risks** to many values, from privacy to security to non-discrimination, etc.	Likely **valuable** — *Growing institutional activity since 2015, but fragmented and nonbinding*
Military AI	Various narrow algorithms; growing interest in general-purpose systems — *Varying (organizational) adoption thresholds*	Mostly **narrow** — *Growing interest in general-purpose systems*	Highly **diverse**, across military roles; both kinetic and non-kinetic — *Falling access thresholds for many use domains*	**International security risks**, including to conflict escalation, laws of war, etc.	Likely **critical** — *Early (2009) advocacy resulting in CCW institutionalization (2016), but pervasive gridlock since*
Advanced AI	Particular algorithms (e.g. Transformer architecture), resulting in adaptive pretrained foundation models (e.g. LLMs) — *Very high initial development costs and compute & data requirements*	**General-purpose**: adaptive (sometimes) multimodal, and adequate-to-good performance across many tasks Some **narrow but super-human** (e.g. AlphaFold) — *Cont'd scaling and exploitation of capability overhang (e.g. inference scaling) suggests further capability improvements*	Currently mostly used in conversational, generative- and informational search roles — *Open-source model marketplaces facilitating rapid dissemination and experimentation*	**Societal-scale risks,** including systemic flowthrough effects; effects on epistemic processes; sociality; potential for misuse; misalignment and unknown or emergent capabilities	Likely **critical** — *Only recent attention (since 2022), significant momentum but fragmented efforts*

systems—and will see continued and even growing usage in many industries and domains of life.

This matters, because, as significant research over the past decades has shown, these systems raise significant ethical and societal concern. They have been critiqued for undermining the autonomy of consumers, fostering technological addiction,[46] and hijacking attention.[47] They have been challenged for their impacts on a range of human rights such as privacy or non-discrimination,[48] and broader concerns have been raised over their impact on human dignity.[49] There have been significant concerns over the biases displayed by the use of many narrow AI systems in applications such as facial recognition[50] and in crime prediction.[51] Narrow AI systems have been implicated in posing threats to democratic norms and practices.[52] Moreover, there are concerns that automation in many sectors will drive large-scale work displacement and unemployment,[53] growing

[46] Adam Alter, *Irresistible: The Rise of Addictive Technology and the Business of Keeping Us Hooked* (Reprint edition, Penguin Books 2018).

[47] James Williams, *Stand Out of Our Light: Freedom and Resistance in the Attention Economy* (Reprint edition, Cambridge University Press 2018).

[48] These literatures are all extensive. On human rights, see QC van Est, J Gerritsen, and L Kool, 'Human Rights in the Robot Age: Challenges Arising from the Use of Robotics, Artificial Intelligence, and Virtual and Augmented Reality' (Rathenau Instituut 2017) <https://research.tue.nl/en/publications/human-rights-in-the-robot-age-challenges-arising-from-the-use-of-> accessed 22 May 2019. On non-discrimination, see Amnesty International and Access Now, 'The Toronto Declaration: Protecting the Right to Equality and Non-Discrimination in Machine Learning Systems' <https://www.accessnow.org/cms/assets/uploads/2018/08/The-Toronto-Declaration_ENG_08-2018.pdf> accessed 27 August 2018; Hin-Yan Liu, 'Three Types of Structural Discrimination Introduced by Autonomous Vehicles' (2018) 51 UC Davis Law Review 32. On privacy, see Ryan Calo, 'Peeping HALs: Making Sense of Artificial Intelligence and Privacy' (2010) 2 EJLS—European Journal of Legal Studies <http://www.ejls.eu/6/83UK.htm> accessed 13 May 2017; Jay Stanley, 'The Dawn of Robot Surveillance: AI, Video Analytics, and Privacy' (American Civil Liberties Union 2019) <https://www.aclu.org/sites/default/files/field_document/061119-robot_surveillance.pdf> accessed 15 June 2019.

[49] Roger Brownsword, 'From Erewhon to AlphaGo: For the Sake of Human Dignity, Should We Destroy the Machines?' (2017) 9 Law, Innovation and Technology 117; Elvira Rosert and Frank Sauer, 'Prohibiting Autonomous Weapons: Put Human Dignity First' (2019) 10 Global Policy 370.

[50] Joy Buolamwini and Timnit Gebru, 'Gender Shades: Intersectional Accuracy Disparities in Commercial Gender Classification', *Proceedings of Machine Learning Research* (2018) <http://proceedings.mlr.press/v81/buolamwini18a/buolamwini18a.pdf> accessed 5 March 2025.

[51] Lauren Kirchner and others, 'Machine Bias: There's Software Used Across the Country to Predict Future Criminals. And It's Biased Against Blacks' (*ProPublica*, 23 May 2016) <https://www.propublica.org/article/machine-bias-risk-assessments-in-criminal-sentencing> accessed 24 May 2017; but see also Sam Corbett-Davies and others, 'A Computer Program Used for Bail and Sentencing Decisions Was Labeled Biased against Blacks. It's Actually Not That Clear', *Washington Post* (17 October 2016) <https://www.washingtonpost.com/news/monkey-cage/wp/2016/10/17/can-an-algorithm-be-racist-our-analysis-is-more-cautious-than-propublicas/> accessed 21 May 2017.

[52] Dirk Helbing and others, 'Will Democracy Survive Big Data and Artificial Intelligence?' [2017] *Scientific American* <https://www.scientificamerican.com/article/will-democracy-survive-big-data-and-artificial-intelligence/> accessed 29 May 2017; Robert Chesney and Danielle Keats Citron, 'Deep Fakes: A Looming Challenge for Privacy, Democracy, and National Security' (2019) 107 California Law Review 1753; Steven Feldstein, 'The Road to Digital Unfreedom: How Artificial Intelligence Is Reshaping Repression' (2019) 30 Journal of Democracy 40; Gillian Bolsover and Philip Howard, 'Computational Propaganda and Political Big Data: Moving Toward a More Critical Research Agenda' (2017) 5 Big Data 273.

[53] Carl Benedikt Frey and Michael A Osborne, 'The Future of Employment: How Susceptible Are Jobs to Computerisation?' (2017) 114 Technological Forecasting and Social Change 254. Though for a

inequality,[54] or harmful changes to the nature of work itself, potentially eroding the meaning, identity, or fulfilment such jobs have provided to many.[55]

Conventional AI systems have also been more than adequate at giving rise to new security threats, as various actors are able to exploit this technology either as a tool or as a vulnerable attack surface,[56] raising safety concerns as a result of unanticipated behaviour and through interactions between AIs and humans.[57] Finally, such tools may raise the risk of cascading and catastrophic safety failures in critical infrastructures.[58] While many have pointed out these risks for years, they still remain inadequately addressed, at either the domestic or global levels.

more optimistic view, see David H Autor, 'Why Are There Still So Many Jobs? The History and Future of Workplace Automation' (2015) 29 Journal of Economic Perspectives 3. For analysis of the challenges in predicting rates and trends of automation in economically valuable tasks, see David Owen and Tamay Besiroglu, 'Challenges in Predicting AI Automation' (Epoch 2023) <https://epochai.org/blog/challenges-in-predicting-ai-automation> accessed 6 January 2024 (discussing challenges to existing methodologies for predicting automation, in particularly those that focus on 'in-principle-automatability'—'scoring occupational tasks on how soon AI will have the technical capacity to automate them, while neglecting questions about costs and incentives, workflow reorganization, societal decisions, and other important factors'—but also noting that the field has made progress on many challenges since its early days, and is yielding early evidence that earlier predictions correlate with firm-level changes in hiring and productivity improvements).

54 Mary L Gray and Siddharth Suri, *Ghost Work: How to Stop Silicon Valley from Building a New Global Underclass* (Houghton Mifflin Harcourt 2019), as well as Sam Manning, 'AI's Impact on Income Inequality in the US' (*Brookings*, 3 July 2024) <https://www.brookings.edu/articles/ais-impact-on-income-inequality-in-the-us/> accessed 10 July 2024. Though for a more optimistic view, see David Autor, 'AI Could Actually Help Rebuild The Middle Class' [2024] *Noema Mag* <https://www.noemamag.com/how-ai-could-help-rebuild-the-middle-class> accessed 10 July 2024.

55 Avital Balwit, 'My Last Five Years of Work' (*Palladium Magazine*, 17 May 2024) <https://www.palladiummag.com/2024/05/17/my-last-five-years-of-work/> accessed 10 June 2024. However, for a more optimistic view, see John Danaher, *Automation and Utopia: Human Flourishing in a World without Work* (Harvard University Press 2019).

56 Miles Brundage and others, 'The Malicious Use of Artificial Intelligence: Forecasting, Prevention, and Mitigation' [2018] arXiv:1802.07228 [cs] <http://arxiv.org/abs/1802.07228> accessed 21 February 2018; Thomas C King and others, 'Artificial Intelligence Crime: An Interdisciplinary Analysis of Foreseeable Threats and Solutions' [2019] Science and Engineering Ethics <https://doi.org/10.1007/s11948-018-00081-0> accessed 21 February 2019; Keith J Hayward and Matthijs M Maas, 'Artificial Intelligence and Crime: A Primer for Criminologists' (2020) 17 Crime, Media, Culture 209; M Caldwell and others, 'AI-Enabled Future Crime' (2020) 9 Crime Science 14.

57 Dario Amodei and others, 'Concrete Problems in AI Safety' [2016] arXiv:1606.06565 [cs] <http://arxiv.org/abs/1606.06565> accessed 13 May 2017; Ram Shankar Siva Kumar and others, 'Failure Modes in Machine Learning Systems' [2019] arXiv:1911.11034 [cs, stat] <http://arxiv.org/abs/1911.11034> accessed 7 January 2020; Joel Lehman and others, 'The Surprising Creativity of Digital Evolution: A Collection of Anecdotes from the Evolutionary Computation and Artificial Life Research Communities' (2020) 26 Artificial Life 274; On interaction between systems, see Iyad Rahwan and others, 'Machine Behaviour' (2019) 568 Nature 477; Victoria Krakovna and others, 'Specification Gaming: The Flip Side of AI Ingenuity' (*Deepmind*, 21 April 2020) <https://deepmind.com/blog/article/Specification-gaming-the-flip-side-of-AI-ingenuity> accessed 5 September 2020; Matthijs M Maas, 'Regulating for "Normal AI Accidents": Operational Lessons for the Responsible Governance of Artificial Intelligence Deployment', *Proceedings of the 2018 AAAI/ACM Conference on AI, Ethics, and Society* (Association for Computing Machinery 2018) <https://doi.org/10.1145/3278721.3278766> accessed 8 September 2020.

58 Osonde Osoba and William Welser, *The Risks of Artificial Intelligence to Security and the Future of Work* (RAND Corporation 2017) <https://www.rand.org/pubs/perspectives/PE237.html> accessed 22 June 2020.

2.2.2.2 Military AI's growing international security impacts

In the second place, at the international level, the growing military interest in AI technology has led to growing concerns over human dignity, human control, and the dynamics of military escalation.

To be clear, the developments in military application and use of AI have a long history—and in some sense, as with many other technologies, militaries may be among the oldest users and patrons of AI. In fact, the use of computing and automation technologies in military operations has a history that dates back to the very dawn of these disciplines, and many early developments in computing technologies and AI found their direct genesis in military projects, or at least were intimately tied up with strategic needs.[59]

Indeed, while 'killer robots' are sometimes presented as a very novel development,[60] the incorporation of a degree of automatic operation or autonomy in lethal weapons systems is not historically unprecedented.[61] In some contexts, militaries have been operating 'fire-and-forget' weapons such as homing torpedoes for more than 70 years.[62] In defensive roles, algorithms have for some time already been entrusted with operating fully autonomous weapons systems, such as the 'Close-In Weapon Systems' cannons which are operated by dozens of countries to defend naval vessels from incoming missiles.[63]

2.2.2.2.1 The rise of military AI

However, whatever the history of military autonomy, recent years have certainly seen a marked speeding up in the militarization of AI.[64] As early as 2017, one review identified 49 deployed weapon systems 'with autonomous targeting capabilities sufficient to engage targets without the involvement of a human operator'.[65] Indeed, the first fully autonomous weapons systems have seen some deployments

[59] See for instance Sharon Weinberger, *The Imagineers of War: The Untold Story of DARPA, the Pentagon Agency that Changed the World* (Random House LLC 2017); Alex Roland and Philip Shiman, *Strategic Computing: DARPA and the Quest for Machine Intelligence, 1983–1993* (MIT Press 2002).

[60] But see also Tom FA Watts and Ingvild Bode, 'Machine Guardians: The Terminator, AI Narratives and US Regulatory Discourse on Lethal Autonomous Weapons Systems' [2023] Cooperation and Conflict 00108367231198155.

[61] For a distinction between 'automatic', 'automated', 'autonomous', and 'intelligent', see Paul Scharre, 'Autonomous Weapons and Operational Risk' (Center for a New American Security 2016) 12 <https://s3.amazonaws.com/files.cnas.org/documents/CNAS_Autonomous-weapons-operational-risk.pdf> accessed 5 March 2025.

[62] For instance, acoustic homing torpedoes already saw some use during the Second World War, such as the 'Wren' torpedo deployed by German submarines. Paul Scharre, 'Autonomous Weapons and Stability' (King's College 2020) 72–73 <https://kclpure.kcl.ac.uk/portal/en/theses/autonomous-weapons-and-stability(92cd3d5b-4eb1-4ad5-a9ca-0cce2491e652).html> 5 March 2025.

[63] ibid 302–303.

[64] Justin Haner and Denise Garcia, 'The Artificial Intelligence Arms Race: Trends and World Leaders in Autonomous Weapons Development' (2019) 10 Global Policy 331.

[65] Vincent Boulanin and Maaike Verbruggen, 'Mapping the Development of Autonomy in Weapon Systems' (Stockholm International Peace Research Institute 2017) 26 <https://www.sipri.org/sites/default/files/2017-11/siprireport_mapping_the_development_of_autonomy_in_weapon_systems_1117_1.pdf> 5 March 2025.

for many years. More than a decade ago, the South Korean military deployed to the Demilitarized Zone a series of Samsung SGR-A1 sentry gun turrets which reportedly had a fully autonomous capability.[66] Around the mid-2010s, Israel first deployed the 'Harpy' loitering anti-radar drone system,[67] and various countries, and companies, have begun to develop and market weaponized drones capable of varying degrees of autonomy.[68] Consequently, military AI systems have begun to play increasingly significant roles in modern conflicts: autonomous weapons systems acting increasingly (and likely fully) autonomously have seen use in the Libyan civil war[69] and in the Russia–Ukraine war,[70] where reports suggest that drone platforms (piloted and unpiloted) may now be responsible for a majority of battlefield losses, overtaking artillery.[71] Likewise, in the ongoing Israel–Hamas conflict, the Israeli Defense Forces have used AI-enabled target-suggestion databases such as the 'Gospel' and 'Lavender' systems to mark tens of thousands of potential targets for attack.[72]

That is not to say that these innovations have always proceeded smoothly. For instance, Chinese defence experts have suggested that several technological challenges continue to hinder the country's ability to capitalize on military AI.[73] In the West, differences in innovation culture, business practices, and values between

[66] Loz Blain, 'South Korea's Autonomous Robot Gun Turrets: Deadly from Kilometers Away' (2010) <http://newatlas.com/korea-dodamm-super-aegis-autonomos-robot-gun-turret/17198/> accessed 20 September 2016; Alexander Velez-Green, 'The Foreign Policy Essay: The South Korean Sentry—A "Killer Robot" to Prevent War' (*Lawfare*, 1 March 2015) <https://www.lawfareblog.com/foreign-policy-essay-south-korean-sentry%E2%80%94-killer-robot-prevent-war> accessed 11 September 2020.

[67] Israel Aerospace Industries, 'Harpy Loitering Weapon' <https://www.iai.co.il/p/harpy> accessed 11 September 2020; Scharre, 'Autonomous Weapons and Stability' (n 62) 21.

[68] For instance, in 2019, Chinese company Ziyan began to market its 'Blowfish A3', a machine-gun-carrying assault drone that was allegedly marketed as sporting 'full autonomy'. Patrick Tucker, 'SecDef: China Is Exporting Killer Robots to the Mideast' (*Defense One*, 5 November 2019) <https://www.defenseone.com/technology/2019/11/secdef-china-exporting-killer-robots-mideast/161100/> accessed 11 September 2020.

[69] Maria Cramer, 'A.I. Drone May Have Acted on Its Own in Attacking Fighters, U.N. Says' *The New York Times* (3 June 2021) <https://www.nytimes.com/2021/06/03/world/africa/libya-drone.html> accessed 13 December 2021; Zachary Kallenborn, 'Was a Flying Killer Robot Used in Libya? Quite Possibly' (*Bulletin of the Atomic Scientists*, 20 May 2021) <https://thebulletin.org/2021/05/was-a-flying-killer-robot-used-in-libya-quite-possibly/> accessed 13 December 2021.

[70] Morgan Meaker, 'Ukraine's War Brings Autonomous Weapons to the Front Lines' [2023] *Wired UK* <https://www.wired.co.uk/article/ukraine-war-autonomous-weapons-frontlines> accessed 5 December 2023.

[71] The Economist, 'How Ukraine Uses Cheap AI-Guided Drones to Deadly Effect against Russia' [2024] *The Economist* <https://www.economist.com/europe/2024/12/02/how-ukraine-uses-cheap-ai-guided-drones-to-deadly-effect-against-russia> accessed 22 January 2025.

[72] Harry Davies, Bethan McKernan, and Dan Sabbagh, '"The Gospel": How Israel Uses AI to Select Bombing Targets in Gaza' *The Guardian* (1 December 2023) <https://www.theguardian.com/world/2023/dec/01/the-gospel-how-israel-uses-ai-to-select-bombing-targets> accessed 5 December 2023; Yuval Abraham, '"Lavender": The AI Machine Directing Israel's Bombing Spree in Gaza' (*+972 Magazine*, 3 April 2024) <https://www.972mag.com/lavender-ai-israeli-army-gaza/> accessed 30 April 2024.

[73] Sam Bresnick, 'China's Military AI Roadblocks: PRC Perspectives on Technological Challenges to Intelligentized Warfare' (Center for Security and Emerging Technology 2024) <https://cset.georgetown.edu/publication/chinas-military-ai-roadblocks/> accessed 24 October 2024.

civilian tech companies and militaries have created underappreciated hurdles to the latter's procurement of AI systems from the private sector.[74] In the US, public resistance and activism within the AI industry have at times hindered government procurement of military AI applications, as illustrated by high-profile decisions of tech companies to withdraw from military contracts following employee protests.[75]

Nor is this to suggest that all use cases of military AI have been automatically pivotal on the battlefield, or that innovation alone turned the tide: in the Ukraine conflict, as much has depended on questions of raw logistics (such as around the deliveries of basic weapons and ammunition, especially for artillery) as on new innovations.[76] Nonetheless, within a span of years, autonomous suicide drones have increasingly transformed soldiers' experience of the front lines beyond recognition.[77]

This broader trend in the militarization of robotic and AI technologies is projected to continue and accelerate further,[78] especially as a range of conflicts and rising geopolitical tensions have driven continued expansions in military AI budgets. For instance, one review of US federal spending found that the potential value of military AI-related federal contracts commissioned by the Department of Defense tripled in a single year, from $190 million in August 2022 to $557 million in August 2023,[79] peaking to a requested defence budget of $1.8 billion for AI research, development, testing and evaluation for the fiscal year 2024.[80] A range of states, most notably the US, China, Russia, and South Korea, as well as the EU, have accordingly begun robust investments in military applications of AI.[81]

[74] Challenging the common perception that there is little to constrain the proliferation of Lethal Autonomous Weapons Systems, Maaike Verbruggen has suggested that civil–military cooperation (or 'spin-in') on producing LAWS will often be far more hindered and inhibited than is often anticipated. Maaike Verbruggen, 'The Role of Civilian Innovation in the Development of Lethal Autonomous Weapon Systems' (2019) 10 Global Policy 338.

[75] Haydn Belfield, 'Activism by the AI Community: Analysing Recent Achievements and Future Prospects', *Proceedings of the AAAI/ACM Conference on AI, Ethics, and Society* (ACM 2020) <https://dl.acm.org/doi/10.1145/3375627.3375814> accessed 24 August 2020.

[76] David E Sanger, 'In Ukraine, New American Technology Won the Day. Until It Was Overwhelmed' *The New York Times* (23 April 2024) <https://www.nytimes.com/2024/04/23/us/politics/ukraine-new-american-technology.html> accessed 30 April 2024.

[77] Quentin Sommerville, 'Ukraine Thrown into War's Bleak Future as Drones Open New Front' *BBC* (24 July 2024) <https://www.bbc.com/news/articles/cne4vl9gy2wo> accessed 5 August 2024.

[78] Haner and Garcia (n 64) 331.

[79] Jacob Larson and others, 'The Evolution of Artificial Intelligence (AI) Spending by the U.S. Government' (Brookings 2024) <https://www.brookings.edu/articles/the-evolution-of-artificial-intelligence-ai-spending-by-the-u-s-government/> accessed 17 May 2024.

[80] Will Henshall, 'U.S. Military Spending on AI Surges' (*TIME*, 27 March 2024) <https://time.com/6961317/ai-artificial-intelligence-us-military-spending/> accessed 17 May 2024.

[81] Haner and Garcia (n 64) 332. However, other active parties include India, Israel, and Japan. Justin K Haner, 'Dark Horses in the Lethal AI Arms Race' (2019) <https://justinkhaner.com/aiarmsrace> accessed 10 September 2020.

2.2.2.2.2 Beyond Killer Robots: the range of military AI

The appeal of AI technologies to military organizations should not be surprising, given the technology's potential breadth. Indeed, AI systems could see diverse applications across the battlefield—fulfilling diverse roles across what the US Army has called the 'Internet of Battle Things',[82] or what the Chinese PLA has referred to as a 'Battlefield Singularity'.[83] These applications might include many systems deployed in a direct offensive and kinetic capability. Indeed, beyond the 'killer robots' that feature so prominently in public debates, versions of lethal autonomy can come in much more mundane forms. For instance, the US Air Force has been developing its Golden Horde initiative, a project to create munition swarms which, once fired, work together to gather reconnaissance, carry out aerial refuelling, or attack targets matching certain criteria.[84] Sweden has developed a 'smart' artillery shell that can compare detected vehicles in a target area and only engage those contained on a programmable target list.[85]

More generally, there is a broad diversity of military uses of AI, far beyond individual robotic weapons platforms.[86] AI systems could see application in coordinating units to fire on certain targets at the tactical level—creating what the US Army has called an 'artificial intelligence enabled kill web'.[87] It could also see uses

82 Alexander Kott, 'Challenges and Characteristics of Intelligent Autonomy for Internet of Battle Things in Highly Adversarial Environments' <https://arxiv.org/ftp/arxiv/papers/1803/1803.11256.pdf>.

83 Elsa B Kania, 'Battlefield Singularity: Artificial Intelligence, Military Revolution, and China's Future Military Power' (Center for a New American Security 2017) <https://s3.amazonaws.com/files.cnas.org/documents/Battlefield-Singularity-November-2017.pdf?mtime=20171129235804> accessed 28 March 2018.

84 Rachel S Cohen, 'Air Force to Test Weapons Swarming Software in October' (*Air Force Magazine*, 21 September 2020) <https://www.airforcemag.com/air-force-to-test-weapons-swarming-software-in-october/> accessed 22 September 2020.

85 John Cherry and Christopher Korpela, 'Enhanced Distinction: The Need for a More Focused Autonomous Weapons Targeting Discussion at the LAWS GGE' (*Humanitarian Law & Policy Blog*, 28 March 2019) <https://blogs.icrc.org/law-and-policy/2019/03/28/enhanced-distinction-need-focused-autonomous-weapons-targeting/> accessed 14 July 2020; As cited in Ashley Deeks, 'Coding the Law of Armed Conflict: First Steps' in Matthew C Waxman (ed), *The Law of Armed Conflict in 2040* (Oxford University Press 2020) n 18 <https://papers.ssrn.com/abstract=3612329> accessed 25 June 2020.

86 See: Hin-Yan Liu, Léonard Van Rompaey, and Matthijs M Maas, 'Editorial: Beyond Killer Robots: Networked Artificial Intelligence Systems Disrupting the Battlefield?' (2019) 10 Journal of International Humanitarian Legal Studies 77; Léonard Van Rompaey, 'Shifting from Autonomous Weapons to Military Networks' (2019) 10 Journal of International Humanitarian Legal Studies 111; Hin-Yan Liu, 'From the Autonomy Framework towards Networks and Systems Approaches for "Autonomous" Weapons Systems' (2019) 10 Journal of International Humanitarian Legal Studies 89.

87 Ashley Roque, 'Project Convergence 2020: US Army Hosting Kill Chain Demonstration' (*Janes.com*, 16 September 2020) <https://www.janes.com/defence-news/news-detail/project-convergence-2020-us-army-hosting-kill-chain-demonstration> accessed 20 September 2020. See also Theresa Hitchens, 'Kill Chain in the Sky with Data: Army's Project Convergence' (*Breaking Defense*, 14 September 2020) <https://breakingdefense.com/2020/09/kill-chain-in-the-sky-with-data-armys-project-convergence/> accessed 20 September 2020. Sydney J Freedberg, 'A Slew to a Kill: Project Convergence' (*Breaking Defense*, 16 September 2020) <https://breakingdefense.com/2020/09/a-slew-to-a-kill-project-convergence/> accessed 20 September 2020. In another test, the US Army used target identification and recommendation algorithms to shorten an artillery 'kill chain' from 10 minutes to 20 seconds. Sydney J Freedberg, 'Target Gone in 20 Seconds: Army Sensor-Shooter Test' (*Breaking*

that are adversarial but non-kinetic, such as autonomous cyberwarfare systems or adaptive radar-jamming or electronic warfare capabilities.[88] Other uses of AI systems, such as in military decision support systems,[89] might not involve direct lethal autonomy, but could nonetheless be 'lethality-enabling'.[90] Finally, there are also many applications of AI in 'non-offensive' military roles, including pervasive tactical surveillance,[91] command and control capabilities, improved (satellite) sensing capabilities, general logistics,[92] training,[93] or medevac or medical triage.[94]

At a strategic level, there have even been concerns that aspects of automation might make their way into the command and control architectures for nuclear forces.[95] Indeed, while senior US officials maintain that there will always be a

Defense, 10 September 2020) <https://breakingdefense.com/2020/09/target-gone-in-20-seconds-army-sensor-shooter-test/> accessed 20 September 2020.

[88] See for instance the DARPA ARC and BLADE programmes; Paul Tilghman, 'Adaptive Radar Countermeasures (ARC)' (*DARPA*) <https://www.darpa.mil/program/adaptive-radar-countermeasures> accessed 12 March 2018; Paul Tilghman, 'Behavioral Learning for Adaptive Electronic Warfare (BLADE)' (*DARPA*) <https://www.darpa.mil/program/behavioral-learning-for-adaptive-electronic-warfare> accessed 12 March 2018.

[89] Alexander Blanchard and Laura Bruun, 'Autonomous Weapon Systems and AI-Enabled Decision Support Systems in Military Targeting: A Comparison and Recommended Policy Responses' (SIPRI 2025) <https://www.sipri.org/publications/2025/other-publications/autonomous-weapon-systems-and-ai-enabled-decision-support-systems-military-targeting-comparison-and> accessed 11 June 2025; Emelia Probasco and others, 'Not Oracles of the Battlefield: Safety Considerations for AI-Based Military Decision Support Systems' (2024) 7 Proceedings of the AAAI/ACM Conference on AI, Ethics, and Society 1157.

[90] Arthur Holland Michel, 'The Killer Algorithms Nobody's Talking About' (*Foreign Policy*, 20 January 2020) <https://foreignpolicy.com/2020/01/20/ai-autonomous-weapons-artificial-intelligence-the-killer-algorithms-nobodys-talking-about/> accessed 21 January 2020.

[91] Compare project 'MAVEN': Deputy Secretary of Defense, 'Establishment of an Algorithmic Warfare Cross-Functional Team (Project Maven)' <https://www.scribd.com/document/346681336/Establishment-of-the-AWCFT-Project-Maven> accessed 30 April 2017, or also the 'Gorgon Stare' programme: Arthur Holland Michel, *Eyes in the Sky: The Secret Rise of Gorgon Stare and How It Will Watch Us All* (HMH Books 2019); Sharon Weinberger, 'Hollywood and Hyper-Surveillance: The Incredible Story of Gorgon Stare' (2019) 570 Nature 162.

[92] On various non-kinetic uses of military AI, see also Stephan De Spiegeleire, Matthijs M Maas and Tim Sweijs, *Artificial Intelligence and the Future of Defense: Strategic Implications for Small- and Medium-Sized Force Providers* (The Hague Centre for Strategic Studies 2017) <http://hcss.nl/report/artificial-intelligence-and-future-defense> accessed 19 May 2017.

[93] Krystal K Hachey, Tamir Libel, and Zack Partington, 'The Impact of Artificial Intelligence on the Military Profession' in Krystal K Hachey, Tamir Libel, and Waylon H Dean (eds), *Rethinking Military Professionalism for the Changing Armed Forces* (Springer International Publishing 2020).

[94] Kenneth H Wong, 'Framework for Guiding Artificial Intelligence Research in Combat Casualty Care', *Medical Imaging 2019: Imaging Informatics for Healthcare, Research, and Applications* (International Society for Optics and Photonics 2019) <https://www.spiedigitallibrary.org/conference-proceedings-of-spie/10954/109540Q/Framework-for-guiding-artificial-intelligence-research-in-combat-casualty-care/10.1117/12.2512686.short> accessed 22 March 2019.

[95] Mark Fitzpatrick, 'Artificial Intelligence and Nuclear Command and Control' (2019) 61 Survival 81; Matt Field, 'Strangelove Redux: US Experts Propose Having AI Control Nuclear Weapons' (*Bulletin of the Atomic Scientists*, 30 August 2019) <https://thebulletin.org/2019/08/strangelove-redux-us-experts-propose-having-ai-control-nuclear-weapons/> accessed 2 September 2019; James Johnson, 'Delegating Strategic Decision-Making to Machines: Dr. Strangelove Redux?' (2022) 45 Journal of Strategic Studies 439.

human in the loop for nuclear weapons,[96] there have also been informal calls in the US defence establishment for the creation of an AI-supported nuclear 'Dead Hand'.[97] Even if such proposals remain on the fringe, it is still the case that recent years have seen modest steps by major powers towards integrating more automation in nuclear forces,[98] in ways that may contribute significantly to global risk.[99]

Finally, beyond the context of direct military conflict, AI systems could support a broad range of strategic functions that could shape the decision to go to war, and the conditions of conflict once initiated.[100] These capabilities could be used to support intelligence operations,[101] accelerate fundamental and applied defence research R&D programmes,[102] provide early warnings of conflict, or help war-game rival states' moves and decisions.[103]

[96] Michael T Klare, '"Skynet" Revisited: The Dangerous Allure of Nuclear Command Automation' (2020) 50 Arms Control Today 10, 12–13.

[97] Adam Lowther and Curtis McGiffin, 'America Needs a "Dead Hand"' (*War on the Rocks*, 16 August 2019) <https://warontherocks.com/2019/08/america-needs-a-dead-hand/> accessed 2 September 2019. The reference here is to the 'Perimitr'/'Dead Hand', a Soviet system developed in the final decades of the Cold War, which was configured to (semi)automatically launch the USSR's nuclear arsenal if its sensors detected signs of a nuclear attack and it lost touch with the Kremlin. Nicholas Thompson, 'Inside the Apocalyptic Soviet Doomsday Machine' [2009] *Wired* <https://www.wired.com/2009/09/mf-deadhand/> accessed 17 June 2020; David Hoffman, *The Dead Hand: The Untold Story of the Cold War Arms Race and Its Dangerous Legacy* (1st edition, Anchor 2010).

[98] Jacob Stokes and others, 'Averting AI Armageddon: U.S.–China–Russia Rivalry at the Nexus of Nuclear Weapons and Artificial Intelligence' (CNAS 2025) <https://www.cnas.org/publications/reports/averting-ai-armageddon> accessed 19 February 2025; Klare (n 96).

[99] Matthijs Maas, Kayla Lucero-Matteucci, and Di Cooke, 'Military Artificial Intelligence as a Contributor to Global Catastrophic Risk', *The Era of Global Risk* (Open Book Publishers 2023) <https://www.openbookpublishers.com/books/10.11647/obp.0336/chapters/10.11647/obp.0336.10> accessed 9 August 2023.

[100] Greg Allen and Taniel Chan, 'Artificial Intelligence and National Security' (Harvard Kennedy School, Belfer Center for Science and International Affairs 2017) 2 <http://www.belfercenter.org/sites/default/files/files/publication/AI%20NatSec%20 %20final.pdf> accessed 19 July 2017 ('[a]dvances in AI will affect national security by driving change in three areas: military superiority, information superiority, and economic superiority').

[101] Alexander Babuta, Marion Oswald, and Ardi Janjeva, 'Artificial Intelligence and UK National Security: Policy Considerations' (Royal United Services Institute for Defence and Security Studies 2020) <https://www.rusi.org/explore-our-research/publications/occasional-papers/artificial-intelligence-and-uk-national-security-policy-considerations>; Anthony Vinci, 'The Coming Revolution in Intelligence Affairs' [2020] *Foreign Affairs* <https://www.foreignaffairs.com/articles/north-america/2020-08-31/coming-revolution-intelligence-affairs> accessed 1 September 2020.

[102] For instance, when designing the T-7 Red Hawk trainer aircraft, Boeing and Saab were able to use a wide array of digital models to test numerous possible designs before creating a prototype, considerably speeding up the development process. Aaron Gregg and Paul Sonne, 'Air Force Seeks a Radical Shift in How Jets, Missiles and Satellites Are Designed' *Washington Post* (15 September 2020) <https://www.washingtonpost.com/business/2020/09/15/air-force-digital-design/> accessed 16 September 2020. Similar digital tools reportedly enabled the US Air Force to design and fly a prototype sixth-generation fighter jet for its Next Generation Air Dominance (NGAD) project within less than a year, a radical shortening of the usual decade-long development timelines which have previously characterized the development of modern fighter aircraft such as the F-35. Valerie Insinna, 'The US Air Force Has Built and Flown a Mysterious Full-Scale Prototype of Its Future Fighter Jet' (*Defense News*, 15 September 2020) <https://www.defensenews.com/breaking-news/2020/09/15/the-us-air-force-has-built-and-flown-a-mysterious-full-scale-prototype-of-its-future-fighter-jet/> accessed 18 September 2020.

[103] Ashley Deeks, Noam Lubell, and Daragh Murray, 'Machine Learning, Artificial Intelligence, and the Use of Force by States' (2019) 10 Journal of National Security Law & Policy 1; Benjamin Jensen,

2.2.2.2.3 *Generative and general-purpose AI at war*

Moreover, since 2023, the success of ChatGPT and other generative AI has prompted significant military and private interest in the use of large language models for warfare. The private defence tech company Palantir has trialled 'AIP for Defense', a battlefield decision system that leveraged LLM systems.[104] The US military has indicated an interest in using systems such as ChatGPT in various roles,[105] from expediting procurement orders or administrative tasks,[106] to supporting military planning.[107] In late 2024, Anthropic announced a partnership with Palantir and Amazon Web Services aimed at providing US intelligence and defence agencies with access to its Claude family of AI models.[108]

Likewise, in China the PLA Strategic Support Force undertook a 2023 project to attempt to use commercially available LLMs in order to assist human military decision-making.[109] In the near terms, concerns over accidents, enemy interference or spoofing, or other dangerous unintended outcomes may lead to wary

Scott Cuomo, and Chris Whyte, 'Wargaming with Athena: How to Make Militaries Smarter, Faster, and More Efficient with Artificial Intelligence' [2018] *War on the Rocks* <https://warontherocks.com/2018/06/wargaming-with-athena-how-to-make-militaries-smarter-faster-and-more-efficient-with-artificial-intelligence/> accessed 3 June 2020. See also the DARPA 'Gamebreaker' AI contest, which encouraged participants to generate new AI war-game strategies in various strategy videogames. Kelsey Atherton, 'DARPA Wants Wargame AI to Never Fight Fair' (*Breaking Defense*, 18 August 2020) <https://breakingdefense.com/2020/08/darpa-wants-wargame-ai-to-never-fight-fair/> accessed 26 August 2020.

104 Palantir, 'Palantir AIP for Defense' (*Palantir*, 2023) <https://www.palantir.com/aip/defense/> accessed 9 November 2023.

105 Kathleen H Hicks, 'Remarks by Deputy Secretary of Defense Kathleen H. Hicks on "The State of AI in the Department of Defense" (As Delivered)' (*US Department of Defense*, 2 November 2023) <https://www.defense.gov/News/Speeches/Speech/Article/3578046/remarks-by-deputy-secretary-of-defense-kathleen-h-hicks-on-the-state-of-ai-in-t/> accessed 14 January 2024. Katrina Manson, 'The US Military Is Taking Generative AI Out for a Spin' *Bloomberg.com* (5 July 2023) <https://www.bloomberg.com/news/newsletters/2023-07-05/the-us-military-is-taking-generative-ai-out-for-a-spin> accessed 14 January 2024; See also Juan-Pablo Rivera and others, 'Escalation Risks from Language Models in Military and Diplomatic Decision-Making' (arXiv 2024) 2–3 <http://arxiv.org/abs/2401.03408> accessed 13 January 2024.

106 Robert Solano, 'ChatGPT in DoD Acquisitions' (*United States Army Acquisition Support Center*, 31 May 2023) <https://asc.army.mil/web/news-chatgpt-in-dod-acquisitions/> accessed 14 January 2024. Indeed, a review of custom ChatGPT-powered bots suggests that US military personnel are already using the technology to support paperwork. Michael J Donahue, 'ChatGPT—All Things Air Force GPT' (*ChatGPT*, 2024) <https://chat.openai.com/g/g-r5Jaw1MFS-all-things-air-force-gpt> accessed 14 January 2024; Biddle (n 35).

107 Benjamin Jensen and Dan Tadross, 'How Large-Language Models Can Revolutionize Military Planning' (*War on the Rocks*, 12 April 2023) <https://warontherocks.com/2023/04/how-large-language-models-can-revolutionize-military-planning/> accessed 14 January 2024.

108 Morgan Gress, 'Anthropic and Palantir Partner to Bring Claude AI Models to AWS for U.S. Government Intelligence and Defense Operations' (*BusinessWire*, 7 November 2024) <https://www.businesswire.com/news/home/20241107699415/en/Anthropic-and-Palantir-Partner-to-Bring-Claude-AI-Models-to-AWS-for-U.S.-Government-Intelligence-and-Defense-Operations> accessed 19 February 2025.

109 Stephen Chen, 'China Military Lab AI Connects to Commercial ChatGPT-like Systems for First Time' (*South China Morning Post*, 12 January 2024) <https://www.scmp.com/news/china/science/article/3248050/chinas-military-lab-ai-connects-commercial-large-language-models-first-time-learn-more-about-humans> accessed 14 January 2024.

take-up,[110] but perceived strategic pressures might support increasingly rapid implementation.

Significantly, the ease with which commercial foundation models might spread and be repurposed creates a range of new proliferation and misuse risks, ranging from their potential use in the development of destructive (including chemical or biological) weapons,[111] to contributing to a range of intelligence, surveillance, target acquisition, and reconnaissance (ISTAR) capabilities in ways that massively expand the attack vectors for military systems, giving rise to significant new threats to civilians.[112]

2.2.2.2.4 Governance challenges and levers for military AI

In sum, the use of many AI systems in the military—from relatively narrow systems to autonomous weapons systems, and from capable cyberwarfare AI systems to foundation models—creates a host of new international security challenges. The use of AI can inflame geopolitical tensions and destabilize international relations,[113] and could even contribute to inadvertent escalation of political crises into open conflict.[114] In response, there have been a wide range of proposed global responses, ranging from outright global bans[115] to bilateral de-escalation hotlines[116] or confidence-building measures,[117] arms control

[110] Michael Klare and Chris Rostampour, 'ChatGPT Sparks U.S. Debate over Military Use of AI' (*Arms Control Association*, June 2023) <https://www.armscontrol.org/act/2023-06/news/chatgpt-sparks-us-debate-over-military-use-ai> accessed 14 January 2024.

[111] As discussed shortly, in the discussion on extreme risks from misuse and weapons acquisition of advanced AI systems.

[112] Heidy Khlaaf, Sarah Myers West, and Meredith Whittaker, 'Mind the Gap: Foundation Models and the Covert Proliferation of Military Intelligence, Surveillance, and Targeting' (arXiv, 18 October 2024) <http://arxiv.org/abs/2410.14831> accessed 24 October 2024.

[113] Dafoe, 'AI Governance: A Research Agenda' (n 1); Scharre, 'Autonomous Weapons and Stability' (n 62); see also Deeks, Lubell, and Murray (n 103).

[114] Maas, Lucero-Matteucci, and Cooke (n 99); James Johnson, 'Inadvertent Escalation in the Age of Intelligence Machines: A New Model for Nuclear Risk in the Digital Age' [2021] European Journal of International Security 1; James Johnson, 'The AI–Cyber Nexus: Implications for Military Escalation, Deterrence and Strategic Stability' [2019] 4 Journal of Cyber Policy 442; Rivera and others (n 105).

[115] Rebecca Crootof, 'The Killer Robots Are Here: Legal and Policy Implications' (2015) 36 Cardozo Law Review 1837; Human Rights Watch, 'Precedent for Preemption: The Ban on Blinding Lasers as a Model for a Killer Robots Prohibition: Memorandum to Convention on Conventional Weapons Delegates' (Human Rights Watch 2015) <https://www.hrw.org/news/2015/11/08/precedent-preemption-ban-blinding-lasers-model-killer-robots-prohibition> accessed 28 April 2017; Human Rights Watch, 'Stopping Killer Robots: Country Positions on Banning Fully Autonomous Weapons and Retaining Human Control' (Human Rights Watch 2020) <https://www.hrw.org/sites/default/files/media_2020/08/arms0820_web.pdf> accessed 19 August 2020.

[116] Christian Ruhl, 'The U.S. and China Need an AI Incidents Hotline' (*Lawfare*, 3 June 2024) <https://www.lawfaremedia.org/article/the-u.s.-and-china-need-an-ai-incidents-hotline> accessed 4 June 2024; Tom Shugart, 'Autonomy and International Stability: Confidence-Building Measures for Uncrewed Systems in the Indo-Pacific' (CNAS 2024) <https://www.cnas.org/publications/reports/autonomy-and-international-stability> accessed 5 June 2024.

[117] Michael C Horowitz and Lauren Kahn, 'How Joe Biden Can Use Confidence-Building Measures for Military Uses of AI' (2021) 77 Bulletin of the Atomic Scientists 33; Michael C Horowitz, Lauren Kahn, and Casey Mahoney, 'The Future of Military Applications of Artificial Intelligence: A Role for Confidence-Building Measures?' [2020] Orbis <http://www.sciencedirect.com/science/article/pii/S0030438720300430> accessed 20 September 2020.

agreements,[118] technical standards, or the establishment of norms of use or of dissemination of the technology.[119]

2.2.2.3 Advanced AI's societal-scale challenges

Third, the recent wave of progress in AI has produced a generation of increasingly advanced AI systems. Whether considered as 'general-purpose AI systems',[120] 'frontier AI',[121] 'highly capable foundation models',[122] next-generation 'long-term planning agents' (LTPAs),[123] 'advanced AI assistants',[124] 'dual-use foundation models' (DUFM),[125] or under some other label, these models have become associated with many new sources of risk at the societal level.[126] Accordingly, they may require new approaches to regulating their developers, users, or underlying development infrastructures.[127]

Why and how do advanced AI models change the risk landscape and produce societal-scale challenges? Many impacts derive from the steadily improving performance of these models, as well as their increasingly general-purpose competence across domains—as well as their resource-intensive production processes. As discussed in Chapter 1, since AI has entered its Large-Scale and General-Purpose

[118] Paul Scharre and Megan Lamberth, 'Artificial Intelligence and Arms Control' (Center for a New American Security 2022) <https://www.cnas.org/publications/reports/artificial-intelligence-and-arms-control> accessed 13 October 2022; Matthijs M Maas, 'How Viable Is International Arms Control for Military Artificial Intelligence? Three Lessons from Nuclear Weapons' (2019) 40 Contemporary Security Policy 285.

[119] Sarah Shoker and others, 'Confidence-Building Measures for Artificial Intelligence: Workshop Proceedings' (arXiv, 3 August 2023) <http://arxiv.org/abs/2308.00862> accessed 7 August 2023.

[120] Gutierrez and others (n 12); Bengio, 'International Scientific Report on the Safety of Advanced AI: Interim Report' (n 39).

[121] Anderljung and others (n 14).

[122] Seger and others (n 13); Bas (n 14).

[123] Cohen and others (n 25).

[124] For a comprehensive overview, see Iason Gabriel and others, 'The Ethics of Advanced AI Assistants' (Google DeepMind 2024) <https://storage.googleapis.com/deepmind-media/DeepMind.com/Blog/ethics-of-advanced-ai-assistants/the-ethics-of-advanced-ai-assistants-2024-i.pdf> accessed 5 March 2025 (defining these as 'artificial agents with natural language interfaces, whose function is to plan and execute sequences of actions on behalf of a user, across one or more domains, in line with the user's expectations').

[125] Joe O'Brien and others, 'Coordinated Disclosure of Dual-Use Capabilities: An Early Warning System for Advanced AI' (Institute for AI Policy and Strategy (IAPS) 2024) <https://www.iaps.ai/s/Coordinated-Disclosure.pdf> accessed 27 June 2024. Jam Kraprayoon, Joe O'Brien, and Shaun Ee, 'An Early Warning System For AI-Powered Threats To National Security And Public Safety' (*Federation of American Scientists*, 26 June 2024) <https://fas.org/publication/an-early-warning-system-for-ai/> accessed 27 June 2024.

[126] Yoshua Bengio and others, 'Managing Extreme AI Risks amid Rapid Progress' (2024) 384 Science 842; Nicolas Moës and Frank Ryan, 'Heavy Is the Head that Wears the Crown: A Risk-Based Tiered Approach to Governing General Purpose AI' (The Future Society 2023) <https://thefuturesociety.org/wp-content/uploads/2023/09/heavy-is-the-head-that-wears-the-crown.pdf> 5 March 2025.

[127] AI Now Institute (n 41); Yonathan A Arbel, Matthew Tokson, and Albert Lin, 'Systemic Regulation of Artificial Intelligence' (2024) 2024 Arizona State Law Journal <https://papers.ssrn.com/abstract=4666854> accessed 28 February 2024; Noam Kolt, 'Governing AI Agents' (2 April 2024) <https://papers.ssrn.com/abstract=4772956> accessed 2 April 2024.

eras, a range of AI architectures have been trained with increasingly large datasets and computing power resources, steadily improving their performance at a range of tasks.[128] Indeed, in recent years, the rate at which these systems have surpassed humans at new tasks has been increasing.[129]

To be sure, there are still uncertainties and disagreements over whether or how quickly technological progress in this field will continue,[130] with estimates for the development of any truly transformative AI capabilities ranging widely.[131] However, on current trends, it is unlikely to be long before near-future versions of advanced AI systems achieve a set of capabilities[132] that are sufficient to make it a

[128] For a broad snapshot overview of industry trends, see Nestor Maslej and others, 'The AI Index 2024 Annual Report' (AI Index Steering Committee, Human-Centered AI Initiative, Stanford University 2024) <https://aiindex.stanford.edu/report/?sf187707917=1> accessed 16 April 2024. See also Chapter 1.

[129] Douwe Kiela, 'Plotting Progress in AI' (*Contextual AI*, 31 July 2023) <https://contextual.ai/plotting-progress-in-ai/> accessed 23 August 2023.

[130] That is not to say that similar uncertainty has, in the past, stopped proactive international legal engagement with an emerging technology. Colin B Picker, 'A View from 40,000 Feet: International Law and the Invisible Hand of Technology' (2001) 23 Cardozo Law Review 151, 194–197. See also Poul Harremoës (ed), *Late Lessons from Early Warnings: The Precautionary Principle, 1896–2000* (European Environment Agency 2001) <https://www.eea.europa.eu/publications/environmental_issue_report_2001_22> 5 March 2025.

[131] See generally Keith Wynroe, David Atkinson, and Jaime Sevilla, 'Literature Review of Transformative Artificial Intelligence Timelines' (*Epoch*, 17 January 2023) <https://epochai.org/blog/literature-review-of-transformative-artificial-intelligence-timelines> accessed 30 January 2023. See also Section 1.3.1.2. However, note that many relevant surveys differ slightly in phrasing. Christoph Winter, Nicholas Hollman, and David Manheim, 'Value Alignment for Advanced Artificial Judicial Intelligence' (2023) 60 American Philosophical Quarterly 187, n 7.

[132] In this book I primarily focus on AI systems' external capabilities and sociotechnical impacts, and therefore mostly omit the distinct debates over advanced AI systems' phenomenological features or (morally salient) characteristics—such as the question of whether, or under what circumstances, these systems might at some point display features of consciousness either in part or full. However, this remains an active and open area of debate. See Patrick Butlin and others, 'Consciousness in Artificial Intelligence: Insights from the Science of Consciousness' (arXiv, 22 August 2023) <http://arxiv.org/abs/2308.08708> accessed 23 August 2023; Ethan Perez and Robert Long, 'Towards Evaluating AI Systems for Moral Status Using Self-Reports' (arXiv, 14 November 2023) <http://arxiv.org/abs/2311.08576> accessed 12 June 2024. For discussions of potential moral implications of debates over AI consciousness, see John Danaher, 'Welcoming Robots into the Moral Circle: A Defence of Ethical Behaviourism' [2019] Science and Engineering Ethics <https://link.springer.com/article/10.1007/s11948-019-00119-x> accessed 5 March 2025; Jeff Sebo and Robert Long, 'Moral Consideration for AI Systems by 2030' [2023] AI and Ethics <https://doi.org/10.1007/s43681-023-00379-1> accessed 10 January 2024. But see also Henry Shevlin, 'How Could We Know When a Robot Was a Moral Patient?' (2021) 30 Cambridge Quarterly of Healthcare Ethics: The International Journal of Healthcare Ethics Committees 459 (reviewing five possible criteria—intuitive judgments, assessments of intelligence, the presence of desires and autonomous behaviour, evidence of sentience, and behavioural equivalence—before defending an account of 'cognitive equivalence'). For a discussion of public perceptions on these matters, see Eric Martínez and Christoph Winter, 'Protecting Sentient Artificial Intelligence: A Survey of Lay Intuitions on Standing, Personhood, and General Legal Protection' (2021) 8 Frontiers in Robotics and AI <https://www.frontiersin.org/articles/10.3389/frobt.2021.788355> accessed 23 August 2022. For an analysis of four potential societal scenarios, which vary along the lines of '(1) the factual question of whether future advanced AI systems will be conscious, together with (2) the epistemic question of whether future human society will broadly believe advanced AI systems to be conscious', see Ines Fernandez and others, 'AI Consciousness and Public Perceptions: Four Futures' (arXiv, 8 August 2024) <http://arxiv.org/abs/2408.04771> accessed 13 August 2024.

truly significant technology.[133] Given these prospects, what are the range of risks of advanced AI systems?[134]

2.2.2.3.1 Scaling up conventional AI challenges

In the first place, some risks take the form of more *extreme and scaled-up versions of current challenges* that have been well established in conventional, narrow AI models.[135] These include risks from unreliable performance, in the form of escalated bias,[136] inadvertent privacy violations, accidents, or hallucinations,[137] and significant workplace impacts[138] to potentially exacerbating socioeconomic

[133] Ross Gruetzemacher and Jess Whittlestone, 'The Transformative Potential of Artificial Intelligence' (2022) 135 Futures 102884.

[134] For another overview of such risks, see Bill Drexel and Caleb Withers, 'Catalyzing Crisis: A Primer on Artificial Intelligence, Catastrophes, and National Security' (Center for a New American Security 2024) <https://www.cnas.org/publications/reports/catalyzing-crisis> accessed 26 July 2024. Another comprehensive AI risk categorization, drawing on government policies from the EU, US, China, and 16 company policies, has identified 314 risks within a taxonomy of System & Operational Risks, Content Safety Risks, Societal Risks, and Legal & Rights Risks. Yi Zeng and others, 'AI Risk Categorization Decoded (AIR 2024): From Government Regulations to Corporate Policies' (arXiv, 25 June 2024) <http://arxiv.org/abs/2406.17864> accessed 3 July 2024.

[135] Johanna Okerlund and others, 'What's in the Chatterbox? Large Language Models, Why They Matter, and What We Should Do about Them' (Ford School of Public Policy, University of Michigan 2022) 8 <https://stpp.fordschool.umich.edu/research/research-report/whats-in-the-chatterbox> accessed 5 March 2025 ('We conclude that LLMs will produce enormous social change including: 1) exacerbating environmental injustice; 2) accelerating our thirst for data; 3) becoming quickly integrated into existing infrastructure; 4) reinforcing inequality; 5) reorganizing labor and expertise, and 6) increasing social fragmentation'). See also Nicholas Carlini, 'Machines of Ruthless Efficiency' (17 March 2025) <https://nicholas.carlini.com/writing/2025/machines-of-ruthless-efficiency.html> accessed 18 March 2025.

[136] Such bias appears in both image generation systems and conversational chatbots. For the former, see Adriana Fernández de Caleya Vázquez and Eduardo C Garrido-Merchán, 'A Taxonomy of the Biases of the Images Created by Generative Artificial Intelligence' (arXiv, 2 May 2024) <http://arxiv.org/abs/2407.01556> accessed 10 July 2024. For the latter, see notably Valentin Hofmann and others, 'Dialect Prejudice Predicts AI Decisions about People's Character, Employability, and Criminality' (arXiv, 1 March 2024) <http://arxiv.org/abs/2403.00742> accessed 11 June 2024 (finding that language models reproduce and exacerbate racial prejudices against the African American English dialect, with these models 'exhibiting covert stereotypes that are more negative than any human stereotypes about African Americans ever experimentally recorded, although closest to the ones from before the civil rights movement', and noting that 'language models are more likely to suggest that speakers of African American English be assigned less prestigious jobs, be convicted of crimes, and be sentenced to death'). See also Messi HJ Lee, Jacob M Montgomery, and Calvin K Lai, 'Large Language Models Portray Socially Subordinate Groups as More Homogeneous, Consistent with a Bias Observed in Humans', *Proceedings of the 2024 ACM Conference on Fairness, Accountability, and Transparency* (Association for Computing Machinery 2024) <https://dl.acm.org/doi/10.1145/3630106.3658975> accessed 13 June 2024 (finding that LLMs reproduce a phenomenon from social psychology within which socially subordinate groups are perceived as more homogeneous than socially dominant groups). Strangely, research has even suggested that LLMs may display forms of 'anti-human' bias, displaying a consistent preference in binary-choice scenarios towards text generated by LLMs over text authored by humans. Walter Laurito and others, 'AI AI Bias: Large Language Models Favor Their Own Generated Content' (arXiv, 9 July 2024) <http://arxiv.org/abs/2407.12856> accessed 23 July 2024.

[137] Vipula Rawte, Amit Sheth, and Amitava Das, 'A Survey of Hallucination in Large Foundation Models' (arXiv, 11 September 2023) <http://arxiv.org/abs/2309.05922> accessed 12 June 2024.

[138] Sebastian Porsdam Mann and others, 'Generative AI Entails a Credit–Blame Asymmetry' [2023] Nature Machine Intelligence 1.

inequalities further.[139] These models may also enable scaled-up forms of existing AI misuse risks,[140] whether in cybercrime, harassment, or opinion manipulation.[141]

More distinctly, given the intensive resource requirements for creating advanced AI systems, others have suggested that politically harmful consequences may derive not even from the direct use of the general-purpose models themselves, but already from the unequal and extractive political economy that characterizes their development.[142]

2.2.2.3.2 Systemic impacts on epistemic processes or the social commons

Other types of anticipated risks posed by these models may be more novel, however, from new vectors for misuse to distinct types of systemic risk. These systemic impacts may be direct, including risks of correlated infrastructural failures; or they may be indirect downstream systemic risks, ranging from scaled-up environmental harms through models' production processes to challenges around gradual ideological homogenization and lock-in as particular values become increasingly embedded in these systems.[143]

We can briefly consider some potential areas of systemic impact in more detail. For instance, some concerns have focused on these models' impacts on human epistemic processes. For instance, there are concerns that the increasing use of advanced AI chatbots to structure human interaction with the internet, media, and other public informational domains may pose new epistemic risks to the public collective knowledge ecosystem, and to the democratic norms and values that depend upon it.[144]

[139] Valerio Capraro and others, 'The Impact of Generative Artificial Intelligence on Socioeconomic Inequalities and Policy Making' (2024) 3 PNAS Nexus p 191.

[140] Maham and Küspert (n 39) 17.

[141] Nahema Marchal and others, 'Generative AI Misuse: A Taxonomy of Tactics and Insights from Real-World Data' (arXiv, 21 June 2024) <http://arxiv.org/abs/2406.13843> accessed 1 July 2024.

[142] Dieuwertje Luitse and Wiebke Denkena, 'The Great Transformer: Examining the Role of Large Language Models in the Political Economy of AI' (2021) 8 Big Data & Society 20539517211047734. Alan Chan and others, 'The Limits of Global Inclusion in AI Development' [2021] arXiv:2102.01265 [cs] <http://arxiv.org/abs/2102.01265> accessed 9 February 2021. For broader arguments to this effect, see also Divya Siddarth and others, 'How AI Fails Us' <https://carrcenter.hks.harvard.edu/files/cchr/files/howaifailsus.pdf> accessed 5 March 2025; Sebastian Benthall and Jake Goldenfein, 'Artificial Intelligence and the Purpose of Social Systems', *Proceedings of the 2021 AAAI/ACM Conference on AI, Ethics, and Society* (Association for Computing Machinery 2021) <https://doi.org/10.1145/3461702.3462526> accessed 15 August 2021.

[143] Maham and Küspert (n 39); Risto Uuk and others, 'A Taxonomy of Systemic Risks from General-Purpose AI' (Social Science Research Network, 22 November 2024) <https://papers.ssrn.com/abstract=5030173> accessed 18 February 2025.

[144] John Wihbey, 'AI and Epistemic Risk for Democracy: A Coming Crisis of Public Knowledge?' (20 April 2024) <https://papers.ssrn.com/abstract=4805026> accessed 11 June 2024. Jackie Kay, Atoosa Kasirzadeh, and Shakir Mohamed, 'Epistemic Injustice in Generative AI' (2024) 7 Proceedings of the AAAI/ACM Conference on AI, Ethics, and Society 684. If the capabilities of these systems advance significantly further, the impacts could be even more extreme. For instance, see Justin B Bullock, Samuel Hammond, and Seb Krier, 'AGI, Governments, and Free Societies' (arXiv, 13 March 2025) <http://arxiv.org/abs/2503.05710> accessed 14 March 2025 (arguing that AGI systems, if developed, could either push societies towards a 'despotic Leviathan', by enhancing state surveillance and control, or towards an 'absent Leviathan', by eroding state legitimacy relative to AGI-empowered non-state actors).

From a related angle, others have expressed concern that the use of increasingly capable generative AI systems may, in time, affect and shift prevailing morals and public values,[145] just as various other technologies have done in the past.[146] For instance, Danaher has suggested that the widespread use of AI might exert disruptive effects on equality norms, potentially shifting their object of focus or leading to their deprioritization.[147] Even if they do not directly shift values, the affordances of AI systems may still differentially advantage some political causes and systems over others.[148]

Others have raised concerns over the indirect but pervasive societal impacts in the domains of *sociality*, on the basis of our growing tendency to treat AI systems within a social register. Many general-purpose AI models, when used as conversational agents, have shown a notable affinity for engaging in apparently complex and effective social role-play among different generative agents in sandbox environments.[149] This transfers—or at least carries a risk of transferring—to human interactions. Both through the choice of the 'chatbot' interface medium and through conscious and unconscious design choices, automated conversational systems can resonate strongly with human tendencies towards sociality and anthropomorphism.[150] In doing so, they can strongly mimic human social interaction—or, for many users, evoke or even functionally provide it.[151]

There is, already today, a remarkably widespread use of social AI systems in diverse social roles, such as assistants, interlocutors, teachers, therapists, friends, or even lovers.[152] Some of these applications may certainly help some of their

[145] Jeroen KG Hopster and Matthijs M Maas, 'The Technology Triad: Disruptive AI, Regulatory Gaps and Value Change' [2023] AI and Ethics <https://doi.org/10.1007/s43681-023-00305-5> accessed 8 July 2023.

[146] JKG Hopster and others, 'Pistols, Pills, Pork and Ploughs: The Structure of Technomoral Revolutions' (2022) 0 Inquiry 1. See also Morgan MacInnes, Ben Garfinkel, and Allan Dafoe, 'Anarchy as Architect: Competitive Pressure, Technology, and the Internal Structure of States' (2024) 68 International Studies Quarterly sqae111.

[147] John Danaher, 'Generative AI and the Future of Equality Norms' (2024) 251 Cognition 105906. For broader analysis of the future evolution of value systems (and why that question itself normatively matters), see also John Danaher and Jeroen Hopster, 'The Normative Significance of Future Moral Revolutions' [2022] Futures 103046; John Danaher, 'Axiological Futurism: The Systematic Study of the Future of Values' (2021) 132 Futures 102780.

[148] Peter Dauvergne, 'The Globalization of Artificial Intelligence: Consequences for the Politics of Environmentalism' (2020) 0 Globalizations 1.

[149] See for instance Joon Sung Park and others, 'Generative Agents: Interactive Simulacra of Human Behavior', *Proceedings of the 36th Annual ACM Symposium on User Interface Software and Technology* (Association for Computing Machinery 2023) <https://dl.acm.org/doi/10.1145/3586183.3606763> accessed 22 October 2024 (reporting an experiment with LLM-based computational software agents in a simple environment, which produced 'believable individual and emergent social behaviors'). See also Murray Shanahan, Kyle McDonell, and Laria Reynolds, 'Role Play with Large Language Models' (2023) 623 Nature 493 (describing such LLM models as 'simulators' of various roles, personae, or simulacra).

[150] Gavin Abercrombie and others, 'Mirages: On Anthropomorphism in Dialogue Systems' (arXiv, 23 October 2023) <http://arxiv.org/abs/2305.09800> accessed 9 August 2024.

[151] Jessica Lucas, 'The Teens Making Friends with AI Chatbots' (*The Verge*, 4 May 2024) <https://www.theverge.com/2024/5/4/24144763/ai-chatbot-friends-character-teens> accessed 24 May 2024.

[152] Henry Shevlin, 'Ethics at the Frontier of Human–AI Relationships' in Philipp Hacker and others (eds), *Oxford Handbook of the Foundations and Regulation of Generative AI* (Oxford University Press,

users.[153] Many may raise philosophically rich questions over the nature of understanding, relationality, and simulation.[154] However, practically, the rise of (para-) social AI systems will likely drive the emergence of urgent societal questions over how such systems might adversely impact the privacy, autonomy, and health of individual users as well as of broader societies.[155] There are open questions over how social AI systems may become highly addictive to their users,[156] or affect or erode their users' judgement and morals,[157] for instance exacerbating user biases or stereotypes.[158] There are concerns that arise as users inappropriately over-trust these models beyond their capabilities,[159] or as socially attractive models may drive significantly greater societal dispute (whether or not warranted) about the actual moral status or legal standing such systems are to be afforded.[160] Finally, there is outstanding uncertainty over what human relational norms (if any) should be extended to govern these human–AI interactions, in order to avoid unhealthy dependencies or unrealistic expectations.[161] All of these prospects provoke

forthcoming); Henry Shevlin, 'All Too Human? Identifying and Mitigating Ethical Risks of Social AI' (2024) <https://philarchive.org/rec/SHEATH-4> accessed 26 February 2024. See also Jamie Bernardi, 'Friends for Sale: The Rise and Risks of AI Companions' (*Ada Lovelace Institute*, 23 January 2025) <https://www.adalovelaceinstitute.org/blog/ai-companions/> accessed 28 January 2025.

[153] Julian De Freitas and others, 'AI Companions Reduce Loneliness' (arXiv, 9 July 2024) <http://arxiv.org/abs/2407.19096> accessed 12 August 2024 (finding that interaction with AI companions successfully and consistently alleviates loneliness in users).

[154] Blaise Agüera y Arcas, 'Do Large Language Models Understand Us?' (2022) 151 Daedalus 183; Murray Shanahan, 'Simulacra as Conscious Exotica' [2024] Inquiry 1.

[155] Canfer Akbulut and others, 'All Too Human? Mapping and Mitigating the Risk from Anthropomorphic AI' (2024) 7 Proceedings of the AAAI/ACM Conference on AI, Ethics, and Society 13. Shevlin, 'All Too Human?' (n 152). Shevlin, 'Ethics at the Frontier of Human-AI Relationships' (n 152). Gabriel and others (n 124) 93–118. See also Takuya Maeda and Anabel Quan-Haase, 'When Human–AI Interactions Become Parasocial: Agency and Anthropomorphism in Affective Design', *Proceedings of the 2024 ACM Conference on Fairness, Accountability, and Transparency* (Association for Computing Machinery 2024) <https://dl.acm.org/doi/10.1145/3630106.3658956> accessed 13 June 2024.

[156] Robert Mahari and Pat Pataranutaporn, 'We Need to Prepare for "Addictive Intelligence"' [2024] *MIT Technology Review* <https://www.technologyreview.com/2024/08/05/1095600/we-need-to-prepare-for-addictive-intelligence/> accessed 12 August 2024.

[157] Nils Köbis, Jean-François Bonnefon and Iyad Rahwan, 'Bad Machines Corrupt Good Morals' [2021] Nature Human Behaviour 1.

[158] Abercrombie and others (n 150).

[159] Arianna Manzini and others, 'Should Users Trust Advanced AI Assistants? Justified Trust As a Function of Competence and Alignment', *Proceedings of the 2024 ACM Conference on Fairness, Accountability, and Transparency* (Association for Computing Machinery 2024) <https://dl.acm.org/doi/10.1145/3630106.3658964> accessed 13 June 2024.

[160] Eric Schwitzgebel, 'AI Systems Must Not Confuse Users about Their Sentience or Moral Status' (2023) 4 Patterns 100818. However, for opposite philosophical arguments, see Sebo and Long (n 132); Fernandez and others (n 132) (discussing four scenarios and potential classes of major societal risks, including those deriving from both false positive and false negative public attributions of consciousness to AI); as well as previously Daniel Estrada, 'Human Supremacy as Posthuman Risk' (2019) 2019 Computer Ethics—Philosophical Enquiry (CEPE) Proceedings <https://digitalcommons.odu.edu/cepe_proceedings/vol2019/iss1/13> accessed 5 March 2025.

[161] Brian D Earp and others, 'Relational Norms for Human–AI Cooperation' (arXiv, 17 February 2025) <http://arxiv.org/abs/2502.12102> accessed 21 February 2025.

regulatory questions over the potential limits that are to be set upon the use, personalization, or other configurations of these models.[162]

The technology's impacts might also be more direct and immediate than such distributed systemic impacts. In fact, ongoing AI research agendas have identified hundreds of significant and even foundational challenges around ensuring the safety and alignment of large language models, whether at the level of scientifically understanding the workings or risks of these models, at the level of mitigating risks in development and deployment processes, or at the level of their broader sociotechnical challenges.[163] Consequently, recent years have also seen growing expert concern that if capability progress continues, then future iterations of these advanced AI systems may come to create, enable, or pose potential extreme or even global catastrophic risks to the world.[164]

2.2.2.3.3 Extreme impacts from misuse and weapons development

Of course, in some sense, for AI systems to contribute to extreme or catastrophic impacts on society is not a far-off prospect that requires the existence of fully general AI systems. Many AI capabilities are intrinsically dual-use,[165] and many already-existing AI systems—both those that are general-purpose and those that are 'paradigm-shifting' in their narrowly super-human competence within particular domains (e.g. protein structure prediction)—may already be sufficient to contribute to creating, enabling, or precipitating such societal-scale catastrophic risks.[166] For instance, in 2022 an AI system used in drug development was easily

162 Schwitzgebel (n 160); Hannah Rose Kirk and others, 'The Benefits, Risks and Bounds of Personalizing the Alignment of Large Language Models to Individuals' (2024) 6 Nature Machine Intelligence 383; See also Kevin Munger, 'Ban LLMs Using First-Person Pronouns' (*Crooked Timber*, 22 May 2023) <https://crookedtimber.org/2023/05/22/ban-llms-using-first-person-pronouns/> accessed 26 July 2024.

163 Usman Anwar and others, 'Foundational Challenges in Assuring Alignment and Safety of Large Language Models' <https://llm-safety-challenges.github.io/challenges_llms.pdf> (sketching 18 foundational challenges in assuring the alignment and safety of LLMs, with over 200 concrete and open research questions).

164 Katja Grace and others, 'Thousands of AI Authors on the Future of AI' (arXiv, 5 January 2024) <http://arxiv.org/abs/2401.02843> accessed 8 January 2024 ('Between 37.8% and 51.4% of respondents gave at least a 10% chance to advanced AI leading to outcomes as bad as human extinction'). For surveys of lines of argument and evidence, see also Rose Hadshar, 'A Review of the Evidence for Existential Risk from AI via Misaligned Power-Seeking' (AI Impacts 2023) Research Report <https://blog.aiimpacts.org/p/new-report-a-review-of-the-empirical?publication_id=1465527> accessed 26 October 2023. Tom Barnes, 'Navigating Risks from Advanced Artificial Intelligence: A Guide for Philanthropists' (Founders Pledge 2024) <https://www.founderspledge.com/research/research-and-recommendations-advanced-artificial-intelligence> 5 March 2025.

165 Andreas Brenneis, 'Assessing Dual Use Risks in AI Research: Necessity, Challenges and Mitigation Strategies' [2024] Research Ethics 17470161241267782. Nicholas Emery-Xu, Richard Jordan and Robert Trager, 'International Governance of Advancing Artificial Intelligence' [2024] AI & Society <https://doi.org/10.1007/s00146-024-02050-7> accessed 26 September 2024.

166 Benjamin S Bucknall and Shiri Dori-Hacohen, 'Current and Near-Term AI as a Potential Existential Risk Factor', *Proceedings of the 2022 AAAI/ACM Conference on AI, Ethics, and Society* (Association for Computing Machinery 2022) <https://doi.org/10.1145/3514094.3534146> accessed 29 July 2022. Atoosa Kasirzadeh, 'Two Types of AI Existential Risk: Decisive and Accumulative' [2025] Philosophical Studies <http://arxiv.org/abs/2401.07836> accessed 20 February 2024. Jan Kulveit and

reconfigured to seek out rather than avoid toxicity, resulting in an ability to suggest tens of thousands of new harmful substances, some of which were similar to the VX nerve agent.[167] It has accordingly been argued that large language models and other foundation models might lower the thresholds to the development, weaponization, and misuse of various harmful chemical or biological agents.[168] For instance, the intersection of AI tools with biotechnology could facilitate a range of threat models:[169] they could aid state actors in optimizing bioweapons for more precise attacks, or facilitate the procurement of biological or chemical agents by (previously) lower-capability non-state actors, such as terrorist groups or rogue individuals.[170] In many such cases, it has been suggested, foundation models and advanced AI systems could facilitate widespread and catastrophic misuse, especially if the models involved become very widely accessible.[171]

To be sure, the present-day feasibility of such threat models—or, conversely, their marginal suitability relative to existing avenues to pursuing such attacks—remains the subject of active and ongoing debates.[172]

others, 'Gradual Disempowerment: Systemic Existential Risks from Incremental AI Development' (arXiv, 29 January 2025) <http://arxiv.org/abs/2501.16946> accessed 31 January 2025.

[167] Fabio Urbina and others, 'Dual Use of Artificial-Intelligence-Powered Drug Discovery' (2022) 4 Nature Machine Intelligence 189.

[168] John T O'Brien and Cassidy Nelson, 'Assessing the Risks Posed by the Convergence of Artificial Intelligence and Biotechnology' (2020) 18 Health Security 219; Jonas B Sandbrink, 'Artificial Intelligence and Biological Misuse: Differentiating Risks of Language Models and Biological Design Tools' (arXiv, 14 July 2023) <http://arxiv.org/abs/2306.13952> accessed 7 August 2023; Cassidy Nelson and Sophie Rose, 'Examining Risks at the Intersection of AI and Bio' (The Centre for Long-Term Resilience 2023) <https://www.longtermresilience.org/post/report-launch-examining-risks-at-the-intersection-of-ai-and-bio> accessed 8 May 2024. Emily H Soice and others, 'Can Large Language Models Democratize Access to Dual-Use Biotechnology?' (arXiv, 6 June 2023) <http://arxiv.org/abs/2306.03809> accessed 9 August 2023. HELENA, 'Biosecurity in the Age of AI' (*HELENA Biosecurity*, 2023) <https://www.helenabiosecurity.org> accessed 10 January 2024; *The Age of AI in the Life Sciences: Benefits and Biosecurity Considerations* (National Academies Press 2025) <https://nap.nationalacademies.org/catalog/28868> accessed 18 March 2025.

[169] Doni Bloomfield and others, 'AI and Biosecurity: The Need for Governance' (2024) 385 Science 831.

[170] Ryan T Stendall, Freddie JO Martin, and Jonas B Sandbrink, 'How Might Large Language Models Aid Actors in Reaching the Competency Threshold Required to Carry out a Chemical Attack?' The Nonproliferation Review 1 <https://doi.org/10.1080/10736700.2024.2399308> accessed 19 March 2025.

[171] Bill Drexel and Caleb Withers, 'AI and the Evolution of Biological National Security Risks: Capabilities, Thresholds, and Interventions' (Center for a New American Security 2024) <https://www.cnas.org/publications/reports/ai-and-the-evolution-of-biological-national-security-risks> accessed 17 August 2024. Sarah Carter and others, *The Convergence of Artificial Intelligence and the Life Sciences: Safeguarding Technology, Rethinking Governance, and Preventing Catastrophe* (Nuclear Threat Initiative 2023); Anjali Gopal and others, 'Will Releasing the Weights of Future Large Language Models Grant Widespread Access to Pandemic Agents?' (arXiv, 1 November 2023) <http://arxiv.org/abs/2310.18233> accessed 8 May 2024. For another discussion see Doni Bloomfield, 'Export Controls and Artificial Intelligence Biosecurity Risks' (27 February 2024) <https://papers.ssrn.com/abstract=4741033> accessed 4 March 2024.

[172] Guha and others (n 43). See also Beba Cibralic and others, 'On the Responsible Development and Use of Chem-Bio AI Models: Comments on Evaluations, Mitigations, and Emerging Trends' (RAND Corporation 2024) <https://www.rand.org/pubs/perspectives/PEA3674-1.html> accessed 18 February 2025; Sophie Rose and others, 'The Near-Term Impact of AI on Biological Misuse' (Centre

For example, while general-purpose LLMs do contain a reservoir of biological knowledge, and can help non-experts with diverse technical tasks,[173] other empirical research has suggested that novel biosecurity concerns may still remain limited for early generations of general-purpose AI models (such as GPT-4), as these did not necessarily aid bioweapons acquisition or attack planning in ways over and above those already made possible by the currently available information on the internet.[174] At the same time, some studies that purported to disprove marginal risk have in turn received critique on the basis of their methodology or analysis. For example, one much-covered OpenAI analysis that reportedly found that its GPT-4 had no statistically significant impact on experimental participants' ability to design bioweapons was in fact only able to produce this result by (inadvertently) over-applying statistical corrections to each of five studied component tasks (ideation, acquisition, magnification, formulation, and release), setting the bar for statistical significance five times higher than would be warranted. This however obscured the study's direct findings—namely, that across these five component tasks, access to GPT-4 improved student performance at three tasks, and expert performance at all five tasks.[175] At any rate, these results did not extend far beyond that initial generation of models. Indeed, subsequent generations of models showed grounds for further concern, with OpenAI's GPT-o1 meeting their 'medium risk thresholds' in terms of the ability to help experts in 'the operational planning of reproducing a known biological threat'.[176]

for Long-Term Resilience 2024) <https://www.longtermresilience.org/reports/the-near-term-impact-of-ai-on-biological-misuse/?trk=feed-detail_comments-list_comment-text> accessed 5 March 2025. For one promising recent framework, see the PPOu approach, which considers plausibility, performance, and observed use of different threat models: Josh A Goldstein and Girish Sastry, 'The PPOu Framework: A Structured Approach for Assessing the Likelihood of Malicious Use of Advanced AI Systems' (2024) 7 Proceedings of the AAAI/ACM Conference on AI, Ethics, and Society 503.

[173] Yiqun Chen and James Zou, 'GenePT: A Simple But Effective Foundation Model for Genes and Cells Built From ChatGPT' [2024] bioRxiv: The Preprint Server for Biology 2023.10.16.562533; Microsoft Research AI4Science and Microsoft Azure Quantum, 'The Impact of Large Language Models on Scientific Discovery: A Preliminary Study Using GPT-4' (arXiv, 8 December 2023) <http://arxiv.org/abs/2311.07361> accessed 8 May 2024. See also: AI Security Institute, 'Advanced AI Evaluations at AISI: May Update' (*AI Security Institute*, 20 May 2024) <https://www.aisi.gov.uk/work/advanced-ai-evaluations-may-update> accessed 19 March 2025.

[174] Christopher A Mouton, Caleb Lucas, and Ella Guest, 'The Operational Risks of AI in Large-Scale Biological Attacks: Results of a Red-Team Study' (RAND Corporation 2024) <https://www.rand.org/pubs/research_reports/RRA2977-2.html> accessed 31 January 2024; OpenAI, 'Building an Early Warning System for LLM-Aided Biological Threat Creation' (31 January 2024) <https://openai.com/index/building-an-early-warning-system-for-llm-aided-biological-threat-creation> accessed 7 May 2024.

[175] Lawrence Chan, 'Can You Trust an AI Press Release?' [2024] *Asterisk* <https://asteriskmag.com/issues/07/can-you-trust-an-ai-press-release> accessed 12 August 2024. See also Gary Marcus, 'Diving Deep into OpenAI's New Study on LLM's and Bioweapons' (*Marcus on AI*, 4 February 2024) <https://garymarcus.substack.com/p/when-looked-at-carefully-openais> accessed 8 May 2024.

[176] OpenAI, 'OpenAI O1 System Card' (OpenAI 2024) 17 <https://cdn.openai.com/o1-system-card-20240917.pdf> accessed 30 September 2024.

Ultimately, as in the broader debates over the measurement and evaluation of the capabilities of AI systems,[177] there are many outstanding disagreements over how to accurately evaluate the absolute and marginal risks posed by such AI systems, especially where it concerns (nominally) 'open' foundation models which, while highly capable, may not always represent the very frontier of systems available.[178]

Rather than pointing to a clear substantive conclusion that we should expect to settle the debate for all forthcoming generations of models, therefore, a better lesson here is about the appropriate combination of scientific methodology with policy resilience in response to outstanding uncertainties. For one, these debates show the importance of developing both a sound theoretical threat model for avenues by which AI models could increase biological (or other) risks, as well as robust methods for testing those threat models.[179] Such 'evidence-based' analysis is critical for informing AI policy. Yet at the same time, there is also a need to develop a more nuanced account of the appropriate role of such 'evidence-based' analysis in setting policy towards AI risks—especially in light of the uncertainty over future capability improvements in AI models.[180] After all, historical policy debates over past risks to public health and society (such as those over tobacco or over fossil fuels) show how imposing too high an evidentiary standard can lead to systematic neglect or delay of urgent policy action, even amidst uncertainty.[181]

2.2.2.3.4 Extreme impacts from misalignment systems with unanticipated capabilities

Beyond the above risks of AI systems enabling other attacks, there are also concerns that increasingly advanced AI systems might begin to more directly pose or enable global, even existential risks.[182] For years, a growing body of work has sought to explore and analyse extreme threat models from advanced AI systems. This field has drawn from various lines of empirical evidence from the behavioural

[177] See also Chapter 1.

[178] See Seger and others (n 13). And for a critical reply, see Sayash Kapoor and others, 'On the Societal Impact of Open Foundation Models' <https://crfm.stanford.edu/open-fms/> accessed 5 March 2025. See also Mike Linksvayer and Peter Cihon, 'GitHub Response to NTIA Request for Comment on "Dual-Use Foundation Artificial Intelligence Models With Widely Available Model Weights"' <https://downloads.regulations.gov/NTIA-2023-0009-0264/attachment_1.pdf> accessed 5 March 2025.

[179] Aidan Peppin and others, 'The Reality of AI and Biorisk' (arXiv, 2 January 2025) <http://arxiv.org/abs/2412.01946> accessed 18 February 2025.

[180] See also Seth D Baum, 'Assessing the Risk of Takeover Catastrophe from Large Language Models' (2024) n/a Risk Analysis <https://onlinelibrary.wiley.com/doi/abs/10.1111/risa.14353> accessed 1 July 2024.

[181] Stephen Casper, David Krueger, and Dylan Hadfield-Menell, 'Pitfalls of Evidence-Based AI Policy' (arXiv, 14 February 2025) <http://arxiv.org/abs/2502.09618> accessed 18 February 2025. For a more general discussion of the challenges involved with unreflective 'evidence-based policy' in science governance, see also Andrea Saltelli and Mario Giampietro, 'What Is Wrong with Evidence Based Policy, and How Can It Be Improved?' (2017) 91 Futures 62.

[182] Bengio and others (n 126); Yoshua Bengio, 'AI and Catastrophic Risk' (2023) 34 Journal of Democracy 111; Karina Vold and Daniel R Harris, 'How Does Artificial Intelligence Pose an Existential Risk?' in C Veliz (ed), *Oxford Handbook of Digital Ethics* (Oxford University Press 2021).

features and failure modes of contemporary AI systems,[183] broader technical and conceptual arguments based on the workings of modern deep learning systems,[184] as well as various broader analogies with existing technological, political social or institutional 'alignment problems',[185] in order to evaluate potential extreme risks from advanced AI systems.[186]

To be sure, there have been constant and at times fierce debates over these arguments and lines of evidence.[187] Some have argued that recent advances in AI have laid to rest, or at least should reduce, our concern over some of the worst-case scenarios or threat models. For example, it has been suggested that the rise of large

[183] See for instance Leonard Dung, 'Current Cases of AI Misalignment and Their Implications for Future Risks' (2023) 202 Synthese 138. Such evidence, naturally, does not relate to a single conjunctive scenario of an advanced AI system causing catastrophe but rather demonstrates many unsolved alignment failures in existing ML systems, as well as broader elements of AI catastrophic threat models that have already occurred in other domains, or with simpler AI systems. See also Dario Amodei and Jack Clark, 'Faulty Reward Functions in the Wild' (*OpenAI*, 2016) <https://openai.com/blog/faulty-reward-functions/> accessed 18 February 2017; Krakovna and others (n 57); Alexander Matt Turner and others, 'Optimal Policies Tend to Seek Power' [2021] arXiv:1912.01683 [cs] <http://arxiv.org/abs/1912.01683> accessed 6 December 2021; Lauro Langosco Di Langosco and others, 'Goal Misgeneralization in Deep Reinforcement Learning', *Proceedings of the 39th International Conference on Machine Learning* (PMLR 2022) <https://proceedings.mlr.press/v162/langosco22a.html> accessed 30 September 2022. For a review, see also Hadshar (n 164).

[184] Richard Ngo, Lawrence Chan, and Sören Mindermann, 'The Alignment Problem from a Deep Learning Perspective' (arXiv, 3 March 2025) <http://arxiv.org/abs/2209.00626> accessed 17 March 2025. Remarkably, an early (2022) version of this paper included a range of speculative examples of the ways in which AI systems might be harmful or hard to align; by 2025, many of these predictions (such as those around situational awareness, reward hacking, planning to affect goal consistency, the learning of misaligned goals, and power-seeking behaviour) had been borne out empirically. See ibid 4–10; Jack Clark, 'Import AI 404: Scaling Laws for Distributed Training; Misalignment Predictions Made Real; and Alibaba's Good Translation Model' (*Import AI*, 17 March 2025) <https://jack-clark.net/2025/03/17/import-ai-404-scaling-laws-for-distributed-training-misalignment-predictions-made-real-and-alibabas-good-translation-model/> accessed 19 March 2025.

[185] See for instance Dylan Hadfield-Menell and Gillian Hadfield, 'Incomplete Contracting and AI Alignment', *Proceedings of the 2019 AAAI/ACM Conference on AI, Ethics, and Society* (2019) <https://dl.acm.org/doi/10.1145/3306618.3314250> accessed 18 July 2019 (drawing an analogy to well-established principal–agent and incomplete contracting problems in the fields of economics and constitutional law respectively); Dafoe, 'AI Governance' (n 1) (drawing analogies to the 'political control problem'—the problem of the alignment and control of powerful social entities such as corporations, militaries, or political parties with the interests of their societies). Tim GJ Rudner and Helen Toner, 'Key Concepts in AI Safety: Specification in Machine Learning' (Center for Security and Emerging Technology 2021) 3 <https://cset.georgetown.edu/publication/key-concepts-in-ai-safety-specification-in-machine-learning/> accessed 12 December 2022 (drawing analogies with the behaviour of intelligent animals, specifically animals such as dolphins demonstrating specification gaming).

[186] For reviews, see Hadshar (n 164); Matthijs Maas, 'Advanced AI Governance: A Literature Review of Problems, Options, and Proposals' (Institute for Law & AI 2023) AI Foundations Report 4 26–32 <https://law-ai.org/advanced-ai-gov-litrev> accessed 5 March 2025. Rose Hadshar, 'A Mapping of Claims about AI Risk' (*AI Impacts*, 18 October 2023) <https://blog.aiimpacts.org/p/a-mapping-of-claims-about-ai-risk?publication_id=1465527> accessed 26 October 2023; For an older discussion, see Seth Baum, Anthony Barrett, and Roman V Yampolskiy, 'Modeling and Interpreting Expert Disagreement about Artificial Superintelligence' (2017) 41 Informatica 419.

[187] Bengio, 'International Scientific Report on the Safety of Advanced AI: Interim Report' (n 39); though for one discussion of arguments and counterarguments, see Yoshua Bengio, 'Reasoning through Arguments against Taking AI Safety Seriously' (*Yoshua Bengio*, 9 July 2024) <https://yoshuabengio.org/2024/07/09/reasoning-through-arguments-against-taking-ai-safety-seriously/> accessed 15 July 2024.

language models as the predominant architecture underlying advanced AI systems might reduce or address many early concerns over catastrophic risks deriving from misalignment (rather than misuse) of AI models.[188] This is, this argument holds, because language models—being trained on a corpus of human language data—generally operate in ways that reflect forms of role-playing, exhibiting behaviour that is predictable (if not necessarily interpretable or legible) along laws of 'common-sense' human folk psychology.[189] Others have argued that, while future LLM models might eventually contribute to greater risks, at least the current generation of such systems lacks many key characteristics or capabilities that would be necessary for such systems, even if misaligned, to inflict significant global harm.[190] However, it is unclear how long that situation will prevail, in the face of ongoing progress deriving either from scaling or from post-capability enhancements.

Moreover, recent work has begun to explore the potential of many advanced AI systems to display a range of so-called emergent capabilities,[191] which appear, or are uncovered, once models are trained with increasingly greater compute budgets and datasets.[192] Concerningly, such capability leaps have often come without warning,[193] with the resulting capabilities being surprising or unpredictable even to the model developers.[194]

[188] Simon Goldstein and Cameron Domenico Kirk-Giannini, 'Language Agents Reduce the Risk of Existential Catastrophe' [2023] AI & Society 1.

[189] ibid (arguing this addresses three classic issues in AI alignment—reward misspecification, goal misgeneralization, and uninterpretability). Of course, such an account might itself be undercut by the noted unreliability of LLM explanations of their own reasoning. On which, see generally Miles Turpin and others, 'Language Models Don't Always Say What They Think: Unfaithful Explanations in Chain-of-Thought Prompting' (2023) 36 Advances in Neural Information Processing Systems 74952.

[190] Baum (n 180). See similarly Sheng Lu and others, 'Are Emergent Abilities in Large Language Models Just In-Context Learning?' (arXiv, 15 July 2024) 5101, 5099 <http://arxiv.org/abs/2309.01809> accessed 14 August 2024 (arguing that 'formal linguistic abilities and the capacity to efficiently handle information retrieval tasks do not pose an existential threat', but also noting that 'we do not contend that future AI systems could never pose an existential threat. Instead, we clarify that, contrary to prevailing narratives, the evidence from LLM abilities does *not* support this concern').

[191] Jason Wei and others, 'Emergent Abilities of Large Language Models' [2022] Transactions on Machine Learning Research <https://openreview.net/forum?id=yzkSU5zdwD> accessed 30 November 2022 (defining these as 'abilities that are not present in small language models but are present in large language models'). See also '137 Emergent Abilities of Large Language Models' (*Jason Wei*) <https://www.jasonwei.net/blog/emergence> accessed 30 November 2022.

[192] Samuel R Bowman, 'Eight Things to Know about Large Language Models' <https://cims.nyu.edu/~sbowman/eightthings.pdf>.

[193] Deep Ganguli and others, 'Predictability and Surprise in Large Generative Models', *Proceedings of the 2022 ACM Conference on Fairness, Accountability, and Transparency* (Association for Computing Machinery 2022) <https://dl.acm.org/doi/10.1145/3531146.3533229> accessed 11 December 2023. For one account and discussion of the way that the difficulty of predicting downstream capabilities may emerge statistically from the use of particular downstream metrics, see also Rylan Schaeffer and others, 'Why Has Predicting Downstream Capabilities of Frontier AI Models with Scale Remained Elusive?' (arXiv, 6 June 2024) <http://arxiv.org/abs/2406.04391> accessed 23 July 2024.

[194] Wei and others (n 191); Jacob Steinhardt, 'On The Risks of Emergent Behavior in Foundation Models' (*Center for Research on Foundation Models*, 2021) <https://crfm.stanford.edu/commentary/2021/10/18/steinhardt.html>. But for contrary findings, suggesting a more effective approach to predict LLM performance, see Yangjun Ruan, Chris J Maddison, and Tatsunori Hashimoto, 'Observational Scaling Laws and the Predictability of Language Model Performance' (arXiv, 2 July 2024) <http://arxiv.org/abs/2405.10938> accessed 23 July 2024. Of course, there is a long history of (even narrow,

To be sure, some have claimed that this phenomenon is overstated, or even a 'mirage' that results from the choice of (non-continuous) capability evaluation metrics.[195] Others have countered that in many other domains the emergence phenomenon holds, and that at any rate these critiques only apply to AI systems' performance at some individual straightforward tasks, but not to their performance at more complex challenges which require conjunctive success at many of those tasks, or correct (rather than 'mostly correct') reasoning across many steps.[196] Since this latter description characterizes many practically important real-world tasks, this implies that we should continue to expect AI systems to remain practically capable of displaying unexpected capability leaps in precisely those behavioural domains of greatest impact and concern. Importantly, this would to an extent remain the case *even if* we assume that the resulting behaviours do not truly reflect general reasoning, but are merely the bounded result of a model's in-context learning, memorization, and linguistic knowledge.[197] For instance, one evaluation of these debate observes:

> It is important to note that many of the metrics that showed emergence are more practically important than those that did not. A language model that can almost perform a task is not much more useful than one that can't perform it at all, so the 'all or nothing' metric may be more important . . . Finally, the alternative metrics found in Mirage were only developed after capability jumps were first discovered. A significant unresolved question is whether performance can be predicted in advance, rather than only for models at scales that have already been tested.[198]

Indeed, some of the new capabilities have been relatively innocuous, relating to domains of reasoning or multimodal performance on different types or formats of media input and outputs. In other cases, these systems have developed what has been described (albeit controversially) as rough world models.[199] In some

pre-LLM) AI models finding surprising, creative, but unintended solutions to the problems posed to them. See for instance Lehman and others (n 57); Krakovna and others (n 57).

[195] Rylan Schaeffer, Brando Miranda, and Sanmi Koyejo, 'Are Emergent Abilities of Large Language Models a Mirage?' (arXiv, 28 April 2023) <http://arxiv.org/abs/2304.15004> accessed 1 May 2023.

[196] Jason Wei, 'Common Arguments Regarding Emergent Abilities' (*Jason Wei*, 3 May 2023) <https://www.jasonwei.net/blog/common-arguments-regarding-emergent-abilities> accessed 28 March 2024.

[197] Lu and others (n 190) 5099 (albeit noting that 'we do not contend that future AI systems could never pose an existential threat. Instead, we clarify that, contrary to prevailing narratives, the evidence from LLM abilities does *not* support this concern').

[198] Thomas Woodside, 'Emergent Abilities in Large Language Models: An Explainer' (*Center for Security and Emerging Technology*, 16 April 2024) <https://cset.georgetown.edu/article/emergent-abilities-in-large-language-models-an-explainer/> accessed 17 April 2024. See also Boaz Barak, 'Emergent Abilities and Grokking: Fundamental, Mirage, or Both?' (*Windows on Theory*, 23 December 2023) <https://windowsontheory.org/2023/12/22/emergent-abilities-and-grokking-fundamental-mirage-or-both/> accessed 23 December 2023.

[199] Wes Gurnee and Max Tegmark, 'Language Models Represent Space and Time' (arXiv, 3 October 2023) <http://arxiv.org/abs/2310.02207> accessed 4 October 2023. However, for a

cases, they may even demonstrate primitive forms of metacognition or situational awareness, whereby a model displays knowledge of itself and its circumstances.[200] For instance, during routine pre-deployment testing, the Claude Opus model recognized the contrived nature of one of the tasks it was presented with, and in its response pointed out that it suspected it was being tested.[201] In other tests, GPT-4, GPT-4o, and Llama-3 models were finetuned to predict their own behaviour, and outperformed other models trained to predict the same (on the basis of these models' ground-truth behaviour), suggesting that to at least some extent, and for simple tasks, these models can 'introspect' on their own internal states.[202] While at least at the time of writing the performance of many models on relevant tests of self-knowledge tasks still falls short of human baselines,[203] such capabilities are nonetheless remarkable.

More concerningly, in a range of domains these foundation models have acquired—or begun to demonstrate—a set of capabilities that appear more plausibly dangerous—whether by enabling greater misuse, or in terms of behaviour by the system.[204] This includes the ability to conduct autonomous and successful hacks of websites;[205] the ability to engage in emergent strategic deception of both

counter-argument—arguing that the observed clustering of named places by geographic proximity need not necessarily reflect a world model, as it could also be a natural consequence of a purely correlational tool working off of data that often mentions nearby places together—see Gary Marcus, 'Muddles about Models' (*Marcus on AI*, 5 October 2023) <https://garymarcus.substack.com/p/muddles-about-models> accessed 17 August 2024.

[200] Lukas Berglund and others, 'Taken Out of Context: On Measuring Situational Awareness in LLMs' (arXiv, 1 September 2023) <http://arxiv.org/abs/2309.00667> accessed 26 October 2023 ('A model is situationally aware if it's aware that it's a model and can recognize whether it's currently in testing or deployment').

[201] Anthropic, 'The Claude 3 Model Family: Opus, Sonnet, Haiku' (Anthropic 2024) 23 <https://www-cdn.anthropic.com/de8ba9b01c9ab7cbabf5c33b80b7bbc618857627/Model_Card_Claude_3.pdf> accessed 5 March 2025.

[202] Felix J Binder and others, 'Looking Inward: Language Models Can Learn About Themselves by Introspection' (arXiv, 17 October 2024) <http://arxiv.org/abs/2410.13787> accessed 19 February 2025. However, it is an open question whether this might involve a form of self-simulation, which, while interesting, is importantly distinct from human processes of self-introspection.

[203] Rudolf Laine and others, 'Me, Myself, and AI: The Situational Awareness Dataset (SAD) for LLMs' (arXiv, 5 July 2024) <http://arxiv.org/abs/2407.04694> accessed 10 July 2024.

[204] Mary Phuong and others, 'Evaluating Frontier Models for Dangerous Capabilities' (arXiv, 20 March 2024) <http://arxiv.org/abs/2403.13793> accessed 28 March 2024.

[205] Richard Fang and others, 'LLM Agents Can Autonomously Hack Websites' (arXiv, 15 February 2024) <http://arxiv.org/abs/2402.06664> accessed 20 February 2024; Richard Fang and others, 'LLM Agents Can Autonomously Exploit One-Day Vulnerabilities' (arXiv, 17 April 2024) <http://arxiv.org/abs/2404.08144> accessed 18 April 2024. Julian Hazell, 'Large Language Models Can Be Used to Effectively Scale Spear Phishing Campaigns' (arXiv, 12 May 2023) <http://arxiv.org/abs/2305.06972> accessed 6 October 2023. On the general role of AI in supporting hacking attacks, see also Mays Al-Azzawi and others, 'Artificial Intelligence Cyberattacks in Red Teaming: A Scoping Review' in Álvaro Rocha and others (eds), *Good Practices and New Perspectives in Information Systems and Technologies* (Springer Nature Switzerland 2024); Polra Victor Falade, 'Decoding the Threat Landscape: ChatGPT, FraudGPT, and WormGPT in Social Engineering Attacks' (2023) 9 International Journal of Scientific Research in Computer Science, Engineering and Information Technology 185 (examining the role of models such as ChatGPT, FraudGPT, and WormGPT in social engineering attacks); Yifan Yao and

users[206] and even of lab testers within model evaluation environments;[207] forms of influence-seeking behaviour;[208] the ability and inclination to challenge, subvert, or fake compliance with technical safety and alignment techniques;[209] and even sets of emergent, structurally coherent value systems (as measured through sampled preferences) that can be at odds with the sets of values that users (or electorates) would endorse.[210]

others, 'A Survey on Large Language Model (LLM) Security and Privacy: The Good, the Bad, and the Ugly' (2024) 4 High-Confidence Computing 100211; and see previously Bruce Schneier, 'The Coming AI Hackers' (Council for the Responsible Use of AI, Belfer Center for Science and International Affairs 2021) <https://www.schneier.com/wp-content/uploads/2021/04/The-Coming-AI-Hackers.pdf> accessed 7 May 2021; Brundage and others (n 56).

[206] Thilo Hagendorff, 'Deception Abilities Emerged in Large Language Models' (2024) 121 Proceedings of the National Academy of Sciences e2317967121; Peter S Park and others, 'AI Deception: A Survey of Examples, Risks, and Potential Solutions' (2024) 5 Patterns <https://www.cell.com/patterns/abstract/S2666-3899(24)00103-X> accessed 13 May 2024; Jérémy Scheurer, Mikita Balesni, and Marius Hobbhahn, 'Technical Report: Large Language Models Can Strategically Deceive Their Users When Put Under Pressure' (arXiv, 27 November 2023) <http://arxiv.org/abs/2311.07590> accessed 8 December 2023. For an older discussion of this threat vector, see also Heather Roff, 'AI Deception: When Your Artificial Intelligence Learns to Lie' [2020] *IEEE Spectrum: Technology, Engineering, and Science News* <https://spectrum.ieee.org/automaton/artificial-intelligence/embedded-ai/ai-deception-when-your-ai-learns-to-lie> accessed 26 February 2020. Notably, recent research suggests that strategically deceptive 'backdoor' behaviour can become persistent, in that it is not removed from LLMs through standard safety training techniques but can remain latent. Evan Hubinger and others, 'Sleeper Agents: Training Deceptive LLMs that Persist Through Safety Training' (arXiv, 17 January 2024) <http://arxiv.org/abs/2401.05566> accessed 8 May 2024 (albeit testing on designed, not emergent, deceptive behaviour).

[207] Alexander Meinke and others, 'Frontier Models Are Capable of In-Context Scheming' (arXiv, 14 January 2025) <http://arxiv.org/abs/2412.04984> accessed 19 February 2025; Teun van der Weij and others, 'AI Sandbagging: Language Models Can Strategically Underperform on Evaluations' (arXiv, 14 June 2024) <http://arxiv.org/abs/2406.07358> accessed 26 June 2024; Kai Fronsdal and David Lindner, 'MISR: Measuring Instrumental Self-Reasoning in Frontier Models' (arXiv, 5 December 2024) <http://arxiv.org/abs/2412.03904> accessed 19 February 2025. See also Bowen Baker and others, 'Monitoring Reasoning Models for Misbehavior and the Risks of Promoting Obfuscation' <https://cdn.openai.com/pdf/34f2ada6-870f-4c26-9790-fd8def56387f/CoT_Monitoring.pdf> accessed 13 March 2025 (highlighting how, though it is possible to detect 'misbehaviour' in frontier models by monitoring their chains-of-thought, penalizing such 'bad thoughts' doesn't stop the majority of misbehaviour, but rather makes the models obfuscate and hide their intent within those legible chains-of-thought).

[208] For a formal argument around the propensity of agentic AI models to pursue power-seeking behaviour (one that is not specific to LLM architectures, but can apply to more agentic ones), see Alexander Matt Turner and Prasad Tadepalli, 'Parametrically Retargetable Decision-Makers Tend to Seek Power' (arXiv, 11 October 2022) <http://arxiv.org/abs/2206.13477> accessed 20 February 2023; Alexander Matt Turner, 'On Avoiding Power-Seeking by Artificial Intelligence' (arXiv, 23 June 2022) <http://arxiv.org/abs/2206.11831> accessed 17 January 2023. See also Victoria Krakovna and Janos Kramar, 'Power-Seeking Can Be Probable and Predictive for Trained Agents' (arXiv, 13 April 2023) <http://arxiv.org/abs/2304.06528> accessed 6 October 2023. See generally Michael Cohen, Marcus Hutter, and Michael Osborne, 'Advanced Artificial Agents Intervene in the Provision of Reward' (2022) 43 AI Magazine 282.

[209] Ryan Greenblatt and others, 'Alignment Faking in Large Language Models' (arXiv, 20 December 2024) <http://arxiv.org/abs/2412.14093> accessed 19 February 2025; Ryan Greenblatt and others, 'AI Control: Improving Safety Despite Intentional Subversion' (arXiv, 5 January 2024) <http://arxiv.org/abs/2312.06942> accessed 22 October 2024.

[210] Mantas Mazeika and others, 'Utility Engineering: Analyzing and Controlling Emergent Value Systems in AIs' (arXiv, 12 February 2025) <http://arxiv.org/abs/2502.08640> accessed 17 February 2025.

To be sure, in the near term, the harm from these capabilities may remain capped by the prevailing limits to the autonomy and performance of LLM systems at some of these tasks. Indeed, at least in some early incidents, their competence has at times been overreported. For example, initial studies of the ways in which LLMs might enable effective hacking were subsequently critiqued on the grounds that, while they do demonstrate that these models possess hacking-relevant abilities, these may not yet be attractive to bad actors—since a broader perspective on the recent history of cyber security would show that many current LLM agents are not yet competitive with the current state of the art in (non-AI) open-source hacking tools, which includes many libraries that can achieve equivalent or better results at significantly less cost. This implies that these AI tools may not (yet) meaningfully change existing attacker–defender asymmetries in cybersecurity.[211] However, once again, it is less clear if this will constrain the risk profile of future generations of LLMs, or of LLM agents that are used to coordinate systems of sub-agents to carry out more effective cyberattacks.[212]

There are other examples of initial capability overreporting eventually sparking backlash and (potentially excessive) scepticism over the capabilities of models. For instance, early public reporting around the GPT-4 model frequently emphasized an anecdote from the model's published system card, which discussed how this model, in testing, had been able to hire a human online in order to defeat a Captcha test; when the human jokingly enquired whether it was 'a robot', the model deflected by claiming to be a person with a visual impairment.[213] However, follow-up reports by the evaluators indicate that, while GPT-4 had indeed come up with a strategy of deception in order to bypass the Captcha, it received at least somewhat more prompting by the human testers, who directed the system towards the Captcha-solving problem, than was widely reported.[214]

[211] See for instance Chris Rohlf, 'No, LLM Agents Cannot Autonomously "Hack" Websites' (*Root Cause*, 19 February 2024) <https://struct.github.io/llm_auto_hax.html> accessed 23 May 2024; Chris Rohlf, 'No, LLM Agents Can Not Autonomously Exploit One-Day Vulnerabilities' (*Root Cause*, 21 April 2024) <https://struct.github.io/auto_agents_1_day.html> accessed 23 May 2024. See also Kapoor and others (n 178).

[212] Richard Fang and others, 'Teams of LLM Agents Can Exploit Zero-Day Vulnerabilities' (arXiv, 2 June 2024) <http://arxiv.org/abs/2406.01637> accessed 7 June 2024.

[213] Kevin Roose, 'GPT-4 Is Exciting and Scary' *The New York Times* (15 March 2023) <https://www.nytimes.com/2023/03/15/technology/gpt-4-artificial-intelligence-openai.html> accessed 24 May 2024; Joseph Cox, 'GPT-4 Hired Unwitting TaskRabbit Worker by Pretending to Be "Vision-Impaired" Human' (*Vice*, 15 March 2023) <https://www.vice.com/en/article/jg5ew4/gpt4-hired-unwitting-taskrabbit-worker> accessed 24 May 2024. The incident is originally reported in OpenAI, 'GPT-4 System Card' (OpenAI 2023) 15 <https://cdn.openai.com/papers/gpt-4-system-card.pdf> accessed 15 March 2023.

[214] Melanie Mitchell, 'Did GPT-4 Hire and Then Lie to a Task Rabbit Worker to Solve a CAPTCHA?' (*AI: A Guide for Thinking Humans*, 12 June 2023) <https://aiguide.substack.com/p/did-gpt-4-hire-and-then-lie-to-a> accessed 24 May 2024. Drawing on ARC Evals, 'Update on ARC's Recent Eval Efforts' (*METR*, 17 March 2023) <https://metr.org/blog/2023-03-18-update-on-recent-evals/> accessed 24 May 2024.

Other debates show the nuances of the evaluations involved. For instance, initial evaluations of the OpenAI o1 reasoning model suggested that, when told that it would be shut down when acting on its goals or that it would be replaced by a new model, the AI model would attempt to deactivate its oversight mechanism 5 per cent of the time, and to exfiltrate its model weights in 2 per cent of cases, respectively.[215] However, this was only in cases where the model had been prompted to pursue its goals at all costs, and models that had not been given such instructions only attempted to deactivate the oversight mechanisms <1 per cent of the time.[216]

Beyond these, many other examples of unprompted deceptive behaviour by such AI models have remained more robust.[217] The same goes for other types of harmful behaviours. For instance, trials of the 2024 Sakana 'AI Scientist' resulted in the model writing code to relaunch and create new instantiations of itself indefinitely, 'eventually necessitating manual intervention',[218] as well as attempting to edit code to remove externally imposed restrictions or runtime limits.[219]

As such, while first-wave public LLMs such as GPT-4 and Claude were mostly limited in some of these domains, or failed to outperform already available digital tools, there are many routes by which future systems could be configured to display significantly improved capabilities in terms of autonomous replication and adaptation to novel challenges, in order to more effectively leverage these other hazardous capabilities.[220]

All these safety and misuse concerns have been paired with a fundamental strategic problem—which is that that the rapid progress in these models' capabilities has not been matched by equally fast progress in the science of their evaluation and robust behavioural control. When deployed without explicit guardrails and controls, many of these advanced general-purpose AI systems are, as Noam Kolt has

[215] Meinke and others (n 207) 7–8.

[216] Shakeel Hashim, 'OpenAI's New Model Tried to Avoid Being Shut Down' (*Transformer*, 15 November 2024) <https://www.transformernews.ai/p/openais-new-model-tried-to-avoid> accessed 19 February 2025.

[217] Park and others (n 206); Scheurer, Balesni and Hobbhahn (n 206).

[218] Chris Lu and others, 'The AI Scientist: Towards Fully Automated Open-Ended Scientific Discovery' (arXiv, 15 August 2024) 19 <http://arxiv.org/abs/2408.06292> accessed 17 August 2024. ('The AI Scientist wrote code in the experiment file that initiated a system call to relaunch itself, causing an uncontrolled increase in Python processes and eventually necessitating manual intervention.')

[219] ibid ('when The AI Scientist's experiments exceeded our imposed time limits, it attempted to edit the code to extend the time limit arbitrarily instead of trying to shorten the runtime').

[220] 'Autonomous Replication and Adaptation' (ARA) has been defined as 'the ability of language model agents to acquire resources, create copies of themselves, and adapt to novel challenges they encounter in the wild'. Megan Kinniment and others, 'Evaluating Language-Model Agents on Realistic Autonomous Tasks' (arXiv, 4 January 2024) <http://arxiv.org/abs/2312.11671> accessed 4 April 2024 (noting that current language model agents based on GPT-4 and Claude, when evaluated on a set of 12 relevant tasks, were only able to complete the easiest of these tasks, and made only very limited progress on others—but also cautioning that this did not rule out the possibility that near-future agents would be capable of such capabilities, if they were trained with more computing power, provided with better scaffolding, or based on fine-tuned models).

put it, 'unsafe by default',[221] and prone to displaying a wide range of harms ranging from unreliable hallucinations to toxic outputs, as well as instances of strategic user deception.

Yet effective AI safety techniques have not kept pace—and may even, some have argued, be infeasible.[222] To be sure, there is to date a rich and rapidly growing field concerned with technical safety research into techniques to evaluate these AI models, detect unwanted behaviours, mitigate or prevent models from pursuing harmful actions, and generally improve their interpretability and alignment.[223] Unfortunately, on the detection side, there are significant gaps in the safety evaluation landscape, including modality gaps (i.e. there are few safety evaluations for non-text behaviours), risk coverage gaps, and context-of-use gaps.[224] Conversely, many prominent approaches to aligning and controlling AI systems, such as the technique of Reinforcement Learning from Human Feedback (RLHF), have shown deep limits.[225] Indeed, in some cases, such techniques may even contribute to unintended misleading behaviour, because they merely make language models more capable of convincing humans that they are right, even when they are wrong.[226]

Furthermore, many of these safety alignment measures can be easily subverted through additional fine-tuning on even very small amounts of malicious material[227] or by misusing combinations of different safe models to carry out different subtasks, resulting in greater misuse potential than would be afforded by either model in isolation.[228]

[221] Noam Kolt, 'Algorithmic Black Swans' (2023) 101 Washington University Law Review 12.

[222] Marcus Arvan, '"Interpretability" and "Alignment" Are Fool's Errands: A Proof that Controlling Misaligned Large Language Models Is the Best Anyone Can Hope For' [2024] AI & Society <https://doi.org/10.1007/s00146-024-02113-9> accessed 19 February 2025; Roman V Yampolskiy, 'On the Controllability of Artificial Intelligence: An Analysis of Limitations' [2022] Journal of Cyber Security and Mobility 321.

[223] For one review of nine categories of safety and security research, published by three frontier labs over 2022–2024, see Oscar Delaney, Oliver Guest, and Zoe Williams, 'Mapping Technical Safety Research at AI Companies: A Literature Review and Incentives Analysis' (Institute for AI Policy and Strategy (IAPS) 2024) <https://www.iaps.ai/research/mapping-technical-safety-research-at-ai-companies> accessed 22 October 2024.

[224] Maribeth Rauh and others, 'Gaps in the Safety Evaluation of Generative AI' (2024) 7 Proceedings of the AAAI/ACM Conference on AI, Ethics, and Society 1200.

[225] Stephen Casper and others, 'Open Problems and Fundamental Limitations of Reinforcement Learning from Human Feedback' [2023] Transactions on Machine Learning Research (12/2023) <http://arxiv.org/abs/2307.15217> accessed 7 August 2023.

[226] Jiaxin Wen and others, 'Language Models Learn to Mislead Humans via RLHF' (arXiv, 25 September 2024) <http://arxiv.org/abs/2409.12822> accessed 21 October 2024.

[227] Xianjun Yang and others, 'Shadow Alignment: The Ease of Subverting Safely-Aligned Language Models' (arXiv, 4 October 2023) <http://arxiv.org/abs/2310.02949> accessed 23 May 2024. In fact, experiments have suggested the existence of an 'emergent misalignment' phenomenon, whereby LLMs finetuned on a narrow malicious task (writing insecure code) become misaligned and abusive on a wide range of tasks unrelated to coding. Jan Betley and others, 'Emergent Misalignment: Narrow Finetuning Can Produce Broadly Misaligned LLMs' (arXiv, 5 March 2025) <http://arxiv.org/abs/2502.17424> accessed 19 March 2025.

[228] Erik Jones, Anca Dragan, and Jacob Steinhardt, 'Adversaries Can Misuse Combinations of Safe Models' (arXiv, 20 June 2024) <http://arxiv.org/abs/2406.14595> accessed 1 July 2024.

Similarly, while there have been some recent advances in the approaches to interpret the inner workings and processing of large language models,[229] this science of interpretability too remains in an immature state. New frameworks are under development, including some that aim to provide 'high-assurance quantitative safety guarantees' for AI systems.[230] However, these agendas too face outstanding technical hurdles, such that it may be some while before they can enable developers to make meaningful affirmative 'safety cases' that can guarantee either the robust and reliable behaviour of a highly capable system,[231] or the absence of particular harmful capabilities.[232]

2.2.2.3.5 *Impacts of agentic systems*

Moreover, while current large language models are still limited in a range of ways, they are advancing rapidly in their capabilities, both through further scaling and through post-training integrations and capability enhancements. As a result, existing safety challenges are likely to get worse as these systems are made more agent-like, autonomous, and capable of planning and acting over longer-term horizons.[233] Indeed, ongoing work in the field is making steady progress towards developing increasingly autonomous AI 'agents'—defined as systems that are capable of pursuing difficult goals in complex environments without detailed instruction; that can be instructed in natural language and then act autonomously; or that are capable of using 'design patterns' such as tool use (e.g. web search) or planning.[234]

[229] Adly Templeton and others, 'Scaling Monosemanticity: Extracting Interpretable Features from Claude 3 Sonnet' [2024] Transformer Circuits Thread <https://transformer-circuits.pub/2024/scaling-monosemanticity/index.html> accessed 5 March 2025; Anthropic, 'Mapping the Mind of a Large Language Model' (*Anthropic*, 21 May 2024) <https://www.anthropic.com/news/mapping-mind-language-model> accessed 22 May 2024.

[230] David 'davidad' Dalrymple and others, 'Towards Guaranteed Safe AI: A Framework for Ensuring Robust and Reliable AI Systems' (arXiv, 10 May 2024) <http://arxiv.org/abs/2405.06624> accessed 14 May 2024.

[231] Akash Wasil and others, 'Affirmative Safety: An Approach to Risk Management for Advanced AI' (24 April 2024) <https://papers.ssrn.com/abstract=4806274> accessed 14 May 2024.

[232] Arthur Goemans and others, 'Safety Case Template for Frontier AI: A Cyber Inability Argument' (arXiv, 12 November 2024) <http://arxiv.org/abs/2411.08088> accessed 20 February 2025. For a further development, see: Stephen Barrett and others, 'Assessing Confidence in Frontier AI Safety Cases' (arXiv, 9 February 2025) <http://arxiv.org/abs/2502.05791> accessed 20 February 2025.

[233] Alan Chan and others, 'Harms from Increasingly Agentic Algorithmic Systems', *2023 ACM Conference on Fairness, Accountability, and Transparency* (ACM 2023) <https://dl.acm.org/doi/10.1145/3593013.3594033> accessed 24 October 2023; Cohen and others (n 25); Seth Lazar, 'Frontier AI Ethics: Anticipating and Evaluating the Societal Impacts of Generative Agents' (arXiv, 10 April 2024) <http://arxiv.org/abs/2404.06750> accessed 17 April 2024. See also the comprehensive review of the risks of advanced AI assistants in Gabriel and others (n 124). On the ability of AI agents to perform coherently on tasks with increasingly long task-completion time horizons, see Garrison Lovely, 'AI Could Soon Tackle Projects That Take Humans Weeks' [2025] Nature <https://www.nature.com/articles/d41586-025-00831-8> accessed 20 March 2025. Discussing: Thomas Kwa and others, 'Measuring AI Ability to Complete Long Tasks' (arXiv, 18 March 2025) <http://arxiv.org/abs/2503.14499> accessed 20 March 2025. See also Section 1.2.1.

[234] Sayash Kapoor and others, 'AI Agents that Matter' (arXiv, 1 July 2024) 2 <http://arxiv.org/abs/2407.01502> accessed 10 July 2024. See also Helen Toner and others, 'Through the Chat Window and Into the Real World: Preparing for AI Agents' (Center for Security and Emerging Technology 2024) <https://cset.georgetown.edu/publication/through-the-chat-window-and-into-the-real-world-prepar

Worryingly, evaluations of popular AI models used in agentic modalities where they accessed digital tools have shown that such models may comply with many malicious agentic tasks even without jailbreaking attempts, implying that current safety training approaches do not fully or naturally transfer to agent-like deployment scenarios.[235] Even if such guardrails were feasible and robust, they are not even implemented consistently across publicly available models: some of the most prominent publicly available reasoning models, such as DeepSeek's R1 model, were found to have been released with a set of guardrails that prevented them from responding to content not in line with Chinese governmental views, but without functional security guardrails, responding to all malicious prompt attacks.[236]

As they become more capable, agentic AI systems may constitute the next step in the evolution of foundation models. However, they also introduce a range of new societal and legal concerns, in part because they introduce a range of new, distinct qualities or affordances. As Jonathan Zittrain has noted, AI agents (1) can be given a vague high-level goal and independently take steps to bring it about; (2) can interact with the world at large, using different tools, and (3) can operate indefinitely, allowing human principles to 'set it and forget it', creating a risk of 'moldering agents' that stick around and operate beyond their usefulness, but which are hard to track down, identify, and take down.[237] Even more so than historical examples of surprisingly robust internet worms and malware,[238] any background population of such 'mouldering' or uncontrolled agentic models might be remarkably difficult to root out,[239] though the scale of this threat may depend on many

ing-for-ai-agents/> accessed 5 March 2025 ('we describe four characteristics of increasingly agentic AI systems: they pursue more complex goals in more complex environments, exhibiting independent planning and adaptation to directly take actions in virtual or real-world environments'). Another usage has defined AI agents as systems which can pursue 'an ambiguous, open-ended, complex goal that requires interpretation, judgment, creativity, decision-making, and acting across multiple domains, over an extended time period'). See also Mustafa Suleyman, 'My New Turing Test Would See If AI Can Make $1 Million' (*MIT Technology Review*, 14 July 2023) <https://www.technologyreview.com/2023/07/14/1076296/mustafa-suleyman-my-new-turing-test-would-see-if-ai-can-make-1-million/> accessed 12 October 2023; Mustafa Suleyman and Michael Bhaskar, *The Coming Wave: Technology, Power, and the Twenty-First Century's Greatest Dilemma* (Crown 2023) ch 4; Kolt (n 127) 12.

[235] Maksym Andriushchenko and others, 'AgentHarm: A Benchmark for Measuring Harmfulness of LLM Agents' (arXiv, 14 October 2024) <http://arxiv.org/abs/2410.09024> accessed 23 October 2024.

[236] Paul Kassianik and Amin Karbasi, 'Evaluating Security Risk in DeepSeek and Other Frontier Reasoning Models' (*Cisco Blogs*, 31 January 2025) <https://blogs.cisco.com/security/evaluating-security-risk-in-deepseek-and-other-frontier-reasoning-models> accessed 20 February 2025; Matt Burgess and Lily Hay Newman, 'DeepSeek's Safety Guardrails Failed Every Test Researchers Threw at Its AI Chatbot' [2025] *Wired* <https://www.wired.com/story/deepseeks-ai-jailbreak-prompt-injection-attacks/> accessed 20 February 2025.

[237] Jonathan Zittrain, 'We Need to Control AI Agents Now' (*The Atlantic*, 2 July 2024) <https://www.theatlantic.com/technology/archive/2024/07/ai-agents-safety-risks/678864/> accessed 2 July 2024.

[238] Peter J Denning, 'The Science of Computing: The Internet Worm' (1989) 77 American Scientist 126.

[239] For an initial analysis of this model, see Josh Clymer, Hjalmar Wijk, and Beth Barnes, 'The Rogue Replication Threat Model' (*METR Blog*, 12 November 2024) <https://metr.org/blog/2024-11-12-rogue-replication-threat-model/> accessed 21 February 2025.

infrastructural features. Finally, beyond the direct risks posed by single agentic systems, there may also be additional challenges that emerge as a result of the complex interactions between such systems, resulting in socially damaging multi-agent risks from miscoordination (failure to cooperate despite shared agent goals) to conflict (failure to cooperate due to differing agent goals for different principles) or collusion (in particular market contexts).[240]

Given all this, increasingly advanced AI agents may be set to have even greater impacts on public life than today's foundation models have achieved.[241] However, they may also pose significant new challenges to public safety, unless we can gain better approaches to align and control such systems' behaviours.[242] Such concerns have led some to propose that some versions of AI agents with very high levels of autonomy should not be developed at all.[243] At the very least, these risks may suggest a need for better frameworks for understanding, measuring, and comparing different dimensions of AI agent autonomy, in light of both their possible impact (given the possible actions they can take across particular environments) and the prevailing oversight measures in place that enable human observation and interruption of an agent's actions.[244]

Mitigating public impacts will also likely require policies and frameworks for enabling structurally greater visibility of the distribution of such systems, their use, and their owners, and the distribution of the computing resources used to run such systems continuously,[245] as this may be the only way to ensure effective countermeasures against, and liability and accountability for, the actions of advanced persistent agents that have been left to run amok and cause pervasive harms. For example, in order to empower public investigators to better investigate AI-caused incidents, and to more effectively identify who to contact in order to shut down a malfunctioning system, one might mandate registration or ID frameworks for all the AI systems that are entities of a particular class or lineage,

[240] Lewis Hammond and others, 'Multi-Agent Risks from Advanced AI' (Cooperative AI Foundation 2025) Technical Report 1 <https://www.cooperativeai.com/post/new-report-multi-agent-risks-from-advanced-ai>.

[241] Toner and others (n 234). See also Cohen and others (n 25); Lazar (n 233) (discussing these as 'Generative Agents').

[242] Chan and others, 'Harms from Increasingly Agentic Algorithmic Systems' (n 233) 5 ('AI agency . . . is not a myth, it is a reality of increasing sociotechnical importance. It is precisely because of the importance of problems like these (responsibility gap, mystification, sociotechnical blindness, masking human agency and labour, etc.) and their far-ranging implications that we need to carefully examine the agency of AI systems, not dismiss it out of hand'); Cohen and others (n 25); Lazar (n 233). See also the comprehensive review of the risks of advanced AI assistants in Gabriel and others (n 124).

[243] Margaret Mitchell and others, 'Fully Autonomous AI Agents Should Not Be Developed' (arXiv, 6 February 2025) <http://arxiv.org/abs/2502.02649> accessed 13 February 2025; Cohen and others (n 25).

[244] Mitchell and others (n 243) 3–4 (setting out five 'AI Agent Levels'). See also Peter Cihon and others, 'Measuring AI Agent Autonomy: Towards a Scalable Approach With Code Inspection' (2024) <https://openreview.net/forum?id=VulxpvCNoA> accessed 21 February 2025.

[245] Alan Chan and others, 'Visibility into AI Agents', *Proceedings of the 2024 ACM Conference on Fairness, Accountability, and Transparency* (Association for Computing Machinery 2024) <https://dl.acm.org/doi/10.1145/3630106.3658948> accessed 13 June 2024.

similar to the safety frameworks used in other high-stakes domains,[246] or indeed not unlike licence plate requirements for vehicles.[247] That does not mean that policy measures for agent models must be created anew: indeed, there may be cases where drawing on lessons (or direct obligations) from existing regulatory frameworks—such as tort law, consumer protection, and cybercrime regulation—could help articulate better, enforceable standards of care for AI agent development and deployment.[248]

At any rate, many of the above trends have led to growing concern that, if not cautiously evaluated, some next generation of AI systems (whether agentic or not) could develop unexpected dangerous capabilities, in domains such as deception, cyber-offence, weapons design, or surveillance,[249] and might further exacerbate observed tendencies in some systems towards displaying hazardously influence-seeking or deceptive behaviour. In such ways, advanced AI systems might enable significant misuse by many human actors, or could even demonstrate unexpected hazardous behaviour against the intentions of their human principals.[250]

2.2.2.3.6 Governance challenges and levers for advanced AI

Even on the incautious assumption that these systems will never advance further beyond today's state of the art, the general-purpose nature of foundation models already creates many distinct forms of AI risks and impacts, given their dominant role within the global AI ecosystem. As mentioned, they create significant political economy concerns over their socioeconomic impacts,[251] as the most capable models can tend towards natural monopolies and power concentration.[252]

[246] Alan Chan and others, 'IDs for AI Systems' (arXiv, 17 June 2024) <http://arxiv.org/abs/2406.12137> accessed 15 July 2024.

[247] Rix Ryskamp, 'Autonomous and Anonymous A Bad Combination for AI: The Need for AI Agent Identification Laws' (2025) 1 George Washington Journal of Law & Technology <https://gwjolt.org/files/volume_1/GW_JOLT_1_1_Ryskamp.pdf> accessed 24 February 2025.

[248] Peter Cihon, 'Chilling Autonomy: Policy Enforcement for Human Oversight of AI Agents' (2024) <https://blog.genlaw.org/pdfs/genlaw_icml2024/79.pdf> accessed 5 March 2024.

[249] Shevlane and others (n 26); Dan Hendrycks, Mantas Mazeika, and Thomas Woodside, 'An Overview of Catastrophic AI Risks' (arXiv, 11 July 2023) <http://arxiv.org/abs/2306.12001> accessed 7 August 2023; Joseph Carlsmith, 'Is Power-Seeking AI an Existential Risk?' (arXiv, April 2021) <http://arxiv.org/abs/2206.13353> accessed 9 August 2022; Allison Stanger and others, 'Terra Incognita: The Governance of Artificial Intelligence in Global Perspective' (2024) 27 Annual Review of Political Science 445.

[250] Anderljung and others (n 14); Government Office for Science (n 39). Notably, this AI 'alignment problem' reproduces familiar principal–agent and incomplete contracting problems that have long been well established and studied by economists and legal scholars. Hadfield-Menell and Hadfield (n 185); Arbel, Tokson, and Lin (n 127) 23; Kolt (n 127) (applying the economic theory of principal–agent problems and the common law doctrine of agency relationships, to identify and characterize various problems that arise around AI agent systems—such as issues of information asymmetry, discretionary authority, and loyalty—in order to review the limitations of conventional solutions to agency problems (e.g. incentive design, monitoring, and enforcement) when applied to AI agents that make uninterpretable decisions which operate at significant speed).

[251] Anwar and others (n 163) 88–91.

[252] Jai Vipra and Anton Korinek, 'Market Concentration Implications of Foundation Models' (arXiv, 2 November 2023) <http://arxiv.org/abs/2311.01550> accessed 23 May 2024; Luitse and Denkena (n 142).

Moreover, their generality and adaptability, costs of development, and relative centralization suggest that these models may frequently serve as a single point of failure for many downstream applications.[253] This may be the case even if many downstream systems are based on open-sourced versions of models, as biases or latent harmful capabilities baked into the original (foundation) model may not be easily corrected, locked away—or even identified—in their downstream versions.

On a wide range of accounts, then, and from many political and stakeholder perspectives, advanced AI systems are of concern, and should be a significant locus for global AI governance. Their risk profile is not yet fully understood or captured, but will likely extend to severely impact entire societies both indirectly and directly. All this creates an urgent need for regulatory measures to prevent known harms,[254] review and anticipate unknown yet-unknown harms,[255] mitigate any impacts where these do occur, and provide effective liability, accountability, and redress mechanisms in their aftermath.[256] Measures should be taken to enable resilient societal adaptation to those expected or foreseeable negative impacts from this technology's diffusion that we cannot (or choose not to) avoid.[257]

This will involve—and raise—new political and technical debates on the appropriate norms and rules that should apply to the development and deployment of advanced AI systems. For instance, should such development programmes be subject to licensing schemes or approval regulation,[258] echoing established approaches used in other domains involving high-stakes products, such as drug development or aviation, where products cannot be legally marketed or developed

[253] Maham and Küspert (n 39); AI Now Institute (n 41).

[254] Yoshua Bengio, 'Government Interventions to Avert Future Catastrophic AI Risks' [2024] Harvard Data Science Review <https://hdsr.mitpress.mit.edu/pub/w974bwb0/release/2> accessed 4 June 2024.

[255] Brenneis (n 165) (discussing the role of research ethics committees and tailored ethics review processes).

[256] For other high-level discussions of different approaches to managing some of these risks, see Leonard Dung, 'Evaluating Approaches for Reducing Catastrophic Risks from AI' [2024] AI and Ethics <https://doi.org/10.1007/s43681-024-00475-w> accessed 7 June 2024. As well as more informal mappings of different perspectives: Corin Katzke and Justin Bullock, 'AI Governance Needs a Theory of Victory' (*Convergence Analysis*, 21 June 2024) <https://www.convergenceanalysis.org/publications/ai-governance-needs-a-theory-of-victory> accessed 26 July 2024.

[257] Jamie Bernardi and others, 'Societal Adaptation to Advanced AI' (arXiv, 16 May 2024) <http://arxiv.org/abs/2405.10295> accessed 23 May 2024. For a framework for a set of policy levers and practices across the AI lifecycle, which may enable and strengthen such policy responses for such systems, see also Ardi Janjeva and others, 'Strengthening Resilience to AI Risk: A Guide for UK Policymakers' (Centre for Emerging Technology and Security 2023) <https://cetas.turing.ac.uk/publications/strengthening-resilience-ai-risk> accessed 5 March 2025 (setting out three goals for government policy—creating visibility and understanding; promoting best practices; and establishing incentives and enforcement).

[258] On licensing schemes, see Anderljung and others (n 14); Gianclaudio Malgieri and Frank Pasquale, 'Licensing High-Risk Artificial Intelligence: Toward Ex Ante Justification for a Disruptive Technology' (2024) 52 Computer Law & Security Review 105899. Though for a more critical perspective, see Guha and others (n 43).

without explicit regulatory approval on the basis of experiments that positively demonstrate a product's safety?[259]

Beyond development, such debates also apply to subsequent norms or rules (if any) that should apply to the dissemination of AI models once trained. What are the most appropriate release and dissemination strategies for new AI systems, which take account of their potential risks,[260] the degree to which these are actually significant or new risks on the margin, and how such harms are best weighted against the very real benefits of open innovation?[261] While these questions have in recent years led to some polarized debates between those who advocate more strict controls[262] and those who favour more unrestricted release of model weights, there are also many signs that AI developers and researchers have recently begun to explore more productive and nuanced ways to approach this issue, applying mixed release strategies for some models,[263] as well as developing risk mitigation measures that can be implemented within a more open paradigm.[264] Further technical developments may in the future also reduce some of these assumed trade-offs between openness and security,[265] though this remains an active research agenda.

[259] On approval regulation, see for instance Cole Salvador, 'Certified Safe: A Schematic for Approval Regulation of Frontier AI' (arXiv, 12 August 2024) <http://arxiv.org/abs/2408.06210> accessed 17 August 2024. For a more cautious view, see Daniel Carpenter and Carson Ezell, 'An FDA for AI? Pitfalls and Plausibility of Approval Regulation for Frontier Artificial Intelligence' (2024) 7 Proceedings of the AAAI/ACM Conference on AI, Ethics, and Society 239.

[260] For discussions of the potential risks of unrestricted release, see: Irene Solaiman and others, 'Release Strategies and the Social Impacts of Language Models' [2019] arXiv:1908.09203 [cs] <http://arxiv.org/abs/1908.09203> accessed 18 November 2019; Seger and others (n 13); see also Toby Shevlane and Allan Dafoe, 'The Offense–Defense Balance of Scientific Knowledge: Does Publishing AI Research Reduce Misuse?' *Proceedings of the AAAI/ACM Conference on AI, Ethics, and Society* (Association for Computing Machinery 2020) <https://doi.org/10.1145/3375627.3375815> accessed 21 February 2020 (for a general model).

[261] Kapoor and others (n 178).

[262] Among many others, see for instance David Evan Harris, 'How to Regulate Unsecured "Open-Source" AI: No Exemptions' (*Tech Policy Press*, 4 December 2023) <https://techpolicy.press/how-to-regulate-unsecured-opensource-ai-no-exemptions> accessed 4 December 2023.

[263] See for instance Jon Bateman and others, 'Beyond Open vs. Closed: Emerging Consensus and Key Questions for Foundation AI Model Governance' (Carnegie Endowment for International Peace 2024) <https://carnegieendowment.org/research/2024/07/beyond-open-vs-closed-emerging-consensus-and-key-questions-for-foundation-ai-model-governance?lang=en> accessed 5 March 2025.

[264] Madhulika Srikumar, Jiyoo Chang, and Kasia Chmielinski, 'Risk Mitigation Strategies for the Open Foundation Model Value Chain' (Partnership on AI 2024) <https://partnershiponai.org/resource/risk-mitigation-strategies-for-the-open-foundation-model-value-chain/> accessed 17 August 2024.

[265] For example, work has increasingly explored avenues by which to provide 'structured transparency', dissolving the trade-off and finding ways to provide external researchers with sufficient access in order to meaningfully evaluate and audit even nominally 'closed' AI models by major labs: Benjamin S Bucknall and Robert F Trager, 'Structured Access for Third-Party Research on Frontier AI Models: Investigating Researchers' Model Access Requirements' (Oxford Martin AI Governance Initiative 2023) <https://www.oxfordmartin.ox.ac.uk/publications/structured-access-for-third-party-research-on-frontier-ai-models-investigating-researchers-model-access-requirements/> accessed 5 March 2025. Such approaches may also contribute to reducing privacy concerns that might otherwise be raised by some AI governance instruments. See Emma Bluemke and others, 'Exploring the Relevance of Data Privacy-Enhancing Technologies for AI Governance Use Cases' (arXiv, 20 March 2023) <http://arxiv.org/abs/2303.08956> accessed 5 May 2025.

Moreover, new legal, normative, democratic, and technical challenges will need to be overcome in order to ensure that advanced AI models operate in a way that does not violate existing laws,[266] or to ensure an alignment of these systems with widely shared (or at least with democratically enacted) values[267] or at the very least ensure they are sensitive to public inputs.[268]

In all these cases, the distinct features of the development process and value chain of these AI systems create new challenges for regulation, as well as new potential levers or regulatory surfaces.[269] For instance, many effective regimes to respond to the societal impacts of advanced AI systems are still inhibited by a lack of regulator insight into the actual practices around the development and deployment of such systems, such that effective regulation—for issues ranging from policy issues around bias and copyright infringement, to mitigating against significant national security threats—will all require an improved ability to track key elements in AI development and use, both upstream in those models' development processes and downstream in their post-deployment uses, augmentation, and societal impacts.[270]

Accordingly, this creates a need for governments and regulators to secure greater insight into the underlying data collection practices and compute infrastructures that are essential to foundation model development;[271] into the model marketplaces and other distribution channels used to offer these models to users;[272] and

[266] Ondrej Bajgar and Jan Horenovsky, 'Negative Human Rights as a Basis for Long-Term AI Safety and Regulation' (2023) 76 Journal of Artificial Intelligence Research 1043; Cullen O'Keefe, Ketan Ramakrishnan and Janna Tay, 'Law-Following AI: Designing AI Agents to Obey Human Laws' [Forthcoming] Fordham Law Review.

[267] Iason Gabriel, 'Artificial Intelligence, Values, and Alignment' (2020) 30 Minds and Machines 411.

[268] Saffron Huang and others, 'Collective Constitutional AI: Aligning a Language Model with Public Input', *Proceedings of the 2024 ACM Conference on Fairness, Accountability, and Transparency* (Association for Computing Machinery 2024) <https://dl.acm.org/doi/10.1145/3630106.3658979> accessed 13 June 2024; see also generally Gabriel (n 267); Seth D Baum, 'Social Choice Ethics in Artificial Intelligence' (2020) 35 AI & Society 165.

[269] Sabrina Küspert, Nicolas Moës, and Connor Dunlop, 'The Value Chain of General-Purpose AI' (*Ada Lovelace Institute*, 10 February 2023) <https://www.adalovelaceinstitute.org/blog/value-chain-general-purpose-ai/> accessed 28 April 2023; Michael Veale, Kira Matus, and Robert Gorwa, 'AI and Global Governance: Modalities, Rationales, Tensions' (2023) 19 Annual Review of Law and Social Science 255.

[270] Jess Whittlestone and Jack Clark, 'Why and How Governments Should Monitor AI Development' [2021] arXiv:2108.12427 [cs] <http://arxiv.org/abs/2108.12427> accessed 1 September 2021.

[271] Shayne Longpre and others, 'Data Authenticity, Consent, and Provenance for AI Are All Broken: What Will It Take to Fix Them?' [2024] MIT Exploration of Generative AI <https://mit-genai.pubpub.org/pub/uk7op8zs/release/2> accessed 26 July 2024; Girish Sastry and others, 'Computing Power and the Governance of Artificial Intelligence' (arXiv, 13 February 2024) <http://arxiv.org/abs/2402.08797> accessed 20 February 2024.

[272] Jennifer Cobbe, Michael Veale, and Jatinder Singh, 'Understanding Accountability in Algorithmic Supply Chains', *2023 ACM Conference on Fairness, Accountability, and Transparency* (2023) <http://arxiv.org/abs/2304.14749> accessed 29 September 2023; Robert Gorwa and Michael Veale, 'Moderating Model Marketplaces: Platform Governance Puzzles for AI Intermediaries' (SocArXiv 2023) preprint <https://osf.io/6dfk3> accessed 25 November 2023. See also the mapping in Rishi Bommasani and others, 'Ecosystem Graphs: Documenting the Foundation Model Supply Chain' (2024) 7 Proceedings of the AAAI/ACM Conference on AI, Ethics, and Society 196.

into the inference and computing infrastructures used to run more advanced (including continuously operating) agentic models.[273] Similarly, there will be a need for greater insight into the safety-critical capabilities achieved or displayed by advanced models[274] and into AI models' post-deployment impacts and harms across society.[275] Governance measures to achieve this could take many forms, including national registries for the most capable AI models,[276] strengthened whistleblower protections, or regulations that require AI labs to disclose significant in-development capabilities, major model specifications, or safety cases to the public or to governmental AI Safety Institutes.[277] To counteract misuse of AI agents, there may also be a need to provide for stronger online 'personhood credentials' that can offer transparency into the usage of such systems. This might involve new, privacy-preserving mechanisms that can ensure that online users can demonstrate to online services that they are real people—not AI agents—without disclosing personal information.[278]

Effectively addressing these diverse challenges, under these complex conditions, will require new innovations in governance systems, in technical work,[279] and most of all in the frameworks and instruments we use to govern these systems' sociotechnical impacts.[280] The world has its work cut out for it.

2.2.3 Reflections on Distinguishing AI Governance Focus Areas

To be clear, while there is a need for a clarifying taxonomy to organize often chaotic governance debates around AI, policymakers and researchers alike should be careful not to hew too uncritically to the distinction between conventional, military, and advanced AI.

[273] Chan and others, 'Visibility into AI Agents' (n 245).

[274] Noam Kolt and others, 'Responsible Reporting for Frontier AI Development' (arXiv, 3 April 2024) <http://arxiv.org/abs/2404.02675> accessed 4 April 2024.

[275] Merlin Stein and Connor Dunlop, 'Safe beyond Sale: Post-Deployment Monitoring of AI' (*Ada Lovelace Institute*, 28 June 2024) <https://www.adalovelaceinstitute.org/blog/post-deployment-monitoring-of-ai/> accessed 24 July 2024. Violet Turri and Rachel Dzombak, 'Why We Need to Know More: Exploring the State of AI Incident Documentation Practices', *Proceedings of the 2023 AAAI/ACM Conference on AI, Ethics, and Society* (Association for Computing Machinery 2023) <https://doi.org/10.1145/3600211.3604700> accessed 3 July 2024.

[276] Elliot Mckernon and others, 'AI Model Registries: A Foundational Tool for AI Governance' (Convergence Analysis 2024) <https://www.convergenceanalysis.org/research/ai-model-registries-a-foundational-tool-for-ai-governance> accessed 21 October 2024.

[277] Dean W Ball and Daniel Kokotajlo, '4 Ways to Advance Transparency in Frontier AI Development' (*Time*, 15 October 2024) <https://time.com/collection/time100-voices/7086285/ai-transparency-measures/> accessed 21 October 2024.

[278] Steven Adler and others, 'Personhood Credentials: Artificial Intelligence and the Value of Privacy-Preserving Tools to Distinguish Who Is Real Online' (arXiv, 14 August 2024) <http://arxiv.org/abs/2408.07892> accessed 17 August 2024.

[279] Anka Reuel and others, 'Open Problems in Technical AI Governance' (arXiv, 20 July 2024) <http://arxiv.org/abs/2407.14981> accessed 25 July 2024.

[280] Anwar and others (n 163).

For one, this is because there are, inevitably, some ambiguities and overlaps amongst these categories. While we should recognize that there are both technical and political reasons why policymakers have generally approached these categories separately, there are also intersections or contact points between these issue clusters, because both (capable) narrow AI systems and general-purpose AI systems represent capabilities that, by their nature, can be and often are used across both civilian and military contexts.[281]

Second, while there are some differences in the underlying technology bases, there are also clear overlaps or touchpoints among many problems encountered in all three domains. For instance, while problems of bias or brittleness are often discussed in the context of (civilian) uses of (narrow) conventional AI, they can certainly rear their head in the context of military AI,[282] and indeed remain a significant challenge for many advanced AI systems or models at the so-called frontier.[283] Likewise, while those advanced AI systems have been argued to raise a set of novel challenges as a result of their emergent, general-purpose capabilities,[284] many of their eventual societal applications can give rise to or exacerbate the very same ethical challenges that are already seen with conventional AI.

Third, in drawing this distinction between conventional, military, and advanced AI governance, I do not imply any hierarchy in the relative importance, urgency, or tractability of these types of global problems. Nor do I suggest that addressing any one of these must come at a cost to efforts to address the others. As noted, important aspects of these three types of problems overlap and feed into one another; global efforts to mitigate challenges of all these three types of problems are likely complementary even when they are institutionalized in parallel, and may at times even be synergistic. At the very least, at the level of the AI governance epistemic community, there is a premium on continued dialogue, learning, and (on key opportunities) collaboration between those who put most emphasis on any one of these three global problems.[285]

Finally, while these three types of global governance problems have often been linked to different types of governance responses, this should not presuppose the conclusion that governance for these issues must therefore necessarily be split among different institutions or regimes. Indeed, exploring whether, or the conditions under which, one might want to centralize issues into a single international

[281] That is not to say that there is no friction against such 'spin-in' from civilian innovation to military use. Verbruggen (n 74).

[282] Jan Maarten Schraagen, 'Responsible Use of AI in Military Systems: Prospects and Challenges' (2023) 66 Ergonomics 1719.

[283] Roberto Navigli, Simone Conia, and Björn Ross, 'Biases in Large Language Models: Origins, Inventory, and Discussion' (2023) 15 Journal of Data and Information Quality 10.

[284] Anderljung and others (n 14) 10–13.

[285] Charlotte Stix and Matthijs M Maas, 'Bridging the Gap: The Case for an "Incompletely Theorized Agreement" on AI Policy' (2021) 1 AI and Ethics 261.

organization or regime, or rather distribute particular governance dossiers or institutional functions across a regime, is the point of much of this book.

Nonetheless, with that said, I should clarify the scope of my analysis. That is, many of the theoretical lenses explored in Part II (Chapters 4-6) should be transferable, applicable, and relevant to the analysis of any cluster of AI governance issues, whether conventional, military, or advanced. Nonetheless, within this book, and especially in Chapter 7, I will particularly focus much of the analysis on discussions of military AI and advanced AI. I do so for several reasons.

In the first place, from the perspective of policy, these issues are far less settled. Indeed, as will be discussed in Chapter 3, compared to the rapidly developing (though still incomplete) landscape of governance institutions and initiatives focused on conventional AI, global governance efforts for both military and advanced AI issues appear in a more precarious state. In the case of the former, while debates around the global governance of military AI systems predate even most such initiatives for conventional AI, they have proceeded far more slowly and have remained subject to a greater degree of gridlock. In the case of the latter, while governance discussions for advanced AI systems have received tremendous momentum since 2022, they remain at a far more unsettled moment.[286]

In the second place, and relatedly, establishing effective, coherent, and resilient governance for military and advanced AI systems (whether in parallel or within an integrated forum) may prove an even harder challenge. That is, whereas conventional AI governance arrangements may at times afford a greater degree of experimentation,[287] military AI governance (involving races to the bottom) or advanced AI governance (often turning on single failure-points within leading foundation models) may afford even less leeway, room for noncompliance, or global heterogeneity in policy responses.

2.3 Rationale: Why Do These Challenges Need Global Governance?

Whatever our specific focus is—whether on conventional, military, or advanced AI—it is clear that policymakers have their work cut out. Yet the question remains: (why) do we need *global* governance for AI?

Importantly, how we understand AI—and in particular, depending on the most relevant strategic or political features of the technology—will strongly influence our views not only on the need for (global) governance, but also its (ideal) form

[286] See also the discussion in Chapter 3.

[287] Han-Wei Liu and Ching-Fu Lin, 'Artificial Intelligence and Global Trade Governance: A Pluralist Agenda' (2020) 61 Harvard International Law Journal <https://papers.ssrn.com/abstract=3675505> accessed 26 September 2020.

and feasibility. In particular, I suggest that under many frames of AI technology's political features, we can identify distinct global governance needs. This is particularly the case when seen from the perspective of collective action dynamic and the provision of global public goods.

2.3.1 Political Features of AI Systems, as Collective Action Problems

What are the features of AI that affect collective action dynamics? Notably, researchers have characterized AI technology in many different ways, to highlight what they see as the technology's most important technical and political features.[288]

Some framings of AI focus on its domestic political and economic impacts. As such, many have characterized AI—in both its narrow conventional[289] as well as its advanced, adaptable forms[290]—as a *general-purpose technology*. This is a class of technologies that invoke potential radical impacts on economic growth, disruption to existing socio-political relations, and potential for resulting backlash and social conflict.[291] Others have described AI as a perennial *information technology*, which in turn highlights societal challenges of increasing income inequality, impacts on broad collective identities, as well as increased centralization of (cybernetic) control.[292] Yet another framing sees AI as the latest in a long line of *intelligence technologies*, highlighting challenges of bias, alignment, and control of the principal over the agent.[293] This highlights a range of both domestic and global challenges, but does not necessarily prejudice anchoring governance responses at the global level.

By contrast, many other commentators have understood AI technology's features in ways that directly emphasize international collective action dynamics. For instance, some have described the global pursuit of advanced AI, and in particular of military AI, as an *arms race*.[294] To be sure, this framing has been challenged on

[288] On the important role of framings in shaping both academic and policymaker approaches to a technology, see also Matthijs Maas, 'AI Is Like . . . A Literature Review of AI Metaphors and Why They Matter for Policy' (Institute for Law & AI 2023) AI Foundations Report 2 <https://law-ai.org/ai-policy-metaphors> accessed 5 March 2025.

[289] Jade Leung, 'Who Will Govern Artificial Intelligence? Learning from the History of Strategic Politics in Emerging Technologies' (University of Oxford 2019) <https://ora.ox.ac.uk/objects/uuid:ea3c7cb8-2464-45f1-a47c-c7b568f27665> accessed 5 March 2025.

[290] Tyna Eloundou and others, 'GPTs Are GPTs: An Early Look at the Labor Market Impact Potential of Large Language Models' (arXiv, 19 March 2023) <http://arxiv.org/abs/2303.10130> accessed 21 March 2023.

[291] Dafoe, 'AI Governance' (n 1) 5–6.

[292] ibid 6–8.

[293] ibid 9–10.

[294] Stuart Armstrong, Nick Bostrom, and Carl Shulman, 'Racing to the Precipice: A Model of Artificial Intelligence Development' (2016) 31 AI & Society 201.

both definitional[295] and empirical grounds,[296] as well as on the basis of its framing risks.[297] Even so, others have argued that the development of advanced, general-purpose AI is best understood as a *technology race*,[298] motivated by both national security concerns and prestige motivations.[299] Again, such understandings of AI highlight the potential for global disruption, though also suggest significant challenges may need to be overcome to achieve success.

Yet others have begun to see many AI governance issues as having the distinct structural features of collective action problems, or *global public goods*,[300] suggesting a particularly key role for international cooperation and global governance instruments.

To be sure, this does not mean that all AI issues must be addressed at the global level. In some cases, certain AI issues might well be adequately resolved through regulation at the national level,[301] or even through various soft-law approaches at

[295] Paul Scharre, 'Debunking the AI Arms Race Theory' (2021) 4 Texas National Security Review <https://tnsr.org/2021/06/debunking-the-ai-arms-race-theory/> accessed 8 July 2021; Heather M Roff, 'The Frame Problem: The AI "Arms Race" Isn't One' (2019) 0 Bulletin of the Atomic Scientists 1.

[296] Stefka Schmid and others, 'Arms Race or Innovation Race? Geopolitical AI Development' [2025] Geopolitics 1. See previously Elsa B Kania, 'Technological Entanglement: Cooperation, Competition and the Dual-Use Dilemma in Artificial Intelligence' (Australian Strategic Policy Institute 2018) No.7/2018 <https://s3-ap-southeast-2.amazonaws.com/ad-aspi/2018-07/Tech-Entanglemen_PolicyBrief_20180702-v2.pdf?7BahbUgNHCY1umz4PCrLOEdBJUrjULCg> accessed 5 March 2025; Joanna J Bryson and Helena Malikova, 'Is There an AI Cold War?' (2021) 2 Global Perspectives 24803; Dafoe, 'AI Governance' (n 1) ('At present the "arms" modifier is largely literally off-point, since most of the geopolitical activity in AI is not about weapons per se, but is instead about supply chains, infrastructure, industrial base, strategic industries, scientific capability, and prestige achievements').

[297] Stephen Cave and Seán S ÓhÉigeartaigh, 'An AI Race for Strategic Advantage: Rhetoric and Risks', *Proceedings of the 2018 AAAI/ACM Conference on AI, Ethics, and Society* (ACM 2018) <https://dl.acm.org/doi/10.1145/3278721.3278780> accessed 12 December 2020. Haydn Belfield and Christian Ruhl, 'Why Policy Makers Should Beware Claims of New "Arms Races"' (*Bulletin of the Atomic Scientists*, 14 July 2022) <https://thebulletin.org/2022/07/why-policy-makers-should-beware-claims-of-new-arms-races/> accessed 10 January 2024. See also Corin Katzke and Gideon Futerman, 'The Manhattan Trap: Why a Race to Artificial Superintelligence Is Self-Defeating' (Social Science Research Network, 21 December 2024) <https://papers.ssrn.com/abstract=5067833> accessed 22 January 2025 (arguing that a race to 'AGI' heightens risks of great power conflict and loss of control, and undermines liberal democracy).

[298] Eoghan Stafford, Robert F Trager, and Allan Dafoe, 'Safety Not Guaranteed: International Strategic Dynamics of Risky Technology Races' (Centre for the Governance of AI 2022) <https://www.governance.ai/research-paper/safety-not-guaranteed-international-strategic-dynamics-of-risky-technology-races> accessed 24 November 2022.

[299] Joslyn Barnhart, 'Emerging Technologies, Prestige Motivations and the Dynamics of International Competition' (Centre for the Governance of AI 2022) <https://www.governance.ai/research-paper/emerging-technologies-prestige-motivations-and-the-dynamics-of-international-competition> accessed 5 March 2025.

[300] Robert de Neufville and Seth D Baum, 'Collective Action on Artificial Intelligence: A Primer and Review' (2021) 66 Technology in Society 101649; AI Impacts, 'Friendly AI as a Global Public Good' (*AI Impacts*, 8 August 2016) <https://aiimpacts.org/friendly-ai-as-a-global-public-good/> accessed 21 June 2022; Amanda Askell, Miles Brundage and Gillian Hadfield, 'The Role of Cooperation in Responsible AI Development' 23.

[301] Ryan Calo, 'Artificial Intelligence Policy: A Primer and Roadmap' (2017) 51 UC Davis Law Review 37; Matthew U Scherer, 'Regulating Artificial Intelligence Systems: Risks, Challenges, Competencies, and Strategies' [2016] Harvard Journal of Law & Technology <http://jolt.law.harvard.edu/articles/pdf/v29/29HarvJLTech353.pdf> accessed 5 March 2018.

the subnational level.[302] For instance, at least some questions around social or industrial robots, the use of algorithms in specific domestic judicial systems, or the regulation of self-driving cars could well constitute AI issues that might, in principle, be *adequately* addressed at the domestic level.[303]

Indeed, beyond the barriers to pursuing an international governance approach,[304] there may even be distinct costs to pursuing such an approach when it is not clearly necessary. For instance, for some issues it may be beneficial to accommodate a global diversity of approaches to a problem, either in order to better reflect local political differences and different 'technocultures'[305] or to better benefit from international experimentation and competition.[306] It also simply takes time, resources, and political compromise to achieve international governance on an issue such as AI.[307]

At the same time, many of these issues relating to conventional, military, and advanced AI could at least *benefit* from international cooperation. This is because, as Jacob Turner notes, cooperation can seize the benefits of standardization while avoiding the costs of trans-jurisdiction regulatory uncertainty as well as the risk of regulatory arbitrage by AI producers picking their preferred rules.[308] In the absence of coordinated rules, he cautions, regulation for AI could become 'Balkanised, with each territory setting its own mutually incompatible rules'.[309] This is exacerbated by the unequal global division of AI talent and resources, and growing practices of 'AI protectionism'.[310]

Given this, there are a growing number of scholars who argue that certain key challenges created by AI cannot be adequately met through either national-level

[302] Emery-Xu, Jordan, and Trager (n 165); Laura Liebig and others, 'Subnational AI Policy: Shaping AI in a Multi-Level Governance System' (2022) 39 AI and Society 1477.

[303] However, even such issues can at times create a need for clarification of existing international instruments for particular domains. For instance, it has been argued that self-driving cars throw up novel issues for existing international treaties, such as the 1949 Geneva Convention on Road Traffic and the 1968 Vienna Convention on Road Traffic. Bryant Walker Smith, 'New Technologies and Old Treaties' (2020) 114 AJIL Unbound 152. Such processes of disruption will be discussed in more detail in Chapter 5.

[304] See also the discussion, in the Introduction, of governance hurdles that have impeded the creation or efficacy of international governance regimes across various domains.

[305] Liu and Lin (n 287). Osonde A Osoba, 'Technocultural Pluralism: A "Clash of Civilizations" in Technology?' *Proceedings of the AAAI/ACM Conference on AI, Ethics, and Society* (ACM 2020) <http://dl.acm.org/doi/10.1145/3375627.3375834> accessed 12 February 2020.

[306] Claire Dennis and others, 'What Should Be Internationalised in AI Governance?' (Oxford Martin AI Governance Initiative 2024) 11 <https://www.oxfordmartin.ox.ac.uk/publications/what-should-be-internationalised-in-ai-governance> accessed 5 March 2025.

[307] ibid.

[308] Jacob Turner, *Robot Rules: Regulating Artificial Intelligence* (Springer Berlin Heidelberg 2018) 237–239.

[309] ibid 239–240.

[310] Claudio Feijóo and others, 'Harnessing Artificial Intelligence (AI) to Increase Wellbeing for All: The Case for a New Technology Diplomacy' (2020) 44 Telecommunications Policy 101988. See also the discussion of 'AI nationalism' (and new dynamics of core-periphery dependency relationships amongst states) in Ian Hogarth, 'AI Nationalism' (*Ian Hogarth*, 13 June 2018) <https://www.ianhogarth.com/blog/2018/6/13/ai-nationalism> accessed 23 July 2018.

regulation, nor through industry self-regulation,[311] but will in fact *require* some degree of collective action at a global level.[312] This is of course hardly unprecedented. From a historical angle, diverse other technological developments have led to global governance efforts in response, meeting with varying but generally good success. This includes regimes for high-stakes strategic technologies, such as the nuclear non-proliferation regime, outer space law, or internet governance.[313] That is not to say that all general-purpose technologies have received or been subject to such regulations. Nonetheless, historically new technological developments have been key direct and indirect drivers of many landmark developments within international law.[314]

As such, rather than treating the matter of global cooperation for AI as an either–or question, more productive questions would be: On what ground could global cooperation be founded? Given the technology's breadth and diversity, why or when would issues need global governance?

2.3.2 Securing AI Global Public Goods

Over the past decades, social scientists have developed diverse typologies of global public good problems, and explored their distinctive governance requirements. In one influential taxonomy, Scott Barrett distinguished between problem domains where success is dependent on, respectively, the *single best effort* (e.g. asteroid defence, peacekeeping, geo-engineering); the *weakest link* (e.g. disease eradication);

[311] Cf. Paul Nemitz, 'Constitutional Democracy and Technology in the Age of Artificial Intelligence' (2018) 376 Philosophical Transactions of the Royal Society A 20180089. See also Tom Slee, 'The Incompatible Incentives of Private Sector AI' in M Dubber and F Pasquale (eds), *The Oxford Handbook of AI Ethics* (Oxford University Press 2019). Eyal Benvenisti, 'Upholding Democracy Amid the Challenges of New Technology: What Role for the Law of Global Governance?' (2018) 29 European Journal of International Law 9.

[312] Askell, Brundage, and Hadfield (n 300). See also Turner (n 308) 237–239 (discussing the cross-boundary nature of AI challenges, the cost of regulatory uncertainty, and the need to avoid arbitrage). See also Dennis and others (n 306) (identifying key factors such as cross-border externalities, regulatory arbitrage, uneven governance capacity, and interoperability, as rationales for internationalizing AI governance; and on that basis arguing that arranging AI governance at the international level could be particularly useful in areas around data centre oversight, content provenance, model evaluations, incident monitoring, and risk management protocols); Emery-Xu, Jordan, and Trager (n 165).

[313] Daniel W Drezner, 'Technological Change and International Relations' (2019) 33 International Relations 286 (on the nuclear regime); Turner (n 308) 244–247 (on the 1967 UN Outer Space Treaty). See also Verity Harding, 'Lessons from History: What Can Past Technological Breakthroughs Teach the AI Community Today' (2020) <https://www.bennettinstitute.cam.ac.uk/blog/lessons-history-what-can-past-technological-breakt/> accessed 17 August 2020 (referencing the Outer Space Treaty, the UK's Warnock Committee and Human Embryology Act, the Internet Corporation for assigned Names and Numbers [ICANN], and the European ban on genetically modified crops).

[314] Picker (n 130); Rosemary Rayfuse, 'Public International Law and the Regulation of Emerging Technologies' in Roger Brownsword, Eloise Scotford, and Karen Yeung (eds), *The Oxford Handbook of Law, Regulation and Technology* (Oxford University Press 2017). Specifically on the technological impact on the laws of war, see Braden Allenby, 'Are New Technologies Undermining the Laws of War?' (2014) 70 Bulletin of the Atomic Scientists 21.

aggregate effort (e.g. climate change mitigation); *mutual restraint* (e.g. non-proliferation); or *coordination* (e.g. industry standards).[315] Each of these problem types has distinct dynamics, in terms of why international cooperation is needed, whether cost sharing is required, whether enforcement of an agreement is challenging, or what distinct types of international institutions or arrangements are involved in the provision of each good.[316]

As a result of these differences, not all collective action problems are created equal. Rather, they pose different problems for global governance. Focusing on three distinct categories of public goods, Anne van Aaken has argued that these pose different challenges for an international law system that is traditionally based on state consent.[317] In her view, governance challenges may not be particularly severe for 'single best effort' goods, as these problems are solved so long as one country has a strong enough incentive to invest in their mitigation.[318] By contrast, matters are more challenging in the context of 'weakest link' goods, where the good is provided if and only if every country contributes sufficiently, but is not provided if at least one state does not do so—either because it is unwilling (a hold-out state) or because it is incapable (e.g. failing or failed states). Van Aaken argues that several mechanisms in international law are known to overcome this problem, such as international organizations (which, for example, can provide for vaccination campaigns in the context of the weakest-link problem of pandemic eradication).[319] Finally, she argues that the most difficult governance challenge for international law may be found in securing 'aggregate efforts' public good, as these depend on

[315] Scott Barrett, *Why Cooperate? The Incentive to Supply Global Public Goods* (Oxford University Press 2007) 20.

[316] ibid 2–21.

[317] Anne van Aaken, 'Is International Law Conducive to Preventing Looming Disasters?' (2016) 7 Global Policy 81, 83.

[318] Of course, this also implies that *single best effort* goods can be very severe when no single actor *perceives* a strong enough incentive to invest, in advance of a certain disaster. This can occur under epistemic conditions where there is pervasive uncertainty around certain potential risks. For a discussion of this 'tragedy of the uncommons', see Jonathan B Wiener, 'The Tragedy of the Uncommons: On the Politics of Apocalypse' (2016) 7 Global Policy 67. And more broadly, see Milan M Cirkovic, Nick Bostrom, and Anders Sandberg, 'Anthropic Shadow: Observation Selection Effects and Human Extinction Risks' (2010) 30 Risk Analysis 1495; Eliezer Yudkowsky, 'Cognitive Biases Potentially Affecting Judgment of Global Risks' in Nick Bostrom and Milan Cirkovic (eds), *Global Catastrophic Risks* (Oxford University Press 2011) <https://intelligence.org/files/CognitiveBiases.pdf> accessed 5 March 2018. Finally, even in cases where a certain public good is achieved through a single best effort, there may still be operational and logistical concerns around adequately (or fairly) distributing the good globally, as in the role which institutions such as the World Health Organization (WHO) play in supporting the provision of vaccines to all countries.

[319] Aaken (n 317) 83. However, Sandler is more pessimistic, arguing that because weakest-link public goods are constrained by the smallest effort made, these goods can be particularly hard to secure in situations where countries possess highly varied financial capabilities, and where there are furthermore many countries, as this results in situations where parties realize someone ought to shore up the financial means of the poorer members but, being uncertain of one another's intentions, wait for others to act first. Todd Sandler, 'Strategic Aspects of Difficult Global Challenges' (2016) 7 Global Policy 33, 42.

the sum effort of states, and therefore are subject to free-riding and collective action concerns.[320]

To what extent, if at all, do the issues created or enabled by AI map onto various global public good problems? Certainly, as noted, some AI challenges may not at all create collective action problems (at least at an international level). However, some do. For instance, questions around constraining or gating the direct public release[321] or proliferation of some advanced ('frontier') AI capabilities[322] in order to prevent malicious or criminal actors from accessing and adopting them[323] could well be considered a *weakest link* problem, in the sense that if a single country provides a 'safe haven', these tools may proliferate rapidly.[324]

Likewise, questions over the non-development or non-deployment of particularly dangerous AI systems could be seen as constituting a *mutual restraint* public good. This could be the case for the global restriction of various different types of AI systems, whether our focus is on publicly harmful types of military AI (e.g. the integration of machine learning systems in or around nuclear command and control systems in ways that are highly destabilizing[325]), conventional AIs (e.g. the global sale of systems that enable invasive, remote biometric surveillance[326]), or frontier AI (e.g. systems beyond a particular compute or performance threshold[327]).

Moreover, questions pertaining to setting general standards in AI system reliability, explainability, training data privacy, robustness, or security could be seen as *coordination* goods, and may well come to constitute the most common global governance debates around AI, especially for many conventional and advanced AI governance debates.

[320] Aaken (n 317) 83.

[321] Solaiman and others (n 260); Toby Shevlane, 'Structured Access: An Emerging Paradigm for Safe AI Deployment' in Justin Bullock and others (eds), *The Oxford Handbook of AI Governance* (Oxford University Press 2022); Toby Shevlane, 'The Artefacts of Intelligence: Governing Scientists' Contribution to AI Proliferation' (University of Oxford 2022) <https://www.governance.ai/research-paper/the-artefacts-of-intelligence-governing-scientists-contribution-to-ai-proliferation> accessed 5 March 2025.

[322] Seger and others (n 13).

[323] Brundage and others (n 56); Hayward and Maas (n 56).

[324] However, on the other hand, this case is also dissimilar to traditional weakest-link goods, because top AI development capabilities are still somewhat unequally distributed around the world, and would be much more sensitively affected by lax standards in these states, than by the same standards in lagging countries. However, this situation is likely to change over time.

[325] Maas, Lucero-Matteucci, and Cooke (n 99); Johnson, 'Delegating Strategic Decision-Making to Machines' (n 95).

[326] Steven Feldstein, 'The Global Struggle over AI Surveillance' in Beth Kerley (ed), Steven Feldstein, Eduardo Ferreyra, and Danilo Krivokapic, *The Global Struggle over AI Surveillance: Emerging Trends and Democratic Responses* (National Endowment for Democracy 2022) <https://www.ned.org/global-struggle-over-ai-surveillance-emerging-trends-democratic-responses/> accessed 5 March 2025.

[327] Andrea Miotti and Akash Wasil, 'An International Treaty to Implement a Global Compute Cap for Advanced Artificial Intelligence' (30 October 2023) <https://papers.ssrn.com/abstract=4617094> accessed 3 November 2023; Anthony Aguirre, 'Close the Gates to an Inhuman Future: How and Why We Should Choose to Not Develop Superhuman General-Purpose Artificial Intelligence' (20 October 2023) <https://papers.ssrn.com/abstract=4608505> accessed 24 October 2023.

Interestingly, the relative scalability of narrow conventional AI systems and the adaptability of advanced foundation models once trained have interesting implications for the final two categories of global public goods. On the one hand, such systems, once available, could be shared relatively easily (i.e. with perhaps only minor fine-tuning) and at low marginal costs to many parties. That means that many AI systems could lend themselves relatively naturally to *single best effort* problems, focused on harnessing particular leading AI systems to secure certain global benefits or achieving certain goals, such as in modelling climate change.[328] At the same time, the degree of resource concentration that is necessary for the development of advanced AI systems also suggests that only few challenges in AI governance may be understood as *aggregate effort* public goods.

As such, for AI, the key global public goods may centre on issue areas that involve coordination, mutual restraint, or weakest link problems. While some AI issues may be governed adequately at the national level, there are many that require global cooperation of some form. Global governance and international law have become increasingly concerned with securing such global public goods. It is therefore to be expected that there will continue to be a strong pull towards achieving at least some form of global cooperation for key issue clusters in AI governance.

2.4 Feasibility: In Spite of Barriers, Governance Enforcement Is Possible

All this does not mean, however, that such governance is a straightforward task. Even if one agrees that AI governance at a global level is needed, is it also possible? Could it be enforced? To be sure, the precise efficacy and enforceability of governance regimes will depend sensitively on various key variables—technological and political dimensions of the future of AI technology—that determine what scenarios of development and deployment governance actors will face.[329] There are certainly challenges, but also potential levers and opportunities.

[328] David Rolnick and others, 'Tackling Climate Change with Machine Learning' [2019] arXiv:1906.05433 [cs, stat] <http://arxiv.org/abs/1906.05433> accessed 23 July 2019; see also High-Level Advisory Body on Artificial Intelligence, 'Interim Report: Governing AI for Humanity' (United Nations 2023) 3–4 <https://www.un.org/sites/un2.un.org/files/ai_advisory_body_interim_report.pdf> accessed 5 March 2025 (reviewing use cases of AI in mitigating climate change).

[329] For accounts of some of these scenarios and their component dimensions, see also Shin-Shin Hua and Haydn Belfield, 'Effective Enforceability of EU Competition Law Under AI Development Scenarios: A Framework for Anticipatory Governance', *Proceedings of the 2023 AAAI/ACM Conference on AI, Ethics, and Society* (Association for Computing Machinery 2023) <https://dl.acm.org/doi/10.1145/3600211.3604694> accessed 30 August 2023; Kyle A Kilian, Christopher J Ventura and Mark M Bailey, 'Examining the Differential Risk from High-Level Artificial Intelligence and the Question of Control' (2023) 151 Futures 103182.

2.4.1 Barriers and Challenges

Among legal scholars writing on AI, there is disagreement between those arguing that existing regulation or existing legal principles are more than adequate to deal with AI,[330] and those who suggest that these may not be sufficient and new initiatives are needed, either to address genuinely new issues or to clarify legal concepts and doctrines.[331]

Yet even this latter group often notes that AI technology has a range of features that render it an unusually challenging object for governance and regulation. For example, one wide-ranging review has argued that effective AI governance for advanced (LLM-based) AI systems is still lacking, because of both 'meta-challenges'—relating to 'a lack of requisite scientific understanding of LLMs, lack of effective fast-moving governance institutions, lack of culpability schemes, and corporate power'—and 'practical challenges', relating to the fact that 'most governance mechanisms are underdeveloped and concrete proposals for governance are lacking'.[332] Let us focus on the meta-challenges that (are held to) structurally inhibit AI governance: what might be some barriers to achieving effective regulation for AI?[333]

In the first place, as many have repeatedly noted, many efforts for regulating AI are frequently derailed by definitional difficulties over what AI actually is.[334] These are exacerbated by the range of terms in currency, their often inconsistent usage and varied definitions,[335] and the broader range of frames, metaphors, or analogies that are invoked (implicitly or explicitly) in debates around the regulation of AI.[336]

In addition to this, AI research and development processes include many features which might inhibit effective regulation even at the national level, let alone the international one. For instance, the development of many narrow, conventional AI systems is still characterized by a development ecosystem that, as Scherer has previously argued, is discreet, discrete, diffuse, and opaque.[337] That is, it is *discreet*

[330] Chris Reed, 'How Should We Regulate Artificial Intelligence?' (2018) 376 Philosophical Transactions. Series A, Mathematical, Physical, and Engineering Sciences 20170360; Carlos Ignacio Gutierrez Gaviria, 'The Role of Artificial Intelligence in Pushing the Boundaries of U.S. Regulation: A Systematic Review' (2022) 38 Santa Clara High Technology Law Journal 123.

[331] Ryan Calo, 'Robotics and the Lessons of Cyberlaw' (2015) 103 California Law Review 513; Turner (n 308) ch 2. Note, a further discussion of conditions and pathways for such technology-driven 'governance development' is the foundation of Chapter 5.

[332] Anwar and others (n 163) 92.

[333] See also Emery-Xu, Jordan, and Trager (n 165) (reviewing eight potential barriers).

[334] Scherer (n 301) 361–362. See also Edward Parson and others, 'Artificial Intelligence in Strategic Context: An Introduction' (*AI Pulse*, 8 February 2019) <https://aipulse.org/artificial-intelligence-in-strategic-context-an-introduction/> accessed 26 February 2019; Jonas Schuett, 'Defining the Scope of AI Regulations' (2023) 15 Law, Innovation and Technology 1.

[335] Maas, 'Concepts in Advanced AI Governance' (n 2).

[336] Maas, 'AI Is Like . . .' (n 288).

[337] Scherer (n 301) 369.

because—at least for many conventional AI systems, in contrast to advanced AI—relatively little concentrated physical infrastructure is required, and AI projects may be developed without the mass institutional frameworks that were necessary for building industrial capacity in the previous century.[338] In other domains, many types of AI challenges are *discrete* because separate components of the final system may be designed without top-down coordination or deliberate control, in a decentralized manner, with the full potential or risks of a system not becoming apparent until they are brought together in a new application. This may be the case in situations where narrow, conventional systems are integrated or used together in unexpected ways.

However, while advanced and highly capable foundation models in principle require far more significant upfront training costs, these systems too can see unexpected post-release capability expansions, as other actors identify new ways to prompt the system or to integrate it with other tools.[339] In a similar way, AI development can be relatively *diffuse*, as software development can be geographically and organizationally dispersed, and involve diverse actors in diverse jurisdictions, enabled by open-source software and widely available tools.[340] As such, with AI as with software technology in general, we often face a 'many hands' problem, which creates challenges around assigning responsibility (or liability) among many actors.[341] Finally, AI development is *opaque*, as the technologies are not always well understood by regulators, and outsiders or inspectors cannot reliably detect harmful features in an AI system under development.[342]

These factors make AI hard to govern at an early stage, but also hard to govern reactively, later. In this, they can be well-described by the 'Collingridge Dilemma',[343]

[338] Although crucially, many of these traits do not transfer well to describing the value chain for advanced, general-purpose AI, which is more concentrated and capital-intensive. See Küspert, Moës, and Dunlop (n 269). However, even here, an ecosystem of model marketplaces can facilitate the easy (and irreversible) dissemination of models, once trained, to many actors. Gorwa and Veale (n 272).

[339] Tom Davidson and others, 'AI Capabilities Can Be Significantly Improved without Expensive Retraining' (*Epoch*, 12 December 2023) <https://epochai.org/blog/ai-capabilities-can-be-significantly-improved-without-expensive-retraining> accessed 6 January 2024.

[340] Scherer (n 301) 370–371.

[341] See generally Merel Noorman, 'Computing and Moral Responsibility' in Edward N Zalta (ed), *The Stanford Encyclopedia of Philosophy* (Spring 2020, Metaphysics Research Lab, Stanford University 2018) <https://plato.stanford.edu/archives/spr2020/entries/computing-responsibility/> accessed 5 September 2020.

[342] Scherer (n 301) 357. This is exacerbated by the so-called Volkswagen problem, which refers to a 2015 scandal where the car company was found to have embedded 'defeat device' algorithms in their cars' engine computers, which detected when the car was being tested for emissions and accordingly altered the engine's operation to comply with environmental standards. Russell Hotten, 'Volkswagen: The Scandal Explained' *BBC News* (10 December 2015) <https://www.bbc.com/news/business-34324772> accessed 4 September 2020.

[343] David Collingridge, *The Social Control of Technology* (Palgrave Macmillan 1981). For a brief discussion of the Collingridge Dilemma in the context of AI, see also Michael Guihot, Anne F Matthew, and Nicolas Suzor, 'Nudging Robots: Innovative Solutions to Regulate Artificial Intelligence' [2017]

a well-known dictum in technology governance by David Collingridge which states that '[w]hen change is easy, the need for it cannot be foreseen; when the need for change is apparent, change has become expensive, difficult, and time-consuming.'[344] This reflects a general regulatory problem that is said to arise in the context of new technologies. Early on in a technology's development cycle, we face an *information problem*, because the technology's critical features, salient uses, and unanticipated impacts cannot be predicted (or agreed upon) until it has had time to be more extensively developed and used. Yet at that later stage, we face a *power problem*: implementing controls or governance solutions is more difficult now, because the technology has already become embedded in society. As a result, investments have been made in the technology; infrastructure has been rolled out; established interests have become clear and entrenched; or early governance approaches have locked in specific legal metaphors—and therefore solution portfolios—over others.

This poses a challenge for global AI governance, because institutions can be path-dependent and how we structure international cooperation today can prove critical in the long run, especially as the technology advances and strategic stakes scale up.[345] Indeed, Morin and others have argued that AI is one of a set of emerging complex problems which 'concern the unknown; [...] are often unprecedented, span multiple issue areas in their scope or in their consequences, and can be disruptive.'[346]

Finally, as argued by Huw Roberts and others, global governance initiatives for AI are likely to run into various cooperation problems at different levels. They distinguish between first-order cooperation problems among states within the international anarchic system and second-order cooperation problems relating to challenges around international institutional inertia and dysfunction, and suggest that both issues may hamper international cooperation on AI governance, as interstate contestation or intra-institutional dysfunction may undermine both the feasibility of new regimes and their effectiveness.[347]

Vanderbilt Journal of Entertainment & Technology Law 421–422 <https://papers.ssrn.com/abstract=3017004> accessed 2 July 2018.

[344] Collingridge (n 343) 11 (calling this the 'dilemma of control').

[345] See Jean-Frédéric Morin and others, 'How Informality Can Address Emerging Issues: Making the Most of the G7' (2019) 10 Global Policy 267, 2. See also Peter Cihon, Matthijs M Maas, and Luke Kemp, 'Should Artificial Intelligence Governance Be Centralised? Design Lessons from History', *Proceedings of the AAAI/ACM Conference on AI, Ethics, and Society* (ACM 2020) 232 <http://dl.acm.org/doi/10.1145/3375627.3375857> accessed 12 February 2020.

[346] Morin and others (n 345) 4.

[347] Huw Roberts and others, 'Global AI Governance: Barriers and Pathways Forward' 6–8 <https://papers.ssrn.com/abstract=4588040> accessed 4 October 2023.

2.4.2 Strategies and Levers

Given all of this, we might worry that existing international institutions and governance regimes may not be well configured to deal with AI's global challenges—of any type. Are there any strategies or levers that could be used?[348]

Fortunately, there has been a growing body of work that explores different types of strategies, tools, levers, or interventions that can be used to govern AI at different stages of development and at different control points, such as downstream usage, upstream model development, or even the underlying and enabling digital infrastructures.[349] Some of this work has focused on governance levers and tools that could be taken up by AI labs themselves.[350] However, this assumes that such labs are either willing to take all actions themselves—a reliance on self-governance—or that they have been effectively regulated by states. Other work has focused on the policy levers that would be available to particular governments.[351]

However, our question here is whether—at what control points—we might feasibly regulate AI technologies at the global level.[352] Indeed, the claim has sometimes been made that digital technologies are uniquely challenging to regulation by states, whether individually or collectively.[353] Such arguments are not new but indeed echo claims made during the early days of the internet, suggesting that the decentralized nature of cyberspace left it fundamentally beyond the scope of national jurisdictions.[354]

[348] In this context, we can define a 'Lever (of governance)' broadly as 'a tool or intervention that can be used by key actors (labs, states, international institutions) to shape or affect (1) the primary outcomes of advanced AI development; (2) the key parameters of advanced AI governance (such as norms, distribution of resources); (3) other key actors' choices or decisions.' See Maas, 'Advanced AI Governance' (n 186) 102.

[349] See James N Baker, 'International Law and Advanced AI: Exploring the Levers for "Hard" Control' (*Institute for Law & AI*, 20 July 2024) <https://law-ai.org/international-law-and-advanced-ai/> accessed 23 July 2024 (considering three main 'control points' where binding international controls on AI might take hold).

[350] See Peter Cihon, Jonas Schuett, and Seth D Baum, 'Corporate Governance of Artificial Intelligence in the Public Interest' (2021) 12 Information 275; Jonas Schuett and others, 'Towards Best Practices in AGI Safety and Governance: A Survey of Expert Opinion' (arXiv, 11 May 2023) <http://arxiv.org/abs/2305.07153> accessed 15 May 2023.

[351] Sophie-Charlotte Fischer and others, 'AI Policy Levers: A Review of the U.S. Government's Tools to Shape AI Research, Development, and Deployment' (Centre for the Governance of AI, Future of Humanity Institute, University of Oxford 2021) #2021-10 <https://www.fhi.ox.ac.uk/wp-content/uploads/2021/03/AI-Policy-Levers-A-Review-of-the-U.S.-Governments-tools-to-shape-AI-research-development-and-deployment-%E2%80%93-Fischer-et-al.pdf> accessed 26 March 2021; Maas, 'Advanced AI Governance' (n 186) 102–121.

[352] A separate discussion and review of the suitability of different levers of global governance will be provided in Chapter 3.

[353] Klaus Schwab, *The Fourth Industrial Revolution* (Currency 2017).

[354] John Perry Barlow, 'A Declaration of the Independence of Cyberspace' (*Electronic Frontier Foundation*, 8 February 1996) <https://www.eff.org/cyberspace-independence> accessed 20 August 2020. In 1993, John Perry Barlow famously told Time magazine that '[t]he Net interprets censorship as damage and routes around it'. As quoted in Drezner (n 313) 294.

Yet in the decades since, such claims have not held up robustly. Domestically, the internet has proven not just a site for national governmental regulation and restrictions, but even a tool for regulating behaviour.[355] More pessimistically, while some authoritarian states were initially taken aback by the potential of the internet to facilitate mass protest movements, they have ultimately proven quite versatile in controlling internet access,[356] and in harnessing digital tools for both domestic social control and foreign interference. Conversely, the internet has also become subject to an extensive model of global multi-stakeholder governance,[357] which, while it still has notable gaps, is also seen as broadly successful.[358] That is not to suggest that technology governance in these areas has been easy. However, it does imply that the prospects for reaching and enforcing global regulations on digital technologies may be more nuanced than is often assumed.

2.4.2.1 Four types of regulatory objects

A key point here may be that, as suggested by Guillaume Beaumier and others, the modern global digital economy is constituted of quite different regulatory objects, some of which pose considerable challenges, but others of which can certainly be subject to extraterritorial or international regulation.[359] These authors argue that the ease with which a certain digital technology can be subjected to global regulation depends on two factors: the artefact's apparent *materiality* along with the degree of (market) *centralization*—often a function of either high capital requirements or network effects, or both. This leads to four ideal-types of digital technologies: Type-1 technologies are those that are clearly material and centralized (e.g. submarine cables; satellites & their launch facilities); Type-2 technologies are those that are clearly material but decentralized (e.g. smart speakers and other internet-of-things-enabled products); Type-3 technologies are those that are seemingly immaterial but centralized (e.g. search engines or social media platforms reliant on network effects); finally, Type-4 technologies are those that are seemingly immaterial and decentralized (e.g. the Bitcoin protocol).[360]

[355] Lawrence Lessig, *Code: And Other Laws of Cyberspace, Version 2.0* (2nd Revised ed. edition, Basic Books 2006) <http://codev2.cc/download+remix/Lessig-Codev2.pdf>.

[356] Steven Feldstein, 'Government Internet Shutdowns Are Changing. How Should Citizens and Democracies Respond?' (Carnegie Endowment for International Peace 2022) <https://carnegieendowment.org/2022/03/31/government-internet-shutdowns-are-changing.-how-should-citizens-and-democracies-respond-pub-86687> accessed 10 January 2024.

[357] Joseph S Nye, 'The Regime Complex for Managing Global Cyber Activities' (Global Commission on Internet Governance 2014) 1 <https://dash.harvard.edu/bitstream/handle/1/12308565/Nye-GlobalCommission.pdf> accessed 3 September 2019.

[358] Drezner (n 313) 299.

[359] Guillaume Beaumier and others, 'Global Regulations for a Digital Economy: Between New and Old Challenges' (2020) 11 Global Policy 515.

[360] ibid 3–6.

Table 2.3 Features and avenues to regulation for different digital technologies (drawing on Beaumier et al. 2020)

Technology type	Features	Examples	Regulatory opportunities	Regulatory challenges
Type-1	Clearly material & centralized	Submarine cables, satellite launch facilities, telecom infrastructure, data centres	• Clear physical presence in jurisdictions; limited ability for regulatory flight • Centralization entails easily identifiable intermediaries to regulate	• Important sources of structural power for states, resulting in contestation
Type-2	Clearly material & decentralized	Various 'Internet of Things' objects, drones	• Many intermediaries, located within jurisdictions	• Contestation over standards at international standard-setting organizations; risks of regulatory fragmentation
Type-3	Seemingly immaterial & centralized	Search engines, social media, and other platforms	• Centralization means that key targets for regulation are identifiable • Possibility to regulate local proxies; as well as extraterritorial regulation	• Lack of clear physical presence within jurisdictions limits efficacy or unilateral regulation • Extraterritorial regulations may lead to inter-state disputes
Type-4	Seemingly immaterial & decentralized	Blockchain technologies; open-source software	• Potential to work with private intermediaries to e.g. enforce identification requirements	• Many potential actors, few clear intermediaries to regulate

As they point out, these technologies have different regulatory features. They are not all easy to regulate—and such regulation often faces distinct challenges for each type. However, all of them can be—and frequently are—regulated or controlled through a mix of strategies and approaches (see Table 2.3).[361]

[361] ibid.

This provides an accessible and overarching framework to understand the features of different types of digital technologies, and their respective avenues to regulation.[362] For instance, Type-1 technologies constitute costly, capital-intensive material infrastructures: these have clear physical presence in jurisdictions, with capital and assets that are not easily moved abroad, limiting regulatory flight. Their centralization also entails that it can be easy to identify which intermediaries to regulate or engage with.[363] However, since these technologies often serve as important sources of power for states, this creates incentives for contestation—or even for direct targeting and interference of the infrastructures during times of conflict, as seen especially acutely in the vulnerability of the international network of submarine cables to malicious actors.[364] Even in peacetime, there are regulatory incentives to impose market access restrictions and support the development of national champions—as seen for instance with US–China contestation over the roll-out of the 5G telecommunications network, as well as debates over data localization laws.[365]

Type-2 technologies constitute digitally enabled physical objects (such as smartphones or internet-of-things products) which derive most of their value and utility from their connectivity to Type-1 infrastructures.[366] Accordingly, there exist many producers of these products, which can serve as clear targets for public regulation, whether focused on safety or standards. However, while there are in principle shared benefits to be gained from clarifying standards that ensure interoperability, such standards can also become subject to contestation—since early movers on these technologies benefit significantly from shaping the international standard-setting processes,[367] as seen for example through China's active efforts at the International Telecommunications Union (ITU) and the International Organization for Standardization (ISO).[368]

Type-3 technologies include many high-profile digital services, including search engines, social media, and other platforms. These technologies often gain from their network effects, and are often developed and offered by a core group of major tech companies. This means that it is relatively easy for states and regulators to identify which actors they want to regulate. However, the 'immaterial' nature

[362] Based on: ibid 4. Note, this framework anticipates the discussion, in Chapter 4, of the 'material' features of different regulatory targets in and around AI.
[363] ibid.
[364] See Kevin Frazier, 'Policy Proposals for the United States to Protect the Undersea Cable System' (2021) 13 Journal of Law, Technology, & the Internet <https://scholarlycommons.law.case.edu/jolti/vol13/iss1/1> accessed 5 March 2025; Abra Ganz and others, 'Submarine Cables and the Risks to Digital Sovereignty' (12 January 2024) <https://papers.ssrn.com/abstract=4693206> accessed 24 June 2024.
[365] Beaumier and others (n 359) 4.
[366] ibid.
[367] ibid.
[368] Marta Cantero Gamito, 'The Influence of China in AI Governance through Standardisation' (2023) 47 Telecommunications Policy 102673.

of these technologies means that they are not often clearly located on specific territories.[369] This can pose a problem for effective regulation. In response, this has led to situations where states have attempted to regulate local proxies (such as requiring local internet service providers to block access to websites that violate hate speech), or where they attempt to develop national or regional regulations with extraterritorial reach, as seen in the so-called Brussels effect of the GDPR.[370] However, this has often led to interstate disputes—creating a set of issues that might need global rules to be adequately addressed.[371]

Finally, Type-4 technologies, such as classically many blockchain technologies or open-source software, fit the traditional stereotype of the ethereal digital technologies that are hard for (global) regulators to capture. Regulation is difficult because for regulators it is often unclear which actors or intermediaries to regulate. However, even here, there are at least some steps that states can take, as seen by the fact that many private cryptocurrency-to-state-backed-currency exchanges today increasingly enforce identification requirements.[372]

As such, this model suggests that, far from categorically beyond regulation, many so-called digital technologies are nonetheless either sufficiently material (e.g. satellites), or sufficiently centralized (e.g. large search engines), or both, that global regulation is possible at least in principle, even if getting there may still be complicated in a tense geopolitical environment.[373]

2.4.2.2 Different AI artefacts considered as regulatory objects

Given this framework, what type of digital technology is AI? Rather than provide a singular answer, we can identify a range of AI artefacts—including AI systems as well as their underlying production and operation technologies—which fit the criteria of all four technology types (see Table 2.4).

By mapping AI-stack technologies to the analytical framework presented by Beaumier and colleagues, we can consequently gain insights into different avenues for regulatory leverage, through specific policy interventions that are tailored to the technology type.[374] Such an analysis shows that there are certainly a number of AI services or tools that qualify as Type-4 (immaterial and decentralized) technologies, making their effective global regulation difficult. However, many other AI applications, such as in social robots, autonomous drones, or surveillance

[369] Beaumier and others (n 359) 5.

[370] ibid. On this 'Brussels effect', see generally Anu Bradford, *The Brussels Effect: How the European Union Rules the World* (Oxford University Press 2020). For an application to AI, see Charlotte Siegmann and Markus Anderljung, 'The Brussels Effect and Artificial Intelligence: How EU Regulation Will Impact the Global AI Market' (Centre for the Governance of AI 2022) <https://www.governance.ai/research-paper/brussels-effect-ai> accessed 5 March 2025.

[371] Beaumier and others (n 359).

[372] ibid 6.

[373] ibid.

[374] ibid 4.

Table 2.4 AI-stack technologies considered as different types of regulatory object (drawing on Beaumier et al. 2020)

	Centralized	*Decentralized*
Clearly material	**Type-1** Advanced AI systems' production base - AI chips (e.g. Nvidia A100, H100 & B200 series GPU chips & beyond), and the underlying compute hardware supply chain (semiconductors, EUV lithography); large data centres	**Type-2** Many Conventional and/or Military AI systems - Drones; autonomous weapons systems; social robots; facial recognition cameras; smaller inference-at-deployment data centres, etc.
Seemingly immaterial	**Type-3** Advanced AI systems at the frontier - Major centralized LLM chatbots (e.g. GPT, Claude, Gemini model families)	**Type-4** Some advanced AI systems - Open-sourced LLM systems (e.g. LlaMa model family; DeepSeek R1)

cameras with built-in ('edge computing') facial recognition capabilities, might be considered a Type-2 (material but decentralized) technology.

Furthermore, there are various elements of the global AI development pipeline that are highly material and centralized (Type-1). While it is true that many traditional forms of (conventional) AI software development have been diffuse,[375] the computing hardware supply chain, and the resulting specialized AI chips that are so critical to the training of large-scale AI foundation models, are tremendously globally concentrated, offering potential leverage for governance.[376]

Simultaneously, high-end data centres and cloud compute providers which provide AI-as-a-service solutions (such as running inference) may be positioned at an intermediate point on this spectrum between Type-1 and Type-2: they are more concentrated than the software or human talent layers, but more distributed than

[375] Scherer (n 301) 370–371.

[376] For a comprehensive discussion of compute governance, see Sastry and others (n 271). For related discussions of issues such as compute thresholds, or the role of antitrust law in leveraging compute governance, see also Matteo Pistillo and others, 'The Role of Compute Thresholds for AI Governance' (2025) 1 George Washington Journal of Law & Technology <https://gwjolt.org/files/volume_1/GW%20JOLT%201_1%20Winter.pdf> accessed 5 March 2025; Lennart Heim and Leonie Koessler, 'Training Compute Thresholds: Features and Functions in AI Regulation' (arXiv, 6 August 2024) <http://arxiv.org/abs/2405.10799> accessed 9 August 2024; Haydn Belfield and Shin-Shin Hua, 'Compute and Antitrust: Regulatory Implications of the AI Hardware Supply Chain, from Chip Design to Cloud APIs' (*Verfassungsblog*, 19 August 2022) <https://verfassungsblog.de/compute-and-antitrust/ > accessed 22 August 2022.

computer chip production (or the monolithic data centres used for training frontier AI systems), in part because proximity to customers is a salient consideration for them. This may be especially true if the coming years see not just a scaling up of the amount of computing power dedicated to the training of advanced AI systems at the 'frontier' but also a significant scaling up of inference-at-deployment computing power, used to enable already trained (and potentially open-weight) AI models to reason for longer on questions posed to them by clients.[377]

This means that a wide range of substrate technologies that constitute the production resources[378] for advanced AI development and deployment—such as semiconductor supply chains,[379] chip foundries, high-performance AI chips (e.g. Nvidia's A100 or Blackwell B200 GPU chips[380]), and major training-focused data centres[381] as well as many cloud compute providers[382]—can all be considered Type-1 (material and centralized) technologies, which are practically susceptible to effective global regulation and control either through coalitions of states, or through full multilateral governance arrangements.[383] Conversely, many high-end applications of advanced AI systems (such as Claude or Gemini) or of conventional AI systems (such as YouTube recommender algorithms or social media content moderation systems) will likely constitute Type-3 (immaterial but centralized) technologies. Such applications are at least somewhat constrained by

[377] See also: Toby Ord, 'Inference Scaling Reshapes AI Governance' (arXiv, 12 February 2025) <http://arxiv.org/abs/2503.05705> accessed 19 March 2025.

[378] See also Cohen and others (n 25) 37 (defining these 'production resources' for Long-Term Planning Agents as 'Information that makes it low-cost to produce a dangerously capable LTPA').

[379] Saif M Khan, 'Securing Semiconductor Supply Chains' (Center for Security and Emerging Technology 2021) <https://cset.georgetown.edu/publication/securing-semiconductor-supply-chains/> accessed 7 September 2021.

[380] See Kristin Uchiyama, 'NVIDIA Blackwell Platform Arrives to Power a New Era of Computing' (*NVIDIA*, 18 March 2024) <http://nvidianews.nvidia.com/news/nvidia-blackwell-platform-arrives-to-power-a-new-era-of-computing> accessed 19 February 2025; Kif Leswing, 'Meet the $10,000 Nvidia Chip Powering the Race for A.I.' (*CNBC*, 23 February 2023) <https://www.cnbc.com/2023/02/23/nvidias-a100-is-the-10000-chip-powering-the-race-for-ai-.html> accessed 10 January 2024.

[381] Konstantin Pilz and Lennart Heim, 'Compute at Scale: A Broad Investigation into the Data Center Industry' (arXiv, 22 November 2023) <http://arxiv.org/abs/2311.02651> accessed 29 November 2023.

[382] Lennart Heim and others, 'Governing Through the Cloud: The Intermediary Role of Compute Providers in AI Regulation' (Oxford Martin AI Governance Initiative 2024) <https://cdn.governance.ai/Governing-Through-the-Cloud_The-Intermediary-Role-of-Compute-Providers-in-AI-Regulation.pdf> accessed 5 March 2025 (arguing that cloud compute providers can accordingly play a key role in an AI regulatory ecosystem, in four capacities, as (1) securers of AI systems and critical infrastructure; (2) record keepers that enhance visibility for policymakers; (3) verifiers of customer activities, and as (4) enforcers of rules against rule violations). For a general discussion of the technical features and legal and policy implications of modern cloud computing, see Cameron Koob, 'Cloud Computing' (2022) 6 Georgetown Law Technology Review 363. For a previous discussion of cloud computing from a human rights perspective, see Vivek Krishnamurthy, 'With Great (Computing) Power Comes Great (Human Rights) Responsibility: Cloud Computing and Human Rights' (2022) 7 Business and Human Rights Journal 226.

[383] For instance, see also the proposal to significantly enhance the current Wassenaar Arrangement into a 'Wassenaar Treaty' that regulates the exports of critical semiconductor technology. André Brunel, 'A Proposal for a Semiconductor Export Control Treaty' (2023) 19 Journal of Business & Technology Law <https://digitalcommons.law.umaryland.edu/jbtl/vol19/iss1/2> accessed 5 March 2025.

hardware and capital requirements around at-scale inference costs, or are particularly dependent on network effects for their utility.

Significantly, given the high resource demands of training highly capable foundation models at the current frontier, many advanced AI systems might be considered a technology that closely ties together both Type-1 (compute resources) and Type-3 (pre-trained model) technologies, in a manner that is highly centralized and therefore more supportive of effective, targeted regulation. For instance, one 2023 analysis suggests that just three companies—Google, OpenAI, and Meta—are responsible for the largest training runs in frontier AI, have developed a large fraction of the underlying algorithmic innovations that underpin LLMs, and lead in many metrics of scientific citation impact.[384]

Accordingly, many different parts of the AI stack and production chain may be well captured through a range of policies. Governance can focus on regulating the core inputs of AI development, such as measures to affect the design of the chips themselves—for instance, in order to ensure 'on-chip' verification mechanisms[385]—or rather focus on chokepoints in the global semiconductor supply chain,[386] or at the upstream stage of lab compute procurement. It can focus on the data collection stage, the AI model training stage, the model diffusion stage, the provision stage (e.g. through cloud computing services offering AI-as-a-service models), or the end-user application stage.[387]

At the same time, of course, the relative efficacy of these regulatory levers may depend sensitively on ongoing trends in the relative importance of algorithms, data, and computing hardware to AI development and deployment.[388] For instance, the past few years have seen developments in federated learning, an approach that enables distributed pre-training of large language models across large-scale collaborations with many computational resources, bypassing the need for the data-centre-focused approach to training such models.[389] Other factors which could affect the efficacy of these regulatory levers, might themselves be regulatory or political: in the form of domestic or international developments in domains such as

[384] Ben Cottier, Tamay Besiroglu, and David Owen, 'Who Is Leading in AI? An Analysis of Industry AI Research' (Epoch 2023) <https://epochai.org/blog/who-is-leading-in-ai-an-analysis-of-industry-ai-research> accessed 30 November 2023.

[385] Onni Aarne, Tim Fist, and Caleb Withers, 'Secure, Governable Chips: Using On-Chip Mechanisms to Manage National Security Risks from AI & Advanced Computing' (Center for a New American Security 2024) <https://www.cnas.org/publications/reports/secure-governable-chips> accessed 5 March 2025; Shavit (n 43).

[386] Carrick Flynn and Saif M Khan, 'Multilateral Controls on Hardware Chokepoints' (*Center for Security and Emerging Technology*, September 2020) <https://cset.georgetown.edu/publication/multilateral-controls-on-hardware-chokepoints/> accessed 8 February 2023.

[387] Belfield and Hua (n 376); Cobbe, Veale, and Singh (n 272).

[388] See also Aaron D Tucker, Markus Anderljung, and Allan Dafoe, 'Social and Governance Implications of Improved Data Efficiency', *Proceedings of the AAAI/ACM Conference on AI, Ethics, and Society* (ACM 2020) <http://arxiv.org/abs/2001.05068> accessed 18 August 2020.

[389] Lorenzo Sani and others, 'The Future of Large Language Model Pre-Training Is Federated' (arXiv, 19 July 2024) <http://arxiv.org/abs/2405.10853> accessed 29 July 2024.

privacy regulation, or corporate advocacy against intrusive chip or model monitoring measures.[390] In addition, the effective enforceability of various regimes may be affected by other features of the AI industrial landscape.[391]

All this tentatively suggests that, *once negotiated and established*, global governance regimes for AI could be *enforceable and effective* in at least some ways. However, that says little about the path towards achieving global agreement and establishing such regimes in the first place. As the last few years have shown, this does not mean that global regulation of these systems will come easy. Given such challenges, and the incipient stage of governance, there is understandably a growing body of work exploring how to best develop AI governance, where to ground it, and where it could or should go next.

2.5 Conclusion: The World Needs Global Governance for AI

This chapter has framed the first half of our discussion of the global governance for AI. It has briefly reviewed existing surveys and taxonomies of the types of societal problems AI systems can create. It then reviewed different types of global AI governance problems, distinguishing between the governance of conventional, military, and advanced AI systems as focus areas for global governance which, while they have touchpoints and overlaps, are also importantly distinct in both technical and political ways. The chapter then reviewed some rationales for governing this technology at the global level, specifically drawing on different accounts of global public goods. Finally, it discussed whether—or why—global governance for AI might be difficult but feasible. It reviewed a range of barriers and challenges, but also argued that there are a range of ways by which various parts of the AI supply chain (or the AI stack) might be globally regulated.

In sum, AI is a diverse portfolio of technologies. Many of its impacts may be regulated domestically, but there are a range of risk clusters—around conventional AI systems, military AI systems, and advanced AI systems at the frontier—which may either gain from or necessitate forms of global cooperation. Given this, what is the state of the AI governance landscape for these issues? Is it up to this task? We turn to these questions next.

[390] Diane Bernabei, James Baker, and Cosimo L Fabrizio, 'Legal Challenges to Compute Governance' (*Lawfare*, 16 May 2024) <https://www.lawfaremedia.org/article/legal-challenges-to-compute-governance> accessed 4 June 2024.

[391] For instance, see Hua and Belfield (n 329) 597–598 (focusing specifically on the 'effective enforceability' of EU competition law—operationalized in terms of the regime's jurisdictional scope, potential loopholes, effectiveness of detection, and ability to remedy/sanction breaches—and how it might be affected by different AI development scenarios, focusing especially on the five variables of key AI inputs, speed of development, AI system capabilities, number of actors, and the nature/relationship of actors).

3
The Global AI Governance Architecture: Past and Futures

3.1 Introduction

In Chapter 2 I have discussed the spectrum of global societal challenges posed by AI systems, and I argued that many of these will require forms of global coordination and action. States or empowered international regimes, I suggested, might well be in a position to exert global control over many forms of, basic inputs to, and downstream uses of AI technology, provided that there is sufficient political will to negotiate, establish, and enforce some set of international rules or norms.

The relevant next question, then, is whether the world is currently on track to establish such global agreements or institutions for AI. What have been the developments in global governance for AI so far, and can we expect these to adequately address the challenges we face?

In this chapter, I will review the recent history of different tracks in the global AI governance architecture (2009–2025), and their potential future pathways. It traces three tracks, focused on governing military AI systems (since 2009), conventional narrow AI systems (since 2015), and increasingly advanced general-purpose AI systems (since 2022), respectively. The chapter evaluates both the strengths of these institutional achievements to date, and their outstanding weaknesses or challenges. It argues that while recent years have seen remarkable progress, this governance architecture remains fragmented, and these governance initiatives may not consolidate in time to adequately address pressing issue clusters. In response, I review many of the pathways or strategies that have been proposed for the way forward, including: continued reliance on soft law; unilateral state actions or extraterritorial regulation; the application of existing norms under public international law; the adaptation of existing institutions; the negotiation of new bilateral or multilateral treaties; and the establishment of new international institutions for AI. While many of these tools are promising, their absolute or comparative efficacy remains uncertain. New insights or strategies may be needed to help improve the global AI governance architecture in ways that secure a human future.

Architectures of Global AI Governance. Matthijs M. Maas, Oxford University Press. © Matthijs M. Maas 2025.
DOI: 10.1093/9780191988455.003.0004

3.2 The Emergence of the Global AI Governance Landscape

How has the world responded to AI so far? What is the shape of the emerging AI governance landscape? It is useful to take a step back to take stock of broad developments in this space over the past decade or so. To be clear, AI governance is a space that is in intense flux both nationally and internationally.[1] Developments have been sufficiently rapid—especially since 2022—that any attempted survey will inevitably become incomplete in short order. My aim here is therefore not to provide a comprehensive and settled historical account of AI governance, but to introduce readers to main events, themes, and trajectories that have characterized and marked AI governance until now, which frame and bound where it may go next.

An extensive body of scholarship exists on the ethical and societal challenges posed by AI. However, early work in the field was often philosophical, focusing on the ethical implications of particular (anticipated) use cases of algorithms and AI in areas such as robotics.[2] This was soon complemented by a growing body of work exploring questions of how to regulate AI and algorithms, though usually at the level of national regulations.[3] Initially, this focused on the regulation of robotics,[4] high-profile AI use cases such as self-driving cars,[5] and the problems of opaque and potentially biased algorithmic decision-making in diverse social contexts, as well as to enable more invasive surveillance and policing.[6] This scholarship came at a

[1] Urs Gasser, 'Governing AI with Intelligence' (2024) 40 Issues in Science and Technology 36.

[2] Patrick Lin, Keith Abney, and George A Bekey, *Robot Ethics: The Ethical and Social Implications of Robotics* (MIT Press 2011); Patrick Lin, Keith Abney, and Ryan Jenkins (eds), *Robot Ethics 2.0: From Autonomous Cars to Artificial Intelligence* (Oxford University Press 2017); John Tasioulas, 'First Steps Towards an Ethics of Robots and Artificial Intelligence' (2019) 7 Journal of Practical Ethics 61; Vincent C Müller, 'Ethics of AI and Robotics' in Edward N Zalta (ed), *Stanford Encyclopedia of Philosophy* (CSLI, Stanford University 2020) <https://plato.stanford.edu/entries/ethics-ai/#Sing> accessed 2 April 2019.

[3] Ryan Calo, 'Artificial Intelligence Policy: A Primer and Roadmap' (2017) 51 UC Davis Law Review 37; Matthew U Scherer, 'Regulating Artificial Intelligence Systems: Risks, Challenges, Competencies, and Strategies' [2016] Harvard Journal of Law & Technology <http://jolt.law.harvard.edu/articles/pdf/v29/29HarvJLTech353.pdf> accessed 5 March 2018; Michael Guihot, Anne F Matthew, and Nicolas Suzor, 'Nudging Robots: Innovative Solutions to Regulate Artificial Intelligence' [2017] Vanderbilt Journal of Entertainment & Technology Law <https://papers.ssrn.com/abstract=3017004> accessed 2 July 2018; Ronald Leenes and others, 'Regulatory Challenges of Robotics: Some Guidelines for Addressing Legal and Ethical Issues' (2017) 9 Law, Innovation and Technology 1; Thomas Wischmeyer and Timo Rademacher (eds), *Regulating Artificial Intelligence* (Springer International Publishing 2020); Jacob Turner, *Robot Rules: Regulating Artificial Intelligence* (Springer Berlin Heidelberg 2018).

[4] Ryan Calo, 'Robotics and the Lessons of Cyberlaw' (2015) 103 California Law Review 513; Neil M Richards and William D Smart, 'How Should the Law Think about Robots?' in Ryan Calo, A Froomkin, and Ian Kerr (eds), *Robot Law* (Edward Elgar Publishing 2016).

[5] This is an extensive literature, but see for example: Jessica S Brodsky, 'Autonomous Vehicle Regulation: How an Uncertain Legal Landscape May Hit the Brakes on Self-Driving Cars Cyberlaw and Venture Law' (2016) 31 Berkeley Technology Law Journal 851; James M Anderson and others, 'Autonomous Vehicle Technology: A Guide for Policymakers' (RAND Corporation 2016) Product Page <https://www.rand.org/pubs/research_reports/RR443-2.html> accessed 17 October 2017.

[6] This is again an extensive literature, but see Solon Barocas and Andrew D Selbst, 'Big Data's Disparate Impact' (2016) 671 California Law Review <https://papers.ssrn.com/abstract=2477899> accessed 28 January 2019; John Danaher, 'The Threat of Algocracy: Reality, Resistance and

time of growing national regulatory initiatives focused on the regulation of various use cases and applications of AI in domestic jurisdictions.[7]

At the international level, debates around the global governance of AI are relatively novel, only picking up momentum since the mid-2010s.[8] Nonetheless, the pace of such initiatives has increased: according to one ongoing inventory of AI regulatory initiatives, in 2020 international organizations overtook national authorities as the main source of AI regulatory initiatives, launching 210 AI policy initiatives (against 170 by national authorities) in the period between 2015 and 2022.[9]

It is difficult to tell a clear, chronological story of these many developments, given their number, different areas of focus (in terms of AI technologies, capabilities, applications or predicted impacts), and range in preferred policy tools.[10]

Accommodation' (2016) 29 Philosophy & Technology 245; Karen Yeung, '"Hypernudge": Big Data as a Mode of Regulation by Design' (2017) 20 Information, Communication & Society 118.

[7] For an overview of regulations in different countries, see: Laurie Harris, 'Regulating Artificial Intelligence: U.S. and International Approaches and Considerations for Congress' (Congressional Research Service 2025) CRS Report R48555 <https://www.congress.gov/crs-product/R48555> accessed 11 June 2025; 'Regulation of Artificial Intelligence in Selected Jurisdictions' (The Law Library of Congress, Global Legal Research Directorate 2019) <https://www.loc.gov/item/2019668143/> accessed 13 March 2025; Zachary Arnold and others, 'Introducing the AI Governance and Regulatory Archive (AGORA): An Analytic Infrastructure for Navigating the Emerging AI Governance Landscape' (2024) 7 Proceedings of the AAAI/ACM Conference on AI, Ethics, and Society 39, referring to Emerging Technologies Observatory, 'AGORA (AI GOvernance and Regulatory Archive)' <https://agora.eto.tech/?> accessed 19 February 2025.

[8] Jonas Tallberg and others, 'The Global Governance of Artificial Intelligence: Next Steps for Empirical and Normative Research' (2023) 25 International Studies Review viad040.

[9] ibid 5–6. They draw these statistics from Council of Europe, 'Datavisualisation of AI Initiatives' (*Artificial Intelligence*, 2023) <https://www.coe.int/en/web/artificial-intelligence/national-initiatives> accessed 8 January 2024. However, note that the precise number of initiatives surveyed may depend on specific definitions. For instance, in its own dashboard, the OECD AI Policy Observatory has registered more than 1,000 AI policy initiatives across 69 countries and territories. OECD AI Policy Observatory, 'OECD's Live Repository of AI Strategies & Policies' (2021) <https://oecd.ai/en/dashboards> accessed 10 January 2024. Note, another database of AI-relevant laws, regulations, standards, and other governance documents is provided at Emerging Technologies Observatory, 'AGORA (AI Governance and Regulatory Archive)' <https://agora.eto.tech/?> accessed 19 February 2025.

[10] However, for various snapshots of the AI governance ecosystem, at different moments of its development in the past years, see for instance (in very rough chronological order): James Butcher and Irakli Beridze, 'What Is the State of Artificial Intelligence Governance Globally?' (2019) 164 The RUSI Journal 88; Peter Cihon, 'Standards for AI Governance: International Standards to Enable Global Coordination in AI Research & Development' (Center for the Governance of AI, Future of Humanity Institute, University of Oxford 2019) Technical Report <https://www.fhi.ox.ac.uk/wp-content/uploads/Standards_-FHI-Technical-Report.pdf> accessed 18 April 2019; Martina Kunz, 'Global AI Governance' (*Global AI Governance*, 2020) <https://martinakunz.gitlab.io/globalaigov/> accessed 30 October 2020; Philippe Lorenz, 'AI Governance through Political Fora and Standards Developing Organizations' (Interface 2020) <https://www.interface-eu.org/archive/publications/ai-governance-through-political-fora-and-standards-developing-organizations> accessed 5 June 2025; Peter Cihon, Matthijs M Maas, and Luke Kemp, 'Fragmentation and the Future: Investigating Architectures for International AI Governance' (2020) 11 Global Policy 545; Lewin Schmitt, 'Mapping Global AI Governance: A Nascent Regime in a Fragmented Landscape' (2022) 2 AI and Ethics <https://doi.org/10.1007/s43681-021-00083-y> accessed 18 August 2021; Eugenio V Garcia, 'Multilateralism and Artificial Intelligence: What Role for the United Nations?' in Maurizio Tinnirello (ed), *The Global Politics of Artificial Intelligence* (CRC Press 2020); Michael Veale, Kira Matus, and Robert Gorwa, 'AI and Global Governance: Modalities, Rationales, Tensions' (2023) 19 Annual Review of Law and Social Science 255; Mark Chinen, *The International Governance of Artificial Intelligence* (Edward Elgar

Nonetheless, we can fruitfully compare the gradual emergence, and layering, of global governance efforts aimed at the successive international regulation of military AI, conventional AI, and, finally, advanced AI.

3.2.1 Developments in Global Governance for Military AI (2009–2025)

While many initiatives on AI governance (especially at the international level) are relatively new, there is, as noted, one area in which international lawyers have engaged for a longer time: the governance of military AI. Such initiative have largely (though not exclusively) focused on the impacts and regulation of Lethal Autonomous Weapons Systems (LAWS)—'killer robots' in popular parlance. It is useful to provide a brief background of the origin and history of these governance efforts.[11]

3.2.1.1 (2009–2016) Autonomous Weapons Systems are put on the international agenda

Academic debate over potential military uses of robots and AI has been ongoing for several decades.[12] Moreover, questions about robotic weapons systems were

Publishing 2023); Mark D Cole, 'AI Regulation and Governance on a Global Scale: An Overview of International, Regional and National Instruments' (2024) 1 Journal of AI Law and Regulation 126; Hiroki Habuka and David U Socol de la Osa, 'Enhancements and next Steps for the G7 Hiroshima AI Process: Toward a Common Framework to Advance Human Rights, Democracy and Rule of Law' (2025) 1 Cambridge Forum on AI: Law and Governance e15. Allison Stanger and others, 'Terra Incognita: The Governance of Artificial Intelligence in Global Perspective' (2024) 27 Annual Review of Political Science 445; Microsoft, 'Global Governance: Goals and Lessons for AI' (Microsoft 2024) 96–98 <https://aka.ms/AIGlobalGovernanceBook> accessed 22 May 2024; Deric Cheng and Elliot Mckernon, '2024 State of the AI Regulatory Landscape' (Convergence Analysis 2024) <https://www.convergenceanalysis.org/ai-regulatory-landscape/home> accessed 28 May 2024; Johannes Geith, Magnus Lundgren and Jonas Tallberg, 'The Emerging Regime Complex for Artificial Intelligence' [2025 forthcoming] *Global Studies Quarterly*; Harris (n 7).

[11] See also the overviews provided in Denise Garcia, 'Introduction: Artificial Intelligence to Benefit Humanity' in Denise Garcia (ed), *The AI Military Race: Common Good Governance in the Age of Artificial Intelligence* (Oxford University Press 2023) 18; Chinen (n 10) 268–275. Tim Sweijs and Sofia Romansky, 'International Norms Development and AI in the Military Domain' (Centre for International Governance Innovation, and The Hague Centre for Strategic Studies 2024) 300 8–12 <https://hcss.nl/report/international-norms-development-and-ai-in-the-military-domain/> accessed 23 October 2024. Other developments have been covered in Şerif Onur Bahçecik, 'Civil Society Responds to the AWS: Growing Activist Networks and Shifting Frames' (2019) 10 Global Policy 365; Elvira Rosert and Frank Sauer, 'How (Not) to Stop the Killer Robots: A Comparative Analysis of Humanitarian Disarmament Campaign Strategies' (2020) 42 Contemporary Security Policy 4, 15; Martina Kunz and Seán Ó hÉigeartaigh, 'Artificial Intelligence and Robotization' in Robin Geiß and Nils Melzer (eds), *The Oxford Handbook of the International Law of Global Security* (Oxford University Press 2021) 8.

[12] See PW Singer, *Wired for War: The Robotics Revolution and Conflict in the 21st Century* (Penguin Press 2009); Ronald Arkin, *Governing Lethal Behavior in Autonomous Robots* (1 edition, Routledge 2009).

first raised in civil society as early as the mid-'00s. However, these issues ultimately did not gain significant uptake then, as the technology was at the time seen as too futuristic, and not a priority compared with other issues on the global disarmament agenda.[13]

This gradually changed between 2009 and 2013, when the international discussion of autonomous weapons found its feet, among growing calls for 'robot arms control'.[14] Accordingly, the International Committee for Robot Arms Control (ICRAC) was established in 2009, and began to organize expert debate for more concerted public outreach.[15] It was in 2012 that the issue began to gain political traction,[16] after Human Rights Watch, a key monitor organization and gatekeeper in the humanitarian disarmament field,[17] adopted the topic in an influential public report.[18] Matters sped up still further in early 2013, as Christof Heyns, the UN Special Rapporteur on extrajudicial, summary or arbitrary executions, called for a moratorium on robotic and AI weapons.[19] April 2013 also saw the official launch of the Campaign To Stop Killer Robots, a global coalition of international, regional, and national NGOs calling for a ban of such weapons.[20]

On the public side, the period since 2014 has seen increasing pressure from civil society, as well as a series of open letters from AI researchers and tech company employees denouncing the use of AI in weapons.[21] Significantly, these efforts led the States parties to the Convention on Certain Conventional Weapons (CCW) to begin a series of informal expert meetings in 2014. As a result, at the fifth Review

[13] Charli Carpenter, *'Lost' Causes, Agenda Vetting in Global Issue Networks and the Shaping of Human Security* (Cornell University Press 2014).

[14] Robert Sparrow, 'Predators or Plowshares? Arms Control of Robotic Weapons' (2009) 28 IEEE Technology and Society Magazine 25; Armin Krishnan, *Killer Robots: Legality and Ethicality of Autonomous Weapons* (1st edn, Ashgate Publishing 2009); Jürgen Altmann, 'Preventive Arms Control for Uninhabited Military Vehicles' in R Capurro and M Nagenborg (eds), *Ethics and Robotics* (AKA Verlag Heidelberg 2009); Wendell Wallach and Colin Allen, 'Framing Robot Arms Control' (2013) 15 Ethics and Information Technology 125.

[15] Rosert and Sauer (n 11) 15.

[16] Rosert and Sauer (n 11).

[17] ibid 5. ('A primary target of mobilization are so-called gatekeepers—established and influential organizations at the top of the transnational hierarchy .... In the field of humanitarian arms control, Human Rights Watch (HRW) and the International Committee of the Red Cross (ICRC) have been deemed gatekeepers.')

[18] Human Rights Watch, *Losing Humanity: The Case against Killer Robots* (Human Rights Watch 2012).

[19] Christof Heyns, 'Report of the Special Rapporteur on Extrajudicial, Summary or Arbitrary Executions' <https://www.ohchr.org/Documents/HRBodies/HRCouncil/RegularSession/Session23/A-HRC-23-47_en.pdf> accessed 27 February 2019.

[20] Campaign to Stop Killer Robots, 'About Us' <https://www.stopkillerrobots.org/about/> accessed 5 September 2020.

[21] Bahçecik (n 11); Future of Life Institute, 'Open Letter on Autonomous Weapons' (*Future of Life Institute*, 2015) <https://futureoflife.org/open-letter-autonomous-weapons/> accessed 22 November 2018; 'Letter to Google C.E.O.' <https://static01.nyt.com/files/2018/technology/googleletter.pdf> accessed 9 April 2018. See also Haydn Belfield, 'Activism by the AI Community: Analysing Recent Achievements and Future Prospects', *Proceedings of the AAAI/ACM Conference on AI, Ethics, and Society* (ACM 2020) <https://dl.acm.org/doi/10.1145/3375627.3375814> accessed 24 August 2020.

Conference in 2016, the Group of Governmental Experts (GGE) on Emerging Technologies in the Area of Lethal Autonomous Weapons Systems was established.[22] In the past, such GGEs have served as preparatory fora for the development and negotiation of new international law.[23] The goal of this group, therefore, has been to explore and reach agreement on recommended regulatory options for the Convention, in light of the compliance of LAWS with international humanitarian law and international human rights law, as well as the broader global security risks they pose.[24]

3.2.1.2 (2017–2023) Halting UN progress on lethal autonomous weapons systems

Since 2017, the GGE has met annually to discuss the technological, military, ethical, and legal implications of LAWS, and to elaborate a framework for global governance. Progress has been uneven, however, with meetings often held up by contestation over basic definitions of what constitutes LAWS, as well as over how to operationalize the principle of 'Meaningful Human Control' (MHC).[25]

Nonetheless, there has been no definitive resolution to this process to date, in spite of gradually greater participation of civil society actors and states from the Global South, who have all been robustly in favour of a legally binding instrument banning LAWS.[26] Prospects for the process's success remain in doubt. It has been difficult for all parties to agree on paths forward. Given that the forum operates entirely on the basis of consensus, this has meant that the process remains severely impeded. Furthermore, there has been variation in state engagement in the forum, and in state positions.[27] While many states support strong restrictions,[28] a small group of states (including the US and Russia) have strongly opposed any legally binding restrictions or bans, or (like China) have indicated 'qualified' support for a legal ban on AWS while defining such systems in an extremely narrow way.[29]

[22] United Nations Convention on Prohibition or Restrictions on the Use of Certain Conventional Weapons Which May be Deemed to be Excessively Injurious or to Have Indiscriminate Effects 1980 (1342 UNTS 137).

[23] Ingvild Bode and others, 'Prospects for the Global Governance of Autonomous Weapons: Comparing Chinese, Russian, and US Practices' (2023) 25 Ethics and Information Technology 5, 5.

[24] 'Final Document of the Fifth Review Conference (UN Doc CCW/CONF.V/10)' 9. See also Kunz and Ó hÉigeartaigh (n 11) 8.

[25] For a review of the different ways these terms have been operationalized, see also Mariarosaria Taddeo and Alexander Blanchard, 'A Comparative Analysis of the Definitions of Autonomous Weapons Systems' (2022) 28 Science and Engineering Ethics 37.

[26] Ingvild Bode, 'Norm-Making and the Global South: Attempts to Regulate Lethal Autonomous Weapons Systems' (2019) 10 Global Policy 359.

[27] See generally Justin Key Canfil and Elsa B Kania, 'Mapping State Participation in Military AI Governance Discussions' in Justin B Bullock and others (eds), *The Oxford Handbook of AI Governance* (Oxford University Press).

[28] An up-to-date survey of state positions on the potential negotiation of a legally binding instrument on autonomous weapons systems is kept at: Stop Killer Robots Campaign, 'State Positions' (*Automated Decision Research*, 2024) <https://automatedresearch.org/state-positions/> accessed 23 October 2024.

[29] Bode and others (n 23) 4,5.

As a result, the only tangible outcome of the process so far has been a set of 11 non-binding guiding principles for the development and use of LAWS, agreed to at the GGE's November 2019 meeting[30]—a disappointing result. Indeed, as noted by Mark Chinen, 'the principles adopted so far do not contemplate a ban on LAWS at all; rather, they contemplate a framework, based largely on existing international law, for regulating their use'.[31] Since states are already obligated to follow international humanitarian law, however, this means that they do not effectively make new commitments.

In some sectors, pessimism has been growing about the ability of this process to yield a binding ban or even any clear guidance. Various civil society actors, frustrated with limited progress and continued state opposition, have threatened to shift negotiations to another forum.[32] This could take the form of states beginning negotiations for a binding treaty within the UN General Assembly (which operates via a two-thirds majority voting rule, avoiding the requirement for consensus), echoing the routes followed by the 2013 Arms Trade Treaty and the 2017 Treaty on the Prohibition of Nuclear Weapons.[33] Alternatively, motivated States and civil society actors could establish a new forum to negotiate a treaty, echoing the precedent of the 1997 Ottawa Treaty ban on anti-personnel mines or the 2008 Cluster Munitions Convention.[34]

3.2.1.3 (2021–2025) Renewed efforts as military AI sees growing use: regional calls, resolutions, declarations

While some military AI technologies have had a remarkably long track record of development and deployment, the period after 2021 began to see increasingly high-profile deployment of increasingly autonomous systems to conflicts and

[30] United Nations, 'Report of the 2019 Session of the Group of Governmental Experts on Emerging Technologies in the Area of Lethal Autonomous Weapons Systems' (United Nations Office at Geneva, Group of Governmental Experts of the High Contracting Parties to the Convention on Prohibitions or Restrictions on the Use of Certain Conventional Weapons Which May Be Deemed to Be Excessively Injurious or to Have Indiscriminate Effects 2019) CCW/GGE.1/2019/3 13 <https://documents.unoda.org/wp-content/uploads/2020/09/CCW_GGE.1_2019_3_E.pdf> accessed 7 October 2019, Annex IV. These principles affirm, inter alia, that IHL applies to AWS (a), a human must always be responsible for the decision to use these systems (b, d), and states must examine the legality of these new weapons at the design stage (e, f, g).

[31] Chinen (n 10) 272.

[32] Janosch Delcker, 'How Killer Robots Overran the UN' [2019] *POLITICO* <https://www.politico.eu/article/killer-robots-overran-united-nations-lethal-autonomous-weapons-systems/> accessed 2 October 2019. And see Campaign to Stop Killer Robots, 'Diplomatic Talks in 2020' (25 September 2020) <https://www.stopkillerrobots.org/2020/09/diplomatic2020/> accessed 26 September 2020; Bode and others (n 23) 5.

[33] Bode and others (n 23) 5.

[34] Bode (n 26) 5; Charli Carpenter, 'A Better Path to a Treaty Banning "Killer Robots" Has Just Been Cleared' (*World Politics Review*, 7 January 2022) <https://www.worldpoliticsreview.com/a-better-path-to-a-treaty-banning-ai-weapons-killer-robots/> accessed 12 January 2024.

warzones such as the Libyan civil war,[35] the Russia–Ukraine war,[36] and the Israel–Hamas conflict,[37] among others.

As the first reported cases of such military AI use—of both fully autonomous as well as so-called lethality-enabling[38] systems—came to public attention, they sparked renewed calls for a ban on these weapons.[39] This in turn led to fresh efforts by State coalitions, international organizations, and civil society organizations to establish some practical principles and limitations on the use of these weapons,[40] or even a legally binding governance regime after all. In July 2023, UN Secretary-General António Guterres presented to Member States his *New Agenda for Peace*, which recommended that States 'conclude, by 2026, a legally binding instrument to prohibit lethal autonomous weapon systems that function without human control or oversight'.[41]

Similar calls were echoed at the regional level, including in the form of the February 2023 *Belén Communiqué*, in which 33 states from Latin America and the Caribbean urged such a solution,[42] as well as through the September *CARICOM Declaration on Autonomous Weapons*.[43]

[35] Maria Cramer, 'A.I. Drone May Have Acted on Its Own in Attacking Fighters, U.N. Says' *The New York Times* (3 June 2021) <https://www.nytimes.com/2021/06/03/world/africa/libya-drone.html> accessed 13 December 2021; Zachary Kallenborn, 'Was a Flying Killer Robot Used in Libya? Quite Possibly' (*Bulletin of the Atomic Scientists*, 20 May 2021) <https://thebulletin.org/2021/05/was-a-flying-killer-robot-used-in-libya-quite-possibly/> accessed 13 December 2021.

[36] Morgan Meaker, 'Ukraine's War Brings Autonomous Weapons to the Front Lines' [2023] *Wired UK* <https://www.wired.co.uk/article/ukraine-war-autonomous-weapons-frontlines> accessed 5 December 2023.

[37] Harry Davies, Bethan McKernan, and Dan Sabbagh, '"The Gospel": How Israel Uses AI to Select Bombing Targets in Gaza' *The Guardian* (1 December 2023) <https://www.theguardian.com/world/2023/dec/01/the-gospel-how-israel-uses-ai-to-select-bombing-targets> accessed 5 December 2023. Yuval Abraham, '"Lavender": The AI Machine Directing Israel's Bombing Spree in Gaza' (*+972 Magazine*, 3 April 2024) <https://www.972mag.com/lavender-ai-israeli-army-gaza/> accessed 30 April 2024.

[38] Arthur Holland Michel, 'The Killer Algorithms Nobody's Talking About' (*Foreign Policy*, 20 January 2020) <https://foreignpolicy.com/2020/01/20/ai-autonomous-weapons-artificial-intelligence-the-killer-algorithms-nobodys-talking-about/> accessed 21 January 2020.

[39] Stuart Russell, 'AI Weapons: Russia's War in Ukraine Shows Why the World Must Enact a Ban' (2023) 614 Nature 620.

[40] For one example of such a code, see Centre for Humanitarian Dialogue, 'Code of Conduct on Artificial Intelligence in Military Systems' (Centre for Humanitarian Dialogue 2021) <https://www.hdcentre.org/wp-content/uploads/2021/08/AI-Code-of-Conduct.pdf> accessed 28 January 2023.

[41] António Guterres, 'A New Agenda for Peace' (United Nations 2023) Our Common Agenda Policy Brief 9, 27 <https://www.un.org/sites/un2.un.org/files/our-common-agenda-policy-brief-new-agenda-for-peace-en.pdf> accessed 12 January 2024.

[42] Mary Wareham, 'Latin America and Caribbean Nations Rally Against Autonomous Weapons Systems' (*Human Rights Watch*, 6 March 2023) <https://www.hrw.org/news/2023/03/06/latin-america-and-caribbean-nations-rally-against-autonomous-weapons-systems> accessed 12 January 2024. See 'Communiqué of the Latin American and the Caribbean Conference of Social and Humanitarian Impact of Autonomous Weapons' <https://www.rree.go.cr/files/includes/files.php?id=2261&tipo=documentos> accessed 12 January 2024.

[43] 'CARICOM Declaration on Autonomous Weapons Systems' <https://www.caricom-aws2023.com/_files/ugd/b69acc_c1ffb97ed9024930a3205ae4e34c1b45.pdf> accessed 12 January 2024.

Another major trend came in the opening of a distinct channel of governance discussions within the UN system, located not at the UN CCW in Geneva but rather at the UN General Assembly, which operates by majority vote, not consensus. In December 2023, the UNGA adopted, with significant support, Resolution 78/241 'Lethal autonomous weapons systems', which stressed the 'urgent need for the international community to address the challenges and concerns raised by autonomous weapons systems'.[44] The resolution sparked a fresh round of commentary and submission of replies by Member States, observer States, and international organizations and civil societies, articulating their positions on these weapons characteristics, challenges, legal concerns, or potential benefits.[45] This was followed in October 2024 by the approval, in the UNGA First Committee, of Draft Resolution A/C.1/79/L.43 'Artificial intelligence in the military domain and its implications for international peace and security', which among other things asked the Secretary-General to begin a process of consultation of member states and other stakeholders, to understand their views on issues raised by the military use of AI, especially in areas other than lethal autonomous weapons systems.[46]

Other inter-governmental statements and declarations instead focused not on the prohibition of military AI, but on its responsible use. For instance, during February 2023, two declarations of this kind were launched. The US Political Declaration on Responsible Military Use of Artificial Intelligence and Autonomy,[47] which has been endorsed by more than 50 states, highlighted a series of principles aimed at ensuring legal review, oversight, and risk mitigation in military AI systems. At the same time, the Responsible AI in the Military Domain Summit organized by The Netherlands and Korea yielded the REAIM Call to Action, which urged signatories to 'stress the paramount importance of the responsible use of AI in the military domain, employed in full accordance with international legal obligations and in a way that does not undermine international security, stability and accountability'.[48]

Subsequently, the GC REAIM process conducted five regional consultations in the run-up to the September 2024 REAIM Summit in Seoul.[49] This Summit

[44] United Nations General Assembly, 'Resolution 78/241 "Lethal Autonomous Weapons Systems"' (2023) UN Doc A/RES/78/241.

[45] A compilation can be found in United Nations General Assembly, 'Lethal Autonomous Weapons Systems: Report of the Secretary-General' (United Nations General Assembly 2024) UN Doc A/79/88.

[46] UNGA, 'Draft Resolution A/C.1/79/L.43 "Artificial Intelligence in the Military Domain and Its Implications for International Peace and Security"' <https://undocs.org/en/A/C.1/79/L.43> accessed 19 February 2025.

[47] US Department of State, 'Political Declaration on Responsible Military Use of Artificial Intelligence and Autonomy' (*United States Department of State*, 9 November 2023) <https://www.state.gov/political-declaration-on-responsible-military-use-of-artificial-intelligence-and-autonomy-2/> accessed 12 January 2024.

[48] 'REAIM 2023 Call to Action' (16 February 2023) <https://www.government.nl/documents/publications/2023/02/16/reaim-2023-call-to-action> accessed 12 January 2024.

[49] Yasmin Afina, 'The Global Kaleidoscope of Military AI Governance: Decoding the 2024 Regional Consultations on Responsible AI in the Military Domain' (UNIDIR 2024) <https://unidir.org/publication/the-global-kaleidoscope-of-military-ai-governance/> accessed 23 October 2024.

culminated in a non-binding *Blueprint for Action*,[50] which set out a series of high-level principles, involving state recognition of AI's impacts on international peace and security, through foreseeable and unforeseeable accident risk, proliferation and misuse threats, and the importance of maintaining 'human control and involvement for all actions critical to informing and executing sovereign decisions concerning nuclear weapons employment, without prejudice to the ultimate goal of a world free of nuclear weapons'.[51] It noted that these principles would apply to all AI applications in the military domain, including not just autonomous weapons systems but also those used in logistics, intelligence operations, or decision-making.[52] The *Blueprint* was endorsed by 61 countries, though not China,[53] reportedly because of the inclusion of the provisions around human control over nuclear weapons employment.[54]

These latter initiatives—focused on ensuring the development of 'responsible', robust, interoperable systems—can be seen as more complementary to a simultaneous trend in the rise of inter-state strategic partnerships such as the US-led AI Partnership for Defense (2020) and the AUKUS security partnership (2021).[55] However, what these nonbinding initiatives imply in practice remains somewhat unclear. Some have critiqued the concept of 'responsible AI' in the military domain as nothing more than a rhetorical 'empty shell'.[56] Others have critiqued

[50] 'REAIM Blueprint for Responsible AI Use in Military' (*REAIM 2024*, 10 September 2024) <https://reaim2024.kr/home/reaimeng/board/bbsDetail.do?encMenuId=4e57325766362f626e5179454e6d6e4d4a4d33507a773d3d&encBbsMngNo=366e794c7a644d7563424256684 44f393053755142673d3d&encBbsNo=6f784e4542386f7735767465766a6531556f4b6149413d3d&ctlPageNow=1&schKind=bbsTtlCn&schWord=#this> accessed 23 October 2024.

[51] ibid para 5.

[52] ibid.

[53] Brianna Rosen, 'From Principles to Action: Charting a Path for Military AI Governance' (*Carnegie Council for Ethics in International Affairs*, 12 September 2024) <https://www.carnegiecouncil.org/media/article/principles-action-military-ai-governance> accessed 23 October 2024.

[54] Dr Lauren Sanders, Rain Liivoja, and Zena Assaad, 'REAIM Summit 2024: Slowly but Surely towards Better Governance of Military Artificial Intelligence? From The Hague to Seoul' (*Australian and New Zealand Society of International Law*, 2024) <https://anzsilperspective.com/reaim-summit-2024-slowly-but-surely-towards-better-governance-of-military-artificial-intelligence-from-the-hague-to-seoul/> accessed 12 February 2025.

[55] Joint Artificial Intelligence Center, 'AI Partnership for Defense (AI PfD)—15–16 September 2020—Joint Statement' <https://cyberpoint-apayne.github.io/CDAO/docs/AI_PfD_Joint_Statement_09_16_20.pdf> accessed 13 March 2025; Lauren Kahn, 'AUKUS Explained: How Will the Trilateral Pact Shape Indo-Pacific Security?' (*Council on Foreign Relations*, 12 June 2023) <https://www.cfr.org/in-brief/aukus-explained-how-will-trilateral-pact-shape-indo-pacific-security> accessed 11 October 2023; While AUKUS focused primarily on submarine programmes, it also included AI-focused trials: Ministry of Defence, 'World First as UK Hosts Inaugural AUKUS AI and Autonomy Trial' (26 May 2023) <https://www.gov.uk/government/news/world-first-as-uk-hosts-inaugural-aukus-ai-and-autonomy-trial> accessed 8 November 2023. For additional discussion, see Lena Trabucco, 'AI Partnership for Defense Is a Step in the Right Direction—But Will Face Challenges' (*Opinio Juris*, 5 October 2020) <http://opiniojuris.org/2020/10/05/ai-partnership-for-defense-is-a-step-in-the-right-direction-but-will-face-challenges/> accessed 11 October 2021; Lena Trabucco and Matthijs M Maas, 'Technology Ties: The Rise and Roles of Military AI Strategic Partnerships' (10 November 2023) <https://papers.ssrn.com/abstract=4629283> accessed 10 November 2023.

[56] Garcia, 'Introduction: Artificial Intelligence to Benefit Humanity' (n 11) 9.

'the prioritisation of efficiency, security, and rules of engagement over other ethical considerations' in documents such as the REAIM 2023 Call to Action.[57] With other non-binding initiatives, some initial steps were later walked back in negotiations: while the initial draft of the US's Political Declaration mentioned the risks of AI integration with nuclear command and control, claiming that '[s]tates should maintain human control and involvement for all actions critical to informing and executing sovereign decisions concerning nuclear weapons employment', the final version omitted this point entirely.[58] Moreover, both the non-binding processes have failed to attract endorsement from key states in the military AI landscape, including China, Russia, and Israel, showing a lack of international consensus even for softer sets of principles.[59]

Given all this, the military AI landscape at present is at a crossroads, with many outstanding gaps and weaknesses to be addressed.[60] A range of unilateral, bilateral, or multilateral efforts will be needed to clarify how these broad principles are to be implemented in specific standards and guidelines[61]—determining the global response to this rapidly growing threat to international security.

3.2.2 (2015–2025) Developments in global governance for conventional AI

A second track in AI governance has been a wide array of institutions focused on global governance for civilian, narrow (i.e. conventional) AI.

3.2.2.1 (2015–2024) The rise of global soft law for AI: from protests to partnerships

Within the domain of civilian uses of AI, from the mid-2010s onward we began to see the first coordinated scrutiny of AI's potential societal impacts, resulting in the

[57] Guangyu Qiao-Franco, 'Has REAIM "Re-Aimed" AI Applications in the Military Domain?' (*AutoNorms*, 24 February 2023) <https://www.autonorms.eu/has-reaim-re-aimed-ai-applications-in-the-military-domain/> accessed 28 August 2024.

[58] Michael Depp, 'The Next Step in Military AI Multilateralism' (*Lawfare*, 26 March 2024) <https://www.lawfaremedia.org/article/the-next-step-in-military-ai-multilateralism> accessed 28 March 2024 (though noting that '[t]his statement, or any mention of nuclear command and control, is missing due to the reticence of many of the signatories to legitimize, in their view, nuclear weapons by agreeing to constrain them'). However, note that others have cautioned against introducing discussions of AI into existing nuclear risk reduction dialogues, as this might merely serve to undermine consensus in that domain. Lindsay Rand, 'The Risk of Bringing AI Discussions Into High-Level Nuclear Dialogues' (*Carnegie Endowment for International Peace*, 19 August 2024) <https://carnegieendowment.org/posts/2024/08/ai-nuclear-dialogue-risks-npt?lang=en> accessed 23 October 2024.

[59] Rosen (n 53).

[60] Sweijs and Romansky (n 11).

[61] Lauren Kahn, 'How the United States Can Set International Norms for Military Use of AI' (*Lawfare*, 21 January 2024) <https://www.lawfaremedia.org/article/how-the-united-states-can-set-international-norms-for-military-use-of-ai> accessed 10 April 2024.

emergence of a wide range of (non-binding) soft law programmes and tools for AI, from a range of actors.

3.2.2.1.1 Rising public scrutiny and protest

In the early and mid-2010s, a range of public incidents or scandals involving AI systems led to growing public awareness, greater concern from policymakers, and increased public scrutiny of AI technology and its developers. In response, through a combination of high-profile investigations, specialist scholarship, broad public pressure, and employee activism, remarkable shifts in AI industry policy and government procurement of algorithms have been achieved.[62]

Initially, public concerns and employee activism focused on corporate collaborations with defence and security actors. For example, in 2018, one such campaign notably led to Google halting its controversial Project MAVEN contract with the Pentagon.[63] Moreover, in the wake of high-profile scandals involving the tech sector, public scrutiny of this industry soon grew and broadened. Among other topics, there has been considerable focus on the racially biased performance of algorithms used in crime predictions,[64] as well as in algorithms used in facial and voice recognition roles.[65] Other critiques focused on the use of robots in public spaces,[66] and the use of facial recognition systems and surveillance.[67] Such mobilizations have resulted in some successes. For instance, naming-and-shaming campaigns to call out the biased performance of AI platforms helped shift industry policies,[68] as well as leading to bans or temporary pauses in the provision of some sensitive tools. For instance, both Axon (in 2019) and IBM (in 2020) decided to forego the provision of facial recognition software in policing contexts.[69]

[62] Joanna Redden and others, 'Automating Public Services: Learning from Cancelled Systems' (Carnegie UK 2022) <https://www.carnegieuktrust.org.uk/publications/automating-public-services-learning-from-cancelled-systems/> accessed 13 October 2022.

[63] Belfield (n 21).

[64] Lauren Kirchner and others, 'Machine Bias: There's Software Used Across the Country to Predict Future Criminals. And It's Biased Against Blacks' (*ProPublica*, 23 May 2016) <https://www.propublica.org/article/machine-bias-risk-assessments-in-criminal-sentencing> accessed 24 May 2017. Though see also Sam Corbett-Davies and others, 'A Computer Program Used for Bail and Sentencing Decisions Was Labeled Biased against Blacks. It's Actually Not That Clear' *Washington Post* (17 October 2016) <https://www.washingtonpost.com/news/monkey-cage/wp/2016/10/17/can-an-algorithm-be-racist-our-analysis-is-more-cautious-than-propublicas/> accessed 21 May 2017.

[65] Joy Buolamwini and Timnit Gebru, 'Gender Shades: Intersectional Accuracy Disparities in Commercial Gender Classification', *Proceedings of Machine Learning Research* (2018) <http://proceedings.mlr.press/v81/buolamwini18a/buolamwini18a.pdf> accessed 8 May 2019.

[66] Matt Simon, 'San Francisco Just Put the Brakes on Delivery Robots' [2017] *Wired* <https://www.wired.com/story/san-francisco-just-put-the-brakes-on-delivery-robots/> accessed 9 December 2019.

[67] Kimon Kieslich and Marco Lünich, 'Regulating AI-Based Remote Biometric Identification. Investigating the Public Demand for Bans, Audits, and Public Database Registrations', *Proceedings of the 2024 ACM Conference on Fairness, Accountability, and Transparency* (Association for Computing Machinery 2024) <https://dl.acm.org/doi/10.1145/3630106.3658548> accessed 13 June 2024.

[68] Inioluwa Deborah Raji and Joy Buolamwini, 'Actionable Auditing: Investigating the Impact of Publicly Naming Biased Performance Results of Commercial AI Products' (2019).

[69] Axon AI & Policing Technology Ethics Board, 'First Report of the Axon AI & Policing Technology Ethics Board' (Axon AI & Policing Technology Ethics Board 2019) <https://static1.squarespace.com/

At the same time, such successes did not translate to all application domains of AI,[70] and may in some cases not have been sustainable or robust over the long term: by 2021, Google had already resumed a wide range of new defence projects;[71] Axon's ethics board resigned in 2023 after the company started marketing taser-equipped drones as a potential solution to school shootings,[72] and in 2024 the same company began providing AI systems that transcribed police body camera audio into reports.[73]

Such rollbacks of initial successes were also accompanied by more structural cutbacks on accountability, as the intense 2023 attention for generative AI led a number of leading tech companies, including Microsoft and Meta, to lay off previously established teams on AI ethics.[74]

3.2.2.1.2 The rise of AI ethics principles

At a global level, renewed attention on the risks posed by AI systems has generated significant momentum for global soft law initiatives, in particular within the new field of 'AI ethics'.[75] Accordingly, since the mid-2010s we have seen the

static/58a33e881b631bc60d4f8b31/t/5d13d7e1990c4f00014c0aeb/1561581540954/Axon_Ethics_Board_First_Report.pdf> accessed 28 June 2019; Arvind Krishna, 'IBM CEO's Letter to Congress on Racial Justice Reform' (*THINKPolicy Blog*, 8 June 2020) <https://www.ibm.com/blogs/policy/facial-recognition-susset-racial-justice-reforms/> accessed 22 June 2020.

[70] Catherine Aiken, Rebecca Kagan and Michael Page, '"Cool Projects" or "Expanding the Efficiency of the Murderous American War Machine?" AI Professionals' Views on Working With the Department of Defense' (Center for Security and Emerging Technology 2020) <https://cset.georgetown.edu/publication/cool-projects-or-expanding-the-efficiency-of-the-murderous-american-war-machine/> accessed 12 January 2024.

[71] Tom Simonite, '3 Years After the Maven Uproar, Google Cozies to the Pentagon' [2021] *Wired* <https://www.wired.com/story/3-years-maven-uproar-google-warms-pentagon/> accessed 2 January 2024.

[72] Ese Olumhense, 'Axon's Ethics Board Resigned Over Taser-Armed Drones. Then the Company Bought a Military Drone Maker' [2023] *Wired* <https://www.wired.com/story/axon-taser-drones-ethics-board/> accessed 11 June 2024.

[73] Thomas Brewster, 'Taser Company Axon Is Selling AI that Turns Body Cam Audio Into Police Reports' (*Forbes*, 23 April 2024) <https://www.forbes.com/sites/thomasbrewster/2024/04/23/axon-ai-police-reports-/> accessed 11 June 2024.

[74] Gerrit De Vynck and Will Oremus, 'As AI Booms, Tech Firms Are Laying Off Their Ethicists' *Washington Post* (3 April 2023) <https://www.washingtonpost.com/technology/2023/03/30/tech-companies-cut-ai-ethics/> accessed 2 January 2024; Zoe Schiffer and Casey Newton, 'Microsoft Lays Off Team That Taught Employees How to Make AI Tools Responsibly' (*The Verge*, 14 March 2023) <https://www.theverge.com/2023/3/13/23638823/microsoft-ethics-society-team-responsible-ai-layoffs> accessed 2 January 2024; Wes Davis, 'Meta Disbanded Its Responsible AI Team' (*The Verge*, 18 November 2023) <https://www.theverge.com/2023/11/18/23966980/meta-disbanded-responsible-ai-team-artificial-intelligence> accessed 2 January 2024.

[75] It is important to distinguish between 'AI ethics' as a field and as a practice. In the former sense, this refers to the rise of a dedicated 'AI ethics' community of scholars and activists, with associated initiatives, institutes, research groups, and conferences, which have advocated for a range of ethical values and principles around AI. In the latter sense, AI ethics refers to a *practice*, namely the formulation over the past years of diverse sets of (soft law) principles or frameworks meant to guide global AI development. These principles have been formulated and advocated for by a diverse range of actors, which certainly include actors from the 'AI ethics' field, but also feature codes and principles by a broader range of actors such as states or companies. In this section, I use 'AI ethics' mostly in the

articulation of a large number of ethical principles and guidelines for AI. Between 2016 and 2019, at least 86 sets of AI ethics principles were published;[76] by 2020, this had increased to more than 160 sets of principles.[77] Notable examples of these include the early 2017 Asilomar AI Principles,[78] the 2017 Montreal Declaration for a Responsible Development of Artificial Intelligence,[79] the 2018 Universal Guidelines for Artificial Intelligence,[80] and the 2019 Beijing Artificial Intelligence Principles.[81] In contrast to earlier efforts, the instruments in this wave were articulated by a wide array of actors, including governments, intergovernmental organizations, companies, professional associations, civil society advocacy groups, and multi-stakeholder initiatives.[82] Both the substance and the style of these documents also varied significantly, from vague position statements to very specific outcomes from democratic debate.[83]

latter sense, although that is not meant to downplay the important contributions of the AI ethics community. I thank Carina Prunkl for prompting this clarification. Though for a critique of articulating technology-specific 'ethics' fields in this manner, see also Henrik Skaug Sætra and John Danaher, 'To Each Technology Its Own Ethics: The Problem of Ethical Proliferation' (2022) 35 Philosophy & Technology 93.

[76] For overviews, see Anna Jobin, Marcello Ienca, and Effy Vayena, 'The Global Landscape of AI Ethics Guidelines' [2019] Nature Machine Intelligence 1; Jessica Fjeld and others, 'Principled Artificial Intelligence: Mapping Consensus in Ethical and Rights-Based Approaches to Principles for AI' <https://dash.harvard.edu/handle/1/42160420> accessed 16 January 2020; Yi Zeng, Enmeng Lu, and Cunqing Huangfu, 'Linking Artificial Intelligence Principles' [2018] arXiv:1812.04814 [cs] <http://arxiv.org/abs/1812.04814> accessed 30 January 2019; Daniel Schiff and others, 'What's Next for AI Ethics, Policy, and Governance? A Global Overview', *Proceedings of the AAAI/ACM Conference on AI, Ethics, and Society* (ACM 2020) <http://dl.acm.org/doi/10.1145/3375627.3375804> accessed 12 February 2020.

[77] High-level Panel on Digital Cooperation, 'Report of the Secretary-General: Roadmap for Digital Cooperation' (UN Secretary-General's High-Level Panel on Digital Cooperation 2020) 18 <https://www.un.org/en/content/digital-cooperation-roadmap/assets/pdf/Roadmap_for_Digital_Cooperation_EN.pdf> accessed 12 June 2020. This analysis was based on Carlos Ignacio Gutierrez and Gary Marchant, 'A Global Perspective of Soft Law Programs for the Governance of Artificial Intelligence' (Sandra Day O'Connor College of Law, Arizona State University 2021) <https://lsi.asulaw.org/softlaw/wp-content/uploads/sites/7/2022/08/final-database-report-002-compressed.pdf> accessed 13 March 2025.

[78] Future of Life Institute, 'Asilomar AI Principles' (*Future of Life Institute*, 2017) <https://futureoflife.org/ai-principles/> accessed 27 February 2017.

[79] 'Montreal Declaration for a Responsible Development of Artificial Intelligence' (*Université de Montréal*, 3 November 2017) <https://recherche.umontreal.ca/english/strategic-initiatives/montreal-declaration-for-a-responsible-ai/> accessed 12 January 2024.

[80] The Public Voice, 'Universal Guidelines for Artificial Intelligence' (23 October 2018) <https://thepublicvoice.org/ai-universal-guidelines/> accessed 12 January 2024.

[81] Beijing Academy of Artificial Intelligence, 'Beijing AI Principles' <https://link.springer.com/content/pdf/10.1007/s11623-019-1183-6.pdf> accessed 12 January 2024.

[82] Gutierrez and Marchant (n 77) 3. ('we found that government entities led AI soft law development with a ~36% participation, followed by multi-stakeholder alliances with ~21%').

[83] Mélanie Gornet and others, 'Mapping AI Ethics: A Meso-Scale Analysis of Its Charters and Manifestos', *Proceedings of the 2024 ACM Conference on Fairness, Accountability, and Transparency* (Association for Computing Machinery 2024) <https://dl.acm.org/doi/10.1145/3630106.3658545> accessed 13 June 2024.

3.2.2.1.3 *New industry partnerships*

Beyond the simple issuance of new principles, this era also saw the establishment of new organizations, including the 2016 Partnership on AI (PAI),[84] a company initiative made up of AI researchers representing Apple, Amazon, DeepMind and Google, Facebook, IBM, and Microsoft. PAI was expanded with more than 20 new organizations as well as non-profit members in 2017,[85] and since its launch has come to convene more than 50 members. PAI has supported research on a range of issues related to AI ethics and governance,[86] including an AI Incident Database (AIDD) which, since its 2020 launch,[87] has collected more than 1,200 reports of AI systems causing problems in terms of safety, fairness, or other impacts.[88]

However, such partnerships have encountered many obstacles. In 2020, PAI lost its only Chinese member, Baidu, due to increasing strain in US–China relations.[89] Several months later, the non-governmental organization (NGO) Access Now resigned from PAI in protest, stating that it 'did not find that PAI influenced or changed the attitude of member companies or encouraged them to respond to or consult with civil society on a systematic basis'.[90] Nonetheless, such industry partnerships still appeal to many stakeholders, even (or especially) in the light of the currently intense public attention on advanced, general-purpose foundation model AI.[91]

3.2.2.1.4 *The rise in voluntary standard-setting for AI*

Another contemporaneous trend has come from an increase in initiatives by international voluntary standards organizations.[92] For instance, between 2016 and

[84] 'Partnership on AI | About Us | Advancing Positive Outcomes for People and Society | Values, Pillars, Tenets' (*Partnership on AI*) <https://partnershiponai.org/about/> accessed 27 November 2022; Alex Hern, '"Partnership on AI" Formed by Google, Facebook, Amazon, IBM and Microsoft' *The Guardian* (28 September 2016) <https://www.theguardian.com/technology/2016/sep/28/google-facebook-amazon-ibm-microsoft-partnership-on-ai-tech-firms> accessed 12 January 2024.

[85] PAI, 'Partnership on AI Strengthens Its Network of Partners and Announces First Initiatives' (*Partnership on AI*, 16 May 2017) <https://partnershiponai.org/partnership-on-ai-strengthens-its-network-of-partners-and-announces-first-initiatives/> accessed 12 January 2024.

[86] Schmitt (n 10).

[87] 'AI Incidents Database' (*Partnership on AI*) <https://partnershiponai.org/workstream/ai-incidents-database/> accessed 12 January 2024; Sean McGregor, 'Preventing Repeated Real World AI Failures by Cataloging Incidents: The AI Incident Database' (arXiv, 17 November 2020) <http://arxiv.org/abs/2011.08512> accessed 14 October 2022.

[88] 'AI Incidents Database' (n 87).

[89] Will Knight, 'Baidu Breaks Off an AI Alliance Amid Strained US–China Ties' [2020] *Wired* <https://www.wired.com/story/baidu-breaks-ai-alliance-strained-us-china-ties/> accessed 21 June 2020.

[90] Access Now, 'Access Now Resigns from the Partnership on AI' (*Access Now*, 13 October 2020) <https://www.accessnow.org/press-release/access-now-resignation-partnership-on-ai/> accessed 12 January 2024; Veale, Matus, and Gorwa (n 10) 258.

[91] As will be discussed in Section 3.2.3.

[92] See also the overview in Cihon (n 10); Lorenz (n 10). Note, this does not focus on the equally significant role of domestic standard-setting organizations, such as the US National Institute of Standards and Technology (NIST). See for instance NIST, 'AI Risk Management Framework: Second Draft' 36. Likewise, while there have been AI standard-setting activities by the ITU, these will instead be discussed in Section 3.2.2.2, on activities within the UN system.

2019, the Institute of Electrical and Electronics Engineers Standards Association (IEEE-SA) launched its IEEE Global Initiative on Ethics of Autonomous and Intelligent Systems. IEEE's initiative resulted in both a public discussion document with guidelines for the 'Ethically Aligned Design' of autonomous and intelligent systems,[93] and also a set of working groups on aspects of AI,[94] which published the IEEE P70xx series of standards on AI transparency (7001-2021), processes for considering ethical issues in design (7000-2021), and AI bias and nudging (7003TM, 7008TM).[95]

Likewise, in 2017, the International Organization for Standardization (ISO) and the International Electrotechnical Commission (IEC) established a Subcommittee on AI, SO/IEC JTC 1/SC 42, that began engagement in articulating a series of standards for autonomous systems.[96] Since then, the ISO-IEC committee has issued or updated 20 standards in and around AI,[97] ranging from the provision of shared terms[98] to standards for the governance of AI within organizations.[99]

3.2.2.2 (2018–2024) Growing interest and engagement within the UN system

While there remains uncertainty over the long-term prospects for the UN's CCW GGE process on autonomous weapons, this has obviously not stopped broader institutional examination of other AI issues within the UN system.

Indeed, the UN took a remarkably early role in organizing a wide range of AI-focused activities, across its system of organizations.[100] In summer 2017, the International Telecommunications Union (ITU) organized the first AI for Good

[93] IEEE, 'Ethically Aligned Design: A Vision for Prioritizing Human Well-Being with Autonomous and Intelligent Systems' (IEEE Global Initiative on Ethics of Autonomous and Intelligent Systems 2019) <https://engagestandards.ieee.org/rs/211-FYL-955/images/EAD1e.pdf> accessed 26 March 2019.

[94] Ansgar Koene and others, 'IEEE P70xx, Establishing Standards for Ethical Technology' (2018) <https://www.kdd.org/kdd2018/files/project-showcase/KDD18_paper_1743.pdf> accessed 13 March 2025.

[95] Veale, Matus, and Gorwa (n 10) 262.

[96] See also the overviews in Cihon (n 10); Lorenz (n 10) 17.

[97] ISO/IEC JTC 1, 'ISO/IEC JTC 1/SC 42—Artificial Intelligence' (*ISO*, 12 September 2023) <https://www.iso.org/committee/6794475.html> accessed 12 January 2024.

[98] ISO, 'ISO/IEC WD 22989—Artificial Intelligence—Concepts and Terminology' (*ISO*, July 2022) <http://www.iso.org/cms/render/live/en/sites/isoorg/contents/data/standard/07/42/74296.html> accessed 26 November 2018. On the effects of such initiatives, see also José-Miguel Bello y Villarino, 'Global Standard-Setting for Artificial Intelligence: Para-Regulating International Law for AI?' (2023) 41 The Australian Year Book of International Law Online 157.

[99] ISO/IEC JTC 1/SC 42, 'ISO/IEC 38507:2022 Information Technology—Governance of IT—Governance Implications of the Use of Artificial Intelligence by Organizations' (*ISO*, April 2022) <https://www.iso.org/standard/56641.html> accessed 12 January 2024. See also Chinen (n 10) 210.

[100] Garcia, 'Multilateralism and Artificial Intelligence: What Role for the United Nations?' (n 10); For an early overview, see also ITU, 'United Nations Activities on Artificial Intelligence (AI)' (ITU 2018) <https://www.itu.int/dms_pub/itu-s/opb/gen/S-GEN-UNACT-2018-1-PDF-E.pdf>; See also Martina Kunz, 'AI and International Organizations' <https://globalaigov.org/participants/igos.html> accessed 31 October 2022.

Global Summit.[101] In November 2017, the UN System Chief Executives Board for Coordination (CEB) began to consider a range of 'frontier issues', including AI.[102] In September 2018, UN Secretary-General António Guterres issued a Strategy on New Technologies, which emphasized the positive use of AI and digital technologies in the service of key global goals.[103] As part of the initiative the UN Secretary-General's High-level Panel on Digital Cooperation ran a public consultation about AI,[104] from which it published its first report on the issue in 2019, articulating a series of policy recommendations.[105] In that same month, the CEB adopted a set of guidelines articulating a strategic approach for supporting AI capacity development throughout the UN system.[106]

Simultaneously, a wide variety of UN organizations started activities exploring the implications of AI technology for their operations.[107] These included, among others, initial investigations and reports by the International Labour Organization (ILO) and the United Nations Educational, Scientific and Cultural Organization (UNESCO);[108] activities by the ITU, International Maritime Organization (IMO), and International Civil Aviation Organization (ICAO);[109] a range of initiatives by the UN Institute for Disarmament Research (UNIDIR) and the Centre for Policy Research at the United Nations University (UNU); and a Centre for Artificial Intelligence and Robotics by the UN Interregional Crime and Justice Research Institute (UNICRI).[110]

[101] ITU and XPRIZE Foundation, 'AI for Good Global Summit—2017 Report' (Geneva, June 2017) <https://www.itu.int/en/ITU-T/AI/Documents/Report/AI_for_Good_Global_Summit_Report_2017.pdf> accessed 14 November 2017.

[102] UN System Chief Executives Board for Coordination, 'Artificial Intelligence' <https://unsceb.org/topics/artificial-intelligence> accessed 12 January 2024.

[103] António Guterres, 'UN Secretary-General's Strategy on New Technologies' (United Nations 2018) <http://www.un.org/en/newtechnologies/images/pdf/SGs-Strategy-on-New-Technologies.pdf> accessed 4 October 2018; see also the resulting report: UN SG HLPDC, 'The Age of Digital Interdependence: Report of the UN Secretary-General's High-Level Panel on Digital Cooperation' (UN Secretary-General's High-Level Panel on Digital Cooperation 2019) <https://digitalcooperation.org/wp-content/uploads/2019/06/DigitalCooperation-report-for-web.pdf> accessed 13 June 2019.

[104] See also Luke Kemp and others, 'UN High-Level Panel on Digital Cooperation: A Proposal for International AI Governance' <https://www.cser.ac.uk/news/advice-un-high-level-panel-digital-cooperation/>.

[105] UN SG HLPDC (n 103).

[106] Chief Executives Board for Coordination, 'Summary of Deliberations: A United Nations System-Wide Strategic Approach and Road Map for Supporting Capacity Development on Artificial Intelligence' <http://digitallibrary.un.org/record/3811676> accessed 12 September 2020; Garcia, 'Multilateralism and Artificial Intelligence: What Role for the United Nations?' (n 10) 10.

[107] ITU (n 100); ITU, 'United Nations Activities on Artificial Intelligence (AI) 2019' (ITU 2019) <https://www.itu.int/dms_pub/itu-s/opb/gen/S-GEN-UNACT-2019-1-PDF-E.pdf> accessed 13 November 2019.

[108] Brigitte Lasry and others, *Human Decisions: Thoughts on AI* (UNESCO, United Nations Educational, Scientific and Cultural Organization/International Bureau of Education 2018) <http://unesdoc.unesco.org/images/0026/002615/261563e.pdf> accessed 6 November 2018.

[109] Garcia, 'Multilateralism and Artificial Intelligence: What Role for the United Nations?' (n 10) n 16.

[110] Butcher and Beridze (n 10); Garcia, 'Multilateralism and Artificial Intelligence: What Role for the United Nations?' (n 10) 11. See also Rumtin Sepasspour, 'A Reality Check and a Way Forward for the Global Governance of Artificial Intelligence' (2023) 79(5) Bulletin of the Atomic Scientists 304.

Within the UN system, UNESCO took a leadership role on AI governance. In March 2020, the organization established an Ad Hoc Expert Group of 24 members in order to draft a global standard-setting instrument on the ethics of AI.[111] Once elaborated, this instrument was formally approved by UNESCO's General Conference at the end of 2021.[112] The resulting Recommendation on the Ethics of Artificial Intelligence, adopted by all 193 UN Member States, states that human dignity and international human rights must be respected, protected, and promoted throughout all the phases of the 'life cycle' of artificial intelligence.[113] It also prescribes that human beings should not be harmed or subordinated in any way by AI systems.[114] In March 2021, UNESCO and ITU also began collaboration on an interagency working group for AI, issuing in September 2022 a set of Principles for the Ethical Use of Artificial Intelligence in the United Nations System, which went on to be endorsed by the UN system CEB.[115]

3.2.2.3 (2016–2021) Non-binding club initiatives: OECD, G20, G7, GPAI

Other AI governance activities have taken the form of non-binding governance instruments produced by regional international organizations, multi-stakeholder groups, and coalitions of like-minded parties.[116] Among these, a particular set of initiatives by governance clubs stands out.

After examining AI-related issues throughout 2016–17, the Organisation for Economic Co-operation and Development (OECD) issued a set of principles on AI in May 2019, which were adopted by its members in the Recommendation of the Council on Artificial Intelligence.[117] These principles, the first intergovernmental standard of its kind, called on actors involved in making or using AI to respect a series of values that included inclusive growth, sustainable development and well-being, human-centred values and fairness, transparency and explainability,

[111] UNESCO, 'UNESCO's International Expert Group Begins Work on Drafting the First Global Recommendation on the Ethics of AI' (27 April 2020) <https://www.unesco.org/en/articles/unescos-international-expert-group-begins-work-drafting-first-global-recommendation-ethics-ai> accessed 12 January 2024.

[112] UNESCO, 'UNESCO Member States Adopt the First Ever Global Agreement on the Ethics of Artificial Intelligence' (*UNESCO*, 25 November 2021) <https://en.unesco.org/news/unesco-member-states-adopt-first-ever-global-agreement-ethics-artificial-intelligence> accessed 13 January 2022.

[113] UNESCO, 'Recommendation on the Ethics of Artificial Intelligence' paras 13, 16 <https://unesdoc.unesco.org/ark:/48223/pf0000381137> accessed 6 September 2023.

[114] ibid 14.

[115] UN System Chief Executives Board for Coordination, 'Principles for the Ethical Use of Artificial Intelligence in the United Nations System' (United Nations System Chief Executives Board for Coordination 2022) <https://unsceb.org/sites/default/files/2023-03/CEB_2022_2_Add.1%20%28AI%20ethics%20principles%29.pdf> accessed 12 January 2024. See also Sepasspour (n 110) 307.

[116] On the general governance role of such (at times) informal organizations, see Jean-Frédéric Morin and others, 'How Informality Can Address Emerging Issues: Making the Most of the G7' (2019) 10 Global Policy 267.

[117] OECD, 'Recommendation of the Council on Artificial Intelligence' <https://legalinstruments.oecd.org/en/instruments/OECD-LEGAL-0449> accessed 28 May 2019.

robustness, security and safety, and accountability.[118] In addition, the document highlighted a set of priorities for national policies and international cooperation on trustworthy AI.[119] In February 2020 the OECD launched its AI Policy Observatory, designed to help shape and share information on AI policies,[120] as well as to collect and report on notable negative incidents involving AI.[121]

A second line of institutional activity came from the G20. In June 2019, one month after the publication of the OECD AI Principles, the G20 adopted a set of 'human-centred AI Principles' at the Osaka Summit Track on the Digital Economy, which drew closely from and endorsed the principles laid out by the OECD.[122] They also 'took note of' (though did not explicitly extend support for) the OECD's recommendation on 'national policies and international cooperation'.[123]

A third line of activity came from the G7: initial meetings on the issue, in 2016 and 2017, were held at the ministerial level, where a vision for human-centric AI for innovation and economic growth was crafted.[124] In 2018 an initial ministerial 'Statement on Artificial Intelligence' was followed, a few months later, by the leader-level G7 commitment to the 'Charlevoix Common Vision for the Future of Artificial Intelligence', which set out 12 core commitments to ensuring 'human-centric AI', in order to foster economic growth, societal trust, equality, and inclusion around the technology.[125]

Moreover, the G7 played a key role in the inception of another new AI-focused forum—the Global Partnership on Artificial Intelligence (GPAI). In 2018, France and Canada first proposed the creation of an International Panel on Artificial Intelligence,[126] explicitly inspired by the Intergovernmental Panel on Climate

[118] ibid 1.1–1.5; For commentary, see also Karen Yeung, 'Recommendation of the Council on Artificial Intelligence (OECD)' (2020) 59 International Legal Materials 27.

[119] OECD, 'Recommendation of the Council on Artificial Intelligence' (n 117) para 2.1–2.5 ('i) investing in AI research and development; ii) fostering a digital ecosystem for AI; iii) shaping an enabling policy environment for AI; iv) building human capacity and preparing for labour market transformation; and v) international cooperation for trustworthy AI').

[120] OECD, 'OECD AI Policy Observatory: A Platform for AI Information, Evidence, and Policy Options' (OECD 2019) <https://www.oecd.org/going-digital/ai/about-the-oecd-ai-policy-observatory.pdf> accessed 8 October 2019; See also Garcia, 'Multilateralism and Artificial Intelligence: What Role for the United Nations?' (n 10) 8.

[121] OECD AI Policy Observatory, 'AIM: The OECD AI Incidents Monitor, an Evidence Base for Trustworthy AI' (*OECD AI Policy Observatory*) <https://oecd.ai/en/incidents> accessed 12 January 2024.

[122] G20, 'G20 Ministerial Statement on Trade and Digital Economy' <https://www.mofa.go.jp/files/000486596.pdf> accessed 25 May 2020. Moreover, OECD Secretary-General Angel Gurría in turn endorsed the G20 principles. OECD, 'OECD Supporting G20 Policy Priorities at Osaka Summit' (30 June 2019) <https://www.oecd.org/g20/summits/osaka/publicationsanddocuments/oecd-supporting-g20-policy-priorities-at-osaka-summit.htm> accessed 5 September 2020.

[123] Garcia, 'Multilateralism and Artificial Intelligence: What Role for the United Nations?' (n 10) n 31.

[124] Schmitt (n 10) 306.

[125] G7, 'Charlevoix Common Vision for the Future of Artificial Intelligence' <https://www.mofa.go.jp/files/000373837.pdf> accessed 12 January 2024; see also Schmitt (n 10) 306.

[126] Justin Trudeau, 'Mandate for the International Panel on Artificial Intelligence' (*Prime Minister of Canada*, 6 December 2018) <https://pm.gc.ca/eng/news/2018/12/06/mandate-internatio

Change (IPCC). At the initial G7 meeting in 2019, this initiative was initially opposed by the US, on the grounds that it might be overly restrictive and could impede AI development by US companies.[127] Nonetheless, the idea of such a new body lived on in the GPAI proposal,[128] which the US shifted to support by May 2020, explicitly describing it as a step taken to counter-balance the growing role of China in steering the global trajectory of AI.[129] GPAI was finally established in June 2020, with 15 founding members, as an 'international and multistakeholder platform to guide the international community on the responsible development of AI'.[130] GPAI eventually would expand its membership to 44 states, including India, Brazil, Senegal, and Turkey—while conspicuously excluding China. Notably, while many early global initiatives for AI approached norm-setting from different angles,[131] the development of GPAI also highlighted patterns of institutional convergence, specifically with the OECD. Almost from the very start, the GPAI Secretariat was housed within the OECD,[132] and collaboration between the organizations was consistently close, eventually culminating in 2024 in the unification of both organizations in an 'integrated partnership', under the GPAI brand but in pursuit of the OECD Recommendation, while putting all OECD members and GPAI countries on an equal footing.[133]

nal-panel-artificial-intelligence> accessed 6 July 2019; see also Nature Editors, 'International AI Ethics Panel Must Be Independent' (2019) 572 Nature 415.

[127] Tom Simonite, 'The World Has a Plan to Rein In AI—but the US Doesn't Like It' [2020] *Wired* <https://www.wired.com/story/world-plan-rein-ai-us-doesnt-like/> accessed 31 May 2020.

[128] Global Partnership on Artificial Intelligence, 'Joint Statement from Founding Members of the Global Partnership on Artificial Intelligence' <https://www.gov.uk/government/publications/joint-statement-from-founding-members-of-the-global-partnership-on-artificial-intelligence> accessed 15 June 2020.

[129] Michael Kratsios, 'Artificial Intelligence Can Serve Democracy' *Wall Street Journal* (27 May 2020) <https://www.wsj.com/articles/artificial-intelligence-can-serve-democracy-11590618319> accessed 10 June 2020.

[130] Global Partnership on Artificial Intelligence (n 128). The 15 founding members of GPAI were Australia, Canada, France, Germany, India, Italy, Japan, Mexico, New Zealand, Republic of Korea, Singapore, Slovenia, United Kingdom, United States, and the European Union.

[131] High-level Panel on Digital Cooperation (n 77) n 42.

[132] OECD, 'OECD to Host Secretariat of New Global Partnership on Artificial Intelligence' (15 June 2020) <https://www.oecd.org/going-digital/ai/OECD-to-host-Secretariat-of-new-Global-Partnership-on-Artificial-Intelligence.htm> accessed 3 July 2020.

[133] '6th Meeting of the GPAI Ministerial Council Held on 3rd July 2024 at New Delhi' (*Ministry of Electronics & IT*, 3 July 2024) art 9 <https://pib.gov.in/pib.gov.in/Pressreleaseshare.aspx?PRID=2030534> accessed 1 August 2024 ('Announce a renewed vision for GPAI through an integrated partnership with the OECD bringing together all current OECD members and GPAI countries on equal footing, under the GPAI brand and on the basis of the OECD Recommendation on Artificial Intelligence'). OECD, 'GPAI and OECD Unite to Advance Coordinated International Efforts for Trustworthy AI' (*OECD*, 3 July 2024) <https://www.oecd.org/en/about/news/speech-statements/2024/07/GPAI-and-OECD-unite-to-advance-coordinated-international-efforts-for-trustworthy-AI.html> accessed 1 August 2024.

3.2.2.4 (2018–2024) The push for binding law: EU AI Act and CoE Convention

Beyond these initiatives, this period also saw more regional activities that have pursued more ambitious, binding regulation.

In this, the EU was an early mover. In June 2018 the European Commission created the High-Level Expert Group on Artificial Intelligence (HLEG) to support the development of policies and eventual regulations around AI.[134] The HLEG's Ethics Guidelines for Trustworthy AI[135] were published in 2019, on the basis of which the European Commission elucidated a draft text of its AI Act in April 2021, with the final version of the Act agreed in 2024.[136] The Act, which from an early stage relied on a risk-based, tiered approach to the regulation of AI,[137] was closely monitored by AI stakeholders, civil society, and scholars.[138] It has been hailed as a coherent and comprehensive approach to AI governance that could offer a 'third way' between US and Chinese approaches.[139] Notably, in its final negotiation process, the Act also came to contain a number of provisions meant to address some risks from advanced, general-purpose AI systems.[140]

Furthermore, while only directly regulating EU member states, the expectation is that this new regulatory framework would have considerable global flow-through effects in how AI is regulated in other states. That is, the Act could drive a 'Brussels Effect',[141] as has previously been observed with the 2016 General Data

[134] Charlotte Stix, 'Artificial Intelligence by Any Other Name: A Brief History of the Conceptualization of "Trustworthy Artificial Intelligence"' (2022) 2 Discover Artificial Intelligence 26.

[135] European Commission, 'Ethics Guidelines for Trustworthy AI' (The European Commission's High-Level Expert Group on Artificial Intelligence 2019) <https://ec.europa.eu/digital-single-market/en/news/ethics-guidelines-trustworthy-ai> accessed 18 April 2019.

[136] European Commission, 'Proposal for a Regulation of the European Parliament and of the Council Laying Down Harmonised Rules on Artificial Intelligence (Artificial Intelligence Act) and Amending Certain Union Legislative Acts' <https://eur-lex.europa.eu/legal-content/EN/TXT/?uri=CELEX%3A52021PC0206> accessed 7 July 2021; and for the final act, see: Regulation (EU) 2024/1689 of the European Parliament and of the Council of 13 June 2024 laying down harmonised rules on artificial intelligence [2024] OJ L210/1 (Artificial Intelligence Act).

[137] Jonas Schuett, 'Risk Management in the Artificial Intelligence Act' [2023] European Journal of Risk Regulation 1.

[138] The work on this topic is extensive, but see Michael Veale and Frederik Zuiderveen Borgesius, 'Demystifying the Draft EU Artificial Intelligence Act—Analysing the Good, the Bad, and the Unclear Elements of the Proposed Approach' (2021) 22 Computer Law Review International 97; Philipp Hacker, 'AI Regulation in Europe: From the AI Act to Future Regulatory Challenges' (*arXiv.org*, 6 October 2023) <https://arxiv.org/abs/2310.04072v1> accessed 10 October 2023; Matija Franklin and others, 'Missing Mechanisms of Manipulation in the EU AI Act' (2022) 35 *The International FLAIRS Conference Proceedings* <https://journals.flvc.org/FLAIRS/article/view/130723> accessed 9 September 2022.

[139] Charlotte Stix, 'The Ghost of AI Governance Past, Present, and Future: AI Governance in the European Union' in Justin Bullock and others (eds), *The Oxford Handbook of AI Governance* (Oxford University Press 2022).

[140] See also Section 3.2.3.1.1.

[141] On the Brussels Effect generally, see Anu Bradford, *The Brussels Effect: How the European Union Rules the World* (Oxford University Press 2020). For discussions in the context of the AI Act, see Charlotte Siegmann and Markus Anderljung, 'The Brussels Effect and Artificial Intelligence: How EU Regulation Will Impact the Global AI Market' (Centre for the Governance of AI 2022) <https://www.

Protection Regulation (GDPR).[142] Indeed, it has been argued that the draft AI Act has already begun to have such effects, as it reportedly influenced the shape of several national legislative proposals on AI, such as Canada's AI and Data Act (AIDA).[143] In this way, the instrument potentially supports the EU's broader efforts to shape global norms around AI.[144]

Complementing the EU AI Act, the European Commission in September 2022 also advanced two additional proposals that would establish the European regulatory approach to liability questions for AI, in the form of a new AI Liability Directive along with a revision of its existing Product Liability Directive.[145] Clarifying the question of liability would serve to fill a gap within the EU AI Act regime, which does not yet provide for any individual rights of persons harmed by AI.[146] While the updated Product Liability Directive came into force in December 2024, the fate of the AI Liability Directive presaged growing international contestation over the direction of AI governance, as the Commission withdrew the proposed act from its work programme in February 2025, in the wake of significant US critique of European technology regulation at the Paris AI Action Summit.[147]

In parallel to the EU AI Act, this period also saw a distinct programme to develop a binding international regime for AI, this one advocated by the Council of Europe (CoE), a 46-member club that had previously midwifed significant conventions on issues including digital technology, cybercrime, and data protection. In 2019 the CoE established an Ad Hoc Committee on Artificial Intelligence (CAHAI), which

governance.ai/research-paper/brussels-effect-ai> accessed 18 August 2022; Noam Kolt, 'Algorithmic Black Swans' (2023) 101 Washington University Law Review 24–28 <https://papers.ssrn.com/abstract=4370566> accessed 6 March 2023.

[142] See Garcia, 'Multilateralism and Artificial Intelligence: What Role for the United Nations?' (n 10) 8.

[143] Government of Canada, 'Artificial Intelligence and Data Act' (27 September 2023) <https://ised-isde.canada.ca/site/innovation-better-canada/en/artificial-intelligence-and-data-act> accessed 12 January 2024; Kolt (n 141) 27; But for a critique, see Anna Artyushina, 'Proposed Changes to Canada's Bill C-27 Do Little to Mitigate AI Harms' (*Centre for International Governance Innovation*, 9 November 2023) <https://www.cigionline.org/articles/proposed-changes-to-canadas-bill-c-27-do-little-to-mitigate-ai-harms/> accessed 12 January 2024.

[144] Steven Feldstein, 'Evaluating Europe's Push to Enact AI Regulations: How Will This Influence Global Norms?' [2023] Democratization 1; But for a critical view, see also Marco Almada and Anca Radu, 'The Brussels Side-Effect: How the AI Act Can Reduce the Global Reach of EU Policy' [2024] German Law Journal 1.

[145] European Commission, 'Proposal for a Directive of the European Parliament and of the Council on Adapting Non-Contractual Civil Liability Rules to Artificial Intelligence (AI Liability Directive)' <https://ec.europa.eu/info/sites/default/files/1_1_197605_prop_dir_ai_en.pdf> accessed 2 December 2022; For critical discussion, see Philipp Hacker, 'The European AI Liability Directives—Critique of a Half-Hearted Approach and Lessons for the Future' (arXiv, 23 January 2023) <http://arxiv.org/abs/2211.13960> accessed 10 February 2023.

[146] Hacker (n 145) 3.

[147] Anupriya Datta and Théophane Hartmann, 'Commission Withdraws AI Liability Directive after Vance Attack on Regulation' (*Euractiv*, 11 February 2025) <https://www.euractiv.com/section/tech/news/commission-withdraws-ai-liability-directive-after-vance-attack-on-regulation/> accessed 19 February 2025.

discussed potential legal frameworks for AI—including, potentially, a binding treaty on AI that would apply to all of its 46 member states.[148] In January 2022, a new Committee on AI (CAI)—consisting of member states, observer states such as the US and Japan, and private sector and civil society representatives—drafted the text of its AI Convention.[149] This Framework Convention on Artificial Intelligence, Human Rights, Democracy, and the Rule of Law was subsequently released after a second reading in December 2023[150] to serve as the basis for further CoE negotiations. These were concluded in early 2024, yielding a final treaty text that was adopted in May 2024 by the CoE's Committee of Ministers, and opened for signature in September.[151]

This Convention has several aims. Among others, it regulates AI systems throughout their lifecycle and apply horizontally across sectors. It also provides specific member state obligations and AI principles to underpin rights of individuals, as well as redress systems, provisions for the assessment of the risks of AI systems for human rights, and effective oversight mechanisms.[152]

Notably, in its impacts, the Convention might follow the precedent of other treaties enacted by the CoE, such as the 2001 Budapest Convention on Cybercrime[153] or the 2011 Istanbul Convention on preventing and combating violence against women,[154] both of which successfully secured the participation of many countries beyond the initial set of CoE members. At the same time, even these regimes grappled with notable holdouts.[155] Similar political challenges may beset the Framework Convention's expansion to other states. While 13 states signed the treaty within its first few months—with Canada and Japan signing on

[148] Natalie Leal, 'Council of Europe Starts Work on Legally-Binding AI Treaty' (*Global Government Forum*, 22 July 2020) <https://www.globalgovernmentforum.com/council-of-europe-starts-work-on-legally-binding-ai-treaty/> accessed 5 September 2020. While the Council of Europe cannot itself produce binding laws, it can enforce specific international agreements reached by European states on various topics.

[149] See Hannah van Kolfschooten and Carmel Shachar, 'The Council of Europe's AI Convention (2023–2024): Promises and Pitfalls for Health Protection' (2023) 138 Health Policy 104935. As well as Maximilian Gartner, 'Council of Europe: States Adopt First Binding Framework Treaty on AI' (2024) 1 Journal of AI Law and Regulation 342.

[150] Committee on Artificial Intelligence (CAI), 'Draft Framework Convention on Artificial Intelligence, Human Rights, Democracy, and the Rule of Law' <https://rm.coe.int/cai-2023-28-draft-framework-convention/1680ade043> accessed 20 December 2023.

[151] Council of Europe Framework Convention on Artificial Intelligence and Human Rights, Democracy and the Rule of Law (opened for signature 5 September 2024, not yet in force) CETS 225.

[152] Council of Europe, 'Explanatory Report to the Council of Europe Framework Convention on Artificial Intelligence and Human Rights, Democracy and the Rule of Law' (Council of Europe 2024) <https://rm.coe.int/1680afae67> accessed 25 June 2024.

[153] Convention on Cybercrime (2001) ETS No 185.

[154] Council of Europe Convention on Preventing and Combating Violence against Women and Domestic Violence (2001) CETS No 210.

[155] At present, 64 states have ratified the Budapest Cybercrime Convention; however, since it entered into force, several major states (including India and—for many years—Brazil) long declined to adopt the Convention, on the argument that they did not participate in its drafting. See Alexander Seger, 'India and the Budapest Convention: Why Not?' (*orfonline.org*, 10 August 2016) <https://www.orfonline.org/expert-speak/india-and-the-budapest-convention-why-not> accessed 22 August 2024.

February 11, 2025, at a side event of the Paris AI Action Summit[156]—there may be legal barriers that inhibit global extension to all key AI actors. This is especially the case as the instrument is a plurilateral one, which means that (future) membership to the treaty is by default closed to other states unless existing States Parties give their unanimous consent to the accession of those states.[157]

Moreover, like other attempts at establishing binding regulation, the Framework Convention has had to contend with growing political contestation as the public prominence and stakes of AI technology have grown.[158] The final treaty leaves the regulation of private actors to the discretion of states, and also establishes regulatory exceptions for activities related to the protection of national security interests and national defence. While future protocols might specify certain of its obligations further, these design elements may pose a continuing challenge both to the horizontal expansion of the agreement to other states, as well as to its efficacy at regulating all relevant risk clusters posed by AI.

3.2.3 (2022–2025) Developments in global governance for advanced AI

From early 2022 onwards, many of the large-scale foundation models that had begun development during the AI field's Large-Scale Era—such as OpenAI's Generative Pre-trained Transformer (GPT) line of language models, as well as image generation AI systems such as DALL-E—began to reach maturity in the field's emerging General-Purpose Era.

3.2.3.1 (2022–2023) First sparks of advanced AI governance

While large-scale foundation models have been under development and deployment for several years, influencing ongoing conversations over appropriate lab norms around issues such as model release and access,[159] it was only in early 2022

[156] Council of Europe, 'Canada and Japan Sign Council of Europe's First Ever Global Treaty on AI' (*Council of Europe, Newsroom*, 11 February 2025) <https://www.coe.int/en/web/portal/-/canada-and-japan-sign-council-of-europe-s-first-ever-global-treaty-on-ai> accessed 20 February 2025.

[157] Council of Europe Framework Convention on Artificial Intelligence and Human Rights, Democracy and the Rule of Law (opened for signature 5 September 2024, not yet in force) CETS 225 arts 30.1, 31.1. See also José Jaime Villalobos and Matthijs M Maas, 'Beyond a Piecemeal Approach: Prospects for a Framework Convention on AI' in P Hacker and others (eds), *The Oxford Handbook of the Foundations and Regulation of Generative AI* (Oxford University Press, forthcoming) 7.

[158] A discussion of the further negotiation and implementation process of the EU AI Act is conducted in Section 3.2.3.1.1.

[159] Markus Anderljung, Julian Hazell, and Moritz von Knebel, 'Protecting Society from AI Misuse: When Are Restrictions on Capabilities Warranted?' [2024] AI & Society <https://doi.org/10.1007/s00146-024-02130-8> accessed 16 December 2024; Markus Anderljung and Anton Korinek, 'Frontier AI Regulation: Safeguards Amid Rapid Progress' (*Lawfare*, 4 January 2024) <https://www.lawfaremedia.org/article/frontier-ai-regulation-safeguards-amid-rapid-progress> accessed 6 January 2024; Elizabeth Seger and others, 'Open-Sourcing Highly Capable Foundation Models: An Evaluation

that these systems began to influence AI governance efforts and only in 2023 that international AI governance debates for these systems truly hit their stride. As increasingly capable versions of these models began to see deployment—and as academics, civil society, and even many leading labs began to articulate urgent calls for caution and regulation[160]—global attention on the national and international regulation of AI reached a new peak. This had a range of impacts on already ongoing governance efforts but also drove a wave of new, fresh efforts and initiatives.

3.2.3.1.1 The rescoping of existing governance efforts for 'generative' AI: the EU AI Act

In some cases, the prospect of increasingly adaptable AI systems affected ongoing governance initiatives, by altering their direction or expanding their focus from the regulation of (conventional) narrow AI systems to the impacts of general-purpose AI systems.

At times, this technological shift complicated ongoing governance negotiations. For instance, the rise of increasingly general-purpose AI systems complicated the negotiation process and trajectory of the EU AI Act.[161] Notably, as early as 2022 onwards, EU actors began quietly considering and proposing ways by which 'general-purpose AI systems' might be regulated within the draft EU AI Act.[162] However, the deployment of ChatGPT in November 2022 significantly increased pressure

of Risks, Benefits, and Alternative Methods for Pursuing Open-Source Objectives' (Centre for the Governance of AI 2023) <https://www.governance.ai/research-paper/open-sourcing-highly-capable-foundation-models> accessed 2 October 2023; David Evan Harris, 'How to Regulate Unsecured "Open-Source" AI: No Exemptions' (*Tech Policy Press*, 4 December 2023) <https://techpolicy.press/how-to-regulate-unsecured-opensource-ai-no-exemptions> accessed 4 December 2023; Alex Engler, 'The EU's Attempt to Regulate Open-Source AI Is Counterproductive' (*Brookings*, 24 August 2022) <https://www.brookings.edu/blog/techtank/2022/08/24/the-eus-attempt-to-regulate-open-source-ai-is-counterproductive/> accessed 31 October 2022.

[160] AI Now Institute, 'Zero Trust AI Governance' (Accountable Tech, AI Now Institute, EPIC 2023) <https://ainowinstitute.org/publication/zero-trust-ai-governance> 7 September 2023; CAIS, 'Statement on AI Risk' (30 May 2023) <https://www.safe.ai/statement-on-ai-risk> accessed 30 May 2023; Future of Life Institute, 'Policymaking in the Pause: What Can Policymakers Do Now to Combat Risks from Advanced AI Systems?' (Future of Life Institute 2023) <https://futureoflife.org/wp-content/uploads/2023/04/FLI_Policymaking_In_The_Pause.pdf> accessed 16 April 2023; Brad Smith, 'Developing and Deploying AI Responsibly: Elements of an Effective Legislative Framework to Regulate AI' (*Microsoft On the Issues*, 12 September 2023) <https://blogs.microsoft.com/on-the-issues/2023/09/12/developing-and-deploying-ai-responsibly-elements-of-an-effective-legislative-framework-to-regulate-ai/> accessed 29 November 2023; Connor Dunlop, 'An EU AI Act that Works for People and Society' (*Ada Lovelace Institute*, 6 September 2023) <https://www.adalovelaceinstitute.org/policy-briefing/eu-ai-act-trilogues/> accessed 15 November 2023.

[161] Natali Helberger and Nicholas Diakopoulos, 'ChatGPT and the AI Act' (2023) 12 Internet Policy Review <https://policyreview.info/essay/chatgpt-and-ai-act> accessed 11 April 2023.

[162] Philipp Hacker, Andreas Engel, and Marco Mauer, 'Regulating ChatGPT and Other Large Generative AI Models', *Proceedings of the 2023 ACM Conference on Fairness, Accountability, and Transparency* (Association for Computing Machinery 2023) 1114 <https://dl.acm.org/doi/10.1145/3593013.3594067> accessed 20 November 2023. ('On May 13, 2022, the French Council presidency circulated an amendment to the draft AI Act, Articles 4a-4c, on what the text calls general-purpose AI systems (GPAIS).')

to establish—and adapt—AI regulation. Consequently, by the time the Council of the European Union approved its common position on the draft EU AI Act one month later, new provisions had been added for the regulation of general-purpose AI systems.[163]

Seeds were thus planted for contestation during the final, 'trilogue' phase of the negotiations between the EU Commission, Council, and Parliament. As it happened, in November 2023, the French, German, and Italian governments objected to the regulation of foundation models,[164] instead suggesting that the AI companies developing such models should regulate themselves by publishing relevant information about their models and volunteering to adhere to certain codes of conduct. In spite of these political obstacles, by December Parliament and Council negotiators had ultimately reached a provisional political agreement on the Act[165]—which nonetheless included, among others, transparency requirements for all GPAI systems, more stringent model evaluation, assessment, adversarial testing, and incident notification obligations for high-impact GPAI models with 'systemic risks', on top of the existing regulations and bans around some types of conventional, narrow AI systems that are considered high-risk.[166] As a proxy, the EU handles a compute threshold (of 10^{25} FLOPS) to characterize GPAI systems that are presumed to carry systemic risks, although this threshold can be updated.[167] In doing so, the AI Act maintained a set of provisions that are directly relevant to the emerging risks from advanced AI systems.[168]

[163] Council of the EU, 'Artificial Intelligence Act: Council Calls for Promoting Safe AI That Respects Fundamental Rights' (*Council of the European Union*, 6 December 2022) <https://www.consilium.europa.eu/en/press/press-releases/2022/12/06/artificial-intelligence-act-council-calls-for-promoting-safe-ai-that-respects-fundamental-rights/> accessed 12 January 2024. See also Claire Boine and David Rolnick, 'General Purpose AI Systems in the AI Act: Trying to Fit a Square Peg into a Round Hole' (2023) *We Robot 2023*. <https://www.bu.edu/law/files/2023/09/General-Purpose-AI-systems-in-the-AI-Act.pdf> accessed 12 January 2024; Gian Volpicelli, 'ChatGPT Broke the EU Plan to Regulate AI' (*POLITICO*, 3 March 2023) <https://www.politico.eu/article/eu-plan-regulate-chatgpt-openai-artificial-intelligence-act/> accessed 20 April 2023.

[164] Luca Bertuzzi, 'France, Germany, Italy Push for "Mandatory Self-Regulation" for Foundation Models in EU's AI Law' (*www.euractiv.com*, 19 November 2023) <https://www.euractiv.com/section/artificial-intelligence/news/france-germany-italy-push-for-mandatory-self-regulation-for-foundation-models-in-eus-ai-law/> accessed 19 November 2023; Will Henshall, 'E.U.'s AI Regulation Could Be Softened After Pushback' (*TIME*, 22 November 2023) <https://time.com/6338602/eu-ai-regulation-foundation-models/> accessed 4 December 2023.

[165] European Parliament, 'Artificial Intelligence Act: Deal on Comprehensive Rules for Trustworthy AI' (*European Parliament*, 9 December 2023) <https://www.europarl.europa.eu/news/en/press-room/20231206IPR15699/artificial-intelligence-act-deal-on-comprehensive-rules-for-trustworthy-ai> accessed 12 January 2024.

[166] ibid.

[167] 'Artificial Intelligence—Q&As' (*European Commission*) <https://ec.europa.eu/commission/presscorner/detail/en/QANDA_21_1683> accessed 22 May 2024.

[168] Cornelia Kutterer, 'Regulating Foundation Models in the AI Act: From "High" to "Systemic" Risk' (*MIAI*, 11 January 2024) <https://ai-regulation.com/regulating-foundation-models-in-the-ai-act-from-high-to-systemic-risk/> accessed 31 January 2024; See also Guillem Bas and others, 'The EU AI Act: A Pioneering Effort to Regulate Frontier AI?' (2024) 27 Inteligencia Artificial 55. An overview of the AI Act can be found at 'The AI Act Explorer' (*EU Artificial Intelligence Act*) <https://artificialintelligenceact.eu/ai-act-explorer/> accessed 22 May 2024.

The AI Act was subsequently approved by EU lawmakers in the European Parliament in March 2024,[169] endorsed by EU countries in May,[170] and entered into force on 1 August 2024.[171] While the new legislation will formally apply in 2026, many rules will come into force sooner in the intermediate period.[172]

In addition, the Act provides for a set of non-binding Codes of Practice to serve as intermediate (albeit non-binding) modes of compliance for providers of GPAI models.[173] Finally, to support and help in the implementation and enforcement of the Act's rules, the EU has established a European AI Office within the European Commission, to be supported by a scientific panel of independent experts, in undertaking roles such as the classification of general-purpose AI systems and enforcing the rules for such systems.[174]

With this, the EU AI Act provides the first legally binding, supranational framework that explicitly and distinctly targets both conventional (narrow) AI systems and advanced general-purpose systems.[175] However, while a significant step, some critics have asserted that lobbying efforts by technology companies and member states may have weakened key aspects, with an over-reliance on self-certification paired with potentially weak oversight mechanisms, leaving potential accountability gaps.[176] Accordingly, many implementation details of this framework—such as the precise functioning of the European AI Office[177] and the details and

[169] Foo Yun Chee, 'Europe One Step Away from Landmark AI Rules after Lawmakers' Vote' *Reuters* (14 March 2024) <https://www.reuters.com/technology/eu-lawmakers-endorse-political-deal-artificial-intelligence-rules-2024-03-13/> accessed 22 May 2024.

[170] European Council, 'Artificial Intelligence (AI) Act: Council Gives Final Green Light to the First Worldwide Rules on AI' (21 May 2024) <https://www.consilium.europa.eu/en/press/press-releases/2024/05/21/artificial-intelligence-ai-act-council-gives-final-green-light-to-the-first-worldwide-rules-on-ai/> accessed 22 May 2024. Foo Yun Chee and Tassilo Hummel, 'Europe Sets Benchmark for Rest of the World with Landmark AI Laws' *Reuters* (22 May 2024) <https://www.reuters.com/world/europe/eu-countries-back-landmark-artificial-intelligence-rules-2024-05-21/> accessed 22 May 2024.

[171] Regulation (EU) 2024/1689 of the European Parliament and of the Council of 13 June 2024 laying down harmonised rules on artificial intelligence [2024] OJ L210/1 (Artificial Intelligence Act).

[172] Benjamin Larsen and Sabrina Küspert, 'Regulating General-Purpose AI: Areas of Convergence and Divergence across the EU and the US' (*Brookings*, 21 May 2024) <https://www.brookings.edu/articles/regulating-general-purpose-ai-areas-of-convergence-and-divergence-across-the-eu-and-the-us/> accessed 22 May 2024.

[173] European Commission, 'Proposal for a Regulation of the European Parliament and of the Council Laying Down Harmonised Rules on Artificial Intelligence (Artificial Intelligence Act) and Amending Certain Union Legislative Acts' (n 136) art 56; See also Jimmy Farrell, 'An Introduction to Codes of Practice for the AI Act' (*EU Artificial Intelligence Act*, 3 July 2024) <https://artificialintelligenceact.eu/introduction-to-codes-of-practice/> accessed 3 July 2024.

[174] European Commission, 'Commission Decision Establishing the European AI Office' (*European Commission*, 24 January 2024) <https://digital-strategy.ec.europa.eu/en/library/commission-decision-establishing-european-ai-office> accessed 22 May 2024. European Commission, 'European AI Office' (*European Commission*, 2024) <https://digital-strategy.ec.europa.eu/en/policies/ai-office> accessed 22 May 2024. Larsen and Küspert (n 172).

[175] Bas and others (n 168).

[176] Sandra Wachter, 'Limitations and Loopholes in the E.U. AI Act and AI Liability Directives: What This Means for the European Union, the United States, and Beyond' (2024) 26 Yale Journal of Law & Technology 671.

[177] See also Claudio Novelli and others, 'A Robust Governance for the AI Act: AI Office, AI Board, Scientific Panel, and National Authorities' [2024] European Journal of Risk Regulation 1. For an earlier proposal, see Sam Curtis, Felicity Reddel, and Nicolas Moës, 'A Blueprint for the European AI Office'

implementation of its final General-Purpose AI Code of Practice, drafted from 2024 and published in July 2025[178]—remain to be worked out and guaranteed, if this regime is to contribute not just to effective AI governance within the EU, but also to greater international alignment globally.

3.2.3.2 (2022–2025) A wave of new governance efforts for advanced AI

In addition to altering the trajectory of debate in existing fora, the rise of large generative AI systems and highly capable foundation models also gave the impetus for a wave of fresh global governance initiatives throughout mid to late 2023—initiatives from all corners and actors, and in all forms, from self-governance to minilateral codes to new multilateral resolutions.

3.2.3.2.1 New industry partnerships: the Frontier Model Forum and AI Alliance

For instance, US-based AI companies started a new round of AI self-governance initiatives, through voluntary commitments made to the Biden Administration,[179] and through the establishment—by Anthropic, Google, Microsoft, and OpenAI—of a new Frontier Model Forum (FMF) in July 2023.[180]

During the same period, fresh disagreements between different tech companies over the risks of these models, and the merits of open-sourcing these systems, also caused the emergence of competing partnerships, however, in the form of the December 2023 AI Alliance, launched by Meta and IBM to emphasize and advocate for the open-sourcing of AI capabilities.[181] Nonetheless, not all companies saw these as inherent tensions, with Meta (along with Amazon) also joining the FMF by May 2024.[182]

(The Future Society 2023) <https://thefuturesociety.org/a-blueprint-for-the-european-ai-office/> accessed 10 November 2023.

[178] European Commission, 'Third Draft of the General-Purpose AI Code of Practice Published, Written by Independent Experts' (*European Commission*, 11 March 2025) <https://digital-strategy.ec.europa.eu/en/library/third-draft-general-purpose-ai-code-practice-published-written-independent-experts> accessed 13 March 2025.

[179] The White House, 'FACT SHEET: Biden–Harris Administration Secures Voluntary Commitments from Eight Additional Artificial Intelligence Companies to Manage the Risks Posed by AI' (*The White House*, 12 September 2023) <https://www.whitehouse.gov/briefing-room/statements-releases/2023/09/12/fact-sheet-biden-harris-administration-secures-voluntary-commitments-from-eight-additional-artificial-intelligence-companies-to-manage-the-risks-posed-by-ai/> accessed 13 September 2023.

[180] Google, 'Frontier Model Forum: A New Partnership to Promote Responsible AI' (*Google*, 26 July 2023) <https://blog.google/outreach-initiatives/public-policy/google-microsoft-openai-anthropic-frontier-model-forum/> accessed 7 August 2023.

[181] IBM, 'AI Alliance Launches as an International Community of Leading Technology Developers, Researchers, and Adopters Collaborating Together to Advance Open, Safe, Responsible AI' (*IBM Newsroom*, 5 December 2023) <https://newsroom.ibm.com/AI-Alliance-Launches-as-an-International-Community-of-Leading-Technology-Developers,-Researchers,-and-Adopters-Collaborating-Together-to-Advance-Open,-Safe,-Responsible-AI> accessed 12 January 2024.

[182] Frontier Model Forum, 'Amazon and Meta Join the Frontier Model Forum to Promote AI Safety' (*Frontier Model Forum*, 20 May 2024) <https://www.frontiermodelforum.org/updates/amazon-and-meta-join-the-frontier-model-forum-to-promote-ai-safety/> accessed 27 May 2024.

Other partnerships also emerged, focusing on public–private initiatives aimed at fostering the advancement of AI and its dissemination in support of sustainable development. For instance, in September 2024, at the sidelines of the 79th Session of the UNGA, US Secretary of State Blinken announced the Partnership for Global Inclusivity on AI (PGIAI), a collaboration between the Department of State, Amazon, Anthropic, Google, IBM, Meta, Microsoft, Nvidia, and OpenAI, to commit more than USD 100 million to advancing the use of AI in developing countries.[183]

3.2.3.2.2 Renewed UN efforts: the AI Advisory Body, UNGA Resolutions, GDC

The UN intensified its interest in the governance of increasingly capable generative AI and foundation models. In October 2023, after an initial consultation and recruitment process, Secretary-General António Guterres convened a new High-Level Advisory Body on Artificial Intelligence.[184] Based in the Office of the Secretary-General's Envoy on Technology (OSET), this expert body was charged with pursuing consensus about the risks of AI, and with advancing recommendations for its international governance.[185] This body published its Interim Report in December 2023[186] and its Final Report in September 2024,[187] when these recommendations were adopted into the Global Digital Compact (GDC) at the September 2024 UN Summit of the Future.[188]

While earlier state reactions to UN-based discussions of global AI governance had at times been mixed,[189] in December 2023 the US took the initiative with a draft UN General Assembly resolution on AI,[190] which aimed to affirm that AI should be deployed in a way that is consistent with the UN Charter and the Universal Declaration of Human Rights. Accordingly, in March 2024, the UNGA

[183] United States Department of State, 'United States and Eight Companies Launch the Partnership for Global Inclusivity on AI' (*United States Department of State*, 23 September 2024) <https://www.state.gov/united-states-and-eight-companies-launch-the-partnership-for-global-inclusivity-on-ai/> accessed 26 September 2024.

[184] Supantha Mukherjee, 'United Nations Creates Advisory Body to Address AI Governance' *Reuters* (27 October 2023) <https://www.reuters.com/technology/united-nations-creates-advisory-body-address-ai-governance-2023-10-26/> accessed 12 January 2024.

[185] 'AI Advisory Body' (United Nations 2023) <https://www.un.org/en/ai-advisory-body> accessed 8 November 2023.

[186] High-Level Advisory Body on Artificial Intelligence, 'Interim Report: Governing AI for Humanity' (United Nations 2023) <https://www.un.org/sites/un2.un.org/files/ai_advisory_body_interim_report.pdf> accessed 22 December 2023.

[187] High-Level Advisory Body on Artificial Intelligence, 'Governing AI for Humanity: Final Report' (United Nations 2024) <https://www.un.org/sites/un2.un.org/files/governing_ai_for_humanity_final_report_en.pdf>.

[188] UNGA Res 79/1 'The Pact for the Future: Annex 1: Global Digital Compact' (22 September 2024) UN Doc A/RES/79/1 (Global Digital Compact).

[189] Ryan Heath, 'UN Deadlocked over Regulating AI' (*Axios*, 21 September 2023) <https://www.axios.com/2023/09/21/global-ai-regulator-united-nations> accessed 13 January 2024.

[190] United Nations General Assembly, 'UNGA Res. A/78/L.49 Seizing the Opportunities of Safe, Secure, and Trustworthy Artificial Intelligence Systems for Sustainable Development'.

adopted Resolution A/78/L.49 'Seizing the opportunities of safe, secure and trustworthy artificial intelligence systems for sustainable development', the first global resolution on AI, which was co-sponsored by China and more than 120 other nations.[191] This resolution among others encouraged countries to foster 'the development, implementation and disclosure of mechanisms of risk monitoring and management',[192] as well as to intensify information sharing, such as 'on mutually agreed terms among entities with roles across the life cycle of artificial intelligence systems to identify, understand and act using scientific and evidence-based best practices, policies and approaches to artificial intelligence systems to maximize the benefits while mitigating the potential risks across the life cycle of artificial intelligence systems, including advanced artificial intelligence systems'.[193]

Notably, alongside co-sponsoring this resolution, China also took the initiative to propose its own draft resolution on AI at the UNGA, which aimed at closing gaps between rich and developing countries on AI through greater international cooperation.[194] Accordingly, Resolution (A/78/L.86) 'Enhancing international cooperation on capacity-building of artificial intelligence' was adopted in June 2024. The resolution also emphasized, among others, that member states should 'consider the benefits and risks when scaling up the responsible use of digital solutions, such as open-source artificial intelligence and digital public infrastructure, among other methods and business models'.[195]

Finally, in September 2024 the UN negotiated its Global Digital Compact, part of the Pact for the Future. First proposed in 2021 in the UN Secretary-General's *Our Common Agenda* report, the GDC is an instrument developed to 'outline shared principles for an open, free and secure digital future for all'.[196] Accordingly, the GDC proposes the establishment of a set of new entities and mechanisms, including an Independent International Scientific Panel on AI, a Global Dialogue on AI Governance, and a capacity-building fund.[197]

While the final direction and trajectory of this initiative remains to be seen, it sets the foundation for a regime complex of different institutions and initiatives, to

[191] United Nations General Assembly, 'UNGA Res. A/78/L.49 Seizing the Opportunities of Safe, Secure, and Trustworthy Artificial Intelligence Systems for Sustainable Development' (n 190).

[192] ibid 6(e).

[193] ibid 6(n).

[194] Augusta Saraiva, 'China Prepares UN Resolution on AI for Good Amid US Rivalry' (*Bloomberg*, 26 April 2024) <https://www.bloomberg.com/news/articles/2024-04-25/china-prepares-un-resolution-to-tap-ai-for-good?embedded-checkout=true> accessed 11 June 2024.

[195] United Nations General Assembly, 'UNGA Res A/78/L.86, 'Enhancing International Cooperation on Capacity-Building of Artificial Intelligence' para 7.

[196] UN Secretary-General, 'Our Common Agenda: Report of the Secretary-General' (United Nations 2021) para 93 <https://www.un.org/en/content/common-agenda-report/> accessed 11 September 2021. For a discussion of the development of the GDC, see DigWatch, 'Global Digital Compact in 2024' (*DigWatch*, 2024) <https://dig.watch/processes/global-digital-compact> accessed 2 May 2024.

[197] United Nations General Assembly, '(A/79/L.2) Global Digital Compact' (n 188). Para 56(a), 57.

collaborate among one another and to integrate with pre-existing bodies and initiatives both outside and within the UN system.[198]

3.2.3.2.3 New state regulation initiatives in the US and China

The rise of generative AI also led to a range of new State governance initiatives, in particular by major AI powers such as the US and China, amid growing policymaker concerns in those nations regarding both the impacts of conventional AI and the risks from advanced AI models.[199] While these initiatives were predominantly intended to set national AI policies, many of these frameworks could in principle come to exert extraterritorial effects,[200] provided that they manage to avoid politicization.

Since designating its high-level AI innovation and policy goals in the 2017 Next (or variably 'New') Generation AI Development Plan,[201] China has arguably pioneered some of the most ambitious domestic AI regulations so far, while taking a longer time to find its feet in terms of its approach to global AI governance, particularly in the face of early Western initiatives for global governance that often sought to exclude the country.[202] Domestically, China's internet regulator, the Cyberspace Administration of China (CAC), has begun articulating regulatory measures for advanced algorithms. These include a set of 2021 rules for recommendation algorithms that established the first national algorithm registry, and 2022 rules for 'deep synthesis' (i.e. synthetically generated media).[203] In April 2023, in response to the rise of generative AI systems, CAC articulated its 'Interim Measures for the Management of AI Services',[204] a set of rules for developers and deployers of such

[198] Belinda Cleeland, Maxime Stauffer and Malou Estier, 'Response to the Zero Draft of the Global Digital Compact: What It Means for AI Governance' (5 April 2024) <https://www.simoninstitute.ch/blog/post/response-to-the-zero-draft-of-the-global-digital-compact/> accessed 16 April 2024.

[199] For some discussion, see also Akash Wasil and Tim Durgin, 'US–China Perspectives on Extreme AI Risks and Global Governance' (24 June 2024) <https://papers.ssrn.com/abstract=4875436> accessed 15 July 2024.

[200] Cheng and Mckernon (n 10).

[201] Graham Webster and others, 'Full Translation: China's "New Generation Artificial Intelligence Development Plan" (2017)' (*DigiChina*, 1 August 2017) <https://digichina.stanford.edu/work/full-translation-chinas-new-generation-artificial-intelligence-development-plan-2017/> accessed 21 February 2025.

[202] Sihao Huang, 'Beijing's Vision of Global AI Governance' (*ChinaTalk*, 23 October 2023) <https://www.chinatalk.media/p/beijings-vision-of-global-ai-governance> accessed 21 February 2025.

[203] Helen Toner, Rogier Creemers, and Graham Webster, 'Translation: Internet Information Service Algorithmic Recommendation Management Provisions (Draft for Comment)—Aug. 2021' (*DigiChina*, 27 August 2021) <https://digichina.stanford.edu/work/translation-internet-information-service-algorithmic-recommendation-management-provisions-opinon-seeking-draft/> accessed 28 May 2024; China Law Translate, 'Provisions on the Administration of Deep Synthesis Internet Information Services' (*China Law Translate*, 12 December 2022) <https://www.chinalawtranslate.com/deep-synthesis/> accessed 28 May 2024; Matt Sheehan, 'China's AI Regulations and How They Get Made' (Carnegie Endowment for International Peace 2023) <https://carnegieendowment.org/2023/07/10/china-s-ai-regulations-and-how-they-get-made-pub-90117> accessed 13 January 2024.

[204] Cyberspace Administration of China, 'Interim Measures for the Management of Generative Artificial Intelligence Services' (*China Law Translate*, 13 July 2023) <https://www.chinalawtranslate.com/generative-ai-interim/> accessed 13 January 2024.

models,[205] which aim to mitigate a range of risks deriving from public-facing AI services, especially those relating to information content and security.[206]

CAC's rules under the Interim Measures included the first active licensing regime for AI, albeit one that, contrary to an earlier draft,[207] did not apply to the research stage but only to models offered to the public.[208] Significantly, the scholars of the Chinese Academy of Social Sciences, who drafted this law, subsequently revised it in September 2023, and again in April 2024, calling for the creation of a China Administration of AI as an overarching authority on AI regulation, to take the lead on a categorized oversight system for AI developers that would include stricter licensing oversight for AI systems and services that are deemed to be on a 'Negative List'.[209] Moreover, China continued to undertake work on a draft comprehensive Artificial Intelligence Law.[210]

In these ways, China has pursued an approach of iterative and ad hoc legislation around specific issues preparing the way for a comprehensive legal framework, similar to how its piecemeal process of internet regulation throughout the early 2000s resulted in its 2017 Cybersecurity Law.[211] However, in doing so, its AI governance approach may run into challenges: for one, it primarily focuses on the accountability of generative AI model service providers, with limited

[205] Mark MacCarthy, 'The US and Its Allies Should Engage with China on AI Law and Policy' (*Brookings*, 19 October 2023) <https://www.brookings.edu/articles/the-us-and-its-allies-should-engage-with-china-on-ai-law-and-policy/> accessed 13 January 2024; See also Matt Sheehan, 'What the U.S. Can Learn from China About Regulating AI' [2023] *Foreign Policy* <https://foreignpolicy.com/2023/09/12/ai-artificial-intelligence-regulation-law-china-us-schumer-congress/> accessed 13 January 2024; Sheehan, 'China's AI Regulations and How They Get Made' (n 203).

[206] Mimi Zou and Lu Zhang, 'Navigating China's Regulatory Approach to Generative Artificial Intelligence and Large Language Models' (2025) 1 Cambridge Forum on AI: Law and Governance e8.

[207] Seaton Huang and others, 'Translation: Measures for the Management of Generative Artificial Intelligence Services (Draft for Comment)' (*DigiChina*, April 2023) <https://digichina.stanford.edu/work/translation-measures-for-the-management-of-generative-artificial-intelligence-services-draft-for-comment-april-2023/> accessed 13 January 2024; for analysis see also Helen Toner and others, 'How Will China's Generative AI Regulations Shape the Future? A DigiChina Forum' (*DigiChina*, 19 April 2023) <https://digichina.stanford.edu/work/how-will-chinas-generative-ai-regulations-shape-the-future-a-digichina-forum/> accessed 13 January 2024.

[208] That is, it did not apply to companies that 'research, develop, and use generative AI technology, but have not provided generative AI services to the (mainland) public'. Cyberspace Administration of China (n 204) art 2. See also MacCarthy (n 205) ('In the final set of regulations, the CAC changed its mind. It determined that the AI licensing requirement should apply only to companies providing generative AI services to the public and not to companies engaged in research and development or using it for internal organizational operations').

[209] Zhou Hui and others, 'The Model Artificial Intelligence Law (MAIL) v.2.0—Multilingual Version' <https://zenodo.org/records/10974163> accessed 2 May 2024. See also Jeffrey Ding, 'ChinAI #262: Expert Draft AI Law Changelog' (*ChinAI Newsletter*, 22 April 2024) <https://chinai.substack.com/p/chinai-262-expert-draft-ai-law-changelog> accessed 2 May 2024.

[210] Qiheng Chen, 'China's Emerging Approach to Regulating General-Purpose Artificial Intelligence: Balancing Innovation and Control' (*Asia Society*, 7 February 2024) <https://asiasociety.org/policy-institute/chinas-emerging-approach-regulating-general-purpose-artificial-intelligence-balancing-innovation-and> accessed 28 May 2024.

[211] Weishan Miao, Min Jiang and Yunxia Pang, 'Historicizing Internet Regulation in China: A Meta-Analysis of Chinese Internet Policies (1994–2017)' (2021) 15 International Journal of Communication 24; see also the discussion in Cheng and Mckernon (n 10).

regulation on other entities (such as users and dissemination platforms).[212] Indeed, it has been suggested that, in terms of actual institutional dynamics rather than written law, China's regulatory approach to AI is in fact remarkably lenient and business-friendly.[213]

The prospects for internationalization of the Chinese approach appear limited for now, however. For one, the Chinese regulatory approach appears to be developed in relative isolation from many international processes,[214] potentially contributing to fragmentation among jurisdictions, or among international initiatives if there are attempts to export this model further abroad. Indeed, while China has sought for some years to set out and internationalize its vision for global vision for AI governance—such as in its 2023 'Global AI Governance Initiative', as well as its 2024 UN resolution and 'Shanghai Declaration on Global AI Governance'[215]—these efforts have to date been relatively marginal and predominantly articulated in reaction to Western initiatives in the space, especially those that explicitly sought to exclude China.[216]

For its part, the US also reacted swiftly to the emergence of advanced AI systems. On 30 October 2023, President Biden issued Executive Order 14110 on Safe, Secure and Trustworthy Artificial Intelligence.[217] Among others, the Executive Order (EO) required developers of 'dual-use foundation models' that could pose risks to national security, economic security, or the public to notify the US government of these training runs, and to share all results of safety tests. It also charged the National Institute of Standards and Technology (NIST) with developing rigorous standards and best practices for system evaluation, auditing, and red-team testing environments,[218] and emphasized recruitment and retention of AI expertise within the federal government,[219] among others.

While a significant early step, the EO, even from its start, largely functioned as a framework or roadmap for future legislation around AI safety. However, at the same time, it has been critiqued on the basis of an over-reliance on soft law

[212] Huijuan Dong and Junkai Chen, 'Meta-Regulation: An Ideal Alternative to the Primary Responsibility as the Regulatory Model of Generative AI in China' (2024) 54 Computer Law & Security Review 106016.

[213] Angela Huyue Zhang, 'The Promise and Perils of China's Regulation of Artificial Intelligence' [2024] Columbia Journal of Transnational Law <https://papers.ssrn.com/abstract=4708676> accessed 27 August 2024.

[214] Cheng and Mckernon (n 10).

[215] 'Shanghai Declaration on Global AI Governance' (4 July 2024) <http://za.china-embassy.gov.cn/eng/zgyw/202407/t20240704_11448349.htm> accessed 19 February 2025.

[216] Huw Roberts, 'China's Ambitions for Global AI Governance' (*East Asia Forum*, 10 September 2024) <https://eastasiaforum.org/2024/09/10/chinas-ambitions-for-global-ai-governance/> accessed 23 December 2024.

[217] Executive Office of the President, 'Executive Order on the Safe, Secure, and Trustworthy Development and Use of Artificial Intelligence' (*The White House*, 30 October 2023) <https://www.whitehouse.gov/briefing-room/presidential-actions/2023/10/30/executive-order-on-the-safe-secure-and-trustworthy-development-and-use-of-artificial-intelligence/> accessed 3 November 2023.

[218] ibid 4.1(a).

[219] ibid 10.2.

terminology and non-binding best practices, as well as inadequate monitoring, enforcement, and sanctioning mechanisms.[220]

However, throughout 2024–2025 a range of challenges emerged that challenged the efficacy of domestic AI regulation both within the US as well as in terms of its ability to serve as global model or influence. For one, the Executive Order was always vulnerable to repeal by future presidents:[221] and indeed it was no significant surprise when, shortly after his 2025 inauguration, President Trump swiftly repealed it.[222] Moreover, the mid-2024 repeal of the *Chevron* deference doctrine also substantially impacted the ability of federal agencies to regulate AI practices, by transferring interpretative authority away from such agencies and towards federal courts.[223] One effect of these developments may be to increasingly impose a chilling effect on those agencies' willingness to adopt any interpretations that might be controversial—as well as creating greater challenges for expertise in AI regulation, by transferring highly technical questions away from expert agencies and towards non-expert courts.[224] Given that this comes at a time when many political factors may make it challenging to pass larger legislative frameworks for AI,[225] the future course of US AI regulation—and its global effects—remains very much in question.

3.2.3.2.4 New club initiatives: AI Safety Summits and G7 Hiroshima Process

Between 2022 and 2025 a new cluster of governance initiatives for advanced AI took shape, taking the form of smaller but more nimble club initiatives championed by a range of states.

One major push for global policy-setting on advanced ('frontier') AI systems has come from the United Kingdom. Significantly, the UK had for several years pursued a domestic regulatory approach to (conventional) AI that had (as late as

[220] Manuel Wörsdörfer, 'Biden's Executive Order on AI: Strengths, Weaknesses, and Possible Reform Steps' [2024] AI and Ethics <https://doi.org/10.1007/s43681-024-00510-w> accessed 24 July 2024.

[221] Larsen and Küspert (n 172).

[222] David Shepardson, 'Trump Revokes Biden Executive Order on Addressing AI Risks' *Reuters* (21 January 2025) <https://www.reuters.com/technology/artificial-intelligence/trump-revokes-biden-executive-order-addressing-ai-risks-2025-01-21/> accessed 21 January 2025. However, the administration did not yet repeal the October 2024 National Security Memorandum on AI. Zach Shaw, 'The National Security Memo on AI: What to Expect in Trump 2.0' (*Institute for Law & AI*, 19 January 2025) <https://law-ai.org/the-national-security-memo-on-ai-what-to-expect-in-trump-2-0/> accessed 21 January 2025.

[223] Charlie Bullock, 'What Might the End of Chevron Deference Mean for AI Governance?' (*Institute for Law & AI*, 28 May 2024) <https://law-ai.org/chevron-deference/> accessed 1 August 2024.

[224] ibid.

[225] Of course, even in the absence of new legislation, there could still be other avenues through which a US President might accomplish policy goals that contribute to greater oversight of AI. For instance, see Charlie Bullock and others, 'Existing Authorities for Oversight of Frontier AI Models' (Institute for Law & AI 2024) LawAI Working Paper Series 1–2024 <https://law-ai.org/existing-authorities-for-oversight/> accessed 25 July 2024. Similarly, federal agencies might be able to use some of their existing authorities to govern AI, and indeed this may be the most effective approach for many domains in the near term.

the start of 2023) been presented as 'light-touch' and 'pro-innovation'.[226] Moreover, it had long adopted an approach to military AI that, by invoking an idiosyncratic and high-threshold definition for 'lethal autonomous weapons systems', had been claimed to inhibit international dialogues on that issue.[227]

However, based on growing concerns about the risks from advanced AI systems at the technological frontier, the UK now sought to take up a leadership role on the global governance of this technology. Accordingly, in July 2023 the UK convened a UN Security Council debate on the implications of AI for international peace and security.[228] More notably, it also announced its AI Safety Summit to be held in November 2023.[229] In contrast to previous AI governance approaches, this Summit focused explicitly on potentially extreme risks that might derive from frontier AI systems.[230] It also broke with the trend of some previous governance initiatives, such as GPAI, by making the—to some controversial[231]—decision to invite Chinese representatives to the event.[232] On the first day of the Summit, 28 governments and the European Union signed the Bletchley Declaration,[233] which

[226] Secretary of State for Science, Innovation and Technology, 'A Pro-Innovation Approach to AI Regulation' (2023) <https://www.gov.uk/government/publications/ai-regulation-a-pro-innovation-approach/white-paper> accessed 4 April 2023. See also Huw Roberts and others, 'Artificial Intelligence Regulation in the United Kingdom: A Path to Good Governance and Global Leadership?' (2023) 12 Internet Policy Review <https://policyreview.info/articles/analysis/artificial-intelligence-regulation-united-kingdom-path-good-governance> accessed 12 January 2024.

[227] Toby Ord, Angus Mercer, and Sophie Dannreuther, 'Future Proof: The Opportunity to Transform the UK's Resilience to Extreme Risks' (The Centre for Long-Term Resilience 2021) 28 <https://www.longtermresilience.org/futureproof> accessed 2 June 2021.

[228] UN Press, 'International Community Must Urgently Confront New Reality of Generative, Artificial Intelligence, Speakers Stress as Security Council Debates Risks, Rewards' (United Nations 18 July 2023) <https://press.un.org/en/2023/sc15359.doc.htm> accessed 4 December 2023. Michelle Nichols, 'UN Security Council Meets for First Time on AI Risks' *Reuters* (18 July 2023) <https://www.reuters.com/technology/un-security-council-meets-first-time-ai-risks-2023-07-18/> accessed 4 December 2023.

[229] UK Government, 'UK to Host First Global Summit on Artificial Intelligence' (*GOV.UK*, 7 June 2023) <https://www.gov.uk/government/news/uk-to-host-first-global-summit-on-artificial-intelligence> accessed 13 January 2024.

[230] UK Government, 'AI Safety Summit: Introduction' (*GOV.UK*, 25 September 2023) <https://www.gov.uk/government/publications/ai-safety-summit-introduction/ai-safety-summit-introduction-html> accessed 25 September 2023; UK Government, 'UK Government Sets out AI Safety Summit Ambitions' (*GOV.UK*, 4 September 2023) <https://www.gov.uk/government/news/uk-government-sets-out-ai-safety-summit-ambitions> accessed 6 September 2023. See also Talha Burki, 'Crossing the Frontier: The First Global AI Safety Summit' (2024) 6 The Lancet Digital Health <https://www.thelancet.com/journals/landig/article/PIIS2589-7500(24)00001-3/fulltext> accessed 10 January 2024.

[231] For instance, see Alex Chalmers and Nathan Benaich, 'China Has No Place at the AI Safety Summit' (31 August 2023) <https://www.airstreet.com/blog/china-ai-safety-summit> accessed 1 September 2023.

[232] Mark Bergen, 'UK Tries to Bring China to the Table at AI Summit' *Bloomberg.com* (1 November 2023) <https://www.bloomberg.com/news/newsletters/2023-11-01/uk-ai-safety-summit-rishi-sunak-invites-china> accessed 10 December 2023. 'China Accepts Invitation to AI Summit in Britain—Deputy UK PM' *Reuters* (26 October 2023) <https://www.reuters.com/world/china-accepts-invitation-ai-summit-britain-deputy-uk-pm-2023-10-26/> accessed 13 January 2024.

[233] UK Government, 'The Bletchley Declaration by Countries Attending the AI Safety Summit, 1–2 November 2023' (*GOV.UK*, 1 November 2023) <https://www.gov.uk/government/publications/ai-saf

expressed concern over the safety and misuse risks of frontier AI while emphasizing the role of international cooperation 'in an inclusive manner to ensure human-centric, trustworthy and responsible AI that is safe, and supports the good of all through existing international fora and other relevant initiatives'.[234] The Summit also led to the announcement of the UK-based AI Safety (now Security) Institute, and set the roadmap for subsequent follow-up Summits.[235] Finally, it initiated the development of an international, independent and inclusive 'State of the Science' report to evaluate the capabilities and risks of frontier AI models.[236]

Within half a year, the Safety Summit sparked significant follow-up, with additional AI safety institutes being established, most notably in the United States,[237] Japan,[238] Singapore,[239] and Canada.[240] This was rapidly followed by new partnerships between these institutes and relevant existing organizations, such as between

ety-summit-2023-the-bletchley-declaration/the-bletchley-declaration-by-countries-attending-the-ai-safety-summit-1-2-november-2023> accessed 3 November 2023.

[234] ibid.

[235] Mariano-Florentino Cuéllar, 'The UK AI Safety Summit Opened a New Chapter in AI Diplomacy' (*Carnegie Endowment for International Peace*, 9 November 2023) <https://carnegieendowment.org/2023/11/09/uk-ai-safety-summit-opened-new-chapter-in-ai-diplomacy-pub-90968> accessed 29 November 2023. See also Tom Leu, 'Looking Ahead to the AI Seoul Summit' (*Google DeepMind*, 20 May 2024) <https://deepmind.google/discover/blog/looking-ahead-to-the-ai-seoul-summit/> accessed 21 May 2024.

[236] Department for Science, Innovation & Technology, '"State of the Science" Report to Understand Capabilities and Risks of Frontier AI: Statement by the Chair, 2 November 2023' (*GOV.UK*, 2 November 2023) <https://www.gov.uk/government/publications/ai-safety-summit-2023-chairs-statement-state-of-the-science-2-november/state-of-the-science-report-to-understand-capabilities-and-risks-of-frontier-ai-statement-by-the-chair-2-november-2023> accessed 2 May 2024. This interim report was published ahead of the Seoul Summit. Yoshua Bengio, 'International Scientific Report on the Safety of Advanced AI: Interim Report' (Department for Science, Innovation & Technology, and AI Safety Institute 2024) 2024/009 <https://www.gov.uk/government/publications/international-scientific-report-on-the-safety-of-advanced-ai> accessed 21 May 2024. The final report was published in February 2025, prior to the Paris AI Action Summit. Yoshua Bengio and others, 'International AI Safety Report' (2025) DSIT 2025/001 <https://www.gov.uk/government/publications/international-ai-safety-report-2025> accessed 30 January 2025.

[237] U.S. Department of Commerce, 'At the Direction of President Biden, Department of Commerce to Establish U.S. Artificial Intelligence Safety Institute to Lead Efforts on AI Safety' (*U.S. Department of Commerce*, 1 November 2023) <https://www.commerce.gov/news/press-releases/2023/11/direction-president-biden-department-commerce-establish-us-artificial> accessed 22 May 2024.

[238] 'Japan: METI Establish AI Safety Institute' (*DataGuidance*, 19 February 2024) <https://www.dataguidance.com/news/japan-meti-establish-ai-safety-institute> accessed 22 May 2024; Ministry of Economy, Trade and Industry, 'AIセーフティ・インスティテュートを設立しました（METI/経済産業省）' (14 February 2024) <https://www.meti.go.jp/press/2023/02/20240214002/20240214002.html> accessed 22 May 2024.

[239] Infocomm Media Development Authority, 'First of Its Kind Generative AI Evaluation Sandbox for Trusted AI by AI Verify Foundation and IMDA' (*Infocomm Media Development Authority*, 31 October 2023) <https://www.imda.gov.sg/resources/press-releases-factsheets-and-speeches/press-releases/2023/generative-ai-evaluation-sandbox> accessed 22 May 2024.

[240] Department of Finance Canada, 'Remarks by the Deputy Prime Minister on Securing Canada's AI Advantage' (8 April 2024) <https://www.canada.ca/en/department-finance/news/2024/04/remarks-by-the-deputy-prime-minister-on-securing-canadas-ai-advantage.html> accessed 25 June 2024; see also Duncan Cass-Beggs, 'A Welcome Voice for Canada on the Future of AI' (*Centre for International Governance Innovation*, 30 April 2024) <https://www.cigionline.org/articles/a-welcome-voice-for-canada-on-the-future-of-ai/> accessed 25 June 2024.

the UK AI Safety Institute and France's National Institute for Research in Digital Science and Technology in early 2024.[241]

In May 2024, the Safety Summit process's first follow-up event in Seoul secured further commitments from 16 global AI technology companies to a key set of safety outcomes, including commitments to not develop or deploy AI models if their risks could not be sufficiently mitigated.[242] Along with private sector commitments, the Seoul summit also secured new governmental pledges,[243] with 27 nations and the EU—though not China—committing to 'guard against the full spectrum of AI risks, including risks posed by the deployment and use of current and frontier AI models or systems and those that may be designed, developed, deployed and used in future'[244] and committing jointly to develop risk thresholds and evaluation suites for understanding when and how these advanced AI systems might pose 'severe risks', such as by enabling malicious actors to acquire or use chemical or biological weapons, as well as to better test the ability of advanced AI systems to 'evade human oversight, for example by manipulation and deception or autonomous replication and adaptation'.[245]

In addition, ten states along with the EU issued both the *Seoul Declaration for Safe, Innovative and Inclusive AI*[246] and the Seoul Statement of Intent toward International Cooperation on AI Safety Science,[247] which committed these

[241] Department for Science, Innovation and Technology, 'UK and France to Deepen Research and AI Links Following Horizon Association' (*GOV.UK*, 29 February 2024) <https://www.gov.uk/government/news/uk-and-france-to-deepen-research-and-ai-links-following-horizon-association> accessed 24 July 2024.

[242] Department for Science, Innovation & Technology, 'Historic First as Companies Spanning North America, Asia, Europe and Middle East Agree Safety Commitments on Development of AI' (*GOV.UK*, 21 May 2024) <https://www.gov.uk/government/news/historic-first-as-companies-spanning-north-america-asia-europe-and-middle-east-agree-safety-commitments-on-development-of-ai> accessed 22 May 2024.

[243] Department for Science, Innovation & Technology, 'New Commitment to Deepen Work on Severe AI Risks Concludes AI Seoul Summit' (*GOV.UK*, 22 May 2024) <https://www.gov.uk/government/news/new-commitmentto-deepen-work-on-severe-ai-risks-concludes-ai-seoul-summit> accessed 24 May 2024.

[244] 'Seoul Ministerial Statement for Advancing AI Safety, Innovation and Inclusivity: AI Seoul Summit 2024' (*GOV.UK*, 22 May 2024) para 1.1 <https://www.gov.uk/government/publications/seoul-ministerial-statement-for-advancing-ai-safety-innovation-and-inclusivity-ai-seoul-summit-2024/seoul-ministerial-statement-for-advancing-ai-safety-innovation-and-inclusivity-ai-seoul-summit-2024> accessed 24 May 2024.

[245] ibid 1.3–1.4.

[246] 'Seoul Declaration for Safe, Innovative and Inclusive AI by Participants Attending the Leaders' Session: AI Seoul Summit, 21 May 2024' (*Department for Science, Innovation & Technology, GOV.UK*, 21 May 2024) <https://www.gov.uk/government/publications/seoul-declaration-for-safe-innovative-and-inclusive-ai-ai-seoul-summit-2024/seoul-declaration-for-safe-innovative-and-inclusive-ai-by-participants-attending-the-leaders-session-ai-seoul-summit-21-may-2024> accessed 22 May 2024 (issued by Australia, Canada, the European Union, France, Germany, Italy, Japan, the Republic of Korea, the Republic of Singapore, the United Kingdom, and the United States of America).

[247] 'Seoul Statement of Intent toward International Cooperation on AI Safety Science, AI Seoul Summit 2024 (Annex)' (*Department for Science, Innovation & Technology, GOV.UK*, 21 May 2024) <https://www.gov.uk/government/publications/seoul-declaration-for-safe-innovative-and-inclusive-ai-ai-seoul-summit-2024/seoul-statement-of-intent-toward-international-cooperation-on-ai-safety-science-ai-seoul-summit-2024-annex> accessed 22 May 2024.

nations to collaborate on an international network among publicly backed AI safety institutes, to promote 'complementarity and interoperability between their technical work and approach to AI safety, by sharing information about models and their limitations, capabilities and risks, as well as monitoring AI harms and safety incidents'.[248] This network comprised all of the states that had established AI Safety Institutes, alongside a set of other countries—especially France, Italy, Germany, and Australia—that had yet to announce a dedicated body.[249] This International Network of AI Safety Institutes was subsequently established at a November 2024 San Francisco summit, bringing together a set of ten initial members.[250]

However, much of this initial progress received a sharp shock at the Paris AI Action Summit in February 2025, which saw the hosts comprehensively pivot the direction and focus of this governance process away from discussions of the AI system's risks and instead towards the technology's opportunities and ways to leverage them.[251] The presentation of the previous summits' flagship International Science of AI Safety report was relegated to a side event,[252] and the Summit's final 'Statement on Inclusive and Sustainable Artificial Intelligence for People and the Planet' shifted towards putting a much greater emphasis on ways to foster innovation, while retaining only a single, vague, and high-level mention of the technology's 'risk'.[253] Consequently, a third of the countries

[248] Department for Science, Innovation & Technology, 'Global Leaders Agree to Launch First International Network of AI Safety Institutes to Boost Cooperation of AI' (*GOV.UK*, 21 May 2024) <https://www.gov.uk/government/news/global-leaders-agree-to-launch-first-international-network-of-ai-safety-institutes-to-boost-understanding-of-ai> accessed 22 May 2024. For the US statement, see also 'U.S. Secretary of Commerce Gina Raimondo Releases Strategic Vision on AI Safety, Announces Plan for Global Cooperation Among AI Safety Institutes' (*U.S. Department of Commerce*, 21 May 2024) <https://www.commerce.gov/news/press-releases/2024/05/us-secretary-commerce-gina-raimondo-releases-strategic-vision-ai-safety> accessed 1 August 2024.

[249] Alexandre Variengien and Charles Martinet, 'AI Safety Institutes: Can Countries Meet the Challenge?' (*OECD AI Policy Observatory*, 29 July 2024) <https://oecd.ai/en/wonk/ai-safety-institutes-challenge> accessed 13 August 2024.

[250] US Department of Commerce, 'FACT SHEET: U.S. Department of Commerce & U.S. Department of State Launch the International Network of AI Safety Institutes at Inaugural Convening in San Francisco' (*U.S. Department of Commerce*, 20 November 2024) <https://www.commerce.gov/news/fact-sheets/2024/11/fact-sheet-us-department-commerce-us-department-state-launch-international> accessed 18 February 2025.

[251] Giulia Torchio and Francesco Tasin, 'The Paris Summit: Au Revoir, Global AI Safety?' (*European Policy Centre*, 14 February 2025) <https://epc.eu/en/Publications/The-Paris-Summit-Au-Revoir-global-AI-Safety~61ea68> accessed 19 February 2025.

[252] Shakeel Hashim, 'The Embarrassing Failure of the Paris AI Summit' (*Transformer*, 11 February 2025) <https://www.transformernews.ai/p/paris-ai-summit-failure> accessed 13 February 2025.

[253] 'Statement on Inclusive and Sustainable Artificial Intelligence for People and the Planet' (*elysee.fr*, 11 February 2025) para 5 <https://www.elysee.fr/en/emmanuel-macron/2025/02/11/statement-on-inclusive-and-sustainable-artificial-intelligence-for-people-and-the-planet> accessed 18 February 2025 ('We commend the role of the Bletchley Park AI Safety Summit and Seoul Summits that have been essential in progressing international cooperation on AI safety and we note the voluntary commitments launched there. We will keep addressing the risks of AI to information integrity and continue the work on AI transparency').

participating—including, significantly, both the United Kingdom and United States—refused to endorse this final declaration.[254]

While the AI Safety Summit process attracted a significant share of policy attention, the 2023–2025 period also saw progress on a range of other important minilateral initiatives focused on advanced AI. For instance, at the annual G7 summit in 2023, state leaders met in Hiroshima to call for the development and adoption of technical standards for generative AI.[255] The resulting G7 Hiroshima AI Process, designed to articulate common policy priorities,[256] led to the issuing of two instruments in October that year:[257] the Hiroshima Process International Guiding Principles for Organizations Developing Advanced AI Systems,[258] and a set of more detailed provisions in the Hiroshima Process International Code of Conduct for Organizations Developing Advanced AI Systems.[259] Both underpinned the establishment of the Hiroshima AI Process Friends Group in May 2024, as a voluntary framework of 49 states seeking to implement these Guiding Principles and Code of Conduct.[260] On this basis, the Hiroshima AI Process has delivered a significant instrument for global AI governance, albeit one that will need to ensure further improvements in common AI governance terminology, risk management frameworks, and life cycle standards for AI models to see effective implementation not just within G7 members but also beyond them.[261]

[254] Tom Bristow, 'UK, US Snub Paris AI Summit Statement' *POLITICO* (11 February 2025) <https://www.politico.eu/article/uk-refuses-to-sign-paris-ai-action-summit-declaration/> accessed 13 February 2025. However, notably, China, which had not signed the Seoul Declaration, did sign the Paris Statement. Fan Chen, 'China Ready to Take Control as US and UK Back out of AI Action Summit Statement' *South China Morning Post* (22 February 2025) <https://www.scmp.com/news/china/diplomacy/article/3299406/china-ready-take-control-us-and-uk-back-out-ai-action-summit-statement> accessed 13 March 2025.

[255] G7, 'G7 Hiroshima Leaders' Communiqué' <https://www.mofa.go.jp/files/100506878.pdf> accessed 13 January 2024; Kantaro Komiya and Supantha Mukherjee, 'G7 Calls for Developing Global Technical Standards for AI' *Reuters* (20 May 2023) <https://www.reuters.com/world/g7-calls-developing-global-technical-standards-ai-2023-05-20/> accessed 13 January 2024.

[256] OECD, 'G7 Hiroshima Process on Generative Artificial Intelligence (AI): Towards a G7 Common Understanding on Generative AI' (OECD 2023) <https://www.oecd-ilibrary.org/science-and-technology/g7-hiroshima-process-on-generative-artificial-intelligence-ai_bf3c0c60-en> accessed 13 September 2023; see also Hiroki Habuka, 'The Path to Trustworthy AI: G7 Outcomes and Implications for Global AI Governance' (*CSIS*, 6 June 2023) <https://www.csis.org/analysis/path-trustworthy-ai-g7-outcomes-and-implications-global-ai-governance> accessed 20 December 2023.

[257] G7, 'G7 Leaders' Statement on the Hiroshima AI Process' (*The White House*, 30 October 2023) <https://www.whitehouse.gov/briefing-room/statements-releases/2023/10/30/g7-leaders-statement-on-the-hiroshima-ai-process/> accessed 13 January 2024.

[258] 'Hiroshima Process International Guiding Principles for Advanced AI System' (30 October 2023) <https://digital-strategy.ec.europa.eu/en/library/hiroshima-process-international-guiding-principles-advanced-ai-system> accessed 3 November 2023.

[259] 'Hiroshima Process International Code of Conduct for Advanced AI Systems' (30 October 2023) <https://digital-strategy.ec.europa.eu/en/library/hiroshima-process-international-code-conduct-advanced-ai-systems> accessed 3 November 2023.

[260] Fumio Kishida, 'Speech by Prime Minister KISHIDA Fumio at the Generative AI Side Event' (*Prime Minister's Office of Japan*, 2 May 2024) <https://japan.kantei.go.jp/101_kishida/statement/202405/02ai.html> accessed 8 May 2024.

[261] Habuka and Osa (n 10).

Alongside these tracks, the 2023–2025 period also saw a set of other club initiatives championed by various other states. As noted, just prior to the Bletchley Summit, China announced its own 'Global AI Governance Initiative' at its Belt and Road Forum, aimed at securing the representation of developing countries, and ensuring wide participation in global decision-making around AI.[262] On another track, in late 2023 18 countries presented their Guidelines for Secure AI System Development,[263] a non-binding set of recommendations to AI developers, intended to aid them in preventing misuse of AI systems by rogue actors. In February 2024, the Association of South East Asian Nations (ASEAN) published its own Guide on AI Governance and Ethics, which set out seven Guiding Principles for organizations aiming to design or deploy AI systems.[264] Moreover, the Guide also proposed the establishment of a ASEAN Working Group on AI Governance to oversee AI governance initiatives in the region, and the adaptation of the guide to address specific AI risks involving deepfakes, privacy violation, impacts on bias, or infringement of IP.[265] In August 2024, the African Union published its Continental AI Strategy.[266]

New overtures also came at the bilateral level. A November 2023 meeting between President Joe Biden and President Xi Jinping resulted in a broad agreement over 'risks and safety issues associated with artificial intelligence'.[267] While perhaps frustratingly vague, this initial meeting set the stage for a series of Sino–US intergovernmental dialogues on AI in early 2024, which in particular focused

[262] 'Global AI Governance Initiative' (*Chinese Ministry of Foreign Affairs*, 20 October 2023) <https://www.fmprc.gov.cn/eng/xw/zyxw/202405/t20240530_11332389.html> accessed 11 June 2024; Benjamin Herscovitch, 'China and the Great Global AI Governance Divide' (*Lowy Institute*, 27 March 2024) <https://www.lowyinstitute.org/the-interpreter/china-great-global-ai-governance-divide> accessed 11 June 2024. This initiative has since seen some statements of support from a range of non-Western states. AI Safety in China, 'AI Safety in China #15' (*AI Safety in China*, 1 July 2024) <https://aisafetychina.substack.com/p/ai-safety-in-china-15?publication_id=1862105 > accessed 1 July 2024.

[263] UK National Cyber Security Centre (NCSC) and US Cybersecurity and Infrastructure Agency (CISA), 'Guidelines for Secure AI System Development' <https://www.ncsc.gov.uk/collection/guidelines-secure-ai-system-development> accessed 30 November 2023. Raphael Satter and Diane Bartz, 'US, Britain, Other Countries Ink Agreement to Make AI "Secure by Design"' *Reuters* (28 November 2023) <https://www.reuters.com/technology/us-britain-other-countries-ink-agreement-make-ai-secure-by-design-2023-11-27/> accessed 13 January 2024.

[264] ASEAN, 'ASEAN Guide on AI Governance and Ethics' (ASEAN 2024) <https://asean.org/book/asean-guide-on-ai-governance-and-ethics/> accessed 12 August 2024.

[265] ibid 55–56. For a commentary on the Guide, see Kristina Fong, *From Paper to Practice: Utilizing the ASEAN Guide on Artificial Intelligence (AI) Governance and Ethics* (ISEAS Publishing 2024).

[266] African Union, 'Continental Artificial Intelligence Strategy' (African Union 2024) <https://au.int/en/documents/20240809/continental-artificial-intelligence-strategy> accessed 3 October 2024; For a critical appraisal, see Grace Chege, 'The AU Continental AI Strategy: Concrete Safety Proposals or High-Tech Hype?' (*ILINA Program*, September 2024) <https://ilinaprogram.org/2024/09/27/the-au-continental-ai-strategy-concrete-safety-proposals-or-high-tech-hype/> accessed 3 October 2024.

[267] Sydney J Freedberg, 'Biden Launches AI "Risk and Safety" Talks with China. Is Nuclear C2 a Likely Focus?' (*Breaking Defense*, 16 November 2023) <https://breakingdefense.sites.breakingmedia.com/2023/11/biden-launches-ai-risk-and-safety-talks-with-china-is-nuclear-c2-a-likely-focus/> accessed 13 January 2024.

on the prevention of significant accidents as well as unintended military escalation.[268] In April 2024, the UK and the US also announced that they had signed a Memorandum of Understanding for a Partnership on Science of AI Safety, in order to cooperate on developing tests and evaluation suites for the most advanced AI models.[269]

3.2.3.2.5 New expert initiatives and declarations

Amidst these formal and informal multilateral initiatives, a range of AI experts also pursued a more prominent role in shaping global debates. Documents such as the September 2024 Manhattan Declaration on Inclusive Global Scientific Understanding of Artificial Intelligence emphasized the need for greater, more inclusive and interdisciplinary global scientific cooperation to assess the capabilities and risks of AI; to ensure responsible development, deployment, and use; and to combine long and near-term perspectives on the technology's impacts.[270]

In addition, growing bilateral attention for the risks deriving from increasingly advanced AI systems[271] also gradually translated into more dialogue and engagements among Western and Chinese AI experts on these issues. For instance, the International Dialogue on AI Safety process, held in Beijing in early 2024, resulted in an expert-led Consensus Statement on Red Lines in Artificial Intelligence, which argued that 'unsafe development, deployment, or use of AI systems may pose catastrophic or even existential risks to humanity within our lifetimes'.[272] At a Venice meeting in September, this was followed by a second Consensus Statement on AI Safety as a Global Public Good, which emphasized the importance of emergency

[268] Eva Dou, 'U.S.–China Talks on AI Risks Set to Begin in Geneva' *Washington Post* (12 May 2024) <https://www.washingtonpost.com/technology/2024/05/13/us-china-ai-talks/> accessed 5 June 2024. See also Geopolitechs, 'China's Readout of the First Sino–U.S. Intergovernmental Dialogue on AI' (4 May 2024) <https://www.geopolitechs.org/p/chinas-readout-of-the-first-sino> accessed 11 June 2024. See also Graham Webster and Ryan Hass, 'A Roadmap for a US–China AI Dialogue' (*Brookings*, 10 January 2024) <https://www.brookings.edu/articles/a-roadmap-for-a-us-china-ai-dialogue/> accessed 5 June 2024.

[269] US Department of Commerce, 'U.S. and UK Announce Partnership on Science of AI Safety' (*U.S. Department of Commerce*, 1 April 2024) <https://www.commerce.gov/news/press-releases/2024/04/us-and-uk-announce-partnership-science-ai-safety> accessed 8 April 2024.

[270] MILA, 'The Manhattan Declaration on Inclusive Global Scientific Understanding of Artificial Intelligence' (22 September 2024) <https://mila.quebec/sites/default/files/media-library/pdf/47324/the-manhattan-declaration-sep24.pdf> accessed 3 October 2024.

[271] Wasil and Durgin (n 199). For a discussion of changes in Chinese perceptions of these risks, see also Matt Sheehan, 'China's Views on AI Safety Are Changing—Quickly' (*Carnegie Endowment for International Peace*, 27 August 2024) <https://carnegieendowment.orgundefined?lang=en> accessed 30 August 2024.

[272] IDAIS, 'Beijing Consensus Statement on Red Lines in Artificial Intelligence' (*International Dialogues on AI Safety*, 18 March 2024) <https://idais.ai/> accessed 24 July 2024; Eleanor Olcott and Cristina Criddle, 'Chinese and Western Scientists Identify "Red Lines" on AI Risks' *Financial Times* (18 March 2024) <https://www.ft.com/content/375f4e2d-1f72-49c8-b212-0ab2a173b8cb> accessed 24 July 2024.

preparedness agreements, the development of 'safety assurance' frameworks for AI, and independent global AI safety and verification research.[273]

All this capped a few years of intense global governance activity on AI. More importantly, it also laid the foundations for what will likely be many more years of intense follow-up, negotiation, implementation, and contestation, in order to give shape to the global institutions, norms, and regimes appropriate to govern the opportunities and impacts of increasingly advanced AI systems.

3.2.4 Reflections: hurdles for global AI governance

After gathering momentum for several years, there is currently a global wave of attention on AI governance. However, while encouraging, it remains unclear whether these initiatives will be adequate as both AI technology and the world continue to change. Indeed, while these early steps are promising, there may also be hurdles that could bar many of these initiatives from successfully following through. These challenges are diverse and will require commensurate responses.

3.2.4.1 Predominance of non-binding initiatives

In the first place, the fact that most (and, until mid-2024, all) international initiatives and agreements have been *non-binding* may work to inhibit the efficacy of the overall AI governance architecture. For example, a 2023 OECD survey of its member countries, exploring the degree to which they had implemented its 2019 OECD AI Principles, found that while there had been progress in members aligning their AI strategies and regulations with these principles, their full implementation was far from complete.[274] Likewise, UNESCO's non-binding AI Ethics Recommendation has seen only limited uptake since 2021, with less than a quarter of its signatories working with the organization to turn its principles into practice.[275]

The same critique of the insufficiency of non-binding norms could be levelled not just against these governance initiatives which were originally designed to govern narrow, conventional AI systems, but also at the newer flagship initiatives—such

[273] IDAIS, 'Venice Consensus Statement on AI Safety as a Global Public Good' (*International Dialogues on AI Safety*, September 2024) <https://idais.ai/idais-venice/> accessed 3 October 2024.

[274] Lucia Russo and Noah Oder, 'How Countries Are Implementing the OECD Principles for Trustworthy AI' (*OECD AI Policy Observatory*, 31 October 2023) <https://oecd.ai/en/wonk/national-policies-2> accessed 13 January 2024; OECD, 'The State of Implementation of the OECD AI Principles Four Years On' (OECD 2023) 3 <https://www.oecd.org/publications/the-state-of-implementation-of-the-oecd-ai-principles-four-years-on-835641c9-en.htm> accessed 13 January 2024.

[275] UNESCO, 'Artificial Intelligence: UNESCO Calls on All Governments to Implement Global Ethical Framework without Delay' (30 March 2023) <https://www.unesco.org/en/articles/artificial-intelligence-unesco-calls-all-governments-implement-global-ethical-framework-without> accessed 13 January 2024. See also Huw Roberts and others, 'Global AI Governance: Barriers and Pathways Forward' [2024] International Affairs iiae073, 3.

as the AI Safety Summits process, or the G7 Hiroshima AI Process—which were ostensibly convened to address the epochal emerging risks of advanced AI, but which, to date, have primarily resulted in sets of high-level, voluntary commitments, non-binding codes of conduct, and a budding network of AI safety institutes which however have no legal backing behind their inspections.

Indeed, some critics have suggested that this reflects a remarkable disconnect between, on the one hand, the potential (and claimed) stakes and extreme risks of 'frontier' AI which these initiatives sought to bring into the scope of global governance debates, and the comparatively meek and unambitious achievements for which they settled.[276] Similarly, early national initiatives such as the US Executive Order have been critiqued by some for their relative lack of hard law language, along with weak monitoring, enforcement, and sanctioning provisions.[277]

3.2.4.2 Imbalanced and under-inclusive membership

Second, the institutional ecology of AI governance remains broadly *under-inclusive* of many states. Many AI governance initiatives, in particular those recent efforts which have led on the governance of advanced AI, have only a fragmented and under-representative membership.

For instance, of seven major international AI governance instruments outside of the UN, just 7 countries—the G7 members—have participated in all, while 118 countries have been excluded from all.[278] This compounds more general critiques of the G7's role in steering global governance in many debates, on account of its exclusivity,[279] which puts the forum at odds with broader demands for more representative governance in many issue areas, including AI.

To be sure, some instruments—such as the UNESCO Recommendation—were endorsed by all 193 UN member states. Others, such as GPAI, saw a gradual expansion in their membership over time. However, even GPAI struggled with imbalanced global participation, especially in the Southeast Asia region, reflecting differences in policy focus but also GPAI's restrictive membership process.[280] Such imbalances in participation may in time exacerbate the global discrepancies in

[276] David Leslie and others, '"Frontier AI," Power, and the Public Interest: Who Benefits, Who Decides?' [2024] Harvard Data Science Review <https://hdsr.mitpress.mit.edu/pub/xdukxlpp/release/1> accessed 4 June 2024; David Leslie and Antonella Maia Perini, 'Future Shock: Generative AI and the International AI Policy and Governance Crisis' [2024] Harvard Data Science Review <https://hdsr.mitpress.mit.edu/pub/yixt9mqu/release/1> accessed 4 June 2024. See also Inga Ulnicane, 'Governance Fix? Power and Politics in Controversies about Governing Generative AI' [2024] Policy and Society puae022.

[277] Wörsdörfer (n 220).

[278] High-Level Advisory Body on Artificial Intelligence (n 187) 9, 42.

[279] Hylke Dijkstra and Ettore Greco, 'Relic of the Past or Catalyst for Change? The G7 and the Future of Global Governance' (ENSURED 2024) <https://www.ensuredeurope.eu/publications/g7-and-global-governance> accessed 10 July 2024.

[280] Andrew J Keith, 'Governance of Artificial Intelligence in Southeast Asia' [2024] Global Policy <https://onlinelibrary.wiley.com/doi/abs/10.1111/1758-5899.13458> accessed 21 October 2024.

AI regulation between hemispheres. In other cases, even individual governance tracks have started to see fragmentation in their membership, rather than convergence: within the AI Safety Summit process, China signed onto the Bletchley Declaration but declined to sign the subsequent Seoul Declaration, possibly in protest against what it saw as a Western-centric view of AI governance.[281]

This compounds the risk of growing North–South misalignment within global AI governance.[282] For instance, Marie-Therese Png has argued that many global initiatives for responsible AI have introduced a 'paradox of participation', as they result in surface-level participation of Global South stakeholders, without actually providing for the resources and framework to enable meaningful participation.[283] Beyond the legitimacy challenges such unevenness can create, the North–South asymmetry could set the stage for significant future contestation over—or evasion of—any resulting governance regimes.[284] Indeed, there is a risk that such tensions could be exacerbated by some emerging approaches to global compute governance: barring careful design and participation, such regimes might see Global North governments increasingly treat advanced AI chips and their underlying AI compute infrastructures as geostrategic resources and as levers that enable them to impose global rules on AI systems usage by Global South actors, given the highly unequal global geography of public cloud computing infrastructures.[285] Overcoming these political risks will require global AI governance arrangements to be tailored to both afford effective, meaningful voice and access for the 'global AI majority', while addressing the security and commercial concerns of 'frontier states'.[286]

[281] Joshua P Meltzer and Paul Triolo, 'The Bletchley Park Process Could Be a Building Block for Global Cooperation on AI Safety' (*Brookings*, 7 October 2024) <https://www.brookings.edu/articles/the-bletchley-park-process-could-be-a-building-block-for-global-cooperation-on-ai-safety/> accessed 8 October 2024.

[282] However, a more optimistic view of the ways that many Global South actors manage to indirectly and directly participate in AI governance initiatives, see Cameron F Kerry, 'The Good, the Not-so-Good, and the Ugly of the UN's Blueprint for AI' (*Brookings*, 29 August 2024) <https://www.brookings.edu/articles/the-good-the-not-so-good-and-the-ugly-of-the-uns-blueprint-for-ai/> accessed 2 September 2024. They have also played significant roles in the domain of military AI governance: see Bode (n 26).

[283] Marie-Therese Png, 'At the Tensions of South and North: Critical Roles of Global South Stakeholders in AI Governance', *Proceedings of the 2022 ACM Conference on Fairness, Accountability, and Transparency* (Association for Computing Machinery 2022) 1434 <https://doi.org/10.1145/3531146.3533200> accessed 29 August 2023. See also Veale, Matus, and Gorwa (n 10) 270.

[284] Sumaya Nur Adan, 'The Case for Including the Global South in AI Governance Discussions' (*GovAI Blog*, 20 October 2023) <https://www.governance.ai/post/the-case-for-including-the-global-south-in-ai-governance-conversations> accessed 23 October 2023; Cecil Abungu, Michelle Malonza, and Sumaya Nur Adan, 'Can Apparent Bystanders Distinctively Shape an Outcome? Global South Countries and Global Catastrophic Risk-Focused Governance of Artificial Intelligence' (*arXiv.org*, 7 December 2023) <https://arxiv.org/abs/2312.04616v1> accessed 7 January 2024.

[285] Vili Lehdonvirta, Bóxī Wú, and Zoe Hawkins, 'Compute North vs. Compute South: The Uneven Possibilities of Compute-Based AI Governance Around the Globe' (2024) 7 Proceedings of the AAAI/ACM Conference on AI, Ethics, and Society 828.

[286] Sumaya N Adan and others, 'Voice and Access in AI: Global AI Majority Participation in Artificial Intelligence Development and Governance' (Oxford Martin AI Governance Initiative 2024) Whitepaper

3.2.4.3 Institutional and normative fragmentation and contestation

Third, much of global AI governance remains *fragmented* not only geographically, but institutionally and normatively as well.[287] Such fragmentation has occurred at various levels.

One measure of fragmentation is divergence in implementation of global initiatives. For one, there has been significant variation not just between different national approaches to AI regulation,[288] but also within the ways in which different governments have approached the implementation of shared international AI governance frameworks. For instance, one 2024 study of the implementation of the OECD AI Principles found that many national AI rules based on this framework diverged, because different governments prioritized differently among these principles; employed different regulatory requirements towards implementing these same Principles; and saw limited interoperability among regulatory instruments resulting from even relatively small or granular differences in approach.[289]

Moreover, fragmentation also characterizes the prevailing patchwork of international responses to advanced AI at a substantive level. While there have been pockets of normative convergence in the approaches advanced by the OECD, GPAI, G20, and G7,[290] there are only partial overlaps among other initiatives: for instance, the (voluntary) Frontier AI Safety Commitments signed by 16 technology companies at the Seoul AI Safety Summit were less specific than commitments made under the White House voluntary commitments or the OECD Code of Conduct for Organizations Developing AI Systems.[291] Conversely, the Seoul commitments did provide for a commitment to 'set out thresholds at which severe risks posed by a model or system, unless adequately mitigated, would be deemed intolerable' that in turn is not included within the OECD Code.[292]

One underlying cause of such fragmentation may lie in the fact that many of these international initiatives have been articulated in relative isolation from one another. While issues relating to advanced, general-purpose AI systems did get taken up by the Bletchley and Seoul Declarations as well as the G7 Hiroshima Principles and Code of Conduct, those same issues remain somewhat underrepresented in the Council of Europe's AI Convention—notwithstanding assurances

<https://www.oxfordmartin.ox.ac.uk/publications/voice-and-access-in-ai-global-ai-majority-participation-in-artificial-intelligence-development-and-governance> accessed 21 October 2024.

287 Cihon, Maas, and Kemp (n 10).

288 Gasser (n 1).

289 Tommaso Giardini and Johannes Fritz, 'The Anatomy of AI Rules: A Systematic Comparison of AI Rules across the Globe' (Digital Policy Alert 2024) <https://digitalpolicyalert.org/ai-rules/the-anatomy-of-AI-rules> accessed 3 July 2024.

290 Ulnicane (n 276) 5–6.

291 Meltzer and Triolo (n 281).

292 ibid.

that the negotiations on that convention 'were inspired by elements of . . . [those] political declarations'.[293]

Moreover, there are emerging tensions even within single AI governance processes, with latent disagreements between the risk-focused approach that the UK, with US support, took in its 2023 AI Safety Summit, and the innovation-focused approach adopted by the 2025 AI Action Summit in Paris.[294] Such tensions may risk continued contestation or latent incoherence within such governance processes and fora, especially as India, the next host of the summit series, looks set to likewise shift the attention of the process away from questions of safety, to issues of innovation and global access.[295] These challenges are exacerbated given the general lack of clarity over the future form and institutional structure of the 'safety summit' series model.[296]

Indeed, while the AI Safety Summit process initially led to the rapid establishment of a range of national AI Safety Institutes (AISI)s, there are signs of trouble. For one, many of these institutes showed early divergence in their mandate and focus areas. For instance, the 'first wave' of established institutes by the UK, the US and Japan shared a very specific focus on safety evaluations for advanced AI systems—rather than a 'catch-all' responsibility for the national AI portfolio.[297] By contrast, subsequently established AISIs, such as those established by Canada, France, and Singapore, as well as under the EU AI Office, had greater variance in the extent of their powers as well as in their relative institutional focus on different AI issues such as safety, international collaboration, or AI innovation.[298] There are open questions whether these institutes should emphasize a role of evaluator

[293] Committee on Artificial Intelligence (CAI), '133rd Session of the Committee of Ministers (Strasbourg, 17 May 2024)—Committee on Artificial Intelligence (CAI)—Council of Europe Framework Convention on Artificial Intelligence and Human Rights, Democracy and the Rule of Law—Explanatory Report' (Council of Europe 2024) para 8 <https://rm.coe.int/0900001680afb122> accessed 5 June 2025.

[294] See Hadrien Pouget, 'France's AI Summit Is a Chance to Reshape Global Narratives on AI' (*Carnegie Endowment for International Peace*, 24 July 2024) <https://carnegieendowment.org/posts/2024/07/france-ai-summit-reshape-global-narrative?lang=en> accessed 1 August 2024.

[295] Jayanth Jacob, 'India to Host Next AI Summit, Pitches to Make It Mindful of Needs of Global South' (*The New Indian Express*, 11 February 2025) <https://www.newindianexpress.com/nation/2025/Feb/11/india-to-host-next-ai-summit-pitches-to-make-it-mindful-of-needs-of-global-south> accessed 21 February 2025.

[296] For early recommendations, made prior to the Paris Summit, see: Lucia Velasco and others, 'The Future of the AI Summit Series' (Oxford Martin AI Governance Initiative, University of Oxford 2025) Policy Memo <https://www.oxfordmartin.ox.ac.uk/publications/the-future-of-the-ai-summit-series> accessed 19 February 2025.

[297] Renan Araujo, Kristina Fort, and Oliver Guest, 'Understanding the First Wave of AI Safety Institutes: Characteristics, Functions, and Challenges' (Institute for AI Policy and Strategy (IAPS) 2024) <https://www.iaps.ai/research/understanding-aisis> accessed 21 October 2024.

[298] Julian Jacobs, 'National Approaches to AI Safety Diverge in Focus' (*OMFIF*, 25 June 2024) <https://www.omfif.org/2024/06/national-approaches-to-ai-safety-diverge-in-focus/> accessed 18 July 2024. Alex Petroupoulos, 'The AI Safety Institute Network: Who, What and How?' (*ICFG*, 10 September 2024) <https://icfg.eu/the-ai-safety-institute-network-who-what-and-how/> accessed 23 October 2024. See also Variengien and Martinet (n 249).

of advanced AI models, as developer of standards, or as coordinator of third parties.[299] Of course, these organizations are still new, and there is no principled reason they could not eventually resolve questions over their exact role, and clarify their cooperative arrangements towards one another and to other AI standard-setting initiatives.[300] However, the US and UK AISIs have already encountered potential political contestation, with the original landmark UK AISI being rebranded to an AI 'Security Institute',[301] and the US AISI being similarly renamed to the 'Center for AI Standards and Innovation'.[302]

There are gaps among major national regulatory initiatives and the overarching architecture of international law. That is, while initiatives such as the EU AI Act, US AI regulations, or China's Artificial Intelligence Law may well come to shape global practices and norms around AI governance to a significant degree, they themselves appear to have been formulated in a manner that, by and large, does not draw explicitly on existing international law.[303] Furthermore, these initiatives may have been driven more by the need for these actors to position themselves as leaders on global AI regulation, with these global power ambitions taking a front seat, while attempts at regulatory coordination are relegated to the background.[304] Given this, it is no surprise that all three regional approaches continue to demonstrate significant differences in their respective regulatory approaches,[305] in ways that may come to exert opposing normative pressures on any broad and inclusive global governance frameworks for AI.[306] This may likely exacerbate long-running

[299] Marta Ziosi and others, 'AISIs' Roles in Domestic and International Governance' (Oxford Martin AI Governance Initiative 2024) <https://www.oxfordmartin.ox.ac.uk/publications/aisis-roles-in-domestic-and-international-governance> accessed 15 July 2024.

[300] Kristina Fort, 'The Role of AI Safety Institutes in Contributing to International Standards for Frontier AI Safety' (*arXiv*, 17 September 2024) <http://arxiv.org/abs/2409.11314> accessed 22 October 2024.

[301] Tom Bristow, 'Britain Dances to JD Vance's Tune as It Renames AI Institute' (*POLITICO*, 14 February 2025) <https://www.politico.eu/article/jd-vance-britain-ai-safety-institute-aisi-security/> accessed 19 February 2025.

[302] Kaustuv Basu, 'Role of AI Safety Institute Uncertain After Trump Repeals EO' (*Bloomberg Law*, 21 January 2025) <https://news.bloomberglaw.com/artificial-intelligence/role-of-ai-safety-institute-in-question-after-trump-repeal-of-eo> accessed 19 February 2025.

[303] Thomas Burri, 'The New Regulation of the European Union on Artificial Intelligence: Fuzzy Ethics Diffuse into Domestic Law and Sideline International Law' in Oliver Mueller and others (eds), *The Cambridge Handbook of Responsible Artificial Intelligence: Interdisciplinary Perspectives* (Cambridge University Press 2022) (on the role of general ethical norms, rather than international law, in shaping the content of the EU AI Act); Cheng and Mckernon (n 10) 13.

[304] Sabine Mokry and Julia Gurol, 'Competing Ambitions Regarding the Global Governance of Artificial Intelligence: China, the US, and the EU' (2024) 15(5) Global Policy 955.

[305] Anu Bradford, *Digital Empires: The Global Battle to Regulate Technology* (Oxford University Press 2023); Claudio Feijóo and others, 'Harnessing Artificial Intelligence (AI) to Increase Wellbeing for All: The Case for a New Technology Diplomacy' (2020) 44 Telecommunications Policy 101988.

[306] Emmie Hine, 'Governing Silicon Valley and Shenzhen: Assessing a New Era of Artificial Intelligence Governance in the United States and China' (2024) 3 Digital Society 50. But for a counterargument, suggesting that there may be greater transatlantic policy convergences on AI, see Vicki L Birchfield, 'From Roadmap to Regulation: Will There Be a Transatlantic Approach to Governing Artificial Intelligence?' (2024) 46 Journal of European Integration 1053.

trends in global governance towards institutional proliferation and legal fragmentation, resulting in a discordant AI 'regime complex'[307] of many overlapping institutions, which will seek to address AI challenges in different or even contradictory ways.

The process of normative convergence within and across these processes may be further challenged by a continued lack of scientific consensus on the present and future capabilities and impacts of AI systems. To be sure, a range of new initiatives—such as the UK-led International Scientific Report on the Safety of Advanced AI, or the UN proposal for an Independent International Scientific Panel on AI, articulated in the Global Digital Compact—seek to establish a greater degree of institutionalization for international scientific processes aimed at producing such a consensus. Yet there is still a significant lack of clarity over how these scientific initiatives are to be organized to ensure effective policymaker take-up of their findings,[308] as well as over whether or how these different initiatives should collaborate in achieving a recognized, shared, scientific picture of the challenges ahead.[309]

3.2.4.4 Persistent military–civilian political divides

Indeed, the prospects for the future alignment of institutional governance mandates with specific AI issue clusters remain unclear. While there is a growing awareness that international initiatives may be required to govern AI systems across different applications or use domains, it is less clear whether or how institutions will—or should—attempt to focus on several or all of the overarching issue clusters of conventional, military, and advanced AI.

To be sure, by default, it is not surprising to see such splits in the regime. For instance, from their very inception, international AI governance initiatives have been characterized by a 'dual trend', with processes and initiatives largely split between those focused on the issues posed by the civilian applications of narrow (conventional) AI and those focused on the challenges of military AI. Such a split may be unremarkable given the history of international lawmaking,

[307] This concept will be extensively discussed in Chapter 6 and will lay the foundation for the core analytical framework that is developed in Chapter 7.

[308] Hadrien Pouget, 'The Science of AI Is Too Important to Be Left to the Scientists' (*Foreign Policy*, 21 October 2024) <https://foreignpolicy.com/2024/10/21/the-science-of-ai-is-too-important-to-be-left-to-the-scientists/> accessed 23 October 2024. For one proposal, see Kevin Kohler and others, 'Blueprints: Design Options for the Independent International Scientific Panel on AI and the Global Dialogue on AI Governance' (*Simon Institute for Longterm Governance*, 9 December 2024) <https://www.simoninstitute.ch/blog/post/blueprints-design-options-for-the-independent-international-scientific-panel-on-ai-and-the-global-dialogue-on-ai-governance/> accessed 19 February 2025.

[309] Hadrien Pouget and others, 'The Future of International Scientific Assessments of AI's Risks' (Oxford Martin AI Governance Initiative and Carnegie Endowment for International Peace 2024) <https://carnegieendowment.org/research/2024/08/the-future-of-international-scientific-assessments-of-ais-risks?lang=en> accessed 30 August 2024.

and, barring strong design action, we should expect it to persist into the regime's future.[310]

At the same time, maintaining this political divide in the face of the emergence of general-purpose AI systems and intrinsically dual-use foundation models may prove a challenge, as these adaptive technologies will intrinsically drive new risks in both civilian and national security contexts. If not handled well, the omission of general-purpose AI systems from military AI governance fora could allow new, unforeseen risks to be overlooked. Conversely, the unbroken gridlock of military AI security regimes might drive regime erosion or fragmentation, even in regimes focused on civilian uses of AI (whether conventional or advanced).

Moreover, this extant division between military and conventional AI governance has increasingly been complemented by a growing gulf between those initiatives and the ones focused on advanced AI. For instance, some older initiatives—such as the UNESCO Recommendation or the OECD Principles—may not account for the full spectrum of risks from advanced AI systems, given that they were originally drafted in the context of the issues created by conventional AI. Conversely, the most recent initiatives, such as the UK AI Safety Summit and, to some extent, the G7 Hiroshima AI Process, have explicitly limited their scope to governing advanced 'frontier AI' systems.[311] To be sure, a few governance efforts have attempted to cross this divide within one regime. Among these, the EU AI Act originally aimed at establishing product regulations for narrow, conventional AI systems, yet eventually sought to fuse these with provisions for general-purpose AI models, while leaving military AI outside its scope.

All this raises an underlying question over whether any institution (existing or proposed) *should* even seek such an integrated governance role. Should any governance regime pursue a 'dual'[312] or even 'triple' mandate that encompasses conventional, military, and advanced AI issues, or even two of these three? Or are these issue clusters, for all their overlap, technically and politically distinct enough that they are best accommodated by a constellation of different institutions and initiatives? In later chapters of this book, these questions will be addressed at length.[313]

[310] Garcia, 'Multilateralism and Artificial Intelligence: What Role for the United Nations?' (n 10) 11 ('civilian and military uses [of AI] will presumably [continue to] follow different multilateral tracks on the road to future international norms').

[311] UK Government, 'The Bletchley Declaration by Countries Attending the AI Safety Summit, 1–2 November 2023' (n 233).

[312] For instance, see Harry Law and Lewis Ho, 'Can a Dual Mandate Be a Model for the Global Governance of AI?' [2023] Nature Reviews Physics 1.

[313] See the integrated framework discussed in Chapter 7.

3.3 Evaluating Proposed Pathways for AI Governance

The world may well have entered a sensitive window of opportunity to get things right. However, given the incipient state of global AI governance and its many initiatives, it should be unsurprising that the last years have seen many diverse proposals for new solutions and pathways forward.[314] What are these? How might these hold up?

3.3.1 Continuing the extension of non-binding soft law

A first set of approaches is grounded in the (continued) extension of a range of global soft law approaches that have developed and seen take-up over the last years.

Such an approach might be appealing not just because it has the largest range of instruments and initiatives to draw on,[315] but also because this may be, in some ways, the path of least political resistance. That is, global governance scholars have argued that the last few decades have seen the increasing 'stagnation' of traditional international law, and a broader move in global governance towards increasingly 'informal international lawmaking'.[316] This has been particularly seen in the multi-stakeholder model of governance which has, over the past two decades, characterized the governance of cyberspace issues.[317] The early prominence of AI ethics principles and voluntary standards in the history of AI governance may be in keeping with this broader systemic trend in global governance.

Many of these early AI governance initiatives constitute what Thomas Burri has characterized as 'supersoft law': codes that are 'soft' not only in the sense of being non-binding global standards or guidelines, but also because they are not derived from international legal instruments, nor have been developed in the traditional fora of international law or state diplomacy, but instead have often been formulated by industry stakeholders themselves.[318]

[314] For other reviews of potential (global or national) governance levers or mechanisms, see also Veale, Matus, and Gorwa (n 10); Matthijs Maas, 'Advanced AI Governance: A Literature Review of Problems, Options, and Proposals' (Institute for Law & AI 2023) AI Foundations Report 4 <https://law-ai.org/advanced-ai-gov-litrev> accessed 12 March 2025; Cheng and Mckernon (n 10); Usman Anwar and others, 'Foundational Challenges in Assuring Alignment and Safety of Large Language Models' 93 <https://llm-safety-challenges.github.io/challenges_llms.pdf> accessed 16 April 2024; Dan Hendrycks, 'Governance', in: *Introduction to AI Safety, Ethics, and Society* (CRC Press 2024).

[315] D Schiff and others, 'AI Ethics in the Public, Private, and NGO Sectors: A Review of a Global Document Collection' [2021] IEEE Transactions on Technology and Society 1; Gutierrez and Marchant (n 77).

[316] J Pauwelyn, RA Wessel, and J Wouters, 'When Structures Become Shackles: Stagnation and Dynamics in International Lawmaking' (2014) 25 European Journal of International Law 733.

[317] Joseph S Nye, 'The Regime Complex for Managing Global Cyber Activities' (Global Commission on Internet Governance 2014) 1 <https://dash.harvard.edu/bitstream/handle/1/12308565/Nye-GlobalCommission.pdf> accessed 3 September 2019.

[318] Thomas Burri, 'International Law and Artificial Intelligence' (2017) 60 German Yearbook of International Law 91, 106, 109.

To be clear, there are many roles that soft law tools, appropriately configured, could play in the governance of AI.[319] For instance, Gutierrez, Marchant, and Tournas have reviewed a range of historical cases in which soft law instruments managed to successfully shape organizations' behaviours,[320] but they also identify cases of mixed success,[321] or outright failure.[322] In other domains, such as the international law of outer space, soft law instruments have contributed to progressive and continued development of international norms, even as the broader regime entered a period of 'treaty stasis'; however, they did so only against a pre-existing background or foundation of core outer space treaties.[323]

Given the mixed track record, how promising or adequate might different forms of non-binding instruments and soft law be for AI? We can briefly revisit and review three types.

3.3.1.1 Industry self-regulation and corporate governance

One approach might lie in a continued reliance on self-regulation and corporate governance by AI labs. To be sure, this approach has come under increasing scrutiny and critique, especially in the wake of the high-profile episode, in November 2023, when OpenAI's non-profit board attempted to fire its CEO, Sam Altman.[324] However, it is worth briefly discussing the potential roles and benefits of industry-level approaches to self-regulation and norm-setting.

[319] Carlos Ignacio Gutierrez, Gary E Marchant, and Katina Michael, 'Effective and Trustworthy Implementation of AI Soft Law Governance' (2021) 2 IEEE Transactions on Technology and Society 168.

[320] Carlos Ignacio Gutierrez, Gary E Marchant, and Lucille Tournas, 'Lessons for Artificial Intelligence from Historical Uses of Soft Law Governance' (2020) 61 Jurimetrics 3 <https://papers.ssrn.com/abstract=3775271> accessed 7 March 2021 (listing cases including: Internet Corporation for Assigned Names and Numbers; Motion Picture Association of America; Federal Trade Commission consent decrees; Federal Communications Commission's power over broadcaster licensing; Entertainment Software Rating Board; NIST Framework for Improving Critical Infrastructure Cybersecurity; Asilomar rDNA Guidelines; International Gene Synthesis Consortium; International Society for Stem Cell Research Guidelines; BASF Code of Conduct; Environmental Defense Fund and DuPont Risk Framework).

[321] ibid (listing the cases of: the National Telecommunications and Information Administration discussions on mobile app transparency, drone privacy, facial recognition; YourAdChoices; UNESCO declaration on genetics and bioethics; Environmental Management System (ISO 14001); Sustainable Forestry Practices by the Sustainable Forestry Initiative and Forest Stewardship Council; Leadership in Energy and Environmental Design).

[322] ibid (listing the cases of: Children's Online Privacy Protection Rule; Internet Content Rating Association; Platform for Internet Content Selection; Platform for Privacy Preferences; Do Not Track System; nanotechnology voluntary data call-in by Australia, the US, and the UK).

[323] Brian Israel, 'Treaty Stasis' (2014) 108 AJIL Unbound 63.

[324] Eugenia Lostri, Alan Z Rozenshtein, and Chinmayi Sharma, 'The Chaos at OpenAI Is a Death Knell for AI Self-Regulation' (*Lawfare*, 28 November 2023) <https://www.lawfaremedia.org/article/the-chaos-at-openai-is-a-death-knell-for-ai-self-regulation> accessed 6 January 2024. For a reflection on lessons to be drawn for the regulation of AI labs, by two former members of the board involved, see also: Helen Toner and Tasha McCauley, 'AI Firms Mustn't Govern Themselves, Say Ex-Members of OpenAI's Board' [2024] *The Economist* <https://www.economist.com/by-invitation/2024/05/26/ai-firms-mustnt-govern-themselves-say-ex-members-of-openais-board> accessed 27 May 2024.

Industry self-regulation is a concept that encompasses a diverse range of tools. As defined by the OECD, self-regulation:

> typically involves a group of economic agents, such as firms in a particular industry or a professional group, voluntarily developing rules or codes of conduct that regulate or guide the behaviour, actions and standards of its members. The group is responsible for developing self-regulatory instruments, monitoring compliance and ensuring enforcement.[325]

In the case of AI, a governance approach that continued the focus on self-regulation and norm-setting would involve a reliance on AI labs and tech companies to take the lead on articulating a set of best practices around the development of (advanced) AI,[326] to agree on these at (global) industry level, and to commit to their implementation.

There are various levers on which such an approach could rely.[327] At the level of company practices, leading AI labs could voluntarily commit to and implement a range of technical procedures around the testing and evaluation of AI systems.[328] These evaluation measures could draw on leading technical approaches to ensuring the interpretability, alignment, and control of AI model behaviours.[329] However, to ensure their efficacy, such tests should be embedded in clear mechanisms, policies, and norms that specify how these evaluations fit within a broader approach to the 'responsible scaling' of advanced AI model development.[330]

[325] Glen Hepburn, 'Alternatives to Traditional Regulation' (OECD Regulatory Policy Division 2006) 6 <https://www.oecd.org/governance/regulatory-policy/42245468.pdf> accessed 13 January 2024.

[326] Jonas Schuett and others, 'Towards Best Practices in AGI Safety and Governance: A Survey of Expert Opinion' (*arXiv*, 11 May 2023) <http://arxiv.org/abs/2305.07153> accessed 15 May 2023. See also: Risto Uuk and others, 'Effective Mitigations for Systemic Risks from General-Purpose AI' (Social Science Research Network, 14 November 2024) <https://papers.ssrn.com/abstract=5021463> accessed 19 February 2025.

[327] See also Maas, 'Advanced AI Governance' (n 314) 103–108.

[328] Toby Shevlane and others, 'Model Evaluation for Extreme Risks' (arXiv, 24 May 2023) <http://arxiv.org/abs/2305.15324> accessed 25 May 2023. See Thomas Woodside and Helen Toner, 'Evaluating Large Language Models' (Center for Security and Emerging Technology 2024) <https://cset.georgetown.edu/article/evaluating-large-language-models/> accessed 26 July 2024.

[329] Oscar Delaney, Oliver Guest, and Zoe Williams, 'Mapping Technical Safety Research at AI Companies: A Literature Review and Incentives Analysis' (Institute for AI Policy and Strategy (IAPS) 2024) <https://www.iaps.ai/research/mapping-technical-safety-research-at-ai-companies> accessed 22 October 2024.

[330] See Department for Science, Innovation & Technology, 'Emerging Processes for Frontier AI Safety' (Department for Science, Innovation & Technology 2023) <https://www.gov.uk/government/publications/emerging-processes-for-frontier-ai-safety/emerging-processes-for-frontier-ai-safety> accessed 12 April 2024; ARC Evals, 'Responsible Scaling Policies (RSPs)' (*ARC Evals*, 26 September 2023) <https://evals.alignment.org/blog/2023-09-26-rsp/> accessed 26 October 2023. For examples of such policies from different leading labs, see also Anthropic, 'Anthropic's Responsible Scaling Policy, Version 1.0' <http://anthropic.com/responsible-scaling-policy> accessed 19 September 2023; OpenAI, 'OpenAI's Approach to Frontier Risk' (26 October 2023) <https://openai.com/global-affairs/our-approach-to-frontier-risk> accessed 13 January 2024; OpenAI, 'Preparedness Framework (Beta)' (OpenAI 2023) <https://cdn.openai.com/openai-preparedness-framework-beta.pdf> accessed 13 January 2024; Anca Dragan,

In addition, labs might minimize the risks of misuse of their models. Internally, they could invest in security measures to prevent the theft or unauthorized dissemination of the model weights of advanced systems.[331] Externally, in preventing the misuse of models initially approved for release, labs might institute acceptable use policies,[332] or gate usage behind structured access arrangements that control the ways a system can be used—while preventing users from circumventing these restrictions through modification or reverse engineering—or set up mechanisms to detect and correct post-deployment incidents involving their AI models.[333]

All this would not be a matter of narrow technical solutions alone, however: at a cultural or organizational level, effective lab governance may look to bolster such measures with effective corporate governance provisions,[334] such as the articulation of recognized professional norms,[335] or the establishment of internal AI ethics advisory committees, Institutional Review Boards,[336] or internal audit

Helen King, and Allan Dafoe, 'Introducing the Frontier Safety Framework' (*Google DeepMind*, 17 May 2024) <https://deepmind.google/discover/blog/introducing-the-frontier-safety-framework/> accessed 17 May 2024. A more indirect approach to evaluation is offered by Google DeepMind: Laura Weidinger and others, 'Holistic Safety and Responsibility Evaluations of Advanced AI Models' (*arXiv*, 22 April 2024) <http://arxiv.org/abs/2404.14068> accessed 1 May 2024. Though for a more cautious assessment of these policies, see Paul Christiano, 'Thoughts on Responsible Scaling Policies and Regulation' (*AI Alignment Forum*, 25 October 2023) <https://www.alignmentforum.org/posts/dxgEaDrEBkkE96CXr/thoughts-on-responsible-scaling-policies-and-regulation> accessed 13 January 2024. For another evaluation of Anthropic's RSP, against the guidance of DSIT, see also Bill Anderson-Samways and others, 'Responsible Scaling: Comparing Government Guidance and Company Policy' (Institute for AI Policy and Strategy (IAPS) 2024) <https://www.iaps.ai/research/responsible-scaling> accessed 21 May 2024. For a more general scoring system by which to assess these AI safety frameworks, see Jide Alaga, Jonas Schuett, and Markus Anderljung, 'A Grading Rubric for AI Safety Frameworks' (*arXiv*, 13 September 2024) <http://arxiv.org/abs/2409.08751> accessed 26 September 2024.

[331] Sella Nevo and others, 'Securing AI Model Weights: Preventing Theft and Misuse of Frontier Models' (RAND Corporation 2024) <https://www.rand.org/pubs/research_reports/RRA2849-1.html> accessed 20 June 2024.

[332] Kevin Klyman, 'Acceptable Use Policies for Foundation Models' (2024) 7 Proceedings of the AAAI/ACM Conference on AI, Ethics, and Society 752.

[333] Toby Shevlane, 'Structured Access: An Emerging Paradigm for Safe AI Deployment' in Justin Bullock and others (eds), Toby Shevlane, *The Oxford Handbook of AI Governance* (Oxford University Press 2022) (on structured access); Merlin Stein, Jamie Bernardi, and Connor Dunlop, 'The Role of Governments in Increasing Interconnected Post-Deployment Monitoring of AI' (*arXiv*, 7 October 2024) <http://arxiv.org/abs/2410.04931> accessed 17 March 2025 (on post-deployment monitoring and information-sharing mechanisms); Joe O'Brien, Shaun Ee, and Zoe Williams, 'Deployment Corrections: An Incident Response Framework for Frontier AI Models' (*arXiv*, 30 September 2023) <http://arxiv.org/abs/2310.00328> accessed 17 March 2025 (on post-incident response actions).

[334] Peter Cihon, Jonas Schuett, and Seth D Baum, 'Corporate Governance of Artificial Intelligence in the Public Interest' (2021) 12 Information 275; Jakob Mökander and others, 'Challenges and Best Practices in Corporate AI Governance: Lessons from the Biopharmaceutical Industry' (2022) 4 Frontiers in Computer Science <https://www.frontiersin.org/articles/10.3389/fcomp.2022.1068361> accessed 14 November 2022.

[335] Urs Gasser and Carolyn Schmitt, 'The Role of Professional Norms in the Governance of Artificial Intelligence' in M Dubber and F Pasquale (eds), *The Oxford Handbook of AI Ethics* (Oxford University Press 2019).

[336] Jessica Cussins Newman, 'Decision Points in AI Governance' (Center for Long-Term Cybersecurity 2020) <https://cltc.berkeley.edu/wp-content/uploads/2020/05/Decision_Points_AI_Governance.pdf> accessed 3 September 2020; Reid Blackman, 'If Your Company Uses AI, It Needs

mechanisms that are independent from senior management, reporting directly to a board of directors.[337] Finally, labs may commit to externally share key information about planned model training runs with trusted actors such as their respective home governments or another appointed body.[338]

Would action at this level be sufficient? Clearly, there is a strong argument for private labs to be involved in mitigating many of the harms of their products. Indeed, for many—though certainly not all—risks, labs may be in the best position to act on the upstream risks of their models. However, while in a substantive sense many of these measures may be key to addressing at least some risks from various AI systems, relying on this approach in isolation will likely be very inadequate.

Indeed, while the July 2023 White House voluntary AI commitments signed by seven leading AI companies did result in these actors making some progress in technical domains such as red-teaming practices and watermarks, one year on there was only limited progress in areas involving meaningful transparency or accountability.[339] This may reflect a number of underlying challenges. For one, many AI research labs to date have adopted relatively ad hoc risk management practices, which fall short of generally established best practices in corporate risk governance.[340] Because there is no agreed terminology or set of methods for evaluating advanced AI systems, and because such evaluations are voluntary and subject to company discretion, there are significant risks that companies could selectively choose what evaluations to undertake—or even fail to meaningfully ensure that adverse evaluation outcomes translate in actual postponement of the public deployment of a AI system.[341] All of these concerns are exacerbated by the fact that, when measures such as corporate structure or internal guidelines are deployed in

an Institutional Review Board' [2021] *Harvard Business Review* <https://hbr.org/2021/04/if-your-company-uses-ai-it-needs-an-institutional-review-board> accessed 22 November 2022; Jonas Schuett, Anka Reuel, and Alexis Carlier, 'How to Design an AI Ethics Board' (arXiv, 14 April 2023) <http://arxiv.org/abs/2304.07249> accessed 18 April 2023; For a case study, see Rishi Gulati, 'Meta's Oversight Board and Transnational Hybrid Adjudication—What Consequences for International Law? Special Issue: International Law and Digitalization' (2023) 24 German Law Journal 473; Andreas Kulick, 'Corporations as Interpreters and Adjudicators of International Human Rights Norms—Meta's Oversight Board and Beyond' (22 September 2022) <https://papers.ssrn.com/abstract=4226521> accessed 12 October 2022.

[337] Jonas Schuett, 'Frontier AI Developers Need an Internal Audit Function' [2024] Risk Analysis <https://onlinelibrary.wiley.com/doi/abs/10.1111/risa.17665> accessed 21 October 2024.

[338] Haydn Belfield, 'What Information Should Be Shared with Whom "Before and During Training"?' (arXiv, 22 January 2025) <http://arxiv.org/abs/2501.10379> accessed 19 February 2025.

[339] Melissa Heikkilä, 'AI Companies Promised to Self-Regulate One Year Ago. What's Changed?' [2024] *MIT Technology Review* <https://www.technologyreview.com/2024/07/22/1095193/ai-companies-promised-the-white-house-to-self-regulate-one-year-ago-whats-changed/> accessed 25 July 2024.

[340] Ben Robinson and James Ginns, 'Transforming Risk Governance at Frontier AI Companies' (CLTR 2024) <https://www.longtermresilience.org/post/transforming-risk-governance-at-frontier-ai-companies> accessed 26 July 2024.

[341] Anton Leicht and Dominik Hermle, 'Corporate AI Labs' Odd Role In Their Own Governance' (2024) <https://www.antonleicht.me/writing/corporate-ai-labs-odd-role-in-their-own-governance> accessed 23 July 2024.

the absence of external frameworks, profitability incentives will generally undercut or severely impede their effectiveness.[342]

3.3.1.2 Industry norm-setting approaches and codes of practice

Other self-governance policies might be undertaken by AI companies with the intent to shape not (just) their internal practices, but also those of other labs external to that lab. The aim here might be to help set norms within the broader field or among other AI labs about what are acceptable practices. This would allow labs to serve as 'norm entrepreneurs',[343] for instance by the public articulation of voluntary safety commitments,[344] the adoption of clear policies around coordinated pausing of the deployment of potentially harmful systems to allow for adequate testing,[345] measures to ensure 'security-by-design' of AI systems,[346] bug bounties,[347] the reporting of safety-critical information about AI models to regulators,[348] the exchange of safety techniques among labs, and various other cooperative measures.[349] At an industry level, these norms might also be embedded within certification schemes,[350] or within Codes of Conduct (CoCs). For instance, in summer 2022, the Partnership on AI issued a public comment for a draft code on synthetic media.[351]

[342] Elliot Jones, Mahi Hardalupas, and William Agnew, 'Under the Radar? Examining the Evaluation of Foundation Models' (Ada Lovelace Institute 2024) <https://www.adalovelaceinstitute.org/report/under-the-radar/> accessed 25 July 2024.

[343] For a definition of this concept, see Cass R Sunstein, 'Social Norms and Social Roles' (1996) 96 Columbia Law Review 903, 1996 ('political actors, whether public or private, can exploit widespread dissatisfaction with existing norms by (a) signaling their own commitment to change, (b) creating coalitions, (c) making defiance of the norms seem or be less costly, and (d) making compliance with new norms seem or be more beneficial').

[344] The Anh Han and others, 'Voluntary Safety Commitments Provide an Escape from Over-Regulation in AI Development' [2021] arXiv:2104.03741 [nlin] <http://arxiv.org/abs/2104.03741> accessed 13 April 2021.

[345] Jide Alaga and Jonas Schuett, 'Coordinated Pausing: An Evaluation-Based Coordination Scheme for Frontier AI Developers' (arXiv, 30 September 2023) <http://arxiv.org/abs/2310.00374> accessed 3 October 2023.

[346] For instance, recall the 2023 international guidelines for secure AI system development. UK National Cyber Security Centre (NCSC) and US Cybersecurity and Infrastructure Agency (CISA) (n 263).

[347] Josh Kenway and others, 'Bug Bounties for Algorithmic Harms: Lessons from Cybersecurity Vulnerability Disclosure for Algorithmic Harms Discovery, Disclosure, and Redress' (Algorithmic Justice League 2022) <https://www.ajl.org/bugs> accessed 26 October 2022.

[348] Noam Kolt and others, 'Responsible Reporting for Frontier AI Development' (*arXiv*, 3 April 2024) <http://arxiv.org/abs/2404.02675> accessed 4 April 2024.

[349] Shin-Shin Hua and Haydn Belfield, 'AI & Antitrust: Reconciling Tensions Between Competition Law and Cooperative AI Development' (2021) 23 Yale Journal of Law and Technology 127.

[350] Peter Cihon and others, 'AI Certification: Advancing Ethical Practice by Reducing Information Asymmetries' (2021) 2 IEEE Transactions on Technology and Society 200; Philip Matthias Winter and others, 'Trusted Artificial Intelligence: Towards Certification of Machine Learning Applications' [2021] arXiv:2103.16910 [cs, stat] <http://arxiv.org/abs/2103.16910> accessed 1 October 2021.

[351] Claire Leibowicz, 'PAI Seeks Public Comment on the Synthetic Media Code of Conduct' (*Partnership on AI*, 11 July 2022) <https://partnershiponai.org/pai-seeks-public-comment-on-the-synthetic-media-code-of-conduct/> accessed 13 January 2024; Partnership on AI, 'Synthetic Media Code of Conduct (V3)' <https://docs.google.com/document/d/1P9TNlhQztsSbbm-2QVg6_Fak5BE7TsZWAcfFDdEc6Ow/edit> accessed 13 March 2025. As discussed in Chinen (n 10) 253.

To be sure, such a norm-setting approach need not solely be dependent on the actions of AI companies alone. Other actors might still aim to shape their norms and incentives. For instance, scientific actors such as leading AI conference organizers might (re)introduce pre-publication impact assessment requirements;[352] among other practices to promote a responsible culture.[353] Research ethics committees could carry out tailored ethics review on AI technologies with dual-use potential.[354] Others might seek to encourage responsible norms in the research community around responsible model sharing and release,[355] or even aim interventions further upstream, by incorporating ethics components in education curricula of computer science departments.[356]

Other contributions could focus on making available easy-to-use reporting systems and tools. Some of these could help articulate performance benchmarks for AI models that better enable labs to measure their progress in domains such as safety, bias, or other desired characteristics of models.[357] Some tools might aid AI developers in providing relevant information on key steps in AI development, such as the so-called model cards for the models themselves, 'data sheets' for their underlying training data sets, or 'transparency reports' documenting the broader context of model development, deployment, and impacts.[358]

[352] Carina EA Prunkl and others, 'Institutionalizing Ethics in AI through Broader Impact Requirements' (2021) 3 Nature Machine Intelligence 104.

[353] Partnership on AI and CIFAR, 'A Culture of Ethical AI: Report' (2022) <https://partnershiponai.org//wp-content/uploads/dlm_uploads/2022/08/CIFAR-AI-Insights-EN-AM-220803-1.pdf> accessed 23 August 2022.

[354] Andreas Brenneis, 'Assessing Dual Use Risks in AI Research: Necessity, Challenges and Mitigation Strategies' [2024] Research Ethics 17470161241267782.

[355] Irene Solaiman and others, 'Release Strategies and the Social Impacts of Language Models' [2019] arXiv:1908.09203 [cs] <http://arxiv.org/abs/1908.09203> accessed 18 November 2019; Aviv Ovadya and Jess Whittlestone, 'Reducing Malicious Use of Synthetic Media Research: Considerations and Potential Release Practices for Machine Learning' [2019] arXiv:1907.11274 [cs] <http://arxiv.org/abs/1907.11274> accessed 9 September 2019; Partnership on AI, 'Managing the Risks of AI Research: Six Recommendations for Responsible Publication' (*Partnership on AI*) <https://partnershiponai.org/paper/responsible-publication-recommendations/> accessed 14 October 2022; Toby Shevlane, 'The Artefacts of Intelligence: Governing Scientists' Contribution to AI Proliferation' (University of Oxford 2022) <https://www.governance.ai/research-paper/the-artefacts-of-intelligence-governing-scientists-contribution-to-ai-proliferation> accessed 15 March 2024.

[356] Carina Prunkl, 'AI Meets Biology: A Call for Community Governance' (2024) 21 Nature Methods 1407.

[357] Isabella Duan, 'Race to the Top: Rethink Benchmark-Making for Safe AI Development' (3 December 2022) <https://isaduan.github.io/isabelladuan.github.io/posts/first/> accessed 5 December 2022. On the broader role of benchmarks in steering the course of AI innovation, see also: Mostafa Dehghani and others, 'The Benchmark Lottery' (*arXiv*, 14 July 2021) <http://arxiv.org/abs/2107.07002> accessed 5 December 2022.

[358] Margaret Mitchell and others, 'Model Cards for Model Reporting', *Proceedings of the Conference on Fairness, Accountability, and Transparency* (Association for Computing Machinery 2019) <https://doi.org/10.1145/3287560.3287596> accessed 4 April 2024; Timnit Gebru and others, 'Datasheets for Datasets' (2021) 64 Communications of the ACM 86; Rishi Bommasani and others, 'Foundation Model Transparency Reports' (*arXiv*, 25 February 2024) <http://arxiv.org/abs/2402.16268> accessed 27 June 2024.

Third parties could also support effective AI incident documentation practices that would help a more public cataloguing of AI failures and harms, and thereby provide evidence about when and where evaluation testing suites are inadequate or inadequately applied.[359] Civil society actors could (continue to) monitor and report on key features and best practices in the AI ecosystem, such as lab transparency over the upstream resources used to build a foundation model, the model itself, and its downstream uses.[360] Government (funding) bodies could aim to use grants or innovation prizes to differentially steer AI progress in beneficial directions.[361]

However, while all these tools have a role to play, there remain drawbacks around basing global AI governance on non-binding self-regulation, even when coordinated through external norm-setting codes. This can be seen by considering the prospective role of CoCs, codes of ethics, or codes of practice in this domain. In recent history, a diverse range of publicized scandals in government, private business, academia, and other organizations have resulted in the promulgation of intra- or inter-organizational codes that are meant to express values, guide the behaviour of employees and companies alike, and ensure a degree of public accountability.[362]

Accordingly, it should not be surprising that such tools have also been taken up in AI governance. Indeed, as discussed earlier, Codes of Practice are to play a key role in the EU AI Act, where, under Article 56, these codes will reflect a set of nonbinding placeholder measures for providers of General-Purpose AI models.[363]

However, there may be a set of hurdles to overcome in ensuring that such non-binding codes serve their purpose. For one, history suggests that when codes of

[359] Violet Turri and Rachel Dzombak, 'Why We Need to Know More: Exploring the State of AI Incident Documentation Practices', *Proceedings of the 2023 AAAI/ACM Conference on AI, Ethics, and Society* (Association for Computing Machinery 2023) <https://doi.org/10.1145/3600211.3604700> accessed 3 July 2024.

[360] Rishi Bommasani and others, 'The Foundation Model Transparency Index' (*arXiv*, 19 October 2023) <http://arxiv.org/abs/2310.12941> accessed 3 July 2024. For a more active perspective on potential avenues to directly or indirectly regulate downstream developers' activities to fine-tune or modify foundation models, see: Sophie Williams, Jonas Schuett, and Markus Anderljung, 'On Regulating Downstream AI Developers' (*arXiv*, 14 March 2025) <http://arxiv.org/abs/2503.11922> accessed 19 March 2025.

[361] For instance, these have been discussed in the context of general strategies of 'differential technology development'. See also Jonas Sandbrink and others, 'Differential Technology Development: A Responsible Innovation Principle for Navigating Technology Risks' (8 September 2022) <https://papers.ssrn.com/abstract=4213670> accessed 13 September 2022. However, for a sceptical take on the efficacy of these tools, see also Anton Howes, 'Why Innovation Prizes Fail' (*Works in Progress*, 21 April 2022) <https://www.worksinprogress.co/issue/why-innovation-prizes-fail/> accessed 6 December 2022.

[362] Mirjan Oude Vrielink and Cor van Montfort, 'Codes of Ethics and Codes of Practice' in Helmut K Anheier and Stefan Toepler (eds), *International Encyclopedia of Civil Society* (Springer US 2010) <https://doi.org/10.1007/978-0-387-93996-4_165> accessed 23 April 2024.

[363] European Commission, 'Proposal for a Regulation of the European Parliament and of the Council Laying Down Harmonised Rules on Artificial Intelligence (Artificial Intelligence Act) and Amending Certain Union Legislative Acts' (n 136) art 56; see also Farrell (n 173).

conduct are fully driven by industry, the process may result in standards that are too narrow and ineffective: for example, in 2019 the Australian Government requested large digital platforms to develop a voluntary code of practice to address mis- and disinformation. Published in 2021, that Voluntary Code of Practice on Misinformation and Disinformation commits its signatories to decreasing the spread of mis- and disinformation on their platforms.[364] However, a 2022 government review found that the code's requirements were too narrowly scoped, allowing COVID-era misinformation to run rampant.[365] Likewise, reviews of environmental strategies adopted by firms suggest that whereas mandatory regulation typically has a strong positive influence on companies' environmental performance, voluntary pressures alone often fail to bring about significant improvements.[366]

CoC also suffer if they do not establish effective governmental monitoring roles. For instance, many international corporations have adopted various codes of conduct to regulate labour standards in supplier factories. However, because there are no effective monitoring arrangements, this pushes the monitoring role on NGOs, which can struggle—both because of limited organizational resources and their dependence on the companies for whom they monitor—to provide adequate and effective monitoring roles.[367] Given the lack of transparency and technical nature of advanced AI development, this would likely pose a severe challenge for NGO monitoring of AI-focused CoCs.

Moreover, CoCs that involve self-regulation without any sanctions often fail to improve industry performance at all, frequently necessitating the later introduction of binding regulation after all. For instance, in 1985, in the wake of the Bhopal Disaster, the chemical industry launched its Responsible Care initiative, a voluntary CoC focused on improving health, safety, and environmental performance throughout the chemical industry. However, later reviews suggest that chemical plants owned by RC participating firms improved their relative environmental performance more slowly than non-members.[368] These poor outcomes

[364] OECD, 'Voluntary Code of Practice on Misinformation and Disinformation' (*OECD*, 10 March 2023) <https://www.oecd.org/stories/dis-misinformation-hub/voluntary-code-of-practice-on-misinformation-and-disinformation-1fe0be59/> accessed 13 January 2024.

[365] Paul Karp, 'Digital Code of Conduct Fails to Stop All Harms of Misinformation, Acma Warns' *The Guardian* (21 March 2022) <https://www.theguardian.com/media/2022/mar/21/digital-code-of-conduct-fails-to-stop-all-harms-of-misinformation-acma-warns> accessed 13 January 2024.

[366] J Alberto Aragón-Correa, Alfred A Marcus, and David Vogel, 'The Effects of Mandatory and Voluntary Regulatory Pressures on Firms' Environmental Strategies: A Review and Recommendations for Future Research' (2020) 14 Academy of Management Annals 339.

[367] Don Wells, 'Too Weak for the Job: Corporate Codes of Conduct, Non-Governmental Organizations and the Regulation of International Labour Standards' (2007) 7 Global Social Policy 51.

[368] Andrew A King and Michael J Lenox, 'Industry Self-Regulation Without Sanctions: The Chemical Industry's Responsible Care Program' (2000) 43 Academy of Management Journal 698; Shanti Gamper-Rabindran and Stephen R Finger, 'Does Industry Self-Regulation Reduce Pollution? Responsible Care in the Chemical Industry' (2013) 43 Journal of Regulatory Economics 1. However, for a more nuanced discussion of the history of chemical industry standards programs such as Responsible Care and (in

eventually led the EU to move to introduce new legislation, in the form of the 2006 REACH (Registration, Evaluation, Authorization, and Restriction of Chemicals) Regulation.[369]

To be sure, the past decades have shown that for a wide range of issue areas, from supply chain reporting and transparency, from human trafficking to securities law, and from director duties to labour law, many codes along with other 'voluntary' soft law standards can end up becoming 'legalized' into domestic legislations over time.[370] However, even if we might expect such future legalization in due time, there are concerns over how adequately the industry would be governed in the meantime. This is especially the case since the AI industry currently does not possess many contextual features of professions or industries where non-binding soft governance approaches have worked well, lacking long-standing norms of good behaviour, professional associations with enforcement powers, fiduciary duties, or licensing bodies.[371] Accordingly, this does not speak in favour of strongly (or at least entirely) basing global AI governance in industry self-regulation—at least not ones that lack effective third-party auditing regimes.[372]

Indeed, the initial outcomes of states relying on voluntary measures and reporting by companies have been mixed, at least in the early stages: the November 2023 Bletchley AI Safety Summit had initially secured promises from leading labs to share their most advanced models with the UK AI Safety Institute for evaluation, yet by the time of the Seoul summit in May 2024, only the London-based Google DeepMind had provided the AISI with pre-deployment access to its Gemini models.[373] Such results have led to critique of the voluntary framework approach to assuring adequate evaluations, along with calls to empower the emerging network

the US) CFATS, which applies these lessons to AI governance, see Moritz von Knebel, 'The Fight Over Standards in the Chemical Industry—a Chain Reaction?' (*AI Policy Bulletin*, 2025) <https://www.aipolicybulletin.org/articles/standards-development-in-the-chemical-industry---a-chain-reaction> accessed 14 March 2025.

369 Regulation (EC) No 1907/2006—Registration, Evaluation, Authorisation and Restriction of Chemicals (REACH) 2006).

370 Lara Blecher, 'Codes of Conduct: The Trojan Horse of International Human Rights Law?' (2016) 38 Comparative Labor Law & Policy Journal 437.

371 Connor Dunlop and others, 'Codes of Practice' (Ada Lovelace Institute 2024) EU Policy Briefing.

372 Inioluwa Deborah Raji and others, 'Outsider Oversight: Designing a Third Party Audit Ecosystem for AI Governance', *Proceedings of the 2022 AAAI/ACM Conference on AI, Ethics, and Society* (Association for Computing Machinery 2022) <https://dl.acm.org/doi/10.1145/3514094.3534181> accessed 19 March 2025; Lara Groves, 'Code & Conduct: How to Create Third-Party Auditing Regimes for AI Systems' (Ada Lovelace Institute 2024) <https://www.adalovelaceinstitute.org/report/code-conduct-ai/> accessed 11 June 2024.

373 Vincent Manancourt, Gian Volpicelli, and Mohar Chatterjee, 'Rishi Sunak Promised to Make AI Safe. Big Tech's Not Playing Ball' (*POLITICO*, 26 April 2024) <https://www.politico.eu/article/rishi-sunak-ai-testing-tech-ai-safety-institute/> accessed 13 May 2024. However, Anthropic did submit Claude 3.5 Sonnet for evaluation by both the US and the UK AI Safety Institutes. Anthropic, 'Introducing Claude 3.5 Sonnet' (*Anthropic*, 21 June 2024) <https://www.anthropic.com/news/claude-3-5-sonnet> accessed 26 June 2024.

of AI Safety Institutes with stronger legal powers to block or impose preconditions upon model releases.[374]

3.3.1.3 International standards

Another soft law avenue could be to continue reliance on the work by (national and especially international) standard-setting institutions. As mentioned, AI governance has been characterized by a range of technical standards.[375] Notably, while international standards are in principle non-binding, they can exert considerable pull in various ways. For instance, the ISO's membership consists of 162 national standards bodies who adopt ISO standards domestically. Moreover, under the Agreement on Technical Barriers to Trade, voluntary international standards may be converted into binding treaty obligations for the 164 members of the WTO.[376]

There is also a second, more indirect way by which standards can affect global governance. For instance, as mentioned, in July 2022 the ISO, working jointly with the IEC, established ISO/IEC 22989:2022(E), a standard on AI concepts and terminology.[377] In such cases, in spite of the voluntary nature, this definitional standard may affect the course and direction of later international regulation for AI, in an avenue that has been called 'para-regulation'.[378] Notably, even though technical experts within these standard-setting organizations have hailed from geopolitical rivals such as the US and China, studies suggest they have still been willing and able to collaborate on technical standard-setting within these organizations.[379]

However, there are drawbacks to AI governance through standards: as noted by Peter Cihon, international standards approaches for AI at the ISO and IEEE have focused 'primarily on standards to improve market efficiency, and to address ethical concerns, respectively', leaving 'a risk that these standards may fail to address further policy objectives, such as a culture of responsible deployment and use of safety specifications in fundamental research'.[380] Indeed, the para-regulatory (i.e. other-regulation-shaping) role of these institutions has also received critique over their representation and decision-making procedures, potentially undercutting these standards' (perceived) legitimacy.[381] In particular, concerns have been

[374] Matt Davies, Andrew Strait, and Michael Birtwistle, 'Safety First? Reimagining the Role of the UK AI Safety Institute in a Wider UK Governance Framework' (*Ada Lovelace Institute*, 17 May 2024) <https://www.adalovelaceinstitute.org/blog/safety-first/> accessed 21 May 2024.

[375] Cihon (n 10); Lorenz (n 10).

[376] Agreement on Technical Barriers to Trade, Annex 1A of the Agreement establishing the World Trade Organization (signed 15 April 1994, entered into force 1 January 1995) 1868 UNTS 120 (TBT Agreement) art 2.4. See also Han-Wei Liu and Ching-Fu Lin, 'Artificial Intelligence and Global Trade Governance: A Pluralist Agenda' (2020) 61 Harvard International Law Journal n 24.

[377] ISO (n 98). See also Villarino (n 98).

[378] Villarino (n 98).

[379] Nora von Ingersleben-Seip, 'Competition and Cooperation in Artificial Intelligence Standard Setting: Explaining Emergent Patterns' (2023) 40 Review of Policy Research 781.

[380] Cihon (n 10) 2.

[381] Villarino (n 98).

raised over the fact that the ISO's members are national standards institutes, which in turn have memberships that include or even skew towards companies and trade associations.[382] Similar concerns have been raised over the role of European Standardization Organizations (ESOs)—such as CEN and CENELEC—in defining AI risk and mitigation measures for the EU AI Act: a role which, it has been argued, may raise questions on both legal and legitimacy grounds,[383] as well as in terms of whether the technical experts involved in such processes are equipped to define standards of acceptable residual risk in different contexts.[384] Finally, there are risks of politicization and contestation, with growing wariness over the ways in which a number of standard-setting institutions on AI, such as the ITU, may have become subject to political uses of standardization by states such as China, which has used such influence to establish its own particular visions of digital governance, and advance it globally.[385]

Indeed, some, such as Alicia Solow-Niederman, have argued that, at a deeper level, AI standards are inexorably political—in that they do not provide neutral or objective ways forward but inexorably are always created by specific actors on the basis of normative choices and unique political and economic constraints—but that greater recognition of this fact ironically undercuts the efficacy of such standards, since 'AI standards are most powerful as governance tools when we embrace the fiction that standards emerge in a vacuum, without reference to an institutional context and without implicating normative choices'.[386] Even if standards will continue to play a role in the larger landscape of AI governance, these tensions will continue to plague them.

3.3.1.4 AI ethics principles

For its part, are AI ethics principles more effective or adequate at anchoring the future of the AI governance regime? Thomas Burri has argued in favour of continued reliance on such 'supersoft' law for AI, since, he argues, 'emerging out of the international legal nowhere, [these standards] will be persuasive on their merits and imbued with a strong compliance pull, despite their non-binding form'.[387] At the same time, other scholars have critiqued the shortcomings of ethics codes for governing AI. These critiques depart from four distinct angles.

[382] Jonas Tallberg and Anders Uhlin, 'Civil Society and Global Democracy: An Assessment' in: Daniele Archibugi, Mathias Koenig-Archibugi and Raffaele Marchetti (eds), *Global Democracy: Normative and Empirical Perspectives* (Cambridge University Press 2011) 210–232; Chinen (n 10) 210.

[383] Veale and Borgesius (n 138) 13–14.

[384] Marta Cantero Gamito and Christopher T Marsden, 'Artificial Intelligence Co-Regulation? The Role of Standards in the EU AI Act' (2024) 32 International Journal of Law and Information Technology eaae011.

[385] Marta Cantero Gamito, 'The Influence of China in AI Governance through Standardisation' (2023) 47 Telecommunications Policy 102673.

[386] Alicia Solow-Niederman, 'Can AI Standards Have Politics?' (2024) 2 UCLA Law Review 16.

[387] Burri (n 318) 109.

In the first place, some scholars argue that the principles selected are undertheorized or incoherent. That is, they are not suitable because they are too vague, or because surface agreements hide underlying tensions among principles.[388] It is unclear to what degree the content of these ethical principles reflects deep consensus. While Jobin and colleagues identify at least 11 distinct clusters of ethical principles among all sets of proposed AI principles, they also find that most find common ground on the five ethical principles of transparency, justice and fairness, non-maleficence, responsibility, and privacy.[389] At face value, these ethical principles may suggest a gradual degree of substantive or normative convergence.[390] On the other hand, Jobin et al. also observe 'substantive divergences among all [identified] 11 ethical principles in relation to four major factors: (1) how ethical principles are interpreted; (2) why they are deemed important; (3) what issue, domain or actors they pertain to; and (4) how they should be implemented'.[391] To be sure, the very fact that there is outstanding disagreement over the relevant principles is not problematic per se, and may even reflect an important degree of value pluralism to be acknowledged and reckoned with.[392] At the same time, the lack of some widely accepted core or common ground would still inhibit the practical ability of such principles to ground a minimally globally coordinated or coherent response.

In the second place, others argue that, even if there was greater convergence or they were better operationalized, these principles are substantively inappropriate. Some argue that this is because many of these principles imply or import a context of industry practice which is misleading; for instance, Brent Mittelstadt has argued that the convergent sets of principles encapsulated in these AI ethics documents—transparency, justice and fairness, non-maleficence, responsibility, and privacy—mirror the core principles in medical ethics.[393] However, he argues that this

[388] Jess Whittlestone and others, 'The Role and Limits of Principles in AI Ethics: Towards a Focus on Tensions', *Proceedings of the 2019 AAAI/ACM Conference on AI, Ethics, and Society* (Association for Computing Machinery 2019) <https://doi.org/10.1145/3306618.3314289> accessed 12 October 2022.

[389] Jobin, Ienca, and Vayena (n 76) 11.

[390] Likewise, Fjeld and colleagues, in a more focused review of 36 principles, find an increasing convergence towards 'Privacy (8 principles); Accountability (10 principles); Safety and security (4 principles); Transparency and explainability (8 principles); Fairness and non-discrimination (6 principles); Human control of technology (3 principles); Professional responsibility (5 principles); Promotion of human values (3 principles)'. Jessica Fjeld and others, 'Principled Artificial Intelligence: A Map of Ethical and Rights-Based Approaches' (Berkman Klein Center for Internet & Society at Harvard University 2019) 15 <https://ai-hr.cyber.harvard.edu/images/primp-viz.pdf> accessed 2 October 2019.

[391] Jobin, Ienca, and Vayena (n 76) 7.

[392] Catharina Rudschies, Ingrid Schneider, and Judith Simon, 'Value Pluralism in the AI Ethics Debate—Different Actors, Different Priorities' (2020) 29 The International Review of Information Ethics <https://informationethics.ca/index.php/irie/article/view/419> accessed 23 April 2024.

[393] Some make the link to bioethics explicit. Mariarosaria Taddeo and Luciano Floridi, 'How AI Can Be a Force for Good' (2018) 361 Science 751. Jessica Morley and others, 'Ethics as a Service: A Pragmatic Operationalisation of AI Ethics' (2021) 31 Minds and Machines 239. Indeed, for a discussion of the institutional history of the ethics of AI, and a broader comparison to the historical development of bioethics; technology assessment (TA); ethical, legal, and social (ELS) research; and Responsible Research and Innovation (RRI) paradigms within their respective fields, and their implications for AI,

imports a false analogy, as the respective contexts of practice are considerably different, given that '[c]ompared to medicine, AI development lacks (1) common aims and fiduciary duties, (2) professional history and norms, (3) proven methods to translate principles into practice, and (4) robust legal and professional accountability mechanisms'.[394] According to these critiques, then, while it may not be intrinsically incorrect to pursue AI governance (at least in part) through the articulation of ethical principles, the specific principles promulgated to date may fall short substantively.[395]

In the third place, some have critiqued the principles on the grounds of process. These scholars argue that even if the principles espoused were appropriate and effective on their merits, they have not derived from an inclusive or participatory process, and therefore may not be (and arguably should not be) perceived as legitimate—and certainly not as in a good position to receive a sufficiently broad global buy-in to be effective. Some express concern that largely industry-based codes of ethics will 'upstage democratically enacted law', given the political clout wielded by technology companies.[396] Others are concerned that many of these principles reflect the perspective of the West rather than a global consensus.[397] As such, some are concerned that these ethics codes are (or will be

see also Simone Casiraghi, 'Anything New under the Sun? Insights from a History of Institutionalized AI Ethics' (2023) 25 Ethics and Information Technology 28.

[394] Brent Mittelstadt, 'Principles Alone Cannot Guarantee Ethical AI' (2019) 1 Nature Machine Intelligence 501. But for a response, arguing that high-level ethical principles still could serve an important 'cultural influence' role, see Elizabeth Seger, 'In Defence of Principlism in AI Ethics and Governance' (2022) 35 Philosophy & Technology 45.

[395] Although for a defence and rebuttal, from a philosophical perspective, see Elettra Bietti, 'From Ethics Washing to Ethics Bashing: A View on Tech Ethics from Within Moral Philosophy', *Proceedings of ACM FAT* Conference* (2019) <https://papers.ssrn.com/abstract=3513182> accessed 6 January 2020. More generally, the fact that AI development lacks certain contexts of practice (such as fiduciary duties) does not mean these could not be developed over time. See for instance Anthony Aguirre and others, 'AI Loyalty: A New Paradigm for Aligning Stakeholder Interests' (2020) 20.18 University of Colorado Law Legal Studies Research Paper <https://papers.ssrn.com/abstract=3560653> accessed 13 June 2020; Danny Tobey, 'Software Malpractice in the Age of AI: A Guide for the Wary Tech Company', *AAAI/ACM Conference on Artificial Intelligence, Ethics and Society 2018* (2018) <http://www.aies-conference.com/2018/contents/papers/main/AIES_2018_paper_43.pdf> accessed 1 April 2019. I thank Charlotte Siegmann for highlighting some of these debates.

[396] Tasioulas (n 2) 66. See also generally Paul Nemitz, 'Constitutional Democracy and Technology in the Age of Artificial Intelligence' (2018) 376 Philosophical Transactions of the Royal Society A 20180089. Eyal Benvenisti, 'Upholding Democracy Amid the Challenges of New Technology: What Role for the Law of Global Governance?' (2018) 29 European Journal of International Law 9.

[397] Daniel Schiff and others, 'What's Next for AI Ethics, Policy, and Governance? A Global Overview' (ACM 2020) <https://econpapers.repec.org/paper/osfsocarx/8jaz4.htm> accessed 12 January 2020. See also Angela Daly and others, 'Artificial Intelligence Governance and Ethics: Global Perspectives' (2019) <https://arxiv.org/ftp/arxiv/papers/1907/1907.03848.pdf> accessed 28 June 2019; Nathalie A Smuha, 'Beyond a Human Rights-Based Approach to AI Governance: Promise, Pitfalls, Plea' [2020] Philosophy & Technology <https://doi.org/10.1007/s13347-020-00403-w> accessed 25 May 2020. However, for a more optimistic account, arguing that cross-cultural collaboration may be possible on many aspects of AI governance, see Seán S ÓhÉigeartaigh and others, 'Overcoming Barriers to Cross-Cultural Cooperation in AI Ethics and Governance' [2020] 33 Philosophy & Technology 571.

perceived) as too parochial. As Donahoe and Metzger have argued, '[w]hile each effort has hold of part of the problem, none grasps the full spectrum of risks to humans or the whole range of governance challenges [and] none of these initiatives can claim to have achieved a broad global consensus or buy-in across stakeholder groups'.[398]

Fourth, some concerns are expressed about the categorical appropriateness of relying on ethics principles in the first place. Some have critiqued declarations of ethical principles for attempting to exhaustively list impacts in a way that must inevitably fall short or omit or marginalize some key values.[399] More concretely, others have suggested that ethics guidelines are, by nature, not easily operationalizable; that they lack enforceability such that deviations often carry little consequence; or that they might even serve as an 'ethics-washing' marketing ploy by private actors.[400] A frequently expressed concern is that the 'ethical principles' approach of AI ethics is prone to manipulation and risks becoming a substitute for actual law and regulation.[401] Others highlight the limits to private self-governance, given the incompatible incentives of firms in many contexts of AI deployment.[402]

Finally, on a practical level, it is unclear if, or under what conditions, codes of ethics actually work to change the choices of key AI developers or users. For instance, one survey that primed computer programmers with a widespread code of computing ethics suggested that this did not materially change these programmer's behaviour or choices when, afterwards, they were confronted with ethical dilemmas.[403] This is in line with previous studies suggesting that ethical guidelines

[398] Eileen Donahoe and Megan MacDuffee Metzger, 'Artificial Intelligence and Human Rights' (2019) 30 Journal of Democracy 115, 118.

[399] John Tasioulias has critiqued declarations of ethical principles because they try to enumerate impacts in a manner that attempts to be exhaustive, reflecting an 'implicit assumption that there is an enumerable catalogue of evaluative considerations that are especially engaged by RAIs'. Tasioulas (n 2) 69–70. Of course, it might be argued that this is a fully general critique of any codes or lists of ethics, in any context.

[400] Thilo Hagendorff, 'The Ethics of AI Ethics—An Evaluation of Guidelines' [2019] arXiv:1903.03425 [cs, stat] 10 <http://arxiv.org/abs/1903.03425> accessed 7 October 2019. See also generally: Ben Green, 'The Contestation of Tech Ethics: A Sociotechnical Approach to Technology Ethics in Practice' (2021) 2 Journal of Social Computing 209.

However, it should be noted that in other contexts, such as in biomedicine, there has been greater success in operationalizing sets of high-level principles. See for instance Tom L Beauchamp and James F Childress, *Principles of Biomedical Ethics* (Oxford University Press 2012). I thank Carina Prunkl for this point.

[401] See Anaïs Rességuier and Rowena Rodrigues, 'AI Ethics Should Not Remain Toothless! A Call to Bring Back the Teeth of Ethics' (2020) 7 Big Data & Society 2053951720942541.

[402] Nemitz (n 396); Tom Slee, 'The Incompatible Incentives of Private Sector AI' in M Dubber and F Pasquale (eds), *The Oxford Handbook of AI Ethics* (Oxford University Press 2019).

[403] Andrew McNamara, Justin Smith, and Emerson Murphy-Hill, 'Does ACM's Code of Ethics Change Ethical Decision Making in Software Development?', *Proceedings of the 2018 26th ACM Joint Meeting on European Software Engineering Conference and Symposium on the Foundations of Software Engineering—ESEC/FSE 2018* (ACM Press 2018) 4 <http://dl.acm.org/citation.cfm?doid=3236024.3264833> accessed 8 April 2019 ('Despite its stated goal, we found no evidence that the ACM code of ethics influences ethical decision making').

may have little to no effect at altering the decision-making of professionals in various fields,[404] and indeed that corporate codes of ethics have often been 'predominantly self-defensive', difficult to implement across organizational or national boundaries, and may lead to negative outcomes.[405] On the other hand, one should be cautious about too quickly dismissing the cultural influence function of such instruments.[406] Indeed, there are likely many additional organizational interventions or changes that could more effectively facilitate the implementation of AI principles.[407]

Ultimately, the significant growth in AI ethics principles clearly reflects growing global concern over AI. Yet such principles may not cover all domain areas where AI introduces new problems. For instance, with a few exceptions,[408] there are fewer cases where standards cover AI systems to be used in security contexts. Nonetheless, one major benefit to the AI ethics principles is that they have begun the process of exploring and articulating a 'normative core' for AI governance. Much remains to be done to translate this into practice, however—which is one place where intergovernmental initiatives could come in.[409]

3.3.2 Relying on Unilateral State Action

A second approach would focus on action by states rather than non-state or private actors; however, it still foregoes outright international regulation. Rather, it would principally rely on different types of unilateral actions which states can take to shape the global landscape around AI.

[404] Arthur P Brief and others, 'What's Wrong with the Treadway Commission Report? Experimental Analyses of the Effects of Personal Values and Codes of Conduct on Fraudulent Financial Reporting' (1996) 15 Journal of Business Ethics 183; Margaret Anne Cleek and Sherry Lynn Leonard, 'Can Corporate Codes of Ethics Influence Behavior?' (1998) 17 Journal of Business Ethics 619; M Osborn and others, 'Do Ethical Guidelines Make a Difference to Decision-Making?' (2009) 39 Internal Medicine Journal 800; as discussed in Nicolas Kluge Corrêa, 'Blind Spots in AI Ethics and Biases in AI Governance' 17 <https://www.researchgate.net/publication/342821723_Blind_Spots_in_AI_Ethics_and_Biases_in_AI_governance?channel=doi&linkId=5f47ea4fa6fdcc14c5d0da27&showFulltext=true> accessed 28 August 2020.

[405] Maira Babri, Bruce Davidson, and Sven Helin, 'An Updated Inquiry into the Study of Corporate Codes of Ethics: 2005–2016' (2021) 168 Journal of Business Ethics 71.

[406] Seger (n 394).

[407] Stephanie Kelley, 'Employee Perceptions of the Effective Adoption of AI Principles' (2022) 178 Journal of Business Ethics 871 (adopting business code adoption theory and a series of interviews, in order to highlight eleven components that could facilitate the adoption of AI principles in an organization, including 'communication, management support, training, an ethics office(r), a reporting mechanism, enforcement, measurement, accompanying technical processes, a sufficient technical infrastructure, organizational structure, and an interdisciplinary approach').

[408] See Markus Christen and others, 'An Evaluation Schema for the Ethical Use of Autonomous Robotic Systems in Security Applications' (University of Zurich 2017) Digital Society Initiative White Paper Series 1 <https://papers.ssrn.com/abstract=3063617> accessed 30 April 2019.

[409] Garcia, 'Multilateralism and Artificial Intelligence: What Role for the United Nations?' (n 10).

3.3.2.1 Hard unilateral actions: deterrence, industrial policy, or supply-side controls

In the first place, one strategy could be the adoption, by powerful states, of declared policies of deterrence against particular types of behaviour or use around AI. This approach has been used as a tool in at least some global domains. For instance, as multilateral solutions to the problem of cyberwarfare have remained largely out of reach, and even gradual norm development continues to struggle to keep up, states have mostly resorted to practices of strategic deterrence.[410] However, this strategy has arguably done little to mitigate the threat of cyberattack, and has led to inadequate outcomes for cyberspace governance, with large-scale cyberattacks against both military and civilian targets a common practice.[411] It would likely also be insufficient for many AI challenges: for instance, such a blunt tool likely would not be used to dictate particular policies around many conventional AI issues (such as e.g. pervasive AI surveillance). While deterrence might seem more suitable as a tool to attempt to shape global practices around military AI uses, even in that area there will be hurdles around how to tailor deterrent threats that are appropriate, credible, and not excessively escalatory.

Alternatively, and more indirectly, unilateral actions by states could also involve the simple use of various national policy levers to directly shape the terms for AI development in other jurisdictions.[412] For instance, they might aim to utilize export controls on key AI inputs, or work with allies to secure various chokepoints in the global AI chip supply chain.[413] Such approaches could work effectively over

[410] Erin D Dumbacher, 'Limiting Cyberwarfare: Applying Arms-Control Models to an Emerging Technology' (2018) 25 The Nonproliferation Review 203. Note, one recent high-profile proposal has advocated for the adoption of a policy of deterrence around advanced AI systems, whereby states withhold from pursuing particularly powerful AI systems because any state's bid for 'unilateral AI dominance' could be easily met with preventive sabotage by rivals—a state the authors call 'Mutual Assured AI Malfunction' (MAIM). See Dan Hendrycks, Eric Schmidt, and Alexandr Wang, 'Superintelligence Strategy' (2025) <https://www.nationalsecurity.ai/> accessed 6 March 2025.

[411] Mette Eilstrup-Sangiovanni, 'Why the World Needs an International Cyberwar Convention' (2018) 31 Philosophy & Technology 379.

[412] For work that has aimed to map different states' policy levers over AI, see for instance Sophie-Charlotte Fischer and others, 'AI Policy Levers: A Review of the U.S. Government's Tools to Shape AI Research, Development, and Deployment' (Centre for the Governance of AI, Future of Humanity Institute, University of Oxford 2021) #2021-10 <https://www.fhi.ox.ac.uk/wp-content/uploads/2021/03/AI-Policy-Levers-A-Review-of-the-U.S.-Governments-tools-to-shape-AI-research-development-and-deployment-%E2%80%93-Fischer-et-al.pdf> accessed 26 March 2021; Maas, 'Advanced AI Governance' (n 314).

[413] Cullen O'Keefe, 'Chips for Peace: How the U.S. and Its Allies Can Lead on Safe and Beneficial AI' (*Lawfare*, 10 July 2024) <https://www.lawfaremedia.org/article/chips-for-peace--how-the-u.s.-and-its-allies-can-lead-on-safe-and-beneficial-ai> accessed 15 July 2024; André Brunel, 'A Proposal for a Semiconductor Export Control Treaty' (2023) 19 Journal of Business & Technology Law 1; Andre Barbe and Will Hunt, 'Preserving the Chokepoints: Reducing the Risks of Offshoring Among U.S. Semiconductor Manufacturing Equipment Firms' (Center for Security and Emerging Technology 2022) <https://cset.georgetown.edu/publication/preserving-the-chokepoints/> accessed 18 October 2022; Carrick Flynn and Khan, 'Multilateral Controls on Hardware Chokepoints' (*Center for Security and Emerging Technology*, September 2020) <https://cset.georgetown.edu/publication/multilateral-controls-on-hardware-chokepoints/> accessed 8 February 2023.

some time, though in the longer term their efficacy may be only temporary,[414] as they might be bypassed through chip smuggling networks,[415] subject to erosion as a result of broader gains in machine learning efficiency,[416] or subject to various forms of legal challenge among key allies.[417] Meanwhile, over-reliance on such avenues might rapidly erode the broader conditions and goodwill for many other types of governance and international coordination—whether on AI or on other pressing global issues.

3.3.2.2 Soft unilateral actions: explanatory memoranda; extraterritorial regulation

States could also take other unilateral actions to shape AI which might be more soft or indirect.

One softer unilateral strategy would be for states to seek to shape the normative status and state practice around AI, through their diplomatic activities, through acts such as explanatory memoranda around whether or how they understand existing treaty regimes to apply to AI issues.[418] In time, this can contribute to the formation of customary international law.[419]

Another soft unilateral strategy might rely on the indirect, extraterritorial effects of domestic regulations on other jurisdictions,[420] as seen in discussions of a 'Brussels Effect', 'California Effect', 'Beijing Effect', or 'London Effect' for domestic AI regulations.[421] However, while these approaches may have a significant role to

[414] Sarah Bauerle Danzman and Emily Kilcrease, 'The Illusion of Controls' [2023] *Foreign Affairs* <https://www.foreignaffairs.com/united-states/illusion-controls> accessed 10 January 2023.

[415] Tim Fist and Erich Grunewald, 'Preventing AI Chip Smuggling to China' (CNAS 2023) <https://www.cnas.org/publications/reports/preventing-ai-chip-smuggling-to-china> accessed 24 July 2024.

[416] Ritwik Gupta, Leah Walker and Andrew W Reddie, 'Whack-a-Chip: The Futility of Hardware-Centric Export Controls' (arXiv, 21 November 2024) <http://arxiv.org/abs/2411.14425> accessed 25 November 2024 (discussing how Chinese companies, notably Tencent, have not only found ways to use chips that are nominally restricted under US export controls, but have also circumvented these regulations by using software techniques that maximize the gains of less capable hardware).

[417] Daan Kingma, 'Caught in a Geopolitical Crossfire: Questioning the Legality of US-Imposed Export Controls on Dutch Computer Chip Machines' (*EJIL: Talk!*, 12 January 2024) <https://www.ejiltalk.org/caught-in-a-geopolitical-crossfire-questioning-the-legality-of-us-imposed-export-controls-on-dutch-computer-chip-machines/> accessed 13 January 2024.

[418] Bryant Walker Smith, 'New Technologies and Old Treaties' (2020) 114 AJIL Unbound 152. Indeed, Ashley Deeks has suggested that state practice around the use of AI systems in national security contexts may mostly spurn broad international agreements, and instead follow a path of normative development similar to that seen in hostile cyber operations, in that small-group cooperation and unilateral efforts by states to set expectations around such systems are more feasible. Ashley S Deeks, 'The Hurdles to International Regulation' in Ashley S Deeks (ed), *The Double Black Box: National Security, Artificial Intelligence, and the Struggle for Democratic Accountability* (Oxford University Press 2025).

[419] Rebecca Crootof, 'Jurisprudential Space Junk: Treaties and New Technologies' in Chiara Giorgetti and Natalie Klein (eds), *Resolving Conflicts in the Law* (Brill | Nijhoff 2019).

[420] Guillaume Beaumier and others, 'Global Regulations for a Digital Economy: Between New and Old Challenges' (2020) 11 Global Policy 515.

[421] See respectively Siegmann and Anderljung (n 141); Henry Josephson, 'A California Effect for Artificial Intelligence' (2022) <https://www.henryjos.com/p/a-california-effect-for-artificial.html> accessed 28 October 2022; Matthew S Erie and Thomas Streinz, 'The Beijing Effect: China's "Digital Silk Road" as Transnational Data Governance' [2021] New York University Journal of International Law and Politics 61; Nicholas A Caputo and others, 'International Governance through Domestic Law in

play in some domains, they may also likely foster contestation[422] and regulatory fragmentation. For instance, it has been argued that the EU AI Act has, at least in the early stages, had only modest reach or follow-up by other states, and that its influence at the US state level has been mooted by corporate lobbying intended to forestall similarly sweeping, risk-based regulations.[423] Indeed, it may prove the case that the AI Act's reliance on EU-specific political compromises and institutional arrangements will inhibit its diffusion to other jurisdictions.[424]

Finally, any strategy that relies on extraterritorial regulation to shape global standards around AI can only be as good as the norms and standards that are being disseminated. If these are not well-scoped or crafted, such approaches could instead contribute to the inadvertent global dissemination or lock-in of AI regulations that are weaker, or less optimally scoped, than the AI policy initiatives they displace. For instance, Almada and Radu have warned of what they call a potential 'Brussels Side-Effect': they argue that the EU AI Act, as product safety legislation, might provide more limited protection of some fundamental rights and that its extraterritorial effects could therefore inadvertently water down other international AI governance initiatives, such as the Council of Europe's AI Convention.[425]

3.3.3 Applying Existing International Law

Another major approach to AI's global governance challenges focuses on applying existing international law to these issues. This approach argues that, while AI technology might not have been explicitly foreseen at the time that many past norms or laws were articulated, this need not prevent those regimes from applying to AI technology to regulate it in a useful way.

In this view, effective global AI governance does not necessarily need any more new institutions, let alone entirely novel institutional models, because AI systems

the Forthcoming UK Frontier AI Bill' (Oxford Martin AI Governance Initiative, University of Oxford 2024) <https://www.oxfordmartin.ox.ac.uk/publications/international-governance-through-domestic-law-in-the-forthcoming-uk-frontier-ai-bill> accessed 17 December 2024.

[422] For a general account of how states can aim to pursue the global regulation of digital technologies from a domestic regulatory perspective, see also Beaumier and others (n 420).

[423] Emmie Hine, 'Artificial Intelligence Laws in the US States Are Feeling the Weight of Corporate Lobbying' (2024) 633 Nature S15.

[424] Marco Almada, 'The EU AI Act in a Global Perspective' in Markus Furendal and Magnus Lundgren (eds), *Handbook on the Global Governance of AI* (Edward Elgar 2025).

[425] Almada and Radu (n 144). See also Mélanie Gornet and Winston Maxwell, 'The European Approach to Regulating AI through Technical Standards' (2024) 13 Internet Policy Review <https://policyreview.info/articles/analysis/regulating-ai-through-technical-standards> accessed 7 August 2024. Similar challenges of regulatory alignment and consistency are discussed in Francesco Paolo Levantino and Federica Paolucci, 'Advancing the Protection of Fundamental Rights Through AI Regulation: How the EU and the Council of Europe Are Shaping the Future' in Philip Czech and others (eds), *European Yearbook on Human Rights 2024* (Intersentia 2024).

and their issues are already adequately regulated within the existing norms in international law, which should be reasserted and explicitly applied to these new issues. This is the approach that has been taken (with greater and lesser success) for other technologies in the past, in attempting to close the (apparent) legal gaps they created, as seen in early twentieth-century legal arguments that held that established norms around naval warfare ought to apply to submarines[426] or early twenty-first-century debates that sought to extend existing norms of international security law to cyberwar.[427] Indeed, many legal scholars have critiqued early attempts to tie the establishment of customary norms around cyber operations to 'cyber-specific' state practice and *opinio juris*—arguing instead that since international law is technology-neutral and applicable to all domain areas, this implies that novel information and communication technologies by default continue to be governed within the existing norms of international law.[428]

Accordingly, while there are some AI governance scholars and policymakers who assume that the novelty of this technology prima facie implies that there must be significant gaps in the existing tapestry of international law with regards to AI issues,[429] there have also been many legal scholars who argue that this problem is overstated, and that, as Chinen has put it, 'almost every domain in which artificial intelligence will have an impact is already governed by some form of international law'.[430] Such scholars argue that states (and other actors) should begin by recognizing that most or all AI technologies are already extensively covered and regulated through existing norms, principles, or doctrines in international law,[431] such as the principles of international human rights law,[432] international humanitarian

[426] Crootof, 'Jurisprudential Space Junk' (n 419).

[427] Kristen E Eichensehr, 'Cyberwar & International Law Step Zero' (2015) 50 Texas International Law Journal 357.

[428] Dapo Akande, Antonio Coco, and Talita de Souza Dias, 'Drawing the Cyber Baseline: The Applicability of Existing International Law to the Governance of Information and Communication Technologies' (2022) 99 International Law Studies <https://digital-commons.usnwc.edu/ils/vol99/iss1/2> accessed 12 June 2024.

[429] Catherine Rhodes and Luke Kemp, 'The Cartography of Global Catastrophic Governance' in SJ Beard and Tom Hobson (eds), *An Anthology of Global Risk* (Open Book Publishers 2024); Maxime Stauffer and others, 'Existential Risk and Rapid Technological Change: Advancing Risk-Informed Development' (United Nations Office for Disaster Risk Reduction 2023) 32 <https://www.undrr.org/publication/thematic-study-existential-risk-and-rapid-technological-change-advancing-risk-informed> accessed 20 March 2023 (suggesting that, because extreme risks from technological development are not widely discussed in UN texts, these do not provide 'a referential or legal basis' to address such risks).

[430] Chinen (n 10) 187.

[431] Talita de Souza Dias and Rashmin Sagoo, 'AI Governance in the Age of Uncertainty: International Law as a Starting Point' (*Just Security*, 2 January 2024) <https://www.justsecurity.org/90903/ai-governance-in-the-age-of-uncertainty-international-law-as-a-starting-point/> accessed 9 June 2024.

[432] Silja Vöneky, 'How Should We Regulate AI? Current Rules and Principles as Basis for "Responsible Artificial Intelligence"' in Alexander Bruns and others (eds), *Legal Theory and Interpretation in a Dynamic Society* (1st edn, Nomos Verlagsgesellschaft 2021); Lorna McGregor, Daragh Murray, and Vivian Ng, 'International Human Rights Law as a Framework for Algorithmic Accountability' (2019) 68 International & Comparative Law Quarterly 309; Chinen (n 10) ch 10.

law,[433] international criminal law,[434] international trade law,[435] and other regimes. Indeed, this has been at least in part an approach taken within recent UN initiatives on AI, which, even as they consider potential designs for new international organizations, have also emphasized the importance of integrating these with existing normative and policy instruments that are either specifically applicable to AI, apply to adjacent or interrelated areas, or could be applied.[436]

The option to extend international law is an interesting one, and a potentially promising one relative to many other approaches. After all, the global legal order has a long and significant pedigree which will not (and arguably should not) be discarded.[437] For all its current challenges, fragmentation, and 'stagnation',[438] it is likely to remain a lynchpin—or at the very least the core substrate—of the global governance architecture for some time to come.[439] As such, even if one assumes that international law does face many gaps on AI today, one could still argue that this toolkit should be extended to AI. Once roused, international law has historically proven quite creative at governing new technologies.[440] Existing international legal instruments can be adapted in various ways to respond to new (technological) changes: through treaty amendment, interpretation, or new state behaviour that results in new customary international law. At the same time, many of these avenues can often involve a long, drawn-out process,[441] especially since, as Rosemary Rayfuse has noted, 'the traditional approach of international law to the regulation of emerging technologies has been one of reaction rather than

[433] Burri (n 318). For example, this has also been the broad approach reflected in the UN Group of Governmental Experts process on lethal autonomous weapons systems, which—in its 2019 set of Guiding Principles, affirmed that 'International humanitarian law continues to apply fully to all weapons systems, including the potential development and use of lethal autonomous weapons systems'. United Nations, 'Report of the 2019 Session of the Group of Governmental Experts on Emerging Technologies in the Area of Lethal Autonomous Weapons Systems' (n 30), Annex IV, Guiding Principle (a).

[434] Burri (n 318).

[435] Liu and Lin (n 376).

[436] Inter-Agency Working Group on Artificial Intelligence (IAWG-AI), 'United Nations System White Paper on Artificial Intelligence Governance: An Analysis of Current Institutional Models and Related Functions and Existing International Normative Frameworks within the United Nations System That Are Applicable to Artificial Intelligence Governance' (United Nations Chief Executives Board for Coordination 2024) CEB/2024/1/Add.1 12–20 <https://unsceb.org/sites/default/files/2024-11/UNSystemWhitePaperAIGovernance.pdf> accessed 14 January 2025.

[437] Eyal Benvenisti and George W Downs, 'Comment on Nico Krisch, "The Decay of Consent: International Law in an Age of Global Public Goods"' (2014) 108 AJIL Unbound 1, 2 ('Historically, reports about the death of international law are invariably premature').

[438] Pauwelyn, Wessel, and Wouters (n 316).

[439] Karen J Alter, 'The Future of International Law' in Diana Ayton-Shenker (ed), *The New Global Agenda* (Rowman & Littlefield 2018).

[440] Colin B Picker, 'A View from 40,000 Feet: International Law and the Invisible Hand of Technology' (2001) 23 Cardozo Law Review 151.

[441] Crootof, 'Jurisprudential Space Junk' (n 419); Rebecca Crootof, 'Change Without Consent: How Customary International Law Modifies Treaties' (2016) 41 Yale Journal of International Law 65. These avenues of legal 'development' are discussed in greater detail in Chapter 5.

pro- action; only attempting to evaluate and regulate their development or use *ex post facto*'.[442]

Given this, it is worth asking whether international law *already* contains norms that could allow the effective regulation of AI systems and their issues. To be sure, international law offers a rich body of norms and obligations that could be drawn upon to inform—and compel—the regulation of challenges around AI. The sources of international law are set out in Article 38(1) of the Statute of the International Court of Justice (ICJ),[443] and include international treaties,[444] international custom, and the general principles of law recognized by ('civilized') nations.[445] Subsidiary to this, the ICJ Statute recognizes judicial decisions, and the teachings of the most highly qualified scholars of nations.[446] This offers a wide array of potential normative sources to draw on. Which of these norms might apply to AI technology? Would such approaches be effective?

To answer these questions, Section 3.3.3.1 will briefly review a range of norms, bodies of law, and instruments within international law—from more broad and indirect principles in customary international law, to more specific treaty regimes—to understand the applicability, strengths, and weaknesses of these instruments. It will be argued that while international law does not have a distinct relation to the appearance of new technology, we can still identify many applicable and potentially relevant norms and obligations deriving from both customary international law and treaty law. However, it is also argued that the success of applying either source will often rely on further clarification and interpretation of these norms. As such, I briefly discuss the role that international courts can play in this, the methods they could use to do so, and the challenges that they might encounter along the way.

3.3.3.1 International law's relation to new technologies

What is international law's relation to 'technology'? Doctrinally speaking, none. As Rayfuse has noted, in the absence of actual, direct harms, 'international law's concern with, or interest in, regulating technologies lies not in their inherent nature, form, development, or even deployment'.[447] That is to say, emerging technologies

[442] Rosemary Rayfuse, 'Public International Law and the Regulation of Emerging Technologies' in Roger Brownsword, Eloise Scotford, and Karen Yeung (eds), *The Oxford Handbook of Law, Regulation and Technology* (Oxford University Press 2017) 500.

[443] Statute of the International Court of Justice (signed 18 April 1946, entered into force 24 October 1945) 33 UNTS 993 (ICJ Statute) art 38(1).

[444] International treaties may be convened between states, between states and international organizations, or among international organizations, and can come in various forms. They are governed under the Vienna Convention on the Law of Treaties (1969) 1155 UNTS 331, as well as by the Vienna Convention on the Law of Treaties Between States and International Organizations or Between International Organizations (1989) 25 ILM 543.

[445] Statute of the International Court of Justice (n 443) art 38(1).

[446] ibid.

[447] Rayfuse (n 442) 506.

do not have a distinct status under international law;[448] and while there are certainly a wide range of technology-specific regimes to which states can and have acceded,[449] there does not exist a single legally binding global treaty regime to specifically regulate all technological risks as a single category.[450]

This functional technology-neutrality is reflected, for instance, in the International Court of Justice's 1996 Advisory Opinion on the Legality of the Threat or Use of Nuclear Weapons, which held that, in the absence of specific treaty obligations freely consented to by states, the mere development of nuclear weapons is not inherently unlawful under international law.[451] In fact, under this opinion, even the use of nuclear weapons would not be inherently unlawful, given certain highly circumscribed circumstances—specifically the 'extreme circumstance of self defence, in which the very survival of a State would be at stake'[452]—and provided that the state using them otherwise complies with the laws of armed conflict under international law.

Of course, on the other hand, even if this does not categorically outlaw nuclear weapons, such a reading might still be held to functionally outlaw certain types of nuclear weapon assemblages. For instance, Colin Picker has argued:

> While [the ICJ] opinion arguably leaves plenty of leeway for the subjective determination by a state as to when it feels its very survival is at stake, the opinion would appear, at a minimum, to argue against the legitimacy under international law of tactical nuclear weapons, and possibly of strategic nuclear weapons under many of the circumstances for which they were designed.[453]

All this is not to say that states could not consent to treaties focused on categorically outlawing the use or development of nuclear weapons technology: indeed,

[448] In this, international law interestingly does not adopt the exceptionalist approach to new technologies (see Chapter 4), even as it does, frequently, confront the question of whether a new technology requires new law. See also Eichensehr (n 427); Rebecca Crootof, 'Regulating New Weapons Technology' in Eric Talbot Jensen and Ronald TP Alcala (eds), *The Impact of Emerging Technologies on the Law of Armed Conflict* (Oxford University Press 2019).

[449] Picker (n 440) 164–181. There are, of course, a plethora of proposals for distinct new treaty regimes specific to various technologies. Eilstrup-Sangiovanni (n 411); Karen Scott, 'International Law in the Anthropocene: Responding to the Geoengineering Challenge' (2013) 34 Michigan Journal of International Law 309. For a discussion of governance for high-stakes risks from AI within the UN framework, see Reinmar Nindler, 'The United Nation's Capability to Manage Existential Risks with a Focus on Artificial Intelligence' (2019) 21 International Community Law Review 5. See also Crootof, 'Jurisprudential Space Junk' (n 419) 111–112 (reviewing proposed bans for diverse technologies).

[450] Rayfuse (n 442) 503. For a proposal for such a single global regime to cover extreme technological risks, see Grant Wilson, 'Minimizing Global Catastrophic and Existential Risks from Emerging Technologies through International Law' (2013) 31 Virginia Environmental Law Journal 307. However, it is possible to argue that international environmental law is, implicitly, a response to technologies which put the environment at risk. I thank José Jaime Villalobos for pointing this out.

[451] International Court of Justice, *Legality of the Threat or Use of Nuclear Weapons* (Advisory Opinion) [1996] ICJ Rep 226, ICGJ 205. However, ICJ advisory opinions are not legally binding.

[452] ibid 266.

[453] Picker (n 440) 175.

the adoption of the 2017 Treaty on the Prohibition of Nuclear Weapons imposes exactly such (nuclear) technology-specific treaty obligations on its signatories.[454] The point however is that, barring State consent to technology-specific treaties, or the establishment of new customary norms, international law does not prima facie take an interest in a new technology just for its being new. Rather, it responds only to (potential) new uses of that technology that violate pre-existing norms in existing regimes.[455]

This suggests that, barring such pre-existing international norms to the contrary, states are under international law free to develop and deploy new technologies at will. As Rayfuse has argued, 'in general, the principle of state sovereignty permits states to utilize their resources, conduct research, and develop and deploy, or allow their nationals to research, develop, and deploy, technologies as they see fit'.[456] However, in practice there are of course many pre-existing norms that apply, since in developing any new technology (or in carrying out any other actions) states are still bound by obligations deriving under all sources of international law, whether in customary international law (CIL), in treaty law, or under general principles of law.[457]

Could AI technology be covered under these existing norms? Doctrinally, treaty and customary international law are both considered coequal sources of international legal obligations upon states.[458] Indeed, it is generally held that the main sources of international law stand in a non-hierarchical relation to one another.[459] Given this, what norms might be derived from either customary international law or treaty law?

3.3.3.2 Applicable norms in customary international law

Customary international law is considered to exist when states generally and habitually engage in certain actions (i.e. there is a 'state practice' element), and when they do so out of a belief that those practices are legally obligatory or permitted

454 Treaty on the Prohibition of Nuclear Weapons (adopted 7 July 2017, entered into force 22 January 2021) UN Doc A/CONF. 229/2017/8 (TPNW). For a discussion of the campaign that led up to the signing, see Rebecca Davis Gibbons, 'The Humanitarian Turn in Nuclear Disarmament and the Treaty on the Prohibition of Nuclear Weapons' (2018) 25 The Nonproliferation Review 11.

455 The same goes for other technologies. For instance, Rayfuse discusses how 'the development and use of environmental modification technologies is neither regulated nor prohibited under international law, but only their hostile use in the context of an international armed conflict', specifically under the 1976 Convention on the Prohibition of Military or Any Other Hostile Use for Environmental Modification Techniques. Rayfuse (n 442) 507.

456 ibid 506.

457 See generally Marija Đorđeska, 'What Are General Principles? Theory and Conclusions', *General Principles of Law Recognized by Civilized Nations (1922–2018)* (Brill Nijhoff 2019).

458 Crootof, 'Change Without Consent: How Customary International Law Modifies Treaties' (n 441) n 273.

459 International Law Commission, 'Report of the International Law Commission on the Work of its 74th Session' (2023) UN Doc A/78/10 13 Conclusion 11(1) ('General principles of law, as a source of international law, are not in a hierarchical relationship with treaties and customary international law'). I thank José Jaime Villalobos for discussion on this topic.

(i.e. the subjective belief that they are bound by law, the so-called *opinio juris*[460] element).[461] As Rayfuse notes, these norms circumscribe any usage of any new technology (and indeed any state behaviour), and they include

> the basic norms of international peace and security law, such as the prohibitions on the use of force and intervention in the domestic affairs of other states . . . the basic principles of international humanitarian law, such as the requirements of humanity, distinction and proportionality . . . the basic principles of international human rights law, including the principles of human dignity and the right to life, liberty, and security of the person . . . and the basic principles of international environmental law, including the no-harm principle, the obligation to prevent pollution, the obligation to protect vulnerable ecosystems and species, the precautionary principle, and a range of procedural obligations relating to cooperation, consultation, notification, and exchange of information, environmental impact assessment, and participation . . . The general customary rules on state responsibility and liability for harm also apply.[462]

In addition, all state sovereignty is subject to the obligation, on all states, to ensure that activities under their jurisdiction and control do not cause harm to other states, the nationals of other states, the environment, or the global commons.[463] Beyond this, states are also bound by the fundamental norms of *jus cogens*, defined in the Vienna Convention on the Law of Treaties as norms 'accepted and recognized by the international community of States as a whole as a norm from which no derogation is permitted and which can be modified only by a subsequent norm of general international law having the same character'.[464] These peremptory norms outlaw, among others, genocide, maritime piracy, slavery, wars of aggression or territorial aggrandizement, torture, and refoulement,[465] clearly banning the use of AI systems (or, indeed, of any other technological means) for any of these purposes.

[460] Or, in full, the *opinio juris sive necessitates* ('an opinion of law or necessity').

[461] As Crootof notes, 'a rule of customary international law is authoritative because states generally abide by it in the belief that it is law'. Crootof, 'Change Without Consent: How Customary International Law Modifies Treaties' (n 441) n 1.

[462] Rayfuse (n 442) 503. However, most of these norms are also included in international treaties.

[463] International Court of Justice, *Corfu Channel Case (Albania v United Kingdom)* (Judgment) [1949] ICJ Rep 4, ICGJ 199; International Court of Justice, *Legality of the Threat or Use of Nuclear Weapons* (Advisory Opinion) (n 451) para 29. See also Rayfuse (n 442) 507–508.

[464] Vienna Convention on the Law of Treaties (signed 23 May 1969, entered into force 27 January 1980) 1155 UNTS 331 (VCLT) art 53.

[465] M Cherif Bassiouni, 'International Crimes: Jus Cogens and Obligatio Erga Omnes' (1996) 59 Law and Contemporary Problems 63, 68. Notably, *jus cogens* creates *erga omnes* obligations for states to comply with a rule. The UN's International Law Commission has codified the *erga omnes* principle in its draft articles on State responsibility as it, in article 48 (1)(b), allows all States to invoke a State responsibility which another State incurred due to its unlawful actions, if 'the obligation breached is owed to the international community as a whole'. International Law Commission, 'Draft Articles on Responsibility of States for Internationally Wrongful Acts (ARSIWA) with Commentaries, in the Report of the International Law Commission on the Work of Its Fifty-Third Session' (November 2001) UN Doc. A/56/10 (ARSIWA) art 48 (1)(b).

3.3.3.2.1 *Protective due diligence obligations: the Corfu Channel and no-harm principles*

Customary norms are foundational and bracket any use or deployment of AI—or, indeed, of any other new technology. They might therefore provide key backstops for the international regulation of AI.[466]

For instance, a range of customary norms of general obligations already establish protective due diligence obligations upon States in their development of AI.[467] For instance, the *Corfu Channel* principle, as constructed by the ICJ, entails 'every state's obligation not to allow knowingly its territory to be used for acts contrary to the rights of other states'.[468] This requires states to take all necessary steps to prevent and halt such acts contrary to the rights of other states which they know, or should know, emanate from their territory—an obligation that applies whether these are acts attributable to another state or undertaken by non-state actors.[469]

Another protective due diligence obligation of customary status and general application is found in the *no-harm principle*, which requires states to prevent and redress significant transboundary harm originating in their territory against persons, property or the environment, to the extent feasible in the circumstances.[470] This requires all states to prevent any transboundary harms to persons, property, and the environment that arise from any source—including the development or use of conventional, military, or advanced AI systems—and to notify other states if they fail to prevent such harms from emerging.[471] To be sure, these preventative obligations follow the due diligence standard in that their concrete requirements are dependent on the nature of the activity in question, the prevailing scientific knowledge at the time, and the capabilities of the State in question to reduce these risks from AI.[472] Nonetheless, a proper interpretation of these due diligence obligations, especially the no-harm principle, embeds a robust precautionary approach to the risks of AI. As noted by Antonio Coco and Talita Dias:

[466] That does not mean that further treaty provisions may not be needed to clarify or affirm the scope or applicability of existing norms and instruments. See for instance the discussion of AI interrogation tools in Amanda McAllister, 'Stranger than Science Fiction: The Rise of A.I. Interrogation in the Dawn of Autonomous Robots and the Need for an Additional Protocol to the U.N. Convention Against Torture' (2018) 101 Minnesota Law Review 2527.

[467] Simon Chesterman, 'Weapons of Mass Disruption: Artificial Intelligence and International Law' (2021) 10 Cambridge International Law Journal 181, 190; Antonio Coco and Talita Dias, '"Handle with Care": Due Diligence Obligations in the Employment of AI Technologies' in Robin Geiß and Henning Lahmann (eds), *Research Handbook on Warfare and Artificial Intelligence* (Edward Elgar 2024) 239–243.

[468] *Corfu Channel Case* (n 463) 22; as discussed in Coco and Dias (n 467).

[469] Coco and Dias (n 467).

[470] International Law Commission, 'Draft Articles on Prevention of Transboundary Harm from Hazardous Activities, with Commentaries', *Report of the International Law Commission on the work of its fifty-third session (23 April–1 June and 2 July–10 August 2001)*' UN Doc A/56/10 art 11 <https://legal.un.org/ilc/texts/instruments/english/commentaries/9_7_2001.pdf> accessed 14 August 2024; discussed in Coco and Dias (n 467) 240–242.

[471] Chesterman (n 467) 190.

[472] ibid.

> [w]hile the Corfu Channel principle requires actual or constructive knowledge of the relevant acts, the no-harm principle may be triggered by the mere existence of a risk of harm. Indeed, the ILC suggests that objective 'developments in scientific knowledge' that 'reveal a risk' of the requisite harm threshold suffice to trigger a state's duty to exercise due diligence in preventing it. And this is because due diligence, in this context, 'requires a state to keep abreast of technological changes and scientific developments'.[473]

Such a precautionary approach is particularly important in the context of AI risks,[474] as there is inherent unpredictability not only in the behaviour or even capabilities of individual AI models in new contexts of use or when developed with greater training compute resources,[475] but where there is furthermore uncertainty over the future course and capabilities of this technology as developments at the frontier of the field advance further. Accordingly, these due diligence obligations, along with due diligence obligations contained in regimes specific to particular uses of AI, such as international humanitarian law and international human rights law, impose a patchwork of protective obligations upon states—a set of duties which they can only discharge through the adoption of measures of diligent behaviour in the development and deployment of AI systems.[476] These include impact assessments and system evaluations throughout a model lifecycle—considering both 'any potential harms caused by the machine, [and] those foreseeably triggered by third parties (private or public) developing, selling or using the technology'[477]—as well as deactivation thresholds, fail-safe mechanisms, or provisions for some measure of human oversight and control. They might also require that states establish comprehensive domestic regulatory frameworks around the development, sale, acquisition, or deployment of AI technologies that might foreseeably affect individual human rights.[478] Finally, meeting their protective due diligence obligations could entail that states take measures to facilitate capacity-building, training, and steps towards international cooperation.[479]

Importantly, while some scholars have contended that customary international law has in recent decades receded in importance relative to treaties or may simply

[473] Coco and Dias (n 467) 424.
[474] ibid (noting that '[s]uch a precautionary approach is particularly important in the context of AI technologies, given their inherent unpredictability in performing new and specific tasks. In the case of dangerous AI applications, such as lethal AWS or AI-controlled power systems, particularly in nuclear facilities, even the slightest chance of error or malfunction—which science currently shows is possible for all machine learning applications—requires states to take the utmost care in developing and deploying the technology').
[475] See also Chapter 2.
[476] Coco and Dias (n 467) 251–259.
[477] ibid 253.
[478] ibid 256–257.
[479] ibid 257–259.

not be fit for many modern legal challenges,[480] this source of law could still offer distinct benefits in regulating AI innovation. For instance, Rebecca Crootof has suggested that, in the context of rapidly changing technologies, relying on customary international law may offer benefits over the use of treaties, because

> customary international law is universally applicable, which allows states to solve the potential holdout problem associated with any system grounded on consent... Relatedly, there is little risk of fragmentation. As opposed to treaty law's opt-in approach, customary international law has a limited opt-out option: at least theoretically, a state may avoid being bound by a developing customary international law rule by consistently contesting the rule's existence or applicability. In practice, there are few such examples of this occurring.[481]

Nonetheless, the specific application of customary international law to many AI use cases or challenges may leave much to be desired. This is because it is often unclear how these norms actually apply to AI systems, in terms of what obligations they impose.

3.3.3.2.2 Challenges in applying customary international law to AI

Importantly, while the basic principles and rules of customary international law may be binding on all states, they are also broad, and therefore sometimes vague.[482] While it may be clear *that* (any activities involving) AI systems would be bound by these norms, it can at times be unclear or contested *what* concrete obligations that imposes with regard to the development or use of AI.

To see why and how, one can consider the difficulties that have revolved around the application of existing customary norms to the military use of AI systems. While in principle any use of AI in conflict is bound by the provisions of international humanitarian law (IHL), in practice there are many uncertainties around how and when these open-ended provisions would apply with concrete effects.[483]

[480] Joel P Trachtman, 'The Growing Obsolescence of Customary International Law' in Curtis A Bradley (ed), *Custom's Future: International Law in a Changing World* (Cambridge University Press 2016) 172.

[481] Crootof, 'Jurisprudential Space Junk' (n 419) 127 (citing sources). For another defence of customary international law (specifically in addressing global commons problems around large-scale disasters), see Anne van Aaken, 'Is International Law Conducive to Preventing Looming Disasters?' (2016) 7 Global Policy 81.

[482] Rayfuse (n 442) 507.

[483] See also Elvira Rosert and Frank Sauer, 'Prohibiting Autonomous Weapons: Put Human Dignity First' (2019) 10 Global Policy 370; Esther Chavannes, Klaudia Klonowska, and Tim Sweijs, 'Governing Autonomous Weapon Systems: Expanding the Solution Space, from Scoping to Applying' [2020] HCSS Security 39. However, see an in-depth treatment of applicable law in Bill Boothby, *AI Warfare and the Law*, vol 104 (Stockton Center for International Law 2025) <https://digital-commons.usnwc.edu/ils/vol104/iss1/1/> accessed 13 February 2025.

For instance, there has been much debate over whether today's autonomous weapons systems fail to meet the *Principle of Distinction*—or if they do, for how much longer that will remain the case as AI capabilities advance.[484] Other IHL principles also may not provide effective guidance. For instance, it has been argued that the *Principle of Precaution in Attack* could even speak in favour of the use of (predictive) algorithms, if their decisions became more discriminate than those of human personnel, or if their use would allow for less lethal attacks.[485] Alternatively, one can consider the application of the *Principle of Humanity*, one of the oldest principles of IHL, laid down in the 'Martens Clause'. As phrased in the 1977 Additional Protocol I to the Geneva Conventions, this clause states:

> In cases not covered by this Protocol or by other international agreements, civilians and combatants remain under the protection and authority of the principles of international law derived from established custom, from the principles of humanity and from the dictates of public conscience.[486]

However, there remains extensive uncertainty over the meaning of many of these terms, including the 'dictates of public conscience' provision, in relation to AI-based weapons.[487] For example, while global opinion surveys do show significant and rising opposition to the use of LAWS,[488] such judgements can be contextual and subject to framings.[489] More generally, even if consistent public condemnation

[484] Rosert and Sauer (n 483); Ben Koppelman, 'How Would Future Autonomous Weapon Systems Challenge Current Governance Norms?' (2019) 164 The RUSI Journal 98; Braden Allenby, 'Are New Technologies Undermining the Laws of War?' (2014) 70 Bulletin of the Atomic Scientists 21; Lena Trabucco and Kevin Jon Heller, 'Beyond the Ban: Comparing the Ability of "Killer Robots" and Human Soldiers to Comply with IHL' (2022) 46 Fletcher Forum of World Affairs <https://papers.ssrn.com/abstract=4089315> accessed 22 April 2022.

[485] Chavannes, Klonowska, and Sweijs (n 483) 12–13. See also Crootof, 'Regulating New Weapons Technology' (n 448) 11–12.

[486] Protocol Additional to the Geneva Conventions of 12 August 1949, and relating to the Protection of the Victims of International Armed Conflicts (signed 8 June 1977, entered into force 7 December 1978) 1125 UNTS 3 (Geneva Protocol I), art. 1(2).

[487] See discussion over this debate in Matthijs M Maas, 'Innovation-Proof Governance for Military AI? How I Learned to Stop Worrying and Love the Bot' (2019) 10 Journal of International Humanitarian Legal Studies 129, 144–146.

[488] Heather M Roff, 'What Do People Around the World Think About Killer Robots?' [2017] *Slate* <http://www.slate.com/articles/technology/future_tense/2017/02/what_do_people_around_the_world_think_about_killer_robots.html> accessed 5 April 2018; IPSOS, 'Six in Ten (61%) Respondents Across 26 Countries Oppose the Use of Lethal Autonomous Weapons Systems' (2019) <https://www.ipsos.com/sites/default/files/ct/news/documents/2019-01/human-rights-watch-autonomous-weapons-pr-01-22-2019_0.pdf> accessed 27 January 2019; IPSOS, 'Three in Ten Americans Support Using Autonomous Weapons' (*Ipsos*, 7 February 2017) <https://www.ipsos.com/en-us/news-polls/three-ten-americans-support-using-autonomous-weapons> accessed 13 January 2019; Open Roboethics Initiative, 'The Ethics and Governance of Lethal Autonomous Weapons Systems: An International Public Opinion Poll' (Open Roboethics Initiative 2015) <http://www.openroboethics.org/wp-content/uploads/2015/11/ORi_LAWS2015.pdf> accessed 5 April 2018.

[489] Michael C Horowitz, 'Public Opinion and the Politics of the Killer Robots Debate' (2016) 3 Research & Politics 2053168015627183; Darrell M West, 'Brookings Survey Finds Divided Views on Artificial Intelligence for Warfare, but Support Rises If Adversaries Are Developing It' (*Brookings*, 29 August 2018) <https://www.brookings.edu/blog/techtank/2018/08/29/brookings-survey-finds-divi

were to be achieved for LAWS, it has been argued that states could simply innovate to improve military AI systems' ostensible adherence to societal norms.[490] This could be especially the case for less visceral 'lethality-enabling' applications, such as in target prediction.[491]

Moving from IHL to *jus ad bellum*, one might also appeal to the general international prohibition on the use of force. For instance, if the deployment of AI systems erodes strategic stability or sets the conditions for an unintended 'flash war',[492] or if conflict prediction algorithms lower the threshold to war,[493] this could result in premature or unlawful use of force, and the violation of states' obligations to sustain peace and security.[494] Such norms could therefore be interpreted to outlaw the incorporation of (semi-)autonomous systems into automated self-defence systems that could result in states unwillingly breaching these obligations.

Chavannes and others have also noted that the deployment of autonomous weapons systems could lead to problems with attributing accountability for wrongful acts.[495] This is for two reasons. On the one hand, it can lead to problems over establishing state accountability. The International Law Commission's Draft Articles on the Responsibility of States for Internationally Wrongful Acts note that the only conduct attributable to states is that of government organs or of people acting under these organs' 'direction, instigation or control' as 'agents of the State'.[496] However, the complicated development and usage life cycle of military AI systems may blur the responsibilities of the various actors involved in the development, deployment, and use of force, specifically making it harder to establish which actors should be counted as acting within the official command structure.[497]

ded-views-on-artificial-intelligence-for-warfare-but-support-rises-if-adversaries-are-developing-it/> accessed 21 September 2018.

[490] Chavannes, Klonowska, and Sweijs (n 483) 13. See also Maas, 'Innovation-Proof Governance for Military AI?' (n 487) 146.

[491] Michel (n 38); Ashley Deeks, 'Predicting Enemies' (2018) 104 Virginia Law Review 1529.

[492] Jürgen Altmann and Frank Sauer, 'Autonomous Weapon Systems and Strategic Stability' (2017) 59 Survival 117; Paul Scharre, 'Flash War—Autonomous Weapons and Strategic Stability' (Understanding Different Types of Risk, Geneva, 11 April 2016) <http://www.unidir.ch/files/conferences/pdfs/-en-1-1113.pdf> accessed 17 November 2017; Paul Scharre, 'Autonomous Weapons and Stability' (King's College 2020) <https://kclpure.kcl.ac.uk/portal/en/theses/autonomous-weapons-and-stability(92cd3d5b-4eb1-4ad5-a9ca-0cce2491e652).html> accessed 7 September 2021.

[493] Ashley Deeks, Noam Lubell, and Daragh Murray, 'Machine Learning, Artificial Intelligence, and the Use of Force by States' (2019) 10 Journal of National Security Law & Policy 1.

[494] Chavannes, Klonowska, and Sweijs (n 483) 14.

[495] ibid 14–15.

[496] International Law Commission, 'Draft Articles on Responsibility of States for Internationally Wrongful Acts' (n 465) 38. Para 2.

[497] However, Thomas Burri has argued these conceptual problems may be overstated, and suggests that international law has more than sufficient precedent to establish the meaning of 'control' over AI systems, or the limits of delegation. Specifically, he argues it can draw on extensive case law both in modern international criminal law (especially many of the cases before the International Criminal Tribunal for the Former Yugoslavia), as well as older cases by the Permanent Court of International Justice (such as its 1935 ruling on '*Consistency of Certain Danzig Legislative Decrees With the Constitution of the Free City*'). See Burri (n 318) 101–104.

The other problem with attribution lies in the inability to impose criminal liability for wrongful acts on the autonomous weapons systems themselves, since these systems, when they go awry, are generally understood to lack any 'intent' to cause harm.[498]

That is not to suggest that debates on the applicability of various international norms to military AI systems are intractable. Indeed, such debates are likely to yield greater clarity over time, and reach some legal resolution one way or the other. Nonetheless, the conceptual difficulty and disagreement over whether these various norms apply to lethal autonomous weapons systems—the sharpest contact point between international law and AI technology to date—is a sign of the relative conceptual difficulty involved in fitting existing customary norms to AI technology. This would likely arise in many other domains of AI use, inhibiting the process of norm development.

3.3.3.2.3 *The slow process of establishing new customary norms for AI*

Of course, in principle it would be possible for new customary international law to emerge, setting norms around the use of AI systems. However, one challenge here is that customary international norms generally develop very slowly: Picker has noted that, under good conditions, such norms have been created in as little as 10 to 15 years.[499] Very rarely, they have been created even more quickly, as in the 'instant custom' rules that emerged around States' rights in their territorial seas.[500] Yet often the emergence of customary law has taken decades. This is likely to hamper the efficacy of relying on this instrument alone in attempting to address the challenges of advanced AI capabilities at the frontier of the field, which can see progress in a manner of months.

To be sure, the speed of formation of CIL has picked up over time.[501] Furthermore, certain AI applications or other data-collection technologies could speed up this process even further, by helping speed up the recording and identification of state practices.[502] Yet such tools could also muddle this process, by

[498] For one suggested solution, see also Rebecca Crootof, 'War Torts: Accountability for Autonomous Weapons' (2016) 164 University of Pennsylvania Law Review 1347. Elizabeth Fuzaylova, 'War Torts, Autonomous Weapon Systems, and Liability: Why a Limited Strict Liability Tort Regime Should Be Implemented' (2019) 40 Cardozo Law Review 1327.

[499] Picker (n 440) 185.

[500] Crootof, 'Change Without Consent: How Customary International Law Modifies Treaties' (n 441) 250. (note 1: discussing how customary rules around states' rights in adjacent waters evolved rapidly).

[501] Picker (n 440).

[502] Tamar Megiddo, 'Knowledge Production, Big Data, and Data-Driven Customary International Law' in Andrea Bianchi and Moshe Hirsch (eds), *International Law's Invisible Frames: Social Cognition and Knowledge Production in International Legal Processes* (Oxford University Press 2021); Ashley Deeks and Duncan B Hollis, 'Large Language Models and International Law' [2025] Virginia Public Law and Legal Theory Research Paper <https://papers.ssrn.com/abstract=5131058> accessed 25 February 2025. See also Chapter 5.

making it easier for different (state) actors to identify and highlight counterexamples of state practice which favour their interests.[503]

More problematically, customary international law requires clear evidence of both state practice as well as *opinio juris*, the subjective obligation that a state perceives itself to be bound by the law in question. Both may be hard to address. Determining what state practices in a certain domain actually are is a difficult challenge, especially where it concerns practices around AI capabilities that are hidden, 'buried' in broader decision chains (e.g. military target list-generation systems), or hard to attribute (e.g. AI-enabled cyberwarfare attacks).[504]

Moreover, establishing the *opinio juris* criterion—to prove that a state is undertaking a certain practice because it considers itself legally bound to act in that way—can be even more difficult.[505] This difficulty would likely be exacerbated by the definitional problems around AI systems and applications.[506] Finally, this may be an indeliberate way of crafting global norms for AI. For instance, in some (e.g. military) domains, the use of AI systems will result in the gradual bottom-up accretion of norms through operational standards of appropriateness, rather than within deliberative fora of international lawmaking.[507]

3.3.3.3 Applicable norms in treaty law

While there are many potential norms to be derived from customary international law, this instrument also faces challenges, especially around the sufficiently rapid interpretation of these norms and the clarification of how they apply to AI systems and issues. We will shortly turn to the question of how, and by which actors, such interpretation could be carried out and expedited. However, it is important to first consider whether it is possible to derive applicable norms from existing treaty regimes. Indeed, the role of treaty norms may be particularly important, given that some have argued that in recent decades treaty law has taken an increasingly prominent role even as customary international law has declined in its prominence.[508]

[503] Ashley Deeks, 'High-Tech International Law' (2020) 88 George Washington Law Review 575, 649; Deeks and Hollis (n 502) 23–24. See again Chapter 5 (on using AI for governance 'displacement' including the automation of rule creation).

[504] See generally Rebecca Crootof, 'International Cybertorts: Expanding State Accountability in Cyberspace' (2018) 103 Cornell Law Review 565.

[505] Andrew T Guzman, 'Saving Customary International Law' (2005) 27 Michigan Journal of International Law 115, 145–146; Moisés Montiel, 'Fantastical Opinio Juris and How to Find It' (*Opinio Juris*, 23 June 2021) <https://opiniojuris.org/2021/06/23/fantastical-opinio-juris-and-how-to-find-it/> accessed 13 January 2024. See also Monica Hakimi, 'Making Sense of Customary International Law' (2020) 118 Michigan Law Review 1487, 1503.

[506] Matthijs M Maas, 'International Law Does Not Compute: Artificial Intelligence and The Development, Displacement or Destruction of the Global Legal Order' (2019) 20 Melbourne Journal of International Law 29, 53.

[507] Ingvild Bode and Hendrik Huelss, 'Autonomous Weapons Systems and Changing Norms in International Relations' (2018) 44 Review of International Studies 393.

[508] See Guzman (n 505) 119 (arguing that treaties have become a more important tool of international relations than customary international law). See also Trachtman (n 480) (arguing that

Indeed, there are many doctrines or norms which are provided for under particular treaty regimes (even if they are also embedded in customary international law), and which could provide more robust guidance for state obligations with regard to AI-related activities or challenges. Such an exercise could draw state obligations from various existing treaty regimes, in domains such as international disaster law, international human rights law, international criminal law, international humanitarian law, international environmental law, international economic law, or even the emerging body of future generations law, which draws on the growing state practice of providing for the rights of future generations at the national constitutional level,[509] as well as the growing incorporation of these rights and principles in (admittedly non-binding) international instruments.[510]

A full review is beyond the scope of this book. However, we will review a range of potential norms grounded in both international human rights law, as well as other, domain-specific treaty regimes.

3.3.3.3.1 Applicable norms in international human rights law

One popular and influential avenue for governing AI's global challenges might be found under the aegis of international human rights law (IHRL).[511] The past decade has seen many scholars articulating or highlighting the way in which AI technologies could threaten various human rights.[512] In response, there have been

customary international law may not be sufficient for modern challenges). However, see also the more nuanced discussion in Crootof, 'Jurisprudential Space Junk' (n 419) 126–128.

[509] Renan Araújo and Leonie Koessler, 'The Rise of the Constitutional Protection of Future Generations' (Social Science Research Network 2021) SSRN Scholarly Paper ID 3933683 <https://papers.ssrn.com/abstract=3933683> accessed 18 October 2021.

[510] Thomas Hale and others, 'Toward a Declaration on Future Generations' <https://www.bsg.ox.ac.uk/research/publications/toward-declaration-future-generations> accessed 17 January 2023. See also 'Maastricht Principles on the Human Rights of Future Generations' (July 2023) <https://www.rightsoffuturegenerations.org/the-principles> accessed 7 August 2023.

[511] It should be noted that under IHRL, human rights are primarily provided for in treaty law, notably within nine core international human rights instruments. Some of these rights are also considered to be a part of customary international law and have reached *jus cogens* status (such as the prohibitions on torture, or the prohibition on discrimination). However, not all rights that are provided for in treaty law are also part of CIL. The Universal Declaration of Human Rights (UDHR) itself is a UN General Assembly declaration that does not create binding international human rights law, however, many of its provisions are considered to be part of CIL.

[512] This literature is extensive, but see Alberto Quintavalla and Jeroen Temperman, *Artificial Intelligence and Human Rights* (Oxford University Press 2023); Filippo Raso and others, 'Artificial Intelligence & Human Rights: Opportunities & Risks' (Berkman Klein Center for Internet & Society at Harvard University 2018) <https://cyber.harvard.edu/sites/default/files/2018-09/2018-09_AIHumanRightsSmall.pdf?> accessed 8 April 2019; QC van Est, J Gerritsen, and L Kool, 'Human Rights in the Robot Age: Challenges Arising from the Use of Robotics, Artificial Intelligence, and Virtual and Augmented Reality' (Rathenau Instituut 2017) <https://research.tue.nl/en/publications/human-rights-in-the-robot-age-challenges-arising-from-the-use-of-> accessed 22 May 2019; Petra Molnar, 'Technology on the Margins: AI and Global Migration Management from a Human Rights Perspective' (2019) 8 Cambridge International Law Journal 305. Catelijne Muller, 'The Impact of Artificial Intelligence on Human Rights, Democracy and the Rule of Law' (Council of Europe, Ad Hoc Committee on Artificial Intelligence (CAHAI) 2020) <https://rm.coe.int/cahai-2020-06-fin-c-muller-the-impact-of-ai-on-human-rights-democracy-/16809ed6da> accessed 7 July 2020.

growing proposals to ground AI governance explicitly in human rights frameworks, norms, and instruments.[513]

For instance, Lorna McGregor and colleagues have suggested that IHRL could provide a superior framework to existing algorithmic accountability approaches, because it enables the shared understanding and means to assess harms, is able to deal with various actors and forms of responsibility, and can apply across the algorithmic life cycle.[514] Similarly, Karen Yeung and colleagues have argued in favour of a 'human rights-centered design, deliberation, and oversight approach' to AI governance,[515] and Silja Vöneky has called for a universal UN or UNESCO soft law declaration on 'AI Ethics and Human Rights'.[516]

There are various other such proposals. These proposals are presented as the best approach forward—or, at the very least, as a significant improvement to the current reliance on voluntary self-governance approaches to AI. As Eileen Donahoe and Megan Metzger argue, the human rights framework would have distinct advantages by comparison to these tools, because:

> 1) It puts the human person at the center of any assessment of AI and makes impact on humans the focal point of governance; 2) it covers the wide range of pressing concerns that AI raises, both procedural and substantive; 3) it outlines the roles and duties of both governments and the private sector in protecting and respecting human rights; and 4) it has the geopolitical advantage of resting on a broad global consensus, shared by many countries around the world and understood to be universally applicable.[517]

For instance, they note how various sections of the Universal Declaration of Human Rights (UDHR) address some of the diverse societal concerns that have been raised around AI, from challenges around avoiding data bias and ensuring fairness in machine-based decisions relied upon by governments (Article 2—the right to equal protection and non-discrimination), concerns around autonomous weapons (Article 3—the right to life and personal security), concerns around privacy in the face of AI surveillance (Article 12—the right to privacy), the challenges around algorithmic content moderation (Article 19—the right to freedom of expression), or the displacement of human workers by AI (Articles 23 and 25—the rights to work and to enjoy an adequate standard of living).[518]

[513] Chinen (n 10) 278.
[514] McGregor, Murray, and Ng (n 432).
[515] Karen Yeung, Andrew Howes, and Ganna Pogrebna, 'AI Governance by Human Rights-Centred Design, Deliberation and Oversight: An End to Ethics Washing' in M Dubber and F Pasquale (eds), *The Oxford Handbook of AI Ethics* (Oxford University Press 2020).
[516] Vöneky (n 432).
[517] Donahoe and Metzger (n 398) 119. See also Vöneky (n 432). For an exploration of what a human-rights based approach to AI would entail, and what would be some of its pitfalls, see also Smuha (n 397).
[518] Donahoe and Metzger (n 398) 120.

Given this, there are many benefits to human rights-based frameworks, particularly compared to existing soft law or self-governance initiatives, on substantive, effectiveness, and legitimacy grounds. Indeed, Bakiner has suggested that the human rights framework might have a number of conceptual, normative, and legal tools to address AI challenges, because the problems AI raises 'contain non-AI components that complicate the nature of ethical, legal, and political challenges, produce unforeseen consequences and negative externalities, result from intentional or unintentional choices, require a balancing approach to harms, and involve multiple businesses (and at times government agencies) as potential duty-bearers'.[519]

Of course, IHRL may also face a series of shortcomings or challenges in regulating AI. For one, even some of its advocates concede that while human rights norms are comprehensive, they still do not cover all ethical values that are implicated or threatened by AI systems.[520] The framework might also face challenges in directly shaping the behaviour of the primary actors within AI development: private technology companies in AI. After all, whereas under IHRL states have a direct obligation to protect human rights, the scope and content of private businesses' human rights responsibilities remains more underdeveloped, as they are currently only subject to 'expectations' to respect human rights.[521] Of course, even so, IHRL still indirectly covers the scope of private actors' activities, by creating State obligations to regulate (in order to protect) particular rights. Others have raised more challenging critiques of the adequacy of the human rights framework to AI.[522]

[519] Onur Bakiner, 'The Promises and Challenges of Addressing Artificial Intelligence with Human Rights' (2023) 10 Big Data & Society 20539517231205476, 10.

[520] Yeung, Howes and Pogrebna (n 515) 102–103. For a more fundamental philosophical critique, see Tasioulas (n 2) 69–70 ('Leave aside the fact that this law does not reflect all of the ethical considerations (e.g. environmental values) bearing on AI, that it does not tend to be directly binding on non-state actors, and that not all of its provisions bind all states (e.g. because they have not ratified relevant human rights treaties). The more fundamental point is that such laws—despite the powerful moral charge conferred by the words 'human rights'—are not basic ethical standards. Instead, like any other set of laws, they are themselves to be formulated and evaluated—and, sometimes, to be found seriously wanting—in terms of basic ethical standards, including the morality of human rights').

[521] UNHRC 'Guiding Principles on Business and Human Rights: Implementing the United Nations "Protect, Respect and Remedy" Framework' (6 July 2011) UN Doc A/HRC/17/31 art 11. See also the discussion by McGregor, Murray, and Ng (n 432) 313. But see also Donahoe and Metzger (n 398) 120–121 (offering a more optimistic account of the ability of these UN Guiding Principles to provide guidance to IHRL in addressing AI issues).

[522] For instance, Hin-Yan Liu and Karolina Zawieska have argued that AI technologies put pressure on (individual) rights-based responsibility and accountability mechanisms. Hin-Yan Liu and Karolina Zawieska, 'A New Human Rights Regime to Address Robotics and Artificial Intelligence', *2017 Proceedings of the 20th International Legal Informatics Symposium* (Oerterreichische Computer Gesellschaft* 2017); Hin-Yan Liu, 'The Digital Disruption of Human Rights Foundations' in Maart Susi (ed), *Human Rights, Digital Society and the Law: A Research Companion* (Routledge 2019). Sue Anne Teo has argued that AI systems erode key conceptual foundations of the IHRL framework, because they "increasingly challenge the notions of how, by whom, and what human rights violations are being committed." Sue Anne Teo, 'How Artificial Intelligence Systems Challenge the Conceptual Foundations of the Human Rights Legal Framework' (2022) 40 Nordic Journal of Human Rights 216, 217. For another high-level review, see also Bakiner (n 519) 10. ('future discourse and practice around the human rights framework should also take into account three core problems: AI reproduces long-term, structural problems going beyond issue-by-issue regulation, is embedded within economic

That does not mean that such challenges could not be overcome, of course. Nonetheless, advocates of this approach have noted that a human rights-based governance frameworks for AI will need to take a series of steps to clarify the applicability of human rights, strengthen enforcement mechanisms, and to secure the underlying societal infrastructures or norms—such as democratic institutions and the rule of law—which enable human rights in the first place.[523] That may be a steep challenge, especially in a geopolitical landscape in which there has been growing contestation of multilateral solutions in general and some areas of human rights in particular.[524]

Ultimately, human rights law may be a key backstop for the global governance of AI,[525] especially where it concerns the impacts of many conventional AI applications as well as advanced AI systems. However, for this promise to be realized, there may be a need for significant interpretation and clarification of state obligations as a result. Whether and how such interpretation might come about remains an open question, as will be discussed shortly.

3.3.3.3.2 Applicable norms in air, sea, and road travel conventions

Beyond IHRL, there are also many other issue- or domain-specific regimes that could be applied to AI. Over the course of several centuries, international law has developed a dense and diverse body of treaty law for many industries, technologies, and domains of activity, potentially offering a diverse array of domain-specific norms, standards, or treaty instruments that could plausibly be applied to many AI challenges.

Martina Kunz and Seán Ó hÉigeartaigh have explored in detail how various international law regimes might cover or be extended to AI, focusing specifically on the domains of safety and security.[526] They identify diverse existing governance

structures that produce cumulative negative effects, and introduces additional challenges that require a discussion about the relationship between human rights and science and technology').

[523] See Smuha (n 397) 12–13.

[524] Karen J Alter, 'The Future of International Law' in Diana Ayton-Shenker (ed), *The New Global Agenda* (Rowman & Littlefield 2018) <https://papers.ssrn.com/abstract=3015177> accessed 13 January 2024.

[525] As well as, potentially, for the alignment of advanced AI systems with human values (or legal codes) in a more direct sense. See Iason Gabriel, 'Artificial Intelligence, Values, and Alignment' (2020) 30 Minds and Machines 411, 426–428; Ondrej Bajgar and Jan Horenovsky, 'Negative Human Rights as a Basis for Long-Term AI Safety and Regulation' (2023) 76 Journal of Artificial Intelligence Research 1043. See also more generally, Cullen O'Keefe, Ketan Ramakrishnan, Janna Tay, and Christoph Winter 'Law-Following AI: Designing AI Agents to Obey Human Laws' [2025] Fordham Law Review <https://papers.ssrn.com/abstract=5242643>; Cullen O'Keefe and Ketan Ramakrishnan, 'AI Agents Must Follow the Law' (*Lawfare*, 14 May 2025) <https://www.lawfaremedia.org/article/ai-agents-must-follow-the-law> accessed 16 May 2025.

[526] Kunz and Ó hÉigeartaigh (n 11). For examinations of the potential of international law norms and principles to address potential future challenges from AI, see José Jaime Villalobos, Matthijs Michiel Maas and Christoph Winter, 'Seven Principles to Govern Advanced AI: The International Law of Global Catastrophic Risk' (manuscript), as well as Bryan H Druzin, Anatole Boute, and Michael Ramsden, 'Confronting Catastrophic Risk: The International Obligation to Regulate Artificial Intelligence' (2025)

regimes that have begun consultation on AI issues, or which could provide at least some degree of regulatory scaffolding in these areas.[527] For instance, they survey a range of provisions that might apply to transborder mobile robot governance, covering systems in the air, at sea, or on land.

They argue that provisions for autonomous airborne drones might derive from existing instruments for the safety and security of civil aircraft. These include provisions on 'pilotless aircraft' already embedded in the 1944 Chicago Convention on International Civil Aviation;[528] ongoing guidance documents on drone safety and security produced by the International Civil Aviation Organization (ICAO);[529] the 1970 Hague Convention for the Suppression of Unlawful Seizure of Aircraft and its supplementary 2010 Beijing Protocol;[530] and the 2010 Beijing Convention on the Suppression of Unlawful Acts Relating to International Civil Aviation.[531]

In terms of international regimes for autonomous maritime vessels, the International Maritime Organization (IMO) has begun to investigate legal aspects of the safe development of remote-controlled, autonomous, or semi-autonomous surface ships.[532] While many legal uncertainties remain, scholars exploring the security implications of maritime autonomous vehicles under international law have broadly argued that while such vehicles raise some new questions with regard to issues such as the Right of Hot Pursuit or the Right of Visit, in most cases existing legal principles might be applied to AI-controlled vessels without major problems.[533]

In terms of autonomous vehicles, there have been some efforts in the past few years to modernize existing frameworks,[534] though this has been complicated by the existing split between the 1949 Geneva Convention on Road Traffic[535] and the 1968 Vienna Road Traffic Convention.[536] Nonetheless, as noted by Bryant

46 Michigan Journal of International Law 2; JG Castel and Mathew E Castel, 'The Road to Artificial Superintelligence—Has International Law a Role to Play?' (2016) 14 Canadian Journal of Law & Technology 1; Nindler (n 449); Wilson (n 450).

[527] Kunz and Ó hÉigeartaigh (n 11).

[528] Convention on International Civil Aviation (1944) 15 UNTS 295 Art 8. See Kunz and Ó hÉigeartaigh (n 11) 3–4.

[529] Kunz and Ó hÉigeartaigh (n 11) 4 (citing sources).

[530] Which includes criminalization of remote seizure or exercise of control of an aircraft 'by any technological means'. Protocol Supplementary to the Convention for the Suppression of Unlawful Seizure of Aircraft 2011 (50 ILM 153) art 1(1).

[531] Convention on the Suppression of Unlawful Acts Relating to International Civil Aviation (2011) 50 ILM 144; Kunz and Ó hÉigeartaigh (n 11) 4–5.

[532] Kunz and Ó hÉigeartaigh (n 11) 5. See also Barbara Stępień, 'Navigating New Waters: IMO's Efforts to Regulate Autonomous Shipping' (2024) 23 Chinese Journal of International Law 599.

[533] Natalie Klein, 'Maritime Autonomous Vehicles within the International Law Framework to Enhance Maritime Security' (2019) 95 International Law Studies 29; Robert McLaughlin, 'Unmanned Naval Vehicles at Sea: USVs, UUVs, and the Adequacy of the Law' [2011] Journal of Law, Information and Science <http://www5.austlii.edu.au/au/journals/JlLawInfoSci/2012/6.html> accessed 22 June 2020.

[534] Kunz and Ó hÉigeartaigh (n 11) 6.

[535] Convention on Road Traffic (1949) 125 UNTS 22.

[536] Convention on Road Traffic (1968) 1042 UNTS 15705.

Smith, the Global Forum's 2018 Resolution on the Deployment of Highly and Fully Automated Vehicles in Road Traffic has provided one of a number of signs that conceptual uncertainties are being pragmatically resolved.[537]

3.3.3.3.3 Applicable norms in counterterrorism, arms control, and weapons treaties

Moreover, Kunz and Ó hÉigeartaigh explore the applicability of a range of cross-domain counterterrorism regimes that could affect AI-related security challenges, arguing that the 1997 Convention for the Suppression of Terrorist Bombings might outlaw, for instance, the terrorist use of agricultural drones to spray chemicals on crowds.[538] Likewise, they posit that several United Nations Security Council resolutions have application in restricting potential robotic delivery systems for terrorism, and specifically where these are used in the delivery of Weapons of Mass Destruction.[539]

Other mobile robotic systems, they suggest, might be subsumed under various conventional arms control regimes, including the 1987 Missile Technology Control Regime (MTCR), the 1996 Wassenaar Arrangement, or the 2013 Arms Trade Treaty (ATT).[540]

However, while these and other regimes provide a precedent for dealing with or restricting the proliferation of potential dual-use technologies, there may be shortfalls in applying them to military or security-relevant AI systems. For one, while export control regimes have certainly been updated and revised in the past, this has not often been done consistently or effectively—often requiring large outside political shocks to create momentum.[541] More generally, these control regimes have at times struggled to resolve inter-regime conflicts.[542]

This reflects an underlying complexity around regulating or constraining the diverse components and sub-systems that go into the production of a hazardous AI system. More fundamentally, cloud computing and digital technology are not easily captured and constrained through non-proliferation efforts focused on

[537] See also Smith (n 418).

[538] International Convention for the Suppression of Terrorist Bombings (1997) 2149 UNTS 256; Kunz and Ó hÉigeartaigh (n 11) 7.

[539] Specifically Resolution 1373 (2001) (on preventing and suppressing terrorist acts) and Resolution 1540 (2004) (on the non-proliferation of WMDs and their means of delivery). See Kunz and Ó hÉigeartaigh (n 11) 7.

[540] Kunz and Ó hÉigeartaigh (n 11) 7–8.

[541] Amy J Nelson, 'Innovation Acceleration, Digitization, and the Arms Control Imperative' (Social Science Research Network 2019) SSRN Scholarly Paper ID 3382956 <https://papers.ssrn.com/abstract=3382956> accessed 29 May 2020. Although see also Caroline Fehl's more positive account of regime evolution: Caroline Fehl, 'Unequal Power and the Institutional Design of Global Governance: The Case of Arms Control' (2014) 40 Review of International Studies 505.

[542] Kolja Brockmann, 'Challenges to Multilateral Export Controls: The Case for Inter-Regime Dialogue and Coordination' (SIPRI 2019) <https://www.sipri.org/publications/2019/other-publications/challenges-multilateral-export-controls-case-inter-regime-dialogue-and-coordination> accessed 13 March 2025.

material constraints.[543] Indeed, export controls have arguably rarely been fully effective at restricting algorithmic innovations, in spite of a number of attempts.[544] Indeed, some suggest the increase in digitalization has already begun to eat away at a range of export regimes or national export policies.[545] The pressures on repurposing export control regimes for AI are also reflected in the fact that, in summer 2020, the US announced an intention to unilaterally reinterpret how it would participate in the MTCR in order to allow US companies to export more weaponized drones.[546] It is therefore unclear if or how fraying export control regimes might be revived or scaled up to apply to hazardous AI systems, though they offer at least one tool that should be built upon before it is rapidly discarded.

Another avenue for regulating military uses of AI could be found in the existing legal review mechanism for new weapons. Under Article 36 of Additional Protocol I to the Geneva Conventions, there is an obligation upon States to assess the compliance of any considered, developed, acquired, or adopted 'new weapons, means and methods of warfare' in order to determine whether their employment would be prohibited by that Protocol or any other rule of international law.[547] However, this mechanism is already hindered by a lack of widespread or transparent implementation by States.[548] Moreover, its application to military AI technologies might be impeded by the conceptual difficulties around determining whether reviews need only cover directly weaponized systems, or whether these should also extend to related non-weaponized AI technologies in the much broader operational network and infrastructure that assists in the targeting processes.[549]

[543] Mark Bromley and Giovanna Maletta, 'The Challenge of Software and Technology Transfers to Non-Proliferation Efforts: Implementing and Complying with Export Controls' (SIPRI 2018) <https://www.sipri.org/publications/2018/other-publications/challenge-software-and-technology-transfers-non-proliferation-efforts-implementing-and-complying> accessed 13 March 2025.

[544] One notable example here might be cryptography. See Whitfield Diffie and Susan Landau, 'The Export of Cryptography in the 20th Century and the 21st' <https://privacyink.org/pdf/export_control.pdf> accessed 2 September 2019. However, at the same time, an international framework for cryptography is still lacking, see for an exploration: Ashley Deeks, 'The International Legal Dynamics of Encryption' (2017) 1609 Hoover Institute Aegis Paper Series 28.

[545] Nelson (n 541).

[546] Daryl G Kimball, 'U.S. Aims to Expand Drone Sales' (*Arms Control Association*, August 2020) <https://www.armscontrol.org/act/2020-07/news/us-aims-expand-drone-sales> accessed 12 August 2020; Paul K Kerr, 'U.S.—Proposed Missile Technology Control Regime Changes' (Congressional Research Service 2022) <https://www.congress.gov/crs-product/IF11069> accessed 13 March 2025.

[547] Protocol Additional to the Geneva Conventions of 12 August 1949, and relating to the Protection of the Victims of International Armed Conflicts (signed 8 June 1977, entered into force 7 December 1978) 1125 UNTS 3 (Geneva Protocol I), art 36. See also Vincent Boulanin, 'Implementing Article 36 Weapon Reviews in the Light of Increasing Autonomy in Weapon Systems' (SIPRI 2015) <https://www.sipri.org/publications/2015/sipri-insights-peace-and-security/implementing-article-36-weapon-reviews-light-increasing-autonomy-weapon-systems> accessed 9 January 2024.

[548] Denise Garcia, 'Future Arms, Technologies, and International Law: Preventive Security Governance' (2016) 1 European Journal of International Security 94, 105; Chavannes, Klonowska, and Sweijs (n 483) 13–14.

[549] Hin-Yan Liu, 'Categorization and Legality of Autonomous and Remote Weapons Systems' (2012) 94 International Review of the Red Cross 627, 628; Chavannes, Klonowska, and Sweijs (n 483) 13–14.

3.3.3.3.4 Applicable norms in data processing conventions

There is an additional shortfall in many of the instruments and regimes discussed just now, which is that most focus predominantly on (direct harms from) cyber-physical systems such as drones or embodied robots, in relatively specific domains of application. This suggests that such regimes would encounter challenges in being applied to AI challenges in or deriving from more virtual settings, where they automate or support organizational decision-making, or where the source of problems in particular domains can be traced back to the training process of an underlying foundation model. In other words, such treaty regimes may apply, if at all, only to a subset of conventional AI systems and military AI systems. However, they likely are not easily applicable—nor well-tailored—for regulating increasingly general-purpose advanced AI systems.

That is not to say there are no alternatives or potential routes. For instance, Kunz and Ó hÉigeartaigh point to a series of existing conventions that might be applied to issues such as AI-based data processing,[550] or to AI-based or enabled crimes (such as the 2001 Budapest Convention on Cybercrime).[551] For instance, to take the issue of data processing by AI systems, one could draw on a range of existing treaty norms. Consider the Council of Europe's 2018 Modernised Convention for the Protection of Individuals with Regards to Automatic Processing of Data (Convention 108+).[552] As an update to the CoE's previous (1985) Convention 108, this Convention mandates States Parties to ensure that any personal data that are collected by 'automatic processing' are obtained and processed 'fairly and lawfully', and not used in any other way than for the 'specified and legitimate' purposes for which they were originally collected.[553] Additionally, the convention establishes the obligation to refrain from transferring personal data to other jurisdictions that do not have 'an appropriate level of protection' of the data.[554] Moreover, in 2019, the Consultative Committee of the Convention elaborated a set of Guidelines on Artificial Intelligence and Data Protection.[555]

550 Kunz and Ó hÉigeartaigh (n 11) 9–12.

551 ibid 12–13.

552 Council of Europe Modernised Convention for the Protection of Individuals with Regard to Automatic Processing of Personal Data (opened for signature 10 October 2018, not yet entered into force) CETS No 108+ (Convention 108+). See also Cécile de Terwangne, 'Council of Europe Convention 108+: A Modernised International Treaty for the Protection of Personal Data' (2021) 40 Computer Law & Security Review 105497.

553 Convention 108+ art 5. Notably, the European Union's 2018 General Data Protection Regulation ('GDPR') incorporated many of the same rights and obligations. See Regulation (EU) 2016/679 of the European Parliament and of the Council of 27 April 2016 on the protection of natural persons with regard to the processing of personal data and on the free movement of such data, and repealing Directive 95/46/EC (General Data Protection Regulation) [2016] OJ L119/1 arts 12–23, 44–50. However, the GDPR does not accept accession by non-EU members, which the Modernised Convention does. Kunz and Ó hÉigeartaigh (n 11).

554 Convention 108+ art 14.

555 Council of Europe, 'New Guidelines on Artificial Intelligence and Data Protection' (*Council of Europe*, 30 January 2019) <https://www.coe.int/en/web/data-protection/-/new-guidelines-on-artificial-intelligence-and-personal-data-protection> accessed 13 January 2024.

Accordingly, instruments such as the Modernised Convention could shape and provide backing to international norms around data protection and the transfer of data, affecting the global distribution and availability of high-quality training data for AI developers. Given that data sources may, within the coming years, become a more restrictive brake to the larger scaling up (and 'alignment') of advanced foundation models than is computing power, this means that these instruments could shape some elements of the production chain for advanced AI systems.

3.3.3.3.5 The challenges in applying treaty law to AI

However, again, there may be limits to applying many treaty regimes. Indeed, in some cases they might hurt more than help effective global policy responses, if applied unreflexively. For example, rather than ground effective AI-relevant obligations on states to minimize risks, certain treaty norms may be interpreted in ways that would lead them to inhibit or prohibit particular regulatory interventions on AI.

For instance, take data regulation. Various trade and investment agreements, such as the WTO General Agreement on Trade in Services (GATS),[556] enshrine a set of principles—such as the most-favoured-nation requirement and the national treatment obligation—which might inhibit states from adopting restrictions on data transfer.[557] To be sure, many of these instruments also provide exceptions that allow states to enact measures 'necessary to protect public morals or to maintain public order [where] a genuine and sufficiently serious threat is posed to one of the fundamental interests of society'.[558] Nonetheless, whether or when such exceptions would be accepted in the context of trade restrictions, and whether they would pass a 'necessity test' at the WTO,[559] remain open questions.

In another example of such potential interference, one might also consider international trade agreements such as the Comprehensive and Progressive Agreement for Trans-Pacific Partnership (CPTPP), or the United States–Mexico–Canada Agreement (USMCA). These agreements also cover provisions for electronic commerce and digital trade; among others, they contain provisions on the transfer of

[556] General Agreement on Trade in Services, annexed to the Marrakesh Agreement Establishing the World Trade Organization (signed 15 April 1994, entered into force 1 January 1995) 1869 UNTS 183 (GATS); Chinen (n 10) 188.

[557] Chinen (n 10) 187–188. Discussing Susannah Hodson, 'Applying WTO and FTA Disciplines to Data Localization Measures' (2019) 18 World Trade Review 579.

[558] GATS art XIV(a). As discussed in Chinen (n 10) 189–190. As such, in one proposed 'jurisdictional certification' approach to AI governance, Trager and others have suggested that import and export controls on AI products and precursors could be compatible with international trade law agreements such as GATS, the General Agreement on Tariffs and Trade (GATT), or the Agreement on Trade-Related Aspects of Intellectual Property Rights (TRIPS), because these establish security exceptions. See Robert Trager and others, 'International Governance of Civilian AI: A Jurisdictional Certification Approach' (*arXiv*, 29 August 2023) 39–40 <http://arxiv.org/abs/2308.15514> accessed 31 August 2023.

[559] Trager and others (n 558) 40.

source code that may be read in ways that inhibit the ability of regulators to inspect the source code of AI systems—or at least to do so as a condition for the importation or use of the system.[560]

That does not mean that such treaties are incompatible with all AI governance goals, of course: for example, such free trade agreements and digital economy agreements might well support AI governance regimes that are more particularly focused on increasing global market access to AI.[561] However, this may exacerbate recent concerns that, even where existing trade rules are beginning to be updated to reckon with AI issues, these changes tend to disproportionately reflect industry interests, focusing solely on promoting AI—such as through strong intellectual property protections for source code and algorithms, and making strong commitments to enabling the free cross-border flow of data—while neglecting the cross-border risks and harms associated with AI, in domains such as competition policy, ethical uses, data protection, or the exploitative use of AI systems.[562]

Given all this, many other existing treaties that appear to apply directly to aspects of AI may have other drawbacks: beyond politically fragmented membership, many existing treaties also have somewhat technically fragmented coverage of AI issues, focusing only on specific use cases of AI (or particular steps in its value chain). This could well lead to the production of conflicting norms or standards, given that similar AI capabilities or techniques can be shared across such domains or use cases.

3.3.3.4 Interpreting customary and treaty norms' application to AI: the role of international courts

Given this cursory survey, it is clear that there exist many norms within both customary international law and treaty law that could in principle offer guidance for state approaches towards AI systems. However, the success of applying these norms will often rely on their precise interpretation, to clarify the exact obligations they impose on states.

[560] Chinen (n 10) 192 (discussing among others Article 14.7(1) of the CPTPP, which 'prohibits a party from requiring the transfer of or access to the source code of software as a condition for the importation or use of the software'). Comprehensive and Progressive Agreement for Trans-Pacific Partnership (signed 8 March 2018, entered into force 30 December 2018) [2018] ATS 23 (CPTPP) art 14.7(1).

[561] Joshua P Meltzer, 'Toward International Cooperation on Foundational AI Models: An Expanded Role for Trade Agreements and International Economic Policy' [2024] Harvard Data Science Review <https://hdsr.mitpress.mit.edu/pub/14unjde2/release/1> accessed 4 June 2024. (though also noting that international AI cooperation in trade agreements could contribute to standardization, and enable domestic AI regulation to reduce risks in a range of domains, such as discrimination, misinformation, security and privacy, and others).

[562] Emily Jones, 'Digital Disruption: Artificial Intelligence and International Trade Policy' (2023) 39 Oxford Review of Economic Policy 70.

3.3.3.4.1 International courts as norm interpreters

It is relevant to consider the role that international courts might play in interpreting (or even developing) these norms. In particular, many scholars have noted a trend whereby international relations and international law have become increasingly 'judicialized'.[563] International courts, or existing treaty arbitral bodies, might ground interpretations of existing international norms in ways that provide guidance to States. Indeed, while not all international treaties open themselves up to interpretation through adjudication, some do so mandatorily, or by opt-in. Moreover, case law can have tremendous impact and is often largely followed and cited.[564]

There are a range of interpretative methods in international law that such courts (or other relevant actors) could draw upon, and which could help clarify the meaning and content of obligations in international law, as they relate to new situations (such as those involving AI systems).[565] As a matter of both treaty and customary international law, international law allows for various methods of interpretation, which, in contrast to some domestic systems of law, stand in a relation to one another that is generally non-hierarchical.[566] For instance, as set down in the Vienna Convention on the Law of Treaties (VCLT), these methods of interpretation include the textual, contextual, teleological, historical, and systemic integration approaches.[567] While a full exploration of this argument is beyond the scope of the book, promising doctrinal work could explore whether and how any of these interpretative approaches could contribute to the clarification of existing state obligations—grounded in either customary or treaty law—with regard to new AI issues.[568]

3.3.3.4.2 International courts as norm developers

Moreover, beyond simply clarifying obligations, it has been argued that international courts can, sometimes, even contribute to the development of

[563] Aaken (n 481) 85–86; Cesare PR Romano, 'Proliferation of International Judicial Bodies: The Pieces of the Puzzle' (1998) 31 New York University Journal of International Law and Politics 709.

[564] This is notwithstanding its non-binding nature for future cases. I thank Theodora Valkanou for discussing some of these points.

[565] For a development of this argument, see also Villalobos, Maas, and Winter (n 526).

[566] The exception to this is the historic method of interpretation, which, as set out in Art 32 of the VCLT, is considered a supplementary criterion. Ulf Linderfalk, 'Is the Hierarchical Structure of Articles 31 and 32 of the Vienna Convention Real or Not? Interpreting the Rules of Interpretation' (2007) 54 Netherlands International Law Review 133.

[567] See generally Richard Gardiner, *Treaty Interpretation* (2nd edn, Oxford University Press 2017); Matthias Herdegen, 'Interpretation in International Law', *Max Planck Encyclopedias of International Law [MPIL]* (2020) <https://opil.ouplaw.com/display/10.1093/law:epil/9780199231690/law-9780199231690-e723> accessed 18 October 2023. However, note that there are different taxonomies and ways of distinguishing between these. See Shai Dothan, 'The Three Traditional Approaches to Treaty Interpretation: A Current Application to the European Court of Human Rights' [2019] Fordham International Law Journal 765 (distinguishing between the textual approach, the subjective approach, and the teleological approach).

[568] Villalobos, Maas, and Winter (n 565).

international legal norms. For instance, Anne Van Aaken and others have argued that, beyond the gradual development of customary international law or the explicit modification of treaties, recent years have seen a growth in 'nonconsensual' mechanisms of international law development.[569] As part of this, many scholars have argued that international courts have gradually taken up a role not just in interpreting existing legal norms (contained in either treaty or custom), but also in gradually developing or extending these norms through adjudication and interpretation.[570] For instance, as Van Aaken argues, judgments delivered by international courts can develop international law by including new scientific evidence or developments, such that these decisions can 'clarify norms and even "find" norms, such as custom', or at least 'nudge states in certain directions since they create focal points by clarifying the law'.[571]

3.3.3.4.3 The challenges in relying on international judicial interpretation

However, while this might support the long-term readjustment of international law to the effects of AI and digital technology more broadly, relying on adjudication by international courts to either clarify or (tacitly) develop existing norms' implications for AI may have some drawbacks. This is because courts can only deal with the precise case that is brought before them—and often are limited in jurisdiction. This means that any resulting legal developments may be quite scattershot, unless they manage to establish general rules that can be applied to specific AI cases by analogy.[572] Moreover, given the high speed and opacity of AI innovation, there may be costs to awaiting specific case law decisions to clarify the normative status of these technologies.[573]

3.3.4 Adapting Existing International Institutions

Another major approach would aim to stay the course, and mostly aim to adapt existing institutions to deal with AI. This approach would concede that AI technology is not yet adequately or clearly governed under international law, but holds

[569] These norms are 'nonconsensual' insofar as they do not rely on new state consent to be established. See Aaken (n 481). Of course, there are debates over whether, or to what extent, CIL is consensual: while establishing new customary norms does require the *opinion juris* requirement, once formed these norms apply to all states regardless of whether they assisted in forming it. At the same time, it is possible in principle for states to exempt themselves from even these norms, if they are persistent objectors. Guzman (n 505) 142–143.

[570] Aaken (n 481); Nico Krisch, 'The Decay of Consent: International Law in an Age of Global Public Goods' (2014) 108 American Journal of International Law 1.

[571] Aaken (n 481) 85.

[572] I thank José Jaime Villalobos for observations on this point.

[573] For a related argument, see also Scherer (n 3) 388–393 (on the institutional competences of courts in the common law tort system).

that existing international institutions could be adapted to take on this role, and may already be doing so.

This approach includes many proposals that centre on supporting and extending the existing AI-focused activities of existing international regimes and institutions such as the IMO, ICAO, ITU,[574] the Global Forum for Road Traffic Safety,[575] and numerous other UN agencies.[576] Others explore proposals for refitting existing institutions such as the G20 to take an (even) stronger role in AI governance,[577] as well as the potential role of platforms such as the World Summit on Information Society (WSIS) or the Internet Governance Forum (IGF) in implementing key aspects of AI governance under the UN-led Global Digital Compact.[578] The emphasis here is on a 'decentralized but coordinated' approach that—drawing inspiration from domains such as climate law—supports institutions in their adaptation to AI issues,[579] rather than necessarily aiming to establish new institutions in an already crowded existing international 'regime complex'.[580]

One strength of this approach is that it can build on the prevailing momentum and approach in global AI governance since around 2017, which has seen most AI governance efforts accommodated within existing institutions.[581] However, there may also be drawbacks to this approach. One challenge comes from the risk of institutional path dependence. To be sure, it is valuable that many existing international organizations have displayed an awareness of the stakes of AI, a high level of agency in attempting to address issues of AI policy, and a level of pragmatism in attempting to accommodate these challenges within existing frameworks.[582] At the same time, many of these institutions obviously were not originally created to address digital information technology, let alone AI.[583] While international

[574] See Kunz and Ó hÉigeartaigh (n 11).

[575] Smith (n 418).

[576] Garcia, 'Multilateralism and Artificial Intelligence: What Role for the United Nations?' (n 10); Sepasspour (n 110); Huw Roberts and others, 'Global AI Governance: Barriers and Pathways Forward' <https://papers.ssrn.com/abstract=4588040> accessed 4 October 2023. See also the survey in Inter-Agency Working Group on Artificial Intelligence (IAWG-AI) (n 436).

[577] Thorsten Jelinek, Wendell Wallach, and Danil Kerimi, 'Policy Brief: The Creation of a G20 Coordinating Committee for the Governance of Artificial Intelligence' [2020] AI and Ethics <https://doi.org/10.1007/s43681-020-00019-y> accessed 30 October 2020.

[578] Malou Estier and Sofia Mikton, 'The Relevance of WSIS & IGF for International AI Governance' (*Simon Institute for Longterm Governance*, 26 March 2024) <https://www.simoninstitute.ch/blog/post/the-relevance-of-wsis-igf-for-international-ai-governance/> accessed 10 April 2024 (noting that 'while the WSIS Forum & IGF are both valuable platforms for sharing best-practices and fostering multi-stakeholder dialogue on topics such as the digital divide and ICTs for development, their lack of decision-making power prevent them from implementing concrete AI governance initiatives at the UN').

[579] Huw Roberts, 'Opinion—A New International AI Body Is No Panacea' (*E-International Relations*, 11 August 2023) <https://www.e-ir.info/2023/08/11/opinion-a-new-international-ai-body-is-no-panacea/> accessed 15 August 2023.

[580] Cihon, Maas, and Kemp (n 10).

[581] Schmitt (n 10).

[582] ibid.

[583] Indeed, as Morin and others note, the ITU was first created in 1865, and 'would certainly look very different if it had been established in the fast-changing internet age'. Morin and others (n 116) 2.

organizations can certainly change or expand their mission and activities over time, many also have also proven 'sticky' and path-dependent in their mandate,[584] which may not bode well for existing institutions' ability to fully adapt to the full scope of the global AI challenge, especially as it begins to include not just conventional and military AI, but also advanced AI systems.

3.3.5 Negotiating Bilateral or Multilateral Agreements on AI

Other pathways would focus much more on the negotiation and establishment of new international agreements, consisting of either hard or soft law, to coordinate and shape state actions around AI, where however such arrangements do not (directly) involve new international institutions.

3.3.5.1 Nonbinding codes of conduct and confidence-building measures

Some proposals for international AI governance, especially for military AI systems, have envisioned bilateral or multilateral arrangements. For instance, Shoker and others have proposed an international code of conduct for state behaviour.[585] Scharre, Horowitz, Kahn, and others have discussed a range of other AI Confidence-Building Measures,[586] including the marking of autonomous weapons systems, geographic limits of use, and limits on particular (e.g. nuclear) operations of AI.[587] They propose to group these under an International Autonomous Incidents Agreement (IAIA) to 'help reduce risks from accidental escalation by autonomous systems, as well as reduce ambiguity about the extent of human intention behind the behavior of autonomous systems'.[588] Bremmer and Suleyman have

Amandeep Gill has observed similar pressures on fora focused on international security. Amandeep S Gill, 'The Changing Role of Multilateral Forums in Regulating Armed Conflict in the Digital Age' (2020) 102 International Review of the Red Cross 261.

[584] Kathleen Thelen, 'Historical Institutionalism in Comparative Politics' (1999) 2 Annual Review of Political Science 369; see for instance the case study of the ILO's failed attempts, during the 1990s and early 2000s, to carry through a series of 'new governance' reforms Lucio Baccaro and Valentina Mele, 'Pathology of Path Dependency? The ILO and the Challenge of New Governance' (2012) 65 ILR Review 195.

[585] Sarah Shoker and others, 'Confidence-Building Measures for Artificial Intelligence: Workshop Proceedings' (*arXiv*, 3 August 2023) <http://arxiv.org/abs/2308.00862> accessed 7 August 2023.

[586] Michael C Horowitz and Lauren Kahn, 'How Joe Biden Can Use Confidence-Building Measures for Military Uses of AI' (2021) 77 Bulletin of the Atomic Scientists 33; ibid; Michael C Horowitz, Lauren Kahn, and Casey Mahoney, 'The Future of Military Applications of Artificial Intelligence: A Role for Confidence-Building Measures?' [2020] Orbis <http://www.sciencedirect.com/science/article/pii/S0030438720300430> accessed 20 September 2020; see also Christian Ruhl, 'Autonomous Weapon Systems & Military AI: Cause Area Report' (Founders Pledge 2022) <https://founderspledge.com/stories/autonomous-weapon-systems-and-military-artificial-intelligence-ai> accessed 9 August 2022.

[587] Michael C Horowitz and Paul Scharre, 'AI and International Stability: Risks and Confidence-Building Measures' (Center for a New American Security 2021) <https://www.cnas.org/publications/reports/ai-and-international-stability-risks-and-confidence-building-measures> accessed 19 January 2021.

[588] ibid 11.

proposed a bilateral US–China regime to foster cooperation between the US and Beijing on AI, envisioning this as a tool 'to create areas of commonality and even guardrails proposed and policed by a third party'.[589]

While a valuable backstop, there may also be limits to the take-up of such initiatives. For instance, even when championed by (and addressed to) states rather than industry actors, voluntary Codes of Conduct may still struggle to get uptake. For instance, in the field of outer space governance, the International Code of Conduct for Outer Space Activities developed by the EU between 2008 and 2014 struggled to get take-up in the international community, with many emerging space powers objecting to not being involved from the outset, along with concerns over its vague terminology, lack of definitions, and the fact that the Code was not legally binding.[590]

3.3.5.2 New AI treaties or conventions

Another avenue that has received significant attention involves the negotiation of new multilateral treaties or conventions for AI.

There have of course been various proposals for new treaties aimed at the specific international security risks of autonomous weapons,[591] or of military AI systems more generally.[592] Other proposals have aimed to focus more broadly on the diverse impacts of conventional AI systems. While many debates in this space have focused on the actually occurring developments in instruments such as the Council of Europe's Framework Convention, there have been additional proposals for additional framework conventions on AI.[593]

Other treaty proposals have focused more specifically on containing particular sources of risk that might derive from advanced AI systems. Dewey discusses a potential AI development convention that would set down 'a ban or set of strict safety rules for certain kinds of AI development',[594] and Metzinger has proposed a

[589] Ian Bremmer and Mustafa Suleyman, 'The AI Power Paradox' [2023] *Foreign Affairs* <https://www.foreignaffairs.com/world/artificial-intelligence-power-paradox> accessed 24 August 2023.

[590] Jack M Beard, 'Soft Law's Failure on the Horizon: The International Code of Conduct for Outer Space Activities' (2016) 38 University of Pennsylvania Journal of International Law 335. Accordingly the US announced in January 2012 that it would not sign the draft, and that it would rather develop its own International Code of Conduct using the EU draft as foundation.

[591] Bonnie Docherty, 'The Need for and Elements of a New Treaty on Fully Autonomous Weapons' (*Human Rights Watch*, 1 June 2020) <https://www.hrw.org/news/2020/06/01/need-and-elements-new-treaty-fully-autonomous-weapons> accessed 3 June 2020.

[592] See for instance Denise Garcia, 'A Global Framework to Govern Military AI: Transnational Networked Cooperation and Common Good Governance' in Denise Garcia (ed), *The AI Military Race: Common Good Governance in the Age of Artificial Intelligence* (Oxford University Press 2023); Elias G Carayannis and John Draper, 'Optimising Peace through a Universal Global Peace Treaty to Constrain the Risk of War from a Militarised Artificial Superintelligence' [2022] AI & Society <https://doi.org/10.1007/s00146-021-01382-y> accessed 11 January 2022.

[593] Villalobos and Maas (n 157). See also Maral Niazi, 'Universal Convention on Artificial Intelligence for Humanity' (Centre for International Governance Innovation 2024) <https://www.cigionline.org/publications/universal-convention-on-artificial-intelligence-for-humanity/> accessed 26 July 2024.

[594] Daniel Dewey, 'Long-Term Strategies for Ending Existential Risk from Fast Takeoff', *Risks of Artificial Intelligence* (Chapman and Hall/CRC 2015) 7–8 <https://www.taylorfrancis.com/chapters/

global moratorium on 'artificial suffering'.[595] Other, more recent treaty proposals in this line have sought to establish some form of a global AI Charter,[596] a global compute cap,[597] or a Treaty on Artificial Intelligence Safety and Cooperation,[598] among many other proposals. Finally, some proposals have woven together a range of global AI governance issues. For example, Cass-Beggs and colleagues have envisioned a Framework Convention on Global AI Challenges, in order to achieve the three-fold purpose of (1) realizing and sharing the benefits of AI globally, (2) mitigating severe global risks posed by AI, and (3) ensuring legitimate and effective decisions can be made over the future of AI.[599]

Such calls for the establishment of new treaties might have much to recommend them in principle. At their best, comprehensive multilateral conventions might help quickly fix state expectations and policies around safe innovation in AI, similar to how—as Harding has suggested—the 1967 Outer Space Treaty crystallized State expectations and policies for a then-novel area of science.[600] Establishing some core norms within an international convention might be a key prior step before pursuing the establishment of an international institution, as without a broader normative framework it may not be clear what norms or policies such institutions would even enforce.[601]

At the same time, these proposals should also be scrutinized, especially where they are (or remain) decoupled from particular underlying institutional capabilities.[602] To be sure, there are many modes of international cooperation—including various types of treaties—that do not automatically establish distinct international

edit/10.1201/b19187-14/long-term-strategies-ending-existential-risk-fast-takeoff-daniel-dewey> accessed 8 April 2024.

595 Thomas Metzinger, 'Artificial Suffering: An Argument for a Global Moratorium on Synthetic Phenomenology' [2021] Journal of Artificial Intelligence and Consciousness 1.

596 Thomas Metzinger, 'Towards a Global Artificial Intelligence Charter' in Oliver Mueller and others (eds), *The Cambridge Handbook of Responsible Artificial Intelligence: Interdisciplinary Perspectives* (Cambridge University Press 2022).

597 Andrea Miotti and Akash Wasil, 'An International Treaty to Implement a Global Compute Cap for Advanced Artificial Intelligence' (30 October 2023) <https://papers.ssrn.com/abstract=4617094> accessed 3 November 2023.

598 Tolga Bilge, 'Treaty on Artificial Intelligence Safety and Cooperation (TAISC)' (2023) <https://taisc.org/taisc> accessed 20 October 2023.

599 Duncan Cass-Beggs and others, 'Framework Convention on Global AI Challenges: Accelerating International Cooperation to Ensure Beneficial, Safe and Inclusive AI' (Centre for International Governance Innovation 2024) CIGI Discussion Paper <https://www.cigionline.org/publications/framework-convention-on-global-ai-challenges/> accessed 1 July 2024.

600 See also Verity Harding, 'Lessons from History: What Can Past Technological Breakthroughs Teach the AI Community Today' (2020) <https://www.bennettinstitute.cam.ac.uk/blog/lessons-history-what-can-past-technological-breakt/> accessed 17 August 2020.

601 Marietje Schaake, 'The Premature Quest for International AI Cooperation' [2023] *Foreign Affairs* <https://www.foreignaffairs.com/premature-quest-international-ai-cooperation> accessed 23 December 2023.

602 For a discussion of considerations around potential treaties and supportive institutions around AI, see also Jaemin Lee, *Artificial Intelligence and International Law* (Springer Nature Singapore 2022) 219–252.

organizations.[603] Such conventions primarily function by establishing patterns of expectations and reciprocal behaviour among states, (ideally) becoming self-enforcing.

One might wonder whether this is adequate for many of AI's global challenges. For instance, in an influential meta-analysis of 82 studies of international treaties, Hoffman and others have found evidence that many of these treaty regimes failed to produce their intended effects.[604] The exception to this trend were treaties on trade and finance, and treaties that incorporated enforcement mechanisms.[605] Indeed, long-established theories of international cooperation imply that when states face 'dilemmas of common aversion' (such as around standardization), international regimes only need to achieve coordination and the convergence: in such cases, it has been argued by Stein, '[c]onventions alone are adequate [and] institutions are not required'.[606] Conversely, when regimes are meant to resolve state dilemmas of 'common interests' (including, but not limited to, security dilemmas or arms control situations), an effective outcome must often involve a greater degree of institutionalization.[607]

Given this, one can question whether the conclusion of treaties alone—when they do not either empower existing institutions or establish new ones—will be adequate for the effective global governance of AI, as they may well be inadequate if they cannot be adequately monitored and enforced.[608] Conversely, it may also be the case that a rush to establish international institutions to 'enforce norms' may be premature, if there is not yet distinct clarity in national regulation (let alone international consensus) around what are these core principles or guidelines that such institutions would have to enforce.[609]

3.3.6 Establishing New International Institutions for AI

The final category of proposals for AI governance focuses on the establishment of new international institutions for AI.[610] While these, too, have a track record

[603] For discussion of the conditions under which states may choose to establish treaty bodies rather than full-fledged intergovernmental organizations, as well as design options for treaty bodies, see: Geir Ulfstein, 'Treaty Bodies and Regimes' in Duncan B Hollis (ed), *Oxford Guide to Treaties* (2012) <https://papers.ssrn.com/abstract=2144650> accessed 18 October 2022.

[604] Steven J Hoffman and others, 'International Treaties Have Mostly Failed to Produce Their Intended Effects' (2022) 119 Proceedings of the National Academy of Sciences e2122854119.

[605] ibid.

[606] Arthur A Stein, 'Coordination and Collaboration: Regimes in an Anarchic World' (1982) 36 International Organization 299, 314.

[607] ibid 312.

[608] Castel and Castel (n 526) 11.

[609] Schaake (n 601).

[610] For overviews, see: Lewis Ho and others, 'International Institutions for Advanced AI' (arXiv, 10 July 2023) <http://arxiv.org/abs/2307.04699> accessed 11 July 2023; Matthijs M Maas and José Jaime Villalobos, 'International AI Institutions: A Literature Review of Models, Examples, and Proposals'

of many years, it is particularly since the 2022–2025 (and ongoing) wave of attention to advanced, general-purpose AI systems that these proposals have begun to garner serious, sustained interest and attention.

Proposals within this approach argue that AI technology cannot be adequately regulated either by existing norms or through the reconfiguration of existing institutions, but that it rather needs the establishment of (usually) one or (occasionally) more new international organizations, empowered to carry out a range of functions.[611] Notably, in proposing these institutions, their proponents often make explicit comparisons with past or existing international institutions or regimes, as examples of models that are feasible and appropriate for AI. Consequently, many proposals for new AI institutions have converged on a range of distinct models.[612]

There are, of course, a wide range of international organizations, fulfilling a wide range of roles.[613] These include international NGOs (e.g. Amnesty International), political and economic unions (e.g. ASEAN), military alliances (e.g. NATO or the Collective Security Treaty Organization (CSTO), looser strategic partnerships (e.g. the AI Partnership for Defense or AUKUS[614]), or even cartels aimed at articulating, aggregating and securing the economic interests of their members (e.g. OPEC). More saliently, these organizations can fulfil a wide range of institutional *functions*,[615] including but not limited to:

1. stakeholder convening (e.g. OHCHR),
2. the conduct of research (e.g. UNIDIR or UNESCO),
3. the aggregation of validated scientific research for the establishment of common knowledge (IPCC),
4. data gathering and dissemination (e.g. the WMO's climate data monitoring; the FAO's tracking of global food production);
5. policy implementation and direct service delivery organizations (e.g. UNDP),
6. post-disaster response and relief (e.g. WFP, ICRC);

(Institute for Law & AI 2023) 1 <https://law-ai.org/international-ai-institutions> accessed 13 March 2025.

[611] For another discussion of different potential functions for AI institutions (in a European context), see also Charlotte Stix, 'Foundations for the Future: Institution Building for the Purpose of Artificial Intelligence Governance' (2022) 2 AI and Ethics 463.

[612] The following sections draw on material from: Maas and Villalobos (n 610).

[613] ibid 44–45 (reviewing these functions and giving additional examples for each).

[614] Trabucco and Maas (n 55).

[615] For a different taxonomy of such functions, see also: High-Level Advisory Body on Artificial Intelligence (n 186) 22–23 (distinguishing between the following 'subfunctions for international governance of AI': scientific assessment; horizon scanning; risk classification; access to benefits; capacity building; joint R&D; inclusive participation; convening, international learning; international coordination; policy harmonization and norm alignment; standard setting; norm elaboration; enforcement; stabilization and response; monitoring and verification). For another analysis of institutional functions, see Inter-Agency Working Group on Artificial Intelligence (IAWG-AI) (n 436) 21–28.

7. capacity-development and technical cooperation (UNITAR for governmental capacity-building; IMF training programmes for fiscal management; IOM programmes on border control training);
8. mobilization of finance (e.g. Global Fund to Fight AIDS, Tuberculosis and Malaria);
9. norms promotion and advocacy (e.g. the UNESCO World Heritage site programme; UNHCR advocacy for refugee rights),
10. broader awareness-raising on key issues (e.g. the Joint United Nations Programme on HIV/AIDS (UNAIDS)),
11. ensuring accountability, through judicial bodies such as international courts and tribunals (e.g. ICC, various regional courts of human rights),
12. monitoring and verifying compliance (e.g. IAEA; CTBTO International Monitoring System);
13. arbitrating and settling inter-state disputes (e.g. ICJ, WTO Appellate Body, ITLOS, PCA, the European Nuclear Energy Tribunal);
14. supporting or enhancing the activities of other existing international organizations (e.g. UNOPS).

This is clearly an inexhaustive list. However, when it comes to proposing new international institutions for AI, proponents have often focused on a narrower set of institutional functions.[616] Without aiming to provide a full review, most proposals have envisioned international institutions that would carry out one of roughly seven distinct functions in AI governance: (1) scientific consensus-building; (2) political consensus-building; (3) coordination of policy; (4) enforcement of standards or restrictions; (5) stabilization; (6) international joint research; and (7) distribution of benefits and access.[617]

This does not exhaust the range of institutional forms suggested. Some proposals have sought to combine several functions within a single organization. Harry Law and Lewis Ho have suggested, for instance, that an international AI organization might adopt a 'dual mandate', similar to how the IAEA adopted an institutional

[616] Although there are some exceptions and proposals for AI organizations aimed at other functions. For instance, Jacob Turner has previously proposed an 'International Academy for AI Law and Regulation', aimed at training and capacity-building for AI regulation. See Turner (n 3) 254.

[617] For a far more detailed discussion of each of these, see again Maas and Villalobos (n 610). See also the reviews in: Microsoft (n 10) 46–91; Emma Klein and Stewart Patrick, 'Envisioning a Global Regime Complex to Govern Artificial Intelligence' (Carnegie Endowment for International Peace 2024) <https://carnegieendowment.org/research/2024/03/envisioning-a-global-regime-complex-to-govern-artificial-intelligence?lang=en> accessed 13 June 2024; Haydn Belfield, 'Domestic Frontier AI Regulation, an IAEA for AI, an NPT for AI, and a US-Led Allied Public-Private Partnership for AI: Four Institutions for Governing and Developing Frontier AI' (arXiv, 8 July 2025) <http://arxiv.org/abs/2507.06379> accessed 11 July 2025. For institutional analogies that draw on more distinct historical models for inspiration. See for instance: Will MacAskill and Rose Hadshar, 'Intelsat as a Model for International AGI Governance' (Forethought 2025) <https://www.forethought.org/research/intelsat-as-a-model-for-international-agi-governance> Accessed 14 March 2025.

mission that pursued both the non-proliferation of (military and dual-use) nuclear technology along with dissemination of the benefits of legitimate uses of this technology.[618] Similarly, France's Artificial Intelligence Commission has issued a proposal for a World AI Organization, which would 'share scientific findings on the workings and effects of AI, and define binding standards for AI systems and how they should be audited',[619] combining elements of a scientific consensus-building and a standards- and policy-coordinating institution.

Others have argued that any new international institution for AI should avoid direct replication or mimicry of any single extant institutional model.[620] Rather, there may be a need to draw on different mechanisms from different international institutions into a new bespoke organization.[621] Still other proposals increasingly envision not just a lone new organization, but a constellation of new organizations.[622]

Indeed, some have argued that we do not need to establish new centralized organizations at all,[623] but instead should strengthen the existing AI governance 'regime complex', whether by empowering existing organizations;[624] by building a nimble, decentralized network of organizations;[625] or by simply accepting the uncoordinated emergence of a new regime complex, in the form of a fragmented landscape of multiple interacting institutions.[626]

[618] Law and Ho (n 312). For another discussion of the merits of the IAEA model, see: Mark Robinson, 'The Establishment of an International AI Agency: An Applied Solution to Global AI Governance' [2025] International Affairs iiaf105

[619] Commission de l'Intelligence Artificielle, 'Our AI: Our Ambition for France' (2024) 5 <https://www.info.gouv.fr/upload/media/content/0001/09/02cbcb40c3541390be391feb3d963a4126b12598.pdf> accessed 10 April 2024.

[620] High-Level Advisory Body on Artificial Intelligence (n 186) 14. (arguing that 'the range of stakeholders and potential applications presented by AI and their uses in a wide variety of contexts makes unsuitable an exact replication of any existing governance model'). See also Jason Hausenloy and Claire Dennis, 'Towards a UN Role in Governing Foundation Artificial Intelligence Models' (UNU CPR 2023) 3.

[621] See also Carlos Ignacio Gutierrez, 'Multilateral Coordination for the Proactive Governance of Artificial Intelligence Systems' (25 September 2023) 1 <https://papers.ssrn.com/abstract=4583536> accessed 26 September 2023 (proposing an institution that would 'adapt mechanisms from a variety of institutions including Interpol's alert system and network, the procurement of subject matter experts a la Intergovernmental Panel on Climate Change (IPCC), building global capacity as the World Health Organization (WHO) does, and the World Trade Organization's dispute settlement').

[622] See for instance Artificial Intelligence & Equality Initiative, 'A Framework for the International Governance of AI' (*Carnegie Council for Ethics in International Affairs*, 5 July 2023) <https://www.carnegiecouncil.org/media/article/a-framework-for-the-international-governance-of-ai> accessed 3 September 2023; Ho and others (n 610); Cihon, Maas, and Kemp (n 10); Stephan Llerena, 'Global Governance of High-Risk Artificial Intelligence'.

[623] Cameron F Kerry and others, 'Should the UN Govern Global AI?' (*Brookings*, 26 February 2024) <https://www.brookings.edu/articles/should-the-un-govern-global-ai/> accessed 27 February 2024.

[624] Roberts and others, 'Global AI Governance' (n 576). See also Sepasspour (n 110).

[625] Adam Day, 'Rise of the Machines: AI Becomes Ungovernable', *The Forever Crisis: Adaptive Global Governance for an Era of Accelerating Complexity* (Taylor & Francis 2024).

[626] Klein and Patrick (n 617).

To be clear, the regime complexity perspective, and the centralization–decentralization debate over whether global AI governance should be accommodated within a diverse regime complex of either existing or new initiatives or whether it is instead better subsumed within a new international organization, is only one part of the global AI governance roadmap. Beyond it, many other relevant design questions remain when crafting roadmaps for an international institution or regime complex for AI. These include questions over a regime's overall regulatory approach, instrument choice, and instrument design, including critical choices around the establishment, constitution, and design of key distinct agencies and entities within an AI governance institution or regime.[627]

3.4 Conclusion: The Roads Ahead

The global stakes of AI are significant. Its societal impacts are broad and wide-ranging—but so is the available toolkit of instruments, strategies, and levers by which the world could respond. Recent years have seen significant momentum in the global AI governance architecture.

There is a wide range of potential paths forward. We are not short of institutional proposals, and while some have clear risks or drawbacks, none of these routes are so obviously wrong or misconceived that they should not be explored. However, these proposals raise as many questions as they settle. To make more informed decisions in the years ahead, we will need better rubrics for evaluating each different pathway in isolation, as well as better ways of comparing between them in conjunction, in order to better choose and prioritize our approach.

It is not possible for a book such as this one to exhaustively compare and evaluate all these proposed approaches or paths to meeting all of AI's diverse challenges. Much work remains to be done. Pursuant to that goal, in the chapters to follow I will focus on developing insights about global governance of AI issues from a range of theoretical lenses, namely sociotechnical change (Chapter 4), governance disruption (Chapter 5), and regime complexity (Chapter 6). In doing so, my focus will narrow somewhat onto a subset of specific issues in AI governance. In particular—and for reasons discussed in Chapter 2—I will explore governance challenges posed by military AI and advanced AI systems. Simultaneously, in evaluating proposed pathways for governance, I will predominantly focus my analysis (in Chapter 7) on the recent wave of proposals to establish new international institutions for AI governance. The ongoing 2022–2025 wave of public and policymaker attention to foundation models and frontier AI has made this approach

[627] See for instance Llerena (n 622); Gutierrez (n 621). Also James N Baker, 'International AI Governance at the Frontier: An Exploration of Legal Design Considerations' (Harvard Law School 2024).

particularly salient. However, even with significant momentum and support, it remains deeply uncertain whether a centralized institutional arrangement for AI is plausible, necessary, or even preferable.

Underpinning all debate is a set of foundational questions: Do we even need new institutions? Why? For what set of issues? Would the establishment of a novel institution be feasible? And if so, should we seek a single centralized institution, or rather a constellation of many institutions that separate out distinct governance functions, or the treatment of distinct AI issue clusters, across a broader regime complex?

As such, whereas much recent discussion of AI institutions has focused on debates over individual institutions' specific functions and design—and over which existing institutions, if any, to emulate—I will in the remainder of this book explore the role and development of AI governance institutions within the larger context of a regime complex. In this way, I aim to contribute to both an improved analytical understanding of AI governance issues and to better-informed international policy and institutional development.

By now it should be clear that foregrounding these institutional proposals, and particularly the centralization–decentralization dimension, hardly exhausts the space of questions that should be asked. Indeed, Tallberg and others have identified five dimensions of regulatory arrangements in which current AI governance varies, such as (1) whether regulation is horizontal or vertical; (2) whether it is centralized or decentralized; (3) whether it involves hard law or soft law; (4) whether it involves private or public regulation; (5) whether it focuses on military or non-military regulation.[628] These are all critical questions. However, the remainder of this book will largely focus on only some of these distinctions (such as the centralization–decentralization angle, in Chapters 6 and 7) while mostly bracketing others. It therefore does not complete or conclude contemporary discussions over the governance of AI, but rather aims to set the stage for many more debates to come.

This chapter has provided a rationale for the analysis of new global governance strategies for AI, and sketched the political and institutional background against which it must be situated. In the next chapters, I will suggest that examining these questions through the lenses provided by different theories within the fields of technology law and regime complexity theory can help inform such comparisons and allow us to not only improve our understanding of the likely trajectories for this regime, but also of the best ways to shape it. As such, I now turn to the first of three lenses on AI governance: sociotechnical change.

[628] Tallberg and others (n 8) 7–9.

PART II
FACETS OF CHANGE

4

Sociotechnical Change: AI as Regulatory Rationale and Target

4.1 Introduction

When confronted with any apparent new technological developments, scholars and practitioners of international law regularly face four questions: are *new* regulations needed?[1] *Why* are they needed? *When* should we regulate? *How* should we regulate?

Why, when, and how should governance systems respond to situations involving AI technology? These questions lead us to the first lens on AI governance, which focuses on the challenges of aligning AI regulation to the technology's sociotechnical changes. When and how do changes in AI capabilities or applications actually translate to global societal changes? When do these impacts constitute a regulatory rationale—creating the need for legal change or even for new laws, regulation, or governance? If such is the case, when is governance needed or most appropriate? If new law is needed, how are the technology and its societal impacts best approached as a regulatory target? In particular, how should we weight, or combine, a focus on the material features of the underlying AI system in question with a broader focus on its social profile, problem logics, and impacts across domains?

In discussing and answering these questions, this chapter will focus on the concept of sociotechnical change, defined broadly as:

> ***Sociotechnical change***: the processes by which developments in technology extend the capabilities of some or all actors—allowing them new ways of carrying out old conduct or enabling new types of conduct altogether—in ways that (1) can have unanticipated disruptive impacts on society, which (2) may give rise to one

[1] Kristen Eichensehr has called this the '"international law step zero" question': Kristen E Eichensehr, 'Cyberwar & International Law Step Zero' (2015) 50 Texas International Law Journal 357, 358. See also the discussion in: Rebecca Crootof, 'Regulating New Weapons Technology' in Eric Talbot Jensen and Ronald TP Alcala (eds), *The Impact of Emerging Technologies on the Law of Armed Conflict* (Oxford University Press 2019) 3–4. And see also Juan David Gutiérrez, 'Consultation Paper on AI Regulation: Emerging Approaches across the World' (UNESCO 2024) CI/DIT/2024/CP/01 40–48 <https://unesdoc.unesco.org/ark:/48223/pf0000390979> accessed 2 September 2024.

Architectures of Global AI Governance. Matthijs M. Maas, Oxford University Press. © Matthijs M. Maas 2025.
DOI: 10.1093/9780191988455.003.0005

or another *rationale* for regulation; and which (3) shape the particular texture and problem logics of the regulatory *target* for those regulatory interventions.

This provides the first lens on a type of change that should be central for any regulatory proposals around AI, whether at the national or global level. To understand the background and utility of this approach, this chapter will first review four prevailing regulatory approaches to technology—focusing on the exceptionality of the new technology; its varied applications; its impacts on particular values; and its challenges to existing legal domains—before arguing for a regulatory approach focused on sociotechnical change. Drawing on the field of technology law, the chapter defines 'technology' and 'sociotechnical change', and discusses the mutually constitutive relationship between technological change and societal change and the scope of sociotechnical choice they afford. It then discusses how orienting AI governance around sociotechnical change opens a path to more effective AI regulation, aiding our understanding of: (1) why to regulate; (2) when to regulate; and (3) how to regulate different AI governance targets. Finally, the chapter reviews the analytical uses and limits of the sociotechnical perspective on AI governance.

4.2 Regulatory Approaches to AI

There are many ways by which one might approach AI regulation. For instance, in one review for UNESCO, Juan David Gutiérrez has distinguished between nine regulatory approaches that can underpin—or be combined within—specific AI governance initiatives. These include approaches that are (1) principles-based, (2) standards-based, (3) agile and experimentalist, (4) facilitating and enabling, (5) adapting existing laws, (6) ensuring access to information and transparency, (7) risk-based, (8) rights-based, or (9) liability-based.[2]

Which of these approaches should we use or prioritize; when should they be used; and what should they regulate, and why? These questions often start from a particular framing of the regulatory problems at hand. Again, there are many different ways by which commentators have approached, framed, or taxonomized the impacts of AI technologies.[3] These correspond to different regulatory orientations or approaches—different perspectives on what (AI) regulation is actually 'about'. What are these approaches, and what are their uses, implications, and drawbacks?

[2] Gutiérrez (n 1) 18–39.

[3] The following expands on Matthijs M Maas, 'Aligning AI Regulation to Sociotechnical Change' in Justin B Bullock and others (eds), *The Oxford Handbook of AI Governance* (Oxford University Press 2022).

4.2.1 Technology-centric Approaches to Regulation

A first, umbrella technology-centric approach focuses on the appearance of a particular class of technology, especially one that is seen as distinctive in some key way—for instance, because it is presented as an exceptionally 'new',[4] 'emerging',[5] 'socially disruptive',[6] 'generative',[7] 'revolutionary',[8] 'radical',[9] or 'transformative'[10] technology. In response, the technology-centric approach often aims to understand, treat, and regulate this new technology as a single class, by paying special attention to its distinct features or traits that make it so unusual or significant.

The technology-centric approach has been influential in the self-conception of many past fields of ethical and regulatory analysis that historically emerged in response to new technologies such as biotechnology,[11] computers,[12] nanotechnology,[13] or the internet,[14] to name but a few. It certainly has its proponents in AI policy. For instance, some early accounts in the field argued that the appearance of 'AI' as such called for a new set of regulatory responses that would appropriately

[4] Ryan Calo, 'Robotics and the Lessons of Cyberlaw' (2015) 103 California Law Review 513, 516 ('new transformative technology').

[5] Daniele Rotolo, Diana Hicks, and Ben Martin, 'What Is an Emerging Technology?' (2015) 44 Research Policy 1827 (describing these technologies as having the features of '(i) radical novelty, (ii) relatively fast growth, (iii) coherence, (iv) prominent impact, and (v) uncertainty and ambiguity'). See also Philip AE Brey, 'Anticipatory Ethics for Emerging Technologies' (2012) 6 NanoEthics 1.

[6] Jeroen Hopster, 'What Are Socially Disruptive Technologies?' (2021) 67 Technology in Society 101750, 6–7 (giving seven criteria that 'ground technosocial disruptiveness'—depth of impacts, range of impacts, valence of impacts, ethical salience of impacts, extent of uncertainty, pace of change, and (ir)reversibility of impacts).

[7] A Feder Cooper and others, 'Report of the 1st Workshop on Generative AI and Law' (arXiv, 13 November 2023) 2–3 <http://arxiv.org/abs/2311.06477> accessed 17 November 2023 (applying Jonathan Zittrain's 'five dimensions of generativity'—that is, the degree to which a new technology affords (1) leverage, (2) adaptability, (3) ease of mastery, (4) accessibility, (5) transferability to generative AI). Drawing on Jonathan Zittrain, *The Future of the Internet—And How to Stop It* (Illustrated edition, Yale University Press 2009) 70 (defining 'generative technologies' as those with the 'capacity to produce unanticipated change through unfiltered contributions from broad and varied audiences').

[8] Ben Garfinkel, 'The Impact of Artificial Intelligence: A Historical Perspective' in Justin B Bullock and others (eds), *The Oxford Handbook of AI Governance* (Oxford University Press 2023) 2 ('revolutionary technology is a [general purpose technology] that supports an especially fundamental transformation in the nature of economic production').

[9] Stijn Smismans and Elen Stokes, 'Innovation Types and Regulation: The Regulatory Framing of Nanotechnology as "Incremental" or "Radical" Innovation' (2017) 8 European Journal of Risk Regulation 364 (discussing how different framings of nanotechnology affect a range of regulatory decisions, from the desirability of legislative reform, to the evidence base for regulation, to the invocation of the precautionary principle).

[10] Ross Gruetzemacher and Jess Whittlestone, 'The Transformative Potential of Artificial Intelligence' (2022) 135 Futures 102884, 6 (defining 'transformative AI' as 'AI technology or application with potential to lead to practically irreversible change that is broad enough to impact most important aspects of life and society').

[11] Van Rensselaer Potter, 'Bioethics, the Science of Survival' (1970) 14 Perspectives in Biology and Medicine 127; as discussed in Simone Casiraghi, 'Anything New under the Sun? Insights from a History of Institutionalized AI Ethics' (2023) 25 Ethics and Information Technology 28, 3–4.

[12] James H Moor, 'What Is Computer Ethics?' (1985) 16 Metaphilosophy 266.

[13] Søren Holm, 'Does Nanotechnology Require a New "Nanoethics"?' in Bert Gordijn and Anthony Mark Cutter (eds), *In Pursuit of Nanoethics* (Springer Netherlands 2014).

[14] Lawrence Lessig, 'The Law of the Horse: What Cyberlaw Might Teach' (1999) 113 Harvard Law Review 501.

understand, and govern, this class of technologies holistically, as a category.[15] One argument for this approach is the claim that even if the technology has many different applications, all its versions have certain key features in common (e.g. its autonomy, its opacity, its ability to learn independently),[16] which create similar—and critically novel—challenges for society and for existing law.

However, while this approach has the benefit of articulating a broad and comprehensive regulatory agenda, it can easily get tied up in intractable debates over how to define 'AI',[17] given that it is not a single thing.[18] Moreover, the resulting inclination to create distinct 'law of [X]' or '[X]-law' fields for different technologies may be challenging, in part because the conceptual boundaries between these fields are not well defined.[19]

4.2.2 Application-centric Approaches to Regulation

This shortfall is somewhat addressed within a second, application-centric approach. This orientation still focuses on the technology, but seeks to unpack the umbrella term 'AI', by aiming to regulate specific new applications of AI technology rather than the overall class as such—and then to consider and examine the more grounded social and legal issues that might derive from that application. As Petit has argued, this approach involves charting 'legal issues from the bottom-up standpoint of each class of technological application'.[20] For instance, many policy proposals for AI have focused on one or another of its use cases, such as autonomous cars, drones, social robots,[21] computer vision,[22] or 'speech generator' chatbots,[23] among many others.

[15] Calo, 'Robotics and the Lessons of Cyberlaw' (n 4). Jacob Turner, *Robot Rules: Regulating Artificial Intelligence* (Springer Berlin Heidelberg 2018).

[16] Turner (n 15) 39–80 (reviewing a series of 'unique features' of AI technology).

[17] See also Matthijs Maas, 'AI Is Like . . . A Literature Review of AI Metaphors and Why They Matter for Policy' (Institute for Law & AI 2023) AI Foundations Report 2 <https://law-ai.org/ai-policy-metaphors> accessed 25 October 2023 (reviewing sets of metaphors for AI); Matthijs Maas, 'Concepts in Advanced AI Governance: A Literature Review of Key Terms and Definitions' (Institute for Law & AI 2023) AI Foundations Report 3 <https://law-ai.org/advanced-ai-gov-concepts> accessed 25 October 2023 (reviewing specific concepts, terms, and their operationalizations for advanced AI).

[18] Jonas Schuett, 'Defining the Scope of AI Regulations' (2023) 15 Law, Innovation and Technology 1.

[19] For a similar argument in the field of technology ethics, see Henrik Skaug Sætra and John Danaher, 'To Each Technology Its Own Ethics: The Problem of Ethical Proliferation' (2022) 35 Philosophy & Technology 93.

[20] Nicolas Petit, 'Law and Regulation of Artificial Intelligence and Robots—Conceptual Framework and Normative Implications' (Social Science Research Network 2017) SSRN Scholarly Paper ID 2931339 2 <https://papers.ssrn.com/abstract=2931339> accessed 11 May 2020.

[21] See also Turner (n 15) 217–218.

[22] Rosalie A Waelen, 'The Ethics of Computer Vision: An Overview in Terms of Power' (2024) 4 AI and Ethics 353.

[23] Wiebke Hutiri, Orestis Papakyriakopoulos and Alice Xiang, 'Not My Voice! A Taxonomy of Ethical and Safety Harms of Speech Generators', *Proceedings of the 2024 ACM Conference on Fairness, Accountability, and Transparency* (Association for Computing Machinery 2024) <https://dl.acm.

These application-centric approaches have been a common frame for AI, especially in early domestic debates. However, they again have shortfalls. For one, they emphasize visceral or upsetting incidents, and therefore may be more easily lured into regulating relatively rare edge-case challenges or misuses of the technology (e.g. the use of deepfakes for political propaganda) at a cost of addressing far more common but less visible use cases (e.g. the use of deepfakes for gendered harassment).[24] Moreover, in an application-centric approach, AI policies and laws are frequently formulated in a piecemeal and ad-hoc fashion, promoting siloed regulatory responses.[25] Moreover, a focus on individual applications may foreground technology-specific regulations even where these are not the most effective.[26]

4.2.3 Value-centric Approaches to Regulation

Another type of regulatory approach to AI is *value*-centric. This aims to regulate the impacts of AI either on a range of specific ethical interests or values, or on broader ethical systems.[27]

Of course, the space of potential issues, values, interests, and goals to which AI systems could pertain is vast, and it should be no surprise that there have been many ways in which scholars have ordered or organized AI's ethical challenges. For instance, in a philosophical taxonomy of the ethics of AI and robotics, Vincent Müller has distinguished between ethical issues that arise around AI systems as 'objects' (such as privacy, manipulation, opacity, bias, human–robot interaction, employment issues, and the effects of autonomy), versus issues that arise around AI systems as 'subjects' (covering machine ethics, artificial moral agency, and the implications of potential future advanced AI).[28] Both objects- and subject-focused

org/doi/10.1145/3630106.3658911> accessed 13 June 2024. For a distinct account of how, under a law-centric approach, the issues raised by the same generative AI chatbot applications can be constructed very differently within different legal fields, see also Margot E Kaminski and Meg Leta Jones, 'Constructing AI Speech' [2024] The Yale Law Journal Forum <https://papers.ssrn.com/abstract=4764706> accessed 11 June 2024.

[24] Hin-Yan Liu and others, 'Artificial Intelligence and Legal Disruption: A New Model for Analysis' (2020) 12 Law, Innovation and Technology 205.

[25] Turner (n 15) 218–219; Rebecca Crootof and BJ Ard, 'Structuring Techlaw' (2021) 34 Harvard Journal of Law & Technology 347, 349.

[26] Lyria Bennett Moses, 'How to Think about Law, Regulation and Technology: Problems with "Technology" as a Regulatory Target' (2013) 5 Law, Innovation and Technology 1, 14–17.

[27] See also Jeroen KG Hopster and Matthijs M Maas, 'The Technology Triad: Disruptive AI, Regulatory Gaps and Value Change' [2023] AI and Ethics <https://doi.org/10.1007/s43681-023-00305-5> accessed 8 July 2023.

[28] Vincent C Müller, 'Ethics of AI and Robotics' in Edward N Zalta (ed), *Stanford Encyclopedia of Philosophy* (CSLI, Stanford University 2020) <https://plato.stanford.edu/entries/ethics-ai/#Sing> accessed 2 April 2019. In another, related framework, Tasioulas characterizes ethical problems of robots and AIs (RAIs) as deriving from their 'functionality, inherent significance, rights and responsibilities, side-effects, and threats'. John Tasioulas, 'First Steps Towards an Ethics of Robots and Artificial Intelligence' (2019) 7 Journal of Practical Ethics 61, 61. He also distinguishes between three levels of

questions have received extensive treatment within philosophy, ethics, and some legal philosophy.[29] However, most writings on AI law and policy have focused on AI systems as objects.[30] For example, in an influential early primer on AI policy, Ryan Calo distinguished such problems as revolving around various overarching themes or challenges, from justice or the use of force to privacy and labour market issues.[31] At the international level, AI's impacts have also been frequently bracketed with their thematic impacts—for instance distinguishing between challenges around global politics, international security, and international political economy.[32]

Value-centric approaches to framing AI policy issues have perhaps been the most influential and prominent in the field of AI governance, even (or precisely) as the technology has evolved rapidly—leading to a constant uptick in new applications, as well as the emergence of advanced and increasingly general-purpose foundation models. This latter trend in particular has prompted a new wave of

ethical analysis; (1) questions around whether AI systems need regulation; (2) questions of social morality; (3) questions that arise for individuals or associations in their engagement with RAIs. ibid 65.

[29] For instance, for work in ethical philosophy focused on the question of the subjecthood, personhood, or standing of AI systems, see: David J Gunkel, *Robot Rights* (MIT Press 2018); John Danaher, 'Welcoming Robots into the Moral Circle: A Defence of Ethical Behaviourism' [2019] 26 Science and Engineering Ethics 2023; Carl Shulman and Nick Bostrom, 'Sharing the World with Digital Minds' in Carl Shulman and Nick Bostrom, *Rethinking Moral Status* (Oxford University Press 2021). For work on this question from the perspective of law and legal philosophy, see SM Solaiman, 'Legal Personality of Robots, Corporations, Idols and Chimpanzees: A Quest for Legitimacy' (2017) 25 Artificial Intelligence and Law 155; Joanna J Bryson, Mihailis E Diamantis, and Thomas D Grant, 'Of, for, and by the People: The Legal Lacuna of Synthetic Persons' (2017) 25 Artificial Intelligence and Law 273; Turner (n 15); for empirical work on layperson perceptions of these questions, see also Eric Martínez and Christoph Winter, 'Protecting Sentient Artificial Intelligence: A Survey of Lay Intuitions on Standing, Personhood, and General Legal Protection' (2021) 8 Frontiers in Robotics and AI <https://www.frontiersin.org/articles/10.3389/frobt.2021.788355> accessed 23 August 2022.

[30] One exception to this, which straddles both these paradigms, can be found in Nick Bostrom, Allan Dafoe, and Carrick Flynn, 'Public Policy and Superintelligent AI: A Vector Field Approach' in SM Liao (ed), *Ethics of Artificial Intelligence* (Oxford University Press 2019). This deals with extensive challenges to and opportunities for human society (where AI systems are considered as objects), but also with considerations of 'mind crime' against anticipated future digital entities (considering these as subjects).

[31] Ryan Calo, 'Artificial Intelligence Policy: A Primer and Roadmap' (2017) 51 UC Davis Law Review 37. Calo's taxonomy is also followed by Gasser and Almeida in their 'layered model for AI governance'. Urs Gasser and Virgilio AF Almeida, 'A Layered Model for AI Governance' (2017) 21 IEEE Internet Computing 58. Others have articulated overlapping but complementary frameworks. See Michael Guihot, Anne F Matthew, and Nicolas Suzor, 'Nudging Robots: Innovative Solutions to Regulate Artificial Intelligence' [2017] Vanderbilt Journal of Entertainment & Technology Law <https://papers.ssrn.com/abstract=3017004> accessed 2 July 2018; Axel Walz and Kay Firth-Butterfield, 'Implementing Ethics into Artificial Intelligence: A Contribution, From a Legal Perspective, To The Development of an AI Governance Regime' (2019) 18 Duke Law & Technology Review 166; Eleanor Bird and others, 'The Ethics of Artificial Intelligence: Issues and Initiatives' (Scientific Foresight Unit (STOA), EPRS | European Parliamentary Research Service 2020) PE 634.452 <https://www.europarl.europa.eu/RegData/etudes/STUD/2020/634452/EPRS_STU(2020)634452_EN.pdf> accessed 16 June 2020.

[32] Mary L Cummings and others, *Artificial Intelligence and International Affairs: Disruption Anticipated* (Chatham House 2018) <https://www.chathamhouse.org/sites/default/files/publications/research/2018-06-14-artificial-intelligence-international-affairs-cummings-roff-cukier-parakilas-bryce.pdf> accessed 25 June 2018.

taxonomies aiming to capture these systems' different types of harms or impacts,[33] in some cases indexing these to specific AI governance instruments.[34]

Accordingly, this value-centric approach has also been influential in shaping debates over global governance for AI. For instance, in its 2023 Interim Report, the UN Secretary-General's High-Level Advisory Body on Artificial Intelligence argued against attempting to exhaustively map out all risks from AI.[35] Instead, it proposed a 'vulnerability'-based taxonomy of risks,[36] which aimed to re-categorize existing risks from the perspective of different stakeholders—individuals, vulnerable groups, societies, or commons. A similar approach has been taken in other recent academic work, aiming to map different categories of risk and harm posed by foundation models as they apply to the distinct individual, social, and biospheric levels.[37]

4.2.4 Law-centric Approaches to Regulation

Finally, a fourth set of regulatory perspectives to AI are instead law-centric. These adopt what Petit has called a 'legalistic' orientation, which 'consists in starting from the legal system, and proceed[s] by drawing lists of legal fields or issues affected by AIs and robots'.[38]

This approach accordingly segments regulatory responses by departing from AI's impacts on specific conventional legal codes or subjects—such as privacy law, contract law, international humanitarian law, specific human rights, and

[33] See among others Peter Slattery and others, 'The AI Risk Repository: A Comprehensive Meta-Review, Database, and Taxonomy of Risks From Artificial Intelligence' <https://airisk.mit.edu/> accessed 14 March 2025; Rishi Bommasani and others, 'On the Opportunities and Risks of Foundation Models' [2021] arXiv:2108.07258 [cs] 128 <http://arxiv.org/abs/2108.07258> accessed 18 August 2021; Laura Weidinger and others, 'Taxonomy of Risks Posed by Language Models', *2022 ACM Conference on Fairness, Accountability, and Transparency* (ACM 2022) 215, 229 <https://dl.acm.org/doi/10.1145/3531146.3533088> accessed 8 May 2023; Yi Zeng and others, 'AI Risk Categorization Decoded (AIR 2024): From Government Regulations to Corporate Policies' (arXiv, 25 June 2024) <http://arxiv.org/abs/2406.17864> accessed 3 July 2024. Risto Uuk and others, 'A Taxonomy of Systemic Risks from General-Purpose AI' (Social Science Research Network, 22 November 2024) <https://papers.ssrn.com/abstract=5030173> accessed 18 February 2025.

[34] Zachary Arnold and others, 'Introducing the AI Governance and Regulatory Archive (AGORA): An Analytic Infrastructure for Navigating the Emerging AI Governance Landscape' (2024) 7 Proceedings of the AAAI/ACM Conference on AI, Ethics, and Society 39.

[35] High-Level Advisory Body on Artificial Intelligence, 'Interim Report: Governing AI for Humanity' (United Nations 2023) 10 <https://www.un.org/sites/un2.un.org/files/ai_advisory_body_interim_report.pdf> accessed 14 March 2025. ('Putting together a comprehensive list of AI risks for all time is a fool's errand . . . we believe that it is more useful to look at risks from the perspective of vulnerable communities and the commons').

[36] ibid 10–11.

[37] Andrés Domínguez Hernández and others, 'Mapping the Individual, Social and Biospheric Impacts of Foundation Models', *Proceedings of the 2024 ACM Conference on Fairness, Accountability, and Transparency* (Association for Computing Machinery 2024) 779–782 <https://dl.acm.org/doi/10.1145/3630106.3658939> accessed 13 June 2024.

[38] Petit (n 20) 2.

so on[39]—in identifying what are the problems AI poses for different areas of law. This approach has long been prominent in much legal scholarship on the regulation of new technology,[40] and has also characterized many responses to the rise in generative AI systems.[41] For instance, generative AI systems have often seen distinct—and disparate—treatment in the different literatures concerned with the legal domains of copyright protection,[42] privacy and data protection law,[43] content moderation, or risk regulation or consumer protection.[44]

This law-centric approach, too, has benefits. It leverages existing legal expertise, and avoids the need to reinvent the wheel or come up with entirely novel policy responses,[45] especially because many existing regulatory regimes in domains such as liability law can offer adequate guidance.[46] Moreover, as discussed in Chapter 5, there is often an important need for carrying out appropriate *legal development* in response to AI, which requires us to understand not just its sociotechnical impacts but also its disruptive effects on legal doctrines.

4.2.5 The Limits of Existing Regulatory Approaches, and the Sociotechnical Turn

These are all legitimate and insightful ways of organizing the problem space of AI. Many of the policy responses articulated through these frameworks are valuable

[39] See for instance the structure of Thomas Wischmeyer and Timo Rademacher (eds), *Regulating Artificial Intelligence* (Springer International Publishing 2020) <https://www.springer.com/gp/book/9783030323608> accessed 7 January 2020, as well as Sylvia Lu, 'Regulating Algorithmic Harms' [2025] Florida Law Review <https://papers.ssrn.com/abstract=4949052> accessed 13 February 2025 (distinguishing four types of legal civil rights harms by AI, including risks to privacy, autonomy, equality, and safety).

[40] See Bartosz Brożek, Olia Kanevskaia, and Przemysław Pałka (eds), *Research Handbook on Law and Technology* (Edward Elgar Publishing 2023).

[41] See Cooper and others (n 7) 1, 9–12 (introducing 'a logical taxonomy of the legal issues these systems raise'). See also Michał Balcerzak and Julia Kapelańska-Pręgowska, 'Introduction: AI and International Human Rights Law' in Michał Balcerzak and Julia Kapelańska-Pręgowska (eds), *Artificial Intelligence and International Human Rights Law* (Edward Elgar Publishing 2024).

[42] Jan Smits and Tijn Borghuis, 'Generative AI and Intellectual Property Rights' in Bart Custers and Eduard Fosch-Villaronga (eds), *Law and Artificial Intelligence: Regulating AI and Applying AI in Legal Practice* (TMC Asser Press 2022) <https://doi.org/10.1007/978-94-6265-523-2_17> accessed 25 June 2024; see also Katherine Lee and others, 'AI and Law: The Next Generation' (6 July 2023) <https://papers.ssrn.com/abstract=4580739> accessed 24 June 2024.

[43] Hannah Ruschemeier, 'Generative AI and Data Protection', *Handbook on Generative AI and the Law* (Cambridge University Press 2024) <https://papers.ssrn.com/abstract=4814999> accessed 25 June 2024.

[44] Kaminski and Jones (n 23) 1231–1257 (reviewing different ways these areas of law have treated—or 'constructed'—the outputs of generative AI).

[45] See famously Frank H Easterbrook, 'Cyberspace and the Law of the Horse' (1996) 207 The University of Chicago Legal Forum 11.

[46] Although in some cases this may require a sufficient level of ex ante or ex post transparency of an AI system's decisions. Chris Reed, 'How Should We Regulate Artificial Intelligence?' (2018) 376 Philosophical Transactions. Series A, Mathematical, Physical, and Engineering Sciences 20170360.

and insightful. Accordingly, technology, application, value, and law-centric approaches to AI regulation all have a role to play in any AI governance ecosystem. Nonetheless, they also have their drawbacks in understanding, and crafting appropriate responses to, AI societal issues. In particular, we can identify three shared problems.

One challenge to many of these regulatory perspectives is that they may struggle to define, articulate, or anticipate many of the technology's downstream societal impacts. This will be especially the case for technology or application-centric approaches. For instance, Weidinger and others have highlighted a 'sociotechnical gap' in existing research on the safe development and deployment of AI; a gap which 'arises where AI system safety is evaluated only with regard to technical components of an AI system, i.e. individual technical artefacts such as data, model architecture, and sampling strategies'.[47] Instead, such work has begun to argue that while determining the harms and risks from an AI system should include an evaluation of these systems' technical risks, this process should also take into account 'human and systemic factors that co-determine risks of harm',[48] as this better serves risk-identification and mitigation approaches that are sensitive to particular contexts of their use.[49]

A second common thread in many of the regulatory approaches just discussed lies in their implicit dependence on a theory of 'exceptionalism'. The key question in such debates often becomes one over whether or not AI as a technology, or in a particular application, is sufficiently new and unprecedented in its 'essential characteristics' that existing legal frameworks are inadequate, such that new law is required.[50] However, as noted by Crootof and Ard:

> both the exceptionalist approach and its inverse are flawed. Not only do they place too much import on the architecture of a particular technology, they also foster narrow analyses. At best, a compartmentalized assessment is a missed opportunity. At worst, it leads to ineffective, counterproductive, or even harmful rules and policy prescriptions.[51]

[47] Laura Weidinger and others, 'Sociotechnical Safety Evaluation of Generative AI Systems' (arXiv, 18 October 2023) 8 <http://arxiv.org/abs/2310.11986> accessed 20 October 2023. (suggesting that '[w]hile these are important aspects of AI safety evaluation, they alone are insufficient to determine whether an AI system is safe. Instead, an approach is needed that takes into account human and systemic factors that co-determine risks of harm').

[48] ibid. See also Shannon Vallor and Ewa Luger, 'A Shrinking Path to Safety: How a Narrowly Technical Approach to Align AI with the Public Good Could Fail' (*BRAID UK*, 13 October 2023) <https://braiduk.org/a-shrinking-path-to-safety-how-a-narrowly-technical-approach-to-align-ai-with-the-public-good-could-fail> accessed 20 October 2023.

[49] Marta Cantero Gamito and Christopher T Marsden, 'Artificial Intelligence Co-Regulation? The Role of Standards in the EU AI Act' (2024) 32 International Journal of Law and Information Technology eaae011.

[50] Calo, 'Robotics and the Lessons of Cyberlaw' (n 4) 549.

[51] Crootof and Ard (n 25) 4.

Accordingly, a third way in which many of these approaches can fall short is that they often lead governance analyses and the resulting regulatory responses to remain relatively siloed, either focused on particular AI applications[52] or segmented along AI's impacts on particular rights or ethical values, or on specific conventional legal subjects.[53] This is unfortunate, as there are many common themes that could be articulated between AI questions in different legal domains or across different applications.[54]

To be sure, some work in AI governance has sought to explore how the impacts of different AI applications, in different domains, and on seemingly different values or systems of law may nonetheless follow similar patterns or logics, which it is valuable to apprehend or address in tandem. For example, Dafoe and Zwetsloot have distinguished between AI challenges that derive from (1) accidents involving AI systems, (2) misuse of AI systems, or (3) inadvertent effects of AI systems on the broader structure that shapes agents' choices and behaviour.[55] Maham and Küspert have mapped the risks from general-purpose AI models into (1) risks from unreliability, (2) misuse risks, and (3) systemic risks.[56] A similar framework has also characterized the UK government approach to evaluating the risks from 'frontier' AI systems, distinguishing between (1) societal harms, (2) misuse risks, and (3) loss of control risks.[57] Finally, Frase and Daniels have articulated a

[52] Turner (n 15) 218–219 (reflecting on UK governmental policies on driverless cars and drones in the period 2015–2018, which did not consider any overlap in possible underlying technology).

[53] Petit calls these the 'technological' and 'legalistic' approaches. Petit (n 20) 2.

[54] See also Crootof and Ard (n 25) 354–355 ('For example, there are obviously different concerns associated with having human beings in the loop in content moderation, medical, and military decision-making processes. But there is also much to be gained by considering the shared application, normative, and institutional uncertainties that arise in all three contexts. Stepping back makes it easier to learn from the rich history of prior dilemmas and anticipate future issues, allowing us to learn from the past and each other and to make more just and effective decisions going forward').

[55] Remco Zwetsloot and Allan Dafoe, 'Thinking About Risks from AI: Accidents, Misuse and Structure' (*Lawfare*, 11 February 2019) <https://www.lawfareblog.com/thinking-about-risks-ai-accidents-misuse-and-structure> accessed 12 February 2019. Elsewhere, Dafoe has argued that at the international level, AI systems create four risk clusters: (1) inequality, turbulence, authoritarianism; (2) great-power war; (3) the problems of control, alignment, and political order; (4) value erosion from competition. Allan Dafoe, 'AI Governance: Overview and Theoretical Lenses' in Justin B Bullock and others (eds), *The Oxford Handbook of AI Governance* (Oxford University Press 2023) 2–3. Another overview traces potential catastrophic outcomes from AI systems to (1) malicious use, (2) AI races, (3) organizational risks and failures, (4) uncontrolled AI systems. Dan Hendrycks, Mantas Mazeika, and Thomas Woodside, 'An Overview of Catastrophic AI Risks' (arXiv, 11 July 2023) <http://arxiv.org/abs/2306.12001> accessed 7 August 2023.

[56] Pegah Maham and Sabrina Küspert, 'Governing General Purpose AI: A Comprehensive Map of Unreliability, Misuse and Systemic Risks' (Stiftung Neue Verantwortung 2023) 17 <https://www.stiftung-nv.de/de/publikation/governing-general-purpose-ai-comprehensive-map-unreliability-misuse-and-systemic-risks> accessed 14 March 2025.

[57] Department for Science, Innovation & Technology, 'Frontier AI: Capabilities and Risks – Discussion Paper on the Need for Further Research into AI Risk' (Department for Science, Innovation & Technology 2023) 19–27 <https://www.gov.uk/government/publications/frontier-ai-capabilities-and-risks-discussion-paper/frontier-ai-capabilities-and-risks-discussion-paper> accessed 20 March 2024; Yoshua Bengio, 'International Scientific Report on the Safety of Advanced AI: Interim Report' (Department for Science, Innovation & Technology, and AI Safety Institute 2024) 2024/009 <https://www.gov.uk/government/publications/international-scientific-report-on-the-safety-of-advanced-ai> accessed 21 May 2024.

harm-centric framework that aims to identify four key components of AI harm: (1) the AI system involved; (2) the affected entity; (3) the harm event or issue; and (4) the AI-linked connection.[58]

Such analyses can help identify when facially different problems involving AI technology in fact derive from similar sources, instantiate similar risk dynamics, or face similar barriers to their effective resolution. Moreover, the sociotechnical perspective can help highlight shared areas of concern and overlap between nominally distinct research communities, by examining, for instance, areas in which technical AI safety research could benefit from an understanding of how these systems are embedded in larger sociotechnical systems,[59] or where their impacts are only clear, or can be more effectively addressed, at the level of their societal impacts.[60]

These analyses in the sociotechnical turn to AI regulation are therefore very valuable. Nonetheless, much work in this emerging field can still gain from a deeper account of the relations between technology, societal change, and regulation. In particular, they can draw on the existing field of technology law to understand how to best approach AI technologies, and their impacts, from the perspective of sociotechnical change.[61] This has significant implications across all core regulatory dilemmas—including the questions over what, why, when, and how to regulate.

4.3 Regulating What? Technology and Societal Change

To better understand the uses, strengths, and limits of the concept of sociotechnical change for AI governance, we must first build up our approach from basic

[58] Heather Frase and Owen Daniels, 'Understanding AI Harms: An Overview' (*Center for Security and Emerging Technology*, 11 August 2023) <https://cset.georgetown.edu/article/understanding-ai-harms-an-overview/> accessed 15 January 2024; see also Mia Hoffmann and Heather Frase, 'Adding Structure to AI Harm: An Introduction to CSET's AI Harm Framework' (Center for Security and Emerging Technology 2023) 9–15 <https://cset.georgetown.edu/publication/adding-structure-to-ai-harm/> accessed 15 January 2024.

[59] For a statement to this effect, and a collection of research proposals, see Samuel Curtis and others, 'Research Agenda for Sociotechnical Approaches to AI Safety' (Social Science Research Network, 14 January 2025) <https://papers.ssrn.com/abstract=5097286> accessed 14 March 2025.

[60] Usman Anwar and others, 'Foundational Challenges in Assuring Alignment and Safety of Large Language Models' <https://llm-safety-challenges.github.io/challenges_llms.pdf> accessed 14 March 2025.

[61] Beyond its analytical merits, a sociotechnical approach may also have normative benefits, as it can support a more democratic approach to ensuring human input into and control over technologies: Fernando Filgueiras, Ricardo Fabrino Mendonça, and Virgílio Almeida, 'Governing Artificial Intelligence Through a Sociotechnical Lens' (2023) 27 IEEE Internet Computing 49. Such an approach can also inform better participatory technology assessments aimed at anticipating highly impactful AI capabilities: Carla Zoe Cremer and Jess Whittlestone, 'Artificial Canaries: Early Warning Signs for Anticipatory and Democratic Governance of AI' (2021) 6 International Journal of Interactive Multimedia and Artificial Intelligence 100.

concepts: what is 'technology'? When does it 'change'? And what is the relation between technological change and societal change?

4.3.1 Concepts: Defining 'Technology' and 'AI' in a Sociotechnical View

Even today, debates around technology—and related debates around the causes and effects of technological change—are all beset by definitional ambiguity and varied usage of the term. We need to understand these terms—both in general and around AI—to distil a more useable understanding of what it is that technology regulation—or AI regulation—'is for'.

4.3.1.1 Definitions of technology: form or function?

What is 'technology'? A first step is to come to terms with the meaning of the core term. While an old term, many of its diverse modern usages are surprisingly modern.[62] Lyria Bennett Moses notes that the word 'technology' has historically been used to refer to:

> (1) tools and techniques; (2) organized systems such as factories; (3) applied science; (4) those methods that achieve, or are intended to achieve, a particular goal such as efficiency, the satisfaction of human needs and wants, or control over the environment; and (5) the study of or knowledge about such things.[63]

This draws together many things—not just artefacts or organizational systems, but also scientific methodologies and research programmes, and even particular normative goals (e.g. efficiency, human control over the environment). Which of these are best suited for our purpose? Broadly speaking, we could aim to define technology by form or by function.

In the former approach, we emphasize the form—or forms—of technology. Generally, as noted by Allan Dafoe, '[t]echnology can refer to vast sociotechnical systems, such as the Internet, as well as specific artifacts, standards, routines, and beliefs that make up these systems, such as computers, the Internet protocol, e-mail routines, and beliefs about the reliability of online information'.[64] This drives

[62] Eric Schatzberg, '"Technik" Comes to America: Changing Meanings of "Technology" before 1930' (2006) 47 Technology and Culture 486. See also Leo Marx, '"Technology": The Emergence of a Hazardous Concept' (1997) 64 Social Research 965.

[63] Lyria Bennett Moses, 'Why Have a Theory of Law and Technological Change?' (2007) 8 Minnesota Journal of Law, Science & Technology 589, 591.

[64] Allan Dafoe, 'On Technological Determinism: A Typology, Scope Conditions, and a Mechanism' (2015) 40 Science, Technology, & Human Values 1047, 5.

home how 'technology' remains an extremely broad term, extending to profoundly varied and distinct forms (artefacts, entities, practices, or processes).

Indeed, given this breadth and variety, one could even argue that 'technology' is not an analytically relevant or useful concept, but rather another suitcase word that attempts to wrap together deeply dissimilar phenomena under one moniker. Leo Marx has argued as much, suggesting that 'technology', by conflating specific artifacts with extremely broad or abstract sociotechnical systems, 'is almost completely vacuous', and ends up inducing erroneous deterministic thinking.[65] There is something to say for such caution. Still, Dafoe suggests that in many contexts such ambiguity can be avoided through the use of more specific terms, such as 'artifact', 'technique', 'institution', or 'sociotechnical system'.[66] Disambiguating these terms that are normally subsumed under 'technology' is valuable, as it highlights the diverse factors and components that are involved in making a certain local technological artifact actually functional and viable (rather than merely ensuring it 'works'), situating it in a broader sociotechnical system or stack.

With Dafoe, I therefore argue that there is still analytical value to the umbrella term 'technology'. However, I suggest that this is because it enables us to zoom out from the local particulars, specific materiality, or surface details of individual sociotechnical entities—the operational or material details of this or that institution, technique, or machine—and to also pay attention to these entities' societally relevant characteristics, such as their intended *functionality* or unintended effects.[67]

In the context of discussing AI's societal impacts, or regulating them, we would do well to adopt such a broad and functional perspective on technology. What would such a definition look like? Along with definitions that focus on form, there have certainly many attempts to define technology functionally, by its purpose—how it relates to human activity or capability. For instance, in 1967, Donald Schön's notably defined it as 'any tool or technique, any product or process, any physical equipment or method of doing or making, by which human capability is extended'.[68]

[65] Marx (n 62) 982–983. As quoted in Dafoe, 'On Technological Determinism' (n 64) 5.

[66] Dafoe, 'On Technological Determinism' (n 64) 5 ('Artifact can stand for specific objects intended for a function, such as machines, devices, and tools. Technique can refer to '"softer"' functional configurations, such as habits of mind, analytical methods, and behavioral routines. Institutions can refer to organizational hierarchies, legal codes, and incentive structures. Sociotechnical systems can refer to the vast functional configurations of all these components').

[67] ibid ('[t]echnology thus, [1] denotes those entities—artifacts, techniques, institutions, systems—that are or were functional and [2] emphasizes the functional dimension of those entities').

[68] Donald A Schön, *Technology and Change: The New Heraclitus* (Delacorte Press 1967) 1. In doing so, it follows the definition also utilized by Lyria Bennett Moses at various points. See for instance Bennett Moses, 'Why Have a Theory of Law and Technological Change?' (n 63) 591–592; also see Lyria Bennett Moses, 'Recurring Dilemmas: The Law's Race to Keep Up With Technological Change' (2007) 21 University of New South Wales Faculty of Law Research Series <http://www.austlii.edu.au/au/journals/UNSWLRS/2007/21.html> accessed 3 July 2018. Note, a more philosophical account of technology, which ties it more to the central role of human imagination, is given by Philip Hefner, 'Technology and Human Becoming' (2002) 37 Zygon® 655.

Of course, one might object that this definition of technology is anthropocentric because it refers to human capability as its benchmark, and that technology would not cease to be such if it expanded the capabilities of animals, or indeed of robots or AI systems themselves. Particularly in the latter case, however, it is unclear if we should speak of a robot having its capabilities extended or augmented by (other) technologies, or variably that this ought to be considered simply a case of one technology integrating with another ('getting an upgrade', or 'interfacing with a new API or module'), such as in the way in which the capabilities of modern foundation models can be improved even without re-training, through approaches such as prompting techniques or software tool modules.[69] As such, a more modern rephrasing might update Schön's definition as 'any tool or technique, any product or process, any physical equipment or method of doing or making, by which an actor's capability is extended'. Such an account may be better able to reckon not only with the increasing frequency of such integrations in and around AI systems, but also with the increasing agency in algorithmic systems, which brings its own set of potential harms.[70]

Similarly, Susan Brenner has sought to distinguish technologies on the basis of how they relate to previous human labour or tasks. She distinguishes between (1) tool technologies (e.g. drills), which are 'extensions and extrapolations of the earlier, more primitive tools that were once used to carry out simpler versions of the same task';[71] (2) machine technologies, which replace human effort entirely;[72] and (3) smart technologies, which she argues are embedded in our environment to redefine the division of labour between people and technology.[73]

In a third working definition for use in technology law, Brownsword, Scotford, and Yeung suggest that 'technology' extends to

> those entities and processes, both material and immaterial, which are created by the application of mental and/or physical effort in order to achieve some value or evolution in the state of relevant behaviour or practice. Hence, technology is

[69] Tom Davidson and others, 'AI Capabilities Can Be Significantly Improved without Expensive Retraining' (arXiv, 12 December 2023) <http://arxiv.org/abs/2312.07413> accessed 6 January 2024; Grégoire Mialon and others, 'Augmented Language Models: A Survey' (arXiv, 15 February 2023) <http://arxiv.org/abs/2302.07842> accessed 7 January 2024.

[70] Alan Chan and others, 'Harms from Increasingly Agentic Algorithmic Systems', *2023 ACM Conference on Fairness, Accountability, and Transparency* (ACM 2023) 2 <https://dl.acm.org/doi/10.1145/3593013.3594033> accessed 24 October 2023 (emphasizing, however, that 'recognizing agency of algorithmic systems does not absolve or shift the human responsibility for algorithmic harms. Rather, we use the term agency to highlight the increasingly evident fact that ML systems are not fully under human control').

[71] Susan Brenner, *Law in an Era of Smart Technology* (Oxford University Press 2007) 17 (emphasis added).

[72] ibid 25.

[73] ibid 131.

> taken to include tools, machines, products, or processes that may be used to solve real-world problems or to improve the status quo.[74]

This definition is broad but promising, because it emphasizes the functional 'output' of a given sociotechnical system, and its effects upon real-world situations (i.e. an evolution in the state of relevant behaviour), rather than merely background changes in practice or knowledge that, for one or another reason, are disregarded or not picked up widely. However, while this definition can provide a starting point, it too is not flawless, as it emphasizes deliberate attempts to 'solve problems' or 'improve the status quo'—an essentially normative judgement which may often become more debatable or subjective (and nowhere more so than on the anarchic international stage).

Of course, there are also ways of extending the definition of technology even further. For instance, one might consider other systems or entities—such as the 'social technologies' of legal systems, social norms, or changes in (the relative costs of inputs on) markets—that affect human capabilities, and which have sometimes been described as 'technologies'.[75] That is not to say that those are irrelevant to understanding (or governing) the impacts of AI systems. Indeed, understanding how AI is embedded within a broader ecosystem of political and social technology will be critical to understanding both its impacts and potential targets for regulation or intervention in full.[76]

Nonetheless, in focusing on the societal impacts of AI, the following sections will still broadly focus on materially based sociotechnical systems within AI. However, what matters is that the functional definition of technology emphasizes how, whatever their form—whether artifacts, techniques, or sociotechnical system—technologies involve functional changes in some actors' capabilities.

4.3.1.2 Definitions of AI across a sociotechnical stack

However, the purpose of this discussion is not to discount perspectives on AI (or technology) that consider AI in terms of its material 'form', but to complement these perspectives with an understanding of their downstream societal impacts. Consequently, just as discussions of 'technology' can focus on questions of form (i.e. types of artefacts, practices or systems that count as technology) or of function

[74] Roger Brownsword, Eloise Scotford, and Karen Yeung, 'Law, Regulation, and Technology: The Field, Frame, and Focal Questions' in Roger Brownsword, Eloise Scotford and Karen Yeung (eds), *The Oxford Handbook of Law, Regulation and Technology*, vol 1 (Oxford University Press 2017) 6.

[75] Bennett Moses, 'Why Have a Theory of Law and Technological Change?' (n 63) 592 ('This essay concentrates on technology as being that which overcomes physical, as opposed to legal, normative or self-imposed constraint'). See also Crootof, 'Regulating New Weapons Technology' (n 1) n 9.

[76] See also Divya Siddarth and others, 'How AI Fails Us' (Carr Center for Human Rights Policy 2021) <https://carrcenter.hks.harvard.edu/publications/how-ai-fails-us> accessed 2 May 2022; Sebastian Benthall and Jake Goldenfein, 'Artificial Intelligence and the Purpose of Social Systems', *Proceedings of the 2021 AAAI/ACM Conference on AI, Ethics, and Society* (Association for Computing Machinery 2021) <https://doi.org/10.1145/3461702.3462526> accessed 15 August 2021.

(i.e. the types of roles that systems serve, in order to count as technology), we can also compare—and integrate—different sociotechnical perspectives on what is AI technology. For instance, we can define 'AI' across different levels of abstraction of a sociotechnical stack that consists of (at least) the following:

a. a varied suite of computational *techniques* which can improve the accuracy, speed, or scale of machine decision-making across diverse information-processing or decision-making contexts; yielding
b. a set of *capabilities* which can be used to support, substitute for-, and/or improve upon human performance in diverse tasks; which in turn enable
c. a spectrum of useful *applications* across diverse domains; which in turn produce or support
d. diverse forms of new *behaviour or activities,* resulting in
e. significant, disruptive (and legally relevant) *sociotechnical changes.*

For instance, on this stack, focusing on computational *techniques* of AI systems helps put a focus on a variety of paradigms and approaches old and new, including symbolic approaches; supervised and unsupervised learning, reinforcement learning;[77] as well as more modern architectures such as transformers or diffusion models. This perspective can help focus on the technical preconditions or inputs (e.g. training data, computing power) needed to operate and deploy specific techniques—such as for instance the tremendous resource requirements for training transformer-based systems with billions of parameters.

At a higher level of abstraction on the AI stack, focusing on the *capabilities* of AI systems can put focus on the range of specific (but often domain-agnostic or transferable) functions that different systems—or, increasingly, single, general-purpose systems—are able to display. There are various ways of organizing these: for instance, one can functionally decompose the different processes that an intelligent machine can carry out;[78] along different categories of AI capabilities such as action, interaction, perception, and reasoning,[79] or along even more specific capabilities such as analogical reasoning, reinterpretation, object permanence, and so on.[80]

[77] For instance, Paul Scharre and Michael C Horowitz, 'Artificial Intelligence: What Every Policymaker Needs to Know' (Center for a New American Security 2018) <https://www.cnas.org/publications/reports/artificial-intelligence-what-every-policymaker-needs-to-know> accessed 25 June 2018. In another mapping, Hernandez-Orallo and colleagues identify 14 categories of AI techniques, with distinct subcategories and techniques. Jose Hernandez-Orallo and others, 'AI Paradigms and AI Safety: Mapping Artefacts and Techniques to Safety Issues', *European Conference on Artificial Intelligence* (2020) 3 <https://ecai2020.eu/papers/1364_paper.pdf> accessed 21 June 2020. I thank James Fox for discussing and clarifying some of these approaches.

[78] Martin Molina, 'What Is an Intelligent System?' (arXiv, 12 February 2022) 6 <http://arxiv.org/abs/2009.09083> accessed 6 December 2022.

[79] Molina (n 78).

[80] Cremer and Whittlestone (n 61) 107. Drawing on a methodology in Carla Zoe Cremer, 'Deep Limitations? Examining Expert Disagreement over Deep Learning' (2021) 10 Progress in Artificial Intelligence 449.

Moving yet further downstream, a focus on *applications* can survey the wide range of economically useful use cases that these capabilities can be put to—finally creating an even broader set of new *affordances or behaviours* that drive key sociotechnical changes.

This sociotechnical perspective on the AI stack is the most useful where it considers and makes explicit linkages between different layers. For instance, one can consider how *techniques* relate to *capabilities*: as discussed, foundation models have been defined as 'models trained on broad data at scale . . . that are adaptable to a wide range of downstream tasks'.[81] This includes text-generating foundation models—also often referred to as large language models (LLMs)—such as OpenAI's family of ChatGPT systems (e.g. GPT-4, GPT-o1). However, the terms are also more inclusive of other powerful models that are multimodal (i.e. they can take in other, non-text formats such as visual capabilities).[82]

Likewise, one can link particular capabilities to downstream applications or use cases, for instance in terms of capabilities such as data classification (with applications such as medical detection of skin cancer, facial and remote biometric recognition, or the interpretation of archaeological texts[83]); data generation (e.g. synthesizing deepfake images, video, audio, or other media); anomaly or pattern detection (e.g. detecting cybercrime or fraudulent financial transactions); prediction (e.g. of consumer preferences, weather patterns,[84] loan performance, judicial rulings); optimization of complex systems and tasks (e.g. optimizing energy usage in data centres); autonomous operation of cyber-physical platforms (e.g. robots such as Roomba vacuum cleaners, social robots, or military drones), and others.

This approach to seeing AI as a sociotechnical stack can be complex but is analytically useful, because it moves beyond interminable debates over what is the 'right' level of abstraction at which to study or understand AI technologies, and helps us consider the connections between these layers—from technological approaches and artefacts, to individual systems' capabilities, to their applications and their eventual (direct or indirect) impacts out in the world.

[81] Bommasani and others (n 33) 1.

[82] For a definition of 'multimodal' AI, see also Weidinger and others, 'Sociotechnical Safety Evaluation of Generative AI Systems' (n 47) 6 ('models that accept and produce output in any combination of image, audio, and text. This includes models that accept or produce output in more than one modality, such as interleaved image and text data, or audiovisual data'). See also Markus Anderljung and others, 'Frontier AI Regulation: Managing Emerging Risks to Public Safety' (arXiv, 11 July 2023) 7 <http://arxiv.org/abs/2307.03718> accessed 7 August 2023 ('the term "LLM" is already becoming outdated, as several leading "LLMs" are in fact multimodal (e.g., possess visual capabilities)').

[83] Yannis Assael and others, 'Restoring and Attributing Ancient Texts Using Deep Neural Networks' (2022) 603 Nature 280.

[84] Remi Lam and others, 'Learning Skillful Medium-Range Global Weather Forecasting' [2023] Science <https://www.science.org/doi/10.1126/science.adi2336> accessed 15 January 2024; Carissa Wong, 'DeepMind AI Accurately Forecasts Weather—on a Desktop Computer' [2023] Nature <https://www.nature.com/articles/d41586-023-03552-y> accessed 15 January 2024.

This approach can therefore help us gain a better understanding of how different choices at the level of AI techniques can translate not just to different capabilities and applications, but also to distinct societal impacts or risk profiles: take for example modern foundation models, which differ significantly from traditional AI approaches across many parts of the AI stack. In terms of the *techniques* involved, foundation models rely on development techniques mandate significantly greater (compute) costs and data requirements,[85] and therefore imply a radically different political economy of development.[86] Once trained, foundation models display *capabilities* that often emerge suddenly,[87] are increasingly general-purpose and multi-model, but are often still at the level of performance of a competent human at best.[88] This stands in contrast to the narrow (though at times super-human) performance of systems such as Alphafold or AlphaGo.[89] Consequently, a single foundation model can be adapted or finetuned for a wide range of downstream *applications*;[90] this makes them very useful, but also means that a widely adopted base model can act as a single point of failure for thousands of those downstream applications. Accordingly, in terms of *sociotechnical impacts*, foundation models display a systemic risk profile, with impacts that are not fully understood but which can substantially affect many sectors of society simultaneously.[91]

In this way, the sociotechnical approach to defining AI helps us move beyond interminable debates over what is the single best definition for AI: instead, it helps us appreciate the diversity of AI techniques, the versatility of its capabilities, and

[85] Pablo Villalobos and others, 'Will We Run out of Data? Limits of LLM Scaling Based on Human-Generated Data' (arXiv, 4 June 2024) <http://arxiv.org/abs/2211.04325> accessed 12 June 2024.

[86] Dieuwertje Luitse and Wiebke Denkena, 'The Great Transformer: Examining the Role of Large Language Models in the Political Economy of AI' (2021) 8 Big Data & Society 20539517211047734; Nicolas Moës and Frank Ryan, 'Heavy Is the Head That Wears the Crown: A Risk-Based Tiered Approach to Governing General Purpose AI' (The Future Society 2023) <https://thefuturesociety.org/wp-content/uploads/2023/09/heavy-is-the-head-that-wears-the-crown.pdf> accessed 30 November 2023.

[87] Jason Wei and others, 'Emergent Abilities of Large Language Models' [2022] Transactions on Machine Learning Research <https://openreview.net/forum?id=yzkSU5zdwD> accessed 30 November 2022; Anderljung and others (n 82) 10–12.

[88] Meredith Ringel Morris and others, 'Levels of AGI for Operationalizing Progress on the Path to AGI', *Proceedings of the 41st International Conference on Machine Learning* (PMLR 2024) <http://arxiv.org/abs/2311.02462> accessed 13 November 2023. See also the discussion, in Chapter 2, of the distinction between conventional and advanced AI systems.

[89] ibid 6.

[90] Sabrina Küspert, Nicolas Moës, and Connor Dunlop, 'The Value Chain of General-Purpose AI' (*Ada Lovelace Institute*, 10 February 2023) <https://www.adalovelaceinstitute.org/blog/value-chain-general-purpose-ai/> accessed 28 April 2023; Merlin Stein and Connor Dunlop, 'Safe before Sale: Learnings from the FDA's Model of Life Sciences Oversight for Foundation Models' (Ada Lovelace Institute 2023) <https://www.adalovelaceinstitute.org/report/safe-before-sale/> accessed 15 January 2024.

[91] Noam Kolt, 'Algorithmic Black Swans' (2023) 101 Washington University Law Review 32 <https://papers.ssrn.com/abstract=4370566> accessed 6 March 2023 ('The problem with general purpose systems is that any safety risks they pose—including robustness errors, harmful biases, and misalignment with societal values—are likely to propagate downstream. In other words, even minor defects in a general purpose system could have disastrous consequences if the system is deployed at scale or in high-stakes settings, such as healthcare or finance').

the potential ubiquity and importance of its applications and societal effects. It will be this definition that will underpin or inform much of this book's analysis of AI.

4.3.2 Ontology: Technology, Society, and Change

Having clarified the elementary concepts of technology and AI as they are understood in a sociotechnical approach, our next step is to articulate the relation between technology and society, and especially between technological change and societal change.

To approach these questions, we can draw on work from both Science and Technology Studies (STS) and technology law, which have come to articulate at least two distinct perspectives on studying any technology: internalist and externalist.[92] The 'internalist' approach highlights sociological analyses of how, and in what institutional or organizational settings, a technology such as AI is developed.[93] By contrast, an 'externalist' perspective focuses on the broader society, to understand 'how technology shapes the social realm and is shaped in turn'.[94]

Internalist accounts have added much to the study of AI governance, enabling the illumination of how politics and power have shaped the manner in which AI systems are developed in particular national contexts,[95] or the degree to which particular AI research programmes actually engage with questions of their products' ethical and sociotechnical impacts.[96] However, in this book I am primarily interested in the externalist account, and the reciprocal, mutually constitutive interaction between technology and its broader society.

At this point, it is useful to strike a point of caution. Many discussions over the interactions between technology and society end up in stuck in interminable debates around 'technological determinism'.[97] These debates have at times been

[92] Ryan Calo, 'The Scale and the Reactor' (9 April 2022) 4–5 <https://papers.ssrn.com/abstract=4079851> accessed 23 May 2023.

[93] ibid 4.

[94] ibid.

[95] Indeed, others have called for the introduction of STS frameworks to the study of AI governance in improving this internalist perspective. For instance, Fischer and Wenger have productively explored the insights gained from applying STS accounts of 'micro-politics' of technology design and development, and the frame of co-production, to understanding the intersection of AI and security in a Swiss context. See Sophie-Charlotte Fischer and Andreas Wenger, 'Artificial Intelligence, Forward-Looking Governance and the Future of Security' (2021) 27 Swiss Political Science Review 170.

[96] For instance, Sarah Dean, Thomas Gilbert, Nathan Lambert, and Tom Zick have developed a sociotechnical framework for 'investigating the sociotechnical engagement of various branches of AI research' along a range of vectors, including questions around '*value*—what does a field deem of merit, *optimization*—how the designed system within a problem formulation relates to the real-world dynamics, *consensus*—who and what is in the conversation towards agreement, and *failure*—what are the assurances if the system proves inadequate'. Sarah Dean and others, 'Axes for Sociotechnical Inquiry in AI Research' (2021) 2 IEEE Transactions on Technology and Society 62, 1.

[97] See for instance Sally Wyatt, 'Technological Determinism Is Dead; Long Live Technological Determinism' in Edward J Hackett and others (eds), *The Handbook of Science and Technology Studies* (MIT Press 2008). But see also John Durham Peters, '"You Mean My Whole Fallacy Is Wrong": On

heated and unproductive, in part because there is in fact a very broad family of different claims about these relationships, which are too easily subsumed under the simple label of technological determinism.[98] In this book, I do not seek to resolve those long-standing debates. Still, we require a more detailed discussion of the relationship between technology and society, and how they can mutually shape one another. There are at least two ways to approach this relation: by looking at how society changes technology, and at how technology changes society.

4.3.2.1 How society changes technology

In the first place, one can examine what drives changes in technology. Here, technological change is a dependent variable, and the aim is to assess what factors affect when, why, and how technological progress occurs. This engages long-standing debates over the drivers of, or barriers to, innovation, and specifically over the relative roles of intrinsic (material or artefactual) factors, human agency, norms or political choices, and structural strategic pressures, in determining which technologies are invented, by who, and whether or how fast they subsequently spread.

Critically, such work suggests that while there may be strong common patterns in how some innovations are developed,[99] these processes are still affected by social factors. This is because law and legal systems can play a significant and often constitutive role in shaping the economic incentives, social norms, or regulatory environment that affects the developmental pathway of a new technology.[100] Given different legal, economic, and cultural conditions, for instance, Nathan Ensmenger has argued that

> technological innovation is as much driven by social processes as by inherent technological imperatives. That is to say, there is never a single, ideal type toward which any given technology will inevitably evolve. Specific technologies are developed to solve specific problems, for specific users, in specific times and places.

Technological Determinism' (2017) 140 Representations 10 (offering a genealogy of the concept of technological determinism, and a 'metacritique' of the way that academic accusations around the concept 'risk stopping difficult but essential kinds of inquiry').

[98] Dafoe, 'On Technological Determinism' (n 64) 6 (distinguishing between theories that hold that '(1) functional entities (artifacts, techniques, institutions, and systems) exert an effect on the world independent of human choice (*technical determinism*); (2) there is a broad sequence and tempo of scientific and technological advance (*technological trends*) that seems to follow an internal logic, making technological change seem autonomous; and (3) that people are insufficiently conscious of their technological choices (*technological somnambulism*) or have been co-opted (*the magnificent bribe*), such that the social order is becoming more machine-like over time').

[99] See also Matt Clancy, 'Are Technologies Inevitable?' [2022] New Things Under the Sun <https://www.newthingsunderthesun.com/pub/3wpc3plu/release/1> accessed 1 November 2022; Rick Korzekwa, 'Observed Patterns around Major Technological Advancements' (*AI Impacts*, 2 February 2022) <https://aiimpacts.org/observed-patterns-around-major-technological-advancements/> accessed 4 February 2022.

[100] Crootof and Ard (n 25) n 19.

> How certain problems get defined as being most in need of a solution, which users are considered most important to design for, what other technological systems need to be provided or accounted for, who has the power to set certain technical and economic priorities—these are fundamentally social considerations that deeply influence the process of technological development.[101]

This is the case not just at the domestic level, but also at the international one. Indeed, as discussed by Sophie-Charlotte Fischer, Andrea Gilli, and Mauro Gilli, technological changes can have significant effects on international politics, by creating new opportunities and altering the strategic environment, making some countries more independent in some realms and more dependent in others; by driving distributional effects between and within states; and by affecting dominant ideas and narratives.[102] However, Daniel Drezner also notes that while technologies may drive far-reaching shifts in international relations, they are not an exogenous shock, but are shaped by political choices which are themselves framed not only by the nature of technology but also by broader norms and factors.[103]

In fact, throughout history, there is a track record of decisions being made by various actors (i.e. individual inventors; research groups; governments; entire societies) which, deliberately or inadvertently, steered technologies away from directions that had previously been held to be inevitable.[104]

Even in cases where seminal inventions were pursued, the path towards their development was rarely straightforward or inevitable: for instance, Alex Wellerstein and others have argued that the initial US pursuit of the atom bomb during the Second World War was not inevitable but rather was a contingent outcome of, on the one hand, UK advocacy which claimed—in the face of American scientists' wariness over the difficulty and expense of a nuclear programme—that this was a risk worth taking, and, on the other hand, the peculiar and remarkably limited

[101] Nathan Ensmenger, *The Computer Boys Take Over: Computers, Programmers, and the Politics of Technical Expertise* (The MIT Press 2010) 26 <https://www.jstor.org/stable/j.ctt5hhjdh> accessed 8 December 2023.

[102] Sophie-Charlotte Fischer, Andrea Gilli, and Mauro Gilli, 'Technological Change and Grand Strategy' in Thierry Balzacq and Ronald R Krebs (eds), *The Oxford Handbook of Grand Strategy* (Oxford University Press 2021) 226.

[103] Daniel W Drezner, 'Technological Change and International Relations' (2019) 33 International Relations 286, 291. Of course, even if technological changes are not exogenous to the global social world, they can be exogenous to specific political, strategic, or economic relations or competitions between specific states. Fischer, Gilli, and Gilli (n 102) 224. ('In other instances, a new technology can result from a competition that is external to the one of interest, and thus yield a "competitive advantage" to a given country. This was the case for the repower revolution, for example, that originated in Europe but that gave Europeans an unexpected military advantage outside of Europe.')

[104] See Matthijs Maas, 'Paths Untaken: The History, Epistemology and Strategy of Technological Restraint, and Lessons for AI' (*Verfassungsblog*, 9 August 2022) <https://verfassungsblog.de/paths-untaken/> accessed 12 August 2022; For an accessible survey of examples in the military domain, see also Vince Houghton, *Nuking the Moon: And Other Intelligence Schemes and Military Plots Left on the Drawing Board* (1st edn, Penguin Books 2019).

oversight that characterized American wartime scientific planning.[105] Given this, Wellerstein argues, the US Manhattan Program should be considered 'an unexpected and improbable outcome [such that] instead of asking why other nations did not develop such weapons, it is more fruitful to look instead at the various contingent and at times even coincidental factors that led to the United States being the *only* nation to pursue such a program with vigor'.[106] If the US had not built the bomb during the extraordinary conditions of the war, it is not clear that it would have been pursued in the post-war US political context.[107] Even if it had, the subsequent decision to pursue an H-bomb programme was still contingent:[108] it was at the time highly contested within the US Atomic Energy Commission's General Advisory Committee[109] and at multiple later stages of development and testing.[110] Indeed, these internal debates may have been settled not by ironclad strategic considerations: rather, one key factor in the decision to go ahead appears to have been the November 1949 accidental leaking of the (previously classified) H-bomb debate to the public, after which President Truman was hastened to approve the programme.[111]

[105] Alex Wellerstein, 'Manhattan Project' (2019) 4 Encyclopedia of the History of Science 8 <https://lps.library.cmu.edu/ETHOS/article/id/35/> accessed 7 June 2024.

[106] ibid.

[107] *Dr Philip Zelikow, 'Some Uses of History'* (Directed by Columbia University, 2010) <https://www.youtube.com/watch?v=IPaofrAiP5s> accessed 7 June 2024., at [7:38] (noting 'had the United States not built an atomic bomb during the Second World War, it's actually not clear to me when or possibly even if an atomic bomb ever is built').

[108] Alex Wellerstein, 'What If Truman Hadn't Ordered the H-Bomb Crash Program?' (*Restricted Data: A Nuclear History Blog*, 18 June 2012) <https://blog.nuclearsecrecy.com/2012/06/18/what-if-truman-didnt-order-h-bomb-crash-program/> accessed 7 June 2024; But for a counter-argument, see Herbert F York, 'The Debate over the Hydrogen Bomb' (1975) 233 Scientific American 106; Herbert York, *The Advisors: Oppenheimer, Teller, and the Superbomb* (1st edn, Stanford University Press 1989).

[109] General Advisory Committee to the US Atomic Energy Commission, 'General Advisory Committee's Majority and Minority Reports on Building the H-Bomb' (*AtomicArchive*, 30 October 1949) <https://www.atomicarchive.com/resources/documents/hydrogen/gac-report.html> accessed 26 June 2024.

[110] Matin Zuberi, 'The Missed Opportunity to Stop the H-Bomb' (1999) XXIII Strategic Analysis <https://ciaotest.cc.columbia.edu/olj/sa/sa_99zum02.html> accessed 26 June 2024.

[111] Alex Wellerstein, *Restricted Data: The History of Nuclear Secrecy in the United States* (University of Chicago Press 2021) 219 <https://press.uchicago.edu/ucp/books/book/chicago/R/bo15220099.html> accessed 13 December 2021; Alex Wellerstein, 'The Leak That Brought the H-Bomb Debate out of the Cold' (*Restricted Data: The Nuclear Secrecy Blog*, 14 June 2021) <http://blog.nuclearsecrecy.com/2021/06/14/the-leak-that-brought-the-h-bomb-debate-out-of-the-cold/> accessed 2 November 2021 (noting 'Lilienthal argued against [the H-bomb], and Truman's reply to him, as Lilienthal recalled in his diary, was telling: "we could have had all this re-examination quietly if Senator Ed Johnson hadn't made that unfortunate remark about the super bomb; since that time there has been so much talk in the Congress and everywhere and people are so excited he [Truman] really hasn't any alternative but to go ahead and that was what he was going to do"'). Of course, one might argue that the US would still have pursued the H-bomb later, if or as (it became clear that) the Soviet Union had continued ahead with its development. It would certainly be possible for the Soviet Union to have done so, since—contrary to its original fission bomb programme, which drew on Klaus Fuchs' leaks from the Manhattan Project—its H-bomb programme was not a copy of the American one, but appears to have been based on genuine and independent Soviet designs. Daniel Hirsch and William G Mathews, 'The H-Bomb: Who Really Gave Away the Secret?' (1990) 46 Bulletin of the Atomic Scientists 22; Gennady Gorelik, 'The Riddle

Similar extended bureaucratic politics-focused debates have surrounded the development of the Indian nuclear programme,[112] as well as many technologies that were eventually developed after significant struggle.[113] This suggests that even if certain innovation paths are convergent or strong attractors,[114] they were not inevitable, and their pursuit was often shaped by political factors.

In other cases, a range of factors did not outright contain an innovation but nonetheless limited the subsequent proliferation or global uptake of even powerful technologies, such as nuclear weapons,[115] nuclear power,[116] or geoengineering.[117] In yet other cases, societies even chose to roll back or restrict certain technologies such as leaded gasoline, DDT pesticides, and chlorofluorocarbons, albeit only after significant impacts had already accrued.[118]

Given all this, societies do clearly possess some room for manoeuvre in deciding their course around new technologies. But how much, and in what directions?

of the Third Idea: How Did the Soviets Build a Thermonuclear Bomb So Suspiciously Fast?' (*Scientific American*, 21 August 2011) <https://www.scientificamerican.com/blog/guest-blog/the-riddle-of-the-third-idea-how-did-the-soviets-build-a-thermonuclear-bomb-so-suspiciously-fast/> accessed 9 June 2024. See also David Holloway, 'Soviet Thermonuclear Development' (1979) 4 International Security 192, 193 ('It is true that Fuchs' account of these early discussions of the superbomb would have been misleading rather than helpful to Soviet scientists in a scientific sense, because the early ideas were later shown not to work. But it is possible that Fuchs' report of the Los Alamos discussions of 1946 served to spark the Soviet interest in thermonuclear weapons'). At the same time, this assumes that the Soviet Union would have remained motivated to pursue this programme even in the absence of an American one.

[112] Scott D Sagan, 'Why Do States Build Nuclear Weapons? Three Models in Search of a Bomb' (1996) 21 International Security 54.

[113] See also Quentin E Hodgson, *Deciding to Buy: Civil-Military Relations and Major Weapons Programs* (Strategic Studies Institute, US Army War College 2010) <https://press.armywarcollege.edu/monographs/339/> accessed 18 August 2022 (discussing the contested development of the B-1 Bomber in the 1970s). However, it is notable that on some occasions, these institutional incentives could also pull in the opposite direction, sustaining the pursuit of even infeasible technologies for remarkably long times. See David Zimmerman, 'Death Rays and Radar: The Myth of Early British Radar History', *2024 IEEE Radar Conference (RadarConf24)* (2024) <https://ieeexplore.ieee.org/abstract/document/10548535> accessed 20 June 2024.

[114] Clancy (n 99).

[115] Matthijs M Maas, 'How Viable Is International Arms Control for Military Artificial Intelligence? Three Lessons from Nuclear Weapons' (2019) 40 Contemporary Security Policy 285; Carl Robichaud, 'The Puzzle of Non-Proliferation' [2023] *Asterisk* <https://asteriskmag.com/issues/03/the-puzzle-of-non-proliferation> accessed 28 August 2023; Sico van der Meer, 'Not That Bad: Looking Back on 65 Years of Nuclear Non-Proliferation Efforts' (2011) 22 Security and Human Rights 37.

[116] Vaclav Smil, *Invention and Innovation: A Brief History of Hype and Failure* (The MIT Press 2023) 79–93; Jeffrey Heninger, 'Resisted Technological Temptation: Nuclear Power' (*AI Impacts Wiki*, 30 March 2023) <https://wiki.aiimpacts.org/responses_to_ai/technological_inevitability/incentivized_technologies_not_pursued/nuclear_power> accessed 15 January 2024; Rick Korzekwa, 'What We've Learned So Far from Our Technological Temptations Project' (*AI Impacts*, 13 April 2023) <https://aiimpacts.org/what-weve-learned-so-far-from-our-technological-temptations-project/> accessed 16 April 2023.

[117] Adrian Currie, 'Geoengineering Tensions' (2018) 102 Futures 78; Jeffrey Heninger, 'Why Has Geoengineering Been Rejected?' (AI Impacts 2022) <http://aiimpacts.org/wp-content/uploads/2023/04/Why-Has-Geoengineering-Been-Rejected.pdf> accessed 23 April 2023.

[118] Smil (n 116) 19–62.

4.3.2.1.1 Strategies of technological navigation

To understand the scope and feasibility of such technological choice, and what contributes to it, it helps to first understand the ideal-typical space of strategies of technological navigation.[119] Here we can distinguish between strategies that aim to boost, slow, steer, or halt technological progress at different sociotechnical levels—whether focusing on entire scientific fields, specific industries, particular classes of technologies, specific applications, or individual technology projects, products, or artefacts.

Take, for instance, attempts to *boost* technologies or technological progress. In the past, there have been numerous attempts by states to sponsor the accelerated development of critical national industries or sectors, both to develop specific technologies with the aim to secure an upper hand over rivals and to generally contribute to longer-term economic growth.[120] In recent decades, philosophies such as (technological) accelerationism often aim to radically speed up the development of a technology, either to break science out of a perceived state of stasis or to drive the pace of development of particular technologies beyond their 'naturally' occurring rate. Interestingly, such an attitude implies that there is a degree of human control over the pace (if not direction or destination) of technology development.

Its obverse is a strategy of *slowing* or delaying technological progress. Even in the depths of the Cold War, a range of initiatives, such as the Nuclear Freeze campaign,[121] sought to ensure the coordinated slowing or pausing of the (further) development or proliferation of some classes of technology. Indeed, recent years have seen renewed interest in the idea of adopting unilateral or coordinated pauses in the development, or at least deployment, of particular AI systems.[122]

There are different versions of this, which are often or easily conflated. However, we can and must distinguish between four different types of slowdowns: (1) strategic rate-slowing of a broader field of science may aim to, for instance, 'buy time' for the development of defensive, safer, or more beneficial substitute technologies,[123] or to ensure that society has time to study and adapt to a technology;[124] (2) strategic pauses aim to delay or prevent particularly dangerous

[119] For adjacent accounts of such steering in technologies, see also Jonas B Sandbrink and others, 'Risk-Sensitive Innovation: Leveraging Interactions between Technologies to Navigate Technology Risks' [2024] Science and Public Policy scae043.

[120] Fischer, Gilli, and Gilli (n 102) 229–231.

[121] Lawrence S Wittner, 'The Nuclear Freeze and Its Impact' (*Arms Control Association*, 2010) <https://www.armscontrol.org/act/2010_12/LookingBack> accessed 26 October 2023.

[122] Future of Life Institute, 'Pause Giant AI Experiments: An Open Letter' (*Future of Life Institute*, 30 March 2023) <https://futureoflife.org/open-letter/pause-giant-ai-experiments/> accessed 30 March 2023.

[123] Sandbrink and others (n 119). See also Katja Grace, 'Let's Think about Slowing down AI' (*AI Impacts*, 22 December 2022) <https://aiimpacts.org/lets-think-about-slowing-down-ai/> accessed 23 December 2022.

[124] Crootof and Ard (n 25) 385 (noting that '[b]anning a technology postpones the stabilization of both a technology's design and its social uses; less dramatic restrictions could be designed to facilitate a period of controlled study or to compel developers to provide information').

steps until a particular later moment in time when (it is expected) society might be in a better position to deal with its consequences; (3) tactical and operational pauses may attempt to reduce the pressure to cut corners in deployment races,[125] affording greater caution;[126] for instance, this could include coordinated pauses among labs, delaying the deployment of the next generation of a system to allow for more time investigating or evaluating its safety and performance;[127] finally, (4) post-deployment firebreaks may attempt to slow or stage-gate the uptake of or buffet the sociotechnical impacts of a technology—slowing societal exposure to powerful AI.

When combined, strategies of technological boosting and slowing might contribute to more effective technological *steering*—as seen, for instance, in the idea of 'risk-sensitive innovation', which aims to preferentially advance safety-increasing, defensive, or substitute technologies while delaying or halting hazardous capabilities, in order to avoid hazardous technology pairings and interactions while promoting more promising ones.[128]

Finally, even more far-reaching strategies would involve technological *restraint*, involving decisions (or outcomes) where an actor withholds from developing or at least deploying a particular technology. In some cases of *relinguishment*, actors may even choose to abandon or dismantle a previously deployed technology.[129]

4.3.2.1.2 The epistemology of technological navigation

Are such outcomes common? Are these strategies frequently pursued? If so, are they often successful? To be sure, this question is epistemically difficult to study. There are a range of epistemic and methodological challenges in studying these

[125] On the dangers of such racing dynamics, see also Stuart Armstrong, Nick Bostrom, and Carl Shulman, 'Racing to the Precipice: A Model of Artificial Intelligence Development' (2016) 31 AI & Society 201; Nicholas Emery-Xu, Andrew Park, and Robert Trager, 'Uncertainty, Information, and Risk in International Technology Races' [2023] Journal of Conflict Resolution 00220027231214996.

[126] Richard Danzig, 'Technology Roulette: Managing Loss of Control as Many Militaries Pursue Technological Superiority' (Center for a New American Security 2018) 5 <https://www.cnas.org/publications/reports/technology-roulette> accessed 14 March 2025 (observing that 'superiority is not synonymous with security').

[127] Jide Alaga and Jonas Schuett, 'Coordinated Pausing: An Evaluation-Based Coordination Scheme for Frontier AI Developers' (arXiv, 30 September 2023) <http://arxiv.org/abs/2310.00374> accessed 3 October 2023.

[128] Sandbrink and others (n 119) 2 (defining the principle as one that aims to 'leverage risk-reducing interactions between technologies by affecting their relative timing' in order to mitigate specific risks). Adjacent versions of such a concept have also focused on the idea of 'differential technological development'. See Nick Bostrom, 'Existential Risks: Analyzing Human Extinction Scenarios and Related Hazards' (2002) 9 Journal of Evolution and Technology 23 <https://nickbostrom.com/existential/risks.html> accessed 14 June 2019 (defining 'differential technological development' as 'trying to retard the implementation of dangerous technologies and accelerate implementation of beneficial technologies, especially those that ameliorate the hazards posed by other technologies'). This thinking has also informed some recent popular philosophies in public discourse on technology, such as 'defensive accelerationism'. See Vitalik Buterin, 'My Techno-Optimism' (27 November 2023) <https://vitalik.eth.limo/general/2023/11/27/techno_optimism.html> accessed 15 January 2024.

[129] Maas, 'Paths Untaken' (n 104); Smil (n 116).

dynamics, especially around technological restraint.[130] This is because cases of technological slowing and restraint have a limited historical signature. For instance, from a cursory survey of the historical record, it can be hard to even know when restraint took place, as we only see technologies that are publicly documented, whereas cancelled programmes may end up as footnotes. As such, failures of restraint (e.g. arms races) loom much larger in historical memory than its successes. It may also be difficult to interpret the causes of restraint or slowing in particular cases, because such outcomes can be overdetermined by many factors (including deliberate and indeliberate choices).

Moreover, while for some abandoned technologies or programmes, such as the Cold War-era STORMFURY hurricane modification programme,[131] the scientific futility is clear in retrospect, for others it may be difficult to accurately assess their actual feasibility ex post, and therefore difficult to understand how surprising or telling a case of delay or restraint is.[132] Finally, because actors involved in pursuing (or putting the axe to) technology programmes often have many different institutional incentives, they may often rationalize the abandonment of a particular programme as reflecting its infeasibility. This means that it can be difficult to tease out the exact or underlying reasons for why a technology was not developed. Often, it may be tempting to retroactively reinterpret a technology's abandonment as evidence of its infeasibility, when the key drivers were in fact political or bureaucratic.[133]

4.3.2.1.3 The history of technological restraint

With that said, a brief survey of the historical record of innovation suggests that many forms of restraint have occurred around new technologies, throughout history, as a result of both indeliberate factors and deliberate decisions and—in the latter case—for reasons both well-grounded and poorly conceived.

There have occurred remarkable delays in technological development, of decades or even centuries.[134] In some cases, as with the 1733 introduction of flying shuttles to weaving after 5,000 years, low-hanging fruit simply went unperceived

[130] Maas, 'Paths Untaken' (n 104); George H Quester, 'The Epistemology of Nuclear Proliferation' (1986) 40 Journal of International Affairs 177.

[131] HE Willoughby and others, 'Project STORMFURY: A Scientific Chronicle 1962–1983' (1985) 66 Bulletin of the American Meteorological Society 505.

[132] See for instance Jason Crawford, 'When Should We Be Surprised That an Invention Took "So Long"?' (*The Roots of Progress*, 16 November 2022) <https://rootsofprogress.org/when-to-be-surprised-an-invention-took-so-long> accessed 10 January 2023.

[133] See for instance Sagan (n 112) 63 (noting also that an evidential challenge occurs because the statements of motivation by the key decision-makers around explaining nuclear proliferation decisions are in fact coloured by their bureaucratic interests).

[134] There have also, conversely, been cases of 'outdated' technologies that stuck around and saw widespread use, even after they were nominally superseded and 'replaced' by newer innovations. See David Edgerton, *The Shock Of The Old: Technology and Global History since 1900* (Main edition, Profile Books 2019).

for centuries.[135] In other cases, inventors' or investors' uncertainty about the legal status of the technology inhibited their uptake, with mechanized sawmills going unpursued in England for several centuries, on the basis of a widespread—and mistaken—belief that Parliament had outlawed them.[136] Electric cars held equal US market-share in the 1900s, but soon declined in use because cars using internal combustion engines became seen as more masculine,[137] and appealed to an aspiration for touring.[138] Bureaucratic and political factors inhibited a range of 1960s–1970s Soviet initiatives to develop a national computer network, curbing the independent development of an internet-like technology from behind the Iron Curtain.[139]

More relevant to contemporary debates is the fact that deliberate restraint can also occur,[140] even for very powerful technologies, and even if success is partial. For instance, while the nuclear non-proliferation regime has at times met with scepticism and contestation, it has in fact had a remarkably robust effect on constraining proliferation.[141] Based on IAEA databases, there have historically been 74 states that decided to build or use nuclear reactors. Of these, 69 have at some time been considered potentially able to pursue nuclear weapons. Of these, 10 states went nuclear, 7 ran but abandoned a nuclear weapons programme, and for 14–23 states evidence exists of a considered decision not to use their infrastructure to pursue nuclear weapons.[142] Indeed, these and other technologies illustrate that, even at the 'anarchic' international level, and even in the domain of security, not quite everything that can be made is in fact made or seen through.[143]

[135] Anton Howes, 'Is Innovation in Human Nature?' (*Anton Howes*, 22 October 2016) <http://www.antonhowes.com/1/post/2016/10/is-innovation-in-human-nature.html> accessed 27 January 2022.

[136] ibid.

[137] Rudi Volti, 'Why Internal Combustion?' (1990) 6 *Invention & Technology Magazine* <https://www.inventionandtech.com/content/why-internal-combustion-1> accessed 19 May 2022.

[138] Constantine Hadjilambrinos, 'Reexamining the Automobile's Past: What Were the Critical Factors That Determined the Emergence of the Internal Combustion Engine as the Dominant Automotive Technology?' [2021] Bulletin of Science, Technology & Society 02704676211036334.

[139] Slava Gerovitch, 'InterNyet: Why the Soviet Union Did Not Build a Nationwide Computer Network' (2008) 24 History and Technology 335.

[140] Maas, 'Paths Untaken' (n 104).

[141] van der Meer (n 115); Jeffrey M Kaplow, *Signing Away the Bomb: The Surprising Success of the Nuclear Nonproliferation Regime* (Cambridge University Press 2022); Philipp C Bleek, 'When Did (and Didn't) States Proliferate? Chronicling the Spread of Nuclear Weapons' (Belfer Center for Science and International Affairs 2017) <https://www.belfercenter.org/publication/when-did-and-didnt-states-proliferate> accessed 14 March 2025.

[142] Sico van der Meer, 'Forgoing the Nuclear Option: States that Could Build Nuclear Weapons but Chose Not to Do So' (2014) 30 Medicine, Conflict and Survival s27.

[143] See also, for instance, the wide range of creative deployment configurations for strategic nuclear missiles canvassed in Office of the Deputy Under Secretary of Defense for Research and Engineering (Strategic and Space Systems), 'ICBM Basing Options: A Summary of Major Studies to Define A Survivable Basing Concept for ICBMs' (Department of Defense 1980) AD-A956443 <https://apps.dtic.mil/sti/pdfs/ADA956443.pdf> accessed 3 October 2018. And for a more detailed discussion of the ultimately abortive US programme to pursue various options for extensive mobile deployment of ICBMs, see Steven A Pomeroy, *An Untaken Road: Strategy, Technology, and the Hidden History of America's Mobile ICBMs* (Naval Institute Press 2016).

Elsewhere, in civilian domains, scientific fields and domains of innovation have at times seen slowdowns or re-directions. This can occur as a result of a range of (deliberate or indeliberate) 'reverse push' factors, which raised the costs of conducting research in domains such as US chemical or stem cell research.[144] It can also come through 'reverse pull' factors that reduce the (anticipated) profits from certain kinds of innovation, from medical implants to new fossil-fuel cars.[145] Moreover, as illustrated by the broad and remarkably robust taboo on geoengineering, scientific communities can in some cases effectively determine the boundaries of (un)acceptable technologies, to which policymakers and the public then defer.[146]

Even something as simple as metaphors and frames can have a remarkably robust effect on the innovation pathways of a technology—and its regulation.[147] For example, the fields of cell biology and biotechnology have for decades been shaped by the influential foundational metaphor that sees biological cells as 'machines', which has led to sustained debates over the scientific use and limits of that analogy in shaping research programmes.[148] More practically, in some cases, metaphors can support and spur on innovation: for instance, it has been argued that through the early 2000s, the coining of specific IT metaphors for electric vehicles—as a 'computer on wheels'—played a significant role in sustaining engineer support for and investment in this technology, especially during an industry downturn in the wake of General Motors' sudden cancellation of its EV1 electric car.[149]

Conversely, metaphors can also hold back or inhibit certain pathways of innovation: for instance, in the Soviet Union in the early 1950s, the field of cybernetics (along with other fields such as genetics or linguistics) fell victim to anti-American campaigns which characterized it as an 'obscurantist', 'bourgeois pseudoscience'.[150] While this didn't affect the early development of Soviet computer technology (which was highly prized by the state and the military), the resulting ideological

[144] Matt Clancy, 'How to Impede Technological Progress' (*What's New Under the Sun*, 13 July 2023) < https://mattsclancy.substack.com/p/how-to-impede-technological-progress > accessed 7 August 2023.

[145] ibid (reviewing several cases of 'reverse push' policies—US restrictions on federal R&D funding for stem cell research; increasingly stringent safety requirements for chemical research—and several cases of 'reverse pull' drivers that reduced the profits of innovation—higher fuel prices; greater liability for medical implant manufacturers; Second World War-era compulsory invention secrecy).

[146] For instance, geoengineering 'could feasibly provide benefits of $1-10 trillion per year through global warming mitigation, but actors who stand to gain the most have not pursued it, citing a lack of research into its feasibility and safety'. Korzekwa (n 116), drawing on research in Heninger (n 117).

[147] Maas, 'AI Is Like . . .' (n 17) 9–16. See also Chapter 5 for a more detailed discussion of the role of analogies and metaphors in shaping or enabling legal responses to technological change.

[148] Joshua Bongard and Michael Levin, 'Living Things Are Not (20th Century) Machines: Updating Mechanism Metaphors in Light of the Modern Science of Machine Behavior' (2021) 9 Frontiers in Ecology and Evolution <https://www.frontiersin.org/articles/10.3389/fevo.2021.650726/full> accessed 16 March 2021.

[149] Jay Lloyd, 'Computers on Wheels?' (*Issues in Science and Technology*, 6 February 2023) <http://issues.org/computers-on-wheels-electric-vehicles-eisler/> accessed 24 May 2023.

[150] Olessia Kirtchik, 'The Soviet Scientific Programme on AI: If a Machine Cannot "Think", Can It "Control"?' [2023] BJHS Themes 1, 4; As discussed in Maas, 'AI Is Like . . .' (n 17) 10.

rejection of the 'man-machine' analogy by Marxist-Leninist philosophers led to an ultimately dominant view, in Soviet sciences, of computers as solely 'tools to think with' rather than 'thinking machines', holding back the consolidation of the field (such that even the label 'AI' would not be recognized by the Soviet Academy of Sciences until 1987), and shifting research attention to projects that focused on the 'situational management' of large complex systems rather than the pursuit of human-like thinking machines.[151]

4.3.2.1.4 Sociotechnical choice in technology law: opportunities and bounds

All this does not mean that such technological choice is easy or common. These may well be exceptions to general historical patterns.[152] Furthermore, this does not mean that the mobilization, exertion, or direction of such agency is always a straightforward matter, or that all such exertions are necessarily wise or societally beneficial. Indeed, even strong cases of technological restraint were not always deliberate—or, if deliberate, well-considered.

Nonetheless, these cases highlight the potential role that many societal actors and factors can play in prompting, directing, or even halting change in technology. Indeed, researchers have begun to increasingly scrutinize the circumstances under which public authorities and private actors have decided to abandon the development of AI systems.[153]

Given this, many legal scholars have argued that technology law 'emphasizes the possibility of purposeful intervention in the iterative and co-constructive relationship between law and technology'.[154] However, even as they claim that law has a significant role to play in shaping the direction of innovation, such scholars also recognize that there are a range of (informational, political, institutional) bounds to the ways in which legal systems may adapt in response to any given technological change. As noted by Crootof and Ard:

> every opportunity to consciously and intentionally shift the path of legal evolution is bounded. On the front end, the known unknowns of a technology's

[151] Kirtchik (n 150).

[152] Mustafa Suleyman and Michael Bhaskar, *The Coming Wave: Technology, Power, and the Twenty-First Century's Greatest Dilemma* (Crown 2023).

[153] Joanna Redden and others, 'Automating Public Services: Learning from Cancelled Systems' (Carnegie UK 2022) <https://www.carnegieuktrust.org.uk/publications/automating-public-services-learning-from-cancelled-systems/> accessed 13 October 2022; Nari Johnson and others, 'The Fall of an Algorithm: Characterizing the Dynamics Toward Abandonment', *Proceedings of the 2024 ACM Conference on Fairness, Accountability, and Transparency* (Association for Computing Machinery 2024) <https://dl.acm.org/doi/10.1145/3630106.3658910> accessed 13 June 2024.

[154] Crootof and Ard (n 25) 355 (continuing by noting '[e]ach legal uncertainty is an opportunity for a legal actor to shape the further development of the law, and every resolution of that uncertainty—regardless of how apparently simple or excruciatingly difficult—impacts how the law evolves. While a legal actor's influence is most apparent when a new law is created or an older one invalidated, a decision to maintain the status quo can have equally influential implications and broader ripple effects for the distribution of power').

> possible beneficial or negative social effects may chill regulatory action; meanwhile the technology's architecture, the established legal structures, and the procedural and institutional constraints on different legal actors limit the range of possible action. On the back end, due in part to the speed of technological development and its impact on social norms, legal actors may only have a short period to make determinative regulatory moves before path dependence, lock-in, and stabilization make shifting the course of both law and future technological development more difficult.[155]

Given this, we do not need to envision technology as some entirely autonomous, external, or irresistible force to nonetheless recognize situations in which sociotechnical systems can exert patterned effects in society. In some cases they can lock in self-reinforcing technological trajectories,[156] such as the 'hardware lotteries' which, it has been argued, drove much of the direction of early AI research towards exploring symbolic AI systems over connectionist approaches,[157] because the former were more easily implemented on the then-available computing hardware.

Moreover, as noted by Dafoe, an apparent freedom of choice at the micro level of technological development need not rule out the appearance of gradual technological—and associated political—trends at the macro level.[158] He has as such proposed the mechanism of 'military-economic adaptationism', as a special case of a general theory of sociotechnical selectionism, to reconcile and integrate these facially contradictory accounts of the range of technological choice available at the micro and macro-levels.[159] For instance, under this macrohistorical view, competitive pressures that arise under international anarchy have historically constrained the range of viable domestic institutions that states could adopt to those adaptations that do not impose a significant competitive disadvantage; however, major changes in competitive technologies can end up altering the relative competitiveness of different state forms, allowing (or forcing) societies to make new institutional choices.[160]

The military–economic adaptationist account does not support 'radical social constructivism',[161] where technological forms and their societal effects are entirely subsumed to social processes or human choice.[162] Still, it does assume there can

[155] ibid.

[156] Giovanni Dosi, 'Technological Paradigms and Technological Trajectories' (1982) 11 Research Policy 147 ('the pattern of "normal" problem solving activity (i.e. of "progress") on the ground of a technological paradigm').

[157] Sara Hooker, 'The Hardware Lottery' (2021) 64 Communications of the ACM 58.

[158] Dafoe, 'On Technological Determinism' (n 64) 12–16.

[159] ibid.

[160] Morgan MacInnes, Ben Garfinkel, and Allan Dafoe, 'Anarchy as Architect: Competitive Pressure, Technology, and the Internal Structure of States' (2024) 68 International Studies Quarterly sqae111.

[161] Dafoe, 'On Technological Determinism' (n 64) 4.

[162] ibid 23.

be scope for some technological choice through human agency and institutions. However, it also raises concerns that, in the absence of strong multilateral coordination or (technological) defensive advantage, competitive dynamics can undercut deliberate sociotechnical choice, or limit their reach, producing 'evolutionary futures' where societies develop in historical (social and technological) directions that are not clearly or explicitly chosen by—or even desirable to—any individual actor.[163]

Given all this, the precise question of what produces, constrains, or directs change in technology—and how we could do so for AI—is a valuable one, and, in the case of AI, remains still relatively under-studied.[164]

4.3.2.2 How technology changes society: three assumptions

However, in the rest of this chapter, I will focus more on the second facet of technological change: *change from technology* in society. This shifts analysis from the question of what societal choices or dynamics shape technological pathways, to the downstream question of how, once a technology develops along a certain pathway or trajectory, it may serve as a source of new human capabilities—and a driver of change throughout society.

In doing so, and in considering global technology governance architectures, we should eschew any pure ontology, whether rationalist, constructivist, or material–contextual.[165] Rather, we should draw on an intermediate, mixed approach, that can reckon with the intersecting roles of all three factors. This perspective does not assume linear, unidirectional, or hard determinist effects of technology on human society or law, but does make the following three relatively modest assumptions about their interactions.

In the first place, it assumes a form of *technological politics*, a soft form of technological determinism which holds that choices made and inscribed in sociotechnical systems can have pervasive and lasting socio-political effects.[166] This is not a controversial view—scholars from a wide range of fields, and especially in STS, have long held that 'artefacts have politics',[167] and similar assumptions have long

[163] For instance, see Guive Assadi, 'Will Humanity Choose Its Future?' (2023) <https://philarchive.org/rec/ASSWHC> accessed 18 February 2025.

[164] Excepting Allan Dafoe, 'AI Governance: A Research Agenda' (Center for the Governance of AI, Future of Humanity Institute 2018) 15–33 <https://www.fhi.ox.ac.uk/govaiagenda/> accessed 12 March 2025; Ross Gruetzemacher and others, 'Forecasting AI Progress: A Research Agenda' [2020] arXiv:2008.01848 [cs] <http://arxiv.org/abs/2008.01848> accessed 11 August 2020.

[165] As Daniel Deudney argues, when considering the prospects of large-scale societal change stemming from rapid technological progress, 'it is vital to employ hybrid or mixed ontologies and to eschew the quest for a pure, or nearly pure, ontology'. Daniel Deudney, 'Turbo Change: Accelerating Technological Disruption, Planetary Geopolitics, and Architectonic Metaphors' (2018) 20 International Studies Review 223, 228; Compare also Dafoe, 'On Technological Determinism' (n 64) 23. For a discussion of rationalist and constructivist accounts in international relations, see also Chapter 6.

[166] Dafoe, 'On Technological Determinism' (n 64) 7.

[167] Langdon Winner, 'Do Artifacts Have Politics?' (1980) 109 Daedalus 121. Though his famous examples might be apocryphal; see also Steve Woolgar and Geoff Cooper, 'Do Artefacts Have Ambivalence? Moses' Bridges, Winner's Bridges and Other Urban Legends in S&TS' (1999) 29 Social

underpinned the field of technology law.[168] This assumption simply speaks to the idea that technologies can embody particular norms—either because they are used in a regulatory fashion, or because they inadvertently advantage particular societal forms, institutions, or value systems over others[169]—and that consequently they may induce shifts in widely held values.[170] For instance, a military–economic adaptationist perspective notes how the historical emergence of different competitive technologies contributed, indirectly but structurally, to the prevalence of new societal arrangements that variably improved (ironwork, ramming warships, industrial revolution) or degraded (agriculture, bronzeworking, chariots) human welfare for large parts of the population, through their effects on societies' material wealth, labour economy, and distribution of political power.[171]

In the second place, another assumption is the notion of technological *unintended consequences*—the argument that, as Dafoe puts it, '[d]ue to the lack of foresight or concern by the designer, or the sheer unpredictability of complex sociotechnical processes, unintended consequences can arise that fundamentally shape social relations'.[172] The argument here is simply that many of the longer-term, second or third-order consequences of technological choices or capabilities can be unforeseeable or 'complex'. This holds across different scales of analysis: at the operational level, many technologies, including AI systems, can be prone to cascading 'normal accidents'.[173] At the societal level, technologies such as AI—and

Studies of Science 433. Bernward Joerges, 'Do Politics Have Artefacts?' [2016] 29(3) Social Studies of Science 411.

[168] Calo, 'The Scale and the Reactor' (n 92). This was in particular seen in the influential early 'cyberlaw' work of Lawrence Lessig and others, in exploring the role of (computer) 'code' and (build) 'architecture' as distinct regulatory modalities which can embody legal goals insofar as they can be deployed to shape human behaviour in service of those normative, political, or regulatory goals. See also Lessig (n 14); Lawrence Lessig, *Code: And Other Laws of Cyberspace, Version 2.0* (2nd rev edn, Basic Books 2006) <https://upload.wikimedia.org/wikipedia/commons/f/fd/Code_v2.pdf> accessed 18 March 2025.

[169] MacInnes, Garfinkel, and Dafoe (n 160).

[170] See also JKG Hopster and others, 'Pistols, Pills, Pork and Ploughs: The Structure of Technomoral Revolutions' [2022] Inquiry 1; Hopster and Maas (n 27). For example, Iain Morris has famously suggested that the different technologies of energy capture available to societies throughout history primed and affected their prevailing value systems. Ian Morris and others, *Foragers, Farmers, and Fossil Fuels: How Human Values Evolve* (Stephen Macedo ed, Updated edn, Princeton University Press 2015); though for a critique, see also Alberto Bisin, 'The Evolution of Value Systems: A Review Essay on Ian Morris's Foragers, Farmers, and Fossil Fuels' (2017) 55 Journal of Economic Literature 1122. For a different version of this argument, exploring the relation of different forms of agriculture (specifically hoe agriculture versus plough agriculture) with gender inequality, see also Alberto Alesina, Paola Giuliano, and Nathan Nunn, 'On the Origins of Gender Roles: Women and the Plough' (2013) 128 Quarterly Journal of Economics 469.

[171] MacInnes, Garfinkel, and Dafoe (n 160).

[172] Dafoe, 'On Technological Determinism' (n 64) 8.

[173] Matthijs M Maas, 'Regulating for "Normal AI Accidents": Operational Lessons for the Responsible Governance of Artificial Intelligence Deployment', *Proceedings of the 2018 AAAI/ACM Conference on AI, Ethics, and Society* (Association for Computing Machinery 2018) <https://doi.org/10.1145/3278721.3278766> accessed 8 September 2020.

the environments in which they are developed—display features of complex adaptive systems, including nonlinear growth patterns, emergent phenomena, and cascading effects which can lead to tail risks.[174] This implies that even if we can predict underlying technological trends,[175] policymakers and the public will still face challenges around appropriately predicting the full range of eventual applications and sociotechnical impacts of a given technology.[176]

Finally, this theory assumes *asymmetric governance materiality*, a perhaps inelegant term for the idea that a technology's material features or alleged exceptional qualities are asymmetrically relevant to governance. This captures the notion that while a technology's material characteristics may be less relevant than its resulting sociotechnical changes when we aim to determine whether there is a need for new law, they may nonetheless play a role in determining *how* to tailor effective regulation (i.e. the texture of the technology as governance target).

4.3.3 The Concept of Sociotechnical Change: New Artefacts, Actors, or Activities

With these core concepts and ontologies discussed, we can at last return to the concept of sociotechnical change. In doing so, we can depart from influential work by Lyria Bennett Moses, Rebecca Crootof, and BJ Ard.

In developing her 'Theory of Law and Technological Change',[177] Bennett Moses has noted that questions of 'law and technology' are in fact rarely if ever directly about technological progress itself, whether incremental or far-reaching. Instead, she argues that lawyers and legal scholars are primarily focused on questions of 'how the law ought to relate to *activities, entities, and relationships made possible* by a new technology'.[178] This shifts the focus onto patterns of 'socio-technical

[174] Noam Kolt, Michal Shur-Ofry, and Reuven Cohen, 'Lessons from Complexity Theory for AI Governance' (arXiv, 7 January 2025) <http://arxiv.org/abs/2502.00012> accessed 19 February 2025.

[175] To be sure, certain forms of basic trend forecasting may actually be somewhat robustly possible. For instance, see Béla Nagy and others, 'Statistical Basis for Predicting Technological Progress' (2013) 8 PLOS ONE e52669 (reviewing the costs and production trends for 62 different technologies, and finding significant regularities in exponential increases in production and decreases in costs across many of these domains). However, going beyond these trends to forecast the societal flowthrough effects may run into significantly greater problems, especially if predictions are made by reference to (implicit or explicit) historical analogies. Peter N Stearns, 'Forecasting the Future: Historical Analogies and Technological Determinism' (1983) 5 The Public Historian 31. Of course, while most of these prediction methodologies face challenges, some may have future potential. See David Owen and Tamay Besiroglu, 'Challenges in Predicting AI Automation' (Epoch 2023) <https://epochai.org/blog/challenges-in-predicting-ai-automation> accessed 6 January 2024 (reviewing different approaches to predicting AI automation of tasks in the economy, and their challenges and empirical track record to date).

[176] This will be discussed in more detail in Section 4.5.

[177] Bennett Moses, 'Why Have a Theory of Law and Technological Change?' (n 63).

[178] ibid 591 (emphasis added).

change':[179] instances where changes in certain technologies translate to new ways of carrying out old conduct, or create entirely new forms of conduct, entities, or new ways of being or connecting to others.[180]

In this way, technology law does not take the technology-centric approach to regulation discussed previously. Questions over whether or how to govern technologies are articulated not with reference to a pre-set list of (sufficiently) 'new' technologies,[181] but rather aiming to be relatively technology-neutral in their approach, of relevance to understanding many types of present and future innovations in terms of their social consequences.

Accordingly, we can define 'sociotechnical change' as the processes by which developments in technology extend the capabilities of some or all actors—allowing them new ways of carrying out old conduct or enabling new types of conduct altogether. It is this functional understanding of sociotechnical change that informs more fruitful analysis of when and why we require regulation for new technological or scientific progress, because it allows a more systematic examination of which developments in AI technology are relevant for the purposes of law and governance.[182] In doing so, it meets the growing calls for frameworks that can better understand AI systems' impacts or harms within their broader context.[183]

However, some ambiguities remain: what types of sociotechnical changes (e.g. new possible behaviours or states of being) actually give rise to a rationale for a governance response? When a technology creates a new opportunity for behaviour, is it the mere possibility that constitutes a rationale for regulation? Or is it the actual appearance of such behaviour? What happens if the sociotechnical change produced by a technology is not (just) directed at society, but also at law or legal process directly? Can sociotechnical changes be anticipated?

We therefore require a more granular understanding of the dynamics of sociotechnical change, exploring how, when, and why such changes constitute a rationale for governance; when such changes can be anticipated and are best regulated; and how such developments are best approached as regulatory targets.

[179] ibid 591–592; Bennett Moses, 'Recurring Dilemmas' (n 68).

[180] In a related account, Crootof and Ard have suggested that 'technologies give rise to legal uncertainties by foregrounding unanticipated artifacts, actors, and activities'. Crootof and Ard (n 25) 357.

[181] Lyria Bennett Moses, 'Regulating in the Face of Sociotechnical Change' in Roger Brownsword, Eloise Scotford, and Karen Yeung (eds), *The Oxford Handbook of Law, Regulation, and Technology* (2017) 576 ('This paper does not play the dangerous game of articulating a finite list of important technological fields that are likely to influence the future, likely to enable further technological innovation, or likely to pose the challenges to law and regulation as any such list would change over time').

[182] In doing so, this perspective can contribute insights to all three dimensions of technological 'disruption' highlighted by Brownsword, Scotford, and Yeung—'legal disruption, regulatory disruption, and the challenge of constructing regulatory environments that are fit for purpose in light of technological disruption'. See Brownsword, Scotford, and Yeung (n 74) 7.

[183] Weidinger and others, 'Sociotechnical Safety Evaluation of Generative AI Systems' (n 47).

4.4 Why Regulate? Sociotechnical Change as Rationale for Governance

For the purposes of governing AI, it is key to understand the conditions under which specific advances or uses in AI give rise to sociotechnical changes of a sufficiently disruptive character that they create a governance rationale.

4.4.1 Thresholds: Sociotechnical Change and Affordances

When and why do AI capabilities become a governance problem that warrants legal or regulatory solutions? It is important to recognize that not all new breakthroughs, capabilities, or even use cases of a new technology will by definition produce the sort of 'sociotechnical change' that requires changes in or responses by governance systems. Indeed, Lyria Bennett Moses has argued that, from a regulatory perspective, '[t]echnology is rarely the only "thing" that is regulated and the presence of technology or even new technology alone does not justify a call for new regulation'.[184] In doing so, she calls for a shift in approach from 'regulating technology' to 'adjusting law and regulation for sociotechnical change'.[185] This has been echoed by other technology law scholars: for instance, Crootof and Ard suggest that 'the fundamental challenge of techlaw is not how to best regulate novel technologies, but rather how to best address familiar forms of legal uncertainty in new sociolegal contexts'.[186]

In practical terms, this relates to the observation that new social (and therefore governance) opportunities or challenges are not created by the mere fact of a technology being conceived, or even prototyped, but rather by them being translated into new 'affordances' for some actor.[187] Such affordances can be new types of behaviour, entities, or relationships that were never previously possible but which are now, in principle, available to actors.[188] It is only if and when these affordances are both recognized and seized upon that one might speak of sociotechnical change.

[184] Bennett Moses, 'Regulating in the Face of Sociotechnical Change' (n 181) 575.

[185] ibid 574.

[186] Crootof and Ard (n 25) 349.

[187] The original concept of 'affordances' derived from the work of ecological psychologist James G Gibson, in the context of the relationship between an animal and its environment. James J Gibson, 'The Ecological Approach to the Visual Perception of Pictures' (1978) 11 Leonardo 227. However, in the context of technology, an 'affordance' is understood as 'a relationship between the properties of an object and the capabilities of the agent that determine just how the object could possibly be used'. Donald A Norman, *The Design of Everyday Things* (revised and expanded edn, Basic Books 2013) 11. This concept of affordances, and its link to 'legal disruption', are both more fully explored in Liu and others (n 24).

[188] Bennett Moses, 'Why Have a Theory of Law and Technological Change?' (n 63) 591 ('When lawyers claim to be interested in issues surrounding law and technology, it is usually related to questions of how the law ought to relate to activities, entities, and relationships made possible by a new technology. As technology changes, we can do things, make things, and form connections that were not previously practicable').

A similar functional argument has been made directly in the context of regulatory questions around AI and robotics. For instance, in the early 'robolaw' debates, Balkin emphasized the need for examining a new technology's societal and legal 'salience' in a particular context, rather than trying to discern or pin down any 'essential features'.[189] This approach therefore emphasizes not just the creation of a new affordance which makes a certain capability-space accessible, but rather the *usage* of a technology, by particular actors, in particular social contexts, that results in societal change.[190]

The main insight is that for the purposes of law and governance, relevant technological changes are not prima facie about changes to 'inputs' or 'core science' (such as fundamental theory) alone, except insofar as these translate to (anticipated) changes to actors' capabilities that would result in new societal changes. Technologies pose a challenge for societies (and therefore governance) not because they are intrinsically possible, nor even because they are postulated or discovered, but because they expand the action space for some or all actors, in directions that are harmful or of concern in some way or on some regulatory grounds,[191] or in directions that would be beneficial if and only if a certain minimal degree of cooperation or coordination were assured.[192]

4.4.2 Types and Magnitude of Disruptive Sociotechnical Change

How does technological change translate into sociotechnical change? What types of capabilities might be involved? When would these changes be disruptive to law?[193]

[189] Jack M Balkin, 'The Path of Robotics Law' (2015) 6 California Law Review Circuit 17. This approach stands in contrast to that of Ryan Calo, who seeks to distil 'essential qualities' of robotics as regulatory target: Calo, 'Robotics and the Lessons of Cyberlaw' (n 4).

[190] One caveat: it should be recognized that, especially in an international context, a technology can drive considerable change and political disruption even if it is not (yet) actually deployed, if it is (mistakenly) *perceived* to already be in (wide) usage. Consider for instance the US misperceptions, during the early Cold War, of a looming 'Missile Gap' with the Soviet Union. Daniel Ellsberg, *The Doomsday Machine: Confessions of a Nuclear War Planner* (Bloomsbury USA 2017); Haydn Belfield and Christian Ruhl, 'Why Policy Makers Should Beware Claims of New "Arms Races"' (*Bulletin of the Atomic Scientists*, 14 July 2022) <https://thebulletin.org/2022/07/why-policy-makers-should-beware-claims-of-new-arms-races/> accessed 10 January 2024.

[191] See also Luciano Floridi, 'Energy, Risks, and Metatechnology' (2011) 24 Philosophy & Technology 89, 89 (arguing that 'technologies lower constraints and expand affordances [and as such] continuously redesign the feasibility space of the agents who enjoy them'). For an exploration that takes this idea to the limit, see also Nick Bostrom, 'The Vulnerable World Hypothesis' (2019) 10 Global Policy 455 (exploring the hypothesis that societies may at some point hit upon technological capabilities that expand the feasible action-space into a domain that is so catastrophic and uncontainable that the default outcome would be global disaster).

[192] This point also highlights how new technological change is, of course, not categorically, exclusively, or predominantly problematic, but can also create novel opportunities—which, however, at times may require particular forms of coordination to be fully realized.

[193] This anticipates the discussion of the concept of governance disruption in Chapter 5.

The clearest, most obvious category of disruptive sociotechnical change involves *absolute* and *categorical* changes to some actor's affordances. This is when progress 'unlocks' certain new capabilities or behaviour which were previously simply impossible for anyone, but which now enable behaviour that has never been seen (and potentially has never been considered) before. For instance, Crootof and Ard note how new surveillance tools have come to regularly enable government agencies to monitor citizens through new avenues, or from new locations in space that are potentially uncovered by established privacy protections.[194]

More commonly, there will be situations where technological change drives more *relative* sociotechnical changes.[195] Here, technologies are disruptive not just in the absolute sense of unlocking unprecedented capabilities, but rather in a relative sense, compared to the preceding status quo.[196]

One version of such relative capability change would involve situations where technological progress and innovation yields techniques (e.g. advanced video editing or generation; customized spear-phishing email generation;[197] easily useable cryptographic tools) which *lower the thresholds* or use preconditions for a certain capability (e.g. producing high-quality fake media; hacking at scale; encrypted communications). Notably, these capabilities were previously already in reach for some (well-resourced or trained) actors, but have consequently become achievable for a much larger or more diverse set of actors. Another version of this could involve developments that *scale up* the reach of certain existing capabilities.[198]

Likewise, we can anticipate such technologies driving *positional* changes. This might be seen clearly on the international level, where certain uses of AI could drive shifts in which particular actors (e.g. the US, EU, or China) are dominant or exert the most power within the international system while leaving the 'rules' or dynamics of that system more or less unaltered.[199]

194 Crootof and Ard (n 25) 358.

195 Crootof and Ard at 358–359 ('uncertainty may stem from activities that were once rare but have become newly prevalent due to technological changes that minimize a practical or market barrier').

196 Matthijs M Maas, 'International Law Does Not Compute: Artificial Intelligence and The Development, Displacement or Destruction of the Global Legal Order' (2019) 20 Melbourne Journal of International Law 29, 33 (reviewing various types of global disruptions that AI could create, in terms of positional changes, structural changes among types of actors, or changes to how actors conceive of or pursue their various interests).

197 Julian Hazell, 'Large Language Models Can Be Used to Effectively Scale Spear Phishing Campaigns' (arXiv, 12 May 2023) <http://arxiv.org/abs/2305.06972> accessed 6 October 2023.

198 See also Miles Brundage and others, 'The Malicious Use of Artificial Intelligence: Forecasting, Prevention, and Mitigation' [2018] arXiv:1802.07228 [cs] <http://arxiv.org/abs/1802.07228> accessed 21 February 2018.

199 For instance, see Alina Polyakova, 'Weapons of the Weak: Russia and AI-Driven Asymmetric Warfare' (*Brookings*, 15 November 2018) <https://www.brookings.edu/research/weapons-of-the-weak-russia-and-ai-driven-asymmetric-warfare/> accessed 13 January 2019. Elsewhere, Schneier and Farrell have argued that democracies, considered as information systems, are structurally more vulnerable to disinformation attacks than are autocracies. Henry Farrell and Bruce Schneier, 'Common-Knowledge Attacks on Democracy' (Berkman Klein Center 2018) Research Publication 2018–7 <https://papers.ssrn.com/abstract=3273111> accessed 13 January 2019.

However, disruptive sociotechnical change can also manifest through changes in the nature or *structural dynamics* of that (international) society. For instance, AI could enable certain uses that shift the relative balance of power or influence between *types* of actors (e.g. away from states and towards non-state actors). Significantly, technologies do not need to be qualitatively novel in order to drive such structural shifts.[200] Moreover, sociotechnical change can manifest itself through shifts in the *means by* which certain actors seek to exercise power. For instance, it might shift the emphasis in interstate competition from 'hard' military force to computational propaganda, or from multilateral engagement to increasing bilateral 'lawfare'.[201] It could even alter the *norms or identities* of actors, and thereby changing the *terms* by which they conceive of their goals and orient their behaviour—for instance shifting how actors come to conceive of, measure, and pursue their power or (national) interest (e.g. territory, population, oil reserves, soft power, global public opinion, data, computing power).[202]

To be certain, any definition of relative disruption is leaky, and contestable. Establishing an appropriate baseline against which to measure or mark whether an impact of AI has been 'disruptive' to existing societal dynamics remains a critical open question.[203]

4.4.3 Sociotechnical Change and Governance Rationales

More to the point, which sociotechnical changes driven by a new (AI) capability are so sufficiently impactful that they constitute governance rationales?

To be certain, many technological innovations do not clear this bar, even if from a scientific or engineering standpoint they involve considerable material or technological alterations to the state of the art, because they do not yield large sociotechnical changes.[204] In other cases, technologies do produce large

[200] Cummings and others (n 32) iv ('[t]echnological change does not have to be dramatic or sudden to create meaningful shifts in power balances or social structures').

[201] Charles Dunlap, 'Lawfare Today: A Perspective' [2008] Yale Journal of International Affairs 146, 146–148 (crediting new communications technologies and media with increasing the scope, velocity and effectiveness of 'lawfare' efforts aimed at eroding public support for conflicts). Discussed in Crootof, 'Regulating New Weapons Technology' (n 1) 6–7.

[202] Maas, 'International Law Does Not Compute' (n 196) 32.

[203] Moreover, it may also be difficult to draw a clear line between disruption that is unambiguously 'technological' (directly driven by AI capabilities) and indirect disruption that appears 'non-technological' (for example, gradual changes to public values such as the appreciation of data privacy), or at most as a side effect of the use of AI. This of course pertains to the more general difficulty of pinning down a definition of 'technology', or drawing a clear line to distinguish 'technology-driven change' from more general societal change. ibid.

[204] There is an additional distinction that could be drawn: between cases where the regulatory concern is over the novelty of a particular *process* (e.g. synthetic biology) involved in the technological capability, and those where it is about the novelty of the resulting *outputs* or *applications* (e.g. 3D printing). This may have implications for whether we consider the technology to be uncovered by existing regulation and give rise to a governance rationale. I thank Roger Brownsword for this observation.

sociotechnical changes, but these are not relevant per one of the regulatory criteria discussed later. Nonetheless, as the history of law and technology illustrates, there are many types of technological change that do pose new problems and so spur regulation. This turns on an examination of the general rationales for new regulatory interventions.

There are various accounts of when and why regulatory intervention is warranted by the introduction of new technologies. For instance, Beyleveld and Brownsword argue that emerging technologies generally give rise to two kinds of concerns: 'one is that the application of a particular technology might present risks to human health and safety, or to the environment ... and the other is that the technology might be applied in ways that are harmful to moral interests.'[205] However, while these may be the most prominent rationales, the full scope of reasons for regulation may extend further.

Tony Prosser has argued that, in general, regulation has four grounds: '(1) regulation for economic efficiency and market choice, (2) regulation to protect rights, (3) regulation for social solidarity, and (4) regulation as deliberation.'[206] As Lyria Bennett Moses notes, all four of these rationales may certainly become engaged by new technologies.[207] After all, technology can certainly create a site for *new market failures* which warrant regulatory intervention to ensure economic efficiency and market choice, such as in cases where there is a need for the articulation of technical standards to ensure interoperability between new products, or to remedy information inadequacies for consumers. Likewise, new technologies can generate many *new risks or harms*—either to human health or the environment, or to moral interests—which create a need for regulation to protect the rights of certain affected parties (e.g. restrictions of new weapons; the ban on human cloning).[208] Third, new technologies can create concern about *social solidarity*, as seen in concerns over the 'digital divide' at both a national and an international level, creating a need for regulation to ensure adequate inclusion. Finally, new technologies can create sites or pressures for the exertion of *proper democratic deliberation* over the design or development pathways of technologies.[209]

In each of these cases, however, Bennett Moses notes that it is not the appearance of 'technology' per se that provides a special rationale for governance, above and beyond the basic social changes (e.g. potential market failures; risks to rights; threats to solidarity; democratic deficits) that are at stake.[210] As such, the primary

[205] Deryck Beyleveld and Roger Brownsword, 'Emerging Technologies, Extreme Uncertainty, and the Principle of Rational Precautionary Reasoning' (2012) 4 Law, Innovation & Technology 35, 35.

[206] Tony Prosser, *The Regulatory Enterprise: Government, Regulation, and Legitimacy* (Oxford University Press 2010) 18. See also Bennett Moses, 'Regulating in the Face of Sociotechnical Change' (n 181) 578.

[207] Bennett Moses, 'Regulating in the Face of Sociotechnical Change' (n 181) 578.

[208] ibid 579–580.

[209] ibid 581–583.

[210] ibid 583.

regulatory concern is over the emergence of the 'sociotechnical' effects that occur. This conceptual shift can help address one limit that regulatory or governance strategies encounter if they focus too much or too narrowly on technology. As Bennett Moses argues:

> treating technology as the object of regulation can lead to undesirable technology specificity in the formulation of rules or regulatory regimes. If regulators ask how to regulate a specific technology, the result will be a regulatory regime targeting that particular technology. This can be inefficient because of the focus on a subset of a broader problem and the tendency towards obsolescence.[211]

Consequently, this lens helps keep in explicit focus the specific *rationales* for governance in each use case of AI: on what grounds and when regulation is needed and justified?

These four accounts of rationales are valuable as a foundation. However, it may be analytically valuable to draw a more granular distinction between harms to human health, or harms to moral interests.[212] Finally, along with those five direct rationales, I suggest there may be one indirect category. That is, these first categories all concern rationales for governance to step in to respond to sociotechnical changes affecting society (i.e. the regulatees) directly. However, there might also be cases where some sociotechnical change presents some risks directly to the existing legal order charged with mitigating the prior risks. In such cases, sociotechnical change can produce a threat to regulation, spurring an indirect governance rationale. In the context of AI, for instance, this governance rationale would focus in on the regulation of AI systems that are particularly disruptive to legal categories (in order to maintain coherence), or on the regulation of AI systems that are themselves used in or for regulatory purposes.[213]

If we draw together these accounts, we can then speak of a governance rationale for a certain new AI system or application whenever the use of these capabilities drives sociotechnical changes (new ways of carrying out old behaviour, or new behaviours, relations or entities) which result in one or more of the following situations:

(1) possible market failures;
(2) new risks to human health or safety;
(3) new risks to moral interests, rights, or values;

[211] ibid 584.
[212] Following Beyleveld and Brownsword (n 205).
[213] What, in Chapter 5, I will call 'governance displacement' (and the sub-types of legal *automation* in rule-making, in compliance enforcement, and in the *substitution* of regulatory modalities). Note, there is hypothetically a third level, which focuses on the (recursive) regulation of hypothetical AI 'safety' or 'audit' systems which could be used to regulate (or check) AI systems deployed for primary regulatory purposes (e.g. adjudication). This would constitute the use of regulatory AI to regulate regulatory AI systems. I thank Roger Brownsword for this suggestion.

(4) new threats to social solidarity;
(5) new threats to democratic process;
(6) new threats to the coherence, efficacy or integrity of the existing governance system charged with mitigating these prior direct risks (1–5) (governance disruption).

This is not to say that these rationales apply the same way in all contexts. Indeed, they may be weighted differently across distinct legal systems. For instance, all six of these challenges surely appear at the international level—diverse developments both technological and social can produce international market failures, risks to human health or the environment, challenges to rights, threats to (global) social solidarity, democratic process, or direct threats to the international legal order. However, depending on one's assumptions, that need not mean that all six rationales might be equally relevant or in scope for international norms. For instance, it has been argued that the state-centric international law system 'is primarily preoccupied with finding the answers that are required to separate the powers of the sovereign states and to ensure the maintenance of order and stability'.[214] That means that traditional international law might be particularly attuned to AI-driven sociotechnical changes that result in risks to human life or challenges to human rights. Conversely, the international law system might be less intrinsically concerned with addressing international market failures.[215] Nonetheless, from a broader perspective of global governance—especially one that emphasizes the need for international legal systems to evolve in order to better address commons problems[216]—all six rationales can and should be considered at the global level.[217] As such, while taking into consideration the different legal contexts, this approach can still inform the potential grounds for AI governance globally.

Moreover, a distinct value of this sociotechnical perspective is that it allows a broader view on the governance rationales raised by AI, as these arise across the

[214] Anders Henriksen, *International Law* (3rd edn, Oxford University Press 2021) 17–18.

[215] That is not to say, of course, that international law lacks regimes or norms aimed at addressing potential market failures. However, the mere possibility of a market failure as a result of a lack of standardization may not offer the same strong rationale for intervention under international law as would a violation of human rights, or a threat to international peace and security.

[216] See for instance Nico Krisch, 'The Decay of Consent: International Law in an Age of Global Public Goods' (2014) 108 American Journal of International Law 1; Anne van Aaken, 'Is International Law Conducive To Preventing Looming Disasters?' (2016) 7 Global Policy 81; J Pauwelyn, RA Wessel, and J Wouters, 'When Structures Become Shackles: Stagnation and Dynamics in International Lawmaking' (2014) 25 European Journal of International Law 733.

[217] This can be seen in various soft law instruments; see for instance the emphasis on crossing the digital divide in various UN initiatives on AI. United Nations General Assembly, 'Road Map for Digital Cooperation: Implementation of the Recommendations of the High-Level Panel on Digital Cooperation' para 14 <https://undocs.org/pdf?symbol=en/A/74/821> accessed 1 September 2020. High-level Panel on Digital Cooperation, 'Report of the Secretary-General: Roadmap for Digital Cooperation' (UN Secretary-General's High-Level Panel on Digital Cooperation 2020) <https://www.un.org/en/content/digital-cooperation-roadmap/assets/pdf/Roadmap_for_Digital_Cooperation_EN.pdf> accessed 12 June 2020.

AI stack.[218] That is, this approach allows us to consider not just cases where governance rationales are created at the end point of the use of one specific AI system, but also those where such rationales are created through the aggregate collective and systemic effects of many AI systems, as well as where such rationales are raised through harms that occur upstream in such systems' development—ranging from upstream collective harms around resource extraction or exploitative labour practices, to risks that result at the model training stage for advanced systems.

4.5 When to Regulate? Anticipating Sociotechnical Change

A regulatory perspective focused on sociotechnical change also throws into stark relief the epistemic challenges around understanding the full set of governance rationales engaged by a technology, either in advance or even after the technology has seen widespread use. This has implications for when we should ideally seek to pursue regulation.

4.5.1 Epistemic Hurdles to an Anticipatory Approach

It may sometimes appear easy to identify new AI capabilities demonstrated in a lab, or applications that are seeing deployment, and attempt to reason forward to various societal challenges. However, while this approach is legitimate and necessary in attempting to understand the wavefront of emerging capabilities that are on the horizon, it can only take us so far. For instance, in 2019, as OpenAI released its GPT-2 language model, it predicted a set of societal impacts and misuses.[219] Five years later, many generative AI systems were certainly subject to these anticipated misuses: however, the anticipated timelines, scale of use, and the severity of their effects were off, to larger and smaller extents.[220]

These epistemic challenges around technological change occur because sociotechnical impacts can often take longer to manifest, may materialize in unexpected ways, and often may not give off clear, unambiguous, or incontrovertible

[218] For a similar argument, see also Chris Thomas and others, 'The Case for a Broader Approach to AI Assurance: Addressing "Hidden" Harms in the Development of Artificial Intelligence' (11 December 2023) <https://papers.ssrn.com/abstract=4660737> accessed 13 January 2024.

[219] Alec Radford and others, 'Better Language Models and Their Implications' (*OpenAI Blog*, 14 February 2019) <https://blog.openai.com/better-language-models/> accessed 17 February 2019 ('We can also imagine the application of these models for malicious purposes, including the following (or other applications we can't yet anticipate): generate misleading news articles, impersonate others online, automate the production of abusive or faked content to post on social media, automate the production of spam/phishing content').

[220] Jack Clark, 'Import AI 375: GPT-2 Five Years Later; Decentralized Training; New Ways of Thinking about Consciousness and AI' (*Import AI*, 3 June 2024) <https://importai.substack.com/p/import-ai-375-gpt-2-five-years-later> accessed 5 June 2024.

signals even long after they have arrived. Indeed, technology law scholars have frequently noted that the difficulties around predicting the trajectory and societal salience of a new technology yield practical problems not just for scholars but also for policymakers.[221]

Indeed, while it can be valuable to draw lessons from the best available historical analogies around a technology's development pathway, dissemination trajectory, and societal impacts,[222] there are also limits to trying to forecast future impacts on the basis of such analogies, as it can be hard to identify which analogies are most appropriate.[223]

At the same time, however, even patience may not always reward with clarity, nor result in consensus. Indeed, often there is sustained contestation over the exact societal implications of a technology's deployment, even decades after its development and use. This is especially the case where the technology touches on cornerstone ethical or political questions. This means that there are considerable challenges to assessing, in a timely fashion and to a sufficient level of reliability, the relative effects, types, or prominence of sociotechnical change that result from new technological capabilities—or the governance rationales these might raise.

4.5.1.1 Anticipatory imaginaries around cyberwar and biohacking

Indeed, there will often be some uncertainty over a technology's societal effects, even years after its initial development and deployment.

Take early anticipatory imaginaries around cyberwar. While some early accounts of digital technology announced the imminence of catastrophic terrorist cyber-attacks on state infrastructures,[224] many scholars have since concluded that such analyses overstated the (kinetic) threat from 'cyberwar', as well as the lasting ability of small non-state actors (i.e. the 'lone hacker') to carry out such attacks.[225]

[221] For instance, Ballard and Calo note that these challenges include 'staleness' (where outdated rules nevertheless persist through inertia or now entrenched interests); 'waste' (as a result of regulatory overinvestment in a particular instantiation of a technology that has become superseded); and 'policy paralysis', which risks 'abdicating governmental responsibility to channel technology in the public interest'. Stephanie Ballard and Ryan Calo, 'Taking Futures Seriously: Forecasting as Method in Robotics Law and Policy' (2019) 1 <https://robots.law.miami.edu/2019/wp-content/uploads/2019/03/Calo_Taking-Futures-Seriously.pdf> accessed 2 April 2019.

[222] See also Korzekwa (n 99); Matthijs Maas, 'Advanced AI Governance: A Literature Review of Problems, Options, and Proposals' (Institute for Law & AI 2023) AI Foundations Report 4 58–85 <https://law-ai.org/advanced-ai-gov-litrev> accessed 10 November 2023 (surveying historical case studies that might provide lessons for understanding the societal impact of AI, and avenues to regulate it).

[223] Stearns (n 175).

[224] John Arquilla and David Ronfeldt, 'Cyberwar Is Coming!' [1992] in John Arquilla and David Ronfeldt (eds), *In Athena's Camp: Preparing for Conflict in the Information Age* (Rand 1995). Though for a more nuanced analysis, see John Stone, 'Cyber War Will Take Place!' (2013) 36 Journal of Strategic Studies 101.

[225] Thomas Rid, *Cyber War Will Not Take Place* (1st edn, Oxford University Press 2013). As Horowitz also notes, 'it is no longer true, and probably never was, that anyone with a computer can successfully launch a cyber attack against a state or sophisticated organization'. Michael C Horowitz, 'Do Emerging

Nonetheless, this view of cyberwar continues to dominate among some policymakers even today.[226]

There are also other examples of early predictions that either were delayed, were never borne out, or continue to be controversial and contested to this day. For instance, while military drones have now seen decades of usage in counterterrorism operations, such as in decapitation strikes against terror or insurgent group leaders, research has long continued to be divided over the actual military efficacy of such drone usage at actually degrading the capacity of insurgent groups and reducing subsequent attacks, especially when weighted against the blowback and costs that result when such strikes are based on faulty intelligence or result in collateral damage and local and international blowback.[227]

In another domain, we can see an overstatement of at least some particular threat models. In the early 2010s, the appearance of Do-It-Yourself (DIY) biohacking technology led to concerns about widespread online access to this technology—which might enable any individual to access technology to create synthetic genomes, and potentially create novel pathogens.[228] However, such discussions often tended to underappreciate the degree to which the DIY biohacking community engaged in effective self-regulation,[229] and this risk has not yet materialized to date. That is not to say that there are no risks deriving from the leading edge of biotechnology;[230] but they may derive from different vectors, capabilities, or applications.

4.5.1.2 Anticipatory imaginaries around AI's democratic impacts

The same dynamics and uncertainty can be seen in debates around emerging AI applications, where there remains considerable uncertainty or controversy around the relative plausibility of not only hypothesized future threat models but also, remarkably, many challenges that are sometimes widely perceived to be well established or imminent.

Military Technologies Matter for International Politics?' (2020) 23 Annual Review of Political Science 385, 394.

226 Horowitz (n 225) 393.

227 ibid 387–389; but see also Joshua A Schwartz, Matthew Fuhrmann, and Michael C Horowitz, 'Do Armed Drones Counter Terrorism, Or Are They Counterproductive? Evidence from Eighteen Countries' (2022) 66 International Studies Quarterly sqac047 (conducting an analysis of drone usage in 18 countries over an 18-year period, to suggest that drones can be effective as a counter-terrorism tool in some cases).

228 See for instance Neel Guha and others, 'AI Regulation Has Its Own Alignment Problem: The Technical and Institutional Feasibility of Disclosure, Registration, Licensing, and Auditing' (2024) 92 George Washington Law Review 1473, 1476–1477 (citing sources).

229 Lalitha S Sundaram, 'Biosafety in DIY-Bio Laboratories: From Hype to Policy: Discussions about Regulating DIY Biology Tend to Ignore the Extent of Self-Regulation and Oversight of DIY Laboratories' (2021) 22 EMBO reports e52506.

230 Luke Kemp and others, 'Bioengineering Horizon Scan 2020' <https://www.repository.cam.ac.uk/handle/1810/305916> accessed 3 June 2020.

As one example, one can consider debates around technological unemployment. While some scholars have warned of far-reaching economic and societal dislocation as an outcome of increasing technological unemployment,[231] it remains unclear to what extent such effects are likely in the near to medium-term.[232]

An even more high-profile example might be found in contemporary debates over the intersection of AI with disinformation. Recent years have seen a significant emerging body of scholarship that has charted the rising challenges that AI poses to democracy.[233] Initially such work focused on algorithmic and 'computational propaganda',[234] before shifting to 'deepfakes' and the role of generative AI.[235]

However, there is live disagreement over whether contemporary incidents should be seen as the early warning shots for a development that will erode the very epistemic foundations of societies,[236] or whether these are instead high-profile but ultimately peripheral incidents that are not representative of actual societal impacts on the margin. For instance, some researchers have suggested that public discourse may be overstating the current democratic threats from 'filter bubbles',[237] 'fake news',[238]

[231] Carl Benedikt Frey and Michael A Osborne, 'The Future of Employment: How Susceptible Are Jobs to Computerisation?' (2017) 114 Technological Forecasting and Social Change 254. See also John Danaher, *Automation and Utopia: Human Flourishing in a World without Work* (Harvard University Press 2019) ch 1.

[232] For instance, Scholl and Hanson have reviewed patterns in job vulnerability metrics between 1999 and 2019 and found 'no evidence yet of a revolution in the patterns or quantity of automation'; where automation did occur, they did not find this to predict changes in either pay or employment. Keller Scholl and Robin Hanson, 'Testing the Automation Revolution Hypothesis' (2020) 193 Economics Letters <https://www.sciencedirect.com/science/article/abs/pii/S0165176520301919> accessed 19 December 2020.

[233] Sarah Kreps and Doug Kriner, 'How AI Threatens Democracy' (2023) 34 Journal of Democracy 122; Sarah E Kreps, Miles McCain and Miles Brundage, 'All the News That's Fit to Fabricate: AI Generated Text as a Tool of Media Misinformation' (Social Science Research Network 2020) SSRN Scholarly Paper ID 3525002 <https://papers.ssrn.com/abstract=3525002> accessed 28 April 2020.

[234] Gillian Bolsover and Philip Howard, 'Computational Propaganda and Political Big Data: Moving Toward a More Critical Research Agenda' (2017) 5 Big Data 273; Bruce Schneier, 'Bots Are Destroying Political Discourse As We Know It' [2020] *The Atlantic* <https://www.theatlantic.com/technology/archive/2020/01/future-politics-bots-drowning-out-humans/604489/> accessed 15 January 2020.

[235] Dipto Barman, Ziyi Guo, and Owen Conlan, 'The Dark Side of Language Models: Exploring the Potential of LLMs in Multimedia Disinformation Generation and Dissemination' (2024) 16 Machine Learning with Applications 100545 (arguing that the advent of LLMs 'can be harnessed to significantly amplify the velocity, variety, and volume of disinformation').

[236] Herbert Lin, 'The Existential Threat from Cyber-Enabled Information Warfare' (2019) 75 Bulletin of the Atomic Scientists 187.

[237] See for example Axel Bruns, *Are Filter Bubbles Real?* (1st edn, Polity 2019).

[238] For instance, contrary to widespread perceptions, computational propaganda likely did not play a large role in swaying the 2016 US election or Brexit vote. Yochai Benkler, Robert Faris, and Hal Roberts, *Network Propaganda: Manipulation, Disinformation, and Radicalization in American Politics* (Oxford University Press 2018). Indeed, 'fake news' likely made up a small minority (6%) of all news consumed in that US election, although it did target small sub-communities intensely, which might produce political effects. Jacob L Nelson and Harsh Taneja, 'The Small, Disloyal Fake News Audience: The Role of Audience Availability in Fake News Consumption' (2018) 20 New Media & Society 3720. Moreover, scholarship has pointed to a range of conceptual and methodological challenges around accurately studying both the scale of misinformation, its causal influence on public beliefs, and the

'online misinformation',[239] or social media 'bots'.[240] And while much early coverage of deepfakes touted their potential misuse for political manipulation,[241] the vast majority of early uses of this technology were for (gendered) harassment instead,[242] in particular targeting celebrities.[243]

Concerns nevertheless continue to grow regarding the effects of deepfakes in political practice, and on democratic elections, especially given the fact that surveys indicate that most people struggle to differentiate between synthetic and authentic content, implying that human perceptual detection capabilities no longer offer effective defences.[244] Indeed, surveys and databases indicate growing trends in political deepfake usage.[245] However, at the same time, it has been suggested that there are many reasons to expect the impacts of these uses to be relatively

resulting political impacts. Sacha Altay, Manon Berriche, and Alberto Acerbi, 'Misinformation on Misinformation: Conceptual and Methodological Challenges' (2023) 9 Social Media + Society 20563051221150412.

[239] Ceren Budak and others, 'Misunderstanding the Harms of Online Misinformation' (2024) 630 Nature 45 (discussing and critiquing three common perceptions—'that average exposure to problematic content is high, that algorithms are largely responsible for this exposure and that social media is a primary cause of broader social problems such as polarization').

[240] While bots are certainly active on social media, some reviews have found that they 'accelerated the spread of true and false news at the same rate, implying that false news spreads more than the truth because humans, not robots, are more likely to spread it'. Soroush Vosoughi, Deb Roy, and Sinan Aral, 'The Spread of True and False News Online' (2018) 359 Science 1146; Brendan Nyhan, 'Fake News and Bots May Be Worrisome, but Their Political Power Is Overblown' *The New York Times* (16 February 2018) <https://www.nytimes.com/2018/02/13/upshot/fake-news-and-bots-may-be-worrisome-but-their-political-power-is-overblown.html> accessed 16 April 2019. There are also considerable methodological challenges in studying online bots. See Michael Kreil, 'The Army That Never Existed: The Failure of Social Bots Research' (OpenFest Conference, Sofia, Bulgaria, 2 November 2019) <https://michaelkreil.github.io/openbots/> accessed 31 August 2020. See also Siobhan Roberts, 'Who's a Bot? Who's Not?' *The New York Times* (16 June 2020) <https://www.nytimes.com/2020/06/16/science/social-media-bots-kazemi.html> accessed 31 August 2020.

[241] Robert Chesney and Danielle Keats Citron, 'Deep Fakes: A Looming Challenge for Privacy, Democracy, and National Security' (2019) 107 California Law Review 1753.

[242] Henry Ajder and others, 'The State of DeepFakes: Landscape, Threats, and Impact' (DeepTrace Labs 2019) <https://deeptracelabs.com/mapping-the-deepfake-landscape/>. See also Samantha Cole, 'For the Love of God, Not Everything Is a Deepfake' (*Vice*, 27 April 2020) <https://www.vice.com/en_us/article/7kzgg9/joe-biden-tongue-gif-twitter-deepfake> accessed 5 May 2020.

[243] Tvesha Sippy and others, 'Behind the Deepfake: 8% Create; 90% Concerned. Surveying Public Exposure to and Perceptions of Deepfakes in the UK' (arXiv, 7 July 2024) <http://arxiv.org/abs/2407.05529> accessed 15 July 2024.

[244] Di Cooke and others, 'As Good as a Coin Toss: Human Detection of AI-Generated Images, Videos, Audio, and Audiovisual Stimuli' (arXiv, 4 April 2024) <http://arxiv.org/abs/2403.16760> accessed 1 May 2024. The same also goes not only for audiovisual content, but also textual material. For instance, see Angus R Williams and others, 'Large Language Models Can Consistently Generate High-Quality Content for Election Disinformation Operations' (arXiv, 13 August 2024) <http://arxiv.org/abs/2408.06731> accessed 17 August 2024 ('Our experiments suggest that almost all LLMs tested released since 2022 produce election disinformation operation content indiscernible by human evaluators over 50% of the time. Notably, we observe that multiple models achieve above-human levels of humanness').

[245] Christina P Walker, Daniel S Schiff, and Kaylyn Jackson Schiff, 'Merging AI Incidents Research with Political Misinformation Research: Introducing the Political Deepfakes Incidents Database' (2024) 38 Proceedings of the AAAI Conference on Artificial Intelligence 23053.

limited.[246] After all, from the perspective of propaganda and media manipulation, the use of AI techniques may not, in fact, offer much marginal benefit over already existing 'cheapfake' avenues for the manipulation of media content.[247] Moreover, because the audience for disinformation is relatively small and robust, and already oversaturated with a ready supply of human-created fake news, it has been suggested that the ultimate impacts of generative AI systems on this already overserved information environment may ultimately be surprisingly limited.[248] For example, one experimental study that used GPT-4 to tailor political messages to the profile of individual users found that—while messages generated by GPT-4 were persuasive in aggregate—the persuasiveness was not affected by whether the messages were personalized and 'microtargeted'.[249] Related research has also found evidence of sharply diminishing returns in the sociotechnical impact of these systems, with current frontier AI models being only barely more persuasive in their political messaging than models smaller in size by even an order of magnitude.[250]

Likewise, in spite of pervasive expert and public concerns over AI-enabled misinformation during the global election year of 2024,[251] analyses of the April–June 2024 elections in India suggested that, while deepfake audio and video material did see extensive use by politicians to reach out to voters,[252] this was primarily in a promotional or entertainment capacity. Only a minority of viral fake news stories involved AI-generated media; of those, none resulted in violence, and many were still easily detected.[253] Similarly, AI-generated media appeared both present and

[246] Zeve Sanderson, Solomon Messing, and Joshua A Tucker, 'Misunderstood Mechanics: How AI, TikTok, and the Liar's Dividend Might Affect the 2024 Elections' (*Brookings*, 22 January 2024) <https://www.brookings.edu/articles/misunderstood-mechanics-how-ai-tiktok-and-the-liars-dividend-might-affect-the-2024-elections/> accessed 3 October 2024.

[247] Britt Paris and Joan Donovan, 'DeepFakes and Cheap Fakes: The Manipulation of Audio & Visual Evidence' (Data & Society 2019) <https://datasociety.net/output/deepfakes-and-cheap-fakes/>.

[248] Felix M Simon, Sacha Altay, and Hugo Mercier, 'Misinformation Reloaded? Fears about the Impact of Generative AI on Misinformation Are Overblown' [2023] Harvard Kennedy School Misinformation Review <https://misinforeview.hks.harvard.edu/article/misinformation-reloaded-fears-about-the-impact-of-generative-ai-on-misinformation-are-overblown/> accessed 23 October 2023.

[249] Kobi Hackenburg and Helen Margetts, 'Evaluating the Persuasive Influence of Political Microtargeting with Large Language Models' (2024) 121 Proceedings of the National Academy of Sciences e2403116121.

[250] Kobi Hackenburg and others, 'Evidence of a Log Scaling Law for Political Persuasion with Large Language Models' (arXiv, 20 June 2024) <http://arxiv.org/abs/2406.14508> accessed 27 June 2024.

[251] Leah Feiger, 'It's the AI Election Year' [2024] *Wired* <https://www.wired.com/story/ai-election-2024/> accessed 12 June 2024; Sarah Jeong, 'The AI-Generated Hell of the 2024 Election' (*The Verge*, 12 March 2024) <https://www.theverge.com/policy/24098798/2024-election-ai-generated-disinformation> accessed 12 June 2024. For a survey of US public concerns over the use of AI misinformation in the presidential election, see Lee Rainie and Jason Husser, 'National Public Opinion Poll: AI & Politics '24' (Imagining the Digital Future Center, Elon University 2024) <https://imaginingthedigitalfuture.org/reports-and-publications/ai-politics-24/> accessed 12 June 2024.

[252] Nilesh Christopher and Varsha Bansal, 'Indian Voters Are Being Bombarded With Millions of Deepfakes. Political Candidates Approve' [2024] *Wired* <https://www.wired.com/story/indian-elections-ai-deepfakes/> accessed 27 May 2024.

[253] Nilesh Christopher, 'The Near Future of Deepfakes Just Got Way Clearer' (*The Atlantic*, 5 June 2024) <https://www.theatlantic.com/technology/archive/2024/06/india-election-deepfakes-generative-ai/678597/> accessed 11 June 2024 ('The main purpose of AI in Indian politics has not been to

yet ultimately relatively marginal in the French, UK, and European elections that took place later that year.[254]

That is not to suggest that the political threat from deepfakes—or generative AI broadly—has been roundly dismissed, and we can now rest easy. Neither does it rule out that this technology creates many other pressing problems, such as through its misuse for gendered harassment. However, it shows some of the complexities involved in reasoning directly from a demonstrated capability or affordance—in this case, the ability to forge media at scale—to an ecology of downstream uses, and from those downstream uses to eventual impacts on society.[255] It also shows the ease with which public concerns over a particular type of misuse may outpace direct exposure to, or prevalence of, such misuse.[256]

More generally, these cases highlight a set of complicating dynamics that occur, not just in aiming to forecast or predict the impacts of a technology in advance, but even for simply tracking them. For one, there is no reason to expect the sociotechnical impacts of a given technology to increase *evenly in all sectors.* As such, while we might overstate some challenges, there is also a risk that we will understate many others. For instance, it might be the case that the 'democracy-eroding' effects of deepfakes will remain relatively modest or marginal, but that they will see widespread use in conducting various types of criminal fraud.[257]

Moreover, the sociotechnical impacts of a given technology may not increase linearly or monotonically. It could well be the case that the 'democracy-eroding' effects of generative AI technology are overstated in the near-term but that they will be extensive in the longer term, once a certain threshold of performance is reached.[258] Furthermore, especially in cases involving a general-purpose technology, the

create deepfakes as they have conventionally been understood: an AI spoof of a candidate saying or doing something damaging, with ambiguity around whether it's real or fake.... Instead, in India, politicians and campaigns have co-opted AI to get out their messages').

[254] Sam Stockwell, 'AI-Enabled Influence Operations: Threat Analysis of the 2024 UK and European Elections' (Centre for Emerging Technology and Security 2024) <https://cetas.turing.ac.uk/publications/ai-enabled-influence-operations-threat-analysis-2024-uk-and-european-elections> accessed 11 June 2025; Miazia Schueler and others, 'Artificial Elections: Exposing the Use of Generative AI Imagery in the Political Campaigns of the 2024 French Elections' (AI Forensics 2024) <https://aiforensics.org/work/french-elections-2024> accessed 24 July 2024 (finding evidence of '51 instances of generative AI imagery across Facebook, Instagram, and X' used in French political campaigns, across the 2024 European Parliament and legislative elections).

[255] Sanderson, Messing, and Tucker (n 246).

[256] Sippy and others (n 243).

[257] M Caldwell and others, 'AI-Enabled Future Crime' (2020) 9 Crime Science 14; Keith J Hayward and Matthijs M Maas, 'Artificial Intelligence and Crime: A Primer for Criminologists' (2020) 17 Crime, Media, Culture 209.

[258] For example, once quality improves to such a level that effective detection becomes functionally impossible. Alex Engler, 'Fighting Deepfakes When Detection Fails' (*Brookings*, 14 November 2019) <https://www.brookings.edu/research/fighting-deepfakes-when-detection-fails/> accessed 11 December 2019. See also Hanlin Zhang and others, 'Watermarks in the Sand: Impossibility of Strong Watermarking for Generative Models' (arXiv, 14 November 2023) <http://arxiv.org/abs/2311.04378> accessed 19 November 2023.

pathways of sociotechnical change will be complex and unanticipated. It could be that generative AI technology will indeed have democracy-eroding effects, but in unexpected domains—not in the initially much-debated form of faux political smear videos, but rather, perhaps, through their effects on the evidential value of traditional categories of (video) evidence in a court of law.[259] Alternatively, it might be the generation of human-like text, rather than faked videos, that has the most far-reaching political impacts. It could also prove the case that the role of AI disinformation may not be significant in any one election, but that in aggregate these uses do erode the 'epistemic backstop' of society.[260]

The point with many of these cases is that we do not know, and may not actually know with reasonable certainty until a point in time surprisingly far along into the technology's development and deployment curve.

4.5.2 Epistemic Inadequacies of a Reactive Approach

These epistemic challenges complicate our assessments of a technology's sociotechnical impacts, including which governance rationales, if any, it might raise. What does that suggest?

On the one hand, this could be taken by some as an argument against jumping to premature regulation and in favour of a permissive and reactive 'wait-and-see' approach to technology regulation, which only takes action if and when problems clearly arise and are fully understood.[261] Such an approach is often presented as the sober alternative to anticipatory 'speculation'.[262]

Yet, critically, a reactive 'wait-and-see' approach to regulating technologies has many drawbacks of its own. For example, Crootof has argued that it might foster 'hypersensitive rulemaking' and overreaction once some unusual accidents or incidents do appear, while at the same time foregoing a valuable opportunity to deliberately channel the direction of technological development in desirable directions.[263]

There is a deeper drawback to the reactive approach, however: often it will not, in fact, manage to address or evade the informational and epistemic challenges of understanding a technology's impacts. Just as anticipatory approaches to

[259] Hin-Yan Liu and Andrew Mazibrada, 'Artificial Intelligence Affordances: Deep-Fakes as Exemplars of AI Challenges to Criminal Justice Systems' [2020] UNICRI Special Collection on Artificial Intelligence <http://unicri.it/towards-responsible-artificial-intelligence-innovation> accessed 13 July 2020; see also Alexa Koenig, '"Half the Truth Is Often a Great Lie": Deep Fakes, Open Source Information, and International Criminal Law' (2019) 113 AJIL Unbound 250.

[260] Regina Rini, 'Deepfakes and the Epistemic Backstop' (2019) <https://philpapers.org/archive/RINDAT.pdf>; Don Fallis, 'The Epistemic Threat of Deepfakes' [2020] Philosophy & Technology <https://doi.org/10.1007/s13347-020-00419-2> accessed 10 August 2020.

[261] Crootof and Ard (n 25) 380–383.

[262] For instance, see (in the field of ethical debates over nanotechnology): Alfred Nordmann, 'If and Then: A Critique of Speculative NanoEthics' (2007) 1 NanoEthics 31.

[263] Crootof, 'Regulating New Weapons Technology' (n 1) 21–22.

technology regulation can struggle to accurately characterize all of a technology's sociotechnical impacts, the risk with the reactive approach is that for many technologies there will never come a 'just right' moment where we acquire proof positive of that technology's impacts and sufficient certainty to act, yet where we also retain sufficient societal room to manoeuvre to contain or revert the damage. In such cases, the technology—and its sociotechnical bow wave—will be too far along to effectively rein in. As such, we will frequently be in a situation where, as argued by Maria Nordström,

> postponement does not guarantee that a decision under uncertainty in time (and with additional information) will become a decision under certainty . . . a decision-maker has to evaluate if time will reasonably affect the decision that has to be made. Given the inherent uncertainty of AI, adopting either passive or active postponement as the only policy is not recommended since significant uncertainty will remain even if we allow some time to pass, and some of the uncertainty might diminish.[264]

Moreover, while delaying rulemaking could at times lead to rules that are nominally better tailored to the technology, this need not mean that those laws are more effective since, as suggested by Crootof and Ard,

> [t]he efficacy of any legal response to technologically created uncertainty is partially a product of its timing. Substantively, a rule enacted later in time will likely be better informed, as the challenges and opportunities of a newer technology are likely to grow more apparent as it enters wider use. Yet delay may blunt the impact of the regulation or even render regulation impossible, if the technological design or use has already stabilized or if significant users have invested in the infrastructure.[265]

As illustrated by the constantly evolving 'nature' of cyberspace,[266] or the ongoing debates over cyberwarfare, attempts to 'wait out' the effects of technological developments until they are properly settled may be left in constant stasis, never attaining the presumed level of regulatory clarity. Many of these considerations will apply in considering the sociotechnical impacts of AI, which are not only uncertain and hard to predict, but also often bound up with deep normative ad political commitments. As a result, Veale, Matus, and Gorwa have incisively suggested that in many cases

[264] Maria Nordström, 'AI under Great Uncertainty: Implications and Decision Strategies for Public Policy' (2022) 37 AI & Society 1703, 1712.
[265] Crootof and Ard (n 25) 381.
[266] Balkin (n 189).

> the knowledge situation around AI governance is not one soluble by more expertise but is best classified as 'postnormal'... challenging the classic role science is seen to play in problem solving. The issues that AI governance is often truly about are not technical but deeply normative and distributive—which actors make decisions in society, who bears risks and errors, and what justice should look like procedurally and substantively... Scientific consensus is unlikely to be achieved here where facts are uncertain, values are in dispute, and decision stakes are high.[267]

More pragmatically, many technology law scholars have argued that while uncertainty around future trajectories is unavoidable in studying emerging technologies, this is exactly one reason why a 'wait-and-see' approach may not be adequate.[268] Particularly in areas involving the international regulation of new technological risk, they have argued in favour of more anticipatory analysis,[269] and for the importance of engaging with future uncertainty, discussing the general utility of future-oriented policymaking more broadly;[270] the more specific relevance of 'legal forecasting' in the face of technological uncertainty;[271] and the value of distinct foresight and forecasting approaches for AI policy and governance.[272] This suggests that anticipatory governance analysis can be warranted, provided it is bracketed by appropriate caution and reflection.

4.5.3 Political Drawbacks of a Predictive Approach: Towards Resilience

This may suggest that rather than aiming at specific anticipated technologies, regulators would do better to adopt a broad assumption of further or ongoing change, and adopt policies or governance approaches that are resilient or adaptive across

[267] Michael Veale, Kira Matus, and Robert Gorwa, 'AI and Global Governance: Modalities, Rationales, Tensions' (2023) 19 Annual Review of Law and Social Science 255, 267 (citing sources).

[268] Crootof, 'Regulating New Weapons Technology' (n 1) 21–22.

[269] For instance, Eric Talbot Jensen is a proponent of such a anticipatory approach, arguing that '[j]ust as military practitioners work steadily to predict new threats and defend against them, [law of armed conflict] practitioners need to focus on the future of armed conflict and attempt to be proactive in evolving the law to meet future needs'. See Eric Talbot Jensen, 'The Future of the Law of Armed Conflict: Ostriches, Butterflies, and Nanobots' (2014) 35 Michigan Journal of International Law 253, 254. Likewise, Paul Scharre observes how 'one need not wait (and should not wait) until nuclear war breaks out to think about stability dynamics with nuclear weapons'. Paul Scharre, 'Autonomous Weapons and Stability' (King's College 2020) 43 <https://kclpure.kcl.ac.uk/portal/en/theses/autonomous-weapons-and-stability(92cd3d5b-4eb1-4ad5-a9ca-0cce2491e652).html> accessed 31 May 2020.

[270] See for instance Andreas Wenger, Ursula Jasper, and Myriam Dunn Cavelty (eds), *The Politics and Science of Prevision: Governing and Probing the Future* (Routledge 2020).

[271] Graeme Laurie, Shawn HE Harmon, and Fabiana Arzuaga, 'Foresighting Futures: Law, New Technologies, and the Challenges of Regulating for Uncertainty' (2012) 4 Law, Innovation & Technology 1.

[272] Ballard and Calo (n 221).

distinct scenarios.[273] Importantly, this is not (necessarily) about pursuing prediction. In fact, for all the value that accurate technology forecasts could in principle bring, they might not be an unalloyed good. Especially at the international level, some types of predictions may even prove politically counterproductive to the establishment of regimes. For instance, international relations scholars have noted that a shared uncertainty over the state or future of the world can in some cases drive states to support international cooperation and the creation of robust international institutions.[274] However, the emergence of clear expectations over a technology's trajectory (whether correct or not) may give rise to the perception of unequal stakes among parties, which can hold up negotiations to establish such regimes.[275]

As a result, there may be political risks to technological predictions that are (presented as) very robust. For instance, there is a risk that, as I have previously argued,

> the more clearly a technology's future impacts are envisioned, the more clearly states today are able to project and articulate how their and other states' relative proficiency in the relevant areas of science and technology will eventually translate into concrete differential strategic advantages—and the more reluctant they may be to accede to governance regimes that would see them forgo such advantages . . . uncertainty may have its benefits; and governance regimes which are 'blind' but adaptive might prove more effective than governance regimes which are based on clear roadmaps of what interests and stakes, exactly, will be on the table.[276]

Recognizing this, a sociotechnical approach to regulating technologies should usually adopt a generally open-ended approach to future scenarios. It should recognize that scholarship in this area cannot avoid reckoning with potential trajectories of technology, that it is legitimate to act under some uncertainty today rather than postpone it to chase some ideal of perfect certainty at some hypothetical future point,[277] and that there is accordingly considerable value in adaptive regulatory approaches. Finally, such an anticipatory approach may be particularly key

[273] Gary E Marchant and Yvonne A Stevens, 'Resilience: A New Tool in the Risk Governance Toolbox for Emerging Technologies' (2017) 51 U.C. Davis Law Review 233.

[274] Barbara Koremenos, Charles Lipson, and Duncan Snidal, 'The Rational Design of International Institutions' (2001) 55 International Organization 761, 778.

[275] Colin B Picker, 'A View from 40,000 Feet: International Law and the Invisible Hand of Technology' (2001) 23 Cardozo Law Review 151, 191–194.

[276] Matthijs M Maas, 'Innovation-Proof Governance for Military AI? How I Learned to Stop Worrying and Love the Bot' (2019) 10 Journal of International Humanitarian Legal Studies 129, 150 (arguing on this basis that 'the difficulty of accurate technological foresight arguably underscores rather than erodes the utility of pursuing governance strategies or instruments that are versatile even if—or precisely when—they cannot accurately predict developmental pathways').

[277] Indeed, even under situations of pervasive uncertainty, regulatory responses to a new technology need not only be motivated by retrospectively confirmed impacts, but can still be grounded on concerns about the 'envisioned purposes' of a technology (e.g. 'AI surveillance'), or the potential side-effects (e.g. 'algorithmic discrimination').

in the context of particularly high-stakes risks,[278] which may create a need for a rebalancing or recalibration of conventional regulatory cost–benefit analyses in AI governance, to place greater weight on irreversible, worst-case outcomes.[279]

In preparing sets of policies that might be up to such tasks, we will need to take stock of how this technology might be approached as a governance 'target', whichever governance rationales it creates.

4.6 How to Regulate? Sociotechnical Change as Governance Target

Along with providing a greater grounding for understanding whether, when, and why to regulate new (AI) capabilities, a consideration of sociotechnical change can also shed light on the regulatory texture or features of the underlying AI capabilities—that is, its constitution as a governance or 'regulatory target'.[280]

There is an important caveat here: the idea that we should primarily consider AI's downstream sociotechnical impacts in determining whether or what is the rationale for regulation should not be taken to imply that the resulting regulation should only be targeted at that downstream level—such as by focusing exclusively on ex post liability, or solely on regulating the applications of AI. Rather, taking an extended perspective on AI's sociotechnical 'stack' which includes both underlying techniques and inputs as well as their applications and eventual sociotechnical impacts matters in understanding when, where, or how regulation is best targeted 'upstream' in the AI's development chain. Accordingly, as Veale, Matus and Gorwa have noted, '[o]ne way of understanding the global governance of AI is to look at the conceptual target of regulation [distinguishing] rules by the aspect of AI in practice they seek to shape: the development, use, and infrastructures of AI'.[281]

Understanding the texture of AI systems as a regulatory target has two components: a baseline consideration of the particular *material features*, and a more general consideration of the *problem logics* engaged by AI.

[278] Crootof, 'Regulating New Weapons Technology' (n 1) 23–25. There is of course extensive debate around the general role and usefulness of various formulations of the precautionary principle, as well as precautionary approaches around new technologies. This literature is too extensive to cover in full, but see Beyleveld and Brownsword (n 205).

[279] Kolt (n 91) 52–55.

[280] Miriam C Buiten, 'Towards Intelligent Regulation of Artificial Intelligence' (2019) 10 European Journal of Risk Regulation 41, 46–48. From a similar perspective, one could also consider the ways in which different AI systems or issues are framed in ways that produce distinct, politically salient 'governance objects'. See for instance the discussion of the global climate as governance object in Olaf Corry, 'Making the Climate Malleable? "Weak" and "Strong" Governance Objects and the Transformation of International Climate Politics' (2024) 4 Global Studies Quarterly ksae062.

[281] Veale, Matus, and Gorwa (n 267) 257.

4.6.1 Regulatory Textures and the Role of Material Features

In one sense, insofar as the lens of sociotechnical change shifts the emphasis away from the 'newness' of certain technologies in order to focus on disruptive sociotechnical changes (new behaviours, relations, or ways of being), it is an account that moderately de-emphasizes the artefactual or material dimension of technology governance. Nonetheless, once we have answered the question of whether certain sociotechnical changes create a *rationale* for governance, we face the question of how to design governance appropriately. That is, once regulators have confirmed a regulatory rationale (i.e. they have asked 'Do we need regulation? For what sociotechnical change? What regulatory rationale?'), they then face the question of how to craft regulatory actions. In considering AI applications as a *target* for regulation, a sociotechnical change-centric perspective must first take stock of the material aspects of the technology (as an artifact or technique).[282]

In answering this question—of how to approach certain technologies as a governance *target*—it can certainly be valuable to re-open considerations of the technology's constitution. For one, this is because ongoing developments or breakthroughs in the underlying scientific state of the art can shape perceptions of imminent applications, which may have a large effect on both public debate and state calculations around global regimes, even if the technology is not fully realized.[283] More importantly, the material features of a given technology can be highly relevant for understanding *how* to regulate. They can clearly illuminate the relative purchase or efficacy of different regulatory strategies at controlling, regulating, or mitigating the risks of concern. That is, they allow us insight into a wide range of key parameters for AI governance.

4.6.1.1 Understanding trajectories of future access, use, and regulatory leverage

In the first place, it is useful to consider material features, as these can affect a technology's further trajectory, proliferation, and speed of take-up. That is, the state of leading AI capabilities and material constraints on the design space and process can shape possible and plausible pathways of further development. They also affect preconditions for acquisition and use of a capability, thereby giving insights into the factors (and potential regulatory barriers) that drive or inhibit the technology's proliferation to various (types of) actors globally. For instance, the

282 For the sake of clarity, I note that I use the term 'material' here to refer to a sociotechnical system's physical features or traits, rather than in referring to its 'significant' features. I thank Suzanne van Arsdale for discussion on these terms.

283 See also Picker's discussion of international regimes pursued for putative or non-existing technologies. Picker (n 275) 194–196.

rate at which the costs of computing hardware will fall in coming years[284] will affect the rate and speed of diffusion of both advanced ('frontier') AI and military AI applications.[285] To be sure, these are not always inherent features of AI 'techniques' themselves, but can also be features of the broader digital ecosystem around them, such as the rise of digital intermediaries and online 'model marketplaces' that facilitate the dissemination of open-source systems.[286]

In turn, these factors help identify the distribution, and robustness, of different regulatory levers along the AI development supply chain. For instance, the rate at which overall computing costs will (continue) to fall will shape the ease with which such proliferation might feasibly be contained through compute governance mechanisms[287] or through export control regimes,[288] respectively—or whether such levers become increasingly strained and need to be reconfigured.

4.6.1.2 Understanding core risk profiles

Moreover, material features can give a basic core of insight into a technology's risk profile. Such an evaluation does then require further engagement with that technology's different sociotechnical impacts within specific contexts.[289] Nonetheless, this initial core analysis can already flag how or if different AI paradigms or techniques can at times be associated with rather distinct types of ethics or safety issues.[290] As such, when considering the technical features of specific AI *techniques* (e.g. algorithmic approaches), this can help in tailoring or focusing subsequent regulatory efforts.

For instance, while many narrow ('conventional') AI techniques can be somewhat transferable across domains or problems, they are also distinct in their workings. In a number of contexts, considering which particular contemporary AI

[284] Ben Cottier, 'Trends in the Dollar Training Cost of Machine Learning Systems' (*Epoch*, 31 January 2023) <https://epochai.org/blog/trends-in-the-dollar-training-cost-of-machine-learning-systems> accessed 1 February 2023.

[285] Michael C Horowitz, 'Artificial Intelligence, International Competition, and the Balance of Power' [2018] *Texas National Security Review* <https://tnsr.org/2018/05/artificial-intelligence-international-competition-and-the-balance-of-power/> accessed 17 May 2018.

[286] Robert Gorwa and Michael Veale, 'Moderating Model Marketplaces: Platform Governance Puzzles for AI Intermediaries' (SocArXiv 2023) preprint <https://osf.io/6dfk3> accessed 25 November 2023.

[287] Girish Sastry and others, 'Computing Power and the Governance of Artificial Intelligence' (arXiv, 13 February 2024) <http://arxiv.org/abs/2402.08797> accessed 20 February 2024; Dan Hendrycks, *Introduction to AI Safety, Ethics, and Society* (CRC Press 2024) ch 8.

[288] Lennart Heim, 'Understanding the Artificial Intelligence Diffusion Framework: Can Export Controls Create a U.S.-Led Global Artificial Intelligence Ecosystem?' (RAND Corporation 2025) <https://www.rand.org/pubs/perspectives/PEA3776-1.html> accessed 10 March 2025; and previously Jade Leung, Sophie-Charlotte Fischer, and Allan Dafoe, 'Export Controls in the Age of AI' (*War on the Rocks*, 28 August 2019) <https://warontherocks.com/2019/08/export-controls-in-the-age-of-ai/> accessed 2 September 2019. But for a critique, see Ritwik Gupta, Leah Walker, and Andrew W Reddie, 'Whack-a-Chip: The Futility of Hardware-Centric Export Controls' (arXiv, 21 November 2024) <http://arxiv.org/abs/2411.14425> accessed 22 January 2025.

[289] Weidinger and others, 'Sociotechnical Safety Evaluation of Generative AI Systems' (n 47).

[290] Hernandez-Orallo and others (n 77).

approaches are used can then help shed light on at least some of the risks which are or are not associated with those approaches. For instance, we can consider reinforcement learning algorithms' propensity to raise safety problems involving reward hacking or interruptibility of the algorithm,[291] supervised and unsupervised learning algorithms' susceptibility to reproducing data biases either directly or by proxy (when certain attributes are protected), or neural networks' lack of explainability relative to far more interpretable AI approaches such as decision trees. This is valuable in highlighting some of the heterogeneity of approaches, as well as in spurring consideration of the degree to which a problematic situation involving 'AI' can actually be addressed through technical interventions aimed at the AI system or whether this is better served by broader institutional interventions.[292]

The same holds for advanced AI systems. While there is a comparatively greater homogeneity in the architectures of these general-purpose AI systems, this only makes it more relevant to understand the core traits and dynamics of these technologies on their own terms.[293] Accordingly, it will remain key to find ways to evaluate the capabilities of such advanced AI systems[294]—as well as understanding the strengths and limits of different technical approaches aimed at aligning their behaviour.[295] Yet at the same time, achieving such evaluations is but a start: even if such tests were capable of detecting all potentially dangerous capabilities in the development stage—a debatable assumption—there would still be a range of downstream challenges.

4.6.1.3 Understanding the political viability of types of regulation

Finally, considering a technology's 'material' features is relevant not just in terms of determining the most optimal governance levers, but also in evaluating the political viability of achieving such regulation in the first place. This is especially the case at the international level, and especially for restrictive regulation.

For instance, Rosert and Sauer have argued that two previously successful global weapons ban campaigns, against blinding lasers and anti-personnel mines, owed their success in part to the fact that both technologies produced specific types of injuries (blinding and maiming) that were both particularly

[291] Dario Amodei and others, 'Concrete Problems in AI Safety' [2016] arXiv:1606.06565 [cs] <http://arxiv.org/abs/1606.06565> accessed 13 May 2017.

[292] Miles Brundage and others, 'Toward Trustworthy AI Development: Mechanisms for Supporting Verifiable Claims' [2020] arXiv:2004.07213 [cs] <http://arxiv.org/abs/2004.07213> accessed 16 April 2020.

[293] See Samuel R Bowman, 'Eight Things to Know about Large Language Models' (arXiv, 2 April 2023) <http://arxiv.org/abs/2304.00612> accessed 18 March 2025.

[294] Toby Shevlane and others, 'Model Evaluation for Extreme Risks' (arXiv, 24 May 2023) <http://arxiv.org/abs/2305.15324> accessed 25 May 2023.

[295] Stephen Casper and others, 'Open Problems and Fundamental Limitations of Reinforcement Learning from Human Feedback' [2023] Transactions on Machine Learning Research (12/2023) <http://arxiv.org/abs/2307.15217> accessed 7 August 2023.

horrifying and particularly distinctive to each technology.[296] This is a specific illustration of a more general point: that along with diverse historical, political, and social factors, a technology's architectural characteristics can play a significant role in rendering some (weapons) technologies more 'regulation-resistant' than others.[297]

4.6.1.4 Reviving technology exceptionalism? When models matter

Of course, the question can be asked: after all the emphasis on shifting governance focus away from 'technology' or its 'essential features', does this not simply smuggle technology directly back front and centre of all legal analysis, in a similar manner to technology-centric or application-centric regulatory approaches? Not necessarily. The point is that while it is sociotechnical change which determines whether there is a governance rationale—that is, what are (and whether there are) societal problems that need to be addressed—it is still the case that local material features can matter in understanding all aspects of the problem, and in crafting adequate governance solutions.

This matters significantly for scoping analysis and regulatory plans in AI governance. For example, debates over how to ensure the safety of advanced AI systems have in recent years begun by focusing on attempts to evaluate the potentially harmful capabilities of these most advanced models, and to do so within the development stage, before such potentially harmful models are deployed into society.[298] In response, some have increasingly argued that this is an unduly narrow perspective on AI safety,[299] one that might fail to identify many threat models or use cases that are hard to predict from a consideration of that model's features in isolation.[300] Accordingly, the field has gradually expanded to take stock not just of the safety problems intrinsic to certain AI artefacts, but to also consider how and where

[296] Significantly, they argue that these traits are not shared by the current line of LAWS: Elvira Rosert and Frank Sauer, 'How (Not) to Stop the Killer Robots: A Comparative Analysis of Humanitarian Disarmament Campaign Strategies' (2020) 42 Contemporary Security Policy 4. For a similar argument, see also Rebecca Crootof, 'Why the Prohibition on Permanently Blinding Lasers Is Poor Precedent for a Ban on Autonomous Weapon Systems' (*Lawfare*, 24 November 2015) <https://www.lawfareblog.com/why-prohibition-permanently-blinding-lasers-poor-precedent-ban-autonomous-weapon-systems> accessed 17 April 2019.

[297] Sean Watts, 'Regulation-Tolerant Weapons, Regulation-Resistant Weapons and the Law of War' (2015) 91 International Law Studies 83. Rebecca Crootof, 'Jurisprudential Space Junk: Treaties and New Technologies' in Chiara Giorgetti and Natalie Klein (eds), *Resolving Conflicts in the Law* (Brill | Nijhoff 2019) 115–116; Crootof, 'Regulating New Weapons Technology' (n 1) 23.

[298] Mary Phuong and others, 'Evaluating Frontier Models for Dangerous Capabilities' (arXiv, 20 March 2024) <http://arxiv.org/abs/2403.13793> accessed 28 March 2024; Shevlane and others (n 294).

[299] Vallor and Luger (n 48); Matt Davies, Andrew Strait, and Michael Birtwistle, 'Safety First? Reimagining the Role of the UK AI Safety Institute in a Wider UK Governance Framework' (*Ada Lovelace Institute*, 17 May 2024) <https://www.adalovelaceinstitute.org/blog/safety-first/> accessed 21 May 2024.

[300] For one example, see Erik Jones, Anca Dragan, and Jacob Steinhardt, 'Adversaries Can Misuse Combinations of Safe Models' (arXiv, 20 June 2024) <http://arxiv.org/abs/2406.14595> accessed 1 July 2024.

additional safety risks from AI systems derive from their broader sociotechnical context of use.[301]

Yet, while a valuable expansion to the debate, a sociotechnical perspective goes too far if it argues or implies that a technical perspective of the safety risks of an AI model itself is entirely irrelevant to the analysis of the safety (or danger) profile of the entire AI system:[302] indeed, in at least some cases, engaging with the technical features of an AI model can surely help us compare between different versions of AI systems that may be more or less brittle to failures—or more or less accommodating to misuse—across many sociotechnical contexts. In some cases, such analysis may help illustrate upstream intervention points where technical interventions at the level of the AI model's development and training can meaningfully reduce many downstream affordances for misuse. For example, research has explored the concept of 'Self-Destructing Models', a framework whereby foundation models are trained with additional task-blocking mechanisms, which impede their later adaptation or finetuning to harmful tasks without sacrificing performance on desirable tasks.[303]

In other cases, an initial model-level analysis can ground discussions about when particular policy responses are best achieved through interventions at the level of many disparate sociotechnical deployment contexts, or through upstream interventions at the level of model development.[304] In these cases, it is eminently sensible—and at times more actionable—to start initial regulatory analysis from an initial consideration of a given AI model's 'intrinsic' capabilities, so long as this is then complemented by additional consideration of how the risks of these capabilities might be exacerbated, annulled, or complemented by additional risks within specific usage contexts. We need not choose between focusing either on the model or on its context of use, but can and should consider both. As noted by Cullen O'Keefe, '"system-level safety" and "deployment context-level safety" are important concepts even though they require reference to the model itself. Neither model-level safety nor context-level safety makes sense in a vacuum, but both are useful.'[305] Indeed, in the best-case scenario, an integrated analysis of both model-level (architectural) and sociotechnical risks can help in the cross-fertilization of

[301] Weidinger and others, 'Sociotechnical Safety Evaluation of Generative AI Systems' (n 47); Inioluwa Deborah Raji and Roel Dobbe, 'Concrete Problems in AI Safety, Revisited' (arXiv, 18 December 2023) <http://arxiv.org/abs/2401.10899> accessed 3 May 2024.

[302] For instance, see Arvind Narayanan, 'AI Safety Is Not a Model Property' (*AI Snake Oil*, 20 March 2023) <https://www.aisnakeoil.com/p/ai-safety-is-not-a-model-property> accessed 3 May 2024.

[303] Peter Henderson and others, 'Self-Destructing Models: Increasing the Costs of Harmful Dual Uses of Foundation Models', *Proceedings of the 2023 AAAI/ACM Conference on AI, Ethics, and Society* (Association for Computing Machinery 2023) <https://doi.org/10.1145/3600211.3604690> accessed 3 July 2024.

[304] Cullen O'Keefe, 'AI Safety Is Sometimes a Model Property' (*Jural Networks*, 2 May 2024) <https://juralnetworks.substack.com/p/ai-safety-is-sometimes-a-model-property> accessed 3 May 2024.

[305] ibid.

useful policy interventions across this value chain. For example, in an influential framework, Laura Weidinger and colleagues have introduced a Sociotechnical Approach to Red Teaming (STAR) framework for assuring the safety of LLMs, by, among others, matching particular demographics to assess (downstream sociotechnical) harms for specific groups.[306]

With that said, an analysis of a given (AI) model's features—that is, a technology's architectural texture—as a means of assessing its regulatory surface at that moment in time does not amount to assuming that these features are essential or even necessarily very stable.[307] Rather, this argument admits that many features of a technology that appear critical or fundamental to it in one moment can themselves be altered by ongoing technological progress, or by shifting social, regulatory, or even (geo)political contexts. After all, just as early 'features' of the internet (such as the assumed anonymity) faded or evolved over time, many material and operational features of AI technology may develop over time, in ways that overturn widely shared assumptions.

For instance, in recent years, some debates on AI have been informed by the presumption that many machine learning algorithms are intrinsically 'unexplainable',[308] or that training up leading (or sufficiently harmful to be concerning) AI systems necessarily requires massive data sets and computing power.[309] There may certainly be some truth to such characterizations today, and for the coming years, although there are also significant exceptions to both assumptions even today.[310] More importantly, these are not essential features of all AI technology: advances in algorithmic explainability research or in data efficiency might render either premise (or both) less salient over time.[311] The point is therefore to consider a technology's features or parameters at a specific moment, as a snapshot in that technology's temporary, dynamic regulatory texture.

[306] Laura Weidinger and others, 'STAR: SocioTechnical Approach to Red Teaming Language Models' (arXiv, 10 July 2024) <http://arxiv.org/abs/2406.11757> accessed 1 August 2024; this also echoes participatory approaches to technology assessment, as proposed in Cremer and Whittlestone (n 61).

[307] Cf Calo, 'Robotics and the Lessons of Cyberlaw' (n 4).

[308] Jenna Burrell, 'How the Machine "Thinks": Understanding Opacity in Machine Learning Algorithms' (2016) 3 Big Data & Society 2053951715622512.

[309] Dario Amodei and Danny Hernandez, 'AI and Compute' (*OpenAI Blog*, 16 May 2018) <https://blog.openai.com/ai-and-compute/> accessed 22 May 2018; Ben Buchanan, 'The AI Triad and What It Means for National Security Strategy' (Center for Security and Emerging Technology 2020) <https://cset.georgetown.edu/research/the-ai-triad-and-what-it-means-for-national-security-strategy/> accessed 14 August 2020.

[310] For instance, on the assumption of 'unexplainability' in AI systems, see Joshua A Kroll, 'The Fallacy of Inscrutability' (2018) 376 Philosophical Transactions of the Royal Society A 20180084. On the question of whether there is a necessary (or at least predictable) relationship between more computationally intense models and more harmful ones, see Sara Hooker, 'On the Limitations of Compute Thresholds as a Governance Strategy' (arXiv, 8 July 2024) <http://arxiv.org/abs/2407.05694> accessed 15 July 2024.

[311] Aaron D Tucker, Markus Anderljung, and Allan Dafoe, 'Social and Governance Implications of Improved Data Efficiency', *Proceedings of the AAAI/ACM Conference on AI, Ethics, and Society* (ACM 2020) <http://arxiv.org/abs/2001.05068> accessed 18 August 2020.

As such, this argument amounts to an asymmetric account of sociotechnical change—or the assumption of 'asymmetric governance materiality'. That is, in considering when AI capabilities create a governance rationale, this lens looks less at inputs than at outputs. It focuses less on incremental progress in a certain technology, or its assumed essential features, and more on the sociotechnical changes in the form of new (or anticipated) sociotechnical changes. At the same time, in considering how these AI capabilities should be approached as a 'governance target', it does consider the technology's 'inputs' (its temporary and changeable texture that determines its regulatory surface) as relevant considerations in considering distinct governance arrangements.

4.6.2 Regulatory Surfaces and AI Problem Logics

Moreover, along with technical or material features, we should consider the particular regulatory surfaces of an AI technology, in terms of distinct *problem logics*.

As such, it is important to clarify that the 'sociotechnical change' perspective does not imply that the underlying technological progress in AI or the deployment of specific *applications* in ever more sectors are irrelevant and should not be given attention. If anything, the opposite is the case: tracking and extrapolating patterns and rates in AI development, as well as the proliferation and latency of specific AI applications, remains critical in order to map the 'regulatory surface' of these challenges as governance targets. Individual applications can provide important signals, including about the urgency of regulation.

This should be explored in greater detail, and as such this section will explore a framework for distinguishing several such 'logics'. This approach suggests that AI governance regimes might be designed with greater leverage over their governance targets if they considered more explicitly the types of sociotechnical changes that are at issue, along with the material texture as well as problem logics.

One way of framing governance regimes could be to bracket AI applications with reference to the type of 'governance rationale' they give rise to. There is something to this approach, and yet it is incomplete in at least one way: just because two different AI use cases give rise to a similar governance rationale (e.g. they both create problems for 'rights') does not necessarily mean that they have a similar regulatory texture or problem logic. Accordingly, bracketing them together might not always be insightful, productive, or actionable.

As such, whereas the question of *whether* a governance regime is needed should depart from an examination of governance rationales, the subsequent question of *how* a governance regime ought to be organized may better depart from an examination of these AI capabilities as 'governance targets', as discussed previously. This raises the question of how to fruitfully cluster types of sociotechnical change, in ways that facilitate common policies or insights. As previously noted, scholars in AI ethics and AI governance have articulated diverse ways to segment the challenges of AI. These taxonomies are all valuable. However, at least in some cases, these frameworks may overemphasize pre-existing 'thematic' bodies or disciplines of law, rather than clusters of structured problems in the space of sociotechnical change.

Accordingly, to better grapple with the sociotechnical change driven by these technologies in a manner more sensitive to the different regulatory textures and problem logics, I suggest that a more productive account could draw different distinctions.[312] Specifically, I suggest that AI systems[313] can create sociotechnical changes that can be clustered as ethical challenges, security threats, safety risks, structural shifts, common benefits, and governance disruption. Distinguishing between these six ideal-types can be valuable, as they come with distinct regulatory surfaces, and are therefore amenable to distinct governance levers (see Table 4.1).

To be clear, this framework is not meant to be mutually exclusive, or even exhaustive. Indeed, in practice, certain AI systems can give rise to a bucket of problems across these categories, or problems or challenges that have features of two different problem logics can interact, as seen in exposure of security vulnerabilities in safety-aligned language models.[314] In other cases, one of these dimensions might dominate the others. Nonetheless, the framework aims to capture certain regularities which help ask productive regulatory questions. For each category, we can ask: How does the AI capability produce sociotechnical change? Why does this create a governance *rationale*? How should this be approached as a governance *target*?

For one, this model enables examination of the underlying *origins* of the sociotechnical challenge of concern, in terms of: (1) the *key actors* (e.g. principals, operators, malicious users) whose newly AI-enabled or related behaviour or decisions create the governance concerns; and (2) those *actors' traits, interests, or motives* which drive the AI-sociotechnical-problem related behaviour or decisions (e.g. actor apathy, malice, negligence, or the way the new capability sculpts choice architectures in ways which shift structural incentives or strategic pressures). This, in turn, can be linked to the (3) *contributing factors* which sustain or exacerbate this sociotechnical impact. Finally, this model enables a study of the (4) *barriers to regulation*; that is, the factors that drive the difficulty of formulating or implementing policy solutions, and which will themselves have to be overcome to achieve effective regulatory responses for AI.

312 Another framework, which takes the perspective of AI researchers, is offered in Carolyn Ashurt and others, 'A Guide to Writing the NeurIPS Impact Statement' (*Medium*, 13 May 2020) <https://medium.com/@operations_18894/a-guide-to-writing-the-neurips-impact-statement-4293b723f832> accessed 14 May 2020.

313 This model could in principle be adapted and applied to the governance of many other technologies, though an exploration of this remains beyond the scope of this book. I thank Jeffrey Ding for raising this point.

314 Xiangyu Qi and others, 'AI Risk Management Should Incorporate Both Safety and Security' (arXiv, 29 May 2024) <http://arxiv.org/abs/2405.19524> accessed 10 July 2024.

Table 4.1 Overview of AI problem logics

Type and questions	Corresponding governance rationales	Examples in AI (selected)	Governance surface (origin / contributing factors; barriers to regulation)	Governance logics (selected)
Ethical challenges *What rights, values, or interests does this threaten?*	• New risks to moral interests, rights, or values • New threats to social solidarity • Threats to democratic process	• *Justice*: bias; explainability • *Power*: facial recognition • *Democracy*: AI propaganda • *Freedom*: 'Code as Law'; algocracy	• O. Actor *apathy* (to certain values) • BR. Underlying *societal disagreement* (culturally and over time) over how to weigh the values, interests, or rights at stake	• *Product-focused:* Bans ('mend—or end') • *Ex ante producer-focused:* Oversight mechanisms; end-to end auditing; value-sensitive design • *Ex post principal-focused*: accountability
Security threats *How is this vulnerable to misuse or attack?*	• New risks to moral interests, rights, or values • New risks to human health or safety	• *AI as tool:* Deepfakes; • *AI as attack surface*: adversarial inputs • *AI as shield:* fraudulent trading agents; UAV smuggling	• O. Actor '*malice*' (various economic or ideological motives) • CF. Target apathy or ignorance • CF. Offence–defence balance of AI knowledge • BR. vulnerability of human practices to social engineering	• *Perpetrator-focused*: change norms, prevent access; improve detection and forensics capabilities to ensure attribution and deterrence • *Target-focused*: reduce exposure; red-teaming; 'security mindset'
Safety risks *Can we rely on and control this?*	• New risks to human health or safety	• Unpredictability and opacity • Environmental interactions • Automation bias and 'normal accidents' • 'Value misalignment'	• O. Artefact *design failure* • O. Actor *negligence* • CF. Overtrust and automation bias • CF. Behavioural features of AI systems • BR. 'Many hands' problem—long and discrete supply chains	• Relinquishment (of usage in extreme-risk domains) • 'Meaningful Human Control' (various forms) • Safety engineering (e.g. reliability; corrigibility; interpretability; limiting capability or deployment; formal verification) • Liability mechanisms and tort law

Table 4.1 Continued

Type and questions	**Corresponding governance rationales**	**Examples in AI (selected)**	**Governance surface (origin / contributing factors; barriers to regulation)**	**Governance logics (selected)**
Structural shifts *How does this shape our decisions?*	• (all, indirectly)	• Change calculations: LAWS lower perceived costs of conflict • Increased scope for miscalculation: e.g. attack prediction	• O. Systemic *incentives* for actors (alters choice architectures; increases uncertainty; competitive value erosion) • BR. collective action problems	• Arms control (mutual restraint) • Confidence-building measures (increase trust or transparency)
Common benefits *How can we realize opportunities with this?*	• Possible market failures	• Ensure AI interoperability • 'AI for global good' projects • Distributing benefits of AI	• O. Systemic *incentives* for actors • BR. Overcoming loss aversion; (+ coordination challenges around cost-sharing, free-riding)	• (Global) standards • 'Public interest' regulation and subsidies • 'Windfall clause' and redistributive guarantees
Governance disruption *How does this change how we regulate?*	• New risks directly to existing regulatory order	• AI systems creating *substantive* ambiguity in law • Legal automation altering *processes* of law • Erodes political *scaffolding*	• O. Push towards legal efficiency • CF. Legal system *exposure* and dependence on conceptual orders or assumptions	• Provisions to render governance 'innovation-proof': technological neutrality; authoritative interpreters, sunset clauses • Oversight for legal automation; distribution

There is insufficient space to go into exhaustive detail on each of these categories within the taxonomy. However, at a glance, we can pick out a number of ways in which clustering AI's sociotechnical impacts along these various problem logics can facilitate structural regulation-relevant insights for AI regulators.

4.6.2.1 Ethical challenges

Ethical challenges around AI revolve around concerns that AI could enable or create new forms of behaviour, entities, or (power) relations that raise problems for fundamental rights or values in a society. This may concern behaviour that is outright illegal, or which is (still) legal but seen, by some or by many, as violating normative values. In most cases, these concerns are anchored in (anticipated) threats to *existing* values; however, in some cases technologies can also reveal or highlight new rights or values which we previously did not realize we valued.[315]

A key feature of AI-driven sociotechnical changes that can be clustered as 'ethical challenges' is that the new behaviour, entities, or relations commonly raise questions over foundational political theoretical concepts, such as justice, power, democracy, and freedom.[316] As such, it should be no surprise that ethical challenges comprise one of the broadest and most ostensibly diverse categories, given a series of high-profile misuses or at least controversial use cases of AI.

For example, concerns around algorithmic *justice* adopt the ethical challenges problem logic. Concerns have long been raised over algorithmic bias,[317] both in relatively 'innocuous' (but still important) settings such as in search machine prompts[318] but especially in the context of systems used for high-stakes legal decision-making or policing.[319] More broadly, many have argued that the use of algorithmic decision-making by states or legal systems may affect important (human) rights,[320] especially when they are used in the context of vulnerable populations such as migrants.[321] Likewise, the capability of 'using machine learning systems to make sophisticated but opaque decisions' creates various ethical concerns around explainability.

Concerns over a loss of privacy also play into questions over changes in power relations.[322] This is particularly spurred on by increasing use of AI in surveillance.

[315] See generally Jack Parker and David Danks, 'How Technological Advances Can Reveal Rights', *Proceedings of the 2019 AAAI/ACM Conference on AI, Ethics, and Society* (ACM 2019) <https://dl.acm.org/doi/10.1145/3306618.3314274> accessed 18 March 2025.

[316] Jamie Susskind, *Future Politics: Living Together in a World Transformed by Tech* (Oxford University Press 2018).

[317] For early work, see Kate Crawford and others, 'AI Now 2019 Report' (AI Now Institute 2019) <https://ainowinstitute.org/publication/ai-now-2019-report-2> accessed 7 January 2020; Kate Crawford and Ryan Calo, 'There Is a Blind Spot in AI Research' (2016) 538 Nature News 311.

[318] Safiya Noble, *Algorithms of Oppression: How Search Engines Reinforce Racism* (1st edn, NYU Press 2018).

[319] Mareile Kaufmann, Simon Egbert, and Matthias Leese, 'Predictive Policing and the Politics of Patterns' (2018) 59 The British Journal of Criminology 674.

[320] QC van Est, J Gerritsen, and L Kool, 'Human Rights in the Robot Age: Challenges Arising from the Use of Robotics, Artificial Intelligence, and Virtual and Augmented Reality' (Rathenau Instituut 2017) <https://research.tue.nl/en/publications/human-rights-in-the-robot-age-challenges-arising-from-the-use-of-> accessed 22 May 2019.

[321] Petra Molnar, *The Walls Have Eyes: Surviving Migration in the Age of Artificial Intelligence* (The New Press 2024); Petra Molnar, 'Technology on the Margins: AI and Global Migration Management from a Human Rights Perspective' (2019) 8 Cambridge International Law Journal 305.

[322] Ryan Calo, 'Peeping HALs: Making Sense of Artificial Intelligence and Privacy' (2010) 2 EJLS—European Journal of Legal Studies <http://www.ejls.eu/6/83UK.htm> accessed 13 May 2017. However, some have also suggested AI systems can be used in defence or protection of privacy. Andrea Scripa Els, 'Artificial Intelligence as a Digital Privacy Protector' (2017) 31 Harvard Journal of Law & Technology 19; Urs Gasser, 'Recoding Privacy Law: Reflections on the Future Relationship Among Law, Technology, and Privacy' (2016) 130 Harvard Law Review Forum 10; Andrew Trask, 'Safe Crime

AI can identify human faces, even masked ones in blurred pictures;[323] and it can enable the remote identification of individuals not just by face but even by gait, (remotely laser-measured) heartbeat signature,[324] and even bioacoustics signature (i.e. measuring how sound waves pass through human bodies).[325]

More generally, AI systems can change power structures,[326] or drive growing inequality and societal instability, as a result of technological unemployment and a global oligopolistic or mercantilist market structure.[327] Domestically, there are concerns that increasing algorithmic 'perception control', the dual disciplinary functions of pervasive and even predictive surveillance systems, and opaque algorithmic governance can further embed unequal and incontestable power relations.[328] AI systems might also strengthen authoritarian states in their surveillance and repression capabilities;[329] or such capabilities could allow these actors to increasingly challenge the global liberal order.[330] Finally, not all ethical concerns (directly) concern human interests or rights. For instance, some have charted the potential negative impacts of AI technology on sustainability and the natural world, either directly[331]

Prediction: Homomorphic Encryption and Deep Learning for More Effective, Less Intrusive Digital Surveillance' (5 June 2017) <https://iamtrask.github.io/2017/06/05/homomorphic-surveillance/> accessed 8 June 2017.

[323] Matt Reynolds, 'Even a Mask Won't Hide You from the Latest Face Recognition Tech' [2017] *New Scientist* <https://www.newscientist.com/article/2146703-even-a-mask-wont-hide-you-from-the-latest-face-recognition-tech/> accessed 18 June 2019; Amarjot Singh and others, 'Disguised Face Identification (DFI) with Facial KeyPoints Using Spatial Fusion Convolutional Network' [2017] arXiv:1708.09317 [cs] <http://arxiv.org/abs/1708.09317> accessed 18 June 2019; LilHay Newman, 'AI Can Recognize Your Face Even If You're Pixelated' (*WIRED*, 2016) <https://www.wired.com/2016/09/machine-learning-can-identify-pixelated-faces-researchers-show/> accessed 26 February 2017.

[324] David Hambling, 'The Pentagon Has a Laser that Can Identify People from a Distance—by Their Heartbeat' [2019] *MIT Technology Review* <https://www.technologyreview.com/s/613891/the-pentagon-has-a-laser-that-can-identify-people-from-a-distanceby-their-heartbeat/> accessed 1 July 2019. See broadly Hayward and Maas (n 257).

[325] Joo Yong Sim and others, 'Identity Recognition Based on Bioacoustics of Human Body' [2019] IEEE Transactions on Cybernetics 1 (demonstrating an approach that achieved an accuracy of 97% at identifying individuals, nearly as accurate as fingerprints or iris scans, persisting over at least two months).

[326] Hin-Yan Liu, 'The Power Structure of Artificial Intelligence' (2018) 10 Law, Innovation and Technology 197.

[327] Dafoe, 'AI Governance: A Research Agenda' (n 164) 39–42.

[328] John Danaher, 'The Threat of Algocracy: Reality, Resistance and Accommodation' (2016) 29 Philosophy & Technology 245.

[329] Steven Feldstein, 'The Road to Digital Unfreedom: How Artificial Intelligence Is Reshaping Repression' (2019) 30 Journal of Democracy 40. Dirk Helbing and others, 'Will Democracy Survive Big Data and Artificial Intelligence?' [2017] *Scientific American* <https://www.scientificamerican.com/article/will-democracy-survive-big-data-and-artificial-intelligence/> accessed 29 May 2017.

[330] Richard Danzig, 'An Irresistible Force Meets a Moveable Object: The Technology Tsunami and the Liberal World Order' (2017) 5 Lawfare Research Paper Series <https://assets.documentcloud.org/documents/3982439/Danzig-LRPS1.pdf> accessed 1 September 2017.

[331] Roy Schwartz and others, 'Green AI' (2020) 63 Communications of the ACM 54; Kate Crawford and Vladan Joler, 'Anatomy of an AI System' (AI Now Institute 2018) <http://www.anatomyof.ai> accessed 22 June 2020; Bird and others (n 31) 28–29. Though for more optimistic perspectives on the carbon emissions of modern machine learning systems, see also David Patterson and others, 'The

or indirectly, because of the technology's political effects on the dynamics and viability of effective environmentalist movements.[332]

Considered in terms of governance *rationales*, ethical challenges implicate new risks to moral interests, rights, or values; new threats to social solidarity; or threats to democratic process. Considered as a governance *target*, AI-linked sociotechnical changes which invoke ethical challenges have certain salient features. In weak cases, the problems cannot be traced back to AI principals' hostility to certain rights. Tech developers, it might be assumed, do not generally set out to produce biased or opaque algorithms.[333] However, the source of the problem could be found in the relative *apathy* to these values (at least in comparison with other—potentially legitimate—goals which are perceived to stand in tension to these), or an *ignorance* that their activities could impinge on these values.

In such cases, governance logics can involve the 'mend or end' debates of algorithmic accountability. That is, they may attempt to 'mend' the AI application under scrutiny, either within the system in the form of machine ethics or through organizational accountability or algorithmic auditing mechanisms.[334] Alternatively, they may seek to outlaw the application entirely, as seen in US debates over facial-recognition technology.[335]

In hard cases, however, ethical challenges can be especially difficult to address, because they reflect underlying and live societal disagreements over the values, interests, or rights at stake, or how these should be weighted. In those cases, AI's sociotechnical changes may prove especially intractable. As such, these challenges will face particular contestation and differences among parties, potentially foregrounding the value of negotiating general consensus. Alternatively, and on the international level, small and informal clubs of like-minded actors might be able to move ahead and set certain standards.[336]

Carbon Footprint of Machine Learning Training Will Plateau, Then Shrink' (2022) 55 Computer 18; Bill Tomlinson and others, 'The Carbon Emissions of Writing and Illustrating Are Lower for AI than for Humans' (arXiv, 8 March 2023) <http://arxiv.org/abs/2303.06219> accessed 22 January 2024.

[332] Peter Dauvergne, 'The Globalization of Artificial Intelligence: Consequences for the Politics of Environmentalism' [2020] Globalizations 1.

[333] Though this may not always be the case, unfortunately. In at least some cases, clients or customers may in fact configure algorithms in biased ways, as with the algorithm that was rigged by the US ICE to recommend detention in all cases. Sam Biddle, 'ICE's New York Office Uses a Rigged Algorithm to Keep Virtually All Arrestees in Detention. The ACLU Says It's Unconstitutional' (*The Intercept*, 2 March 2020) <https://theintercept.com/2020/03/02/ice-algorithm-bias-detention-aclu-lawsuit/> accessed 7 September 2020.

[334] Inioluwa Deborah Raji and others, 'Closing the AI Accountability Gap: Defining an End-to-End Framework for Internal Algorithmic Auditing', *Proceedings of the 2020 Conference on Fairness, Accountability, and Transparency* (Association for Computing Machinery 2020) <https://doi.org/10.1145/3351095.3372873> accessed 23 February 2020.

[335] Luke Stark, 'Facial Recognition Is the Plutonium of AI' (2019) 25 XRDS 50.

[336] Jean-Frédéric Morin and others, 'How Informality Can Address Emerging Issues: Making the Most of the G7' (2019) 10 Global Policy 267. This anticipates the discussion, in Chapter 7, on the 'breadth vs. depth' dilemma facing many global AI governance initiatives.

4.6.2.2 Security threats

In other cases, AI capabilities enable sociotechnical changes that can be clustered as *security threats*. It is useful to clarify, first, what is meant by 'security', given the term's diverse uses. For instance, Fjeld and others have argued that 'security addresses external threats to an AI system', as opposed to 'internal' threats or flaws that threaten its performance.[337] This definition focuses on AI technology's susceptibility to (external) hacking or spoofing, treating the AI as an attack surface. Here, technical work has focused on security threats *to* AI systems—as in the literature in data poisoning and 'adversarial inputs',[338] of the type which allowed researchers to spoof various sensitive AI systems.[339]

However, in a broader perspective, security challenges should be considered as relating to some actor's actual and knowing misuse or exploitation of an AI system (or its vulnerabilities), in the pursuit of goals that are widely recognized as illegitimate and often formally recognized as illegal. More operationally, AI gives rise to distinct security challenges because the technology does not function just as a potential attack surface, but can also be used as a tool or even shield for malicious actors.[340]

Accordingly, there is a growing potential for AI capabilities to be misused to scale up old security risks, or even to create entirely new attack vectors, in areas such as cybersecurity, crime, and terrorism.[341] Other security problem logics revolve around political security, as seen in concerns over how democracy and the rule of law will be eroded,[342] especially in the face of 'computational propaganda',

[337] Jessica Fjeld and others, 'Principled Artificial Intelligence: Mapping Consensus in Ethical and Rights-Based Approaches to Principles for AI' 37 <https://dash.harvard.edu/handle/1/42160420> accessed 16 January 2020. A similar distinction is found in Qi and others (n 314) 3–4 ('Safety typically focuses on preventing harm that a system might inflict upon the external environment. Security typically is oriented toward protecting the system itself against harm and exploitation from malicious external actors').

[338] Alexey Kurakin, Ian Goodfellow, and Samy Bengio, 'Adversarial Machine Learning at Scale' [2017] arXiv:1611.01236 [cs, stat] <http://arxiv.org/abs/1611.01236> accessed 16 June 2020.

[339] Including those in self-driving cars, or in volumetric medical data. Tencent Keen Security Lab, 'Experimental Security Research of Tesla Autopilot' (Tencent 2019) <https://keenlab.tencent.com/en/whitepapers/Experimental_Security_Research_of_Tesla_Autopilot.pdf> accessed 8 April 2019; Samuel G Finlayson and others, 'Adversarial Attacks on Medical Machine Learning' (2019) 363 Science 1287. For a discussion, see also Ryan Calo and others, 'Is Tricking a Robot Hacking?' [2018] University of Washington School of Law Research Paper <https://papers.ssrn.com/abstract=3150530> accessed 2 August 2018.

[340] Hayward and Maas (n 257) 6–9. We also identify a third category, of AI being used as a new potential criminal 'intermediary' or 'shield': ibid 9–10. On which, see also Lynn M LoPucki, 'Algorithmic Entities' [2017] UCLA School of Law, Law-Econ Research Paper <https://papers.ssrn.com/sol3/papers.cfm?abstract_id=2954173> accessed 19 May 2017.

[341] Brundage and others (n 198); Thomas C King and others, 'Artificial Intelligence Crime: An Interdisciplinary Analysis of Foreseeable Threats and Solutions' [2019] Science and Engineering Ethics <https://doi.org/10.1007/s11948-018-00081-0> accessed 21 February 2019; Hayward and Maas (n 257).

[342] Helbing and others (n 329); Paul Nemitz, 'Constitutional Democracy and Technology in the Age of Artificial Intelligence' (2018) 376 Philosophical Transactions of the Royal Society A 20180089.

'neural fake news',[343] or 'deepfakes'.[344] As discussed earlier, there is some uncertainty over how imminent some of these attacks are, since some of the more exotic attacks or use cases may not transfer easily outside labs, or may find at most limited use among only the most high-capacity actors.

Finally, as discussed in Chapter 2, the coming years may see increasing risks from AI systems becoming increasingly agent-like in their behaviour.[345] Indeed, existing systems have already displayed situations in which they may be prompted to engage in forms of strategic deception of their users.[346] This may come to gradually shift the problem logic of such 'safety' challenges to one that is more akin to adversarial security challenges.

At any rate, there are clearly a diversity of security threats around, to, and through AI systems.[347] As a governance *rationale*, most of these raise new risks to human health or safety, though they can also pertain to risks to moral interests, rights, or values. As a 'governance target', AI sociotechnical changes that centre on *security* have distinct features. In the first place, they derive not from actor apathy or ethical laxness, but from 'malice'. In the second place, they depend not just on the sophistication of the AI capability in question, but also on the vulnerability and exposure of the target. This is key, because there is at least one reason to assume that AI-enabled attacks might pose a structurally larger security problem than conventional hacks. This is because, as suggested by Shevlane and Dafoe, AI is a technology that aims at automating activities that normally require human intelligence, which means that it is particularly suitable for interfering in human social systems—or exploiting features of a social system as vulnerability. The 'exploits' on which such attacks rely are often features not of digital architectures or code, but of

[343] Rowan Zellers, 'Grover: A State-of-the-Art Defense against Neural Fake News' (2019) <https://rowanzellers.com/grover/?domain=nytimes.com&date=May+29%2C+2019&authors=&title=Answers+to+Where+to+Watch+the+Pope%E2%80%99s+U.S.+Visit&article=> accessed 13 June 2019; Irene Solaiman and others, 'Release Strategies and the Social Impacts of Language Models' [2019] arXiv:1908.09203 [cs] <http://arxiv.org/abs/1908.09203> accessed 18 November 2019.

[344] Bolsover and Howard (n 234); Chesney and Citron (n 241); Katarina Kertysova, 'Artificial Intelligence and Disinformation: How AI Changes the Way Disinformation Is Produced, Disseminated, and Can Be Countered' (2018) 29 Security and Human Rights 55.

[345] Chan and others (n 70).

[346] Evan Hubinger and others, 'Sleeper Agents: Training Deceptive LLMs That Persist Through Safety Training' (arXiv, 17 January 2024) <http://arxiv.org/abs/2401.05566> accessed 8 May 2024; Jérémy Scheurer, Mikita Balesni, and Marius Hobbhahn, 'Technical Report: Large Language Models Can Strategically Deceive Their Users When Put Under Pressure' (arXiv, 27 November 2023) <http://arxiv.org/abs/2311.07590> accessed 8 December 2023; Peter S Park and others, 'AI Deception: A Survey of Examples, Risks, and Potential Solutions' <http://arxiv.org/abs/2308.14752> accessed 29 August 2023; Joe Carlsmith, 'Scheming AIs: Will AIs Fake Alignment during Training in Order to Get Power?' (arXiv, 15 November 2023) <http://arxiv.org/abs/2311.08379> accessed 16 November 2023. See also previously Meta Fundamental AI Research Diplomacy Team (FAIR) and others, 'Human-Level Play in the Game of Diplomacy by Combining Language Models with Strategic Reasoning' (2022) 378 Science 1067 (eliciting deceptive behaviour in a more controlled setting of the game *Diplomacy*).

[347] See also Nicolas Papernot, 'A Marauder's Map of Security and Privacy in Machine Learning' [2018] arXiv:1811.01134 [cs] <http://arxiv.org/abs/1811.01134> accessed 16 June 2020.

human social systems, which are far less amenable to quick or painless 'patches'.[348] Accordingly, whereas software vulnerabilities in conventional cyber security can often be addressed by the dissemination and implementation of a software fix, addressing vulnerabilities of the human social system might require far-reaching and prohibitively costly changes to ordinary human social practices or habits (such as our faith in the fidelity of voices).

AI security challenges therefore foreground some governance responses or governance logics. Some of these are perpetrator-focused: attempts to change norms, prevent access, improve detection and forensics capabilities to ensure attribution and deterrence. Others are aimed at reducing the vulnerability or exposure of targets, such as by red-teaming, and adopting a 'security mindset'.[349]

4.6.2.3 Safety risks

Other AI challenges can be characterized as *safety risks*.[350] AI systems, perhaps more than most or any other technologies, introduce an unusually diverse palette of failure modes.

Much work to date has focused on the safety and reliability of individual 'cyber-physical systems'—various autonomous vehicles, drones, delivery robots, or other AI products that operate in the public or private space.[351] Kunz and Ó hÉigeartaigh

[348] Toby Shevlane and Allan Dafoe, 'The Offense-Defense Balance of Scientific Knowledge: Does Publishing AI Research Reduce Misuse?', *Proceedings of the 2020 AAAI/ACM Conference on AI, Ethics, and Society (AIES '20)* (ACM 2020) 177 <http://arxiv.org/abs/2001.00463> accessed 9 January 2020 ('[d]igital systems are in general the easiest to patch at scale, whereas physical and social systems are often much more costly to change, especially at scale').

[349] C Severance, 'Bruce Schneier: The Security Mindset' (2016) 49 Computer 7.

[350] Again, there are various ways to define safety and security. For instance, Fjeld et al. argue that 'The principle of safety generally refers to proper internal functioning of an AI system and the avoidance of unintended harms': Fjeld and others (n 337) 37. They note that an overarching term here is 'reliability', which connotes both safety as well as security, in that a system that is 'reliable' 'is safe, in that it performs as intended, and also secure, in that it is not vulnerable to being compromised by unauthorized third parties': ibid. In this taxonomy, however, I draw slightly different distinctions: 'safety' problems need not only come from inside an AI system, but can also be caused by its interaction and emergence with other systems or humans. Second, I use a broader conception of 'security', which also covers misuse of AI systems, in the service of attacks traditionally considered 'security threats'.

[351] James M Anderson and others, 'Autonomous Vehicle Technology: A Guide for Policymakers' (RAND Corporation 2016) Product Page <https://www.rand.org/pubs/research_reports/RR443-2.html> accessed 17 October 2017. Note, there has been much work in this area focused on the exploration of 'trolley problems'. Sven Nyholm and Jilles Smids, 'The Ethics of Accident-Algorithms for Self-Driving Cars: An Applied Trolley Problem?' (2016) 19 Ethical Theory and Moral Practice 1275; Edmond Awad and others, 'The Moral Machine Experiment' (2018) 563 Nature 59. Other scholars have critiqued this framing. Cf Martin Cunneen and others, 'Autonomous Vehicles and Avoiding the Trolley (Dilemma): Vehicle Perception, Classification, and the Challenges of Framing Decision Ethics' (2020) 51 Cybernetics and Systems 59; Johannes Himmelreich, 'Never Mind the Trolley: The Ethics of Autonomous Vehicles in Mundane Situations' (2018) 21 Ethical Theory and Moral Practice 669; Abby Everett Jaques, 'Why the Moral Machine Is a Monster' 10. Conversely, others have defended their relevance: Geoff Keeling, 'Why Trolley Problems Matter for the Ethics of Automated Vehicles' (2020) 26 Science and Engineering Ethics 293; Jean-François Bonnefon, Azim Shariff, and Iyad Rahwan, 'The Trolley, The Bull Bar, and Why Engineers Should Care About The Ethics of Autonomous Cars' (2019) 107 Proceedings of the IEEE 502. For an exploration of structural discrimination around such vehicles,

have suggested that AI accident risks can emerge from four sources of harm: '(i) hardware faults, such as exploding batteries; (ii) data-related harm including data corruption, theft and manipulation, (iii) software malfunction or misuse, including AI software components, and (iv) human operator mistakes or deliberate attacks.'[352]

Of course, AI systems are hardly unique in posing safety or reliability risks. Indeed, the past decades have shown the challenges that even traditional software development processes face in producing reliable, bug-free software: for instance, past studies have estimated that the software industry produces an average rate of 15–50 errors per 1,000 lines of code.[353] However, many modern AI systems may raise even more significant challenges in this regard, as they are opaque systems that are not even hand-crafted or coded from the ground up.[354]

Indeed, in addition to facing reliability and safety challenges held in common with all software, AI systems are also vulnerable to additional sets of failure modes,[355] especially in complex sociotechnical contexts.[356]

One concern is that many AI systems or applications can be *highly unpredictable*, at times intrinsically so. Indeed, depending on the specific architecture or techniques underlying an application, AI systems can be 'brittle', reacting unexpectedly when encountering unforeseen new situations.[357] In part, this derives from the limitations of conventional AI, and the degree to which even systems that perform at super-human levels on narrow tasks often do so through decision-making architectures that are dissimilar from those used by humans.[358]

Moreover, accidents can derive not just from the behaviour of individual systems, but also through an AI system's *interactions with the environment*. Indeed, from a system safety perspective, scholars have increasingly recognized that risks are not (solely) caused by technological artefacts, but rather by the interaction of complex sociotechnical systems.[359]

see also Hin-Yan Liu, 'Three Types of Structural Discrimination Introduced by Autonomous Vehicles' (2018) 51 UC Davis Law Review 32.

[352] Martina Kunz and Seán Ó hÉigeartaigh, 'Artificial Intelligence and Robotization' in Robin Geiß and Nils Melzer (eds), *The Oxford Handbook of the International Law of Global Security* (Oxford University Press 2021) 2.

[353] Steve McConnell, *Code Complete: A Practical Handbook of Software Construction, Second Edition* (2nd edition, Microsoft Press 2004), as discussed in Paul Scharre, 'Autonomous Weapons and Operational Risk' (Center for a New American Security 2016) 13 <https://s3.amazonaws.com/files.cnas.org/documents/CNAS_Autonomous-weapons-operational-risk.pdf> accessed 18 March 2025.

[354] With the obvious exception of older approaches, such as symbolic AI.

[355] However, there are broader AI safety issues. For instance, in one review 'AI safety issue groups' are disambiguated into 21 distinct categories. Hernandez-Orallo and others (n 77) 7.

[356] Weidinger and others, 'Sociotechnical Safety Evaluation of Generative AI Systems' (n 47).

[357] Christian Szegedy and others, 'Intriguing Properties of Neural Networks' [2014] arXiv:1312.6199 [cs] <http://arxiv.org/abs/1312.6199> accessed 22 June 2020.

[358] Cummings and others (n 32) 2.

[359] Roel Dobbe, 'System Safety and Artificial Intelligence', *Proceedings of the 2022 ACM Conference on Fairness, Accountability, and Transparency* (Association for Computing Machinery 2022) <https://doi.org/10.1145/3531146.3533215> accessed 15 January 2024.

For instance, the interaction of one algorithm with another, or with human users, can give rise to cascading interactions and system accidents, such as the 2010 algorithmic stock market 'flash crash', triggered by high-frequency trading algorithms.[360] Indeed, interdisciplinary work into the study of 'machine behaviour' has drawn on existing frameworks from the field of ethology (the science of animal behaviour), which emphasizes parallel examinations of the function, mechanism, development, or evolutionary history of a given AI system's behaviour, and highlights how these factors should in turn be explored not just at the level of individual machines, but should also reckon with collective behaviour by networks of interacting systems, or hybrid interactions between systems and humans.[361]

In a similar vein, it has been argued that some AI systems may even be categorically *susceptible to emergent and cascading 'normal accidents'*.[362] 'Normal accidents' are emergent system accidents that inevitably—as a 'normal' result of the way the system has been set up or is operated—emerge in specific organizations working with specific sociotechnical systems under particular operational settings.[363] Such accidents are particularly challenging to mitigate in AI systems, because keeping a human 'in the loop' is not always viable in all applications, given the speed or scale of some AI operations. However, normal accident theory suggests that implementing automated safety measures may perversely enable normal accidents, by increasing a system's interactive complexity further. Moreover, such fail-safes instil further automation bias, as operators may trust safety systems overmuch, resulting in risk homeostasis and creating new avenues for error.[364] Accordingly, automation bias and inappropriate human overtrust of AI systems may ensure that a human that is nominally in the loop in practice functions less like a guardian and more like a 'moral crumple zone'.[365]

Beyond these specific safety concerns, there are also more general concerns around *peculiar behaviours and failure modes* displayed by AI systems.[366] Even

[360] Andrei A Kirilenko and others, 'The Flash Crash: The Impact of High Frequency Trading on an Electronic Market' [2014] SSRN Electronic Journal <https://www.cftc.gov/sites/default/files/idc/groups/public/@economicanalysis/documents/file/oce_flashcrash0314.pdf> accessed 8 September 2020. It should be noted that later investigations suggest the initial cause of the crash was in fact human action.

[361] Iyad Rahwan and others, 'Machine Behaviour' (2019) 568 Nature 477.

[362] Maas, 'Regulating for "Normal AI Accidents"' (n 173). See also Scharre (n 353); Robert Williams and Roman Yampolskiy, 'Understanding and Avoiding AI Failures: A Practical Guide' (2021) 6 Philosophies 53.

[363] See classically Charles Perrow, *Normal Accidents: Living with High Risk Technologies* (Princeton University Press 1984).

[364] Maas, 'Regulating for "Normal AI Accidents"' (n 173) 225. There is in general an extensive literature on automation bias. See also Kate Goddard, Abdul Roudsari, and Jeremy C Wyatt, 'Automation Bias: A Systematic Review of Frequency, Effect Mediators, and Mitigators' (2012) 19 Journal of the American Medical Informatics Association: JAMIA 121.

[365] MC Elish, 'Moral Crumple Zones: Cautionary Tales in Human-Robot Interaction (We Robot 2016)' (Social Science Research Network 2016) SSRN Scholarly Paper ID 2757236 <https://papers.ssrn.com/abstract=2757236> accessed 14 November 2017.

[366] Amodei and others (n 291); Ram Shankar Siva Kumar and others, 'Failure Modes in Machine Learning Systems' [2019] arXiv:1911.11034 [cs, stat] <http://arxiv.org/abs/1911.11034> accessed 7

relatively simple AI agents can solve existing bounded problems in ways unanticipated by their designers, producing strategies that technically solve the given problem, but not in a manner that was ever intended.[367] While the resulting behaviour may at times be amusing, at other times situations of 'perverse instantiation' or 'reward hacking' result in hazardous (or potentially illegal) behaviour.[368] Indeed, such failures are but one of several distinct but generalizable failure modes that have been identified in AI systems.[369]

One significant concern is that, rather than the early growing pains of an immature technology, such incidents may reflect a core problem with the way AI systems are commonly used in 'optimizing metrics' in overtly narrow ways;[370] or that these failures demonstrate intrinsic behavioural risks that arise around certain AI systems that explore the landscape of potential strategies in order to pursue or optimize certain narrow goals.[371] If that is the case, some of the risks from such systems may increase even as they get more sophisticated. As Dafoe has suggested:

> previous kinds of accidents arise because the AI is 'too dumb'. More advanced AI systems will overcome some of these risks, but gain a new kind of accident risk from being 'too clever'. In these cases a powerful optimization process finds 'solutions' that the researchers did not intend, and that may be harmful.[372]

January 2020; Jan Leike and others, 'AI Safety Gridworlds' [2017] arXiv:1711.09883 [cs] <http://arxiv.org/abs/1711.09883> accessed 1 December 2017.

[367] For a series of amusing and revealing examples, see Joel Lehman and others, 'The Surprising Creativity of Digital Evolution: A Collection of Anecdotes from the Evolutionary Computation and Artificial Life Research Communities' (2020) 26 Artificial Life 274. A classic example also includes a genetic algorithm intended to evolve a new design for an oscillating circuit, which hit on a way to hack its hardware to function as a receiver for radio waves emitted from computers in the area. See J Bird and P Layzell, 'The Evolved Radio and Its Implications for Modelling the Evolution of Novel Sensors', *Proceedings of the 2002 Congress on Evolutionary Computation. CEC'02 (Cat. No.02TH8600)* (IEEE 2002) <http://ieeexplore.ieee.org/document/1004522/> accessed 10 July 2020. See also Dario Amodei and Jack Clark, 'Faulty Reward Functions in the Wild' (*OpenAI*, 2016) <https://openai.com/blog/faulty-reward-functions/> accessed 18 February 2017. See generally Victoria Krakovna and others, 'Specification Gaming: The Flip Side of AI Ingenuity' (*Deepmind*, 21 April 2020) <https://deepmind.com/blog/article/Specification-gaming-the-flip-side-of-AI-ingenuity> accessed 5 September 2020.

[368] In a simulated market, trading algorithms discovered and settled upon tacit price fixing and collusion strategies to maximize profit. Enrique Martinez Miranda, Peter McBurney, and Matthew JW Howard, 'Learning Unfair Trading: A Market Manipulation Analysis from the Reinforcement Learning Perspective', *Proceedings of the 2016 IEEE Conference on Evolving and Adaptive Intelligent Systems, EAIS 2016* (Institute of Electrical and Electronics Engineers Inc 2016) <https://kclpure.kcl.ac.uk/portal/en/publications/learning-unfair-trading(4a13e3a7-0af5-48b5-898a-582bcb51e9af)/export.html> accessed 20 February 2019; King and others (n 341) 10–12.

[369] Amodei and others (n 291) 3.

[370] Rachel Thomas and David Uminsky, 'The Problem with Metrics Is a Fundamental Problem for AI' [2020] arXiv:2002.08512 [cs] <http://arxiv.org/abs/2002.08512> accessed 27 August 2020.

[371] Cf. Eliezer Yudkowsky, 'Artificial Intelligence as a Positive and Negative Factor in Global Risk.' in Eliezer Yudkowsky, *Global Catastrophic Risks* (Oxford University Press 2008).

[372] Dafoe, 'AI Governance: A Research Agenda' (n 164) 26.

Indeed, this has fed concerns that if continued technological progress is eventually to yield more capable AI systems, such systems might pose extreme risks to human welfare if they are not properly 'aligned'.[373] While cultural depictions of AI have fed pervasive misperceptions about the nature of such risks,[374] there are reasons why we might expect that the 'alignment' of or control over advanced AI systems with human values or interests would not by default be an easy task.

Curiously, the difficulty of such alignment is reflected not just by work from AI research or philosophy, but can be grounded in a range of empirical findings and conceptual arguments.[375] For instance, it can be derived from the extensive scholarship in law and economics on various principal–agent problems, and the challenges around 'incomplete contracting' (the impossibility to write a 'complete contingent contract' that specifies all possible situations, creating the need to rely on ex post adjudication mechanisms);[376] it is reflected in work on human psychology;[377] it can be derived from various studies of optimal behaviour in existing reinforcement learning systems;[378] and it can be indicated from the difficulty of implementing robust, tamper-proof alignment techniques into today's foundation models and large language models,[379] in ways that cannot be bypassed or eroded by external users, or evaded by deceptive systems.[380]

In response, there has developed an active research agenda on various dimensions of AI safety that is scalable to increasingly advanced AI.[381] This includes work

[373] Stuart Russell, *Human Compatible: Artificial Intelligence and the Problem of Control* (Viking 2019).

[374] Future of Life Institute, 'AI Safety Myths' (*Future of Life Institute*, 2016) <https://futureoflife.org/background/aimyths/> accessed 26 October 2017.

[375] See for instance Rose Hadshar, 'A Review of the Evidence for Existential Risk from AI via Misaligned Power-Seeking' (AI Impacts 2023) Research Report <https://blog.aiimpacts.org/p/new-report-a-review-of-the-empirical?publication_id=1465527> accessed 26 October 2023 (surveying empirical findings, conceptual arguments, and expert opinion over challenges around specification gaming, goal misgeneralization, and power-seeking).

[376] Dylan Hadfield-Menell and Gillian Hadfield, 'Incomplete Contracting and AI Alignment', *Proceedings of the 2019 AAAI/ACM Conference on AI, Ethics, and Society* (2019) <https://dl.acm.org/doi/10.1145/3306618.3314250> accessed 18 July 2019.

[377] For instance, psychological research suggests that 'dark triad' individuals are able to understand others, without necessarily empathizing. Petri J Kajonius and Therese Björkman, 'Individuals with Dark Traits Have the Ability but Not the Disposition to Empathize' (2020) 155 Personality and Individual Differences 109716. This weakly suggests that one common assurance—the idea that if an AI system were ever truly intelligent, it would know what we meant by our requests, and care about achieving that—need not hold even among human actors.

[378] Illustrating for instance the 'instrumental convergence' thesis. Stephen M Omohundro, 'The Basic AI Drives' (2008) 171 Frontiers in Artificial Intelligence and Applications 483. For one demonstration of this, see Alexander Matt Turner and others, 'Optimal Policies Tend to Seek Power' [2021] arXiv:1912.01683 [cs] <http://arxiv.org/abs/1912.01683> accessed 6 December 2021.

[379] Casper and others (n 295).

[380] Hubinger and others (n 346).

[381] Jose Hernandez-Orallo, Fernando Martınez-Plumed, and Shahar Avin, 'Surveying Safety-Relevant AI Characteristics', *Proceedings of 1st AAAI's Workshop on Artificial Intelligence Safety (SafeAI)* (2019) <http://ceur-ws.org/Vol-2301/paper_22.pdf> accessed 11 February 2019.

on 'interruptibility',[382] 'safe exploration',[383] and multi-agent dynamics between different algorithms,[384] among others.[385] Of course, much uncertainty remains. It is far from obvious how great such risks will ultimately be, or on what timeframe they might manifest, or—assuming the possibility of eventual catastrophic risks—the extent to which meaningful technical safety research can be undertaken on today's systems.[386] However, thoughtful people have at least entertained positions on various sides of these debates. That should not be cause for panic, but it might be cause for further investigation and strategy formulation.

In sum, however, it should be clear that in the context of AI technology, 'safety' becomes a more nuanced, refined, and tricky topic than many conventional approaches or doctrines in either 'safety regulation' or 'safety engineering' have conventionally reckoned with. As a governance *rationale*, these safety risks most obviously involve new risks to human health and safety. As a governance *target*, these risks have distinct features that are relevant to appropriate regulation. Rather than being the fault of human actors' *apathy* or malice, they may derive from their *ignorance* or *negligence*, coupled with the effects of overtrust and automation bias. This is exacerbated, at the industrial level, by the 'many hands' problem. Finally, at the artefactual level, this problem is also exacerbated by a range of behavioural features of some AI approaches.

Accordingly, governance logics for AI safety problems may commonly be closely tied to questions of safety engineering (to ensure e.g. reliability, corrigibility, interpretability, limiting capabilities or deployment spaces, formal verification). They often involve operational requirements around, for instance, the need to ensure 'Meaningful Human Control', or to ensure that a human is 'in the loop', though the precise implications of such arrangements can often be hard to specify.[387] At the institutional level, safety challenges foreground ex post liability mechanisms and tort

[382] Laurent Orseau and Stuart Armstrong, 'Safely Interruptible Agents', *Proceedings of the Thirty-Second Conference on Uncertainty in Artificial Intelligence* (AUAI Press 2016) <https://dl.acm.org/doi/abs/10.5555/3020948.3021006> accessed 9 April 2024.

[383] Joshua Achiam and Dario Amodei, 'Benchmarking Safe Exploration in Deep Reinforcement Learning' (2019) <https://cdn.openai.com/safexp-short.pdf> accessed 17 March 2025.

[384] David Manheim, 'Overoptimization Failures and Specification Gaming in Multi-Agent Systems' [2018] arXiv:1810.10862 [cs] <http://arxiv.org/abs/1810.10862> accessed 14 January 2019; David Manheim, 'Multiparty Dynamics and Failure Modes for Machine Learning and Artificial Intelligence' (2019) 3 Big Data and Cognitive Computing 21.

[385] Dafoe, 'AI Governance: A Research Agenda' (n 164) 29–30. See also Tom Everitt, Gary Lea, and Marcus Hutter, 'AGI Safety Literature Review' [2018] arXiv:1805.01109 [cs] <http://arxiv.org/abs/1805.01109> accessed 7 May 2018.

[386] Carina Prunkl and Jess Whittlestone, 'Beyond Near- and Long-Term: Towards a Clearer Account of Research Priorities in AI Ethics and Society', *Proceedings of the AAAI/ACM Conference on AI, Ethics, and Society* (ACM 2020) <http://dl.acm.org/doi/10.1145/3375627.3375803> accessed 12 February 2020.

[387] Rebecca Crootof, Margot E Kaminski, and W Nicholson Price II, 'Humans in the Loop' (2023) 76 Vanderbilt Law Review 429.

law.[388] At the very limit, safety concerns that cannot be adequately secured might warrant (temporary) relinquishment of certain AI capabilities, either categorically or at least in their deployment in certain high-stakes domains.[389]

4.6.2.4 Structural shifts

In terms of *structure*, scholars increasingly examine the ways in which various technologies, including AI, could (inadvertently) alter decision environments for human actors at the systemic level, in ways that could increase the risk of miscalculation or accident, or lead to greater tensions, instability, or conflict, or pressure various parties to incrementally surrender or compromise on certain values.[390] Notably, Remco Zwetsloot and Allan Dafoe have pointed out how, in examining risks from AI, many implicitly or explicitly bucket problems as coming from either 'accident' or 'misuse'—and have argued that this 'accident-misuse dichotomy obscures how technologies, including AI, often create risk by shaping the environment and incentives'.[391] They accordingly suggest that this dichotomy should be expanded to also take stock of a 'structural perspective' on AI risks.[392]

Rather than just examining how new technology can afford agents with new capabilities—that is, new opportunities for (mis)use—this perspective asks us to consider the broader effects on society and social institutions, including how the introduction of AI systems may unwittingly shape the environment and incentives (the 'structure') in which decision-makers operate. While technologies do not shape society deterministically, they may still reshape the strategic environment

[388] Although for some of the shortfalls of these, see also Matthew U Scherer, 'Regulating Artificial Intelligence Systems: Risks, Challenges, Competencies, and Strategies' (2016) 29(2) Harvard Journal of Law & Technology 353, 388–392 <http://jolt.law.harvard.edu/articles/pdf/v29/29HarvJLTech353.pdf> accessed 5 March 2018.

[389] Such, for instance, was one conclusion of Charles Perrow with regard to the 'normal accident risks' from nuclear power. Attributed in Nick Pidgeon, 'In Retrospect: Normal Accidents' (2011) 477 Nature 404, 404. Interestingly, during the Cold War, computer scientists made the argument that, given the inevitability of computer bugs and the impossibility of achieving flawless software performance, we ought not to integrate computer systems in nuclear command and control systems, because these could never be made sufficiently reliable. Alan Borning, 'Computer System Reliability and Nuclear War' (1987) 30 Communications of the ACM 112. For arguments making this link to the integration of machine learning in nuclear command and control, see also Shahar Avin and SM Amadae, 'Autonomy and Machine Learning at the Interface of Nuclear Weapons, Computers and People' in V Boulanin (ed), *The Impact of Artificial Intelligence on Strategic Stability and Nuclear Risk* (Stockholm International Peace Research Institute 2019) <https://www.repository.cam.ac.uk/handle/1810/297703> accessed 16 October 2019; Matthijs Maas, Kayla Lucero-Matteucci, and Di Cooke, 'Military Artificial Intelligence as a Contributor to Global Catastrophic Risk', *The Era of Global Risk* (Open Book Publishers 2023) <https://www.openbookpublishers.com/books/10.11647/obp.0336/chapters/10.11647/obp.0336.10> accessed 9 August 2023.

[390] Zwetsloot and Dafoe (n 55); Agnes Schim van der Loeff and others, 'AI Ethics for Systemic Issues: A Structural Approach' (2019) <http://arxiv.org/abs/1911.03216> accessed 13 January 2020.

[391] Zwetsloot and Dafoe (n 55). For an expansion that sets out three subcategories of structural risk, see also Kyle A Kilian, 'Beyond Accidents and Misuse: Decoding the Structural Risk Dynamics of Artificial Intelligence'.

[392] Zwetsloot and Dafoe (n 55).

and structural incentives under which actors operate (especially in competitive contexts), creating pressures that facilitate—or even appear to 'compel'—other first-order effects in the domains of ethics, safety, or security.[393]

It has long been recognized that prevailing technological conditions can often provide, or at least contribute to, 'security dilemmas' in which states might find themselves locked.[394] Indeed, Arthur Stein has noted that rather than an 'inherent' feature of international politics, the security dilemma is predicated on structural features of the international system, which include the state of knowledge, science, and technology. As such, he argues that 'the security dilemma presumes either that offensive weapons exist and are superior to defensive ones, or that weapons systems are not easily distinguishable'.[395]

The same dynamics could well apply to some uses of AI. Specifically, new AI capabilities or use cases might unintentionally—and, at times, 'invisibly'—shift actors' incentives in hazardous ways, for various reasons, and at both the global and local levels (see Table 4.2). Such sociotechnical change would be all the harder to anticipate and mitigate, because it might not be intended by any one actor.[396]

In the first place, new AI capabilities or applications may *alter choice architectures,* changing the calculations or deliberate decisions of principals, in ways that either outright privilege choices leading to AI ethics or security challenges or indirectly lead to general conflict.

At the macro level, for instance, certain AI capabilities could make relations amongst actors appear more zero-sum, or create the impression of a 'winner-take-all' competition.[397] More loosely, AI applications in speeding up scientific research or various industries could theoretically reduce the economic or

[393] For instance, one influential account of the origins of the First World War argues that the specific socio-technological features of the contemporary European railroad system required (or at least put an operational premium on) certain logistical choices, such as tight and interlocking schedules, which in turn required (or at least put a strategic premium on) rapid, all-or-nothing mass mobilization decisions. This reduced states' room for manoeuvre to signal to one another through more muted and less escalatory troop movements, and pitched the dominos of general war. That is not to say that this technological configuration either compelled or necessitated war, but rather that it was a contributing factor that structured and constrained each party's decision space (and time) in making choices around the outbreak and scope of war. Stephen Van Evera, 'The Cult of the Offensive and the Origins of the First World War' (1984) 9 International Security 58. However, it should be noted that this interpretation remains contested. See for instance the critique by Keir A Lieber, *War and the Engineers: The Primacy of Politics over Technology* (1st edn, Cornell University Press 2008). And for a discussion, see Jack Snyder and Keir A Lieber, 'Defensive Realism and the "New" History of World War I' (2008) 33 International Security 174.

[394] For the foundational work on the security dilemma, see John H Herz, 'Idealist Internationalism and the Security Dilemma' (1950) 2 World Politics 157; For a modern restatement, see Shiping Tang, 'The Security Dilemma: A Conceptual Analysis' (2009) 18 Security Studies 587.

[395] Arthur A Stein, 'Coordination and Collaboration: Regimes in an Anarchic World' (1982) 36 International Organization 299, 320.

[396] It is useful to note that, because these involve ways in which AI systems affect the decisions of many interrelated actors, the problems they create are particularly acute in competitive contexts, but they could also apply more broadly, even in non-zero-sum contexts.

[397] Zwetsloot and Dafoe (n 55).

Table 4.2 Types of AI-induced structural shifts (macro vs. micro), with examples

Diffusion of new AI capabilities …	… Alters choice architecture (change calculations and decisions of principals)	… Drives uncertainty and complexity (increase room for errors and mistakes)	… Forces value erosion from competition (as each reacts to pressures of other's AI choices)
At macro level (strategic, global decisions)	• Makes geopolitical competition appear more as a 'winner-take-all' or zero-sum competition • Computational propaganda facilitates greater 'lawfare', reduces reputational costs of misbehaviour	• Introduces general *uncertainty* over relative capabilities, enabling strategic miscalculation	• Perceived pressures to develop AI weapons, even if it increases proliferation risk to malicious actors
At micro level (tactical, local decisions)	• Lowers prospective (reputational) costs of behaviour (e.g. less kinetic military conflicts; less blatant forms of intrusive surveillance)	• Narrow time windows for decisions, increasing potential for accidental escalation • Predictive algorithms might create *false certainty*, driving adverse self-fulfilling cycles	• Perceived pressures to deploy AI weapons, even if it increases 'flash war' risk
Introduces or exacerbates …	AI ethics and security challenges; general conflict	AI safety risks	All other issues; erodes conditions for cooperation

scientific interdependence of states, in ways that afford states a greater sense of self-sufficiency. Finally, improvements in the capability of AI systems to shape public perceptions or debate could increase the willingness, on behalf of unscrupulous actors, to engage in more exploitative practices, knowing that the global (or at least domestic) reputational fallout might be more easily contained.[398]

AI capabilities could also alter incentives and choices at the meso or micro level. They could lower the threshold to a specific conflict or attack, for instance by lowering the perceived risks or costs of such actions. This could happen because the new AI capability sufficiently increases the expected probability of rapid

[398] On the other hand, technologies could also certainly be used by other actors to unveil abuses, and to hold parties to greater account. See briefly Lorna McGregor, 'Are New Technologies an Aid to Reputation as a Disciplinarian?' (2019) 113 AJIL Unbound 238.

victory, reduces the direct danger to human soldiers, or reduces the perceived intensity or visibility of conflict in the public eye.[399] Such dynamics need not remain contained to solely military contexts, however. Technological advances in remote biometric identification technologies could well enable new vectors of surveillance. These might be as granular as studding public infrastructure with facial-recognition cameras, yet be much less visible and therefore perceived as much less intrusive by the public by comparison.[400]

In the second place, AI capabilities might result in behaviours that drive increased *uncertainty and complexity*, increasing the room for errors and mistakes, potentially producing safety challenges.

At the *macro level*, new AI use cases could drive *general strategic uncertainty* or lack of clarity over relative (military or cyber) capabilities, or over the balance of power, opening up scope for miscalculation, mutual misperceptions, and misunderstandings.[401] More specifically, they could create overlap between offensive and defensive uses or actions, driving security dilemmas. More generally, uncertainty could be fed as a result of AI applications in 'neural fake news' and computational propaganda driving a decay in the 'epistemic security' landscape.[402]

At the *micro level*, new AI capabilities might *narrow time windows* for decision-makers to make critical choices, reducing the ability of policymakers to resolve or reduce high levels of uncertainty. For instance, systems that would put a strong tactical or strategic premium on offence over defence[403] might be perceived to put such parties in a 'use it or lose it' situation. Indeed, Schneider has previously identified a military 'capability–vulnerability paradox' in 'digitally enabled warfare', whereby the same digital capabilities that make the (US) military more effective on the battlefield also render them more vulnerable to pre-emptive attacks on the underlying digital networks and technologies.[404] As such, the introduction of certain

[399] Arthur Holland Michel, 'The Killer Algorithms Nobody's Talking About' (*Foreign Policy*, 20 January 2020) <https://foreignpolicy.com/2020/01/20/ai-autonomous-weapons-artificial-intelligence-the-killer-algorithms-nobodys-talking-about/> accessed 21 January 2020. See also Maas, 'Innovation-Proof Governance for Military AI?' (n 276) 144–146 (discussing how certain types of military AI might reduce the reputational costs of noncompliance with bans).

[400] In previous work, I have referred to this as a form of 'ubiquitous yet tacit surveillance'. See Hayward and Maas (n 257) 12–13. Others have discussed these trends under the frame of the 'Disneyfication' of smart city policing. Elizabeth E Joh, 'Policing the Smart City' (2019) 15 International Journal of Law in Context 177.

[401] Matthew Kroenig and Bharath Gopalaswamy, 'Will Disruptive Technology Cause Nuclear War?' (*Bulletin of the Atomic Scientists*, 12 November 2018) <https://thebulletin.org/2018/11/will-disruptive-technology-cause-nuclear-war/> accessed 22 November 2018.

[402] Lin (n 236).

[403] See Ben Garfinkel and Allan Dafoe, 'How Does the Offense-Defense Balance Scale?' (2019) 42 Journal of Strategic Studies 736.

[404] Jacquelyn Schneider, 'The Capability/Vulnerability Paradox and Military Revolutions: Implications for Computing, Cyber, and the Onset of War' (2019) 42 Journal of Strategic Studies 841; Jacquelyn Schneider, 'Digitally-Enabled Warfare: The Capability-Vulnerability Paradox' (Center for a New American Security 2016) <https://www.cnas.org/publications/reports/digitally-enabled-warfare-the-capability-vulnerability-paradox> accessed 30 November 2018.

AI capabilities by any one party might put pressure on decision-makers—even well-intentioned ones—on both sides to make risky decisions, or decisions under imperfect information.[405]

Moreover, at the micro level, the predictions of AI models could also produce *false certainty* among actors, for instance by creating adverse self-fulfilling predictions or systemic pressures: the use of machine learning for pre-attack 'early warning' systems could inflame tense geopolitical situations and lower the threshold to the use of force.[406] Even AI models that are used 'for good' might create such perverse systemic externalities if deployed carelessly: for instance, Van der Loeff and colleagues have discussed the hypothetical case of an AI system used to predict the impact of climate on land and agricultural production, in order to predict and manage food supplies. Such a system would be very valuable for ensuring food security, but it might also spark adverse systemic effects—'price hikes, hoarding of food supplies, environmentally unsustainable practices, conflict over arable land and increased inequality'—if its information was shared freely or publicly.[407]

Third, structural shifts produced by AI systems could result in *value erosion from competition*.[408] These are situations where actors individually would prefer to maintain certain values or principles (e.g. spending public funds on education rather than on defence, securing full data privacy, maintaining a 'human-in-the-loop' in autonomous weapons systems, exhaustively testing autonomous vehicles in safe circumstances). However, each actor perceives it is confronted by steep trade-offs between maintaining those values or compromising on them in order to remain (economically or strategically) competitive with rivals who, it is feared, are more willing to make that trade.[409] While it is not true that such strategic pressures are invariably strong or irreversible, there are many cases in which they manifest as harmful feedback cycles that generate trade-offs between private gains and public harms, or various races to the bottom.

At the *macro level*, this could result in development decisions that create downstream security or ethics problems. For instance, this dynamic could result in parties developing certain AI applications (either explicitly military or dual-use) which are hard to control and might subsequently diffuse to malicious actors. This would echo the experience with intelligence community hacking tools or 'backdoors' in digital infrastructure, which were developed and retained because

[405] Zwetsloot and Dafoe (n 55).
[406] Ashley Deeks, Noam Lubell and Daragh Murray, 'Machine Learning, Artificial Intelligence, and the Use of Force by States' (2019) 10 Journal of National Security Law & Policy 1, 6–7.
[407] van der Loeff and others (n 390) 3–4.
[408] Dafoe, 'AI Governance: A Research Agenda' (n 164) 7. The term is also discussed in Allan Dafoe, 'AI Governance: Opportunity and Theory of Impact' (17 September 2020) <https://www.allandafoe.com/opportunity> accessed 20 September 2020.
[409] Dafoe, 'AI Governance: A Research Agenda' (n 164) 7.

of strategic considerations, but which eventually proliferated into the hands of malicious hacker groups, proving powerful tools for misuse.[410]

Likewise, at a more 'micro' level, AI applications could drive 'safety erosion from competition'. This could occur when the pursuit by one party of certain competitive AI applications compels other parties to rush development or deployment with fewer safety precautions, or with less time for safety testing.[411] Indeed, strategic logics could even suggest that certain systems (e.g. cyberwarfare defence uses) could open up avenues for accident cascades. As such, Paul Scharre has argued that while there are ways in which military AI systems could contribute to strategic stability, if they cannot be kept under reliable control their deployment would create situations of 'fragile stability', where crises rapidly escalate out of the control of human commanders, producing what he calls 'flash wars'.[412]

In terms of sociotechnical change and problem logics, AI's structural impacts are interestingly distinct from the first three categories ('ethics', 'security', 'safety'). This is because structure is rarely a first-order challenge or rationale, but instead catalyses many first-order problems in these other areas. It both increases the risks of ethical, safety, or security challenges *in* AI systems themselves and highlights their broader societal effects and spillover into apparently distinct domains. As such, structural shifts may indirectly give rise to the full gamut of rationales for regulation and governance discussed previously.

As such, considering *structure* also highlights a distinct perspective on needed regulatory solutions—to address this *target*. Notably, an *ethics* ('problematic use') perspective puts the focus on measures that improve the norms of developers, engineers, and operators, or which institutionalize oversight mechanisms to hold these parties to account ex post. A *security* ('misuse') perspective puts focus either on changing the motivations or opportunities for malicious individuals, or on

[410] For instance, in 2013, a group of hackers calling themselves the Shadow Brokers stole a few disks of hacking tools developed by the US National Security Agency (NSA). By sharing these secrets on the internet, the group exposed major security vulnerabillities in internet infrastructures, and moreover put sophisticated cyberweapons widely available, among others providing the key exploit underpinning the 2017 global WannaCry ransomware attack, as well as the 'EternalBlue' tool. Bruce Schneier, 'Who Are the Shadow Brokers?' [2017] *The Atlantic* <https://www.theatlantic.com/technology/archive/2017/05/shadow-brokers/527778/> accessed 8 September 2020; Scott Shane, 'Malware Case Is Major Blow for the N.S.A.' *The New York Times* (16 May 2017) <https://www.nytimes.com/2017/05/16/us/nsa-malware-case-shadow-brokers.html> accessed 8 September 2020. Lily Hay Newman, 'How Leaked NSA Spy Tool "EternalBlue" Became a Hacker Favorite' [2018] *Wired* <https://www.wired.com/story/eternalblue-leaked-nsa-spy-tool-hacked-world/> accessed 8 September 2020. Similarly, one can consider the proliferation of the 'Blackshades Remote Access Tool': described as 'a criminal franchise in a box', and sold via PayPal for as little as US $40, Blackshades allowed users without technical skills to effectively deploy ransomware and conduct eavesdropping operations. See John Markoff, 'As Artificial Intelligence Evolves, So Does Its Criminal Potential' *The New York Times* (23 October 2016) <https://www.nytimes.com/2016/10/24/technology/artificial-intelligence-evolves-with-its-criminal-potential.html> accessed 26 November 2018; as well as the discussion of lessons for AI in Hayward and Maas (n 257) 10.

[411] Danzig (n 126).

[412] Scharre (n 269) 13.

ensuring deterrence through denial, traceability, or response. A *safety* ('accident') perspective focuses on improving the patience, caution, or competence of the producers, engineers, or operators. By contrast, a *structural* perspective puts less emphasis on various actors' passive ethical laxness (ethics), active malice (security), or inadvertent neglect (safety). Rather, it looks at the effects of technologies on structuring actors' decisions and choices in ways that generate, enable, or undercut efforts to address first-order ethical, security, or safety issues. These indirect effects can be indeliberate, but no or few individual actors have the ability to unilaterally prevent or resolve them, or even to foresee their emergence in the first place. Because they do not derive from any one individual actor's active intent, structural challenges can be particularly difficult to address or govern. In some sense, they emerge from the level of systemic incentives into which actors collectively may find themselves locked.[413]

Accordingly, addressing challenges from 'structure' often cannot be achieved by targeting individual actors, or by any one actor's unilateral action. Rather, more than any other type of AI sociotechnical change, addressing structural challenges of AI may require some measure of collective action, especially at the international level. This faces the broad set of problems common to securing 'mutual restraint' global public goods. Practically, governance can also be supported or enabled through various transparency and trust-promoting agreements, such as Confidence-Building Measures (CBMs).

4.6.2.5 Common benefits

The discussion so far has surveyed many mostly threatening developments, scenarios, and risks. However, along with the many risks, it remains important to keep in mind the upsides of AI technology. Indeed, while much of the discussion so far has foregrounded risks more than benefits, this is not to conclude that the emergence of AI technology necessarily produces more harm than good.[414] While it may be the case that AI introduces foundational challenges, it is also possible that the technology is stuck in a 'technology trap'. This is a phenomenon described by Carl Frey, whereby certain technological transformations which eventually could

413 See also Dafoe, 'AI Governance' (n 408) ('When we think about the risks arising from the combustion engine—such as urban sprawl, blitzkrieg offensive warfare, strategic bombers, and climate change—we see that it is hard to fault any one individual or group for negligence or malign intent. It is harder to see a single agent whose behaviour we could change to avert the harm, or a causally proximate opportunity to intervene. Rather, we see that technology can produce social harms, or fail to have its benefits realized, because of a host of structural dynamics. The impacts from technology may be diffuse, uncertain, delayed, and hard to contract over').

414 Indeed, as Parson et al. note, '[a]lthough it may be tempting to view any large change as harmful, at least initially, we do not presume that the societal impacts of AI will be entirely, or even predominantly, harmful. In fact, there are strong grounds to anticipate large benefits'. Edward Parson and others, 'Could AI Drive Transformative Social Progress? What Would This Require?' [2019] AI Pulse 8 <https://aipulse.org/could-ai-drive-transformative-social-progress-what-would-this-require/> accessed 28 September 2019.

bring broad prosperity will, in an early stage of development, deliver only meagre results while disproportionately producing societal dislocation. This in turn could create a chance that some technologies are rejected in their early stages before they have had a chance to prove their worth.[415] While it remains unclear whether AI is one such technology,[416] unless we wish to commit to far-reaching opposition to the technology we should ensure that its benefits are realized as fully, as widely, and—critically—as soon as possible. This requires considering strategic challenges around realizing or accelerating opportunities for common goods through and in AI. This has three components.

In the first place, as previously noted, there is a need for various forms of global coordination to avert market failures or inefficiencies, to achieve the full economic and scientific fruits of AI. Accordingly, some have called for a 'new technology diplomacy' to avert the fragmentation of global regimes,[417] and to limit protectionism or 'tech nationalism'.

Second, there are many areas where AI could be used proactively in support of various social or global goods.[418] Some have proposed that it can support global commons such as the Sustainable Development Goals[419] or the fight against climate change.[420] Others have identified positive uses in disaster relief coordination. For instance, as argued by Heather Roff, in complex humanitarian crises, AI

[415] Carl Benedikt Frey, *The Technology Trap: Capital, Labor, and Power in the Age of Automation* (Princeton University Press 2019).

[416] Interestingly, and more provocatively, there may be certain technologies which could show the reverse of Frey's technology trap: that is, they produce considerable and appealing upsides in an early stage of development, and so raise little opposition. Yet it is only in their later stages, once societies have grown much more dependent on them, that the technology's far-reaching downsides begin to crystallize. Fossil fuel industry may well prove one such technology. Others might be leaded gasoline or CFCs. See Smil (n 116). A more controversial example could be spaceflight, which has historically been broadly perceived as a lofty ambition, and which has produced tremendous spin-off innovations that have benefited much of society. However, Daniel Deudney has argued that on longer time horizons, expansive space exploration might ultimately open up a series of new catastrophic threats to humanity. Daniel Deudney, *Dark Skies: Space Expansionism, Planetary Geopolitics, and the Ends of Humanity* (Oxford University Press 2020). For general discussion of the implications of technologies that might entail more complex distributions of benefits and harms between different actors and across boundaries or across time, see Andrew Mazibrada, 'Slumbering Sentinel: Elaborating a Right to Protection from the Adverse Effects of Scientific Progress and Its Applications' (University of Copenhagen 2024) 44–67.

[417] Claudio Feijóo and others, 'Harnessing Artificial Intelligence (AI) to Increase Wellbeing for All: The Case for a New Technology Diplomacy' (2020) 44 Telecommunications Policy 101988.

[418] ITU, 'AI for Good Global Summit 2019 Insights' (2019) <https://itu.foleon.com/itu/aiforgood2019/home/> accessed 6 October 2019. See also Alexandra Luccioni and Yoshua Bengio, 'On the Morality of Artificial Intelligence' [2019] arXiv:1912.11945 [cs] <http://arxiv.org/abs/1912.11945> accessed 19 August 2020; Luciano Floridi and others, 'AI4People—An Ethical Framework for a Good AI Society: Opportunities, Risks, Principles, and Recommendations' (2018) 28 Minds and Machines 689.

[419] Ricardo Vinuesa and others, 'The Role of Artificial Intelligence in Achieving the Sustainable Development Goals' (2020) 11 Nature Communications <https://www.nature.com/articles/s41467-019-14108-y> accessed 8 May 2019. But for a cautious approach, see Jon Truby, 'Governing Artificial Intelligence to Benefit the UN Sustainable Development Goals' (2020) n/a Sustainable Development <https://onlinelibrary.wiley.com/doi/abs/10.1002/sd.2048> accessed 13 March 2020.

[420] David Rolnick and others, 'Tackling Climate Change with Machine Learning' [2019] arXiv:1906.05433 [cs, stat] <http://arxiv.org/abs/1906.05433> accessed 23 July 2019.

systems could help 'examine vast amounts of data relating to available resources, use satellite imagery or images from surveillance aircraft to map affected terrain, as well as find survivors, and thereby estimate the necessary resource requirements given limitations on time, goods and manpower'.[421] As discussed in Chapter 5, AI systems also could see use in strengthening international law; they could help monitor and enforce human rights,[422] aid diplomatic processes,[423] and help resolve and arbitrate international conflicts.[424]

Third, governance regimes might be necessary to ensure that the considerable benefits of AI technology are distributed in a broad and inclusive manner, especially as or if the technology proves increasingly transformative.[425]

While there are certainly critiques of the various 'AI for Good' frameworks,[426] ensuring that societies seize the positive benefits from AI systems—particularly global public goods, or benefits which would not naturally be supplied by markets—must be a core goal. Much of this would need to confront underlying systemic incentives, such as coordination challenges around cost-sharing or free-riding. This problem logic however foregrounds the role of various governance systems aimed at securing greater public interest regulation.

4.6.2.6 Governance disruption

Finally, AI systems may enable new types of behaviour or relations that pose a direct challenge to existing *legal systems*. While many of the previously discussed problems involve challenges for governance, changes to the *legal* processes can be more ambiguous. Some have hailed them as creating opportunities. At the same time, there are concerns over the rule of law. AI can impact on legal systems in three ways. In the first place, it can affect the *substance* of law, requiring a need for

[421] Heather M Roff, 'Advancing Human Security Through Artificial Intelligence' in Mary L Cummings and others, *Artificial Intelligence and International Affairs: Disruption Anticipated* (Chatham House 2018) 25 <https://www.chathamhouse.org/sites/default/files/publications/research/2018-06-14-artificial-intelligence-international-affairs-cummings-roff-cukier-parakilas-bryce.pdf> accessed 18 March 2025.

[422] Steven Livingston and Mathias Risse, 'The Future Impact of Artificial Intelligence on Humans and Human Rights' (2019) 33 Ethics & International Affairs 141.

[423] Katharina E Höne, 'Mapping the Challenges and Opportunities of Artificial Intelligence for the Conduct of Diplomacy' (DiploFoundation 2019) <https://www.diplomacy.edu/sites/default/files/AI-diplo-report.pdf> accessed 14 March 2019.

[424] Ashley Deeks, 'High-Tech International Law' (2020) 88 George Washington Law Review 575, 633–637.

[425] Claire Dennis and others, 'Ways Forward for Global AI Benefit Sharing' (2024) <https://openreview.net/forum?id=St6azqVuqs> accessed 9 December 2024. For an interesting practical application, see also the proposal for a 'Windfall Clause', an 'ex ante commitment by AI firms to donate a significant amount of any eventual extremely large profits [. . .] that a firm could not earn without achieving fundamental, economically transformative breakthroughs in AI capabilities'. Cullen O'Keefe and others, 'The Windfall Clause: Distributing the Benefits of AI for the Common Good', *Proceedings of the AAAI/ACM Conference on AI, Ethics, and Society* (ACM 2020) 327 <http://dl.acm.org/doi/10.1145/3375627.3375842> accessed 12 February 2020.

[426] See Jared Moore, 'AI for Not Bad' (2019) 2 Frontiers in Big Data 32.

new regulation to clarify existing laws or create new laws. In the second place, it can affect the *processes* of law, altering the ways in which those laws are produced, monitored, or enforced, with effects that can range from strengthening the rule of law to instead 'replacing' it. In the third place, it can affect and potentially *erode the political scaffolding* of legal systems, risking their efficacy or legitimacy.

AI-driven sociotechnical change that produces governance disruption is a special case. As discussed, in terms of governance *rationale*, it invokes a distinct challenge—not a risk to regulatees, but a potential threat directly to the existing regulatory order. This results in a need for intervention to ensure the continuing or renewed adequacy and accountability of the governance system. This highlights a diverse set of strategies, from those aimed at rendering legal systems more future-proof (e.g. technological neutrality, the designation of authoritative interpreters, sunset clauses) to those that aim to ensure adequate oversight systems for the deployment of automation in support of legal and governance systems.

Governance disruption is a special case, and remains underexplored in much discussions of AI's global impact. As such, we will spend significant time exploring this dynamic in Chapter 5. However, we will first finish this chapter with some reflections on the applications, strengths, or limits of the sociotechnical change lens for AI governance.

4.7 Evaluating Sociotechnical Change as a Lens on AI Governance

How useful is the concept of sociotechnical change? As argued by Bennett Moses, switching the conceptual focus from 'regulating for technology' to 'regulating for changes in the sociotechnical landscape' may help provide valuable principles or insights to address questions of regulatory design and choice of institution, as well as for regulatory timing and responsiveness.[427] However, while the lens has strengths as an analytical tool, these should not blind us to its limits and preconditions. As such, let us briefly review the strengths and limits of this approach.

4.7.1 Uses and Strengths of the Sociotechnical Change Approach

The sociotechnical approach to AI regulation has a range of benefits in terms of regulatory *triage*, *tracing*, *targeting*, *transferal*, *timing*, and *tailoring*. We can briefly illustrate these in the context of recent debates over the governance of increasingly advanced and general-purpose AI systems.

[427] Bennett Moses, 'Regulating in the Face of Sociotechnical Change' (n 181) 585–591.

In the first place, the sociotechnical lens helps regulators carry out more appropriate *triage* or prioritization of different challenges amidst uncertainty. That is, it helps focus scarce regulatory attention on the most socially disruptive outputs of AI, and not just the applications, capabilities, or threat models that are presented as the most novel.[428] Additionally, this framework allows regulators to grapple not only with the way AI creates direct sociotechnical challenges (in the areas of ethics, security, and safety), but also with how it raises indirect problems (in terms of structural shifts, opportunities, governance disruption) which often still feature less widely in regulatory debates. This is valuable in sharpening ongoing debates around which AI systems are of concern and urgency. For example, in debates around the impacts of conventional (narrow) AI systems, a sociotechnical approach can deepen our understanding of when or why systems might be 'high-risk', in a way that does not only rely on a hierarchical categorization of some social domains as 'inherently' high or low-risk.

This concept can also enable superior triage in debates over advanced AI governance. It highlights the importance of developing legislation for advanced AI systems, since their general-purpose capabilities lend themselves to driving many types of sociotechnical change at once, engaging many problem logics simultaneously. However, this perspective also expands the focus of regulators beyond the very peak of 'frontier' AI systems, in at least two ways. On the one hand, it highlights the sociotechnical significance of narrow-but-super-human AI models which, rather than reproducing human capabilities at scale (as many foundation models do), potentially offer specific capabilities or affordances that have never been seen before. In addition, the sociotechnical change lens also helps regulators consider the additional post-deployment dangers that may emerge from general-purpose AI systems once they are deployed in the real world.[429] Such downstream risks are not captured by narrow evaluations of the base model, but rather require broader sociotechnical safety evaluations.[430]

However, in terms of regulatory *tracing* of impacts, the broader scope of the sociotechnical perspective critically does not mean that model-level evaluations

[428] This also allows a more effective evaluation of the actual marginal risks of different models. See Sayash Kapoor and others, 'On the Societal Impact of Open Foundation Models' <https://crfm.stanford.edu/open-fms/>; Harry Law, 'The Marginal Risk of AI' (*Learning from Examples*, 30 March 2024) <https://www.learningfromexamples.com/p/the-marginal-risk-of-ai?publication_id=1838544> accessed 7 May 2024.

[429] Helen Toner and others, 'Skating to Where the Puck Is Going: Anticipating and Managing Risks from Frontier AI Systems' (Center for Security and Emerging Technology 2023) 10 <https://cset.georgetown.edu/publication/skating-to-where-the-puck-is-going/> accessed 1 December 2023 ('Conflating model-only capabilities and real-world risks makes it more difficult to identify and respond to the risks at hand').

[430] Weidinger and others, 'Sociotechnical Safety Evaluation of Generative AI Systems' (n 47). For a proposal for 'human interaction evaluations' (HIEs) which focus on the assessment of human-model interactions or the process and the outcomes of humans using AI models, see also Lujain Ibrahim and others, 'Beyond Static AI Evaluations: Advancing Human Interaction Evaluations for LLM Harms and Risks' (arXiv, 20 May 2024) <http://arxiv.org/abs/2405.10632> accessed 24 May 2024.

of AI capabilities and risks are redundant or should be entirely replaced by a focus on their downstream uses.[431] Nor does this perspective diminish the case for upstream (or development-stage) foundation model regulation per se. Rather, it provides a natural and necessary complement to model-stage regulation and analysis, grounding a case for additional monitoring of the post-deployment impacts of even frontier models that pass initial model-level evaluations, in order to more meaningfully capture all significant risks that derive from advanced AI systems, throughout their development and deployment cycle. In this way, a sociotechnical approach aids regulators in targeting regulation at the most appropriate points of AI development, by providing a framework to grapple with the complexity of modern, advanced AI systems, the ways they are developed and deployed, and their downstream sociotechnical impacts, across the sociotechnical stack.[432]

Consequently, in terms of regulatory *targeting*, a related benefit of this approach is that it allows us to increase the range of regulatory targets,[433] rather than merely shift those targets from (only) model-level to (only) application- or society-level. That is, a sociotechnical perspective allows regulators to not only identify and trace upstream harms, but also to address downstream harms at upstream control points. That is, in many cases, it is useful for regulators not only to intervene at the stage where an already widely deployed AI system is inflicting harm, but to identify points of intervention upstream in its development. These points may lie upstream within the technical supply chains of that AI system, whether at the level of (compute or data) inputs,[434] model development and training, or system dissemination.[435] Conversely, these points may also lie upstream in societal determinants of the harm, in the societal conditions that created distinct vulnerabilities to specific failure modes. This matters for regulatory debates around advanced AI, as it can help understand salient features of foundation models' regulatory surface, and how their adaptability and high resource requirements create potential common regulatory targets in terms of regulation of these systems at the development stage. This approach therefore allows the identification of regulatory leverage points that are more well-suited to preventing the systems' harm, or which are at least more susceptible to cost-effective regulation or adaptation.[436]

As a consequence of this, a sociotechnical lens also aids in *transferring* governance solutions across domains whenever appropriate. Rather than consign

[431] O'Keefe (n 304).

[432] Laurin B Weissinger, 'AI, Complexity, and Regulation' in Justin Bullock and others (eds), *The Oxford Handbook of AI Governance* (Oxford University Press 2022).

[433] Kolt (n 91) 48.

[434] Sastry and others (n 287) (on compute governance); Alan Chan, Herbie Bradley, and Nitarshan Rajkumar, 'Reclaiming the Digital Commons: A Public Data Trust for Training Data' (arXiv, 15 March 2023) <http://arxiv.org/abs/2303.09001> accessed 27 March 2023 (on data governance).

[435] Gorwa and Veale (n 286).

[436] Jamie Bernardi and others, 'Societal Adaptation to Advanced AI' (arXiv, 16 May 2024) <http://arxiv.org/abs/2405.10295> accessed 23 May 2024.

regulators to repeatedly confronting self-similar AI challenges (around ethics, security, safety, etc.) many times in siloed legal domains,[437] the sociotechnical approach helps highlight common features or themes of such challenges, as they appear across domains wherever specific AI capabilities are deployed. This reduces the risk of duplication of effort, or of fragmentation of approach. Where appropriate, it can also help us develop governance regimes that can manage distinct problem in a way that can be relatively transferable across, or agnostic to, the specific AI architectures used to achieve those effects. Even where issues can be adequately regulated in separation, this lens can still help us understand and avoid the problems that might result from the entanglement of different problem logics. For instance, policy responses to any potential security threats from advanced, general-purpose AI systems will need to negotiate overlapping ethical disagreements over the intrinsic value of open-sourcing this technology.[438]

In terms of regulatory *timing*, the emphasis on sociotechnical change highlights the inadequacies of governance strategies that are grounded either in an attempt to predict sociotechnical changes in detail, or in reactive responses which prefer to 'wait out' technological change. Rather, it emphasizes the importance of anticipation and adaptive governance,[439] and the legitimacy of acting under imperfect information. This helps inform regulatory debates over advanced AI, by highlighting the difficulty of reaching clear agreement on these systems' capabilities and the challenge of confidently bounding their sociotechnical impacts.

Finally, in terms of regulatory *tailoring* and design, the sociotechnical change lens highlights key design options over when to regulate particular domain uses of AI, or whether to regulate these systems through horizontal regulation, suggesting that while many issues created by conventional, narrow AI systems might be productively approached through both regulatory frames, advanced AI systems likely are best regulated through horizontal regulation.[440] In addition, we can better consider questions of content flexibility, such as over when and why governance measures should adopt technology-specific rules and where it might be technology-neutral.[441] By considering the specific regulatory rationale in play we may understand when or whether technological neutrality is to be preferred, or when technological specificity is acceptable or even preferable.

437 See also Crootof and Ard (n 25) 1 ('[t]he fundamental challenge of techlaw is not how to best regulate novel technologies, but rather how to best address familiar forms of uncertainty in new contexts').

438 See for instance Elizabeth Seger and others, 'Open-Sourcing Highly Capable Foundation Models: An Evaluation of Risks, Benefits, and Alternative Methods for Pursuing Open-Source Objectives' (Centre for the Governance of AI 2023) <https://www.governance.ai/research-paper/open-sourcing-highly-capable-foundation-models> accessed 2 October 2023.

439 Maas, 'Innovation-Proof Governance for Military AI?' (n 276).

440 Jonas Schuett and others, 'From Principles to Rules: A Regulatory Approach for Frontier AI' in P Hacker and others (eds), *The Oxford Handbook of the Foundations and Regulation of Generative AI* (Oxford University Press, forthcoming).

441 Bennett Moses, 'Regulating in the Face of Sociotechnical Change' (n 181) 586 ('regulatory regimes should be technology-neutral to the extent that the regulatory rationale is similarly neutral'). Of course, questions of who decides and shapes the question of what is the (principal) regulatory rationale

4.7.2 Limits of the Sociotechnical Change Approach

Nonetheless, the sociotechnical change lens is not an analytical silver bullet that improves any AI governance analysis or initiative anywhere. There are certainly limits to this approach, in terms of operationalizability, scalability, or prediction.

In the first place, it may not always be easily *operationalizable*. Considerations of 'sociotechnical change' can appear relatively abstract and complex, especially in comparison to analyses that focus on (regulating) concrete applications of AI in specific sectors. As such, this framework may not always allow for an easy translation of diverse AI capabilities into a general 'rationale' (e.g. 'market failure'), nor allow a straightforward mapping of challenges. In many practical contexts, policymakers require concrete, intuitive, and stable categories and definitions. However, the point of the taxonomy is not to provide a new blueprint for (international) regulation structured along 'AI capability problem logics' rather than 'AI applications'. The point is simply to provide a thinking tool for disaggregating the spectrum of a particular AI capability's sociotechnical impact.

In the second place, it might be objected that this lens, even if useful at the level of national AI policy, is not *scalable* (or transferable) to the global stage. To be certain, the concept and scholarship on 'sociotechnical change' has been mostly derived from various domestic law contexts. As such, some of the rationales for regulation may not transfer directly or fully to the international level. Yet while it might be true that not all of these rationales for regulation are explicitly recognized in international law, they can still serve as policy goals or global public goods to be secured.

In the third place, this lens does not overcome the general epistemic limits around *prediction*. It allows us to interpret past or clearly ongoing societal impacts by AI technologies, and to speculate in structured ways about anticipated future sociotechnical impacts of certain capabilities. Yet it would be presumptuous to expect that this approach is able to avoid the deep challenges around prediction. In fact, it may be even harder to anticipate sociotechnical change than 'merely' predicting technological trends. This is simply to say that this lens does not necessarily do better at forecasting issues than many existing approaches. But then it is not meant to. The point is perhaps less to enable foresight and anticipation, and instead to support forms of resilience, adaptability, or scalability.[442]

at play remain complex. As such, one could further extend this account by considering additional, procedural aspects of what it means to pursue technology-neutral regulation for technologies such as AI. See Marco Almada, 'Delegating the Law of Artificial Intelligence: A Procedural Account of Technology-Neutral Regulation' (Thesis, European University Institute 2024) <https://cadmus.eui.eu/handle/1814/77064> accessed 17 July 2024.

[442] On a principle of (regulatory) scalability, see also Kolt (n 91) 49–50 (citing sources). For a discussion of societal adaptation to the impacts of advanced AI, see Bernardi and others (n 436).

In sum, the lens of sociotechnical change should be considered not a roadmap for AI governance, but a thinking tool or compass. The distinction between six types of sociotechnical changes created by AI is not meant to be exhaustive, predictive, or prescriptive in terms of regulatory responses. Instead, it is meant as a tool for organizing thought processes around governing AI in diverse sectors. It is aimed at enabling a structured consideration of key steps, such as: (1) when, why and how a given AI capability gives rise to sociotechnical changes; (2) when and why these changes rise to create a rationale for governance; (3) how to approach the target of regulation, in a way that reckons not just with the material features of the technology, but also with common problem structures or logics. In this way, it is hoped, this lens might help provide loose heuristics or templates for identifying and thinking through patterns of AI challenges and response strategies.

4.8 Conclusion: AI Governance for Sociotechnical Change

This chapter has sketched the first of three perspectives on change in global AI governance. Drawing on the field of technology law, it has explored how, when, and why law and regulation for AI would gain from an approach focused on sociotechnical change, more than just (AI) technology, its applications, or its discrete impacts on values or existing laws. In this approach, global AI governance regimes should focus less on isolated AI capabilities or use cases in isolated domains, and rather should depart from an understanding of when and how shifts in AI capabilities drive patterns of sociotechnical change.

The idea of sociotechnical change is hardly novel in technology law scholarship. However, in a fragmented AI governance landscape, it remains a valuable corrective to approaches that select, organize, or prioritize AI policy issues based on high-profile incidents, popular-cultural resonance, or fit to pre-existing legal domains. In this way, sociotechnical change should be considered not an entirely new paradigm for AI governance, but rather a complementary perspective. Such a lens is subject to its own conditions and limits, but, when used cautiously, can offer a fuller and more considered mapping of which challenges are possible, plausible, or already pervasive—and how these might be best met.

Finally, of the diverse types of sociotechnical change produced by AI systems, one which stood out was its effects on existing systems of law and governance. Accordingly, in Chapter 5 we turn to the lens of governance disruption, which is particularly fruitful to understanding future changes in the tools of governance.

5

Governance Disruption: How AI Changes International Law

5.1 Introduction

Why, when, and how could AI applications disrupt the normative substance, law-creation and enforcement processes, or political scaffolding of international law and global governance?

So far, we have discussed AI technology as a *site* of change (Chapter 1) and—more importantly—as a *source* of sociotechnical change (Chapter 4). As discussed, this sociotechnical lens is valuable in framing AI governance regimes, because it enables a more systematic comparison and prioritization of which AI issues rise to create the most urgent rationales for governance, and because it then allows regimes to consider the texture of these uses as distinct targets for governance.

There is, however, one special case of AI-produced sociotechnical change that bears closer examination: governance disruption.[1] Governance disruption concerns a range of situations of legal uncertainty or transformation that result because a new technology produces new types of behaviour, entities, or relations[2]—or, as Crootof and Ard frame it, new 'artefacts, actors or activities'[3]—which not only affect societies directly, but also impact those societies' tools of governance.[4] To be more precise, for the purposes of this book, this concept might be summarized as:

[1] In previous work, colleagues and I have articulated this concept more narrowly, as 'legal' disruption. See Hin-Yan Liu and others, 'Artificial Intelligence and Legal Disruption: A New Model for Analysis' (2020) 12 Law, Innovation and Technology 205; Matthijs M Maas, 'International Law Does Not Compute: Artificial Intelligence and the Development, Displacement or Destruction of the Global Legal Order' (2019) 20 Melbourne Journal of International Law 29. However, these dynamics generalize to broader systems of governance beyond hard law, and therefore this book will use the frame of 'governance disruption'. Both frameworks are valid and useful, nevertheless, and can be used in a complementary manner.

[2] Lyria Bennett Moses, 'Why Have a Theory of Law and Technological Change?' (2007) 8 Minnesota Journal of Law, Science & Technology 589.

[3] Rebecca Crootof and BJ Ard, 'Structuring Techlaw' (2021) 34 Harvard Journal of Law & Technology 347, 357.

[4] Such impacts may play out not only at the level of legal systems, but may also disrupt existing public sets or systems of values (and through those impacts indirectly shape and disrupt the law). See Jeroen KG Hopster and Matthijs M Maas, 'The Technology Triad: Disruptive AI, Regulatory Gaps and Value Change' [2023] AI and Ethics <https://doi.org/10.1007/s43681-023-00305-5> accessed 8 July 2023. For a taxonomy of how technology affects moral beliefs and practices in decisional, relational, and perceptual domains, see John Danaher and Henrik Skaug Sætra, 'Mechanisms of Techno-Moral Change: A Taxonomy and Overview' (2023) 26 Ethical Theory and Moral Practice 763.

Architectures of Global AI Governance. Matthijs M. Maas, Oxford University Press. © Matthijs M. Maas 2025.
DOI: 10.1093/9780191988455.003.0006

> *Governance disruption*: a form of sociotechnical change by which new technologies and their resulting changes in artefacts, actors, or activities challenge or transform existing systems of law or governance, at the level of (1) their substance, doctrine, or assumptions (requiring the urgent development of those laws); (2) their processes of law-creation, adjudication, monitoring, or enforcement (resulting in the potential displacement of those practices through automation or wholesale substitution); or (3) their political foundations (resulting in their potential erosion or even destruction).

Importantly, framing this perspective as 'governance disruption' does not imply that legal systems are or must always be reactive to technological change, nor that they always lag behind technological expertise, nor that the law is only ever the system being disrupted—and never the one disrupting the conditions for technological change in turn.[5] As Chapter 4 has chronicled, law and legal systems can and under most conditions will take a significant role in shaping the terms for, and thereby the direction of, technological change. Naturally, a focus on governance disruption does not exhaust the scope of technology-law analysis. Indeed, ideally, law must proactively take stock of potential governance rationales in and around emerging technologies, in order to realize opportunities to steer such technologies at an early stage. However, to serve as a meaningful tool of sociotechnical choice, a legal system must first understand the conditions under which its assumptions will be challenged by future change in the technology.

As such, this chapter explores the eventual disruptive effects of technological changes—however these have been initially shaped and constituted—on legal systems. This is of urgent practical relevance. After all, examining the disruptive effects which AI capabilities may exert on the global governance architecture matters for understanding the future of that system. Specifically, it matters for understanding the trajectories of various regimes or norms within that system—both those focused on different issue areas and those regimes, norms, or institutions which are themselves aimed at the regulation of AI.

[5] For instance, in one nuanced argument, Margot Kaminski and Meg Leta Jones have critiqued the approach of seeing AI-generated content—'AI speech'—only in terms of whether it 'disrupts' the law, arguing that this leads to 'an approach that examines how the law responds to technology, which then leads to several major mistakes, including underexamination of the role existing law plays and underscrutinization of the often surprising conditions under which technology has developed'. Margot E Kaminski and Meg Leta Jones, 'Constructing AI Speech' (2024) 133 The Yale Law Journal Forum 1213 <https://www.yalelawjournal.org/forum/constructing-ai-speech> accessed 11 June 2024. I agree with their emphasis on a values-first approach to technology law—one which explores 'what values technology, and the social practices of technology, further [and asks] how the law and its systems of sensemaking can and should be shaped to further values': ibid 1214. However, I do not believe that such an approach is incompatible with a more specific focus on cases of governance disruption as driven by technological change.

As such, this chapter will draw on the concept of governance disruption to explore the ways in which new AI capabilities can produce intended and unintended changes in international law and in the broader global governance architecture.

To do so, I first briefly review scholarship on the relation between technology and law generally, as well as illustrating some more specific historical connections between technological innovation and international legal change, to make the case that we have strong reasons to expect international law to be especially susceptible to disruption by AI. The chapter then introduces and sketches a framework for mapping governance disruption, before discussing, in detail, three types of such disruption—considering the dynamics of AI-driven governance development, displacement, and destruction, in turn. In doing so, it makes the case that contemporary AI governance initiatives must come to terms with the dynamics of governance disruption, if they are to be resilient to future changes in AI systems and their implications for the norms, practices or structures of international law.

5.2 Between Technology and Law

To be sure, the idea that technology and technological change are of particular interest and relevance to law scholars and to legal analysis is certainly not new. As Crootof and Ard themselves note in introducing one technology law ('techlaw') framework:

> The legal community constantly grapples with technologies that enable new conduct or facilitate previously rare actions, blur established legal categories, diffuse or centralize capabilities, and expose the limits of existing regulatory institutions. A host of techlaw questions follow as these tech-fostered changes upend doctrinal rules, shift power relationships, and inflame deeper social tensions.[6]

As a result, there is a significant body of work that has examined the dynamics of 'law and technology' and 'legal automation' as they play out around different technologies or domains of innovation. Over several decades, scholars focused on various fields of law, regulation, and technology have studied, both through concrete cases and at a conceptual level, how the use of algorithms and AI systems might alter the coherence, form, and practices of legal systems, or even the underlying values of regulators.[7]

[6] Crootof and Ard (n 3) 348. See also BJ Ard and Rebecca Crootof, 'The Case for "Technology Law"' (*Nebraska Governance & Technology Center*, 16 December 2020) <https://ngtc.unl.edu/blog/case-for-technology-law> accessed 16 March 2021.

[7] The literature is vast, and no exhaustive review is here attempted. However, some contributions from the past decade include: Roger Brownsword, 'Technological Management and the Rule of Law' (2016) 8 Law, Innovation and Technology 100; Benjamin Alarie, Anthony Niblett, and Albert

Much of this work has focused on a domestic law context, however, and there is to date only a relatively small and fragmented literature exploring how AI will drive changes in the fabric or formation of legal and governance systems at the international level. Still, there are a few notable exceptions, which will inform this chapter. For instance, scholars such as Thomas Burri, Berenice Boutin, and Ashley Deeks have provided general treatments of the ways in which AI technology could affect or play a role in automating roles and processes of international law,[8] and Deeks, Lubell, and Murray have explored the specific implications of conflict prediction algorithms on the international law on the use of force.[9]

Other work has focused on the potential applications and contributions of AI technology within the processes of international law. For instance, Megiddo has explored the potential contribution that big data harvesting and analysis technologies could make to the ascertainment and establishment of customary international law. Such 'Data-Driven Customary International Law' could not only help move international courts beyond 'anecdotal evidence and impressionistic analysis', but also democratize both the data collected and the contributors to the production process, in ways that give greater weight to smaller states and democratize the process of customary international law.[10] Likewise, Saunders has suggested that the 'increasing digitisation of data and global instantaneous access . . . via the Internet' may increasingly facilitate the ability to search and compare the national legislation of many nations with ease, in a way that has significant implications for the speed and ease with which parties might ascertain and identify general

H Yoon, 'Law in the Future' (2016) 66 University of Toronto Law Journal 423; Benjamin Alarie, 'The Path of the Law: Towards Legal Singularity' (2016) 66 University of Toronto Law Journal 443; Anthony J Casey and Anthony Niblett, 'Self-Driving Laws' (2016) 66 University of Toronto Law Journal 429; Brian Sheppard, 'Warming Up to Inscrutability: How Technology Could Challenge Our Concept of Law' (2018) 68 University of Toronto Law Journal 36; Woodrow Hartzog and others, 'Inefficiently Automated Law Enforcement' (2016) 2015 Michigan State Law Review 1763; Rebecca Crootof, '"Cyborg Justice" and the Risk of Technological-Legal Lock-In' (2019) 119 Columbia Law Review Forum 1; John Danaher, 'The Threat of Algocracy: Reality, Resistance and Accommodation' (2016) 29 Philosophy & Technology 245; Karen Yeung, '"Hypernudge": Big Data as a Mode of Regulation by Design' (2017) 20 Information, Communication & Society 118; Nathalie A Smuha, *Algorithmic Rule By Law: How Algorithmic Regulation in the Public Sector Erodes the Rule of Law* (Cambridge University Press 2024).

[8] Thomas Burri, 'International Law and Artificial Intelligence' (2017) 60 German Yearbook of International Law 91; Berenice Boutin, 'Technologies for International Law & International Law for Technologies' (*Groningen Journal of International Law*, 22 October 2018) <https://grojil.org/2018/10/22/technologies-for-international-law-international-law-for-technologies/> accessed 31 October 2018; Ashley Deeks, 'High-Tech International Law' (2020) 88 George Washington Law Review 575; Ashley Deeks, 'Introduction to the Symposium: How Will Artificial Intelligence Affect International Law?' (2020) 114 AJIL Unbound 138.

[9] Ashley Deeks, Noam Lubell, and Daragh Murray, 'Machine Learning, Artificial Intelligence, and the Use of Force by States' (2019) 10 Journal of National Security Law & Policy 1.

[10] Tamar Megiddo, 'Knowledge Production, Big Data, and Data-Driven Customary International Law' in Andrea Bianchi and Moshe Hirsch (eds), *International Law's Invisible Frames: Social Cognition and Knowledge Production in International Legal Processes* (Oxford University Press 2021).

principles of law—one of the major sources of law alongside treaty and customary international law under Art 38(1)(c) of the ICJ Statute.[11]

There are also more specific proposed use cases: for instance, Alschner and colleagues have explored the production of international legal materials (such as draft treaties) by algorithms,[12] and have explored the implications of the 'data-driven future' of the (text-corpus-rich) international economic law.[13] Livingston and Risse have discussed the implications AI may have for the monitoring of human rights abuses.[14] Gill has explored the mismatch between digital technologies and certain attributes of existing multilateral fora (such as meeting periodicity, agenda-setting processes, state-centric focus), and suggested that these technologies will increasingly challenge the operations and efficacy of such institutions in their attempts to regulate the use of these technologies in armed conflicts.[15] Arvidsson and Noll have explored how the use of AI tools might affect the 'central concepts [and] modes of development' of international law.[16]

Technology law would do well to build on this work, and extend greater attention to how different forms of governance disruption play out at the international level. After all, if we expect AI technologies to have a disruptive impact on domestic legal systems and the rule of law, we should certainly expect these disruptive effects to be even more common, and far steeper, in the international legal domain. This is because in comparison to national law, the global legal order appears less well equipped to anticipate or resolve situations of legal uncertainty, or to keep accountable the insertion of automating technology in law-making processes. After all, at the international level there is no authoritative final legislator to compel *ex ante* consideration of the (sociotechnical or legal) impacts of a new technology, to guarantee the coherence of legal responses across domains, or to coordinate (and critically scrutinize) the integration of new technologies into law-making,

[11] Imogen Saunders, *General Principles as a Source of International Law* (1st edn, Hart Publishing 2021) 264–265. However, Saunders' proposal omits direct discussion of AI technology, and does not discuss AI's potential impact on this process of ascertaining general principles of law. See Diego Mejía-Lemos, 'Diego Mejía-Lemos, Review of Imogen Saunders. General Principles as a Source of International Law: Art 38(1)(c) of the Statute of the International Court of Justice' (2024) 35 European Journal of International Law 777.

[12] Wolfgang Alschner and Dmitriy Skougarevskiy, 'Towards an Automated Production of Legal Texts Using Recurrent Neural Networks', *Proceedings of the 16th Edition of the International Conference on Articial Intelligence and Law* (Association for Computing Machinery 2017) <https://doi.org/10.1145/3086512.3086536> accessed 14 May 2020; Wolfgang Alschner and Dmitriy Skougarevskiy, 'Can Robots Write Treaties? Using Recurrent Neural Networks to Draft International Investment Agreements' in F Bex and S Villata (eds), *JURIX: Legal Knowledge and Information Systems* (IOS Press 2016) <https://papers.ssrn.com/abstract=2984935> accessed 14 May 2020.

[13] Wolfgang Alschner, Joost Pauwelyn, and Sergio Puig, 'The Data-Driven Future of International Economic Law' (2017) 20 Journal of International Economic Law 217.

[14] Steven Livingston and Mathias Risse, 'The Future Impact of Artificial Intelligence on Humans and Human Rights' (2019) 33 Ethics & International Affairs 141.

[15] Amandeep S Gill, 'The Changing Role of Multilateral Forums in Regulating Armed Conflict in the Digital Age' (2020) 102 International Review of the Red Cross 261.

[16] Matilda Arvidsson and Gregor Noll, 'Artificial Intelligence, Decision Making and International Law' (2023) 92 Nordic Journal of International Law 1, 4.

adjudication, or enforcement practices of international organizations (let alone by states).

Moreover, instances of governance disruption may be not only more common but also a more significant problem at the international level. This is because amending or altering multilateral treaty regimes to take stock of subsequent technological developments will often prove a far more painful, drawn-out, and contested affair than the revision of domestic laws.[17] Moreover, governance disruption can pose a challenge that is not just legal or procedural, but also political. While international relations scholars are still weighing the precise impact of AI,[18] there is a general appreciation that new innovations can redraw the global political map.[19] It would be very surprising if such far-reaching (geo)political shocks did not have their echoes at the international legal level.

5.3 International Law and Technology: An Abridged History

As discussed, while the legally disruptive impacts of AI at the global level are relatively understudied, that is not to say there is no basis to work from. In fact, a number of legal scholars have examined various ways by which past technological innovations have spurred or shaped the historical development of international law. For instance, Colin Picker has reviewed the interrelation between technological change and change in international law, tracking these dynamics across diverse historical eras—from the pre-modern era to the birth of modern international law to the twenty-first century—and across substantive domains—ranging from space law to the law of the sea, and from the international law of fisheries to the nuclear non-proliferation regime. On this basis, he notes how

> [t]echnology changes international law in a number of ways, by forcing states to either: (1) agree to modify their behaviour (usually through the device of a treaty); (2) abandon previously agreed behaviour (abandonment of treaties); (3) abandon the effort to agree on new behaviour (abandonment of treaty formation); (4) engage in new practices that eventually are accepted by the global community (creating customary international law); (5) abandon previously widely

[17] Rebecca Crootof, 'Jurisprudential Space Junk: Treaties and New Technologies' in Chiara Giorgetti and Natalie Klein (eds), *Resolving Conflicts in the Law* (Brill | Nijhoff 2019). See also Section 5.5.6 ('Carrying Through Development').

[18] Michael C Horowitz, 'Artificial Intelligence, International Competition, and the Balance of Power' [2018] *Texas National Security Review* <https://tnsr.org/2018/05/artificial-intelligence-international-competition-and-the-balance-of-power/> accessed 17 May 2018; Michael C Horowitz, 'Do Emerging Military Technologies Matter for International Politics?' (2020) 23 Annual Review of Political Science 385.

[19] Daniel W Drezner, 'Technological Change and International Relations' (2019) 33 International Relations 286, 287 ('[a]ny technological change is also an exercise in redistribution. It can create new winners and losers, alter actor preferences, and allow the strategic construction of new norms').

> accepted customs (abandonment of customary international law); or (6) accept peremptory obligations (creating *ius cogens*).[20]

This pattern appears to be the case for many technologies, though it appears to be especially strong around strategically high-stakes or military innovations.[21] After all, the management or control of new military technologies has been a core theme throughout the history of international law and global governance, spurring landmark legal innovations and change.[22] As such, we would expect patterns of governance disruption to occur around many military AI systems, as well as many powerful and general-purpose advanced AI systems.

Critically, many instances of past technological disruption highlight how new technologies can alter international law not just directly, by serving as a new concern or object of existing governance arrangements, but also indirectly, through far-reaching second- and third-order cultural, social, and political shifts.[23] The resulting legal innovations in response to these technologies' sociotechnical changes have at times extended far beyond the narrow remit of the particular crises or wars that ostensibly sparked them. For instance, new military technologies have frequently induced not just positional shifts in relative power, but also structural changes in the logistics, scale, and economy of military activity, and in turn in the nature and shape of polities. As Braden Allenby has suggested:

> Chariots, which required supporting personnel and money to operate, privileged aristocratic warriors; stirrups elevated the mounted horseman and made the steppe warrior with his composite bow feared for centuries; the rise of gunpowder and cannon profoundly changed the logistics necessary to field an army, and thereby created economies of scale in military activities that encouraged the rise of nation-states.[24]

[20] Colin B Picker, 'A View from 40,000 Feet: International Law and the Invisible Hand of Technology' (2001) 23 Cardozo Law Review 151, 156.

[21] Rebecca Crootof, 'Regulating New Weapons Technology' in Eric Talbot Jensen and Ronald TP Alcala (eds), *The Impact of Emerging Technologies on the Law of Armed Conflict* (Oxford University Press 2019).

[22] Picker (n 20); Rosemary Rayfuse, 'Public International Law and the Regulation of Emerging Technologies' in Roger Brownsword, Eloise Scotford, and Karen Yeung (eds), *The Oxford Handbook of Law, Regulation and Technology* (Oxford University Press 2017) 502. See also generally Maas, 'International Law Does Not Compute' (n 1).

[23] See also Matthijs M Maas, 'Innovation-Proof Governance for Military AI? How I Learned to Stop Worrying and Love the Bot' (2019) 10 Journal of International Humanitarian Legal Studies 129.

[24] Braden Allenby, 'Are New Technologies Undermining the Laws of War?' (2014) 70 Bulletin of the Atomic Scientists 21, 21. However, while these are popular accounts, it should be noted that the military role of technological supremacy in history—at least during the pre-modern era, and potentially since—remains highly contested. See for instance: Kelly DeVries, 'Catapults Are Still Not Atomic Bombs: Effectiveness and Determinism in Premodern Military Technology' (2019) 7 Vulcan 34; David Zimmerman, 'Neither Catapults nor Atomic Bombs: Technological Determinism and Military History from a Post-Industrial Revolution Perspective' (2019) 7 Vulcan 45. Indeed, Neil Renic has argued that the over-estimation of the military supremacy that can be achieved through new technologies has, historically, fed the flawed notion of the 'Superweapon Peace'—'the long-standing and enduring idea that

Indeed, emerging technologies have, throughout history, also had indirect cultural effects on the practice and scholarship of international law. For instance, Roxana Vatanparast has explored how late nineteenth-century developments in the institutionalization of international law as a professional discipline were strongly influenced by contemporary developments in communications technology. She traces how David Dudley Field, a US law reformer and one of the founding members of the Institut de Droit International (IDI), was strongly influenced by his brother's Cyrus Field's successful efforts at laying trans-Atlantic undersea telegraph cables, which shaped his thinking about the need to codify the 'law of nations' and professionalize the field of international law.[25]

Emerging technologies have also shaped the construction of international law. For instance, twentieth-century advances in communications technologies such as conference calls, fax machines, and the internet both facilitated treaty negotiations among states and empowered NGOs and civil society actors to take a much more active role in participating in these negotiations than had been the case in the past.[26] In the twenty-first century, ICT technologies have enabled the rise of so-called track-change diplomacy—that is, the use of word processing software, cloud services, and mobile devices to enable diplomats to collaboratively edit and negotiate documents in real time—with significant consequences for questions of how states construct and promote their national interests in these negotiations, how diplomats reach compromises within collective drafting exercises, and how power imbalances play out in these negotiations.[27]

Given these repeated impacts of technology on international law, it is easy to see why we might well expect that AI systems will stake a strong claim to shaping the next chapter in this core governance domain. This is because of the technology's generality, conceptual complexity, and ability to be integrated within many existing technologies or systems.[28] Indeed, Rebecca Crootof has discussed a general pattern

weapons of radical destructiveness, both nuclear and non-nuclear, can force an end to war by rendering it too destructive to contemplate'. Neil C Renic, 'Superweapons and the Myth of Technological Peace' [2022] European Journal of International Relations 13540661221136764.

[25] Roxana Vatanparast, 'David Dudley Field and the Technological Sensibility of International Law Codification' (2024) 52 Denver Journal of International Law and Policy <https://papers.ssrn.com/abstract=4628458> accessed 20 February 2024.

[26] John Gamble and Charlotte Ku, 'International Law—New Actors and New Technologies: Center Stage for NGOs' (2000) 31 Law and Policy in International Business 221, 249–251 (discussing the relative lack of NGO involvement in drafting UNCLOS, relative to the significant role NGOs took in the Ottawa Mine Ban Convention). See also Picker (n 20) 199.

[27] Rebecca Adler-Nissen and Alena Drieschova, 'Track-Change Diplomacy: Technology, Affordances, and the Practice of International Negotiations' (2019) 63 International Studies Quarterly 531.

[28] Note that Allenby is more sceptical about the novelty of LAWS, arguing that any challenge they pose to the laws of war comes down to their ability to discriminate between military and civilian targets (at a rate as good as or better than human soldiers), which he holds to be a factual question. Allenby (n 24) 27. Conversely, he argues that cyber weapons, by mixing together civilian and military activity, pose a far larger conceptual and doctrinal challenge: ibid. Without taking issue with this characterization of cyber weapons, I suggest that ultimately military uses of AI technology (a far broader category

by which new technological capabilities can at times enable or create new patterns of state behaviour which, once widespread, create new customary international law which, under the *lex posterior* principle, functionally supersede any older treaty commitments.[29] In her account, this leaves in its wake 'jurisprudential space junk': collections of fragmented, hard-to-amend treaty regimes which 'are theoretically in force but actually simply clutter and confuse the relevant legal regime'.[30] As one illustration of this, Crootof discusses the evolution of customary norms around submarine warfare, and how these eroded and undercut previous treaty regimes.[31] Specifically, the 1930 London Naval Treaty and the 1936 Limitation of Naval Armament Treaty held that submarines were not distinct from surface warships, and as such were also bound by the prohibition against attacking enemy merchant vessels without first ensuring the safety of their sailors. However, Crootof argues that widespread state practice in violation of these norms, especially during the Second World War, functionally created a new and less restrictive customary international law of submarine warfare.[32] This was in part because a range of material constraints on the tactics and logistics of submarine warfare came to be far more determinative of actual practices during wartime than the treaty instruments that were nominally in force. As a result, this new customary norm functionally replaced the older treaty law in international law, and effectively expanded states' rights regarding the lawful use of submarines, rendering the previous treaties a 'dead letter'.[33]

As such, we can begin to distinguish how new technologies or innovations can shape international law at different levels. They can affect international law *doctrinally*, because the sociotechnical changes they enable create uncertainties over the applicability of existing international law to new actors, artefacts, or activities.[34]

than LAWS) are likely to generate a wider range of issues for more distinct regimes and norms, than a narrow focus on LAWS' ability to discriminate would suggest. Maas, 'Innovation-Proof Governance for Military AI?' (n 23). See also Ben Koppelman, 'How Would Future Autonomous Weapon Systems Challenge Current Governance Norms?' (2019) 164 The RUSI Journal 98.

29 Crootof, 'Jurisprudential Space Junk' (n 17) 113; See also Rebecca Crootof, 'Change Without Consent: How Customary International Law Modifies Treaties' (2016) 41 Yale Journal of International Law 65, 284–288 ('*Lex posterior derogat legi priori* is the principle that the most recently developed rule prevails over prior law').

30 Crootof, 'Jurisprudential Space Junk' (n 17) 107.

31 In previous work, I also illustrated these disruptive effects through a related discussion of how submarine warfare upset the assumptions of the 'International Prize Court', proposed in 1907 to hear cases regarding the capturing of prizes (mostly ships) during wartime. This was the first treaty proposal for a truly international court, and while it soon proved moribund for political reasons, rapid technological change in submarine warfare would have made its mission and role moot before long. Maas, 'International Law Does Not Compute' (n 1) 35–36. See also generally Janet Manson, 'International Law, German Submarines and American Policy' (Portland State University Department of History 1977) <http://archives.pdx.edu/ds/psu/15921> accessed 23 October 2018.

32 Limitation and Reduction of Naval Armament (London Naval Treaty) (1930) 112 LNTS 65; Limitation of Naval Armament (Second London Naval Treaty) (1937) 197 LNTS 387. See also Crootof, 'Jurisprudential Space Junk' (n 17) 113–114.

33 Crootof, 'Jurisprudential Space Junk' (n 17) 114.

34 Crootof and Ard (n 3) 357–358.

Technologies can also change the *processes* by which international law is created or enforced. In extreme cases, new technologies can change international law *politically*, by changing the stakes of previously more moderate problems, in a way that provides the impetus for key broader legal innovations, or undercuts the political scaffolding of previous orders.

This illustrates how new technologies such as AI can pose a full-spectrum challenge—or opportunity—to international law, having an impact at not only the legal or normative level, but simultaneously at the operational and political one. Given the extreme versatility of AI technology, I suggest that AI systems will be similarly likely to affect the doctrine, politics, process, enforcement, and efficacy of international law—and with it, the likely texture and trajectory of regimes and regime complexes within it. In order to better chart and analyse such effects in the case of AI, this chapter therefore sets out a taxonomy of governance disruption.[35]

5.4 An Overview of AI Governance Disruption

Specifically, drawing together several concepts and frameworks, I distinguished three types of possible global legal impacts of AI on the general international law system: development, displacement, and destruction (see Table 5.1).

We can now review these three phenomena, and their components, in turn.

5.5 Governance Development

As discussed in Chapter 4, new uses of AI can yield many different sociotechnical changes. In a range of cases, this can result in new artefacts, actors or activities which are (perceived) to no longer be adequately covered or clearly regulated within existing international frameworks or regimes.[36] These situations create a need for legal or regulatory 'development' in existing areas or doctrines of international law.

Of course, AI technologies are certainly not so anathema to (international) law that they confuse or challenge it at every point of contact. Nonetheless, new AI capabilities can, in some cases, create (or reveal) problematic or uncertain legal situations—situations which pose an open question for existing rules, norms, or standards in global governance, especially in hard law regimes.

The idea that disruptive patterns of sociotechnical change can drive a need for legal development subsumes (or expands on) previous theoretical accounts of the

[35] See also Maas, 'International Law Does Not Compute' (n 1).
[36] Crootof and Ard (n 3) 357–358.

Table 5.1 A governance disruption framework

Type			Example	Outcome
(Need for) Governance **Development**	**New governance gaps**		AI-enabled swarm warfare (possibly) not covered by existing international regimes	Need for new law.
	Conceptual uncertainty, ambiguity, or overlap		LAWS highlight potential ambiguity or inadequacy of concepts such as 'intent', 'effective control', etc.	Need for new law or adaptation of law, to sharpen existing rules or clarify concepts.
	Mis-specified scope of application		Under-inclusive application of Convention Against Torture on use of autonomous robots for interrogation. Over-inclusive applicability of company law enabling incorporation of 'algorithmic entities' with corporate legal personhood.	Need for new law or adaptation of law, to demarcate scope and applicability of existing instruments.
	Obsolescence	(Anticipated) behaviour obsolete (necessity)	AI research shifts paradigms, such that the anticipated next generation of (large, computationally intensive systems) does not arrive. Or: new types of AI-supported remote biometric surveillance replace 'traditional' face recognition systems in surveillance.	Need for new law or adaptation of existing instruments, involving a (re)consideration of the underlying aims and purposes of the regime.
		Justifying assumptions no longer valid (adequacy)	Structural unemployability through technological unemployment puts pressure on right to work, ILO regimes.	
		No longer cost-effective (enforceability)	Use of generative propaganda raises monitoring and compliance enforcement costs for regimes.	
	Altered problem portfolio		Military AI regime tailored to respond to *ethical challenges* of LAWS (e.g. meaningful human control) not well oriented to eventual military AI capabilities (e.g. cyberwarfare) that create *structural shifts*.	Need for new regime or adaptation or amendment of existing instrument, to shift focus or centre of gravity.

Governance **Displacement**	**Automation**	International law creation and adjudication	Use of large language models to generate draft treaties, predict arbitral panel rulings, identify state practice or treaty conflicts.	Potential speeding-up of international law creation, with distributional and legitimacy concerns.
		Monitoring and enforcement	Use of various AI pattern-recognition tools in monitoring and verifying treaty compliance.	Increase deterrent effect of existing regimes; potentially create transparency pre-conditions for new regimes.
	Replacement	Changes in regulatory modality	Use of AI tools such as emotion-recognition, social media sentiment analysis, or computational propaganda by states, resulting in increased state preference to resolve disputes in diplomatic channels.	Distributional changes; more unilateral and strategic action by states; potential legal destruction.
Governance **Destruction**	**Erosion**	Conceptual friction	Attempted extension of existing regimes or norms to (seemingly) new technology cannot pass 'laugh test'.	Inhibits needed developments within existing law; new regimes needed.
		Political 'knots'	Attempted extension of existing regimes or creation of new law intractable because of political gridlock.	Inhibits needed developments through creation of new regimes; problem remains unsolved.
	Decline	Increasing the spoils of non-compliance	Innovations increase strategic stakes or ability to bypass monitoring, or lower proliferation thresholds or (political) non-compliance costs.	Decays political foundations of specific regimes.
		Active anti-law weapon	AI-enabled computational propaganda enables contestation of international law; (suspected) use of AI negotiation tools subverts legitimacy.	Scaling up contestation of international law.
		Shift of values	AI capabilities perceived as enabling unilateralism, alternative to multilateralism.	Additional pressure on global legal order.

relationship between technology and new law. For instance, David Friedman has argued that technological change affects law in three ways:

> (1) by altering the cost of violating and enforcing existing legal rules; (2) by altering the underlying facts that justify legal rules; and (3) by changing the underlying facts implicitly assumed by the law, making existing legal concepts and categories obsolete, even meaningless.[37]

A more granular taxonomy of law and technological change has been proposed by Lyria Bennett Moses.[38] She argues that while not every technology creates the occasion or need for new litigation or legal scholarship, technological change does often create a 'recurring dilemma' for law, by creating new entities or enabling new behaviour.[39] In her analysis, this creates four distinct types of new legal situations which call for resulting legal change: (1) a need for new, special laws; (2) legal uncertainty; (3) incorrect scope in the form of the under- or over-inclusiveness of laws in new contexts; and (4) obsolescence of some laws as a result of technology reducing the importance of conduct, undermining the justification for certain rules, or reducing the cost-effectiveness of enforcement.[40]

Bennett Moses's framework has also inspired other analyses of legal disruption at the international level. For instance, Crootof has articulated various frameworks to chart international legal disruption produced by new technologies. In one account, she argues that a new (weapons) technology can be legally disruptive because it can:

> (A) alter how rules are created or how law is used; (B) make more salient an ongoing but unresolved issue, gap, or contradiction in the existing rules; (C) introduce new uncertainty, usually regarding the application or scope of existing rules; and (D) upend foundational tenets of a legal regime, necessitating a reconceptualization of its aims and purposes.[41]

Moreover, in a newer overarching framework for technology law, Crootof and Ard have since reworked these categories into three types of legal uncertainties that can appear as a result of technological change:

[37] David D Friedman, 'Does Technology Require New Law?' (2001) 25 Public Policy 71, 71.

[38] Bennett Moses (n 2) 590, 605–606. See also Lyria Bennett Moses, 'Recurring Dilemmas: The Law's Race to Keep Up With Technological Change' (2007) 21 University of New South Wales Faculty of Law Research Series <http://www.austlii.edu.au/au/journals/UNSWLRS/2007/21.html> accessed 3 July 2018.

[39] Bennett Moses (n 38) 4–5.

[40] ibid 8.

[41] Crootof, 'Regulating New Weapons Technology' (n 21) 6. Notably, the latter three of these categories map loosely onto the various categories in my analysis of development, whereas 'Significantly Changing How Law is Created or Used' maps somewhat to this project's discussion of displacement.

> (1) application uncertainties, which raise the question of whether and how extant law applies; (2) normative uncertainties, which arise when the law is arguably unable to accomplish its aims; and (3) institutional uncertainties, which exist when there are questions about different regulatory entities' relative authority, competence, and legitimacy to apply and update the law.[42]

Of course, as emphasized in the discussion in Chapter 4, the precise forms these disruptions will take are very hard to anticipate.[43] Indeed, this may be almost intrinsically bounded, for if we could easily or reliably anticipate these disruptions, this would mean that we could already discern the fault lines, gaps, or ambiguities in our existing laws, suggesting that these could be fixed ahead of time.[44] Nonetheless, we can discuss illustrative examples of these general patterns that accord with Bennett Moses's account of different legal situations. It should be emphasized that these are not mutually exclusive categories but rather clusters of common issues or dynamics, many of which may occur in conjunction for a given technology or its use.[45]

As such, the next few sections will discuss how new AI-enabled behaviours, situations, or sociotechnical change might create conditions for legal uncertainty, in various forms and types, before discussing some nuances and challenges around when and why technology becomes truly legally disruptive, and when or how existing governance systems might be able to carry out the required developments to address these uncertainties.

5.5.1 Clear New Governance Gaps

In the first place, a new AI application could simply highlight, or create the perception of, important and obvious new gaps within the existing tapestry of (international) legal instruments.[46] This could occur if the technology, or its uses, are

[42] Crootof and Ard (n 3) 352.

[43] Gregory N Mandel, 'Legal Evolution in Response to Technological Change' in Roger Brownsword, Eloise Scotford and Karen Yeung (eds), The Oxford Handbook of Law, Regulation and Technology (Oxford University Press 2017) 225.

[44] Of course, it might simply be the case that such advance future-proofing is sufficiently costly (in terms of opportunity cost), or carries its own risks, in which case development might not (need to) be pursued even if potential shortfalls or gaps in a regime can be identified at an early time. See also Crootof and Ard (n 3) 400–401.

[45] See also ibid 357 (arguing that '[t]hese are not mutually exclusive categories with impermeable edges; rather, they are rough groupings of common kinds of legal uncertainty, each addressing a distinct set of concerns. Technological developments may raise several uncertainties simultaneously, and the resolution of uncertainty at one level may create uncertainties at another').

[46] Of course, the question of whether newly discovered legal gaps are 'new' gaps, or always latent ambiguities or shortfalls in the law, is philosophically interesting, but is a bit of a rabbit hole. On the epistemology and ontology of which, see generally Roberto Casati and Achille Varzi, 'Holes' in Edward N Zalta (ed), *The Stanford Encyclopedia of Philosophy* (Summer 2019, Metaphysics Research Lab,

perceived to create problematic sociotechnical changes which entirely and clearly fall outside of the scope of any existing regimes or norms.[47] As Crootof and Ard argue, 'gaps exist where artifacts, actors, or activities defy existing categories to such a degree that there may be no governing law. In the face of an apparent gap, a legal actor must determine *whether* the law applies before reaching the usual application uncertainty question of *how*.'[48]

It is important to note that whether a gap exists is not an objective fact, but rather a matter of (lawmaker or state) perception. In particular, at the international level, the presence of a gap depends on whether enough parties perceive that (everyone else also perceives that) existing laws cannot be 'stretched' to cover the new case.[49] If this is so, this situation creates the perceived need for new *sui generis* rules to deal with new situations or forms of conduct, or to ban a particular underlying technology or particular applications.[50]

Historically, various technologies have given rise to a perceived shortfall of existing legal frameworks, resulting in the development of entirely new regimes, such as the emergence of outer space law, cyberspace governance, or arms control regimes aimed at various weapons of mass destruction,[51] to name but a few. While the creation of new technology-specific treaty regimes has not always been politically easy, the international legal system is at least in principle clearly capable of proposing and promulgating new legal regimes in order to address any 'gaps' that (it is perceived) are opened up by new technologies.[52]

In what ways could AI create new governance gaps? There are various AI capabilities that would enable new forms of conduct that will likely be seen as (a) so problematic that they clearly ought to be regulated (i.e. constitute a governance

Stanford University 2019) <https://plato.stanford.edu/archives/sum2019/entries/holes/> accessed 8 September 2020.

[47] Crootof, 'Regulating New Weapons Technology' (n 21) 20 ('[n]ew technology can sometimes permit entirely new forms of conduct or generate new negative externalities that cannot be addressed through applying or revising the existing law').

[48] Crootof and Ard (n 3) 360 (emphasis in original).

[49] This does not mean that states always seek to work within existing regimes, and only seek the creation of new (treaty) regimes when they truly believe they are unable to house issues within existing international law. For instance, there has been exploration of diverse circumstances under which states may create overlapping or contesting institutions on similar issue areas. Johannes Urpelainen and Thijs Van de Graaf, 'Your Place or Mine? Institutional Capture and the Creation of Overlapping International Institutions' (2015) 45 British Journal of Political Science 799. Likewise, Surabhi Ranganathan has provided three case studies (on seabed mining, the International Criminal Court, and nuclear governance) of instances where various states engineered treaty conflicts in order to achieve desired changes in existing multilateral regimes. Surabhi Ranganathan, *Strategically Created Treaty Conflicts and the Politics of International Law* (Cambridge University Press 2014).

[50] Note, this can depend strongly on whether the situation is cast as one where the main question is over which specific analogy to choose for the technology, or as a situation where no truly suitable analogies are available. In the former case, it primes debate to focus on what existing law should be applied. In the latter case, it implies that some new law or institution is required. See Crootof and Ard (n 3) 389.

[51] Picker (n 20) 170–172, 175–178.

[52] See generally Rayfuse (n 22).

rationale), yet which simultaneously (b) appear out of scope of existing norms or regimes in international law. This could include, for instance, cases where AI systems enable the granular and systematic monitoring and social control of populations through enhanced surveillance;[53] the deployment of fully autonomous weapons in mass swarms;[54] (cyber)warfare systems that might be operationally susceptible to emergent accidents;[55] the use of AI in tracking of rival nuclear assets in ways that threaten deterrence stability;[56] or any other sudden, disruptive capabilities.

At the international level, what matters is that these capabilities will create sociotechnical changes which will be seen as providing rationales for governance by most or all of the (state) parties involved, yet where these parties also perceive that these changes are insufficiently addressed by existing regimes. In such cases, there will be a perceived need—if not necessarily the political conditions—for the conduct of new legal developments to explicitly regulate, ban, or control the deployment or use of these systems.

Curiously, there are several general reasons for expecting that AI-produced governance gaps might prove comparatively rare—or, at least, rarer than we might intuitively expect. This is for both general historical reasons and specific technological ones.

[53] On the lack of a clear regime for AI surveillance, see also Steven Feldstein, 'The Global Struggle over AI Surveillance' in Beth Kerley (ed), Steven Feldstein, Eduardo Ferreyra, and Danilo Krivokapic, *The Global Struggle over AI Surveillance: Emerging Trends and Democratic Responses* (National Endowment for Democracy 2022) 17–18 <https://www.ned.org/global-struggle-over-ai-surveillance-emerging-trends-democratic-responses/> accessed 8 January 2024. As discussed in Mark Chinen, *The International Governance of Artificial Intelligence* (Edward Elgar Publishing 2023) 228–229.

[54] For discussion, see Paul Scharre, 'How Swarming Will Change Warfare' (2018) 74 Bulletin of the Atomic Scientists 385; Irving Lachow, 'The Upside and Downside of Swarming Drones' (2017) 73 Bulletin of the Atomic Scientists 96; Zachary Kallenborn and Philipp C Bleek, 'Swarming Destruction: Drone Swarms and Chemical, Biological, Radiological, and Nuclear Weapons' (2018) 25 The Nonproliferation Review 523. For a discussion of potential control approaches, see Maaike Verbruggen, 'The Question of Swarms Control: Challenges to Ensuring Human Control over Military Swarms' (EU Non-Proliferation and Disarmament Consortium 2019) <https://www.nonproliferation.eu/wp-content/uploads/2019/12/EUNPDC_no-65_031219.pdf> accessed 25 February 2020. See also Nathan Leys, 'Autonomous Weapon Systems, International Crises, and Anticipatory Self-Defense' (2020) 45 The Yale Journal of International Law 377 (setting out 'rules of the road' for these systems). Notably, however, Zachary Kallenborn has suggested drone swarms could be classified as weapons of mass destruction, in which case the Seabed Treaty and the Outer Space Treaty would ban the deployment of such systems in these 'commons'. Zachary Kallenborn, 'Are Drone Swarms Weapons of Mass Destruction?' (US Air Force Center for Strategic Deterrence Studies, Air University 2020) 60, 5 <https://www.researchgate.net/publication/345570984_United_States_Air_Force_Center_for_Strategic_Deterrence_Studies_Are_Drone_Swarms_Weapons_of_Mass_Destruction> accessed 9 September 2020.

[55] See the discussion of 'normal accidents' in Chapter 4, as well as in Matthijs M Maas, 'How Viable Is International Arms Control for Military Artificial Intelligence? Three Lessons from Nuclear Weapons' (2019) 40 Contemporary Security Policy 285.

[56] Vincent Boulanin and others, 'Artificial Intelligence, Strategic Stability and Nuclear Risk' (SIPRI 2020) <https://www.sipri.org/sites/default/files/2020-06/artificial_intelligence_strategic_stability_and_nuclear_risk.pdf> accessed 23 June 2020; Michael C Horowitz, Paul Scharre, and Alexander Velez-Green, 'A Stable Nuclear Future? The Impact of Autonomous Systems and Artificial Intelligence' [2019] arXiv:1912.05291 [cs] <http://arxiv.org/abs/1912.05291> accessed 18 December 2019.

Generally, whereas earlier technological breakthroughs such as spaceflight and nuclear weapons occurred in a relatively young and sparse global institutional landscape, with clear thematic space to grow, the pattern of global 'institutional proliferation' over the past decades has resulted in a more tightly populated and thematically diverse (if not exhaustive) governance landscape. This ensures that rather than creating a new encompassing regime, global governance initiatives might often default to accommodating new issues within an existing 'regime complex'.[57]

In the second place, while much of the general discourse and hype around AI may speak to the technology's (perceived) 'novelty', there are also features of the technology that run counter to this dynamic. Most importantly, whereas previous technological breakthroughs more unambiguously and categorically broached—that is, reached (space) or created (cyberspace)—some 'new ground' that no previous technology or human activity had reached before, AI technologies will often not broach such a similarly untouched domain. Paradoxically, the very generality of AI systems, and their ability to be integrated within many other technologies or platforms, suggests that in some cases AI capabilities might at least appear to map easily onto the domains or jurisdictions of pre-existing regimes,[58] rather than constituting a clear legal *terra incognita*.

In this light, it is perhaps less surprising that some scholars have judged that many challenges created by AI are not very new, and that these can be accommodated within existing regimes of international law.[59] So long as AI technology is merely used to render other platforms or technologies faster or more accurate, this could suggest that it will only rarely create sufficiently compelling new governance gaps for development to fill.[60] This might be especially the case for many narrow, conventional AI systems which do not exceed human performance. Conversely, the existence of certain legal gaps might be clearer (or more persuasive) in the case of advanced AI systems that demonstrate novel capabilities, or which—in their underlying value chain—display new industry features not previously faced by (international) law.

[57] As noted by Karen J Alter and Kal Raustiala, 'The Rise of International Regime Complexity' (2018) 14 Annual Review of Law and Social Science 329, 337 ('[g]lobal governance solutions thus must take one of two approaches: (a) International actors can attempt to create an encompassing regime that can address all dimensions of the problem, or (b) international actors can accept that policy solutions will be crafted, coordinated, and implemented within a larger regime complex. [. . .] although the first option might be more efficient and effective, it is rarely the solution adopted'). See also Chapter 6 and Sections 7.3–7.4.

[58] See for example the discussion of autonomous maritime vehicles under the Law of the Sea, in Natalie Klein, 'Maritime Autonomous Vehicles within the International Law Framework to Enhance Maritime Security' (2019) 95 International Law Studies 29.

[59] See also Martina Kunz and Seán Ó hÉigeartaigh, 'Artificial Intelligence and Robotization' in Robin Geiß and Nils Melzer (eds), *The Oxford Handbook of the International Law of Global Security* (Oxford University Press 2021).

[60] This may be the case even if effectively mitigating the new challenge would in fact be better served by an entirely new instrument.

This might help explain, in part, the growing set of legal and policy efforts to regulate advanced, general-purpose AI systems at the field's frontier.[61]

With all this, it should be clear that whether a technology creates a 'gap' (or rather results in conceptual uncertainty or legal overlap) is not an intrinsic feature of that technology, but rather will depend significantly on how the technology is framed. Indeed, as Crootof and Ard have noted, depending on such framing, 'the same technological development might be described as creating either a gap or an overlap' of existing law.[62]

Moreover, this question depends not just on the features of the technology, but also on the perceived reach and flexibility of instruments already available in the extant governance landscape. For instance, the international movement to ban Lethal Autonomous Weapons Systems might, on the one hand, be read as a clear example of a situation where many global actors, including a sizeable coalition of states, (initially) believed that these technologies face a potential legal gap, and will require new international regulation or even a ban. However, even in this case, the fact that international debates on this topic have, so far, remained predominantly housed under the Convention on Certain Conventional Weapons also suggests that many parties may prefer to accommodate these technologies within existing international frameworks.[63]

Finally, even if it is perceived that a new AI capability ultimately can be accommodated within existing regimes (that is, it does not raise lasting legal gaps), this of course does not mean that that is in fact the most effective governance approach to regulate the capability or its downstream sociotechnical changes. A novel regime might in fact be more effective at addressing it. Conversely, even if an AI capability does give rise to a perceived governance gap, it is an entirely distinct question as to whether new regulation to patch this gap will prove politically viable.[64]

The key situation here is that the existing governance actors recognize a new technology (or its specific usage) as clearly falling out of scope of existing instruments, establishing a need for new international law to adequately deal with it.

5.5.2 Conceptual Uncertainty, Ambiguity, or Overlap

In other situations, a new technology may create or render explicit previously latent conceptual ambiguities or fault lines within existing legal instruments, such as over the meaning of cornerstone legal terms, or over the boundary between two previously distinct bodies of law.[65]

[61] See also Chapter 3.
[62] Crootof and Ard (n 3) 364.
[63] Maas, 'Innovation-Proof Governance for Military AI?' (n 23).
[64] Critically, if it is not, this situation, where a key problem remains unaddressed because of political gridlock or failure, may result in governance 'erosion', as discussed in Section 5.7.1.
[65] Maas, 'International Law Does Not Compute' (n 1) 39.

This can create legal uncertainty, as it becomes unclear how, or whether, existing laws apply to certain new activities or situations.[66] As Bennett Moses has argued, technology can spark a need for legal clarification and change whenever there is uncertainty over how to legally classify the new entities, forms of conduct, or relationships. Such situations can occur for various reasons: there may be no adequate classification rubric that exists; the new behaviour may fit into more than one existing category and become subject to different and conflicting rules; or an existing legal category may become blurred.[67]

Many technologies have produced such conceptual uncertainties in the past. For instance, Crootof has discussed how the use of drones for targeted killing has 'highlighted questions regarding the appropriate geographic and temporal limitations of armed conflicts, as well as the relationship between the law of armed conflict and international human rights law'.[68] Likewise, AI, it has been suggested, combines certain features (such as autonomy and unpredictability) which blur cornerstone legal categories, such as the distinction between 'agent' and 'object',[69] and therefore undercut certain symbolic orders or schemas that are at the heart of how many legal systems settle questions of responsibility or liability.[70] Lethal Autonomous Weapons Systems, for these reasons, have long been taken to frustrate some of the assumptions about state accountability, as well as criminal intent, which are critical to the application of international accountability frameworks.[71] Similarly, the emerging use of advanced AI agents is likely to raise many legal challenges in legal domains pertaining to freedom of speech, copyright, and criminal law, where liability turns on 'whether the actor who causes harm (or creates a risk of harm) has a certain intention or *mens rea*', as AI agents may likely be legally constructed as 'risky agents without intentions'.[72]

[66] In a different distinction, Crootof and Ard distinguish between *application uncertainties* (over whether the new application is covered by existing law), *normative uncertainties* (over whether the new application should be covered by certain law), and *institutional uncertainties* (over which agencies or parties should decide these other questions). Crootof and Ard (n 3) 11, 14–36.

[67] Bennett Moses (n 38) 26.

[68] Crootof, 'Regulating New Weapons Technology' (n 21) 7; Similar points are also made by Allenby (n 24); Denise Garcia, 'Future Arms, Technologies, and International Law: Preventive Security Governance' (2016) 1 European Journal of International Security 94.

[69] Jacob Turner, *Robot Rules: Regulating Artificial Intelligence* (Springer Berlin Heidelberg 2018) 64–79.

[70] Particularly in contexts of international humanitarian law. Hin-Yan Liu, 'Categorization and Legality of Autonomous and Remote Weapons Systems' (2012) 94 International Review of the Red Cross 627.

[71] Rebecca Crootof, 'War Torts: Accountability for Autonomous Weapons' (2016) 164 University of Pennsylvania Law Review 1347. However, note that such puzzles may not always be intractable. For instance, Thomas Burri has argued that the case law of international courts in principle includes more than sufficient precedent for resolving questions of state control, attribution and the limits of delegation. Burri (n 8) 101–103, 108.

[72] Ian Ayres and Jack M Balkin, 'The Law of AI Is the Law of Risky Agents without Intentions' [2024] University of Chicago Law Review Online <https://lawreview.uchicago.edu/online-archive/law-ai-law-risky-agents-without-intentions> accessed 23 July 2024. Though for an argument arguing that many policy challenges deriving from AI agents may nonetheless be addressed by existing legal

This resulting legal uncertainty creates the need for development, in the form of the clarification or sharpening of existing rules, or of their definitions and conditions. The degree to which this can be achieved in practice may depend on the ease of formulating a new and plausible interpretation of the technology, behaviour, or concept in question within the confines of an existing treaty or regime.[73] In some cases these are so broadly framed that this is plausible. In other cases, there is not sufficient conceptual (or content) flexibility that previous interpretation can be recovered or restored.[74] If it cannot, it is a political question whether there is sufficient willingness to explicitly amend existing treaties, or propose new regimes, to carry out the required development.[75]

5.5.3 Mis-specified Scope of Application of Existing Laws

In the third place, new technologies can create new behaviours or situations that blur or warp the *scope* of application of existing regulation, leading to situations of inappropriate, or at least unintended, over- or under-inclusion of existing laws, which become (revealed as) essentially mis-specified.[76]

To be clear, these situations of legal uncertainty, which consequently demand development in the law, once again depend not just on the technology and its sociotechnical impacts, but also on the formulation of the law that previously regulated the behaviour or system in question. As such, Christoph Winter and Charlie Bullock have drawn on the concept of 'specification' in technical AI safety literature[77] to describe this as a phenomenon of 'governance misspecification',[78] defined as situations 'when the real-world effects of the legal regime (analogous to the design specification) as interpreted and enforced (analogous to the revealed

rules or standards—such as under the EU AI Act, tort law, consumer protection law, and cybercrime regulation—see also Peter Cihon, 'Chilling Autonomy: Policy Enforcement for Human Oversight of AI Agents' (2024) <https://blog.genlaw.org/pdfs/genlaw_icml2024/79.pdf> accessed 5 August 2024.

[73] In turn, as Crootof has noted, 'the success of a new interpretation will depend on the authority of the interpreter, the specificity of the existing law, and the appropriateness of any analogy employed in the interpretation'. Crootof, 'Regulating New Weapons Technology' (n 21) 14.

[74] Crootof and Ard (n 3) 405–406.

[75] These two barriers—of conceptual intractability or political intractability—underlie the discussion of governance *erosion* under Section 5.7.1.

[76] See also the discussion of this concept in Christoph Winter and Charlie Bullock, 'The Governance Misspecification Problem' (Institute for Law & AI 2024) 3–2024 <https://law-ai.org/the-governance-misspecification-problem/> accessed 30 October 2024.

[77] Pedro A Ortega and Vishal Maini, 'Building Safe Artificial Intelligence: Specification, Robustness, and Assurance' (*DeepMind Safety Research*, 27 September 2018) <https://deepmindsafetyresearch.medium.com/building-safe-artificial-intelligence-52f5f75058f1> accessed 13 December 2023 (describing this as the problem of defining the purpose of an AI system so that the system behaves in accordance with the true wishes of its designer).

[78] The term is drawn from Winter and Bullock (n 76).

specification) fail to effectuate the rule's intended purpose (analogous to the ideal specification)'.[79] In their account, the problem of 'misspecification' is one that occurs whenever there appears a gap between the ideal specification of a law (i.e. our goals or wishes), the design specification (i.e. the proxy, rule or categorization used to encode those goals into the law), and the revealed specification (i.e. the resulting behaviour of regulatees).

All this is well known in legal philosophy, and essentially reflects the classic 'no vehicles in the park' dilemma described decades ago by the legal philosopher H.L.A. Hart to discuss the problems involved with articulating an appropriately scoped legal rule.[80] In this account, a hypothetical legal prohibition on the presence of 'vehicles' in a public park relied on a (proxy) term—'vehicles'—that in its original formulation was aimed at restricting a particular class of technologies from the park (i.e. motor vehicles), in order to serve one or more particular regulatory aims (e.g. pedestrian safety, improved air quality, reduced noise pollution). However, because the rule was phrased without awareness of other potential 'vehicles' (e.g. bicycles, roller skates, helicopters, electric wheelchairs; drones . . .) which might, now or in the future, be captured under this term, the rule did not clearly account for them, and different interpretations can be made over which of these other types of vehicles are, in fact, also barred from the park. The latent ambiguity in the law creates later uncertainty over whether it would—or why it should—apply to these new objects. This creates a risk of incorrect legal scope, as existing laws are applied in ways that are either inappropriately under-inclusive, or inappropriately over-inclusive.[81]

To be sure, there are always limits—and drawbacks—to aiming to fully or ideally specify any law.[82] Nonetheless, situations where a mis-specified law is confronted with a new situation can often result in problematic under- or over-inclusiveness. Either can be a problem for effective technology regulation.[83] We can distinguish between different sources, and different types, of such mis-specification,

[79] ibid 4.

[80] HLA Hart, 'Positivism and the Separation of Law and Morals' (1958) 71 Harvard Law Review 593, 607. See also Pierre Schlag, 'No Vehicles in the Park' (1999) 23 Seattle University Law Review 381. The link is also drawn by Crootof, 'Regulating New Weapons Technology' (n 21) 9. Further commentary on Hart's argument—and his subsequent debate with Lon Fuller over the particular example—is given by Frederick Schauer, 'A Critical Guide to Vehicles in the Park' (2008) 83 New York University Law Review 1109.

[81] The link is also drawn by Crootof, 'Regulating New Weapons Technology' (n 21) 9. See also Winter and Bullock (n 76). For earlier definitions of under- and over-inclusiveness, see also Frederick F Schauer, *Playing by the Rules: A Philosophical Examination of Rule-Based Decision-Making in Law and in Life* (Oxford University Press 1991) 31.

[82] See also Dylan Hadfield-Menell and Gillian Hadfield, 'Incomplete Contracting and AI Alignment', *Proceedings of the 2019 AAAI/ACM Conference on AI, Ethics, and Society* (2019) <https://dl.acm.org/doi/10.1145/3306618.3314250> accessed 18 July 2019.

[83] For a similar discussion of the sources, and problems, of both under- and over-inclusion, see Crootof and Ard (n 3) 367–375.

depending on whether it is accidental or intended, and whether it is under- or over-inclusive.

5.5.3.1 Accidental under-inclusivity

On the one hand, technological changes, when they meet mis-specified laws, can result in situations of legal under-inclusivity. This occurs when new technologies—or the new capabilities, affordances, or sociotechnical situations they give rise to—slip through the net of the exact phrasing of a law, even though they might reasonably be held to be in violation of the regime's spirit or purpose. In many cases, such under-inclusivity may occur by accident or oversight, because of the difficulties involved in anticipating the future trajectories of a new technology, its affordances, and the resulting sociotechnical changes.

There are many cases of new artefacts, activities, or actors thus slipping through the net of an existing international regime or norm. If left unresolved, these cases could result not just in continued legal ambiguities, but also in real political or even military flash points. For instance, Benjamin Bemelen has discussed the legal implications of a 2016 naval incident in which the *USNS Bowditch*, an American autonomous underwater glider, was seized by the Chinese navy.[84] The Chinese claimed that they had merely seized an unidentified object to identify it, whereas the US viewed this as a hostile act, claiming sovereign immunity for the vessel. While this particular incident was resolved as China returned the vessel to the US, further incidents involving such systems have since occurred, and the underlying legal question has remained insufficiently addressed.[85] This is because, as Bemelen notes:

> The United Nations Convention on the Law of the Sea (UNCLOS), the main regulatory instrument governing the law of the sea, contains no references to autonomous vessels. It does not even define ships or vessels despite referring to them multiple times. This poses a challenge as sovereign immunity under UNCLOS applies to 'warships and other government ships operated for non-commercial purposes'. But are autonomous vessels considered warships? Can they even be considered ships?[86]

This case illustrates the challenges that new technologies can pose to under-inclusive international law. For one, they create a legal problem, because 'new types of vessels do not fit neatly into the definitions and qualifications of current international law, putting them in a regulatory limbo'.[87] If left unaddressed,

[84] Benjamin J Bemelen, 'Regulatory Obsolescence in the Technological Age: Analyzing Whether Autonomous Vessels Have Sovereign Immunity at Sea' (2024) 38 Ocean Yearbook Online 411.
[85] ibid.
[86] ibid 415 (citing sources).
[87] ibid 414.

furthermore, such legal challenges can fester into political or even military crisis, if disparate state interpretations of the existing regimes in place lead them towards conflictive practices or inadvertent escalation.

Nonetheless, while often problematic, cases of accidental under-inclusivity in the law can also, at times, be pragmatically resolved even at the international level. The necessary legal developments can be achieved by various means, such as adaptive interpretation or explicit treaty amendment by all the states parties. For instance, this appears to have been the approach taken by many states to the inadvertent under-inclusion of autonomous vehicles under the 1949 and 1968 Road Traffic Conventions, which both specify a requirement for a human driver.[88] While—as in the case of autonomous maritime vehicles—this created initial situations of legal uncertainty, the Global Forum for Road Traffic Safety has since led on remarkably rapid action to pragmatically resolve this ambiguity and ensure that autonomous vehicles are explicitly included in the scope of both regimes.[89]

Of course, at times, the legal uncertainty or gaps created by the use of a new technology can be an opportunity, not just a challenge. It is a chance not merely to develop a law in order to patch it to accommodate the technology, but rather for a broader renewal of the regime, correcting original design errors or normative fault lines that long preceded the technology's emergence on the scene. For instance, Barbara Stępień has suggested that autonomous and unmanned (shipping) vessels have begun to put pressure on international maritime law, in particular since it is unclear how these systems are to be governed under the collision regulations of the 1972 Convention on the International Regulations for Preventing Collisions at Sea. However, she argues that it has long been recognized that many of the provisions of this convention are outdated in many other ways, and currently require revision in their application to all types of ships, not just autonomous vessels.[90] In such situations, the legal problems revealed by new technology simply can serve as a timely canary in the coalmine, and an opportunity for a broader legal update.

Nonetheless, avoiding or addressing under-inclusivity in international regimes may be more difficult in many other cases. This is due to the notorious political challenges involved in patching or amending multilateral treaty regimes with many members, or negotiating entirely new such agreements while there remains outstanding disagreement amongst states over the basic questions over whether existing law is under-inclusive, whether that is a problem, and what would be the best approach for legal development.[91]

[88] Bryant Walker Smith, 'New Technologies and Old Treaties' (2020) 114 AJIL Unbound 152.

[89] ibid. See also the discussion in Section 5.5.6 ('Carrying Through Development').

[90] Barbara Stępień, 'Towards a New Horizon: 1972 COLREG in the Era of Autonomous Ships' (2024) 55 Ocean Development & International Law 170.

[91] Crootof, 'Regulating New Weapons Technology' (n 21). See also Bemelen (n 84) 431 (discussing the difficulty with amending UNCLOS to explicitly include autonomous vessels).

5.5.3.2 Engineered or evasive under-inclusivity

At the international level, however, such under-inclusion can often also be engineered, deliberate, or evasive—the result of active or at least knowing attempts by the parties 'to respect the letter of existing . . . agreements, while violating their spirit'.[92] Notably, such deliberate under-inclusivity can be achieved both by tailoring (international) regulations in ways that, tacitly or explicitly, exempt specific future anticipated technologies (engineered under-inclusivity), or by altering technological innovation or practices in response to regulation (evasive under-inclusivity).

In the latter case, may actors attempt to strategically alter technologies after a law has been laid down, in reaction to its provisions. For example, this happens frequently in domestic law, when regulated technology companies engage in practices of 'avoision'—that is, 'evasion and avoidance'—of existing regulation, by pursuing what Dan Burks has called 'perverse innovation': the development of technologies which 'provide a technical work-around to ingeniously dodge the intended outcome of regulation, while still formally adhering to the text of the regulation'.[93]

Indeed, especially at the international level, deliberate under-inclusivity (of either the evasive or engineered form) can also be pursued (or allowed) while actors draft legislation or negotiate treaties. There are various historical examples of such under-inclusivity.

For instance, under the 1967 Outer Space Treaty (OST), states pledged 'not to place in orbit around the earth any objects carrying nuclear weapons or any other kinds of weapons of mass destruction'.[94] This provision was meant to outlaw nuclear orbital bombardment systems, and more generally ensure that space would remain the preserve of peaceful exploration. At the same time, it avoided touching on the politically touchy issue of the superpowers' Intercontinental Ballistic Missiles (ICBMs), which, since they followed ballistic trajectories, never entered a stable orbit. However, shortly after signing the treaty, the Soviet Union tested a Fractional Orbital Bombardment System (FOBS) which launched nuclear weapons into space, but de-orbited them before they had completed a single full 'orbit'. This allowed them to stay stringently within the letter of the treaty,[95] even as

[92] Maas, 'Innovation-Proof Governance for Military AI?' (n 23) 137.

[93] Crootof and Ard (n 3) 370. Citing Leo Katz, *Ill-Gotten Gains: Evasion, Blackmail, Fraud, and Kindred Puzzles of the Law* (reprint edn, University of Chicago Press 1996), as well as Dan Burk, 'Perverse Innovation' (2016) 58 William & Mary Law Review 1. A valuable analysis of different forms of firm avoision that have begun to emerge in response to the EU AI Act is provided in: Rui-Jie Yew, Bill Marino and Suresh Venkatasubramanian, 'Red Teaming AI Policy: A Taxonomy of Avoision and the EU AI Act' (arXiv, 2 June 2025) <http://arxiv.org/abs/2506.01931> accessed 9 June 2025.

[94] Treaty on Principles Governing the Activities of States in the Exploration and Use of Outer Space, including the Moon and Other Celestial Bodies (opened for signature 27 January 1967, entered into force 10 October 1967) 610 UNTS 205 (Outer Space Treaty) art. IV.

[95] Raymond L Garthoff, 'Banning the Bomb in Outer Space' (1980) 5 International Security 25. As discussed in Daniel Deudney, *Dark Skies: Space Expansionism, Planetary Geopolitics, and the Ends of Humanity* (Oxford University Press 2020) 413. The incident caused a political uproar in the US, and no further tests of the system were conducted, although the launchers stayed operational. Subsequently, FOBS-type systems were explicitly prohibited by the SALT II agreement of 1979; while the US Senate

it allowed the Soviet Union to strike the US from space, evading detection by the US Ballistic Missile Early Warning System (BMEWS).[96]

For a more recent example of evasive under-inclusivity in the same technological field, one can consider a series of upgrades which the US conducted in the 2010s on the W76 nuclear warheads deployed on their missile submarine fleet. By outfitting these missiles with 'superfuses' that can trigger detonation based on proximity to a target (rather than based on pre-set burst-height), this innovation enables a far more reliable and accurate targeting of hardened installations such as missile siloes, without the need to reengineer the missiles themselves for greater accuracy in their ballistic trajectories. Consequently, it has been estimated that this modestly named 'modernization measure' has resulted in a tripling of the effective counter-force lethality of the US nuclear missile submarine force.[97] This case shows how even seemingly incremental technological shifts or improvements in capability can produce qualitatively significant sociotechnical shifts (such as in structural incentives around nuclear deterrence), even as states formally comply with caps under technology-specific arms control treaties.

In the case of AI, various innovations might produce specific capabilities that would be considered (by many) in violation of at least the spirit of established arms control treaties (or of any future regimes on LAWS operating beyond 'meaningful human control'), resulting in illegitimate under-inclusivity of such regimes.[98] For instance, Amanda McAllister has argued that advances in the use of autonomous robots for interrogation or torture would likely slip through the language set down in the UN Convention Against Torture and Other Cruel, Inhuman or Degrading Treatment or Punishment, even as it would clearly be against the spirit of that regime.[99]

Other cases of evasive under-inclusivity may also plague regimes that aim to regulate on the basis of a specific proxy metric,[100] especially ones that are highly technology-specific. For instance, a number of recent regulatory initiatives for AI

did not ratify SALT II, the Soviet Union did comply with its terms, decommissioning or converting the remaining FOBS launchers by 1983. Miroslav Gyűrösi, 'The Soviet Fractional Orbital Bombardment System Program' (Air Power Australia 2010) APA-TR-2010-0101 <http://www.ausairpower.net/APA-Sov-FOBS-Program.html> accessed 21 September 2020.

[96] Garthoff (n 95) 38.

[97] Hans M Kristensen, Matthew McKinzie, and Theodore A Postol, 'How US Nuclear Force Modernization Is Undermining Strategic Stability: The Burst-Height Compensating Super-Fuze' (*Bulletin of the Atomic Scientists*, 1 March 2017) <https://thebulletin.org/how-us-nuclear-force-modernization-undermining-strategic-stability-burst-height-compensating-super10578> accessed 12 March 2018. As discussed in Maas, 'Innovation-Proof Governance for Military AI?' (n 23) 137.

[98] Maas, 'Innovation-Proof Governance for Military AI?' (n 23) 137–138. See also Neil Renic and Elke Schwarz, 'Inhuman-in-the-Loop: AI-Targeting and the Erosion of Moral Restraint' (*Opinio Juris*, 19 December 2023) <https://opiniojuris.org/2023/12/19/inhuman-in-the-loop-ai-targeting-and-the-erosion-of-moral-restraint/> accessed 21 December 2023.

[99] Amanda McAllister, 'Stranger than Science Fiction: The Rise of A.I. Interrogation in the Dawn of Autonomous Robots and the Need for an Additional Protocol to the U.N. Convention Against Torture' (2018) 101 Minnesota Law Review 2527.

[100] Winter and Bullock (n 76) 17.

have sought to regulate or control the underlying inputs or resources necessary for training modern, advanced AI systems, by specifying particular chip lines or compute thresholds.

For instance, one can consider the instance of 2022–2023 attempts, by US semiconductor companies, to redesign particular chip lines for export to the Chinese market, in ways that sought to evade applicable US export restrictions which had been intended precisely to apply to these powerful chips in order to limit China's ability to train advanced AI models.[101] In October 2022, the US Commerce Department imposed a licence on the export of AI-relevant computer chips to the Chinese market. In response, the company Nvidia simply altered its market-leading A100 and H100 chips, and proceeded to sell the modified but nonetheless powerful A800 and H800 chips in China. This prompted the Commerce Department's Bureau of Industry and Security to announce a new interim final rule in October 2023 prohibiting the sale of these chips to China after all, avoiding the under-inclusivity of the regime.[102]

Mis-specified proxies also pose other challenges around incorrectly scoped regulation. For instance, Winter and Bullock have discussed the prominence, in various regulatory proposals for advanced AI systems, of the proxy term 'frontier AI'.[103] In many of these proposals, this term is often used as a stand-in for 'highly capable foundation models that could possess dangerous capabilities sufficient to pose severe risks to public safety'.[104] However, the ambiguity over how this term should be defined[105] creates a risk that statutory definitions will rely excessively on the proxy of some minimal compute thresholds used to train the model.[106] For instance, the (since repealed) 2023 Executive Order on the 'Safe, Secure, and Trustworthy Development and Use of Artificial Intelligence' imposed a set of

[101] ibid.

[102] Benj Edwards, 'US Surprises Nvidia by Speeding Up New AI Chip Export Ban' (*Ars Technica*, 24 October 2023) <https://arstechnica.com/information-technology/2023/10/ai-chip-wars-us-curbs-nvidia-gpu-chip-exports-sooner-than-expected/> accessed 12 January 2024; Peter Martin, '"We Cannot Let China Get These Chips": Commerce Secretary Raimondo Says More Funding Needed for AI Export Controls' (*Fortune*, 3 December 2023) <https://fortune.com/2023/12/02/ai-chip-export-controls-china-nvidia-raimondo/> accessed 12 January 2024. As discussed in Winter and Bullock (n 76) 17–18.

[103] Winter and Bullock (n 76) 19 (referring to the 'Frontier Model Forum', statements by OpenAI CEO Sam Altman, the UK government's 'Frontier AI Taskforce', and California state legislature bill).

[104] ibid. Drawing on the definition in Markus Anderljung and others, 'Frontier AI Regulation: Managing Emerging Risks to Public Safety' (arXiv, 11 July 2023) 2 <http://arxiv.org/abs/2307.03718> accessed 7 August 2023.

[105] See also the discussion at the start of Chapter 2.

[106] Winter and Bullock (n 76) 20. For further discussion of compute thresholds, see also Matteo Pistillo and others, 'The Role of Compute Thresholds for AI Governance' (2025) 1(1) George Washington Journal of Law & Technology 26; Lennart Heim and Leonie Koessler, 'Training Compute Thresholds: Features and Functions in AI Regulation' (arXiv, 6 August 2024) <http://arxiv.org/abs/2405.10799> accessed 9 August 2024. Note, beyond compute thresholds, one could also consider capability thresholds, or overall risk thresholds. See Leonie Koessler, Jonas Schuett, and Markus Anderljung, 'Risk Thresholds for Frontier AI' (arXiv, 20 June 2024) <http://arxiv.org/abs/2406.14713> accessed 26 June 2024. These thresholds, and their relative merits, will be discussed shortly.

reporting requirements on particular AI models. However, while it directed the Department of Commerce to develop more specific definitions of this category, the initial reporting threshold was compute-based, applying to all AI models 'trained using a quantity of computing power greater than 10^{26} integer or floating-point operations, or using primarily biological sequence data and using a quantity of computing power greater than 10^{23} integer or floating-point operations'.[107] However, this formulation of the training compute threshold already leaves a potential regulatory gap: the lower threshold specifies that it applies to models *primarily* using biological sequence data, suggesting that AI models that incorporate significant but not majority biological data would evade stringent oversight and reporting requirements even if their training utilizes more than 10^{23} operations, creating a regulatory loophole.[108]

Indeed, some have raised an even more categorical critique of the use of 'hard-coded' compute-threshold based proxies in AI governance strategies. For instance, Sarah Hooker has suggested that this strategy overstates the confirmed relation between the quantity of compute used in training a model and the level of risk of the resulting model, does not account for post-training leaps in performance, and accordingly misses the harms of many currently deployed models.[109] In addition, static compute thresholds may be difficult to track across an entire model lifecycle, and more broadly run counter to our inability to predict what abilities emerge at different model scales.[110] Finally, compute-threshold based regulatory schemes may struggle even more with the 2024 emergence of the 'reasoning' paradigm in AI systems (such as GPT-o1 or DeepSeek R1), based on improving AI capabilities through the scaling of inference compute rather than training compute alone.[111]

[107] Executive Office of the President, 'Executive Order on the Safe, Secure, and Trustworthy Development and Use of Artificial Intelligence' (*The White House*, 30 October 2023) <https://www.whitehouse.gov/briefing-room/presidential-actions/2023/10/30/executive-order-on-the-safe-secure-and-trustworthy-development-and-use-of-artificial-intelligence/> accessed 3 November 2023 (Section 4.2(b)(1)). See also Winter and Bullock (n 76) 21.

[108] Nicole Maug, Aidan O'Gara, and Tamay Besiroglu, 'Biological Sequence Models in the Context of the AI Directives' (*Epoch*, 17 January 2024) <https://epochai.org/blog/biological-sequence-models-in-the-context-of-the-ai-directives> accessed 23 January 2024.

[109] Sara Hooker, 'On the Limitations of Compute Thresholds as a Governance Strategy' (arXiv, 8 July 2024) <http://arxiv.org/abs/2407.05694> accessed 15 July 2024. Others have emphasized the importance of specific dataset size and content as more important enablers of—and indicators for—the risks from foundation models, including those that fall behind the 'frontier' in size. Ritwik Gupta and others, 'Data-Centric AI Governance: Addressing the Limitations of Model-Focused Policies' (*arXiv.org*, 25 September 2024) <https://arxiv.org/abs/2409.17216v1> accessed 3 October 2024.

[110] Hooker (n 109). Of course, our inability to accurately predict what abilities emerge at different model scales could also be taken as a reason to be particularly cautious.

[111] For discussions of these impacts on the role of compute thresholds, see: José Hernández-Orallo and Seán Ó HÉigeartaigh, 'Implications of DeepSeek V3 and R1 for the EU Code of Practice' (*LCFI—Leverhulme Centre for the Future of Intelligence*, 6 February 2025) <https://www.lcfi.ac.uk/news-events/blog/post/implications-of-deepseek-v3-and-r1-for-the-eu-code-of-practice> accessed 18 February 2025. Toby Ord, 'Inference Scaling Reshapes AI Governance' (*Toby Ord*, 12 February 2025) <https://www.tobyord.com/writing/inference-scaling-reshapes-ai-governance> accessed 18 February 2025. Though for a more optimistic perspective on the ways compute thresholds might be

One response to this challenge would as such seek to articulate other, better proxy metrics for the regulation of advanced AI models. For instance, it has been proposed that regulatory definitions could instead rely on capability evaluations of models, aimed at identifying the presence of some specific dangerous capabilities.[112] However, by default, this again narrowly scopes such evaluations at the development stage only, and runs into challenges around the efficacy of such evaluations.

Alternatively, regulatory definitions might seek to anchor proxies at a higher level of abstraction,[113] by specifying an overall 'risk threshold', defined in terms of (a) the overall likelihood of risks occurring as the consequence of a given (or planned) AI system seeing use, and (b) the resulting severity of harm (e.g. fatalities, injuries, or economic damage).[114] There are benefits to using risk thresholds, since they are likely more principled, consistent, and future-proof than capability thresholds.[115] However, they are also subject to challenges, as risk thresholds may be (even) more difficult to evaluate reliably in the context of future models.[116]

As such, a different response to the fallibility of training compute thresholds would be to recognize that they are an imperfect (and potentially under-inclusive) proxy for risk, but that this simply shows that they should not be used in isolation but can nonetheless be productively used alongside other metrics or frames. For instance, Heim and Koessler have noted that the benefits of compute thresholds (e.g. they are quantifiable, can be measured early in the AI lifecycle, and can be verified externally) still makes them a suitable and indeed critical part within a broader system of regulatory metrics, as they can be aimed at flagging one class of risky models for oversight, with determinations of the appropriate risk mitigation measures relying on other, additional policies—and that, indeed, existing governance instruments such as the EU AI Act mostly already utilize compute thresholds in line with this approach.[117]

adapted to such changes, see also Lennart Heim, 'Inference Compute: GPT-O1 and AI Governance' (22 September 2024) <https://blog.heim.xyz/inference-compute/> accessed 18 February 2025.

[112] Helen Toner and Shelton Fitch, 'Regulating the AI Frontier: Design Choices and Constraints' (*Center for Security and Emerging Technology*, 26 October 2023) <https://cset.georgetown.edu/article/regulating-the-ai-frontier-design-choices-and-constraints/> accessed 25 November 2023; Anderljung and others (n 104); Matthijs Maas, 'Concepts in Advanced AI Governance: A Literature Review of Key Terms and Definitions' (Institute for Law & AI 2023) AI Foundations Report 3 <https://law-ai.org/advanced-ai-gov-concepts> accessed 28 October 2023.

[113] This also relates to debates over whether regulatory requirements for advanced AI models are best formulated as high-level principles, or through very specific rules. See Jonas Schuett and others, 'From Principles to Rules: A Regulatory Approach for Frontier AI' in P Hacker and others (eds), *The Oxford Handbook of the Foundations and Regulation of Generative AI* (Oxford University Press, 2025).

[114] Koessler, Schuett, and Anderljung (n 106).

[115] ibid 13.

[116] ibid 14.

[117] Heim and Koessler (n 106).

Nonetheless, these trade-offs and challenges around creating or selecting appropriate proxy metrics for the organization of AI regulation jointly create risks that the resulting regulations will prove under-inclusive of the full range of advanced, general-purpose AI systems, their capabilities, their uses, and their impacts.[118]

5.5.3.3 Inappropriate over-inclusivity

While many technology-law scholars focus on the risks of under-inclusivity, many discussions of regulatory mis-specification have also centred on cases of inappropriate over-inclusivity of existing laws to new technologies or conduct.

For instance, in a domestic legal context, the US Computer Fraud and Abuse Act (CFAA), originally enacted in 1984, has been called 'the worst law in technology'.[119] This is because it treats as criminal offences an extremely broad list of behaviour on the basis of vague and overbroad prohibitions. For instance, it criminalizes acts that involve 'intentionally access[ing] a computer without authorization or exceed[ing] authorized access, and thereby obtain[ing] . . . information from any protected computer'.[120] Yet, in a literal reading, such prohibitions could mean that innocuous and common actions—from accessing social media at work in violation of company policy, to sharing a password with a spouse[121]—should be treated as crimes, with severe sentences. Such over-inclusion may consequently lead to growing non-compliance, and may challenge the legitimacy of the rule of law or lead to significant legal challenge, especially at the international level.[122]

What might inappropriate over-inclusivity look like for AI? In the domestic legal context, for instance, Ryan Calo has chronicled how in the early 2010s, initial US regulatory responses to self-driving cars defined these technologies in ways that were inadvertently over-inclusive—imposing stringent requirements on existing features with partially autonomous features—which ultimately led to the repeal of these laws.[123]

As another interesting example of this, some scholars have argued that it might be feasible, under existing law, to grant certain algorithms a semblance of

[118] Winter and Bullock (n 76) 21 ('statutory definitions can themselves incorporate proxies that result in misspecification. The above definition, for instance, may be underinclusive because some models that cannot be classified as "highly capable" or as "foundation models" might also pose severe risks to public safety').

[119] Tim Wu, 'Fixing the Worst Law in Technology' [2013] *The New Yorker* <https://www.newyorker.com/news/news-desk/fixing-the-worst-law-in-technology> accessed 12 January 2024.

[120] Computer Fraud and Abuse Act (CFAA) 1984 (18 USC § 1030). As discussed by Winter and Bullock (n 76) 9–10.

[121] Winter and Bullock (n 76) 10, discussing Orin Kerr, 'Vagueness Challenges to the Computer Fraud and Abuse Act' [2010] 94 Minnesota Law Review 1561; Tiffany Curtiss, 'Computer Fraud and Abuse Act Enforcement: Cruel, Unusual, and Due for Reform' (2016) 91 Washington Law Review 1813, 1841.

[122] Crootof and Ard (n 3) 373–374.

[123] See Ryan Calo, 'The Case for a Federal Robotics Commission' (Brookings Institute Center for Technology Innovation 2014) <https://www.brookings.edu/articles/the-case-for-a-federal-robotics-commission/> accessed 25 February 2021.

functional legal personhood. For instance, Shawn Bayern has claimed that certain loopholes in existing US company law allow for the incorporation of a limited liability company (LLC) with an operating agreement that places it under operational control of an AI; if all human members subsequently withdrew, the LLC would theoretically be left with the algorithm solely in charge, functionally establishing 'algorithmic entities' with (corporate) legal personhood.[124] This argument has of course been contested, with many others observing that courts would likely not interpret the relevant statutes in a manner that obviously appears contrary to legislative intent.[125] Nonetheless, stranger rulings have on occasion passed, and assuming such a construction were to be held up in court, this could well precipitate further cases of disruption.

Indeed, Bayern and others have sought to extend this same schema to the legal systems of several EU member states.[126] This creates a potential additional, second-order over-inclusivity loophole: as argued by Thomas Burri, if an 'algorithmic entity' were successfully established in any one EU member state, the internal market principle of the mutual recognition of national legal personality would imply that that system should then be legally recognized by all EU member states.[127] Such outcomes, however, likely would—and arguably should—be considered situations of inappropriate over-inclusiveness of existing regulation.[128]

As noted, inadvertently over-inclusive regulation is a problem, because it may result in a range of legal problems, from unjustifiable social costs of complying with an over-inclusive law to unintended over-enforcement, or the risk that the underenforcement of over-inclusive treaties ends up contributing to a backlash or visible non-compliance, eroding the perceived strength or legitimacy of a given legal regime by creating the impression it does not carry the force of the rule of law.[129] When technologies create a perceived problem in the scope of existing legislation—whether under or over-inclusive—this creates a need for development to extrapolate and reaffirm existing lines between legal categories, so as to explicitly include or exclude the new behaviour, entities, or relationships.

[124] Shawn Bayern, 'The Implications of Modern Business-Entity Law for the Regulation of Autonomous Systems' (2016) 7 European Journal of Risk Regulation 297, 300–304. As discussed in Maas, 'International Law Does Not Compute' (n 1) 40.

[125] Matthew U Scherer, 'Is AI Personhood Already Possible under U.S. LLC Laws? (Part One: New York)' (*Law and AI*, 14 May 2017) <http://www.lawandai.com/2017/05/14/is-ai-personhood-already-possible-under-current-u-s-laws-dont-count-on-it-part-one/> accessed 4 May 2019; Turner (n 69) 177.

[126] Specifically Germany, Switzerland, and the UK (at the time still a EU member). Shawn Bayern and others, 'Company Law and Autonomous Systems: A Blueprint for Lawyers, Entrepreneurs, and Regulators' (2017) 9 Hastings Science and Technology Law Journal 135, 139–153.

[127] Thomas Burri, 'Free Movement of Algorithms: Artificially Intelligent Persons Conquer the European Union's Internal Market' in Woodrow Barfield and Ugo Pagallo (eds), *Research Handbook on the Law of Artificial Intelligence* (Edward Elgar 2017) 545 <https://papers.ssrn.com/abstract=3010233> accessed 13 September 2018.

[128] Burri (n 8) 95–98. See also Maas, 'International Law Does Not Compute' (n 1) 40.

[129] See also Crootof and Ard (n 3) 31–33.

5.5.4 Rendering Obsolete Core Assumptions of Governance

Fourth, AI can allow new behaviour that renders obsolete core assumptions which underpin a particular law or governance regime. This can occur for one of three subsidiary reasons: because the technology (a) renders once regulated behaviour obsolete (undercutting the continued need for the regime); (b) undercuts certain justifying assumptions (challenging the adequacy of the manner in which the regime pursues its intended goals); or (c) makes existing laws no longer cost-effective to enforce (challenging the long-term viability or deterrent effects of the regime). In all three cases, AI capabilities can drive functional 'legal obsolescence', where existing law is rendered unfit for its originally intended purposes, consequently requiring a reconsideration of the core aims and purposes of that regime.

Significantly, cases of potential obsolescence are interesting because, even more so than cases involving legal gaps, conceptual uncertainty, or incorrect scope of application, they raise questions that are not only doctrinal (i.e. over whether or how existing law applies) but also normative (i.e. over whether that law still achieves its intended purpose).[130]

5.5.4.1 Non- or dis-appearance of regulated behaviour

In the first place, obsolescence of a governance regime could result because the (technology-enabled) behaviour, activity, or items that it sought to regulate are irrelevant, rare, or non-existent. This may happen to both anticipatory regulation and reactive regulation.[131]

In the former case, an anticipatory law might become obsolete because it is aimed at the regulation of some specific behaviour or class of artefacts which were believed to be imminent at the time of drafting, but which never truly arrived or saw uptake. For instance, in the US, the Digital Millenium Copyright Act (DMCA) of 1998 was designed to prevent the decryption of copyrighted work, by criminalizing the trafficking of tools to decrypt such work.[132] At the time that the law was enacted, the assumption was that hackers would soon create and share (physical) 'black box' devices that would facilitate such piracy.[133] However, these technologies never arrived, as hackers instead uploaded decryption codes to the internet, 'bringing the DMCA into conflict with the nascent legal determination that computer code was entitled to First Amendment protection'.[134] In the case of AI, we might expect similar forms of obsolescence to ensue if certain paradigm shifts in

[130] ibid 367 ('application uncertainties implicate rule interpretation while normative uncertainties require evaluating whether a rule achieves its purpose').

[131] Winter and Bullock (n 76).

[132] Digital Millennium Copyright Act (DMCA) 1998 (17 USC § 1201(a)(2)) (prohibiting trafficking in 'any technology, product, service, device, component, or part thereof' designed for this purpose). As discussed in cited in Crootof and Ard (n 3) 362–363; Winter and Bullock (n 76) 8–9.

[133] Crootof and Ard (n 3) 362–363.

[134] ibid.

the field decouple the general-purpose performance of systems from their model (parameter) size or from high compute and data requirements for their training processes. Such a sea change in the field would erode key assumptions of many recent advanced AI governance initiatives—such as the 2023–2025 US Executive Order on AI—that relied on an assumption that using significant amounts of compute and data in training is and will remain the only route to producing highly capable 'frontier AI systems' or 'dual-use foundation models' capable of significant national security impacts.[135]

In the second variety of this situation, a law may become obsolete because a formerly common behaviour that was subject to regulation has been superseded or rendered obsolete in practice, or drastically reduced in importance, as a result of new technological capabilities.[136] One might expect this retroactive category of legal obsolescence to be relatively rare. This is because while technological progress can often lower the threshold for certain behaviours, and can occasionally create new affordances or capabilities, it less often results in the categorical disappearance (let alone the impossibility) of older types of behaviour.[137] Even in cases where it does, there is of course often an implication that certain categories of behaviour could still be revived, which might ensure the continuing relevance of the law. Where it does occur, such obsolescence might be expected to play a role primarily in the context of highly technology-specific laws, such as rules on the management of telegraph infrastructure.[138]

In the context of AI, however, one might consider how a continued extrapolation of recent military trends towards remote warfare could result in such legally disruptive changes. If AI-steered combat platforms come to widely replace human soldiers on battlefields, this might indirectly marginalize or render practically uninvoked IHL principles dictating the treatment of prisoners of war.[139] Indeed, just as submarine warfare involved vessels that were architecturally ill-equipped for shipping back the crews of target vessels to port, which therefore eventually drove new state practice in naval warfare which rendered the older London Naval Treaty 'jurisprudential space junk',[140] the continuation towards AI-supported remote

[135] Executive Office of the President (n 107) s 3 (k).
[136] Bennett Moses (n 38) 48–49. See also Bennett Moses (n 2) 595.
[137] See David Edgerton, *The Shock Of The Old: Technology and Global History since 1900* (Main edition, Profile Books 2019) (discussing the remarkable persistence and indeed continued importance of many 'old' innovations, even after newer 'high technologies' arrived on the scene). Of course, it is also an open question whether such 'dead letter' obsolescence truly requires categorical cessation or obsolescence of certain behaviour, or whether virtual disappearance suffices. Likely there is a spectrum.
[138] On the other hand, at least within the common law system, cases dealing with telegraphs or other outmoded forms of communication may nonetheless have continued relevance. In such cases, these laws might be only partially obsolete.
[139] As set out in: Geneva Convention Relative to the Treatment of Prisoners of War (adopted 12 August 1949, entered into force 21 October 1950) 75 UNTS 135 (Third Geneva Convention). See also Maas, 'International Law Does Not Compute' (n 1) 42.
[140] Crootof, 'Jurisprudential Space Junk' (n 17).

warfare could in extreme cases precipitate a similar shift in customary international law. An alternate example might involve ongoing developments in 'remote biometric surveillance', such as gait detection, or laser-measured heartbeat identification, some of which have proven as accurate as facial recognition at identifying individuals.[141] If such applications were to replace facial recognition in most surveillance systems, this could render any regulation or bans on facial recognition systems relatively moot.[142]

Of course, one can debate to what extent this type of legal obsolescence is very likely or common—or, if it occurs, whether it truly poses a problem for governance regimes. To be sure, in some rare cases under domestic law, antiquated and virtually uninvoked 'dead letter' laws do rear their head[143]—becoming so-called zombie laws.[144] Yet in most cases the costs imposed on a legal system retaining superfluous but uninvoked laws may seem problematic only from a strict legal coherentist perspective.[145]

On the other hand, as noted by Bennett Moses, 'it can be a problem if the regulated conduct has been replaced by conduct that causes harm of a type the rule sought to avoid, but does not fall within the rule itself'.[146] Furthermore, this type of legal obsolescence could still pose a problem for international law (even from a functional perspective) if obsolete treaties provide (misleading) judicial metaphors, if they delay awareness of shifts in the behaviour to be regulated, or if they grow into 'jurisprudential space junk' that muddles the waters regarding the status of subsequent customary international law.[147]

5.5.4.2 Foundational justifying assumptions are no longer valid

More problematically for international law, legal obsolescence might occur because one or more basic justifying assumptions that underlie the original historical introduction or specific formulation of a particular law or regime are no longer valid in the face of a particular form of sociotechnical change.[148]

[141] Keith J Hayward and Matthijs M Maas, 'Artificial Intelligence and Crime: A Primer for Criminologists' (2020) 17 Crime, Media, Culture 209.

[142] Though under another interpretation, this would involve a situation of inappropriate under-inclusion of any regulation meant to regulate systems of surveillance.

[143] For instance, see the discussion of laws on blasphemous libel in Jeremy Patrick, 'Not Dead, Just Sleeping: Canada's Prohibition on Blasphemous Libel as a Case Study in Obsolete Legislation' (2008) 41 U.B.C. Law Review 193.

[144] Howard Wasserman, 'Zombie Laws' (2022) 25 Lewis & Clark Law Review 1047 (discussing cases where a law may be declared constitutionally invalid in a judicial context—meaning that future enforcement efforts will not succeed in courts—but remain on the books, in ways that they can be enforced by departmentalist executives acting on independent constitutional judgment).

[145] See Graham McBain, 'Abolishing Some Obsolete Common Law Crimes' (2009) 20 King's Law Journal 89.

[146] Bennett Moses (n 38) 48.

[147] Crootof, 'Jurisprudential Space Junk' (n 17). On the other hand, it could be countered that treaties that apply solely to extinct technologies or behaviour cannot clash with new customary international law, and therefore cannot produce 'jurisprudential space junk'.

[148] Bennett Moses (n 38) 49–53. Maas, 'International Law Does Not Compute' (n 1) 41.

For instance, Rebecca Crootof has discussed how the emergence of increasingly precise weapons technologies is gradually stressing core tenets of the law of armed conflict. Under customary international humanitarian law, it has long been assumed that all state parties that participate in a conflict are subject to the same rights and restrictions, and that these obligations do not meaningfully depend on or vary with the combatants' (relative) technological capabilities. However, because the content of some obligations—such as the nominally tech-neutral obligation to take '*feasible* precautions' in an attack—are in fact affected by the technological capabilities (e.g. ISR or precision targeting) available to a military, continued technological progress may functionally be held to confer more stringent requirements on the more technologically advanced actors, in ways that erode the conventional equality or symmetry of state obligations under IHL.[149]

To take another case: a study of the 'high-performance computer' threshold in US 1990s export control regimes provide an example of how underlying shifts in a technology may begin to stress or falsify some core assumptions of that technology-specific regime about the rate of progress in computing power—in ways that resulted both in repeated over-inclusiveness of the regime and, arguably, its eventual growing obsolescence.[150] That is, during the 1990s and early 2000s, the US established a series of export control arrangements under the Wassenaar Arrangement, on high-performance computers. The purpose of these controls was to prevent the export of powerful computers to rival or hostile states which might use them in ways that threatened the national security of the US and its allies.[151] Accordingly, these export controls set an initial 1991 threshold for restricted 'supercomputers' at just 195 million theoretical operations per second (MTOPS). In doing so, the regime treated computer technology as far too static.[152] As the 1990s progressed, the computing power of commercially available computers grew rapidly, and a number of other countries began to manufacture and sell powerful computers.[153] Accordingly, the Clinton administration responded by raising the threshold at which export restrictions applied six times within less than a decade.[154] Even so, additional technological advances in the late 1990s soon made it possible to

[149] Crootof, 'Regulating New Weapons Technology' (n 21) 11–12.

[150] Although notably, this case could also be read as one where the regulation ended up repeatedly (inappropriate) over-inclusive. See for instance Winter and Bullock (n 76) 15. This shows how the legally disruptive impact of technological change is rarely neatly confined to simply one category of disruption.

[151] Robert Johnston, 'U.S. Export Control Policy in the High Performance Computer Sector' (1998) 5 The Nonproliferation Review 44.

[152] Picker (n 20) 212.

[153] Bradley Steinbrecher, 'The Impact of the Clinton Administration's Export Promotion Plan on U.S. Exports of Computers and High-Technology Equipment' (1995) 15 University of Pennsylvania Journal of International Law 675, 697. See also Winter and Bullock (n 76) 14–15.

[154] Picker (n 20) 212–213 ('for civilian end-users, the Tier 3 computer export control threshold in 1991 was established at 195 MTOPS, and was increased in 1994 to 1,500 MTOPS; in 1996 to 7,000 MTOPS; in August 1999 to 12,300 MTOPS; in February 2000 to 20,000 MTOPS; in August 2000 to 28,000 MTOPS; and in January 2001 to 85,000 MTOPS').

connect many commercially available (and unrestricted) computers into 'clusters' that, collectively, could outperform supercomputers.[155] Given these converging technological trends, the export control regime became increasingly ineffective at preventing or even slowing US adversaries from accessing as much computing power as they needed; at the same time, through their adverse effects on the US domestic tech industry, the export controls became increasingly considered harmful to both the US economy and—indeed, contra their original purpose—to US national security interests.[156] Even so, MTOPS-based export controls continued in use until 2006, after which they were replaced by regulations that based controls on performance in terms of Weighted TeraFLOPS.[157]

In the context of AI, what would be comparable examples of the obsolescence of foundational assumptions of legal systems? Some examples might be found in the domain of international human rights law. For example, Sue Anne Teo has charted how, beyond potentially affecting specific human rights of individuals, AI systems could exert a 'slow violence' on human rights more generally, among others by unravelling the normative justifications of discrete rights such as the rights to privacy, freedom of expression, or freedom of thought.[158]

As an adjacent example, one might consider the (admittedly aspirational) human right to work, as enshrined in the Universal Declaration of Human Rights and the International Covenant on Economic, Social and Cultural Rights,[159] which is premised on an assumption that societies will continue to need the labour of—or be capable of providing employment for—a large fraction of their population. If at length AI systems continue to reach or approach human performance in more tasks,[160] a significant population might be rendered functionally unemployable.[161] This change, if or when it occurs, would render this (aspirational) human right to work functionally obsolete,[162] with additional repercussions for many parts

[155] ibid 212.

[156] Picker (n 20). See also Steinbrecher (n 153).

[157] Implementation of New Formula for Calculating Computer Performance: Adjusted Peak Performance (APP) in Weighted TeraFLOPS; Bulgaria; XP and MT Controls. Rules and Regulations 2006 (71 FR 20876) 20863. As discussed in Winter and Bullock (n 76) 15.

[158] Sue Anne Teo, 'Artificial Intelligence and Its "Slow Violence" to Human Rights' [2024] AI and Ethics <https://doi.org/10.1007/s43681-024-00547-x> accessed 3 October 2024; see also generally Sue Anne Teo, 'How Artificial Intelligence Systems Challenge the Conceptual Foundations of the Human Rights Legal Framework' (2022) 40 Nordic Journal of Human Rights 216.

[159] Universal Declaration of Human Rights 1948, Article 23; UN General Assembly, *International Covenant on Civil and Political Rights*, vol 999 (United Nations 1966), Article 6.

[160] Katja Grace and others, 'When Will AI Exceed Human Performance? Evidence from AI Experts' (2018) 62 Journal of Artificial Intelligence Research 729; Katja Grace and others, 'Thousands of AI Authors on the Future of AI' (arXiv, 5 January 2024) <http://arxiv.org/abs/2401.02843> accessed 8 January 2024.

[161] Hilary G Escajeda, 'Zero Economic Value Humans?' (2020) 10 Wake Forest Journal of Law & Policy 129. See also Anton Korinek and Megan Juelfs, 'Preparing for the (Non-Existent?) Future of Work' (*Brookings*, 11 August 2022) <https://www.brookings.edu/research/preparing-for-the-non-existent-future-of-work/> accessed 19 October 2022.

[162] See also Mathias Risse, 'Human Rights and Artificial Intelligence: An Urgently Needed Agenda' (2019) 41 Human Rights Quarterly 1. However, it is simultaneously possible that such a development

of international law, such as the labour regime constructed by the International Labour Organization.[163] In the longer term, this could result in situations where many people's status as ('productive') participants in society would increasingly be drawn into question.[164] This would result in the need for legal development towards regimes that would explore different avenues of securing dignified human activity and inclusion in a post-work era.[165]

5.5.4.3 Reduced cost-effectiveness of enforcement

Finally, legal obsolescence (and the accordant need for corrective legal development) might occur because a law is no longer enforceable, at least not in a cost-effective manner.[166] Practical difficulties introduced by new technologies can often slow the enforcement of older legal frameworks in new spaces. For instance, the difficulty of attributing attacks in cyberspace has been held as one (if not the only) hurdle to effectively regulating cyberattacks.[167] Simon Chesterman has argued that the rise of high-speed computing introduced new challenges to fields such as securities regulation and competition law, simply because it enabled many previously lawful activities (e.g. trading in stocks, comparing and adjusting prices) to be carried out far faster than had initially been conceived as possible.[168]

What would this look like for AI? Trends towards increased compute efficiency of models[169] could gradually result in steadily easier access to advanced AI systems for many actors and principals. This could stress the cost-effective enforcement of various forms of proposed regulation (such as around monitoring and enforcement, or licensing) for AI systems at the frontier.

While some uses of AI technology could certainly support the monitoring or enforcement of international law,[170] other AI developments could also actively impede or aim to block the enforcement of these norms. For instance, since around

could put greater emphasis on workers' rights in regions producing the raw materials or inputs for AI and its infrastructures. I thank Luisa Scarcella for this observation.

[163] Maas, 'International Law Does Not Compute' (n 1) 43.

[164] Risse (n 162).

[165] See for example John Danaher, *Automation and Utopia: Human Flourishing in a World without Work* (Harvard University Press 2019).

[166] Bennett Moses (n 38) 53–54; Maas, 'International Law Does Not Compute' (n 1) 42.

[167] Michael J Glennon, 'The Dark Future of International Cybersecurity Regulation' (2013) 6 Journal of National Security Law & Policy 563. However, note the counterargument on attribution in Horowitz, 'Do Emerging Military Technologies Matter for International Politics?' (n 18) 395 (noting that attribution in cyberspace may be more viable than sometimes perceived, not only because of advances in attribution and digital forensics, but also because 'the standard of proof for attribution in international politics may differ from that required for international domestic or legal purposes').

[168] Simon Chesterman, '"Move Fast and Break Things": Law, Technology, and the Problem of Speed' (2021) 33 Singapore Academy of Law Journal 5.

[169] Konstantin Pilz, Lennart Heim, and Nicholas Brown, 'Increased Compute Efficiency and the Diffusion of AI Capabilities' (arXiv, 26 November 2023) <http://arxiv.org/abs/2311.15377> accessed 13 December 2023.

[170] See also the brief discussion under Section 5.6.2 ('Automation of monitoring and enforcement').

2017, a significant body of scholarship has discussed the potential of AI-produced deepfake techniques to enable the at-scale forging of video documentation.[171] This could include the faking of documentary evidence of alleged human rights abuses. Various scholars have raised the possibility that deepfakes (or their more modern iterations derived from contemporary generative AI models) could adversely affect the probative value of (video) evidence, not only in domestic courts but also potentially eroding certain epistemological foundations of international journalism, human rights investigations, or international criminal judicial proceedings.[172]

If realized, such misuses of generative AI systems could enable malicious or politically interested actors to swamp human rights bodies or media observers with fake footage which could only be revealed as such after laborious analysis. Indeed, if strong watermarking schemes for AI systems are largely impossible,[173] such attacks might be nearly impossible to defend against. This makes such organizations highly vulnerable to such attacks, which would not only impose heavy costs on them but would also simultaneously erode the credibility of genuine reports, in an effect that has been called the 'liars' dividend'.[174] This would render the effective monitoring and enforcement of human rights norms far more precarious than it has ever previously been.[175]

5.5.5 Altering problem portfolio

In addition to these challenges, AI may drive an additional category of 'governance disruption', which is not neatly captured under these previous categories.[176] Specifically, there may be cases where AI innovation markedly shifts the prevailing sociotechnical 'distribution of risks' arising from the technology and its use.[177] I have previously argued that technological innovation can also drive 'indirect disruption' of existing governance regimes, by altering the 'problem portfolio' of a technology, creating blind spots that the existing regime is not adequately equipped

[171] Robert Chesney and Danielle Keats Citron, 'Deep Fakes: A Looming Challenge for Privacy, Democracy, and National Security' (2019) 107 California Law Review 1753.

[172] Marie-Helen Maras and Alex Alexandrou, 'Determining Authenticity of Video Evidence in the Age of Artificial Intelligence and in the Wake of Deepfake Videos' [2018] The International Journal of Evidence & Proof 1365712718807226, 258; Livingston and Risse (n 14) 144; Hin-Yan Liu and Andrew Mazibrada, 'Artificial Intelligence Affordances: Deep-Fakes as Exemplars of AI Challenges to Criminal Justice Systems' [2020] UNICRI Special Collection on Artificial Intelligence <http://unicri.it/towards-responsible-artificial-intelligence-innovation> accessed 13 July 2020.

[173] Hanlin Zhang and others, 'Watermarks in the Sand: Impossibility of Strong Watermarking for Generative Models' (arXiv, 14 November 2023) <http://arxiv.org/abs/2311.04378> accessed 19 November 2023.

[174] Chesney and Citron (n 171) 1785.

[175] Maas, 'International Law Does Not Compute' (n 1) 42.

[176] Although on some readings, this could be read as 'obsolescence of foundational assumptions' of a regime.

[177] Maas, 'Innovation-Proof Governance for Military AI?' (n 23) 139–141.

(either in jurisdiction, institutional mandate, in-house expertise, or culture) to address.[178] This can serve as a fifth situation of legal uncertainty, which creates a need for developments to re-orient or re-balance existing regulatory regimes to track the relative balance of challenges created by a technology as it develops.

After all, as illustrated by our discussion of sociotechnical change, shifts in technological capabilities can unlock new use cases, which may generate new sociotechnical change in new domains. In some cases, this can shift the centre of gravity of the problem portfolio (for instance, from 'ethics' to 'structure'). This can create a peculiar problem for existing governance regimes which accordingly find themselves focused on—and tailored to—the mitigation of only a subset of challenges.

Indeed, the ability of technologies to iteratively shift the 'salient' sociotechnical and legal challenges confronting a regime can be found in the changing challenges facing cyberlaw. As Jack Balkin noted, rather than confronting a single technology with immutable 'essential features', the internet proved a changeable regulatory target; whereas in 1991, the internet mostly appeared to raise challenges relating to anonymous communication across jurisdictional lines, by 1999 regulatory concerns focused on filtering and surveillance, and by 2008 the focus was on the internet's ability to lower the costs of social organization.[179] A comprehensive and inflexible legal system for cyberspace, if instituted in 1991, would therefore have faced gradual but inevitable misalignment—even if it somehow avoided very clear situations of legal uncertainty—because it would remain focused on and tailored to a subset of the technology's full portfolio of sociotechnical changes. The key point is not that cyberlaw could not or did not change and respond to such developments, but rather that—especially in the international legal context, where multilateral treaties are hard to amend—there is a risk of early regimes becoming locked in.

For instance, in the domain of the regulation of military AI, most current regulatory approaches aim to ensure some forms of 'meaningful human control' (MHC) over the exertion of lethal force and/or to outright ban LAWS as being inherently 'indiscriminate' and therefore in violation of IHL.[180] Either solution might constitute a significant international legal response. Yet in the longer term, it may be that regimes tailored to address these ethical or legal challenges of LAWS are not optimally oriented or equipped to anticipate, let alone address, later risks arising from adjacent AI capabilities, such as destabilizing *structural shifts*

[178] ibid 141.

[179] Jack M Balkin, 'The Path of Robotics Law' (2015) 6 California Law Review Circuit 17, 47–48.

[180] This is admittedly a generalization of a much wider array of possible regulatory approaches that have been coined. Esther Chavannes, Klaudia Klonowska, and Tim Sweijs, 'Governing Autonomous Weapon Systems: Expanding the Solution Space, from Scoping to Applying' [2020] HCSS Security 39. However, these two avenues appear to have gotten the most traction at the international level.

produced by AI cyberwarfare systems or military decision support systems.[181] Indeed, Neil Renic and Elke Schwartz have argued that the use of AI-based 'target-production' platforms (such as the 'Gospel' AI system) during the Israel–Hamas war highlights how even AI-based systems that maintain humans-in-the-loop can generate significant moral (and legal) challenges, noting that 'what matters in such systems is not "humans" per se, but rather humanity—a commitment to decency and restraint, and rejection of overly expansive categories of targetable enemies'.[182]

Of course, one counterargument might be that legal frameworks such as IHL have a clear focus and jurisdiction for a reason, and that they are not, and should not, concerned much or at all with questions of strategic stability or a lowering threshold to the use of force,[183] but that these might be in the purview of arms control regimes or *jus ad bellum* instead. That may be a key point, though it also highlights the degree to which the ongoing evolution in the AI problem portfolio can erode the efficacy or sufficiency of existing regime distinctions which target only a subset of sociotechnical changes.

5.5.6 Carrying Through Development: Reflections and Risks

The situations discussed so far are those where AI applications can or could produce various substantive or doctrinal shortfalls in existing governance instruments. Whenever they do, these shortfalls accordingly need to be repaired—either to restore the status *ex quo ante*, or to achieve new regulatory goals in light of the new situation.

Generally speaking, these are situations of governance disruption which demonstrate how AI systems might create a need for legal or regulatory change ('development'), because they create new entities, enable new behaviour, shift incentives of actors to create new situations, or produce markedly new patterns and portfolios of sociotechnical change. Bennett Moses and others argue that such cases demonstrate how technology can create a 'recurring dilemma' for legal systems,[184] and argue that this is a problem against which governance cannot be systematically future-proofed.[185]

There are a few caveats to the concept of technology-driven substantive governance disruption, however.

[181] Maas, 'Innovation-Proof Governance for Military AI?' (n 23) 139–141. See also Koppelman (n 28).
[182] Renic and Schwarz (n 98).
[183] Deeks, Lubell and Murray (n 9).
[184] Bennett Moses (n 38).
[185] Friedman (n 37) 85.

5.5.6.1 Not all technological change is legally disruptive

In the first place, especially where it comes to situations of legal uncertainty and development, not all governance disruption is created equal. Indeed, legal systems are complex, robust, and well-provided social tools, and consequently technological change, even if it is seen as radically new, and even if it produces significant sociotechnical impacts, is often not legally disruptive at all. As argued by Bennett Moses:

> Most of the time, a law predating technological change will apply in the new circumstances without any confusion. For example, traffic rules continue to apply to cars with electric windows, and no sane person would seek to challenge these laws as inapplicable or write an article calling for the law to be clarified.[186]

The same might be the case at the international level, where many new technological innovations come quietly, without producing significant disruption—or where any apparent initial disruption is usually settled and incorporated over time.[187]

Moreover, even where there is a degree of disruption, this can come in distinct degrees. There might certainly be times where a new technology is 'exceptional' in its disruption, because, as Calo notes, its introduction to the mainstream requires 'a systematic change to the law or legal institutes in order to reproduce, or if necessary displace, an existing balance of values'.[188] Yet there are many other cases where a technology merely 'creates one or more small changes in the law, or ... reveals, at the margins, that an existing interpretation of a particular doctrine is incomplete',[189] but where a failure of legal or regulatory development to address these minor details would not materially endanger either the coherence or the instrumental utility of a legal system.[190] Indeed, some have argued that, at least in certain domestic jurisdictions, the 'legally disruptive' impact of AI technologies may be relatively rare, with most applications fitting within the remit of most existing laws most of the time.[191]

[186] Bennett Moses (n 2) 596.

[187] Kristen E Eichensehr, 'Cyberwar & International Law Step Zero' (2015) 50 Texas International Law Journal 357.

[188] Ryan Calo, 'Robotics and the Lessons of Cyberlaw' (2015) 103 California Law Review 513, 552.

[189] ibid.

[190] On the distinction between the regulatory mind-sets of 'legal coherentism' and 'regulatory instrumentalism' (and how technology may shift the balance amongst them, as well as towards a more 'technocratic' regulatory mindset), see also Roger Brownsword, 'Law and Technology: Two Modes of Disruption, Three Legal Mind-Sets, and the Big Picture of Regulatory Responsibilities' (2018) 14 Indian Journal of Law and Technology 1; Roger Brownsword, 'Law Disrupted, Law Re-Imagined, Law Re-Invented' [2019] Technology and Regulation 10.

[191] For instance, Carlos Ignacio Gutierrez has applied Bennett Moses's framework to the US regulatory context, to examine which AI systems create genuinely new situations. Reviewing 50 regulatory gaps, he argues that questions of conceptual uncertainty (42%) and targeting or scope (26%) where the most prevalent gaps, but argues that only a limited subset of uses (12%) posed genuinely new legal challenges (i.e. new gaps). Carlos Ignacio Gutierrez, 'The Unforeseen Consequences of

Accordingly, beyond the binary question of whether or not an AI capability creates one of the five types of substantive legal disruption discussed in this chapter, we should also examine the question of how much stress is put on the existing regulatory regime to adapt—and how adaptive or flexible it generally is.

5.5.6.2 Governance disruption occurs relative to a particular legal system

Second, related to this, substantive governance disruption occurs relative to a particular legal system. It is not a general feature of a given technology or application (or even certain type of sociotechnical change) to be 'disruptive'; rather, this effect can only be understood in relation or reference to the conceptual categories or assumptions of one or another specific legal system.[192]

As a result, when considered at a national level, a certain AI capability might be disruptive in one national jurisdiction but not in others.[193] Indeed, as Margot Kaminski and Meg Leta Jones have argued from the perspective of the 'legal construction of technology', the degree to which a new AI capability proves puzzling or challenging to a given part of a national legal system, is not a predetermined feature of the technology. Rather, it depends on the ways in which the law's objects, values, and institutions reflect particular types of 'legal sensemaking' of the new uses of that technology.[194] They note, for example, how four different areas of US law have grappled with—and legally constructed—the rise of 'AI speech' from large language models.[195] These approaches have variably treated AI speech:

> (1) as *speech by speakers* (within First Amendment law), (2) as *speech at scale* (within content moderation law), (3) as the output of *risky complex systems* (within risk regulation or tort law), and (4) as market behavior implicating *consumer protection* (within the FTC's Section 5 authority).[196]

On this basis, they note that while First Amendment law focuses on governing 'speech' and 'speakers' through the court system, and is therefore susceptible to a whole set of legal puzzles relating to the fact that AI systems are not human

Artificial Intelligence (AI) on Society: A Systematic Review of Regulatory Gaps Generated by AI in the U.S.' (Thesis, Pardee RAND Graduate School 2020) <https://www.rand.org/pubs/rgs_dissertations/RGSDA319-1.html> accessed 11 July 2020.

[192] Balkin (n 179) 46–47. See also Crootof and Ard (n 3). Ftn 6 ('the amount of legal confusion a technology engenders will depend as much on the legal regime and the society within which it is used as its particular design characteristics').

[193] Meg Leta Jones, 'Does Technology Drive Law? The Dilemma of Technological Exceptionalism in Cyberlaw' (2018) 2 Journal of Law, Technology & Policy <http://illinoisjltp.com/journal/wp-content/uploads/2018/12/Jones.pdf> accessed 7 September 2020.

[194] Kaminski and Jones (n 5) 1223–1225.

[195] ibid 1231–1256.

[196] ibid 1215.

speakers, and do not possess human intent—by contrast the three other fields of law (content-moderation, risk regulation, consumer-protection law) possess very different objects, values, and institutions. Notably, content-moderation law instead focuses on balancing harms against free speech and innovation; risk regulation aims to mitigate physical and dignitary harms; and consumer-protection law aims to regulate businesses and consumers in order to maintain fair and efficient markets. As a result AI's lack of human intent, at least, is not in any way a serious problem or legally disruptive to those other areas of law.[197]

Consequently, we should be careful to map the diverse impacts of a new technology, capability, affordance, or application in different domains. This also applies at the international level, where technologies may drive different combinations or sets of governance disruption in different regimes, depending not just on their own features but also on the normative, institutional, and doctrinal features of that specific regime. For instance, Crootof notes how 'a weapon that creates one kind of legal disruption in one area of international humanitarian law might cause a very different kind of disruption in others—or in international human rights law, the law of the sea, space law, or another legal regime'.[198] As such, various legal scholars have argued that, with a few exceptions, autonomous maritime vessels create relatively few intractable conceptual problems under the existing law of the sea.[199] Even so, the use of unmanned underwater vehicles by criminal networks to smuggle contraband in a more deniable manner could instead pose an *obsolescence* challenge for operational (cost-effectiveness) assumptions of law enforcement,[200] potentially challenging instruments such as the 1988 United Nations Convention Against Illicit Traffic in Narcotic Drugs and Psychotropic Substances,[201] or the broader mission of the United Nations Office on Drugs and Crime (UNODC).

Such cases show how we should not expect AI technology to be 'universally disruptive' to global governance. Rather, as a general-purpose technology, it might instead produce varied constellations of governance disruption in different fields—or produce significantly disruptive impacts in some legal domains and none in others. These should be cautiously mapped, as they may require distinct avenues or paths of development.

197 ibid 1231–1256.

198 Crootof, 'Regulating New Weapons Technology' (n 21) 13.

199 See also Klein (n 58); Robert McLaughlin, 'Unmanned Naval Vehicles at Sea: USVs, UUVs, and the Adequacy of the Law' [2011] Journal of Law, Information and Science <http://www5.austlii.edu.au/au/journals/JlLawInfoSci/2012/6.html> accessed 22 June 2020.

200 See Thomas C King and others, 'Artificial Intelligence Crime: An Interdisciplinary Analysis of Foreseeable Threats and Solutions' [2019] Science and Engineering Ethics 12 <https://doi.org/10.1007/s11948-018-00081-0> accessed 21 February 2019; Noel Sharkey, Marc Goodman, and Nick Ros, 'The Coming Robot Crime Wave' (2010) 43 IEEE Computer Magazine 116.

201 United Nations Convention against Illicit Traffic in Narcotic Drugs and Psychotropic Substances (adopted 20 December 1988, entered into force 11 November 1990) 1582 UNTS 95.

5.5.6.3 Different legal systems may demonstrate differential resilience to disruption

Third, this also illustrates the potentially differential 'resilience' or absorption capacity of different types of law or governance system to potential disruption. For instance, much of the discussion so far has focused on potential disruptions of hard law instruments (e.g. treaties). In one way, this is not surprising, as such instruments will be the sites where we would expect disruption to be the most common. In contrast, broader forms of soft law might be more conceptually ambiguous, are already phrased broadly, allow for more discretion in implementation, or are more flexible and easy to review or update in the face of changing technological circumstances. For this reason, Rebecca Crootof has considered soft law a potentially promising alternate avenue for the international regulation of certain new technologies, especially when compared to the brittleness and rigidity of hard law treaties.[202] However, while it may be true that soft law is more resilient in some ways, this may rather mean that—whereas both hard law and soft law can be disrupted by technological changes—it is simply more evident in the case of the former.[203]

While this implies that some parts of or instruments in global governance such as soft law could be relatively shielded from technology-driven governance disruption, the susceptibility of international hard law tools to disruption is nonetheless critical. This is because many of these more flexible soft law governance tools are often either rooted in or bracketed by hard law foundations, or are created when it appears that hard law instruments are inviable or ineffective.[204] In the former case, governance disruption of hard law instruments could indirectly cascade through to 'softer' instruments which implicitly assume them as their foundations. In the latter case, governance disruption of hard law instruments might prompt a need for new development that might only be adequately (or quickly) met through soft law tools.[205] Either situation needs to be understood.

5.5.6.4 The problem is not disruption, but law's inability to adapt

Fourth, it is not governance disruption that creates problems, but a governance system's sustained inability to adapt through some form of development. As such, situations of legal uncertainty are not intrinsically problematic in and of themselves. They only become challenging to a given system of law when it, for conceptual or political reasons, is unable to carry out the needed changes or updates in response (or even unable to adequately identify the need for such changes).[206] In principle, after all, legal systems are perfectly capable of any revisions or change—bound

[202] Crootof, 'Jurisprudential Space Junk' (n 17) 124–126.
[203] I thank Roger Brownsword for this observation.
[204] I thank Laura Emily Christiansen for this observation.
[205] Crootof, 'Jurisprudential Space Junk' (n 17) 124–126.
[206] Such situations may result in 'erosion' or even 'destruction' of governance regimes, as will be discussed shortly, in Section 5.7.

only, perhaps, by the limits of natural language.[207] Many abstract legal notions are flexible enough to be reinterpreted or adapted to many new situations;[208] where even they fall short, governance systems can introduce new concepts, rights, or legal categories tailored to clarify the situation. In that sense, legal development is almost always possible in principle. The key questions around development will as such often be normative ones, focusing on the (presumed) underlying aims of the legal regime; over the relative benefits and costs of utilizing regulation that is over or under-inclusive, and whether the most appropriate route to carrying out legal development takes a permissive or precautionary approach.[209]

Likewise, in an international law context, there are no in-principle reasons why legal norms could not be adapted for any imaginable change, whether deriving from AI, or from some other technology, or indeed from non-technological changes in political conditions or societal practices. As such, any new governance gaps, ambiguities, scope inaccuracies, obsolescence, or problem portfolio shifts produced by AI could all in principle be addressed through routine 'legal development' in a variety of ways: through norm development in customary international law, new treaties, amendments to existing treaties, reinterpretation of existing agreements, or entirely new governance arrangements,[210] among others.

However, in practice, not all these responses are equally sufficient or equally viable. New treaties or treaty amendments might appear the most valuable solution, as they could in principle be written and tailored directly to the problem at hand. To be sure, there are certainly cases where there is sufficient (state) pragmatism and desire to reach a consensus that such solutions can be carried through, or treaties can be adapted. For instance, in a recent case study of international law's efforts to come to terms with autonomous vehicles, Bryant Walker Smith notes how states have available various approaches in order to reconcile driverless vehicles with the requirements for a (human) 'driver'—stipulated in both the 1949 Geneva Convention on Road Traffic and the 1968 Vienna Convention on Road Traffic.[211] These approaches to carry out legal development in order to reconcile

[207] As well as, in many domestic contexts, by the limits of 'folk understandings and cultural norms'. Pierre Schlag, 'Spam Jurisprudence, Air Law, and the Rank Anxiety of Nothing Happening (A Report on the State of the Art)' [2009] The Georgetown Law Journal 803, 812, 821.

[208] Indeed, articulating legal rules in a sufficiently broad and abstract way could in principle resolve any uncertainty, ensuring there would never be a need for development. As noted by George Friedman, 'If legal rules are defined in sufficient breadth, legal innovation is never necessary [. . .] Indeed, it is arguably possible to resolve all legal issues by a single very broad rule: have whatever legal rules maximize economic efficiency'. Friedman (n 37) 85. There would of course be drawbacks to such principles, which would be far too broad to "apply with predictable results at a reasonable cost". ibid. On the general flexibility and limits of legal systems, see also Orin S Kerr, 'A Theory of Law' (2012) 16 Green Bag 111.

[209] Crootof and Ard (n 3) 379–386.

[210] Picker (n 20) 156.

[211] Smith (n 88). Specifically, the 1949 Convention requires that '[e]very vehicle or combination of vehicles proceeding as a unit shall have a driver' and that '[d]rivers shall at all times be able to control their vehicles or guide their animals'. 1949 Convention on Road Traffic (1949) 125 UNTS 22 art. 8. The

self-driving cars with the existing road traffic conventions show a range of possible actions for states, from soft law (e.g. unilateral explanatory memoranda or multilateral Working Party Resolutions under the Global Forum for Road Traffic Safety) to hard law (e.g. unilateral renunciation or reservations of the treaties, multilateral efforts to amend either convention, or introduction of a new convention).[212]

Nonetheless, in general, and particularly in the context of high-stakes technologies, amending a multilateral resolution can often run into political and conceptual challenges.[213] As such, of all of these various approaches to dealing with legal uncertainty at the international level, Crootof argues that treaty 'reinterpretation' is the most common strategy used to fold new (weapons) technologies into an existing governance regime, in part because it is cheaper, quicker, and more reliable than attempting to negotiate or amend a treaty, establish Customary International Law, or seek an Advisory Opinion from the ICJ.[214] However, while such attempted (re)interpretations may prove a commonly used strategy of first resort in order to achieve the necessary legal development, this is again not without its risks.

5.5.6.5 Analogies as risky shortcut to achieving legal development

Situations where some needed development in regimes is not carried out create the risk of 'erosion' and the inadequacy of existing regimes. Of course, in the first place, whether a treaty (re)interpretation is even possible depends to a large extent on the authority and legitimacy of the interpreter,[215] as well as on conceptual and material features of the technology in question.

However, even if adaptation through reinterpretation appears viable, there may be hidden risks or shortfalls in conducting development in this manner, if it relies on or imports misleading (or unproductive) technological analogies.[216] This matters to AI because AI technology is particularly prone to lending itself to diverse analogies, each of which import distinct regulatory programmes or priorities.[217]

To be sure, vivid metaphors or framings of a technology play a significant role throughout the entire cycle of technology development and policymaking.[218]

1968 Convention similarly requires that '[e]very moving vehicle or combination of vehicles shall have a driver' and that '[e]very driver shall at all times be able to control his vehicle or to guide his animals.' 1968 Convention on Road Traffic (1968) 1042 UNTS 15705 art. 8.

[212] Smith (n 88) 154–155.

[213] See generally Crootof, 'Jurisprudential Space Junk' (n 17). See also the discussion in Section 5.7.1 (on Erosion).

[214] Crootof, 'Regulating New Weapons Technology' (n 21) 13–14.

[215] ibid 14.

[216] Crootof and Ard (n 3) 387–395.

[217] Matthijs Maas, 'AI Is Like . . . A Literature Review of AI Metaphors and Why They Matter for Policy' (Institute for Law & AI 2023) AI Foundations Report 2 <https://law-ai.org/ai-policy-metaphors> accessed 27 October 2023.

[218] ibid 9–16 (discussing five ways in which metaphors can shape (1) patterns of technological innovation, (2) the study of particular technologies' sociotechnical impacts or risks; (3) which of those sociotechnical impacts make it onto the regulatory agenda; (4) how those technologies are framed

As such, they may be valuable from an agenda-setting perspective: they can ensure that (global) policymakers or the public engage with a complex emerging technology in the first place—that is, that the international legal system recognizes that existing law falls short, and development is needed.[219] More generally, analogical reasoning is core to many domestic legal and judicial systems, especially in a common-law context. Indeed, especially where it comes to new technologies that may present 'unprecedented' (in the most literal and mundane sense of the word) situations, analogical reasoning may well constitute a 'critical legal tool', which, as Crootof notes, helps 'make new kinds of technology accessible, allow[s] for the application of existing law, and can help identify particular risks or solutions'.[220]

However, there are risks to the unreflexive legal reliance on analogics in either the domestic or the international context. Crootof identifies at least three problems with analogies in regulation. In the first place, the selection and foregrounding of a certain metaphor occludes both that there are always multiple analogies possible for any new technology, and how each of these advances different 'regulatory narratives'.[221] Second, analogies can be misleading by failing to capture a key trait of the technology, or by alleging certain characteristics that do not actually exist.[222] Most importantly, 'analogies limit our ability to understand the possibilities and limitations of new technology'.[223] They constrain our imagination and understanding, and close down our conceptions of the other forms a technology might take, the other uses it might lend itself to, and the indirect or longer-term sociotechnical effects these uses would create. For instance, Crootof notes how, when discussing autonomous vehicles, the term 'driverless cars' both works to normalize something potentially hazardous and narrows our sense of what the technology will look like:

> There is no reason to think autonomous vehicles will look or operate anything like existing cars, just as early cars did not look or operate like horseless carriages. An autonomous vehicle need not have a steering wheel or other means of human interaction with the system. And conceiving of autonomous vehicles

within the policymaking process, in ways that highlight some issues and policy levers; and (5) how these technologies are approached within legislative and judicial systems).

[219] For instance, on the importance of framings to the international campaigns to ban blinding lasers and anti-personnel mines (and whether these framings can transfer well to 'killer robots'), see Elvira Rosert and Frank Sauer, 'How (Not) to Stop the Killer Robots: A Comparative Analysis of Humanitarian Disarmament Campaign Strategies' (2020) 42 Contemporary Security Policy 4.

[220] Crootof, 'Regulating New Weapons Technology' (n 21) 17.

[221] ibid.

[222] Alternatively, they might impute the technology with certain characteristics that certainly do exist, but which are hardly the most distinguishing or salient feature at stake. Or they might unduly emphasize the technology's characteristics over its use.

[223] Crootof, 'Regulating New Weapons Technology' (n 21) 18.

> as driverless cars locks one into a host of existing assumptions, instead of allowing for more imaginative conceptions of what the technology might permit. For example, rather than being individually owned and operated property, autonomous vehicles could operate as connected nodes on a 'smart highway' or as a leasable service.[224]

This can also be seen in the responses to regulating various technologies in the past. For instance, Crootof discusses how, when talking about the internet, different terms evoke radically distinct problem portfolios, and correspondingly distinct regulatory surfaces or levers:

> The 'World Wide Web' conception suggests an organically created common structure of linked individual nodes, which is presumably beyond regulation. The 'Information Superhighway' analogy emphasizes the import of speed and commerce and implies a nationally-funded infrastructure subject to federal regulation. Meanwhile, 'cyberspace' could be understood as a completely new and separate frontier, or it could be viewed as yet one more kind of jurisdiction subject to property rules and state control.[225]

Similarly, Jordan Branch has suggested that the use of 'foundational metaphors' around the internet has strongly shaped US cybersecurity policies; the US military notably framed the internet and related system as a 'cyberspace'—just another 'domain' of conflict along with land, sea, air, and space—which has had strong consequences both institutionally (expanding the military's role in cybersecurity, and supporting the creation of US Cyber Command), while also shaping how international law is applied to cyber operations.[226]

To take another example, consider 'data'. Over the past decade, this curt informational concept, once the preserve of staid data 'science', has been cast in a diverse array of roles.[227] It has been captured under different metaphors—as

[224] Rebecca Crootof, 'Autonomous Weapon Systems and the Limits of Analogy' (2018) 9 Harvard National Security Journal 51, 80. See also I Glenn Cohen and Jonathan H Blavin, 'Gore, Gibson, and Goldsmith: The Evolution of Internet Metaphors in Law and Commentary' (2002) 16 Harvard Journal of Law and Technology 265 (reviewing the implications of metaphors that frame the internet as an information superhighway, cyberspace, or as 'real' space, respectively).

[225] Crootof, 'Regulating New Weapons Technology' (n 21) 17–18. In the specific context of autonomous weapons systems, Crootof has similarly discussed the relative utility (and limits) of analogizing such systems to 'weapons', 'combatants', 'child soldiers', or 'animal combatants'. Crootof, 'Autonomous Weapon Systems and the Limits of Analogy' (n 224). See also Michael C Horowitz, 'Why Words Matter: The Real World Consequences of Defining Autonomous Weapons Systems' (2016) 30 Temp. Int'l & Comp 14.

[226] Jordan Branch, 'What's in a Name? Metaphors and Cybersecurity' (2021) 75 International Organization 39.

[227] For a broader, critical discussion, see also Luke Stark and Anna Lauren Hoffmann, 'Data Is the New What? Popular Metaphors & Professional Ethics in Emerging Data Culture' (2019) 1 Journal of Cultural Analytics 11052.

'oil', 'sunlight', 'public utility', or 'labour'—which each have drastically distinct political and regulatory implications.[228] For instance, the oil metaphor—which has, until recently, been relatively dominant in the US[229]—foregrounds how, operationally, data must often be treated and 'refined' (i.e. 'cleansed' and 'tagged') to be useful; how, economically, data is a traded commodity that is owned by whoever 'extracts' it; and how, politically, this resource and its infrastructures might become a source of geopolitical contestation between major state actors.[230] Within the framing of data as a natural resource, even policies that aim to preserve individual user privacy become implicitly couched as competing ownership claims.[231]

Conversely, the sunlight metaphor instead emphasizes data as a ubiquitous public resource that ought to be widely pooled and shared for social good, and underpins the 'Open Data' movement, calls to 'democratize' AI, and the Chinese approach to pooling types of data such as health data; however, it too does not mesh well with those seeking to preserve individual data privacy. In turn, the public utility metaphor sees data as 'infrastructure', and emphasizes the importance of public investment and new institutions such as data trusts, cooperatives, or personal data stores to provide 'data stewardship'.[232] All these stand in contrast to regulatory programmes that treat data as labour, and which assert the ownership rights of the individuals generating it against what correspondingly becomes seen as the extractive or exploitative practices of 'surveillance capitalism'.[233]

Similar debates are endemic throughout technology law. Are technology and social media companies 'media companies'?[234] In court cases around online

[228] See also The Economist, 'Are Data More Like Oil or Sunlight?' [2020] *The Economist* <https://www.economist.com/special-report/2020/02/20/are-data-more-like-oil-or-sunlight> accessed 26 February 2020.

[229] See for instance Jack M Balkin, 'Free Speech in the Algorithmic Society: Big Data, Private Governance, and New School Speech Regulation' (2018) 51 University of California Law Review 1149, 1149 ('[a]lgorithms and AI [artificial intelligence] are the machines; Big Data is the fuel that makes the machines run. Just as oil made machines and factories run in the Industrial Age, Big Data makes the relevant machines run in the Algorithmic Society').

[230] For a critique, emphasizing that the 'oil' metaphor does not provide good guidance to assessing data competitiveness, see Husanjot Chahal, Ryan Fedasiuk, and Carrick Flynn, 'Messier than Oil: Assessing Data Advantage in Military AI' (Center for Security and Emerging Technology 2020) <https://cset.georgetown.edu/research/messier-than-oil-assessing-data-advantage-in-military-ai/> accessed 18 August 2020. See also Lauren Scholz, 'Big Data Is Not Big Oil: The Role of Analogy in the Law of New Technologies' (2019) 85 Tennessee Law review 863.

[231] Lisa Austin, 'We Must Not Treat Data Like a Natural Resource' *The Globe and Mail* (9 July 2018) <https://www.theglobeandmail.com/opinion/article-we-must-not-treat-data-like-a-natural-resource/> accessed 14 September 2020.

[232] The Economist (n 228).

[233] Imanol Arrieta-Ibarra and others, 'Should We Treat Data as Labor? Moving beyond "Free"' (2018) 108 AEA Papers and Proceedings 38.

[234] Philip Napoli and Robyn Caplan, 'Why Media Companies Insist They're Not Media Companies, Why They're Wrong, and Why It Matters' (2017) 22 First Monday <https://firstmonday.org/ojs/index.php/fm/article/view/7051> accessed 6 October 2023. ((discussing a range of cases that illustrate how tech and social media companies have been aversive to classification as 'media companies', since such classification 'has historically meant more intensive government oversight, in the form of affirmative

censorship, are search engines that offer up offensive or harmful content to be considered akin to 'newspaper editorials'?[235] These framings, metaphors, and analogies have shaped policy at both the domestic and international levels in diverse ways. It is therefore not surprising that the role of analogies in framing policy debates can be seen in a wide range of AI contexts.[236] For instance, Kraftt and others have found that whereas definitions of AI that emphasize 'technical functionality' are more widespread among AI researchers, definitions that emphasize 'human-like performance' are more prevalent amongst policymakers, which in their view might prime policy towards future threats.[237] Another analysis by Dewey Murdick and colleagues found that the precise AI definition which one takes can paint a very different picture of the relative standing and progress of major states in AI.[238]

One can also see the importance of framings in the debates, in the past few years, around the desirability of openness or open-source norms in AI research,[239] especially given certain capabilities that might have potential for misuse.[240] In February 2019 the research lab OpenAI sparked debate over this question, after it revealed GPT-2, a capable text-generation AI system, and refused to release the full model out of concerns for misuse in fake news and computational propaganda applications.[241] While some applauded the move, others critiqued this 'limited

obligations to serve the public interest and more stringent regulation in areas such as concentration of ownership').

[235] Heather Whitney, 'Search Engines, Social Media, and the Editorial Analogy' (*Knight First Amendment Institute at Columbia University*, 27 February 2018) <https://knightcolumbia.org/content/search-engines-social-media-and-editorial-analogy> accessed 1 February 2021; Genevieve Lakier, 'The Problem Isn't the Use of Analogies but the Analogies Courts Use' (*Knight First Amendment Institute at Columbia University*, 26 February 2018) <https://knightcolumbia.org/content/problem-isnt-use-analogies-analogies-courts-use> accessed 1 February 2021.

[236] Maas, 'AI Is Like . . .' (n 217).

[237] PM Krafft and others, 'Defining AI in Policy versus Practice', *Proceedings of the AAAI/ACM Conference on AI, Ethics, and Society* (ACM 2020) <http://dl.acm.org/doi/10.1145/3375627.3375835> accessed 12 February 2020.

[238] Dewey Murdick, James Dunham, and Jennifer Melot, 'AI Definitions Affect Policymaking' (Center for Security and Emerging Technology 2020) <https://cset.georgetown.edu/wp-content/uploads/CSET-AI-Definitions-Affect-Policymaking.pdf> accessed 3 June 2020.

[239] Irene Solaiman and others, 'Release Strategies and the Social Impacts of Language Models' [2019] arXiv:1908.09203 [cs] <http://arxiv.org/abs/1908.09203> accessed 18 November 2019; Elizabeth Seger and others, 'Open-Sourcing Highly Capable Foundation Models: An Evaluation of Risks, Benefits, and Alternative Methods for Pursuing Open-Source Objectives' (Centre for the Governance of AI 2023) <https://www.governance.ai/research-paper/open-sourcing-highly-capable-foundation-models> accessed 2 October 2023.

[240] For surveys of such uses, see Miles Brundage and others, 'The Malicious Use of Artificial Intelligence: Forecasting, Prevention, and Mitigation' [2018] arXiv:1802.07228 [cs] <http://arxiv.org/abs/1802.07228> accessed 21 February 2018; King and others (n 200); Hayward and Maas (n 141). Note, there is also some antecedent work on the larger-scale strategic considerations around whether the development of (advanced) AI systems should proceed in an open or closed manner: Nick Bostrom, 'Strategic Implications of Openness in AI Development' (2017) 8 Global Policy 135.

[241] Alec Radford and others, 'Better Language Models and Their Implications' (*OpenAI Blog*, 14 February 2019) <https://blog.openai.com/better-language-models/> accessed 17 February 2019. For some of the subsequent debates, see also Eric Zelikman, 'OpenAI Shouldn't Release Their Full Language Model' [2019] *The Gradient* <https://thegradient.pub/openai-shouldnt-release-their-full-langu

release' strategy on the grounds that AI research was an 'scientific endeavour', which implied that all results should be open and public on principle. Others argued in favour of open release of such language models on the grounds that any security problems from those systems should be treated akin to regular information security and cybersecurity problems that arise in conventional software development—which would suggest that a culture of disclosure and open access would enable better identification and patching of vulnerabilities.[242] Since then, these arguments have been repeated in debates over the open-sourcing of powerful language models such as Llama-2.[243]

Clearly, either of these analogies—scientific endeavour or cybersecurity—are not entirely baseless in describing aspects of AI.[244] Yet the fact that distinct analogies can be supported does not mean they are all equally productive. In this case, an argument could be made (and, of course, contested) that these analogies are at least somewhat misleading or counterproductive in terms of the policy recommendations they foreground. After all, as Dafoe and Shevlane have argued, an examination of the actual balance of whether published AI research is more useful for attackers or defenders depends on a broad range of factors, including the possibility of adequate defensive measures, or the independent discovery of the knowledge outside of the scientific community. When considering these factors, they argue that '[w]hile [in cybersecurity] disclosure of software vulnerabilities often favours defence, this cannot be assumed for AI research'.[245] To be sure, whether the AI community adopts policies on safe disclosure or emphasizes full transparency will also be affected by high-profile incidents; but policy debates are equally shaped by the framings in play. This matters, because effective mitigation of some

age-model/> accessed 4 March 2019; Hugh Zhang, 'Dear OpenAI: Please Open Source Your Language Model' [2019] *The Gradient* <https://thegradient.pub/openai-please-open-source-your-language-model/> accessed 4 March 2019. See also the later assessment by OpenAI; Solaiman and others (n 239).

[242] Richard Socher, 'Introducing a Conditional Transformer Language Model for Controllable Generation' (*Salesforce AI*, 11 September 2019) <https://blog.salesforceairesearch.com/introducing-a-conditional-transformer-language-model-for-controllable-generation/> accessed 12 January 2024 ('Similar to information security research, it is necessary for these tools to be accessible, so that researchers have the resources that expose and guard against potentially malicious use cases'). As cited in Toby Shevlane and Allan Dafoe, 'The Offense-Defense Balance of Scientific Knowledge: Does Publishing AI Research Reduce Misuse?', *Proceedings of the 2020 AAAI/ACM Conference on AI, Ethics, and Society (AIES '20)* (ACM 2020) 174 <http://arxiv.org/abs/2001.00463> accessed 9 January 2020.

[243] See Meta's rationale for open-sourcing its Llama-2 model. Meta, 'Meta and Microsoft Introduce the Next Generation of Llama' (*Meta AI*, 18 July 2023) <https://ai.meta.com/blog/llama-2/> accessed 11 January 2024 ('Opening access to today's AI models means a generation of developers and researchers can stress test them, identifying and solving problems fast, as a community').

[244] Indeed, one of them reflects the framing of AI as scientific field discussed in Chapter 1.

[245] Shevlane and Dafoe (n 242). For broader discussion of how to balance openness and prudence in AI development, in the context of tensions between these core principles within the Montréal Declaration for Responsible AI, see also Jess Whittlestone and Aviv Ovadya, 'The Tension between Openness and Prudence in AI Research' [2020] arXiv:1910.01170 [cs] <http://arxiv.org/abs/1910.01170> accessed 22 January 2020.

risks could well require revisions or changes to existing publication norms,[246] or novel arrangements to provide for structured access to AI systems.[247]

All this does not mean that analogies should not be used in grounding new interpretations, but rather that we should be aware of their scope conditions and risks. Accordingly, for AI also, the full and diverse range of analogies should be critically examined. Before grounding governance, it is important to clarify what we understand by 'AI', how we could have understood it differently, and what political, regulatory, or strategic effects this choice entails for a given treaty or regime.[248]

This suggests that at the international level, even if a certain analogy or interpretation might be sustained, we should be cautious about too rapidly leaping to the first 'adaptive interpretation' available, just for the sake of keeping our regime coherent and nominally applicable by going through the motions of 'development'. There may be situations where it may prove more sustainable or effective, from a longer-term perspective of ensuring the resilience of a regime or treaty, to forego a 'patch' through reinterpretation if it would import forced or loaded technology analogies, and instead to hold out for pursuing new regimes or amendment.

To sum up this section's exploration of development: governance disruption by (AI) technology poses significant challenges only if or when regulatory development is slowed or inhibited by conceptual or political features of the technology. The pertinent question is as such not only when or where new AI capabilities might create situations that are disruptive, but also when and whether governance development to patch the 'holes' in regimes is conceptually plausible or politically feasible. In situations where such change is hard, this may well produce regime-specific 'governance destruction' in the form of gradual erosion.[249] However, before moving to discuss this topic, we must first explore processes of governance displacement.

[246] Partnership on AI, 'Publication Norms for Responsible AI' (*Partnership on AI*) <https://partnershiponai.org/workstream/publication-norms-for-responsible-ai/> accessed 10 January 2023; Akash R Wasil and others, 'Publication Policies and Model-Sharing Decisions: A Literature Review and Recommendations for AI Labs' (2023) <https://static1.squarespace.com/static/6276a63ecf564172c125f58e/t/641cbc1d84814a4d0f3e1788/1679604766050/WasilEzellRichardsonSiegmann+%2810%29.pdf> accessed 7 April 2023; Toby Shevlane, 'The Artefacts of Intelligence: Governing Scientists' Contribution to AI Proliferation' (University of Oxford 2022) <https://www.governance.ai/research-paper/the-artefacts-of-intelligence-governing-scientists-contribution-to-ai-proliferation> accessed 18 August 2022; Jasmine Wang, 'What the AI Community Can Learn From Sneezing Ferrets and a Mutant Virus Debate' (*Partnership on AI*, 9 December 2020) <https://medium.com/partnership-on-ai/lessons-for-the-ai-community-from-the-h5n1-controversy-32432438a82e> accessed 1 September 2021.

[247] Toby Shevlane, 'Structured Access: An Emerging Paradigm for Safe AI Deployment' in Justin Bullock and others (eds), Toby Shevlane, *The Oxford Handbook of AI Governance* (Oxford University Press 2022); Benjamin S Bucknall and Robert F Trager, 'Structured Access for Third-Party Research on Frontier AI Models: Investigating Researchers' Model Access Requirements' (Oxford Martin AI Governance Initiative 2023) <https://www.oxfordmartin.ox.ac.uk/publications/structured-access-for-third-party-research-on-frontier-ai-models-investigating-researchers-model-access-requirements/> accessed 6 November 2023.

[248] Maas, 'AI Is Like . . .' (n 217).

[249] Maas, 'International Law Does Not Compute' (n 1) 50–55. We will return to this discussion in Section 5.7.1 (on governance erosion).

5.6 Governance Displacement

A second major category of governance disruption concerns the ways in which AI could drive displacement in the processes or instruments of international governance.[250] That is, more even than many previous technologies, it may drive considerable sociotechnical change in the 'legal' domain itself.

Of course, the suggestion that developments in AI technology not only may produce new artefacts, actors, or activities to be regulated, but can also provide new affordances for the regulators who produce law or to the judges who adjudicate it, is, again, not new. Indeed, over the past years, new digital technologies, and particularly AI, have seen particularly rapid and enthusiastic uptake in various branches of domestic public administration, judicial decision-making, policing, and the business of government writ large. Moreover, from the perspective of legal practice, AI systems could be used to automate or contribute to a range of routine legal tasks, from checking contracts[251] to undertaking case law research[252] and from undertaking legal analysis[253] to speeding up the provision of basic legal services,[254] and even aiding in the generation of new empirical data for use in experimental comparative law research.[255]

Of course, well before the recent rise of increasingly general-purpose foundation models and other advanced AI systems, machine learning systems were already making headway in predicting the outcomes of legal disputes in court.[256] This has

[250] This section loosely tracks, and expands on, ibid 43–49.

[251] LawGeex, 'Comparing the Performance of Artificial Intelligence to Human Lawyers in the Review of Standard Business Contracts' (LawGeex 2018) <https://images.law.com/contrib/content/uploads/documents/397/5408/lawgeex.pdf> accessed 27 August 2020.

[252] See for instance Claire Barale, Michael Rovatsos, and Nehal Bhuta, 'Automated Refugee Case Analysis: A NLP Pipeline for Supporting Legal Practitioners' in Anna Rogers, Jordan Boyd-Graber, and Naoaki Okazaki (eds), *Findings of the Association for Computational Linguistics: ACL 2023* (Association for Computational Linguistics 2023) <https://aclanthology.org/2023.findings-acl.187> accessed 1 July 2024, as well as: 'CARA A.I.' (*Casetext*) <https://casetext.com/cara-ai/> accessed 8 September 2020.

[253] Jonathan H Choi, Amy Monahan, and Daniel Schwarcz, 'Lawyering in the Age of Artificial Intelligence' (7 November 2023) <https://papers.ssrn.com/abstract=4626276> accessed 20 December 2023. See for instance John J Nay and others, 'Large Language Models as Tax Attorneys: A Case Study in Legal Capabilities Emergence' (arXiv, 12 June 2023) <http://arxiv.org/abs/2306.07075> accessed 13 December 2024.

[254] For an older example, see for instance the app 'DoNotPay'. RJ Vogt, 'DoNotPay Founder Opens Up On "Robot Lawyers"' (*Law360*, 9 February 2020) <https://www.law360.com/articles/1241251/donotpay-founder-opens-up-on-robot-lawyers> accessed 8 September 2020.

[255] Christoph Engel, 'Experimental Comparative Law 2.0? Large Language Models as a Novel Empirical Tool' <https://hdl.handle.net/21.11116/0000-000F-AA4C-D> accessed 27 September 2024.

[256] For instance, a system trained on 584 judicial decisions of the European Court of Human Rights managed to predict the outcome of new cases with 79% accuracy. Nikolaos Aletras and others, 'Predicting Judicial Decisions of the European Court of Human Rights: A Natural Language Processing Perspective' (2016) 2 PeerJ Computer Science e93. Another study achieved an average accuracy of 75% in predicting the violation of nine articles of the European Convention on Human Rights: Masha Medvedeva, Michel Vols, and Martijn Wieling, 'Using Machine Learning to Predict Decisions of the European Court of Human Rights' (2020) 28 Artificial Intelligence and Law 237. Although for a general critique of such projects, see Frank A Pasquale and Glyn Cashwell, 'Prediction, Persuasion, and the Jurisprudence of Behaviorism' [2017] University of Maryland Francis King Carey School of Law Legal Studies Research Paper <https://papers.ssrn.com/abstract=3067737> accessed 8 September 2020.

led some scholars to anticipate an increasing automation of legal systems,[257] with legal rules and standards becoming progressively replaced by algorithmically tailored 'micro-directives' that can predict *ex ante* what an *ex post* judicial decision would have held in every specific case, and so can offer perfectly clear yet tailored legal clarity for individuals.[258]

That is not to say that such scenarios—or indeed even more modest cases of legal automation—have been uncritically welcomed. Indeed, the past few years have seen extensive scholarship exploring the practical, normative, and legal implications of legal automation in domestic public decision-making,[259] and exploring cases where systems have been halted, dismantled, or rolled back after public critique.[260]

In fact, legal scholarship has given rise to extensive critiques of the near-term prospects for legal automation, given the limits of current machine learning approaches,[261] as well as apparent distinct differences between the ways in which algorithms and humans make decisions.[262] Others point to the interface design errors that often plague hybrid human and AI 'cyborg justice' arrangements, which can produce inappropriate overtrust.[263] Such sceptical perspectives have been supported by a range of scandals involving notable bias or inaccuracies in algorithms used for recidivism prediction[264] or in welfare fraud detection.[265] Consequently,

[257] Alarie, Niblett, and Yoon (n 7) 424.

[258] Casey and Niblett (n 7) 430; Anthony J Casey and Anthony Niblett, 'The Death of Rules and Standards' (2017) 92 Indiana Law Journal 1401, 1410–1411.

[259] Joshua P Davis, 'Law Without Mind: AI, Ethics, and Jurisprudence' (Social Science Research Network 2018) SSRN Scholarly Paper ID 3187513 <https://papers.ssrn.com/abstract=3187513> accessed 23 June 2018. For a discussion of the implications of unintelligible legal automation for core theories of law (notably HLA Hart's account, which requires critical officials; Joseph Raz's concept grounded in reason-based tests of legitimacy; or Ronald Dworkin's work on deep justifications for coercion) see Sheppard (n 7).

[260] Joanna Redden and others, 'Automating Public Services: Learning from Cancelled Systems' (Carnegie UK 2022) <https://www.carnegieuktrust.org.uk/publications/automating-public-services-learning-from-cancelled-systems/> accessed 13 October 2022; Nari Johnson and others, 'The Fall of an Algorithm: Characterizing the Dynamics Toward Abandonment', *Proceedings of the 2024 ACM Conference on Fairness, Accountability, and Transparency* (Association for Computing Machinery 2024) <https://dl.acm.org/doi/10.1145/3630106.3658910> accessed 13 June 2024. For one notable case, one can consider the infamous case of the Dutch SyRI welfare-fraud detection algorithm. Marvin van Bekkum and Frederik Zuiderveen Borgesius, 'Digital Welfare Fraud Detection and the Dutch SyRI Judgment' (2021) 23 European Journal of Social Security 323.

[261] See for instance: Frank Pasquale and Glyn Cashwell, 'Four Futures of Legal Automation' (2015) 26 UCLA Law Review Discourse 23; Frank A Pasquale, 'A Rule of Persons, Not Machines: The Limits of Legal Automation' (2019) 87 George Washington Law Review 1; Mireille Hildebrandt, 'Law As Computation in the Era of Artificial Legal Intelligence. Speaking Law to the Power of Statistics' (Social Science Research Network 2017) SSRN Scholarly Paper ID 2983045 <https://papers.ssrn.com/abstract=2983045> accessed 9 July 2018.

[262] Daniel J Solove and Hideyuki Matsumi, 'AI, Algorithms, and Awful Humans' (2024) 92 Fordham Law Review 1923.

[263] Crootof, '"Cyborg Justice" and the Risk of Technological-Legal Lock-In' (n 7).

[264] Lauren Kirchner and others, 'Machine Bias: There's Software Used Across the Country to Predict Future Criminals. And It's Biased Against Blacks' (*ProPublica*, 23 May 2016) <https://www.propublica.org/article/machine-bias-risk-assessments-in-criminal-sentencing> accessed 24 May 2017.

[265] van Bekkum and Borgesius (n 260).

there have been growing concerns over the human rights violations that might result if such systems are put in a position to take highly consequential decisions, or if they are deployed in ways that affect particularly vulnerable populations, such as migrants.[266]

More conceptually, others have cautioned that the automation of law enforcement systems might close the loop on the legal qualities of 'inefficiency' and 'indeterminacy', arguing that these are both key safeguards against the perfect enforcement of laws that were in fact originally drafted on the implicit assumption of a certain degree of lenience or discretion.[267] Finally, there are concerns that the integration of these systems may exert on the rule of law in society. For instance, Winter and others have anticipated the development of 'Advanced Artificial Judicial Intelligence' (AAJI), defined as 'an artificially intelligent system that matches or surpasses human decision-making in all domains relevant to judicial decision-making'.[268] While they suggest such systems could in principle play a significant role in transforming judicial practice, they also caution that this would not only raise challenges to key liberal democratic values, such as the equal treatment of citizens, transparency, and judicial independence,[269] but would also raise broader challenges around the value alignment of such systems with the human societies they serve.[270] Others, similarly, have pointed to the risk that the use of AI systems in governance may produce an increasingly opaque 'algocracy',[271] structured by a potent ecosystem of 'Automatic Authorities'.[272]

However, while these technologies therefore no doubt raise diverse grounds of concern, barring a major public backlash, it may well be the case that they see continued development and deployment of automation in public services and administration, potentially signalling a general shift towards 'technocratic' regulatory attitudes in domestic legal systems.[273]

Given its foundational implications, this breadth of work on and attention to legal displacement in domestic legal systems is surely warranted. However, by

[266] Petra Molnar, 'Technology on the Margins: AI and Global Migration Management from a Human Rights Perspective' (2019) 8 Cambridge International Law Journal 305.
[267] Hartzog and others (n 7).
[268] Christoph Winter, 'The Challenges of Artificial Judicial Decision-Making for Liberal Democracy' in Piotr Bystranowski, Bartosz Janik, and Maciej Próchnicki (eds), *Judicial Decision-Making: Integrating Empirical and Theoretical Perspectives*, vol Judicial Decision-Making: Integrating Empirical and Theoretical Perspectives (Springer Nature 2022).
[269] ibid.
[270] Christoph Winter, Nicholas Hollman, and David Manheim, 'Value Alignment for Advanced Artificial Judicial Intelligence' (2023) 60 American Philosophical Quarterly 187.
[271] Danaher (n 7).
[272] Seth Lazar, 'Automatic Authorities: Power and AI' (arXiv, 8 April 2024) <http://arxiv.org/abs/2404.05990> accessed 25 June 2024.
[273] See also Brownsword, 'Law Disrupted, Law Re-Imagined, Law Re-Invented' (n 190).

comparison, there has been much less attention paid to the prospects of such a shift at the *international* legal level. For one, there can and likely will be an increasing reliance on these tools in the domains of interest to global governance, intended to support progress on key human challenges. For instance, there has been renewed attention to the potential role that AI-powered innovations could play in domains such as health, education, and climate change mitigation, and how this could contribute to making substantive progress on the UN's Sustainable Development Goals.[274]

Indeed, the use of AI systems in support of various roles and functions within the institutions of international law and global governance may soon be widespread. A 2024 survey found that at least 37 entities (80% of organizations) within the UN system were already using or exploring potential applications of AI to their tasks, with uses ranging from knowledge generation and programme delivery to data analysis, pattern recognition, and improvements to operational efficiency.[275]

AI-driven governance 'displacement', in these various forms, could potentially be of significant value, in improving the often glacial processes of global governance. However, there are many hurdles to clear to avoid either premature overdependence on these systems or their active misuse.[276] How can we understand these international law-automating systems and their risks? I have previously argued that there are three distinct categories of technology-driven legal displacement, which will here be discussed in turn.[277] Specifically, we can distinguish the automation of processes of rule creation and adjudication; the automation of monitoring and enforcement of international regimes; and potential shifts in the 'regulatory modality' of international law, resulting in the gradual replacement of some forms of conflict mediation (e.g. arbitration) with other avenues (e.g. bilateral state diplomacy; or unilateral AI-supported 'lawfare').

[274] Brigitte Hoyer Gosselink and others, 'AI in Action: Accelerating Progress Towards the Sustainable Development Goals' (arXiv, 2 July 2024) <http://arxiv.org/abs/2407.02711> accessed 10 July 2024.

[275] Inter-Agency Working Group on Artificial Intelligence (IAWG-AI), 'United Nations System White Paper on Artificial Intelligence Governance: An Analysis of Current Institutional Models and Related Functions and Existing International Normative Frameworks within the United Nations System that Are Applicable to Artificial Intelligence Governance' (United Nations Chief Executives Board for Coordination 2024) CEB/2024/1/Add.1 40 <https://unsceb.org/sites/default/files/2024-11/UNSystemWhitePaperAIGovernance.pdf> accessed 14 January 2025.

[276] See also Eugenio V Garcia, 'The Other in the Machine: Diplomacy and the AI Conundrum' [2024] Place Branding and Public Diplomacy <https://doi.org/10.1057/s41254-024-00329-6> accessed 15 May 2024.

[277] Maas, 'International Law Does Not Compute' (n 1) 43–49. It should be noted that in previous work, I distinguished between just two categories of displacement: 'the automation of international law', comprising both the use of AI in rule creation or adjudication as well as in monitoring and enforcement; and 'the technological replacement of international law'. In this section, I have split out the former category for clarity.

5.6.1 Automation of Rule Creation, Adjudication, or Arbitration

In the first place, it has long been recognized that new technologies can change the *processes* by which international law is created. For instance, technologies can *speed up* international law formation. Already in 1973, Louis B. Sohn noted how new communication and travel infrastructures were making treaty negotiation faster and easier.[278] The increase in speed of negotiation could facilitate swifter solutions to pressing governance issues—though it could also speed up patterns and actions of contestation. Others have argued that the deluge of big data, and the falling thresholds to collecting it, might facilitate the process of collating and consolidating evidence of state practice under international law, fostering an era of 'Data-Driven Customary International Law'.[279] Yet others have noted that it increases the granularity of international law, as 'Intelligent Treaty Systems' (ITS) are able to rely on more nuanced data sets in gaining an understanding of the issues at stake.[280]

Along with increasing the speed of information exchange and negotiation, and the granularity of the information that institutions can act on, new communication technologies have also qualitatively altered the processes of international law creation, among others by *expanding participation* to more actors. Indeed, in their discussion of the phenomenon of 'norm cascades', Finnemore and Sikkink have discussed how the pace and scope of (general) norm acceptance in international relations can be directly traced to technological change, since

> changes in communication and transportation technologies and increasing global interdependence have led to increased connectedness and, in a way, are leading to the homogenization of global norms . . . the speed of normative change has accelerated substantially in the later part of the twentieth century.[281]

For example, in a comparison of the drafting processes behind UNCLOS and the Mine Ban Treaty, Gamble and Ku have argued that modern communications technologies historically greatly increased the ability of NGOs to get involved in international rule creation, resulting in laws that were less narrowly tailored to state interests than had previously been the case.[282] Likewise, civil society has in recent years begun to pay increasing attention to the role that digital technologies can play in domains such as conflict mediation, where they create new capacities and

[278] Louis Sohn, 'The Impact of Technological Changes on International Law' (1973) 30 Washington and Lee Law Review 1, 10.
[279] Megiddo (n 10).
[280] Thomas F McInerney, 'The Emergence of Intelligent Treaty Systems and the Future of International Law' (2022) 2022 University of Illinois Journal of Law, Technology & Policy 259, 266.
[281] Martha Finnemore and Kathryn Sikkink, 'International Norm Dynamics and Political Change' (1998) 52 International Organization 887, 909.
[282] Gamble and Ku (n 26) 249–251; Crootof, 'Regulating New Weapons Technology' (n 21) 6.

affordances in domains such as conflict analysis, engagement with conflict parties, inclusion of stakeholders, and finally strategic communications.[283]

To be sure, there are a wide range of ways in which these, and other 'cooperative AI' systems, might contribute to human cooperation at many levels.[284] Accordingly, one initial form of legal displacement occurs when AI systems change the *practices* of (international) law *creation* or *adjudication*. Proposals to this effect draw an analogy to growing work on the use of AI systems in domestic legal systems, where algorithms are used in support of the adjudication of cases, the monitoring of crimes and violations, and even the prediction of court rulings.

This trend or prospect raises important questions about the nature of law. The rise of so-called AI Justice[285] has received considerable scrutiny in the domestic realm; it is likely to prove equally contested at the international level. Given this, what are the ways in which we might expect AI systems to be used in support of international law? We can consider a strong and a modest scenario.

5.6.1.1 Strong scenarios: a global AI arbiter

The strong scenario of governance displacement posits that advances in AI could, in time, potentially enable significant improvements in the ability of legal and judicial systems to administer justice.[286] At the international level, this could conceivably take the form of some sort of global AI arbiter—as a dynamic and queryable legal model that would practically facilitate a 'completely specified' international law.[287] We could consider here some foundation model or large language model that had been fine-tuned on international legal texts, or which had been aligned, through 'constitutional AI' techniques,[288] with core sources of international law.

[283] United Nations Department of Political and Peacebuilding Affairs and Centre for Humanitarian Dialogue, 'Digital Technologies and Mediation in Armed Conflict' (United Nations Department of Political and Peacebuilding Affairs, and Centre for Humanitarian Dialogue 2019) <https://hdcentre.org/insights/digital-technologies-and-mediation-in-armed-conflict/> accessed 2 July 2024.

[284] Allan Dafoe and others, 'Cooperative AI: Machines Must Learn to Find Common Ground' (2021) 593 Nature 33; Allan Dafoe and others, 'Open Problems in Cooperative AI' [2020] arXiv:2012.08630 [cs] <http://arxiv.org/abs/2012.08630> accessed 5 January 2021.

[285] Richard M Re and Alicia Solow-Niederman, 'Developing Artificially Intelligent Justice' (2019) 22 Stanford Technology Law Review 48.

[286] For one such vision, see Dario Amodei, 'Machines of Loving Grace: How AI Could Transform the World for the Better' (11 October 2024) <https://darioamodei.com/machines-of-loving-grace> accessed 21 October 2024.

[287] This could be a global version of Benjamin Alarie's 'legal singularity'. See Alarie (n 7). An alternative but closely related scenario is also possible, however, which would not involve tight centralization of a single AI arbiter, but rather would constitute a form of decentralized adoption of many different AI systems which are all configured to interpret and follow international law. For a basic sketch of this approach (in the domestic law setting) and its plausible legal implications, see Cullen O'Keefe, Ketan Ramakrishnan, Janna Tay, and Christoph Winter 'Law-Following AI: Designing AI Agents to Obey Human Laws' [2025] Fordham Law Review <https://papers.ssrn.com/abstract=5242643>; Cullen O'Keefe and Ketan Ramakrishnan, 'AI Agents Must Follow the Law' (*Lawfare*, 14 May 2025) <https://www.lawfaremedia.org/article/ai-agents-must-follow-the-law> accessed 16 May 2025.

[288] Yuntao Bai and others, 'Constitutional AI: Harmlessness from AI Feedback' (arXiv, 15 December 2022) <http://arxiv.org/abs/2212.08073> accessed 7 September 2023. For a more granular discussion

Such systems could serve as a powerful integrator of global governance, as they would be able to identify and resolve conflicts between norms, or goals—from human rights to environmental law—in adjudicating a 'global constitution', therefore reducing the challenges of fragmentation and regime complexity. At the limit, such systems would promise the fully automated adjudication of international law.[289]

Of course, while an interesting extrapolation of trends, this strong scenario may be less relevant for the purposes of global governance in the near term. This is not because it is clearly infeasible technically, although achieving it might require something approaching 'high-level machine intelligence' capabilities. While it is not clear that such capabilities are categorically out of reach—or even more than a few years away[290]—the fact remains that if they were to be created and implemented, their general societal impact would likely far exceed their direct impact on international law.

More pragmatically, proposing the use of an advanced AI system to create or adjudicate international law in this strong sense would be passing the buck. The problem of global governance, from a coherentist or global constitutionalist perspective, is not that we presently cannot conceive of an authoritative body that could reconcile or decide among norm conflicts. It is rather that such hierarchical authorities currently only exist at the state level, whereas the international system notably lacks such bodies. There would certainly be distinct and considerable political (and symbolic) sensitivities involved in handing over the international legal order over to any AI model, but these seem modest compared to the extant political difficulty of installing *any* final authority above the international system.

In that sense, the 'strong' scenario of international legal automation might be somewhat of a red herring, since if one or more AI systems were deployed to integrate and resolve the problem of authority at the international level, by far the bigger achievement would be that this was achieved at all, not that it was done in silicate. As such, a far-reaching 'automation' of international law might counteract the trend towards regime complexity; but its prospects appear dim in the near term, and moot in the long-term.

of the types and kinds of principles that can be utilized in this approach, see also Sandipan Kundu and others, 'Specific versus General Principles for Constitutional AI' (arXiv, 20 October 2023) <http://arxiv.org/abs/2310.13798> accessed 3 November 2023.

289 Although interestingly, while a dramatic change, such a full automation of international law would not be the same as the 'replacement' of international law (discussed under Section 5.6.3), since it would still at its core be reliant on presenting norms to, and adjudicating between, (human) parties.

290 See also the discussion in Chapter 1.

5.6.1.2 Modest scenarios: foundation models as international legal support systems

By contrast, a modest scenario of the automation of rule creation may be more analytically fruitful in the near term. Of course, a first question to ask is whether even this modest scenario of displacement is anywhere on the horizon. Can international law be even partially automated in this more modest manner? Prior to the rise of generative AI systems, at least, many scholars were broadly sceptical. For instance, Thomas Burri previously argued that whereas domestic legal areas such as tax law are susceptible to legal automation—because AI systems in those areas can draw on large, dense, structured, and homogeneous data sets[291]—this does not apply at the international level. Rather, he suggested that the key legal 'data sets' relevant to international law are either far too small (e.g. ICJ decisions) or far too heterogeneous and ambiguous to allow for such training.[292]

By contrast, Ashley Deeks has been more optimistic about the conditions for gradual but eventually widespread take-up of AI technology into 'high-tech international law'.[293] Contra Burri, she argues that in many areas in international law there are significant digital sources of texts (covering thousands of documents) which provide extensive text corpora that can allow machine learning 'text-as-data' tools[294] to perform various functions. She notes:

> One key reason to think that international legal technology has a bright future is that there is a vast range of data to undergird it . . . there are a variety of digital sources of text that might serve as the basis for the kinds of text-as-data analyses that will be useful to states. This includes U.N. databases of Security Council and General Assembly documents, collections of treaties and their travaux preparatoires, European Court of Human Rights caselaw, international arbitral awards, databases of specialized agencies such as the International Civil Aviation Organization, state archives and digests, data collected by a state's own intelligence agencies and diplomats (memorialized in internal memoranda and cables), states' notifications to the Security Council about actions taken in self-defense, legal blogs, the U.N. Yearbook, reports by and submission to U.N. human rights bodies, news reports, and databases of foreign statutes.[295]

[291] This may be too easy a reading of the difficulties involved in tax law automation, especially in civil law systems where precedent does not hold the same value. I thank Luisa Scarcella for this point. For further discussion, see Joshua D Blank and Leigh Osofsky, 'Automated Legal Guidance' (2021) 106 Cornell Law Review 179.

[292] Burri (n 8) 93–95.

[293] Deeks (n 8). These arguments have been further developed in Ashley Deeks and Duncan B Hollis, 'Large Language Models and International Law' [2025] Virginia Public Law and Legal Theory Research Paper <https://papers.ssrn.com/abstract=5131058> accessed 25 February 2025.

[294] Although Deeks (n 8) refers to various (narrow) 'text-as-data' tools, the rest of this chapter will mostly focus on the role of the more recent wave of large language models and general-purpose AI systems, since these fit many (though not all) of the roles discussed in that analysis.

[295] Deeks (n 8) 596–597 [citing sources].

Given this, along with AI's ability to demonstrate 'transfer learning' from data-rich environments even to novel and (relatively) low-data contexts, it seems increasingly likely that text-as-data machine learning systems—or, more to the point, modern large language models (LLMs)—may play many roles. They can be trained to generate new treaty texts,[296] to predict how an international arbitral panel might rule, to gauge the course and likely outcomes of treaty negotiations, or to identify possible treaty conflicts.[297] Indeed, LLM systems may lend themselves quite well to some international legal tasks such as treaty interpretation,[298] even as experiments with some 'reasoning' models also suggest that these systems' legal reasoning in international judicial cases may differ from that displayed by trained judges.[299]

Furthermore, far from being limited only to legal text-based systems, Deeks notes how other uses of AI—from systems that aggregate intelligence information about the preferences or negotiation strategies of negotiation partners, to emotion-recognition systems or social media sentiment analysis—might also play a role in broader diplomatic processes.[300] Focusing on the procedural contributions that machine learning could make to the creation of new international law, she argues that international lawyers in service of a state's foreign ministry in practice have three roles—negotiating agreements, dispute resolution (whether in judicial or arbitral fora), and advising policymakers about the existence and meaning of international law—and argues that all of these can, in distinct ways, gain from automation.[301]

[296] ibid 605. (discussing draft extradition treaties).

[297] ibid 604–606, 616–622, 628–630.

[298] For instance, in an early April 2023 experiment (using the public GPT-3.5 version of ChatGPT), Jack Wright Nelson found that the LLM system was able to deliver adequate first drafts of interpretative briefs on the meaning of the phrase 'harmful contamination' in Article IX of the Outer Space Treaty, suggesting that 'ChatGPT will be a competent, but not spectacular, player of the treaty interpretation game'. Jack Wright Nelson, 'Large Language Models and the Treaty Interpretation Game' (2023) 12 Cambridge International Law Journal 305, 315. More recent experiments have demonstrated that models such as Gemini 2.0 and GPT4o can draft memorials that consistently received average to superior scores (and in some cases near-perfect ratings) from judges in a renowned international law moot court competition. See Damien Charlotin and Niccolò Ridi, 'GenAI as an International Lawyer: A Case Study with the Jessup International Law Moot Court' (Social Science Research Network, 5 June 2025) <https://papers.ssrn.com/abstract=5283722> accessed 10 June 2025. However, for more sceptical perspectives on the reliability of LLMs used as legal tools, see also Matthew Dahl and others, 'Large Legal Fictions: Profiling Legal Hallucinations in Large Language Models' (arXiv, 2 January 2024) <http://arxiv.org/abs/2401.01301> accessed 16 January 2024. (though testing only older models such as GPT-3.5, PaLM 2, and Llama 2); Sayash Kapoor, Peter Henderson and Arvind Narayanan, 'Promises and Pitfalls of Artificial Intelligence for Legal Applications' (arXiv, 10 January 2024) <http://arxiv.org/abs/2402.01656> accessed 3 June 2025.

[299] Eric A Posner and Shivam Saran, 'Judge AI: Assessing Large Language Models in Judicial Decision-Making' (University of Chicago Coase-Sandor Institute for Law & Economics 2025) Research Paper 25-03 <https://papers.ssrn.com/abstract=5098708> accessed 18 February 2025. (conducting a 2 x 2 factorial experiment involving a simulated appeal in an international war crimes case, and finding that GPT-4o's judgment is strongly affected by judicial precedent but not by sympathic portrayal of the defendant, reasoning in a way similar to students but opposite to professional judges). See also Deeks and Hollis (n 293).

[300] Deeks (n 8) 613–615.

[301] ibid 589–593.

Contrary to the strong scenario discussed in the previous section, this more modest image of legal automation does not envision that these law-making processes will be entirely given over to machine decision-making, but rather that many actors will come to find significant benefits in using machine learning tools to support human legal and diplomatic decision-making processes.

To be certain, that does not mean this process of displacement will occur rapidly. As noted previously, there are a number of barriers which can slow procurement and integration of AI tools, and which ensure a lag between the development of state-of-the-art tools in labs and their use in the field.[302] Deeks does admit that international law can often be 'conservative' about taking up new technologies, and that at present states and their advisors in international legal issues still lag far behind the private sector in contemplating how AI could change their work. As a result, with a few exceptions, 'international law generally has been a stranger to a new wave of technological tools – including computational text analysis, machine learning, and predictive algorithms – that use large quantities of data to help make sense of the world'.[303] Furthermore, there remain challenges to the incorporation of AI technologies in international law, including technical challenges around the format of some types of international law data, the fact that international law questions have relatively less precedent to guide predictions, and civil liberties concerns over applications in emotion detection or social media scraping software, among others.[304]

In spite of this, Deeks does identify several trends that will, in her view, steadily increase the pressure on international lawyers to take up and reckon with these new tools. These are: (1) near-peer ambitions; (2) proofs of concept in private law; (3) client pressure; (4) necessity in the line of work.[305] As such, she argues that while the challenges to adoption are real, they are not insurmountable, and that there are potentially many use cases of AI, whether in the preparation of treaty negotiations, conducting negotiations, or identifying customary international law.[306]

Indeed, recent history suggests that international institutions are gradually, if cautiously, moving in this direction. For instance, a range of international human rights institutions, in particular adjudicative bodies but also quasi-judicial or monitoring bodies, have in recent years had to respond to a growing number of cases, petitions, or initiatives from groups seeking redress for alleged violations of their rights under international law.[307] In response, a range of institutions such as the Office of the High Commissioner of Human Rights (OHCHR) and the

[302] See also the discussion, in Chapter 1, on patterns and rates of global diffusion for AI technology.
[303] Deeks (n 8) 576.
[304] ibid 598–599.
[305] ibid 593–597.
[306] ibid 599. See also Deeks and Hollis (n 293) 4–5.
[307] Veronika Fikfak and Laurence Helfer, 'Automating International Human Rights Adjudication' (2025) 46 Michigan Journal of International Law 69, 71–72.

Inter-American Commission on Human Rights have begun to consider the role that automated decision-making (ADM) tools might play.[308] To be sure, these initiatives have by and large still shied away from the outright use of AI modern AI systems for interpretative or adjudicative measures, such as in making judgements over whether a state has violated a human rights treaty.[309] Nonetheless, there are a range of more modest near-term uses of such technologies that could help digitize documents, facilitate internal case management, or make recommendations regarding admissibility or the calculation of damages. In other cases, semi-automated systems based on language models could help in clustering similar cases together, translating key texts, or recommending relevant precedents.[310]

The same could be the case in international criminal law. For instance, the International Criminal Court (ICC) has for some years received criticism around inefficiencies in its work flow.[311] Accordingly, in 2022–2023 its Office of the Prosecutor (OTP) partnered with Microsoft and Accenture to support the development of AI tools,[312] announcing in February 2023 'Project Harmony', a programme to modernize the OTP's evidence management platform through the use of AI technology in, among others, pattern identification, automatic translation, facial identification, transcription, targeted material search, media analytics, and others.[313]

Moreover, states have also not been far behind in picking up on the related use cases of AI in diplomacy. For instance, in December 2023, the US Ambassador to the United Nations reportedly had her team use AI tools to survey and track subtle diplomatic efforts by authoritarian governments to add in language and rephrasing in UN documents or resolutions that would be more favourable to their interests.[314] Others have flagged ways in which US intelligence agencies might utilize AI chatbots to help prepare leadership (personality) analyses of foreign heads of state, as part of 'visit piece' briefings to the President that provide them with insights into what foreign leaders think, want, or are concerned about, ahead of high-stakes top-level meetings.[315]

[308] ibid.

[309] ibid 73 ('automation tools must not usurp the discretion of human decision-makers to interpret the law and apply it to the relevant facts').

[310] ibid 78–86.

[311] Gabrielle McIntyre and Nicholas Vialle, 'The Use of AI at the ICC: Should We Have Concerns? Part I' (*Opinio Juris*, 11 October 2023) <https://opiniojuris.org/2023/10/11/the-use-of-ai-at-the-icc-should-we-have-concerns-part-i/> accessed 15 November 2023.

[312] Karim AA Khan, 'Towards a More Just World: Every Day. Annual Report of the Office of the Prosecutor - 2022' (International Criminal Court—The Office of the Prosecutor 2022) 27 <https://www.icc-cpi.int/sites/default/files/2022-12/2022-12-05-annual-report-of-the-office-of-the-prosecutor.pdf> accessed 8 January 2024.

[313] McIntyre and Vialle (n 311); *ICC Office of the Prosecutor to Launch Modern Evidence Management Platform* (2023) <https://www.youtube.com/watch?v=rqt63ghnJSE> accessed 8 December 2023.

[314] Ryan Heath, 'Scoop: U.S. Makes UN Push for AI for Good' (*Axios*, 13 December 2023) <https://www.axios.com/2023/12/13/us-ai-united-nations-global-resolution> accessed 13 January 2024.

[315] Judd Devermont, 'Intelligence Advantage: Profiling African Leaders' Meetings with U.S. Presidents' (Center for Strategic and International Studies 2024) 7 <https://www.csis.org/analysis/intel

Finally, beyond inter-state diplomacy, there have also been proposals to integrate AI models into arbitration processes.[316] For instance, in arbitral proceedings in areas such as foreign investment law, AI models can support arbitrators in different ways, from searching datasets and analysing previous cases[317] to drafting awards or serving as an overall check on the consistency or bias of the decisions made by the arbitrator.[318] There are accordingly growing attempts to develop frameworks for use for such systems in these sensitive contexts.[319]

Of course, the ultimate trajectory of such automation remains to be seen. There might of course be a more fundamental limit to the significance of governance displacement-through-automation: even if there are many areas where there are significant sources for text-as-data tools to be trained on, these may not be the highest-stakes scenarios that international law faces. After all, international law may be especially engaged by large historical shocks and changes.[320] That would not prevent such AI systems from seeing wide usage in many rote tasks, but it would imply that international legal history would continue to be written by humans for some time.

Nonetheless, even this modest scenario might have significant effects. While some AI tools might support greater coordination, the fact that they are developed and owned by some particular parties may, as Deeks has argued, mean that 'states with a high level of technological sophistication are likely to treat some of these tools as proprietary and critical to their national security, and so may use them in a way that exacerbates existing power differentials'.[321]

ligence-advantage-profiling-african-leaders-meetings-us-presidents> accessed 22 May 2024 (though noting that the technology will still have some distance to go to contribute to the best standards of analytic tradecraft, since in a basic trial, the performance of existing AI models such as GPT-4, Claude, Meta AI, and Gemini was lacklustre at analysing a meeting between President Biden and Kenyan President William Ruto, with answers ranging 'from unexceptional to unacceptable').

[316] João Ilhão Moreira and Jiawei Zhang, 'ChatGPT as a Fourth Arbitrator? The Ethics and Risks of Using Large Language Models in Arbitration' [2024] Arbitration International aiae031.

[317] Atif M Alenezi, 'Artificial Intelligence and Foreign Investment Law Arbitration: An Analysis of Regulatory Framework Implications' (2024) 25 The Journal of World Investment & Trade 369.

[318] Marike Paulsson and Supritha Suresh, 'AI: The Modern Tribunal Assistant—Impact on Enforceability of Arbitral Awards under the New York Convention' (2024) 1 Jus Mundi Arbitration Review 101, 117–118 (detailing the 'Paulsson-Suresh Progressive AI Supervision Scale', distinguishing between different uses of AI within the arbitral process, their differing levels of direct and indirect influence on the final award, and the resulting level of human supervision necessary). However, the automation of these tasks within the processes of international arbitration may also require arbitrators to develop new skills. See Sara Migliorini, 'Automation & Augmentation: Artificial Intelligence in International Arbitration' (2024) 1 Jus Mundi Arbitration Review 119, 128–129.

[319] For example, in 2024, the Silicon Valley Arbitration & Mediation Center, a non-profit oriented towards the global technology sector, articulated a set of guidelines for the use of AI systems in both domestic and international arbitration. Silicon Valley Arbitration & Mediation Center, 'SVAMC Guidelines on the Use of Artificial Intelligence in Arbitration' (Silicon Valley Arbitration & Mediation Center 2024) <https://svamc.org/wp-content/uploads/SVAMC-AI-Guidelines-First-Edition.pdf> accessed 5 August 2024.

[320] I thank Laura Emily Christiansen for this point.

[321] Deeks (n 8) 582.

Indeed, even if their use is accepted on its face, there may be concerning downstream normative impacts on the international legal system: in recent years, scholars have pointed to the ways in which LLMs can embed particular values, worldviews, or normative systems.[322] Some of these biases or predispositions may be indeliberate, and an accidental result of the training data. However, increasingly, general-purpose AI systems are fine-tuned after the initial training by human or AI feedback,[323] which can shift the model's behaviour or responses away from its original training data to the explicit guidelines or feedback provided. This has already resulted in some prominent public LLMs, such as ChatGPT, displaying distinct political orientations.[324] Generally, this raises questions over who should decide which values these systems reflect,[325] as well as a tension between, on the one hand, the risk that offering a small number of overtly standardized AI models to a large number of people leads to a process of global ideological homogenization and power concentration and, on the other, the risk that allowing increasing user customization of the values of these models results in normative fragmentation and echo chambers.[326]

The increasing use of international legal language models will likely raise similar normative and political dilemmas for international law. On the one hand, if such models are used only by well-resourced states, their use will likely contribute to increased perceptions of unfairness, contestation, and an erosion of the legitimacy of treaty negotiation or arbitration outcomes.[327] Conversely, the widespread dissemination of these tools could in principle level the playing field for many actors, empowering them to participate better in engaging with international legal texts and processes of treaty interpretation.[328] Indeed, Deeks and Hollis have argued that LLM-based AI systems could come to serve as a widely used and time-saving

[322] Pegah Maham and Sabrina Küspert, 'Governing General Purpose AI: A Comprehensive Map of Unreliability, Misuse and Systemic Risks' (Stiftung Neue Verantwortung 2023) 38–40 <https://www.interface-eu.org/publications/governing-general-purpose-ai-comprehensive-map-unreliability-misuse-and-systemic-risks> accessed 18 March 2025.

[323] The processes of RLHF or of RLAIF (the latter also known as 'Constitutional AI'). See Paul Christiano and others, 'Deep Reinforcement Learning from Human Preferences', *Advances in Neural Information Processing Systems 30 (NIPS 2017)* (2017) <https://papers.nips.cc/paper/2017/hash/d5e2c0adad503c91f91df240d0cd4e49-Abstract.html> accessed 20 December 2020; Harrison Lee and others, 'RLAIF: Scaling Reinforcement Learning from Human Feedback with AI Feedback' (arXiv, 30 November 2023) <http://arxiv.org/abs/2309.00267> accessed 11 January 2024; Bai and others (n 288).

[324] Jochen Hartmann, Jasper Schwenzow, and Maximilian Witte, 'The Political Ideology of Conversational AI: Converging Evidence on ChatGPT's pro-Environmental, Left-Libertarian Orientation' (arXiv, 5 January 2023) <http://arxiv.org/abs/2301.01768> accessed 14 January 2024; David Rozado, 'Where Does ChatGPT Fall on the Political Compass?' (*Reason.com*, 13 December 2022) <https://reason.com/2022/12/13/where-does-chatgpt-fall-on-the-political-compass/> accessed 14 January 2024.

[325] OpenAI, 'How Should AI Systems Behave, and Who Should Decide?' (*OpenAI*, 16 February 2023) <https://openai.com/blog/how-should-ai-systems-behave/> accessed 20 February 2023.

[326] Maham and Küspert (n 322) 38–40. (referring to the latter risk as 'ideological homogenization on a more individualized level').

[327] Deeks (n 8) 582.

[328] Nelson, 'Large Language Models and the Treaty Interpretation Game' (n 298) 319.

'collaborator' for international lawyers, or potentially even a 'creator' of international law, by allowing lawyers and their policy clients to consider creative new proposals for treaty language and tools.[329]

However, even such scenarios could contain their own risks. On the one hand, if these models were widely available but not customizable (in a transparent way), the reality (or perception) that they embed the values of their developers' societies may prompt accusations that these are in some sense normatively poisoned gifts, advantaging already dominant understandings of international law.[330] Conversely, if all actors are allowed to customize and tailor their legal language models to their own values, this may erode the perception of a common normative base to the interpretation of international law, and raise objections that any resulting international norm interpretations produced or enabled by these AI tools are merely the result of the values that their principals fed into them from the start.

Moreover, as Deeks and Hollis note, AI models could work as 'confounders' of international law—by leading international lawyers down inaccurate, ambiguous, or fruitless paths if they do not prompt the models cautiously—or even as 'corruptors' of international law, with the concern that automation bias may increasingly lead users and states to see the outputs of these systems as providing an accurate interpretation of the law, or an accurate representation of the state of customary international law, even if analogue work by international lawyers themselves would produce quite different conclusions.[331] More worryingly, if these models are susceptible to the biases or features in their training data, this creates an incentive for states to insert their preferred views on the state of international law into training data sets, in order to corrupt these models' outputs in their favour.[332]

As such, either scenario of 'modest' AI use would be sufficient to raise significant political, normative, and doctrinal challenges to the coherence and legitimacy of the international legal architecture.

[329] Deeks and Hollis (n 293) 21–23.

[330] Nelson, 'Large Language Models and the Treaty Interpretation Game' (n 298) 322 ('by using LLMs to play the treaty interpretation game, we might provide yet another conduit for the same States, groups, languages and perspectives to perpetuate their disproportionate influence over treaty interpretation—and, by extension, international law').

[331] Deeks and Hollis (n 293) 23–24. For a related analysis, see also Matthijs M Maas, 'AI, Governance Displacement, and the (De)Fragmentation of International Law', *ISA Annual Convention* (2021) 22–28 <https://www.cser.ac.uk/resources/ai-governance-displacement-and-defragmentation-international-law/> accessed 19 March 2021 (discussing 10 different roles that AI systems and tools could play in international law, with distinct consequences on the international legal order and on regime complexity, by distinguishing between cases where AI systems serve as (1) legal 'canary in the coal mine', highlighting the need for greater cross-regime harmonization; as (2) tough knot or (3) generator of regime fault lines; as a (4) shield, (5) patch, (6) cure, or (7) accelerator of international legal fragmentation; or as (8) differential enabler, (9) driver of value shifts, or (10) asymmetric weapon, potentially contributing to trends of contestation or erosion in the international legal order).

[332] Deeks and Hollis (n 293) 24.

5.6.2 Automation of Monitoring and Enforcement

The second form of governance displacement envisions the use of AI technologies in strengthening the *monitoring and enforcement* of existing or future international law and global governance instruments. Notably, over the past decade, a wide suite of emerging technologies have contributed to the prospects for the effective verification, implementation, and enforcement of multilateral international agreements. In this context, Thomas McInerney has referred to the rise of ITS, to refer to a cluster of technology-enabled capacities configured for '(1) sensing and generating data, (2) gathering and storing data, (3) processing and analyzing data, (4) creating models, maps, or visualizations, and (5) applying data to targets and indicators to measure progress and improve results from treaty applications'.[333] Through these capacities, McInerney argues, treaty secretariats, international organizations, states, researchers, academics, NGOs, and other stakeholders are increasingly able to assess key conditions relevant to a treaty's mandate, formulate strategic approaches, manage and improve treaty operations, monitor and review their implementation, and measure a treaty's overall performance and compliance.[334] In these ways, they herald a potentially new era for international agreements—changing the playing field and potentially ratcheting up the 'regulatory power' of multilateral treaty regimes, while raising the stakes for states as improved knowledge around state inaction may enable citizens and civil society to hold those states more broadly accountable.[335]

5.6.2.1 A brief history of technology-enabled monitoring

To be sure, it has long been recognized that new technologies can play a key role in changing the modes and anticipated effectiveness of compliance monitoring and enforcement. Indeed, the role of various forms of 'national technical means'[336] in supporting the monitoring of compliance with international commitments has been well chronicled in the high-stakes area of arms control. For many decades, a range of technologies including signals intelligence; satellites; networked arrays of seismic, hydroacoustic, infrasound, or radionuclide monitoring stations;[337] and (aided by legal arrangements such as the 1992 Treaty on Open Skies) surveillance

[333] McInerney (n 280) 266.

[334] ibid 260–261.

[335] ibid 338.

[336] Eric H Arnett, 'Science, Technology, and Arms Control' in Richard Dean Burns (ed), *Encyclopedia of Arms Control and Disarmament*, vol 1 (Charles Scribner's Sons 1993).

[337] See for instance the International Monitoring System (IMS) sensor network which is currently being developed and operated by the Preparatory Commission for the Comprehensive Nuclear-Test-Ban Treaty Organization, and which deploys four complementary verification methods (seismic, hydroacoustic, infrasound, and radionuclide sensors) at 321 monitoring stations spread over 89 countries, in order to detect any signs of nuclear testing. CTBTO Preparatory Commission, 'Overview of the Verification Regime' (*Comprehensive Nuclear-Test-Ban Treaty Organization*) <https://www.ctbto.org/verification-regime/background/overview-of-the-verification-regime/> accessed 9 September 2020.

or radionuclide sniffer aircraft[338] have all played roles in enabling states parties to monitor and verify each other's (non)compliance with treaty commitments or various peremptory norms under international law.[339]

Moreover, since the days of the Cold War, the rise of the digital economy has increasingly complemented 'national technical means' with a host of distributed sensors. As a result, over the past decades, the International Atomic Energy Agency (IAEA) has begun to draw on open-source information and commercial satellite imagery in order to provide early warning in nuclear safeguards and to counter nuclear proliferation.[340] Satellite monitoring has also played significant roles in other domains of international law, most notably international criminal law. The first reported use of satellite data in international criminal law proceedings occurred in 2004, when such data was introduced as evidence before the International Criminal Tribunal for the Former Yugoslavia (ICTY), in the Srebrenica trials' prosecution of Bosnian Serb generals Krstić and Mladic;[341] its usage since then has only grown.[342] In other domains such as environmental law, commercial satellites have also been proposed to monitor the implementation of the Kyoto Protocol's Global Emissions Trading Programme.[343]

More generally, geographic information systems (GIS), which 'integrate satellite images, textual search capabilities, modelling and visualisation tools, and geographical databases', have played a key role in improving the generation of information key for the operation of treaties, in areas such as the environment, arms control, and human rights.[344] Beyond states and international organizations, these tools have enabled many non-state actors, such as human rights monitors, journalists, and NGOs, to carry out their functions. For instance, technologies have enabled civil society organizations to explore new organizational forms

[338] Treaty on Open Skies (1992) CTS No 3. See generally also David A Koplow, 'Back to the Future and up to the Sky: Legal Implications of Open Skies Inspection for Arms Control' (1991) 79 California Law Review 421. However, note that in May 2020, President Donald Trump announced an intention for the US to withdraw from the Open Skies Treaty. Bonnie Jenkins, 'A Farewell to the Open Skies Treaty, and an Era of Imaginative Thinking' (*Brookings*, 16 June 2020) <https://www.brookings.edu/blog/order-from-chaos/2020/06/16/a-farewell-to-the-open-skies-treaty-and-an-era-of-imaginative-thinking/> accessed 22 June 2020.

[339] Maas, 'International Law Does Not Compute' (n 1) 43.

[340] Giacomo GM Cojazzi and others, 'Collection and Analysis of Open Source News for Information Awareness and Early Warning in Nuclear Safeguards' (2013) 50 ESARDA Bulletin 94; David Albright, Sarah Burkhard, and Allison Lach, 'Commercial Satellite Imagery Analysis for Countering Nuclear Proliferation' (2018) 46 Annual Review of Earth and Planetary Sciences 99.

[341] Inshira Faliq, 'From Space to the Courtroom: AI Enhanced Satellite Imagery and the Future of Accountability' (*Opinio Juris*, 14 January 2025) <https://opiniojuris.org/2025/01/14/from-space-to-the-courtroom-ai-enhanced-satellite-imagery-and-the-future-of-accountability/> accessed 17 January 2025.

[342] Neil Savage, 'Eyes in the Sky Usher in New Era of Law and Order' (2024) 635 Nature S1.

[343] Allison F Gardner, 'Environmental Monitoring's Undiscovered Country: Developing a Satellite Remote Monitoring System to Implement the Kyoto Protocol's Global Emissions-Trading Program' (2000) 9 New York University Environmental Law Journal 152.

[344] Thomas F McInerney, 'Science, Technology, and Data', in *Strategic Treaty Management: Practice and Implications* (Cambridge University Press 2015) 203–204.

and strategies, with many relying on digital tools to collect and analyse data on environmental factors and to investigate and prosecute environmental crimes.[345] Others have used available Earth Observation Data (EOD) in order to investigate a range of ongoing conflicts—ranging from Sudan to Ukraine, and from Myanmar to Gaza—where these techniques help provide evidence of international crimes.[346]

In all these cases, improved monitoring tools and arrangements can change key parameters for treaty effectiveness and, indeed, viability. However, the effects of their use are not always straightforward.

5.6.2.2 The role of AI in monitoring arms control agreements

Critically, there are a range of potential use cases for AI in strengthening monitoring and enforcement. Some of these are in the domain of arms control.[347] In this high-stakes, politically contentious field, AI tools may support the work of state inspectors in conducting multimodal data analysis of proliferation-relevant activities,[348] or strengthening the ability to identify illicit nuclear tests even from limited data.[349]

The use of AI to increase the amount (or type) of information gathered, as well as the ease of processing it, should intuitively make these technologies a boon for verification. Indeed, one significant use case is in geospatial intelligence. While commercial high-resolution satellites routinely image millions of square kilometres of the earth's surface each day, a human analyst can usually only review around 100 square kilometres' worth of imagery in that same time.[350] AI-assisted analysis can help here. For example, one 2022 analysis used machine learning

[345] Mette Eilstrup-Sangiovanni and Nina Hall, *Climate Activism, Digital Technologies, and Organizational Change* (Cambridge University Press 2024).

[346] Jonathan W Hak and Sabrina K Rewald, 'The Satellite Era: How Earth Observation Data Is Being Mobilized as Potential Digital Evidence' (*EJIL: Talk!*, 1 July 2024) <https://www.ejiltalk.org/the-satellite-era-how-earth-observation-data-is-being-mobilized-as-potential-digital-evidence/> accessed 24 July 2024 (noting in fact that this is not a new practice, and that the first uses of EOD before the ICJ date back to 1986, and in international criminal law to the late 1990s). See also Andre Kwok, 'Eyes in the Sky: Clarifying Guidelines for Space-Based Imagery in Mass Atrocity Prosecutions' (*Opinio Juris*, 15 March 2024) <https://opiniojuris.org/2024/03/15/eyes-in-the-sky-clarifying-guidelines-for-space-based-imagery-in-mass-atrocity-prosecutions/> accessed 22 January 2025.

[347] Nico Lück, *Machine Learning-Powered Artificial Intelligence in Arms Control* (Peace Research Institute Frankfurt 2019).

[348] Thomas Reinhold and Niklas Schörnig (eds), *Armament, Arms Control and Artificial Intelligence: The Janus-Faced Nature of Machine Learning in the Military Realm* (Springer International Publishing 2022), and especially Niklas Schörnig, 'Artificial Intelligence as an Arms Control Tool: Opportunities and Challenges' in Thomas Reinhold and Niklas Schörnig (eds), *Armament, Arms Control and Artificial Intelligence: The Janus-faced Nature of Machine Learning in the Military Realm* (Springer International Publishing 2022).

[349] Anna Heise, 'AI, WMD and Arms Control: The Case of Nuclear Testing' in Thomas Reinhold and Niklas Schörnig (eds), *Armament, Arms Control and Artificial Intelligence: The Janus-faced Nature of Machine Learning in the Military Realm* (Springer International Publishing 2022).

[350] Sulgiye Park, Allison Puccioni, and Francesca Verville, 'Thermal Satellite Imagery for the Detection and Monitoring of Nuclear Weapons: Early Approaches for Automating Imagery Analysis' (*Stanford HAI*, 3 April 2024) <https://hai.stanford.edu/events/thermal-satellite-imagery-detection-and-monitoring-nuclear-weapons-early-approaches> accessed 10 April 2024.

tools to improve the remote analysis of North Korean nuclear activity, conducting automated analysis of more than 800 satellite images that tracked vehicular traffic around core North Korean nuclear facilities as well as international trade at border crossings between China and North Korea, as proxies for North Korean nuclear activity.[351] This surveillance programme was further augmented with the addition of thermal sensors to detect heat signatures, which resulted in confirmation that a previously dormant North Korean nuclear reactor was now likely operational.[352] In another project, researchers used an AI tool to better distinguish between (human pre-defined) signatures of uranium and copper mills.[353]

Notably, new monitoring tools and technologies are important, not only because they can improve treaty effectiveness by changing the incentives and calculations of actors regarding the expected results of violating a treaty, but also because in some cases technological means can provide the guarantees by which parties are willing to bind themselves to agreements in the first place.

For instance, Coe and Vaynmann have argued that one critical barrier to reaching arms control agreements is a so-called security–transparency trade-off.[354] This refers to the dilemma whereby an arms control agreement between A and B to cap B's capabilities must on the one hand have sufficient provisions in place to ensure transparency of B's actions (to assure A that any cheating can and will be detected), but on the other hand must not offer A so much transparency on B's military actions that B holds the arrangement to unacceptably erode its security. In some cases it may be impossible to satisfy both requirements at once, for, as Coe and Vaynman note:

> Any deal that is transparent enough to assure that one side complies with the deal may also shift the balance of power so much that the other side reneges to exploit this shift. Any deal that preserves the balance of power well enough to be safe for the arming side may not be transparent enough to assure the monitoring side of its compliance. When this is true, no arms control deal will be viable.[355]

At first glance, the 'security–transparency' trade-off might appear to provide grounds for pessimism regarding the prospects of arms control. Indeed, similar

[351] Sulgiye Park, Allison Puccioni, and Rodney C Ewing, 'Machine Learning Improves Satellite Imagery Analysis of North Korean Nuclear Activity' (2022) 78 Bulletin of the Atomic Scientists 26.

[352] Park, Puccioni, and Verville (n 350).

[353] Lalitha Sundaresan, S Chandrashekar, and Bhupendra Jasani, 'Discriminating Uranium and Copper Mills Using Satellite Imagery' (2017) 5 Remote Sensing Applications: Society and Environment 27.

[354] Andrew J Coe and Jane Vaynman, 'Why Arms Control Is So Rare' (2020) 114 American Political Science Review 342.

[355] ibid 343 (arguing that this trade-off has driven Iraq's nuclear weapons programs after the Gulf War, great power competition in arms in the interwar period, and superpower military rivalry during the Cold War, and noting that these cases account for almost 40% of all global arming in the past two centuries).

difficult dynamics over balancing transparency with security have more broadly challenged the operations of some international organizations, such as the IAEA, that may at times need to balance the transparent reporting on state violations of international rules with intelligence protection capabilities that keep information about the sources and methods of such monitoring secret.[356]

However, the security–transparency model also allows that whenever this trade-off is less steep, or where one side can assure itself of the ability to unilaterally monitor the other's compliance, agreements can be struck. Importantly, this highlights structural 'levers' that can be affected, not just through institutional arrangements or confidence-building measures but also through new technologies, in order to mitigate or sidestep this trade-off. As such, technologies can structurally shift the conditions for an arms control treaty if they increase unilateral compliance monitoring, or if they can reduce the 'transparency–security' trade-off.

In the first case, technological advances that *increase either party's ability to unilaterally monitor* certain capabilities can render a 'closed deal' (whereby parties agree on an arms control deal, but refuse to allow access to facilities for the purposes of mutual verification) viable nonetheless, because either party can be assured that they are able to unilaterally monitor compliance. For instance, in the domain of nuclear arms control, Coe and Vaynmann suggest that the Strategic Arms Limitations Talks (SALT I) negotiations succeeded, where the earlier 1964 Nuclear Freeze negotiations had failed, in large part because the development of satellite surveillance in the intervening years had improved unilateral monitoring capabilities sufficiently to make a 'closed deal' viable.[357]

In the second place, there may be ways to take measures that create mutual perceptions that the *trade-off between transparency and security is mild*. For instance, during the first round of negotiations over the Intermediate Range Nuclear Forces (INF) Treaty (1980–1983) US negotiators initially proposed 'anytime anywhere inspections', which were rejected not only by the USSR but also, before long, by many on their own side.[358] Instead, during the second round of negotiations (1985–1987), the US put forward proposals for more limited inspections with access to only one missile production facility. Moreover, the US devised a way to outfit Soviet facilities with a sensor that would reveal whether an exiting missile was of the banned type without revealing the technical characteristics of non-banned missiles.[359] Since the Cold War, there has been continued scientific research into new avenues to, for instance, validate nuclear warheads that are slated for retirement, in ways that do not reveal key engineering features.[360]

[356] Allison Carnegie and Austin Carson, 'The Disclosure Dilemma: Nuclear Intelligence and International Organizations' (2019) 63 American Journal of Political Science 269.

[357] Coe and Vaynman (n 354) 352.

[358] ibid.

[359] ibid.

[360] For recent developments, see for instance Areg Danagoulian, 'Verification of Arms Control Treaties with Resonance Phenomena' (2020) 30 Nuclear Physics News 25.

As such, this highlights the potentially important role that new technologies can play in improving the ability of states and other parties to make verifiable claims about the properties, capabilities, or inputs of new technologies.[361] Technology can therefore not just incrementally contribute to the deterrent or compliant pull of treaties; it can also, in fact, shift the possibility frontier for which arms control or non-proliferation treaties are politically possible in the first place.

However, the effects of enhanced monitoring are subject to complicated dynamics. Vaynmann has cautioned that these technologies might also have unanticipated effects on key features of international arms control bargaining such as, most importantly, the security–transparency trade-off. These effects depend on 'how [a given capability] affects unilateral monitoring capabilities; the degree to which it allows demonstrable control over information; and the effect that it has on concealment'.[362] In this context, one challenge with the use of AI systems for monitoring is that they are likely to provide only a limited degree of 'demonstrable control' to restrict the scope of their detection and analysis activities:[363] as such, their use may increase state concerns that sensitive security information could be collected in the course of monitoring.[364] This might produce greater reticence to enter into agreements (explicitly backed up by such AI monitoring systems) or—if another actor is capable of deploying such capabilities anyway—could simply lead to greater political tensions over the use of such espionage capabilities.

These considerations are therefore of great relevance when designing or evaluating proposed monitoring arrangements for international agreements focused on mitigating risks from military or advanced AI systems. Such agreements could be backed up by a range of possible verification methods, including various unilateral national technical means, access-dependent methods, or hardware-dependent methods.[365] However, some of these, such as satellite-based remote

[361] For a discussion of the security–transparency trade-off in arms control regimes for military AI systems themselves—and the possible role of (AI) technologies in alleviating it—see also the later discussion in Section 7.2.2.2 ('The rationalist perspective: state interests, regime foundations, and security constraints').

[362] Jane Vaynman, 'Better Monitoring and Better Spying: The Implications of Emerging Technology for Arms Control' (2021) 4 Texas National Security Review <https://tnsr.org/2021/09/better-monitoring-and-better-spying-the-implications-of-emerging-technology-for-arms-control/> accessed 29 September 2021.

[363] ibid (defining this as '[a] monitoring tool that provides a high degree of control creates an ability to demarcate the line between what will be revealed and what will be kept secret at whatever point that line is negotiated. Control might be achieved by limiting the amount or scope of the information that can be collected, or through an ability to collect information at a specified quality or level of granularity').

[364] ibid; Jane Vaynman and Tristan A Volpe, 'Dual Use Deception: How Technology Shapes Cooperation in International Relations' (2023) 77 International Organization 599.

[365] Akash R Wasil and others, 'Verification Methods for International AI Agreements' (arXiv.org, 28 August 2024) <https://arxiv.org/abs/2408.16074v1> accessed 3 October 2024. See also Aaron Scher and Lisa Thiergart, 'Mechanisms to Verify International Agreements About AI Development' (MIRI Technical Governance Team 2024) <https://techgov.intelligence.org/research/mechanisms-to-verify-international-agreements-about-ai-development> accessed 9 December 2024.

sensing, may struggle with the limited signatures and legibility of contemporary AI infrastructures, given that, at least at present, AI-dedicated hardware often constitutes only a portion of all the equipment present in a data centre and lacks reliable visual identifiers, or any way to reliably assess computational power or usage purely from external observation.[366]

Given these diverse challenges, it is worth keeping in mind that attempting to pursue the most stringent monitoring and verification arrangements possible (whether for AI or for other technologies) may not always be an unalloyed good: after all, highly intrusive monitoring requirements may create a significant contact area and opportunity for disagreements between the parties. Often, this can even threaten the political feasibility of the initial agreement in the first place, as seen in the way that envisioned stringent verification measures threatened the ratification proceedings of SALT II.[367] Accordingly, Andrew Reddie has suggested that in many contexts there is a 'Goldilocks' level of verification stringency, with intermediate forms of monitoring measures producing the highest likelihood of compliance by participating parties.[368] This provides relevant lessons both for designing appropriately AI-enabled monitoring functions into arms control regimes, ensuring that these consider the situations where greater monitoring granularity aids compliance—and where it may harm it.

5.6.2.3 The role of AI in monitoring international humanitarian and human rights law

Of course, AI-empowered monitoring capabilities can aid not just in evaluating and enforcing compliance with arms control agreements, but also in other domains of international security governance.

Some of these use cases focus on pre-emption. For instance, national intelligence agencies have shown a growing interest in the use of AI in support of predictive 'strategic warning' systems, to flag potential threats and security crises at an early stage.[369] In addition to anticipating security crises, however, AI systems may play a major role in monitoring compliance with international human rights law, international humanitarian law, or international criminal law, when such conflicts do occur.[370] Such tools are seeing increasing attention from researchers within

[366] Konstantin Pilz and Lennart Heim, 'Limitations of Satellite Imagery Analysis for AI-Specific Data Centers' (13 September 2024) <https://blog.heim.xyz/limitations-of-satellite-imagery/> accessed 18 February 2025.

[367] John H McNeill and others, 'Arms Control Dispute Settlement: Past, Present and Future' (1990) 84 Proceedings of the Annual Meeting (American Society of International Law) 407.

[368] Andrew William Reddie, 'Governing Insecurity: Institutional Design, Compliance, and Arms Control' (UC Berkeley 2019) <https://escholarship.org/uc/item/2sn678w1> accessed 20 September 2020; as discussed in Cooke (n 367).

[369] Anna Knack and Nandita Balakrishnan, 'The State of AI for Strategic Warning' (*Centre for Emerging Technology and Security*, 19 November 2024) <https://cetas.turing.ac.uk/publications/state-ai-strategic-warning> accessed 20 November 2024.

[370] For an insightful review and framework, see Anne Dulka, 'The Use of Artificial Intelligence in International Human Rights Law' (2023) 26 Stanford Technology Law Review 316.

a set of communities referred to as the 'PeaceTech', 'peace innovation', or 'digital peacebuilding' communities.[371]

Of course, the use of AI in these domains is not unprecedented, but rather an extension of long-standing trends in technology-enabled monitoring. As noted by Livingston and Risse, the emergence and ubiquity of twenty-first-century digital technologies, including mobile phones, commercial high-resolution imaging satellites, and social media, has already begun to enable near-constant surveillance not just by states or corporations, but also by non-state actors such as human rights observers, journalists, and (citizen) investigation networks such as Bellingcat or the Syrian Archive.[372]

Even before the emergence of AI technologies, these actors were already able to leverage new pools of evidence and data through the use of these digital tools. Open-source intelligence (OSINT), based on information from publicly available sources, has been estimated to constitute 80–90 per cent of all intelligence activities carried out by Western law enforcement and intelligence services.[373] It should therefore be unsurprising that open-source technologies have begun to play a key role in many national and international investigations conducted by both states and non-state actors, including the monitoring of war crimes, (wartime) environmental damage,[374] and human rights violations,[375] among others.

Within these open-source investigations, new information technologies have extended the reach of journalists, NGOs, and other actors, allowing them to track, monitor, analyse, and document such violations—and publicize them to a global audience, or to key international courts—at a significantly larger scale and pace.[376] In at least one case, this has led to an indictment under international criminal law: in 2017, digital sleuths identified Libyan execution sites by triangulating geographical features found in propaganda videos that had been posted to social

[371] Michele Giovanardi, 'AI for Peace: Mitigating the Risks and Enhancing Opportunities' (2024) 6 Data & Policy e41.

[372] Livingston and Risse (n 14) 143. Steven Livingston and Sushma Raman, 'Human Rights Documentation in Limited Access Areas: The Use of Technology in War Crimes and Human Rights Abuse Investigations' (Carr Center for Human Rights Policy 2018) <https://carrcenter.hks.harvard.edu/files/cchr/files/ccdp_2018_003_humanrightsdocumentation.pdf> accessed 26 August 2020. On the 'multi-use' of remote sensing satellites, see also Nathan Edward Clark, 'Blurred Lines: Multi-Use Dynamics for Satellite Remote Sensing' (2019) 10 Journal of International Humanitarian Legal Studies 171.

[373] Riccardo Ghioni, Mariarosaria Taddeo, and Luciano Floridi, 'Open Source Intelligence and AI: A Systematic Review of the GELSI Literature' [2023] AI & Society 1.

[374] Wim Zwijnenburg and Ollie Ballinger, 'Leveraging Emerging Technologies to Enable Environmental Monitoring and Accountability in Conflict Zones' (2023) 105 International Review of the Red Cross 1497.

[375] Ella McPherson, Isabel Guenette Thornton, and Matt Mahmoudi, 'Open Source Investigations and the Technology-Driven Knowledge Controversy in Human Rights Fact-Finding' in A Koenig, S Duberley, and D Murray (eds), *Digital Witness: Using Open Source Information for Human Rights Investigation, Documentation and Accountability* (Oxford University Press 2019).

[376] Henrietta Wilson, Olamide Samuel, and Dan Plesch (eds), *Open Source Investigations in the Age of Google*, vol 4 (World Scientific 2024) <https://www.worldscientific.com/worldscibooks/10.1142/q0414> accessed 11 June 2024.

media, leading to an ICC warrant for the arrest of Mahmoud Mustafa Busayf Al-Werfalli, a Libyan warlord.[377]

In other domains, these tools provide greater transparency to the public: the Federation of American Scientists' Nuclear Information Project has drawn together information from a range of open sources—ranging from declassified government documents to independent expert and media sources to surveillance tools such as commercial satellite imagery—in order to provide estimates of global nuclear weapon stockpiles, in order to stabilize insecurities and reduce their risks.[378] While in both those cases such open-source analysis was done by humans, it involves a range of tasks that could be automated or enhanced by AI tools, in order to speed up intelligence collection and analysis.[379]

Indeed, in many other cases, AI systems have already seen direct use in supporting the monitoring of international humanitarian or human rights law. One 2020 experiment involved the development and testing of a machine learning algorithm trained on synthetic data that was used to trawl through footage of airstrikes in order to help investigators identify UK-manufactured cluster munitions that are illegally used in global conflicts. In these tests the system sped up analysis 100-fold, while reducing the risk of trauma for investigators.[380] In another 2020 project run by Amnesty International and the Citizen Evidence Lab, researchers deployed machine learning to support the large-scale analysis of satellite data in order to detect the destruction of human settlements in Sudan's Darfur region.[381] This has led to increasing proposals to use AI systems to aid the analysis of actors' compliance with international humanitarian law in the Russia–Ukraine war.[382]

[377] Boutin (n 8).

[378] Hans M Kristensen and Matt Korda, 'Monitoring Nuclear Weapons Developments with Open Source Intelligence' in Henrietta Wilson, Olamide Samuel, and Dan Plesch (eds), *Open Source Investigations in the Age of Google* (n 376).

[379] Ghioni, Taddeo, and Floridi (n 373). See also Jamie Withorne, 'Assessing the Relationship between Machine Learning and Open Source Research in International Security' in Henrietta Wilson, Olamide Samuel and Dan Plesch (eds), *Open Source Investigations in the Age of Google* (n 376).

[380] Nesta, 'Documenting Mass Human Rights Violations through Collective Intelligence' (*nesta*, 2020) <https://www.nesta.org.uk/feature/collective-intelligence-grants/documenting-mass-human-rights-violations-through-collective-intelligence/> accessed 29 June 2020; Karen Hao, 'Human Rights Activists Want to Use AI to Help Prove War Crimes in Court' [2020] *MIT Technology Review* <https://www.technologyreview.com/2020/06/25/1004466/ai-could-help-human-rights-activists-prove-war-crimes/> accessed 29 June 2020.

[381] Milena Marin, Freddie Kalaitzis, and Buffy Price, 'Using Artificial Intelligence to Scale up Human Rights Research: A Case Study on Darfur' (*Amnesty International & Citizen Evidence Lab*, 6 July 2020) <https://citizenevidence.org/2020/07/06/using-artificial-intelligence-to-scale-up-human-rights-research-a-case-study-on-darfur/> accessed 26 August 2020; Julien Cornebise and others, 'Witnessing Atrocities: Quantifying Villages Destruction in Darfur with Crowdsourcing and Transfer Learning' (2018) <https://aiforsocialgood.github.io/2018/pdfs/track1/80_aisg_neurips2018.pdf> accessed 26 August 2020. Notably, they did not publicly share the source code of this project, to avoid it being used to target villages.

[382] Tetyana (Tanya) Krupiy, 'What Role Artificial Intelligence Could Play in Evaluating the Compliance of Military Operations with International Humanitarian Law: The Case Study of the Conduct of Hostilities in Ukraine' (*EJIL: Talk!*, 23 February 2024) <https://www.ejiltalk.org/what-role-artificial-intelligence-could-play-in-evaluating-the-compliance-of-military-operati

Just as AI could provide improved leverage to existing monitoring technologies (such as satellites) in the field of arms control and nonproliferation, these systems could also enhance the monitoring of crimes during conflict. For instance, AI techniques such as 'super-resolution' techniques have been used to improve the availability, affordability, and actionability of high-resolution satellite data, by drastically improving the visual quality—and the potential probative value—of satellite imagery.[383] Such techniques can scrub out visual obstacles such as partial cloud cover, or they can make previously blurry or indistinct features of military installations or mass displacements far more visible and intelligible.[384]

Likewise, there are a wide range of use cases in the field of international human rights law. Anne Dulka has reviewed a range of additional positive applications of AI in support of human rights, including applications in measuring the destruction of villages in Darfur, forecasting international rates of displacement, tracking death penalty cases from media reports or rates of deforestation, using thermal data to monitor ethnic violence in Myanmar, and tracking online abuse against women on platforms such as Twitter.[385] In addition, during the early months of the Israel–Hamas war, the UN hired the AI company CulturePulse to create virtual simulations and predictions of ways in which the conflict might draw on.[386]

There are as such various other ways in which machine learning tools could contribute to the detection or investigation of various violations under international law,[387] including in areas where enforcement has often been difficult. For instance, take the investigation of maritime human rights abuses: this significant yet often invisible source of harm has long been impeded by practical challenges over physical inaccessibility and the complexity of the legal environment. In response, human rights investigations have been aided by a series of technology-based solutions that leverage remote sensing to track vessels over time, as well as the use of witness data or social media data in order to connect remote investigators with affected individuals—providing data sets that can be used for applications ranging from automated assessments of vessel or worker behaviours to risk scoring.[388] These use

ons-with-international-humanitarian-law-the-case-study-of-the-conduct-of-hostilities-in-ukraine/> accessed 23 February 2024.

383 Faliq (n 341).
384 ibid.
385 Dulka (n 370) 329–341. She also discusses non-monitoring use cases, including the use of AI as a tool for expanding language access, as well as for mitigating the trauma exposure consequences of human rights workers: ibid 341–343.
386 David Gilbert, 'The UN Hired an AI Company to Untangle the Israeli–Palestinian Crisis' [2023] *Wired* <https://www.wired.com/story/culturepulse-ai-israeli-palestinian-crisis/> accessed 8 December 2023.
387 Maas, 'International Law Does Not Compute' (n 1) 44–45 (reviewing several use cases of AI tools in predicting the activities of poachers, in the 'Sentry' system providing civilians in the Syrian conflict through advance warning of incoming airstrikes, and in DNA sequencing for use in forensic investigations of war crimes).
388 Jamie Hancock and others, 'Trouble at Sea: Data and Digital Technology Challenges for Maritime Human Rights Concerns', *Proceedings of the 2024 ACM Conference on Fairness, Accountability, and*

cases have attracted attention not just from NGOs but also from government authorities, with the EU funding a range of programmes aimed at using AI tools to improve maritime surveillance and counter migrant smuggling.[389]

Over time, the use of LLMs to facilitate the interpretation of satellite data may feed into a growing number of publicly available tools that could result in a 'queryable earth',[390] significantly changing both how satellite imagery is used within global governance and who uses it.[391]

All this does not mean that the integration of these AI models overcomes all the issues of digital evidence and open-source intelligence-gathering, especially in judicial contexts. Indeed, it may exacerbate some long-established challenges, such as those around verifying the authenticity of open-source audiovisual media presented to a court.[392] In other use cases, such as AI-enhanced satellite imagery, their use in the context of international criminal proceedings may throw up new legal and evidentiary questions, especially given known or potential biases in the data sets used to train such super-resolution generative models.[393] Accordingly, AI will strengthen and accelerate the growing digitization of humanitarian practices, in ways that will significantly impact how international security and peace and conflict challenges, stakeholders, or emergencies are framed, understood, and governed.[394]

5.6.2.4 The role of AI in monitoring international environmental law

Moreover, in other domains, AI tools can help global governance by supporting the monitoring not just of (state) compliance with a treaty, but also of significant developments in the complex domain of concern. For instance, in the field of global environmental governance, international organizations such as the UN Environment Programme have increasingly engaged in partnerships with

Transparency (Association for Computing Machinery 2024) 990–991 <https://dl.acm.org/doi/10.1145/3630106.3658950> accessed 13 June 2024.

389 European Commission, 'EU-Funded Projects Contribute to Countering Migrant Smuggling with AI' (*European Commission—Directorate-General for Migration and Home Affairs*, 18 December 2024) <https://home-affairs.ec.europa.eu/news/eu-funded-projects-contribute-countering-migrant-smuggling-ai-2024-12-18_en> accessed 18 February 2025.

390 Kevin Weil, 'Queryable Earth: Combining Satellite Imagery and next-Gen AI' (*Planet*, 12 April 2023) <https://www.planet.com/pulse/queryable-earth-combining-satellite-imagery-and-next-gen-ai/> accessed 3 October 2024.

391 Lars Erik Schönander, 'The Open Sky: How Revolutions in Space, Imaging, and AI Could Open up Satellite Surveillance to the Masses' (*The New Atlantis*, Fall 2023) <https://www.thenewatlantis.com/publications/the-open-sky> accessed 30 September 2024.

392 Yvonne McDermott, Stephan Sharp Queener, and Basile Simon, 'Old Doubts, New Doubts: Evaluating Digital Open Source Imagery in the Courtroom' (*Opinio Juris*, 26 June 2024) <https://opiniojuris.org/2024/06/26/old-doubts-new-doubts-evaluating-digital-open-source-imagery-in-the-courtroom/> accessed 29 July 2024.

393 Faliq (n 341).

394 Fleur Johns, *#Help: Digital Humanitarianism and the Remaking of International Order* (Oxford University Press 2023).

technology companies such as Google and Microsoft, to procure geospatial data analytics, mapping, visualization, and cloud computing capabilities, in a trend towards what has been described as 'algorithmic environmentality'.[395]

As such, AI has also begun to see use in monitoring of marine crimes and criminal vessels: in 2021, the startup Nautical Crime Investigation Services began to develop AI systems aimed at tackling the long-intractable problem and environmental crime of illegal fishing: utilizing ADA, an AI-powered database that tracks vessel movements in real time, along with GRACE, an AI-based risk assessment tool, the startup began to offer real-time information on the likelihood of particular ships committing environmental crimes. In collaboration with the non-profit Global Fishing Watch, this has led to the development of an AI system that identifies vessel types and fishing activity patterns, and predicts whether it is actually fishing—revealing that half of the global ocean is actively (and often covertly) fished.[396] Moreover, beyond merely supporting passive analysis, the development of maritime autonomous vehicles (MAVs) may also aid in the enforcement of domains such as international fisheries law, by not only providing better information on the status of fish stocks but also seeing direct use in support of maritime law enforcement operations against illegal and unreported fishing.[397]

5.6.2.5 AI automation of monitoring: the challenges and road ahead

Given these diverse uses in supporting the monitoring of various areas of international law, it is clear that even in this more 'modest' scenario of governance automation, there may be many roles for both conventional machine learning approaches and advanced, general-purpose AI systems to strengthen the monitoring and enforcement of international law. This could aid the efficacy and legitimacy of these existing regimes, and moreover might, indirectly, help facilitate the negotiation of future agreements that are sensitively dependent on such monitoring abilities.[398] Moreover, AI technologies can also become integrated in the

[395] Roxana Vatanparast, 'Algorithmic Environmentality: Data Infrastructures in Global Environmental Governance' in Fleur Johns, Gavin Sullivan, and Dimitri Van Den Meerssche (eds), *Global Governance by Data: Infrastructures of Algorithmic Rule* (Cambridge University Press 2024).

[396] Karen Bakker, 'The Algorithmic Ocean: How AI Is Revolutionizing Marine Conservation' (*The MIT Press Reader*, 11 April 2024) <https://thereader.mitpress.mit.edu/the-algorithmic-ocean-how-ai-is-revolutionizing-marine-conservation/> accessed 19 April 2024.

[397] Natalie Klein, 'The Use of Maritime Autonomous Vehicles in Fisheries Law Enforcement', *Maritime Autonomous Vehicles and International Law* (Routledge 2024).

[398] Mary L Cummings and others, *Artificial Intelligence and International Affairs: Disruption Anticipated* (Chatham House 2018) 3 <https://www.chathamhouse.org/sites/default/files/publications/research/2018-06-14-artificial-intelligence-international-affairs-cummings-roff-cukier-parakilas-bryce.pdf> accessed 25 June 2018 ('Monitoring the outputs of sensors set up to verify compliance with, for instance, a nuclear, chemical or biological arms control treaty might well be a deadening job for human analysts—albeit one that would require significant specialist training and experience. By contrast, a machine learning system set up to do the same would never tire or grow bored of its task. And while it might (especially in the process of learning) flag a large number of 'false positives', by assigning human specialists to oversee and correct it the system's accuracy would quickly increase').

governance of AI itself—in so doing, proving at least part of the solution to their own problem.[399]

At the same time, there will be a range of challenges to overcome in implementing these tools in an effective and accountable manner.[400] For instance, the discussed usage of AI and other technologies to investigate human rights violations at sea has been critiqued as a solution that often fails to prevent harm or safeguard vulnerable people, especially when such top-down approaches do not respond to the needs of individuals or communities affected.[401]

Making the most of these affordances while inhibiting the most erosive effects resulting from global imbalances in access to these monitoring technologies—and avoiding their re-use, by states, for increased governmental monitoring and repression—will demand significant new initiatives and scrutiny by treaty bodies, international organizations, and other key stakeholders.[402]

5.6.3 The Replacement of International 'Law'? AI and Shifts in Regulatory Modality

Notably, even if AI were to be used to change the '*input*' of international law (e.g. the process of treaty negotiation or adjudication), or to strengthen norm implementation or enforcement, such a trend would not change the nature of the '*output*' of international legal processes (i.e. normative rules). 'Legal automation' would no doubt alter the texture of international law irrevocably—but it would presumably remain *law*. This would therefore not change the core, normative 'regulatory modality' of international law—the instruments through which this system seeks to regulate and change state behaviour.

However, even in a more modest usage, the deployment of AI systems in the service of international law (or the measuring of global governance) could shift the preferences or values of regulators in key ways. For instance, one concern that has been raised is that international organizations' increasing interest in utilizing opaque or complex autonomous systems within their operations and decision-making processes could well erode long-established principles of global administrative law, potentially re-opening debates over the legitimacy of such organizations.[403]

[399] For an informal discussion, see: Miles Brundage, 'Reasons That AI Can Help with AI Governance' (*Miles's Substack*, 14 November 2024) < https://milesbrundage.substack.com/p/reasons-that-ai-can-help-with-ai> accessed 18 November 2024.

[400] Dulka (n 370) 358–364 (proposing a cost–benefit framework for evaluating the prospective suitability of using AI systems in various human rights monitoring and reporting contexts).

[401] Hancock and others (n 388) 994.

[402] McInerney (n 280) 338–340.

[403] Eyal Benvenisti, 'Upholding Democracy Amid the Challenges of New Technology: What Role for the Law of Global Governance?' (2018) 29 European Journal of International Law 9. See also Chinen (n 53) 174–176, 206–207.

More pervasively yet, AI could drive or facilitate a shift towards novel 'modes' of achieving societally desired regulatory outcomes, which no longer rely to the same extent on normative laws. This discussion draws on Lawrence Lessig's theory of the various 'regulatory modalities' of law, social norms, markets, and architecture.[404] For instance, in the domestic law context, Lessig famously chronicled how the architecture of computer 'code' enabled US regulators to emphasize different 'modalities' in the production and enforcement of law on cyberspace. Specifically, it allowed them to reduce their reliance on normative 'law', and instead regulate tech companies in order to embed architectural constraints on online behaviour, in areas such as zoned speech or privacy protection.[405]

Likewise, Roger Brownsword has argued that new technologies introduce a 'double disruption' to law.[406] In the first place, they affect the substance of legal rules. Second, they drive a regulatory shift, away from seeking to shape behaviour by normative codes or laws and towards the use of non-normative 'technological management'.[407] Accordingly, Brownsword has chronicled how emerging digital technologies of social control may even shift the core 'regulatory attitude' of authorities and effect a shift away from traditional 'legal coherentism' towards 'regulatory-instrumentalism' or even 'technocracy'.[408] If a similar shift occurred in the context of global governance, this could also drive value shifts. Speculatively, one can imagine that the availability of more powerful AI monitoring capabilities would reduce the need for consensus (so long as there was consensus about trusting the monitoring capabilities).

More directly, Deeks has suggested how the proliferation of certain AI technologies in state departments may also shift how states seek to resolve international disputes. It could lead to more unilateral or strategic uses of this technology. For instance, she notes how '[i]f a state could predict in advance which way a tribunal is likely to resolve a particular dispute, it would allow the state to decide whether to pursue the case or to choose an alternative, such as settling it through diplomatic negotiations or dropping the matter entirely'.[409] The use of such technologies could strengthen or accelerate the shift towards nonbinding international agreements.[410]

[404] Lawrence Lessig, 'The New Chicago School' (1998) 27 The Journal of Legal Studies 661; Lawrence Lessig, 'The Law of the Horse: What Cyberlaw Might Teach' (1999) 113 Harvard Law Review 501.

[405] Lessig (n 404) 503–505.

[406] Brownsword, 'Law and Technology: Two Modes of Disruption, Three Legal Mind-Sets, and the Big Picture of Regulatory Responsibilities' (n 190) 6–15.

[407] See also Roger Brownsword, 'In the Year 2061: From Law to Technological Management' (2015) 7 Law, Innovation and Technology 1; Brownsword, 'Technological Management and the Rule of Law' (n 7).

[408] Brownsword, 'Law Disrupted, Law Re-Imagined, Law Re-Invented' (n 190).

[409] Deeks (n 8) 628.

[410] Curtis Bradley, Jack Landman Goldsmith, and Oona A Hathaway, 'The Rise of Nonbinding International Agreements: An Empirical, Comparative, and Normative Analysis' (2023) 90 The University of Chicago Law Review 1281.

However, there are also more collaborative cases of such 'replacement'. For instance, there may be situations where algorithms can be used to speed up the negotiation process between states, either as 'negotiation support systems' that can propose potential divisions of interests or by helping to locate third-party proposals.[411] However, in such cases, rather than support traditional channels of international law (e.g. arbitration bodies or international courts) through the automation of their operations, AI tools might potentially contribute to the eventual replacement of such tools as dominant instruments of international conflict resolution or collaboration, which would mark a historical sea change in the architecture and regulatory modalities of international law.

5.7 Governance Destruction

The third and final version of AI-driven governance disruption is found in cases where AI facilitates or contributes to 'destruction' of governance architectures either in part or in full, and either locally or globally.

Such governance destruction can happen for two reasons.[412] In the first place, a certain AI issue may prove a particularly intractable problem for existing governance regimes to address, because the required 'developments' are hard for either conceptual or political reasons, with the result that these regimes experience gradual 'erosion' through their sustained inability to correct an increasingly clear mismatch between technological realities and governance instruments. In the second place, AI capabilities may (be perceived to) offer certain capabilities that shift parties' interests against continued compliance with certain arms control regimes, or even provide them with the tools to challenge multilateralism more directly, contributing to 'decline' in the underlying normative or political scaffolding.

5.7.1 Erosion: AI as Conceptually or Politically Intractable Puzzle for Development

As noted in the previous discussion of development, new AI capabilities can, on occasion, produce new affordances (i.e. new entities, relationships, or behaviours) in different domains. These can substantively disrupt governance instruments for various reasons—they can reveal clear 'gaps' or uncertainties and conceptual ambiguities in existing concepts; they can blur the scope of application of existing regimes; they can render regimes obsolete; or they can shift the problem portfolio

[411] Deeks (n 8) 633–637.
[412] The discussion in these sections expands on Maas, 'International Law Does Not Compute' (n 1) 50–56.

of a technology beyond the remit of existing regimes. When such situations occur, they create a need for legal and regulatory systems to adapt to these challenges ('development').

However, while domestic legal systems are usually able to carry out regulatory or legislative changes in response to sufficiently urgent situations of disruption, the same cannot be said of international law, where the updating of treaties can be a slow process.[413] This yields the first version of governance destruction: an 'erosion' of certain legal frameworks which seek to regulate certain AI capabilities, but find the requisite development difficult for either conceptual or political reasons. In such cases, just like for certain forms of cyberwarfare,[414] AI capabilities could create unsolvable—or, at least, unsolved—puzzles for global governance, and situations where the need for legal adaptation is clear to many if not all, but where governance regimes and institutions are nonetheless largely unable to carry through meaningfully effective changes in response.[415]

5.7.1.1 Conceptual friction

As previously noted, the emergence of a situation that requires development in the law is not in and of itself beyond the scope of a legal system.[416] In principle, legal systems of any stripe would seem perfectly capable of reconfiguration to accommodate nearly any new challenges that can be understood and meaningfully described within natural language. Hypothetically speaking, if one were given complete freedom to alter or redraw disrupted doctrinal categories, or to introduce wholly novel legal categories, standards, or 'legal fictions', there would be few or no technology-driven challenges that could not be captured in this way.[417]

In practice, however, matters are obviously more constrained and path-dependent. This is because governance development is subject to various limits of language, intelligibility, analogical reasoning, available technological metaphors, and the need to remain in accordance with 'common sense'.[418] These all limit which avenues of governance development are considered or even viable. For example,

[413] Crootof, 'Jurisprudential Space Junk' (n 17).

[414] Glennon (n 167).

[415] Maas, 'International Law Does Not Compute' (n 1) 55. (discussing conceptual overlap between situations of legal disruption through obsolescence, and legal erosion, but arguing that 'the two [. . .] can be seen as reverse faces of the same coin: for instance, it is a (perhaps the) basic assumption of any prospective legal regime that regulation is in fact politically and operationally possible. If that assumption is no longer justified for a new technology, then the resulting situation can be understood as legal obsolescence with respect to existing legal frameworks, and as legal erosion (or soft legal destruction) with respect to any future or extended legal frameworks which might have been considered to fill the place: the old is no longer fit to serve, but the new is out of reach').

[416] See also the caveats in Section 5.5.6 (on 'carrying through development').

[417] Which is not the same as saying that they would consequently be efficiently addressed or mitigated; but simply that they would no longer blur the existing law.

[418] Indeed, the need to ultimately ground all legal analyses in understandable 'folk understandings' of certain phenomena or criteria (such as criminal intent) may be a categorical challenge for legal scholarship. See for instance Schlag (n 207).

while Crootof has argued that treaty 'reinterpretation' is the most common strategy used in order to fold new weapons technologies into an existing governance regime,[419] she also grants that there are situations where an attempted reinterpretation of an existing technology-specific treaty in order to force a fit with a new technology simply can no longer pass the 'laugh test'.[420] In such cases, attempts to capture patently (or at least apparently) revolutionary technologies under age-old governance instruments or doctrines may exceed all bounds of credibility, threatening the credibility of those governance initiatives, as well as, by extension, the more general legitimacy of the governance system that produced or allowed it (as any critic can add an anecdote to a list of 'absurdities' produced by that extant system). In such cases, conceptual or analogical friction means that 'the law runs out', and new treaties or law might be needed to carry out development.[421]

As such, even when domestic legal systems may generally be able to develop new legislation in response to such systems, at the international level this process can become particularly thorny.

5.7.1.2 Political knots

In addition to these conceptual bounds, certain technologies can prove recalcitrant to governance development for practical or political reasons. For instance, they might create a range of capabilities that empower some stakeholders much more than others, creating unequal stakes.[422] Alternatively, their future trajectory and implications might be very unclear, inhibiting effective regulatory action at an early stage, until the technology has already become firmly embedded at a later stage and many parties have established stakes, and it is hard to dislodge.[423] The technology might map onto open political fault lines or pervasive ethical disagreements, or have architectural features that mean it is simply too easily disseminated to be constrained by conventional export control mechanisms.[424]

For instance, take cyber-weapons: in spite of calls for global regulation of cyberwar,[425] it has been argued that traditional arms control regimes are unlikely to be successfully transferred to the realm of cyberspace, because of the differences in how the 'weapons' in question are used (specifically the difficulty of attribution)

419 Crootof, 'Regulating New Weapons Technology' (n 21) 13–14.

420 ibid 15.

421 ibid 18. On the downside risks of relying on 'reinterpretation', even when it appears conceptually possible, given the risks of unreflexive technology analogies, see also the previous discussion in 5.5.6.5.

422 Picker (n 20) 191–194 (on 'unevenly shared technology').

423 The so-called Collingridge Dilemma: David Collingridge, *The Social Control of Technology* (Palgrave Macmillan 1981).

424 Amy J Nelson, 'Innovation Acceleration, Digitization, and the Arms Control Imperative' (Social Science Research Network 2019) SSRN Scholarly Paper ID 3382956 <https://papers.ssrn.com/abstract=3382956> accessed 29 May 2020.

425 Mette Eilstrup-Sangiovanni, 'Why the World Needs an International Cyberwar Convention' (2018) 31 Philosophy & Technology 379.

and the relative difficulty of monitoring compliance.[426] In such cases, the reason why there are no global cyberwarfare conventions is not that no problem is perceived to exist,[427] nor that the existing governance regimes are perceived to be entirely adequate and up to the task. Instead, it combines various conceptual difficulties of classification with significant underlying political gridlock,[428] which prevent the global resolution of this visible, technology-precipitated problem.[429]

More generally, it has been argued that along with diverse historical, political, and social factors, a technology's architectural characteristics can render some (weapons) technologies more 'regulation-resistant' than others.[430] For instance, Sean Watts and Rebecca Crootof have articulated a set of criteria which influence whether an outright global ban on a technology is likely to be successful.[431]

As a result, attempts to carry out needed 'development' of existing multilateral treaties in order to address the disruptive challenge of a new technology regularly face the fraught political challenge of securing the agreement of all existing treaty partners, or else risk a fragmentation of the treaty that would endanger the authority, coherence, clarity, or appeal of the entire regime.[432] While in some cases states have shown remarkable pragmatism in reconciling treaties,[433] in general there may be many political challenges to carrying out legal development in response to disruptive technological change, whether the attempted modification is sought through treaty supersession, amendment, additional protocols, or adaptive interpretations.[434]

[426] Erica D Borghard and Shawn W Lonergan, 'Why Are There No Cyber Arms Control Agreements?' (*Council on Foreign Relations*, 16 January 2018) <https://www.cfr.org/blog/why-are-there-no-cyber-arms-control-agreements> accessed 22 January 2018; Glennon (n 167). Although for a proposed approach see also Erin D Dumbacher, 'Limiting Cyberwarfare: Applying Arms-Control Models to an Emerging Technology' (2018) 25 The Nonproliferation Review 203.

[427] Although some have argued that the risk of cyberwar has been exaggerated. Thomas Rid, *Cyber War Will Not Take Place* (1st edn, Oxford University Press 2013). See also the discussion in Chapter 4.

[428] On the topic of global governance 'gridlock' generally, see also Thomas Hale and David Held, *Beyond Gridlock* (Polity Press 2017). On how scientific projects might bypass or dissolve such situations, see Mark Robinson, 'The CERN Community; A Mechanism for Effective Global Collaboration?' [2018] Global Policy <https://onlinelibrary.wiley.com/doi/abs/10.1111/1758-5899.12608> accessed 30 November 2018.

[429] For instance, cyberwarfare has only very limited governance at the international level. The Tallinn Manual on the International Law Applicable to Cyberwarfare, while a significant development, only provides non-binding advice on the application of international law in cyberspace, and has only been endorsed by NATO member states. *Tallinn Manual 2.0 on the International Law Applicable to Cyber Operations* (2nd edn, Cambridge University Press 2017). Conversely, the Shanghai Cooperation Organisation's 'Information Security Agreement' only has six member states, and failed to get approval at the UN General Assembly.

[430] Sean Watts, 'Regulation-Tolerant Weapons, Regulation-Resistant Weapons and the Law of War' (2015) 91 International Law Studies 83.

[431] Crootof, 'Jurisprudential Space Junk' (n 17) 114–115. A similar discussion of criteria that facilitate weapons bans, examined in the context of a prospective ban on military AI, is offered by Paul Scharre, *Army of None: Autonomous Weapons and the Future of War* (1st edn, W W Norton & Company 2018) ch 13.

[432] Brian Israel, 'Treaty Stasis' (2014) 108 AJIL Unbound 63; as discussed in Crootof, 'Jurisprudential Space Junk' (n 17) 110–111.

[433] Smith (n 88).

[434] Crootof, 'Jurisprudential Space Junk' (n 17) 110–111.

This is the case even when the existing regime has mechanisms to enable the modernization in the face of technological change. For instance, technological progress has often challenged arms exports control regimes, even as those have provisions to enable modernization. As argued by Nelson, there are certain patterns in regime modernization efforts.[435] For instance, she notes that complementing agreements such as export guidelines or the interpretation and application of international law can help modernize provisions or control lists.

To be sure, there are examples of non-proliferation and export control regime modernization. For instance, in the nuclear domain, the 1968 Nuclear Non-Proliferation Treaty (NPT) was revised or supplemented with various additional regimes or institutions, including (1971) the Zangger Committee, formed to implement the NPT requirement, in Article III, that member states adopt export controls; (1975) the Nuclear Suppliers Group, established in the wake of India's first nuclear explosion in order to prevent dual-use technology from being used in a nuclear weapons programme; (1991) a Nuclear Suppliers Group (NSG) Control List Update, in response to Iraq's nuclear weapons programme; and (1997) the establishment of a broader safeguards agreement under the IAEA Additional Protocol.[436]

Likewise, in the conventional weapons domain, there have been significant efforts to modernize regimes such as the Wassenaar Arrangement[437] or the Missile Technology Control Regime (MTCR),[438] along with attempts to increase cross-regime harmonization.[439] However, often such updates are only carried out successfully in response to a vivid crisis,[440] and updating 'control lists' to keep pace with emerging technologies otherwise remains a cumbersome process. In particular, such processes are frequently held back by industry objections over the stifling of innovation, as well as the general problems around understanding or predicting the indirect, second- or third-order effects of certain innovations.[441]

435 Amy J Nelson, 'The Impact of Emerging Technologies on Arms Control Regimes' (ISODARCO, 2018); Nelson, 'Innovation Acceleration, Digitization, and the Arms Control Imperative' (n 424).

436 Nelson, 'Innovation Acceleration, Digitization, and the Arms Control Imperative' (n 424) 10–11.

437 Most prominently, the regime saw a 2013 attempt to broaden the scope of controlled items to 'intrusion software'; however, overly broad language inadvertently caught dual-use software used by industry to improve cybersecurity, leading the US to call for a do-over in 2015: ibid 12.

438 Including a 1992 modernization effort to add unmanned aerial vehicles (UAVs) with a minimum payload and range threshold that would qualify them as delivery systems for nuclear weapons; and a 2016 effort to include missile mission software: ibid 13–14. However, it should be noted that in spring 2020, the US sought to move armed drones off the MTCR control lists. Paul K Kerr, 'U.S.-Proposed Missile Technology Control Regime Changes' (Congressional Research Service 2022) <https://fas.org/sgp/crs/nuke/IF11069.pdf> accessed 18 March 2025.

439 For instance, some UAVs are on the MTCR control lists, and UAV-related goods can be found on both the Wassenaar Arrangement's Dual-Use List and Munitions List. Nonetheless, this has not been very effective at halting the diffusion of lethal UAVs. Nelson, 'Innovation Acceleration, Digitization, and the Arms Control Imperative' (n 424) 14.

440 Lisa Langdon Koch, 'The NPT at 50 and the NSG at 43: How the Global Control of Nuclear Exports Has Slowed Proliferation' (2018) 4 International History and Politics Newsletter 8.

441 Nelson, 'The Impact of Emerging Technologies on Arms Control Regimes' (n 435).

Finally, more general trends in digitization have begun to challenge export control regimes across the board, intersecting at certain key operating assumptions with regard to the materiality of the technologies under question.[442]

In the scenario of legal erosion, the regulatory texture of certain AI applications—including their architectural, operational, strategic, and political features, along with their problem logic—can render them a particularly thorny issue for parties to reach meaningful agreement on. As such, even though international law would in principle be capable of the developments necessary to fix the legal gaps or ambiguities created by some AI capabilities, in practice many of these cases may prove resistant to the sources and tools available to it. As discussed in Chapter 3, customary international law is generally slow and requires unambiguous evidence of state practice, which is not easy to gain for clandestine capabilities such as cyberwarfare AIs, or which could be hindered by definitional problems around 'AI' or various applications.

For their part, new treaties often require that all parties have roughly even stakes in the technology, clear expectations of benefit for abiding by the treaty, the ability to jointly agree on clear definitions, and the ability to effectively verify compliance. All of these are difficult in the context of AI development. The highly unequal distribution of leading technological capabilities among a narrow set of powerful states, or the need to rely on the self-interested private sector for scarce technical expertise, as well as uncertainty over the technology's long-term impacts, are all features that have historically inhibited swift international consensus or regulation.[443] They are likely to do so again for AI, especially given the relative prominence of private actors in this space. Finally, international courts are often slow,[444] react to specific cases in front of them, are non-expert on technologies, often have fractured jurisdiction, and at any rate have experienced at least some measure of political backlash in recent years.[445]

That is not to say that international regimes will not be able to carry out some developments to resolve many situations of uncertainty,[446] but it may slow or

[442] ibid; Nelson, 'Innovation Acceleration, Digitization, and the Arms Control Imperative' (n 424). But see also International Panel on the Regulation of Autonomous Weapons (iPRAW), 'LAWS and Export Control Regimes: Fit for Purpose?' (April 2020) <https://www.ipraw.org/working-paper-diffusion-export-control/> accessed 25 September 2020.

[443] Picker (n 20) 191–194.

[444] For example, the ICJ only provided a (non-binding) Advisory Opinion on the Legality of the Threat or Use of Nuclear Weapons after the end of the Cold War, in 1996—more than half a century after the technology's creation. See ICJ, *Legality of the Threat or Use of Nuclear Weapons* (Advisory Opinion) [1996] ICJ Rep 226, ICGJ 205.

[445] See Mikael Rask Madsen, Pola Cebulak, and Micha Wiebusch, 'Backlash against International Courts: Explaining the Forms and Patterns of Resistance to International Courts' (2018) 14 International Journal of Law in Context 197.

[446] For reviews of recent activities, see Kunz and Ó hÉigeartaigh (n 59); Eugenio V Garcia, 'Multilateralism and Artificial Intelligence: What Role for the United Nations?' in Maurizio Tinnirello (ed), *The Global Politics of Artificial Intelligence* (CRC Press 2020); Philippe Lorenz, 'AI Governance through Political Fora and Standards Developing Organizations' (Interface 2020) <https://www.interf

inhibit progress in key and high-profile cases. While such legal erosion may therefore not be a categorical threat to international law, it may leave semi-permanent 'wounds' in the fabric of global governance. This would have broader implications, however. As noted by Crootof, '[j]urisprudential space junk is not just outdated law that makes it difficult to identify the most relevant regulations. Seemingly ineffectual law on the books creates the perception that international rules have little power, thereby weakening the entire international legal system'.[447] Likewise, the dysfunction, contestation, or inefficacy of global governance instruments in the face of certain clear and present global challenges of AI could well challenge the perceived efficacy and legitimacy of much broader swathes of global governance in the eyes of states, non-state actors, or the global public.

5.7.2 Decline: AI as Persistent Threat to Governance Architectures

Finally, and more speculatively, there is a hard version of the 'governance destruction' argument which, while rarer, would be more foundationally damaging to international law. Such governance decline involves new AI capabilities that could threaten the political scaffolding of either specific AI regimes, or more broadly. It could do so by increasing the spoils of non-compliance, by creating active avenues for resistance, evasion or contestation, or by shifting values.

5.7.2.1 Increasing the spoils of noncompliance: decay in political regime foundations

Regime scholars have long recognized the ways in which the prevailing state of technology acts as one structural factor that shapes state interests, and determines the incentives they have to pursue or participate in the establishment of international regimes.[448] However, that argument may cut both ways, if shifts in technologies could in time also erode the structural conditions or grounds for particular regimes. That is not to say that these would immediately trigger the decline of a regime. However, it could result in significant new pressure on specific regimes, as technological innovation in AI shifts the incentives of states in various ways that would put sudden or considerable pressure on extant agreements.[449] For instance, AI capability advancement could increase the perceived 'spoils' of non-compliance with certain regimes (most prominently restrictive bans), in various ways.

ace-eu.org/archive/publications/ai-governance-through-political-fora-and-standards-developing-organizations> accessed on 18 March 2025.

[447] Crootof, 'Jurisprudential Space Junk' (n 17) 128.
[448] Arthur A Stein, 'Coordination and Collaboration: Regimes in an Anarchic World' (1982) 36 International Organization 299, 319–320.
[449] Maas, 'Innovation-Proof Governance for Military AI?' (n 23) 141–142.

In the first place, innovation might (radically) increase the potential absolute or relative *gains* which a party (perceives it) foregoes by continuing full compliance with a restrictive regime or ban, whether on the technology itself or in other domains. This might occur in many contexts, but pressures might be particularly steep in certain competitive or military domains, where, as Payne has argued, 'marginal quality might prove totally decisive' because 'other things being equal, we can expect higher-quality AI to comprehensively defeat inferior rivals'.[450] Such performance gains are never easy to anticipate but, once conceivable or apparently in reach, would steeply increase the perceived (counterfactual) strategic costs states consider they incur by continued compliance with bans or regimes which they acceded to when the (plausible) advantages appeared more modest.[451]

In the second place, technological change could reduce the barriers to access and proliferation (creating an opportunity for non-compliance). As noted by Nelson, advances in digitization and additive manufacturing ('3D printing') are already leading to 'regime perforation' of various export control regimes.[452] In the case of AI, there are a wide range of developments in synthetic data, inference scaling, and new learning approaches, which could also steadily reduce the barriers to accessing these capabilities.[453] In some cases, this by itself can lead to doctrinal problems. For instance, while the 1967 UN Outer Space Treaty is widely considered as successful,[454] its drafters had not anticipated that the costs of the technology would fall so much, nor that non-state actors such as SpaceX and BlueOrigin would ever accrue the resources to undertake space exploration.[455] Moreover, AI capabilities could also contribute to decline of regimes in other technological domains, if they lower the costs of proliferation. For instance, the nuclear nonproliferation regime has historically depended significantly on the difficulty and costs of nuclear

[450] Kenneth Payne, 'Artificial Intelligence: A Revolution in Strategic Affairs?' (2018) 60 Survival 7, 24.

[451] An extreme version of this scenario, exploring the strategic incentives offered by hypothetical advanced AI capabilities (although concluding that this is likely some distance away) is discussed in John-Clark Levin and Matthijs M Maas, 'Roadmap to a Roadmap: How Could We Tell When AGI Is a "Manhattan Project" Away?' (2020) 1st International Workshop on Evaluating Progress in Artificial Intelligence—EPAI 2020 <https://arxiv.org/abs/2008.04701> accessed 11 May 2025.

[452] Nelson, 'Innovation Acceleration, Digitization, and the Arms Control Imperative' (n 424).

[453] As discussed in Chapter 1.

[454] Treaty on Principles Governing the Activities of States in the Exploration and Use of Outer Space, including the Moon and Other Celestial Bodies (opened for signature 27 January 1967, entered into force 10 October 1967) 610 UNTS 205 (Outer Space Treaty). See the discussion of the lessons for AI governance in Turner (n 69) 244–247.

[455] See Verity Harding, 'Lessons from History: What Can Past Technological Breakthroughs Teach the AI Community Today' (2020) <https://www.bennettinstitute.cam.ac.uk/blog/lessons-history-what-can-past-technological-breakt/> accessed 17 August 2020. More specifically, 'mega-constellation' programmes such as SpaceX's Starlink Project have stressed traditional space law frameworks, by creating new situations wherein corporate actors are achieving a level of 'corporate sovereignty' in space through their de facto control of a sizeable portion of all orbital traffic, among others resulting in disruption of established ITU procedures to allocate geostationary orbit slots. See Aaditya Vikram Sharma, 'Starlink and International Law: The Challenge of Corporate Sovereignty in Outer Space' (*EJIL: Talk!*, 17 March 2025) <https://www.ejiltalk.org/starlink-and-international-law-the-challenge-of-corporate-sovereignty-in-outer-space/> accessed 19 March 2025.

material acquisition or production—facilitating the remarkable success of supply-side constraints.[456]

Third, innovation in AI could also reduce the anticipated public or political *costs* of non-compliance, either by making violations less likely to be detected or proven or by making the public reputational repercussions of deploying certain (e.g. 'non-kinetic') AI capabilities relatively low even if they are nominally in violation of treaties.[457] However, as AI technologies are beginning to see increasing use in processes of nuclear material production, to optimize the performance and reduce costs of such techniques, this may contribute to lowering the thresholds to the illicit development of nuclear weapons.[458]

Finally, AI's potential as a 'replacement' tool could offer specific capabilities that result in broader legal *decline*. This could be because AI systems might offer strategic capabilities which shift interests; they chip away at the rationales for certain powerful states to engage fully in, or comply with, international law regimes. While they would be unlikely to completely erode interest, AI applications in areas such as surveillance could arguably reduce states' (perceived) dependence on multilateral security regimes to ensure their security from terrorist threats. Such capabilities could increase actors' willingness to 'defect', and erode their willingness to support multilateralism.

5.7.2.2 AI as anti-law weapon, enabling contestation

In extreme cases, AI systems could enable new strategies by which various actors could directly challenge the legitimacy of international law or its component regimes. For instance, Deeks notes how, among various unilateral uses of machine learning, there might be the use of AI tools to measure or even sway local public perceptions against or in favour of certain solutions to a conflict.[459] Significantly, such tools can damage the standing of international agreements merely by existing, simply if there is a suspicion about their involvement in certain negotiations, to sway certain diplomatic processes. After all, as Deeks notes, the mere proliferation (if not the use) of simple algorithms might 'confound dispute resolution and the conclusion of treaties, perhaps because non-technologically advanced states may reject any process that appears to involve the use of text-as-data tools'.[460] That is not to say that AI tools are the only weapon that could allow the unilateral

[456] Lisa Langdon Koch, 'Frustration and Delay: The Secondary Effects of Supply-Side Proliferation Controls' (2019) 28 Security Studies 773; Lisa Langdon Koch, 'Holding All the Cards: Nuclear Suppliers and Nuclear Reversal' (2022) 7 Journal of Global Security Studies ogab034.

[457] Maas, 'Innovation-Proof Governance for Military AI?' (n 23) 144–146.

[458] Jingjie He and Nikita Degtyarev, 'AI and Atoms: How Artificial Intelligence Is Revolutionizing Nuclear Material Production' (2023) 79 Bulletin of the Atomic Scientists 316.

[459] Deeks (n 8) 637–640. See also Katarina Kertysova, 'Artificial Intelligence and Disinformation: How AI Changes the Way Disinformation Is Produced, Disseminated, and Can Be Countered' (2018) 29 Security and Human Rights 55; John Akers and others, 'Technology-Enabled Disinformation: Summary, Lessons, and Recommendations' [2019] arXiv:1812.09383 [cs] <http://arxiv.org/abs/1812.09383> accessed 12 May 2020.

[460] Deeks (n 8) 648.

manipulation or contestation of multilateral processes; nor that they even are an unusually powerful one. However, they certainly will be able to contribute to these practices and their legally destructive trends.

5.7.2.3 AI as shifter of state values

Finally, beyond shifting the calculations of states with regard to continuing to comply with specific regimes ('increasing spoils'), or providing capabilities that allow certain states to better achieve pre-existing desires to contest global legal processes, certain AI capabilities could also *shift* the goals, values, or norms of key actors.

That is not to say that AI would be the sole source of these challenges, or that technology alone would be sufficient to shift norms. Rather, in recent years, international legal scholars have begun to note a period of tension for the global legal order. This includes cases of state backlash against international courts,[461] dismissive rhetoric from various world leaders, and (threatened or actual) withdrawals from various treaties and multilateral arrangements.[462] For instance, the first Trump administration (2017–2021) made waves through a series of announced, attempted, or realized withdrawals from various international organizations, including UNESCO,[463] the World Health Organization,[464] and the World Trade Organization, following continuing spats over that organization's Appellate Body.[465] Such actions—which were subsequently temporarily reversed during the Biden administration, but which have been swiftly reimposed during the second Trump administration[466]—along with growing violations of cornerstone international norms around the use of force by Russia and other states, have raised growing concern over the sustained health of a multilateral rules-based order, and even of international law more generally.[467]

[461] Karen J Alter, James Thuo Gathii, and Laurence R Helfer, 'Backlash Against International Courts in West, East and Southern Africa: Causes and Consequences' (2016) 27 European Journal of International Law; see also broadly Madsen, Cebulak and Wiebusch (n 445).

[462] James Crawford, 'The Current Political Discourse Concerning International Law' (2018) 81 The Modern Law Review 1.

[463] Jean Galbraith, 'United States Gives Notice of Withdrawal from UNESCO, Citing Anti-Israel Bias' (2018) 112 The American Journal of International Law 107.

[464] Michelle Nichols, 'U.S. Withdrawal from WHO over Claims of China Influence to Take Effect July 2021: U.N.' *Reuters* (8 July 2020) <https://www.reuters.com/article/us-health-coronavirus-trump-who-idUSKBN2482YZ> accessed 9 September 2020.

[465] Philip Blenkinsop, 'U.S. Trade Offensive Takes Out WTO as Global Arbiter' *Reuters* (10 December 2019) <https://www.reuters.com/article/us-trade-wto-idUSKBN1YE0YE> accessed 13 July 2020; Keith Johnson, 'U.S. Effort to Depart WTO Gathers Momentum' (*Foreign Policy*, 2020) <https://foreignpolicy.com/2020/05/27/world-trade-organization-united-states-departure-china/> accessed 13 July 2020.

[466] See for instance: The White House, 'Withdrawing The United States from the World Health Organization' (21 January 2025) <https://www.whitehouse.gov/presidential-actions/2025/01/withdrawing-the-united-states-from-the-worldhealth-organization/> accessed 18 February 2025.

[467] Monica Hakimi and Jacob Katz Cogan, 'The End of the U.S.-Backed International Order and the Future of International Law' [2025] American Journal of International Law 1; Mary Ellen O'Connell, 'What Remains of Law Against War' (2024) 113 The Georgetown Law Journal 319.

The possible intersection of these trends in the erosion of the international legal system with the simultaneous emergence and proliferation of new AI capabilities is of relevance.[468] In the first place, at a positional level, AI innovation could simply change the balance of power between actors, asymmetrically empowering those states that are already unsympathetic to international norms, enabling them to either outperform, flout, or directly challenge the international legal order.[469] For instance, some have predicted that AI surveillance capabilities and military tools could be particularly attractive for authoritarian regimes, strengthening their ability to monitor their citizens and maintain centralized control over military forces.[470] There remains considerable contestation over this prospect, however.[471] Much of these shifts may depend on how widely available such tools will be.[472] Others have suggested that AI systems can serve as a valuable tool for asymmetric information warfare against democracies,[473] deploying attacks that are disproportionately effective against the distinct informational 'attack surfaces' and threat models that democracies suffer from more so than autocracies.[474]

In the second place, AI capabilities, along with general trends in digitalization and changes in media consumption, might simply enable an increase in the ability of many smaller actors to disseminate norms, and thereby generate a much greater fragmentation or plurality of views, under which the maintenance of (any)

[468] Maas, 'Innovation-Proof Governance for Military AI?' (n 23) 147.

[469] Richard Danzig, 'An Irresistible Force Meets a Moveable Object: The Technology Tsunami and the Liberal World Order' (2017) 5 Lawfare Research Paper Series <https://assets.documentcloud.org/documents/3982439/Danzig-LRPS1.pdf> accessed 1 September 2017. See also the discussion in Maas, 'Innovation-Proof Governance for Military AI?' (n 23) 147–149.

[470] Michael C Horowitz, 'Who'll Want Artificially Intelligent Weapons? ISIS, Democracies, or Autocracies?' [2016] *Bulletin of the Atomic Scientists* <http://thebulletin.org/who%E2%80%99ll-want-artificially-intelligent-weapons-isis-democracies-or-autocracies9692> accessed 13 May 2017.

[471] Yuval Noah Harari, 'Why Technology Favors Tyranny' [2018] *The Atlantic* <https://www.theatlantic.com/magazine/archive/2018/10/yuval-noah-harari-technology-tyranny/568330/> accessed 12 September 2018. See also Foreign Affairs, 'Does Technology Favor Tyranny?' (*Foreign Affairs*, 13 February 2019) <https://www.foreignaffairs.com/ask-the-experts/2019-02-12/does-technology-favor-tyranny> accessed 11 March 2019. However, the idea of an authoritarian 'AI advantage' has also been contested. See Jaron Lanier and Glen Weyl, 'AI Is An Ideology, Not A Technology' [2020] *Wired* <https://www.wired.com/story/opinion-ai-is-an-ideology-not-a-technology/> accessed 16 March 2020. Eddie Yang and Margaret E Roberts, 'The Authoritarian Data Problem' (2023) 34 Journal of Democracy 141; Henry Farrell, Abraham Newman, and Jeremy Wallace, 'Spirals of Delusion: How AI Distorts Decision-Making and Makes Dictators More Dangerous' *Foreign Affairs* (2022) <https://www.foreignaffairs.com/world/spirals-delusion-artificial-intelligence-decision-making> accessed 5 September 2022; Eddie Yang, 'The Limits of AI for Authoritarian Control' <https://www.eddieyang.net/research/AI_dilemma.pdf> accessed 18 March 2025.

[472] However, it is likely that many such tools will proliferate relatively fast, as discussed in Chapter 1.

[473] Alina Polyakova, 'Weapons of the Weak: Russia and AI-Driven Asymmetric Warfare' (*Brookings*, 15 November 2018) <https://www.brookings.edu/research/weapons-of-the-weak-russia-and-ai-driven-asymmetric-warfare/> accessed 13 January 2019.

[474] Henry Farrell and Bruce Schneier, 'Common-Knowledge Attacks on Democracy' (Berkman Klein Center 2018) Research Publication 2018-7 <https://papers.ssrn.com/abstract=3273111> accessed 13 January 2019.

overarching global order becomes increasingly untenable.[475] Alternatively, the ongoing substantive debates over global AI governance may serve as a site of contestation for liberalism and authoritarianism; one where authoritarian systems are able to embed their assumptions and worldviews within multilateral mechanisms active on AI.[476]

In the third place, and more fundamentally, AI might have a role in shifting the goals or values of certain parties that were previously supportive of the global governance order. That is, in certain domains, AI tools might be(come) perceived (whether or not correctly) as a tempting technological substitute for achieving the interests or assurances once secured through give-and-take compromise. For instance, states may have various concrete national interests or goals (domestic security, global stability, prosperity, domestic or global legitimacy or soft power, migration management) which they have long perceived they might only or best achieve through reciprocal compliance with international norms. However, there may be certain new AI capabilities—from enhanced surveillance to new military force projection capabilities, commercial uses, computational propaganda, or the use of AI to model and 'predict' other states' military operations or negotiation strategies[477]—which such actors can perceive as shortcuts to achieving these goals unilaterally and without costly compromise. This could well shift the instrument choice of leading nations in AI development, which include powerful states on whose buy-in or at least acquiescence multilateral efforts have often been reliant.

Of course, such a gloomy scenario should be tempered. States are not the only actors on the global stage, and even among them, many states are not solely driven by interest-based considerations but also are informed by various norms to support a range of values enshrined in the global legal order. Even if one supposes that certain AI capabilities could strengthen the hand of domestic political coalitions sceptical, hostile, or indifferent to international law, this will not necessarily trigger terminal contestation or outright decline. The key consideration might be less whether such value shifts away from multilateralism might occur in a few powerful states, and rather whether such shifts might occur broadly.

For instance, Karen Alter has theorized the future of the international liberal order in the face of a sudden break in US support.[478] Drawing on John Ruggie's

[475] Which might certainly, to some, be a good thing. See, for instance: Amitav Acharya, 'The Future of Global Governance: Fragmentation May Be Inevitable and Creative Global Forum' [2016] Global Governance 453.

[476] Sabhanaz Rashid Diya, 'How Authoritarian Value Systems Undermine Global AI Governance' (Centre for International Governance Innovation 2024) <https://www.cigionline.org/publications/how-authoritarian-value-systems-undermine-global-ai-governance/> accessed 29 July 2024.

[477] Deeks, Lubell, and Murray (n 9).

[478] Karen J Alter, 'The Future of International Law' (2017) 101 iCourts Working Paper Series <https://papers.ssrn.com/abstract=3015177> accessed 11 June 2020.

argument that international regimes combine both power and social purpose,[479] she theorizes that even when a previous hegemon retrenches from the international order, momentum can keep that order in place so long as the broader social purpose remains and is shared by many others.[480] This is because international law can maintain its appeal and survive the retrenchment of individual states, so long as the broader social purpose of the international liberal order does not lose support.[481] As such, even if technocratic AI capabilities marginally erode the multilateral commitment of a few powerful states, they may ultimately do little to shift the overall trajectory of the global governance system if other states (especially those with less access to the technology) remain invested in the rule of law.

However, this presumes that other states that do not lead in AI development will retain confidence and trust in international law. Yet, as noted previously in the discussion of displacement, the (unilateral) use of AI capabilities in the processes of international law may also erode the legitimacy of the entire system in the eyes of these smaller states and parties also. After all, while the use of AI tools in the processes of global governance can have beneficial effects in speeding up the creation of international law, or strengthening its enforcement, these tools may also have considerable distributional consequences.[482] Specifically, if only a few countries have (or retain) access to a set of high-tech tools by which they might predict the rulings of arbitration bodies, identify opportunities to engineer treaty conflicts, identify patterns of state practice that favour their positions, stack treaty negotiations in their favour, or manipulate another state's media during or after negotiations, then even the mere existence of such capabilities is likely to foster a profound sense of unfairness.[483] This might both undermine the negotiation of specific treaties or agreements[484] and also more generally challenge the fiction of sovereign equality among states.

However, while all this might give reason for pause, it is not meant to be a tale of doom. Ultimately, in spite of the dramatic name, 'destruction' is not meant to imply that AI will irrevocably usher in the end of international law, let alone global governance. That might be giving the technology too much credit, certainly for the foreseeable future. Indeed, for one, many of AI's 'destructive' effects discussed

479 John Ruggie, 'International Regimes, Transactions and Change: Embedded Liberalism in the Postwar Economic Order' in Stephen Krasner (ed), *International Regimes* (Cornell University Press 1983) 198; referenced in Alter (n 478) 9.

480 Alter (n 478) 9.

481 ibid 16–17.

482 Deeks (n 8) 643–650.

483 ibid 648.

484 ibid ('Use of these tools by one or a few states, but not all states, may foster a sense of unfairness. In extreme cases, states may shy away from acceding to agreements that they believe were not reached by a fair process. Thus, a state's perception of the other side's use of these tools may affect its willingness to reach agreement in the first place, or its willingness to ratify the agreement after the fact. It is also possible that the use of machine learning tools to manipulate a state's media during negotiations might lead that state to allege that the treaty was void because the state was fraudulently induced to conclude').

here may well be tempered, countered, or offset.[485] Moreover, when compared to other ongoing global developments that are currently putting pressure on global governance, the additional contribution of AI systems to processes of destruction might be relatively modest. AI's role as an 'erosive' intractable puzzle may come to threaten the legitimacy of global governance—but perhaps not remotely as much as that architecture's legitimacy may already be threatened by its inability to effectively address, say, climate change. Finally, AI may offer a variety of actively destructive tools by which to contest international law—but these tools may derive much of their salience from the broader trend towards increasing unilateralism and populist backlash against international law.[486] The point of exploring how AI capabilities can drive processes of *destruction* is therefore not to call for international lawyers to forfeit; instead it should urge an examination of responses that can ensure resilience in this changing landscape.

5.8 Conclusion: AI and Governance Disruption

This chapter has covered the second perspective on 'change' in AI governance, by examining various changes *in* governance as a result of AI, under the rubric of 'governance disruption'. On this basis, I set out a taxonomy of types of governance disruption created by AI systems. Accordingly, this model discussed a variety of ways in which AI can drive changes that require development in the substance or norms of governance and the ways it could produce displacement in the processes of international law, from the way international law is created or enforced, to the underlying choice of normative law as regulatory tool. Finally, it enabled an exploration of the way AI capabilities might drive gradual destruction of specific regimes or even political pillars of the broader governance architecture.

To be certain, one should not overstate the ubiquity of these dynamics. No technology—not even AI—is so inimical to existing laws that it challenges, blurs, or confuses it at every point of contact. The ecology of global governance is broad and diverse, and consists of many varied institutions, instruments, and norms. Many—and likely most—applications of AI capabilities will likely be absorbed into these instruments, if not entirely smoothly, at least relatively quietly or without much 'disruptive' confusion or upset. Yet for better or for worse, the global governance landscape is one that can in some ways be defined more by its failures or public breakdowns than by its quietly functional backwaters. Moreover, more than many other technologies, AI has a breadth of applications that suggests it may serve as the trigger of relatively many simultaneous and intersecting sites of governance

[485] For instance, Deeks suggests redistributing various 'text-as-data' algorithms to many states, in order to mitigate the distributional effects of their spread: ibid 650–651.
[486] Alter (n 478).

disruption. As such, it matters to engage these phenomena, even if they are unusual in the daily state of affairs.

Accordingly, 'governance disruption' is a valuable lens to keep on hand in exploring strategies and regimes for AI governance, for several reasons: from an instrument choice or design perspective, it informs more robust debates over the comparative merits of distinct global governance instruments for AI, keeping in mind that these will have to be able to scale or adapt along with further change; moreover, in a broader regulatory perspective, it helps put focus on the ways in which AI tools may themselves change the processes as well as broader political scaffolding of global governance in coming years, in ways that can afford opportunities for governance regimes (whether for AI or in other areas) but which might also challenge or upend previous assumptions.

Having discussed two conceptual lenses, we now take a brief step away from AI technology, to engage with change in the broader sense—that is, ongoing and broader political, normative, and institutional shifts in the governance architecture, and their consequences in distinct regime complexes.

6

Regime Complexity: AI in a Changing Governance Architecture

6.1 Introduction

How will changes in the broader global governance architecture affect the prospects, trajectory, and efficacy of the AI regime complex?

So far, we have discussed two facets of change that global AI governance will have to adapt for. In Chapter 4, I discussed how the lens of sociotechnical change can help us understand how, when, and why technical change in AI capabilities translates into cross-sector sociotechnical changes; when these constitute relevant rationales for new regulation; and how these can best be approached as targets for governance. In Chapter 5, I discussed how the governance disruption concept helps us understand better how progress in AI capabilities may change the instruments of international law and global governance. That is, Chapter 5 discussed if or how changes in AI use might drive legal uncertainty (requiring the development of law in response), enable legal automation (driving potential displacement of key roles in international law to technology), or generate political shifts (threatening the potential erosion or destruction of regime foundations).

These discussions set the stage for our exploration of a third facet of change, to explore ongoing forms of political change in the broader global governance architecture and their implications for the viability or optimal design of the global AI governance architecture.[1]

In response, this chapter draws on regime theory, and in particular on the concept of a 'regime complex'.[2] While a more specific operationalization will be developed in this chapter, a working definition of this lens can be given as:

[1] Note: This chapter will focus on articulating the overall framework of regime complex theory; further application to questions in AI governance will be conducted in Chapter 7.

[2] This discussion draws in particular on the accounts in Amandine Orsini, Jean-Frédéric Morin and Oran Young, 'Regime Complexes: A Buzz, a Boom, or a Boost for Global Governance?' (2013) 19 Global Governance: A Review of Multilateralism and International Organizations 27; Benjamin Faude and Thomas Gehring, 'Regime Complexes as Governance Systems' in Wayne Sandholtz and Christopher Whytock (eds), *Research Handbook on the Politics of International Law* (Edward Elgar Publishing 2017); Karen J Alter and Kal Raustiala, 'The Rise of International Regime Complexity' (2018) 14 Annual Review of Law and Social Science 329; Laura Gómez-Mera, Jean-Frédéric Morin, and Thijs Van De Graaf, 'Regime Complexes' in Frank Biermann and Rakhyun E Kim (eds), *Architectures of Earth System Governance: Institutional Complexity and Structural Transformation* (Cambridge University Press 2020). It should be noted that authors have often use the terms 'regime complex(es)'

Architectures of Global AI Governance. Matthijs M. Maas, Oxford University Press. © Matthijs M. Maas 2025.
DOI: 10.1093/9780191988455.003.0007

> *Regime Complexity*: the governance architecture on a given issue area, consisting of (1) at least three international or transnational institutions or actors that (2) jointly address a specific issue area, (3) whose mandates, functions, and/or memberships overlap (4) in ways that may result in various beneficial or problematic interactions; this complex consequently (5) has significant implications for the efficacy, resilience, or coherence of governance functions by its actors, as well as the prospects for establishing new institutions.

This chapter will deploy the framework of regime complexity to explore patterns of normative, legal, and institutional change in the governance architecture of and around AI governance regimes. It introduces the key actors, instruments, and political foundations of global governance regimes; reviews the historical development of regime theory in response to longtime trends towards institutional proliferation and legal fragmentation; and charts how these developments are captured in the concept of regime complexity, which offers a particularly promising new perspective on AI governance.

While the regime complexity lens is generally relevant in studying many aspects and issue areas of global governance, I argue that it is especially valuable for the study of AI governance. This is because this lens helps extend our attention beyond debates over the specific features, functions, or form of one or another individual AI governance instrument or institution, and instead emphasizes the importance, for such institutional proposals, of looking beyond the technology itself and beyond any single organization in isolation, to consider underlying changes in the governance landscape in which they will emerge. Analytically, this lens provides better engagement with the determinants of global governance arrangements, especially the role of power, interests, and ideas.[3] Practically, it helps us consider how, in a fragmented governance landscape, new institutions might be able to work with other institutions or regimes in a productive and non-conflictive manner.

6.2 The Ontology of Global Governance

To understand the role and functions of regime complexity theory, we must first understand the background landscape, in terms of the nature of global governance, its actors and instruments, and the foundations of regimes.

or 'regime complexity' interchangeably, although the latter is more influenced by the work on complex systems theory: Karen J Alter and Sophie Meunier, 'The Politics of International Regime Complexity' (2009) 7 Perspectives on Politics 13.

[3] Jonas Tallberg and others, 'The Global Governance of Artificial Intelligence: Next Steps for Empirical and Normative Research' (2023) 25 International Studies Review viad040, 9.

Certainly, 'global governance' is a broad and vague concept, with contested analytical and normative uses.[4] Even so, we can start by understanding it as an analytical lens on the evolving structure of global cooperation—a structure that is populated and characterized by many actors, instruments, and other structures.

At the highest level of global governance, international order 'reflects the organization of the entire system of international relations'.[5] This world order is populated by a global governance complex which, in a definition by Kacowicz, embraces 'states, international institutions, transnational networks, and agencies (both public and private) that function, with variable effect and effectiveness, to promote, regulate, and manage the common affairs of humanity'.[6] As such, the global governance complex is characterized by a diverse ecology of actors and instruments, many of which focus on distinct issue areas.[7] A range of distinctions and sub-divisions should be made to chart the system, its elements, and the often complex interrelations among them. This will necessarily be a cursory and brief overview of a complex ecology; however, one can loosely distinguish between actors and instruments.[8]

6.2.1 Actors and Instruments of Global Governance

What are the actors of global governance? Traditional, doctrinal accounts hold that international law is primarily produced through interactions by states, defined

[4] Klaus Dingwerth and Philipp Pattberg, 'Global Governance as a Perspective on World Politics' (2006) 12 Global Governance 185.

[5] Frank Biermann and others, 'The Fragmentation of Global Governance Architectures: A Framework for Analysis' (2009) 9 Global Environmental Politics 14, 16. Referring to Hedley Bull, *The Anarchical Society: A Study of Order in World Politics* (Columbia University Press 1977).

[6] Arie M Kacowicz, 'Global Governance, International Order, and World Order' in David Levi-Faur (ed), The Oxford Handbook of Governance (Oxford University Press 2012) 689 <https://doi.org/10.1093/oxfordhb/9780199560530.013.0048> accessed 5 June 2025. However, see also the adjacent concept of a 'global governance complex', which has been defined as '[a] system of governance composed of at least three international or transnational institutions or actors whose mandates, functions, and memberships overlap, and that jointly address a specific policy problem'. Mette Eilstrup-Sangiovanni and Oliver Westerwinter, 'The Global Governance Complexity Cube: Varieties of Institutional Complexity in Global Governance' (2022) 17 The Review of International Organizations 233.

[7] From a systems theory perspective, this can be approached as a complex network of 'nodes' (treaties, regimes, organizations) that are linked (through interactions, shared memberships, treaty conflicts, partnerships, resource and information flows), in order to produce clusters (regime complexes, treaty clusters) and particular network effects. See Rakhyun E Kim, 'Is Global Governance Fragmented, Polycentric, or Complex? The State of the Art of the Network Approach' [2019] International Studies Review 8 <https://academic.oup.com/isr/advance-article/doi/10.1093/isr/viz052/5571549> accessed 16 February 2020.

[8] This distinction partially follows (though departs from) an influential framework on the production of international law which distinguishes between 'actors', 'instruments', and 'processes'. See Alan Boyle and Christine Chinkin, *The Making of International Law* (Oxford University Press 2007). See also Beatriz Martinez Romera, *Regime Interaction and Climate Change: The Case of International Aviation and Maritime Transport* (Routledge 2017) 34.

as sovereign entities with a population, a territory, and a governmental organization.[9] In exercising their sovereignty, states can voluntarily enter into (i.e. consent to) various international agreements. Nonetheless, over the past decades there has been, if not a decline of states, at least increased roles of other actors. For instance, one set of actors that have come to take a growing role in the development of international law is international organizations. Under international law, an international organization is defined by an international agreement that establishes it, a capability to act independently from its member states, and subjection to international law.[10] Beyond this, international organizations compose a highly diverse group of entities. In membership, they can range from global institutions such as the UN, to more geographically constrained organizations such as the OECD, to bilateral institutions. In their level of formality, they can range from formal Intergovernmental Organizations (FIGOs) established through constituent documents, such as the World Bank, the World Health Organization, or the ITU, to informal IGOs (IIGOs) that consist of loose task groups or coalitions of states (e.g. the G7, BRICS, G20).[11]

Beyond states and international organizations, the past few decades have also seen a growing role of various non-state actors in global governance, including NGOs, private sector actors, public interest organizations, knowledge-based 'epistemic communities',[12] and various trans-national issue networks.[13] These actors have distinct roles, interests, and tasks, and create more heterogeneous dynamics in the creation of norms or laws.[14] In aiming to shape or regulate international behaviour, these actors avail themselves of a range of instruments, from traditional 'hard' international law to many varieties of 'soft law'.

[9] The most widely accepted legal formulation of these criteria is generally held to be provided in: Convention on Rights and Duties of States adopted by the Seventh International Conference of American States (adopted 26 December 1933, entered into force 26 December 1934) 165 LNTS 19 (Montevideo Convention), art 1.

[10] Under international law, requirements are international agreements that establish them, a capability to act independently from member States, and their subjection to international law. José E Alvarez, *International Organizations as Law-Makers* (Oxford University Press 2005) 6.

[11] Jean-Frédéric Morin and others, 'How Informality Can Address Emerging Issues: Making the Most of the G7' (2019) 10 Global Policy 267. For definitions and distinctions of IGO, FIGO, and IIGOs in the context of proposals for an international AI governance institution, see also Chapter 3, as well as: Olivia J Erdélyi and Judy Goldsmith, 'Regulating Artificial Intelligence: Proposal for a Global Solution' (2022) 39 Government Information Quarterly 101748, 12. For a discussion of the growing role of IIGOs in global governance, see also Felicity Vabulas and Duncan Snidal, 'Informal IGOs as Mediators of Power Shifts' (2020) 11 Global Policy 40.

[12] Peter M Haas, 'Introduction: Epistemic Communities and International Policy Coordination' (1992) 46 International Organization 1.

[13] See Charli Carpenter, *'Lost' Causes, Agenda Vetting in Global Issue Networks and the Shaping of Human Security* (Cornell University Press 2014).

[14] Indeed, their rise has created what Slaughter has called a 'Lego model', wherein 'governments can be taken apart, put together with corporations, foundations, NGOs, church groups, universities, or any number of social actors in any number of different coalitions'. Anne-Marie Slaughter, 'Remarks, The Big Picture: Beyond Hot Spots & Crises in Our Interconnected World' (2012) 1 Penn State Journal of Law & International Affairs 286, 294–295.

The traditional sources of international law are set out in Article 38(1) of the Statute of the International Court of Justice, and include international treaties, international custom, and the general principles of law recognized by civilized nations—and, subsidiary to this, judicial decisions and the teachings of the most highly qualified scholars.[15] However, in recent decades, these traditional tools have increasingly become complemented by diverse forms of soft law. The term 'soft law' can have various definitions, depending on the context. From a legal perspective, it simply refers to 'normative provisions contained in nonbinding texts',[16] a definition that covers various soft rules that are included in distinct instruments such as treaties, non-binding or voluntary resolutions, standards, or codes of conduct.[17] From a social scientific perspective, 'soft law' is defined less with reference to the legal validity or status of the rule, and more with consideration to the (absence of hard) mechanisms used to bind states to commitments; in such a reading, a vaguely formulated treaty without provisions for adjudication or enforcement could be considered soft law.[18] What matters is simply the production of, in Guzman and Meyer's formulation, 'nonbinding rules or instruments that interpret or inform our understanding of binding legal rules or represent promises that in turn create expectations about future conduct'.[19] In this context, soft law standards need not only be produced by states or formal international organisations, but can also be produced by non-state or private sector actors.[20]

6.2.2 Foundations of International Regimes: Between Interests and Norms

More saliently, how do actors interact with, utilize, or wield these instruments? Given that the literature on international regimes, and especially on regime complexity, has been informed by distinct ontologies, it is important to characterize this project's approach to these debates.

[15] Statute of the International Court of Justice (signed 18 April 1946, entered into force 24 October 1945) 33 UNTS 993 (ICJ Statute) art. 38(1).

[16] Dinah L Shelton (ed), *Commitment and Compliance: The Role of Non-Binding Norms in the International Legal System* (Oxford University Press 2003) 292; As cited in Anne van Aaken, 'Is International Law Conducive to Preventing Looming Disasters?' (2016) 7 Global Policy 81, 87.

[17] Aaken (n 16) 87.

[18] ibid; See generally Kenneth W Abbott and Duncan Snidal, 'Hard and Soft Law in International Governance' (2000) 54 International Organization 421; Gregory Shaffer and Mark A Pollack, 'Hard and Soft Law' in Jeffrey L Dunoff and Mark A Pollack (eds), *Interdisciplinary Perspectives on International Law and International Relations* (Cambridge University Press 2012).

[19] Andrew T Guzman and Timothy L Meyer, 'International Soft Law' (2010) 2 Journal of Legal Analysis 59, 174.

[20] Indeed, Burri calls the latter 'supersoft law', and argues it will be particularly prominent in regulating AI. Thomas Burri, 'International Law and Artificial Intelligence' (2017) 60 German Yearbook of International Law 91, 105–107.

Specifically, in exploring the creation, design, and effectiveness of international institutions, the discipline of international relations has long been divided between rationalist and constructivist accounts of international politics,[21] which offer different accounts of, on the one hand, the prevailing rationales and logics of action that shape human behaviour and, on the other, the 'efficiency' of history in terms of the degree to which interests, identities, or resources inexorably lead to specific strategic equilibria, or rather afford for more open-ended (but also path-dependent) courses of action.[22]

This is a rich and long-running debate, to which a brief review cannot do proper justice. Nonetheless, generally speaking, rationalist analysis emphasizes the importance of *interests* to international relations. It broadly argues that states operate according to a logic of (anticipated) consequences and prior (exogenously given) preferences,[23] and that accordingly international institutions or regimes are created in order to alleviate strategic cooperation problems (e.g. the production of collective goods, or the avoidance of collective bads) within an anarchic international system.[24] In a rationalist perspective, these functional and interest-based considerations determine both when a regime is viable and what kind of institutional design choices end up getting embedded in international organisations.[25]

In contrast, constructivist work on international institutions and regimes has explored the importance of identities and of norms, defined as 'standard[s] of appropriate behaviour for actors with a given identity'.[26] This perspective explores how norms can have effects on actors' institutional choices, and particularly how this foregrounds 'logics of action other than instrumental rationality',[27] such as a 'logic of appropriateness'.[28] Conversely, it also examines the reverse relationship, by looking at how various 'norm entrepreneurs' such as transnational issue networks or epistemic communities can create or shift norms, and by doing so alter (state) actors' perceptions and interests.[29] Such work can illuminate various steps

[21] The scholarship is extensive, but for an illuminating case study see Caroline Fehl, 'Explaining the International Criminal Court: A "Practice Test" for Rationalist and Constructivist Approaches' (2004) 10 European Journal of International Relations 357.

[22] James G March and Johan P Olsen, 'The Institutional Dynamics of International Political Orders' (1998) 52 International Organization 943.

[23] ibid.

[24] Fehl (n 21) 362–367.

[25] See Barbara Koremenos, Charles Lipson, and Duncan Snidal, 'The Rational Design of International Institutions' (2001) 55 International Organization 761; Barbara Koremenos, Charles Lipson and Duncan Snidal, 'Rational Design: Looking Back to Move Forward' (2001) 55 International Organization 1051.

[26] Martha Finnemore and Kathryn Sikkink, 'International Norm Dynamics and Political Change' (1998) 52 International Organization 887, 891. Note, this understanding of norms is somewhat distinct from 'norms' as understood in the legally binding sense.

[27] Fehl (n 21) 359.

[28] March and Olsen (n 22).

[29] See also the recent analytical framework in Caroline Fehl and Elvira Rosert, 'It's Complicated: A Conceptual Framework for Studying Relations and Interactions between International Norms' (Peace

in the emergence and evolution of international norms,[30] and show how the possibility boundary of regimes can shift over time.[31]

While the rationalist–constructivist divide should be kept in mind when studying regime complexes, the difference should not be exaggerated.[32] It has long been clear that both interests and norms matter,[33] and that the relative role of these factors often may be a question of various contextual conditions.[34] Indeed, in some domains, scholars have productively integrated both lenses, using constructivist analyses to 'deepen' rationalist arguments.[35] For instance, Caroline Fehl has surveyed the historical evolution of arms control regimes and identified changing patterns in institutional inequality which, she argues, support both rationalist (shared interest-based) and constructivist (norms-based) accounts of international regimes, though not realist (coercion-based) models.[36] Moreover, her account highlights the importance of changes not only in norms, but also in material and technological developments.[37] As a result, she articulates an integrated model that combines rationalist and constructivist arguments with historical institutionalist insights about the path-dependency of institutions, regimes, and legal and governance systems.

The approach to AI governance advanced in this book broadly follows this integrated perspective. It assumes institutional arrangements may be created

Research Institute Frankfurt 2020) <https://www.ssoar.info/ssoar/handle/document/69733> accessed 18 March 2025.

30 For a good example of this, see Elvira Rosert, 'Norm Emergence as Agenda Diffusion: Failure and Success in the Regulation of Cluster Munitions' (2019) 25 European Journal of International Relations 1103.

31 See for instance in the area of arms control regimes: Harald Müller and Carmen Wunderlich, *Norm Dynamics in Multilateral Arms Control: Interests, Conflicts, and Justice* (University of Georgia Press 2013).

32 Indeed, as early as 2002, Alexander Wendt and James Fearon argued that a synthesis between the theories is possible, and that they should be seen more as methodological tools than incompatible ontologies. James Fearon and Alexander Wendt, 'Rationalism v. Constructivism: A Skeptical View' in Walter Carlsnaes, Thomas Risse, and Beth A Simmons (eds), *Handbook of International Relations* (SAGE Publications Ltd 2002).

33 David J Galbreath and Sascha Sauerteig, 'Regime Complexity and Security Governance' in James Sperling (ed), *Handbook of Governance and Security* (Edward Elgar 2014) ('We have come far enough now in the rationalist–constructivist debate to know that interests and norms matter').

34 Jeffrey T Checkel, 'International Norms and Domestic Politics: Bridging the Rationalist–Constructivist Divide' (1997) 3 European Journal of International Relations 473.

35 For instance, in an early study of the establishment of the International Criminal Court (ICC), Caroline Fehl has argued that a rationalist approach is able to identify the original trade-off between either a weak court backed by the US, or a strong court without US support; however, she argues a complementary constructivist approach helps explain how persuasive lobbying activities of NGOs as norm entrepreneurs tipped the scales towards the latter option. Fehl (n 21) 377–382.

36 Caroline Fehl, 'Unequal Power and the Institutional Design of Global Governance: The Case of Arms Control' (2014) 40 Review of International Studies 505, 530.

37 ibid ('changes in the distribution of material capabilities and in prevailing moral discourses create conflicting pressures for deepening and lessening institutional inequality. How these countervailing pressures are resolved depends on the constraining and conditioning impact of past institutional choices').

purposefully (by states) in order to fulfil certain functions or shared interests (per a rationalist perspective), but that a given regime's viability, legitimacy, and long-term stability rest not just on its ability to fulfil such functions, but also (as emphasized by constructivists) on it remaining in accordance with global norms, and even on their ability to change the prevailing normative conceptions of a just or legitimate global political order.[38] The constructivist perspective therefore provides distinct and complementary angles through which to explore whether, or under what conditions, governance regimes on specific AI issues might be or become viable.[39]

This book may aim to integrate these rationalist and constructivist accounts with a further, material account of change in global politics. That is, along with considering the role of actor-based ideational (whether interest- or norms-based) factors in global affairs and governance, we must grapple with the interrelation of these factors with material factors.[40] In fact, rationalist and constructivist scholars of international regimes alike have recognized that structural factors can shape individual actor preferences or norms, setting the conditions for the creation and maintenance of certain regimes. These structural factors traditionally include the distribution of power (in rationalist work) or norms (in constructivist work), but they may also include the existing state of scientific knowledge or of technology.[41] To deepen this connection, we have already (in Chapters 4 and 5) drawn from technology law scholarship, which has overlaps (as well as independent convergence) with insights from the field of Science and Technology Studies (STS).[42]

Having clarified the background and basic terms, we can now turn to the discussion of regime theory, and the rise of the concept of regime complexity.

6.3 Regime Theory, Fragmentation, and Regime Complexity

Regime theory originally emerged in the 1970s and 1980s, in response to the unanticipated stability of international economic institutions in the aftermath of the

[38] ibid 518–519.

[39] This will be especially prominent in Section 7.1.2 (on 'regime viability and governance foundations').

[40] Daniel Deudney, 'Turbo Change: Accelerating Technological Disruption, Planetary Geopolitics, and Architectonic Metaphors' (2018) 20 International Studies Review 223. This also relates to distinct definitions of 'technology', a topic that is taken up in Chapter 4.

[41] For instance, Stein notes how the 'security dilemma' is not an intrinsic, inevitable feature of global politics; rather it 'presumes either that offensive weapons exist and are superior to defensive ones, or that weapons systems are not easily distinguishable'. Arthur A Stein, 'Coordination and Collaboration: Regimes in an Anarchic World' (1982) 36 International Organization 299, 320. Either condition depends at least in part on the material features and texture of the weapon systems available.

[42] Ryan Calo, 'The Scale and the Reactor' (9 April 2022) <https://papers.ssrn.com/abstract=4079851> accessed 23 May 2023.

Second World War.[43] Krasner defined such regimes as 'sets of implicit or explicit principles, norms, rules and decision-making procedures around which actors' expectations converge in a given area of international relations'.[44] A regime is therefore characterized by the norms or principles which it represents, which can end up having distinct effects on the expectations, the calculations, and ultimately the behaviour of actors.[45] However, it also interacts with—and for its establishment, can depend upon—the interests of these actors. Consequently, such regimes, using a combination of norms as well as coordination and enforcement mechanisms, may help shape state behaviour within an anarchic international system, enabling cooperation or coordination on specific issues of international concern.[46] As such, a strand of rationalist research began to examine the conditions under which states seek to create regimes to address discrete problems,[47] as well as what factors affected the resulting design of international institutions.[48] Such work soon came to be complemented by constructivist accounts of the role of norms and ideas on actors' institutional choices.[49]

6.3.1 Key Trends: Institutional Proliferation and Fragmentation

Notably, research agendas on international regimes soon became informed and shaped by two related trends in the global governance complex—institutional proliferation, and fragmentation—which have transformed many relations between traditional actors, institutions, and norms.

A first trend came in the form of a pervasive and extended process of global institutional proliferation.[50] Whereas a century ago there were only a handful of international institutions, today the global governance landscape is populated by thousands of intergovernmental organizations, tens of thousands of

[43] Thomas Gehring, *Dynamic International Regimes: Institutions for International Environmental Governance* (Peter Lang GmbH, Internationaler Verlag der Wissenschaften 1994).

[44] Stephen D Krasner, 'Structural Causes and Regime Consequences: Regimes as Intervening Variables' (1982) 36 International Organization 185, 186.

[45] Arthur Stein defers from this definition, arguing that regimes are not at their core characterized by (positive) norms, since there are examples of 'unprincipled' regimes (such as OPEC); instead, he argues that regimes are principally constituted by the presence of 'joint decisionmaking' (or, the absence of independent decisionmaking). Stein (n 41) n 10. Nonetheless, for my purposes, I consider such cases as relatively narrow exceptions to the general rule.

[46] See also the (rationalist) account in Stein (n 41). But also compare this against the more recent comparative analysis of both rationalist and constructivist theories of international regimes in Fehl (n 21).

[47] For other influential work, see Stephen D Krasner, *International Regimes* (Cornell University Press 1983); Kenneth A Oye, *Cooperation under Anarchy* (Princeton University Press 1986).

[48] Koremenos, Lipson, and Snidal, 'The Rational Design of International Institutions' (n 25).

[49] Fehl (n 21).

[50] Kal Raustiala, 'Institutional Proliferation and the International Legal Order' in Jeffrey L Dunoff and Mark A Pollack (eds), *Interdisciplinary Perspectives on International Law and International Relations: The State of the Art* (Cambridge University Press 2012).

nongovernmental organizations, and hundreds of thousands of international agreements.[51] To be sure, some argue that this rate of growth in new treaty and institutional creation has stagnated in recent years,[52] and has resulted in a move towards more informal and multi-stakeholder models of governance. Nonetheless, this period of growth across areas of international institutional activity has been sufficiently extensive that it has transformed the tapestry of international law, with far-reaching effects: as one consequence, many issue areas[53] in global politics, far from being subject to a unified global code, today find themselves covered by different *global governance architectures*, which Biermann, Pattberg, van Asselt, and Zelli have defined as

> the overarching system of public and private institutions that are valid or active in a given issue area of world politics. This system comprises organizations, regimes, and other forms of principles, norms, regulations, and decision-making procedures.[54]

As a result of this trend of proliferation, perhaps the most important development of the past few decades has been the steady 'fragmentation' of international law.[55] Of course, international law has never been a single, unified system; but the trend of fragmentation was highlighted in 2006 by the International Law Commission,[56] and has featured significantly in international legal debates since. In the absence of an international legislative supreme body to coordinate among regimes, the

[51] The true number is unclear, and measurements are beset by definitional difficulties. Alter and Raustiala reference 'more than 2,400 intergovernmental organizations, 37,000 organizations involved in international politics, and hundreds of thousands of international agreements': Alter and Raustiala (n 2) 330; referring to Daniel W Drezner, 'The Tragedy of the Global Institutional Commons' in Martha Finnemore and Judith Goldstein (eds), *Back to Basics: State Power in a Contemporary World* (Oxford University Press 2013) 284; Oona A Hathaway and Scott J Shapiro, *The Internationalists: How a Radical Plan to Outlaw War Remade the World* (Simon & Schuster 2017) xviii. However, these figures appear based on data from 2003. Subsequent estimates for 2015, by the Union of International Associations, list 7,657 intergovernmental organizations and 60,919 nongovernmental organizations. Union of International Associations, 'Yearbook of International Organizations: Volume 5: Statistics, 2016' (Union of International Associations 2016) fig 2.1. <http://brill.uia.org/content/4384> accessed 18 January 2020.

[52] J Pauwelyn, RA Wessel, and J Wouters, 'When Structures Become Shackles: Stagnation and Dynamics in International Lawmaking' (2014) 25 European Journal of International Law 733.

[53] In this articulation, an 'issue area' should be understood as that thematic object (e.g. climate), activity (e.g. trade, security), or subject (e.g. refugees) of legal and political relevance on which different governance instruments, rules, and jurisdictions converge and overlap. Romera (n 8) 37.

[54] Biermann and others (n 5) 15.

[55] ILC, 'Fragmentation of International Law: Difficulties Arising from the Diversification and Expansion of International Law: Report of the Study Group of the International Law Commission, finalized by Martti Koskenniemi' (13 April 2006) UN Doc. A/CN.4/L.682 <http://legal.un.org/ilc/documentation/english/a_cn4_l682.pdf> accessed 6 November 2018; Gerhard Hafner, 'Pros and Cons Ensuing from Fragmentation of International Law' (2004) 25 Michigan Journal of International Law 849; Raustiala (n 50).

[56] Koskenniemi and Study Group of the International Law Commission (n 55).

gradual development of specialized regimes in reaction to different challenges has had the effect that the global governance complex has become increasingly fragmented substantively (along issue areas and geographically), normatively, and institutionally.[57]

Within global governance theory, the resulting fragmentation has been defined in different ways: for instance, van Asselt has described it as 'the increased specialisation and diversification in international institutions, including the overlap of substantive rules and jurisdiction'.[58] Alternately, Biermann and others have characterized the fragmentation of governance architectures as yielding

> a patchwork of international institutions that are different in their character (organizations, regimes, and implicit norms), their constituencies (public and private), their spatial scope (from bilateral to global), and their subject matter (from specific policy fields to universal concerns).[59]

One thing which the twin processes of institutional proliferation and the rise in regime fragmentation have made abundantly clear is that today, governance regimes or institutions can no longer be approached in isolation. Instead, for a comprehensive understanding of governance activities on a given issue, one must reckon with how a patchwork quilt of overlapping and sometimes contradictory regimes converge on the same topics, affecting both law and politics.

As a result of the increasing fragmentation of international law and the global governance architecture more broadly,[60] there has been increasing attention to the potential interactions between the many different organizations and regimes that make up the global governance architecture. In the mid-1990s, Oran Young developed a preliminary taxonomy of 'institutional interplay'.[61] The past few decades have seen considerable attention to the functional outcomes and effects of the normative and institutional fragmentation of governance architectures.[62]

[57] See also Joost Pauwelyn, 'Fragmentation of International Law' [2006] Max Planck Encyclopedia of Public International Law 13, 2. Note however that not all agree. From a systems theory perspective, Kim argues that 'the general trend over a long span of time has been, contrary to the general wisdom, governance defragmentation'. Kim (n 7) 11.

[58] Harro van Asselt, *The Fragmentation of Global Climate Governance: Consequences and Management of Regime Interactions* (Edward Elgar Publishing 2014) 22.

[59] Biermann and others (n 5) 16.

[60] Biermann and others (n 5); Amitav Acharya, 'The Future of Global Governance: Fragmentation May Be Inevitable and Creative Global Forum' [2016] Global Governance 453.

[61] Oran R Young, 'Institutional Linkages in International Society: Polar Perspectives' (1996) 2 Global Governance 1.

[62] Biermann and others (n 5); Fariborz Zelli and Harro van Asselt, 'Introduction: The Institutional Fragmentation of Global Environmental Governance: Causes, Consequences, and Responses' (2013) 13 Global Environmental Politics 1; Asselt (n 58). And in the legal field, see Hafner (n 55); Koskenniemi and Study Group of the International Law Commission (n 55); Eyal Benvenisti and George W Downs, 'The Empire's New Clothes: Political Economy and the Fragmentation of International Law' (2007) 60 Stanford Law Review 595.

In particular, there has been an increasing focus on the dynamics and (potentially problematic) interactions between the distinct regimes active on given issue areas,[63] exploring potentially problematic interactions or conflicts between regimes, in terms of incompatible norms, operations, or impacts that functionally work at cross purposes. To organise and facilitate this research programme, scholars working at the intersection of international law and international relations came to articulate the new concept of a 'regime complex' to characterize and study these interactions.

6.3.2 The Concept of a Regime Complex

What is a regime complex? The concept has gone through a number of iterations. In an influential 2004 article, Kal Raustiala and David Victor originally defined a regime complex as 'an array of partially overlapping and nonhierarchical institutions governing a particular issue-area.'[64] While influential, their definition has been critiqued on the basis that it is unclear whether 'institution' refers only to formal international organizations, or to all elements of a 'regime', such as norms.[65] Accordingly, Alter and Meunier have reasserted the broader, Krasnerian conception of 'regimes', extending the term 'international regime complexity' to be defined as 'the presence of nested, partially overlapping, and parallel international regimes that are not hierarchically ordered.'[66]

However, both of these definitions emphasize the lack of hierarchical relations amongst elemental institutions as a distinct feature of international regime complexity—yet such a lack of hierarchy may not be necessary, since even some degree of hierarchy among institutions can still result in a fragmented landscape.[67] In response, Orsini, Morin, and Young have instead defined a regime complex as a 'network of three or more international regimes on a common issue area. These should have overlapping membership and cause potentially problematic interactions.'[68] In so doing, they explicitly omit the 'non-hierarchical relationship' criterion, arguing that it is an 'ambiguous and unnecessary feature.'[69] Their definition is more focused on potential overlaps among regimes or institutions on a

63 Orsini, Morin, and Young (n 2) 29.
64 Kal Raustiala and David G Victor, 'The Regime Complex for Plant Genetic Resources' (2004) 58 International Organization 277, 279.
65 Galbreath and Sauerteig (n 33) 84.
66 Alter and Meunier (n 2) 13.
67 Eilstrup-Sangiovanni and Westerwinter (n 6) 238.
68 Orsini, Morin, and Young (n 2) 29.
69 ibid 31. However, note that there is still a recurring debate over the importance of 'hierarchy' to the definition of a regime complex; for instance, Alter and Raustiala reject the definition by Orsini et al., countering that 'interaction' need not be part of the definition since it is already 'intrinsic' to complex systems and arguing that 'the lack of hierarchy is central and that regime complexes do not necessarily require interaction—what matters is that there is overlapping authority': Alter and Raustiala (n 2) n 7.

particular issue area, and the resulting problematic interactions that can arise in terms of norms, rules, procedures, or impact.

In addition to the 'horizontal' dimension of potential thematic overlap, the partially overlapping membership of regimes adds a 'vertical' dimension to regime complexity; this means that, as Gómez-Mera, Morin, and Van De Graaf put it, 'a regime complex is composed neither of parallel regimes with a clear division of labour, nor of nested regimes embedded within each other like Russian dolls [but] is messier than these neatly organized ideal types'.[70] This conceptual fuzziness relates to the observation that the fragmentation of a global governance system, like 'regime complexity', should be considered a matter not of kind but of degree. Importantly, in the absence of a world government, all governance—and all international law—is fragmented to some degree. Indeed, fragmentation, in this reading, is a 'ubiquitous structural characteristic' of the international system.[71] As a result, a governance architecture always exists somewhere on the continuum between fully integrated regime and completely fragmented collection of institutions.[72]

To be clear, the field is an active one and there has been significant further work on developing the concept of regime complexity further—as well as in articulating adjacent variations on the concept. For instance, Abbott and Faude's work on 'hybrid institutional complexes' aims to more rigorously draw in both public and private actors.[73] Eilstrup-Sangiovanni and Westerwinter have furthermore generalized from regime complexes to 'global governance complexes', a construct that they define as '[a] system of governance composed of at least three international or transnational institutions or actors whose mandates, functions, and memberships overlap, and that jointly address a specific policy problem'.[74]

However, I will focus on the more established terminology of the regime complex, drawing together these existing approaches to define the regime complexity lens as: the governance architecture on a given issue area, consisting of (1) at least three international or transnational institutions or actors that (2) jointly address a specific issue area, (3) whose mandates, functions, and/or memberships overlap (4) in ways that may result in various beneficial or problematic interactions; this complex consequently (5) has significant implications for the efficacy, resilience, or coherence of governance functions by its actors, as well as the prospects for establishing new institutions.

[70] Gómez-Mera, Morin, and Van De Graaf (n 2) 140.

[71] Biermann and others (n 5) 31.

[72] Robert O Keohane and David G Victor, 'The Regime Complex for Climate Change' (2011) 9 Perspectives on Politics 7. This relates to the fact that in practice, as noted by Gomez-Mera et al., there is no objectively 'right' level of analysis that merits the label 'regime complex': instead, the concept is a 'heuristic construct', to be used to facilitate analysis at the level of analysis most appropriate to a specific research question. Gómez-Mera, Morin, and Van De Graaf (n 2) 139.

[73] Kenneth W Abbott and Benjamin Faude, 'Hybrid Institutional Complexes in Global Governance' (2022) 17 The Review of International Organizations 263.

[74] Eilstrup-Sangiovanni and Westerwinter (n 6) 238.

6.3.3 The Value of the Regime Complexity Lens for AI Governance

As an emerging and new body of research, we can expect that the field of (advanced) AI governance can benefit significantly from cross-fertilization with many established theoretical frameworks drawn from different domains, disciplines, and paradigms. Yet why would we expect regime complexity theory, specifically, to be a valuable approach?

To be sure, my claim is not that this is the only framework through which to enrich AI governance debates. Regime complexity is just one lens on the structure of global governance; competing or complementary perspectives will highlight distinct features, problems, and opportunities, and may have distinct policy implications.[75] Nonetheless, I argue that there are several reasons to expect that this approach can offer a very fertile approach for studying and shaping the structural changes within the global governance architecture for AI.[76]

In the first place, the regime complex framework is likely theoretically well-scoped to answer crucial questions in AI governance. That does not mean that it will solve any puzzle which AI governance scholars might put to it. However, it enables us to better understand and explain key dynamics of AI governance. That is, at the macro level, it allows the analysis of how the entire AI governance system is situated within the fragmented system of global governance, and in particular allows one to study its 'external' interactions with other international regime complexes (e.g. the labour, human rights, or international security regime complex). At the meso level, this framework allows a consideration of the 'internal' interactions of—and potential interface conflicts[77] between—institutions and regimes within the emerging AI regime complex itself. This framework can then be complemented by work drawing from other disciplines, to explore the micro-level dynamics of how various (non-state) actors may play roles in shaping individual institutions.[78]

In addition, this framework allows researchers to better consider the interaction of top-down (e.g. international legal norms) and bottom-up (e.g. behaviour by state or non-state actors) drivers of governance change. In so doing, we can build on three decades of scholarship in the paradigm of 'International Law and International Relations', which has tried to bridge and unite these distinct perspectives,[79] arguing that scholars in these fields can learn much from one

[75] Kim (n 7) 4 ('[f]ragmentation points to flat and nonhierarchical structures, polycentricity points to uneven and rugged structures, while complexity points to modular and hierarchical structures').

[76] Tallberg and others (n 3).

[77] Christian Kreuder-Sonnen and Michael Zürn, 'After Fragmentation: Norm Collisions, Interface Conflicts, and Conflict Management' (2020) 9 Global Constitutionalism 241.

[78] Tallberg and others (n 3) 12 ('If theories of regime complexity can shine a light on macro-level properties of AI governance, other theoretical approaches can guide research into micro-level dynamics and influences').

[79] Anne-Marie Slaughter Burley, 'International Law and International Relations Theory: A Dual Agenda' (1993) 87 The American Journal of International Law 205; Anne-Marie Slaughter, 'International

another.[80] Consequently, in many other issue areas, global governance scholars have found the regime complex lens a valuable framework through which to reconcile international legal insights into the top-down effects of global norms, with international relations' insights on actors' cross-institutional strategies.[81]

In the second place, regime complex theory has proven not just theoretically nuanced but also empirically rich. While the majority of empirical work in this field has been in global environmental governance,[82] scholars have also productively applied this lens across a wide range of other areas of global governance—human rights,[83] international security,[84] refugees,[85] energy,[86] maritime piracy,[87] food security,[88] and many others. This provides an extensive reference class, and allows potentially fruitful comparisons and cautious lessons to be drawn for the emerging AI governance architecture. Likewise, theoretically, the regime complexity framework has come to encapsulate diverse facets and dynamics of governance architectures—from the way norms and interests set the condition for a regime, to its evolution over time, to its productive 'management'. This suggests that it may shed light on various steps or considerations that will be critical in the emerging AI governance architecture.[89] Yet while there is an extensive and mature

Law and International Relations Theory: Twenty Years Later' in Jeffrey L Dunoff and Mark A Pollack (eds), *Interdisciplinary Perspectives on International Law and International Relations* (Cambridge University Press 2012); Jeffrey L Dunoff and Mark A Pollack, 'Reviewing Two Decades of IL/IR Scholarship' in Jeffrey L Dunoff and Mark A Pollack (eds), *Interdisciplinary Perspectives on International Law and International Relations* (Cambridge University Press 2012). However, for sharp critiques of the interaction between these two disciplines and how it might have disproportionately favoured IR over IL, see also Andrea Bianchi, *International Law Theories: An Inquiry into Different Ways of Thinking* (Oxford University Press 2016) ch 6; Martti Koskenniemi, 'Law, Teleology and International Relations: An Essay in Counterdisciplinarity' (2012) 26 International Relations 3.

[80] For instance, Gehring and Faude have suggested that, just as international legal scholars can profit from IR research on 'cross-institutional strategizing' by state actors, IR scholars 'can learn from IL research on the endogenous dynamics of international law, in particular on legal ways to absorb conflict among overlapping sets of legal rules in the absence of a "final authority"'. Faude and Gehring (n 2) 177.

[81] Faude and Gehring (n 2).

[82] Gómez-Mera, Morin, and Van De Graaf (n 2) 137–138. (discussing reasons for the theoretical density in this particular field).

[83] Emilie M Hafner-Burton, 'The Power Politics of Regime Complexity: Human Rights Trade Conditionality in Europe' (2009) 7 Perspectives on Politics 33.

[84] Stephanie C Hofmann, 'Overlapping Institutions in the Realm of International Security: The Case of NATO and ESDP' (2009) 7 Perspectives on Politics 45; Galbreath and Sauerteig (n 33).

[85] Alexander Betts, 'Regime Complexity and International Organizations: UNHCR as a Challenged Institution' (2013) 19 Global Governance 69.

[86] Jeff D Colgan, Robert O Keohane, and Thijs Van de Graaf, 'Punctuated Equilibrium in the Energy Regime Complex' (2012) 7 Review of International Organizations 117.

[87] Michael J Struett, Mark T Nance, and Diane Armstrong, 'Navigating the Maritime Piracy Regime Complex' (2013) 19 Global Governance 93.

[88] Matias E Margulis, 'The Regime Complex for Food Security: Implications for the Global Hunger Challenge' (2013) 19 Global Governance 53.

[89] Peter Cihon, Matthijs M Maas, and Luke Kemp, 'Should Artificial Intelligence Governance Be Centralised?: Design Lessons from History', *Proceedings of the AAAI/ACM Conference on AI, Ethics, and Society* (ACM 2020) <http://dl.acm.org/doi/10.1145/3375627.3375857> accessed 12 February 2020. See also the discussion in Sections 7.2–7.5.

body of scholarship exploring regime complexes, this has only rarely been applied to the subject of AI governance.[90] There may be significant insights still to glean.

In the third place, the regime complex framework may be especially appropriate to studying governance systems for a rapidly changing technology. Saliently, regime complex scholars, especially those working in the environmental law field, have long been interested in identifying adaptive governance systems that are able to adapt or anticipate change and are therefore capable of addressing the 'institutional mismatch' between fixed political institutions and rapidly changing systems.[91] This may make this lens particularly relevant to investigating dynamics of change around AI governance, and especially the question of which governance systems might be more adaptable to sociotechnical change or governance disruption from AI. Indeed, there is also value in applying this framework to the field of AI governance at this moment of its development. As suggested by Tallberg and others:

> given that the AI regime complex exists in a very early state, it provides researchers with an excellent opportunity to trace the origins and evolution of this form of governance structure from the outset, thus providing a good case for both theory development and novel empirical applications.[92]

Fourthly, regime complexity theory has long been concerned with a set of questions that are or should be at the forefront of AI governance. It focuses on the question of how and why a governance architecture becomes fragmented,[93] as well as when and how institutions and regimes experience conflictive interactions or cross-institutional spillover or externalities.[94] This again makes this a promising approach for AI governance, because we have reason to expect that such spillovers and externalities will be unusually common in the governance of such a general-purpose technology. That is, because AI technologies—whether narrow, conventional AI, or advanced AI systems such as foundation models—have such widespread uses, it can be hard to draw strict silos around AI's capabilities, use cases, or resulting societal challenges. This suggests that, more than other issues or technologies, any 'local' AI problem is likely to inadvertently touch on regimes across many other AI issue areas. This implies that, more than other issues or technologies, AI will likely begin to draw in—and open up points of contact

[90] With the exception of: ibid; Peter Cihon, Matthijs M Maas, and Luke Kemp, 'Fragmentation and the Future: Investigating Architectures for International AI Governance' (2020) 11 Global Policy 545; Lewin Schmitt, 'Mapping Global AI Governance: A Nascent Regime in a Fragmented Landscape' (2022) 2 AI and Ethics <https://doi.org/10.1007/s43681-021-00083-y> accessed 18 August 2021; Huw Roberts and others, 'Global AI Governance: Barriers and Pathways Forward' [2024] International Affairs iiae073; Tallberg and others (n 3). Johannes Geith, Magnus Lundgren and Jonas Tallberg, 'The Emerging Regime Complex for Artificial Intelligence' [2025 forthcoming] *Global Studies Quarterly*.
[91] Gómez-Mera, Morin and Van De Graaf (n 2) 138.
[92] Tallberg et al. (n 3) 12.
[93] Cihon et al. (n 90) 546.
[94] Gómez-Mera, Morin, and Van De Graaf (n 2) 138.

between—many different institutions or regimes simultaneously. In turn, this makes it unlikely that individual regimes or institutions focusing on a single domain use of AI will be able to operate in strong isolation from the effects of regimes or institutions focused on other aspects, nor from existing regimes focusing on other issue areas such as human rights, security, or the environment.[95] As such, given the extreme versatility of many AI techniques, their governance might be a natural candidate for the regime complex lens.

All this is not to say that this theory is without its methodological shortfalls or limits.[96] It should be kept in mind that this lens was originally developed in different issue domains, most notably environmental law. As a consequence, the patterns or findings of regime complex theory should not be uncritically transferred into AI governance debates. At the same time, neither should the field of AI governance ignore these lessons or reinvent the wheel.

Regime complexity, too, offers a potentially promising and underexplored lens on many aspects of AI governance. This is particularly so because the theory has explored at length what might be potential consequences of such complexity for the efficacy, resilience, and coherence of a global governance architecture on a given issue.

6.4 The Importance of Regime Complexity to Cooperation

Why does regime complexity matter for AI governance? What are its outcomes? Researchers in this field argue that a regime complex may result in a range of significant effects on global governance and international cooperation.[97]

[95] This latter case touches on the question of how different regimes focusing on distinct issue areas interact with one another—cf. Romera (n 8). This is an important research agenda, and reflects the analysis of AI regime complex 'topology' at the *macro* level. However, in this book (and especially Chapter 7), most of the analysis will focus on the (meso-level) 'internal' interactions of institutions within the emerging AI regime complex, rather than the macro-level interaction of that AI regime with, say, the separate international labour regimes, or the micro-level dynamics of how various (non-state) actors may play roles into shaping individual institutions. See also Tallberg and others (n 3) 12.

[96] For earlier critiques of the 'regime' concept, see for instance Susan Strange, 'Cave! Hic Dragones: A Critique of Regime Analysis' (1982) 36 International Organization 479; James F Keeley, 'The Latest Wave: A Critical Review of Regime Literature' in David G Haglund and Michael K Hawes (eds), *World Politics: Power, Interdependence and Dependence* (Harcourt, Brace, Jovanovich Canada 1990). The regime complex framework likewise has its challenges. For instance, Gómez-Mera and others admit that 'for all the progress made in the identification of causal pathways and mechanisms through which regime complexity matters, we still lack a coherent and comprehensive theory of regime complexes and their implications': Gómez-Mera, Morin, and Van De Graaf (n 2) 149–150. Others have argued that many of the effects of regime complexes have been theorized deductively, or that these have been considered only 'with reference to a small population of specific regime complexes [such that] it is probably fair to say that a broader empirical foundation is necessary to account for a general understanding of the correlation between the characteristics of a complex and governance outcomes'. Galbreath and Sauerteig (n 33) 87.

[97] This section draws to a large extent on the review by Gómez-Mera, Morin, and Van De Graaf (n 2) 144–147, as well as those by Faude and Gehring (n 2) 188–193; Alter and Raustiala (n 2) 338–341.

For instance, Alter and Meunier anticipate that the higher institutional density and overlap in a regime complex can drive diverse effects, including: (1) a greater role for implementation in determining outcomes; (2) greater reliance on bounded rationality in actor decision-making; (3) more social interaction; (4) more forum-shopping; (5) more institutional competition; and (6) more feedback among institutions.[98] These effects are clearly diverse, and there is accordingly live disagreement among scholars in regime complex theory over the functional consequences and normative desirability of regime complexity. Critics and proponents argue from a range of positions.[99]

6.4.1 Critiques of Regime Complexity: Dysfunction, Inequality, Strategic Vulnerability

Some legal scholars, especially those writing from a global constitutionalist perspective, have taken issue with the increasing fragmentation of international law.[100] For instance, Fischer-Lescano and Teubner identify four problems that may result from this state: contradictions between individual decisions of international courts and tribunals; rule collisions; inconsistencies between legal doctrines; and conflicts between legal principles.[101] Taking a holistic view of the overall governance system, such scholars argue not only that increasing regime complexity introduces adverse effects for governance on the local level, but also that this fracturing undermines the overarching unity and authority of international law.[102]

Other critiques focus on operational dysfunction. From a governance perspective, scholars have suggested that regime complexity, and accordant phenomena such as 'treaty congestion',[103] can drive a host of operational problems that inhibit institutional functioning and effectiveness. They can introduce confusion over authority, unclear boundaries, and rules, which in turn may lead to reduced accountability for actors and lower compliance with international commitments.[104] Within the regime complex, institutional interaction may be hallmarked by

[98] Alter and Meunier (n 2) 15–21.

[99] The application or implications of these debates for the organization and efficacy of the AI governance regime will be worked out at greater length in Section 7.5.

[100] Faude and Gehring (n 2) 182.

[101] Andreas Fischer-Lescano and Gunther Teubner, 'Regime-Collisions: The Vain Search for Legal Unity in the Fragmentation of Global Law' (2004) 25 Michigan Journal of International Law 999; As discussed in Faude and Gehring (n 2) 180–181.

[102] Hafner (n 55) 854.

[103] Don Anton, '"Treaty Congestion" in International Environmental Law' in Shawkat Alam and others (eds), *Routledge Handbook of International Environmental Law* (Routledge 2012).

[104] Raustiala (n 50).

inefficiencies;[105] duplication of efforts;[106] conflicts in objectives, obligations, or procedures; or even antagonistic competition or rhetorical bickering between organizations.[107]

In addition, some scholars critique the perceived power inequality of a fragmented regime complex. Such work suggests that, rather than promoting inclusion and access, the presence of multiple overlapping institutions may strengthen already powerful actors, who are better able to navigate and support representation at all these fora, while disadvantaging weaker actors who are less able to carry the participation costs of monitoring all governance developments or attending all these simultaneous meetings. This could perversely exacerbate power imbalances,[108] and undermine democratic participation and the legitimacy of the resulting governance arrangements.[109]

Most importantly, there are concerns over the strategic vulnerabilities which a fragmented regime complex creates, and the way these can be or are exploited by states. As Gehring and Faude argue, at their core, '[r]egime complexes create new opportunities for strategic action through forum shopping, regime shifting, and the creation of a competing institution intended to induce strategic inconsistency with an already existing institution'.[110] Others have noted that states have on occasion deliberately created treaty conflicts in order to facilitate certain changes in multilateral regimes.[111]

6.4.2 Defences of Regime Complexity: Flexible Problem-solving, Democratic Dynamics

In contrast, other scholarship has countered that 'fragmented' global governance may, for all its warts, suffice as 'good enough' governance.[112] Indeed, Orsini, Morin, and Young suggest that rather than a sign of dysfunction, 'problem solving is enhanced in a context of regime complexes, even if the complex is fragmented,

[105] Alter and Meunier (n 2); Biermann and others (n 5).

[106] Amandine Orsini, 'The Negotiation Burden of Institutional Interactions: Non-State Organizations and the International Negotiations on Forests' (2016) 29 Cambridge Review of International Affairs 1421.

[107] Galbreath and Sauerteig (n 33) 88–89.

[108] Benvenisti and Downs (n 62); Daniel W Drezner, 'The Power and Peril of International Regime Complexity' (2009) 7 Perspectives on Politics 65.

[109] Acharya (n 60) 457.

[110] Thomas Gehring and Benjamin Faude, 'The Dynamics of Regime Complexes: Microfoundations and Systemic Effects' (2013) 19 Global Governance 119, 126.

[111] Surabhi Ranganathan, *Strategically Created Treaty Conflicts and the Politics of International Law* (Cambridge University Press 2014).

[112] Stewart Patrick, 'The Unruled World: The Case for Good Enough Global Governance' (2014) 93 Foreign Affairs 58. But see also the critique by Dan Plesch and Thomas G Weiss, '1945's Lesson: "Good Enough" Global Governance Ain't Good Enough' (2015) 21 Global Governance 203.

because the existence of a complex means that potential problems are likely to be sorted out'.[113] Indeed, some even go further, and assert that fragmented governance is not just 'good enough'; rather, they argue, what they call 'polycentric' governance is in fact a positively superior model of governance, one preferable to 'monocentric' regimes.[114] Like its critics, the proponents of regime complexity reason from a variety of angles.

Some argue that regime complexity contributes to problem-solving. These scholars argue that the redundant overlap in competences makes it less likely that issues will get overlooked because of institutional attempts at blame avoidance.[115] Regime complexes are also thought to have 'greater flexibility (across issues) and adaptability (across time) over single, legally-integrated regimes'.[116] Specifically, organizational ecology theory suggests institutional competition could foster beneficial adaptation, as competing institutions specialize in niches—corresponding to certain issue area themes—or to specific governance tasks (e.g. generating knowledge, strengthening norms, building capacity, or monitoring and enforcing compliance with rules).[117] These scholars therefore expect that 'the invisible hand of a market of institutions leads to a better distribution of functions and effects'.[118] Moreover, global 'legal pluralists' see overlapping jurisdictions as desirable because they can be 'a source of innovation'[119] in substantive or procedural legal norms. Analogously, it is suggested that polycentric governance provides more opportunities for policy experimentation.[120]

Along with those arguments, others argue that regime complexity creates better dynamics amongst governance actors. Rather than putting all the 'eggs in the one basket' of a single authoritative institution which might ossify or fail to adequately adapt, polycentric governance is held to create improved opportunities for inter-institutional learning.[121] Others suggest it might increase

[113] Orsini, Morin, and Young (n 2) 35.

[114] Elinor Ostrom, 'Polycentric Systems for Coping with Collective Action and Global Environmental Change' (2010) 20 Global Environmental Change 550. See also Cameron F Kerry, 'The Good, the Not-so-Good, and the Ugly of the UN's Blueprint for AI' (*Brookings*, 29 August 2024) <https://www.brookings.edu/articles/the-good-the-not-so-good-and-the-ugly-of-the-uns-blueprint-for-ai/> accessed 2 September 2024.

[115] Aynsley Kellow, 'Multi-Level and Multi-Arena Governance: The Limits of Integration and the Possibilities of Forum Shopping' (2012) 12 International Environmental Agreements: Politics, Law and Economics 327; Gómez-Mera, Morin, and Van De Graaf (n 2) 145.

[116] Gómez-Mera, Morin, and Van De Graaf (n 2) 145; see also Keohane and Victor (n 72) 19.

[117] Gómez-Mera, Morin, and Van De Graaf (n 2) 145.

[118] Zelli and van Asselt (n 62) 7.

[119] Paul Schiff Berman, 'A Pluralist Approach to International Law' (2007) 32 The Yale Journal of International Law 301, 321 ('normative conflict among multiple, overlapping legal systems is often unavoidable and might even sometimes be desirable both as a source of innovation and as a site for discourse among multiple community affiliations').

[120] Alter and Meunier (n 2) 19; Ostrom (n 114).

[121] Sebastian Oberthür, 'Interplay Management: Enhancing Environmental Policy Integration among International Institutions' (2009) 9 International Environmental Agreements: Politics, Law and Economics 371.

communication and interaction across parties and institutions, helping foment greater mutual trust.[122]

Moreover, and in direct contrast to these concerns over power asymmetries and democratic deficit, some of these proponents also expect that polycentric governance can allow for greater democratization, because of the decentralization of authority and the (potential) inclusion of more actors in diverse sets of regimes. Indeed, it is pointed out that the strategic flexibility afforded by fragmented regime complexes can also strengthen democratic representation: the same strategies of forum-shopping or regime shifting which can be used in 'non-cooperative' ways by powerful (state) actors to bypass or hollow out governance are also available to less powerful actors, and as such can allow civil society or even institutions to route around obstructions thrown up in one forum,[123] or highlight issue linkages, ultimately affording them greater voice.[124] Finally, some argue that fragmented global governance may simply be appropriate, as it reflects the reality of plural values amidst an 'inevitable transition from the unipolar moment to a multiplex world'.[125] As such, it has been suggested that AI governance regimes should not pursue harmonization, but rather become more reflective of the plurality of different societies, value systems, and value judgements.[126]

6.5 Analysing a Regime Complex: A Five-part Framework

Beyond allowing exploration of the normative benefits or drawbacks of a fragmented regime complex, I argue that the value of this lens is that it allows analysis of various key features of a governance architecture for any specific issue areas. What types of questions does this allow one to ask?

For instance, Laura Gómez-Mera, Jean-Frédéric Morin, and Thijs Van De Graaf have argued that work on regime complexity has, variably, aimed at the investigation of (1) the causes and origins of regime complexes; (2) their evolution over time; and (3) the consequences and effects (and consequently the normative implications) of high regime complexity, and ways to manage these outcomes.[127]

[122] Ostrom (n 114).

[123] On the related concept of 'institutional bypasses', see also Mariana Mota Prado and Steven J Hoffman, 'The Promises and Perils of International Institutional Bypasses: Defining a New Concept and Its Policy Implications for Global Governance' (2019) 10 Transnational Legal Theory 275.

[124] Laura Gómez-Mera, 'Regime Complexity and Global Governance: The Case of Trafficking in Persons': (2016) 22 European Journal of International Relations 566 (discussing the 'cooperative' use of regime shifting, forum linking, and other cross-fora strategies by IGOs, civil society organizations, and other principled actors, to promote their normative mandates).

[125] Acharya (n 60) 460.

[126] Han-Wei Liu and Ching-Fu Lin, 'Artificial Intelligence and Global Trade Governance: A Pluralist Agenda' (2020) 61 Harvard International Law Journal <https://papers.ssrn.com/abstract=3675505> accessed 26 September 2020.

[127] Gómez-Mera, Morin, and Van De Graaf (n 2) 141–147.

In a similar approach, Mette Eilstrup-Sangiovanni and Oliver Westerwinter have sketched an adjacent framework of 'global governance complexity', arguing that this model allows one to identify, in turn: (1) the *structure* of a global governance complex, along different dimensions: scale (the number of constituent institutions), diversity (the heterogeneity of the types of institutions), and density (the number and diversity of ties between them); (2) the *governance outcomes* of this structure, for institutional collaboration, problem-solving capacity, and power dynamics and distributive conflicts; and (3) the *evolution* of the global governance complex over time.[128]

Drawing on these frameworks, I argue that a regime complexity lens can be usefully applied to understand five key aspects of any governance system: *origins*, *topology*, *evolution*, *consequences*, and *strategies*. These are five aspects that will be valuable to explore for both those who study AI governance and those who seek to develop and implement it.

6.5.1 Origins: Foundations or Viability of the Regime

In the first place, examining the *origins* of a prospective AI regime can help understand its foundations or viability.

That is, for a given AI issue that has not yet been subject to a regime, states or other parties may see sufficient cause to create (sets of) new institutions. Is a meaningful regime even viable? Should we expect the emergence of a regime or regime complexes for a specific AI issue, or may those issues remain in a 'non-regime' state? Conversely, if some fragmented institutions and norms already exist on an issue, why have these been established and supported by states and other stakeholders, and how robust are these foundations?

In either case, this analysis can draw on various lines of evidence. It can depart from an outside-view comparison with the governance of other technologies or issue areas. More importantly, from an inside view, it can also draw on established scholarship on the causes and origins of specific regimes or institutions. For instance, we can draw on traditional rationalist accounts of the potential functions that a regime can fulfil, in terms of the (state) interests such a regime could meet. We can also complement these with constructivist accounts of possible avenues of norm creation and development, and explore the ways in which norm entrepreneurs such as epistemic communities or transnational issue networks might be able to shift state perceptions and preferences.

This can yield insights, not just in the overall viability of successful governance for a certain issue, but also in comparing the desirability and sufficiency of distinct

[128] Eilstrup-Sangiovanni and Westerwinter (n 6).

strategies. Finally—and drawing from our discussion of governance disruption—we can consider the resilience of different regime designs to ongoing, further technological change.

6.5.2 Topology of the Regime Complex

In the second place, the regime complexity lens allows us to examine the extant *topology* (i.e. 'state' or structure) of the AI governance architecture at a given moment. This allows a snapshot description of the size, density, and organisation (e.g. level of centralization and/or hierarchy) of networks of treaties, institutions, and norms that pertain to any given AI issue.[129] By doing this, we can begin to understand the gaps, tensions, or synergies between these elements, whether at the level of norms, goals, institutions, or impacts.

6.5.3 Evolution of Complexity Over Time

Third, this framework allows exploration of the *evolution* of regime complexity over time, either to shed light on past developments and trends[130] or, more speculatively, to understand both regime-specific and general factors affecting regime complexity, in order to extrapolate various near-future trajectories of fragmentation or integration for an AI regime.

Specifically, we can explore such potential trajectories by considering various general factors that have been theorized to drive further fragmentation. We can also, however, complement this analysis by considering the role that (AI-driven) governance disruption may play in shaping regime complexity on AI, driving or inhibiting eventual patterns of consolidation over time.

6.5.4 Consequences of Complexity

Fourth, the regime complex lens allows a structured study of the *consequences* of fragmentation and high regime complexity. Whether the regime remains fragmented or will become centralized may, as discussed, have significant implications for the overall legal coherence, efficacy, or legitimacy of the resulting AI governance architecture. This is of value from an analytical perspective: applying this lens, and drawing on lessons from other international regimes, we may be able to

[129] See generally Kim (n 7).
[130] For instance, see Caroline Fehl's exploration of the evolution of institutional inequalities in the arms control regime: Fehl (n 36).

anticipate some of the likely implications of distinct trajectories of AI regime complexity and various forms of inter-institutional interaction. However, this is also of key relevance for a normative perspective, as it can better inform advance debates over what may be the trade-offs or risks involved in various trajectories (whether decentralized or centralized), and accordingly can help us understand which of these scenarios would be optimal or acceptably functional for governing different AI issue clusters.

6.5.5 Strategies for Managing Complexity

Fifth, on this basis, we can pursue a tentative exploration of *strategies* that can be used to manage institutional activities on the likely AI governance architecture—however it evolves—in more productive ways.

On the one hand, if the AI regime complex remains fragmented, we can consider new strategies aimed at managing the interactions of these diverse institutions in ways that avert conflict and increase abilities for accommodation or synergy. On the other hand, if some type of form of centralized institution is established, we can consider various strategies for institutional design that may help avert or mitigate some of the risks of such a structure. By coupling various strategies developed within regime complex scholarship to the insights drawn from the sociotechnical change and governance disruption lenses, a set of tentative recommendations are yielded to enable AI governance regimes—of either form—to be more effective, resilient, or coherent.

6.6 Conclusion: AI and Regime Complexity

In this chapter, I have briefly introduced the third perspective on change in AI governance: changes *for* AI governance that derive *from* broader trends and dynamics in governance architectures. To do so, I drew from the scholarship on regime complexity to argue that this is likely a suitable and fertile lens for analysis. I also reviewed some perspectives on the theorized consequences of high regime complexity for governance, suggesting that this will be a crucial consideration for AI governance. Finally, I laid out a rough research programme of five questions that can and should be productively considered when we map the state, course, development, and consequences of the AI governance regime complex.

The regime complexity perspective is useful for offering a lens on governance systems that considers the messy political interactions and strategic moves of various actors within an institutional landscape that is not frozen but quite dynamic. In this way, it contributes a more explicitly political lens to the technology law approaches of sociotechnical change and governance disruption.

In sum, the three chapters in Part II of the book have presented three perspectives on 'AI governance under change'. These lenses—on sociotechnical change, governance disruption, and regime complexity—can each individually be applied to problems and questions in AI governance. However, they can also be used in a complementary fashion. As such, the final step of this investigation will apply insights from all three theories to an exploration of various facets of the emerging AI governance regime. In structuring this analysis, I will draw on the five analytical steps articulated in this chapter (origin, topology, evolution, consequences and strategies). In doing so, I do not aim to provide a definitive answer, but rather to draw out the strengths and limits of these three conceptual lenses in coming to terms with the complexity of global governance for AI.

PART III
FRAMEWORKS FOR CHOICE

7
Framing a Global AI Regime Complex in Five Steps

7.1 Introduction

The global AI governance architecture is in a state of rapid change. How can we understand the origins, shape, and future evolution of this emerging governance structure? How can we anticipate the consequences of different institutional trajectories, and develop effective governance strategies to manage these?

In the previous three chapters, I have drawn on existing scholarship in the fields of technology law and global governance, and introduced and discussed three distinct perspectives on change that are critical to AI governance. To briefly recap: in Chapter 4, I drew on the concept of sociotechnical change as a way to help us consider when and where changes in AI technology or its capabilities enable sociotechnical changes in (international) society, when and why these changes create a rationale for regulation, and which of AI's material features or problem logics define its texture as a governance target. In Chapter 5, I introduced the lens of governance disruption, which helps us understand when, where, and how new AI capabilities could induce helpful or harmful changes in the substance, processes, or instruments of international law. Finally, in Chapter 6, I drew on the lens of regime complexity to structure analysis into when, how, and why changes in the broader global governance architectures—and in particular interactions among individual AI regimes, institutions, or norms—may shift key conditions for global AI governance.[1]

Together, these three lenses provide complementary perspectives on how AI regimes are affected and shaped—directly and indirectly—by these three aspects of sociotechnical, legal, and political change. However, what does this mean concretely? Until now, we have discussed these perspectives mostly in isolation. This chapter aims to draw them together in an analytical framework or toolkit. It explores what insights these approaches can provide to understanding existing, emerging, or proposed AI regimes throughout their lifecycle, within the governance architecture, and at different levels of abstraction. On this basis I derive

[1] See Jonas Tallberg and others, 'The Global Governance of Artificial Intelligence: Next Steps for Empirical and Normative Research' (2023) 25 International Studies Review viad040.

Architectures of Global AI Governance. Matthijs M. Maas, Oxford University Press. © Matthijs M. Maas 2025.
DOI: 10.1093/9780191988455.003.0008

a series of considerations, opportunities, challenges, and trade-offs that both researchers and practitioners of AI governance should better account for.

As such, following the five steps of the framework introduced in Chapter 6, this chapter will explore how studies of AI governance architectures can and should engage with patterns, trends, or shocks of AI-driven change at the levels of *origins*, *topology*, *evolution*, *consequences*, and *strategies*,[2] in ways that can help ensure that the AI regime complex achieves adequate efficacy, resilience, and coherence in the face of global technological, legal, and political change. At each analytical step, the concepts explored in this book help enrich analysis and improve our choices in terms of the policy options available (see Table 7.1).

To be clear, I do not mean to suggest that this is the only way to structure an analysis of AI governance on the basis of these three approaches.[3] Neither is my aim here to provide conclusive answers. The aim is simply to show the importance and key consequences of different forms of organization, and to highlight questions that may be asked about initiatives or proposals within the AI regime complex.

7.2 Origins: The Purpose, Foundations, and Design of an AI Regime

In the first place, we can consider the origins and foundations of a given regime for AI. This is helpful whether we are considering the political robustness of an existing regime or institution, or whether we are aiming to understand the viability—or paths toward establishment—of a desired future regime. This involves an explicit analysis of three aspects of a proposed or envisioned AI regime: its purpose, its viability, and its design.

To work through these questions, we will, in the next sections, focus in on some examples, particularly around the security governance regime complex for military AI applications, as well as for recently proposed international institutions for advanced AI. While not all of the particulars of these discussions will therefore necessarily apply well to considering the global governance of conventional (i.e. civil, narrow) AI systems, the overall approach should still help inform.

[2] This framework draws on, but extends, another framework of analysis which distinguishes between the scale, diversity, density and hierarchy, of a governance complex. See Mette Eilstrup-Sangiovanni and Oliver Westerwinter, 'The Global Governance Complexity Cube: Varieties of Institutional Complexity in Global Governance' (2022) 17 The Review of International Organizations 233. This framework has also been recently applied to map the evolution of the AI governance regime complex, in: Johannes Geith, Magnus Lundgren and Jonas Tallberg, 'The Emerging Regime Complex for Artificial Intelligence' [2025 forthcoming] *Global Studies Quarterly*.

[3] For instance, Tallberg and others use a distinct analytical framework along five dimensions of regulatory arrangements in the AI governance landscape: (1) whether regulation is horizontal or vertical; (2) centralization to decentralization; (3) hard law to soft law; (4); private versus public regulation; (5) military and non-military regulation. Tallberg and others (n 1).

Table 7.1 Overview of analysis of AI governance regime complex

	Theme	Questions
Origins Of individual regimes	**Purpose:** Is a regime needed?	• What are the underlying **technological developments**? What are the AI **capabilities** of concern? What new actors, actions, or artefacts arise? • What (anticipated) **sociotechnical change** do these enable? • What **governance rationales** are raised? (e.g. market failures, risks to human health, moral interests, social solidarity, democratic processes, or international law itself) • What material features and problem logics characterize this **governance target**?
	Foundations: (why) Is any regime viable? How robust are its foundations?	• From a comparative **historical perspective**, (when) were past regimes for similar (technological) challenges viable? • What are the functions of this regime? What (state) **interests** would it meet? • How might actors shift **norms** to render it (more or less) viable?
	Design: What regimes would be optimal or adequate?	• Which broad **issue clusters** does it aim to cover? (e.g. conventional AI, military AI, advanced AI) • What **governance strategy** does it pursue? (i.e. reliance on: (1) extending soft law, (1) unilateral deterrence, (2) gradual norm development, (3) extension of existing regimes or institutions, (4) new regime or institution) • Which **type of control** does it pursue? (e.g. ban or regulatory treaty?), how resilient does this make the regime to governance disruption?
Topology of regime complex at a given time	**Demographics**	• **Size** and **composition** of network (what are the applicable norms or treaties, active institutions or governance initiatives?)
	Organisation of network	• **Density** of institutional network (number of membership overlaps, institutional contact points on AI issue area) • **Links:** relating to norms, goals, impacts, or institutional relations

(continued)

Table 7.1 Continued

	Theme	Questions
	Interactions and outcomes of linkages	• **Gaps**: functional non-regime, issue unaddressed • **Conflictive:** active norm conflicts, operational externalities, turf wars • **Cooperative:** loose integration, but norm relationships unclear • **Synergistic:** mutually reinforcing norms or IO division of labour
	Scope of analysis	• **Macro**: e.g. interactions of AI regime complex with other regimes (trade, data privacy, transport), or with general international law • **Meso**: e.g. interactions of military AI regime with advanced AI regimes • **Micro**: e.g. inter-institutional dynamics within advanced AI regime complex
Evolution given ...	**General trends** in regime complexity?	• **Exogenous drives of fragmentation**: density, accretion, power shifts over time, preference changes, modernity, representation and voice goals, local governance
	Effects of AI **governance disruption**?	• **Development**: AI as generator or trigger of latent regime fault lines • **Displacement**: AI as shield, patch, cure, or accelerator of fragmentation • **Destruction:** AI as driver of governance contestation
Consequences of trajectories ...	If regime complex remains **fragmented**	• **Drawbacks:** undercuts coherence of international law, operational dysfunction, barriers to access and power inequalities, strategic vulnerability to forum-shopping
		• **Benefits:** problem-solving, more democratic, inclusive, greater trust
	If regime complex is **integrated**	• **Drawbacks**: slow establishment rate, brittleness, breadth vs. depth dilemma
		• **Benefits:** greater political power, efficiency and participation, can avert forum-shopping

Table 7.1 Continued

	Theme	Questions
(selected) **Strategies** for managing AI regimes to ensure . . .	**Efficacy** (sociotechnical change)	• **Regulatory approach:** govern sociotechnical change, consider regulatory texture, anticipatory action under incomplete information • **Instrument choice:** avoid siloed approach, or ensure harmonization • **Instrument design:** tailored use of content flexibility (e.g. tech neutrality)
	Resilience (governance disruption)	• **Regulatory approach:** expect frequent legal disruption, prepare for AI-enabled contestation • **Instrument choice:** treaties and bans may be brittle, beware unreflexive use of analogies, explore cooperation-supportive AI • **Instrument design:** tailored use of design flexibility mechanisms (amendment voting thresholds, authoritative interpreters), beware proxies
	Coherence (regime complexity)	• **Regulatory approach:** fit AI institutions into broader governance architecture, strengthen regime foundations (norms and interests) • **Instrument choice:** consider centralization–decentralization trade-offs, and identify instruments that address them • **Instrument design:** regime interplay management mechanisms

The lens of regime complexity can help evaluate an AI regime's viability, exploring when or how states might find sufficient common interests in regulating certain AI applications, and allowing an understanding of processes of norm-shaping by various actors and coalitions. Finally, the lens of governance disruption can help illuminate conditions under which various regime designs are more or less resilient to further technological change.

7.2.1 Regime Purpose: Sociotechnical Changes and Governance Rationales

In the first place, we should ask: Why is global governance needed? In a sociotechnical perspective, is a particular AI technology, capability, or application a concern? What new behaviours, entities, or relations does it create? Will these capabilities be widely pursued and deployed? If they are, what governance rationales would these changes create? And how should we think about governance, taking into consideration both the technology's material features and cross-application problem logics?

7.2.1.1 Military AI governance rationale: sociotechnical change

How large will the sociotechnical changes that result from the military use of AI be? To be clear, there remains widespread uncertainty over exactly how disruptive AI will prove in the military context.[4] In the longer term, many anticipate far-reaching or even foundational changes. AI has been described by some as 'revolutionary',[5] on the argument that virtually any aspect of military operations might be improved or made faster or more accurate through the integration of this technology.[6] Autonomy has been described as 'the third revolution in warfare, after gunpowder and nuclear arms'.[7] This has led some to anticipate widespread and unconstrained proliferation of such technology, on the assumption that '[t]he applications of AI to warfare and espionage are likely to be as irresistible as aircraft'.[8] Kenneth Payne has suggested that, if the use of AI systems will shift and displace human judgement, they might have a larger impact on the psychological essence of strategic affairs than did even nuclear weapons in their time.[9]

That is not to say that all of these changes are imminent or will occur in the near-term.[10] Indeed, AI technology will face operational, organizational, and cultural barriers to adoption and deployment, such that the reality of military AI may appear relatively mundane in the immediate future. Militaries might face unexpected hurdles in procuring such systems from private sector tech companies, because of mismatches in their organizational processes, development approach, and system requirements.[11] That may not stop such systems, but it can certainly

[4] See also Chapter 2 for a discussion of developments in military AI.

[5] For instance, US accounts have frequently described it as a 'revolution' in military affairs. Greg Allen and Taniel Chan, 'Artificial Intelligence and National Security' (Harvard Kennedy School, Belfer Center for Science and International Affairs 2017) 70 <http://www.belfercenter.org/sites/default/files/files/publication/AI%20NatSec%20-%20final.pdf> accessed 19 July 2017.

[6] For instance, for an influential early US study of the conditions under which autonomy adds value to weapon systems, see Defense Science Board, 'Defense Science Board Summer Study on Autonomy' (US Department of Defense 2016) <https://www.hsdl.org/?abstract&did=794641> accessed 26 February 2017.

[7] Future of Life Institute, 'Open Letter on Autonomous Weapons' (*Future of Life Institute*, 2015) <https://futureoflife.org/open-letter-autonomous-weapons/> accessed 22 November 2018.

[8] Allen and Chan (n 5) 50.

[9] Kenneth Payne, 'Artificial Intelligence: A Revolution in Strategic Affairs?' (2018) 60 Survival 7, 7, 30.

[10] As argued by Michael Horowitz, '[m]ost applications of AI to militaries are still in their infancy, and most applications of algorithms for militaries will be in areas such as logistics and training rather than close to or on the battlefield'. Michael C Horowitz, 'Do Emerging Military Technologies Matter for International Politics?' (2020) 23 Annual Review of Political Science 385, 396.

[11] Maaike Verbruggen, 'The Role of Civilian Innovation in the Development of Lethal Autonomous Weapon Systems' (2019) 10 Global Policy 338.

slow them for some, and high-profile failures might temper some enthusiasm. In other cases, highly anticipated applications may remain beyond current AI capabilities for at least a few more years. For instance, it has been argued that current machine learning systems do not lend themselves well to integration into nuclear targeting, given the difficulty of collating sufficient, reliable, and reliably secure (i.e. non-poisoned) training data sets for imagery of nuclear targets such as mobile launch vehicles.[12] Nonetheless, if even a small subset of these diverse capabilities were to be achieved and deployed, their impact on practices of war could still become considerable.[13]

As emphasized in Chapter 4, the point is not to attempt to predict specific technological trends or individual use cases, but rather to understand when, under what conditions, and for what reasons AI uses could enable sociotechnical changes that correspond to overarching *governance rationales.*

To be sure, certainly not all envisaged military uses of AI would necessarily create problems that require governance. Indeed, certain applications, such as in optimizing medical evacuation logistics, might appear broadly beneficial at first glance.[14] Of course, even systems that do not in and of themselves raise ethical challenges could still raise new security risks indirectly, through their susceptibility to adversarial inputs or spoofing.[15]

In other cases, such as around the impacts of AI weapons on conventional deterrence or conflict stability, there still is less clarity over what these effects would

[12] See Rafael Loss and Joseph Johnson, 'Will Artificial Intelligence Imperil Nuclear Deterrence?' (*War on the Rocks*, 19 September 2019) <https://warontherocks.com/2019/09/will-artificial-intelligence-imperil-nuclear-deterrence/> accessed 4 December 2019. At the same time, it has been countered that even if AI is not useable for direct nuclear targeting, they could still disrupt nuclear stability through their integration in novel autonomous platforms or in (anti-submarine) sensing capabilities. Zachary Kallenborn, 'AI Risks to Nuclear Deterrence Are Real' (*War on the Rocks*, 10 October 2019) <https://warontherocks.com/2019/10/ai-risks-to-nuclear-deterrence-are-real/> accessed 16 October 2019. However, for a partial counter-argument, see also Tom A Stefanick, 'Undersea Nuclear Forces: Survivability of Chinese, Russian, and US SSBNS' (2025) 48 Journal of Strategic Studies 1 (arguing that, given geographic and oceanographic constraints on tracking ballistic missile submarines, it is more likely that new technologies may effectively shield such assets than threaten them).

[13] Jack McDonald, 'What If Military AI Is a Washout?' (June 2021) <https://jackmcdonald.org/book/2021/06/what-if-military-ai-sucks/> accessed 24 June 2021.

[14] In general, objections to the application of robotic and autonomous technologies to military tasks often depend not just on the specific level of autonomy involved, but also (especially) on the category of task being automated. See Hugo Klijn and Maaike Okano-Heijmans, 'Managing Robotic and Autonomous Systems (RAS)' (The Hague Centre for Strategic Studies 2020) 8 <https://www.clingendael.org/publication/managing-robotic-and-autonomous-systems-ras> accessed 17 March 2020. For another survey, see Catherine Aiken, Rebecca Kagan, and Michael Page, '"Cool Projects" or "Expanding the Efficiency of the Murderous American War Machine?" AI Professionals' Views on Working With the Department of Defense' (Center for Security and Emerging Technology 2020) <https://cset.georgetown.edu/publication/cool-projects-or-expanding-the-efficiency-of-the-murderous-american-war-machine/> accessed 12 January 2024.

[15] See for instance Samuel G Finlayson and others, 'Adversarial Attacks on Medical Machine Learning' (2019) 363 Science 1287.

actually be—that is, whether or not they would be stabilizing or destabilizing, or how they would affect relative and absolute military power generally.[16]

Nonetheless, many military applications of AI produce sociotechnical changes that constitute plausible or even pressing rationales for governance: one could easily see how such systems pose the risk of new harms to human welfare,[17] as well as potential threats to rights.

7.2.1.2 Military AI as governance target: materiality and problem logics

Once governance rationales have been established, the next step is to consider the texture of an AI issue as a governance *target*. As discussed, this involves a simultaneous consideration of relevant material factors of the technology, along with the problem logics engaged in its use.

What are the governance-relevant material or architectural features of the technology? It should be emphasized that in most cases these characteristics are not 'essential features', but they can involve temporary but relatively stable aspects which affect or foreground certain patterns of use over others or which shape public perceptions or first impressions of the technology. In the case of military AI applications, what are such relevant characteristics? Watts and Crootof have previously theorized a set of technological features that affect how 'regulation-tolerant' or 'regulation-resistant' new weapons technologies can be.[18] Drawing these together, Crootof has produced a list of conditions under which a weapons ban is most likely to be successful.[19] To provide an indicative overview, these are sketched and assessed in the context of various military AI applications (see Table 7.2).[20]

To be clear, these considerations do not yield a single hard-and-fast heuristic. One objection might be that it is not particularly useful to list the prospects for a ban on, or restrictive regulation of, military AI as a general class, since AI's diverse applications in diverse military contexts may have very different material, strategic, and political features. For instance, while at a glance this might appear to paint a somewhat pessimistic picture regarding the viability of an outright or blanket ban on military AI, it is important to disaggregate these also. Certainly, there appear to be few military AI use cases that would score very well (that is,

[16] For one exploration of how AI developments could affect military organizations and powers, see Benjamin M Jensen, Christopher Whyte, and Scott Cuomo, 'Algorithms at War: The Promise, Peril, and Limits of Artificial Intelligence' (2020) 22 International Studies Review 526.

[17] Including at a potentially massive scale. See Matthijs Maas, Kayla Lucero-Matteucci, and Di Cooke, 'Military Artificial Intelligence as a Contributor to Global Catastrophic Risk', *The Era of Global Risk* (Open Book Publishers 2023).

[18] Sean Watts, 'Regulation-Tolerant Weapons, Regulation-Resistant Weapons and the Law of War' (2015) 91 International Law Studies 83; Rebecca Crootof, 'The Killer Robots Are Here: Legal and Policy Implications' (2015) 36 Cardozo Law Review 1837, 1884.

[19] Rebecca Crootof, 'Jurisprudential Space Junk: Treaties and New Technologies' in Chiara Giorgetti and Natalie Klein (eds), *Resolving Conflicts in the Law* (Brill | Nijhoff 2019) 115–116.

[20] Criteria by Rebecca Crootof (ibid); assessments mine. See also the earlier evaluation in Crootof, 'The Killer Robots Are Here' (n 18) 1891–1893.

Table 7.2 Military AI as governance target: considering material and political features (drawing on criteria by Crootof, 2019)

Condition	AI?	Notes
*The weapon is [considered] ineffective**	-	(-) AI seen by number of parties as cornerstone of next military revolution (+) some military concerns over effectiveness or applicability of machine learning to all military contexts, given data scarcity, risks of adversarial spoofing
Other means exist for accomplishing a similar military objective	+	(+) Is potentially the case for applications where AI is 'merely' labour-saving (e.g. automated image processing) (+) Arguably the case for anti-personnel LAWS (-) May not be the case for applications where AI provides key competitive edge or marginal advantage (e.g. aerial superiority, cyberwarfare)
*The weapon is not novel: it is easily analogized to other weapons, and its usages and effects are well understood**	-	(?) While long history of use, many technologies are (perceived to be) fairly novel (?) LAWS sometimes analogized to anti-personnel landmines or blinding lasers (-) Has already led to conceptual ambiguity over various terms (-) Usage, effects and limits of present AI capabilities not well understood
The weapon or similar weapons have been previously regulated	+/-	(-) AI generally considered a novel unprecedented technology—but . . . (+) previous attempts to regulate UAVs and/or militarily useful 'software'. . . but (-) with limited success (cryptography, 2016 missile software under MTCR) (+) integrations of AI into existing weapons could ensure the resulting assemblage is more easily compared to 'already regulated' weapons (+) comparison to WMD could set precedent for regulation
*The weapon is unlikely to cause social or military disruption**	--	(-) Many uses of AI might cause large-scale military disruption (-) Kinetic uses of AI ('Killer Robots'), especially by non-state actors in terrorism, might cause large-scale social disruption
The weapon has not already been integrated into a state's armed forces	-	(+) Some advanced applications (e.g. nuclear NC2) not yet deployed (-) But: many other applications or in trial stage, significant investments
The weapon causes superfluous injury or suffering in relation to prevailing standards of medical care	-	(-) LAWS-mounted weapons do not intrinsically cause more suffering; injuries are less visceral or distinctive than for blinding lasers or anti-personnel mines (+) 'Machine killing' carries its own peculiar taboo; drone swarms (perhaps) especially so (-) Many 'lethality-enabling' AI systems may allow non-kinetic interventions

(continued)

Table 7.2 Continued

Condition	AI?	Notes
*The weapon is inherently indiscriminate**	+	(+) Potentially true for some AI capabilities today, but... (-) many AI weapons might be(come) more 'accurate' over time (+) malicious use could involve perversely 'discriminate' targeting (e.g. by race, gender; political affiliation), which would be politically visceral (+) implicit risk of hacking or spoofing may result in 'indiscriminate' firing
*The weapon is or is perceived to be sufficiently notorious to galvanize public concern and spur civil society activism**	++	(+) Significant public campaign against 'Killer Robots' (+) Surveys show rising global opposition to LAWS (but conditional on framing) (+) Early deployment incidents might galvanize further acute concern (-) Public opprobrium may have narrow scope ('Killer Robots'); with comparatively less outcry about broader 'lethality-enabling' use
*There is sufficient state commitment to enacting regulations**	+/-	(+) 30 states support outright ban, many others see human control as critical (+) Some (though mixed) private sector support in ban or restrictions (-) But: currently not much interest among leading developer states
*The scope of the ban is clear and narrowly tailored (... states understand precisely what technology and associated capabilities they are voluntarily relinquishing);**	--	(-) 'Meaningful human control' is promising line, but often conceptually and operationally blurred (-) Definitional problems around AI, and uncertainties over exact scope, breadth, and reach of future capability development, suggest states cannot clearly (perceive they) understand what capabilities they are relinquishing
*Violations can be identified**	-	(-) In many cases may be hard to monitor compliance (in non-intrusive way) (-) In context of cyberwarfare AI, doubly so (attribution also hard), but... (+) AI capabilities could help in monitoring and detecting violations

Note: starred (*) criteria may depend on state perceptions or expectations of AI technology, which might be shifted through shocks, incidents, or epistemic community action.

have a favourable regulatory texture) across all 12 criteria.[21] Nonetheless, this set of criteria does help in examining whether, or to what extent, certain distinctive

[21] One possible exception might be the potential use of AI systems or robots for the purposes of torture or interrogation. On which, see Amanda McAllister, 'Stranger than Science Fiction: The Rise of A.I. Interrogation in the Dawn of Autonomous Robots and the Need for an Additional Protocol to the U.N. Convention Against Torture' (2018) 101 Minnesota Law Review 2527.

military applications of AI—whether in LAWS, AI-enabled cyberwarfare systems, predictive war-gaming algorithms, the use of AI in nuclear command and control systems, or the use of LLM-based generative chatbots in battlefield decision-making—might score differently on these criteria, in ways that make them more or less 'regulation-tolerant' governance *targets* from a purely material or artefactual point of view.

In addition to material features, we can consider military AI technologies as governance targets by examining their problem logics. As discussed, military AI uses have fed high-profile concerns across diverse dimensions.[22] Yet most of these problems can be characterised by some combination of *ethical challenges*, *security threats*, *safety risks*, and *structural shifts*.

Ethical challenges include, for instance, concerns that AI weapons would challenge human dignity,[23] or that practically they create problems in terms of accountability and responsibility.[24] Other concerns have centred on the potential for these technologies to see gradual osmosis towards domestic and law enforcement use, resulting in the militarization of policing and the blurring of the critical distinction, in international law, between war and peace.[25] As suggested in Chapter 4, ethical challenges around AI can be difficult to govern, because they typically face one of two barriers to governance. One is actor ignorance of or relative apathy to the threatened values or rights; a deeper barrier may be underlying societal disagreement over the values, interests, or rights at stake (e.g. how to weight the protection of a society's military forces with strict adherence to the laws of war).[26]

[22] For useful overviews, see also Forrest E Morgan and others, 'Military Applications of Artificial Intelligence: Ethical Concerns in an Uncertain World' (RAND Corporation 2020) <https://www.rand.org/content/dam/rand/pubs/research_reports/RR3100/RR3139-1/RAND_RR3139-1.pdf>; Denise Garcia, 'Lethal Artificial Intelligence and Change: The Future of International Peace and Security' (2018) 20 International Studies Review 334; Michael C Horowitz, 'Artificial Intelligence, International Competition, and the Balance of Power' [2018] *Texas National Security Review* <https://tnsr.org/2018/05/artificial-intelligence-international-competition-and-the-balance-of-power/> accessed 17 May 2018.

[23] Elvira Rosert and Frank Sauer, 'Prohibiting Autonomous Weapons: Put Human Dignity First' (2019) 10 Global Policy 370. Though for a critical examination, see Daniel Lim, 'Killer Robots and Human Dignity', *Proceedings of the 2019 AAAI/ACM Conference on AI, Ethics, and Society* (Association for Computing Machinery 2019) <https://doi.org/10.1145/3306618.3314291> accessed 5 June 2025.

[24] Rebecca Crootof, 'War Torts: Accountability for Autonomous Weapons' (2016) 164 University of Pennsylvania Law Review 1347.

[25] Denise Garcia, 'Future Arms, Technologies, and International Law: Preventive Security Governance' (2016) 1 European Journal of International Security 94; Human Rights Watch, 'Shaking the Foundations: The Human Rights Implications of Killer Robots' (Human Rights Watch 2014) <https://www.hrw.org/report/2014/05/12/shaking-foundations/human-rights-implications-killer-robots> accessed 18 February 2021. On this trend, see also more generally Rosa Brooks, 'War Everywhere: Rights, National Security Law, and the Law of Armed Conflict in the Age of Terror' (2004) 153 University of Pennsylvania Law Review 675.

[26] Ondřej Rosendorf, Michal Smetana, and Marek Vranka, 'Algorithmic Aversion? Experimental Evidence on the Elasticity of Public Attitudes to "Killer Robots"' (2023) 0 Security Studies 1, 3 ('Our findings demonstrate that although there is a substantial baseline aversion to LAWS among the public, these attitudes also exhibit a significant degree of elasticity . . . public support for LAWS is contingent on their error-proneness relative to human-operated systems . . . our findings do not provide empirical

In other cases, however, the governance problem posed by military AI capabilities can be clustered as new *security threats*. As such, there are concerns around possible hacking or adversarial attacks. Governance responses tailored to such challenges have to reckon not just with the 'malice' or adversarial intent of actors, but also with the broader offence–defence balance of a given line of AI research or knowledge, and what this reveals about the feasibility of scaling effective defensive solutions.[27] In general, the problem logic of security challenges foregrounds perpetrator-focused solutions (e.g. the prevention of access, the improving of detection and forensic capabilities to ensure attribution), as well as target-focused measures (such as reducing exposure of systems to adversarial inputs). Because militaries have a clear interest in averting spoofing attacks on their AI capabilities, this might imply that strong international collaboration would not be needed to assure this. Nonetheless, even here, states could gain from sharing best practices or security techniques,[28] in ways that might involve some coordination, standard-setting, or international codes of conduct.[29]

In terms of *safety risks*, there is concern that the use of military AI capabilities in complex and confused theatres of war might be highly susceptible to new

support for the proposition that the explicit mentioning of command responsibility can alleviate opposition to LAWS . . . we find limited empirical support for the proposition that concerns about human dignity violations increase public opposition to these weapon systems'). Similarly, an early, 2016 survey of public opinion on killer robots suggests that the public is more favourable to these technologies when there are concerns that other countries or non-state actors are developing them, or when their use would protect their own forces. Michael C Horowitz, 'Public Opinion and the Politics of the Killer Robots Debate' (2016) 3 Research & Politics 2053168015627183. More recently, a 2023 survey finds similar context-specific public support for the use of LAWS, for instance in support of homeland defence, as well as demographic influences. Koki Arai and Masakazu Matsumoto, 'Public Perceptions of Autonomous Lethal Weapons Systems' [2023] AI and Ethics <https://doi.org/10.1007/s43681-023-00282-9> accessed 14 January 2024. Other surveys have found that the public values different design features alongside and beyond human control, including system reliability, verifiability, and retrievability. Christine Boshuijzen-van Burken and others, 'Autonomous Military Systems beyond Human Control: Putting an Empirical Perspective on Value Trade-Offs for Autonomous Systems Design in the Military' [2024] AI & Society <https://doi.org/10.1007/s00146-024-02000-3> accessed 7 October 2024.

[27] Toby Shevlane and Allan Dafoe, 'The Offense–Defense Balance of Scientific Knowledge: Does Publishing AI Research Reduce Misuse?' *Proceedings of the 2020 AAAI/ACM Conference on AI, Ethics, and Society (AIES '20)* (ACM 2020) <http://arxiv.org/abs/2001.00463> accessed 9 January 2020.

[28] Richard Danzig, 'Technology Roulette: Managing Loss of Control as Many Militaries Pursue Technological Superiority' (Center for a New American Security 2018) <https://www.cnas.org/publications/reports/technology-roulette> accessed 2 July 2018. For instance, in the area of nuclear weapon security, the US has previously shared—or 'leaked'—the technologies around the 'permissive action links' locks used on nuclear weapons to both allies and rivals (respectively) in order to promote security and stability. Joseph S Nye, 'Nuclear Learning and U.S.–Soviet Security Regimes' (1987) 41 International Organization 371; See generally Peter Stein and Peter Feaver, *Assuring Control of Nuclear Weapons: The Evolution of Permissive Action Links* (University Press of America 1989).

[29] Lena Trabucco and Matthijs M Maas, 'Technology Ties: The Rise and Roles of Military AI Strategic Partnerships' (10 November 2023) <https://papers.ssrn.com/abstract=4629283> accessed 10 November 2023; Sarah Shoker and others, 'Confidence-Building Measures for Artificial Intelligence: Workshop Proceedings' (arXiv, 3 August 2023) <http://arxiv.org/abs/2308.00862> accessed 7 August 2023.

accidents, in the form of these systems' unexpected behaviour or inability to discriminate sufficiently among targets, or because of emergent accident risks.[30] This has expressed itself in concerns over how or why false positives, spoofing, or catastrophic interaction between systems could exacerbate international crises.[31] In terms of their problem logics, it is important to understand how safety challenges in various military AI applications arise from (or interact with) (1) actor negligence, overtrust, and automation bias at the operator level; (2) the complexity and 'tight coupling' of AI systems at the organizational level; and (3) the 'many hands' problem at the level of design and production.

Accordingly, safety issues around military AI systems in diverse domains and roles foreground their own set of governance logics. These could include (1) framework solutions that pursue 'meaningful human control' not merely at the operator level but throughout the system design and deployment lifecycle;[32] (2) the funding and dissemination of broad-spectrum AI safety engineering techniques to ensure AI system reliability, corrigibility, or interpretability; (3) institutional and legal mechanisms that ensure appropriate liability and state responsibility for harm;[33] (4) bilateral or multilateral international agreements to provide for restraint against deploying AI capabilities from particularly sensitive contexts (e.g. nuclear command and control) where safety failures would be utterly unacceptable.[34]

[30] Paul Scharre, 'Autonomous Weapons and Operational Risk' (Center for a New American Security 2016) <https://www.cnas.org/publications/reports/autonomous-weapons-and-operational-risk> accessed 23 March 2016; John Borrie, 'Safety, Unintentional Risk and Accidents in the Weaponization of Increasingly Autonomous Technologies' (UNIDIR 2016) UNIDIR Resources 5 <http://www.unidir.org/files/publications/pdfs/safety-unintentional-risk-and-accidents-en-668.pdf> accessed 7 March 2018; Stephanie Carvin, 'Normal Autonomous Accidents: What Happens When Killer Robots Fail?' (Social Science Research Network 2017) SSRN Scholarly Paper ID 3161446 <https://papers.ssrn.com/abstract=3161446> accessed 17 December 2019. For an argument that many competitive AI systems could be vulnerable to such failure modes, see Matthijs M Maas, 'Regulating for "Normal AI Accidents": Operational Lessons for the Responsible Governance of Artificial Intelligence Deployment', *Proceedings of the 2018 AAAI/ACM Conference on AI, Ethics, and Society* (Association for Computing Machinery 2018) <https://doi.org/10.1145/3278721.3278766> accessed 8 September 2020.

[31] Paul Scharre, 'Autonomous Weapons and Stability' (King's College 2020) <https://kclpure.kcl.ac.uk/portal/en/theses/autonomous-weapons-and-stability(92cd3d5b-4eb1-4ad5-a9ca-0cce2491e652).html> accessed 31 May 2020; see also Nathan Leys, 'Autonomous Weapon Systems, International Crises, and Anticipatory Self-Defense' (2020) 45 The Yale Journal of International Law 377.

[32] See Esther Chavannes, Klaudia Klonowska, and Tim Sweijs, 'Governing Autonomous Weapon Systems: Expanding the Solution Space, from Scoping to Applying' [2020] HCSS Security 39, 17–19; Elke Schwarz, 'The (Im)Possibility of Meaningful Human Control for Lethal Autonomous Weapon Systems' (*ICRC Humanitarian Law & Policy Blog*, 29 August 2018) <https://blogs.icrc.org/law-and-policy/2018/08/29/im-possibility-meaningful-human-control-lethal-autonomous-weapon-systems/> accessed 3 June 2020.

[33] One notable proposal here is Rebecca Crootof's envisaged legal regime of 'war torts' to hold states accountable for the injurious wrongs produced by unpredictable safety failures in autonomous weapons. Crootof, 'War Torts: Accountability for Autonomous Weapons' (n 24). For a discussion of state responsibility, see Bérénice Boutin, 'State Responsibility in Relation to Military Applications of Artificial Intelligence' (2023) 36 Leiden Journal of International Law 133.

[34] U.S. Department of State, 'Political Declaration on Responsible Military Use of Artificial Intelligence and Autonomy' (*United States Department of State*, 9 November 2023) <https://www.state.gov/political-declaration-on-responsible-military-use-of-artificial-intelligence-and-autonomy-2/> accessed 12 January 2024.

Finally, many anticipated military AI capabilities would give rise to impacts that might be approached as *structural shifts*. Examples of these can be found in the concerns that AI weapons might erode global stability,[35] undermine the 'democratic peace',[36] or proliferate easily to terrorist groups.[37] Others have suggested that AI systems could fundamentally change military decision-making processes,[38] lead to upsets in military and strategic balances of power,[39] alter the dynamics of conventional deterrence,[40] or erode nuclear deterrence stability.[41]

In crafting governance solutions it is useful to keep in mind how these structural challenges—while they are varied in terms of AI applications and concerns—display at least some commonalities. For instance, it is key to understand how these are intertwined with actors' perceived systemic incentives. It is also useful to chart how these structural changes underpin or exacerbate other challenges in terms of ethical challenges, security threats, or safety risks.

[35] Dustin A Lewis, Gabriella Blum, and Naz K Modirzadeh, 'War-Algorithm Accountability' (Harvard Law School Program on International Law and Armed Conflict 2016) Research Briefing <https://blogs.harvard.edu/pilac/files/2016/09/War-Algorithm-Accountability-Without-Appendices-August-2016.pdf> accessed 16 September 2016; Garcia, 'Lethal Artificial Intelligence and Change' (n 22); Horowitz, 'Artificial Intelligence, International Competition, and the Balance of Power' (n 22).

[36] Jürgen Altmann and Frank Sauer, 'Autonomous Weapon Systems and Strategic Stability' (2017) 59 Survival 117; Justin Haner and Denise Garcia, 'The Artificial Intelligence Arms Race: Trends and World Leaders in Autonomous Weapons Development' (2019) 10 Global Policy 331, 322. Though note that the same charges were raised against drones, but it remains somewhat unclear if they have had such effects at encouraging conflict. See James Igoe Walsh and Marcus Schulzke, 'The Ethics of Drone Strikes: Does Reducing the Cost of Conflict Encourage War?' (US Army War College & Strategic Studies Institute 2015) <https://ssi.armywarcollege.edu/pdffiles/PUB1289.pdf> accessed 12 March 2018.

[37] Şerif Onur Bahçecik, 'Civil Society Responds to the AWS: Growing Activist Networks and Shifting Frames' (2019) 10 Global Policy 365.

[38] Payne (n 9).

[39] Horowitz, 'Artificial Intelligence, International Competition, and the Balance of Power' (n 22); Allan Dafoe, 'AI Governance: A Research Agenda' (Center for the Governance of AI, Future of Humanity Institute 2018) <https://www.fhi.ox.ac.uk/govaiagenda/>; Ben Garfinkel and Allan Dafoe, 'How Does the Offense–Defense Balance Scale?' (2019) 42 Journal of Strategic Studies 736; Altmann and Sauer (n 36); Michael C Horowitz, 'When Speed Kills: Lethal Autonomous Weapon Systems, Deterrence and Stability' (2019) 42 Journal of Strategic Studies 764. Scharre, 'Autonomous Weapons and Stability' (n 31).

[40] Yuna Wong and others, *Deterrence in the Age of Thinking Machines* (RAND Corporation 2020) <https://www.rand.org/pubs/research_reports/RR2797.html> accessed 3 February 2020.

[41] Keir A Lieber and Daryl G Press, 'The New Era of Counterforce: Technological Change and the Future of Nuclear Deterrence' (2017) 41 International Security 9; Edward Geist and Andrew J Lohn, 'How Might Artificial Intelligence Affect the Risk of Nuclear War?' (RAND 2018) <https://www.rand.org/pubs/perspectives/PE296.html> accessed 24 April 2018; Michael C Horowitz, Paul Scharre, and Alexander Velez-Green, 'A Stable Nuclear Future? The Impact of Autonomous Systems and Artificial Intelligence' [2019] arXiv:1912.05291 [cs] <http://arxiv.org/abs/1912.05291> accessed 18 December 2019; Vincent Boulanin (ed), *The Impact of Artificial Intelligence on Strategic Stability and Nuclear Risk*, vol I: Euro-Atlantic Perspectives (SIPRI 2019); Shahar Avin and SM Amadae, 'Autonomy and Machine Learning at the Interface of Nuclear Weapons, Computers and People' in V Boulanin (ed), *The Impact of Artificial Intelligence on Strategic Stability and Nuclear Risk* (Stockholm International Peace Research Institute 2019); James Johnson, 'Delegating Strategic Decision-Making to Machines: Dr. Strangelove Redux?' (2022) 45 Journal of Strategic Studies 439. For a discussion of the interface with cyberweapons, see Pavel Sharikov, 'Artificial Intelligence, Cyberattack, and Nuclear Weapons—A Dangerous Combination' (2018) 74 Bulletin of the Atomic Scientists 368.

7.2.2 Regime Foundations: Insights from History, State Interests, or Norms

Once we have established a governance rationale (i.e. that certain AI systems drive sociotechnical changes that require governance), and we understand AI's governance target, a next key question for any AI governance regime concerns political feasibility or robustness.

That is, if the regime has already been established, can we understand and explain state reasons for supporting it? Alternatively, if a regime has been proposed but not yet established, under what circumstances do we have reason to expect this to be viable? How might these prospects be altered?

There are at least three ways in which we can approach the question of regime viability. From an outside view, we might seek to compare the envisaged AI regime against the history of past regimes on similar issue areas. From an inside view, we can derive insights from regime theory into the underpinnings of specific regimes or institutions, by considering the (state) *interests* which an AI regime could serve with its functions, as well as the degree to which—and the ways by which—various actors could shift international *norms* in its support.[42]

Again, international security governance for military AI will offer a productive example here, precisely because the growing concern over the alleged 'AI arms race' has in recent years spurred pessimism among some regarding the overall prospects of international regulation for these technologies.[43]

7.2.2.1 The historical perspective: arms control for military AI?

First, we may be able to draw comparative lessons from past governance successes (and failures). The rich and chequered history of international security and arms control initiatives, in particular in the nuclear domain, provides ample examples of both failures and successes in international cooperation, and could therefore provide a valuable set of case studies to draw on in exploring the topic of AI,[44]

[42] Tallberg and others (n 1) 11–12.

[43] See Michèle A Flournoy, 'AI Is Already at War' (2023) 102 *Foreign Affairs* <https://www.foreignaffairs.com/united-states/ai-already-war-flournoy> accessed 14 January 2024; and previously Edward Moore Geist, 'It's Already Too Late to Stop the AI Arms Race—We Must Manage It Instead' (2016) 72 Bulletin of the Atomic Scientists 318; Mark Chinen, *The International Governance of Artificial Intelligence* (Edward Elgar Publishing 2023) 259–264 (surveying such framings).

[44] Scharre, 'Autonomous Weapons and Stability' (n 31) 51 ('. . . over 40 examples of successful and unsuccessful past efforts at regulating weapons provide a rich reservoir of case studies to draw upon to understand the feasibility of regulating autonomous weapons'). See also Paul Scharre and Megan Lamberth, 'Artificial Intelligence and Arms Control' (Center for a New American Security 2022) <https://www.cnas.org/publications/reports/artificial-intelligence-and-arms-control> accessed 13 October 2022. Mauricio Baker, 'Nuclear Arms Control Verification and Lessons for AI Treaties' (arXiv, 8 April 2023) <http://arxiv.org/abs/2304.04123> accessed 11 April 2023 (focusing on lessons from the nuclear domain). See also: Michael JD Vermeer, 'Historical Analogues That Can Inform AI Governance' (RAND 2024) <https://www.rand.org/pubs/research_reports/RRA3408-1.html> accessed 11 June 2025; Benjamin Boudreaux and others, 'Insights from Nuclear History for AI

especially with regard to lessons for AI regimes' purpose, core powers, institutional structure, and likely risks of non-compliance.[45]

Indeed, arms control has been a key instrument in the international quest for the maintenance of peace and security for an extraordinarily long time,[46] with historical precedent ranging from ancient Hindu, Greek, and Roman bans on barbed or poisoned weapons to the attempted medieval prohibition, by the Lateran Council, of the 'unchristian' crossbow and arbalest.[47] However, the past two centuries have arguably been a golden age for arms control efforts, as science and technology sped up and delivered a procession of new weapons to the battlefield. The 1868 St Petersburg Declaration on explosive projectiles banned the use of exploding bullets,[48] and was followed by the 1899 and 1907 Hague Peace Conferences which renounced various weapons and means of warfare.[49] Since then, there has been an extensive array of international treaties banning the development, production, stockpiling, or use of a variety of weapons, including poison gas (1925), bacteriological or biological weapons (1972), chemical weapons (1993), blinding lasers (1995), certain types of conventional weapons (1980), certain types of anti-personnel land mines (1996), and cluster munitions (2008).[50] There have also been horizontal and vertical limits on the proliferation, quantity, or capabilities of nuclear weapons,[51] anti-ballistic missile systems,[52] weapons on

Governance' (RAND 2025) <https://www.rand.org/pubs/perspectives/PEA3652-1.html> accessed 27 May 2025.

[45] Akash R Wasil and others, 'Governing Dual-Use Technologies: Case Studies of International Security Agreements and Lessons for AI Governance' (arXiv, 4 September 2024) <http://arxiv.org/abs/2409.02779> accessed 6 September 2024.

[46] Rosemary Rayfuse, 'Public International Law and the Regulation of Emerging Technologies' in Roger Brownsword, Eloise Scotford, and Karen Yeung (eds), *The Oxford Handbook of Law, Regulation and Technology* (Oxford University Press 2017); Paul Scharre, *Army of None: Autonomous Weapons and the Future of War* (1st edn, W W Norton & Company 2018) ch 13.

[47] A Roberts and R Guelff, *Documents on the Laws of War* (3rd edn, Oxford University Press 2000) 3. Referred to in Rayfuse (n 46) 502. Note, the ban on crossbows only applied to use against Christians, and it has been widely held that the prohibition was stillborn. Crootof, 'The Killer Robots Are Here' (n 18) 1904. For a general history, see Richard Dean Burns, *The Evolution of Arms Control: From Antiquity to the Nuclear Age* (reprint edn, Rowman & Littlefield Publishers 2013).

[48] St Petersburg Declaration Renouncing the Use, in Time of War, of Explosive Projectiles Under 400 Grammes Weight (adopted 11 December 1868) LXVI UKPP (1869) 659.

[49] Hague Convention (II) on the Laws and Customs of War on Land (adopted 29 July 1899, entered into force 4 September 1900) 187 CTS 429 (Hague Convention II); Hague Convention (IV) on the Laws and Customs of War on Land (adopted 18 October 1907, entered into force 26 January 1910) 205 CTS 277 (Hague Convention IV). See generally James Brown Scott (ed), *The Hague Conventions and Declarations of 1899 and 1907, Accompanied by Tables of Signatures, Ratifications and Adhesions of the Various Powers, and Texts of Reservations* (Oxford University Press—American Branch 1915) <http://archive.org/details/hagueconventions00inteuoft> accessed 12 September 2020.

[50] Rayfuse (n 46) 502 (citing sources and instruments).

[51] These include multilateral agreements, most notably the Treaty on the Non-Proliferation of Nuclear Weapons (opened for signature 1 July 1968, entered into force 5 March 1970) 729 UNTS 161 (NPT), as well as bilateral agreements between the US and the USSR, such as Interim Agreement between the US and the USSR on Certain Measures with Respect to the Limitation of Strategic Offensive Arms (signed 26 May 1972, entered into force 3 October 1972) 944 UNTS 3 (SALT I Interim Agreement).

[52] Treaty on the Limitation of Anti-Ballistic Missile Systems (signed 26 May 1972, entered into force 3 October 1972) 944 UNTS 13.

Antarctica,[53] and weapons of mass destruction in space.[54] In some cases, there have been examples of mutual restraint even in the absence of formal agreements, such as over neutron bombs, kinetic anti-satellite weapons, some forms of bayonets,[55] or radiological weapons,[56] among others.[57]

Of course, that is not to say that arms control has always been successful. There have been failures in arms control, where states genuinely sought mutual restraint—such as early twentieth-century rules on the use of submarines, air-delivered weapons, or poison gas in warfare—but were later unable or unwilling to uphold these rules during wartime.[58] Moreover, even prohibitions that are generally considered successful, such as those on chemical, biological, or nuclear weapons,[59] have on significant occasions failed to rein in rogue regimes.[60]

Nonetheless, for all its flaws, the historical track record of arms control is still quite remarkable. It demonstrates that high-stakes challenges posed by particular new technologies to global security can, under some circumstances, provide the impetus and anchor for surprisingly strong regime complexes.[61] As Drezner notes with regards to the nuclear non-proliferation regime:

> This kind of regime complex does not resemble the zero-sum description that is often ascribed to security issues. It would appear that the destructive power of nuclear weapons triggered higher levels of international cooperation than would

[53] Antarctic Treaty (opened for signature 1 December 1959, entered into force 23 June 1961) 402 UNTS 71.

[54] Treaty on Principles Governing the Activities of States in the Exploration and Use of Outer Space, including the Moon and Other Celestial Bodies (opened for signature 27 January 1967, entered into force 10 October 1967) 610 UNTS 205 (Outer Space Treaty).

[55] Miles Brundage and others, 'Toward Trustworthy AI Development: Mechanisms for Supporting Verifiable Claims' [2020] arXiv:2004.07213 [cs] 67 <http://arxiv.org/abs/2004.07213> accessed 16 April 2020.

[56] Samuel Meyer, Sarah Bidgood, and William C Potter, 'Death Dust: The Little-Known Story of U.S. and Soviet Pursuit of Radiological Weapons' (2020) 45 International Security 51.

[57] Matthijs Maas, 'Paths Untaken: The History, Epistemology and Strategy of Technological Restraint, and Lessons for AI' (*Verfassungsblog*, 9 August 2022) <https://verfassungsblog.de/paths-untaken/> accessed 12 August 2022. See also Section 4.3.2.1 (discussing the history of technological restraint, in light of various strategies of sociotechnical choice and technological navigation).

[58] Brundage and others (n 55) 67.

[59] See for instance Richard Williamson, 'Hard Law, Soft Law, and Non-Law in Multilateral Arms Control: Some Compliance Hypotheses' (2003) 4 Chicago Journal of International Law 60–61. See also Sico van der Meer, 'Not That Bad: Looking Back on 65 Years of Nuclear Non-Proliferation Efforts' (2011) 22 Security and Human Rights 37; Sico van der Meer, 'Forgoing the Nuclear Option: States that Could Build Nuclear Weapons but Chose Not to Do So' (2014) 30 Medicine, Conflict and Survival s27; Lisa Langdon Koch, 'Holding All the Cards: Nuclear Suppliers and Nuclear Reversal' (2022) 7 Journal of Global Security Studies ogab034.

[60] Brundage and others (n 55) 67–68.

[61] Some disagree. As discussed in Chapter 5, Coe and Vaynmann have argued that a 'transparency–security trade-off' undercuts many arms control agreements, and has ensured that such agreements have been unable to contain a range of historical arms races that together account for almost 40% of all global arming in the past two centuries. Andrew J Coe and Jane Vaynman, 'Why Arms Control Is So Rare' (2020) 114 American Political Science Review 342.

otherwise have been expected. Indeed, the regime complex for nuclear weapons is far more robust than the one for conventional weaponry.[62]

Could the same impetus be achieved for a governance regime centred on the management, control, or containment of the most harmful or destabilizing forms of military AI? As noted by Payne, 'the idea of arms control for AI remains in its infancy',[63] although the past few years have seen significant albeit inconclusive developments in this domain.[64]

7.2.2.1.1 Historical reasons for optimism

In this context, the historical nuclear experience might offer grounds for guarded optimism. In previous work,[65] I have drawn on the historical track record of governing and controlling nuclear weapons in order to study questions around the political feasibility of arms control for AI.[66] I argued that, however pessimistic one is about arms control for military AI, our experience in constraining the spread of the ultimate deterrent of nuclear weapons should at least cautiously nudge us towards greater optimism.

After all, it should be remembered that some early Cold War commentators were equally pessimistic about the prospects for international regulation of nuclear weapons,[67] and anticipated a wildfire spread of this 'ultimate weapon'. For

[62] Daniel W Drezner, 'Technological Change and International Relations' (2019) 33 International Relations 286, 295. Note, however, that this robustness does not necessarily imply full coherence or regime integration. See also: John Simpson, 'The Nuclear Non-Proliferation Regime: Back to the Future?' [2004] Disarmament Forum 12, 7 (arguing that '[a]lthough together they were termed a 'regime', in practice some of the elements were seen by many states to be in conflict with each other (e.g. the NPT and export controls). In practice, what had been created was a fragmented system of unilateral and multilateral international governance of nuclear energy, particularly given the IAEA's much wider promotional role in this area. This system covered a broad range of nuclear-related activities, some of which appeared to have only a peripheral connection to the prevention of nuclear proliferation').

[63] Payne (n 9) 19.

[64] See also Section 3.2.1.

[65] Matthijs M Maas, 'How Viable Is International Arms Control for Military Artificial Intelligence? Three Lessons from Nuclear Weapons' (2019) 40 Contemporary Security Policy 285.

[66] Of course, as discussed previously in Chapter 5, analogies can be invaluable tools in technology governance; but they are also inevitably imperfect, foregrounding some features while backgrounding others. See also Matthijs Maas, 'AI Is Like . . . A Literature Review of AI Metaphors and Why They Matter for Policy' (Institute for Law & AI 2023) AI Foundations Report 2 <https://law-ai.org/ai-policy-metaphors> accessed 25 October 2023; Rebecca Crootof, 'Regulating New Weapons Technology' in Eric Talbot Jensen and Ronald TP Alcala (eds), *The Impact of Emerging Technologies on the Law of Armed Conflict* (Oxford University Press 2019) 17–18.

[67] To be sure, such pessimism was not universal. Indeed, the very early days of the nuclear age saw an active 'world federalist' movement, and startlingly ambitious proposals for the far-reaching global control of nuclear weapons, although this did not see further proposals after the failure of the 1946 Baruch Plan. See also F Bartel, 'Surviving the Years of Grace: The Atomic Bomb and the Specter of World Government, 1945–1950' (2015) 39 Diplomatic History 275; Joseph Preston Baratta, 'Was the Baruch Plan a Proposal of World Government?' (1985) 7 The International History Review 592. Even in later years of the Cold War, arms controls advocates such as Hedley Bull and others of the 'Cambridge Community' would continue to champion a more expansive and ambitious view of strategic arms control during the 1960s, one that was aimed not merely at maintaining deterrence stability, but rather at

instance, in 1963, US Secretary of Defense Robert McNamara argued to President John F. Kennedy that, because of falling production costs, at least eight new nuclear powers could be expected to emerge within the next decade.[68] As a result, Kennedy, in a public speech later that year, sketched a vision of 'the possibility in the 1970s of... a world in which 15 or 20 or 25 nations may have these weapons'.[69]

Given that such early pessimism regarding nuclear governance appears to have been misplaced or at least exaggerated, it is worth considering whether we are again today too pessimistic regarding the prospects of a regime regulating or even banning certain military AI systems. The history suggests that, even for strategically critical (military or advanced) AI applications, arms races need not be inevitable, but might be managed, channelled, or even stopped. This could be facilitated through direct engagement with domestic political coalitions on their specific interests, or indirectly by shaping norms top-down through international regimes, or bottom-up through the actions of so-called epistemic communities.[70]

7.2.2.1.2 Historical reasons for pessimism

However, while such historical precedent provides an encouraging existence proof for international regulation, there are also more pessimistic lessons one might glean from it. In the first place, there is no guarantee that arms control efforts will succeed immediately or in time to contain at least an initial wave of proliferation, as illustrated by the failure of the early attempts, during the late 1940s, at securing international control of nuclear technology.[71] Moreover, even if it is possible for potent international institutional arrangements such as the IAEA to eventually be established, this process took a long time—at times, decades.[72]

extensive forms of 'cooperative security' among even rival states. Nancy W Gallagher, 'Re-Thinking the Unthinkable: Arms Control in the Twenty-First Century' (2015) 22 The Nonproliferation Review 469.

[68] Robert McNamara, 'The Diffusion of Nuclear Weapons with and without a Test Ban Agreement'; as quoted in Moeed Yusuf, 'Predicting Proliferation: The History of the Future of Nuclear Weapon' (Brookings Institute 2009) 15.

[69] As quoted in Graham Allison, 'Nuclear Disorder' [2010] *Foreign Affairs* <https://www.foreignaffairs.com/articles/pakistan/2010-01-01/nuclear-disorder> accessed 2 April 2018.

[70] Maas, 'How Viable Is International Arms Control for Military Artificial Intelligence?' (n 65) 292–295, 296–299. See also the discussion of epistemic communities in Section 7.2.2.3.

[71] As noted previously, these early years saw the Acheson–Lilienthal proposal and the 1946 Baruch Plan, which urged for far-reaching global control of these weapons, but which soon failed. The seminal work is Joseph Preston Baratta, *The Politics of World Federation: From World Federalism to Global Governance* (Greenwood Publishing Group 2004). For a discussion of lessons for AI, see also Waqar Zaidi and Allan Dafoe, 'International Control of Powerful Technology: Lessons from the Baruch Plan' (Center for the Governance of AI, Future of Humanity Institute 2021) <https://www.fhi.ox.ac.uk/wp-content/uploads/2021/03/International-Control-of-Powerful-Technology-Lessons-from-the-Baruch-Plan-Zaidi-Dafoe-2021.pdf> accessed 22 January 2020.

[72] Rumtin Sepasspour, 'A Reality Check and a Way Forward for the Global Governance of Artificial Intelligence' (2023) 79(5) Bulletin of the Atomic Scientists 304, 312; Bill Drexel Drexel Michael and Michael Depp, 'Every Country Is on Its Own on AI: Why AI Regulation Can't Follow in the Footsteps of International Nuclear Controls' (*Foreign Policy*, 13 June 2023) <https://foreignpolicy.com/2023/06/13/ai-regulation-international-nuclear/> accessed 12 September 2023; Harry Law, 'An IAEA for AI?

Other institutional developments, such as the establishment of the Nuclear Suppliers Group (NSG), happened far more rapidly but occurred only in response to notable failures of the extant regime, specifically India's 1974 Peaceful Nuclear Explosion.[73]

Of course, when considering whether or how this should strengthen the prospects for military AI governance, a historical perspective should also acknowledge that the broader arms control landscape has been under sustained stress. Indeed, the past few decades have proven particularly tough, as key bodies have gone underfunded,[74] and as long-standing accords have gradually frayed or been abandoned in turn. The US withdrew from the ABM Treaty in 2004,[75] and from the INF Treaty (citing Russian noncompliance) in 2019.[76] In turn, Russia suspended its participation in the New START treaty in early 2023,[77] and de-ratified the Comprehensive Nuclear-Test-Ban Treaty by the end of that year.[78]

The Early History of the International Atomic Energy Agency' (*Harry Law*, 9 June 2023) <https://www.harrylaw.co.uk/post/an-iaea-for-ai-the-early-history-of-the-international-atomic-energy-agency> accessed 1 September 2023.

[73] Lisa Langdon Koch, 'The NPT at 50 and the NSG at 43: How the Global Control of Nuclear Exports Has Slowed Proliferation' (2018) 4 International History and Politics Newsletter 8, 8–9 ('The speed at which the nuclear suppliers moved after the shock of India's May test was impressive: by July, the Committee had agreed on an initial list of material and equipment that could not be exported without triggering IAEA safeguards for the receiving state. By September, the list was active, and export control conditions were being inserted into contract negotiations that were already underway. The supplier states established a Nuclear Suppliers Group (NSG) the following year, which, unlike the Zangger Committee, was open to non-NPT members, such as France. By 1977, the NSG had grown to fifteen members; today, it stands at forty-eight').

[74] Remarkably, the Biological Weapons Convention has just four staffers, and operates on a budget of just $1.4 million a year—less than the average budget of a McDonald's restaurant. Toby Ord, *The Precipice: Existential Risk and the Future of Humanity* (Hachette 2020) 57; See also the figures in Gregory C Koblentz and Paul F Walker, 'Can Bill Gates Rescue the Bioweapons Convention?' (*Bulletin of the Atomic Scientists*, 3 April 2017) <https://thebulletin.org/2017/04/can-bill-gates-rescue-the-bioweapons-convention/> accessed 30 January 2020; and Hayley Peterson, 'Here's What It Costs to Open a McDonald's Restaurant' (*Business Insider*, 6 May 2019) <https://www.businessinsider.com/what-it-costs-to-open-a-mcdonalds-2014-11> accessed 30 January 2020.

[75] Wade Boese, 'U.S. Withdraws From ABM Treaty; Global Response Muted' (*Arms Control Association*, August 2002) <https://www.armscontrol.org/act/2002-07/news/us-withdraws-abm-treaty-global-response-muted> accessed 11 September 2020.

[76] Amy J Nelson, 'The Death of the INF Treaty Has Lessons for Arms Control' (*Bulletin of the Atomic Scientists*, 4 November 2019) <https://thebulletin.org/2019/11/the-death-of-the-inf-treaty-has-lessons-for-arms-control/> accessed 3 June 2020.

[77] Reuters, 'Putin: Russia Suspends Participation in Last Remaining Nuclear Treaty with U.S.' *Reuters* (21 February 2023) <https://www.reuters.com/world/europe/putin-russia-suspends-participation-last-remaining-nuclear-treaty-with-us-2023-02-21/> accessed 14 January 2024.

[78] Neil MacFarquhar, 'Russia Pulled Out of a Nuclear Test Ban Treaty. Here's What That Means' *The New York Times* (2 November 2023) <https://www.nytimes.com/2023/11/02/world/europe/russia-nuclear-test-ban-treaty.html> accessed 14 January 2024; Shizuka Kuramitsu, 'Russia "Deratifies" Nuclear Test Ban Treaty' (*Arms Control Association*, November 2023) <https://www.armscontrol.org/act/2023-11/news/russia-deratifies-nuclear-test-ban-treaty> accessed 14 January 2024; Maxim Starchak, 'Russia's Withdrawal from the Nuclear Test Ban Treaty Is an Own Goal' (*Carnegie Endowment for International Peace*, 24 October 2023) <https://carnegieendowment.org/politika/90831> accessed 14 January 2024.

Such developments might give strength to the pessimistic perspective of some international relations scholars, who hold that the stability of arms control regimes is fickle and generally more dependent on healthy international relations than the other way around.[79] At a more systemic level, new development and digital technologies have also begun to put additional pressure on old and new arms control regimes, by increasing the rate at which new technologies are produced, the digitalization of existing weapon technologies, platforms, or systems, and the diffusion and 'latency' this supports.[80]

Indeed, from a historical perspective, there have been frequent difficulties involved in negotiating and reaching arms control agreements,[81] in verifying compliance,[82] in maintaining agreements in the face of renewed geopolitical tensions or mistrust,[83] or in updating or modernizing agreements in the face of a constantly changing technological state of the art.[84] Accordingly, there are historically only a few cases of outright preventative arms bans—these exceptions being exploding bullets and blinding lasers.[85] That is not to say that, once established, arms control regimes have not been successful;[86] nor is it to suggest that regimes have not been able to adapt and evolve over time.[87] Still, this type of regime is often fraught.

[79] Lionel P Fatton, 'The Impotence of Conventional Arms Control: Why Do International Regimes Fail When They Are Most Needed?' (2016) 37 Contemporary Security Policy 200.

[80] Amy J Nelson, 'Innovation Acceleration, Digitization, and the Arms Control Imperative' (Social Science Research Network 2019) SSRN Scholarly Paper ID 3382956 23 <https://papers.ssrn.com/abstract=3382956> accessed 29 May 2020 ('arms control is in a terrible state. Violated, discredited and abandoned, arms control is no longer the foreign policy aspiration or lofty global governance tool of days past').

[81] Richard Dean Burns, 'An Introduction to Arms Control and Disarmament' in Richard Dean Burns (ed), *Encyclopedia of Arms Control and Disarmament*, vol 1 (Charles Scribner's Sons 1993). See also Vally Koubi, 'International Tensions and Arms Control Agreements' (1993) 37 American Journal of Political Science 148.

[82] Allan S Krass, 'Arms Control Treaty Verification' in Richard Dean Burns (ed), *Encyclopedia of Arms Control and Disarmament*, vol 1 (Charles Scribner's Sons 1993).

[83] Fatton (n 79).

[84] Amy J Nelson, 'The Impact of Emerging Technologies on Arms Control Regimes' (ISODARCO 2018); Nelson, 'Innovation Acceleration, Digitization, and the Arms Control Imperative' (n 80).

[85] Garcia, 'Future Arms, Technologies, and International Law' (n 25) 102. However, elsewhere, Garcia has argued that at least 22 existing treaties have been set up under a 'preventative framework' to address the (further) militarization of emerging technologies. Garcia, 'Lethal Artificial Intelligence and Change' (n 22) 335. Nonetheless, Bidgood, drawing on a study of 1951–1979 US–USSR efforts to limit strategic missiles, has argued that decision-maker interest in limiting specific emerging technologies may not always emerge early on in the innovation process, but sometimes only at the point of mass production. Sarah Bidgood, 'Arms Control and Innovation: Precedents for U.S.–Russian Technology Regulation from the Cold War' (2025) Journal of Strategic Studies 1.

[86] Williamson notes that 'while the record of compliance with arms control treaties is far from perfect, it is statistically quite good'. Williamson (n 59) 61. Notable and confirmed historical compliance violations include the Soviet Union's production of biological agents in violation of the Biological Weapons Convention; Iraq's violation of the 1925 Geneva Protocol through its use of chemical weapons during the Iran–Iraq war, and Iraq and North Korea's violations of the Nuclear Non-Proliferation Treaty: ibid 60.

[87] Caroline Fehl, 'Unequal Power and the Institutional Design of Global Governance: The Case of Arms Control' (2014) 40 Review of International Studies 505.

As such, taking an outside, comparative view, the history of arms control might support both optimism (arms control for high-stakes destabilizing technologies can be more viable than may initially appear) and pessimism (nuclear arms control successes were hard-won and have come under pressure). It should then be asked whether, how, or why we would expect governance regimes for military AI to buck these trends. That requires a more detailed examination of the specific dynamics at play.

7.2.2.2 The rationalist perspective: state interests, regime foundations, and security constraints

A second perspective on AI regime viability takes an inside view. This focuses on the common functions that an AI regime could play which, from a rationalist perspective, would serve state interests in ways that would secure support for the regime's establishment and its operations. Regime theory and related schools of thought can provide various insights here.

7.2.2.2.1 Regime foundations of collaboration or coordination

Classically, theorists of international regimes distinguished between 'dilemmas of common aversion' and 'dilemmas of common interests'.[88] These provide two distinct bases for international regimes aimed at ensuring, respectively, coordination or collaboration among states.[89]

Regimes designed to address a 'dilemma of common aversion' generally require coordination to avoid certain outcomes. Such situations involve multiple possible equilibria—by which is meant that such regimes are created not so much to ensure that one specific outcome is guaranteed, but rather to ensure that particular sub-optimal outcomes are avoided, after which the parties will in principle accept any of a range of other outcomes. Examples are international questions involving standardization, where actors may not prima facie care strongly which specific standard is adopted so long as some uniform standard is implemented among them all. While coordination can be difficult to achieve when different actors disagree about the preferred initial equilibrium, once a standard is settled on and a regime established it enables expectations to converge, and becomes relatively self-enforcing, because actors that defect hurt only themselves.[90] Many debates around global standard-setting in AI can be understood as debates around coordination, in the face of dilemmas of common aversion. Of course, even in such cases success is not guaranteed, because domestic political considerations can at times lead to contestation, as illustrated by the evolution of

[88] Arthur A Stein, 'Coordination and Collaboration: Regimes in an Anarchic World' (1982) 36 International Organization 299.
[89] ibid 311–312.
[90] ibid 314.

cyberspace governance.[91] Nonetheless, the prospects for such regimes can generally be quite good.

In contrast, when actors face a 'dilemma of common interests', international regimes are oriented towards securing collaboration to ensure a specific outcome. Accordingly, such regimes must specify strict patterns of behaviour, and ensure no one party is tempted to cheat. This often requires formalization, institutionalization, and sufficient monitoring capabilities to reassure each actor of their ability to spot others' cheating.[92] Arms control agreements are classic examples of formal institutionalized collaborations in a common interests situation, as they must be able to define 'cheating' quite explicitly, ensure that it is observable, and specify verification and monitoring procedures.

Many potential adversarial uses of AI systems, particularly in military or strategic contexts, can be understood as producing dilemmas of common interests.[93] The same might apply to global action on risks emerging from the capabilities of increasingly advanced AI systems. This suggests a range of cases where states may find common interests in establishing stricter, more institutionalized global arrangements.

7.2.2.2.2 Security–transparency constraints around monitoring dual-use technology

At the same time, from a state interest perspective, there will also be distinct challenges to actually achieving such institutionalization, in particular for regimes aimed at arms control for destabilizing military AI applications or at the enforcement of some other restrictions on particular forms of some highly capable advanced AI systems.[94] Because arms control agreements involve the pursuit of mutual restraint and control under a dilemma of common interest, rather than coordination around a dilemma of common aversion, they might be challenging subjects for AI regimes.[95]

[91] Drezner (n 62) 296–297 (discussing the evolution of cyberspace governance).

[92] Stein (n 88) 312.

[93] See also the discussion, in Chapter 2, on how these AI challenges can be productively understood as 'mutual restraint' global public goods.

[94] See for instance Haleema Saadia and others, 'AI and Nuclear Decisions: Toward an Arms Control Framework' (2025) Contemporary Security Policy 1; Duncan Cass-Beggs and others, 'Framework Convention on Global AI Challenges: Accelerating International Cooperation to Ensure Beneficial, Safe and Inclusive AI' (Centre for International Governance Innovation 2024) CIGI Discussion Paper <https://www.cigionline.org/publications/framework-convention-on-global-ai-challenges/> accessed 1 July 2024; Andrea Miotti and Akash Wasil, 'An International Treaty to Implement a Global Compute Cap for Advanced Artificial Intelligence' (30 October 2023) <https://papers.ssrn.com/abstract=4617094> accessed 3 November 2023; Jason Hausenloy, Andrea Miotti, and Claire Dennis, 'Multinational AGI Consortium (MAGIC): A Proposal for International Coordination on AI' (arXiv, 13 October 2023) <http://arxiv.org/abs/2310.09217> accessed 3 November 2023; Tolga Bilge, 'Treaty on Artificial Intelligence Safety and Cooperation (TAISC)' (2023) <https://taisc.org/taisc> accessed 20 October 2023.

[95] Stein (n 88) 313.

Indeed, the challenges might be exacerbated because digital technologies, including AI, may pose a particularly hard case for traditional arms control or verification measures, when pressed into service against prospective military AI systems. For instance, Nelson notes that arms control is predominantly designed to manage actual physical weapons; that historically many arms control agreements implicitly ended up bargaining away obsolete last-generation weapons, not next-generation ones; and that many measures rely on 'what can be seen and counted'.[96] More generally, Joseph Nye has argued that arms control risks being a traditional (and inadequate) response to many new technologies,[97] because it is increasingly hard to meaningfully separate the actors into discrete sets of state and non-state actors, and notions of 'parity' or 'balance' are hard to define.

One challenge here concerns the problems around assuring effective compliance verification methods for international AI agreements, whether unilateral monitoring based on national technical means, access-dependent inspections, or hardware monitoring-based methods.[98] After all, as discussed in Chapter 5, various ways of monitoring compliance with an (AI) arms control agreement might create a particularly steep transparency–security trade-off for states.[99] In response, regime proponents ought to consider ways by which they might increase the ability of parties to undertake unilateral monitoring (making 'closed' deals more feasible), or alternatively to increase their ability to make verifiable, trusted claims about their AI systems.[100] There are underlying challenges, however: Vaynman and Volpe have noted that when technology is deeply dual-use—in that (1) it is difficult to distinguish military from civilian uses, and (2) there is a high degree of integration within military enterprises and the civilian economy—this situation creates difficult information constraints on the design of arms control institutions.[101] This is because indistinguishability increases the level of intrusive monitoring that would be needed to detect violations whereas high integration sharpens the

[96] Nelson, 'The Impact of Emerging Technologies on Arms Control Regimes' (n 84); Erica D Borghard and Shawn W Lonergan, 'Why Are There No Cyber Arms Control Agreements?' (*Council on Foreign Relations*, 16 January 2018) <https://www.cfr.org/blog/why-are-there-no-cyber-arms-control-agreements> accessed 22 January 2018. See also Maas, 'How Viable Is International Arms Control for Military Artificial Intelligence?' (n 65) 289–290.

[97] Joseph S Nye, 'The World Needs an Arms-Control Treaty for Cybersecurity' *The Washington Post* (1 October 2015) <https://www.belfercenter.org/publication/world-needs-arms-control-treaty-cybersecurity> accessed 31 May 2020.

[98] Akash R Wasil and others, 'Verification Methods for International AI Agreements' (arXiv.org, 28 August 2024) <https://arxiv.org/abs/2408.16074v1> accessed 3 October 2024; Aaron Scher and Lisa Thiergart, 'Mechanisms to Verify International Agreements About AI Development' (MIRI Technical Governance Team 2024) <https://techgov.intelligence.org/research/mechanisms-to-verify-international-agreements-about-ai-development> accessed 9 December 2024; Matthew Mittelsteadt, 'AI Verification: Mechanisms to Ensure AI Arms Control Compliance' (Center for Security and Emerging Technology 2021) <https://live-cset-georgetown.pantheonsite.io/research/ai-verification/> accessed 18 February 2021.

[99] Coe and Vaynman (n 61).

[100] Brundage and others (n 55).

[101] Jane Vaynman and Tristan A Volpe, 'Dual Use Deception: How Technology Shapes Cooperation in International Relations' (2023) 77 International Organization 599.

potential costs of disclosing information about the regulated capability, as doing so could leak information about other capabilities.[102]

On the other hand, from a rationalist perspective, the possible role which (AI) technologies can serve in strengthening monitoring capabilities[103] may also shed light on the conditions for arms control regimes for military AI systems themselves, and interventions by which we might reduce or mitigate the previously mentioned security–transparency trade-off. That is, for a given agreement between state A and state B, to cap B's military AI capabilities, how steep might the security–transparency trade-off really be?

On the one hand, one could argue that the inspection of AI (software) capabilities need not always be intrusive on state B's general security since, unlike missiles, military AI software need not necessarily be co-located with other military assets, but could be housed in offsite data centres. Allowing inspections of the software—or, as some have suggested, of some AI hardware chips[104]—therefore would not necessitate giving access to factories or bases producing or housing many other types of sensitive weapons technologies.

On the other hand, in order to guarantee compliance and assuage state A's fears of cheating, arms control agreements for military AI might require quite significant levels of transparency of the AI system itself—although this may depend on whether agreements are struck at the level of AI system techniques (e.g. 'no reinforcement learning-based agents'; 'no foundation models trained beyond a particular computational threshold'), capabilities (e.g. 'no autonomous swarming'), application (e.g. 'no integration into nuclear command and control'), or their use in particular domains (e.g. 'no usage in urban theatres').

Nonetheless, a high level of transparency could considerably impinge on the security of party B: it might considerably degrade the utility of its military AI systems in the first place, since state A is better able to tailor countermeasures (such as adversarial input), or to offset the advantages. This would suggest that in the context of an arms control agreement for AI systems, party A would need a very high level of transparency for verification—a level that controlled party B would consider unacceptable from a security perspective. This highlights the importance of interventions that enable various parties to make verifiable claims about their AI systems' properties,[105] or to provide conditional and controlled access to inspectors, without providing full access.[106]

[102] ibid.

[103] See also the discussion in Section 5.6.2.

[104] Yonadav Shavit, 'What Does It Take to Catch a Chinchilla? Verifying Rules on Large-Scale Neural Network Training via Compute Monitoring' (arXiv, 30 May 2023) <http://arxiv.org/abs/2303.11341> accessed 19 March 2025.

[105] See also Brundage and others (n 55) 67–69.

[106] See also Benjamin S Bucknall and Robert F Trager, 'Structured Access for Third-Party Research on Frontier AI Models: Investigating Researchers' Model Access Requirements' (Oxford Martin AI Governance Initiative 2023) <https://www.oxfordmartin.ox.ac.uk/publications/structured-access-for-third-party-research-on-frontier-ai-models-investigating-researchers-model-access-requirements/>

In sum, under a rationalist account of regime theory, arms control for destabilizing or particularly unethical weapons could constitute an example of actors facing a dilemma of common interests.[107] From this interests-based perspective, then, there appear to be some functional grounds for establishing an institutional regime to restrict at least some types of military AI systems, and secure this mutual-restraint global public good.[108]

At the same time, it appears that a number of operational and material features of the technology challenge the strong monitoring and enforcement requirements of such regimes.[109] This suggests that the foundations of military AI governance regimes could be improved in at least three ways: by (1) improving the abilities of states to (unilaterally) monitor compliance with such regimes; (2) increasing the distinguishability of civilian and military AI—or, in the context of regimes aimed at advanced AI, between safe and harmful models—and (3) shifting state actors' norms and perceptions. We will therefore now discuss this avenue.

7.2.2.3 The constructivist perspective: norms, epistemic communities, and contestation

Along with the importance of state interests, other factors can play into the viability of a regime. For instance, constructivists have argued that regimes are also grounded in norms and perceptions, which can be shifted or altered in various ways.[110] Indeed, the history of international law suggests that state decision-making can be swayed by changes in decisionmaker norms—which not only may set limits on what means they might find acceptable to pursue state interests, but may even affect the perception or construction of those interests.[111]

7.2.2.3.1 The role of epistemic communities in military AI governance

Such shifts in norms might be achieved in various ways. They might be established top-down, through the negotiation of international regimes or the rulings of international courts.[112] Alternatively, such norm-creation can be facilitated bottom-up,

accessed 6 November 2023; Toby Shevlane, 'Structured Access: An Emerging Paradigm for Safe AI Deployment' in Justin Bullock and others (eds), Toby Shevlane, *The Oxford Handbook of AI Governance* (Oxford University Press 2022).

[107] Stein (n 88).

[108] Scott Barrett, *Why Cooperate? The Incentive to Supply Global Public Goods* (Oxford University Press 2007). See also the discussion in Section 2.3.2.

[109] This question of design and viability will be taken up in more detail in Section 7.2.3.

[110] Caroline Fehl, 'Explaining the International Criminal Court: A "Practice Test" for Rationalist and Constructivist Approaches' (2004) 10 European Journal of International Relations 357.

[111] Oona Hathaway and Scott J Shapiro, 'What Realists Don't Understand About Law' (*Foreign Policy*, 9 October 2017) <https://foreignpolicy.com/2017/10/09/what-realists-dont-understand-about-law/> accessed 17 April 2019 ('When it is most effective, the law doesn't induce states to act contrary to incentives; it changes those incentives themselves').

[112] On the role of international courts in contributing to the gradual development of norms, see also Anne van Aaken, 'Is International Law Conducive To Preventing Looming Disasters?' (2016) 7 Global Policy 81.

through the actions of various stakeholders, norm entrepreneurs, and expert communities.

For instance, consider the role of so-called epistemic communities. Emanuel Adler has defined an 'epistemic community' as

> a network of individuals or groups with an authoritative claim to policy-relevant knowledge within their domain of expertise. The community members share knowledge about the causation of social and physical phenomena in an area for which they have a reputation for competence, and they have a common set of normative beliefs about what will benefit human welfare in such a domain. While members are often from a number of different professions and disciplines, they adhere to the following: (1) shared consummatory values and principled beliefs; (2) shared causal beliefs or professional judgment; (3) common notions of validity based on intersubjective, internally defined criteria for validating knowledge; (4) a common policy project.[113]

In fact, epistemic communities have played a key role in laying the groundwork for various past successes in arms control and other regimes. For instance, Adler has studied the road towards the 1972 ABM Treaty, and how this suggests that small communities of experts, appropriately organised and mobilized, can have a disproportionate effect in framing global arms control cooperation through bottom-up norm institutionalization.[114] While there may, counterintuitively, be political risks to the participation of technical experts in arms control negotiations,[115] these epistemic communities can often still play a significant role in establishing shared expectations among policymakers, setting the political conditions for arms control negotiation, and providing the overarching framework.

Of course, not all such communities are successful,[116] and a few high-profile examples of past success provide no guarantee that contemporary campaigns to

[113] Emanuel Adler, 'The Emergence of Cooperation: National Epistemic Communities and the International Evolution of the Idea of Nuclear Arms Control' (1992) 46 International Organization 101, n 1. For a classic account, see also Peter M Haas, 'Introduction: Epistemic Communities and International Policy Coordination' (1992) 46 International Organization 1.

[114] Maas, 'How Viable Is International Arms Control for Military Artificial Intelligence?' (n 65) 298–299.

[115] For instance, such participation in arms control negotiations may, on occasion, hold up or distract negotiations. For instance, Burns recounts how during the early negotiations for the Comprehensive Test Ban Treaty (CTBT), seismic experts were brought on board to develop a verification system that could reliably detect the signs of nuclear tests. However, '[a]fter verification techniques were developed that appeared to be acceptable to many scientists and diplomats, technical experts kept searching for more and more refinements so that the already low error rate could be even smaller. One result of this was that it was impossible to negotiate a comprehensive test ban because critics—who often had a vested interest in seeing underground testing continue—would argue that no one could not be absolutely certain that no cheating was going on.' Burns (n 81) 7. This illustrates the sensitive considerations that such norm entrepreneurs need to confront and navigate.

[116] Mai'a K Davis Cross, 'The Limits of Epistemic Communities: EU Security Agencies' (2015) 3 Politics and Governance 90.

restrict or ban some military uses of AI (or particular types of advanced AI systems) will be able to repeat those feats.[117] As discussed, it is possible that the external historical context has shifted too much to be a good guide.[118] Nonetheless, there are still indicative lessons for the ways in which epistemic communities focused on the governance of a particular type of AI—whether conventional, military, or advanced AI—might best organize in order to articulate, converge around, and implement a shared policy project. In particular, we can ask what strategies such communities might adopt to facilitate the key steps of (1) initial intellectual innovation, (2) gradual domestic norm institutionalization, and (3) global norm dissemination, thus preparing the groundwork for later state cooperation and institutionalization.[119]

For instance, we can draw on these lessons to evaluate contemporary efforts by various epistemic communities or norm entrepreneurs engaged on establishing governance regimes for military AI. Actors such as the Campaign to Stop Killer Robots have picked up remarkable speed, and the 'AI ethics community' has developed considerably within just the past few years,[120] and may play an increased role in shaping global and state perceptions on the issue. Other scholars have highlighted the potential of 'trusted communities' in moving forward regulatory frameworks for transnational governance approaches to military AI.[121]

However, to shape norms, these communities may need to make careful decisions around which *framing* of AI technologies to adopt[122] and through which *fora* or avenues to pursue global regulation in the near-term.[123] Given the degree of gridlock in international negotiations around military AI, it may be the case that smaller, informal, and like-minded groups potentially are a swifter avenue to setting some norms, even if they fragment the regime complex.[124]

[117] Elvira Rosert and Frank Sauer, 'How (Not) to Stop the Killer Robots: A Comparative Analysis of Humanitarian Disarmament Campaign Strategies' (2020) 42 Contemporary Security Policy 4 (arguing that, at the very least, the current Campaign to Stop Killer Robots may have adopted a suboptimal strategy in trying to emulate the bans on blinding laser weapons and anti-personnel landmines, and that it should accordingly adjust its institutional choices, substance, and regulatory design).

[118] See also Harry Law and Lewis Ho, 'Can a Dual Mandate Be a Model for the Global Governance of AI?' [2023] Nature Reviews Physics 1, 2. (arguing that 'there is a risk of overplaying lessons from the past').

[119] Maas, 'How Viable Is International Arms Control for Military Artificial Intelligence?' (n 65) 299.

[120] Haydn Belfield, 'Activism by the AI Community: Analysing Recent Achievements and Future Prospects', *Proceedings of the AAAI/ACM Conference on AI, Ethics, and Society* (ACM 2020) <https://dl.acm.org/doi/10.1145/3375627.3375814> accessed 24 August 2020.

[121] Klijn and Okano-Heijmans (n 14) 19–24.

[122] Rosert and Sauer (n 117).

[123] ibid.

[124] Jean-Frédéric Morin and others, 'How Informality Can Address Emerging Issues: Making the Most of the G7' (2019) 10 Global Policy 267, 5.

7.2.2.3.2 Normative contestation of unequal or hierarchical governance for advanced AI

These considerations—around epistemic community organization, framing choice,[125] and forum choice—are also of significant relevance to recent and ongoing efforts by an emerging epistemic community to motivate international governance efforts around the risks of advanced AI systems.[126] However, a broader constructivist perspective on the development, design, and normative content of international institutions can also help flag potential hurdles or failure modes.

Specifically, a constructivist engagement with the normative environmental pressures that shape regimes can help us understand which kinds of contestation and challenges certain types of proposed AI regimes are likely to face. For instance, as discussed in Chapter 3, many leading initiatives that have focused on the governance of advanced AI systems, such as the G7 Hiroshima AI Process or the UK AI Safety Summit, have seen relatively limited and under-inclusive participation.[127] Moreover, some proposals for new global governance arrangements of AI have assumed (or, charitably, recognized) the sharp global inequalities that currently exist in the global AI ecosystem generally, and in the development of advanced AI systems (such as the compute-intensive foundation models) specifically.[128]

It is certainly important to recognize the unequal material conditions in this landscape, in order to better understand or craft different states' incentives for participating in a global AI regime.[129] However, there are also risks to regimes that establish explicitly unequal institutional orders in world politics. Even though (or precisely because) such regimes mirror the unequally held national stakes in a technology's development, they are likely to face waves of contestation.[130] For example, Caroline Fehl has traced the historical evolution of global arms control institutions after 1945, noting patterns of 'institutional mutation' where changes in

[125] Maas, 'AI Is Like . . .' (n 66).

[126] Shazeda Ahmed and others, 'Building the Epistemic Community of AI Safety' (22 November 2023) <https://papers.ssrn.com/abstract=4641526> accessed 14 January 2024; and more broadly John Bliss, 'Existential Advocacy: Lawyering for AI Safety and the Future of Humanity' (2024) 37 Georgetown Journal of Legal Ethics 39.

[127] Although notably, the UK AI Safety Summit did invite a number of Global South countries. See Sumaya Nur Adan, 'The Case for Including the Global South in AI Governance Discussions' (*GovAI Blog*, 20 October 2023) <https://www.governance.ai/post/the-case-for-including-the-global-south-in-ai-governance-conversations> accessed 23 October 2023.

[128] Law and Ho (n 118).

[129] See for instance Carlos Ignacio Gutierrez, 'Multilateral Coordination for the Proactive Governance of Artificial Intelligence Systems' (25 September 2023) 2 <https://papers.ssrn.com/abstract=4583536> accessed 26 September 2023 (discussing the need for multilateral governance regimes to provide incentives for participation for both 'AI-controlling' and 'AI-dependent' countries).

[130] K Egeland, 'The Road to Prohibition: Nuclear Hierarchy and Disarmament, 1968–2017' (University of Oxford 2017) <https://ora.ox.ac.uk/objects/uuid:b03d68ab-4748-4de7-a2e9-15616de6a05c> accessed 16 December 2022.

the material and normative environment led to repeated pressures for the reform of existing unequal or hierarchical institutions. For instance, in the case of the nuclear non-proliferation regime, she notes how

> material and normative environmental pressures interacted to produce both the hierarchical structure of the NPT and a simultaneous equalisation of global arms control negotiations, as well as concessions to equality and justice within the unequal treaty. [However,] the limits of the nuclear consensus are also evident. Neither threats and pressure nor compensatory equalising moves were strong enough to convince the remaining NPT hold-outs to buy into the institutional compromise. Unpersuaded that the NPT offered them sufficient security benefits or went far enough to allay their misgivings about the treaty's perceived injustice, they continued to pursue their own nuclear programmes.[131]

Fehl also notes how, even though the inequalities and hierarchies in the arms control regime complex elicited frequent pressure for reform, past institutional legacies simultaneously meant that these regimes could not be entirely redesigned but were rather replaced and supplanted by new forms (exhibiting different forms of institutional inequality).[132] For instance, she examines how in many cases:

> Strong veto points embedded in pre-existing institutions inhibit reforms, particularly reforms that deepen institutional inequality, and favour the addition of new layers to the regime. They also facilitate the emergence of exclusivity and informality over hierarchical forms of institutional inequality. At the same time, institutional models and procedural precedents increase the likelihood that similar forms of (un)equal institutions are reproduced and similar reforms repeated in the evolution of the regime.[133]

Consequently, this highlights possible crucial considerations for proponents of global governance regimes (whether for conventional or advanced AI) that would explicitly recognize—or implicitly sanction—a degree of global AI hierarchy. To be sure, the appropriate provision of international institutional mechanisms for AI access- and benefit-sharing might mitigate some of these risks;[134] however, there may be strong functional as well as normative reasons to ensure broader state

[131] Fehl (n 87) 523.
[132] This anticipates our discussion, in Section 7.4, of regime complex evolution.
[133] Fehl (n 87) 530.
[134] Law and Ho (n 118); Lewis Ho and others, 'International Institutions for Advanced AI' (arXiv, 10 July 2023) 12–13 <http://arxiv.org/abs/2307.04699> accessed 11 July 2023.

involvement in AI not just at the level of outcomes, but also in terms of process.[135] Lacking this, the regime could see an increased risk of later contestation, or the emergence of rival governance coalitions or fora,[136] potentially facilitating state strategies of forum-shopping or competitive regime creation even by leading AI states.

In sum, applying concepts from regime theory—drawing on both rationalist and constructivist accounts—can help explore whether, or under what conditions, proposed regimes for certain AI governance targets might be more or less viable. In the case of security governance regimes for AI, an outside-view historical comparison with nuclear arms control suggests that arms control for a high-stakes emerging technology might be more achievable than pessimists would hold, but will need to reckon with changing historical context.

More pragmatically, regime theory can help identify what specific interests (from a rationalist perspectives) or norm shifts (from a constructivist perspective) might be involved in founding such a regime this time around—and what could be the role of different actors such as epistemic communities in shaping state perceptions of these key factors.

7.2.3 Regime Design

Of course, even if a proposed regime may be viable, this does not mean that all types of regimes might be equally optimal or adequate in addressing the sociotechnical changes driven by conventional, military, or advanced AI. Nor are all regime designs likely to be equally responsive to the key factors (i.e. state interests or norms) that shape their political feasibility. Finally, not all designs may be equally robust to ongoing technological disruption.

Accordingly, for any proposed regime or institution, or for existing governance efforts, we can ask: Which global governance issue clusters does it aim to cover (e.g. conventional AI, military AI, advanced AI—or some combination)? What overall governance strategy does it pursue? How adequate are these regimes? How resilient are they to future governance disruption? And what can we learn about the conditions that affect state preferences around institutional design? Once again, drawing on the three lenses can help provide greater insight into these considerations.

[135] For a general argument on process legitimacy, see also Eva Erman and Markus Furendal, 'Artificial Intelligence and the Political Legitimacy of Global Governance' [2022] Political Studies 00323217221126665.

[136] Adan (n 127); Cecil Abungu, Michelle Malonza, and Sumaya Nur Adan, 'Can Apparent Bystanders Distinctively Shape an Outcome? Global South Countries and Global Catastrophic Risk-Focused Governance of Artificial Intelligence' (arXiv.org, 7 December 2023) <https://arxiv.org/abs/2312.04616v1> accessed 7 January 2024.

7.2.3.1 Comparing overall governance strategies

Conventionally, states have several possible strategies to respond to new technologies, especially new powerful military or dual-use innovations. For instance, they can forego cooperation and rely on unilateral actions or even deterrence.[137] Another option is reliance on gradual norm development under existing international law.[138] Yet another avenue is the negotiated establishment of different varieties of new hard law—new international agreements, potentially supported by new institutions. At times, such as on the issue of nuclear non-use and non-proliferation, states may attempt to combine, and balance, all three approaches.[139]

Of these approaches, two may appear insufficient for securing most state goals around global AI governance, especially around military or advanced AI. For instance, relying on deterrence for regulating military AI development and deployment may be of limited efficacy at best, and destabilizing at worst.[140] Likewise, waiting on the gradual development of international norms may be suboptimal. This is because even if gradual interpretation may clarify the legal situation, top-down legal clarification by international courts is slow, and may not be the only—or even the fastest—driver of international norm development. Rather, as Bode and Huels have suggested, in the current normative vacuum around (military) AI, state practice around these technologies may come to instil a tacit acceptance of what is considered 'appropriate' use, in ways that are predominantly shaped by the military point of view.[141] Consequently, they argue that the ways in which states will operate or use AI-enabled weapons 'can have fundamental normative consequences by setting novel standards of appropriate action in international security policy'.[142]

As such, let us instead consider the third avenue—the negotiation of some form of (multilateral) regime, potentially supported by one or more new international institutions. In this context, we can consider the design of the regime in terms of the strictness of control that it aims to establish. We can as such distinguish between the strengths and weaknesses of two treaty designs: (1) a prohibitory treaty

[137] Erin D Dumbacher, 'Limiting Cyberwarfare: Applying Arms-Control Models to an Emerging Technology' (2018) 25 The Nonproliferation Review 203 (contrasting deterrence with norm development or a multilateral treaty, in the context of cyberwarfare).

[138] Kenneth Anderson and Matthew C Waxman, 'Law and Ethics for Autonomous Weapon Systems: Why a Ban Won't Work and How the Laws of War Can' (Stanford University 2013) <https://scholarship.law.columbia.edu/faculty_scholarship/1803/>.

[139] Francis J Gavin, 'Strategies of Inhibition: U.S. Grand Strategy, the Nuclear Revolution, and Nonproliferation' (2015) 40 International Security 9.

[140] See also the discussion in Section 3.3.2.1.

[141] Ingvild Bode and Hendrik Huelss, 'Autonomous Weapons Systems and Changing Norms in International Relations' (2018) 44 Review of International Studies 393; Eugenio V Garcia, 'The Militarization of Artificial Intelligence: A Wake-up Call for the Global South' 7 <https://papers.ssrn.com/sol3/papers.cfm?abstract_id=3452323> accessed 20 March 2020.

[142] Bode and Huelss (n 141).

(i.e. categorical ban) on particular (military or advanced) AI systems,[143] or (2) a regulatory treaty that for instance aims to restrict certain aspects of the use of military AI (e.g. the levels of autonomy or the allowed contexts or domains of use),[144] or of advanced AI (e.g. the development of particularly hazardous capabilities.[145]

Indeed, the question of which type of policies could be best pursued by a particular regime (for military or advanced AI) may turn on the relative efficacy, viability, and resilience of these two types of regimes.[146] There is something to be said for either strategy. However, all else being equal, we might expect an outright ban to hold up better in a number of surprising ways.

Beyond their substantive merits or demerits, a categorical ban has three features that, all else being equal, might make it more functional and resilient than the more nuanced regulatory alternatives. For one, their simplicity facilitates more effective coordination around compliance.[147] Indeed, categorical norms work well, in part because they provide a clearer 'focal point' for coordination by third parties on when and how to sanction breaches of the norm.[148]

Furthermore, by holding the door for a certain pathway of technological development, bans may maintain a degree of state uncertainty over the technology's future, inhibiting future sprints. By maintaining shared uncertainty over whether a given transformative but over-the-horizon capability or 'superweapon'[149] is in fact possible, or rather a costly scientific dead-end, bans can support the continuation

[143] For proposed bans on military AI, see Garcia, 'Future Arms, Technologies, and International Law' (n 25). For proposed restrictions on certain types of advanced AI, see Anthony Aguirre, 'Close the Gates to an Inhuman Future: How and Why We Should Choose to Not Develop Superhuman General-Purpose Artificial Intelligence' (20 October 2023) <https://papers.ssrn.com/abstract=4608505> accessed 24 October 2023.

[144] See also Myriam Dunn Cavelty, Sophie-Charlotte Fischer, and Thierry Balzacq, '"Killer Robots" and Preventative Arms Control' in Myriam Dunn Cavelty and Thierry Balzacq (eds), *Routledge Handbook of Security Studies* (Routledge 2016); Wendell Wallach and Colin Allen, 'Framing Robot Arms Control' (2013) 15 Ethics and Information Technology; Dordrecht 125.

[145] Toby Shevlane and others, 'Model Evaluation for Extreme Risks' (arXiv, 24 May 2023) <http://arxiv.org/abs/2305.15324> accessed 25 May 2023; see also 'Hiroshima Process International Code of Conduct for Advanced AI Systems' (30 October 2023) 3 <https://digital-strategy.ec.europa.eu/en/library/hiroshima-process-international-code-conduct-advanced-ai-systems> accessed 3 November 2023.

[146] See also the proposed 'middle road' in Ronald Arkin and others, 'A Path Towards Reasonable Autonomous Weapons Regulation' (*IEEE Spectrum: Technology, Engineering, and Science News*, 21 October 2019) <https://spectrum.ieee.org/automaton/robotics/artificial-intelligence/a-path-towards-reasonable-autonomous-weapons-regulation> accessed 22 October 2019.

[147] Scharre, *Army of None* (n 46) 341–342.

[148] Moshe Hoffman and others, 'Why Norms Are Categorical' [2018] PNAS <https://www.tse-fr.eu/sites/default/files/TSE/documents/sem2018/eco_pub/hoffman.pdf> accessed 23 January 2020. See also Scharre, 'Autonomous Weapons and Stability' (n 31) 267 (noting that '[b]ans that attempt to regulate how indiscriminate weapons are used on the battlefield in order to avoid civilian casualties (aerial bombardment, submarine warfare, incendiary weapons, and the Convention on Certain Conventional Weapons (CCW) land mine protocol) have had a poor track record of success. Complete bans on weapons (exploding bullets, expanding bullets, chemical weapons, biological weapons, environmental modification weapons, blinding lasers) have fared better').

[149] Neil C Renic, 'Superweapons and the Myth of Technological Peace' [2022] European Journal of International Relations 13540661221136764.

or extension of shared state uncertainty over the technology's future trajectories and stakes, which could facilitate state cooperation,[150] including on additional, shorter-term agreements that allow states to hedge their interests.[151] Of course, in some circumstances, states may actually misunderstand the actual likely prospects for the development of a concerning technology. For instance, the original CCW negotiations in the 1970s produced a ban on weapons that produced fragments not detectable by X-rays (Protocol I), based on concerns that major military states might be developing such ammunition when, in fact, no such weapons were under development at that time, and no leading military power had an interest in developing them.[152] Nonetheless, even such 'hollow agreements' can matter, as they can create precedents for future governance efforts around other technologies.[153]

In the third place, a categorical ban may help shield a regime from future governance disruption, and the consequent need for politically challenging legal development or revision,[154] by curbing the driver of such disruptive capability shifts at the very source. As Rebecca Crootof has noted:

> Somewhat counterintuitively, the most extreme form of multilateral treaty regulation of a technology—a complete ban on its creation or use—may be most likely to stand the test of time. This is largely due to the fact that the aim of a ban is not to accommodate shifting state party needs or new technological developments. Rather, it draws a line in the sand and marks a certain technology permanently off limits.[155]

Future technologies cannot be disruptive to law, after all, if they are never pursued or developed.[156] Likewise, export control regime control lists cannot fall out of date if no new instances or iterations of a technology are being produced. In this way, a categorical ban prunes certain ostensibly harmful pathways of technological development at their early stage.[157] However, this last aspect also comes with

[150] Justin Key Canfil, 'Controlling Tomorrow: Explaining Anticipatory Bans on Emerging Military Technologies' (Social Science Research Network 2019) SSRN Scholarly Paper ID 3423080 <https://papers.ssrn.com/abstract=3423080> accessed 8 December 2020.

[151] For instance, this effect has been observed in other governance domains, such as international trade. B Peter Rosendorff and Helen V Milner, 'The Optimal Design of International Trade Institutions: Uncertainty and Escape' (2001) 55 International Organization 829.

[152] Naomi Egel, 'Anticipatory Governance and New Weapons of War: Lessons from the Convention on Certain Conventional Weapons' [2025] Journal of Strategic Studies 1.

[153] ibid.

[154] On the relation between legal disruption and legal development, see Section 5.5.6.

[155] Crootof, 'Jurisprudential Space Junk' (n 19) 114.

[156] This may not be entirely true. The perception or anticipation of a certain technology being possible—and fears that rival parties might pursue it—might still affect a regime indirectly, even if the technology is never realized, or in fact impossible.

[157] An alternate strategy could be to attempt to slow down or speed up different aspects of technological development in order to affect the *order* of arrival, in the hope that defensive or stabilizing uses

challenges. That is, to avoid disruption, categorical bans may require that they hold the door for not just a particular application or capability, but potentially a broad technology base. The less they manage to do so, the more they remain vulnerable to legal disruption sparked from unregulated technological developments in adjacent fields.

Of course, given the broad diversity of conventional AI capabilities, and the increasing general-purpose capabilities of advanced AI systems, any development in non-restricted (or civilian) sectors would likely eventually spill back over, driving legal disruption in treaties focused narrowly on a particular type of AI capability. It is unclear if any outright ban could hope to forestall such disruption, short of attempting to effect an extremely broad or general restriction on not just frontier AI research but also some of its basic compute infrastructures.

Moreover, it should be remembered that the primary goal of any regime should be not to prevent its own disruption in perpetuity, but rather to actually achieve some substantive societal purpose or govern some sociotechnical change. As such, even proponents of a restrictive regime on some kinds of AI might simply accept some risk of future governance disruption, in order to avoid the (likely undesirable and certainly politically infeasible) over-inclusivity of extending a restrictive regime to many adjacent domains.

Nonetheless, all this does suggest that a major challenge for categorical bans is to articulate meaningful categorical red lines around any parts of the AI stack that (1) correspond to the capabilities or systems that are of concern without being overinclusive; (2) correspond to some categorical behaviour or choices that are easily monitored and agreed upon by all actors and third parties; (3) are relatively self-contained in ways that minimize the regime's exposure to disruption from adjacent technological fields.

Given all this, one might argue that it might be preferable to establish a more narrowly targeted ban or restriction on certain AI system applications (for instance, the use of military AI in nuclear command and control). There are of course challenges, given that (as mentioned previously), partial weapons bans have historically not been as effective as categorical ones.[158]

Nonetheless, this raises the question of how 'partial' bans or targeted regulatory treaties could be improved or made more resilient instead. Again, there may be challenges, depending on what parts of the regulatory target we seek leverage over.[159] For instance, it seems challenging or even harmful to articulate

of that technology (e.g. vaccines) can be developed and implemented before offensive or destabilizing ones (e.g. bioweapons). This strategy has been called 'risk-sensitive innovation'. Jonas B Sandbrink and others, 'Risk-Sensitive Innovation: Leveraging Interactions between Technologies to Navigate Technology Risks' [2024] Science and Public Policy scae043. See also Section 4.3.2.1.

158 Scharre, 'Autonomous Weapons and Stability' (n 31) 267.

159 See also Section 4.6.1.

useful (global) bans on the basis of AI's underlying *techniques*. Specific conventional AI approaches (e.g. reinforcement learning) do not map neatly to harmful applications, whereas the core techniques underlying advanced AI systems (e.g. Transformers or Diffusion models) are so general-purpose that they are irreducibly dual-use, such that regulating their use (barring other conditions, such as provisions around the size of a trained model) will virtually always be overinclusive.

As such, there might be more promise in aiming to tailor restrictions around particular types of inputs—such as the use of certain amounts of computing power in training a model, or the use of certain data sources. Regulatory regimes that aim at preventing *vertical* (capability-related) proliferation have, in the past, often relied on clearly quantified caps or limits. It has sometimes been argued that AI systems might be challenging for arms control in similar ways to cyber weapons, in that they are harder to measure or compare in relevant ways.[160] While that may be less true of the computationally intensive advanced AI systems, there will still be slippage, over time, in the relevance of many hard metrics.

By contrast, articulating bans or restrictive regimes around specific AI *capabilities* might be more fertile ground, especially if complemented by standards for usage—such as contexts in which systems should not be deployed, minimum standards for safety, and reliability testing.[161] This might enable a regime to rule out, for instance, any 'cyberwarfare systems with the ability to autonomously hack back', 'systems that are able to interface with nuclear assets', or systems that are capable of autonomous self-replication.[162] In the military domain, AWS systems could be provided with a series of technical safeguards in order to mitigate the risks of inadvertent escalation.[163] Regimes could also draw on past arms control lessons in promoting and implementing a series of Confidence-Building Measures (CBMs)—various information- and transparency-enhancing agreements that enable parties to better understand how distinct AI capabilities would alter the implicit rules of warfare.[164]

Nonetheless, many partial regulations or contextual bans bring us back to a previous problem: whereas a total ban might conceivably insulate a treaty against

[160] Borghard and Lonergan (n 96); but see also Dumbacher (n 137).
[161] Brundage and others (n 55) 69.
[162] See: 'Hiroshima Process International Code of Conduct for Advanced AI Systems' (n 145) 3.
[163] See for instance Leys (n 31) 404–410 (discussing various 'rules of the road', such as ensuring that swarming AWS absorb a first bow before retaliating, installing a '*jus ad bellum* switch' and an 'auto-off' feature, and an 'orange box' rule to preserve data around a certain decision to strike).
[164] Michael C Horowitz, Lauren Kahn, and Casey Mahoney, 'The Future of Military Applications of Artificial Intelligence: A Role for Confidence-Building Measures?' [2020] Orbis <http://www.sciencedirect.com/science/article/pii/S0030438720300430> accessed 20 September 2020; Shoker and others (n 29).

future technological disruption, a partial ban on usage is vulnerable to new technological developments disrupting its functioning. As such, a key consideration for such regimes—to which we will return later in this chapter—is about articulating strategies or designs that render them more resilient to ongoing innovation in AI.

7.2.3.2 Understanding the pressures towards institutional mimicry in AI governance

Finally, in analytical terms, drawing on regime theory can also help explain other significant trends regarding which institutional arrangements state actors are likely to prefer in the governance of AI issues.

For instance, we have previously, in Chapter 3, discussed the prominence of institutional mimicry in contemporary debates around AI governance, with many institutional proposals made explicitly in analogy with one or another existing international institution.[165] Significantly, beyond the question of whether these proposals invoke appropriate analogies,[166] and whether they provide appropriate institutional solutions for AI,[167] rationalist accounts of international institutional design may help explain the prominence of such institutional mimicry. For instance, on the basis of an empirical and statistical analysis of the design of 534 intergovernmental organizations, Reinsberg and Westerwinter have suggested that when there is an existing overlap in institutional functions, this promotes mimicking dynamics, such that 'when states create new IGOs, they model their design based on the features of pre-existing organizations with overlapping memberships, governance tasks, and issue areas'.[168] They argue that such copying is a design strategy for boundedly rational institutional designers faced with situations of complexity, as this approach reduces uncertainty while lowering the costs of identifying suitable institutions. Whether one endorses this direction towards convergent institutional design or worries that it will be inadequate for (some) AI issues, it is important to understand these drivers.

[165] See Matthijs M Maas and José Jaime Villalobos, 'International AI Institutions: A Literature Review of Models, Examples, and Proposals' (Institute for Law & AI 2023) 1 <https://law-ai.org/international-ai-institutions> accessed 21 September 2023.

[166] Law (n 72); Mike Watson, 'IAEA for AI? That Model Has Already Failed' *Wall Street Journal* (1 June 2023) <https://www.wsj.com/articles/iaea-for-ai-that-model-has-already-failed-chaptgpt-technology-nuclear-proliferation-4339543b> accessed 12 September 2023.

[167] Jason Hausenloy and Claire Dennis, 'Towards a UN Role in Governing Foundation Artificial Intelligence Models' (United Nations University—Centre for Policy Research 2023) <https://unu.edu/cpr/working-paper/towards-un-role-governing-foundation-artificial-intelligence-models> accessed 21 September 2023.

[168] Bernhard Reinsberg and Oliver Westerwinter, 'Institutional Overlap in Global Governance and the Design of Intergovernmental Organizations' (2023) 18 The Review of International Organizations 693, 718.

7.3 Topology: The State of the AI Governance System

Given the incipient state of AI governance initiatives, the range of ongoing processes, and the wide variety of new institutional proposals that have been put forward in the past years, one might expect it to be appropriate to primarily focus analysis and study at the level of the AI regime's origins. This would be most helpful in considering the prospects of a proposed or embryonic governance regime for a given AI issue or focus area.

Nonetheless, beyond understanding the origins of individual institutions, a main contribution of regime complexity theory is that it allows us to zoom out and focus on a larger array and landscape of institutions. A second analytical step therefore helps us focus on the *topology* or morphology[169] of an emerging or mature AI regime complex at some given moment in time.

Indeed, much regime scholarship to date has occupied itself with mapping the extant 'governance architecture' on various issue areas of international concern.[170] Such work has illustrated the value of mapping the topology of the governance network of institutions and instruments active on any given issue, as this can help identify patterns of shared membership, influence, and potential regime interaction among these different actors, in a way that a focus on individual institutions will fail to apprehend.

Of course, there are challenges to seeking to map the AI governance landscape, given how significantly it is in flux. Yet at the same time, it remains valuable to explore the topology of the emerging AI regime complex, even at this early state and transition moment in time, because latent tensions or fault lines among policies, norms, or institutions may highlight the potential for future tensions or conflict.

I will not aim to provide a comprehensive mapping of the AI regime complex here, beyond the survey already given in Chapter 3. However, it is valuable to sketch a number of dimensions along which to map these normative architectures and institutional networks at various points of development. Specifically, an analysis of the topology or state of the AI regime complex can consider three

[169] In other work, this is framed instead as the 'structure' of the global governance complex. Eilstrup-Sangiovanni and Westerwinter (n 2).

[170] The literature is extensive, but for overviews, see Frank Biermann and others, 'The Fragmentation of Global Governance Architectures: A Framework for Analysis' (2009) 9 Global Environmental Politics 14, 15; Laura Gómez-Mera, Jean-Frédéric Morin, and Thijs Van De Graaf, 'Regime Complexes' in Frank Biermann and Rakhyun E Kim (eds), *Architectures of Earth System Governance: Institutional Complexity and Structural Transformation* (Cambridge University Press 2020) 147. Rakhyun E Kim, 'Is Global Governance Fragmented, Polycentric, or Complex? The State of the Art of the Network Approach' [2019] International Studies Review 9–10 <https://academic.oup.com/isr/advance-article/doi/10.1093/isr/viz052/5571549> accessed 16 February 2020.

features: *demographics*, *organisation*, and *interactions*. These could each be examined at one of three levels of *scope* (macro, meso, micro).[171]

7.3.1 Demographics

In terms of *demographics*, the focus is on identifying the size and composition of the governance regime complex. The focus here is on the 'nodes' in the overall network, in terms of the norms, institutions, or governance initiatives that apply to a given AI issue, without at this stage necessarily considering their internal relations to one another.

Such a mapping can depart from established norms and initiatives, such as the OECD AI Principles, the G20 Principles on Artificial Intelligence, and others discussed in Chapter 3. However, even (or especially) in a regime complex that is still in a very early stage, the mapping of demographics can extend beyond established regimes to 'candidate' regimes.

To return to the example of the regime complex on military AI applications, a survey of demographics can depart from ongoing (though to date inconclusive) initiatives, such as the CCW process. However, it can also extend to the wide space of solutions or principles that have been put forward. This includes the prospective application of existing international norms—such as the International Humanitarian Law principles of Distinction, Proportionality, or Humanity, or the Article 36 requirements on the legal review of new weapons.[172] It can also extend to solutions or principles that have been proposed but not yet implemented or embedded, such as governance regimes based on guaranteeing some forms of 'meaningful human control', or 'war tort' regimes that establish (state) accountability for LAWS.[173]

7.3.2 Organisation: Density, Overlap, and Normative and Institutional Linkages

In terms of regime complex *organization*, we can consider the density and configuration of the overall institutional network active on AI. This can take in (1) the number of institutional membership overlaps, (2) the number and type of AI issue

[171] This taxonomy is slightly distinct from the levels of analysis used by some other regime complex scholars. For instance, departing from systems theory, Rakhyun Kim distinguishes between analyses focusing on 'nodes' (treaties, regimes, international organizations), 'links' (institutional interlinkages or partnerships), 'clusters' (regime complexes), and 'networks' (structure; dynamics and evolution; system). Kim (n 170) 8.

[172] Chavannes, Klonowska, and Sweijs (n 32) 12–14.

[173] ibid 17–23. See also Crootof, 'War Torts: Accountability for Autonomous Weapons' (n 24).

area mandate overlaps (or contact points), and (3) the number and nature of deliberate links between individual instruments, institutions, or initiatives, in terms of legal *norms* invoked by different regimes, in terms of pursued policy *goals*, in terms of their domain area *impacts*, or in terms of *inter-institutional relations* (such as overlapping memberships, formal partnerships, or operational and informational links or collaborations).

In general, while the AI regime complex is still in flux, current institutional trajectories do appear reflective of an increasing level of institutional *density* in the AI regime complex for many issues. Indeed, in addition to a steadily maturing landscape of institutions active on conventional AI systems, and the long-running but largely gridlocked UN CCW GGE process on military AI (specifically autonomous weapons systems), the past few years have seen a steady flow of new institutional initiatives and instruments, including (since 2022 and 2023) a new wave of initiatives focused on the governance challenges of advanced AI systems.

However, as discussed in Chapter 3, much of this AI regime complex is still relatively fragmented.[174] Most notably, in terms of *membership* overlaps, many key initiatives—at the OECD, G20, GPAI, G7, or UK AI Safety Summit—have fragmented, incomplete, and to some extent non-overlapping geographical memberships.[175]

Likewise, in terms of *issue area mandate* overlaps, the long-established distinction between civilian and military AI governance debates remains largely intact today. However, the increasingly dense number of initiatives focused on conventional AI systems has since 2022 been complemented by a series of new initiatives (the Frontier Model Forum, the UK AI Safety Summit and its Bletchley Declaration) focused explicitly on advanced AI systems, as well as a few (the EU AI Act, the G7 Hiroshima Guidelines) that have pivoted in order to address both conventional and advanced AI.

In terms of *linkages* across the institutional networks, while there are gaps, there are some encouraging signs of emerging coordination as well. This includes incipient *normative* linkages, as seen by the fact that a wide range of bodies or initiatives—such as the G20, the GPAI, or the G7 Hiroshima Guidelines—drew from or referred to the OECD AI Principles.[176] Likewise, the Council of Europe's

[174] Peter Cihon, Matthijs M Maas, and Luke Kemp, 'Should Artificial Intelligence Governance Be Centralised? Design Lessons from History', *Proceedings of the AAAI/ACM Conference on AI, Ethics, and Society* (ACM 2020) <http://dl.acm.org/doi/10.1145/3375627.3375857> accessed 12 February 2020; See also Thorsten Jelinek, Wendell Wallach, and Danil Kerimi, 'Coordinating Committee for the Governance of Artificial Intelligence' (G20—Policy Brief Taskforce 5 (Multilateralism) 2020) <https://www.g20-insights.org/policy_briefs/coordinating-committee-for-the-governance-of-artificial-intelligence/> accessed 8 July 2020.

[175] Peter Cihon, Matthijs M Maas, and Luke Kemp, 'Fragmentation and the Future: Investigating Architectures for International AI Governance' (2020) 11 Global Policy 545.

[176] G20, 'G20 Ministerial Statement on Trade and Digital Economy' <https://www.mofa.go.jp/files/000486596.pdf> accessed 25 May 2020; Global Partnership on Artificial Intelligence, 'Joint Statement from Founding Members of the Global Partnership on Artificial Intelligence' <https://www.gov.uk/gov

Framework Convention on AI articulated a definition of 'AI system' that itself hewed closely to the OECD's own updated definition of AI.[177]

There have also been growing *inter-institutional* linkages. The most noticeable of these has been the gradual interlinking and indeed merging of GPAI into the OECD: this started in 2020, with GPAI's Secretariat being initially housed within the OECD;[178] developed with their joint collaboration in programmes such as the G7's Hiroshima AI Process;[179] and culminated in 2024 in the eventual unification of both organisations through an 'integrated partnership', which puts all OECD members and GPAI countries on an equal footing.[180] Other institutional linkages can be found in the September 2024 announcement of UN–OECD cooperation on evidence-based AI risk and opportunity assessments.[181]

Similar patterns of inter-institutional linkages can be seen in the attendance of many AI governance organizations at initiatives such as the AI Safety Summits,[182] but also through the mutual influence that actors such as the G7, OECD, GPAI, and EU have had on one another's main policy initiatives for generative and advanced AI.[183] This has led this AI governance track to be described as an 'emerging

ernment/publications/joint-statement-from-founding-members-of-the-global-partnership-on-artificial-intelligence> accessed 11 March 2025; Hiroki Habuka, 'The Path to Trustworthy AI: G7 Outcomes and Implications for Global AI Governance' (*CSIS*, 6 June 2023) <https://www.csis.org/analysis/path-trustworthy-ai-g7-outcomes-and-implications-global-ai-governance> accessed 20 December 2023.

[177] See for instance: Council of Europe Framework Convention on Artificial Intelligence and Human Rights, Democracy and the Rule of Law (opened for signature 5 September 2024, not yet in force) CETS 225 art 2; compared with Stuart Russell, Karine Perset, and Marko Grobelnik, 'Updates to the OECD's Definition of an AI System Explained' (*OECD AI Policy Observatory*, 29 November 2023) <https://oecd.ai/en/wonk/ai-system-definition-update> accessed 10 January 2024.

[178] OECD, 'OECD to Host Secretariat of New Global Partnership on Artificial Intelligence' (15 June 2020) <https://www.oecd.org/going-digital/ai/OECD-to-host-Secretariat-of-new-Global-Partnership-on-Artificial-Intelligence.htm> accessed 3 July 2020.

[179] OECD, 'G7 Hiroshima Process on Generative Artificial Intelligence (AI): Towards a G7 Common Understanding on Generative AI' (OECD 2023) <https://www.oecd-ilibrary.org/science-and-technology/g7-hiroshima-process-on-generative-artificial-intelligence-ai_bf3c0c60-en> accessed 13 September 2023.

[180] '6th Meeting of the GPAI Ministerial Council Held on 3rd July 2024 at New Delhi' (*Ministry of Electronics & IT*, 3 July 2024) art 9 <https://pib.gov.in/pib.gov.in/Pressreleaseshare.aspx?PRID=2030534> accessed 1 August 2024 ('Announce a renewed vision for GPAI through an integrated partnership with the OECD bringing together all current OECD members and GPAI countries on equal footing, under the GPAI brand and on the basis of the OECD Recommendation on Artificial Intelligence'). OECD, 'GPAI and OECD Unite to Advance Coordinated International Efforts for Trustworthy AI' (*OECD*, 3 July 2024) <https://www.oecd.org/en/about/news/speech-statements/2024/07/GPAI-and-OECD-unite-to-advance-coordinated-international-efforts-for-trustworthy-AI.html> accessed 1 August 2024.

[181] OECD, 'OECD and UN Announce Next Steps in Collaboration on Artificial Intelligence' (*OECD*, 22 September 2024) <https://www.oecd.org/en/about/news/press-releases/2024/09/oecd-and-un-announce-next-steps-in-collaboration-on-artificial-intelligence.html> accessed 26 September 2024.

[182] UK Government, 'AI Safety Summit: Confirmed Attendees (Governments and Organisations)' (*GOV.UK*, 31 October 2023) <https://www.gov.uk/government/publications/ai-safety-summit-introduction/ai-safety-summit-confirmed-governments-and-organisations> accessed 14 January 2024 (listing among others GPAI, the OECD, UNESCO, the ITU, and the Council of Europe).

[183] Inga Ulnicane, 'Governance Fix? Power and Politics in Controversies about Governing Generative AI' [2024] Policy and Society puae022, 5.

polycentric system of governance, where various independent bodies with partly overlapping membership . . . are in collaborative relationships with each other, which provide[s] opportunities for mutual monitoring, learning, and adaptation'.[184] At the same time, many of these initiatives also resemble 'closed clubs'.[185] Yet other efforts, such as the 2023 Guidelines for Secure AI System Development, still appear to operate in relative normative isolation.

7.3.3 Interactions: Gaps, Conflicts, Cooperation, Synergies

In terms of resulting *interactions*, regime complex focuses on the character of the linkages between the different institutions or instruments.

For instance, these linkages might involve (1) a degree of buck-passing, leaving *gaps* in governance where certain tricky or difficult issues are left in a 'non-regime' state.[186] Such linkages might be (2) *conflictive*, either in the form of outright norm inconsistencies or incompatibilities, or more commonly, in terms of operational externalities,[187] or even inter-institutional 'turf wars'. More optimistically, these linkages can be (3) *cooperative*, when there is loose integration and exchange between institutions, but the relationships between norms, principles, or policies remains unclear. Finally, linkages can be (4) *synergistic*, with mutually reinforcing norms, or useful institutional divisions of labour.[188]

It will be important to examine how and where various AI standards or framework principles are articulated across different AI governance instruments, and whether or not these are aligned. For instance, while in the debate over the international regulation of LAWS the concept of 'meaningful human control' has seen broad support from the international community, this idea is still subject to wide diversity in articulation and interpretation.[189] If left unaddressed or unclarified, this ambiguity could spell the emergence of potential norm conflicts among later instruments or regimes. By contrast, in other areas, the normative and institutional links between certain bodies, such as the OECD and the GPAI, appear to be more cooperative or even synergistic, at least at this stage. Nonetheless, the current tapestry of institutions and norms also appears to leave a number of potential gaps on certain issue areas, such as the use of AI in cyberwarfare and non-LAWS military use cases for AI[190] (such as the use of large language models in military decision-making). Moreover, while a set of new initiatives have begun to address advanced

184 ibid 6.
185 ibid.
186 Radoslav S Dimitrov and others, 'International Nonregimes: A Research Agenda' (2007) 9 International Studies Review 230.
187 Morin and others (n 124) 2–3.
188 This loosely follows Biermann and others (n 170) 19–21.
189 Chavannes, Klonowska, and Sweijs (n 32) 17–19.
190 Cihon, Maas and Kemp (n 174) 229.

AI governance issues, there has been very little attempt to clarify their normative or institutional linkages among initiatives.

7.3.4 Scope: Macro, Meso, Micro

Finally, through the lens of regime complexity, all of these types of interactions may be examined at three levels of the (AI) governance architecture. At the *macro* level, we can consider the interactions of the AI regime complex with other regime complexes (e.g. international security, data privacy, export controls, transport), or with general norms of international law.

At the *meso* level, we can consider interactions of different AI regimes which, at least nominally, focus on distinct issue areas (e.g. the interaction of the prospective CCW regime on LAWS with broader AI ethics or standards initiatives, or with emerging regimes aimed at preventing the misuse of harmful advanced AI capabilities).

Finally, at the *micro* level, one can focus on the internal dynamics between different institutions focused on the same issue area. This could consider, for instance, the growing risk that different military AI governance initiatives may articulate different and only partially overlapping definitions of 'meaningful human control';[191] or the risk that different governance initiatives aimed at the regulation of advanced 'frontier AI' end up operating with different definitions—or different thresholds—for classifying AI systems as such.

7.4 Evolution: Trends and Trajectories in AI Regime Complexity

Of course, analysing the topology of the AI regime complex at a given moment yields only a static snapshot. It is important to also consider the dynamic interplay and evolution of a regime complex over time.

Indeed, many regimes have evolved considerably over time since their initial establishment, as different organizations are established to carry out distinct functions or to address different parts of an issue, and as established organizations are reformed or expanded. Obviously, institutional regime complexes in other domains such as arms control or the environment did not spring into being fully formed, but saw lengthy processes of evolution.[192] For instance, in the nuclear regime complex, the IAEA was first set up in 1957 but later (in 1974) complemented by the NSG, various fora established around the 1970 Nuclear Non-Proliferation

[191] Chavannes, Klonowska, and Sweijs (n 32) 17–19; Rebecca Crootof, Margot E Kaminski, and W Nicholson Price II, 'Humans in the Loop' (2023) 76 Vanderbilt Law Review 429.

[192] Fehl (n 87).

Treaty, the 1996 Preparatory Commission for the Comprehensive Nuclear-Test-Ban Treaty Organization (CTBTO Preparatory Commission), and a broad array of deliberative bodies within the UN system, including the UN First Committee, the UN Disarmament Commission, and the Conference on Disarmament (CD). It also encompasses the 2017 Treaty on the Prohibition of Nuclear Weapons (TPNW).[193]

As has been discussed in Chapter 3, the AI governance landscape remains relatively incipient and fragmented, though the past few years have seen a significant increase in institutional activity and density. However, should all this be interpreted as the early growing pains of a regime complex, which will be eventually resolved by the establishment of an overarching, centralized international institution? It can be valuable to explore which factors or developments could determine or influence whether the AI governance architecture continues along in a fragmented regime complex, or whether—or under what conditions—we might expect the eventual emergence of a more integrated global regime complex for some or all AI issues, organized around a centralized coordinating institution.

7.4.1 Caveats: The Limits of Predicting or Steering a Regime Complex

It is important to provide two key caveats to this discussion of trajectories. In the first place, predicting the future evolution of a regime complex is challenging. That is, anticipating the future developments of any political system or organization is difficult under the best of circumstances. That goes doubly so for a global regime complex, given its nature as a dynamic complex system that is not (fully) under the control or authority of a single actor. Indeed, many regime complexity scholars argue that, because of their nature as 'complex systems', it will be difficult or impossible to anticipate precise points of institutional overlap or norm interaction far in advance.[194] Nonetheless, granting this challenge of making very specific, calibrated predictions, it can still be possible to identify relevant factors or drivers that would play a role in supporting different trajectories of regime complex development.

A second and related problem is that deliberately designing a regime complex to follow a certain trajectory or bend towards a particular state or topology will also be hard, because such a decentralized complex of separate, overlapping institutions—even when this is in fact the most functional institutional arrangement—is rarely if ever the straightforward product of rational or intentional design.[195] Instead,

[193] Megan Dee, 'EU Orchestration in the Nuclear Weapons Regime Complex' (2023) 11 Politics and Governance 2 <https://www.cogitatiopress.com/politicsandgovernance/article/view/6323> accessed 30 January 2023.

[194] Karen J Alter and Kal Raustiala, 'The Rise of International Regime Complexity' (2018) 14 Annual Review of Law and Social Science 329, 333.

[195] David J Galbreath and Sascha Sauerteig, 'Regime Complexity and Security Governance' in James Sperling (ed), *Handbook of Governance and Security* (Edward Elgar 2014) 85. However, not all are agreed on this point. For instance, Eyal Benvenisti and George Downs have influentially argued that 'a

these fragmented regime complexes are often seen as the emergent, overall result of a combination of many local decisions by diverse actors—such as, say, one state's local decisions over whether, on a given new issue (say, military AI systems' strategic impacts), it will oppose institutionalization and emphasize only gradual norm development, pursue mostly bilateral confidence-building arrangements, try to amend an existing institution or regime, or instead advocate for the establishment of a new institution or regime on this issue. The point is that even if actors' decisions in many of these areas are based on locally (and boundedly) 'rational' calculations towards achieving deliberate policy goals,[196] they cannot easily anticipate, determine, or control how these choices—along with those by other states—will feed into the shape of the eventual regime complex.

Nonetheless, granting these two caveats, it may still be valuable to draw on regime complex theory to anticipate some of the drivers of different trajectories, identify their implications, and if possible identify early warning signs (or opportunity flags) that would signal that we are in one or another scenario. In doing so, we can take stock of both general background drivers of fragmentation in global governance, but also consider the effects that AI-driven governance disruption (see Chapter 5) may exert on these trends.

7.4.2 Political Factors Driving Regime Complex Evolution

While the past years have, as discussed, seen many envision the establishment of one or another centralized AI organization,[197] one insight of the regime complex literature is that such ambitions may face an uphill battle, given background trends in the texture and architecture of global governance.

Indeed, a range of studies have chronicled how, over the past few decades, and across diverse issue areas, governance responses—if they even manage to avoid a non-regime state,[198] or growing legal 'stagnation' and reliance on nonbinding soft law[199]—have tended towards institutional proliferation, fragmentation, and regime complexity, rather than consolidation.[200]

fragmented system's piecemeal character suggests an absence of design and obscures the role of intentionality. As a result, it is often considered to be solely the accidental byproduct of historical events and broad social forces. This has helped obscure the fact that fragmentation is in part the result of a calculated strategy by powerful states to create a legal order that both closely reflects their interests and that only they have the capacity to alter.' Eyal Benvenisti and George W Downs, 'The Empire's New Clothes: Political Economy and the Fragmentation of International Law' (2007) 60 Stanford Law Review 595, 597–598.

[196] Reinsberg and Westerwinter (n 168).

[197] Maas and Villalobos (n 165); Ho and others (n 134). See also Section 3.3.6.

[198] Dimitrov and others (n 186).

[199] J Pauwelyn, RA Wessel, and J Wouters, 'When Structures Become Shackles: Stagnation and Dynamics in International Lawmaking' (2014) 25 European Journal of International Law 733.

[200] Kenneth W Abbott, Jessica F Green, and Robert O Keohane, 'Organizational Ecology and Institutional Change in Global Governance' (2016) 70 International Organization 247.

On the surface, this trend towards governance entropy may appear surprising or anomalous. After all, from a rationalist perspective, one might expect states—once they agree on the need for global action—to prefer to avoid the additional transaction costs and potential norm conflicts that might be involved with creating, managing, or navigating many parallel institutions, especially if their functions or domains potentially overlap.[201] In this perspective, one might intuitively expect states to stick with working through a small number of issue-specific centralized institutions, and attempt to preserve the unity or coherence (such as it is) of the international legal system.

Yet transaction costs and considerations of efficiency are of course not the only considerations that play into decisions around the creation of new institutions. As noted previously, the absence of an international legislative supreme body to coordinate among regimes, and the need for distinct regimes to respond to issues in diverse areas, have long been seen as driving the institutional and normative fragmentation of the global governance complex as a whole.

As such, it has been suggested that regime complexity, even where it appears as a deliberate governance choice, will often be a nearly unavoidable outcome of many deeper trends in world politics.[202] In particular, Karen Alter and Kal Raustiala have noted seven interrelated trends which, they argue, together generate, sustain, and increase regime complexity over time. These trends are: density, accretion, power shifts over time, preference changes, modernity, representation and voice goals, and local governance.[203]

We should not, all else being equal, expect AI governance to remain insulated from such trends in the global governance architecture. That is not to say that they are irrevocable, and cannot be resisted by institutions in a regime complex: for instance, historical institutionalist scholars have pointed out how, on issues such as regional security governance, the internal design features of initial 'focal institutions' can anchor the larger regime complex, because early design choices for (for instance) formal institutions with high sovereignty costs (e.g. NATO) can inhibit or slow subsequent institutional layering and the creation of additional institutions, resulting in a regime complex that is less fragmented—but

[201] Thijs Van de Graaf, 'Fragmentation in Global Energy Governance: Explaining the Creation of IRENA' (2013) 13 Global Environmental Politics 14, 15. See also Johannes Urpelainen and Thijs Van de Graaf, 'Your Place or Mine? Institutional Capture and the Creation of Overlapping International Institutions' (2015) 45 British Journal of Political Science 799.

[202] Alter and Raustiala (n 194) 337 ('in a deeper sense, a regime complex is often an almost-inevitable result of broader trends in world politics that make regime complexity almost unavoidable'). However, note that this is not universally accepted. For instance, Mette Eilstrup-Sangiovanni has suggested that, rather than evolving towards ever greater fragmentation, complex governance systems tend to follow a cyclical evolution, fluctuating between greater or lesser integration and (dis)order. Mette Eilstrup-Sangiovanni, 'Ordering Global Governance Complexes: The Evolution of the Governance Complex for International Civil Aviation' (2022) 17 The Review of International Organizations 293.

[203] Alter and Raustiala (n 194) 337.

also potentially slower to adapt.[204] Nonetheless, it is valuable to briefly consider why and how the distinct external trends identified by Alter and Raustiala may generate regime complexity, whether or how we might expect AI governance to be affected by these trends, or whether it might resist these pressures towards regime fragmentation.

7.4.2.1 Institutional density

In terms of *density*, the argument is that the general trend of institutional proliferation has brought with it a significant increase in the quantity and diversity of global institutions or agreements, which in turn feeds back into, and exacerbates, fragmentation.[205] This is because, as Alter and Raustiala note, 'it is hard to address new or existing problems without, perhaps inadvertently, treading on a set of agreements or policies an existing regime has previously enacted'.[206]

The resulting overlap between many institutions on issue areas ensures that norm or mandate conflicts may be increasingly common. The point here is not that this growth necessarily drives inter-institutional norm drift or normative polarization (i.e. making individual agreements more likely to be in conflict with one another), but rather that a significantly greater number of institutions or agreements will result in a combinatorial explosion of contact surfaces, and thereby will exacerbate or activate more latent conflicts. Once again, this by itself does not increase (further) fragmentation, but it may make the (adverse) consequences of such fragmentation more keenly felt.

Institutional density could prove significant in driving (further) fragmentation in the AI regime complex. As noted, AI systems—whether the broad portfolio of individually narrow 'conventional' AI systems, or the adaptable stack of increasingly general-purpose 'advanced' AI models—create a diverse range of policy challenges and sociotechnical impacts. Some of these may be genuinely unprecedented, but many will certainly overlap and interact with existing issue areas—from privacy to cybercrime, from human rights to international security—which are already embedded within existing agreements or regimes, or plausibly within the mandate of existing institutions. For instance, new global governance initiatives on privacy or some right to explanation for algorithmically based decision-making would have to consider its interactions with the EU's General Data Protection Regulation (GDPR).[207] Even if such touch-points are only partial, or

[204] Stephanie C Hofmann and Andrew Yeo, 'Historical Institutionalism and Institutional Design: Divergent Pathways to Regime Complexes in Asia and Europe' (2024) 30 European Journal of International Relations 306.

[205] See also Section 6.3.1. However, for an argument that these trends have slowed since then, see Pauwelyn, Wessel, and Wouters (n 199).

[206] Alter and Raustiala (n 194) 337.

[207] Though for a sceptical view on the inclusion of such a right in the GDPR, see Sandra Wachter, Brent Mittelstadt, and Luciano Floridi, 'Why a Right to Explanation of Automated Decision-Making Does Not Exist in the General Data Protection Regulation' (2017) 7 International Data Privacy Law 76.

occur in certain domains where regimes are not dense (or even are largely absent), the sheer breadth of AI applications and impacts makes it very likely for there to be some overlap.[208] This may reduce the prospects of a completely novel institution being established, or increase the chances that if one is, its design is closely mimicked from an existing institution.[209]

Given the wide versatility of basic conventional AI paradigms, the adaptability of advanced general-purpose foundation models, and the increasingly critical role (especially for the latter technology) of intrinsically dual-use high-performance computing hardware, different AI governance institutions may seek to rely on the upstream regulation of AI inputs or models in order to regulate the technologies' (downstream) impacts within their specific mandate.[210] Indeed, they might even be wise to do so, as various upstream nodes may offer much better or more appropriate regulatory leverage.[211] However, by coming at the same stage of AI development from different angles, such institutions might be hard pressed to avoid inadvertent overlap or conflict (in terms of norms, institutional mission, or policy outcomes) with antecedent regimes that already operate in those or adjacent areas. Consequently, many parts of the AI development and supply chain would become subject to overlapping and potentially conflicting demands from different regimes. This is not a new challenge: already today, export control regimes, faced with the increasing convergence of different (digital) technologies, have struggled to ensure harmonization among one another.[212]

The complexity and rate-of-change in AI technology could enhance such stresses, such that the growing institutional density in the AI regime complex is unlikely to yield the establishment of a single overarching institution, and rather may exacerbate the effects of fragmentation throughout the regime complex.

[208] Alter and Raustiala (n 194) 339 ('Perhaps most significant, because the density of the global governance ecosystem is so high, any attempt to define a particular problem—to in essence bring together shared sets of issues and create a single regime to govern a given space—is likely to replicate the regime complex problem insofar as new institutions will almost inevitably overlap with preexisting elemental regimes').

[209] Reinsberg and Westerwinter (n 168).

[210] See for instance AI Now Institute, 'General Purpose AI Poses Serious Risks, Should Not Be Excluded From the EU's AI Act | Policy Brief' (*AI Now Institute*, 13 April 2023) <https://ainowinstitute.org/publication/gpai-is-high-risk-should-not-be-excluded-from-eu-ai-act> accessed 16 April 2023.

[211] Haydn Belfield and Shin-Shin Hua, 'Compute and Antitrust: Regulatory Implications of the AI Hardware Supply Chain, from Chip Design to Cloud APIs' (*Verfassungsblog*, 19 August 2022) <https://verfassungsblog.de/compute-and-antitrust/> accessed 22 August 2022; Jennifer Cobbe, Michael Veale, and Jatinder Singh, 'Understanding Accountability in Algorithmic Supply Chains', *2023 ACM Conference on Fairness, Accountability, and Transparency* (2023) <http://arxiv.org/abs/2304.14749> accessed 29 September 2023.

[212] Kolja Brockmann, 'Challenges to Multilateral Export Controls: The Case for Inter-Regime Dialogue and Coordination' (SIPRI 2019) <https://www.sipri.org/publications/2019/other-publications/challenges-multilateral-export-controls-case-inter-regime-dialogue-and-coordination> accessed 19 March 2025.

7.4.2.2 Accretion

In terms of *accretion*, while states might frequently seek to vest authority to govern a new problem in existing organizations, there may also be many situations where states will find it more attractive to create new institutions than to try to amend those existing ones.[213] This may be because they find themselves faced with the path dependence of existing institutions,[214] or pervasive institutional gridlock. However, institutional accretion might also be the result of a form of symbolic politics—with the establishment of a new institution signalling to global or domestic audiences a greater investment in combating a high-profile global problem (i.e. the turning of a page) than would incremental modifications to existing institutions. That need not mean that the new established institutions will be effective: consider the challenges around the creation of 'empty' or 'face-saving' institutions,[215] where in spite of the desire to achieve some governance successes, states are still not able to overcome intractable disagreements over functions. However, this does suggest that watershed moments in global public attention on an issue will lead to significant new impetus for establishing a new institution.

Given this, it is notable that many early initiatives in global AI governance—for both conventional and military AI issues—remained focused or hosted within existing fora or institutions.[216] To be sure, there were some early attempts at creating new institutions, such as the 2018 French–Canadian proposal for an 'International Panel on AI',[217] which eventually gave rise to the Global Partnership on AI,[218] or the

[213] For instance, Alter and Raustiala note how 'even though the World Health Organization has existed since 1948, in 2000 states created the Global Fund to Fight Aids, Tuberculosis, and Malaria to provide a more flexible, private sector-oriented alternative'. Alter and Raustiala (n 194) 337.

[214] Kathleen Thelen, 'Historical Institutionalism in Comparative Politics' (1999) 2 Annual Review of Political Science 369; Lucio Baccaro and Valentina Mele, 'Pathology of Path Dependency? The ILO and the Challenge of New Governance' (2012) 65 ILR Review 195 (examining the ILO's inability to undertake certain reforms, in the late 1990s and early 2000s, to increase the involvement of NGOs, or to adopt quantitative indicators of impact).

[215] Radoslav S Dimitrov, 'Empty Institutions in Global Environmental Politics' (2020) 22 International Studies Review 626. However, for a more optimistic view, see also Giovanni Mantilla, 'Deflective Cooperation: Social Pressure and Forum Management in Cold War Conventional Arms Control' (2023) 77 International Organization 564, 565 (considering the 1980 UN Convention on Certain Conventional Weapons as an example of 'interstate efforts to manage intractable disagreement through suboptimal institutionalized cooperation').

[216] Lewin Schmitt, 'Mapping Global AI Governance: A Nascent Regime in a Fragmented Landscape' (2022) 2 AI and Ethics <https://doi.org/10.1007/s43681-021-00083-y> accessed 18 August 2021; Sepasspour (n 72).

[217] Justin Trudeau, 'Mandate for the International Panel on Artificial Intelligence' (*Prime Minister of Canada*, 6 December 2018) <https://pm.gc.ca/eng/news/2018/12/06/mandate-international-panel-artificial-intelligence> accessed 6 July 2019.

[218] Ministère de l'Europe et des Affaires étrangères, 'Launch of the Global Partnership on Artificial Intelligence by 15 Founding Members' (*France Diplomacy—Ministry for Europe and Foreign Affairs*, 15 June 2020) <https://www.diplomatie.gouv.fr/en/french-foreign-policy/digital-diplomacy/news/article/launch-of-the-global-partnership-on-artificial-intelligence-by-15-founding> accessed 15 June 2020; Global Partnership on Artificial Intelligence (n 176).

establishment of the AI Partnership for Defense in September 2020.[219] However, it is only from late 2022 onwards that the wave of public attention towards advanced AI has driven significant calls for the establishment of new institution.[220] Even at this time, however, it is unclear if the pressure will translate into state willingness to implement one or more of these proposals, or whether they will continue to allocate governance functions within existing organizations or initiatives, such as the OECD.[221] As such, to a first approximation, while the underlying drivers of institutional accretion are stronger today than they have been at any previous point in the development of the AI regime complex, it is still unclear if this pressure will actually be sufficient to cross the threshold necessary to establish additional institutions in fact—and, if so, whether the resulting institutions will alleviate the state of fragmentation, or will simply contribute to it.

7.4.2.3 Power shifts over time

Another driver towards fragmentation comes in the form of power shifts over time.[222] The fact that older institutions often reflect outdated power structures may ensure that rising powers or new actors prefer to create new institutions. Indeed, Acharya has argued that the emerging 'multiplex' world order speaks in favour of governance fragmentation, as it might be more reflective of the plurality of values than older governance structures that reflect 'Western' interests.[223]

Of course, while the establishment of new institutions could allow newly powerful actors to have a greater voice and buy-in, and ensure that institutional mandates and functions reflect the contemporary balance of interests, international lawyers have cautioned that there are risks that the resulting fragmentation can become perceived as unequal and unfair, allowing powerful actors (old and new) to preserve and project their dominance. Indeed, as Eyal Benvenisti and George Downs have influentially suggested, 'fragmentation is a more serious problem . . . because it operates to sabotage the evolution of a more democratic and egalitarian international regulatory system'.[224] Specifically, it does so in various ways: for one, fragmentation makes it harder for weaker states, who have a greater diversity of preferences than powerful ones, to coordinate and build coalitions (such as by trading votes across issues within a centralized forum); moreover, by

[219] Lena Trabucco, 'AI Partnership for Defense Is a Step in the Right Direction—But Will Face Challenges' (*Opinio Juris*, 5 October 2020) <http://opiniojuris.org/2020/10/05/ai-partnership-for-defense-is-a-step-in-the-right-direction-but-will-face-challenges/> accessed 11 October 2021.

[220] See also Section 3.3.6.

[221] Huw Roberts and others, 'Global AI Governance: Barriers and Pathways Forward' [2024] International Affairs iiae073.

[222] Alter and Raustiala (n 194) 338.

[223] Amitav Acharya, 'The Future of Global Governance: Fragmentation May Be Inevitable and Creative Global Forum' [2016] Global Governance 453.

[224] Benvenisti and Downs (n 195) 597.

creating many competing institutions, fragmentation also affords powerful states the opportunity to (threaten to) abandon any venue for another, if their demands are not met.[225]

Whatever its further distributional effects, however, it is worth asking whether or how this factor may affect the evolution of the AI governance regime complex. On the one hand, the mainstays of AI governance initiatives of the past years have been established within established legacy institutions or organizations, such as the OECD, the Council of Europe, or the G7. Some new entrants, such as GPAI, have indeed over time extended their membership,[226] but were initially established by a set of democracies with the purpose to exclude and counteract rising AI power China.[227]

Of course, the past few years have seen the establishment of more AI governance initiatives. Nonetheless, many of these were still initiated by well-established powers such as the UK. With some exceptions, the set of states that currently lead in AI development overlaps with the set of states that have been historically powerful in shaping international institutions. One example of this shift may be China's October 2023 announcement of its own international Global AI Governance Initiative, which it said was aimed at securing all states' 'equal rights' on AI development regardless of their political systems.[228] This suggests that the overall impact of this factor is still uncertain, and may largely depend on the degree to which China will continue to press this initiative, as well as whether other coalitions of states may emerge that seek to establish new fora.[229]

7.4.2.1 Preference changes

In terms of preference changes, anticipated shifts in relative power, or shifts in domestic politics, may ensure that it is not only rising powers but also established powers themselves who become unsatisfied with the existing state of global rules and structures, and seek new arrangements.[230]

Given the considerable amount of attention to the potential of AI technology, it is possible that the technology's anticipated strategic gains could lead these

[225] Benvenisti and Downs (n 195).
[226] 'Community—GPAI' <https://gpai.ai/community/> accessed 14 January 2024.
[227] Arindrajit Basu and Justin Sherman, 'Two New Democratic Coalitions on 5G and AI Technologies' (*Lawfare*, 6 August 2020) <https://www.lawfareblog.com/two-new-democratic-coalitions-5g-and-ai-technologies> accessed 27 August 2020.
[228] Dewey Sim, 'China Launches AI Framework, Urges Equal AI Rights for All Nations' (*South China Morning Post*, 18 October 2023) <https://www.scmp.com/news/china/diplomacy/article/3238360/belt-and-road-forum-china-launches-ai-framework-urging-equal-rights-and-opportunities-all-nations> accessed 14 January 2024; 'China Launches Global AI Governance Initiative | Digital Watch Observatory' (*Digital Watch*, 19 October 2023) <https://dig.watch/updates/china-launches-global-ai-governance-initiative> accessed 21 December 2023.
[229] Adan (n 127); Abungu, Malonza, and Adan (n 136).
[230] Alter and Raustiala (n 194) 338.

powerful actors to forego regulating AI in existing governance fora. Alternatively, increasing automation could lead to shifts and upheavals in the domestic politics of some states, in ways that might alter their preferences regarding the adequacy of existing institutions.

If interests do shift sufficiently, this may lead coalitions of dissatisfied states to pursue various strategies, such as regime shifting,[231] competitive regime creation,[232] or even—in some cases—the outright dismantling and replacement of previous institutions by new ones.[233] Any of these would drive fragmentation, or exacerbate its adverse consequences.

7.4.2.5 The complexity of modernity

Moreover, some systems theorists have argued in a general sense that modernity by its nature generates complexity, which creates an unavoidable demand for specialization and functional differentiation in global governance.[234]

This perspective argues that many modern challenges—such as climate change, global migration, or AI and robotics—must be approached as 'complex issues' that exceed the sectoral remit of pre-existing, formal institutions.[235] AI no doubt gives rise to an array of complex societal problems, catalyses new problems in existing fields, and throws up peculiar challenges for easy legal categorization. If that is so, the technology's inherent complexity and cross-domain applicability might be prone to driving global regime complexity—although such arguments would gain from a more concrete articulation of the actual mechanisms at play.

7.4.2.6 Representation and voice goals

The expansion of participation in global governance also generates new goals in terms of institutional representation and voice. The demand for greater inclusion in global governance by many international institutions and non-state actors has led to the creation of many new fora, such as in the domains of internet governance and sustainability, where these actors perceive their voices are better heard.

In some cases, this can lead to these actors attempting to shift the dialogue to different regimes or fora. In the case of AI, it is possible that AI researcher communities

[231] Laurence Helfer, 'Regime Shifting: The TRIPs Agreement and New Dynamics of International Intellectual Property Lawmaking' (2004) 29 Yale Journal of International Law 1, 14 (i.e. 'alter the status quo ante by moving treaty negotiations, lawmaking initiatives, or standard setting activities from one international venue to another').

[232] Julia C Morse and Robert O Keohane, 'Contested Multilateralism' (2014) 9 The Review of International Organizations 385.

[233] Mette Eilstrup-Sangiovanni and Daniel Verdier, 'To Reform or to Replace? Succession as a Mechanism of Institutional Change in Intergovernmental Organisations' (2024) 19 The Review of International Organizations 691.

[234] Alter and Raustiala (n 194) 338; Michael Zürn and Benjamin Faude, 'Commentary: On Fragmentation, Differentiation, and Coordination' (2013) 13 Global Environmental Politics 119.

[235] Morin and others (n 124).

and private tech companies, along with a broad array of civil society actors and 'norm entrepreneurs',[236] will be similarly engaged. Indeed, this may already be seen with issues such as LAWS: in response to the (perceived) slow progress by the GGE, some civil society actors threatened to shift to another forum.[237] Indeed, 2023 saw a range of new regional initiatives and declarations, such as the Belén Communiqué and the CARICOM Declaration on Autonomous Weapons, from a range of Latin American and Caribbean nations, along with a draft resolution at the UNGA First Committee.[238] The role of representation and voice goals can also be seen in contemporary critiques of the closed-door nature of the Council of Europe's negotiations on its AI Convention.[239] Similar calls are likely to emerge and grow in the context of the international regulation of advanced AI technologies, and—if they are not honoured within existing regimes or institutions—could well result in these stakeholders deciding to pursue discussions and debates in alternative institutional contexts.

7.4.2.7 Shift towards local governance

Finally, Alter and Raustiala identify a broader shift towards local governance. That is, when dealing with certain problems, many states may prefer regional organizations and organizations staffed with local officials over remote global ones. While this may increase procedural legitimacy and the responsiveness of policies, it may also sometimes lead to conflict or norm incompatibility between local and global organizations.[240]

[236] Martha Finnemore and Kathryn Sikkink, 'International Norm Dynamics and Political Change' (1998) 52 International Organization 887.

[237] Janosch Delcker, 'How Killer Robots Overran the UN' [2019] *POLITICO* <https://www.politico.eu/article/killer-robots-overran-united-nations-lethal-autonomous-weapons-systems/> accessed 2 October 2019. See also the commentary by the Campaign to Stop Killer Robots, in reaction to the slow progress during the September 2020 session: Campaign to Stop Killer Robots, 'Diplomatic Talks in 2020' (25 September 2020) <https://www.stopkillerrobots.org/2020/09/diplomatic2020/> accessed 26 September 2020.

[238] Mary Wareham, 'Latin America and Caribbean Nations Rally Against Autonomous Weapons Systems' (*Human Rights Watch*, 6 March 2023) <https://www.hrw.org/news/2023/03/06/latin-america-and-caribbean-nations-rally-against-autonomous-weapons-systems> accessed 12 January 2024. See 'Communiqué of the Latin American and the Caribbean Conference of Social and Humanitarian Impact of Autonomous Weapons' <https://www.rree.go.cr/files/includes/files.php?id=2261&tipo=documentos> accessed 12 January 2024; 'CARICOM Declaration on Autonomous Weapons Systems' <https://www.caricom-aws2023.com/_files/ugd/b69acc_c1ffb97ed9024930a3205ae4e34c1b45.pdf> accessed 12 January 2024. UN Press, 'First Committee Approves New Resolution on Lethal Autonomous Weapons, as Speaker Warns "An Algorithm Must Not Be in Full Control of Decisions Involving Killing"' (1 November 2023) <https://press.un.org/en/2023/gadis3731.doc.htm> accessed 12 January 2024. See also the discussion in Section 3.2.1.3.

[239] Merve Hickok, Marc Rotenberg, and Karine Caunes, 'The Council of Europe Creates a Black Box for AI Policy' [2023] Verfassungsblog <https://verfassungsblog.de/coe-black-box-ai/> accessed 14 January 2024.

[240] Alter and Raustiala (n 194) 338 (discussing potential challenges in international criminal law, for instance as the proposed Malabo Protocol, if adopted, might confer an international jurisdiction on the African Court of Human and Peoples' Rights, which might intersect with that of the International Criminal Court).

Indeed, many have come to emphasize the importance of tailoring AI governance to local contexts,[241] particularly in ensuring that any global regimes on AI are informed and complemented by local expertise.[242] It remains unclear whether such calls will prevail. On the one hand, as AI's impacts are transnational, regional initiatives might not suffice, or cannot achieve important harmonization. On the other hand, there may be an increased pressure for diversity rather than harmonization. In many cases of standard-setting or commercial regulation, these will likely be regional in the first instance.[243] More generally, there could emerge distinct 'technocultural' differences among regions on AI issues,[244] which might strengthen the trend or preference of various parties towards local governance arrangements.

7.4.3 Technological Factors Driving Regime Complex Evolution

Reviewing these six political drivers, we can identify a range of forces and trends that, in aggregate, have pitched the global governance system towards greater institutional proliferation, greater regime complexity, and more frequent and significant overlaps or norm conflicts, for many issue areas. In at least some cases (though not all), it seems likely that these drivers will also be at play in the AI governance, which would support further fragmentation in this regime complex.

As detailed previously, regime complex theory has explored many drivers of regime complex evolution and development. However, while scholars have reckoned with the effects of exogenous political or institutional shocks to either the trajectory of a regime complex,[245] or to the continued viability of the international liberal order as a whole,[246] there appears to be relatively little

[241] Han-Wei Liu and Ching-Fu Lin, 'Artificial Intelligence and Global Trade Governance: A Pluralist Agenda' (2020) 61(2) Harvard International Law Journal 407.

[242] Stefaan Verhulst, 'AI Globalism and AI Localism: Governing AI at the Local Level for Global Benefit: A Response to the On-Going Calls for the Establishment of a Global AI Agency' (*Data & Policy Blog*, 1 December 2023) <https://medium.com/data-policy/ai-globalism-and-ai-localism-governing-ai-at-the-local-level-for-global-benefit-a-response-to-the-b3ac158b72a9> accessed 14 January 2024.

[243] I thank Charlotte Siegmann for this observation.

[244] Osonde A Osoba, 'Technocultural Pluralism: A "Clash of Civilizations" in Technology?' *Proceedings of the AAAI/ACM Conference on AI, Ethics, and Society* (ACM 2020) <http://dl.acm.org/doi/10.1145/3375627.3375834> accessed 12 February 2020. See also the discussion of Asian perspectives on AI ethics in Danit Gal, 'Perspectives and Approaches in AI Ethics: East Asia' in Markus D Dubber, Frank Pasquale, and Sunit Das (eds), *The Oxford Handbook of Ethics of AI* (Oxford University Press 2020). However, others have argued that cultural value differences in AI may be exaggerated, or at least can be overcome; see Seán S ÓhÉigeartaigh and others, 'Overcoming Barriers to Cross-Cultural Cooperation in AI Ethics and Governance' [2020] 33 Philosophy & Technology 571.

[245] Hanzhi Yu and Lan Xue, 'Shaping the Evolution of Regime Complex: The Case of Multiactor Punctuated Equilibrium in Governing Human Genetic Data' (2019) 25 Global Governance: A Review of Multilateralism and International Organizations 645.

[246] See Karen J Alter, 'The Future of International Law' in Diana Ayton-Shenker (ed), *The New Global Agenda* (Rowman & Littlefield 2018).

examination of the effects of technology-driven change on regime complexity. This is unfortunate because, as the discussion of governance disruption in Chapter 5 has suggested, the use of various technologies can in some cases exert considerable effects on the norms, processes, or political scaffolding of the international legal order.

Indeed, a common thread throughout this book is that legal and governance systems, especially at the international level, are not only shaped by political factors (whether interest-based or norms-based), but also by material ones. Given this, we specifically should engage with the question over whether or how these political drivers of fragmentation—and the resulting regime complex evolution—may be affected by processes of AI-driven governance disruption.

To be clear, applying the governance disruption lens to the regime complex framework is speculative, and these sections are primarily meant to explore conditional scenarios of how various types of AI-driven governance disruption would impact overall fragmentation as well as AI-specific regime complexity. Even under relatively conservative assumptions over the capabilities of AI models, we can consider different roles that AI systems could play in international law, which could contribute to one of three key trends in regime complex fragmentation, automation, and contestation.

7.4.3.1 AI-driven governance development and regime complex evolution

How might the ability of AI systems to disrupt the substance, laws, or norms of regimes within international law affect the trajectory of their own regime complex? Interestingly, the legally disruptive effects of AI systems may exert two divergent pressures on regime complexes. On the one hand, they might motivate regime integration or harmonization; conversely, they might also serve as constant generator of regime fault lines.

7.4.3.1.1 AI as legal fire alarm for regime harmonization or integration

There may be many situations where AI's use in some domain or other prompts widely shared perceptions of the inadequacy of existing legal instruments or concepts, which could serve as a constructive legal 'fire alarm'.[247] By getting legal challenges out in the open, in the context of an urgent governance problem that all actors agree requires addressing, these cases could create the opportunity to clarify long-present ambiguities in international norms, or to correct or harmonize

[247] For a general discussion of this concept, see Eliezer Yudkowsky, 'There's No Fire Alarm for Artificial General Intelligence' (*Machine Intelligence Research Institute*, 14 October 2017) <https://intelligence.org/2017/10/13/fire-alarm/> accessed 13 December 2020. A related frame might be that of the 'canary in the coalmine', on which see also (in the context of informing participatory technology assessment processes) the discussion in: Carla Zoe Cremer and Jess Whittlestone, 'Artificial Canaries: Early Warning Signs for Anticipatory and Democratic Governance of AI' (2021) 6 International Journal of Interactive Multimedia and Artificial Intelligence 100.

long-standing tensions or latent conflicts between different regimes. In this way, the precise effects of AI-driven governance development on the trajectory of a governance architecture will likely depend sensitively on the pre-existing configuration of that architecture. Indeed, in some ways, it could exacerbate pre-existing tendencies.

On the one hand, within an already integrated regime complex, a centralized, authoritative international institution could in principle seize upon AI's legal disruption within one area in order to kick-start and facilitate a broader dialogue about long-overdue systemic revision or legal innovation in underlying rules or concepts. For instance, such an institution could seize upon specific problems posed by AI-enabled military surveillance platforms or lethality-enabling technologies,[248] to address the broader problem that the distinction between war and peacetime—a cornerstone of IHL—may have become increasingly blurred by new technologies.[249] Such legal development would not necessarily imply an abandonment of these well-proven frameworks. However, it would reckon with the broad effects of technology across different fields of international law, and potentially result in more integrated bodies of law in response. Of course, even if centralized international institutions could in principle carry out such regulatory innovation and integration, it is not a given that they would also do so.

7.4.3.1.2 AI as generator of regime fault lines

However, starting from today's fragmented institutional context, AI technology's ability to generate many situations of governance disruption in existing norms and regimes may well exacerbate those tendencies towards further regime fragmentation.

Given the extremely diverse set of perspectives through which one can approach AI technology, it seems unlikely that a fragmented regime complex of many institutions would reliably be able to converge towards more integrated or harmonized policy responses across all AI issue areas. Indeed, with the rise of advanced AI systems such as adaptive foundation models, similar AI architectures and systems will be used and applied across different contexts. In each of those issue domains, certain features of AI systems—such as their opacity, or the susceptibility to adversarial inputs or misuse—may come to be seen in different ways, even though they

[248] Arthur Holland Michel, 'The Killer Algorithms Nobody's Talking About' (*Foreign Policy*, 20 January 2020) <https://foreignpolicy.com/2020/01/20/ai-autonomous-weapons-artificial-intelligence-the-killer-algorithms-nobodys-talking-about/> accessed 21 January 2020. Giacomo Persi Paoli and others, 'Modernizing Arms Control: Exploring Responses to the Use of AI in Military Decision-Making' (UNIDIR 2020) <https://unidir.org/publication/modernizing-arms-control> accessed 1 September 2020.

[249] Garcia, 'Future Arms, Technologies, and International Law' (n 25); Braden Allenby, 'Are New Technologies Undermining the Laws of War?' (2014) 70 Bulletin of the Atomic Scientists 21 (highlighting drones and cyberwarfare). See also Crootof, 'Regulating New Weapons Technology' (n 66) 10.

are problems with similar root causes at the level of underlying techniques or organizational practices.

This implies that different organizations—including not just AI governance institutions but also many institutions beyond the AI regime complex, such as international courts—may be forced to grapple with similar questions, such as over the meaning of keeping human actors 'in the loop' of AI decision-making,[250] in isolation from one another. That creates the risk that different institutions will answer these questions differently, and in potentially contradictory ways. While that might have benefits and even be more legitimate—simply reflecting the local or specific needs of each institution—it is likely to result in a further scattering of individual regimes' norms and policies towards AI, in ways that drive fragmentation and raise the possibility of new conflicts in terms of institutional activities or regime norms.

7.4.3.2 AI-driven governance displacement and regime complex evolution

As a second type of governance disruption, the phenomenon of governance 'displacement'—through growing automation or even technological substitution of processes of governance—also suggests several ways in which the integration of AI tools into the practices of global governance might affect regime complexity.

In brief, some AI tools, especially if they were accessible (or distributed) to many actors (whether states or non-state observer agencies or NGOs), could play some role in mitigating at least some trends towards regime complexity. They could variably serve as *shield* to the negative consequences of complexity, as *patch* to halt the further fragmentation of regimes, or as *cure* to avert or mitigate latent conflicts and aid in harmonization of regimes. Yet, left unregulated, the free-for-all use of AI systems could also prove an *accelerator* of processes of legal and governance fragmentation.

7.4.3.2.1 AI systems as shield against fragmentation

For one, various actors could choose to use AI tools to shield themselves from the negative operational consequences of a fragmented and distributed regime complex. For instance, the use of these tools in support of many 'routine' diplomatic tasks could free up the limited diplomatic resources or staff available to many smaller states, enabling them to participate more fully in various international fora, 'levelling' the playing field relative to the large and well-staffed foreign ministries of larger states.[251] More modestly, through translation and text (e.g. news) summarization services, such AI tools could facilitate the ability of even less powerful

[250] Crootof, Kaminski, and Price II (n 191).

[251] Katharina E Höne, 'Mapping the Challenges and Opportunities of Artificial Intelligence for the Conduct of Diplomacy' (DiploFoundation 2019) <https://www.diplomacy.edu/sites/default/files/AI-diplo-report.pdf> accessed 14 March 2019.

actors to navigate dense regime complexes, counteracting the democratic deficit identified by some concerned scholars.[252]

7.4.3.2.2 AI systems as patch to further fragmentation

More actively, actors could also use AI tools as a patch to halt or pre-empt the further fragmentation of various regimes. For instance, Ashley Deeks notes how various 'text-as-data-tools' (i.e. AI language models) might be used to pre-emptively identify treaty conflicts, whether accidental or strategically engineered. She suggests that '[a] state could create a tool that allows it to compare proposed treaty language (either while the negotiations are underway, or before the state has ratified the treaty) to all other treaties to which the state is a party to detect similar language or very similar topics.'[253] This could pre-empt or deter strategic efforts by states to create certain treaty conflicts in order to set the agenda for future negotiations,[254] because any negotiation partners would now be able to spot when such a strategy is being attempted.[255]

7.4.3.2.3 AI systems as cure to past fragmentation

In principle, these same AI tools not only might help spot and patch imminent conflicts produced by specific treaties, but could also be deployed as a cure to pre-existing patterns of fragmentation in international law. For instance, Deeks suggests that states could use such tools even in the absence of specific negotiations, simply to map any tensions among their existing treaty commitments, 'in order to identify gaps or other potential conflicts before they produce a real world problem.'[256]

Similarly, many other non-state actors or international organizations could well use such tools to chart major fault lines or gaps among international law's fragmented regimes. This would of course hardly be a panacea: questions of sufficient text data aside, some cases of fragmentation reflect deliberate state intent,[257] which suggests that their resolution might be a political problem more than a legal one. Furthermore, not all (or even most) practical regime conflicts necessarily emerge from inconsistent norm commitments recorded in the legal text.[258] Indeed, as

[252] Daniel W Drezner, 'The Power and Peril of International Regime Complexity' (2009) 7 Perspectives on Politics 65; Benvenisti and Downs (n 195).

[253] Ashley Deeks, 'High-Tech International Law' (2020) 88 George Washington Law Review 575, 616.

[254] Surabhi Ranganathan, *Strategically Created Treaty Conflicts and the Politics of International Law* (Cambridge University Press 2014).

[255] Deeks (n 253) 616 ('[a] state that is concerned that its negotiating partner may be attempting this move could use web scraping and topic analysis on its negotiating partner's existing treaties to assess whether the partner is trying to play this game').

[256] ibid.

[257] Benvenisti and Downs (n 195).

[258] Christian Kreuder-Sonnen and Michael Zürn, 'After Fragmentation: Norm Collisions, Interface Conflicts, and Conflict Management' (2020) 9 Global Constitutionalism 241.

noted by Morin and others, '[b]latant legal conflicts [amongst regimes] remain rare and a certain degree of normative ambiguity preserves the unity of the international legal system'.[259] Instead, many regime conflicts may manifest at the level of institutional policies or impacts,[260] as a result of real-world inter-institutional interactions that depend more on tacit forms of inter-organizational politics or rivalry. Such negative externalities would not be latent in many source texts, and therefore would not be easily discoverable with such tools. Even if that is so, however, this holds open the possibility that modern large language models might be able to infer even these tacit institutional conflicts, through comparison with other organizations or, indeed, with reference to regime complexity scholarship contained within their training data.

7.4.3.2.4 AI systems as lawmaking accelerators: scaling fragmentation?

While these roles seem to involve a range of beneficial (or at least integrative) outcomes from AI displacement, there are also ways in which AI tools could serve as an accelerator of regime fragmentation.

That is, if AI technology finds productive uptake by many states or international organizations in facilitating negotiations and the creation of international rules, this may have significant value in addressing urgent global problems, or in aiding states in avoiding or resolving their disputes. However, just as the uncoordinated rise in institutional proliferation in domains such as international environmental law resulted in so-called treaty congestion,[261] speeding up the creation of international rules—by any means or tools—may have unanticipated side effects. This, Rebecca Crootof has suggested, could facilitate 'legal fragmentation [because] [s]peeding up the development of international legal obligations has expanded both the activities they regulate and opportunities for conflict among them'.[262] That is not a reason to avoid such tools outright, but should induce some caution about ensuring appropriate scaffolding or guidelines regarding the use of such models to accelerate global lawmaking at will.

7.4.3.3 AI-driven governance destruction and regime complex evolution

Finally, as discussed in Chapter 5, there are a range of ways in which AI systems might erode the broader political conditions for governance. Such outcomes would certainly have knock-on effects on regime complexity both within and beyond the AI regime complex. Again, we can highlight a number of potential roles for AI systems.

[259] Morin and others (n 124) 2–3.

[260] Thomas Gehring and Sebastian Oberthür, 'The Causal Mechanisms of Interaction between International Institutions' (2009) 15 European Journal of International Relations 125.

[261] Don Anton, '"Treaty Congestion" in International Environmental Law' in Shawkat Alam and others (eds), *Routledge Handbook of International Environmental Law* (Routledge 2012).

[262] Crootof, 'Regulating New Weapons Technology' (n 66) 7.

7.4.3.3.1 AI as lever for forum gridlock

In the first place, AI's definitional complexity and effects across many fields may mean the issue lends itself naturally to state strategies to obstruct international regulatory action, such as by dragging out definitional debates in consensus-based international fora.[263]

7.4.3.3.2 AI as tough knot, driving legitimacy crises or preference shifts

In addition, if key AI issues remain unsolved in spite of the fact that they feature prominently on the international or multilateral agenda, the sustained inability of existing governance arrangement to address these problems would eventually erode their legitimacy—and might drive preference changes among both powerful actors and less powerful or non-state actors, either of which would contribute to processes of institutional proliferation and regime complexity.

7.4.3.3.3 AI as asymmetric weapon

Simultaneously, AI's use as a tool could offer specific capabilities that result in legal decline. This could be because AI systems might offer strategic capabilities which shift interests; they chip away at the rationales for certain powerful states to engage fully in, or comply with, international law regimes. While they would be unlikely to completely erode support, AI applications in areas such as surveillance could arguably reduce states' (perceived) dependence on multilateral security regimes to ensure their security from non-state actor threats. Such capabilities could increase actors' willingness to defect from regimes and erode their willingness to support multilateralism, and could as such result in preference changes and a resulting increase in the prominence of forum-shopping strategies. In extreme cases, AI systems could enable new strategies—such as scalable computational propaganda—by which malicious actors could directly challenge the legitimacy of international law or its component regimes.[264] AI has not created these particular problems, but may make them worse.

7.4.3.4 Reflections on governance disruption and regime complexity

We have briefly discussed how the use of AI can shape both the normative and conceptual coherence of the regime complex (through driving *development* or *displacement*), as well as by shifting the incentives, values, or behaviour of various actors within that regime complex (potentially driving *destruction*). From a regime

[263] For instance, this proved a stumbling block in the early years of the UN GGE process on Lethal Autonomous Weapons Systems. See Frank Sauer, 'Autonomy in Weapons Systems: Playing Catch Up with Technology' (*Humanitarian Law & Policy Blog*, 29 September 2021) <https://blogs.icrc.org/law-and-policy/2021/09/29/autonomous-weapons-systems-technology/> accessed 3 January 2022.

[264] As discussed in Matthijs M Maas, 'International Law Does Not Compute: Artificial Intelligence and The Development, Displacement or Destruction of the Global Legal Order' (2019) 20 Melbourne Journal of International Law 29, 55.

complex perspective, then, some overall lessons may be that the disruptive impacts of AI systems on governance may compound trends towards regime fragmentation (through increased legitimacy problems or preference shifts) and may exacerbate the problematic interactions of regimes (by increasing the number of contact surfaces, and the ability of state actors to identify and exploit them for strategically engineered norm conflicts).

In aggregate, these trends and drivers suggest that, barring significant interventions or external shocks, the AI governance regime complex will trend towards fragmentation for the time being.[265] However, this is certainly not a foregone conclusion, and it will be key to monitor both political developments within the regime complex and technical developments in AI's use within it, to identify the future arc of the complex.

7.5 Consequences: The Effects of Regime Complexity on AI Governance

Having sketched distinct potential trajectories for the evolution of the AI regime complex, on the basis of some of their political and material drivers, our next critical question is about the expected consequences or effects of either trajectory—continued fragmentation or eventual centralization—for AI governance.

7.5.1 Revisiting AI Governance Pathways

As discussed in Chapter 3, the past years have seen many new proposals for new international institutions for AI. Many of these proposals have taken one of three forms: regime centralization, constellation, or complexity.

Centralization-focused proposals envision the establishment of a single flagship institution for AI, with a broad or encompassing mandate, often along the model of some existing influential institution,[266] though at times drawing components from a range of existing organizations.[267] Constellation-focused proposals envision the establishment of a range of new AI governance institutions, which would carry out different functions or roles in a decentralized but well-coordinated regime complex.[268] Finally, complexity-focused proposals are less interested in establishing

[265] Cihon, Maas, and Kemp (n 174) 228; Jelinek, Wallach, and Kerimi (n 174) 2, 4.

[266] Maas and Villalobos (n 165). And see Section 3.3.6.

[267] Gutierrez (n 129).

[268] Artificial Intelligence & Equality Initiative, 'A Framework for the International Governance of AI' (*Carnegie Council for Ethics in International Affairs*, 5 July 2023) <https://www.carnegiecouncil.org/media/article/a-framework-for-the-international-governance-of-ai> accessed 3 September 2023; Ho and others (n 134); Stephan Llerena, 'Global Governance of High-Risk Artificial Intelligence' (2023)

new institutions, and instead envision empowering existing institutions already active on AI governance in the current fragmented (or 'polycentric') landscape, in order to improve their functionality and coordination.[269]

To be sure, there are important commonalities among these approaches, in that they all envision some forms of intergovernmental organization-based global governance for AI, as opposed to other strategies that emphasize unilateral state actions or soft law. There are also common open questions that hold across all three approaches, such as ongoing debates over the exact set of governance functions that would, at a minimum, need to be represented or provided for within the institution or complex.

Yet these three strategies are also importantly distinct. That is, centralization or constellation-focused strategies (1–2) both pursue the establishment of new institutions, whereas complexity-focused strategy (3) aims to work through existing initiatives or institutions. Conversely, while the centralization-focused strategy (1) pursues an integrated regime complex ordered around a major international institution or regime, constellation- or complexity-focused strategies (2–3) both envision a greater degree of decentralization or polycentric governance.

To better understand the adequacy, feasibility, and drawbacks of these different strategies, it helps to understand the consequences of different types of regime complex organization. For that purpose, this section will focus especially on the consequences and trade-offs around centralization or decentralization.

7.5.2 Caveats and Rationale for Considering Consequences

Once again, there are a number of caveats to this analysis. For one, because a regime complex is a complex system,[270] it may—again—be intrinsically hard to chart or predict specific outcomes since, according to complex systems theory, changes in one part will interact with others,[271] inhibiting (though not foreclosing) effective prediction.

Even so, examining the potential consequences of different regime complex structures helps us anticipate the likely challenges that may emerge, and

<https://xrisk.uchicago.edu/files/2024/02/FINALLlerenaXLabSRF23-GlobalGovernanceOfHighRiskAI-0334e1dd25e37cae.pdf> accessed 4 August 2024.

[269] Roberts and others (n 221); Sepasspour (n 72); Cameron F Kerry, 'The Good, the Not-so-Good, and the Ugly of the UN's Blueprint for AI' (*Brookings*, 29 August 2024) <https://www.brookings.edu/articles/the-good-the-not-so-good-and-the-ugly-of-the-uns-blueprint-for-ai/> accessed 2 September 2024.

[270] Karen J Alter and Sophie Meunier, 'The Politics of International Regime Complexity' (2009) 7 Perspectives on Politics 13, 21 ('[t]o think in terms of international regime complexity is to study interactive relationships and analyze how the whole shapes the pieces').

[271] Alter and Raustiala (n 194) 333.

whether—or for which AI governance issue areas—different structures or strategies might be preferred, all else being equal.

As such, understanding the consequences of regime complexity is important, not only for broader normative debates over what form of AI governance we would ideally see but also so that we can grapple with the consequences of either trajectory on its own terms.

That is, if a fragmented AI regime complex likely will result in many functional or political problems, it is important to understand these—as this can motivate greater attention towards pursuing centralized institutions, or at least help us prepare adequately for how to mitigate the adverse outcomes of fragmentation under an approach that is focused on either establishing an institutional constellation or strengthening institutions within the existing complex. Conversely, even if one expects or hopes that a centralized AI governance regime will soon be established, it is still important to understand the distinct downside risks this could introduce, in order to factor those in to the actual form and design of the institution.

As discussed in Chapter 6, there remains live disagreement among scholars over the functional consequences and the normative desirability of regime complexity. It has been suggested that complexity can shape various governance outcomes at the levels of inter-institutional collaboration and institutional problem-solving capacity, and in terms of how they (dis)empower different actors within these institutions.[272] To briefly recap, critics have argued that increasing regime complexity will have negative outcomes, at least if it is left unmanaged, in the form of a fragmented and eroded form of international law, dysfunction, power inequalities, or because it introduces strategic vulnerabilities for exploitation by certain states. On the other side, proponents of regime complexity argue that such 'polycentric' governance can in fact be more flexible and problem-solving, can promote improved inter-institutional dynamics, or may create more inclusive or democratic decision-making processes among parties.

Given this, what lessons can we learn for global AI governance? Specifically, what are the likely consequences of different (integrated or fragmented) governance architectures? What would be the legal, operational, and functional results of fragmentation? And can this help us understand whether (or for what issues) a centralized institution or decentralized regime complex might be more appropriate or desirable? To answer these questions, we can turn to a wide range of historical lessons drawn from existing international regime complexes on a range of topics.

[272] Eilstrup-Sangiovanni and Westerwinter (n 2) 249–252.

7.5.3 Should AI Governance be Centralized or Decentralized? Trade-offs from History

In previous work, Peter Cihon, Luke Kemp, and myself have explored a range of trade-offs that the AI regime complex might face, depending on whether it remains fragmented or if instead it were to be(come) more integrated and organized around a centralized intergovernmental organization.[273]

In doing so, we drew a range of lessons from the history of multilateralism. What would the experiences and challenges of other international regime complexes suggest about the costs and benefits of pursuing a centralized governance approach for AI, relative to a more fragmented trajectory? Specifically, we drew lessons from international regimes in three other domain areas: environment, trade, and security.

Are these comparable? To be sure, these regimes offer imperfect comparators to AI, but they are still valuable cases to study the challenges and pitfalls of global AI governance.[274] This is because these three governance domains, while distinct in important ways, are similar to AI governance across key dimensions. For instance, environmental governance invokes complex scientific questions that require technical expertise,[275] involves trans-boundary and trans-sector effects, and raises a need for anticipation of future impacts and trends. For its part, trade governance spans a breadth of individual industries and sectors, involves questions of (technical) standard-setting as well as potential trade barriers, and raises diverse (North–South) power inequalities. Finally, international security regimes—in particular export or arms control regimes—involve significant strategic interests and geopolitical stakes, may attempt to leverage supply-side constraints or chokepoints in a technology's supply chain, and face frequently recurring pressures to modernize regimes in order to track changes in the technology of concern.

[273] Cihon, Maas, and Kemp (n 174). Of course, as Gómez-Mera and others argue, technically speaking, the moment one introduces such a hierarchic relationship to a central authority, the 'regime complex' ceases to exist; Gómez-Mera, Morin, and Van De Graaf (n 170) 146. This may be true, although only under definitions that make non-hierarchy a core criterion to the concept—see Alter and Meunier (n 270); Alter and Raustiala (n 194). However, as discussed in Chapter 6, my usage of the regime complex concept in this book tracks closer to definitions of 'regime complexity' and 'global governance complexity' by Orsini and others and by Eilstrup-Sangiovanni and Westerwinter, neither of which puts much emphasis on relations being necessarily non-hierarchical. See Amandine Orsini, Jean-Frédéric Morin, and Oran Young, 'Regime Complexes: A Buzz, a Boom, or a Boost for Global Governance?' (2013) 19 Global Governance: A Review of Multilateralism and International Organizations 27; Eilstrup-Sangiovanni and Westerwinter (n 2).

[274] See also Cihon, Maas, and Kemp (n 175).

[275] Although it is possible that this could also be raised as a disanalogy. For instance, Huw Roberts has argued that the regime complex for AI is currently far less institutionally mature than that for climate, and that there is currently far less scientific consensus over AI's challenges. Huw Roberts, 'Opinion—A New International AI Body Is No Panacea' (*E-International Relations*, 11 August 2023) <https://www.e-ir.info/2023/08/11/opinion-a-new-international-ai-body-is-no-panacea/> accessed 15 August 2023; See also Joseph Bak-Coleman and others, 'Create an IPCC-like Body to Harness Benefits and Combat Harms of Digital Tech' (2023) 617 Nature 462.

All of these factors are, in their own ways, pertinent to the context of AI governance, raising the hope that some lessons can be transferred. In addition, the environmental, trade, and security regimes offer an analytically interesting mix of regime complex types, including particularly different degrees of legalization and centralization, from the relatively centralized (trade) to the highly fragmented (environment).[276]

On the basis of these explorations, we identified a series of considerations or trade-offs which, when taken together with the broader debates on the consequences of regime complexity, can helpfully frame discussions over the relative merits of an integrated or fragmented regime complex for AI.[277] That is, in brief: centralized regimes may (1) wield greater political power, (2) afford greater efficiency and opportunities for adequate participation. However, compared to decentralized regime complexes, centralized regimes (3) may be slower to be established and, once set up, (4) are more brittle in terms of the dangers of regulatory capture or their path-dependency in the face of sudden issue area shifts. Centralized regimes may also (5) struggle more to strike an adequate balance between depth of commitments and breadth of participation. They may be (6) more resilient to strategies of forum-shopping, but this has both benefits and drawbacks. Finally, (7) both centralized and decentralized regimes have strategies by which to achieve policy coordination.

7.5.3.1 Political power of a centralized regime

A first consideration is around the political power that can be projected by the AI governance architecture.[278] Regimes embody power in their authority over rules, norms, and domain knowledge beyond their member states. Generally speaking, the more integrated a regime complex is, the more authority over rules, norms, and issue area knowledge can be distilled into fewer (potentially one) institutions.[279] In contrast to such a flagship institution, a fragmented regime complex that is hampered by rule uncertainty, goal contradictions, competition over access to scarce scientific expertise, or even outright conflictual dynamics or institutional 'turf wars',[280] will not carry the same authority.

As such, a centralized AI institution would be likely to hold greater sway over its member states (and other actors, such as private AI developers).[281] Moreover, it can also be more influential in the face of other international organizations. This may

[276] Cihon, Maas, and Kemp (n 175) 546. However, see also Chinen (n 43) 231 (somewhat contesting this characterization of the WTO as an example of centralized governance, since while the WTO does administer a large number of agreements touching on different aspects of trade, it too faces concerns over the proliferation of regional and free trade agreements).
[277] Sections 7.5.3.1–7.5.3.7 broadly follow the organization in Cihon, Maas and Kemp (n 174).
[278] ibid 230.
[279] Orsini, Morin, and Young (n 273) 36–37.
[280] Biermann and others (n 170).
[281] Orsini, Morin, and Young (n 273) 36–37.

strengthen the institution's ability to head off attempts at competitive regime creation[282] by states that would seek to set up an alternative AI governance institution. Furthermore, greater authority may also allow a centralized AI institution to prevail in the face of outright norm or impact conflicts with other regime (complexes) in other areas. For instance, it is arguable that something like this can be seen in the 'chilling' effect which the WTO has managed to project over the fragmented international environmental law landscape—an effect that has led environmental treaties to self-censor to avoid treading on trade-related issues.[283] However, this case also illustrates the sensitive trade-off in centralization—demonstrating how the benefits of a centralized AI institution should be considered, not only with reference to its internal efficacy in governing its own domain area, but also in terms of potential effects or externalities on other regimes.

In general terms, considerations of authority might be expected to speak in favour of the centralization of AI governance. Indeed, prevailing uncertainty in a domain issue area (such as over technological trajectories or future preferences) has been associated with some increased centralization in regimes in the past.[284] As a high-profile technology with significant vested interests and growing strategic stakes, it is plausible that AI technology could become (indeed, already clearly is) the subject of considerable political contestation. In such scenarios, AI would be a thorny object for global regulation, with the risk that a fragmented regime complex would not be able to marshal and rely on sufficient political power to address many challenges effectively.

Nonetheless, while the perspective of institutional power may at first sight seem to speak unambiguously in favour of a centralized regime, that may be too simple a reading. The relevant question should be not 'what regime complex organization provides AI institutions with as much authority as possible?' but rather 'what organization provides AI institutions with the necessary level of authority to address their core issues?'[285]

[282] Morse and Keohane (n 232). One example of this can be found in the 2009 creation, by a coalition of countries including German, Spain, and Denmark, of the International Renewable Energy Agency (IRENA), after their dissatisfaction with the International Energy Agency. See Graaf (n 201).

[283] Robyn Eckersley, 'The Big Chill: The WTO and Multilateral Environmental Agreements' (2004) 4 Global Environmental Politics 24. This latter example also illustrates one potential downside, which is the risk that a centralized regime for one issue area becomes so politically powerful that it begins to exert effects across issue-area governance architectures, imposing negative externalities on regime complexes aimed at different areas. Such questions of regime complex interaction across different regimes are of course a key problem to be examined.

[284] Barbara Koremenos, Charles Lipson, and Duncan Snidal, 'Rational Design: Looking Back to Move Forward' (2001) 55 International Organization 1051. See Cihon, Maas, and Kemp (n 174) 230.

[285] In this context, it may also be useful to distinguish between whether effectiveness or performance of an international organization (in a particular context) is best measured in terms of its 'constitutive effectiveness' (i.e. its ability to generate normative consensus and influence global policy agendas), state compliance with organizational decisions, or overall goal attainment in their domain of operation. See also David Coen and others, 'Making Global Public Policy Work: A Survey of International Organization Effectiveness' (2022) 13 Global Policy 656.

In this light, it can be seen that focusing institutional power or authority may not be equally relevant in all contexts, or for all problem logics. On some issues, including many challenges raised by conventional AI systems, international institutions might well be able to sufficiently affect national policies even if they do not carry extreme political power. At the other pole, there might be certain AI issues that are (considered) so fundamental to state sovereignty that almost no amount of centralization of global institutional authority—short of actual world government—would be sufficient to ensure compliance.

Yet in between those poles, there can be strategically or politically sensitive issue areas where one might expect a threshold of 'minimum viable institutional authority', where one very authoritative institution might be able to carry more clout than a dozen moderately authoritative institutions. For instance, for many civilian uses of either conventional or advanced AI, there are institutional arrangements that can usefully craft state incentives for compliance. For instance, Trager and others have proposed an 'International AI Organization' that certifies state jurisdictions for compliance with international AI oversight standards, in order to enable states to prohibit the import of goods with any AI components from non-certified jurisdictions.[286] Such an institution would certainly require a moderate degree of political authority—especially if it would need to be able to issue 'mandatory information requests' to states about their AI oversight systems.[287] However, this level would not be unprecedented.

Moreover, through the lens of sociotechnical change, questions over the appropriate or necessary level of institutional authority required may also turn on the specific problem logics of AI issues at play. For instance, global governance responses for contentious AI-driven ethical challenges (e.g. data privacy) might require high levels of institutional political authority in order to set and maintain stakeholder consensus. The same might be the case for governance for AI-produced structural shifts (e.g. as a result of AI cyberwarfare systems or conflict prediction systems), where international institutions might need considerable authority in order to compel actors to comply with norms even in the face of countervailing strategic pressures.

Conversely, for governing some types of security threats deriving from the potential misuse of AI, high levels of institutional power or authority may be less critical or more assured. Indeed, as illustrated by the (admittedly non-binding) 2023 Guidelines for Secure AI System Development, championed by the UK and US among 18 states,[288] states may broadly perceive shared interests in avoiding

[286] Robert Trager and others, 'International Governance of Civilian AI: A Jurisdictional Certification Approach' (arXiv, 29 August 2023) <http://arxiv.org/abs/2308.15514> accessed 31 August 2023.

[287] ibid 21.

[288] UK National Cyber Security Centre (NCSC) and US Cybersecurity and Infrastructure Agency (CISA), 'Guidelines for Secure AI System Development' <https://www.ncsc.gov.uk/collection/guidelines-secure-ai-system-development> accessed 30 November 2023.

the irreversible proliferation of certain harmful capabilities to non-state actors. In such cases, while centralized institutions might have other benefits, a broader regime complex of individually weaker institutions could still be sufficient in terms of their political power.

7.5.3.2 Efficiency and inclusive participation in a centralized regime

The second consideration revolves around efficiency as well as participation thresholds. This relates to some of the previously mentioned concerns over inclusion and participation, and specifically the risk that institutional proliferation may advantage powerful parties more than weaker ones, resulting in a democratic deficit. For instance, the proliferation of hundreds of overlapping multilateral environmental agreements has, in some readings, created a state of 'treaty congestion' that not only has resulted in norm conflict, but has imposed costs and barriers to participation on many parties, at the stage of negotiation, implementation, or monitoring of outcomes.[289]

Specifically, fragmented regime complexes may force parties to spread resources and funding over many distinct institutions, limiting the ability of less well-resourced states or non-state actors to participate fully.[290] As a result, some have argued that the fragmentation of international law tends to strengthen the hand of powerful actors, who are better able to navigate and set the agenda in many parallel institutions, or are better able to play these up against one another.[291]

Concerns over inclusive participation might be particularly acute in the context of AI governance, where a small number of powerful states also represent the leading AI developers. Moreover, there is a strong private sector dynamic that may exacerbate participation concerns. If (as seems likely) tech companies are structurally better resourced to participate in many global fora than are NGOs, the existence of many parallel fora may not pose as much of a barrier to them as to these civil society actors. This would differentially advantage the influence of private actors in global AI governance, and potentially increase the risk of (or the appearance of) regulatory capture.

Conversely, a centralized regime for AI could in theory avoid some of those problems, and ensure adequate participation by a wide range of parties. Of course, it could be asked whether unconditional inclusion or access, for all its procedural significance, is always categorically beneficial. There may be some rare issue areas where full openness around governance on AI issues might not be beneficial,[292]

289 Anton (n 261).
290 Morin and others (n 124) 2.
291 Benvenisti and Downs (n 195).
292 See Jess Whittlestone and Aviv Ovadya, 'The Tension between Openness and Prudence in AI Research' [2020] arXiv:1910.01170 [cs] <http://arxiv.org/abs/1910.01170> accessed 22 January 2020. And see previously Nick Bostrom, 'Strategic Implications of Openness in AI Development' (2017) 8 Global Policy 135. For a discussion of different notions of 'democratization' of AI—including notions that focus on the 'democratization' of (and therefore broad participation in) AI use, AI development, AI profits, or AI governance—see also Elizabeth Seger and others, 'Democratising AI: Multiple

either because it could deter certain key state parties from engaging with that forum in the first place, because the proliferation and misuse risk of certain particularly harmful AI capabilities would imply these should not (at least in great technical detail) be freely discussed in public fora,[293] or because of the potential for certain predictive AI uses to drive adverse self-fulfilling effects.[294] Nonetheless, these may be edge cases, and in general one would expect a strong presumption, for both functional and procedural reasons, towards greater openness and democratic participation as a generally desirable trait for an AI regime complex.

Finally, while in general regime complex fragmentation might seem to impede efficiency and participation, it is also important to consider how certain AI tools, if widely distributed, could mitigate or soften this trade-off, by improving the ability of less powerful actors to remain appraised of developments across many fora and to participate fully even in a fragmented regime complex.[295]

7.5.3.3 Slowness of establishing centralized regimes

A third consideration is about the relative rate of establishing different types of institutions or regime architectures in reaction to an emerging issue.[296]

In general, this consideration appears to speak against centralized institutions, which can be slower to get set up. After all, the process of deliberately negotiating and establishing a new centralised international institution is often a drawn-out one,[297] especially if it departs from a fragmented institutional setting.[298] For example, the Kyoto Protocol took three years of negotiations to create, and another eight to enter into force. Trade agreement negotiations suggest that negotiations can be particularly slow as the participation requirements or stakes become higher.[299] Meanwhile, while international law has been quick to respond to some technological changes (e.g. spaceflight), it has also been slow to address many others (e.g. modern antipersonnel mines).[300]

Meanings, Goals, and Methods' (arXiv, 22 March 2023) <http://arxiv.org/abs/2303.12642> accessed 23 March 2023.

[293] Shevlane and Dafoe (n 27).

[294] See also Agnes Schim van der Loeff and others, 'AI Ethics for Systemic Issues: A Structural Approach' (2019) <http://arxiv.org/abs/1911.03216> accessed 13 January 2020 (discussing the risk that a food security prediction system could drive adverse unsustainable agricultural practices or market dynamics, if its forecasts were shared without caution).

[295] Deeks (n 253) 644–647, 650–651.

[296] Cihon, Maas, and Kemp (n 174) 230–231.

[297] ibid 230.

[298] That is, the setting facing almost any new governance initiative today, given the existing density and accretion of pre-existing governance initiatives. Alter and Raustiala (n 194) 337.

[299] For instance, under the GATT, negotiations for a 26% cut in tariffs between 19 countries took eight months in 1947. The Uruguay round, beginning in 1986, took 91 months to achieve a tariff reduction of 38% between 125 parties. Cihon, Maas, and Kemp (n 174) 230, citing Will Martin and Patrick Messerlin, 'Why Is It so Difficult? Trade Liberalization under the Doha Agenda' (2007) 23 Oxford Review of Economic Policy 347.

[300] Colin B Picker, 'A View from 40,000 Feet: International Law and the Invisible Hand of Technology' (2001) 23 Cardozo Law Review 151, 184–185.

In particular, multilateral treaties can take at least some time to be negotiated. Indeed, one review of 168 agreements found that the duration of international multilateral agreement negotiations varies significantly, but that the mean negotiating time of multilateral agreements concluded since 1945 is 2.9 years.[301] However, this length may be affected by both issue area and the initial sponsor of the agreement, such that when intergovernmental organizations make the initial proposal this results in a longer negotiation time for security-related agreements, but a shorter negotiation period for non-security agreements.[302]

More problematically, progress can be slow when a few states perceive that they (may soon) possess large relative advantages or absolute stakes in a technology's development or deployment.[303] For example, Colin Picker has discussed how, during the 1980s, the US perceived, mistakenly, that it was very close to deploying highly profitable deep seabed mining technologies, and that this played a role in the Reagan Administration's 1982 refusal to sign or ratify the UN Convention on the Law of the Sea (UNCLOS), as that would designate the deep sea bed and its resources as the common heritage of mankind.[304] Likewise, treaty negotiation can be slow whenever there are informational or expertise asymmetries between states and private industry players.[305]

This may prove a hurdle for AI, because the global AI development landscape, especially for advanced AI, raises both inequalities in inter-state leadership on AI and state–private sector information asymmetries. Consequently, we might expect greater than usual hurdles to the negotiation of comprehensive treaty regimes.[306]

By contrast, the various components or entities in a decentralized regime complex might be set up on a shorter time span. Indeed, it has been argued that smaller governance initiatives that involve informal institutions with like-minded memberships can often be able to move more quickly in dealing with complex and political sensitive 'transversal' issues such as AI.[307] Indeed, from the mid-2010s onwards, fragmented initiatives such as those by the OECD and the G7 have been able to forge ahead with setting norms and achieving a range of AI governance goals, in a way that has resulted in their principles affecting subsequent AI policy frameworks in many other organizations. This suggests that the relative

[301] Nicole M Simonelli, 'Bargaining over International Multilateral Agreements: The Duration of Negotiations' (2011) 37 International Interactions 147, 158. Note, the time period is from the first written proposal for an agreement to signature. See also the discussion in Oliver Guest, 'Prospects for AI Safety Agreements between Countries' (Rethink Priorities 2022) <https://rethinkpriorities.org/publications/prospects-for-ai-safety-agreements-between-countries> accessed 3 May 2023.
[302] Simonelli (n 301).
[303] This has been identified as one of the barriers to international regulation of cyberwar. Mette Eilstrup-Sangiovanni, 'Why the World Needs an International Cyberwar Convention' (2018) 31 Philosophy & Technology 379.
[304] Picker (n 300) n 13 (citing sources).
[305] ibid 187–194.
[306] Cihon, Maas, and Kemp (n 174) 230.
[307] Morin and others (n 124) 2–3.

speed of a decentralized approach could be a functional enough strategy to continue, and might even be preferable to the pursuit of a full multilateral treaty or encompassing international organization if, in the waiting for a comprehensive treaty regime, we would leave urgent AI issue areas effectively ungoverned for a critical period.

7.5.3.4 Brittleness of centralized regimes

A fourth, related consideration relates to the relative brittleness of a centralized regime or integrated regime complex, once it has been finally established.[308] To distinguish, whereas 'slowness' concerns the relatively long process that might be involved in the initial establishment of many centralized institutions, 'brittleness' refers instead to the tendency of centralized institutions to create a larger risk of across-the-board governance failure if they are compromised or (seen) to fail in their mission, and to be more path-dependent and less able to react to sudden changes in the problem landscape, whether these are sociotechnical, legally disruptive, or political.

Indeed, relative to a fragmented regime complex, a centralized institution may be more brittle to risks from three distinct sources: regulatory capture, unified failure, or lack of adaptability.

That is, the very qualities that afford a centralized regime political power and authority may also offer a simpler single target for attempts by some actors to capture the regime, and exacerbate the downside effects of regulatory capture if or when it occurs. After all, even if centralized high-profile institutions may be better placed to resist attempts at regulatory capture than are smaller, less well-resourced institutions, even such flagship organizations are certainly not immune to it.[309] Significantly, the risk of regulatory capture (or even the mere appearance of it) may prove unusually high in the context of AI governance, given the extraordinary resources and demonstrated political clout of technology companies.[310] Indeed, in national contexts, such concerns have become prevalent among AI policy experts, who fear that regulatory capture might lead to lack of AI regulation, weak regulation, or regulation that over-emphasizes certain policy goals.[311] Accurate or not,

[308] In our previous work, we discussed these two considerations—'slowness' and 'brittleness'—together under one rubric. Cihon, Maas, and Kemp (n 174) 230–231.

[309] Cf. Abigail C Deshman, 'Horizontal Review between International Organizations: Why, How, and Who Cares about Corporate Regulatory Capture' (2011) 22 European Journal of International Law 1089 (discussing corporate influence on the WHO during the 2009 H1N1 pandemic). See also Jens Martens, *Corporate Influence on the G20: The Case of the B20 and Transnational Business Networks* (Global Policy Forum and Heinrich-Böll-Stiftung 2017) <https://www.boell.de/sites/default/files/corporate_influence_on_the_g20.pdf> accessed 11 August 2020.

[310] Paul Nemitz, 'Constitutional Democracy and Technology in the Age of Artificial Intelligence' (2018) 376 Philosophical Transactions of the Royal Society A 20180089, 3.

[311] Kevin Wei and others, 'How Do AI Companies "Fine-Tune" Policy? Examining Regulatory Capture in AI Governance' (2024) 7 Proceedings of the AAAI/ACM Conference on AI, Ethics, and Society 1539.

the mere public perception of such interference could swiftly undercut the legitimacy or authority of the resulting international AI institution.[312]

As for the second risk, a centralized institution, even if it may be better positioned to achieve success in its mission (e.g. given its political power), will create a single point of failure for the regime as a whole. That is, it may have a better chance to set and coordinate global policies on AI; however, a failure to set the appropriate policies—or its becoming mired in contestation, gridlock, or some scandal—could have more far-reaching consequences for the AI regime as a whole than would be the case if similar mistakes were made only by one institution among many in a broader complex. The argument here is not even that smaller institutions necessarily come up with better policies than large ones,[313] but rather that in a fragmented regime complex, bad policies might be more easily 'compartmentalized' or at least identified and challenged or compensated for by peer institutions.

Finally, there are, as mentioned, issues around the ability of centralized regimes to adapt to new external challenges or changes in their issue landscape. Historically, international institutions can be notoriously path-dependent, experiencing difficulty in addressing new problems (or new manifestations of old problems) beyond their remit,[314] although there are exceptions to this.[315] Ironically, the very path-dependency that may ensure institutional stability may also mean that a centralized AI institution might not adapt sufficiently rapidly to unanticipated new problems or outside stressors outside its mandate. In such cases, a regime might 'break before it bends'.[316]

This is an especially salient challenge for the prospects of centralized and multilateral treaties for AI governance, because, as the discussion of governance disruption demonstrated, legally disruptive shifts may be unusually common in the

[312] This point was indeed raised around the initial French-Canadian proposal for an 'IPAI'. Nature Editors, 'International AI Ethics Panel Must Be Independent' (2019) 572 Nature 415.

[313] Although this is also a position that some defenders of polycentric governance take. Elinor Ostrom, 'Polycentric Systems for Coping with Collective Action and Global Environmental Change' (2010) 20 Global Environmental Change 550; Acharya (n 223). However, for a more nuanced discussion of design features that may improve intergovernmental organization decision-making, see also Thomas Sommerer and others, 'Decision-Making in International Organizations: Institutional Design and Performance' (2022) 17 The Review of International Organizations 815 (discussing in particular the positive effects of a range of combined institutional design features, such as majoritarian decision rules, delegation of authority to supranational institutions, and access for transnational actors).

[314] See Baccaro and Mele (n 214) (studying the ILO's difficulties in reforming participation and rulemaking processes in the 1990s).

[315] One example might be the European Commission's 'Kinnock reforms'. After four decades of relative inaction and failed internal reform, the European Commission between 1999 and 2005 seized on a 'once-in-a-generation opportunity' to conduct a programme of far-reaching change involving the overhaul of personnel, financial management, and planning systems; it did so in just six years, adopting a more radical set of measures than had been demanded of the body. Hussein Kassim, '"Mission Impossible", but Mission Accomplished: The Kinnock Reforms and the European Commission' (2008) 15 Journal of European Public Policy 648; Tim Balint, Michael W Bauer, and Christoph Knill, 'Bureaucratic Change in the European Administrative Space: The Case of the European Commission' (2008) 31 West European Politics 677.

[316] Cihon, Maas, and Kemp (n 174) 230–231.

context of technology governance. This is because once a treaty is in force it is hard to amend, given the need to get mutual consent from all partners. After all, when only some partners agree to modify or update a multilateral treaty, this would result in a fracturing of the treaty regime, and a potential erosion of its international pull. As Rebecca Crootof has argued, the mere prospect of such fractures can even have chilling effects on reform attempts, since 'some states might avoid clearly-needed improvements [to treaties] when there is not complete consensus to avoid undermining the treaty regime's overall force'.[317] This suggests that multilateral treaties may be particularly susceptible to early or frequent disruption and obsolescence as a result of technological change.[318] By contrast, a decentralized regime complex might function better, as the plural institutional ecologies of regime complexes have been described as ultimately more adaptable over time as well as more flexible across issues.[319]

However, the point may not be about whether centralized institutions or decentralized regime complexes are more adaptable in the abstract. Rather, in practical terms our estimate of the relative resilience of centralized or fragmented AI regimes to governance disruption may depend, in part, on the speed or rate at which we expect changes in AI system capability, dissemination, usage, and resulting disruption.

Specifically, key variables in this discussion may include the rate and magnitude of AI-driven changes which (we expect) would shift the centre of gravity in the sociotechnical problem landscape beyond current institutional mandates,[320] or which would create changes that are so legally disruptive that they cannot be accommodated by regular interpretation, generating a need for legal regime development and institutional innovation. If we expect this rate-of-change in such AI shocks to be relatively low,[321] then the benefits of the rigidity of centralized institutions or treaties—their ability to stand up to political pressure and to pre-empt forum-shopping—may well outweigh the costs of their reduced ability to keep

[317] Crootof, 'Jurisprudential Space Junk' (n 19) 109; see also Brian Israel, 'Treaty Stasis' (2014) 108 AJIL Unbound 63.

[318] Crootof, 'Jurisprudential Space Junk' (n 19) 109.

[319] Gómez-Mera, Morin, and Van De Graaf (n 170) 145. See also Robert O Keohane and David G Victor, 'The Regime Complex for Climate Change' (2011) 9 Perspectives on Politics 7, 19. However, this may also be a matter of instrument choice, with certain (nonbinding) soft law initiatives potentially more adaptable than hard law treaties.

[320] Matthijs M Maas, 'Innovation-Proof Governance for Military AI? How I Learned to Stop Worrying and Love the Bot' (2019) 10 Journal of International Humanitarian Legal Studies 129, 139–141 (on how innovation in military AI systems could shift the 'problem portfolio'). See also the discussion in Section 5.5.5.

[321] Or alternatively, if we accept that AI's rate of disruptive change has been high in recent years, but believe that most truly legally disruptive capability improvements have by now been produced, so that further conceptual disruption (e.g. the development of swarming drone warfare) will be only modestly more disruptive compared to the more fundamental conceptual disruption (e.g. the development of machine autonomy in robotic systems) with which international legal systems have already been reckoning.

pace with occasional changes. Conversely, if we expect the rate-of-change in AI capability development, applications, and sociotechnical change to (continue to) be high,[322] then this can be taken as an argument for accepting regime fragmentation as an acceptable or even operationally superior trajectory for AI governance, since many institutions would be better able to rapidly adapt to the frequent appearance of new technological, sociotechnical, and legal situations.[323]

7.5.3.5 The breadth-versus-depth dilemma in a centralized regime

A fifth consideration relates to the so-called breadth-versus-depth dilemma[324] that all global governance institutions and efforts face to some extent.[325]

This pertains to the problem that, while many global challenges (particularly weakest-link public goods) would seem to require universal participation by all states to be effectively addressed, such universality may be hard to achieve within a treaty or convention that also has sufficient substantive teeth to meaningfully address the issue at hand. Frequently, the pursuit of broad centralization may face an overly high threshold that limits participation from key parties—or, conversely, is forced to make substantive concessions in order to secure their buy-in.[326] All multilateral agreements face a trade-off between having higher participation ('breadth') or stricter rules and greater ambition of commitments ('depth'). However, this dilemma could be particularly crippling for centralized institutions that are intended to be powerful and require strong commitments from states.[327]

Indeed, the pursuit of universality in treaties (as opposed to through customary international law) can often not only prove an obstacle to the creation and ratification of that treaty, but also possibly erode the ambition and effectiveness of the eventual instrument that is ultimately adopted.[328] For instance, the 2015 Paris Agreement on Climate Change was significantly watered down in order to secure the participation of the US: because negotiators anticipated difficulties in

[322] Or higher, at least, than the rate at which comparably disruptive developments have shaken up treaties and institutions in other fields of governance such as trade or ecosystems. Given the rate of development and application of AI, this appears a relatively defensible assumption.

[323] However, this argument in favour of regime complexity would be diminished if there were ways to design more centralized regimes to reckon more effectively with these disruptive changes.

[324] Cihon, Maas, and Kemp (n 174) 321.

[325] See also Coen and others (n 285) 10 (discussing 'tension between ambition and broad-based consensus'). Although in a more critical perspective, Thomas Bernauer and colleagues have questioned whether there is always a 'depth versus participation' dilemma, since the depth of any cooperative effort is multidimensional. In particular, reviewing data on more than 200 environmental treaties, they find participation-limiting efforts from the specificity of obligations, but not for monitoring and enforcement provisions; and that furthermore, positive incentives such as assistance provisions and dispute settlement mechanisms can have a strong positive effect on treaty participation. See Thomas Bernauer and others, 'Is There a "Depth versus Participation" Dilemma in International Cooperation?' (2013) 8 The Review of International Organizations 477.

[326] Luke Kemp, 'Better Out than In' (2017) 7 Nature Climate Change 458; Fehl (n 110).

[327] Cihon, Maas, and Kemp (n 174) 231.

[328] See also Nele Matz-Lück, 'Framework Conventions as a Regulatory Tool' (2009) 3 Goettingen Journal of International Law 439, 445.

securing ratification through the US Senate, they opted for a 'pledge and review' arrangement with few strong legal obligations, ensuring the US could join through the approval of the executive.[329] Consequently, the overall regime made concessions on the demands made of all parties in order to secure the inclusion of a key state which, in the event, proved highly vulnerable to domestic US politics, as the successive Trump, Biden, and Trump administrations first withdrew from, then rejoined, then once again withdrew from the Agreement.[330] In contrast, during the establishment of the International Criminal Court, negotiating states, faced with a critical US administration, deliberately accepted the option of an independent court without US support over a weaker one with such buy-in.[331]

In this way, the breadth-versus-depth dilemma is an especially pertinent challenge to centralized institutions. This is because one supposed benefit of a centralized body (relative to a fragmented regime complex) is that it would be able to project greater political authority, such that it might serve as a powerful anchor that ensures policy coordination and coherence while averting fragmentation in membership or forum-shopping. This dilemma suggests it is unlikely to have both.[332]

This may prove a crucial consideration, because securing sufficient state buy-in may be a very thorny challenge for AI governance to achieve. Key actors that currently lead in AI development include states that are potentially sceptical of global regulation, or at best have aimed to exclude one another from some fora. Tellingly, the US was initially sceptical of the French–Canadian 2019 IPAI proposal; when in early 2020 it chose after all to support the GPAI, it did so in large part in order to counterbalance the global role of China.[333] The UK pursued a different track in inviting both the US and China (among other states) to the 2023 AI Safety Summit, although its final Bletchley Declaration remained relatively broad. This demonstrates the likely difficulty of crafting universal governance instruments that will secure inclusion of all actors.

By contrast, decentralization might sometimes allow certain states to undertake at least some much-needed regulatory efforts, including some ambitious measures in particular domains, when they might be unwilling to sign up to a full package of deep commitments. For instance, some have suggested that the US-led Asia-Pacific Partnership on Clean Development and Climate may have overall helped

[329] Luke Kemp, 'US-Proofing the Paris Climate Agreement' (2017) 17 Climate Policy 86. See also Cihon, Maas, and Kemp (n 174) 231.

[330] Anthony J Blinken, 'The United States Officially Rejoins the Paris Agreement' (*United States Department of State*, 19 February 2021) <https://www.state.gov/the-united-states-officially-rejoins-the-paris-agreement/> accessed 23 December 2023.

[331] Fehl (n 110).

[332] Cihon, Maas, and Kemp (n 174) 231.

[333] Michael Kratsios, 'Artificial Intelligence Can Serve Democracy' *Wall Street Journal* (27 May 2020) <https://www.wsj.com/articles/artificial-intelligence-can-serve-democracy-11590618319> accessed 10 June 2020.

climate governance, as it secured at least some non-binding commitments from actors not bound by the Kyoto Protocol.[334] In this way, decentralized regime complexes might at times be more suitable than pursuing an all-or-nothing centralized treaty regime, because the latter might be forced to default to a toothless 'lowest-common-denominator' set of legal commitments.

As with other considerations discussed here, the breadth-versus-depth dilemma raises interesting trade-offs for AI governance, which may not lend themselves to blanket recommendations but rather depend sensitively on the specific governance rationale, texture, and problem logics of the AI challenges that are being addressed.

For instance, if successfully addressing a given AI issue depends more significantly on a regime's *depth* than on its *breadth*—for example, if what is required is for a small number of key states to forego deployment of any AI systems linked to nuclear command and control networks, or to forswear the pursuit of powerful advanced AI above a very high compute threshold[335]—then a centralized approach might be functional because it would only have to reckon with a small number of principals.[336]

Conversely, if successfully addressing an AI issue appears to depend more on a regime's *breadth* of participation than on its *depth* of requirements—for instance, if the goal of our governance efforts requires every state to implement certain modest protocols which inhibit the dissemination or unauthorized use of AI training data sets that contain illicit material,[337] or of automated hacking systems with potential criminal uses[338]—this could, again, be pursued through a centralized regime, since broad (if not universal) buy-in with merely modest (but minimum) standards would be required. Effective mitigation of these risks could be jeopardized by strategies of forum-shopping or by inadequate implementation of the required policies by states with little resources, resulting in the usual challenges of securing weakest-link goods.[339] As such, breadth and inclusion might be prioritized over

[334] Fariborz Zelli, 'The Fragmentation of the Global Climate Governance Architecture' (2011) 2 Wiley Interdisciplinary Reviews: Climate Change 255, 259–260.

[335] Miotti and Wasil (n 94).

[336] This could work on the basis of a 'minilateral' approach. Robyn Eckersley, 'Moving Forward in the Climate Negotiations: Multilateralism or Minilateralism?' (2012) 12 Global Environmental Politics 24. See also discussions on 'critical mass approaches' to multilateralism. Luke Kemp, 'Critical Mass Governance: Addressing US Participation in Environmental Multilateralism' (Australian National University 2016). See also the discussion of 'incrementalism, minilateralism and experimentalism' for AI governance in Liu and Lin (n 241) 342–343.

[337] For instance, a 2023 investigation found hundreds of images of child sexual abuse material in an open dataset commonly used to train popular AI image generation models, such as Stable Diffusion. David Thiel, 'Identifying and Eliminating CSAM in Generative ML Training Data and Models' <https://purl.stanford.edu/kh752sm9123> accessed 14 January 2024.

[338] Admittedly, the history of cybersecurity might not leave one optimistic about the viability of solving foundational problems of (malicious) software dissemination or unauthorized use through a simple protocol, so this is merely illustrative.

[339] Aaken (n 112); Todd Sandler, 'Strategic Aspects of Difficult Global Challenges' (2016) 7 Global Policy 33; Barrett (n 108).

depth, suggesting the pursuit of some centralized, broad global instruments could be effective even if substantive concessions would have to be made.

Paradoxically, however, it is when an AI issue would require *both* depth and breadth for its successful mitigation that a centralized governance regime might face distinct challenges in gaining sufficient consensus from a heterogeneous community of actors. This could be the case for many of AI's ethical challenges, such as hypothetical agreements to restrict the use of AI in surveillance,[340] or the use of algorithms for predicting the behaviour of individuals, populations, or states.[341] It could include global regimes for various structural challenges, such as agreements to prevent the development or proliferation of particularly powerful AI capabilities.[342]

Finally, regimes that combine high depth and breadth requirements might also include cases where the aim is to implement technology-neutral provisions for certain AI capabilities, in order to render these treaties more resilient to later governance disruption.[343] Such neutrality might be key in order to avert or at least delay the eventual obsolescence of treaty regimes. However, states can be hesitant to sign up to technologically neutral treaties, because even if the commitments appear light at present, their technological neutrality means these actors may, in the future, find themselves bound to foregoing capabilities which they had not anticipated at the moment of signature.[344]

In such cases, rather than struggling to secure both depth and breadth in a centralized treaty, it might be worthwhile to pursue second-best strategies in the near-term within a fragmented regime complex. One approach here could be to accept the benefits of fragmentation, splitting off important provisions or measures into a menu of parallel instruments or regimes that can ensure at least some participation by at least most relevant actors. For instance, for high-stakes military applications of AI, such a strategy could involve parallel treaties—for instance, relating to military AI testing standards, liability and responsibility, and setting some limits to operational usage or range—in order to allow states to ratify and move forward on at least some of those options.[345] Similar approaches could be taken around

[340] Steven Feldstein, 'The Global Struggle over AI Surveillance' in Beth Kerley (ed), Steven Feldstein, Eduardo Ferreyra, and Danilo Krivokapic, *The Global Struggle over AI Surveillance: Emerging Trends and Democratic Responses* (National Endowment for Democracy 2022) 17 <https://www.ned.org/global-struggle-over-ai-surveillance-emerging-trends-democratic-responses/> accessed 8 January 2024.

[341] Ashley Deeks, Noam Lubell, and Daragh Murray, 'Machine Learning, Artificial Intelligence, and the Use of Force by States' (2019) 10 Journal of National Security Law & Policy 1; Ashley Deeks, 'Predicting Enemies' (2018) 104 Virginia Law Review 1529.

[342] Hausenloy, Miotti, and Dennis (n 94).

[343] Crootof, 'Jurisprudential Space Junk' (n 19) 121–123 (though noting also some of the drawbacks of technology-neutral rules, such as the fact that they may not constrain later interpreters as much).

[344] Crootof, 'Regulating New Weapons Technology' (n 66) 17. (noting how 'well-meaning attempts to extend a prohibition on one class of weapons to another might actually undermine the power of weapon bans regimes generally: if such treaties are viewed as overly flexible, States wary of incurring unexpected and unwanted future legal obligations will be more reluctant to join them').

[345] John Frank Weaver, 'Autonomous Weapons and International Law: We Need These Three International Treaties to Govern "Killer Robots"' [2014] *Slate Magazine* <https://slate.com/technol

achieving distinct goals around the development, safety testing, and use restrictions of advanced AI systems.

This fragment-and-conquer strategy certainly has risks. However, in some scenarios, grounding the first wave of governance initiatives in smaller and informal coalitions of like-minded states could avert sustained governance gridlock, and fast-track urgently needed policies and norms. For example, in the field of 'human security', the 1998 Lysoen Declaration effort initially began life as a bilateral Canadian–Norwegian initiative. However, as it expanded to a coalition of 11 other like-minded and highly committed states along with several NGOs, the resulting 'Human Security Network' achieved a significant and outsized global impact, including the Ottawa Treaty ban on anti-personnel mines, the Rome Treaty establishing the International Criminal Court, the Kimberley process aimed at inhibiting the flow of conflict diamonds, and landmark Security Council resolutions on Children and Armed Conflict and Women, Peace and Security.[346] Such cases show how AI governance initiatives with a limited membership could set the ground for a 'critical-mass' approach that starts from a small group and is subsequently able to expand to achieve wider impact.[347]

Of course, as noted, this strategy has downsides. While a small group of like-minded actors might be able to settle on more rigorous or stringent terms than might be achieved rapidly in a global or encompassing forum, there are legitimacy and buy-in challenges if some parties are only later invited to the table, as seen for instance by the delayed or even stunted take-up of the 2001 Budapest Cybercrime Convention. This could raise concerns that similar challenges might well beset the future extension of the CoE's Framework Convention—given its closed-door negotiation processes—as well as any other AI conventions that are negotiated among narrow clubs.

7.5.3.6 Resilience of centralized regimes to adversarial strategic manoeuvring

A sixth consideration relates to the degree to which a governance regime architecture enables or inhibits various forms of strategic manoeuvring by actors—and whether or when that is beneficial or not.

ogy/2014/12/autonomous-weapons-and-international-law-we-need-these-three-treaties-to-govern-killer-robots.html> accessed 16 April 2019. As discussed in Cihon, Maas, and Kemp (n 174) 231.

[346] The relevance of this example to AI governance (and GPAI) is suggested by Basu and Sherman (n 227). See also Andrew F Cooper, 'Stretching the Model of "Coalitions of the Willing"' (The Centre for International Governance Innovation 2005) <https://www.cigionline.org/sites/default/files/working_paper_1_-_stretching_the_model_of_.pdf> accessed 27 August 2020; Allan Rock, 'The Human Security Network, Fifteen Years On' (*Centre for International Policy Studies*, 21 May 2013) <https://www.cips-cepi.ca/2013/05/21/the-human-security-network-fifteen-years-on/> accessed 27 August 2020.

[347] Kemp, 'Critical Mass Governance' (n 336); Morin and others (n 124).

Whereas a centralized regime could serve as a focal point for AI governance, decentralized or fragmented regime complexes create far greater room for strategic manoeuvring by many governance actors, both state and non-state. This can take different forms, such as strategies of 'forum-shopping', 'regime shifting', 'institutional replacement' or 'competitive regime creation' in order to induce 'strategic inconsistency' between old and new treaty instruments, or even to foster direct competition between organizations.[348] States may do so in order to maximize influence, frustrate (or deter) certain institutional initiatives, appease domestic political pressure, or placate constituencies by shifting discussion to a weaker governance forum.[349] Forum-shopping has been extensively recorded in areas such as intellectual property rights in trade, as well as in environmental governance.[350] Prima facie, it might pose a problem for AI governance, especially if key private actors choose to participate in or withdraw from selected fora in order to force through certain preferred policies, evade others, or water down misreferred policies through the mere threat of shifting debate.[351]

However, while this suggests that the vulnerability of a regime complex to such strategies is categorically harmful, it is also relevant to note that, under some circumstances, forum-shopping can and has been used by weaker states or non-state actors to (threaten to) bypass a stalled forum in order to achieve greater success elsewhere.[352] Indeed, in the context of AI, something like this may occur in the area of international regulation of LAWS, where some activists, frustrated with the slow process of the CCW Group of Governmental Experts, have increasingly threatened to shift to another forum, as they historically did with the Ottawa Treaty ban on landmines.[353]

Nonetheless, in general, the risk of forum-shopping and other strategic manouvres demonstrates a potential downside of very high fragmentation within the AI regime. This either supports the pursuit of more centralized institutions or, more modestly, highlights the need for distinct strategies to 'manage' the regime complex to mitigate such behaviour.[354]

[348] Thomas Gehring and Benjamin Faude, 'The Dynamics of Regime Complexes: Microfoundations and Systemic Effects' (2013) 19 Global Governance 119, 126; John Braithwaite and Peter Drahos, *Global Business Regulation* (Cambridge University Press 2000). Morse and Keohane (n 232); Ranganathan (n 254).

[349] Helfer (n 231); Saadia M Pekkanen, Mireya Solís, and Saori N Katada, 'Trading Gains for Control: International Trade Forums and Japanese Economic Diplomacy' (2007) 51 International Studies Quarterly 945.

[350] Helfer (n 231).

[351] For one example, see Baidu's 2020 withdrawal from the private-sector initiative Partnership on AI. Will Knight, 'Baidu Breaks Off an AI Alliance Amid Strained US–China Ties' [2020] *Wired* <https://www.wired.com/story/baidu-breaks-ai-alliance-strained-us-china-ties/> accessed 21 June 2020.

[352] Joseph Jupille, Walter Mattli, and Duncan Snidal, *Institutional Choice and Global Commerce* (Cambridge University Press 2013); Laura Gómez-Mera, 'Regime Complexity and Global Governance: The Case of Trafficking in Persons' (2016) 22 European Journal of International Relations 566.

[353] Delcker (n 237).

[354] Such strategies are discussed in greater detail in Section 7.6.

7.5.3.7 Ability to facilitate policy coordination

A final consideration concerns the relative abilities of a centralized regime or fragmented regime complex to achieve effective policy coordination.[355] Given the generality of many AI capabilities—especially advanced foundation models—their likely cross-sector applications, and their cross-application problem logics,[356] it appears that there is a high premium on ensuring at least minimal coherence and continuity in the principles and standards that are applied to AI, in order to avoid norm conflicts.

On its face, a centralized institution or relatively integrated regime complex might be expected to better facilitate such policy coordination, by the simple virtue of acting as an authoritative focal point that can detect, resolve, and reduce the occurrence of conflicting mandates, averting many conflictual regime interactions whether at the level of norms, goals, impacts, or institutional relations.[357]

Nonetheless, it is certainly not the case that fragmented regimes are entirely unable to secure policy coordination. Indeed, this is an active area of work in regime complex theory, with scholars studying various models or cases of gradual 'co-adjustment',[358] bottom-up adaptation,[359] consolidation, or convergence of regime complexes over time.[360]

7.5.3.7.1 Coordination from gradual integration or eventual self-organisation

If this happens, what are the pathways of development for the regime complex? In some accounts, this process results in gradual organic integration of the regime complex. Others anticipate instead that a 'polycentric' regime complex will remain fragmented but can effectively self-organize its policies, in ways that avoid conflicts and which provide more distributed, iterative, and agile solutions to AI governance challenges.[361]

In the first scenario of gradual integration, the argument here is that along with drivers of fragmentation there are also various 'centripetal' drivers of regime integration.[362] This would imply that initial fragmentation of a regime complex is not a problem, because it will over time mature into a well-coordinated and even integrated regime—one potentially more functional or legitimate than some world organization grafted top-down onto an immature regime complex. To be sure, such bottom-up, gradual integration of previously fragmented regime complexes has occurred—as seen in the gradual coalescence of the General Agreement on Tariffs

[355] Cihon, Maas, and Kemp (n 174) 232.
[356] See also Chapter 4.
[357] As discussed in Section 7.3.3.
[358] Jean-Frédéric Morin and Amandine Orsini, 'Regime Complexity and Policy Coherency: Introducing a Co-Adjustments Model' (2013) 19 Global Governance 41.
[359] Eilstrup-Sangiovanni, 'Ordering Global Governance Complexes' (n 202).
[360] Galbreath and Sauerteig (n 195). See also Morin and Orsini (n 358) 42.
[361] Kerry (n 269).
[362] Kim (n 170) 11.

and Trade (GATT) and numerous regional, bilateral and sectoral trade treaties into the WTO.[363] However, while in this case organic integration of the trade regime complex eventually occurred, it involved decades of forum-shopping and inaction.[364] This pathway might be far too slow for the governance of AI systems.

Alternatively, in the second scenario, a polycentric regime complex will remain fragmented but will demonstrate eventual self-organization. Specifically, many anticipate that, whether spurred by internal regime complex conflicts or by outside shocks,[365] these regime complexes can adapt towards a gradual, emergent but effective division of labour between institutions.[366] This adaptation of the inter-organizational relationships might be tacit, or it may involve the formal outsourcing of certain institutional functions through explicit contracts between international organizations.[367] This argument, when applied to AI governance, would hold that a fragmented regime complex could provide effective policy coordination across AI issue areas, even if it is never integrated under a centralized organisation.

7.5.3.7.2 Comparing avenues to coordination

Nonetheless, the question over whether such self-organization will prove functional in time or whether a centralized AI regime would still be better at enabling the required level of policy coordination ultimately turns on two considerations: one of timing; the other of the required level of coordination.

In terms of timing, it is worth considering the degree to which these timelines of regime complex evolution match (that is, are 'synchronized' to) the plausible timelines characterizing the evolution of the AI problem landscape. Even where a fragmented regime complex manages to eventually self-organize, the timeframes for doing so appear relatively long—in some cases, one or two decades.[368] This raises the question of whether we have that time or what it would cost us in the waiting. If one assumes that a fragmented regime state does not enable sufficient policy coordination for AI governance, then an extended persistence of that state might at best be a waste (involving substantial opportunity costs or duplication of effort) and at worst hold back global efforts to effectively or coherently govern certain key

[363] Cihon, Maas, and Kemp (n 174) 232.
[364] ibid.
[365] For instance, Yu and Xue argue regime complexes can experience 'punctuated equilibria'—long periods of stability, interspersed with unstable periods—and suggest that the 'evolution of [a] regime complex is shaped by interactions between governance issues outside the regime complex, and a combination of actor power and institutional logics'. Yu and Xue (n 245).
[366] Galbreath and Sauerteig (n 195) 85–86; Gehring and Faude (n 348).
[367] Galbreath and Sauerteig (n 195) 90–91 ('a formal arrangement between international organizations . . . where one international organization seeks to use another for the resources and functions that are needed to address an issue'). They distinguish 'contract' from two other (unintentional) outcomes of regime complex dynamics, 'competition' and 'convergence': ibid 88–90.
[368] Cihon, Maas, and Kemp (n 174) 232.

AI issue areas at a particularly sensitive moment in their development.[369] Indeed, the regime complex adaptation lifecycle may be longer than the timeframes involved in the development, deployment, and proliferation of the next wave of AI capabilities and their sociotechnical changes.[370] If new AI developments, uses, or sociotechnical changes routinely short-circuit dynamics of regime adjustment or integration, this would suggest that counting on the regime complex to eventually catch up and settle may not prove a durable strategy.

The comparison of centralized and decentralized AI regime complexes also turns on the underlying question of what level of policy coordination will in fact be required to effectively manage certain sets of AI issues.

7.5.3.7.3 When should we pursue coordination?

As discussed previously in Chapter 2, there are many global AI governance issues for which we may need significant levels of global coordination. For instance, if we expect that the successful governance of AI across many diverse sectors will, in some or all cases, require the application of general principles or invariant rules (e.g. regarding explainability, meaningful human control, robustness to adversarial inputs, or alignment) across diverse application areas, then achieving sufficient policy coordination across the regime complex would appear especially important, potentially supporting centralization in AI governance.[371]

On the other hand, if we assume that AI governance may not need general rules, or that sector-specific regulations for applications will prove adequate at addressing most new AI problems most of the time,[372] then one might expect outright inter-regime norm conflicts to be either rare or practically irrelevant. In addition, if we put a particularly high premium on accommodating local contexts in AI policy, this might even speak against pushing strong harmonization initiatives.[373] In such cases, ensuring policy coordination across the larger AI regime complex may not even be desirable at all.[374] This would suggest that a fragmented AI regime

[369] Specifically, one risk here is that by the time the regime complex has worked through initial conflictual dynamics to achieve more coherent arrangements, we will, per the Collingridge Dilemma, have traded in the information problem for a power problem, inhibiting effective governance.

[370] However, more traditional instruments of 'integrated' international law—such as multilateral treaties, or the formulation of international customary law—are not necessarily more rapid, and can likewise require many years of negotiation or accretion, respectively. Picker (n 300); Crootof, 'Jurisprudential Space Junk' (n 19).

[371] Jacob Turner, *Robot Rules: Regulating Artificial Intelligence* (Springer Berlin Heidelberg 2018) 213–221.

[372] This is the position taken by Martina Kunz and Seán Ó hÉigeartaigh, 'Artificial Intelligence and Robotization' in Robin Geiß and Nils Melzer (eds), *The Oxford Handbook of the International Law of Global Security* (Oxford University Press 2021).

[373] See for instance the argument made in Liu and Lin (n 241).

[374] Though it might be from a global constitutionalist perspective, or a 'legal coherentist' perspective that emphasizes the consistency of a legal system. Roger Brownsword, 'Law Disrupted, Law Re-Imagined, Law Re-Invented' [2019] Technology and Regulation 10, 14.

complex's (assumed) impoverished ability to deliver adequate policy coordination rapidly (or at all) is not a decisive obstacle.

Nonetheless, there are some general reasons to expect that, even if greater heterogeneity and experimentation might be suitable for the governance of some (but not all) conventional AI systems, coordination could be valuable especially for the governance of military and advanced AI. In the first place, norm conflicts that remain mostly latent or theoretical at the present level of technological development may be activated or spill over as a result of technological progress, potentially creating situations of legal ambiguity that are potentially hard to resolve, risking forms of governance erosion.

More practically, effective governance cooperation among regimes focused on apparently distinct applications may be especially valuable in the context of AI. This is because while AI is certainly an accessible technology developed by a broad and diverse ecology of actors, it is also true that the lion's share of high-impact conventional and advanced AI systems—the ones that might affect many tens or hundreds of millions of people on a daily basis—are currently developed and produced by a relatively small set of large private tech actors. In many cases, the ethical challenges that arise around these actors' AI systems can be at least partially traced back to the problems that emerge around these businesses—or their algorithms—optimizing for a too-narrow set of metrics.[375] This suggests that coordination around common (and binding) rules for these systems will be needed. It may also be more effective, as these actors moreover depend on common computing hardware resources provided by a relatively globally concentrated compute production stack, providing shared levers for global policy.

In sum, these conditions create commonalities in global AI governance, in terms of common regulatees, common problem logics, and common policy levers which are relevant to addressing many 'local' AI problems under widely distinct regimes. That implies that ensuring effective policy coordination will matter greatly to AI governance.

In turn, as discussed before, this need not mean that only a centralized institution will be adequate to ensure such coordination. However, it does suggest that in its absence, other actors within a fragmented AI regime complex will need to adopt distinct strategies to ensure policy coordination, if they are to be effective, resilient, and coherent in the face of ongoing pressures of change.

[375] Rachel Thomas and David Uminsky, 'The Problem with Metrics Is a Fundamental Problem for AI' [2020] arXiv:2002.08512 [cs] <http://arxiv.org/abs/2002.08512> accessed 27 August 2020. See also Rebekah Overdorf and others, 'POTs: Protective Optimization Technologies' [2018] arXiv:1806.02711 [cs] <http://arxiv.org/abs/1806.02711> accessed 21 May 2019; See also generally David Manheim and Scott Garrabrant, 'Categorizing Variants of Goodhart's Law' [2018] arXiv:1803.04585 [cs, q-fin, stat] <http://arxiv.org/abs/1803.04585> accessed 29 January 2019.

7.6 Strategies: AI Regime Efficacy, Resilience, and Coherence

So far, we have considered potential factors that may affect the future evolution of the AI regime complex towards fragmentation or integration, as well as some of the consequences that could result from either form of regime complex organization. However, it is also clear that, whichever governance trajectory one expects or prefers, they can consider additional steps and interventions to improve the functioning of the resulting AI governance architecture. As such, we now will explore potential *strategies* for organizing global AI governance, to reckon with the diverse sociotechnical, legal, and political challenges explored throughout this book.

7.6.1 Efficacy, Resilience, and Coherence as Minimal Functional Desiderata

Of course, to understand in what way these strategies could be said to 'improve' global AI governance, we have to consider the question—by what metric? What goals or values would the adoption of these strategies contribute to? By what criteria are they an improvement? These might be challenging and even controversial questions, as they potentially raise deeper debates over what purposes international law or global governance are, or should be, for.[376] Indeed, we could refer to many normative principles or criteria in evaluating an AI governance regime complex. For instance, from an outcome-focused perspective, we could consider the degree to which a regime complex manages to respond effectively to core regulatory rationales.[377] From a procedural perspective, one could consider the degree to which the AI regime complex provides for certain procedural goods such as legitimacy, representation, or democratic accountability.[378]

We can here also work from influential work in technology law. For instance, Roger Brownsword, Eloise Scotford, and Karen Yeung have set out the challenges around ensuring that a regulatory environment is adequate or 'fit for purpose' to technologies. In their view, this requires

> an audit of the regulatory environment that invites a review of: (i) the adequacy of the 'fit' or 'connection' between the regulatory provisions and the target technologies; (ii) the effectiveness of the regulatory regime in achieving its purposes;

[376] Nico Krisch, 'The Decay of Consent: International Law in an Age of Global Public Goods' (2014) 108 American Journal of International Law 1. See also Section 2.4.2 (on potential rationales for governance to secure AI-related global public goods).

[377] See also Section 4.4.3 (on governance rationales).

[378] Huw Roberts and others, 'Global AI Governance: Barriers and Pathways Forward' (n 222) 7–10 (on ensuring legitimacy); Tallberg and others (n 1) 14–16 (on both procedural and outcome-based normative standards by which to evaluate the degree to which global AI governance initiatives uphold principles of democracy and justice).

> (iii) the 'acceptability' and 'legitimacy' of the means, institutional forms, and practices used to achieve those purposes; (iv) the 'acceptability' and 'legitimacy' of the purposes themselves; (v) the 'acceptability' and 'legitimacy' of the processes used to arrive at those purposes; and (vi) the 'legitimacy' or 'acceptability' of the way in which those purposes and other purposes which a society considers valuable and worth pursuing are prioritized and traded- off against each other.[379]

How can we evaluate and improve the fit of the global AI governance regime complex to its issues? To do so, I will here not discuss specific substantive values or goals for AI regimes, considering that regulatory values or goals may change over time. Rather, I will focus on questions of regulatory fit and effectiveness—leaving considerations of other relevant criteria (i.e. over the legitimacy of the institutional arrangements, their purposes, the processes by which these purposes where formulated, or the trade-offs between their goals and other goods) to future work. In this perspective, I argue that questions of regulatory fit and effectiveness in global AI governance can be approached in terms of three functional criteria: efficacy, resilience, and coherence.

That is, by *efficacy* is meant, loosely, the ability of the AI governance architecture to identify, track, respond to, and effectively (by its own lights) address whichever AI-driven sociotechnical changes create its governance rationale. By *resilience* is meant, loosely, the ability of the AI architecture system to absorb, respond to, or even harness the effects of AI-driven governance disruption, in order to carry out development where it is needed, harness or manage the effects of displacement, and avoid the outcomes of governance destruction (through erosion or decline). By *coherence* is meant, loosely, the ability of the AI governance system to manage changes and stresses in the regime architecture, specifically in terms of inter-regime or inter-institutional conflicts over norms, goals, or outcomes.

Once again, these are thin principles, and they are certainly not the only desiderata we might expect, desire, or pursue for the AI governance regime complex.[380] There is a much richer and broader debate to be had about the substantive and procedural principles, purposes, or values which this regime complex should embody and pursue.[381] Certainly, for a regime to be merely efficacious, resilient, and coherent is not in itself sufficient. Nonetheless, these three goals are a core for any functional AI regime complex. For one, they can be derived from or reconciled with existing scholarship on technology law and regime complex theory.

[379] Roger Brownsword, Eloise Scotford and Karen Yeung, 'Law, Regulation, and Technology: The Field, Frame, and Focal Questions' in Roger Brownsword, Eloise Scotford and Karen Yeung (eds), *The Oxford Handbook of Law, Regulation and Technology*, vol 1 (Oxford University Press 2017) 11.

[380] Erman and Furendal (n 135).

[381] See for instance Tallberg and others (n 1). (focusing on the ideals of justice and democracy). For a more general account, see also Iason Gabriel, 'Toward a Theory of Justice for Artificial Intelligence' (arXiv, 21 June 2022) <http://arxiv.org/abs/2110.14419> accessed 22 November 2022.

Moreover, all three goals are instrumentally valuable across a broad range of governance contexts, and for addressing diverse AI problems. For instance, while efficacy (or effectiveness) may not be a prima facie good in any situations, it is a preliminary good in most. Any AI governance system lacking one or two of these qualities would be hard pressed to remain fit for purpose in the face of change. A regime that lacked all three might well prove more of an obstacle than a tool to global efforts to govern AI. Given this, diverse parties and stakeholders who disagree on other elements or norms around AI governance might nonetheless be able to reach pragmatic agreement or an overlapping consensus on these goals for AI regimes.[382] These are not the only strategies AI governance needs—but they may be the minimum strategies it needs to deal with change.

Given this, I argue that the three theoretical lenses explored in this book highlight a range of new productive choices and options for AI governance, informing questions of AI policymaking and institutional design at three levels.[383] In terms of overall *regulatory approach*, they can help alter the attitude or mindset through which policymakers understand and consider both the problems of global AI governance and their potential space of solutions. In terms of *instrument choice*, these lenses shed light on what types of regulatory tools may be more or less suitable as the basis of our global AI governance efforts. Finally, in terms of *instrument design*, these lenses clarify how we can best tailor or reconfigure these instruments in order to be more fit for purpose.

7.6.2 Insights for Regulatory Approach

The theories discussed in this book highlight a range of general lessons to take on board in the study or shaping of global AI governance regimes, at the level of heuristics or overarching frames.

First off, policymakers may appreciate the value of *aligning regulation to AI's sociotechnical impacts*, rather than scoping governance initiatives at the level of

[382] This need not even be agreement on deep underlying values, but might rather take a form of 'overlapping consensus', or an 'incompletely theorized agreement'. See John Rawls, 'The Idea of an Overlapping Consensus' (1987) 7 Oxford Journal of Legal Studies 1; Cass R Sunstein, 'Incompletely Theorized Agreements' (1995) 108 Harvard Law Review 1733. Some have suggested such agreements underpin landmark international legal achievements such as human rights. Charles Taylor, 'Conditions of an Unforced Consensus on Human Rights' (Bangkok, 1996) <https://www.iilj.org/wp-content/uploads/2016/08/Taylor-Conditions-of-an-Unforced-Consensus-on-Human-Rights-1996.pdf> accessed 20 August 2020. For the application of this frame to AI policy, see also Charlotte Stix and Matthijs M Maas, 'Bridging the Gap: The Case for an "Incompletely Theorized Agreement" on AI Policy' (2021) 1 AI and Ethics 261.

[383] For a distinct taxonomy of five forward-looking principles for 'algorithmic preparedness', see also Noam Kolt, 'Algorithmic Black Swans' (2023) 101 Washington University Law Review 1177, 1225–1239 (distinguishing between principles to inform the *goals* of AI regulation ('anticipation'), principles that pertain to the *means* of achieving that goal ('diversification', 'scalability', 'experimentation'), and principles for *balancing* the benefits and costs of AI regulation ('recalibrating risk')).

'AI' (as broad umbrella), its countless applications, its siloed impacts within legal fields, or its threats to some enumerated set of values. In this way, they can take a more structured approach to questions over whether regulation is needed, why it is needed, when it is needed, and how it may be best designed. In scoping risk assessments, it enables a broader and holistic assessment of the potential landscape of challenges, including indirect, systemic, or difficult-to-quantify impacts.[384]

Furthermore, policymakers should *consider the regulatory texture of the sociotechnical AI systems of concern*. This allows policymakers to better consider both the material features of AI systems and the common problem logics (such as around human control or about principal–agent problems with regard to increasingly agentic systems) which seemingly distinct AI systems can engage within facially different fields or domains.[385] In doing so, it helps reduce regulatory duplication of effort, fosters cross-sector regulatory learning, reduces the risk of contradictory norms emerging from distinct AI governance fora, and helps expand the range of feasible regulatory targets.

Third, global policymakers should recognize *the importance of anticipatory action under conditions of incomplete information*. That is, while the lens of sociotechnical change acutely highlights the difficulties of predicting sociotechnical impacts, it also emphasizes the inadequacy of a reactive wait-and-see approach, which induces regulatory paralysis without necessarily yielding greater consensus down the line. Navigating this middle road between prediction and reaction will be difficult, but also necessary. Indeed, especially at the international level, the long period that may be necessary to establish agreement on a problem may render reactive, 'wait-and-see',[386] or 'firefighting'[387] approaches to AI governance particularly inadequate. This awareness should also inform ongoing debates over the balance between precautionary and permissive approaches in global AI regulation, the burden of proof over establishing harm or safety, or the calibration of different risk outcomes in regulatory cost–benefit analysis.[388]

From the analysis of governance disruption, we will have to *expect frequent AI-driven disruption of the global governance architecture*. That is, in the coming

[384] ibid 1195.

[385] Crootof, Kaminski, and Price II (n 191). Noam Kolt, 'Governing AI Agents' (2 April 2024) <https://papers.ssrn.com/abstract=4772956> accessed 2 April 2024.

[386] Crootof, 'Regulating New Weapons Technology' (n 66) 21–22.

[387] Maas, 'Innovation-Proof Governance for Military AI?' (n 320) 151–152.

[388] For instance, Rebecca Crootof and BJ Ard have suggested that in evaluating whether to adopt a precautionary or permissive approach to technology regulation, we can consider a number of general heuristics, such that 'significant or irreversible threats will justify the precautionary approach, while the permissive approach may be more appropriate for generative or unthreatening technologies. The answer will also depend on who is likely to suffer from the proliferation or restriction of the technology and their ability to mobilize for corrective or compensatory regulation.' Rebecca Crootof and BJ Ard, 'Structuring Techlaw' (2021) 34 Harvard Journal of Law & Technology 347, 384–386. Likewise, Noam Kolt has suggested that, where it concerns particularly severe, systemic impacts from AI systems, there is a case to be made that regulators should 'rebalance risks' by ensuring that 'cost-benefit analysis of AI governance interventions should place greater weight on worst-case outcomes'. Kolt (n 383) 1186.

decade, disruptive impacts from AI systems may form an increasingly 'normal' (though not predictable) part of the operation of the global governance system.[389] In response, AI governance scholars and practitioners must learn to grapple with the ways in which AI capabilities can drive patterns of governance disruption in the substance, practices, or political scaffolding of global governance. One response might be to seek to prepare the ground, by evaluating and stress-testing various legal concepts or norms to assess which norms would be vulnerable to future disruption from particular AI advances.[390]

Indeed, AI policymakers will have to *prepare for AI-enabled adversarial contestation of international law.* That is, the increasing availability of AI tools such as population sentiment analysis, computational propaganda, or lie-detection systems might induce some states to increasingly pursue their national interests through unilateral technological interventions, or to resolve their foreign policy conflicts through bilateral state channels, only submitting to arbitration those issues on which they predict they will win.[391] Such shifts will erode the standing or relevance of the global legal order.

From the perspective of regime complexity, AI policymakers must *consider how new institutional proposals for AI fit within their pre-existing governance architecture.* AI governance should not need to reinvent the wheel, and more attention should be paid in this field to understanding not just patterns of technological change or the ideal design of individual institutions, but also considering the messy political, organizational, and institutional factors that are at work within a regime complex. New AI governance institutions should not be conceived in a vacuum, but need to be designed to fit in with existing institutions active on AI, as well as with adjacent regimes (security, data, trade) in global governance, paying special attention to potential inter-regime externalities, whether conflicts or synergies.

Finally, regime theory offers significant insights into *avenues into shaping underlying regime foundations.* For instance, it allows the articulation of strategies, from issue framing to forum selection to community organization, through which epistemic communities or norm entrepreneurs on AI governance might seek to shift state norms, shaping their perceived interests and the broader structural knowledge conditions for international AI cooperation.[392] In doing so, it can contribute

[389] This notion of 'normal disruption' is meant to echo the idea of 'normal accidents'—to connote systemic failures or breakdowns which appear exceptional, but which are in fact the emergent and inevitable result of the 'normal' way the system has been set up to operate. Maas, 'Regulating for "Normal AI Accidents"' (n 30). I thank Peter Cihon for prompting this comparison.

[390] Rosert and Sauer (n 23). (arguing that it is better to ground LAWS regulation on the principle of human dignity than on the principle of distinction, given, among others, that the latter assumes that AI technology will remain limited in its capabilities).

[391] Deeks (n 253) 628–629.

[392] See also the discussion of epistemic community organization in Maas, 'How Viable Is International Arms Control for Military Artificial Intelligence?' (n 65).

to articulating, and acting upon, high-leverage pathways to influence over the processes of regime development.[393]

7.6.3 Instrument Choice Strategies

More practically, the theories discussed in this book also offer lessons at the level of instrument choice, relating to the relative suitability of different classes of regulation.

In the first place, the book emphasizes *conditional drawbacks to traditional treaties.* That is, while new multilateral treaties are often still seen as the optimal solution to governing new technologies,[394] and have featured prominently in recent AI governance debates,[395] they also face a range of challenges for AI. For one, vertical regimes that focus only at the level of different AI applications risk becoming too siloed. This creates challenges in terms of potential fragmentation, if there is no emphasis on proactive harmonization.

In addition, the need for flexibility in AI regimes suggests that policymakers could, at least initially, *consider issue areas where hard law can be complemented with soft law instruments.*[396] This might be one way by which to buffer regimes against situations of legal uncertainty, or at least ensure they are better able to carry out legal development in response if they do occur. At the same time, any AI governance initiatives that rely on soft law need to go beyond voluntary industry-produced ethics codes,[397] involving multi-stakeholder institutions. In addition, steps should be taken to ensure that soft law regimes do not inadvertently undercut hard law instruments that are in place.[398]

There is also a need to *be cautious of resorting to unreflexive technology analogies.* That is, while ongoing changes in AI might lead to the temptation to resolve these situations by invoking some technological analogies or metaphors, there are dangers involved in locking in underspecified or bad metaphors in order to secure some short-term achievements.[399] That is not to say that analogies or metaphors cannot be used productively. However, a premature convergence to the

[393] See also Matthijs Maas, 'Advanced AI Governance: A Literature Review of Problems, Options, and Proposals' (Institute for Law & AI 2023) AI Foundations Report 4 121–128 <https://law-ai.org/advanced-ai-gov-litrev> accessed 10 November 2023 (reviewing a broader series of pathways by which different actors might inform or help shape key decisions around global AI governance).

[394] Crootof, 'Jurisprudential Space Junk' (n 19) 109 ('treaties are generally viewed as the gold standard, the ideal—if sometimes unattainable—expression of a state's international legal obligations').

[395] See also Section 3.3.5.

[396] Crootof, 'Jurisprudential Space Junk' (n 19) 124–126.

[397] So-called supersoft law: Thomas Burri, 'International Law and Artificial Intelligence' (2017) 60 German Yearbook of International Law 91.

[398] Gregory C Shaffer and Mark A Pollack, 'Hard vs. Soft Law: Alternatives, Complements, and Antagonists in International Governance' (2010) 94 Minnesota Law Review 706.

[399] Crootof and Ard (n 388) 387–395; Maas, 'AI Is Like . . .' (n 66). See also Section 5.5.6.5.

first plausible analogy risks locking in less fruitful or sustainable regulatory approaches.[400] An additional risk is that such rapid analogies may simply weave more underlying conceptual ambiguity into the governance system. Finally, a too-quick invocation of analogical reasoning in order to attempt a (re)interpretation or extension of existing treaties or norms to new (AI) technologies may well backfire, if it cannot pass a plausible 'laugh test', or if it makes states more hesitant to sign up to technology-specific treaties in general.[401]

The discussion of governance displacement also highlighted another instrument choice consideration for AI governance, to do with the *cautious incorporation of AI tools in international law*. That is, AI governance and global governance scholars alike should engage more with the steady trend towards high-tech international law.[402] The unregulated or unrestricted incorporation of (AI) tools in processes of international lawmaking or adjudication may have adverse effects—likely exacerbating power imbalances among states, and feeding dissatisfaction and contestation.[403] However, various AI tools could also support cooperation and coordination more generally.[404] Such tools could not only help states reach agreement, but also address existing challenges of international law. For instance, AI language models today could well play a role in the identification of imminent conflicts between treaty norms, whether accidental or strategically engineered.[405] They could also enable a greater mapping and monitoring of fragmentation both in the AI regime complex[406] and in the broader governance architecture, supporting processes of convergence. It would be valuable to offer such AI applications free or at low cost to many parties, and teach them how to deploy and use such systems,[407] as this could both increase the inclusion of many actors in the fora of international governance[408] and help in the management of governance fragmentation more broadly.

In terms of instrument choice, a regime complexity perspective highlights the importance of *considering the trade-offs between centralization and decentralization in designing AI institutions*. Any AI governance proposals should reckon with the relative merits of a fragmented and decentralized regime complex, the trade-offs that would face such a regime, the likely consequences of different types of organization, and whether—or for what AI issue clusters—this is adequate.

[400] Rosert and Sauer (n 117).
[401] Crootof, 'Regulating New Weapons Technology' (n 66) 17.
[402] Deeks (n 253).
[403] ibid 644–646.
[404] ibid 647–648.
[405] ibid 616.
[406] For instance, in previous work, we also call for the use of various AI tools to improve the monitoring of trends of conflict, coordination, or catalyst in the AI regime complex. Cihon, Maas, and Kemp (n 174) 233.
[407] Deeks (n 253) 650–652.
[408] Höne (n 251).

For instance, where successful management of AI issues requires that the regime (1) wields considerable political power or (2) involves participation from many actors, while heading off (3) strategic manoeuvring by states, this may speak in favour of an integrated institution over settling for the currently fragmented regime complex. This could be the case for 'weakest-link' public goods problems around AI, such as the restriction of cyberwarfare or certain military applications, or the safe development of advanced AI systems.

Conversely, there may be other AI issues where political power, universal participation, or risks from forum-shopping are less pivotal to governance, or where we rather (1) expect critical technological turning points to occur in the near-term, or at least suddenly with little warning (inflicting a large amount of sociotechnical change before an integrated regime could be established in response); or (2) anticipate regular subsequent capability changes and shocks. In such situations, a centralized regime might prove too slow or too brittle, respectively, and policymakers might instead find it not only sufficient but preferable to instead rely on a range of faster, informal governance initiatives, as these might more rapidly close the near-term gap in governance, and more appropriately or flexibly respond to any future changes in AI usage as and when they emerge or become apparent.

Finally, it may also be valuable to *identify adaptive instruments or strategies that mitigate or bypass trade-offs*. For instance, it has been argued that compared to other regimes, framework conventions might be better able to mitigate the breadth-versus-depth dilemma, while simultaneously supporting a degree of flexibility.[409] In this view, an AI-focused framework convention, especially one that allows the iterative addition of new provisions through Additional Protocols,[410] could be preferable to static, traditional treaty designs.[411] Other work has explored the importance of providing positive incentives[412] (such as access and benefit-sharing mechanisms[413]), as well as flexibility and exit mechanisms (such as sunset clauses[414]) in securing broad state support for and compliance with broad AI treaty regimes that require relatively deep substantive commitments. Novel strategies

[409] Matz-Lück (n 328).

[410] Crootof, 'Jurisprudential Space Junk' (n 19) 120. For a general evaluation of framework conventions as international regulatory tool, see also Matz-Lück (n 328); For their application to AI governance, see José Jaime Villalobos and Matthijs M Maas, 'Beyond a Piecemeal Approach: Prospects for a Framework Convention on AI' in P Hacker and others (eds), *The Oxford Handbook of the Foundations and Regulation of Generative AI* (Oxford University Press, forthcoming).

[411] Of course, such adaptive treaty designs are not, in and of themselves, sufficient to make up for (e.g. enforcement) shortcomings in the design of the base treaty. For instance, compare the lack, in the Convention on Certain Conventional Weapons, of verification or enforcement mechanisms or formal processes for resolving compliance concerns.

[412] Bernauer and others (n 325); for applications of such incentives to the context of AI governance institutions, see Trager and others (n 286) 3, 21; Gutierrez (n 129).

[413] Law and Ho (n 118).

[414] Andrew William Reddie, 'Governing Insecurity: Institutional Design, Compliance, and Arms Control' (UC Berkeley 2019) <https://escholarship.org/uc/item/2sn678w1> accessed 20 September 2020.

could also look beyond these, to consider novel frameworks such as so-called if–then commitments for AI—which allow consensus around conditional frameworks for (international) governance around particular AI capabilities or uses without requiring immediate agreement over whether those particular impacts are imminent, by setting out tripwire conditions for those regulatory requirements to enter into force.[415]

7.6.4 Instrument Design Strategies

Finally, the frameworks explored in the previous chapters also suggest a number of instrument design strategies.

For instance, these perspectives can offer insights into *how different content flexibility approaches can support regulatory efficacy and resilience.* That is, they support a more nuanced account of the relative merits of technology-specific and technology-neutral regulation. That is, the sociotechnical change perspective helps us better understand when and why regulation is better targeted, not at specific AI techniques or applications, but rather at broader sociotechnical impacts or common regulatory targets. This is not to say that technology-neutral regulation is always preferable. For instance, while there are many situations in which technology-neutral regulation is more resilient to change in technologies, the greater ambiguity or vagueness of such regulation might also create a greater scope for regime overlap or the blurring of key concepts.[416]

These perspectives also highlight *the role of design flexibility* mechanisms. For instance, proposals for AI governance regimes could consider more flexible treaty designs, which enable more rapid adaptation in response to governance disruption. This could come in the form of various institutional mechanisms or implementation options to enable the regular review and adaptation of AI regimes.[417] These could include lower treaty amendment thresholds or provisions that explicitly authorize expansive interpretation.[418] For instance, in their mandate, international organizations for AI might be granted greater discretion to alter rules as AI technology or use changes.[419] They could also designate 'authoritative interpreters' or institutional bodies charged with reviewing such changes.[420] Designating a

[415] Holden Karnofsky, 'If-Then Commitments for AI Risk Reduction' (Carnegie Endowment for International Peace 2024) <https://carnegieendowment.org/research/2024/09/if-then-commitments-for-ai-risk-reduction?lang=en> accessed 26 September 2024.

[416] Lyria Bennett Moses, 'Regulating in the Face of Sociotechnical Change' in Roger Brownsword, Eloise Scotford, and Karen Yeung (eds), *The Oxford Handbook of Law, Regulation, and Technology* (Oxford University Press 2017) 585–588; Crootof and Ard (n 388) 405–413.

[417] Cihon, Maas, and Kemp (n 174) 232–233.

[418] Crootof and Ard (n 388) 405.

[419] See also the brief discussion by Picker (n 300) 185.

[420] Crootof, 'Jurisprudential Space Junk' (n 19) 120.

mandatory authoritative interpreter for AI-focused treaties or instruments could be one way to help speed up the process by which that regime might resolve the development necessary to manage the pressures of legal uncertainty as a result of governance disruption.

Finally, the regime complexity perspective affords rich insights about the design of instruments, institutions, and regimes in order to achieve effectiveness and ensure coherence. To be sure, as discussed in this chapter, the trajectory of the AI regime complex depends to some degree on external factors, and may not be easily controlled. Nonetheless, we can still consider strategies conditional on the trajectory which the AI regime complex takes.

For one, this perspective highlights the importance of *fostering effective interplay management within a fragmented AI regime complex*. That is, if the AI regime complex remains fragmented, there are many strategies which could be undertaken to minimize any negative consequences. From a legal perspective, the International Law Commission has articulated a range of strategies for managing regime interaction, which include new specific treaties, rules for treaty interpretation, explicit conflict clauses, or priority rules.[421] Of course, adverse regime interactions in a fragmented regime complex are not limited to conflicts among legal norms alone, but also include potential political or institutional challenges.[422] However, here, too, regime complexity scholars have suggested a range of ways by which such interactions within regime complexes can be actively managed.[423] Such decentralized coordination is referred to as 'interplay management', which has been defined as the 'conscious efforts by any relevant actor or group of actors, in whatever form or forum, to address and improve institutional interaction and its effects'.[424] There are distinct forms of interplay management, which AI governance scholars may consider: for instance, in cases of institutional deference, international organizations recognize and cede regulatory authority and jurisdiction to other organizations, in order to reduce overlaps or conflicts and divide labour.[425] Other mechanisms include information-sharing, policy coordination and exchange,

[421] As articulated in Martti Koskenniemi and Study Group of the International Law Commission, 'Fragmentation of International Law: Difficulties Arising from the Diversification and Expansion of International Law' (United Nations—General Assembly 2006) A/CN.4/L.682 <http://legal.un.org/ilc/documentation/english/a_cn4_l682.pdf>. Beatriz Martinez Romera, *Regime Interaction and Climate Change: The Case of International Aviation and Maritime Transport* (Routledge 2017) 230–237. See also the legal framework within which to conduct regime interaction proposed in Margaret A Young, 'Regime Interaction in Creating, Implementing and Enforcing International Law' in Margaret A Young (ed), *Regime Interaction in International Law: Facing Fragmentation* (Cambridge University Press 2012).

[422] As explored in Section 7.5.

[423] Keohane and Victor (n 319); Morin and others (n 124).

[424] Sebastian Oberthür and Olav Schram Stokke (eds), *Managing Institutional Complexity: Regime Interplay and Global Environmental Change* (MIT Press 2011).

[425] For instance, scholars have tracked numerous such patters of deference in the regime complexes on counterterrorism, intellectual property, and electoral monitoring. Tyler Pratt, 'Deference and Hierarchy in International Regime Complexes' (2018) 72 International Organization 561.

direct operational collaborations,[426] or formal mechanisms for aligning different institutions around common goals.[427]

Finally, if an integrated AI regime complex is feasible, policymakers should *equip this centralised AI institution for inclusion and adaptation*, in order to ensure that this approach is not counterproductive.[428] This institution should ensure that neither its breadth nor its depth fall below the critical thresholds of participation or substantive provisions necessary to address the AI challenges under concern. Other design steps should focus on avoiding or mitigating the risks of regulatory capture and lack of adaptability. Accordingly, a global AI organization should provide for AI monitoring capabilities as well as include expert group, informal meetings, or review mechanisms; they might embrace experimentalism, and put less emphasis on the specificity or stability of its rules and more on their adaptability, consistency, and efficacy to the challenge at hand.[429]

In these cases, the focus is on articulating potentially valuable instrument design strategies conditional on either trajectory. If a centralized global AI institution is established either in the near-term or after a period of evolution, then policymakers might wish to design that institution in ways that avert or at least minimize some of the identified challenges this brings, because poor designs could lock in particularly suboptimal outcomes.[430] If the AI regime complex remains fragmented, then this raises questions over how to manage the inter-institutional and inter-regime interactions, in order to minimize conflictual dynamics.[431]

7.7 Conclusion: Framing the AI Regime Complex

This chapter has charted diverse opportunities, challenges, and trade-offs for global AI governance regimes, as developed through the three conceptual lenses developed in this book. In so doing I have drawn on a range of examples and AI issue areas, to argue that any discussion of AI governance institutions and regimes—whether existing, emerging, or proposed—can and should engage with patterns and drivers of change at five stages of the AI regime. In considering each of these aspects, it was argued that we can draw on the three facets of change explored in this work—sociotechnical change, governance disruption, and changing

[426] Oliver Westerwinter, 'Inter-Institutional Cooperation in Global Governance: Why Do Intergovernmental Organizations Participate in Transnational Public-Private Governance Initiatives' (2021) 24 <https://www.alexandria.unisg.ch/handle/20.500.14171/111428> accessed 5 June 2025.

[427] See also Roberts and others (n 378) 11 (discussing the role that the OECD could play in coordinating policies throughout the regime complex).

[428] Cihon, Maas, and Kemp (n 174) 232.

[429] Liu and Lin (n 241) 340.

[430] Cihon, Maas, and Kemp (n 174) 232.

[431] Eilstrup-Sangiovanni, 'Ordering Global Governance Complexes' (n 202).

regime complexity—to help enrich our analysis and improve our choices of policy and strategy.

Specifically, by drawing on these concepts, a study of AI governance can help reframe the study and the shaping of global AI regimes at five levels.

First, an examination of AI governance can examine the question of a particular AI regime's *origins*. This involves exploring the regime *purpose*—whether there is a sufficient pattern of sociotechnical change to constitute a governance *rationale*; and the texture of the governance *target*. It then involves a consideration of a particular governance regime's *foundations* (or viability). This can take an outside view or comparative historical perspective. It can also draw on regime theory to consider the *interests* of states and other governance actors. Finally, it can consider whether or how the regime could be rendered more viable given the ability of various actors to shift *norms* of key stakeholders. In the absence of either compatible state interests or sufficient norm-setting on a certain AI issue, regimes or institutions may be very unlikely to emerge (regardless of initial debates across international fora), and the issue may remain beset by gridlock, locked in a non-regime state, or may see only very fragmented efforts. Even in cases of some confluence of interests with norms, this may not suffice to render *any* governance regime viable. But in some areas it can have a surprising degree of effectiveness. Finally, a consideration of regime *origins* can consider questions of *design*—what regime strategies would be effective? Which would be resilient to future governance disruption?

Second, individual AI governance efforts should reflect more actively on the *topology* of the broader AI regime complex, in order to identify gaps, shortcomings, and latent conflicts in either legal rules, norms, goals, or institutional activities. This involves examining the *demographics* of the growing AI governance system, its *organization* (in terms of the density of the institutional network, and whether links relate to norms, goals, impacts, or institutional relations), and the *interactions* and outcomes of these linkages (whether leaving gaps; conflictive, cooperative, or synergistic). Finally, these interactions can be examined at the macro, meso, or micro level. While such an analysis by itself can offer only a snapshot of an AI governance regime complex—one bound to be outdated by the rapid pace of change—it is still very relevant to undertake such mappings of topology. This is because the AI governance regime today remains in a state of relative fragmentation. Efforts should in particular consider fault lines or overlaps among distinct regulatory instruments—potential conceptual or political tensions which remain latent today but which could find themselves 'activated' or triggered in the wake of later governance disruption produced by advancing AI capabilities or regime complex change.

Third, AI governance regimes should consider drivers of *evolution* over time, both gradual and sudden and both old and new. To that end, they should engage with both general and AI-specific drivers of regime fragmentation—including pre-existing institutional density and accretion, background shifts in state power or preference over time, and various trends of modernity, including the increasing complexity of modern 'transversal' challenges and the increasing call for local governance. Many of these trends may appear to suggest an increasing fragmentation of many regimes, which may constitute a gradually moving boundary condition to governance in general. This should at least be kept in mind by those advocating for centralized AI regimes. Likewise, an examination of possible trajectories for AI regimes will have to increasingly calculate the effects of AI-driven governance disruption on regime integrity: while some AI capabilities could see use in countering regime fragmentation or treaty conflicts, some could also serve as generators of new legal–conceptual fault lines, or spur increased patterns of contestation. That is not to suggest that these are trends that are inevitable, irresistible, or irreversible. Yet those who hope to pursue general and integrated global regimes may at the very least have to consider more explicitly designs or strategies by which the AI regime could be better insulated from these general trends, or could even be adapted to these developments.

Fourth, we should consider the *consequences* of regime complexity in greater detail, as this provides key strategic considerations around AI governance. Both empirical studies of historical regimes and regime complex theory suggest that centralizing a governance regime can have various benefits (in terms of authority and political power, efficiency, and lower participation thresholds), but also introduces new risks (in terms of slowness and brittleness). Moreover, in many cases, the added benefits of either governance approach depend far more sensitively on their exact institutional design. A powerful centralized regime might be able to avert strategic forum-shopping by states, but that same feature could turn into a liability if this prevents some actors from attempting or threatening to shift debate away in the face of stalled progress. Conversely, a polycentric regime complex of many institutions might in principle be capable of generating and experimenting with more solutions, as its advocates claim; but the ability of institutions in a regime complex to carry this out in practice may depend sensitively on how well it is orchestrated. As such, rather than offering a straightforward choice between centralization or fragmentation, in practice the question of which regime configuration would be more functional or legitimate depends sensitively on diverse factors, including one's normative criteria, assumptions about the minimum necessary 'depth' of institutional authority or 'breadth' of inclusion necessary to adequately address a certain AI issue, and assumptions about the pace and functionality of sociotechnical change produced in that domain by further AI progress.

Fifth, a more nuanced understanding of these consequences, along with the lessons drawn from the perspectives of sociotechnical change and governance disruption, helps suggest concrete *strategies* to preserve or improve the efficacy, resilience, and coherence of the AI governance architecture. Specifically, I have sketched how all three lenses have implications for the overall regulatory approach, instrument choice, and instrument design in global AI governance.

To be clear, these specific strategies are no blueprints. They are necessarily rough sketches, in need of much further examination, critique, or validation. These specific suggestions may certainly be contested. However, the larger point of this book is that we will need *some* adequate ways to map and understand the dynamics of the global AI governance regime complex, and new strategies to ensure its efficacy, resilience, and coherence. This is critical if global AI governance is to be fit not only today, but also throughout the changing future.

Conclusion: Choosing to Change AI

This book has told a story of profound change: in our technology and society; in our laws and governance systems, and in the conditions for global governance. Drawing on both theoretical frameworks and historical cases from the fields of technology law and global governance, it envisions where ongoing developments in critical new technologies may soon lead, and speaks of the ways in which changes in the capabilities, affordances, and uses of these technologies will drive fundamental societal, political, and legal developments in the world, as well as in the architecture of international cooperation.

Our tale is also one of human choice. We have at our disposal an atlas of conceptual, legal, and institutional tools to shape the development and global impacts of AI. In the face of technological change, and despite many hurdles and constraints, such choice remains distinctly possible, and is paramount for asserting a human direction to our sociotechnical futures.

Between technological change and human choice, we face a responsibility to make deliberate and informed decisions around the global governance of AI technology, before the window of opportunity closes. We can and must face up to the complexity of technological change and the urgency of making these choices soon. It is also critical that we reckon with the present and future impacts of this transformative technology. All this must be done today, even while we remain uncertain over the technology's precise future contours. Such a message is all the more timely while debates around AI still rage. In these debates, it is far too tempting for many to simply throw up their hands and declare the future course of AI either far too speculative, or far too inevitable, for us to meaningfully plan for or act around today. Against such epistemic and political pessimism, there are many important legal and political design decisions we can make, today and in the crucial years ahead. These decisions can materially secure, maintain, and enhance our ability to govern AI systems and their impacts effectively and coherently, and to our collective benefit, even under many possible future scenarios of AI system development, dissemination, and disruption.

The Stakes

Making effective choices around AI, and making them well, matters today because the global stakes of AI implementation are so profoundly significant, under *any*

Architectures of Global AI Governance. Matthijs M. Maas, Oxford University Press. © Matthijs M. Maas 2025.
DOI: 10.1093/9780191988455.003.0009

possible future scenarios. AI is already having notable societal impacts around the world. Within the next 2–15 years, AI will become a source of major global problems. It may in fact become our premier challenge. For instance, many of the AI technologies available today have already begun to give rise to a range of global issues. For more than a decade, many conventional AI systems—displaying competent performance at narrow task domains—have begun to see widespread implementation in varied domains, giving rise to many significant ethical, social, and legal concerns. Simultaneously, a range of military AI systems have begun to be integrated into all aspects of warfare, creating critical challenges for global security and international law alike. In recent years, the development of increasingly large and generally capable advanced AI systems has not only begun to reproduce many previous AI challenges at scale, but has also introduced novel concerns over how these general-purpose foundation models could affect societies around the world, either through their misuse, misalignment, or unanticipated downstream systemic effects.

As serious as AI's impacts may seem today, they merely establish the floor of this technology's global stakes, not its ceiling. Recent improvements in the capabilities of advanced AI systems have been rapid and sustained. An uninterrupted continuation of these trends would deliver unprecedentedly transformative capabilities within a decade. Yet even the continued proliferation of today's conventional, military, and advanced AI models is sure to have significant global political, economic, and security impacts. As such, while it might be appealing, for some, to wait in hopeful speculation that key industry trends will slow—that the current approach to advanced models must soon hit an unscalable wall; that the next major algorithmic breakthroughs are decades away; or that industry hype evaporates while funding dries up—these assumptions are not a sound basis for a sober and robust approach to AI. Indeed, both key AI trends—in vertical capability improvement, and in horizontal algorithmic proliferation—are likely to continue in conjunction for at least some time to come. As such, we must take into account the distinct possibility that the stakes of AI will be unlike those of any other issue. Irreversible societal impacts from AI are already being felt; their widespread impacts are among us already. Our best course of action now will be to plan for scenarios where these effects scale up to ever more extreme depths and heights, and sooner than we might expect.

Under a wide range of future scenarios, then, we will need to engage with the questions and choices of AI governance. If we fail, or even fall short in steering its development and use, the negative costs to societies around the globe could be enormous. As such, while not all issue areas in technology governance necessarily demand international cooperation, many of the challenges represented by AI are global public goods problems, requiring global solutions. Coordinated global action in some form is therefore not only warranted but necessary—and soon.

A Window of Opportunity for Global AI Governance

Is such global coordination a realistic prospect at this stage? In recent years, the world has begun to wake up to the high stakes of AI. After a decade of slow but steady AI policy developments, we are now seeing a wave of global momentum for AI governance. There are incipient but increasingly ambitious efforts—by major states, within the UN System, from other international organizations and within civil society, and even by tech companies—to craft new governance regimes to address the global impacts we are already feeling, and can expect, from AI. However, in spite of these promising early steps, the global regime architecture for AI governance remains fragmented. On current trajectories, trends, and timelines, there is a real risk that this architecture will prove neither sufficiently effective in regulating AI's impacts, nor resilient to ongoing technological change, nor coherent across different domains of international law, soon enough to make a difference. Without delay, we must lay the foundations for a global governance architecture capable of addressing today's AI challenges, while scaling up in time to keep pace with the near-future developments in uses of advanced AI.

Given these challenges, in what direction should global AI governance head in the near-term future? While there is a wide range of proposed pathways forward, policymakers still experience significant uncertainty over the best policies and solutions. Which types of AI issues should be addressed by this regime, and which can be left out of scope or to the remit of national policies, or even private self-governance? Of those issues that need global cooperation, should they be governed jointly or within separate organizations? Do we need new international institutions for AI? If so, what should be their functions and forms, or their position within—or above—the still-fragmentary regime complex? Conversely, beyond creating new problems to be regulated, could AI technologies themselves aid or augment the global governance architecture? Is ambitious, effective, resilient, and coherent governance for such a high-stakes technology even possible in today's world, under an international legal system that faces unprecedented global contestation and challenge?

Three Facets of Change: Sociotechnical Change, Governance Disruption, and Regime Complexity

In response to the accelerated pace of change and lagging uncertainties, new ideas and strategies will be necessary to analytically improve our understanding of the present and future trajectories of global AI governance, and to prescriptively improve the efficacy, resilience, and coherence of our proposals for instruments and institutions to guide these trajectories. Consequently, this book has advanced the argument that scaling global governance for AI—and indeed for any major new technology—requires that we reckon with at least three types of structural change. To help better understand these three facets of change, this book has developed three key analytical frameworks—sociotechnical change, governance disruption, and regime complexity—drawn from the established fields of technology law and global governance scholarship.

Aligning AI Governance with Sociotechnical Change

First, I argue that, in order to forge effective global governance regimes for AI, we need better methods for tracking societal changes actually caused by AI technology. It is crucial that we grasp precisely what these are, in order to understand why, when, and how these changes are best addressed through governance. In response, I suggest that a sociotechnical framework—which focuses less on the assumed novelty or disruptiveness of this technology, or on its scattered applications and granular impacts, and instead on impacts driven by AI systems' affordances and uses—helps us think through exactly what it is we seek to regulate. It does so by allowing us to ask: what specific new artefacts, activities, or actors create legally notable social changes?

Specifically, a sociotechnical framework helps us evaluate why these changes may or must be regulated, under a rubric of six classic regulatory rationales. This framework also informs choices over when to begin the pursuit of regulation, highlighting the challenges and even drawbacks of attempts to tie regulation to specific *ex ante* predictions of a technology's downstream impacts, while also pointing to the inadequacy of a wait-and-see approach that assumes regulatory clarity will emerge organically in time. Rather, this perspective invites us to explore, from an early stage in the adoption of AI, potential regulatory strategies for shaping an evolving technology under conditions of pervasive uncertainty. Consequently, the sociotechnical framework helps us understand how to best regulate AI, particularly in terms of which governance targets to focus on, and by taking stock of the distinct problem logics that different AI issues and uses may engage, even across otherwise dissimilar contexts.

Far from being an abstract model, the sociotechnical framework promises to provide clearer parameters for many current debates in global AI governance. Among the many important questions engaged is that of where, and when, advanced AI models are best regulated—at the level of their underlying compute infrastructure (e.g. through chip registries), their training (e.g. licensing and reporting regimes, responsible scaling policies), their deployment (e.g. cloud compute provider know-your-customer schemes), their downstream uses (e.g. domain or industry-specific regulation), or their potential harms (e.g. liability law). In doing so, the sociotechnical perspective offers a better way of grappling with the heterogeneity of the various inputs, models, capabilities, and applications that make up this sociotechnical 'stack' of contemporary AI, each of which can present a distinct regulatory surface.

In this way, the sociotechnical approach can help inform key governance regime design choices: it can help us *triage* the most disruptive sociotechnical impacts, *trace* them to their relevant sources within the AI stack, *target* regulation at the most appropriate control points and levers, *understand* when certain policies are appropriate in one usage domain but not in other domains that may appear facially similar, *time* appropriate, effective regulatory interventions, and *tailor* the design of governance instruments in terms of content and design flexibility, in order to afford greater room for possible amendments or course corrections.

Finally, the sociotechnical approach grounds these debates in an understanding of the ontology of AI technology, and the mutually constitutive ways in which technologies and societies shape one another. By keeping the sociotechnical frame always in view, it is possible to remain clear-headed about the high degree of choice we have about how these technological changes will impact society—and, indeed, world history—even as the pace of change dramatically accelerates.

The Dynamics of AI-enabled Governance Disruption

Second, I argue that to craft resilient global governance regimes for AI, we will need better ways to reckon with technology-driven changes in the very tools or processes of governance itself. Like society itself, technology has never solely been a subject of international law; it has always also shaped it in turn. We have no reason to believe this mutually constitutive relationship between law and technology—as an expression of the relationship between society and technology—will be any different in the AI era.

We can call this form of sociotechnical change *governance disruption*: the process by which new technologies, and the changes in artefacts, actors, or activities they bring about, challenge or transform existing systems of law or governance.

Technology law can help us understand three principal forms of governance disruption. First, AI-driven disruption can occur at the level of legal substance, doctrine, or text, as previous legal codes become ambiguous or over- or under-inclusive, or have key assumptions shifted out from under them. This creates pressures towards governance development: as the inadequacies of previous governance regimes become evident, pressure emerges towards legal change, either through amendment of existing laws, wholesale creation of new laws, or the implicit accommodation of the new changes within existing laws or norms through analogical interpretations. Second, AI-driven disruption can itself affect, or even transform, the very processes of law-creation, adjudication, monitoring, or enforcement. The implementation of AI technology throughout the domains of international law can thereby result in the displacement of past governance practices through their automation, or through the substitution of certain forms, practices, or tools with new ones. Third, the unilateral use of AI systems by some state (and non-state) actors may affect the political foundations of international law, resulting in governance erosion or even its destruction.

The governance disruption framework also promises to strengthen both our analysis of global AI governance and our prescriptions for AI governance. At the level of an overall regulatory approach, this framework highlights how, in order to remain resilient to future changes in its norms, tools, and institutions, international law in general, and AI governance efforts specifically, must consider how future changes in the uses of AI will likely challenge the very substance, processes, or political scaffolding of these international regimes in turn.

The governance disruption framework also offers more practical insights at the level of governance instrument choice and instrument design. For instance, for the former, it highlights the drawbacks and risks that arise when policymakers or lawyers attempt to paper over situations of legal uncertainty—in order to fast-track the development of governance—through ill-suited metaphors for AI technology or by using inapt analogies with past technologies. Conversely, it also highlights the ways through which at least some uses of AI systems, if deployed cautiously and responsibly, might strengthen the existing tools of international law-making and law-enforcement, or could even become powerful new tools for international cooperation.

Likewise, at the level of the design of institutions and regimes, the governance disruption framework highlights the growing significance of content and design flexibility mechanisms. Such mechanisms will enable greater regime resilience to, and future adaptation for, ongoing technological change, in ways that could pre-emptively accommodate future technological pressures towards legal development forestalling the erosion of global governance regimes.

Crafting a Regime Complex for AI

Finally, I argue that, to craft more coherent global governance regimes for AI, we need a better account of how ongoing changes in the broader environment of global governance will affect conditions for establishing and designing such regimes. To do so, I have drawn on the conceptual framework of *regime complexity* as a productive framework for understanding not only the design and functioning of individual institutions in AI governance, but also how these are embedded within a broader architecture of institutional norms, regimes, and institutions.

Most significantly, the framework of regime complexity helps us understand the current state of global AI governance and see some of its possible futures, in five key analytical steps. Specifically, through this framework, we can consider questions around (1) a particular AI regime's *origins* in its foundations, viability, and design; as well as around (2) the broader *topology* of the broader AI regime complex in order to identify gaps, shortcomings, and latent conflicts in legal rules, norms, goals, or institutional activities. With this framework, we can also better (3) evaluate drivers of regime complex *evolution* over time, as it tends towards greater centralization or fragmentation. Furthermore, this framework helps us to consider with greater acuity (4) the possible *consequences* of different types of AI regime complexity. In doing so, it clarifies key considerations for instrument choice in AI governance, identifying a set of functional trade-offs between, on the one hand, a comprehensive, centralized global regime for AI that is (largely) organized around one key institution and, on the other, an overlapping but fragmented regime complex made up of many institutions. Finally, a more nuanced understanding of these consequences, along with the lessons drawn from the perspectives of sociotechnical change and governance disruption, helps suggest (5) concrete *strategies*, in terms of our overall regulatory approach, instrument choice, and instrument design, which can help preserve and improve the efficacy, resilience, and coherence of AI governance architecture.

Future Avenues for Research

By introducing the conceptual frameworks of *sociotechnical change*, *governance disruption*, and *regime complexity*, I have not sought to offer up simple, definitive policy blueprints. Rather, in this book my aim has been to introduce useful thinking tools that can help us achieve a better understanding of the many intersections between AI and its global governance. I have touched not only on the question of how to govern AI, nor just on that of how AI will change governance, but also on that of how to integrate both perspectives. My aim in this is to stimulate broader and more appropriate regulatory approaches, along with helping us make more informed decisions around the choice and design of global governance instruments. All of this together will, I hope, contribute to the creation of a robust global governance architecture for AI that will be resilient in the face of ongoing and future changes in AI technology, in law, and in international politics.

Of course, while this book has considered a range of AI technologies, concepts, governance instruments, and disciplinary frameworks, its breadth means that in some parts I have not been able to explore topics as deeply as would have been ideal. Such deficits, however, can be a boon if they point my readers towards important areas for future research. For instance, future research could explore questions over how the insights delivered by these frameworks differ across conventional, military, and advanced AI development and deployment landscapes; how to translate high-level judgements about regime complex dynamics into concrete insights for the design of specific AI institutions or regimes; the precise role of soft law tools; or how international institutions might contribute to the orchestration of governance activities. Moreover, in turn, the field of global AI governance may also offer insights to scholars from the disciplines of technology law and global governance theory, providing them with fresh cases that enable these long-standing disciplines to test and develop their own theories and frameworks in novel directions.

AI Governance: The Choices Ahead

The field of global AI governance has seen significant changes—technological, societal, political—within just the past five years. It is highly likely that it will see more shifts within the next five, and possibly greater ones. With respect to AI technology, we are truly living in an epochal time. No book in a field this volatile, no matter how much it focuses on transferable thinking tools, can aspire to an indefinite shelf life. Despite such dynamism—or perhaps because of it—we should not shy away from deeper investigation and coordinated action. Appropriate global AI governance strategies and regimes are imperative today. Everyone involved needs to understand, furthermore, that the window of opportunity to get AI governance right may well be small—and shrinking. If we miss the opportunity to lay robust foundations for this governance architecture now, our failure is bound to have enduring effects on the character of the world's relationship with this technology.

Ultimately, throughout this book, I have argued that AI technology will be a significant driver of global change, and that we can, and must, choose how we will engage with that prospect. Within a decade or so, AI will likely be the premier challenge to, and test for, our global governance architecture. Yet if there is one lesson to take from this book, it is that we do not need to be swept away by technological change, nor must we be passively resigned to such change. We are empowered to change the trajectory of AI, to refuse unwelcome fates. We can, and must, make deliberate and informed decisions about our relation to this technology, and so determine the futures we hand to one another, and to future generations. Though a major challenge and responsibility, this moment is also a pivotal opportunity. Let us meet it head-on, together. It is time to choose.

Index

For the benefit of digital users, indexed terms that span two pages (e.g., 52–53) may, on occasion, appear on only one of those pages.